ENSER'S FILMED BOOKS AND PLAYS

ENSER'S FILMED BOOKS AND PLAYS

A list of books and plays from which films have been made,
1928 – 1991

Compiled by

ELLEN BASKIN and MANDY HICKEN

*a*SHGATE

Published by
Ashgate
Ashgate Publishing Limited
Gower House
Croft Road
Aldershot
Hants GU11 3HR
England

Ashgate Publishing Company
Old Post Road
Brookfield
Vermont 05036
USA

British Library Cataloguing-in-Publication Data.
A catalogue record for this book is available from the British Library.

ISBN 1 85742 026 8

Typeset in 9 point Century Old Style by Poole Typesetting and printed in Great
Britain by the University Press, Cambridge.

CONTENTS

FROM THE COMPILERS

The first motion pictures were just that: moving images of such simple scenes as trains pulling into stations, waves crashing on a sandy shore, or crowds walking down streets. These larger-than-life visuals were enough to satisfy early audiences. But film-makers soon realized that the pictures they were capturing on celluloid could be edited together to tell a story, and ever since, the cinema has been searching for narrative material to present to its screen audience.

From the inception of the motion picture industry, books and plays have been used as a prime source of story material, from the early silent screen classic *The Birth of a Nation* (based on the novel *The Clansmen* by Thomas Dixon) to Hollywood's 'golden era' in the 1930s, which offered adaptations of such renowned works as Charles Dickens' *David Copperfield, Pygmalion* by George Bernard Shaw and Margaret Mitchell's *Gone With the Wind*, through to more recent films, such as adaptations of Mario Puzo's *The Godfather, Driving Miss Daisy*, from Alfred Uhry's Pulitzer Prize-winning play, and the 1992 multiple Academy Award-winning *The Silence of the Lambs*, based on the novel by Thomas Harris.

Since the 1950s, television also has drawn on books and plays for dramatic material; the appetite of both cinema and television for dramatic stories continues to be insatiable. As we write, screen or television treatments are being prepared of such currently popular works as John Grisham's novel *The Firm*, the non-fiction work *Barbarians at the Gate*, by Brian Burrough, and David Mamet's play *Glengarry Glen Ross*.

However, the entertainment industry is not exclusively interested in newly-written works; in recent years there has been a boom in film adaptations of classics. Several of E.M. Forster's novels have been made into popular and critically-acclaimed films, most recently *Howard's End* and *Where Angels Fear to Tread*. A new film version of Emily Bronte's *Wuthering Heights* is imminent and *Dracula* is soon again to wreak night-time havoc on the cinema-going audience.

Enser's Filmed Books and Plays is the only comprehensive compendium of motion picture and television adaptations of books and plays. Covering more than 60 years – from 1928 through to 1991 – there are more than 6000 listings in this current edition, incorporating live-action and animated films made since the advent of sound, television movies and mini-series, and the television serials produced to worldwide acclaim by the BBC and other British television networks. An essential reference tool for the serious film buff or literary researcher, *Enser's Filmed Books and Plays'* cross-indexed information on films made in the United States, Great Britain, Canada, Australia, and non-English-speaking countries makes it easy to trace a particular film, a particular author, or, where applicable, the various adaptations of a particular book or play.

We have endeavoured to be as thorough and accurate as possible in this expanded edition of *Enser's Filmed Books and Plays,* and this new edition sets a standard for future volumes of this respected reference work. We welcome any suggestions or corrections, if found, for the information contained here.

To gather such extensive data required an enormous effort. Sincere appreciation goes to Rene Kirby for her valuable contribution. Many thanks also to the staff of The Margaret Herrick Library of the Academy of Motion Picture Arts and Sciences, without whose comprehensive archives and generous assistance this new edition of the book would not have been possible.

Ellen Baskin
Santa Monica

Mandy Hicken
Brimington

INTRODUCTION

Enser's Filmed Books and Plays 1928-1991 is a new and enlarged edition of a work which for the last 25 years has guided readers to the fascinating link between books, plays and films. *Enser* has always been considered a valuable work of reference for film enthusiasts, students and scholars. This new edition has over 6000 entries (up 2000 from the last edition), and has a far wider coverage of US, Canadian, Australian and foreign language material.

The book has more useful lists and specialist indexes than ever before, such as a *list of production studios and distribution companies* with abbreviated names, and their addresses where available. *A list of feature length films, mini-series and serials made for television* has been compiled, following a boom in TV adaptations of books and plays. Since many people are interested in musicals, another index lists musical films. Animated films have often been made from books and plays: the *animated films index* provided in this edition restricts itself to feature-length works.

Comments made in earlier editions hinted that more information could be given about the films and the books. Therefore this time round film directors' names have been added to the entries, as has the country of origin and in most cases the place of publication of the book or play. A list of codes at the end of each entry allows the reader to see other facts about the film, such as whether it was made for television, was aimed at children, is available on video or was shown as a series or mini-series.

Like any other complicated work of this sort, criteria have to be set up to control the inclusion of data. Anything that is a close adaptation of a book or play has been included, but we excluded anything that is so loosely based on the original as to be unrecognizable. In those instances where the film's release year was different in the US from the UK, the earlier date has been taken as the country of origin. Also the film is listed according to its title in the country of origin, with a note of the title in the other country's version if different. Another situation that presented itself a number of times was when a filmed version of a stage play was itself based on another work. In such cases an attempt was made to include the original source and the stage version.

In addition to adding new material and information to this edition, a thorough clearing out of the previous edition also took place. Because of the habit of film companies to announce films far in advance of production, many titles in the old edition were in fact never produced. These have been taken out as has much of the fringe pre-1930 material where neither the book nor film is now obtainable.

Enser aims to be correct and complete up to December 1991. Unfortunately, complete information for 1992 was not available when we went to press; we have included the few that we identified. There will inevitably be some omissions in this fast-moving field, with new videos appearing continually, so the publishers would encourage all readers to inform us of any missing items, so that they can be incorporated into the next edition. Also welcome would be general comments and suggestions about the structure and content of the book.

HOW TO USE THIS BOOK

The book is divided into three main sections with additional lists and indexes.

Film Title Index

This listing is the heart of the book, assuming that the reader has the name of a film in mind and wants to find out certain basic facts about it; but more importantly, whether it is based on a book or a play, which they can then read.

The index is arranged alphabetically under the film's title and gives much information about the film and its published source, such as country of origin, the director, distribution or production company, whether the title of the book and film are different, or whether the filmed version is perhaps a musical, a made-for-TV series, or available on video.

Remember that the articles 'The', 'A' or 'An' are not taken as being part of the film's main title, but are placed at the end of the title. Foreign language films are listed most frequently under their English titles.

An example of an entry from the Film Title Index is shown below. The sample entry is repeated at the beginning of the Film Title Index.

Title of film ——— **Kiss Me Kate** ————— Date of release

Studio name and ——— MGM (US) 1953 dir. George Sidney ——— Director's name
country of origin   **M**

MILBERG (US) 1958 dir. George Schaefer

British, etc, title, ——— GB title:
where applicable   **TV (US), V**

    Shakespeare, W. *Taming of* ——— Author and title of
Abbreviations   *the Shrew, The*   book (if title is different
    P   from film title)

    Spewack, S. and Spewack, B.
Means adapted   **P**   Author of film
from a play

Author Index

This listing is for the use of readers who want to see whether their favourite authors' books have been made into a feature film or a film for television. The Index is arranged alphabetically by author with a further alphabetical arrangement of each author's works.

The publisher of the work is often added in this section; the general term 'various' has been used in the case of classic authors such as Shakespeare, whose works have been published by many different companies.

An example of an entry from the Author Index appears below. The sample entry is repeated at the beginning of the Author Index.

Author's name —— **Spewack, B. and Spewack, S.**
Book or play title —— **Kiss Me Kate** Means adapted from
P —————————————— a play
Name and location —— Various
of publisher MGM (US) 1953 dir. George Sidney —— Film title (if different)
M, V Director's name
Studio name and MILBERG (US) 1958 dir. George Schaefer
country of origin **TV (US)** —————————————— Date of release
GB title:
British, etc, title Abbreviations
(if different)

Change of Title Index

It happens very often that a new title is given to a book or play when it appears as a film. This index pulls out all those books and plays where this has occurred.

An example of a Change of Title Index entry is shown below. The sample entry is repeated at the beginning of the Change of Title Index.

Book or play title —— **Taming of the Shrew, The** —— Film title
Author's name —— Shakespeare, W.
Kiss Me Kate
Studio name, location MGM (US) 1953 dir. George Sidney —— Director's name
and release date MILBERG (US) 1958 dir. George Schaefer
GB title:
British, etc, title
(if different)

In addition to these three main sections there are three supplementary indexes which reflect reader interest in made-for-TV films, musical films and animated films. Each of these indexes is arranged in alphabetical order and the reader can then refer back to the main entry for that film, to obtain details of it and its original published source material.

Two lists which give general help to an understanding of the book are included. The *List of Production and Distribution Companies*, at the end of the book, will be useful for identification and research purposes. It has proved difficult to keep an exact record of companies within this fast-moving industry, particularly with regard to the production of films made for television or foreign language films, and the companies linked to some of the older films. However, wherever possible the abbreviated name and full name have been supplied, with addresses included for major motion picture studios and several production companies. The *List of Country Abbreviations* (overleaf) lists the names of the countries in which films have been made, both in their abbreviated form (as it appears in the main entries) and in full.

———— Country Abbreviations ————

Alg	Algeria
Arg	Argentina
Aus	Australia
Austria	Austria
Bel	Belgium
Braz	Brazil
Can	Canada
China	China
Den	Denmark
Eire	Eire
Fr	France
GB	Great Britain
Ger	Germany
Greece	Greece
HK	Hong Kong
Hun	Hungary
Ind	India
Iran	Iran
Ire	Ireland
Israel	Israel
It	Italy
Jap	Japan
Kor	Korea
Mex	Mexico
Neth	Netherlands
Nor	Norway
NZ	New Zealand
Pan	Panama
Phil	Philippines
Pol	Poland
Port	Portugal
Sp	Spain
Swe	Sweden
Tai	Taiwan
Tur	Turkey
US	United States of America
USSR	USSR
Yugo	Yugoslavia
Zam	Zambia

FILM TITLE INDEX

Title of film — **Kiss Me Kate** — Date of release

Studio name and — MGM (US) 1953 dir. George Sidney — Director's name
country of origin — **M**

British, etc, title, — MILBERG (US) 1958 dir. George Schaefer
where applicable — GB title. — Author and title
TV (US), V — of book (if title is
Abbreviations as — **Shakespeare, W.** *Taming of* — different from
listed below — *the Shrew, The* — film title)
P

Means adapted — **Spewack, S. and Spewack, B.** — Author of film
from a play — **P**

A = Animated film

Ch = Made for children

M = Based on a musical

TV (GB, US, etc) = Made for British, American, etc, television
TVSe = Made-for-television series or mini-series
V = Available on video

Aaron Slick from Punkin Crick
PAR (US) 1952 dir. Claude Binyon
GB title: Marshmallow Moon
Benjamin, W.
P

Abdication, The
WAR (GB) 1974 dir. A. Harvey
Wolff, R.
P

Abduction of St. Anne
Q. MARTIN (US) 1975 dir. Harry Falk
TV(US), V
McMahon, T. P. *Issue of the Bishop's Blood, The*

Abe Lincoln in Illinois
RKO (US) 1940 dir. John Cromwell
V
COMPASS (US) 1964
dir. George Schaefer
TV(US)
Sherwood, R. E. *Abe Lincoln of Illinois*
P

Abie's Irish Rose
UA (US) 1952 dir. Edward A. Sutherland
Nichols, A.
P

About Face
WAR (US) 1952 dir. Roy del Ruth
Monks, J. and Finklehoffe, F. F.
Brother Rat
P

About Last Night . . .
TRI-STAR (US) 1986 dir. Edward Zwick
V
Mamet, D. *Sexual Perversity in Chicago*
P

About Mrs. Leslie
PAR (US) 1954 dir. Daniel Mann
Delmar, V.

Above Suspicion
MGM (US) 1943 dir. Richard Thorpe
MacInnes, H.

Above us the Waves
GFD (GB) 1955 dir. Ralph Thomas
V
Warren, C. E. T. and Benson, J.

Absolute Beginners
VIRGIN (GB) 1985 dir. Julien Temple
V
MacInnes, C.

Accent on Youth
PAR (US) 1935 dir. Wesley Ruggles
Raphaelson, S.
P

Accident
MON (GB) 1967 dir. Joseph Losey
V
Mosley, N.

1

Accidental Tourist, The
WAR (US) 1988 dir. Lawrence Kasdan
V

Tyler, A.

Acorn People, The
NBC ENT (US) 1981
dir. Joan Tewkesbury
TV(US), V

Jones, R.

Account Rendered
RANK (GB) 1957
dir. Peter Graham Scott

Barrington, P.

Across Five Aprils
LCA (US) 1990 dir. Kevin Meyer
TV(US)

Hunt, I.

Act of Love
PAR TV (US) 1980 dir. Jud Taylor
TV(US)

Mitchell, P.

Act of Vengeance
LORIMAR (US) 1986
dir. John MacKenzie
TV(US)

Armbrister, T.

Accused, The
PAR (US) 1948 dir. William Dieterle
V

Truesdell, J. *Be Still My Love*

Accused of Murder
REP (US) 1956 dir. Joe Kane

Burnett, W. R. *Vanity Row*

Aces High
EMI (GB/Fr) 1976 dir. Jack Gold
V

Sherriff, R. C. *Journey's End*
P

Across 110th Street
UA (US) 1972 dir. Barry Shear
V

Ferris, W.

Across the Bridge
RANK (GB) 1957 dir. Ken Annakin
V

Greene, G.

Across the Wide Missouri
MGM (US) 1951 dir. William Wellman
De Voto, B.

Action for Slander
UA (GB) 1938 dir. Tim Whelan
V

Borden, M.

Action in the North Atlantic
WAR (US) 1943 dir. Lloyd Bacon
Gilpatric, G.

Action of the Tiger
MGM (GB) 1957 dir. Terence Young
Wellard, J.

Act of Love
UA (US) 1954 dir. Anatole Litvak
Hayes, A. *Girl on the Via Flaminia, The*

Act of Murder, An
UN (US) 1948 dir. Michael Gordon
Lothar, E. *Mills of God, The*

Act of Will
PORTMAN (US) 1989
TVSe, V
Bradford, B. T.

Act One
WAR (US) 1963 dir. Dore Schary
Hart, M.

Actor's Revenge, An
DAIEI (Jap) 1963 dir. Kon Ichikawa
Otokichi, M

Actress, The
MGM (US) 1953 dir. George Cukor
Gordon, R. *Years Ago*
P

Ada
MGM (US) 1961 dir. Daniel Mann
Williams, W. *Ada Dallas*

Adam had Four Sons
COL (US) 1941 dir. Gregory Ratoff
V
Bonner, C. *Legacy*

Adding Machine, The
RANK (GB) 1968 dir. Jerome Epstein
Rice, E.
P

Address Unknown
COL (US) 1944
dir. William Cameron Menzies
Taylor, K.

Admirable Crichton, The
COL (GB) 1957 dir. Lewis Gilbert
US title: Paradise Lagoon
COMPASS (US) 1968
dir. George Schaefer
TV(US)
Barrie, Sir J. M.
P

Adolf Hitler — My Part in his Downfall
UA (GB) 1972 dir. Norman Cohen
Milligan, S.

Adorable Julia
ETOILE (Austria/Fr) 1962
dir. Alfred Weidenmann
GB title: Seduction of Julia, The
Maugham W. S.
P

À Double Tour
PARIS/PANI (Fr/It) 1959
dir. Claude Chabrol
Gegauff, P. *La Clé de la Rue Saint Nicolas*

Advance to the Rear
MGM (US) 1964 dir. George Marshall
Chamberlain, W. *Company of Cowards, The*

Adventure
MGM (US) 1945 dir. Victor Fleming
Davis, C. B. *Anointed, The*

Adventure in Iraq
WAR (US) 1943 dir. D. Ross-Lederman
Archer, W. *Green Goddess, The*
P

Adventure in the Hopfields
ABP (GB) 1954 dir. John Guillermin
Lavin, N. and Thorp, M. *Hop Dog, The*

Adventure Island
PAR (US) 1947 dir. Peter Stewart
Stevenson, R. L. *Ebb Tide*

Adventurers, The
PAR (US) 1970 dir. Lewis Gilbert
Robbins, H.

Adventures of Baron Munchausen, The
COL (GB) 1988 dir. Terry Gilliam
V
Raspe, R. E. *Twelve Adventures of the Celebrated Baron Munchausen*

3

Adventures of Bullwhip Griffin, The

DISNEY (US) 1965 dir. James Neilson
V

Fleischman, S. *By the Great Horn Spoon*

Adventures of Captain Fabian, The

REP (US) 1951 dir. William Marshall
V

Shannon, R. *Fabulous Ann Medlock*

Adventures of Gerard, The

UA (GB) 1970 dir. Jerzy Skolimowski

Doyle, Sir A. C. *Exploits of Brigadier Gerard, The*

Adventures of Hajji Baba, The

FOX (US) 1954 dir. Don Weis

Morier, J. J. *Adventures of Hajji Baba of Ispahan*

Adventures of Huckleberry Finn, The

MGM (US) 1960 dir. Michael Curtiz
V
TAFT (US) 1981 dir. Jack B. Hively
TV(US)

Twain, M.

Adventures of Martin Eden, The

COL (US) 1942 dir. Sidney Salkow

London, J. *Martin Eden*

Adventures of Quentin Durward, The

MGM (GB) 1955 dir. Richard Thorpe
US title: Quentin Durward

Scott, Sir W. *Quentin Durward*

Adventures of Robinson Crusoe, The

UA (Mex/US) 1954 dir. Luis Bunuel

Defoe, D. *Robinson Crusoe*

Adventures of Sherlock Holmes, The

FOX (US) 1939 dir. Alfred Werker
GB title: Sherlock Holmes
GRANADA (GB) 1984 dir. Paul Annett
TVSe,V

Doyle, Sir A. C.

Adventures of Tom Sawyer, The

UA (US) 1938 dir. Norman Taurog
V

Twain, M.

Advise and Consent

COL (US) 1962 dir. Otto Preminger

Drury, A.

Aerodrome, The

BBC (GB) 1983 dir. Giles Foster
TV, V

Warner, R.

Affair in Mind, An

BBC (GB) 1988 dir. Clive Luke
TV

Rendell, R.

Affairs of Cellini, The

FOX (US) 1934 dir. Gregory La Cava

Mayer, E. J. *Firebrand*
P

African Queen, The

ROMULUS (US/GB) 1951
dir. John Huston
V

Forester, C. S.

After Dark, My Sweet
AVENUE (US) 1990 dir. James Foley
Thompson, J.

After Julius
YTV (GB) 1979
TV(GB)
Howard, E. J.

Aftermath: A Test of Love
COL (US) 1991 dir. Glenn Jordan
TV (US)
Kinder, G. *Victim: The Other Side of Murder*

After Office Hours
BI (GB) 1935 dir. Thomas Bentley
Druten, J. van *London Wall*
P

After the Ball
BL (GB) 1957 dir. Compton Bennett
De Frece, Lady *Recollections of Vesta Tilly*

After Tomorrow
FOX (US) 1932 dir. Frank Borzage
Golden, J., and Strange, H.
P

Against all Odds
COL (US) 1984 dir. Taylor Hackford
V
Homes, G. *Build My Gallows High*

Agency
CAROLCO (Can) 1981
dir. George Kaczender
V
Gottlieb, P.

Age of Consent
COL (Aust) 1969 dir. Michael Powell
V
Lindsay, N.

Age of Innocence
RKO (US) 1934 dir. Philip Moeller
Wharton, Mrs E.

Agitator, The
BRIT NAT (GB) 1944 dir. John Harlow
Riley, W. *Peter Pettinger*

Agnes of God
COL (US) 1985 dir. Norman Jewison
V
Pielmeier, J.
P

Agony and the Ecstacy, The
FOX (US) 1965 dir. Carol Reed
V
Stone, I.

Ah, Wilderness
MGM (US) 1935 dir. Clarence Brown
M. ALBERG (US) 1959
dir. Robert Mulligan
TV(US)
O'Neill, E. G.
P

Air America
TRI-STAR (US) 1990
dir. Roger Spottiswoode
Robbins, C.

Airport
UN (US) 1970 dir. George Seaton
V
Hailey, A.

Akenfield
ANGLIA (GB) 1975 dir. Peter Hall
Blythe, R.

Alamo: 13 Days to Glory, The
FRIES (US) 1987 dir. Burt Kennedy
TV(US)
Tinkle, J. L. *Thirteen Days to Glory: The Seige of the Alamo*

Alan and Naomi
Triton Films (US) 1992
dir. Sterling van Wagenen
Levoy, M.

Albert RN
DIAL (GB) 1953 dir. Lewis Gilbert
US title: Break to Freedom
Morgan, G.
P

Albuquerque
PAR (US) 1948 dir. Ray Enright
Short, L.

Alex and the Gypsy
TCF (US) 1976 dir. John Korty
Elkin, S. *The Bailbondsman*

Alex: The Life of a Child
MANDY (US) 1986
dir. Robert Markowitz
TV (US)
Deford, F.

Alfie
PAR (GB) 1966 dir. Lewis Gilbert
V
Naughton, B.
P

Alf's Button Afloat
GAINS (GB) 1938 dir. Marcel Varnel
Darlington, W.A. *Alf's Button*

Algiers
WANGER (US) 1938 dir. John Cromwell
d'Ashelbe, R. *Pépé le Moko*

Alibi
CORONA (GB) 1942
dir. Brian Desmond Hirst
Archard, M.

Alibi Ike
WAR (US) 1935 dir. Ray Enright
Lardner, R.

Alice
HEMDALE (Bel/Pol/GB) 1980
dir. Jerry Gruza
V
Carroll, L. *Alice's Adventures in Wonderland*

Alice Adams
RKO (US) 1933 dir. George Stevens
Tarkington, B.

Alice in Wonderland
PAR (US) 1933 dir. Norman Z. McLeod
Ch
DISNEY (US) 1951
dir. Clyde Geronomi, HamiltonLuske, Wilfred Jackson
A, Ch
M. EVANS (US) 1955
dir. George Schaefer
TV (US)
COL TV (US) 1985 dir. Harry Harris
Ch, TV(US)
Carroll, L. *Alice's Adventures in Wonderland*

Alice's Adventures in Wonderland (V)
FOX (GB) 1972 dir. William Sterling
A, Ch, V
Carroll, L.

Allan Quatermain and the Lost City of Gold
CANNON (US) 1987 dir. Gary Nelson
V
Haggard, H. R. *Allan Quatermain*

All Creatures Great and Small
EMI (GB) 1974 dir. Claude Whatham
V
BBC (GB) 1980
TV(GB)
Herriot, J. *If Only They Could Talk; It Shouldn't Happen to a Vet; Lord God Made Them All, The*

Allegheny Uprising
RKO (US) 1939 dir. William A. Seiter
GB title: First Rebel, The
V
Swanson, N. H. *First Rebel, The*

All Fall Down
MGM (US) 1961
dir. John Frankenheimer
Herlihy, J. L.

All for Mary
RANK (GB) 1955 dir. Wendy Toye
Brook, H. and Bannerman, K.
P

All Hands on Deck
TCF (US) 1961 dir. Norman Taurog
M
Morris, D. R.

Alligator Named Daisy, An
RANK (GB) 1955 dir. J. Lee Thompson
Terrot, C.

All Men are Enemies
FOX (US) 1934 dir. George Fitzmaurice
Aldington, R.

All My Sons
UI (US) 1948 dir. Irving Reis
BBC (GB) 1990 dir. Jack O'Brien
TV
Miller, A.
P

All Neat in Black Stockings
WAR (GB) 1968
dir. Christopher Morahan
Gaskell, J.

All of Me
PAR (US) 1934 dir. James Flood
Porter, R. *Chrysalis*
P

All of Me
UN (US) 1984 dir. Carl Reiner
V
Davis, E. *Me Two*

All Over the Town
RANK (GB) 1948 dir. Dereck Twist
Delderfield, R. F.
P

All Passion Spent
BBC (GB) 1986
TV
Sackville-West, V.

All Quiet on the Western Front
UN (US) 1930 dir. Lewis Milestone
V
M ARCH (US) 1979 dir. Delbert Mann
TV(US), V
Remarque, E. M.

All that Money can Buy
RKO (US) 1941 dir. William Dieterle
Benet, S.V. *Devil and Daniel Webster, The*

All The Brothers were Valiant
MGM (US) 1953 dir. Richard Thorpe
Williams, B.A.

All the Fine Young Cannibals
MGM (US) 1960 dir. Michael Anderson
Marshall, R. *Bixby Girls, The*

All the King's Men
COL (US) 1949 dir. Robert Rossen
V

Warren, R.P.

All the President's Men
WAR (US) 1976 dir. Alan J. Pakula
V

Bernstein, C. and Woodward, R.

All the Rivers Run
Crawford (Aus) 1983 dir. George Miller,
Pino Amenta
TV(Aus)

Cato, N.

All the Way Home
PAR (US) 1963 dir. Alex Segal
PAR (US) 1971 dir. Fred Coe
TV (US)

Agee, J. *Death in the Family, A*

All the Way Up
GRANADA/EMI (GB) 1970
dir. James MacTaggart

Turner, D. *Semi Detached*
P

All This and Heaven Too
WAR (US) 1940 dir. Anatole Litvak
V

Field, R.

Almost Married
FOX (US) 1932
dir. W. Cameron Menzies

Soutar, A. *Devil's Triangle*

Aloha Means Goodbye
UN TV (US) 1974 dir. David Lowell Rich
TV(US)

Hintze, N.

Along Came a Spider
FOX TV (US) 1970 dir. Lee H. Katzin
TV(US)

Lee, L. *Sweet Poison*

Along Came Jones
UA (US) 1945 dir. Stuart Heisler
V

LeMay, A. *Useless Cowboy, The*

Alphabet Murders, The
MGM (GB) 1966 dir. Frank Tashlin

Christie, A. *ABC Murders, The*

Altered States
WAR (US) 1980 dir. Ken Russell
V

Chayefsky, P.

Always in My Heart
WAR (US) 1942 dir. Joe Graham

Bennett D. and White, I. *Fly Away
Home*
P

Amadeus
ORION (US) 1984 dir. Milos Forman
V

Shaffer, P.
P

Amants, Les
NEF (Fr) 1958 dir. Louis Malle

Vivant, D. *Point de Lendemain*

Amateur, The
FOX (Can) 1982 dir. Charles Jarrot
V

Littell, R.

Amateur Gentlemen, The
UA (GB) 1936 dir. Thornton Freeland

Farnol, J.

Amazing Dr. Clitterhouse, The
WAR (US) 1938 dir. Anatole Litvak

Lyndon, B.
P

Amazing Howard Hughes, The
EMI TV (US) 1977
dir. William A. Graham
TVSe (US), V

Dietrich, W. and Thomas, B.
Howard: The Amazing Mr. Hughes

Amazing Mr Blunden, The
HEMDALE (GB) 1972
dir. Lionel Jeffries
Ch, V

Barber, A. *Ghosts, The*

Amazing Quest of Ernest Bliss, The
KLEMENT (GB) 1936 dir. Alfred Zeisler
US title: Romance & Riches

Oppenheim, E. P. *Amazing Quest of Mr Ernest Bliss, The*

Ambassador, The
CANNON (US) 1984
dir. J. Lee Thompson
V

Leonard, E. *52 Pick-Up*

Ambush
MGM (US) 1949 dir. Sam Wood

Short, L.

Ambushers, The
COL (US) 1967 dir. Harry Levin
V

Hamilton, D.

Ambush Murders, The
FRIES (US) 1982
dir. Steven Hilliard Stern
TV(US)

Bradlee, Jr, B.

America, America
WAR (US) 1964 dir. Elia Kazan
GB title: Anatolian Smile, The

Kazan, E.

Americana
CROWN (US) 1983 dir. David Carradine
V

Robinson, H. M. *Perfect Round, The*

American Christmas Carol, An
SM HEM (US) 1979 dir. Eric Till
TV(US)

Dickens, C. *Christmas Carol, A*

American Dream, An
WAR (US) 1966 dir. Robert Gist
GB title: See You in Hell, Darling
V

Mailer, N.

American Friend, The
CINEGATE (W. Ger) 1977
dir. Wim Wenders
V

Highsmith, P. *Ripley's Game*

American Geisha
INTERSCOPE (US) 1986
dir. Lee Philips
TV(US)

Dalby, L. *Geisha*

American Guerilla in the Philippines, An
TCF (US) 1950 dir. Fritz Lang
GB title: I Shall Return

Wolfert, I.

Americanization of Emily, The
MGM (US) 1964 dir. Arthur Hiller

Huie, W. B.

American Tragedy, An
PAR (US) 1931 dir. Josef von Sternberg

Dreiser, T.

Amityville Horror, The
AIP (US) 1979 dir. Stuart Rosenberg
V

Anson, J.

Amityville II: The Possession
ORION (US) 1982
dir. Damiano Damiani
V

Holzer, H. *Murder in Amityville*

Amongst Barbarians
BBC (GB) 1990 dir. Jane Howell
TV(GB)

Wall, M.

Among the Cinders
NEW WORLD (US) 1985
dir. Rolf Haedrich
V

Shadbolt, M.

L'Amore
TEVERE (It) 1948
dir. Roberto Rossellini

Cocteau, J.
P

Amorous Adventures of Moll Flanders, The
PAR (GB) 1965 dir. Terence Young

Defoe, D. *Fortunes and Misfortunes of the Famous Moll Flanders, The*

Amorous Prawn, The
BL (GB) 1962 dir. Anthony Kimmins
US title: Playgirl and the War Minister, The

Kimmins, A.
P

Amos
BRYNA (US) 1985 dir. Michael Tuchner
TV(US), V

West, S.

Amsterdam Affair
LIP/TRIO/GROUP W (GB) 1968
dir. Gerry O'Hara
V

Freeling, N. *Love in Amsterdam*

Anastasia
FOX (GB) 1956 dir. Anatole Litvak
V
COMPASS (US) 1967
dir. George Schaefer
TV(US)

Maurette, M. & Bolton, G.
P

Anastasia: The Mystery of Anna
TELECOM (US) 1986
dir. Marvin Chomsky
TVSe(US)

Kurth, P. *Anastasia: The Riddle of Anna Anderson*

Anatomy of a Murder
COL (US) 1959 dir. Otto Preminger
V

Traver, R.

Anatomy of an Illness
CBS ENT. (US) 1984
dir. Richard Heffron
TV(US)

Cousins, N.

Anderson Tapes, The
COL (US) 1971 dir. Sidney Lumet
V

Sanders, L.

And I Alone Survived
OSL (US) 1978 dir. William Graham
TV(US), V

Elder, L. and Streshinsky, S.

And Now Miguel
UI (US) 1965 dir. James B. Clark

Krumgold, J.

And Now the Screaming Starts
AMICUS (GB) 1973
dir. Roy Ward Baker
V

Case, D. *Fengriffen*

And Now Tomorrow
PAR (US) 1944 dir. Irving Pichel
Field, R.

And One Was Wonderful
MGM (US) 1940 dir. Robert Sinclair
Miller, A.D.

Androcles and the Lion
RKO (US) 1952 dir. Chester Erskine
V

Shaw, G. B.
P

Andromeda Strain, The
UN (US) 1971 dir. Robert Wise
V

Crichton, M.

And Then There Were None
ABP (US) 1945 dir. Rene Clair
GB title: Ten Little Niggers
V
EMI (GB) 1974 dir. Peter Collinson
Christie, A. *Ten Little Niggers*

And the Sea will Tell
COL (US) 1991 dir. Tommy L. Wallace
TVSe(US)
Bugliosi, V., and Henderson, B. B.

Angel
PAR (US) 1937 dir. Ernest Lubitsch
Lengyel, M.
P

Angel at My Table, An
FINE LINE (Aus) 1991
dir. Jane Campion
Frame, J.

Angel Baby
CONT DIS (US) 1960 dir. Paul Wendkos
Barber, E.O. *Jenny Angel*

Angel City
FAC-NEW (US) 1980 dir. Philip Leacock
TV(US)
Smith, P.

Angel Dusted
NRW (US) 1981 dir. Dick Lowry
TV(US)
Etons, U.

Angele
INTERAMA (FR) 1934
dir. Marcel Pagnol
Giono, J.

Angel from Texas, An
WAR (US) 1940 dir. Ray Enright
Kaufman, G. S. *The Butter and Egg Man*

Angel Heart
TRI-STAR (US) 1987 dir. Alan Parker
V

Hjortsberg, W. *Falling Angel*

Angelique
FRANCOS (Fr/W.Ger/It) 1964
dir. Bernard Borderie
Golon, S.

Angel Levine, The
UA (US) 1970 dir. Jan Kadar
Malamud, B.

Angel Who Pawned Her Harp, The
BL (GB) 1954 dir. Alan Bromly
Terrot, C.

Angel with the Trumpet, The
BL (GB) 1949 dir. Anthony Bushell
Lothar, E.

Angry Harvest
CCC (Ger) 1986 dir. Agneiszka Holland
V

Field, H. and Mierzenski, S.

Angry Hills, The
MGM (GB) 1959 dir. Robert Aldrich
Uris, L.

Animal Crackers
PAR (US) 1930 dir. Victor Heerman
V

Ryskind, M. and Kaufman, G.S.
P

Animal Farm
ABP (GB) 1955 dir. John Halas and Joy Batchelor
A,V
Orwell, G.

Animal Kingdom, The
RKO (US) 1932 dir. Edward H. Griffith
GB title: Woman in His House, The
Barry, P.
P

Anna and the King of Siam
FOX (US) 1946 dir. John Cromwell
Landon, M.

Annabelle's Affairs
FOX (US) 1931 dir. Alfred Werker
Kummer, C. *Good Gracious Annabelle*
P

Anna Christie
MGM (US) 1930 dir. Clarence Brown
V
O'Neill, E. G.
P

Anna Karenina
MGM (US) 1935 dir. Clarence Brown
BL (GB) 1947 dir. Julien Duvivier
RASTAR (US) 1985 dir. Simon Langton
TV(GB/US)
Tolstoy, L. N.

Anna Lucasta
COL UA(US) 1949 dir. Irving Rapper
UA (US) 1958 dir. Arnold Laven
Yordan, P.
P

Anna of the Five Towns
BBC (GB) 1985
TVSe(GB)
Bennett, A.

L'Année des Meduses
AT (Fr) 1987 dir. Christopher Frank
V
Frank, C.

Anne of Green Gables
RKO (US) 1934 dir. George Nicholls
SULLIVAN (GB) 1985
TVSe(GB), V
Montgomery, L. M.

Anne of the Thousand Days
UN (GB) 1969 dir. Charles Jarrot
V
Anderson, M.
P

Anne of Windy Poplars
RKO (US) 1940 dir. Jack Hively
Montgomery, L. M. *Anne of Windy Willows*

Annie
COL (US) 1982 dir. John Huston
M, V
Meehan, T.
P

Annie Get Your Gun
MGM (US) 1950 dir. George Sidney
M
Fields, H. and Fields, D.
P

Annie's Coming Out
ENT (Aust) 1984 dir. Gil Brealey
V
Crossley, R.

Anniversary, The
WAR (GB) 1968 dir. Roy Ward Baker
MacIlwraith, W.
P

Ann Vickers
RKO (US) 1933 dir. John Cromwell
V
Lewis, S.

Another Country
GOLD (GB) 1984 dir. Marek Kanievska
V
Mitchell, J.
P

Another Language
MGM (US) 1933 dir. Edward H. Griffith
Franken, R.
P

Another Man's Poison
EROS (GB) 1951 dir. Irving Rapper
Sands, L. *Deadlock*
P

Another Part of the Forest
UN (US) 1948 dir. Michael Gordon
Hellman, L.F.
P

Another Shore
EAL (GB) 1948 dir. Charles Crichton
Reddin, K.

Another Time, Another Place
PAR (GB) 1958 dir. Lewis Allen
Coffee, L. *Weep No More*

Another Time, Another Place
CINEGATE (GB) 1983
dir. Michael Radford
V
Kesson, J.

Anthony Adverse
WAR (US) 1936 dir. Mervyn Le Roy
V
Allen, H.

Antony and Cleopatra
RANK (GB) 1972 dir. Charlton Heston
V
ITV (GB) 1974 dir. Jon Scoffield
Shakespeare, W.
P

Any Number Can Play
MGM (US) 1949 dir. Mervyn Le Roy
Heth, E. H.

Anything Can Happen
PAR (US) 1952 dir. George Seaton
M
Papashvily, G. and Papashvily, H.

Anything Goes
PAR (US) 1936 dir. Lewis Milestone
M
PAR (US) 1956 dir. Robert Lewis
M
Bolton, G., Wodehouse, P. G.,
Lindsay, H., Crouse, R.
P

Anything to Survive
SABAN/SCHERICK (US) 1990
dir. Zale Dalen
TV(US)
Wortman, E. *Almost Too Late*

Any Wednesday
WAR (US) 1966 dir. Robert Ellis Miller
GB title: Bachelor Girl Apartment
V

Resnik, M.
P

Anzio
PAN (It) 1968 dir. Edward Dmytryk
GB title: Battle for Anzio, The
V

Thomas, W. V.

Apache
UA (US) 1954 dir. Robert Aldrich
V

Wellman, P. I. *Bronco Apache*

Ape, The
MON (US) 1940 dir. William Nigh
V

Shirk, A.
P

Ape and Essence
BBC (GB) 1966 dir. David Benedictus
TV(GB)

Huxley, A.

Appaloosa, The
UN (US) 1968 dir. Sidney J. Furie
GB title: Southwest to Sonora
V

MacLeod, R.

Apple Dumpling Gang, The
DISNEY (US) 1974 dir. Norman Tokar

Bickham, J. M.
Ch, V

Appointment with Death
CANNON (US) 1989
dir. Michael Winner
V

Christie, A.

Appointment with Venus
GFD (GB) 1951 dir. Ralph Thomas
US title: Island Rescue

Tickell, J.

Apprenticeship of Duddy Kravitz, The
RANK (Can) 1974 dir. Ted Kotcheff
V

Richler, M.

April Love
TCF (US) 1957 dir. Henry Levin

Chamberlain, G.A.

April Morning
S GOLD TV (US) 1988
dir. Delbert Mann
TV(US)

Fast, H.

Arabesque
UN (US) 1966 dir. Stanley Donen
V

Votler, G. *The Cipher*

Arch of Triumph
UA (US) 1948 dir. Lewis Milestone
HTV (GB) 1984 dir. Waris Hussein
TV(GB), V

Remarque, E. M.

Are Husbands Necessary?
PAR (US) 1942 dir. Norman Taurog

Rorick, I. S. *Mr and Mrs Cugat*

Aren't Men Beasts!
AB (GB) 1937 dir. Graham Cutts

Sylvaine, V
P

Aren't We All?
PAR (GB) 1932
dir. Harry Lachman & Rudolf Maté

Lonsdale, F.
P

Ashanti

Are You In The House Alone
FRIES PRODS (US) 1978
dir. Walter Grauman
M,TV(US),V
Peck, R. H.

Are You With It?
UN (US) 1948 dir. Jack Hively
M
Perrin, S. and Balzer, G.
P

L'Argent
EOS (Switz/Fr) 1983
dir. Robert Bresson
Tolstoy, L. *False Note, The*

Ariana
UN TV (US) 1989 dir. Paul Krasny
TV(US)
Raab, S.

Arizona
COL (US) 1940 dir. Wesley Ruggles
Kelland, C. B.

Arms And The Man
WARDOUR (GB) 1932 dir. Cecil Lewis
ARGENT (GB) 1982
TV
Shaw, G. B.
P

Around the World in Eighty Days
UA (US) 1956 dir. Michael Anderson, Kevin McClory
HARMONY GOLD (US) 1989
dir. Buzz Kulik
TVSe(US), V
Verne, J.

Arrangement, The
WAR (US) 1969 dir. Elia Kazan
V
Kazan, E.

Arrowhead
PAR (US) 1953
dir. Charles Marquis Warren
Burnett, W. R. *Adobe Walls*

Arrow in the Dust
ABP (US) 1954 dir. Lesley Selander
Foreman, L. L. *Road to San Jacinto*

Arrowsmith
UA (US) 1931 dir. John Ford
V
Lewis, S.

Arsene Lupin
MGM (US) 1932 dir. Jack Conway
LeBlanc. M. and de Croisset, F.
P

Arsenic and Old Lace
WAR (US) 1944 dir. Frank Capra
V
COMPASS (US) 1962
dir. George Schaefer
TV(US)
Kesselring, J. O.
P

Artists in Crime
BBC (GB) 1990 dir. Silvio Narizzano
TV
Marsh, N.

Art of Crime, The
UN TV (US) 1975 dir. Richard Irving
TV(US)
Smith, M. *Gypsy in Amber*

Arturo's Island
MGM (It) 1962 dir. Damiano Damiani
Morante, E.

Ashanti
COL (Switz) 1979 dir. Richard Fleischer
Vasquez-Figueroa, A. *Ebano*

Ashes and Diamonds
POLSKI (Pol) 1958 dir. Andrzej Wajda
V
Andrzejewski, J.

As Husbands Go
FOX (US) 1934 dir. Hamilton McFadden
Crothers, R.
P

As Is
BRANDMAN (US) 1986
dir. Michael Lindsay-Hogg
TV(US)
Hoffman, W. H.
P

Ask Any Girl
MGM (US) 1959 dir. Charles Walters
Wolfe, W.

As Long As They're Happy
GFD (GB) 1955 dir. J. Lee Thompson
Sylvaine, V.
P

Aspen
UN TV (US) 1977 dir. Douglas Heyes
TVSe(US)
Hirschfeld, B.

Aspern
CONN (Port) 1981
dir. Eduardo de Gregorion
James, H. *Aspern Papers, The*

Asphalt Jungle, The
MGM (US) 1950 dir. John Huston
V
Burnett, W. R.

Assassination Bureau, The
PAR (GB) 1969 dir. Basil Dearden
London, J. and Fish, R.

Assault
RANK (GB) 1971 dir. Sidney Hayers
V
Young, K. *Ravine, The*

Assault, The
CANNON (Neth) 1986
dir. Fons Rademakers
Mulisch, H.

Assault and Matrimony
NBC (US) 1987 dir. James Frawley
TV(US)
Anderson, J.

Assault on a Queen
PAR (US) 1966 dir. Jack Donohue
Finney, J.

Assignment in Brittany
MGM (US) 1943 dir. Jack Conway
MacInnes, H.

Assignment 'K'
COL (GB) 1968 dir. Val Guest
Howard, H.

Assignment Paris
COL (US) 1952 dir. Robert Parrish
Gallico, P. *Trial by Terror*

Assisi Underground, The
CANNON (GB) 1985
dir. Alexander Ramati
V
Ramati, A.

As Summers Die
TELEPIC (US) 1986
dir. Jean-Claude Tramont
TV(US)
Groom, W.

As the Earth Turns
WAR (US) 1934 dir. Alfred E. Green
Carroll, G.

Astonished Heart, The
GFD (GB) 1949 dir. Terence Fisher, Anthony Darnborough

Coward, N.
P

As You Desire Me
MGM (US) 1932
dir. George Fitzmaurice

Pirandello, L.
P

As You Like It
FOX (GB) 1936 dir. Paul Czinner
V

Shakespeare, W.
P

At Bertram's Hotel
BBC (GB) 1986 dir. Mary McMurray
TV(GB)

Christie, A.

Atlantic
BI (GB) 1929 dir. E. A. Dupont

Raymond, E. *Berg, The*
P

Atlantis, The Lost Continent
MGM (US) 1961 dir. George Pal

Hargreaves, Sir G.
P

At Mother's Request
VISTA (US) 1987 dir. Michael Tuchner
TVSe(US)

Coleman, J.

At Play in the Fields of the Lord
UN (US) 1991 dir. Hector Babenco

Matthiessen, P.

Attack
UA (US) 1956 dir. Robert Aldrich

Brooks, N. *Fragile Fox*
P

Attack on Fear
TOM (US) 1984 dir. Mel Damski
TV(US)

Mitchell, D., Mitchell, C., Ofshe, R.
Light on Synanon, The

Attack on Terror: The FBI Versus The Ku Klux Klan
WAR TV (US) 1975
dir. Marvin Chomsky
TVSe(US)

Whitehead, D. *Attack on Terror: The FBI Against The Ku Klux Klan inMississippi*

Attempt to Kill
AA (GB) 1961 dir. Royston Murray

Wallace, E. *Lone House Mystery, The*

At the Earth's Core
BL (GB) 1976 dir. Kevin Connor
V

Burroughs, E. R.

At the Villa Rose
AB (GB) 1939 dir. Walter Summers
US title: House of Mystery

Mason, A. E. W.

Attica
ABC (US) 1980 dir. Marvin J. Chomsky
TV(US),V

Wicker, T. *Time to Die, A*

Attic, The: Hiding of Anne Frank, The
TELECOM/YTV (US/GB) 1988
dir. John Erman
TV(GB/US)

Gies, M. and Gold, A. L. *Anne Frank Remembered: The Story of the Woman Who Helped To Hide the Frank Family*

17

At War with the Army
PAR (US) 1951 dir. Hal Walker
V

Allardice, J.
P

Audrey Rose
UA (US) 1977 dir. Robert Wise
V

De Felitta, F.

Aunt Clara
BL (GB) 1954 dir. Anthony Kimmins
Streatfeild, N.

Auntie Mame
WAR (US) 1958 dir. Morton da Costa
V

Dennis, P.

Austeria
POLSKI (Pol) 1988
dir. Jerzy Kawaterowicz
Stryzkowski, J.

Autobiography of Miss Jane Pittman, The
TOM (US) 1974 dir. John Korty
TV(US), V
Gaines, E. J.

Autumn Crocus
BI (GB) 1934 dir. Basil Dearden
Anthony, C.L.
P

Avalanche Express
FOX (Eire) 1979 dir. Mark Robson
V

Forbes, C.

Avanti!
UA (US) 1972 dir. Billy Wilder
V

Taylor, S.
P

Avengers, The
REP (US) 1950 dir. John Auer
Beach, R. E. *Don Careless*

L'Aveu
CORONA (Fr) 1970 dir. Costa-Gavras
London, A. and London, L. *On Trial*

Aviator, The
MGM/UA (US) 1985 dir. George Miller
Gann, E.

Awakening, The
EMI (GB) 1980 dir. Mike Newell
V

Stoker, B. *Jewel of the Seven Stars*

Awakening Land, The
WAR TV (US) 1978 dir. Boris Sagal
TVSe(US)
Richter, C.

Awakenings
COL (US) 1990 dir. Penny Marshall
V

Sacks, O.

Away All Boats
UI (US) 1956 dir. Joseph Pevney
V

Dodson, K.

Awful Truth, The
COL (US) 1937 dir. Leo McCarey
Richman, A.
P

Babbit
WAR (US) 1934 dir. William Keighley

Lewis, S.

Babe
MGM TV (US) 1975 dir. Buzz Kulik
TV(US)

Zaharias, B. D. and Paxton, H. *This Life I've Led: My Autobiography*

Babe Ruth
LYTTLE (US) 1991 dir. Mark Tinker
TV(US)

Cramer, R. W. *Babe: The Legend Comes to Life*

Wagenheim, K. *Babe Ruth, His Life and Legend*

Babette's Feast
DAN FI (Den) 1987 dir. Gabriel Axel

Blixen, K. aka Dinesen, I.

Baby and the Battleship, The
BL (GB) 1956 dir. Jay Lewis
V

Thorne, A.

Baby Doll
WAR (US) 1956 dir. Elia Kazan
V

Williams, T.
P

Baby Love
AVCO (GB) 1969 dir. Alistair Reid
V

Christian, T.C.

Baby, The Rain Must Fall
COL (US) 1965 dir. Robert Mulligan
V

Foote, H. *Travelling Lady, The*
P

Bachelor Flat
TCF (US) 1961 dir. Frank Tashlin

Grossman, B.
P

Bachelor in Paradise
MGM (US) 1961 dir. Jack Arnold

Caspary, V.

Bachelor Party, The
UA (US) 1957 dir. Delbert Mann
V

Chayefsky, P.
P

Back from the Dead
FOX (US) 1957
dir. Charles Marquis Warren

Turney, C. *Other One, The*

Background
ABP (GB) 1953 dir. Daniel Birt
US title: Edge of Divorce

Chetham-Strode, W.
P

Background to Danger
WAR (US) 1943 dir. Raoul Walsh

Ambler, E. *Uncommon Danger*

Back Home
DISNEY (US) 1990 dir. Piers Haggard
TV(US)
Magorian, M.

Backstairs at the White House
FRIENDLY PRODS (US) 1979
dir. Michael O'Herlihy
TVSe(US)
Parks, L.R. *My Thirty Years Backstairs at the White House*

Back Street
UN (US) 1932 dir. John M. Stahl
UN (US) 1941 dir. Robert Stevenson
UN (US) 1961 dir. David Miller
V
Hurst, F.

Back to God's Country
UN (US) 1953 dir. Joseph Pevney
Curwood, J. O.

Bad Day at Black Rock
MGM (US) 1954 dir. John Sturges
Breslin, H. *Bad Time at Honda*

Bad for Each Other
COL (US) 1954 dir. Irving Rapper
McCoy, H.

Bad Little Angel
MGM (US) 1939 dir. William Thiele
Turnbull, M. *Looking After Sandy*

Bad Man, The
MGM (US) 1940 dir. Richard Thorpe
GB title: Two Gun Cupid
Brown, P. E.
P

Bad Medicine
TCF (US) 1985 dir. Harvey Miller
V
Horowitz, S. *Calling Dr. Horowitz*

Bad Men of Tombstone
ABP (US) 1949 dir. Kurt Neumann
Monaghan, J. *Last of the Badmen*

Bad Ronald
LORIMAR (US) 1974 dir. Buzz Kulik
TV(US)
Vance, J. H.

Badge of the Assassin
BLATT/SINGER (US) 1985
dir. Mel Damski
TV(US)
Tannenbaum, R. K. and Rosenberg, P.

Bad Seed, The
WAR (US) 1956 dir. Mervyn Le Roy
V
WAR (US) 1985 dir. Paul Wendkos
TV(US)
March, W.

Bahama Passage
PAR (US) 1941 dir. Edward H. Griffith
Hayes, N. *Dildo Cay*

Bait, The
ABC (US) 1973 dir. Leonard Horn
TV(US)
Uhnak, D.

Baja Oklahoma
HBO (US) 1988 dir. Bobby Roth
TV(US)
Jenkins, D.

Balalaika
MGM (US) 1939 dir. Reinhold Schunzel
Maschwitz, E.
P

Balcony, The
BL (US) 1963 dir. Joseph Strick
Genet, J.
P

Ballad of Gregorio Cortez, The
EMBASSY (US) 1983
dir. Robert M. Young
V

Parades, A. *With a Pistol in His Hand*

Ballad of Narayama
ROEI (Jap) 1983 dir. Shohei Imamura

Fukazawa, S.

Ballad of the Sad Café, The
MERCHANT IVORY/HOBO (US/GB)
1991 dir. Simon Callow

McCullers, C.; Albee, E.
P (only Albee version)

Ballroom of Romance, The
BBC (GB) 1980 dir. Patrick O'Connor
TV

Trevor, W.

Bambi
DISNEY (US) 1942 dir. David Hand
A, Ch

Salten, F.

Banana Ridge
ABP (GB) 1941 dir. Walter C. Mycroft

Travers, B.
P

Bande à Part
ANOUCHKA/ORSAY (Fr) 1964
dir. Jean-Luc Godard

Hitchens, D. and Hitchens, B.
Fool's Gold

Bandit of Sherwood Forest, The
COL (US) 1946
dir. George Sherman/Henry Levin

Castleton, P. A. *Son of Robin Hood*

Band of Angels
WAR (US) 1957 dir. Raoul Walsh

Warren, R. P.

Bang the Drum Slowly
PAR (US) 1973 dir. John Hancock
V

Harris, M.

Banjo on my Knee
TCF (US) 1936 dir. John Cromwell

Hamilton, H.

Bank Shot, The
UA (US) 1974 dir. Gower Champion
V

Westlake, D. E.

Barabbas
COL (It) 1962 dir. Richard Fleischer
V

Lagerkvist, P.

Barbarella
PAR (Fr/It) 1967 dir. Roger Vadim
V

Forest, J-C.

Barbarian, The
MGM (US) 1933 dir. Sam Wood
GB title: Night in Cairo, A

Selwyn, E.
P

Barchester Chronicles, The
BBC (GB) 1982 dir. David Giles
TVSe(GB)

Trollope, A. *Barchester Towers:
Warden, The*

Bare Essence
WAR TV (US) 1982 dir. Walter Grauman
TVSe(US)

Rich, M.

Barefoot in Athens
COMPASS (US) 1966
dir. George Schaefer
TV(US), V

Anderson, M.
P

Barefoot in the Park
PAR (US) 1967 dir. Gene Saks
V

Simon, N.
P

Barefoot Mailman, The
COL (US) 1951 dir. Earl McEvoy

Pratt, T.

Baroness and the Butler, The
FOX (US) 1938 dir. Walter Lang

Bus-Fekete, L. *Lady Has a Heart, A*
P

Baron Munchhausen
CESK (Czech) 1962 dir. Karel Zeman

Burger, G.

Barretts of Wimpole Street, The
MGM (US) 1934 dir. Sidney Franklin
MGM (US) 1956 dir. Sidney Franklin

Besier, R.
P

Barry Lyndon
WAR/HAWK (GB) 1975
dir. Stanley Kubrick
V

Thackeray, W. M.

Bas-Fonds, Les
ALB (Fr) 1936 dir. Jean Renoir

Gorky, M.
P

Bastard, The
UN TV (US) 1978 dir. Lee Katzin
TVSe(US)

Jakes, J.

Bat, The
ALLIED (US) 1959 dir. Crane Wilbur
V

Rinehart, M. R.
P

Bates Motel
UN TV (US) 1987 dir. Richard Rothstein
TV(US)

Bloch, R. *Psycho*

Battle, The
GAU (Fr) 1934 dir. Nicolas Farkas

Farrere, C.

Battle Cry
WAR (US) 1954 dir. Raoul Walsh
V

Uris, L.

Battle of Britain
UA (GB) 1969 dir. Guy Hamilton
V

Wood, D. and Dempster, D. *Narrow Margin, The*

Battle of the River Plate, The
RANK (GB) 1956 dir. Michael Powell
and Emeric Pressburger
US title: Pursuit of the Graf Spee
V

Powell, M. *Graf Spee*

Battle of the Sexes, The
PROM (GB) 1960 dir. Charles Crichton

Thurber, J. *Catbird Seat, The*

Battle of the V1
MAY-SEW (GB) 1958 dir. Vernon Sewell
US title: Unseen Heroes

Newman, B.

Battle of Villa Fiorita, The
WAR (GB) 1964 dir. Delmer Daves
US title: Affair at the Villa Fiorita
Godden, R.

BAT 21
TRI STAR (US) 1988 dir. Peter Markle
V
Angerson, W. C.

Bat Whispers, The
UA (US) 1930 dir. Roland West
Rinehart, M. R. *Bat, The*
P

Bawdy Adventures of Tom Jones, The
UN (GB) 1976 dir. Cliff Owen
M, V
Fielding, H. *History of Tom Jones, A; Foundling, The*

Baxter!
EMI (GB) 1972 dir. Lionel Jeffries
Ch
Platt, K. *Boy Who Could Make Himself Disappear, The*

Beachcomber, The
GFD (GB) 1954 dir. Muriel Box
Maugham, W.S. *Vessel of Wrath*

Beaches
TOUCH (US) 1988 dir. Garry Marshall
V
Dart, I. R.

Beachhead
UA (US) 1954 dir. Stuart Heisler
Hubler, R. G. *I've Got Mine*

Bear, The
TRI-STAR (Fr) 1989
dir. Jean-Jacques Annaud
Curwood, J. O. *Grizzly King, The*

Bear Island
COL (Can/GB) 1979 dir. Don Sharp
V
MacLean, A.

Bears and I, The
DISNEY (US) 1974
dir. Bernard McEveety
Ch, V
Leslie, R. F.

Beast, The
COL (US) 1988 dir. Kevin Reynolds
Mastrosimone, W. *Nanawatai*
P

Beast From 20,000 Fathoms, The
WAR (US) 1953 dir. Eugene Lourie
Bradbury, R. *Foghorn, The*

Beast with Five Fingers, The
WAR (US) 1946 dir. Robert Florey
V
Harvey, W. F.

Beast Within, The
MGM/UA (US) 1982 dir. Philippe Mora
V
Levy, E.

Beat the Devil
ROMULUS (GB) 1953 dir. John Huston
V
Helvick, J.

Beau Brummell
MGM (GB) 1954 dir. Curtis Bernhardt
Fitch, C.
P

Beau Geste
PAR (US) 1939 dir. William A. Wellman
V
UI (US) 1966 dir. Douglas Heyes
V
BBC (GB) 1984
TVSe(GB)
Wren, P. C.

Beau Ideal
RKO (US) 1931 dir. Herbert Brenon
Wren, P. C.

Beau James
PAR (US) 1957 dir. Melville Shavelson
Fowler, G.

Beauty and the Beast
LOPERT (Fr) 1947 dir. Jean Cocteau
V
PALM (US) 1976 dir. Fielder Cook
TV(US)
CANNON (US) 1987
dir. Eugene Marner
DISNEY (US) 1991
dir. Gary Trousdale, Kirk Wise
A, Ch, M
de Villeneuve, Mme.

Beauty for Sale
MGM (US) 1933
dir. Richard Boleslawski
Baldwin, F. *Beauty*

Because They're Young
COL (US) 1960 dir. Paul Wendkos
Farris, J. *Harrison High*

Becket
PAR (GB) 1963 dir. Peter Glenville
V
Anouilh, J.
P

Becky Sharp
RKO (US) 1935 dir. Rouben Mamoulian
V
Thackeray, W. M. *Vanity Fair*

Bedelia
GFD (GB) 1946 dir. Lance Comfort
Caspary, V.

Bedford Incident, The
COL (GB) 1965 dir. James B. Harris
V
Rascovich, M.

Bedknobs and Broomsticks
DISNEY (US) 1971
dir. Robert Stevenson
Ch, V
Norton, M. *Bed-Knob and Broomstick*

Bed of Lies
WOLPER TV(US) 1992
dir. William A. Graham
Salerno, S. *Deadly Blessing*

Bedroom Window, The
DELAUR (US) 1987 dir. Curtis Hanson
Holden, A. *Witness, The*

Bed Sitting Room, The
UA (GB) 1969 dir. Richard Lester
Milligan, S. and Antrobus, J.
P

Bedtime Story, A
PAR (US) 1933 dir. Norman Taurog
Horniman, R. *Bellamy the Magnificent*

Beecham
YTV (GB) 1990 dir. Vernon Lawrence
TV(GB)
Brahms, C. and Sherrin, N.

Before Winter Comes
COL (GB) 1968 dir. J. Lee Thompson
Keefe, F. L. *Interpreter, The*

Beggarman, Thief
UN TV (US) 1979 dir. Lawrence Doheny
TVSe(US)

Shaw, I.

Beggars of Life
PAR (US) 1928 dir. William Wellman

Tully, J.

Beggar's Opera, The
BL (GB) 1952 dir. Peter Brook
M, V

Gay, J.
P

Beggar's Opera, The
BARRANDOV (Czech) 1991
dir. Jiri Menzel

Gay, J.
P

Havel, V.
P

Beguiled, The
UN (US) 1971 dir. Don Siegel
V

Cullinan, T. *Bedeviled, The*

Behind that Curtain
FOX (US) 1929 dir. Irving Cummings

Biggers, E. D.

Behind the Headlines
RANK (GB) 1956 dir. Charles Saunders

Chapman, R.

Behind the Mask
BL (GB) 1958 dir. Brian Desmond Hurst

Wilson, J. R. *Pack, The*

Behind the Rising Sun
RKO (US) 1943 dir. Edward Dmytryk
V

Young, J. R.

Behold a Pale Horse
COL (US) 1964 dir. Fred Zinnemann
V

Pressburger, E. *Killing a Mouse on Sunday*

Behold my Wife
PAR (US) 1934 dir. Mitchell Leisen

Parker, G. *Translation of a Savage, The*

Being There
LORIMAR (US) 1979 dir. Hal Ashby
V

Kosinski, J.

Bejewelled
DISNEY CH (US/GB) 1991
dir. Terry Marcel
TV(GB/US)

Babson, M. *Bejewelled Death*

Believers, The
ORION (US) 1987 dir. John Schlesinger
V

Conde, N. *Religion, The*

Bell, The
BBC (GB) 1982 dir. Barry Davis
TV

Murdoch, I.

Belladonna
OLY (GB) 1934 dir. Robert Milton

Hichens, R.

Bell'Antonio, Il
CINA (It/Fr) 1960 dir. Piero Piccioni

Brancati, V.

Bell, Book and Candle
COL (US) 1958 dir. Richard Quine
V

Druten, J. van
P

Belle de Jour
CURZON (Fr/It) 1967 dir. Luis Bunuel
Kessel, J.

Belle Noiseuse, La
FR3 (Fr) 1991 dir. Jacques Rivette
de Balzac, H.

Belle of New York, The
MGM (US) 1952 dir. Charles Walters
M, V
McLellan, C. M. S. and Morton, H.
P

Bell for Adano, A
FOX (US) 1945 dir. Henry King
Hayward (US) 1967 dir. Mel Ferber
TV(US)
Hersey, J. R.

Bell Jar, The
AVCO (US) 1979 dir. Larry Peerce
V
Plath, S.

Bellman and True
HANDMADE (GB) 1987
dir. Richard Loncraine
V
Lowden, D.

Bells are Ringing
MGM (US) 1960 dir. Vincente Minnelli
M, V
Comden, B. and Green, A.
P

Belles on Their Toes
FOX (US) 1952 dir. Henry Levin
Gilbreth, Jr., F. B. and Carey, E.

Beloved Bachelor, The
PAR (US) 1931 dir. Lloyd Corrigan
Peple, E. H.
P

Beloved Infidel
FOX (US) 1959 dir. Henry King
Graham, S. and Frank, G.

Beloved Vagabond, The
COL (GB) 1936 dir. Curtis Bernhardt
Locke, W. J.

Below the Belt
ATLANTIC (US) 1982
dir. Robert Fowler
V
Drexler, R. *To Smithereens*

Belstone Fox, The
RANK (GB) 1973 dir. James Hill
V
Rook, D. *Ballad of the Belstone Fox, The*

Bend of the River
UI (US) 1952 dir. Anthony Mann
GB title: Where the River Bends
V
Gulick, W. *Bend of the Snake*

Bengal Brigade
UI (US) 1954 dir. Laslo Benedek
GB title: Bengal Rifles
Hunter, H. *Bengal Tiger*

Ben Hur
MGM (US) 1926 dir. Fred Niblo
MGM (US) 1959 dir. William Wyler
V
Wallace, L.

Benvenuta
NI (Bel/Fr) 1982 dir. André Delvaux
Lilar, S. *Confession Anonyme La*

Bequest to the Nation
UN (GB) 1973 dir. James Cellan Jones
Rattigan, T.
P

Berkeley Square
FOX (US) 1933 dir. Frank Lloyd
MILBERG (US) 1959
dir. George Schaefer
TV(US)

Balderston, J. L.
P

Berlin Affair, The
CANNON (It/Ger) 1985
dir. Liliana Cavani
V

Tanizaki, J. *Buddhist Cross, The*

Berlin Alexanderplatz
TELECUL/CH 4 (Fr/GB) 1985
dir. RainerWernerFassbinder
TVSe(Fr/GB)

Doblin, A.

Berlin, Tunnel 21
FILMWAYS (US) 1981
dir. Richard Michaels
TV(US), V

Lindquist, D.

Bernardine
FOX (US) 1957 dir. Henry Levin

Chase, M.
P

Best Defense
PAR (US) 1984 dir. Willard Huyck

Grossbach, R. *Easy and Hard Ways Out*

Best Foot Forward
MGM (US) 1943 dir. Edward Buzzell
M, V

Holmes, J. C.
P

Best Little Girl in the World, The
A. SPELLING (US) 1981
dir. Sam O'Steen
TV(US)

Levenkron, S.

Best Little Whorehouse in Texas
UN (US) 1982 dir. Colin Higgins
M, V

King, L. L. and Masterson, P.
P

Best Man, The
UA (US) 1964 dir. Franklin Schaffner

Vidal, G.
P

Best Man Wins, The
COL (US) 1934 dir. Erle C. Kenton
V

Kohn, B. G.

Best of Everything, The
FOX (US) 1959 dir. Jean Negulesco

Jaffe, R.

Best Place To Be, The
R. HUNTER (US) 1979 dir. David Miller
TVSe(US)

van Slyke, H.

Best Years of Our Lives, The
GOLDWYN (US) 1946
dir. William Wyler
V

Kantor, M. *Glory for Me*

Bête Humaine, La
PARIS (Fr) 1938 dir. Jean Renoir
V

Zola, E.

Betrayal
VIRGIN (GB) 1982 dir. David Jones
V

Pinter, H.
P

Betrayal
METRO (US) 1974 dir. Gordon Hessler
TV(US)
Disney, D. M. *Only Couples Need Apply*

Betrayal
EMI TV (US) 1978 dir. Paul Wendkos
TV(US), V

Freeman, L. and Roy, J.

Betrayal from the East
RKO (US) 1945 dir. William Beake
Hynd, A.

Betsy, The
UA (US) 1978 dir. Daniel Petrie
V

Robbins, H.

Betty
MK2 (Fr) 1992 dir. Claude Chabrol
Simenon, G.

Betty Blue
GAU (Fr) 1986 dir. Jean-Jacques Beineix
V

Dijan, P. *372 Le Matin*

Betty Ford Story, The
WAR TV (US) 1987 dir. David Greene
TV(US)
Ford, B. and Chase, C. *Times Of My Life, The*

Between Friends
HBO (US) 1983 dir. Lou Antonio
V

List, S. *Nobody Makes Me Cry*

Between Heaven and Hell
FOX (US) 1956 dir. Richard Fleischer
Gwaltney, F. I. *Day the Century Ended, The*

Between Two Women
J. AVNET (US) 1986 dir. Jon Avnet
TV(US)
Martin, G. *Living Arrows*

Between Two Worlds
WAR (US) 1944 dir. Edward A. Blatt
Vane, S. *Outward Bound*
P

Between Us Girls
UN (US) 1942 dir. Henry Koster
Gignoux, R. *Le Fruit Vert*
P

Beulah Land
COL TV (US) 1980 dir. Virgil Vogel, Harry Falk
TVSe(US)
Coleman, L.

Beware My Lovely
RKO (US) 1952 dir. Harry Horner
Dineli, M. *Man, The*
P

Beware of Pity
TC (GB) 1946 dir. Maurice Elvey
Zweig, S.

Beyond Mombasa
COL (GB) 1955 dir. George Marshall
Eastwood, J. *Mark of the Leopard*

Beyond Reasonable Doubt
J & M (NZ) 1980 dir. John Laing
V

Yallop, D.

Beyond the Curtain
RANK (GB) 1960 dir. Compton Bennett
Wallis, A. J. and Blair, C. E.
Thunder Above

Beyond the Forest
WAR (US) 1949 dir. King Vidor
Engstrandt, S. D.

Beyond Therapy
NEW WORLD (US) 1987
dir. Robert Altman
V
Durang, C.
P

Beyond the Reef
UN (US) 1981 dir. Frank C. Clark
Richer, C. *Tikoyo and his Shark*

Beyond this Place
REN (GB) 1959 dir. Jack Cardiff
Cronin, A. J.

B.F.'s Daughter
MGM (US) 1948 dir. Robert Z. Leonard
Marquand, J. P.

Bhowani Junction
MGM (GB) 1955 dir. George Cukor
Masters, J.

Bicycle Thief, The
MGM (It) 1949 dir. Vittorio de Sica
V
Bartolini, L.

Big Boodle, The
UA (US) 1957 dir. Richard Wilson
GB title: Night in Havana
Sylvester, R.

Big Bounce, The
WAR (US) 1969 dir. Alex March
Leonard, E.

Big Broadcast, The
PAR (US) 1932 dir. Frank Tuttle
Manley, W. F. *Wild Waves*

Big City, The
R. D. BANSAL (Ind) 1963
dir. Satyajit Ray
Mitra, N. M.

Big Clock, The
PAR (US) 1947 dir. John Farrow
Fearing, K.

Big Country, The
UA (US) 1958 dir. William Wyler
V
Hamilton, D.

Big Fella
FORTUNE (GB) 1937 dir. J. E. Wills
McKay, C. *Banjo*

Big Fisherman, The
CENT (US) 1959 dir. Frank Borzage
Douglas, L. C.

Big Fix, The
UN (US) 1978 dir. Jeremy Paul Kagan
V
Simon, R. L.

Big Hand for the Little Lady, A
WAR (US) 1966 dir. Fielder Cook
GB title: Big Deal at Dodge City
Carroll, S.
P

Big Heat, The
COL (US) 1953 dir. Fritz Lang
V
McGivern, W. P.

Big Knife, The
UA (US) 1955 dir. Robert Aldrich
Odets, C.
P

Big Land, The
WAR (US) 1957 dir. Gordon Douglas
GB title: Stampeded
V
Gruber, F. *Buffalo Grass*

Big Man, The
PALACE (GB) 1990 dir. David Leland
McIlvanney, W.

Big Night, The
UA (US) 1951 dir. Joseph Losey
Ellin, S. *Dreadful Summit*

Big Pond, The
PAR (US) 1930 dir. Hobart Henley
Middleton, G. and Thomas, A. E.
P

Big Red
DISNEY (US) 1962 dir. Norman Tokar
A, Ch, V
Kjelgaard, J. A.

Big Sky, The
RKO (US) 1952 dir. Howard Hawks
V
Guthrie, A. B.

Big Sleep, The
WAR (US) 1946 dir. Howard Hawks
V
ITC (GB) 1977 dir. Michael Winner
Chandler, R.

Big Street, The
RKO (US) 1942 dir. Irving Reis
V
Runyon, D. *Little Pinks*

Big Town, The
COL (US) 1987 dir. Ben Bolt
Howard, C. *The Arm*

Billie
UA (US) 1965 dir. Don Weis
Alexander, R. *Time Out for Ginger*
P

Billionaire Boys Club, The
ITC (US) 1987 dir. Marvin Chomsky
TVSe(US)
Horton, S.

Billion Dollar Brain
UA (GB) 1967 dir. Ken Russell
V
Deighton, L.

Bill of Divorcement, A
RKO (US) 1932 dir. George Cukor
RKO (US) 1940 dir. John Farrow
GB title: Never to Love
V
Dane, C.
P

Billy Bathgate
TOUCH (US) 1991 dir. Robert Benton
Doctorow, E. L.

Billy Budd
AAL (GB) 1962 dir. Peter Ustinov
V
Melville, H.

Billy Liar
WAR (GB) 1963 dir. John Schlesinger
V
Waterhouse, K

Billy: Portrait of a Street Kid
CARLINER (US) 1977
dir. Steven Gethers
TV(US), V
Downs, R. C. S. *Peoples*

Billy the Kid
MGM (US) 1930 dir. King Vidor
MGM (US) 1941 dir. David Millar

Burns, W. N. *Saga of Billy the Kid, The*

Biloxi Blues
UN (US) 1988 dir. Mike Nichols
V

Simon, N.
P

Bingo
BBC (GB) 1990 dir. Don Taylor
TV

Bond, E.

Bingo Long Travelling All-Stars and Motor Kings, The
UN (US) 1976 dir. John Badham
V

Brashler, W.

Biography (of a Bachelor Girl)
MGM (US) 1935 dir. Edward H. Griffith

Behrman, S. N. *Biography*
P

Birch Interval
GAMMA III (US) 1976
dir. Delbert Mann

Crawford, J.

Birdman of Alcatraz
UA (US) 1961 dir. John Frankenheimer

Gaddis, T. E.

Birds, The
UN (US) 1963 dir. Alfred Hitchcock
V

Du Maurier, D.

Birdy
TRI-STAR (US) 1984 dir. Alan Parker
V

Wharton, W.

Birthday Party, The
CINERAMA (GB) 1968
dir. William Friedkin
V
BBC (GB) 1988
TV

Pinter, H.
P

Bishop Misbehaves, The
MGM (US) 1935 dir. E. A. Dupont
GB title: Bishop's Misadventures, The

Jackson, F.
P

Bishop Murder Case, The
MGM (US) 1930 dir. Nick Grinde and
David Burton

van Dine, S. S.

Bishop's Wife, The
RKO (US) 1947 dir. Henry Koster
V

Nathan, R. *In Barley Fields*

Bitch, The
BW (GB) 1979 dir. Gerry O'Hara
V

Collins, J.

Bitter Harvest
RANK (GB) 1963
dir. Peter Graham Scott
V

Hamilton, P. *Street Has a Thousand Eyes, The*

Bitter Harvest
FRIES (US) 1981 dir. Roger Young
TV(US)

Halbert, F. and Halbert, S.

Bitter Sweet
UA (GB) 1933 dir. Herbert Wilcox
MGM (US) 1940 dir. W. S. Van Dyke II
M

Coward, N.
P

Bitter Tea of General Yen, The
COL (US) 1932 dir. Frank Capra
Stone, Mrs G.

Black Aces
UN (US) 1937 dir. Buck Jones
Payne, S.

Black Angel
UN (US) 1946 dir. Roy William Neill
Woolrich, C.

Black Arrow
COL (US) 1948 dir. Gordon Douglas
GB title: Black Arrow Strikes, The
TOWER (US) 1985 dir. John Hough
TV(US/GB), V

Stevenson, R. L.

Blackbeard's Ghost
DISNEY (US) 1968
dir. Robert Stevenson
V, Ch

Stahl, B.

Black Beauty
FOX (US) 1946 dir. Max Nosseck
TIGON (GB) 1971 dir. James Hill
UN (US) 1978 dir. Daniel Haller
Ch, TVSe(US)

Sewell, A.

Blackboard Jungle, The
MGM (US) 1955 dir. Richard Brooks
Hunter, E.

Black Camel
FOX (US) 1931
dir. Hamilton-MacFadden
Biggers, E. D.

Black Candle, The
TYNE-TEES (GB) 1991
dir. Roy Battersby
TV

Cookson, C.

Black Cauldron, The
DISNEY (US) 1985 dirs. Ted Berman
and Richard Rich
A, Ch

Alexander, L. *Chronicles of Prydain, The*

Black Eye
WAR (US) 1974 dir. Jack Arnold
Jacks, J. *Murder on the Wild Side*

Black Fury
WAR (US) 1935 dir. Michael Curtiz
V

Irving, H. R. *Bohunk*
P

Black Jack
ENT (GB) 1979 dir. Kenneth Loach
V

Garfield, L.

Black Joy
WINCAST/WEST ONE (GB) 1977
dir. Anthony Simmons
Ali, J. *Dark Days and Light Nights*
P

Black Limelight
ABPC (GB) 1938 dir. Paul Stein
Sherry, G.
P

Black Magic
UA (US) 1949 dir. Gregory Ratoff
Dumas, A. *Memoirs of a Physician*

Blackmail
BI (GB) 1929 dir. Alfred Hitchcock
V

Bennett, C.
P

Blackmailed
GFD (US) 1950 dir. Marc Allegret

Myers, E. *Mrs Christopher*

Black Marble, The
AVCO EMBASSY (US) 1980
dir. Harold Becker
V

Wambaugh, J.

Black Market Baby
BRUT (US) 1977 dir. Robert Day
GB title: Don't Steal My Baby
TV(US)

Christman, E. *Nice Italian Girl, A*

Black Narcissus
ARC (GB) 1946 dir. Michael Powell
V

Godden, R.

Black Rain
ART EYE (Jap) 1988
dir. Shohei Imamura

Ibuse, M.

Black Robe
ALLIANCE (Can/Aust) 1991
dir. Bruce Beresford

Moore, B.

Black Rose, The
FOX (US) 1950 dir. Henry Hathaway

Costain, T. B.

Black Shield of Falworth, The
UI (US) 1954 dir. Rudolph Maté

Pyle, H. *Men of Iron*

Black Stallion, The
UA (US) 1979 dir. Carroll Ballard
Ch, V

Farley, W.

Black Stallion Returns, The
MGM (US) 1983 dir. Robert Dalva
Ch, V

Farley, W.

Black Sunday
PAR (US) 1977 dir. John Frankenheimer
V

Harris, T.

Black Swan, The
FOX (US) 1942 dir. Henry King

Sabatini, R.

Black Tower, The
ANGLIA (GB) 1985
TVSe(GB)

James, P. D.

Black Tulip, The
CINERAMA (Fr) 1963
dir. Christian-Jaque
V

Dumas, A.

Black Velvet Gown, The
TYNE-TEES (GB) 1991
dir. Norman Stone
TV

Cookson, C.

Black Widow
FOX (US) 1954 dir. Nunnally Johnson

Quentin, P. *Fatal Woman*

Black Windmill, The
PAR (GB) 1974 dir. Don Siegel
V

Egleton, C. *Seven Days to a Killing*

Blade Runner
WAR (US) 1982 dir. Ridley Scott
V

Dick, P. K. *Do Androids Dream of Electric Sheep?*

Blanche
TELEPRESSE (Fr) 1971
dir. Walerian Borowczyk
Slowacki, J. *Mazepa*

Blanche Fury
CIN (GB) 1948 dir. Marc Allégret
Shearing, J.

Blaze
TOUCHSTONE (US) 1989
dir. Ron Shelton
Starr, B. and Perry, H. *Blaze Starr: My Life as Told to Huey Perry*

Blaze of Noon
PAR (US) 1947 dir. John Farrow
Gann, E. K.

Bleak House
BBC (GB) 1985 dir. Ross Devenish
TVSe(GB), V
Dickens, C.

Blessed Event
WAR (US) 1932 dir. Roy del Ruth
Seff, M. and Wilson, F.
P

Bless the Beasts and Children
COL (US) 1971 dir. Stanley Kramer
V
Swarthout, G.

Blind Alley
COL (US) 1939 dir. Charles Vidor
Warwick, J.
P

Blind Ambition
TIME-LIFE (US) 1979
dir. George Schaefer
TVSe(US)
Dean, J.
Dean, M. *Mo: A Woman's View of Watergate*

Blind Date
RANK (GB) 1959 dir. Joseph Losey
US title: Chance Meeting
V
Howard, L.

Blinded by the Light
TIME-LIFE (US) 1980
dir. John A. Alonzo
TV(US), V
Brancato, R. F.

Blind Faith
NBC (US) 1990 dir. Paul Wendkos
TVSe(US)
McGinniss, J.

Blindfold
UI (US) 1965 dir. Philip Dunne
Fletcher, L.

Blind Goddess, The
FOX (GB) 1947 dir. Harold French
Hastings, Sir P.
P

Bliss
NSW (Aust) 1984 dir. Ray Lawrence
V
Carey, P.

Blithe Spirit
CIN (GB) 1945 dir. David Lean
COMPASS (US) 1966
dir. George Schaefer
TV(US)
Coward, N.
P

Blockhouse, The
GALACTUS (GB) 1973 dir. Clive Rees
V
Clebert, J. P. *Blockhaus, Le*

Blondes for Danger
WILCOX (GB) 1938 dir. Jack Raymond
Price, E. *Red for Danger*

Blood Alley
WAR (US) 1955 dir. William Wellman
Fleischman, A. S.

Blood and Orchids
LORIMAR (US) 1986 dir. Jerry Thorpe
TVSe(US)
Katkov, N.

Blood and Sand
FOX (US) 1941 dir. Rouben Mamoulian
Ibanez, V. B.

Bloodbrothers
WAR (US) 1978 dir. Robert Mulligan
V
Price, R.

Blood from the Mummy's Tomb
MGM-EMI (GB) 1971 dir. Seth Holt
V
Stoker, B. *Jewel of the Seven Stars*

Bloodhounds of Broadway
FOX (US) 1952 dir. Harmon Jones
COL (US) 1989 dir. Howard Brookner
Runyon, D.

Blood Hunt
BBC (GB) 1986
TV(GB)
Gunn, N.

Bloodline
PAR (US) 1979 dir. Terence Young
V
Sheldon, S.

Blood of Others, The
HBO PREMIERE (Can/Fr) 1984 dir. Claude Chabrol
TV,V
De Beauvoir, S.

Blood on the Moon
RKO (US) 1948 dir. Robert Wise
V
Short, L *Gunman's Choice*

Blood Red Roses
CHANNEL 4 (GB) 1987
TVSe(GB)
McGrath, J.

Blood Relatives
FILMCORD (Can/Fr) 1981 dir. Claude Chabrol
McBain, E.

Blood Rights
BBC (GB) 1991 dir. Leslie Manning
TV(GB)
Phillips, M.

Blood Sport
DLT (US) 1989 dir. Harvey Hart
TV(US)
Francis, D.

Blood Wedding
LIBRA (Sp) 1981 dir. Carlos Saura
V
Lorca, F. G.
P

Blott on the Landscape
BBC (GB) 1985 dir. Roger Bamford
TVSe(GB)
Sharpe, T.

Blue and the Gray, The
COL TV (US) 1982
dir. Andrew McLaglen
TVSe(US), V
Catton, B.

Blue Angel, The
PAR (Ger) 1930 dir. Josef von Sternberg
FOX (US) 1959 dir. Edward Dmytryk
V
Mann, H. *Professor Unrath*

Bluebeard's Eighth Wife
PAR (US) 1938 dir. Ernst Lubitsch
Savoir, A.
P

Bluebell
BBC (GB) 1986
TVSe(GB)
Perry, G.

Blue Bird, The
FOX (US) 1940 dir. Walter Lane
FOX (US/Rus) 1976 dir. George Cukor
V
Maeterlinck, M.
P

Blue Blood
MIQ (GB) 1973 dir. Andrew Sinclair
V
Thynne, A. *Carry Cot, The*

Blue City
PAR (US) 1986 dir. Michelle Manning
MacDonald, R.

Blue Denim
TCF (US) 1959 dir. Philip Dunne
GB title: Blue Jeans
Herlihy, J. L. and Noble, W.
P

Blue Fin
S. AUS (Aus) 1978 dir. Carl Schultz
V
Thiele, C.

Bluegrass
LAN (US) 1988 dir. Simon Wincer
TVSe(US)
Deal, B.

Blue Knight, The
LORIMAR (US) 1973 dir. Robert Butler
TVSe(US)
Wambaugh, J.

Blue Lagoon, The
GFD (GB) 1949 dir. Frank Launder
COL (US) 1980 dir. Randal Kleiser
V
Stacpoole, H. D.

Blue Max, The
FOX (US) 1966 dir. John Guillermin
V
Hunter, J. D.

Blues in the Night
WAR (US) 1941 dir. Anatole Litvak
Gilbert, E. *Hot Nocturne*
P

Boat, The
COL (Ger) 1981 dir. Wolfgang Petersen
V
Buchheim, L-G.

Bobby Deerfield
WAR (US) 1977 dir. Sydney Pollack
V
Remarque, E. M. *Heaven has no Favourites*

Bobo, The
WAR (US) 1978 dir. Robert Parrish
V
Cole, B. *Olimpia*

Body in the Library, The
BBC (GB) 1984 dir. George Gallaccio
TV(GB)
Christie, A.

Body Parts
PAR (US) 1991 dir. Eric Red
Boileau, P. and Narcejac, T. *Choice Cuts*

Body Snatcher, The
RKO (US) 1945 dir. Robert Wise
V
Stevenson, R. L.

Boeing-Boeing
PAR (US) 1965 dir. John Rich
Camoletti, M.
P

Bofors Gun, The
RANK (GB) 1968 dir. Jack Gold
McGrath, J. *Events whilst Guarding the Bofors Gun*
P

Bogie
FRIES (US) 1980 dir. Vincent Sherman
TV(US)
Hyams, J.

Bohème, La
NEW YORKER/ERATO (Fr/It) 1989 dir. Leo Conencini
M
Puccini, G.

Bohemian Life
FILMS A2/PYRAMIDE PRODS. (Fr) 1992 dir. Aki Kaurismaki
Murger, H. *Scènes de la Vie Bohème*

Bomb, The
CHANNEL 4 (Ger) 1987 dir. H. C. Gorlitz
Molin, L.

Bombay Mail
UN (US) 1933 dir. Edwin L. Martin
Blochman, L. G.

Bombshell
MGM (US) 1933 dir. Victor Fleming
GB title: Blonde Bombshell
Franke, C. and Crane, M.
P

Bonfire of the Vanities, The
WAR (US) 1990 dir. Brian De Palma
V
Wolfe, T.

Bonjour Tristesse
COL (GB) 1957 dir. Otto Preminger
V
Sagan, F.

Bonne Soupe, La
BELSTAR (Fr/It) 1963 dir. Robert Thomas
Marceau, F.
P

Bon Voyage
DISNEY (US) 1962 dir. James Neilson
V
Hayes, M. and Hayes, J. A.

Bon Voyage
BBC (GB) 1985 dir. Mike Vardy
TV, V
Coward, N.

Boom!
UI (GB) 1968 dir. Joseph Losey
Williams, T. *Milk Train Doesn't Stop Here Anymore, The*
P

Boost, The
HEMDALE (US) 1988 dir. Harold Becker
Stein, B. *Ludes*

Bordertown
WAR (US) 1934 dir. Archie Mayo

Graham, C.

Born Again
AVCO (US) 1978 dir. Irving Rapper
V

Colson, C.

Born Free
COL (GB) 1965 dir. James Hill
V

Adamson, J.

Born on the Fourth of July
UN (US) 1989 dir. Oliver Stone

Kovic, R.

Born Reckless
FOX (US) 1930 dir. John Ford

Clarke, D. H. *Louis Beretti*

Born to be Bad
RKO (US) 1950 dir. Nicholas Ray
V

Parrish, A. *All Kneeling*

Born to be Sold
SAMUELS (US) 1981
dir. Burt Brinckerhoff
TV(US)

McTaggart, L. *Baby Brokers, The*

Born to Kill
RKO (US) 1947 dir. Robert Wise
GB title: Lady of Deceit
V

Gunn, J. E. *Deadlier than the Male*

Born Yesterday
COL (US) 1950 dir. George Cukor
V
MILBERG (US) 1956 dir. Garson Kanin
TV (US)

Kanin, G.
P

Borrowers, The
FOX TV (US) 1973 dir. Walter C. Miller
Ch, TV(US)

Norton, M.

Bostonians, The
RANK (GB) 1984 dir. James Ivory
V

James, H.

Boston Strangler, The
FOX (US) 1968 dir. Richard Fleischer
V

Frank, G.

Botany Bay
PAR (US) 1952 dir. John Farrow
V

Nordhoff, C. and Hall, J. N.

Bottom of the Bottle, The
TCF (US) 1956 dir. Henry Hathaway
GB title: Beyond the River

Simenon, G.

Boudu Sauvé des Eaux
M. SIMON (Fr) 1932 dir. Jean Renoir
V

Fauchois, R.
P

Bought
WAR (US) 1931 dir. Archie Mayo

Henry, H. *Jackdaws Strut*

Bound for Glory
UA (US) 1976 dir. Hal Ashby
V

Guthrie, W.

Bounty, The
ORION (GB) 1984 dir. Roger Donaldson
V

Hough, R. *Captain Bligh and Mr Christian*

Bouquet of Barbed Wire
LWT (GB) 1976 dir. Tony Wharmby
TVSe(GB), V
Newman, A.

Bourne Identity, The
WAR TV (US) 1988 dir. Roger Young
TVSe(US)
Ludlum, R.

Boxer and Death, The
(Czech/Ger) 1962 dir. Peter Solan
V
Hen, Jozef

Box of Delights, The
BBC 1984 dir. Renny Rye
Ch, TVSe(GB), V
Masefield, J.

Boyd's Shop
RANK (GB) 1960 dir. Henry Cass
Ervine, St. J. G.
P

Boy Friend, The
MGM (GB) 1971 dir. Ken Russell
M, V
Wilson, S.
P

Boy in the Bush, The
CHANNEL 4 (GB) 1984
dir. Rob Stewart
TV(GB)
Lawrence, D. H. and Skinner, M. L.

Boy Meets Girl
WAR (US) 1938 dir. Lloyd Bacon
Spewack B. and Spewack, S.
P

Boy on a Dolphin, The
FOX (US) 1957 dir. Jean Negulesco
Divine, D.

Boys from Brazil, The
ITC (US/GB) 1978
dir. Franklin Shaffner
V
Levin, I.

Boys from Syracuse, The
UN (US) 1940 dir. E. A. Sutherland
M
Abbott, G.
Shakespeare, W. *Comedy of Errors, The*
P

Boys in Brown
GFD (GB) 1949 dir. Montgomery Tully
Beckwith, R.
P

Boys in the Band, The
WAR (US) 1970 dir. William Friedkin
V
Crowley, M.
P

Boy who Drank Too Much, The
MTM (US) 1980 dir. Jerrold Freedman
TV(US)
Greene, S.

Bramble Bush
WAR (US) 1960 dir. Daniel Petrie
Mergendahl, C.

Branded
PAR (US) 1950 dir. Rudolph Maté
Evans, E.

Brandy for the Parson
MGM (GB) 1952 dir. John Eldridge
Household, G.

Brasher Doubloon, The
FOX (US) 1946 dir. John Brahm
GB title: High Window, The
Chandler, R. *High Window, The*

Brass Bottle, The
RANK (US) 1964 dir. Harry Keller
Anstey, F.

Brass Target
UN (US) 1978 dir. John Hough
V
Nolan, F. *Algonquin Project, The*

Brat Farrar
PHILCO (US) 1950 dir. Gordon Duff
TV(US)
BBC (GB) 1986
TVSe(GB)
Tey, J.

Bravados, The
FOX (US) 1958 dir. Henry King
V
O'Rourke, F.

Brave Bulls, The
COL (US) 1951 dir. Robert Rossen
Lea, T.

Brave Little Toaster, The
HYP (US) 1989 dir. Jerry Rees
A
Disch, T. M.

Brave New World
UN (US) 1980 dir. D. B. Brinckerhoff
TV
Huxley, A.

Breaker Morant
S. AUST (Aust) 1980
dir. Bruce Beresford
V
Ross, K.
P

Breakfast at Tiffany's
PAR (US) 1961 dir. Blake Edwards
V
Capote, T.

Breakheart Pass
UA (US) 1975 dir. Tom Gries
V
MacLean, A.

Breaking Point, The
WAR (US) 1950 dir. Michael Curtiz
Hemingway, E. *To Have and Have Not*

Breaking Point, The
BUTCHER (GB) 1961
dir. Lance Comfort
Meynell, L.

Break in the Circle
EXC (GB) 1955 dir. Val Guest
Loraine, P.

Breakout
COL (US) 1975 dir. Tom Gries
V
**Asinof, E., Hinckle, W. & Turner,
W.** *Ten-Second Jailbreak, The*

Break Out
CFTF (GB) 1984 dir. Frank Godwin
GB title: Break Out
Ch
Gillham, B. *Place to Hide, A*

Break the News
GFD (GB) 1938 dir. Rene Clair
de Gouriadec, L. *Mort en fuite, La*

Breath of French Air, A
YTV (GB) 1991 dir. Robert Tronson
TV
Bates, H. E.

Breath of Scandal, A.
PAR (US) 1960 dir. Michael Curtiz and
Mario Russo
V

Molnar, F. *Olympia*
P

Brewster's Millions
UA (US) 1945 dir. Allan Dwan
BRITISH & DOMINION (GB) 1935
dir. Thornton Freeland
UN (US) 1985 dir. Walter Hill
V

McCutcheon, G. B.

Brian's Song
COL TV (US) 1971 dir. Buzz Kulik
TV(US), V

Sayers, G. and Silverman, A. *I am
Third*

Bridal Path, The
BL (GB) 1959 dir. Frank Launder

Tranter, N.

Brides are Like That
WAR (US) 1936 dir. William McGann

Conners, B. *Applesauce*
P

Bride in Black, The
NEW WORLD (US) 1990
dir. James Goldstone
TV(US)

Woolrich, C.

Bride of Re-Animator
WILDSTREET (US) 1991
dir. Brian Yuzna

Lovecraft, H. P. *Herbert West — The
Re-Animator*

Bride Wore Black, The
UA (Fr/It) 1967 dir. François Truffaut

Irish, W.

Bride Wore Red, The
MGM (US) 1937 dir. Dorothy Arzner

Molnar, F. *Girl from Trieste, The*
P

Brideshead Revisited
GRANADA (GB) 1981
dir. Charles Sturridge
TVSe(GB), V

Waugh, E.

Bridge, The
FONO (W. Ger) 1959
dir. Bernhard Wicki

Gregor, M.

Bridge at Remagen, The
UA (US) 1969 dir. John Guillermin
V

Hechler, K.

Bridge in the Jungle, The
UA (US/Mexico) 1970
dir. Pancho Kohner

Traven, B.

Bridge of San Luis Rey, The
UA (US) 1944 dir. Rowland V. Lee
V

Wilder, T.

**Bridge on the River Kwai,
The**
COL (GB) 1957 dir. David Lean
V

Boulle, P.

Bridges at Toko-Ri, The
PAR (US) 1954 dir. Mark Robson
V

Michener, J. A.

Bridge Too Far, A
UA (GB/US) 1977
dir. Richard Attenborough
V

Ryan, C.

Bridge to the Sun
MGM (Fr/US) 1961 dir. Etienne Périer

Terasaki, G.

Brief Encounter
CIN (GB) 1945 dir. David Lean
V
ITC (US) 1974 dir. Alan Bridges
TV(US)
Coward, N. *Still Life*
P

Brigadoon
MGM (US) 1954 dir. Vincente Minnelli
M, V
Lerner, A. J. and Loewe, F.
P

Bright Leaf
WAR (US) 1950 dir. Michael Curtiz

Fitz-Simons, F.

Bright Lights, Big City
MGM/UA (US) 1988 dir. James Bridges
V
McInerney, J.

Brighton Beach Memoirs
UN (US) 1986 dir. Gene Saks
V
Simon, N.
P

Brighton Rock
AB (GB) 1947 dir. John Boulting
US title: Young Scarface
V
Greene, G.

Bright Victory
UI (US) 1951 dir. Mark Robson
GB title: Lights Out

Kendrick, B. H. and W. H. Allen

Brimstone and Treacle
NAMARA (GB) 1982
dir. Richard Loncraine
V
Potter, D.
P

Britannia Mews
TCF (GB) 1948 dir. Jean Negulescu
US title: Forbidden Street, The
Sharp, M.

British Agent
WAR (US) 1934 dir. Michael Curtiz
Lockhart, Sir. R. II. B. *Memoirs of a British Agent*

British Intelligence
WAR (US) 1940 dir. Terry Morse
GB title: Enemy Agent
Kelly, A. P.
P

Broadway
UN (US) 1942 dir. Seiter, W. A.
Dunning, P. and Abbott, G.
P

Broken Arrow
FOX (US) 1950 dir. Delmer Daves
V
Arnold, E. *Blood Brother*

Broken Cord, The
UNTV (US) 1992 dir. Ken Olin
Dorris, M.

Broken Lullaby
PAR (US) 1931 dir. Ernst Lubitsch
Rostand, M. *L'Homme Que J'ai Tué*
P

Broken Promise
EMI TV (US) 1981 dir. Don Taylor
TV(US)
Hayes, K. and Lazzarino, A.

Broken Vows
R. HALMI (US) 1987 dir. Jud Taylor
TV(US)
Davis, D. S. *Where the Dark Streets Go*

Brotherhood of the Rose
NBC (US) 1989 dir. Marvin Chomsky
TVSe(US)
Morrell, D.

Brotherly Love
CBS (US) 1985 dir. Jeff Bleckner
TV(US), V
Blankenship, W. D.

Brother Orchid
WAR (US) 1940 dir. Lloyd Bacon
Connell, R. E.

Brother Rat
FOX (US) 1938 dir. William Keighley
Monks, J. and Finklehoffe, F. R.
P

Brothers, The
GFD (GB) 1947 dir. David MacDonald
Strong, L. A. G.

Brothers in Law
BL (GB) 1957 dir. Ray Boulting
Cecil, H.

Brothers Karamazov, The
MGM (US) 1957 dir. Richard Brooks
V
(USSR) 1980 dir. Ivan Pyriev
Dostoevski, F.

Brothers Rico, The
COL (US) 1957 dir. Phil Karlson
Simenon, G.

Brother's Tale, A
GRANADA (GB) 1983 dir. Les Chatfield
TVSe(GB)
Barstow, S.

Broth of a Boy
E. DALTON (Eire) 1958
dir. George Pollack
Leonard, H. *Big Birthday, The*
P

Browning Version, The
GFD (GB) 1951 dir. Anthony Asquith
V
Rattigan, T.
P

Brown on 'Resolution'
GB (GB) 1935 dir. Walter Forde
US title: Born for Glory
Forester, C. S.

Brute, La
(Fr) 1987 dir. Claude Guillemot
desCars, G.

Buccaneer, The
PAR (US) 1937 dir. Cecil B. de Mille
PAR (US) 1958 dir. Anthony Quinn
V
Saxon, L. *LaFitte the Pirate*

Bud and Lou
BANNER (US) 1978
dir. Robert C. Thompson
TV(US)
Thomas, B.

Buddies
TOHO/SHOCHIKU (Jap) 1990
dir. Yasuo Furuhata
Mukoda, K.

Buddy Buddy
MGM (US) 1981 dir. Billy Wilder
V
Veber, F.
P

Buffalo Bill and the Indians
UA (US) 1976 dir. Robert Altman
V

Kopit, A. *Indians*
P

Bug
PAR (US) 1975 dir. Jeannot Szwarc
V

Page, T. *Hephaestus Plague, The*

Bugles in the Afternoon
WAR (US) 1952 dir. Roy Rowland
V

Haycox, E.

Bulldog Drummond
GOLDWYN (US) 1929
dir. F. Richard Jones
V

McNeile, H. C. *Sapper*

Bullitt
WAR (US) 1968 dir. Peter Yates
V

Pike, R. L. *Mute Witness*

Bump in the Night
RHI (US) 1991 dir. Karen Arthur
TV(US)

Holland, I.

Bunker, The
TIME-LIFE (US) 1981
dir. George Schaefer
TV(US)

O'Donnell, J. P.

Bunker Bean
RKO (US) 1936
dir. William Hamilton/Edward Kelly

Wilson, H. L.

Bunny Lake is Missing
COL (GB) 1965 dir. Otto Preminger

Piper, E.

Burden of Proof, The
ABC Prods. TVS(US) 1992
dir. Mike Robe

Turow, S.

Burglar, The
COL (US) 1957 dir. Paul Wendkos

Goodis, D.

Burglar
WAR (US) 1987 dir. Hugh Wilson
V

Block, L.

Burglars, The
COL (Fr/It) 1971 dir. Henri Verneuill
V

Goodis, D. *Burglar, The*

Buried Alive
AIRTIME (GB) 1983
TVSe(GB)

Bennett, A.

Burmese Harp, The
NIKKATSU (Jap) 1956
dir. Kon Ichikawa
V

Takeyama, M.

Burn 'em up O'Connor
MGM (US) 1938 dir. Edward Sedgwick

Campbell, Sir M. *Salute to the Gods*

Burning Bed, The
TA (US) 1984 dir. Robert Greenwald
TV(US), V

McNulty, F.

Burning Bridges
LORIMAR TV (US) 1990
dir. Sheldon Larry
TV(US)

Miller, I.

Burning Glass, The
ATV (GB) 1956 dir. Cyril Coke
TV(GB)
ATV (GB) 1960 dir. David Boisseau
Morgan, C.

Burning Hills, The
WAR (US) 1956 dir. Stuart Heisler
GB title: Apache Territory
L'Amour, L.

Burning Secret
VESTRON (GB/Ger) 1988
dir. Andrew Birkin
V
Zweig, S. *Brennendes Geheimnis*

Burnt Offerings
UA (US) 1976 dir. Dan Curtis
V
Marasco, R.

Busman's Honeymoon
MGM (GB) 1940 dir. Arthur Woods
US title: Haunted Honeymoon
BBC (GB) 1988
TVSe(GB)
Sayers, D. L.

Bus Stop
FOX (US) 1956 dir. Joshua Logan
V
Inge, W.
P

Busy Body, The
PAR (US) 1967 dir. William Castle
Westlake, D. E.

Butley
Seven Kings (GB/US) 1973
dir. Harold Pinter
Gray, S.
P

But Not For Me
PAR (US) 1959 dir. Walter Lang
Raphaelson, S. *Accent on Youth*
P

Buttercup Chain, The
COL (GB) 1969 dir. Robert Ellis Miller
Elliot, J.

Butterfield 8
MGM (US) 1960 dir. Daniel Mann
O'Hara, J.

Butterflies are Free
COL (US) 1972 dir. Milton Katselas
V
Gershe, L
P

Butterfly
J & M (US) 1982 dir. Matt Cimber
V
Cain, J. M.

But the Flesh is Weak
MGM (US) 1932 dir. Jack Conway
Novello, I. *Truth Game, The*
P

By Candlelight
UN (US) 1933 dir. James Whale
Geyer, S.
P

By Dawn's Early Light
HBO (US) 1990 dir. Jack Sholder
TV (US)
Prochnau, W. *Trinity's Child*

Bye Bye Birdie
COL (US) 1963 dir. George Sidney
M, V
Stewart, M.
P

Bye Bye Braverman
WAR (US) 1968 dir. Sidney Lumet
Markfield, W. *To an Early Grave*

By Love Possessed
UA (US) 1961 dir. John Sturges
Cozzens, J. G.

By the Light of the Silvery Moon
WAR (US) 1953 dir. David Butler
Tarkington, B. *Penrod*

Cabaret
CINERAMA (US) 1972 dir. Bob Fosse
M, V
Druten, J. van *I am a Camera*
P

Cabin in the Cotton
WAR (US) 1932 dir. Michael Curtiz
Knoll, H. H.

Cabin in the Sky
MGM (US) 1943 dir. Vincente Minnelli
M, V
Root, L.
P

Cactus Flower
COL (US) 1969 dir. Gene Saks
V
Burrows, A.
P

Caddie
HEMDALE (Aust) 1976
dir. Donald Crombie
V
Brink, C. R. *Caddie Woodlawn*

Cadence
New Line (US) 1990 dir. Martin Sheen
Weaver, G. *Count a Lonely Cadence*

Caesar and Cleopatra
RANK (GB) 1945 dir. Gabriel Pascal
V
TALENT ASS. (US) 1976
dir. James Cellan Jones
TV(US)
Shaw, G. B.
P

Cage Aux Folles, La
UA (Fr/It) 1978 dir. Edouard Molinaro
V
Poiret, J.
P

Caine Mutiny, The
COL (US) 1954 dir. Edward Dmytryk
V
Wouk, H.

Caine Mutiny Court-Martial, The
MALTESE (US) 1988
dir. Robert Altman
TV(US)

Wouk, H.
P

Cairo
MGM (GB) 1963 dir. Wolf Rilla
Burnett, W. R. *Asphalt Jungle, The*

Cal
WAR (GB) 1984 dir. Pat O'Connor
V

MacLaverty, B.

Calendar, The
GFD (GB) 1948 dir. Arthur Crabtree
Wallace, E.

California Gold Rush
TAFT (US) 1981 dir. Jack Hively
TV(US), V
Harte, B. *Luck of Roaring Camp, The;
Outcasts of Poker Flat, The*

California Suite
COL (US) 1975 dir. Herbert Ross
V

Simon, N.
P

Callan
EMI (GB) 1974 dir. Don Sharp
V

Mitchell, J. *Red File for Callan, A*

Call Her Savage
PAR (US) 1932 dir. John Francis Dillon
Thayer, T.

Calling Philco Vance
WAR (US) 1939 dir. William Clemens
van Dine, S. S. *Kennel Murder Case,
The*

Call it a Day
WAR (US) 1937 dir. Archie Mayo
Smith, D.
P

Call me Anna
FINNEGAN (US) 1990
dir. Gilbert Cates
TV(US)
Duke, P. and Turan, K. *My Name is
Anna: The Autobiography of Patty Duke*

Call me Madam
TCF (US) 1953 dir. Walter Lang
M

Lindsay, H. and Crouse, R.
P

Call of the Wild
UA (US) 1935 dir. William Wellman
MASSFILMS (GB/Fr/It/Ger) 1972
dir. Ken Annakin
V
FRIES (US) 1976 dir. Jerry Jameson
TV(US)
London, J.

Came a Hot Friday
ORION (Nz) 1985 dir. Ian Mune
V

Morrieson, R. H.

Camelot
WAR (US) 1967 dir. Joshua Logan
M, V
Lerner, A. J. and Loewe, F.
P

White, T. H. *Once and Future King,
The*

Cameron's Closet
SVS (US) 1989 dir. Armand Mastroianni
V

Brandner, G.

Camille
MGM (US) 1936 dir. George Cukor
ROSEMONT (US/GB) 1984
dir. Desmond Davis
TV(GB/US), V
Dumas, A. fils *Dame aux Camélias, La*

Camille Claudel
GAU BR (Fr) 1989 dir. Bruno Nuytten
Paris, R-M.

Campbell's Kingdom
RANK (GB) 1957 dir. Ralph Thomas
V
Innes, H.

Can Can
TCF (US) 1960 dir. Walter Lang
M, V
Burrows, A.
P

Cancel My Reservation
MGM-EMI (US) 1972 dir. Paul Bogart
L'Amour, L. *Broken Gun, The*

Candleshoe
DISNEY (GB) 1977 dir. Norman Tokar
V
Innes, M. *Christmas at Candleshoe*

Candy
CINERAMA (US) 1968
dir. Christian Marquand
Southern, T. and Hoffenberg, M.

Cannery Row
MGM (US) 1982 dir. David S. Ward
V
Steinbeck, J.

Canterbury Tales, The
UA (It/Fr) 1972 dir. Pier Paolo Pasolini
V
Chaucer, G.

Canterville Ghost, The
MGM (US) 1943 dir. Jules Dassin
HTV (GB/US) 1986 dir. Paul Bogart
TV(GB/US), V
Wilde, O.

Canyon Passage
UN (US) 1946 dir. Jacques Tourneur
Haycox, E.

Cape Fear
UI (US) 1962 dir. J. Lee Thompson
V
UN (US) 1991 dir. Martin Scorsese
MacDonald, J. D. *Executioners, The*

Caper of the Golden Bulls, The
EMBASSY (US) 1966 dir. Russel Rouse
GB title: Carnival of Thieves
V
McGivern, W. P.

Captain Apache
BENMAR (US/Sp) 1971
dir. Alexander Singer
V
Whitman, S. E.

Captain Blood
WAR (US) 1935 dir. Michael Curtiz
V
Sabatini, R.

Captain Boycott
INDIVIDUAL (GB) 1947
dir. Frank Launder
Rooney, P.

Captain Brassbound's Conversion
COMPASS (US) 1960
dir. George Schaefer
TV(US)
Shaw, G. B.
P

Captain Carey USA
PAR (US) 1950 dir. Mitchell Leisen
GB title: After Midnight
Albrand, M. *Dishonoured*

Captain Caution
UA (US) 1940 dir. Richard Wallace
V
Roberts, K.

Captain from Castille
FOX (US) 1947 dir. Henry King
Shellabarger, S.

Captain Horatio Hornblower, R. N.
WAR (GB) 1951 dir. Raoul Walsh
Forester, C. S. *Captain Hornblower, R. N.*

Captain is a Lady, The
MGM (US) 1940 dir. Robert Sinclair
Crothers, R. *Old Lady 31*
P

Captain January
FOX (US) 1936 dir. David Butler
Ch, V
Richards, L. E.

Captain Lightfoot
UI (US) 1955 dir. Douglas Sirk
Burnett, W. R.

Captain Newman, M.D.
UI (US) 1963 dir. David Mil S)
V
Rosten, L.

Captain Pirate
COL (US) 1952 dir. Ralph Murphy
GB title: Captain Blood, Fugitive
Sabatini, R. *Captain Blood Returns*

Captains and the Kings
UN TV (US) 1976 dir. Douglas Heyes,
Allen Reisner
TVSe(US)
Caldwell, T.

Captains Courageous
MGM (US/GB) 1937
dir. Victor Fleming
V
ROSEMONT (US) 1977
dir. Harvey Hart
TV(GB/US)
Kipling, R.

Captain's Doll, The
BBC (GB) 1982
TV(GB)
Lawrence, D. H.

Captain's Table, The
RANK (GB) 1958 dir. Jack Lee
V
Gordon, R.

Captive in the Land, A
GLORIA/GORKY (US/USSR) 1991
dir. John Berry
Aldridge, J.

Capture of Grizzly Adams, The
TAFT (US) 1982 dir. Don Kessler
TV(US)
Sellier, Jr., C. E.

Caravan
BL (GB) 1946 dir. Arthur Crabtree
Smith, Lady E.

Caravans
BORDEAUX (US/Iran) 1978
dir. James Fargo
V
Michener, J. A.

Caravan to Vaccares
RANK (GB/Fr) 1974
dir. Geoffrey Reeve
V

MacLean, A.

Card, The
GFD (GB) 1952 dir. Ronald Neame
US title: Promoter, The
V

Bennett, A.

Cardinal, The
COL (US) 1963 dir. Otto Preminger
V

Robinson, H. M.

Career
PAR (US) 1959 dir. Joseph Anthony
Lee, J.
P

Career
RKO (US) 1939 dir. Leigh Jason
Stong, P. D.

Careful, He Might Hear You
SYME (Aust) 1983 dir. Carl Schultz
V

Elliott, S. *Signs of Life*

Care of Time, The
ANGLIA (GB) (1990)
TV
Ambler, E.

Caretaker, The
BL (GB) 1963 dir. Clive Donner
US title: Guest, The
Pinter, H.
P

Caretakers, The
UA (US) 1963 dir. Hall Bartlett
GB title: Borderlines
Telfer, D.

Carey Treatment, The
MGM (US) 1972 dir. Blake Edwards
V

Hudson, J. *Case of Need, A*

Caribbean Mystery, A
WAR (US) 1983 dir. Robert Lewis
TV(US)
BBC (GB) 1988 dir. Christopher Pettit
TV(GB)
Christie, A.

Carmen
TRIUMPH (Fr) 1984 dir. Francesco Rosi
V

Merimée, P.
Bizet, G.

Carnival
RANK (GB) 1946 dir. Stanley Haynes
MacKenzie, Sir C.

Carolina
FOX (US) 1934 dir. Henry King
GB title: House of Connelly
Green, P. *House of Connelly, The*
P

Carolina Skeletons
KUSHNER-LOCKE (US) 1991
dir. John Erman
TV (US)
Stout, D.

Caroline?
B&E (US) 1990 dir. Joseph Sargent
TV(US)
Konigsburg, E. L. *Father's Arcane Daughter*

Caroline Chérie
GAU (Fr) 1951 dir. Richard Pottier
Saint-Laurent, C.

Carousel
TCF (US) 1956 dir. Henry King
M
Molnar, F. *Liliom*
P

Carpetbaggers, The
PAR (US) 1964 dir. Edward Dmytryk
V
Robbins, H.

Carrie
PAR (US) 1952 dir. William Wyler
Dreiser, T. *Sister Carrie*

Carrie
UA (US) 1976 dir. Brian de Palma
V
King, S.

Carrington, V. C.
BL (GB) 1954 dir. Anthony Asquith
US title: Court Martial
V
Christie, D. and Christie, C.
P

Carry on, Admiral
REN (GB) 1957 dir. Val Guest
Hay, I. and King-Hall, S. *Off the Record*
P

Carry on Sergeant
AAM (GB) 1958 dir. Gerald Thomas
Delderfield, R. F. *Bull Boys, The*
P

Carve Her Name with Pride
RANK (GB) 1958 dir. Lewis Gilbert
V
Minney, R. J.

Casablanca
WAR (US) 1943 dir. Michael Curtiz
V
Burnett, M. and Alison, J. *Everybody Comes to Rick's*
P

Casanova Brown
INTERNAT (US) 1944 dir. Sam Wood
Dell, F. *Bachelor Father*
P

Case Against Mrs Ames, The
PAR (US) 1936 dir. William A. Seiter
Roche, A. S.

Case of Deadly Force, A
TELECOM (US) 1986
dir. Michael Miller
TV(US)
O'Donnell, Jr., L. *Deadly Force: The Story of How a Badge Can Become a License to Kill*

Case of Sergeant Grischa, The
RKO (US) 1930 dir. Herbert Brenon
Zweig, A.

Case of the Black Cat, The
WAR (US) 1936 dir. William McGann
Gardner, E. S. *Case of the Caretaker's Cat, The*

Case of the Curious Bride, The
WAR (US) 1935 dir. Michael Curtiz
Gardner, E. S.

Case of the Frightened Lady, The
BL (GB) 1940 dir. George King
US title: Frightened Lady, The
Wallace, E.

Case of the Hillside Stranglers, The
FRIES (US) 1989 dir. Steven Gethers
TV(US)

O'Brien, D. *Two of a Kind: The Hillside Stranglers*

Case of the Howling Dog, The
WAR (US) 1934 dir. Alan Crosland

Gardner, E. S.

Case of the Lucky Legs, The
WAR (US) 1935 dir. Archie Mayo

Gardner, E. S.

Case of the Stuttering Bishop, The
WAR (US) 1937 dir. William Clemens

Gardner, E. S.

Case of the Velvet Claws, The
WAR (US) 1936 dir. William Clemens

Gardner, E. S.

Cash McCall
WAR (US) 1960 dir. Joseph Pevney

Hawley, C.

Cash on Demand
COL (GB) 1963 dir. Quentin Lawrence

Gillies, J.
P

Casino Murder Case, The
MGM (US) 1935 dir. Edwin Marin

Dine, S. S. van

Casino Royale
COL (GB) 1967 dir. John Huston
V

Fleming, I.

Cass Timberlane
MGM (US) 1947 dir. George Sidney

Lewis, S.

Cast a Dark Shadow
EROS (GB) 1955 dir. Lewis Gilbert

Green, J. *Murder Mistaken*
P

Cast a Giant Shadow
UA (US) 1966 dir. Melville Shavelson
V

Berkman, T.

Cast a Long Shadow
UA (US) 1959 dir. Thomas Carr

Overholser, W. D.

Castaway
VIRGIN (GB) 1986 dir. Nicolas Roeg
V

Irvine, L.

Castle in the Air
ABP (GB) 1952 dir. Henry Cass

Melville, A.
P

Castle Keep
COL (US) 1969 dir. Sydney Pollack

Eastlake, W.

Castle of Adventure
TVS (GB) 1990
Ch, TV(GB)

Blyton, E.

Casual Sex?
UN (US) 1988 dir. Genevieve Robert
V

Goldman, W. *Casual Sex*
P

Casualties of War
COL (US) 1989 dir. Brian de Palma

Lang, D.

Casualty of War, A
BLAIR (US) 1990 dir. Tom Clegg
TV(GB/US)
Forsyth, F.

Catacombs
BL (GB) 1964 dir. Gordon Hessler
US title: Woman Who Wouldn't Die, The
Bennett, J.

Cat and Mouse
EROS (GB) 1958 dir. Paul Rotha
V
Halliday, M.

Cat and the Canary, The
PAR (US) 1939 dir. Elliot Nugent
GALA (GB) 1978 dir. Radley Metzger
V
Willard, J.
P

Cat Ballou
COL (US) 1965 dir. Eliot Silverstein
V
Chanslor, R. *Ballad of Cat Ballou, The*

Cat Chaser
VESTRON (US) 1989 dir. Abel Ferrara
Leonard, E.

Catch me a Spy
RANK (GB) 1971 dir. Dick Clement
V
Marton, G. and Meray, T.

Catch-22
PAR (US) 1970 dir. Mike Nichols
V
Heller, J.

Cat Creeps, The
UN (US) 1930 dir. Rupert Julian
Willard, J. *Cat and the Canary, The*
P

Catered Affair, The
MGM (US) 1956 dir. Richard Brooks
Chayefsky, P.
P

Cathedral
UNICORN 1984
TV
Macaulay, D.

Catherine the Great
KORDA (GB) 1934 dir. Paul Czinner
V
Lengyel, M. *The Czarina*
P

Catholics
Glazier (US) 1973 dir. Jack Gold
TV(US), V
Moore, B.

Catlow
MGM (GB) 1971 dir. Sam Wanamaker
V
L'Amour, L.

Cat on a Hot Tin Roof
MGM (US) 1958 dir. Richard Brooks
V
GRANADA TV (GB) 1976
dir. Robert Moore
TV(GB/US)
Williams, T.
P

Cattle Annie and Little Britches
UN (US) 1981 dir. Lamont Johnson
V
Ward, R.

Caught
MGM (US) 1948 dir. Max Ophuls
V
Block, L. *Wild Calendar*

Cavalcade
FOX (US) 1932 dir. Frank Lloyd
Coward, N.
P

Caviar Rouge, Le
GALAXY (Fr/Switz) 1988
dir. Robert Hossein
Hossein, R. and Dard, F.

Cease Fire
CINEWORLD (US) 1985
dir. David Nutter
V
Fernandez, G. *Vietnam Trilogy*
P

Ceiling Zero
WAR (US) 1935 dir. Howard Hawks
Wead, F.
P

Cela S'Appelle L'Aurore
MARCEAU/LAE (Fr/It) 1955
dir. Luis Bunuel
Robles, E.

Celebration Family
VSS (US) 1987 dir. Robert Day
TV(US)
Nason, D. and Etchison, B.

Celebrity
NBC (US) 1984 dir. Paul Wendkos
TVSe(US), V
Thompson, T.

Celeste
PEL (W. Ger) 1981 dir. Percy Adlon
Albaret, C. *Monsieur Proust*

Cell 2455, Death Row
COL (US) 1955 dir. Fred F. Sears
Chessman, C.

Centennial
UN TV (US) 1979 dir. Virgil Vogel,
PaulKrasny,Harry Falk, Bernard
McEveety
TVSe(US)
Michener, J. A.

Centennial Summer
FOX (GB) 1946 dir. Otto Preminger
Idell, A. E.

Ceremony, The
UA (US/Sp) 1963 dir. Laurence Harvey
Grendel, F.

Certain Smile, A.
FOX (US) 1958 dir. Jean Negulesco
Sagan, F.

Cervantes
PRISMA (Sp/It/Fr) 1968
dir. Vincent Sherman
Frank, B.

Chad Hanna
FOX (US) 1940 dir. Henry King
Edmonds, W. D.

Chalk Garden, The
RANK (GB) 1963 dir. Ronald Neame
V
Bagnold, E.

Challenge to Lassie
MGM (US) 1949 dir. Richard Thorpe
Atkinson, E. *Greyfriar's Bobby*

Chamade, La
ARIANE (Fr) 1969 dir. Alain Cavalier
US title: Heartkeeper, The
Sagan, F.

Champion
UA (US) 1949 dir. Mark Robson
V
Lardner, R.

Champions
Embassy (GB) 1983 dir. John Irvin
V

Champion, B. and Powell, J.
Champion's Story: A Great Human Triumph

Chanel Solitaire
GARDENIA (Fr/GB) 1981
dir. George Kaczender
V

Dulay, C.

Changes
NBC (US) 1991 dir. Charles Jarrot
TV(US)

Steel, D.

Changes, The
BBC (GB) 1975 dir. John Prowse
Ch, TV(GB)

Dickinson, P.

Chant of Jimmie Blacksmith, The
FOX (Aust) 1979 dir. Fred Schepisi
V

Keneally, T.

Chapman Report, The
WAR (US) 1962 dir. George Cukor

Wallace, I.

Chapter Two
COL (US) 1979 dir. Robert Moore
V

Simon, N.
P

Charley and the Angel
DISNEY (US) 1974
dir. Vincent McEveety
V

Stanton, W. *Golden Evenings of Summer, The*

Charley Moon
BL (GB) 1956 dir. Guy Hamilton

Arkell, R.

Charley's Aunt
FOX (US) 1941 dir. Archie Mayo
GB title: Charley's American Aunt
V

Thomas, B.
P

Charley Varrick
UN (US) 1973 dir. Don Siegel
V

Reese, J. *Looters, The*

Charlie Chan Carries On
FOX (US) 1931 dir. Hamilton McFadden

Biggers, E. D.

Charlie Muffin
EUSTON (GB) 1979 dir. Jack Gold
V

Freemantle, B. *Charlie, M.*

Charlotte's Web
SCOTIA-BARBER (US) 1972
dir. Charles A. Nichols
A, Ch, V

White, E. B.

Charly
CINERAMA (US) 1968
dir. Ralph Nelson
V

Keyes, D. *Flowers for Algernon*

Charters and Caldicott
BBC (GB) 1985 dir. Julian Amyes
TVSe(GB)

Bingham, S.

Chase, The
NERO (US) 1947 dir. Arthur Ripley

Woolrich, C. *Black Path of Fear, The*

Chase, The
COL (US) 1966 dir. Arthur Penn
V

Foote, H.

Chasing Yesterday
RKO (US) 1935 dir. George Nicholls, Jr.

France, A. *Crime of Sylvester Bonnard, The*

Cheaper by the Dozen
FOX (US) 1950 dir. Walter Lang

Gilbreth, F. B. and Carey, E. G.

Cheating Cheaters
UN (US) 1934 dir. Richard Thorpe

Marcin, M.
P

Checkers
FOX (US) 1937
dir. H. Bruce Humberstone

Young, R. J.
P

Cheers for Miss Bishop
PAR (US) 1941 dir. Tom Garnett
V

Aldrich, Mrs B. *Miss Bishop*

Cheetah
DISNEY (US) 1989 dir. Jeff Blyth
Ch

Caillou, A. *Cheetahs, The*

Chernobyl: The Final Warning
CAROLCO (US/USSR) 1991
dir. Anthony Page
TV(US/USSR)

Gale, R. P. and Hauser, T. *Final Warning: The Legacy of Chernobyl*

Cherry Picker, The
FOX-RANK (GB) 1974 dir. Peter Curran
V

Phillips, M. *Pick up Sticks*

Cheyenne Autumn
WAR (US) 1964 dir. John Ford

Sandoz, M.

Chicken Chronicles, The
AVCO (US) 1977 dir. Francis Simon
V

Diamond, P.

Chicken Every Sunday
FOX (US) 1948 dir. George Seaton

Taylor, R.

Chicken-Wagon Family
FOX (US) 1939 dir. Herbert I. Leeds

Benefield, B.

Chienne, La
BRAU (Fr) 1931 dir. Jean Renoir

de la Fouchardière, G.

Chiefs
HIGHGATE (US) 1983
dir. Jerry London
TVSe(US)

Woods, S.

Child in the House
EROS (GB) 1956 dir. C. Baker Endfield

McNeill, J.

Child is Born, A
WAR (US) 1939 dir. Lloyd Bacon

Axelson, Mrs M. M.
P

Child of Darkness, Child of Light
WIL COURT (US) 1991
dir. Marina Sargenti
TV(US)

Patterson, J. *Virgin*

Children Are Watching Us, The
MAGLI (It) 1942 dir. Vittorio de Sica
V

Viola, C. G. *Prico*

Children of a Lesser God
PAR (US) 1986 dir. Randa Haines
V

Medoff, M.
P

Children of Dynmouth, The
BBC (GB) 1987 dir. Peter Hammond
TV(GB)

Trevor, W.

Children of Hiroshima
KEL (Jap) 1952 dir. Kaneto Shindo

Osada, A.

Children of Sanchez, The
HALL BARTLETT (US/Mex) 1978
dir. Hall Bartlett
V

Lewis, O.

Children of the Corn
NEW WORLD (US) 1984
dir. Fritz Kiersch

King, S.

Children's Hour, The
UA (US) 1961 dir. William Wyler
GB title: Loudest Whispers, The

Hellman, L. F.
P

Child's Play
PAR (US) 1972 dir. Sidney Lumet
V

Marasco, R.
P

Chilly Scenes of Winter *also known as* Head Over Heels
UA (US) 1979 dir. Joan Micklin Silver
V

Beattie, A.

Chiltern Hundreds, The
TC (GB) 1949 dir. John Paddy Carstairs

Home, W. D
P

Chimera
Anglia (GB) 1991 dir. Nicholas Gillott
TV(GB)

Gallagher, S.

China
PAR (US) 1943 dir. John Farrow

Forbes, R. *Fourth Brother, The*

China Cry
PENLAND (US) 1990
dir. James F. Collier

Lam, N. and Burke, I.

China Seas
MGM (US) 1935 dir. Tay Garnett
V

Garstin, C.

China Sky
RKO (US) 1945 dir. Ray Enright

Buck, P.

Chinese Ghost Story II
GORDON (China) 1990
dir. Ching Siu-Tung

Ling, P. S. *Strange Tales of Liao Zhai*

Chisholms, The
LAN (US) 1979 dir. Mel Stuart
TVSe(US)

Hunter, E.

Chitty, Chitty Bang Bang
UA (GB) 1968 dir. Ken Hughes
Ch, V
Fleming, I.

Chocky
THAMES (GB) 1984 dir. Chris Hodson
Ch, TVSe(GB), V
Wyndham, J.

Chocolate Soldier, The
MGM (US) 1941 dir. Roy Del Ruth
M
Molnar, F. *Guardsman, The*
P

Chocolate War, The
MCEG (US) 1988 dir. Keith Gordon
V
Cormier, R.

Choirboys, The
LORIMAR (US) 1977 dir. Robert Aldrich
V
Wambaugh, J.

Chorus Line, A
COL (US) 1985
dir. Richard Attenborough
M, V
Dante, N., Kirkwood, J. and Hamlisch, M.
P

Chorus of Disapproval, A.
HOBO (GB) 1989 dir. Michael Winner
Ayckbourn, A.
P

Chosen, The
CONTEM (US) 1981
dir. Jeremy Paul Kagan
V
Potok, C.

Choses de la Vie, Les
LIRA/FIDA (Fr/It) 1969
dir. Claude Sautet
Guimard, P.

Christiane F
FOX (Ger) 1981 dir. Ulrich Edel
V
Hermann, K. and Rieck, H.

Christine
COL (US) 1983 dir. John Carpenter
V
King, S.

Christine Jorgensen Story, The
UA (US) 1970 dir. Irving Rapper
Jorgensen, C.

Christmas Carol, A
MGM (US) 1938 dir. Edwin L. Marin
V
ENTERTAINMENT PARTNERS (US)
1984 dir. Clive Donner
TV(US), V
Dickens, C.

Christmas Festival, A
COMPASS (US) 1959
dir. Albert McCleery
TV(US)
Bemelmans, L. *Borrowed Christmas, A*

Christmas Holiday
UN (US) 1944 dir. Robert Siodmak
Maugham, W. S.

Christmas Present, A
CHANNEL 4 (GB) 1985
TV(GB)
Dickens, C. *Christmas Carol, A*

Christmas Story, A
MGM/UA (US) 1983 dir. Bob Clark
V

Shepherd, J. *In God We Trust, All Others Pay Cash*

Christmas to Remember, A
ENGLUND (US) 1978
dir. George Englund
TV(US), V

Swarthout, G. *Melodeon, The*

Christmas Tree, The
FOX (Fr/It) 1969 dir. Terence Young
V

Bataille, M.

Christopher Bean
MGM (US) 1933 dir. Sam Wood
Howard, S. *Late Christopher Bean, The*
P

Christopher Strong
RKO (US) 1933 dir. Dorothy Arzner
V

Frankau, G.

Christ Stopped At Eboli
ART EYE (It/Fr) 1979
dir. Francesco Rosi
V

Levi, C.

Chronicle of a Death Foretold
ITAL/MEDIA (It/Fr) 1987
dir. Francesco Rosi
V

Marquez, G. G.

Chu Chin Chow
GAU (GB) 1934 dir. Walter Forde
M

Asche, O. and Norton, F.
P

Chuka
PAR (US) 1967 dir. Gordon Douglas
Jessup, R.

Cimarron
RKO (US) 1930 dir. Wesley Ruggles
MGM (US) 1960 dir. Anthony Mann
Ferber, E.

Cincinnati Kid, The
MGM (US) 1965 dir. Norman Jewison
V
Jessup, R.

Cinderella Liberty
FOX (US) 1974 dir. Mark Rydell
Ponicsan, D.

Circle of Children, A
FOX (US) 1977 dir. Don Taylor
TV(US), V
MacCracken, M.

Circle of Deceit
BIOSKOP/ARTEMIS (Fr/W. Ger)
1981 dir. Volker Schlondorff
Born, N.

Circle of Deception
FOX (GB) 1960 dir. Jack Lee
Waugh, A. *Guy Renton, A London Story*

Circle of Two
BORDEAUX (Can) 1980
dir. Jules Dassin
V
Baird, M. T. *Lesson in Love, A*

Circus Queen Murder
COL (US) 1933 dir. Roy William Neill
Abbot, A. *Murder of the Circus Queen, The*

Citadel, The
MGM (GB) 1938 dir. King Vidor
V
BBC (GB) 1983 dir. Peter Jefferies
TVSe(GB)
Cronin, A. J.

City Across The River
UI (US) 1949 dir. Maxwell Shane
Shulman, I. *Amboy Dukes, The*

City and the Dogs, The
INCA (Peru) 1985
dir. Francisco J. Lombardi
V
Llosa, M. V.

City for Conquest
WAR (US) 1940 dir. Anatole Litvak
V
Kandel, A.

City of Joy
TRI-STAR (US) 1992 dir. Roland Joffe
Lapierre, D.

City Streets
PAR (US) 1931 dir. Rouben Mamoulian
Boothe, E. *Ladies of the Mob*

Clair de Femme
GAU (Fr/It/Ger) 1979 dir. Costa-Gavras
Gary, R.

Clairvoyant, The
GB (GB) 1935 dir. Maurice Elvey
V
Lothar, E.

Clan of the Cave Bear, The
WAR (US) 1986 dir. Michael Chapman
V
Auel, J. M.

Clara's Heart
WB (US) 1988 dir. Robert Mulligan
Olshan, J.

Clash by Night
RKO (US) 1952 dir. Fritz Lang
V
Odets, C.
P

Class Enemy
SFB (Ger) 1984 dir. Peter Stein
Williams, N.
P

Classified Love
CBS ENT (US) 1986 dir. Don Taylor
TV(US)
Foxman, S.

Class of Miss MacMichael, The
GALA (GB) 1978 dir. Silvio Narizzano
V
Hutson, S. *Eff Off*

Class Relations
ART EYE (Ger/Fr) 1983
dir. Jean Marie Straub/Daniele Huillet
Kafka, F. *Amerika*

Claudelle Inglish
WAR (US) 1961 dir. Gordon Douglas
GB title: Young and Eager
Caldwell, E.

Claudia
FOX (US) 1943 dir. Edmund Goulding
Franken, R.

Claudia and David
FOX US 1946 dir. Walter Lang
Franken, R.

Clayhanger
ATV (GB) 1976 dir. John Davies, David Reid
TVSe(GB)
Bennett, A.

Clearcut
TELEFILM (Can) 1991
dir. Richard Bugajski
Kelly, M. T. *Dream Like Mine, A*

Cleopatra
FOX (US) 1963
dir. Joseph L. Manciewicz
V

Franzero, C. M. *Life and Times of Cleopatra, The*

Climax, The
UN (US) 1944 dir. George Waggner
Cochran, E.
P

Clive of India
FOX (US) 1935 dir. Richard Boleslawski
Lipscombe, W. P. and Minney, R. J.
P

Clochemerle
BLUE RIBBON (Fr) 1948
dir. Pierre Chénal
Chevalier, G.

Clockwork Orange, A
WAR (GB) 1971 dir. Stanley Kubrick
V
Burgess, A.

Closely Watched Trains
CESK (Czech) 1966 dir. Jiri Menzel
V
Hrabal, B.

Closer, The
ION (US) 1990 dir. Dimitri Logothetis
Larusso, II, L. *Wheelbarrow Closers*
P

Cloud Waltzing
AVV/YTV (US/GB) 1987
dir. Gordon Flemyng
TV(GB/US)
Gates, T.

Cluny Brown
FOX (US) 1946 dir. Ernst Lubitsch
Sharp, M.

Coal Miner's Daughter
UN (US) 1980 dir. Michael Apted
V
Lynn, L. and Vecsey, G.

Cobra
WAR (US) 1986 dir. G. P. Cosmatos
V
Gosling, P. *Fair Game*

Cobweb, The
MGM (US) 1955 dir. Vincente Minnelli
Gibson, W.

Coca-Cola Kid, The
CINECOM (Aus) 1985
dir. Dusan Makevejev
V
Moorhouse, F. *Americans, Baby, The; Electrical Experience, The*

Cocaine and Blue Eyes
COL TV (US) 1983
dir. E. W. Swackhamer
TV(US)
Zackel, F.

Cockeyed Miracle, The
MGM (US) 1946 dir. S. Sylvan Simon
Seaton, G.
P

Cockfighter
EMI (US) 1974 dir. Monte Hellman
V
Willeford, C.

Cocktail
TOUCH (US) 1988
dir. Roger Donaldson
V
Gould, H.

Cocoon
FOX (US) 1985 dir. Ron Howard
V
Saperstein, D.

Code Name: Emerald
MGM/UA (US) 1985
dir. Jonathan Sanger
V
Bass, R. *Emerald Illusion, The*

Codename: Kyril
INCITO/HTV (US/GB) 1988
dir. Ian Sharp
TV(GB/US)
Trenhaile, J. *Man Called Kyril, A*

Code of the Woosters
Central (GB) 1991 dir. Simon Langton
TV
Wodehouse, P. G.

Coffee, Tea or Me?
CBS ENT. (US) 1983
dir. Norman Panama
TV(US)
Baker, T. and Jones, R.

Coiffeur Pour Dames
HOCHE (Fr) 1952 dir. Jean Boyer
GB title: Artist with Ladies, An
Armont, P. and Gerbidon, M.
P

Cold Heaven
HEMDALE (US) 1992 dir. Nicolas Roeg
Moore, B.

Colditz Story, The
BL (GB) 1954 dir. Guy Hamilton
V
Reid, R. P.

Cold Moon
GAU (Fr) 1991 dir. Luc Besson, Andrée
Martinez
French title: Lune Froide
Bukowski, C. *Copulating Mermaid of Venice; Trouble with the Battery*

Cold River
PACIFIC (US) 1982 dir. Fred G. Sullivan
V
Judson, W.

Cold Room, The
HBO PREM (US) 1984
dir. James Dearden
TV(US), V
Caine, J.

Cold Sassy Tree
TNT (US) 1989 dir. Joan Tewkesbury
TV(US)
Burns, O. A.

Cold Sweat
CORONA/FAIRFILM (It/Fr) 1974
dir. Terence Young
V
Matheson, R. *Ride the Nightmare*

Cold Turkey
UA (US) 1970 dir. Norman Lear
Rau, M. and Rau, N. *I'm Giving Them Up For Good*

Cold Wind in August
UA (US) 1961 dir. Alexander Singer
Wohl, B.

Collector, The
BL (US) 1965 dir. William Wyler
V
Fowles, J.

Colonel Effingham's Raid
FOX (US) 1945 dir. Irving Pichel
GB title: Man of the Hour
V

Fleming, B.

Colour of Money, The
DISNEY (US) 1986 dir. Martin Scorcese
V

Tevis, W.

Colour Purple, The
WAR (US) 1986 dir. Steven Spielberg
V

Walker, A.

Coma
MGM (US) 1978 dir. Michael Crichton
V

Cook, R.

Comancheros, The
FOX (US) 1961 dir. Michael Curtiz
V

Wellman, P. I.

Come and Get It
UA (US) 1936
dir. Howard Hawks/William A. Wellman
V

Ferber, E.

Come and See
MOSFILM (USSR) 1985
dir. Elem Klimov

Adamovich, A. *Story of Khatyn, The*

Comeback, The
CBS ENT (US) 1989
dir. Jerrold Freedman
TV(US)

Epstein, S. *Eye of the Beholder*

Come Back Charleston Blue
WAR (US) 1972 dir. Mark Warren

Himes, C. *Heat's On, The*

Come Back, Little Sheba
PAR (US) 1952 dir. Daniel Mann
GRANADA (US) 1977
dir. Silvio Narizzano
TV(GB/US)

Inge, W.
P

Come Back to the Five and Dime, Jimmy Dean, Jimmy Dean
SANDCASTLE (US) 1982
dir. Robert Altman
V

Graczyk, E.
P

Come Blow Your Horn
PAR (US) 1963 dir. Bud Yorkin

Simon, N.
P

Comedians, The
MGM (US/Fr) 1967 dir. Peter Glenville

Greene, G.

Comedy Man, The
BL (GB) 1964 dir. Alvin Rakoff

Hayes, D.

Come Fill the Cup
WAR (US) 1951 dir. Gordon Douglas

Ware, H.

Come Fly with Me
MGM (US) 1963 dir. Henry Levin

Glemser, B. *Girl on a Wing*

Come Home Charlie and Face Them
LWT (GB) 1990 dir. Roger Bamford
TV

Delderfield, R. F.

Come in Spinner
BBC (GB) 1991 dir. Ray Marchand
TV(GB)
Cusack, D.

Comfort of Strangers, The
SOVEREIGN (US/It) 1990
dir. Paul Schrader
McEwan, I.

Coming Out of the Ice
KONIGSBERG (US) 1982
dir. Waris Hussein
TV(US), V
Herman, V.

Command, The
WAR (US) 1954 dir. David Butler
Bellah, J. W.

Command Decision
MGM (US) 1948 dir. Sam Wood
Haines, W. W.

Commissar
GORKY (USSR) 1988
dir. Alexander Askoldov
Grossman, V. *City of Bardish, A*

Common Ground
LORIMAR TV (US) 1990
dir. Michael Newell
TVSe(US)
Lukas, J. A.

Common Touch, The
BN (GB) 1941 dir. John Baxter
Ayres, H.

Communion
NEW LINE (US) 1989
dir. Philippe Mora
Streiber, W.

Company Limited
CHILRANGALI (Ind) 1971
dir. Satyajit Ray
V
Shankar

Company of Wolves, The
PALACE (GB) 1984 dir. Neil Jordan
V
Carter, A.

Compromising Positions
PAR (US) 1985 dir. Frank Perry
V
Isaacs, S.

Compulsion
FOX (US) 1959 dir. Richard Fleischer
Levin, M.

Conagher
IMAGINE (US) 1991
dir. Reynaldo Villalobos
TV(US)
L'Amour, L.

Condemned
UA (US) 1929 dir. Wesley Ruggles
Niles, B. *Condemned to Devil's Island*

Condemned of Altona, The
FOX (Fr/It) 1962 dir. Vittorio di Sica
Sartre, J-P.
P

Condominium
UN TV (US) 1980 dir. Sidney Hayers
TVSe(US)
MacDonald, J. D.

Condorman
DISNEY (US) 1981 dir. Charles Jarrot
V
Sheckley, R. *Game of X, The*

Conduct Unbecoming
BL (GB) 1975 dir. Michael Anderson
V

England, B.
P

Cone of Silence
BL (GB) 1960 dir. Charles Frend
US title: Trouble in the Sky
Beatty, D.

Confessional
HG/GRANADA (US) 1990
dir. Gordon Flemyng
TVSe(GB/US)
Higgins, J.

Confessions from a Holiday Camp
COL (GB) 1977 dir. Norman Cohen
V

Lea, T.

Confessions of a Driving Instructor
COL (GB) 1976 dir. Norman Cohen
V

Lea, T.

Confessions of a Pop Performer
COL (GB) 1975 dir. Norman Cohen
V

Lea, T.

Confessions of a Window Cleaner
COL (GB) 1974 dir. Val Guest
V

Lea, T.

Confessions of Felix Krull, The
FILMAUFBAU (Ger) 1958
dir. Kurt Hoffman
V

Mann, T.

Confidential Agent
WAR (US) 1945 dir. Herman Shumlin
Greene, G.

Confidentially Yours
IS (Fr) 1984 dir. François Truffaut
V

Williams, C. *Long Saturday Night, The*

Conflict of Wings
BL (GB) 1953 dir. John Eldridge
US title: Fuss Over Feathers
Sharp, D.

Conformist, The
CURZON (It/Fr/W.Ger) 1969
dir. Bernardo Bertolucci
Moravia, A.

Connecticut Yankee, A
FOX (US) 1931 dir. David Butler
Twain, M. *Connecticut Yankee at the Court of King Arthur, A*

Connecticut Yankee in King Arthur's Court, A
PAR (US) 1948 dir. Tay Garnett
GB title: Yankee in King Arthur's Court, A
M, V
CONSOL (US) 1989 dir. Mel Damski
TV(US)
Twain, M. *Connecticut Yankee at the Court of King Arthur, A*

Connection, The
CONT (US) 1961 dir. Shirley Clarke
V

Gelber, J.
P

Connecting Rooms
TELSTAR (GB) 1969
dir. Franklin Gollings
V

Hart, M. *The Cellist*
P

Conquering Horde
PAR (US) 1931 dir. Edward Sloman

Hough, E. *North of 36*

Conquest
MGM (US) 1937 dir. Clarence Brown
GB title: Marie Walewska

Jerome, H.
P

Conquest of Space
PAR (US) 1955 dir. Byron Haskin
V

Bonestell, C. and Ley, W.
P

Conrack
FOX (US) 1974 dir. Martin Ritt
V

Conroy, P. *Water is Wide, The*

Consenting Adult
STARGER (US) 1985 dir. Gilbert Cates
TV(US)

Hobson, L. Z.

Consider Your Verdict
CHARTER (GB) 1938 dir. Roy Boulting

Housman, L.
P

Conspiracy of Terror
LORIMAR (US) 1975
dir. John Llewellyn Moxey
TV(US)

Delman, D.

Conspirator
MGM (GB) 1949 dir. Victor Saville

Slater, H.

Conspirators, The
WAR (US) 1944 dir. Jean Negulesco

Prokosch, F. *City of Shadows*

Constant Nymph, The
GAU (GB) 1933 dir. Basil Dean
WAR (US) 1943 dir. Edmund Goulding

Kennedy, M.

Consuming Passions
GOLDWYN (GB) 1988 dir. Giles Foster
V

Palin, M. and Jones, T. *Secrets*
P

Contract on Cherry Street
COL TV (US) 1977
dir. William A. Grahan
TV(US)

Rosenberg, P.

Convicted
COL (US) 1950 dir. Henry Levin

Flavin, M. *One Way Out*
P

Convicts Four
ALLIED (US) 1962 dir. Millard Kaufman
GB title: Reprieve

Resko, J. *Reprieve*

Cool Breeze
MGM (US) 1972 dir. Barry Pollack
V

Burnett, W. R. *Asphalt Jungle, The*

Cool Hand Luke
WAR (US) 1967 dir. Stuart Rosenberg
V

Pearce, D.

Cool World, The
WISEMAN (US) 1963
dir. Shirley Clarke
V

Miller, W.

Cop
ATLANTIC (US) 1988
dir. James B. Harris
V

Ellroy, J. *Blood on the Moon*

Corn is Green, The
WAR (US) 1945 dir. Irving Rapper
V
M. EVANS (US) 1956
dir. George Schaefer
TV(US)
WAR (US) 1979 dir. George Cukor
TV(US)

Williams, E.
P

Coroner Creek
COL (US) 1948 dir. Ray Enright

Short, L.

Corpse Came C.O.D., The
COL (US) 1947 dir. Henry Levin

Starr, J.

Corridor of Mirrors
GFD (GB) 1948 dir. Terence Young

Massie, C.

Corrupt
NEW LINE (It) 1983 dir. Robert Faenza
V

Fleetwood, H. *Order of Death, The*

Corsican Brothers, The
UA (US) 1942 dir. Gregory Ratoff
ROSEMONT (US) 1985 dir. Ian Sharp
TV(US), V

Dumas, A. *Deux Frères*

Cottage to Let
GFD (GB) 1941 dir. Anthony Asquith
US title: Bombsight Stolen

Kerr, G.
P

Cotton Comes to Harlem
UA (US) 1969 dir. Ossie Davis

Himes, C.

Couch Trip, The
ORION (US) 1988 dir. Michael Ritchie
V

Kolb, K.

Counsellor at Law
UN (US) 1933 dir. William Wyler

Rice, E.
P

Counsel's Opinion
KORDA (GB) 1933 dir. Allan Dwan

Wakefield, G.
P

Counterattack
COL (US) 1945 dir. Zoltan Korda
GB title: One Against Seven

Stevenson, J. and Stevenson, P.
P

Counterfeit Traitor, The
PAR (US) 1962 dir. George Seaton

Klein, A.

Counterpoint
UI (US) 1968 dir. Ralph Nelson

Sillitoe, A. *General, The*

Count of Monte Cristo, The
UA (US) 1934 dir. Rowland V. Lee
ROSEMONT (GB) 1975
dir. David Greene
TV(GB)
(Fr/GB) 1987 dir. D. de la Patellière
TV(Fr/GB)

Dumas, A.

Country Girl, The
PAR (US) 1954 dir. George Seaton
V
PAR (US) 1974 dir. Paul Bogart
TV(US)
Odets, C.
P

Country Girls, The
LONDON (GB) 1983
dir. Desmond Davis
V
O'Brien, E.

Country Dance
MGM (GB) 1969 dir. J. Lee Thompson
Kennaway, J. *Household Ghosts*

Count Your Blessings
MGM (US) 1959 dir. Jean Negulesco
Mitford, N. *Blessing, The*

Coup de Torchon
FT (Fr) 1981 dir. Bertrand Tavernier
GB title: Clean Slate
Thompson, J. *POP: 1280*

Courage of Kavik, the Wolf Dog, The
PANTHEON (US) 1980 dir. Peter Carter
TV(US)
Morey, W. *Kavik the Wolf Dog*

Court Martial of George Amstrong Custer, The
HALLMARK (US) 1977
dir. Glenn Jordan
TV(US)
Jones, D. C.

Courtneys of Curzon Street, The
BL (GB) 1947 dir. Herbert Wilcox
US title: Courtney Affair, The
Tranter, F.

Courtship of Eddie's Father, The
MGM (US) 1963 dir. Vincente Minnelli
Toby, M.

Covenant with Death, A
WAR (US) 1966 dir. Lamont Johnson
Becker, S.

Cover Her Face
ANGLIA (GB) 1985
TVSe(GB)
James, P. D.

Cowboy
COL (US) 1957 dir. Delmer Daves
Harris, F. *On the Trail: My Reminiscences as a Cowboy*

Cowboys, The
WAR (US) 1972 dir. Mark Rydell
V
Jennings, W. D.

Cow Country
ABP (US) 1953 dir. Lesley Selander
Bishop, C. *Shadow Range*

Crabe Tambour, Le
AMLF (Fr) 1977
dir. Pierre Schoendoerffer
Schoendoerffer, P.

Cracker Factory, The
EMI (US) 1979 dir. Burt Brinckerhoff
TV(US), V
Rebeta-Burditt, J.

Crack in the Mirror
FOX (US) 1960 dir. Richard Fleischer
Haedrich, M.

Cradle Song, The
M. EVANS (US) 1956
dir. George Schaefer
TV(US)
COMPASS (US) 1960
dir. George Schaefer
TV(US)
Sierra, G. M.
P

Cradle will Fall, The
P&G PRODS (US) 1983
dir. J. Llewellyn Moxey
TV(US)
Clark, M. H.

Craig's Wife
COL (US) 1936 dir. Dorothy Arzner
V
Kelly, G.
P

Crash
FRIES (US) 1978 dir. Barry Shear
TV(US)
Elder, R. and Elder, S.

Crawlspace
TITUS (US) 1972 dir. Joan Newland
TV(US)
Lieberman, H.

Craze
EMI (GB) 1973 dir. Freddie Francis
V
Seymour, H. *Infernal Idol*

Creator
UN (US) 1985 dir. Ivan Passer
V
Leven, J.

Crime and Punishment
COL (US) 1935 dir. Josef von Sternberg
GAU (Fr) 1935 dir. Pierre Chenal
AA (US) 1958 dir. Denis Sanders
Dostoevski, F. M.

Crime by Night
WAR (US) 1944 dir. William Clemens
Homes, G. *Forty Whacks*

Crime in the Streets
AA (US) 1956 dir. Don Siegel
Rose, R.
P

Crimes of the Heart
DELAUR (US) 1986
dir. Bruce Beresford
V
Henley, B.
P

Crimson Circle, The
NEW ERA (GB) 1929 dir. Fred Zelnick
WAINRIGHT (GB) 1936
dir. Reginald Denham
Wallace, E.

Crisis at Central High
TIME-LIFE (US) 1981
dir. Lamont Johnson
TV(US), V
Huckaby, E. P.

Criss Cross
UI (US) 1949 dir. Robert Siodmak
V
Tracy, D.

Critical List, The
MTM INC (US) 1978 dir. Lou Antonio
TVSe(US)
Goldberg, Dr. M.

Critic's Choice
WAR (US) 1963 dir. Don Weis
Levin, I.
P

Crooked Road, The
GALA (GB/Yugo) 1964 dir. Don Chaffey
West, M. L. *Big Story, The*

Crooked Hearts, The
LORIMAR (US) 1972 dir. Jay Sandrich
TV(US)
Watson, C. *Miss Lonelyhearts 4122*

Cross and the Switchblade, The
FOX (US) 1970 dir. Don Murray
V
Wilkerson, D.

Cross Country
NEW WORLD (Can) 1983
dir. Paul Lynch
V
Kastle, H.

Cross Creek
UN (US) 1983 dir. Martin Ritt
V
Rawlings, M. K.

Crossfire
RKO (US) 1947 dir. Edward Dmytryk
V
Brooks, R. *Brick Foxhole, The*

Crossing Delancey
WAR (US) 1988 dir. Joan Micklin Silver
V
Sandler, S.
P

Crossings
A. SPELLING (US) 1986
dir. Karen Arthur
TVSe(US)
Steel, D.

Crossing to Freedom
TELECOM/GRANADA (GB/US) 1990
dir. Norman Stone
TV(GB/US)
Shute, N. *Pied Piper, The*

Cross of Iron
AVCO (GB/Ger) 1977
dir. Sam Peckinpah
Henrich, W.

Crosswinds
PAR (US) 1951 dir. Lewis R. Foster
Burtis, T. *New Guinea Gold*

Crouching Beast, The
OLY (GB) 1935 dir. Victor Hanbury
Williams, V. *Clubfoot*

Crowded Sky, The
WAR (US) 1960 dir. Joseph Pevney
Searls, H.

Crown Matrimonial
TALENT (US) 1974 dir. Alan Bridges
TV(US)
Ryton, R.
P

Crucifer of Blood
AGAMEMNON (US) 1991
dir. Fraser Heston
TV(US)
Giovanni, P.
P

Cruel Passion
TARGET (GB) 1977 dir. Chris Boger
De Sade, Marquis *Justine*

Cruel Sea, The
GFD (GB) 1952 dir. Charles Frend
V
Monsarrat, N.

Cruising
LORIMAR (US) 1980
dir. William Friedkin
V
Walker, G.

Crusoe
ISLAND (US) 1989 dir. Caleb Deschanel
V

Defoe, D. *Robinson Crusoe*

Cry for Happy
COL (US) 1961 dir. George Marshall

Campbell, G.

Cry for Love, A
FRIES/SACKS (US) 1980
dir. Paul Wendkos
TV(US)

Robinson, J. S. *Bedtime Story*

Cry for the Strangers
MGM (US) 1982 dir. Peter Medak
TV(US)

Saul, J.

Cry Freedom
UN (GB) 1987
dir. Richard Attenborough
V

Woods, D. *Biko*

Cry from the Streets, A
EROS (GB) 1958 dir. Lewis Gilbert

Coxhead, E. *Friend in Need, The*

Cry Havoc
MGM (US) 1943 dir. Richard Thorpe

Kenward, A. R. *Proof Thru' the Night*
P

Cry in the Dark, A
CANNON (US) 1988 dir. Fred Schepisi
V

Bryson, J. *Evil Angels*

Cry in the Night, A
WAR (US) 1956 dir. Frank Tuttle
V

Masterson, W. *All Through the Night*

Cry in the Wild, A
CONCORDE (US) 1990
dir. Mark Griffiths

Paulsen, G. *Hatchet*

Cry of Battle
WAR (US) 1964 dir. Irving Lerner
V

Appel, B. *Fortress in the Rice*

Cry of the City
FOX (US) 1948 dir. Robert Siodmak

Helseth, H. E. *Chair for Martin Rome, The*

Cry of the Innocent
NBC ENT. (US) 1980
dir. Michael O'Herlihy
V

Forsyth, F. *In No Comebacks*

Cry, The Beloved Country
BL (GB) 1951 dir. Zoltan Korda

Paton, A.

Cry Tough
UA (US) 1959 dir. Paul Stanley

Shulman, I. *Children of the Dark*

Cry Wolf
WAR (US) 1947 dir. Peter Godfrey
V

Carleton, Mrs M. C.

Cuckoo in the Nest, A
GB (GB) 1938 dir. Tom Walls

Travers, B.
P

Cujo
WAR (US) 1982 dir. Lewis Teague
V

King, S.

Cure for Love, The
BL (GB) 1949 dir. Robert Donat
Greenwood, W.
P

Curse of Frankenstein, The
WAR (GB) 1957 dir. Terence Fisher
V
Shelley, Mrs M. W. *Frankenstein*

Curse of the Werewolf, The
RANK (GB) 1961 dir. Terence Fisher
V
Endore, G. *Werewolf of Paris, The*

Curtain Up
GFD (GB) 1952 dir. Ralph Smart
V
King, P. *On Monday Next*
P

Custard Boys, The
FOREST HALL (GB) 1979
dir. Colin Finbow
Rae, J.

Cutter and Bone
UA (US) 1981 dir. Ivan Passer
GB title: Cutter's Way
V
Thornburg, N.

Cynara
GOLDWYN (US) 1933 dir. King Vidor
Harwood, H. M.
P

Cyrano de Bergerac
UA (US) 1950 dir. Michael Gordon
V
COMPASS (US) 1962
dir. George Schaefer
TV(US)
UGC (Fr) 1990 dir. Jean-Paul Rappeneau
Rostand, E.
P

Da
FILM DALLAS (US) 1988
dir. Matt Clarke
V
Leonard, H.
P

Dad
UN (US) 1989 dir. Gary D. Goldberg
Wharton, W.

Daddy
NBC (US) 1991 dir. Michael Miller
Steel, D.

Daddy Long Legs
FOX (US) 1931 dir. Alfred Santell
FOX (US) 1955 dir. Jean Negulesco
M
Webster, J.

Daddy's Dyin' . . . Who's Got the Will?
MGM/UA (US) 1990 dir. Jack Fisk
Shores, D.
P

Dain Curse, The
POLL (US) 1978 dir. E. W. Swackhamer
TVSe(US), V
Hammett, D.

Daisy Kenyon
FOX (US) 1947 dir. Otto Preminger
Janeway, Mrs E.

Daisy Miller
PAR (US) 1974 dir. Peter Bogdanovich
V
James, H.

Dam Busters, The
ABP (GB) 1954 dir. Michael Anderson
V
Brickhill, P.

Damnation Alley
FOX (US) 1977 dir. Jack Smight
V
Zalazny, R.

Damned, The
BL (GB) 1961 dir. Joseph Losey
US title: These Are The Damned
Lawrence, H. L. *Children of the Light, The*

Damned Don't Cry, The
WAR (US) 1950 dir. Vincent Sherman
Walker, G. *Case History*

Damn Yankees
WAR (US) 1958 dir. George Abbott, Stanley Donen
GB title: What Lola Wants
M, V
Adler, R. and Ross, J.
P
Wallop, D. *Year the Yankees Lost the Pennant, The*

Damsel in Distress, A
RKO (US) 1937 dir. George Stevens
M, V
Wodehouse, P. G.

Dance Hall
FOX (US) 1941 dir. Irving Pichel
V
Burnett, W. R.

Dance of Death, The
PAR (GB) 1968 dir. David Giles
Strindberg, A.
P

Dance of the Dwarfs
DOVE (Phil/US) 1982 dir. Gus Trikonis
V
Household, G.

Dance Pretty Lady
BI (GB) 1932 dir. Anthony Asquith
Mackenzie, Sir C. *Carnival*

Dances with Wolves
ORION (US) 1990 dir. Kevin Costner
V
Blake, M.

Dancing in the Dark
FOX (US) 1949 dir. Irving Reis
Kaufman, G. S., Dietz, H. and Schwarz, A. *Bandwagon, The*
P

Dancing in the Dark
CAN BC (Can) 1986 dir. Leon Marr
V

Barfoot, J.

Dancing Lady
MGM (US) 1933 dir. Robert Z. Leonard
M, V

Bellah, J. W.

Dancing Years, The
ABPC (GB) 1949 dir. Harold French
ATV (GB) 1979
TV(GB)

Novello, I.

Dandy in Aspic, A.
COL (GB) 1968 dir. Anthony Mann

Marlowe, D.

Danger Ahead
MON (GB) 1940 dir. Ralph Staub

Erskine, L. Y. *Renfrew's Long Trail*

Dangerous Company
FINNEGAN (US) 1982
dir. Lamont Johnson
TV(US)

Johnson, R. and McCormick, M.
Too Dangerous to be at Large

Dangerous Corner
RKO (US) 1934 dir. Phil Rosen

Priestley, J. B.
P

Dangerous Davies — The Last Detective
INNER CIRCLE (GB) 1980
dir. Val Guest
V

Thomas, L.

Dangerous Days of Kiowa Jones, The
MGM (US) 1966 dir. Alex March
TV(US)

Adams, C.

Dangerous Exile
RANK (GB) 1957
dir. Brian Desmond Hurst

Wilkins, V. *King Reluctant, A*

Dangerous Journey
CHANNEL 4 (GB) 1985
TVSe (GB)

Bunyan, J. *Pilgrim's Progress*

Dangerous Liaisons
WAR (US) 1988 dir. Stephen Frears
V

de Laclos, P. *Liaisons Dangereuses, Les*
Hampton, C. *Liaisons Dangereuses, Les*
P

Dangerous to Know
PAR (US) 1938 dir. Robert Florey

Wallace, E. *On The Spot*
P

Danger Route
UA (GB) 1967 dir. Seth Holt

York, A. *Eliminator, The*

Danger Signal
WAR (US) 1945 dir. Robert Florey

Bottome, P.

Danger Within
BL (GB) 1958 dir. Don Chaffey
US title: Breakout

Gilbert, M. *Death in Captivity*

Daniel
PAR (GB) 1983 dir. Sidney Lumet
V

Doctorow, E. L. *Book of Daniel, The*

Danny Jones
CINERAMA (GB) 1972
dir. Jules Bricken
V

Collier, J. L. *Fires of Youth*

Danny the Champion of the World
COL (GB) 1989 dir. Gavin Millar
Ch
Dahl, R.

Danton
GAU/TFI (Fr/Pol) 1982
dir. Andrzej Wajda
Przybyszewska, S. *Danton Affair, The*
P

Darby's Rangers
WAR (US) 1957 dir. William Wellman
GB title: Young Invaders, The
Altieri, Major J.

Dark Angel, The
GOLDWYN (US) 1935
dir. Sidney Franklin
Bolton, G.
P

Dark Angel, The
BBC (GB) 1991 dir. Peter Hammond
TV(GB)
Le Fanu, S. *Uncle Silas*

Dark at the Top of the Stairs, The
WAR (US) 1960 dir. Delbert Mann
Inge, W. M.
P

Dark Command
REP (US) 1940 dir. Raoul Walsh
V
Burnett, W. R.

Darker than Amber
FOX (US) 1970 dir. Robert Clouse
MacDonald, J. D.

Dark Eyes
EXCELSIOR (It) 1987
dir. Nikita Mikhalkov
V
Chekhov, A. *Stories*

Dark Holiday
ORION TV (US) 1989 dir. Lou Antonio
TV(US)
LePere, G. *Never Pass This Way Again*

Dark Journey
LONDON GBN (US) 1937
dir. Victor Saville
Biro, L.
P

Dark Night
GOODYEAR (Tai/HK) 1986
dir. Fred Tan
Li-Eng, S.

Dark Passage
WAR (US) 1947 dir. Delmer Daves
V
Goodis, D.

Dark Secret of Harvest Home, The
UN TV (US) 1978 dir. Leo Penn
TVSe(US), V
Tryon, T. *Harvest Home*

Dark Tower, The
WAR (GB) 1943 dir. John Harlow
Woolcott, A. and Kaufman, G. S.
P

Dark Victory
WAR (US) 1939 dir. Edmund Goulding
V
UN (US) 1976 dir. Robert Butler
TV(US)

Brewer, G. E. and Bloch, B.
P

Dark Waters
UA (US) 1944 dir. André de Toth
V

Cockrell, F. M. and Cockrell, M.

Darling Buds of May, The
YTV (GB) 1991 dir. Robert Tronson
TV(GB)

Bates, H. E.

Darling, How Could You
PAR (US) 1951 dir. Mitchell Leisen
GB title: Rendezvous

Barrie, Sir J. M. *Alice Sit-by-the-Fire*
P

Darlings of the Gods
THAMES (GB) 1991
dir. Catherine Millar
TVSe(GB)

O'Connor, G.

Daughter of the Dragon
PAR (US) 1931 dir. Lloyd Corrigan

Rohmer, S. *Daughter of Fu Manchu*

Daughter of the Mind
FOX (US) 1969 dir. Walter Grauman
TV(US)

Gallico, P. *Hand of Mary Constable,
The*

Daughters Courageous
WAR (US) 1939 dir. Michael Curtiz

Bennett, D. *Fly Away Home*
P

David
KINO (W.Ger) 1982 dir. Peter Lilienthal

Konig, J.

David
ITC (US) 1988 dir. John Erman
TV(US)

Rothenberg, M. and White, M.

David and Lisa
BL (US) 1963 dir. Frank Perry
V

Rubin, T. I. *Lisa and David*

David Copperfield
MGM (US) 1935 dir. George Cukor
V
OMNIBUS (GB) 1970
dir. Delbert Mann
TV(GB), V
BBC GB 1986
TVSe(GB)

Dickens, C.

Dawning, The
(TVS) (GB) 1988 dir. Robert Knights
TVSe(GB)

Johnston, J. *The Old Jest*

Daybreak
GFD (GB) 1946 dir. Compton Bennett

Hoffe, M.

Day in the Death of Joe Egg, A
COL (GB) 1971 dir. Peter Medak
V

Nichols, P.
P

Day of the Dolphin, The
AVCO (US) 1973 dir. Mike Nichols
V

Merle, R.

Day of the Jackal, The
UN (Fr/GB) 1973 dir. Fred Zinnemann
V

Forsyth, F.

Day of the Locust, The
PAR (US) 1975 dir. John Schlesinger
V

West, N.

Day of the Outlaw, The
UA (US) 1958 dir. André de Toth

Wells, L. E.

Day of the Triffids, The
RANK (GB) 1962 dir. Steve Sekely
V
BBC (GB) 1982 dir. Ken Hannam
TVSe(GB)

Wyndham, J.

Day One
A. SPELLING (US) 1989
dir. Joseph Sargent
TV(US)

Wyden, P. *Day One: Before Hiroshima and After*

Day the Bubble Burst, The
FOX (US) 1982 dir. Joseph Hardy
TV(US)

Thomas, G. and Witts, M.

Day the Loving Stopped, The
MONASH-ZEITMAN (US) 1981
dir. Delbert Mann
TV(US)

List, J. A.

Day They Robbed the Bank of England, The
MGM (GB) 1959 dir. John Guillermin

Brophy, J.

Day to Remember, A
GFD (GB) 1953 dir. Ralph Thomas

Tickell, J. *Hand and the Flower, The*

D-Day the Sixth of June
FOX (US) 1956 dir. Henry Koster
V

Shapiro, L. *Sixth of June, The*

Dead, The
VESTRON (US) 1987 dir. John Huston
V

Joyce, J.

Dead Calm
WAR (Aus) 1989 dir. Philip Noyce

Williams, C.

Dead Cert
UA (GB) 1974 dir. Tony Richardson

Francis, D.

Dead End
UA (US) 1937 dir. William Wyler
V

Kingsley, S.
P

Deadfall
FOX (GB) 1968 dir. Bryan Forbes

Cory, D.

Deadline at Dawn
RKO (US) 1946 dir. Harold Clurman
V

Irish, W.

Deadly Affair, The
COL (GB) 1966 dir. Sidney Lumet
V

Le Carré, J. *Call for the Dead*

Deadly Companions, The
WAR (US) 1961 dir. Sam Peckinpah
V

Fleischman, A. S. *Yellowleg*

Deadly Duo
UA (US) 1962 dir. Reginald LeBorg

Jessup, R.

Deadly Eyes
WAR (US) 1983 dir. Robert Clouse
V
Herbert, J.

Deadly Friend
WAR (US) 1986 dir. Wes Craven
V
Henstell, D. *Friend*

Deadly Harvest
CBS ENT (US) 1972
dir. Michael O'Herlihy
TV(US), V
Household, G. *Watcher in the Shadows*

Deadly Hunt, The
FOUR STAR (US) 1971
dir. John Newland
TV(US)
Stadley, P. *Autumn of a Hunter*

Deadly Intentions
GREEN-EPSTEIN (US) 1985
dir. Noel Black
TVSe(US)
Stevens, W. R.

Deadly is the Female
UA (US) 1949 dir. Joseph Lewis
Kantor, M. *Gun Crazy*

Deadly Record
AA (GB) 1959 dir. Lawrence Huntington
Hooke, N. W.

Deadly Silence, A.
R. GREENWALD (US) 1989
dir. John Patterson
TV(US)
Kleiman, D.

Deadly Trap, The
NAT GEN (Fr/It) 1971
dir. René Clément
V
Cavanaugh, A. *Children are Gone, The*

Dead Men Tell No Tales
ALL (GB) 1938 dir. David MacDonald
Beeding, F. *Norwich Victims, The*

Dead Men Tell No Tales
FOX (US) 1971 dir. Walter Grauman
TV(US)
Roos, K. *To Save His Life*

Dead Man's Folly
WAR (US) 1986 dir. Clive Donner
TV(US)
Christie, A.

Dead of Jericho, The
CENTRAL (GB) 1989
dir. Edward Bennett
TV(GB)
Dexter, C.

Dead on the Money
INDIEPROD (US) 1991
dir. Mark Cullingham
TV(US)
Ingalls, R. *End of Tragedy, The*

Dead Ringers
FOX (Can) 1988 dir. David Cronenberg
V
Wood, B. & Geasland, J. *Twins*

Dead Solid Perfect
HBO (US) 1988 dir. Bobby Roth
TV(US)
Jenkins, D.

Dead Zone, The
PAR (US) 1983 dir. David Cronenberg
V
King, S.

Dealing: or The Berkeley-to-Boston-Forty-Brick-Lost-Bag-Blues
WAR (US) 1972 dir. Paul Williams
Douglas, M.

Dear Brigitte
FOX (US) 1965 dir. Henry Koster
V

Haase, J. *Erasmus with Freckles*

Dear Heart
WAR (US) 1964 dir. Delbert Mann

Mosel, T.

Dear Inspector
ARIANE/MONDEX (Fr) 1977
dir. Philippe de Broca

Rouland, J-P and Olivier, C. *Tendre Poulet*

Dear John
SANDREW (Swe) 1964
dir. Lars Magnus Lindgren

Lansburg, O.

Dear Mr Prohack
GFD (GB) 1949 dir. Thornton Freeland

Bennett, A. *Mr Prohack*

Dear Murderer
GFD (GB) 1947 dir. Arthur Crabtree

Clowes, St. J. L.

Dear Octopus
GFD (GB) 1943 dir. Harold French
US title: Randolph Family, The

Smith, D.
P

Dear Ruth
PAR (US) 1947 dir. William D. Russell

Krasna, N.
P

Death at Broadcasting House
PHOENIX (GB) 1934
dir. Reginald Denham

Gielgud, V. H.

Death Be Not Proud
WESTFALL (US) 1975 dir. Donald Wrye
TV(US), V

Gunther, J.

Death Dreams
D. CLARK (US) 1991
dir. Martin Donovan
TV(US)

Katz, W.

Death in California, A.
LORIMAR (US) 1985 dir. Delbert Mann
TVSe(US)

Barthel, J.

Death in Canaan, A.
WAR (US) 1978 dir. Tony Richardson
TV(US)

Barthel, J.

Death in Venice
WAR (It) 1971 dir. Luchino Visconti
V

Mann, T.

Death is Part of the Process
BBC (GB) 1986
TV(GB)

Bernstein, H.

Death of a Gunfighter
UI (US) 1969 dir. Robert Totten, Don Siegel
V

Patten, L. B.

Death of an Expert Witness
ANGLIA (GB) 1983 dir. Herbert Wise
TVSe(GB)

James, P. D.

Death of a Salesman
COL (US) 1951 dir. Laslo Benedek
PUNCH (US) 1985
dir. Volker Schlondorff
TV(US), V

Miller, A.
P

Death of a Schoolboy
NEUE STUDIO (Austria) 1991
dir. Peter Patzak

Konig, H.

Death of Innocence, A
CARLINER (US) 1971
dir. Paul Wendkos
TV

Popkin, Z.

Death of Me Yet, The
A. SPELLING (US) 1971
dir. John Llewellyn-Moxey
TV(US)

Masterson, W.

Death of Richie, The
H. JAFFE (US) 1977 dir. Paul Wendkos
TV(US), V

Thompson, T.

Death of the Heart, The
GRANADA (GB) 1985
TV(GB)

Bowen, E.

Death on the Nile
EMI (GB) 1978 dir. John Guillermin
V

Christie, A.

Death Sentence
SPELLING-GOLDBERG (US) 1974
dir. E. W. Swackhamer
TV, V

Roman, E. *After the Trial*

Death Stalk
D. WOLPER (US) 1975 dir. Robert Day
TV(US), V

Chastain, T.

Death Takes a Holiday
PAR (US) 1934 dir. Mitchell Leisen
UN TV (US) 1971 dir. Robert Butler
TV(US)

Anderson, M. and Casella, A.
P

Deathtrap
WAR (US) 1982 dir. Sidney Lumet

Levin, I.
P

Deathwatch
CONTEM (Fr/Ger) 1979
dir. Bertrand Tavernier
V

Compton, D. *Unsleeping Eye, The*

Death Wish
CANNON (US) 1974
dir. Michael Winner
V

Garfield, B.

Decameron, The
UA (It/Fr/W.Ger) 1970
dir. Pier Paolo Pasolini
V

Boccaccio, G.

Decameron Nights
EROS (GB) 1952 dir. Hugo Fregonese
V

Boccaccio, G. *Decameron, The*

Deceivers, The
MERCHANT IVORY (GB/Ind) 1988
dir. Nicholas Meyer

Masters, J.

Deception
WAR (US) 1946 dir. Irving Rapper
V

Verneuil, L. *Jealousy*
P

Deceptions
COL (US) 1985 dir. Robert Chenault
TVSe(US)

Michael, J.

Decision Before Dawn
FOX (US) 1951 dir. Anatole Litvak

Howe, G. L. *Call it Treason*

Decision of Christopher Blake, The
WAR (US) 1948 dir. Peter Godfrey

Hart, M. *Christopher Blake*
P

Decline and Fall . . . of a Birdwatcher
FOX (GB) 1968 dir. John Karsh

Waugh, E. *Decline and Fall*

Decoration Day
M. REES (US) 1990
dir. Robert Markowitz
TV(US)

Corrington, J. W.

Deep, The
COL-WAR (US) 1977 dir. Peter Yates
V

Benchley, P.

Deep Blue Sea, The
FOX (GB) 1955 dir. Anatole Litvak

Rattigan, T.
P

Deep in my Heart
MGM (US) 1954 dir. Stanley Donen
M, V

Arnold, E.

Deep Six, The
WAR (US) 1958 dir. Rudolph Maté
V

Dibner, M.

Deep Valley
WAR (US) 1947 dir. Jean Negulesco

Totheroh, D.

Deep Waters
FOX (US) 1948 dir. Henry King

Moore, R. *Spoonhandle*

Deerslayer, The
FOX (US) 1957 dir. Kurt Neumann
V
SCHICK SUNN (US) 1978
dir. Dick Friedenberg
TV(US), V

Cooper, J. F.

Defector, The
PECF (Fr/W.Ger) 1966 dir. Raoul Levy

Thomas, P. *Spy, The*

Déjà Vu
CANNON (GB) 1985
dir. Anthony Richmond

Meldal-Johnson, T. *Always*

Delavine Affair, The
MON (GB) 1954 dir. Douglas Pierce

Chapman, R. *Winter Wears a Shroud*

Deliberate Stranger, The
LORIMAR (US) 1986
dir. Marvin Chomsky
TVSe(US)

Larsen, R. W. *Bundy: The Deliberate Stranger*

Delicate Balance, A
SEVEN KEYS (US) 1975
dir. Tony Richardson

Albee, E.
P

Delinquents, The
GR UN (Aust) 1990 dir. Chris Thomson
Rohan, C.

Deliverance
WAR (US) 1973 dir. John Boorman
V
Dickey, J.

Deluge, The
POLSKI (Pol) 1974 dir. Jerzy Hoffman
Sienkiewicz, H.

Demon Seed
MGM (US) 1977 dir. Donald Cammell
V
Koontz, D.

Dempsey
FRIES (US) 1983 dir. Gus Trikonis
TV(US)
Dempsey, J. and Dempsey, B. P.

Dentist in the Chair
REN (GB) 1960 dir. Don Chaffey
Finch, M.

Dernier Tournant, Le
LUX (Fr) 1939 dir. Pierre Chenal
Cain, J. M. *Postman Always Rings Twice, The*

Desert Fox, The
FOX (US) 1951 dir. Henry Hathaway
GB title: Rommel, Desert Fox
V
Young, D. *Rommel, The Desert Fox*

Desert Fury
PAR (US) 1947 dir. Lewis Allen
Stewart, R. *Desert Town*

Desert Gold
PAR (US) 1936 dir. James Hogan
V
Grey, Z.

Desert Hearts
MGM (US) 1986 dir. Donna Deitch
V
Rule, J. *Desert of the Heart*

Desert Pursuit
ABP (US) 1952 dir. George Blair
Perkins, K. *Desert Voices*

Desert Sands
UA (US) 1955 dir. Lesley Selander
Robb, J. *Punitive Action*

Desert Song
WAR (US) 1943 dir. Robert Florey
M
WAR (US) 1953
dir. Bruce Humberstone
M
Harbach, O., Schwab, L. and Mandel, F.
P

Design for Living
PAR (US) 1933 dir. Ernst Lubitsch
Coward, N.
P

Desire
PAR (US) 1936 dir. Frank Borzage
Szekely, H. and Stemmple, R. A.
P

Desirée
FOX (US) 1954 dir. Henry Koster
V
Selinko, A.

Desire in the Dust
TCF (US) 1960 dir. William F. Claxton
Whittington, H.

Desire Me
MGM (US) 1947 dir. George Cukor
Frank, L. *Carl and Anna*

Desire Under the Elms
PAR (US) 1958 dir. Delbert Mann

O'Neill, E. G.
P

Desk Set, The
TCF (US) 1957 dir. Walter Lang
GB title: His Other Woman

Marchant, W.
P

Despair
GALA (Ger) 1978
dir. Rainer Werner Fassbinder
V

Nabokov, V.

Desperate Characters
ITC (US) 1971 dir. Frank D. Gilroy
V

Fox, P.

Desperate Hours, The
PAR (US) 1955 dir. William Wyler
MGM (US) 1990 dir. Michael Cimino
V

Hayes, J.

Desperate Man, The
AA (GB) 1959 dir. Peter Maxwell

Somers, P. *Beginner's Luck*

Desperate Moment
GFD (GB) 1953 dir. Compton Bennett

Albrand, M.

Desperate Ones, The
AMERICAN (Sp/US) 1968
dir. Alexander Ramati
V

Ramati, A. *Beyond the Mountains*

Desperate Search
MGM (US) 1952 dir. Joseph Lewis

Mayse, A.

Desperate Voyage
WIZAN (US) 1980
dir. Michael O'Herlihy
TV(US)

Kytle, R. *Last Voyage of the Valhalla*

Destination Tokyo
WAR (US) 1943 dir. Delmer Daves
V

Fisher, S. G.

Destiny of a Spy
UN TV (US) 1969 dir. Boris Sagal
TV(US)

Blackburn, W. J. *Gaunt Women, The*

Destry
UI (US) 1954 dir. George Marshall

Brand, M. *Destry Rides Again*

Destry Rides Again
UN (US) 1939 dir. George Marshall
V

Brand, M.

Detective, The
FOX (US) 1968 dir. Gordon Douglas
V

Thorp, R.

Detective, The
BBC (GB) 1985 dir. Don Leaver
TVSe(GB)

Ferris, P.

Detective Story
PAR (US) 1951 dir. William Wyler

Kingsley, S.
P

Detour
PRC (US) 1946 dir. Edgar G. Ulmer

Goldsmith, M. M.

Devil and the Nun, The
KADR (Pol) 1960
dir. Jerzy Kawalerowicz
Iwaszkiewicz, J.

Devil at 4 O'Clock, The
COL (US) 1961 dir. Mervyn Le Roy
V
Catto, M.

Devil Commands, The
COL (US) 1941 dir. Edward Dmytryk
Sloane, W. *Edge of Running Water, The*

Devil Dogs of the Air
WAR (US) 1935 dir. Lloyd Bacon
Saunders, J. M.

Devil Doll, The
MGM (US) 1936 dir. Tod Browning
V
Merritt, A. *Burn, Witch, Burn*

Devil in the Flesh
TRANS (Fr) 1947
dir. Claude Autant-Lara
ORION (It/Fr) 1987
dir. Marco Bellocchio
V
Radiguet, R.

Devil is a Woman, The
PAR (US) 1935 dir. Josef von Sternberg
Louys, P. *Femme et le Pantin, La*

Devil Makes Three, The
MGM (US) 1952 dir. Andrew Marton
Bachmann, L. *Kiss of Death*

Devil Never Sleeps, The
FOX (GB) 1962 dir. Leo McCarey
Buck, P.

Devil Rides Out, The
ABP (GB) 1971 dir. Terence Fisher
US title: Devil's Bride, The
Wheatley, D.

Devils, The
WAR (GB) 1971 dir. Ken Russell
V
Huxley, A. *Devils of Loudon, The*

Devil's Advocate, The
RANK (Ger) 1977 dir. Guy Green
West, M.

Devil's Brigade, The
UA (US) 1968 dir. Andrew V. MacLaglen
Adleman, R. H. and Walton, G.

Devil's Daffodil, The
BL (GB) 1962 dir. Akos Rathony
Wallace, E. *Daffodil Mystery, The*

Devil's Disciple, The
M. EVANS (US) 1955
dir. George Schaefer
TV(US)
UA (GB) 1959 dir. Guy Hamilton
Shaw, G. B.
P

Devil's General, The
RYAL (W Ger) 1955 dir. Helmut Kautner
Zuckmayer, C.
P

Devil's Own, The
FOX (GB) 1967 dir. Cyril Frankel
Curtis, P.

Devotion
RKO (US) 1931 dir. Robert Milton
Wynne, P. *Little Flat in the Temple, A*

Diaboliques, Les
FILMSONOR (Fr) 1954
dir. Henri-Georges Clouzot
V

Boileau, P. and Narcejac, T. *Woman Who Was, The*

Dial 'M' for Murder
WAR (US) 1954 dir. Alfred Hitchcock
V
MILBERG (US) 1958
dir. George Schaefer
TIME-LIFE PRODS (US) 1981
dir. Boris Sagal
TV(US)
Knott, F.
P

Diamond Head
COL (US) 1962 dir. Guy Green
V
Gilman, P.

Diamond Horseshoe
FOX (US) 1945 dir. George Seaton
Nicholson, K. *Barker, The*
P

Diamond Jim
UN (US) 1935 dir. A. Edward Sutherland
Morell, P.

Diamonds are Forever
UA (GB) 1971 dir. Guy Hamilton
V
Fleming, I.

Diamond's Edge
KINGS (US) 1990 dir. Stephen Bayly
Horowitz, A. *Falcon's Malteser, The*

Diamond Trap, The
COL TV (US) 1988 dir. Don Taylor
TV(US)
Minahan, J. *Great Diamond Robbery, The*

Diana
BBC (GB) 1983 dir. David Tucker
TVSe(GB)

Delderfield, R. F. *There was a Fair Maid Dwelling: The Unjust Skies*

Diary of a Chambermaid, The
B. BOGEAUS (US) 1946
dir. Jean Renoir
V
Mirbeau, O.

Diary of a Country Priest, The
GGT (Fr) 1950 dir. Robert Bresson
V
Bernanos, G.

Diary of a Mad Housewife
UI (US) 1970 dir. Frank Perry
V
Kaufman, S.

Diary of Anne Frank, The
FOX (US) 1959 dir. George Stevens
V
FOX (US) 1980 dir. Boris Sagal
TV(US)
BBC (GB) 1988
TVSe(GB)

Frank, A. *Anne Frank: The Diary of a Young Girl*

Diary of Major Thompson, The
GALA (Fr) 1955 dir. Preston Sturges
US title: French They are a Funny Race, The

Daninos, P. *Notebooks of Major Thompson, The*

Dick Turpin
STOLL-STAFFORD (GB) 1933
dir. Victor Hanbury, John Stafford
Ainsworth, H. *Rookwood*

Died in the Wool
ITV (GB) 1978 dir. Brian McDuffie
TVSe(GB)
Marsh, N.

Die Hard
FOX (US) 1988 dir. John McTiernan
V
Thorp, R.

Die Hard 2
FOX (US) 1990 dir. Renny Harlin
Wager, W. *58 Minutes*

Die, Monster, Die!
AIP (US/GB) 1965 dir. Daniel Haller
Lovecraft, H. P. *Color Out of Space, The*

Dieu à Besoin des Hommes
TRANS (Fr) 1950 dir. Jean Delannoy
Quefflec, H. *Recteur de l'Ile de Sein, Un*

Digby — The Biggest Dog in the World
RANK (GB) 1973 dir. Joseph McGrath
Ch, V
Key, T.

Dimenticare Palermo
PENTA (It/Fr) 1990 dir. Francesco Rosi
Charles-Roux, E.

Dinner at Eight
MGM (US) 1933 dir. George Cukor
V
TNT (US) 1989 dir. Ron Lagomarsino
TV(US)
Kaufman, G. S. and Ferber, E.
P

Diplomatic Courier
FOX (US) 1952 dir. Henry Hathaway
Cheyney, P. *Sinister Errand*

Dirty Dingus Magee
MGM (US) 1970 dir. Burt Kennedy
V
Markson, D. *Ballad of Dingus Magee, The*

Dirty Dozen, The
MGM (US) 1967 dir. Robert Aldrich
V
Nathanson, E. M.

Dirty Mary, Crazy Larry
FOX (US) 1974 dir. John Hough
V
Unekis, R. *Chase, The*

Dirty Tricks
FILMPLAN (Can) 1980 dir. Alvin Rakoff
V
Gifford, T. *Glendower Legacy, The*

Dirty Work
GAU (GB) 1934 dir. Tom Walls
Travers, B.
P

Disappearance, The
CINEGATE (GB/Can) 1977 dir. Stuart Cooper
V
Marlowe, D. *Echos of Celandine*

Discarnates, The
SHOCHIKU (Jap) 1989 dir. Nobuhiko Obayashi
Yamada, T.

Dishonoured Lady
MARS (US) 1947 dir. Robert Stevenson
V
Sheldon, E. and Barnes, M. A.
P

Disputed Passage
PAR (US) 1939 dir. Frank Borzage
Douglas, L. C.

Disraeli
WAR (US) 1929 dir. Alfred E. Green
Parker, L. N.
P

Distant Trumpet, A.
WAR (US) 1964 dir. Raoul Walsh
Horgan, P.

Dites-Lui que Je L'Aime
ART EYE (Fr) 1977 dir. Claude Miller
GB title: This Sweet Sickness
US title: Tell Her I Love Her
Highsmith, P.

Diva
GALAXIE (Fr) 1981
dir. Jean-Jacques Beineix
V
Delacorta

Divorcee, The
MGM (US) 1930 dir. Robert Z. Leonard
Parrott, U. *Ex-Wife*

Divorce of Lady X, The
LONDON (GB) 1938 dir. Tim Whelan
V
Wakefield, G. *Counsel's Opinion*
P

Doc Hollywood
WAR (US) 1991
dir. Michael Caton-Jones
Shulman, N.B. *What? . . . Dead Again?*

Doc Savage — Man of Bronze
WAR (US) 1975 dir. Michael Anderson
V
Robeson, K.

Dock Brief, The
MGM (GB) 1962 dir. James Hill
US title: Trial & Error
Mortimer, J.
P

Doctor, The
TOUCH (US) 1991 dir. Randa Haines
Rosenbaum, E. *Taste of my own Medicine, A*

Doctor and the Girl, The
MGM (US) 1949 dir. Curtis Bernhardt
van der Meersch, M. *Bodies and Souls*

Doctor Dolittle
FOX (US) 1967 dir. Richard Fleischer
Ch, M, V
Lofting, H.

Doctor Faustus
COL (GB) 1967 dir. Richard Burton,
Neville Coghill
V
Marlowe, C. *Tragical History of Doctor Faustus*
P

Doctor Fisher of Geneva
BBC (GB) 1984
dir. Michael Lindsay-Hogg
TV(GB)
Greene, G.

Doctor in the House
GFD (GB) 1954 dir. Ralph Thomas
V
Gordon, R.

Doctor in the Village
NFM (Neth) 1958 dir. Fons Rademakers
Coolen, A.

Doctor's Dilemma, The
MGM (GB) 1958 dir. Anthony Asquith
Shaw, G. B.
P

Doctor's Wives
COL (US) 1971 dir. George Schaefer
V
Slaughter, F. G.

Doctor, You've got to be Kidding
MGM (US) 1967 dir. Peter Tewkesbury
Mahan, P. W.

Doctor Zhivago
MGM (US) 1965 dir. David Lean
V
Pasternak, B.

Dodsworth
UA (US) 1936 dir. William Wyler
V
Lewis, S.

Dog of Flanders, A
FOX (US) 1959 dir. James B. Clark
V
Ouida

Dogs of War, The
UA (GB) 1980 dir. John Irvin
V
Forsyth, F.

Doing Life
PHOENIX (US) 1986
dir. Gene Reynolds
TV(US)
Bello, S.

Doktor Faustus
SAFIR (Ger) 1982 dir. Franz Seitz
Mann, T.

Dollmaker, The
IPC (US) 1984 dir. Daniel Petrie
TV(US), V
Arnow, A.

Doll's House, A
COMPASS (US) 1959
dir. George Schaefer
TV(US), V
BL (GB) 1973 dir. Patrick Garland
V
Ibsen, H.
P

Dombey and Son
BBC (GB) 1984
TVSe(GB)
Dickens, C.

Dominant Sex, The
AB (GB) 1937 dir. Herbert Brenon
Egan, M.
P

Dominique
GRAND PRIZE (GB) 1978
dir. Michael Anderson
Lawlor, H. *What Beckoning Ghost*

Domino Principle, The
ITC (US) 1977 dir. Stanley Kramer
V
Kennedy, A.

Dona Flor and her Two Husbands
FD (Braz) 1977 dir. Bruno Barretto
V
Amado, J.

Dona Herlinda and her Son
CLASA (Mex) 1986 dir. J. H. Hermosillo
V
Paez, J. L.

Don Camillo's Last Round
Rizzoli (Italy) 1955
dir. Carmine Guareschi
Guareschi, G.

Don Chicago
BN (GB) 1945 dir. Maclean Rogers
Roberts, C. E. B.

Don is Dead, The
UN (US) 1973 dir. Richard Fleischer
V
Albert, M. H.

Do Not Disturb
FOX (US) 1965 dir. Ralph Levy
Fairchild, W.
P

Do not Fold, Spindle or Mutilate
L. RICH (US) 1971 dir. Ted Post
TV(US)
Disney, D. M.

Donovan's Brain
UA (US) 1953 dir. Felix Feist
V
Siodmak, C.

Don Quixote
VANDOR (Fr) 1933 dir. G. W. Pabst
LENFILM (USSR) 1957
dir. Grigori Kozintsev
V
EUSTON (GB) 1985
TV
Cervantes, M. de

Don's Party
Double Head (Aust) 1976
dir. Bruce Beresford
Williamson, D.

Don't Bother to Knock
FOX (US) 1952 dir. Roy Ward Baker
V
Armstrong, C. *Mischief*

Don't Bother to Knock
WAR (GB) 1961 dir. Cyril Frankel
US title: Why Bother to Knock
Hanley, C. *Love From Everybody*

Don't Drink the Water
AVCO EMBASSY (US) 1969
dir. Howard Morris
V
Allen, W.
P

Don't go Near the Water
MGM (US) 1957 dir. Charles Walters
Brinkley, W.

Don't Just Lie There, Say Something
RANK (GB) 1973 dir. Bob Kellet
V
Pertwee, M.
P

Don't Just Stand There
UN (US) 1967 dir. Ron Winston
Williams, C. *Wrong Venus, The*

Don't Look Back
TBA (US) 1981 dir. Richard Colla
TV(US)
Paige, L. and Lipman, D. *Maybe I'll Pitch Forever*

Don't Look Now
BL (GB) 1973 dir. Nicolas Roeg
V
Du Maurier, D.

Don't Make Waves
MGM (US) 1967
dir. Alexander Mackendrick
Wallach, I. *Muscle Beach*

Don't Raise the Bridge, Lower the River
BL (GB) 1967 dir. Jerry Paris
V

Wilk, M.

Don't Tell Her It's Me
HEMDALE (US) 1990
dir. Malcolm Mowbray
Bird, S. *Boyfriend School, The*

Don't Touch My Daughter
P-K (US) 1991 dir. John Pasquin
TV(US)
Dorner, M. *Nightmare*

Door in the Wall, The
ABP (GB) 1956 dir. Glenn H. Alvey, Jr.
Wells, H. G.

Dorian Gray
AIP (It/Ger) 1970
dir. Massimo Dallamano
V

Wilde, O. *Picture of Dorian Gray, The*

Double Confession
ABP (GB) 1950 dir. Ken Annakin
Garden, J. *All on a Summer's Day*

Double Indemnity
PAR (US) 1944 dir. Billy Wilder
V
UN (US) 1973 dir. Jack Smight
TV(US)
Cain, J. M.

Double Man, The
WAR (GB) 1967 dir. Franklin Schaffner
V

Maxfield, H. S. *Legacy of a Spy*

Double Negative
QUADRANT (Can) 1980
dir. George Bloomfield
Macdonald, R. *Three Roads, The*

Double Standard
FRIES (US) 1988 dir. Louis Rudolph
TV (US)
Ellison, J. W.

Doubletake
TITUS (US) 1985 dir. Jud Taylor
TVSe(US)
Bayer, W. *Switch*

Double Wedding
MGM (US) 1937 dir. Richard Thorpe
Molnar, F. *Great Love*
P

Doubting Thomas
FOX (US) 1935 dir. David Butler
Kelly, G. *The Torch Bearers*
P

Doughgirls, The
WAR (US) 1944 dir. James V. Kern
Fields, J.
P

Dove, The
EMI (US) 1974 dir. Charles Jarrot
V

Graham, R. L. and Gill, D.

Down and Out in Beverly Hills
TOUCH (US) 1986 dir. Paul Mazursky
V

Fauchois, R. *Boudu Sauvé des Eaux*
P

Downhill Racer
PAR (US) 1969 dir. Michael Ritchie
V

Hall, O. *Downhill Racers*

Down the Long Hills
DISNEY CH (US) 1986
dir. Burt Kennedy
TV(US)
L'Amour, L.

Down 3 Dark Streets
UA (US) 1954 dir. Arnold Laven
Gordon, M. and Gordon G. *Case File F.B.I.*

Do You Like Women?
FRANCORITZ (Fr/It) 1964 dir. Jean Leon
Bardawil, G.

Dracula
UN (US) 1931 dir. Tod Browning
V
UI (GB) 1958 dir. Terence Fisher
US title: House of Dracula
EMI (It) 1973 dir. Paul Morrissey
UN (US) 1974 dir. Dan Curtis
TV (US), V
Stoker, B.

Dracula
CIC (GB) 1979 dir. John Badham
V
Stoker B.
Balderston, J. and Deane, H.
P

Dracula's Daughter
UN (US) 1936 dir. Lambert Hillyer
V
Stoker, B. *Dracula's Guest*

Dragon Seed
MGM (US) 1944 dir. Jack Conway
V
Buck, P.

Dragonwyck
FOX (US) 1946 dir. Joseph L. Mankiewicz
Seton, A.

Dramatic School
MGM (US) 1938 dir. Robert B. Sinclair, Jr.
Szekely, H. *School of Drama*
P

Dr. Bull
FOX (US) 1933 dir. John Ford
Cozzens, J. G. *Last Adam, The*

Dr. Cook's Garden
PAR TV (US) 1971 dir. Ted Post
TV(US)
Levin, I.
P

Dreamer of Oz, The: L. Frank Baum Story, The
ADAM (US) 1990 dir. Jack Bender
TV(US)
Hearn, M. P.

Dream Girl
PAR (US) 1947 dir. Mitchell Leisen
M. EVANS (US) 1955 dir. George Schaefer
TV(US)
Rice, E.
P

Dreaming Lips
TRAFALGAR (GB) 1936 dir. Paul Czinner, Lee Garmes
Bernstein, H.
P

Dream Merchants, The
COL TV (US) 1980 dir. Vincent Sherman
TVSe(US)
Robbins, H.

Dream of Kings, A
WAR (US) 1969 dir. Daniel Mann
Petrakis, H. M.

Dreams Lost, Dreams Found
ATLANTIC/YTV (US/GB) 1987 dir. Willi Patterson
TV(GB/US)
Wallace, P.

Dream West
SCHICK SUNN (US) 1986
dir. Dick Lowry
TVSe(US)
Nevin, D.

Dresser, The
COL (GB) 1983 dir. Peter Yates
V

Harwood, R.
P

Dress Gray
WAR TV (US) 1986 dir. Glenn Jordan
TVSe(US)
Truscott IV, L. K.

Dressmaker, The
FILM 4 (GB) 1988 dir. Jim O'Brien

Bainbridge, B.

Drive, He Said
COL (US) 1970 dir. Jack Nicholson

Larner, J.

Driving Miss Daisy
WAR (US) 1989 dir. Bruce Beresford

Uhry, A.
P

Dr Jekyll and Mr Hyde
PAR (US) 1931 dir. Rouben Mamoulian
MGM (US) 1941 dir. Victor Fleming
V

Stevenson, R. L.

Dr No
UA (GB) 1962 dir. Terence Young
V

Fleming, I.

Drop Dead Darling
SEVEN ARTS (GB) 1966
dir. Ken Hughes
US title: Arrivederci Baby

Deming, R. *Careful Man, The*

Drowning Pool, The
WAR (US) 1975 dir. Stuart Rosenberg
V

Macdonald, R.

Dr. Socrates
WAR (US) 1935 dir. William Dieterle

Burnett, W. R.

Dr Strangelove; Or How I Learned to Stop Worrying and Love the Bomb
COL (GB) 1963 dir. Stanley Kubrick
V

George, P. *Red Alert*

Dr Syn
GAU (GB) 1937 dir. Roy. William Neill
V

Thorndike, R. *Christopher Syn*

Dr. Syn, Alias the Scarecrow
DISNEY (US) 1962 dir. James Neilson
V

Thorndike, R. *Christopher Syn*

Drugstore Cowboy
AVENUE (US) 1989 dir. Gus van Sant

Fogle, J.

Drug Wars: The Camarena Story
ZZY INC. (US) 1990 dir. Brian Gibson
TVSe(US)

Shannon, E. *Desperados: Latin Drug Lords, US Lawmen and the War America Can't win*

Drum
PAR (US) 1976 dir. Steve Carver
V

Onstott, K.

Drum, The
UA (GB) 1938 dir. Zoltan Korda
US title: Drums
Mason, A. E. W.

Drums Along the Mohawk
FOX (US) 1939 dir. John Ford
V
Edmonds, W. D.

Drums in the Deep South
RKO (GB) 1952
dir. William Cameron Menzies
V
Noble, H. *Woman with a Sword*

Drums of Fu Manchu
REP (US) 1940
dir. William Witney/John English
V
Rohmer, S.

Dr. X
WAR (US) 1932 dir. Michael Curtiz
V
Comstock, H. W.
P

Dry Rot
BL (GB) 1956 dir. Maurice Elvey
Chapman, J.
P

Dry White Season, A
MGM (US) 1989 dir. Euzhan Palcy
Brink, A.

Dubai
ACI (US) 1980
TVSe(US)
Moore, R.

Dubarry was a Lady
MGM (US) 1943 dir. Roy deRuth
M
Fields, H.
P

Dublin Nightmare
RANK (GB) 1957 dir. John Pomeroy
Loraine, P.

Duel at Diablo
UA (US) 1966 dir. Ralph Nelson
Albert, M. H. *Apache Rising*

Duel in the Sun
MGM (US) 1946 dir. King Vidor
V
Busch, N.

Duel of Hearts
TNT (US/GB) 1992 dir. John Hough
TV(US/GB)
Cartland, B.

Duellists, The
CIC (GB) 1977 dir. Ridley Scott
V
Conrad, J. *Point of Honour, The*

Duet for One
CANNON (GB) 1987
dir. Andrei Konchalovsky
V
Kempinski, T.
P

Duffy of San Quentin
WAR (US) 1954 dir. Walter Doniger
Duffy, C. T. and Jennings, D. *San Quentin Story, The*

Dulcima
EMI (GB) 1971 dir. Frank Nesbitt
Bates, H. E.

Dulcy
MGM (US) 1940 dir. S. Sylvan Simon
Kaufman, G. S. and Connelly, M.
P

Dumbo
DISNEY (US) 1941 dir. Ben Sharpsteen
A, Ch, V
Aberson, H. and Pearl, H. *Dumbo, the Flying Elephant*

Dummy
WAR TV (US) 1979 dir. Frank Perry
TV(US)
Tidyman, E.

Dune
UN (US) 1984 dir. David Lynch
V
Herbert, F.

Dunkirk
MGM (GB) 1958 dir. Leslie Norman
Trevor, E. *Big Pick-Up, The*

Dunwich Horror, The
AMERICAN (US) 1970
dir. Daniel Haller
V
Lovecraft, H. P. *Shuttered Room, The*

Duped Till Doomsday
DEFA (Ger) 1957 dir. Kurt Jung-Alsen
Fuhmann, F. *Kamaraden*

Dust
DASKA (Bel/Fr) 1985
dir. Marion Hansel
V
Coetzee, J. M. *In the Heart of the Country*

Dusty Ermine
TWICKENHAM (GB) 1938
dir. Bernard Vorhaus
Grant, N.
P

Dying Young
TCF (US) 1991 dir. Joel Schumacher
Leimbach, M.

Dynasty
PARADINE TV (US) 1976
dir. Lee Philips
TV
Michener, J. A.

Each Dawn I Die
WAR (US) 1939 dir. William Keighley
V
Odlum, J.

Eagle has Landed, The
ITC (GB) 1976 dir. John Sturges
V
Higgins, J.

Earl of Chicago
MGM (US) 1940 dir. Richard Thorpe
Williams, B.

Earth v. The Flying Saucers
COL (US) 1956 dir. Fred F. Sears
V
Keyhoe, D. E. *Flying Saucers from Outer Space*

Easiest Way, The
MGM (US) 1931 dir. Jack Conway
Walter, E.
P

East Lynne
FOX (US) 1931 dir. Frank Lloyd
Wood, Mrs. H.

East of Eden
WAR (US) 1954 dir. Elia Kazan
V
NEUFELD PRODS (US) 1980
dir. Harvey Hart
TVSe(US)
Steinbeck, J.

East of Piccadilly
ABPC (GB) 1940 dir. Hardol Huth
Beckles, G.

East of Sumatra
UI (US) 1953 dir. Budd Boetticher
L'Amour, L.

East Side, West Side
MGM (US) 1949 dir. Mervyn Le Roy
Davenport, M.

Easy Come, Easy Go
PAR (US) 1947 dir. John Farrow
McNulty, J. L. *Third Avenue, New York*

Easy Living
PAR (US) 1937 dir. Mitchell Leisen
Caspary, V.

Easy Money
GFD (GB) 1948 dir. Bernard Knowles
Ridley, A.
P

Easy to Love
WAR (US) 1933 dir. William Keighley
Buchanan, T.
P

Eat a Bowl of Tea
COL (US) 1989 dir. Wayne Wang
Chu, L.

Ebb Tide
PAR (US) 1937 dir. James Hogan
Stevenson, R. L.

Ebony Tower, The
GRANADA (GB) 1984
dir. Robert Knights
TV(GB), V
Fowles, J.

Echoes in the Darkness
NEW WORLD TV (US) 1987
dir. Glenn Jordan
TVSe(US)
Wambaugh, J.

Echo of Barbara
RANK (GB) 1961 dir. Sidney Hayers
Burke, J.

Eclipse
GALA (GB) 1976 dir. Simon Perry
Wolaston, N.

Eddie and the Cruisers
EMBASSY (US) 1983
dir. Martin Davidson
V
Kluge, P. F.

Eddie Macon's Run
UN (US) 1983 dir. Jeff Kane
V
McLendon, J.

Edge of Darkness
WAR (US) 1943 dir. Lewis Milestone
Woods, W. H.

Edge of Doom
RKO (US) 1950 dir. Mark Robson
GB title: Stronger than Fear
Brady, L.

Edge of Fury
UA (US) 1958 dir. Robert Gurney,
Irving Lerner
Coates, R. M. *Wisteria Cottage*

Edge of the City
MGM (US) 1957 dir. Martin Ritt
GB title: Man is Ten Feet Tall, A.
Arthur, R. A.
P

Edith's Diary
ZDF (W Ger) 1986
dir. Hans W. Geissendoerfer
Highsmith, P.

Educating Rita
RANK (GB) 1983 dir. Lewis Gilbert
V
Russell, W.
P

Edward, My Son
MGM (GB) 1949 dir. George Cukor
Morley, R. and Langley, N.
P

Edward II
WORK TITLE (GB) 1991
dir. Derek Jarman
Marlowe, C.
P

Effect of Gamma Rays on Man-in-the-Moon Marigolds, The
FOX-RANK (US) 1972 dir. Paul Newman
Zindel, P.
P

Egg and I, The
UN (US) 1947 dir. Chester Erskine
V
Macdonald, B.

Egyptian, The
FOX (US) 1954 dir. Michael Curtiz
Waltari, M.

Eiger Sanction, The
UN (US) 1975 dir. Clint Eastwood
V
Trevanian

Eight Iron Men
COL (US) 1952 dir. Edward Dmytryk
Brown, H. *Sound of Hunting, A*
P

Eight Men Out
ORION (US) 1988 dir. John Sayles
V
Asinof, E.

8 Million Ways to Die
TRI-STAR (US) 1986 dir. Hal Ashby
V
Block, L. *Stab in the Dark*

84 Charing Cross Road
COL (US/GB) 1987 dir. David Jones
V
Hanff, H.

80,000 Suspects
RANK (GB) 1963 dir. Val Guest
Trevor, E. *Pillars of Midnight, The*

E1
NACIONAL (Mex) 1952
dir. Luis Bunuel

Pinto, M. *Pensamientos*

El Dorado
PAR (US) 1966 dir. Howard Hawks
V

Brown, H. *Stars in their Courses, The*

Eleanor and Franklin
TALENT (US) 1976 dir. Daniel Petrie
TVSe(US)

Lash, J. P.

Eleanor and Franklin: The White House Years
TALENT (US) 1977 dir. Daniel Petrie
TV(US)

Lash, J. P. *Eleanor and Franklin*

Electra
UA (Greece) 1962
dir. Michael Cacoyannis

Sophocles
P

Eleni
WAR (US) 1985 dir. Peter Yates
V

Gage, N.

Elephant Boy
UA (GB) 1937 dir. Robert Flaherty,
Zoltan Korda
V

Kipling, R. *Toomai of the Elephants*

Elephant Man, The
PAR (GB) 1980 dir. David Lynch

Treves, Sir F. *Elephant Man and Other Reminiscences, The*

Elephant Walk
PAR (US) 1954 dir. William Dieterle

Standish, R.

11 Harrowhouse
FOX (GB) 1974 dir. Aram Avakian
V

Browne, G. A.

Elizabeth the Queen
COMPASS (US) 1968
dir. George Schaefer
TV(US), V

Anderson, M.
P

Ellery Queen: Don't Look Behind You
UN TV (US) 1971 dir. Barry Shear
TV(US)

Queen, E. *Cat of Many Tales*

Ellery Queen: Too Many Suspects
UN TV (US) 1975 dir. David Greene
TV(US)

Queen, E. *Fourth Side of the Triangle, The*

Ellis Island
Telepics (US) 1984 dir. Jerry London
TVSe(US)

Stewart, F. M.

Elmer Gantry
UA (US) 1960 dir. Richard Brooks
V

Lewis, S.

Elusive Pimpernel, The
BL (GB) 1950 dir. Michael Powell

Orczy, Baroness E.

Elvis and Me
NEW WORLD TV (US) 1988
dir. Larry Peerce
TVSe(US)

Presley, P. and Harman, S.

Embassy
HEMDALE (GB) 1972
dir. Gordon Hessler
Coulter, S.

Emigrants, The
SVENSK (Swe) 1970 dir. Jan Troell
Moberg, V.

Emil and the Detectives
UFA (Ger) 1931 dir. Gerhard Lamprecht
Ch
DISNEY (US) 1964
dir. Peter Tewkesbury
Ch, V
Kastner, E.

Emlyn's Moon
HTV (GB) 1990 dir. Pennant Roberts
Ch, TVSe(GB)
Nimmo, J.

Emma: Queen of the South Seas
FRIES (US) 1988 dir. Bryan Forbes
TVSe(US)
Dutton, G. *Queen Emma of the South Seas*

Emmanuelle
SF (Fr) 1975 dir. Just Jacklin
V
Arsan, E.

Emperor Jones, The
UA (US) 1933 dir. Dudley Murphy
V
O'Neill, E. G.
P

Emperor's Candlesticks, The
MGM (US) 1937
dir. George Fitzmaurice
Orczy, Baroness E.

Emperor's New Clothes, The
CANNON (US) 1987 dir. David Irving
Ch
Andersen, H. C.

Empire of Passion
PARIS/OSHIMA (Jap) 1980
dir. Magisa Oshima
Nakamura, I.

Empire of the Ants
AIP (US) 1977 dir. Bert I. Gordon
V
Wells, H. G. *Valley of the Ants, The*

Empire of the Sun
WAR (US) 1987 dir. Steven Spielberg
V
Ballard, J. G.

Employee's Entrance
WAR (US) 1933 dir. Roy del Ruth
Boehm, D.
P

Empty Canvas, The
CC (It/Fr) 1964 dir. Damiano Damiani
V
Moravia, A.

Empty Saddles
UN (US) 1937 dir. Les Selander
Wilson, C.

En Cas de Malheur
UCIL (Fr/It) 1958
dir. Claude Autant-Lara
Simenon, G.

Enchanted April
RKO (US) 1935 dir. Harry Beaumont
'Elizabeth'

Enchanted Cottage, The
RKO (US) 1945 dir. John Cromwell

Pinero, Sir A. W.
P

Enchanted Island
WAR (US) 1958 dir. Allan Dwan
V

Melville, H. *Typee*

Enchantment
RKO (US) 1948 dir. Irving Reis

Godden, R. *Fugue in Time, A*

Encore
GFD (GB) 1951 dir. Harold French, Pat Jackson, Anthony Pellissier
V

Maugham, W. S. *Ant and the Grasshopper, The; Winter Cruise; Gigolo and Gigolette*

Endless Love
UN (US) 1981 dir. Franco Zeffirelli
V

Spencer, S.

Endless Night
BL (GB) 1971 dir. Sidney Gilliat
V

Christie, A.

End of August, The
QUARTET (US) 1981 dir. Bob Graham
V

Chopin, K. *Awakening, The*

End of the Affair, The
COL (GB) 1954 dir. Edward Dmytryk

Greene, G.

End of the Game
TCF (US/Ger) 1976
dir. Maximilian Schell

Durrenmatt, F. *Judge and his Hangman, The*
P

End of the River, The
GFD (GB) 1947 dir. Derek Twist

Holdridge, D. *Death of a Common Man*

End of the Road
ALLIED (US) 1970 dir. Aram Avakian
V

Barth, J.

Enemies, A Love Story
FOX (US) 1989 dir. Paul Mazursky

Singer, I. B.

Enemy Below, The
FOX (US) 1957 dir. Dick Powell

Rayner, D. A. *Escort*

Enemy Mine
FOX (US) 1986 dir. Wolfgang Petersen
V

Longyear, B.

Enemy of the People, An
ENT (US) 1978 dir. George Schaefer
V

Ibsen, H.
P

Enfants Terribles, Les
MELVILLE (Fr) 1950
dir. Jean-Pierre Melville
V

Cocteau, J.

England Made Me
HEMDALE (GB) 1972 dir. Peter Duffell

Greene, G.

Enigma
EMBASSY (GB/Fr) 1983
dir. Jeannot Szwarc
V

Barak, M.

Enola Gay
VIACOM (US) 1980
dir. David Lowell Rich
TV(US), V
Thomas, G. and Witts, M. M.

Ensign Pulver
WAR (US) 1964 dir. Joshua Logan
Logan, J. and Heggen, T. *Mister Roberts*
P

Entente Cordiale
FLORA (Fr) 1939 dir. Marcel l'Herbier
Maurois, A. *Edward VII and his Times*

Enter Laughing
COL (US) 1967 dir. Carl Reiner
V
Reiner, C.
P

Entertainer, The
BL (GB) 1960 dir. Tony Richardson
RSO FILMS (US) 1976 dir. Donald Wrye
TV(US)
Osborne, J.
P

Entertaining Mr. Sloane
PAR (GB) 1969 dir. Douglas Hickox
V
Orton, J.
P

Entity, The
FOX (US) 1982 dir. Sidney J. Furie
V
De Felitta, F.

Equus
UA (GB) 1977 dir. Sidney Lumet
V
Shaffer, P.
P

Eric
LORIMAR (US) 1975
dir. James Goldstone
TV(US)
Lund, D.

Ernesto
CLESI (It) 1978 dir. Salvatore Samperi
V
Saba, U.

Eroica
KADR (Pol) 1957 dir. Andrzej Munk
Stawinski, J. S.

Escapade
EROS (GB) 1955 dir. Philip Leacock
MacDougall, R.
P

Escapade in Florence
DISNEY (US) 1962 dir. Steve Previn
Ch, V
Fenton, E. *Golden Doors, The*

Escape
RKO (GB) 1930 dir. Basil Dean
FOX (US) 1948
dir. Joseph L. Mankiewicz
Galsworthy, J.
P

Escape
MGM (US) 1940 dir. Mervyn Le Roy
Vance, E.

Escape
H. JAFFE (US) 1980
dir. Robert Michael Lewis
TV(US)
Worker, D., and Worker, B.

Escape Artist, The
ORION (US) 1982 dir. Caleb Deschanel
V
Wagoner, D.

Escape from Alcatraz
PAR (US) 1979 dir. Don Siegel
V

Bruce, J. C.

Escape from Sobibor
ZENITH (US) 1987 dir. Jack Gold
TV(US)

Rashke, R.

Escape from Zahrein
PAR (US) 1962 dir. Ronald Neame

Barrett, M. *Appointments in Zahrein*

Escape in the Desert
WAR (US) 1945 dir. Edward A. Blatt

Sherwood, R. E. *Petrified Forest, The*
P

Escape Me Never
UA (GB) 1935 dir. Paul Czinner
WAR (US) 1947 dir. Peter Godfrey

Kennedy, M.
P

Escape to Witch Mountain
DISNEY (US) 1974 dir. John Hough
Ch, V

Key, A.

Espionage
MGM (US) 1937 dir. Kurt Neumann

Hackett, W.
P

Esther Waters
WESSEX (GB) 1948 dir. Jan Dalrymple

Moore, G.

L'Etat Sauvage
FILMS 1966 (Fr) 1990 dir. Francis Girod

Conchon, G.

L'Etoile du Nord
UA (Fr) 1982
dir. Pierre Granier-Deferre

Simenon, G. *Locataire, La*

Eureka!
MGM/UA (GB/US) 1982
dir. Nicolas Roeg
V

Leasor, J. *Who Killed Sir Harry Oakes?*

Europeans, The
GB (GB) 1979 dir. James Ivory
V

James, H.

Eve
Gala (Fr/It) 1963 dir. Joseph Losey

Chase, J. H.

Evelyn Prentice
MGM (US) 1934 dir. William K. Howard

Woodward, W. E.

Evening in Byzantium
UN TV (US) 1978 dir. Jerry London
TVSe(US)

Shaw, I.

Evensong
GAU (GB) 1934 dir. Victor Saville

Nichols, B.
P

Eve of St. Mark, The
FOX (US) 1944 dir. John M. Stahl

Anderson, M.
P

Evergreen
GAU (GB) 1934 dir. Victor Saville
M

Levy, B. W.
P

Evergreen
METRO (US) 1985 dir. Fielder Cook
TVSe(US)
Plain, B.

Everlasting Secret Family, The
FGH (Aus) 1989 dir. Michael Thornhill
Moorhouse, F. *Everlasting Secret Family and Other Secrets, The*

Everybody's All-American
WAR (US) 1988 dir. Taylor Hackford
Deford, F.

Every Little Crook and Nanny
MGM (US) 1972 dir. Cy Howard
Hunter, E.

Every Morning of the World
BAC FILMS (Fr) 1992 dir. Alan Corneau
Quignard, P.

Everything is Thunder
GB (GB) 1936 dir. Milton Rosmer
Hardy, J. B.

Everything you Ever Wanted to Know about Sex but were Afraid to Ask
UA (US) 1972 dir. Woody Allen
V
Reuben, D.

Evil That Men Do, The
TRI-STAR (US) 1984
dir. J. Lee Thompson
V
Hill, R. L.

Evil Under the Sun
UN (GB) 1982 dir. Guy Hamilton
V
Christie, A.

Evita Peron
ZEPHYR (US) 1981
dir. Marvin Chomsky
TVSe(US)
Barnes, J. *Evita: First Lady*
Fraser, N. *Eva Peron*

Excalibur
ORION (US) 1981 dir. John Boorman
Malory, Sir T. *Morte d'Arthur, Le*

Execution, The
COMWORLD (US) 1985
dir. Paul Wendkos
TV(US), V
Crawford, O.

Execution of Private Slovik, The
UN TV (US) 1974 dir. Lamont Johnson
TV(US)
Huie, W. B.

Executioner's Song, The
FCI (US) 1982 dir. Lawrence Schiller
TVSe(US), V
Mailer, N.

Executive Suite
MGM (US) 1954 dir. Robert Wise
Hawley, C.

Ex-Flame
Tiffany (US) 1930 dir. Victor Halperin
Wood, Mrs H. *East Lynne*

Exile, The
UN (US) 1948 dir. Max Ophuls
Hamilton, C. *His Majesty the King*

Exodus
UA (US) 1960 dir. Otto Preminger
V
Uris, L.

Exorcist, The
WAR (US) 1973 dir. William Friedkin
V

Blatty, W. P.

Exorcist III, The
TCP (US) 1990 dir. William Peter Blatty
Blatty, W. P. *Legion*

Experiences of an Irish RM
CHANNEL 4 (GB) 1982
TVSe(GB)
Somerville, E. and Ross, M.

Experiment in Terror
COL (US) 1962 dir. Blake Edwards
GB title: The Grip of Fear
V

Gordon M. and Gordon, G. The
Operation Terror

Experiment Perilous
RKO (US) 1944 dir. Jacques Tourneur
V

Carpenter, M.

Expresso Bongo
BL (GB) 1959 dir. Val Guest
M

Mankowitz, W.

Extraordinary Seaman, The
MGM (US) 1969
dir. John Frankenheimer
Rock, P.

Extremities
ATLANTIC (US) 1986
dir. Robert M. Young
V

Mastrosimone, W.
P

Eye for an Eye, An
UGC (Fr/It) 1956 dir. André Cayatte
Katcha, V.

Eye of the Devil
MGM (GB) 1967 dir. J. Lee-Thompson
Loraine, P. *Day of the Arrow*

Eye of the Needle
UA (GB) 1981 dir. Richard Marquand
V

Follett, K.

Eyes in the Night
MGM (US) 1942 dir. Fred Zinnemann
Kendrick, B. H. *Odour of Violets*

Eyes Without A Face
CH ELYSEE (Fr/It) 1959
dir. George Franju
Redon, J.

Eyewitness
MGM (GB) 1970 dir. John Hough
US title: Sudden Terror
Hebden, M. *Eye-witness*

Fabian
UA (Ger) 1982 dir. Wolf Gremm
Kastner, E.

Fabian of the Yard
EROS (GB) 1954
dir. Edward Thommen,
Anthony Beauchamp
Fabian, R.

Face at the Window
PENNANT (GB) 1939 dir. George King
Warren, F. B.
P

Face Behind the Mask, The
COL (US) 1941 dir. Robert Florey
O'Connell, T.
P

Face in the Crowd, A
WAR (US) 1957 dir. Elia Kazan
V
Schulberg, B. W. *Your Arkansas Traveller*

Face in the Night
GN (GB) 1956 dir. Lance Comfort
Graeme, B. *Suspense*

Face of Fear, The
Q. MARTIN (US) 1971
dir. George McCowan
TV(US)
Cunningham, E. V. *Sally*

Face of Fear, The
WAR TV (US) 1990 dir. Farhad Mann
TV(US)
Koontz, D.

Faces in the Dark
RANK (GB) 1960 dir. David Eady
Boileau, P. and Narcejac, T.

Face to Face
RKO (US) 1952
dir. John Brahm/Bretaigne Windust
Crane, S. *Bride Comes to Yellow Sky, The*
Conrad, J. *Secret Sharer, The*

Fahrenheit 451
UI (GB) 1966 dir. François Truffaut
V
Bradbury, R.

Fail Safe
COL (US) 1963 dir. Sidney Lumet
V
Burdick, E. and Wheeler, H.

Fair Wind to Java
REP (US) 1952 dir. Joseph Kane
V
Roark, G.

Faithless
MGM (US) 1932 dir. Harry Beaumont
Cram, M. *Tinfoil*

Falcon and the Snowman, The
ORION (US) 1985 dir. John Schlesinger
Lindsey, R.

Fall, The
ARG SONO (Arg) 1958
dir. Leopoldo Torre Nilsson
Guido, B.

Fallen Angel
FOX (US) 1945 dir. Otto Preminger
Holland, M.

Fallen Idol, The
FOX (GB) 1948 dir. Carol Reed
US title: Lost Illusion, The
V
Greene, G. *Basement Room, The*

Fallen Sparrow, The
RKO (US) 1943 dir. Richard Wallace
Hughes, D. B.

Fall of the House of Usher, The
TAFT (US) 1982 dir. James Conway
TV(US)
Poe, E. A.

False Witness
NEW WORLD TV (US) 1989
dir. Arthur Allan Seidelman
TV(US)
Uhnak, D.

Fame is the Name of the Game
UN TV (US) 1966 dir. Stuart Rosenberg
TV(US)
Thayer, T. *One Woman*

Fame is the Spur
TC (GB) 1947 dir. Roy Boulting
BBC (GB) 1982 dir. David Giles
TVSe(GB)
Spring, H.

Family, The
PUBLIC (Jap) 1974
dir. Karei Naru Ichikozo
Yamazaki, T.

Family Affair, A
MGM (US) 1937 dir. George B. Seitz
Rouverol, A. *Skidding*
P

Family Business
EUROPEAN (Fr) 1987 dir. Costa-Gavras
Ryck, F.

Family Business
TRI-STAR (US) 1989 dir. Sidney Lumet
Patrick, V.

Family Game, The
TOHO (Jap) 1983
dir. Yoshimitsu Morita
V
Honma, Y.

Family Honeymoon
UN (US) 1948 dir. Claude Binyon
Croy, H.

Family Life
EMI (GB) 1971 dir. Ken Loach
V
Mercer, D. *In Two Minds*
P

Family Man, The
TIME-LIFE (US) 1979 dir. Glenn Jordan
TV(US), V
Gallagher, T. *Monogamist, The*

Family Nobody Wanted, The
UN TV (US) 1975 dir. Ralph Senensky
TV(US)
Doss, H.

Family Plot
UN (US) 1976 dir. Alfred Hitchcock
V
Canning, V. *Rainbird Pattern, The*

Family Rico, The
CBS (US) 1972 dir. Paul Wendkos
TV(US)
Simenon, G. *Brothers Rico, The*

Family Way, The
BL (GB) 1966 dir. Roy Boulting
Naughton, B. *All in Good Time*
P

Fan, The
FOX (US) 1949 dir. Otto Preminger
GB title: Lady Windemere's Fan
Wilde, O. *Lady Windemere's Fan*
P

Fan, The
PAR (US) 1981 dir. Edward Bianchi
V
Randall, B.

Fanatic
COL (GB) 1965 dir. Silvio Narizzano
US title: Die! Die! My Darling
Blaisdell, A. *Nightmare*

Fancy Pants
PAR (US) 1950 dir. George Marshall
Wilson, H. L. *Ruggles of Red Gap*

Fanny
WAR (US) 1960 dir. Joshua Logan
Behrman, S. N. and Logan, J.
P

Fanny by Gaslight
GFD (GB) 1944 dir. Anthony Asquith
US title: Man of Evil
V
BBC (GB) 1981 dir. Peter Jefferies
TVSe(GB)
Sadleir, M.

Fanny Hill
GALA (Ger) 1965 dir. Russ Meyer
BW (GB) 1983 dir. Gerry O'Hare
V
Cleland, J.

Fantasist, The
BLUE DOLPHIN (Ire) 1987
dir. Robin Hardy
McGinley, P. *Goosefoot*

Fantasticks, The
COMPASS (US) 1964
dir. George Schaefer
M, TV(US)
Jones, T. and Schmidt, H.
P

Farewell, My Lovely
RKO (US) 1944 dir. Edward Dmytryk
V
AVCO (US) 1975 dir. Dick Richards
V
Chandler, R.

Farewell to Arms, A
PAR (US) 1932 dir. Frank Borzage
V
FOX (US) 1957 dir. Charles Vidor
V
Hemingway, E.

Farewell to Manzanar
UN TV (US) 1976 dir. John Korty
TV(US)
Wakatsuki, J. and Houston, J. D.

Farewell to the King
ORION (US) 1989 dir. John Milius
Schoendoerffer, P.

Far from the Madding Crowd
WAR (GB) 1967 dir. John Schlesinger
V
Hardy, T.

Far Horizons, The
PAR (US) 1955 dir. Rudolph Maté
Emmons, D. G. *Sacajawea of the Shoshones*

Farmer Takes a Wife, The
FOX (US) 1935 dir. Victor Fleming
FOX (US) 1953 dir. Henry Levin
M
Edmonds, W. D. *Rome Haul*

Farmer's Wife, The
AB (GB) 1940 dir. Norman Lee
Philpotts, E.
P

Far Pavilions, The
GOLD (GB) 1983 dir. Peter Duffell
TVSe(GB), V
Kaye, M. M.

Fast and Loose
GFD (GB) 1954 dir. Gordon Parry
Travers, B. *Cuckoo in the Nest, A*
P

Fast Times at Ridgemont High
UN (US) 1982 dir. Amy Heckerling
V
Crowe, C.

Fast-Walking
PICKMAN (US) 1982
dir. James B. Harris
V
Brawley, E. *Rap, The*

Fatal Vision
NBC ENT (US) 1984 dir. David Greene
TVSe(US), V
McGinniss, J.

Fat City
COL (US) 1972 dir. John Huston
V
Gardner, L.

Fate is the Hunter
FOX (US) 1964 dir. Ralph Nelson
Gann, E. K.

Father, The
BBC (GB) 1985
TV(GB)
Strindberg, A.
P

Father Brown
COL (GB) 1954 dir. Robert Hamer
Chesterton, G. K. *Blue Cross, The*

Father Brown, Detective
PAR (US) 1935 dir. Edward Sedgwick
ATV (GB) 1974 dir. Robert Tronson
TVSe(GB)
Chesterton, G. K. *Wisdom of Father Brown, The*

Father Figure
TIME-LIFE (US) 1980 dir. Jerry London
TV(US), V
Peck, R.

Father of the Bride
MGM (US) 1950 dir. Vincente Minnelli
V
DISNEY (US) 1991 dir. Charles Shyer
Streeter, E.

Father's Doing Fine
ABP (GB) 1952 dir. Henry Cass
Langley, N. *Little Lambs Eat Ivy*
P

Father Sergius
MOSFILM (USSR) 1978
dir. Igor Talankin
Tolstoy, L.

Father was a Fullback
FOX (US) 1949 dir. John M. Stahl
Goldsmith, C.
P

Fathom
FOX (GB) 1967 dir. Leslie Martinson
Forrester, L. *Girl Called Fathom, A*

Favorite Son
NBC (US) 1988 dir. Jeff Bleckner
TVSe(US)
Sohmer, S.

FBI Story, The
WAR (US) 1959 dir. Mervyn LeRoy
V
Whitehead, D.

FDR — The Last Year
TITUS PRODS (US) 1980
dir. Anthony Page
TV(US)
Bishop, J. *FDR's Last Year*

Fear is the Key
EMI (GB) 1972 dir. Michael Tuchner
V
MacLean, A.

Fearmakers, The
PACEMAKER (US) 1958
dir. Jacques Tourneur
Teilhet, D.

Fear on Trial
LAN (US) 1975 dir. Lamont Johnson
TV(US)
Faulk, J. H.

Fedora
MAINLINE (Ger/Fr) 1978
dir. Billy Wilder
V
Tryon, T. *Crowned Heads*

Feet of the Snake, The
WELLER/MYERS (GB) 1985
TV(GB)
Chubin, B.

Fellini Satyricon
UA (It) 1969 dir. Federico Fellini
V
Petronius *Satyricon*

Feminine Touch, The
RANK (GB) 1956 dir. Pat Jackson
Russell, S. M. *Lamp is Heavy, A*

Femme du Boulanger, La
PAGNOL (Fr) 1938 dir. Marcel Pagnol
Giono, J. *Jean le Bleu*

Ferry to Hong Kong
RANK (GB) 1959 dir. Lewis Gilbert
V
Catto, M.

Feud, The
CASTLE HILL (US) 1990 dir. Bill D'Elia
Berger, T.

Feu Follet, Le
ARCO (Fr/It) 1963 dir. Louis Malle
La Rochhelle, P. D.

Fever in the Blood, A
WAR (US) 1960 dir. Vincent Sherman
Pearson, W.

Few Days in Weasel Creek, A.
WAR TV (US) 1981 dir. Dick Lowry
TV(US)
Brent, J.

Few Days With Me, A
GALAXY (Fr) 1989 dir. Claude Sautet
Josselin, J. F.

Fiancée, The
(Ger) 1984 dir. Gunter Reisch, Gunther
Rucker
Lippold, E. *House with the Heavy
Doors, The*

Fiddler on the Roof
UA (US) 1971 dir. Norman Jewison
M, V
Stein, J.
P

Field, The
AVENUE (GB) 1990 dir. Jim Sheridan
Keane, J. B.
P

Field of Dreams
UN (US) 1989 dir. Phil A. Robinson
Kinsella, W. P. *Shoeless Joe*

Fiercest Heart, The
FOX (US) 1961 dir. George Sherman
Cloete, S.

Fifteen Streets, The
TYNE-TEES (GB) 1991
dir. David Wheatley
TV(GB)
Cookson, C.

Fifth Missile, The
MGM/UA TV (US) 1986
dir. Larry Peerce
TV(US)
Scortia, T. N. and Robinson, F. M.
Gold Crew, The

Fifth Musketeer, The
SASCH WIEN FILMS (Austria) 1978
dir. Ken Annakin
V
Dumas, A. *Man in the Iron Mask, The*

52 Pick-Up
CANNON (US) 1986
dir. John Frankenheimer
V
Leonard, E.

Fighter, The
UA (US) 1952 dir. Herbert Kline
V
London, J. *Mexican, The*

Fighting Back
MTM (US) 1980 dir. Robert Lieberman
TV(US)
Bleier, R. and O'Neil, T.

Fighting Caravans
PAR (US) 1931 dir. Otto Brower, David
Burton
V
Grey, Z.

Fighting Guardsman, The
COL (US) 1945 dir. Henry Levin
Dumas, A. *Companions of Jehu, The*

Fighting O'Flynn, The
UN (US) 1949 dir. Arthur Pierson
McCarthy, J. H.

**Fighting Prince of Donegal,
The**
DISNEY (GB) 1966
dir. Michael O'Herlihy
V
Reilly, R. T. *Red Hugh, Prince of
Donegal*

Figures in a Landscape
CINECREST (GB) 1970
dir. Joseph Losey
England, B.

File on Devlin, The
COMPASS (US) 1969
dir. George Schaefer
TV(US)
Gaskin, C.

Final Days, The
SAMUELS (US) 1989
dir. Richard Pearce
TV(US)
Woodward, B. and Bernstein, C.

Finally, Sunday
FILMS A2 (Fr) 1983
dir. François Truffaut
Williams, C. *Long Saturday Night, The*

Final Notice
SHARMHILL (US) 1989
dir. Steven Hilliard Stern
TV(US)
Valin, J.

Final Option, The
MGM/UA (GB) 1983 dir. Ian Sharp
V
Markstein, G. *Tiptoe Boys, The*

Final Programme, The
MGM-EMI (GB) 1973 dir. Robert Fuest
US title: Last Days of Man on Earth,
The
V
Moorcock, M.

Final Verdict, The
TURNER (US) 1991 dir. Jack Fisk
TV(US)
St. John, A. R. *Final Verdict*

Finders Keepers
RANK (US) 1984 dir. Richard Lester
V
Dennis, C. *Next-to-Last Train Ride, The*

Finding the Way Home
MGM/UA TV (US) 1991
dir. Rob Holcomb
TV(US)
Small, G. R. *Mittelmann's Hardware*

Fine Madness, A
WAR (US) 1966 dir. Irvin Kershner
V
Baker, E.

Fine Things
NBC (US) 1990 dir. Tom Moore
TV(US)
Steel, D.

Finian's Rainbow
WAR (US) 1968
dir. Francis Ford Coppola
M, V
Harburg, E. Y. and Saidy, F.
P

Finn and Hattie
PAR (US) 1930 dir. Norman Taurog,
Norman McLeod
Stewart, D. O. *Mr and Mrs Haddock
Abroad*

Fire and Rain
WIL COURT (US) 1989
dir. Jerry Jameson
TV(US)
Chandler, J. G.

Fire Down Below
COL (GB) 1957 dir. Robert Parrish
V
Catto, M.

Firefox
WAR (US) 1982 dir. Clint Eastwood
V
Thomas, C.

Fire on the Mountain
CARSON (US) 1981 dir. Donald Wrye
TV(US)
Abbey, E.

Fire Over England
UA (GB) 1937 dir. William K. Howard
V
Mason, A. E. W.

Fire Sale
FOX (US) 1977 dir. Alan Arkin
Klane, R.

Fires on the Plain
DAIEI (Jap) 1959 dir. Kon Ichikawa
V
O-Oka, Shohei

Firestarter
UN (US) 1984 dir. Mark L. Lester
V
King, S.

First Among Equals
ITV (GB) 1986
TV(GB)
Archer, J.

First Blood
ORION (US) 1982 dir. Ted Kotcheff
V
Morell, D.

First Born
BBC (GB) 1988 dir. Philip Saville
TVSe(GB)
Duffy, M. *Gor Saga, The*

First Comes Courage
COL (US) 1943 dir. Dorothy Arzner
Arnold, E. *Commandos, The*

First Deadly Sin, The
CIC (US) 1980 dir. Brian G. Hutton
V
Sanders, L.

First Gentleman, The
COL (GB) 1948 dir. Alberto Cavalcanti
US title: Affairs of a Rogue
Ginsbury, N.
P

First Great Train Robbery, The
UA (GB) 1978 dir. Michael Crichton
V
Crichton, M. *Great Train Robbery, The*

First Lady
WAR (US) 1937 dir. Stanley Logan
Kaufman, G. S. and Dayton, K.
P

First Legion, The
UA (US) 1951 dir. Douglas Sirk
V
Lavery, E. G.
P

First Men in the Moon
Col (GB) 1963 dir. Nathan Juran
Wells, H. G.

First Monday in October
PAR (US) 1981 dir. Ronald Neame
V
Lawrence, J. and Lee, R. E.
P

First Name: Carmen
IS (Fr) 1984 dir. Jean-Luc Godard
Merimée, P. *Carmen*

First Year, The
FOX (US) 1932 dir. William K. Howard
Craven, F.
P

111

First You Cry
MTM (US) 1978 dir. George Schaefer
TV(US)
Rollin, B.

Fitzwilly
UA (US) 1967 dir. Delbert Mann
GB title: Fitzwilly Strikes Back
Tyler, P. *Garden of Cucumbers, A*

Five Against the House
COL (US) 1955 dir. Phil Karlson
Finney, J.

Five and Ten
MGM (US) 1931 dir. Robert Z. Leonard
GB title: Daughter of Luxury
Hurst, F.

Five Boys from Barska Street
POLSKI (Pol) 1953 dir. Aleksander Ford
Kozniewski, K.

Five Branded Women
PAR (It/US) 1960 dir. Martin Ritt
Pirro, U.

Five Card Stud
PAR (US) 1968 dir. Henry Hathaway
V
Gaulden, R.

Five Children And It
BBC (GB) 1991 dir. Marian Fox
Ch, TVSe(GB)
Nesbit, E.

Five Days One Summer
WAR (US) 1982 dir. Fred Zinnemann
V
Boyle, K. *Maiden Maiden*

Five Finger Exercise
COL (US) 1962 dir. Delbert Mann
Shaffer, P.
P

Five Fingers
FOX (US) 1952
dir. Joseph L. Mankiewicz
Moyzisch, L. C. *Operation Cicero*

Five Graves to Cairo
PAR (US) 1943 dir. Billy Wilder
Biro, L.
P

Five Have A Mystery to Solve
CFF (GB) 1964 dir. Ernest Morris
Ch
Blyton, E.

Five Little Peppers and How They Grew
COL (US) 1939 dir. Charles Barton
Sidley, M.

Five of Me, The
FARREN (US) 1981 dir. Paul Wendkos
TV(US)
Hawksworth, H. and Schwarz, T.

Five on a Treasure Island
BL (GB) 1957 dir. Gerald Landau
Ch
Blyton, E.

Five Star Final
WAR (US) 1931 dir. Mervyn LeRoy
Weitzenkorn, L.
P

Five Steps to Danger
UA (US) 1956 dir. Henry S. Kesler
Hamilton, D.

Five Weeks in a Balloon
FOX (US) 1962 dir. Irwin Allen
V
Verne, J.

Fixer, The
MGM (US) 1969
dir. John Frankenheimer
Malamud, B.

Flambards
YTV (GB) 1979
TVSe(GB)
Peyton, K. M.

Flame and the Flesh, The
MGM (US) 1954 dir. Richard Brooks
Bailly, A.

Flame in the Streets
RANK (GB) 1961 dir. Roy Baker
Willis, T. *Hot Summer Night*
P

Flame is Love, The
NBC ENT (US) 1979
dir. Michael O'Herlihy
TV(US), V
Cartland, B.

Flamingo Road
WAR (US) 1949 dir. Michael Curtiz
Wilder, R.

Flaming Star
FOX (US) 1960 dir. Don Siegel
V
Huffaker, C. *Flaming Lance*

Flap
WAR (US) 1970 dir. Carol Reed
GB title: Last Warrior, The
Huffaker, C. *Nobody Loves a Drunken Indian*

Flashpoint
TRI-STAR (US) 1984
dir. William Tannen
V
La Fontaine, G.

Flash the Sheepdog
CFF (US) 1967 dir. Laurence Henson
Ch
Fidler, K.

Flaxfield, The
COURIER (Bel/Neth) 1983
dir. Jan Gruyaert
Streuvels, S.

Flea in her Ear, A
FOX (US/Fr) 1968 dir. Jacques Charon
Feydeau, G.
P

Flesh and Blood
BL (GB) 1951 dir. Anthony Kimmins
Bridie, J. *Sleeping Clergyman, A.*
P

Flesh and Blood
PAR TV (US) 1979 dir. Jud Taylor
TVSe(US)
Hamill, P.

Flesh and Fantasy
UN (US) 1943 dir. Julien Duvivier
Wilde, O. *Lord Arthur Savile's Crime*

Fleshburn
CROWN (US) 1984 dir. George Gage
V
Garfield, B. *Fear in a Handful of Dust*

Fletch
UIP (US) 1985 dir. Michael Ritchie
V
McDonald, G.

Flight from Ashiya
UA (US/Jap) 1963
dir. Michael Anderson
Arnold, E.

Flight from Destiny
WAR (US) 1941 dir. Vincent Sherman
Berkeley, A.
P

Flight of the Doves
COL (US) 1971 dir. Ralph Nelson
V
Macken, W.

Flight of the Eagle
SUMMIT (Swe) 1983 dir. Jan Troell
V
Sundman, P. O.

Flight of the Intruder
PAR (US) 1991 dir. John Milius
Coonts, S.

Flight of the Phoenix, The
FOX (US) 1965 dir. Robert Aldrich
V
Trevor, E.

Flim-Flam Man, The
FOX (US) 1967 dir. Irvin Kershner
V
Owen, G. *Ballad of the Flim-Flam Man, The*

Floating Dutchman, The
AA (GB) 1953 dir. Vernon Sewell
Bentley, N.

Floods of Fear
RANK (GB) 1958 dir. Charles Crichton
Hawkins, J. and Hawkins, W.

Florentine Dagger, The
WAR (US) 1935 dir. Robert Florey
Hecht, B.

Florian
MGM (US) 1940 dir. Edwin L. Marin
Salten, F.

Flotsam and Jetsam
ATV (GB) 1960
TV(GB)
Maugham, W. S. *Stories*

Flower Drum Song
UI (US) 1961 dir. Henry Koster
M, V
Lee, C. Y.

Flowers in the Attic
NEW WORLD (US) 1987
dir. Jeffrey Bloom
V
Andrews, V. C.

Flowing
East-West (Jap) 1956 dir. Mikio Naruse
Koda, A.

Fly, The
FOX (US) 1958 dir. Kurt Neumann
FOX (US) 1986 dir. David Cronenberg
V
Langelaan, G.

Fly Away Peter
GFD (GB) 1948 dir. Charles Saunders
Dearsley, A. P.
P

Flying Down to Rio
RKO (US) 1933 dir. Thornton Freeland
V
Caldwell, A.
P

Fog Over Frisco
WAR (US) 1934 dir. William Dieterle
Dyer, G.

Folies Bergère
FOX (US) 1935 dir. Roy del Ruth
GB title: Man from the Folies Bergère,
The

Lothar, R. and Adler, H. *Red Cat,*
The
P

Follow Me
UN (GB) 1972 dir. Carol Reed
US title: Public Eye, The

Shaffer, P. *Public Eye, The*
P

Follow Me Boys!
DISNEY (US) 1966 dir. Norman Tokar
V

Kantor, M. *God and My Country*

Follow that Dream
UA (US) 1962 dir. Gordon Douglas
V

Powell, R. *Pioneer Go Home*

Follow that Horse!
WAR (GB) 1959 dir. Alan Bromly

Mason, H. *Photo Finish*

Follow the Fleet
RKO (US) 1936 dir. Mark Sandrich
M, V

Osborne, H. and Scott, A. *Shore*
Leave
P

Follow Your Heart
NBC (US) 1990 dir. Noel Nosseck
TV(US)

Everett, P. *Walk Me to the Distance*

Folly to be Wise
BL (GB) 1952 dir. Frank Launden

Bridie, J. *It Depends what you Mean*
P

Fontane Effi Briest
TANGO (W Ger) 1974
dir. Rainer Werner Fassbinder

Fontane, T.

Fool for Love
CANNON (US) 1985 dir. Robert Altman
V

Shepard, S.
P

Fools for Scandal
WAR (US) 1938 dir. Mervyn LeRoy

Hamilton, N., Casey, R. and Shute,
J. *Return Engagement*
P

Fools of Fortune
PALACE (GB) 1990 dir. Pat O'Connor

Trevor, W.

Fools Parade
COL (US) 1971
dir. Andrew V. McLaglen
GB title: Dynamite Man from Glory Jail

Grubb, D. *Fools Paradise*

Fools Rush In
RANK (GB) 1949
dir. John Paddy Carstairs

Horne, K.
P

Footsteps in the Dark
WAR (US) 1941 dir. Lloyd Bacon

Fodor, L. *Blondie White*
P

Footsteps in the Fog
COL (GB) 1955 dir. Arthur Lubin

Jacobs, W. W. *Interruption, The*

For Better, For Worse
ABP (GB) 1954 dir. J. Lee Thompson
V

Watkyn, A.
P

Forbidden
ENT (GB/Ger) 1984 dir. Anthony Page
TV(GB)

Gross, L. *Last Jews in Berlin, The*

Forbidden Fruit
CAMEO-POLY (Fr) 1952
dir. Henri Verneuil

Simenon, G. *Act of Passion*

Forbidden Territory
GAU (GB) 1934 dir. Phil Rosen

Wheatley, D.

Forbidden Valley
UN (US) 1938 dir. Wyndham Gittens

Hardy, S.

Forbin Project, The
UN (US) 1970 dir. Joseph Sargent
GB title: Colossus, the Forbin Project

Jones, D. F. *Colossus*

Force of Evil
MGM (US) 1948 dir. Abraham Polonsky
V

Wolfert, I. *Tucker's People*

Force 10 from Navarone
COL (GB) 1978 dir. Guy Hamilton
V

MacLean, A.

Ford: The Man and the Machine
LANTANA (US) 1987 dir. Allan Eastman
TVSe(US)

Lacey, R.

Foreign Body
ORION (GB) 1986 dir. Ronald Neame

Mann, R.

Foreign Correspondent
UA (US) 1940 dir. Alfred Hitchcock
V

Sheean, V. *Personal History*

Foreign Exchange
ABC (US) 1970 dir. Roy Baker
TV(US)

Sangster, J.

Forever
EMI (US) 1978 dir. John Korty
TV(US)

Blume, J.

Forever Amber
FOX (US) 1947 dir. Otto Preminger

Winsor, K.

Forever Female
PAR (US) 1953 dir. Irving Rapper

Barrie, Sir J. M. *Rosalind*
P

Forgotten Story, The
HTV (GB) 1982
TV(GB)

Graham, W.

For Heaven's Sake
FOX (US) 1950 dir. George Seaton

Segall, H.
P

Forlorn River
PAR (US) 1937 dir. Charles Barton

Grey, Z.

For Love Alone
WARRANTY (Aus) 1986
dir. Stephen Wallace
V

Stead, C.

Formula, The
MGM (US) 1980 dir. John G. Avildsen
V

Shagan, S.

Forsaking All Others
MGM (US) 1934 dir. W. S. Van Dyke

Roberts, E. B. and Cavett, F. M.
P

Forsyte Saga, The
BBC (GB) 1967 dir. David Giles
TVSe(GB), V

Galsworthy, J.

Fort Apache
RKO (US) 1948 dir. John Ford
V

Bellah, J. W. *Massacre*

For Them That Trespass
ABP (GB) 1949 dir. Alberto Cavalcanti

Raymond, E.

For the Term of his Natural Life
FILMO (Aus) 1985 dir. Rob Stewart
TVSe(Aus)

Clarke, M.

For Those I Loved
GALA (Can/Fr) 1983 dir. Robert Enrico
V
BBC (GB) 1991 dir. Robert R. Enrico
TV(GB)

Gray, M. and Gallo, M.

Fortress
HBO PREM (US) 1985
dir. Arch Nicholson
TV(US), V

Lord, G.

Fortunate Pilgrim, The
NBC (US) 1988 dir. Stuart Cooper
TVSe(US)

Puzo, M.

Fortune and Men's Eyes
MGM (US/Can) 1971 dir. Harvey Hart

Herbert, J.
P

Fortune is a Woman
COL (GB) 1956 dir. Sidney Gilliatt
US title: She Played with Fire

Graham, W.

Fortunes of Captain Blood, The
COL (US) 1950 dir. Gordon Douglas

Sabatini, R.

Forty Carats
COL (US) 1973 dir. Milton Katselas

Barillet, P. and Gredy, J-P.
P

Forty Days of Musa Dagh
HIGH INV (US/Tur) 1987
dir. Sarky Mouradia
V

Werfel, F.

Forty-Second Street
WAR (US) 1933 dir. Lloyd Bacon
M, V

Ropes, B.

For Whom the Bell Tolls
PAR (US) 1943 dir. Sam Wood
V

Hemingway, E.

Foster and Laurie
FRIES (US) 1975
dir. John Llewellyn Moxey
TV(US)

Silverman, A.

Fountain, The
RKO (US) 1934 dir. John Cromwell

Morgan, C.

Fountainhead, The
WAR (US) 1949 dir. King Vidor
V
Rand, A.

Four Daughters
WAR (US) 1938 dir. Michael Curtiz
Hurst, F. *Sister Act*

Four Days Wonder
UN (US) 1936 dir. Sidney Salkow
Milne, A. A.

Four Faces West
UA (US) 1948 dir. Alfred E. Green
V
Rhodes, E. M. *Paso Por Aqui*

Four Feathers, The
PAR (US) 1929 dir. Lothar Mendes
UA (GB) 1939 dir. Zoltan Korda
V
ROSEMONT (GB) 1978 dir. Don Sharp
TV(GB), V
Mason, A. E. W.

Four Frightened People
PAR (US) 1934 dir. Cecil B. de Mille
Robertson, E. A.

Four Horsemen of the Apocalypse, The
MGM (US) 1961 dir. Vincente Minnelli
V
Blasco-Ibanez, V.

Four Hours to Kill
PAR (US) 1935 dir. Mitchell Leisen
Krasna, N. *Small Miracle*
P

Four Just Men, The
EAL (GB) 1939 dir. Walter Forde
US title: Secret Four, The
Wallace, E.

Four Men and a Prayer
FOX (US) 1938 dir. John Ford
Garth, D.

Four Musketeers, The
FOX-RANK (Pan/Sp) 1974
dir. Richard Lester
V
Dumas, A. *Three Musketeers, The*

Four-Poster, The
COL (GB) 1952 dir. Irving Reis
Hartog, J. de
P

Four-Sided Triangle
HAMMER (GB) 1952
dir. Terence Fisher
Temple, W. F.

Fourth Man, The
VER NED (Neth) 1984
dir. Paul Verhoeven
V
Reve, G.

Fourth Protocol, The
RANK (GB) 1987 dir. John MacKenzie
V
Forsyth, F.

Fourth War, The
CANNON (US) 1990
dir. John Frankenheimer
Peters, S.

Fox, The
WAR (US/Can) 1967 dir. Mark Rydell
Lawrence, D. H.

Fox and the Hound, The
DISNEY (US) 1981 dir. Art Stevens
A, Ch
Mannix, D.

Foxes of Harrow, The
FOX (US) 1947 dir. John M. Stahl
Yerby, F.

Foxfire
UI (US) 1955 dir. Joseph Pevney
Seton, A.

Foxfire
M. REES (US) 1987 dir. Jud Taylor
TV(US)
Cooper, S. and Cronyn, H.
P

Foxhole in Cairo
BL (GB) 1960 dir. John Moxey
V
Mosley, L. *Cat and the Mice, The*

Fragment of Fear
COL (GB) 1969 dir. Richard C. Sarafian
V
Bingham, J.

Framed
PAR (US) 1975 dir. Phil Karlson
V
Powers, A. and Misenheimer, M.

Franchise Affair, The
ABP (GB) 1951
dir. Lawrence Hurtington
BBC (GB) 1988
TVSe(GB)
Tey, J.

Francis
UI (US) 1949 dir. Arthur Lubin
Stern, D.

Francis Gary Powers: The True Story of the U-2 Spy Incident
FRIES (US) 1976 dir. Delbert Mann
TV(US), V
Powers, F. G. and Gentry, C.
Operation Overflight

Frankenstein
UN (US) 1931 dir. James Whale
DAN CURTIS PRODS (US) 1973
dir. Glenn Jordan
TV(US), V
Shelley, Mrs M. W.

Frankenstein: The True Story
UN TV (US) 1973 dir. Jack Smight
TVSe(US)
Shelley, Mrs M. W. *Frankenstein*

Frankenstein Unbound
TCF (US) 1990 dir. Roger Corman
V
Aldiss, B.

Frankie and Johnny
PAR (US) 1991 dir. Garry Marshall
McNally, T. *Frankie and Johnny in the Clair de Lune*
P

Fraulein
FOX (US) 1957 dir. Henry Koster
McGovern, J.

Freaks
MGM (US) 1932 dir. Tod Browning
V
Robbins, T. *Spurs*

Freaky Friday
DISNEY (US) 1976 dir. Gary Nelson
Ch, V
Rodgers, M.

Freckles
RKO (US) 1935 dir. Edward Killy
FOX (US) 1960 dir. Harry Spalding
Porter, G. S.

Freedom Fighter
COL TV (US/GB) 1987
dir. Desmond Davis
TV(GB/US)
Galante, P. *Berlin Wall, The*

Freedom Road
BRAUN (US) 1980 dir. Jan Kadar
TVSe(US), V
Fast, H.

Freejack
WAR (US) 1992 dir.Geoff Murphy
Sheckley, R. *Immortality, Inc.*

Free Soul, A
MGM (US) 1931 dir. Clarence Brown
St. John, A. R.

Freeway
NEW WORLD (US) 1988
dir. Francis Delia
Barkley, D.

French Atlantic Affair, The
MGM TV (US) 1979 dir. Douglas Heyes
TVSe(US)
Lehman, E.

French Connection, The
FOX (US) 1971 dir. William Friedkin
V
Moore, R.

French Leave
AB (GB) 1930 dir. Jack Raymond
Berkeley, R.
P

French Lieutenant's Woman, The
UA (GB) 1981 dir. Karel Reisz
V
Fowles, J.

Frenchman's Creek
PAR (US) 1944 dir. Mitchell Leisen
Du Maurier, D.

French Mistress, A
BL (GB) 1960 dir. Roy Boulting
Monro, R.
P

French Without Tears
PAR (GB) 1939 dir. Anthony Asquith
Rattigan, T.
P

Frenzy
RANK (GB) 1971 dir. Alfred Hitchcock
V
La Bern, A. J. *Goodbye Piccadilly, Farewell Leicester Square*

Fresh Horses
WEINTRAUB (US) 1988
dir. David Anspaugh
V
Ketron, L.
P

Frieda
EAL (GB) 1947 dir. Basil Dearden
Millar, R.
P

Fried Green Tomatoes
UN (US) 1991 dir. Jon Avnet
Flagg, F. *Fried Green Tomatoes at the Whistle Stop Cafe*

Friendly Fire
M. ARCH (US) 1979 dir. David Greene
TV(US), V
Bryan, C. D. B.

Friendly Persuasion
MGM (US) 1956 dir. WIlliam Wyler
V
AA (US) 1975 dir. Joseph Sargent
TV(US)
West, J.

Friend or Foe
CFF (GB) 1982 dir. John Krish
Ch, V
Morpurgo, M.

Friends and Lovers
RKO (US) 1931 dir. Victor Schertzinger
Dekobra, M. *Sphinx has Spoken, The*

Friendship in Vienna, A
DISNEY CH (US) 1988
dir. Arthur Allan Seidelman
TV(US)
Orgel, D. *Devil in Vienna, The*

Friendships, Secrets and Lies
WAR TV (US) 1979
dir. Ann Zane Shanks, Marlena Laird
TV(US)
Deal, B. H. *Walls Came Tumbling Down, The*

Friends of Eddie Coyle, The
PAR (US) 1973 dir. Peter Yates
Higgins, G. V.

Frightened Lady, The
BL (GB) 1932 dir. T. Hayes Hunter
Wallace, E. *Case of the Frightened Lady, The*

Fringe Dwellers, The
OZFILMS (Aus) 1986
dir. Bruce Beresford
Gare, N.

Frog, The
WILCOX (GB) 1937 dir. Jack Raymond
Wallace, E. *Fellowship of the Frog, The*

From Beyond
EMPIRE (US) 1986 dir. Stuart Gordon
V
Lovecraft, H. P.

From Beyond the Grave
EMI (GB) 1973 dir. Kevin Connor
V
Chetwynd-Hayes, R. *Elemental, The; Gate Crasher, The; Act of Kindness, An; Door, The*

From Here to Eternity
COL (US) 1953 dir. Fred Zinnemann
V
COL (US) 1979 dir. Buzz Kulik
TVSe(US)
Jones, J.

From Noon Till Three
UA (US) 1976 dir. Frank D. Gilroy
V
Gilroy, F. D.

From Russia With Love
UA (GB) 1963 dir. Terence Young
V
Fleming, I.

From the Dead of Night
PHOENIX (US) 1989 dir. Paul Wendkos
TVSe(US)
Brandner, G. *Walkers*

From the Earth to the Moon
WAR (US) 1958 dir. Byron Haskin
V
Verne, J.

From the Terrace
FOX (US) 1960 dir. Mark Robson
O'Hara, J.

From This Day Forward
RKO (US) 1946 dir. John Berry
Bell, T. *All Brides are Beautiful*

Frontier Marshall
FOX (US) 1933 dir. Lew Seiler
FOX (US) 1939 dir. Allan Dwan
Lake, S. *Wyatt Earp, Frontier Marshall*

Front Page, The
UA (US) 1931 dir. Lewis Miles
U-I (US) 1974 dir. Billy Wilder
V
Hecht, B. and MacArthur, C. C.
P

Front Page Story
BL (GB) 1953 dir. Gordon Parry
Gaines, R. *Final Night*

Fruits of Passion
(Fr/Jap) 1982 dir. Shuji Terayama
Réage, P. *Return to the Château*

Fugitive Among Us
ABC PRODS. (US) 1992
dir. Michael Toshiyuki Uno
TV(US)
Cochran, M. *And Deliver Us From Evil*

Fugitive, The
RKO (US) 1947 dir. John Ford
V
Greene, G. *Power and the Glory, The*

Fugitive Kind, The
UA (US) 1960 dir. Sidney Lumet
V
Williams, T. *Orpheus Descending*
P

Fulfillment of Mary Gray, The
INDIAN NECK (US) 1989
dir. Piers Haggard
TV(US)
Spencer, L. *Fulfillment, The*

Full Circle
PAR (GB/Can) 1976
dir. Richard Loncraine
Straub, P. *Julia*

Full Fathom Fire
CONCORDE (US) 1990
dir. Carl Franklin
Davis, B.

Full Metal Jacket
WB (US) 1987 dir. Stanley Kubrick
V
Hasford, G. *The Short Timers*

Full of Life
COL (US) 1956 dir. Richard Quine
Fante, J.

Full Treatment, The
COL (GB) 1960 dir. Val Guest
US title: Stop Me Before I Kill
Thorn, R. S.

Funeral in Berlin
PAR (GB) 1966 dir. Guy Hamilton
V
Deighton, L. *Berlin Memorandum, The*

Funny Dirty Little War
CINEVISTA (Sp) 1986
dir. Hector Olivera
V
Sorino, O.

Funny Farm
WAR (US) 1988 dir. George Roy Hill
Cronley, J.

Funny Girl
COL (US) 1968 dir. William Wyler
M, V
Lennart, I.
P

Funny Thing Happened on the Way to the Forum, A
UA (GB) 1966 dir. Richard Lester
V
Shevelove, B. and Gelbart, L.
P

Furies, The
PAR (US) 1950 dir. Anthony Mann
Busch, N.

Fury, The
FOX (US) 1978 dir. Brian De Palma
V
Farris, J.

Fuzz
UA (US) 1972 dir. Richard A. Colla
V
McBain, E.

Fuzzy Pink Nightgown, The
UA (US) 1957 dir. Norman Taurog
Tate, S.

Gabriela
MGM/UA (Port) 1984
dir. Bruno Barreto
V
Amado, J. *Gabriela, Clove and Cinnamon*

Gabriel Over the White House
MGM (US) 1933 dir. Gregory LaCava
Tweed, T. F. *Rinehard*

Gaby
MGM (US) 1956 dir. Curtis Bernhardt
Sherwood, R. E. *Waterloo Bridge*
P

Gaily, Gaily
UA (US) 1969 dir. Norman Jewison
GB title: Chicago, Chicago
Hecht, B.

Galileo
CINEVISION (GB) 1975
dir. Joseph Losey
Brecht, B.
P

Gambit
UI (US) 1966 dir. Ronald Neame
V
Lane, K.

Gambler, The
LENFILM (USSR) 1982
dir. Alexei Batalov
Dostoevski, F.

Game for Vultures
NEWLINE (GB) 1979 dir. James Fargo
V
Hartmann, N. M.

Game is Over, The
COL (Fr/It) 1967 dir. Roger Vadim
V
Zola, E. *Kill, The*

Games, The
FOX (GB) 1969 dir. Michael Winner
V
Atkinson, H.

Game Set and Match
GRANADA TV (GB) 1987
TV
Deighton, L.

Games Mother Never Taught You
CBS ENT (US) 1982 dir. Lee Philips
TV(US)
Harragan, B. L.

Ganashatru
ELECTRIC (Ind) 1989 dir. Satyajit Ray
Ibsen, H. *An Enemy of the People*
P

Gang That Couldn't Shoot Straight, The
MGM (US) 1971 dir. James Goldstone
Breslin, J.

Garden of Allah, The
UA (US) 1936 dir. Richard Boleslawski
V
Hichens, R.

Garden of the Finzi-Continis, The
DOCUMENTO (It/Ger) 1970
dir. Vittorio de Sica
V
Bassani, G.

Gardens of Stone
TRI-STAR (US) 1987
dir. Francis Ford Coppola
V
Proffitt, N.

Gas, Food and Lodging
IRS (US) 1992 dir. Allison Anders
Peck, R. *Don't Look and it Won't Hurt*

Gaslight
BN (GB) 1939 dir. Thorold Dickinson
US title: Angel Street
MGM (US) 1944 dir. George Cukor
GB title: Murder in Thornton Square, The
V
Hamilton, P. *Angel Street*
P

Gate of Hell
DAIEI (Jap) 1953
dir. Teinosuke Kinugasa
V
Kikuchi, K.

Gathering of Old Men, A
CONSOL (US) 1987
dir. Volker Schlondorff
TV(US)
Gaines, E. J.

Gathering Storm, The
BBC (GB/US) 1974 dir. Herbert Wise
TV(GB/US), V
Churchill, Sir W.

Gaunt Stranger, The
NORTHWOOD (GB) 1938
dir. Walter Forde
US title: Phantom Strikes, The
Wallace, E. *Ringer, The*

Gawain and the Green Knight
THAMES (GB) 1990 dir. J. M. Phillips
TV(GB)
Anon. *Sir Gawain and the Green Knight*

Gay Sisters, The
WAR (US) 1942 dir. Irving Rapper
Longstreet, S.

Gazebo, The
MGM (US) 1959 dir. George Marshall
Coppel, A.

Gemini Man
UN TV (US) 1976 dir. Alan J. Levi
TV(US)
Wells, H. G. *Invisible Man, The*

General Crack
WAR (US) 1930 dir. Alan Crosland
Preedy, G.

General Died at Dawn, The
PAR (US) 1936 dir. Lewis Milestone
Booth, C. G.

Generation
POLSKI (Pol) 1954 dir. Andrzej Wajda
Czeszko, B.

Generation
AVCO (US) 1969 dir. George Schaefer
GB title: Time for Giving, A
V
Goodhart, W.
P

Gentle Annie
MGM (US) 1944 dir. Andrew Marton
Kantor, M.

Gentle Giant, The
PAR (US) 1967 dir. James Neilson
Ch, V
Morley, W. *Gentle Ben*

Gentle Gunman, The
GFD (GB) 1952 dir. Basil Dearden
MacDougall, R.
P

Gentleman Jim
WAR (US) 1942 dir. Raoul Walsh
Corbett, J. J. *Roar of the Crowd, The*

Gentleman's Agreement
FOX (US) 1947 dir. Elia Kazan
Hobson, L. Z.

Gentlemen Marry Brunettes
UA (US) 1955 dir. Richard Sale
Loos, A. *But Gentlemen Marry
Brunettes*

Gentlemen Prefer Blondes
FOX (US) 1953 dir. Howard Hawks
V
Loos, A.

Geordie
BL (GB) 1955 dir. Frank Launder
US title: Wee Geordie
Walker, D.

George and Margaret
WAR (GB) 1940 dir. George King
Savory, G.
P

George Washington
MGM TV (US) 1984 dir. Buzz Kulik
TVSe(US)
Flexner, J. T.

**George Washington II: The
Forging of a Nation**
MGM/UA TV (US) 1986
dir. William A. Graham
TVSe(US)
Flexner, J. T.

**George Washington Slept
Here**
WAR (US) 1942 dir. William Keighley
Kaufman, G. S. and Hart, M.
P

Georgy Girl
COL (GB) 1966 dir. Silvio Narizzano
V
Forster, M.

Gertrud
PATHE (Den) 1966 dir. C. T. Dreyer
V

Soderberg, H.
P

Gervaise
CLCC (Fr) 1956 dir. René Clément
V

Zola, E. *L'Assommoir*

Getaway, The
CINERAMA (US) 1972
dir. Sam Peckinpah
V

Thompson, J.

Get Carter
MGM (GB) 1971 dir. Mike Hodges
Lewis, T. *Jack's Return Home*

Get Christy Love!
WOLPER (US) 1974
dir. William A. Graham
TV(US)
Uhnak, D. *Ledger, The*

Get Off My Foot
WAR (GB) 1935 dir. William Beaudine
Paulton, E. *Money by Wire*
P

Getting it Right
MEDUSA (US) 1989 dir. Randal Kleiser
Howard, E. J.

Getting of Wisdom, The
TEDDERWICK (Aus) 1979
dir. Bruce Beresford
V

Richardson, H. H.

Getting Straight
COL (US) 1970 dir. Richard Rush
V

Kolb, K.

Ghost and Mrs Muir, The
FOX (US) 1947
dir. Joseph L. Mankiewicz
Dick, R. A.

Ghost Breakers, The
PAR (US) 1940 dir. George Marshall
Dickey, P.
P

Ghost in Monte Carlo, A
GRADE (GB) 1990 dir. John Hough
TV(GB)
Cartland, B.

Ghost of Flight 401, The
PAR TV (US) 1978
dir. Steven Hilliard Stern
TV(US)
Fuller, J. G.

Ghosts of Berkeley Square, The
BN (GB) 1947 dir. Vernon Sewell
V

Brahms, C. and Simon, S. J. *No Nightingales*

Ghost Story
UN (US) 1981 dir. John Irvin
V

Straub, P.

Ghost Train, The
GFD (GB) 1931 dir. Walter Forde
GFD (GB) 1941 dir. Walter Forde
V

Ridley, A.
P

Ghoul, The
GAU (GB) 1933 dir. T. Hayes Hunter
King, F.

Giant
WAR (US) 1956 dir. George Stevens
V
Ferber, E.

Gideon's Day
COL (GB) 1958 dir. John Ford
US title: Gideon of Scotland Yard
Creasey, J.

Gideon's Trumpet
WORLDVISION (US) 1980
dir. Robert Collins
TV(US), V
Lewis, A.

Gidget
COL (US) 1959 dir. Paul Wendkos
V
Kohner, F.

Gidget Grows Up
COL TV (US) 1969 dir. James Sheldon
TV(US)
Kohner, F. *Gidget Goes to New York*

Gift, The
GOLDWYN (Fr) 1983 dir. Michel Lang
V
Valme and Terzolli *Bankers Also Have Souls*
P

Gift, The
PAR TV (US) 1979 dir. Don Taylor
TV(US)
Hamill, P.

Gift of Love, The: A Christmas Story
TELECOM (US) 1983
dir. Delbert Mann
TV(US)
Aldrich, B. S. *Silent Stars Go By, The*

Gigi
(Fr) 1948 dir. Jacqueline Audry
MGM (US) 1958 dir. Vincente Minnelli
M, V
Colette

Girl/Boy
HEMDALE (GB) 1971 dir. Bob Kellett
Percival, D. *Girlfriend*
P

Girl Called Hatter Fox, The
EMI (US) 1977 dir. George Schaefer
TV (US)
Harris, M. *Hatter Fox*

Girl Crazy
MGM (US) 1943 dir. Norman Taurog
M, V
Bolton, G., McGowan, J.
P

Girl from Hunan, The
CHINA (China) 1986 dir. Xie Fei, U Lan
Congwen, S. *Xiao, Xiao*

Girl from Petrovka, The
UN (US) 1974 dir. Robert Ellis Miller
V
Feifer, G.

Girl from Tenth Avenue, The
WAR (US) 1935 dir. Alfred E. Green
GB title: Men on her Mind
Davies, H. H.
P

Girl He Left Behind, The
WAR (US) 1956 dir. David Butler
Hargrove, M.

Girl Hunters, The
FOX (GB) 1963 dir. Roy Rowland
V
Spillane, M.

Girl in a Swing, The
J&M (GB/US) 1989 dir. Gordon Hessler
Adams, R.

Girl in the Headlines, The
BL (GB) 1963 dir. Michael Truman
US title: Model Murder Case, The
Payne, L. *Nose on my Face, The*

Girl in the News, The
FOX (GB) 1940 dir. Carol Reed
Vickers, R.

Girl in White, The
MGM (US) 1952 dir. John Sturges
GB title: So Bright the Flame
Barringer, E. D. *Bowery to Bellevue*

Girl Must Live, A
UN (GB) 1939 dir. Carol Reed
Bonett, E.

Girl Named Sooner, A
FOX TV (US) 1975 dir. Delbert Mann
TV(US)
Clauser, S.

Girl Named Tamiko, A
PAR (US) 1962 dir. John Sturges
Kirkbride, R.

Girl of the Limberlost, A
MON (US) 1934 dir. Christy Cabanne
FREEDOM PRODS. (US) 1990
dir. Burt Brinckerhoff
TV(US)
Porter, G. S.

Girl of the Night
WAR (US) 1960 dir. Joseph Cates
Greenwald, H. *Call Girl, The*

Girl on the Boat, The
UA (GB) 1962 dir. Henry Kaplan
Wodehouse, P. G.

Girl on a Motorcycle
BL (GB/Fr) 1968 dir. Jack Cardiff
US title: Naked Under Leather
V
Mandiargues, A. P. de *Motocyclette, La*

Girls, Les
MGM (US) 1957 dir. George Cukor
M, V
Caspary, V.

Girls of Huntington House, The
LORIMAR (US) 1973 dir. Alf Kjellin
TV(US)
Elfman, B.

Girls of Pleasure Island, The
PAR (US) 1953
dir. F. Hugh Herbert & Alvin Ganzer
Maier, W. *Pleasure Island*

Girl, The Gold Watch and Everything, The
PAR TV (US) 1980 dir. William Wiard
TV(US)
MacDonald, J. D.

Girl who Couldn't Quit, The
MON (GB) 1950 dir. Norman Lee
Marks, L.
P

Girl Who Had Everything, The
MGM (US) 1953 dir. Richard Thorpe
St. John, A. R.

Girl With Green Eyes
UA (GB) 1964 dir. Desmond Davis
V
O'Brien, E. *Lonely Girl, The*

Girl with the Red Hair, The
UA (Neth) 1983 dir. Ben Verbong
DeVries, T.

Give me a Sailor
PAR (US) 1938 dir. Elliott Nugent
Nichols, A.
P

Give Me Your Heart
WAR (US) 1936 dir. Archie Mayo
GB title: Sweet Aloes
Mallory, J. *Sweet Aloes*
P

Give Us the Moon
GFD (GB) 1944 dir. Val Guest
Brahms, C. and Simon, S. J.
Elephant is White, The

Give Us This Day
GFD (GB) 1949 dir. Edward Dmytryk
US title: Salt to the Devil
Di Donata, P. *Christ in Concrete*

Glad Tidings
EROS (GB) 1953 dir. Wolf Rilla
Delderfield, R. F.
P

Glamorous Night
ABP (GB) 1937
dir. Brian Desmond Hurst
M
Novello, I.
P

Glass Cell, The
SOLARIS (Ger) 1981
dir. Hans C. Geissendoerfer
Highsmith, P.

Glass Full of Snow, A
CIN IT (It) 1988 dir. Florestano Vancini
Rossi, N.

Glass House, The
TOM (US) 1972 dir. Tom Gries
TV(US), V
Capote, T. and Cooper, W.

Glass Key, The
PAR (US) 1935 dir. Frank Tuttle
PAR (US) 1942 dir. Stuart Heisler
Hammett, D.

Glass Menagerie, The
WAR (US) 1950 dir. Irving Rapper
TALENT (US) 1973
dir. Anthony Harvey
TV(US)
CINEPLEX (US) 1987 dir. Paul Newman
V
Williams, T.
P

Glitter Dome, The
HBO (US) 1984 dir. Stuart Margolin
TV(US), V
Wambaugh, J.

Glitz
LORIMAR (US) 1988 dir. Sandor Stern
TV(US)
Leonard, E.

Glory
TRI-STAR (US) 1989 dir. Edward Zwick
Burchard, P. *One Gallant Rush*
Kirstein, L. *Lay this Laurel*

Glory Boys, The
YTV (GB) 1984 dir. Michael Ferguson
V, TV(GB)
Seymour, G.

Glory Guys
UA (US) 1965 dir. Arnold Laven
Birney, H. *Dice of God, The*

Gnome-Mobile, The
DISNEY (US) 1967
dir. Robert Stevenson
Ch, V
Sinclair, U.

Go-Between, The
EMI (GB) 1970 dir. Joseph Losey
V
Hartley, L. P.

Goddess of Love, The
NEW WORLD TV (US) 1988
dir. James Drake
TV(US)
Anstey, F. *Tinted Venus*

Godfather, The
PAR (US) 1972
dir. Francis Ford Coppola
V
Puzo, M.

Godfather Part II, The
PAR (US) 1974
dir. Francis Ford Coppola
V
Puzo, M. *Godfather, The*

God is my Co-Pilot
WAR (US) 1945 dir. Robert Florey
Scott, R. L.

God's Country and the Woman
WAR (US) 1936 dir. William Keighley
Curwood, J. O.

Godsend, The
CANNON (US) 1980
dir. Gabrielle Beaumont
V
Taylor, B.

God's Little Acre
UA (US) 1958 dir. Anthony Mann
V
Caldwell, E.

Godspell
COL (US) 1973 dir. David Greene
M
Tebelak, J. M.
P

Going Bananas
CANNON (US) 1988 dir. Boaz Davidson
Borenstein, T. *Kofiko*

Gold
HEMDALE (GB) 1974 dir. Peter Hunt
Smith, W. *Gold Mine*

Gold Diggers of Broadway
WAR (US) 1939 dir. Roy del Ruth
Hopwood, A. *Gold Diggers, The*
P

Golden Arrow
WAR (US) 1936 dir. Alfred E. Green
Arlen, M.
P

Golden Boy
COL (US) 1939 dir. Rouben Mamoulian
V
Odets, C.
P

Golden Ear-Rings
PAR (US) 1947 dir. Mitchell Leisen
Foldes, Y.

Goldeneye
ANGLIA (GB) 1990 dir. Don Boyd
TV(GB)
Pearson, J. *Life of Ian Fleming, The*

Goldengirl
AVCO (US) 1979 dir. Joseph Sargent
V
Lear, P.

Golden Hawk, The
COL (US) 1952 dir. Sidney Salkow
Yerby, F.

Golden Head, The
CINERAMA (US/Hun) 1965
dir. Richard Thorpe
Pilkington, R. *Nepomuk of the River*

Golden Rendezvous
RANK (US) 1977 dir. Ashley Lazarus
V
MacLean, A.

Goldenrod
TALENT (US) 1977 dir. Harvey Hart
TV(US), V
Harker, H.

Golden Salamander, The
GFD (GB) 1949 dir. Ronald Neame
Canning, V.

Golden Seal, The
GOLDWYN (US) 1983 dir. Frank Zuniga
V
Marshall, J. V. *River Ran out of Eden,
A*

Goldfinger
UA (GB) 1964 dir. Guy Hamilton
V
Fleming, I.

Gold for the Caesars
MGM (US) 1964 dir. Andre de Toth
Seward, F. A.

Gold of the Seven Saints
WAR (US) 1961 dir. Gordon Douglas
Frazee, S. *Desert Guns*

Go Naked in the World
MGM (US) 1960
dir. Ronald MacDougall
Chamales, T.

Gone to Earth
BL (GB) 1950
dir. Michael Powell/Emeril Pressburger
US title: Wild Heart, The
Webb, M.

Gone with the Wind
MGM (US) 1939 dir. Victor Fleming
V
Mitchell, M.

Goodbye Again
UA (US) 1961 dir. Anatole Litvak
Sagan, F. *Aimez-vous Brahms?*

Goodbye Charlie
FOX (US) 1964 dir. Vincente Minnelli
Axelrod, G.
P

Goodbye Columbus
PAR (US) 1969 dir. Larry Peerce
V
Roth, P.

Goodbye Gemini
CINDERAMA (GB) 1970
dir. Alan Gibson
Hall, J. *Ask Agamemnon*

Goodbye, Miss 4th of July
FINNEGAN/PINCHUK (US) 1988
dir. George Miller
TV(US)
Janus, C. G. *Miss 4th of July, Goodbye*

Goodbye Mr Chips
MGM (GB) 1939 dir. Sam Wood
V
Hilton, J.

Goodbye Mr Chips
MGM (GB) 1969 dir. Herbert Ross
M

Hilton, J. and Burnham, B.
P

Goodbye, My Fancy
WAR (US) 1951 dir. Vincent Sherman
Kanin, F.
P

Goodbye, My Lady
WAR (US) 1956 dir. William Wellman
Street, J. H.

Goodbye People, The
EMBASSY (US) 1984 dir. Herb Gardner
V

Gardner, H.
P

Good Companions, The
GAU (GB) 1932 dir. Victor Saville
ABP (GB) 1956 dir. J. Lee Thompson
Priestley, J. B.

Good Cops, Bad Cops
KUSHNER-LOCKE (US) 1990
dir. Paul Wendkos
TV(US)
Clemente, G. W. and Stevens, K.
Cops are Robbers, The

Good Earth, The
MGM (US) 1937 dir. Sidney Franklin
V

Buck, P.

Good Fairy, The
UN (US) 1935 dir. William Wyler
HALLMARK (US) 1956
dir. George Schaefer
TV(US)
Molnar, F.
P

Good Father, The
FILM 4 (GB) 1986 dir. Mike Newell
Prince, P.

Goodfellas
WAR (US) 1990 dir. Martin Scorsese
Pileggi, N. *Wiseguy: Life in A Mafia Family*

Good Morning, Miss Dove
FOX (US) 1955 dir. Henry Koster
Patton, F. G.

Good Mother, The
TOUCH (US) 1988 dir. Leonard Nimoy
V

Miller, S.

Good Neighbour Sam
COL (US) 1964 dir. David Swift
V

Finney, J.

Good Old Boy
DISNEY CH (US) 1988
dir. Tom G. Robertson
TV(US)
Morris, W. *Good Old Boy: A Delta Summer*

Good Old Soak
MGM (US) 1937 dir. J. Walter Ruben
Marquis, D. *Old Soak, The*
P

Good-Time Girl
GFD (GB) 1948 dir. David MacDonald
La Bern, A. J. *Night Darkens the Streets*

Gor
CANNON (US) 1989 dir. Fritz Kiersch
Norman, J. *Tarnsman of Gor*

Gore Vidal's Lincoln
FINNEGAN/PINCHUK (US) 1988
dir. Lamont Johnson
TVSe(US)
Vidal, G. *Lincoln*

Gorgeous Hussy, The
MGM (US) 1936 dir. Clarence Brown
Adams, S. H.

Gorilla, The
FOX (US) 1939 dir. Allan Dwan
V
Spence, R.
P

Gorillas in the Mist
WAR/UN (US) 1988 dir. Michael Apted
V
Fossey, D.

Gorky Park
ORION (GB) 1983 dir. Michael Apted
V
Smith, M. C.

Go Tell It On The Mountain
PRICE (US) 1985 dir. Stan Latham
TV
Baldwin, J.

Go Toward the Light
CORAPEAKE (US) 1988 dir. Mike Robe
TV(US)
Polson, B.

Goupi Mains Rouges
MINERVA (Fr) 1943
dir. Jacques Becker
US title: It Happened at the Inn
Very, P.

Go West Young Man
PAR (US) 1936 dir. Henry Hathaway
Riley, L. *Personal Appearance*
P

Gracie Allen Murder Case, The
PAR (US) 1939 dir. Alfred E. Green
Dine, S. S. van

Graduate, The
UA (US) 1967 dir. Mike Nichols
V
Webb, C.

Grambling's White Tiger
INTERPLAN (US) 1981
dir. Georg Stanford Brown
TV(US), V
Behrenberg, B. *My Little Brother is Coming Tomorrow*

Grand Canary
FOX (US) 1934 dir. Irving Cummings
Cronin, A. J.

Grand Central Murder
MGM (US) 1942 dir. S. Sylvan Simon
McVeigh, S.

Grand Hotel
MGM (US) 1932 dir. Edmund Goulding
V
Baum, V.

Grand Isle
TURNER (US) 1992 dir. Mary Lambert
TV(US)
Chopin, K. *Awakening, The*

Grand National Night
REN (GB) 1953 dir. Bob McNaught
US title: Wicked Wife, The
Christie, D. and Christie, C.
P

Grand Slam
WAR (US) 1933 dir. William Dieterle
Herts, B. R.

Grapes of Wrath, The
FOX (US) 1940 dir. John Ford
V

Steinbeck, J.

Grasshopper, The
NGL (US) 1969 dir. Jerry Paris

McShane, M. *Passing of Evil, The*

Grass is Always Greener over the Septic Tank, The
J. HAMILTON (US) 1978
dir. Robert Day
TV(US), V

Bombeck, E.

Grass is Greener, The
UI (GB) 1960 dir. Stanley Donen
V

Williams, H. and Williams, M.
P

Grass is Singing, The
MAINLINE (Zam/Swe) 1981
dir. Michael Raeburn

Lessing, D.

Grass Roots
JBS PRODS. (US) 1992
dir. Jerry London
TVSe(US)

Woods, S.

Graveyard Shift
PAR (US) 1990 dir. Ralph S. Singleton

King, S.

Gray Lady Down
UN (US) 1978 dir. David Greene
V

Lavallee, D. *Event One Thousand*

Grease
PAR (US) 1978 dir. Randal Kleiser
M

Jacobs, J. and Casey, W.
P

Great Balls of Fire
ORION (US) 1989 dir. Jim McBride

Lewis, M.

Great Bank Robbery, The
WAR (US) 1969 dir. Hy Averback

O'Rourke, F.

Great Catherine
WAR (GB) 1968 dir. Gordon Flemyng

Shaw, G. B.
P

Great Day
RKO (GB) 1945 dir. Lance Comfort

Storm, L.

Great Day in the Morning
RKO (US) 1955 dir. Jacques Tourneur
V

Andrew, R. H.

Great Escape, The
UA (US) 1963 dir. John Sturges
V

Brickhill, P.

Greatest, The
COL-WAR (US/GB) 1977 dir. Tom Gries
V

Ali, M.

Greatest Gift, The
UN TV (US) 1974 dir. Boris Sagal
TV(US)

Farris, J. *Ramey*

Greatest Story Ever Told, The
UA (US) 1965 dir. George Stevens
V

Oursler, F.

Greatest Thing That Almost Never Happened, The
FRIES (US) 1977 dir. Gilbert Moses
TV(US)
Robertson, D.

Great Expectations
UN (US) 1934 dir. Stuart Walker
RANK/CINEGUILD (GB) 1946
dir. David Lean
V
SCOTIA BARBER/ITC (GB) 1974
dir. Joseph Hardy
V
PRIMETIME/HTV (GB/US) 1989
dir. Kevin Connor
TV(GB/US)
Dickens, C.

Great Game, The
ADELPHI (GB) 1952 dir. Maurice Elvey
Thomas, B. *Shooting Star*
P

Great Gatsby, The
PAR (US) 1949 dir. Elliot Nugent
PAR (US) 1974 dir. Jack Clayton
V
Fitzgerald, F. S.

Great Impersonation, The
UN (US) 1935 dir. Alan Crosland
UN (US) 1942 dir. John Rawlins
Oppenheim, E. P.

Great Imposter, The
UI (US) 1961 dir. Robert Mulligan
V
Crichton, R.

Great Jasper, The
RKO (US) 1933 dir. J. Walter Ruben
Oursler, F.

Great Lie, The
WAR (US) 1941 dir. Edmund Goulding
Banks, P. *January Heights*

Great Man, The
UI (US) 1956 dir. Jose Ferrer
Morgan, A.

Great Man's Whiskers, The
UN TV (US) 1973 dir. Philip Leacock
TV(US)
Scott, A.
P

Great Meadow, The
MGM (US) 1931 dir. Charles Brabin
Roberts, E. M.

Great Moment, The
PAR (US) 1944 dir. Preston Sturges
Fulop-Miller, R. *Triumph*

Great Mouse Detective, The
DISNEY (US) 1986
dir. Burny Mattinson
A, Ch
Titus, E. *Basil of Baker Street*

Great Mr. Handel, The
RANK (GB) 1942 dir. Norman Walker
Peach, L. D.

Great Santini, The
ORION (US) 1979
dir. Lewis John Carlino
V
Conroy, P.

Great Sinner, The
MGM (US) 1949 dir. Robert Siodmak
Dostoevski, F. *Great Gambler*

Great White Hope, The
FOX (US) 1970 dir. Martin Ritt
V
Sackler, H.
P

135

Greeks had a Word for Them, The
UA (US) 1932 dir. Lowell Sherman

Atkins, Z.
P

Green Berets, The
WAR (US) 1968
dir. John Wayne/Ray Kellogg
V

Moore, R.

Green Dolphin Street
MGM (US) 1947 dir. Victor Saville
V

Goudge, E.

Green Fingers
BN (GB) 1946 dir. John Harlow

Arundel, E. *Persistent Warrior, The*

Green for Danger
INDIVIDUAL (GB) 1946
dir. Sidney Gilliat
V

Brand, C.

Greengage Summer, The
RANK (GB) 1961 dir. Lewis Gilbert
US title: Loss of Innocence

Godden, R.

Green Goddess, The
WAR (US) 1930 dir. Alfred E. Green

Archer, W.
P

Green Grass of Wyoming
FOX (US) 1949 dir. Louis King

O'Hara, M.

Green Grow the Rushes
BL (GB) 1951 dir. Derek Twist

Clewes, H.

Green Helmet, The
MGM (GB) 1960 dir. Michael Forlong

Cleary, J.

Green Ice
ITC (GB) 1981 dir. Ernest Day
V

Browne, G. A.

Green Light, The
WAR (US) 1937 dir. Frank Borzage

Douglas, L. C.

Green Man, The
BL (GB) 1956 dir. Robert Day
V

Launder, F. and Gilliat, S. *Meet a Body*
P

Green Man, The
BBC (GB) 1991 dir. Elijah Moshinsky
TV(GB)

Amis, K.

Green Mansions
MGM (US) 1959 dir. Mel Ferrer

Hudson, W. H.

Green Pastures, The
WAR (US) 1936
dir. William Keighley/Marc Connelly
V
MILBERG (US) 1957
dir. George Schaefer
TV(US)

Connelly, M.
P

Green Scarf, The
BL (GB) 1954
dir. George More O'Ferrall

Cars, G. des *Brute, The*

Green Years, The
MGM (US) 1946 dir. Victor Saville

Cronin, A. J.

Greystoke: The Legend of Tarzan, Lord of the Apes
WAR (GB) 1984 dir. Hugh Hudson
V

Burroughs, E. R. *Tarzan of the Apes*

Grifters, The
MIRAMAX (US) 1990
dir. Stephen Frears

Thompson, J.

Grissom Gang, The
CINERAMA (US) 1971
dir. Robert Aldrich
V

Chase, J. H. *No Orchids for Miss Blandish*

Groundstar Conspiracy, The
UN (US) 1972 dir. Lamont Johnson
V

Davies, L. P. *Alien, The*

Group, The
UA (US) 1966 dir. Sidney Lumet
V

McCarthy, M.

Guadalcanal Diary
FOX (US) 1943 dir. Lewis Seiler

Tregaskis, R. W.

Guardian, The
UN (US) 1990 dir. William Friedkin

Greenburg, D. *Nanny, The*

Guardian Angel, The
SANDREW (Swe) 1990
dir. Suzanne Osten

Huch, R. *Der Letste Sommer*

Guardsman, The
MGM (US) 1931 dir. Sidney Franklin

Molnar, F.
P

Guess Who's Sleeping in my Bed?
ABC (US) 1973 dir. Theodore J. Flicker
TV(US)

Chais, P. H. *Six Weeks in August*

Guest in the House
UA (US) 1944 dir. John Brahm
V

Wilde, H. and Eunson, D.
P

Guide for the Married Man, The
FOX (US) 1967 dir. Gene Kelly
V

Tarloff, F.

Guilt is my Shadow
ABP (GB) 1950 dir. Roy Kellino

Curtis, P. *You're Best Alone*

Guilty?
GN (GB) 1956 dir. Edmund Greville

Gilbert, M. *Death has Deep Roots*

Guilty as Hell
PAR (US) 1932 dir. Erle C. Kenton

Rubin, D. *Riddle Me This*
P

Guinea Pig, The
PILGRIM-PATHE (GB) 1948
dir. Roy Boulting
US title: Outsider, The

Strode, W. S.
P

Gulliver's Travels
PAR (US) 1939 dir. Dave Fleischer
EMI (GB) 1976 dir. Peter Hunt
A, V

Swift, J.

Gun and the Pulpit, The
CINE TV (US) 1974 dir. Daniel Petrie
TV(US)
Ehrlich, J.

Gunfighters
COL (US) 1947 dir. George Waggner
Grey, Z. *Twin Sombreros*

Gun Fury
COL (US) 1953 dir. Raoul Walsh
V
Granger, K. R. G. *Ten Against Caesar*

Gun Glory
MGM (US) 1957 dir. Roy Rowland
Yordan, P. *Man of the West*

Gun Runners, The
UA (US) 1958 dir. Don Siegel
Hemingway, E. *To Have and Have Not*

Guns at Batasi
FOX (GB) 1964 dir. John Guillermin
Holles, R. *Siege of Battersea, The*

Gunsmoke
UN (US) 1953 dir. Nathan Juran
Fox, N. A. *Roughshod*

Guns of Darkness
WAR (GB) 1962 dir. Anthony Asquith
Clifford, F. *Act of Mercy*

Guns of Diablo
MGM (US) 1964 dir. Boris Sagal
V
Taylor, R. L. *Travels of Jaimie McPheeters, The*

Guns of Navarone, The
COL (GB) 1961 dir. J. Lee Thompson
V
MacLean, A.

Guns of the Timberland
WAR (US) 1960 dir. Robert D. Webb
V
L'Amour, L.

Guts and Glory: The Oliver North Story
PAPAZIAN-HIRSCH (US) 1989
dir. Mike Robe
TVSe(US)
Bradlee, Jr., B. *Guts and Glory: The Rise and Fall of Oliver North*

Guyana Tragedy: The Story of Jim Jones
KONIGSBERG (US) 1980
dir. William A. Graham
TVSe(US), V
Krause, C. A. *Guyana Massacre: The Eyewitness Account*

Guy Named Joe, A
MGM (US) 1943 dir. Victor Fleming
Cairn, J.

Guys and Dolls
MGM (US) 1955
dir. Joseph L. Mankiewicz
M, V
Runyon, D. *Idyll of Miss Sarah Brown, The*
Burrows, A., Loesser, F. and Swerling, J.
P

Gymkata
MGM/UA (US) 1985 dir. Robert Clouse
V
Moore, D. T.

Gypsy
WAR (US) 1962 dir. Mervyn LeRoy
M, V
Lee, G. R.
Laurents, A.
P

Gypsy and the Gentleman, The
RANK (GB) 1957 dir. Joseph Losey
Hooke, N. W. *Darkness I Leave You*

Gypsy Moths, The
MGM (US) 1969
dir. John Frankenheimer
Drought, J.

Hail Hazana
STILLMAN (Sp) 1978
dir. Jose Maria Guttierez
de Soto, J. M. V. *Infierno y la Brisa, El*

Hail, Hero!
CIN CEN (US) 1969 dir. David Miller
Weston, J.

Hair
UA (US) 1979 dir. Milos Forman
M, V
MacDermot, G., Ragni, G. and Rado, J.
P

Hairy Ape, The
UA (US) 1944 dir. Alfred Santell
O'Neill, E. G.
P

Half a Sixpence
PAR (GB) 1967 dir. George Sidney
M
Cross, B.
P
Wells, H. G. *Kipps*

Half Moon Street
RKO (US) 1986 dir. Bob Swaim
V
Theroux, P.

Halfway House, The
EAL (GB) 1944 dir. Basil Dearden
Ogden, D.
P

Hallelujah Trail, The
UA (US) 1965 dir. John Sturges
Gulick, B.

Hamlet
TC (GB) 1948 dir. Laurence Olivier
M. EVANS (US) 1953
dir. Albert McCleery
TV(US)
CLASSIC (USSR) 1964
dir. Grigori Kozintsev
V
COL (GB) 1969 dir. Tony Richardson
V
ATV/UN (GB/US) 1970 dir. Peter Wood
TV(GB/US)
WAR/GUILD (US/GB) 1990
dir. Franco Zeffirelli
V
Shakespeare, W.
P

Hammerhead
COL (GB) 1968 dir. David Miller
Mayo, J.

Hammer the Toff
BUTCHER (GB) 1952
dir. Maclean Rogers
Creasey, J.

Hammett
WAR (US) 1982 dir. Wim Wenders
V
Gores, J.

Hand, The
ORION/WAR (US) 1981
dir. Oliver Stone
Brandel, M. *Lizard's Tail, The*

Handful of Dust, A
NEW LINE (GB) 1988
dir. Charles Sturridge
V
Waugh, E.

Handmaid's Tale, The
CINECOM (US) 1990
dir. Volker Schlondorff
Atwood, M.

Hands of a Stranger
TAFT (US) 1987 dir. Larry Elikann
TV(US)
Daley, R.

Hands of Cormac Joyce, The
CRAWFORD PRODS (US) 1972
dir. Fielder Cook
TV(US)
Wibberley, L.

Handy Andy
FOX (US) 1934 dir. David Butler
Beach, L. *Merry Andrew*
P

Hangar 18
SCHICK SUNN (US) 1980
dir. James L. Conway
V
Weverka, R. and Sellier, Jr., C.

Hanged Man, The
UN (US) 1964 dir. Don Siegel
TV(US)
Hughes, D. B. *Ride the Pink Horse*

Hanging Tree, The
WAR (US) 1958 dir. Delmer Daves
Johnson, D. M.

Hangover Square
FOX (US) 1945 dir. John Brahm
Hamilton, P.

Hanna's War
CANNON (US) 1988
dir. Menahem Golan
V
Senesh, H. *Diaries of Hannah Senesh, The*
Palgi, Y. *Great Wind Cometh, A*

Hans Brinker, or the Silver Skates
MILBERG (US) 1957 dir. Sidney Lumet
TV(US)
Dodge, M. M.

Hansel and Gretel
CANNON (US) 1987 dir. Len Talan
Ch, V
Grimm, J. L. K. and Grimm, W. K.

Happiest Days of Your Life, The
BL (GB) 1950 dir. Frank Launder
Dighton, J.
P

Happiest Millionaire, The
DISNEY (US) 1967 dir. Norman Tokar
M, V
Biddle, C. D. and Crichton, K.
P

Happiness of Three Women, The
ADELPHI (GB) 1954 dir. Maurice Elvey
Evans, E. *Wishing Well*
P

Happy Anniversary
UA (US) 1959 dir. David Miller
Fields, J. and Chodorov, J.
Anniversary Waltz
P

Happy Birthday, Gemini
UA (US) 1980 dir. Richard Benner
Innaurato, A. *Gemini*
P

Happy Birthday, Turke!
SENATOR FILMS (Ger) 1992
dir. Dorris Dorrie
Arjourni, J.

Happy Birthday, Wanda Jane
COL (US) 1971 dir. Mark Robson
Vonnegut, K.
P

Happy Family, The
APEX (GB) 1952 dir. Muriel Box
US title: Mr. Lord Says No
Hutton, M. G.
P

Happy Hooker, The
SCOTIA BARBER (US) 1975
dir. Nicholas Sgarro
V
Hollander, X.

Happy is the Bride
BL (GB) 1957 dir. Roy Boulting
McCracken, E. *Quiet Wedding*
P

Happy Land
FOX (US) 1943 dir. Irving Pichel
Kantor, M.

Happy Thieves, The
UA (US) 1962 dir. George Marshall
Condon, R. *Oldest Confession, The*

Happy Time, The
COL (US) 1952 dir. Richard Fleischer
Fontaine, R. L.; Taylor, S. A. *Happy Time, The* is based on both book and play
P

Harder They Fall
COL (US) 1956 dir. Mark Robson
V
Schulberg, B. W.

Hard, Fast and Beautiful
RKO (US) 1951 dir. Ida Lupino
Tunis, J. R.

Hard Steel
GFD (GB) 1942 dir. Norman Walker
Dataller, R. *Steel Saraband*

Hard Times
GRANADA (GB) 1977 dir. John Irvin
TVSe(GB), V
Dickens, C.

Hard Travelling
NEW WORLD (US) 1986
dir. Dan Bessie
V
Bessie, A. *Bread and a Stone*

Harlow
PAR (US) 1965 dir. Gordon Douglas
V

Shulman, I.

Harper
WAR (US) 1966 dir. Jack Smight
GB title: Moving Target, The
V

Macdonald, R. *Moving Target, The*

Harrad Experiment, The
CINERAMA (US) 1973 dir. Ted Post
V

Rimmer, R. H.

Harriet Craig
COL (US) 1950 dir. Vincent Sherman

Kelly, G. *Craig's Wife*
P

Harry and Son
ORION (US) 1984 dir. Paul Newman
V

DeCapite, R. *Lost King, A*

Harry Black and the Tiger
FOX (GB) 1958 dir. Hugo Fregonese
US title: Harry Black

Walker, D.

Harry's Game
YTV (GB) 1982
dir. Lawrence Gordon Clark
TVSe(GB), V

Seymour, G.

Harvest
M. PAGNOL (Fr) 1937
dir. Marcel Pagnol
V

Giono, J.

Harvey
UN (US) 1950 dir. Henry Koster
TALENT ASS. (US) 1972
dir. Fielder Cook
TV(US)

Chase, M.
P

Hasty Heart, The
ABP (GB) 1949 dir. Vincent Sherman

Patrick, J.
P

Hatful of Rain, A
FOX (US) 1957 dir. Fred Zinnemann

Gazzo, M. V.
P

Hatter's Castle
PAR (GB) 1941 dir. Lance Comfort

Cronin, A. J.

Haunted, The
FOX TV (US) 1991 dir. Robert Mandel
TV(US)

Curran, R.

Haunted Palace, The
AMERICAN (US) 1963
dir. Roger Corman

Lovecraft, H. P. *Case of Charles Dexter, The*

Haunted Summer
CANNON (US) 1988 dir. Ivan Passer
V

Edwards, A.

Haunting, The
MGM (GB) 1963 dir. Robert Wise
V

Jackson, S. *Haunting of Hill House, The*

Haunting of Morella, The
CONCORDE (US) 1990
dir. Jim Wynorski
Poe, E. A.

Hauser's Memory
UN (US) 1970 dir. Boris Sagal
TV(US)
Siodmak, C.

Having Wonderful Crime
RKO (US) 1945 dir. Eddie Sutherland
Rice, C.

Having Wonderful Time
RKO (US) 1938 dir. Alfred Santell
V
Kober, A.
P

Hawaii
UA (US) 1966 dir. George Roy Hill
V
Michener, J. A.

Haywire
WAR (US) 1980 dir. Michael Tuchner
TV(US)
Hayward, B.

Hazard
PAR (US) 1948 dir. George Marshall
Chanslor, R.

Hazard of Hearts, A
MGM (GB) 1987 dir. John Hough
TV(GB)
Cartland, B.

Heads or Tails
CASTLE HILL (Fr) 1983
dir. Robert Enrico
Harris, A. *Follow the Widower*

Heart Beat
WAR (US) 1979 dir. John Byrum
V
Cassady, C.

Heartbreak Kid, The
FOX (US) 1972 dir. Elaine May
V
Friedman, B. J. *Change of Plan, A*

Heartburn
PAR (US) 1986 dir. Mike Nichols
Ephron, N.

Heart is a Lonely Hunter, The
WAR (US) 1968 dir. Robert Ellis Miller
V
McCullers, C.

Heart of a Child
RANK (GB) 1958 dir. Clive Donner
Bottome, P.

Heart of Dixie
ORION (US) 1989 dir. Martin Davidson
Siddons, A. R. *Heartbreak Hotel*

Heart of New York
WAR (US) 1932 dir. Mervyn LeRoy
Freedman, D. *Mendel Inc.*
P

Heart of the Matter
BL (GB) 1953
dir. George More O'Ferrall
Greene, G.

Heartsounds
EMBASSY (US) 1984 dir. Glenn Jordan
TV(US)
Lear, M. W.

Heat
NEW CENTURY (US) 1987
dir. Dick Richards
V

Goldman, W.

Heat and Dust
UN/ENT (GB) 1983 dir. James Ivory
V

Jhabvala, R. P.

Heat Lightning
WAR (US) 1934 dir. Mervyn Le Roy

Abbott, G. and Abrams, L.
P

Heaven Can Wait
FOX (US) 1943 dir. Ernst Lubitsch

Bus-Fekete, L. *Birthday*
P

Heaven Can Wait
PAR (US) 1978 dir. Warren Beatty,
Buck Henry
V

Segall, H. *Halfway to Heaven*
P

Heaven Fell That Night
IENA (Fr/It) 1958 dir. Roger Vadim

Vidalie, A.

Heaven Knows Mr. Allison
FOX (US) 1957 dir. John Huston

Shaw, C.

Hedda
SCOTIA BARBER (GB) 1977
dir. Trevor Nunn
V

Ibsen, H. *Hedda Gabler*
P

Heidi
FOX (US) 1937 dir. Allan Dwan
V
NBC (US) 1968 dir. Delbert Mann
TV(US)
BBC (GB) 1974
dir. June Wyndham-Davies
TVSe(GB)

Spyri, J.

Heidi's Song
HANNA-BARBERA (US) 1982
dir. Robert Taylor
A, V

Spyri, J. *Heidi*

Heiress, The
PAR (US) 1949 dir. William Wyler
V

James, H. *Washington Square*

Helden
SOKAL/GOLDBAUM (Ger) 1959
dir. Franz Peter Wirth

Shaw, G. B. *Arms and the Man*
P

Helen Keller — The Miracle Continues
FOX TV (US) 1984 dir. Alan Gibson
TV(US)

Lash, J. P. *Helen and Teacher*

Hell Below
MGM (US) 1933 dir. Jack Conway

Ellsberg, E. *Pigboats*

Hell Below Zero
COL (GB) 1954 dir. Mark Robson

Innes, H. *White South, The*

Hellcats of the Navy
COL (US) 1957 dir. Nathan Juran
V

Lockwood, C. A. and Adamson, H. C. *Hellcats of the Sea*

Heller in Pink Tights
PAR (US) 1960 dir. George Cukor
V

L'Amour, L. *Heller With A Gun*

Hell Hath No Fury
BAR-GENE (US) 1991
dir. Thomas J. Wright
TV(US)
Battin, B. W. *Smithereens*

Hell is a City
WAR (GB) 1959 dir. Val Guest
Procter, M.

Hell is Empty
RANK (Czech/GB) 1967
dir. John Ainsworth and
Bernard Knowles
V

Straker, J. F.

Hell is Sold Out
EROS (GB) 1951 dir. Michael Anderson
Dekobra, M.

Hello Dolly
FOX (US) 1969 dir. Gene Kelly
M, V
Steward, M. and Herman, J.
P
Wilder, T. *Matchmaker, The*
P

Hell on Frisco Bay
WAR (US) 1955 dir. Frank Tuttle
V
McGivern, W. P. *Darkest Hour*

Hello Sister
FOX (US) 1933 dir. Erich von Stroheim
Powell, D.

Hellraiser
CINEMARQUE (GB) 1987
dir. Clive Barker
V
Barker, C. *Hellbound Heart, The*

Hell's Heroes
UN (US) 1930 dir. William Wyler
Kyne, P. B. *Three Godfathers, The*

Hell Without Limits
AZTECA (Mex) 1978
dir. Arturo Ripstein
Donoso, J.

Helter Skelter
LORIMAR (US) 1976 dir. Tom Gries
TVSe(US), V
Bugliosi, V. and Gentry, C.

Hemingway
WILSON (US) 1988
dir. Bernhard Sinkel
TVSe(US)
Baker, C. *Ernest Hemingway: A Life Story*

Henry and June
UN (US) 1990 dir. Philip Kaufman
Nin, A.

Henry V
TC (GB) 1944 dir. Laurence Olivier
V
RENAISSANCE (GB) 1989
dir. Kenneth Branagh
Shakespeare, W.
P

Henry's Leg
TVS (GB) 1990 dir. Michael Kerrigan
TVSe(GB), V
Pilling, A.

He Ran All The Way
UA (US) 1951 dir. John Berry
Ross, S.

Her Cardboard Lover
MGM (US) 1942 dir. George Cukor
Deval, J.
P

Here Comes Mr. Jordan
COL (US) 1941 dir. Alexander Hall
V
Segall, H. *Halfway to Heaven*
P

Here Come the Littles
ATLANTIC (US) 1985
dir. Bernard Deyries
A, V
Peterson, J.

Here we go Round the Mulberry Bush
UA (GB) 1967 dir. Clive Donner
Davies, H.

Hero Ain't Nothing but a Sandwich, A
NEW WORLD (US) 1977
dir. Ralph Nelson
Childress, A.

Hero and the Terror
CANNON (US) 1988
dir. William Tanner
Blodgett, M.

Heroes, The
TVS FILMS (Aus) 1990
dir. Donald Crombie
TV(Aus)
McKie, R.

Heroes of the Telemark
RANK (GB) 1965 dir. Anthony Mann
V
Drummond, J. D. *But for These Men*

Herr Puntila and his Servant Matti
BAUERFILM (Austria) 1955
dir. Alberto Cavalcanti
Brecht, B.
P

Her Sister's Secret
PRC (US) 1946 dir. Edgar G. Ulmer
Kaus, G. *Dark Angel*

Her Twelve Men
MGM (US) 1954 dir. Robert Z. Leonard
Baker, L.

He Stayed for Breakfast
COL (US) 1940 dir. Alexander Hall
Duran, M. *Liberté Provisoire*
P

Hester Street
CONN (US) 1975
dir. Joan Micklin Silver
V
Cahen, A. *Yekl*

He Who Must Die
KASSLER (Fr/It) 1957 dir. Jules Dassin
Kazantzakis, N. *The Greek Passion*

Hey, I'm Alive!
FRIES (US) 1975 dir. Lawrence Schiller
TV(US)
Klaben, H. and Day, B.

Hidden Homicide
RANK (US) 1959 dir. Tony Yound
Capon, P. *Murder at Shinglestrand*

Hideaways, The
UA (US) 1973 dir. Fielder Cook
V
Konigsburg, E. L. *From the Mixed-up Files of Mrs Basil E. Frankwester*

Hide in Plain Sight
UA (US) 1980 dir. James Caan
V
Waller, L.

Hiding Place, The
WORLD WIDE (US) 1974
dir. James F. Collier
V
Boom, C. Ten

High and Low
TOHO (Jap) 1963 dir. Akira Kurosawa
McBain, E. *King's Ransom, The*

High and the Mighty, The
WAR (US) 1954 dir. William Wellman
Gann, E. K.

High Barbaree
MGM (US) 1947 dir. Jack Conway
Nordhoff, C. B. and Hall, J. N.

High Bright Sun, The
RANK (GB) 1965 dir. Ralph Thomas
US title: McGuire Go Home
Black, I. S.

High Command, The
ABFD (GB) 1936 dir. Thorold Dickinson
V
Strueby, K. *General Goes Too Far, The*

Higher and Higher
RKO (US) 1943 dir. Tim Whelan
M, V
Hurlbut, G. and Logan, J.
P

High Noon
UA (US) 1952 dir. Fred Zinnemann
V
Cunningham, J. M. *Tin Star, The*

High Pressure
WAR (US) 1932 dir. Mervyn LeRoy
Kandel, A. *Hot Money*
P

High Price of Passion, The
TAFT (US) 1986 dir. Larry Elikann
TV(US)
Glitman, R. M. *Ruling Passion, The*

High Road to China
WAR (US) 1983 dir. Brian G. Hutton
V
Cleary, J.

High Sierra
WAR (US) 1941 dir. Raoul Walsh
V
Burnett, W. R.

High Society
MGM (US) 1956 dir. Charles Walters
M, V
Barry, P. *Philadelphia Story, The*
P

High Wind in Jamaica, A
FOX (GB) 1965
dir. Alexander Mackendrick
Hughes, R.

Hilda Crane
FOX (US) 1956 dir. Philip Dunne
Raphaelson, S.
P

Hill, The
MGM (GB) 1965 dir. Sidney Lumet
Rigby, R. and Allen, R. S.
P

Hill in Korea, A
BL (GB) 1956 dir. Julian Aymes
US title: Hell in Korea
Catto, M.

Hindenburg, The
UN (US) 1975 dir. Robert Wise
V

Mooney, M. M.

Hindle Wakes
GB (GB) 1931 dir. Victor Saville
MON (GB) 1952 dir. Arthur Crabtree

Houghton, S.
P

Hireling, The
COL (GB) 1973 dir. Alan Bridges
V

Hartley, L. P.

His Double Life
PAR (US) 1933 dir. Arthur Hopkins
V

Bennett, A. *Buried Alive*

His Excellency
GFD (GB) 1951 dir. Robert Hamer

Christie, D. and Christie, P.
P

His Girl Friday
COL (US) 1940 dir. Howard Hawks
V

Hecht, B. and MacArthur, C. *Front Page, The*
P

His Glorious Night
MGM (US) 1929 dir. Lionel Barrymore
GB title: Breath of Scandal

Molnar, F. *Olympia*
P

His Majesty O'Keefe
WAR (GB) 1954 dir. Byron Haskin

Kingman, L. and Green, G.

History
SACIS (It) 1988 dir. Luigi Comencina
Morante, E.

History Man, The
BBC (GB) 1981 dir. Robert Knights
TVSe(GB)

Bradbury, M.

His Woman
PAR (US) 1931 dir. Edward Sloman

Collins, D. *Sentimentalists, The*

History of Mr. Polly, The
GFD (GB) 1949 dir. Anthony Pelissier

Wells, H. G.

Hitch-Hiker's Guide to the Galaxy, The
BBC (GB) 1981 dir. Alan Bell
TVSe(GB)

Adams, D.

Hitler: A Career
GTO (Ger) 1987
dir. Christian Herrendoerfer,
Joachim C. Fest
V

Fest, J.

Hitler's Children
RKO (US) 1943 dir. Edward Dmytryk
V

Ziemer, G. *Education for Death*

Hitler's Daughter
WIL COURT (US) 1990
dir. James A. Contner
TV(US)

Benford, T.

Hit the Deck
MGM (US) 1955 dir. Roy Rowland
M

Fields, H.
P

Osborne, H. *Shore Leave*

H.M. Pulham, Esq
MGM (US) 1940 dir. King Vidor
Marquand, J. P.

H.M.S. Defiant
COL (GB) 1962 dir. Lewis Gilbert
US title: Damn the Defiant
Tilsley, F. *Mutiny*

Hobson's Choice
BL (GB) 1931 dir. Thomas Bentley
BL (GB) 1953 dir. David Lean
V
CBS ENT (US) 1983 dir. Gilbert Cates
TV(US)
Brighouse, H.
P

Hoffman
ABP (GB) 1970 dir. Alvin Rackoff
V
Gebler, E. *Shall I Eat You Now?*
P

Holcroft Covenant, The
UN (GB) 1985 dir. John Frankenheimer
V
Ludlum, R.

Hold Back The Dawn
PAR (US) 1941 dir. Mitchell Leisen
Frings, Mrs. K.

Hold Back The Night
ABP (US) 1956 dir. Allan Dwan
Frank, P.

Hold the Dream
TAFT (GB) 1986 dir. Don Sharp
TVSe(GB), V
Bradford, B. T.

Hole, The
PLAY ART (Fr/It) 1959
dir. Jacques Becker
Giovanni, J.

Hole in the Head, A
UA (US) 1959 dir. Frank Capra
Schulman, A.
P

Holiday
PATHE (US) 1930
dir. Edward H. Griffith
COL (US) 1938 dir. George Cukor
GB title: Free to Live
V
Barry, P.
P

Hollow Triumph
EL (US) 1948 dir. Steve Sekely
Forbes, M.

Holly and the Ivy, The
BL (GB) 1952
dir. George More O'Ferrall
Browne, W.
P

Hollywood Wives
WAR (US) 1985 dir. Robert Day
TVSe(US), V
Collins, J.

Holy Innocents, The
GANESH (Sp) 1985 dir. Mario Camus
Spanish title: Los Santos Inocentes
V
Delibes, M.

Holy Matrimony
PAR (US) 1943 dir. John Stahl
Bennett, A. *Buried Alive*

Hombre
FOX (US) 1967 dir. Martin Ritt
V
Leonard, E.

Home and the World, The
NFC (Ind) 1985 dir. Satyajit Ray
V

Tagore, R.

Home at Seven
BL (GB) 1952 dir. Ralph Richardson
US title: Murder on Monday

Sherriff, R. C.
P

Home Before Dark
WAR (US) 1958 dir. Mervyn LeRoy

Bassing, E.

Homecoming, The
SEVEN KEYS (GB) 1973 dir. Peter Hall

Pinter, H.
P

Homecoming, The — A Christmas Story
LORIMAR (US) 1974 dir. Fielder Cook
TV(US), V

Hamner, Jr., E.

Home Fires Burning
M. REES (US) 1989 dir. Glenn Jordan
TV(US)

Inman, R.

Home from the Hill
MGM (US) 1959 dir. Vincente Minnelli
V

Humphrey, W.

Home in Indiana
TCF (US) 1944 dir. Henry Hathaway

Chamberlain, G. A. *Phantom Filly, The*

Home of the Brave
UA (US) 1949 dir. Mark Robson
V

Laurents, A.
P

Home Sweet Homicide
FOX (US) 1946 dir. Lloyd Bacon

Rice, C.

Home to Stay
TIME-LIFE INC. (US) 1978 dir. Delbert Mann
TV(US), V

Majerus, J. *Grandpa and Frank*

L'Homme au Chapeau Rond
ALCINA (Fr) 1946 dir. Pierre Billon

Dostoevski, F. *Eternal Husband, The*

L'Homme de Nulle Part
CG (Fr) 1987 dir. Pierre Chenal

Pirandello, L.

Hondo
WAR (US) 1953 dir. John Farrow

L'Amour, L.

Honey
PAR (US) 1930 dir. Wesley Ruggles

Miller, A. D. and Thomas, A. E. *Come out of the Kitchen*
P

Honeymoon for Three
WAR (US) 1941 dir. Lloyd Bacon

Scott, A. and Haight, G. *Goodbye Again*
P

Honeymoon Machine, The
MGM (US) 1961 dir. Richard Thorpe

Semple, L. *Golden Fleecing, The*
P

Honeymoon with a Stranger
TCF (US) 1969 dir. John Peyser
TV(US)

Thomas, R. *Piège Pour un Homme Seul*
P

Honey Pot, The
UA (US) 1966 dir. Joseph L. Mankiewicz
Sterling, T. *Evil of the Day, The*

Honey Siege, The
HTV (GB) 1988
Ch, TVSe(GB)
Buhet, G.

Honkytonk Man
WAR (US) 1982 dir. Clint Eastwood
V
Carlile, C.

Honor Thy Father
METRO (US) 1973 dir. Paul Wendkos
TVSe(US), V
Talese, G.

Honorary Consul, The
PAR (GB) 1983 dir. John Mackenzie
US title: Beyond the Limit
V
Greene, G.

Hook, The
MGM (US) 1962 dir. George Seaton
Katcham, V. *Hameçon, The*

Hopalong Cassidy
PAR (US) 1935 dir. Howard Bretherton
Mulford, C. E.

Hopscotch
AVCO (US) 1980 dir. Ronald Neame
V
Garfield, B.

Horizontal Lieutenant, The
MGM (US) 1962 dir. Richard Thorpe
Cotler, G. *Bottletop Affair, The*

Horse in the Grey Flannel Suit, The
DISNEY (US) 1968 dir. Norman Tokar
Ch, V
Hatch, E. *Year of the Horse, The*

Horsemen, The
COL (US) 1970
dir. John Frankenheimer
V
Kessel, J.

Horse of Pride, The
FILM FORUM (Fr) 1980
dir. Claude Chabrol
V
Helias, P-J.

Horse's Mouth, The
UA (GB) 1958 dir. Ronald Neame
V
Cary, J.

Horse Soldiers, The
UA (US) 1959 dir. John Ford
V
Sinclair, H.

Horse Without a Head, The
DISNEY (GB) 1963 dir. Don Chaffey
Ch
Berna, P. *Hundred Million Frames, A*

Hors La Vie
BAC (Fr/It/Bel) 1991
dir. Maroun Bagdadi
Auque, R. and Forestier, P.

Hostage Heart, The
MGM (US) 1977 dir. Bernard McEverty
TV(US)
Green, G.

Hostages
PAR (US) 1943 dir. Frank Tuttle
Heym, S.

Hostile Witness
UA (GB) 1968 dir. Ray Milland

Roffey, J.
P

Hotel
WAR (US) 1967 dir. Richard Quine
V

Hailey, A.

Hotel Berlin
WAR (US) 1945 dir. Peter Godfrey

Baum, V. *Berlin Hotel*

Hotel du Lac
BBC (GB) 1986 dir. Giles Foster
TV(GB), V

Brookner, A.

Hotel Imperial
PAR (US) 1939 dir. Robert Florey

Biro, L.
P

Hotel New Hampshire, The
ORION (US) 1984 dir. Tony Richardson
V

Irving, J.

Hotel Paradiso
MGM (US) 1966 dir. Peter Glenville

Feydeau, G. and Desvallieres, M.
P

Hotel Reserve
RKO (GB) 1944 dir. Victor Hanbury

Ambler, E. *Epitaph for a Spy*

Hot Enough for June
RANK (GB) 1963 dir. Ralph Thomas

Davidson, L. *Night Before Wenceslas, The*

Hot Rock, The
TCF (US) 1972 dir. Peter Yates
GB title: How to Steal a Diamond in Four Uneasy Lessons

Westlake, D. E.

Hot Spell
PAR (US) 1958 dir. Daniel Mann

Coleman, L. *Next of Kin*
P

Hot Spot, The
ORION (US) 1990 dir. Dennis Hopper

Williams, C. *Hell Hath no Fury*

Houdini
PAR (US) 1953 dir. George Marshall

Kellock, H.

Hound-Dog Man
FOX (US) 1959 dir. Don Siegel

Gipson, F. B. *Circles Round the Wagon*

Hound of the Baskervilles, The
ID (GB) 1932 dir. V. G. Gundrey
FOX (US) 1939 dir. Sidney Lawfield
UA (GB) 1959 dir. Terence Fisher
UN (US) 1972 dir. Barry Crane
TV(US)
HEMDALE (GB) 1977
dir. Paul Morrissey
V
EMBASSY (GB) 1983
dir. Douglas Hickox

Doyle, Sir A. C.

Hour Before the Dawn, The
PAR (US) 1944 dir. Frank Tuttle

Maugham, W. S.

Hour of the Star, The
RAIZ (Braz) 1987 dir. Suzana Amaral

Lispector, C.

Hour of Thirteen, The
MGM (GB) 1952 dir. Harold French

MacDonald, P. *X vs Rex*

House by the River
REP (US) 1950 dir. Fritz Lang

Herbert, Sir A. P.

House Divided, A
UN (US) 1932 dir. William Wyler

Edens, O. *Heart & Hand*

House in Marsh Road, The
GN (GB) 1960 dir. Montgomery Tully

Meynell, L.
P

House in the Square, The
FOX (GB) 1951 dir. Roy Baker
US title: I'll Never Forget You

Balderston, J. L. *Berkeley Square*
P

House is Not a Home, A
PAR (US) 1964 dir. Russel Rouse

Adler, P.

Housekeeper's Daughter, The
UA (US) 1939 dir. Hal Roach

Clarke, D. H.

Housekeeping
COL (US) 1987 dir. Bill Forsyth
V

Robinson, M.

Houseman's Tale, A
BBC (GB) 1985
TV(GB)

Douglas, C.

Housemaster
ABPC (GB) 1938 dir. Herbert Brenon

Hay, I. *Bachelor Born*
P

House of a Thousand Candles, The
REP (US) 1936 dir. Arthur Lubin

Nicolson, M.

House of Bernada Alba, The
GALA (Sp) 1990 dir. Mario Camus
CHANNEL 4 (GB) 1992
dir. Nuria Espert and StuartBurge
TV(GB)

Lorca, F. G.
P

House of Cards
UN (US) 1968 dir. John Guillerman

Ellin, S.

House of Cards
BBC (GB) 1991 dir. Paul Seed
TVSe(GB)

Dobbs, M.

House of Fear
UN (US) 1945 dir. Roy William Neill
V

Doyle, Sir A. C. *Adventure of the Five Orange Pips*

House of God, The
UA (US) 1984 dir. Donald Wrye

Shem, S.

House of Numbers
MGM (US) 1957 dir. Russell Rouse

Finney, J.

House of Rothschild, The
FOX (US) 1934 dir. Alfred Werker

Hembert, G.
P

House of Secrets
RANK (GB) 1956 dir. Guy Green
US title: Triple Deception

Noel, S.

House of Strangers
FOX (US) 1949
dir. Joseph L. Mankiewicz
Weidman, J.

House of the Angel, The
ARG SONO (Arg) 1957
dir. Leopoldo Torre Nilsson
Guido, B.

House of the Arrow, The
AB (GB) 1930 dir. Leslie Hiscott
AB (GB) 1940 dir. Harold French
ABP (GB) 1953 dir. Michael Anderson
Mason, A. E. W.

House of the Long Shadows, The
CANNON (GB) 1983 dir. Pete Walker
V
Biggers, E. D. *Seven Keys to Baldpate*

House of the Seven Gables
UN (US) 1940 dir. Joe May
Hawthorne, N.

House of the Seven Hawks, The
MGM (GB) 1959 dir. Richard Thorpe
Canning, V. *House of the Seven Flies, The*

House of Usher, The
AIP (US) 1960 dir. Roger Corman
GB title: Fall of the House of Usher, The
21st CENTURY (US) 1988
dir. Alan Birkinshaw
V
Poe, E. A. *Fall of the House of Usher, The*

House on Garibaldi Street, The
ITC (US) 1979 dir. Peter Collinson
TV(US), V
Harel, I.

House on Telegraph Hill, The
FOX (US) 1951 dir. Robert Wise
Lyon, D. *Tentacles*

House That Would Not Die, The
A. SPELLING (US) 1980 dir. J. L. Moxey
TV(US)
Michaels, B. *Ammie, Come Home*

Howards' End
MERCHANT IVORY (GB) 1992
dir. James Ivory
Forster, E. M.

Howards of Virginia, The
COL (US) 1940 dir. Frank Lloyd
GB title: Tree of Liberty, The
V
Page, E. *Tree of Liberty, The*

How Awful About Allan
A. SPELLING (US) 1970
dir. Curtis Harrington
TV(US)
Farrell, H.

How Do I Love Thee?
ABC (US) 1970 dir. Michael Gordon
V
De Vries, P. *Let Me Count the Ways*

How Green Was My Valley
FOX (US) 1941 dir. John Ford
Llewellyn, R.

How He Lied to Her Husband
BI (GB) 1931 dir. Cecil Lewis
Shaw, G. B.
P

How I Won the War
UA (GB) 1967 dir. Richard Lester
V
Ryan, P.

Howling, The
AVCO (US) 1981 dir. Joe Dante
V

Brandner, G.

Howling III
SQUARE (Aus) 1987 dir. Philippe Mora

Brandner, G.

Howling in the Woods, A
UN (US) 1971 dir. Daniel Petrie
TV(US)

Johnston, V.

How Sweet It Is
WAR (US) 1968 dir. Jerry Paris

Resnik, M. *Girl in the Turquoise Bikini, The*

How to Make Love to a Negro Without Getting Tired
ANGELIKA (Fr) 1990
dir. Jacques Benoit

Laferrière, D. *Comment faire l'amour avec un nègre sans se fatiguer*

How to Succeed in Business Without Really Trying
UA (US) 1967 dir. David Swift
M

Mead, S., Burrows, A., Weinstock, J., Gilbert, W. & Loesser, F.
P

Huckleberry Finn
PAR (US) 1931 dir. Norman Taurog
MGM (US) 1939 dir. Richard Thorpe
V
UA (US) 1974 dir. J. Lee Thompson
M, V
ABC (US) 1975 dir. Robert Totten
TV(US)

Twain, M. *Adventures of Huckleberry Finn, The*

Hucksters, The
MGM (US) 1947 dir. Jack Conway

Wakeman, F.

Hud
PAR (US) 1963 dir. Martin Ritt
V

McMurtry, L. *Horseman, Pass By*

Huis Clos
MARCEAU (Fr) 1954
dir. Jacqueline Audry

Sartre, J-P.
P

Human Comedy, The
MGM (US) 1943 dir. Clarence Brown
V

Saroyan, W.

Human Desire
COL (US) 1954 dir. Fritz Lang

Zola, E. *La Bête Humaine*

Human Factor, The
RANK (GB) 1979 dir. Otto Preminger
V

Greene, G.

Humoresque
WAR (US) 1946 dir. Jean Negulesco

Hurst, F.

Hunchback of Notre Dame, The
RKO (US) 1939 dir. William Dieterle
V
RANK (Fr/It) 1956 dir. Jean Delannoy
BBC (GB) 1977 dir. Alan Cooke
TV(GB)
COL (US/GB) 1982
dir. Michael Tuchner
TV(GB/US)

Hugo, V. *Notre Dame de Paris*

Hungarians
IFEX (Hun) 1981 dir. Zoltan Fabri
Balazs, J.

Hunger, The
MGM/UA (US) 1983 dir. Tony Scott
V
Strieber, W.

Hungry Hill
TC (GB) 1947 dir. Brian Desmond Hurst
Du Maurier, D.

Hunter, The
PAR (US) 1980 dir. Buzz Kulik
V
Keane, C.

Hunters, The
FOX (US) 1958 dir. Dick Powell
Salter, J.

Hunter's Blood
CONCORDE (US) 1987
dir. Robert C. Hughes
Cunningham, J.

Hunt for Red October, The
PAR (US) 1990 dir. John McTiernan
Clancy, T.

Hurricane, The
UA (US) 1937 dir. John Ford
ITC (US) 1979 dir. Jan Troell
V
Nordhoff, C. B. and Hall, J. N.

Hurricane
METRO (US) 1974 dir. Jerry Jameson
TV(US)
Anderson, W. C. *Hurricane Hunters*

Hurry Sundown
PAR (US) 1967 dir. Otto Preminger
Gilden, K. B.

Husband's Holiday
PAR (US) 1931 dir. Robert Milton
Pascal, E. *Marriage Bed, The*

Hustler, The
FOX (US) 1961 dir. Robert Rossen
V
Tevis, W.

I am a Camera
BL (GB) 1955 dir. Henry Cornelius
V
Druten, J. van
P

I am a Cat
TOHO (Jap) 1982 dir. Kenichi Kawa
Natsume, S.

I am a Fugitive from a Chain Gang
WAR (US) 1932 dir. Mervyn LeRoy
V
Burns, R. E.

I am the Cheese
ALMI (US) 1983 dir. Robert Jiras
V
Cormier, R.

I Believe in You
EAL (GB) 1952 dir. Basil Dearden

Stokes, S. *Court Circular*

I Can Get It For You Wholesale
FOX (US) 1951 dir. Michael Gordon
GB title: This is My Affair

Weidman, J.

Ice Cold in Alex
ABP (GB) 1958 dir. J. Lee Thompson
US title: Desert Attack
V

Landon, C.

Ice House
UPFRONT/CACTUS (US) 1989
dir. Eagle Pennell

Brinkman, B. *Ice House Heat Waves*
P

Iceman Cometh, The
AFT (US) 1973 dir. John Frankenheimer

O'Neill, E. G.
P

Ice Palace
WAR (US) 1960 dir. Vincent Sherman
V

Ferber, E.

Ice Station Zebra
MGM (US) 1968 dir. John Sturges
V

MacLean, A.

I, Claudius
BBC (GB) 1976 dir. Herbert Wise
TVSe(GB), V

Graves, R.

I Confess
WAR (US) 1953 dir. Alfred Hitchcock
V

Anthelme, P.
P

I'd Climb the Highest Mountain
FOX (US) 1951 dir. Henry King

Harris, C.

Ideal Husband, An
BL (GB) 1948 dir. Alexander Korda
V

Wilde, O.
P

I Died a Thousand Times
WAR (US) 1955 dir. Stuart Heisler

Burnett, W. R. *High Sierra*

Idiot's Delight
MGM (US) 1939 dir. Clarence Brown
V

Sherwood, R. E.
P

Idle on Parade
COL (GB) 1959 dir. John Gilling

Camp, W.

I Don't Give a Damn
ROLL (Israel) 1988
dir. Shmuel Imberman
V

Ben Amitz, D.

If . . .
PAR (GB) 1968 dir. Lindsay Anderson
V

Sherwin, D. and Howlett, J.
Crusaders

If a Man Answers
UN (US) 1962 dir. Henry Levin

Wolfe, W.

If I Were Free
RKO (US) 1933 dir. Elliot Nugent

Druten, J. van *Behold We Live*
P

If I Were King
PAR (US) 1938 dir. Frank Lloyd
McCarthy, J. H.

If Tomorrow Comes
CBS ENT (US) 1986 dir. Jerry London
TVSe(US)
Sheldon, S.

If Winter Comes
MGM (US) 1948 dir. Victor Saville
Hutchinson, A. S. M.

If You Could See What I Can Hear
SCHICK SUNN (US) 1982 dir. Eric Till
V
Sullivan, T. and Gill, D.

I Hate Actors!
GALAXY (Fr) 1988
dir. Gerald Krawczyk
Hecht, B.

I Heard the Owl Call My Name
TOMORROW INC. (US) 1973
dir. Daryl Duke
TV(US), V
Craven, M.

Ike
ABC (US) 1979 dir. Melville Shavelson,
Boris Sagal
TVSe(US), V
Morgan, K. S. *Past Forgetting*

I Killed The Count
GN (GB) 1939 dir. Fred Zelnik
Coppel, A.
P

I Know Why the Caged Bird Sings
TOMORROW INC. (US) 1979
dir. Fielder Cook
TV(US)
Angelou, M.

I Lived With You
GB (GB) 1933 dir. Maurice Elvey
Novello, I.
P

I'll Be Seeing You
SELZNICK (US) 1944
dir. William Dieterle
Martin, C.

I'll Cry Tomorrow
MGM (US) 1955 dir. Daniel Mann
V
Roth, L., Frank, G.

Illegal Traffic
PAR (US) 1938 dir. Louis King
Hoover, J. E. *Persons in Hiding*

I'll Get You For This
BL (GB) 1950 dir. Joseph M. Newman
US title: Lucky Nick Cain
V
Chase, J. H. *High Stakes*

Ill Met By Moonlight
RANK (GB) 1956 dir. Michael Powell/
Emeric Pressburger
US title: Night Ambush
V
Moss, W. S.

I'll Take Manhattan
S. KRANTZ (US) 1987
dir. Douglas Hickox, Richard Michaels
TVSe(US)
Krantz, J.

Illustrated Man, The
WAR (US) 1969 dir. Jack Smight
V
Bradbury, R.

Illustrious Corpses
PEA/LAA (It) 1976 dir. Francesco Rosi
Sciascia, L. *The Context*

I Loved You Wednesday
TCF (US) 1933 dir. Henry King,
WilliamCameronMenzies
Ricardei, M. and Dubois, W.
P

I Love Trouble
COL (US) 1948 dir. S. Sylvan Simon
Huggins, R. *Double Take, The*

I'm All Right Jack
BL (GB) 1959 dir. John Boulting
V
Hackney, A. *Private Life*

I Married a Doctor
WAR (US) 1936 dir. Archie Mayo
Lewis, S. *Main Street*

I Married an Angel
MGM (US) 1942 dir. W. S. Van Dyke
M
Janos, V.
P

I Married A Shadow
IS (Fr) 1983 dir. Robin Davis
Irish, W. *I Married A Dead Man*

I Married a Witch
UA (US) 1942 dir. Rene Clair
V
Smith, T. *The Passionate Witch*

I'm Dancing as Fast as I Can
PAR (US) 1982 dir. Jack Hofsiss
V
Gordon, B.

I'm Dangerous Tonight
MCA TV (US) 1990 dir. Tobe Hooper
TV(US)
Woolrich, C.

I Met My Love Again
WANGER (US) 1937 dir. Joshua Logan,
Arthur Ripley
Corliss, A. *Summer Lightning*

I'm From Missouri
PAR (US) 1939 dir. Theodore Reed
Croy, H. *Sixteen Hands*

Imitation General
MGM (US) 1958 dir. George Marshall
Chamberlain, W. *Trumpets of Company K*

Imitation of Life
UN (US) 1934 dir. John Stahl
UN (US) 1959 dir. Douglas Sirk
V
Hurst, F. *Anatomy of Me*

Immigrants, The
UN (US) 1978 dir. Alan J. Levi
TVSe(US)
Fast, H.

Immortal Sergeant, The
FOX (US) 1943 dir. John Stahl
V
Brophy, J.

Immortal Story
ORTF (Fr) 1968 dir. Orson Welles
Blixen, K.

Impatient Maiden
UN (US) 1932 dir. James Whale

Clarke, D. H. *Impatient Virgin, The*

Importance of Being Earnest, The
RANK/GFD (GB) 1952
dir. Anthony Asquith
V

Wilde, O.
P

Impossible Years, The
MGM (US) 1968 dir. Michael Gordon

Fisher, B. and Marx, A.
P

Inadmissible Evidence
PAR (GB) 1968 dir. Anthony Page

Osborne, J.
P

In a Lonely Place
COL (US) 1950 dir. Nicholas Ray
V

Hughes D. B.

In a Shallow Grave
SKOURAS (US) 1988
dir. Kenneth Bowser

Purdy, J.

In Broad Daylight
NEW WORLD (US) 1991
dir. James Steven Sadwith
TV(US)

MacLean, H.

In Celebration
SEVEN KEYS (GB) 1974
dir. Lindsay Anderson

Storey, D.
P

Incense for the Damned
GN (GB) 1970
dir. Robert Hartford-Davis

Raven, S. *Doctors Wear Scarlet*

Incident in San Francisco
ABC TV (US) 1971 dir. Don Medford
TV(US)

Brown, J. E. *Incident at 125th Street*

In Cold Blood
COL (US) 1967 dir. Richard Brooks
V

Capote, T.

Inconvenient Woman, An
ABC (US) 1991 dir. Larry Elikann
TVSe(US)

Dunne, D.

In Country
WAR (US) 1989 dir. Norman Jewison
V

Mason, B. A.

Incredible Journey, The
DISNEY (US) 1963 dir. Fletcher Markle
A, Ch, V

Burnford, S.

Incredible Mr. Limpet, The
WAR (US) 1964 dir. Arthur Lubin
A

Pratt, T.

Incredible Shrinking Man, The
UN (US) 1957 dir. Jack Arnold
V

Matheson, R. *Shrinking Man, The*

Incubus, The
NEW REALM (Can) 1982
dir. John Hough
V

Russell, R.

Indecent Obsession, An
PBL (Aus) 1985 dir. Lex Marinos
V

McCullough, C.

Indict and Convict
UN TV (US) 1974 dir. Boris Sagal
TV(US)

Davidson, B.

Indiscreet
WAR (GB) 1958 dir. Stanley Donen
V
REPUBLIC (US) 1988
dir. Richard Michaels
TV(US)

Krasna, N. *Kind Sir*
P

I Never Promised you a Rose Garden
NEW WORLD (US) 1977
dir. Anthony Page
V

Greenberg, J.

I Never Sang for my Father
COL (US) 1970 dir. Gilbert Cates
V

Anderson, R. W.
P

Infamous Life, An
LC/CINEMAX (It/Fr/Ger) 1990
dir. Giacomo Battiato

Cellini, B.

Informer, The
RKO (US) 1935 dir. John Ford
V

O'Flaherty, L.

Informers, The
RANK (GB) 1963 dir. Ken Annakin
US title: Underworld Informers

Warner, D. *Death of a Snout*

L'Ingenue Libertine
CODO (Fr) 1950 dir. Jacqueline Audry

Colette

In Harm's Way
PAR (US) 1965 dir. Otto Preminger

Bassett, J. *Harm's Way*

Inheritance
GRANADA (GB) 1967
TV(GB)

Bentley, P.

Inherit the Wind
UA (US) 1960 dir. Stanley Kramer
V
COMPASS (US) 1965
dir. George Schaefer
TV(US)
VINCENT (US) 1988 dir. David Greene
TV(US)

Lawrence, J. and Lee, R. E.
P

In Love and War
FOX (US) 1958 dir. Philip Dunne

Myrer, A. *Big War, The*

In Love and War
TA (US) 1987 dir. Paul Aaron
TV(US)

Stockdale, J. and Stockdale, S.

In Love With an Older Woman
FRIES (US) 1982 dir. Jack Bender
TV(US)

Kaufelt, D. *Six Months With an Older Woman*

In Name Only
RKO (US) 1939 dir. John Cromwell
V

Brewer, B. *Memory of Love*

Innocent Bystanders
SCOTIA-BARBER (GB) 1972
dir. Peter Collinson
Munro, J.

Innocent Sinners
RANK (US) 1957 dir. Philip Leacock
Godden, R. *Episode of Sparrows, An*

Innocents, The
FOX (GB) 1961 dir. Jack Clayton
James, H. *Turn of the Screw, The*

Innocents with Dirty Hands
FOX-RANK (Fr/It/Ger) 1975
dir. Claude Chabrol
Neely, R.

Inn of the Sixth Happiness, The
FOX (GB) 1958 dir. Mark Robson
V
Burgess, A. *Small Woman, The*

In Old Chicago
FOX (US) 1937 dir. Henry King
Busch, N. *We the O'Leary's*

In Person
RKO (US) 1935 dir. William A. Seiter
V
Adams, S. H.

In Praise of Older Women
ASTRAL (Can) 1977
dir. George Kaczender
V
Vizinczey, S.

Inquest
CHARTER (GB) 1939 dir. Roy Boulting
Barringer, M.
P

Inquisitor, The
GALA (Fr) 1981 dir. Claude Miller
Wainwright, J. *Brainwash*

In Search of the Castaways
DISNEY (GB) 1961
dir. Robert Stevenson
Ch, V
Verne, J. *Captain Grant's Children*

Inside Daisy Clover
WAR (US) 1965 dir. Robert Mulligan
Lambert, G.

Inside Moves
BARBER (US) 1980 dir. Richard Donner
V
Walton, T.

Inside the Third Reich
ABC (US) 1982 dir. Marvin J. Chomsky
TVSe(US), V
Speer, A.

Inspector, The
FOX (GB) 1962 dir. Philip Dunne
US title: Lisa
Hartog, J. de

Inspector Calls, An
BL (GB) 1954 dir. Guy Hamilton
V
Priestley, J. B.
P

Inspector General, The
WAR (US) 1949 dir. Henry Koster
V
Gogol, N. V.
P

Insurance Man, The
BBC (GB) 1986
TV(GB)
Kafka, F. *Trial, The*

Intent to Kill
FOX (GB) 1958 dir. Jack Cardiff
Bryan, M.

International Airport
A. SPELLING (US) 1985
dir. Charles Dubin, Don Chaffey
TV(US)
Hailey, A. *Airport*

Internecine Project, The
MACLEAN (GB) 1974 dir. Ken Hughes
V
Elkind, M.

Interns, The
COL (US) 1962 dir. David Swift
Frede, R.

Interpol
COL (GB) 1957 dir. John Gilling
US title: Pickup Alley
Forrest, A. J.

In the Cool of the Day
MGM (US) 1962 dir. Robert Stevens
Ertz, S.

In the Doghouse
RANK (GB) 1961 dir. Darcy Conyers
Duncan, A. *It's a Vet's Life*

In the Frame
DLT (US) 1989 dir. Wigbert Wicker
TV(US)
Francis, D.

In the French Style
COL (US/Fr) 1963 dir. Robert Parrish
Shaw, I.

In the Good Old Summertime
MGM (US) 1949 dir. Robert Z. Leonard
M, V
Laszlo, N. *Shop Around the Corner, The*
P

In the Heat of the Night
UA (US) 1967 dir. Norman Jewison
V
Ball, J.
V

In the Line of Duty: Manhunt in the Dakotas
P-K (US) 1991 dir. Dick Lowry
TV(US)
Corcoran, J. *Bitter Harvest: Murder in the Heartland*

In the Secret State
BBC (GB) 1985
TV(GB)
McCrum, R.

In the Wake of a Stranger
BUTCHER (GB) 1959 dir. David Eady
Black, I. S.

In this House of Brede
TOMORROW (US) 1975
dir. George Schaefer
TV(US), V
CHANNEL 4 (GB) 1984
TV(GB)
Godden, R.

In This Our Life
WAR (US) 1942 dir. John Huston
Glasgow, E.

Intruder, The
BL (GB) 1953 dir. Guy Hamilton
V
Maugham, R. *Line on Ginger*

Intruder, The
FILMGROUP (US) 1961
dir. Roger Corman
GB title: Stranger, The
Beaumont, C.

Intruder in the Dust
MGM (US) 1949 dir. Clarence Brown
Faulkner, W.

Invasion of Privacy, An
EMBASSY TV (US) 1983
dir. Mel Damski
TV(US)
Taylor, J. *Asking for It*

Invasion of the Body Snatchers, The
ALLIED (US) 1956 dir. Don Siegel
UA (US) 1978 dir. Philip Kaufman
V
Finney, J. *Body Snatchers, The*

Investigation
QUARTET (Fr) 1978 dir. Etienne Perier
V
Laborde, J. *Lesser of Two Evils, The*

Investigation, The: Inside a Terrorist Bombing
GRANADA (US/GB) 1990
dir. Mike Beckham
TV(GB/US)
Mullin, C. *Error of Judgment: The Birmingham Bombings*

Invincible Six, The
MOULIN ROUGE (US/Iran) 1970
dir. Jean Negulesco
Barrett, M. *Heroes of Yucca, The*

Invisible Man, The
UN (US) 1933 dir. James Whale
V
UN (US) 1975 dir. Robert Michael Lewis
TV(US)
BBC (GB) 1984 dir. Brian Lightill
TV(GB)
Wells, H. G.

Invisible Stripes
WAR (US) 1939 dir. Lloyd Bacon
Lawes, L. E.

Invitation au Voyage
TRIUMPH (Fr) 1983
dir. Peter Del Monte
V
Barry, J. *Moi, Ma Soeur*

I Ought to be in Pictures
TCF (US) 1982 dir. Herbert Ross
V
Simon, N.
P

I Passed for White
WAR (US) 1960 dir. Fred M. Wilcox
Bradley, M. H.

Ipcress File, The
RANK (GB) 1965 dir. Sidney J. Furie
V
Deighton, L.

Iphighenia
UA (Greece) 1978
dir. Michael Cacoyannis
V
Euripides
P

I Remember Mama
RKO (US) 1948 dir. George Stevens
V
Druten, J. van
P

Irene
RKO (US) 1940 dir. Herbert Wilcox
Montgomery, J. H.
P

Irezumi: The Spirit of Tattoo
DAIEI (Jap) 1983
dir. Yoichi Takabayashi
V
Akae, B.

Irishman, The
S AUST (Aust) 1978
dir. Donald Crombie
V
O'Connor, E.

Iron Curtain
FOX (US) 1948 dir. William Wellman
Gouzenko, I. *This was my Choice*

Iron Duke, The
GAU BR (GB) 1935 dir. Victor Saville
V
Harwood, H. M.
P

Iron Man
UN (US) 1931 dir. Tod Browning
UI (US) 1951 dir. Joseph Pevney
V
Burnett, W. R.

Iron Mistress, The
WAR (US) 1952 dir. Gordon Douglas
Wellman, P. I.

Ironweed
TRI-STAR (US) 1987
dir. Hector Babenco
V
Kennedy, W.

Iron Maze
TRANS-TOKYO (US/Jap) 1991
dir. Hiroaki Yoshida
Kutagawa, R. A. *In the Grove*

Isadora
UI (GB) 1969 dir. Karel Reisz
US title: Loves of Isadora, The
V
Duncan, I. *My Life*
Stokes, S. *Isadora Duncan, An Intimate Portrait*

I Saw What You Did
UN (US) 1965 dir. William Castle
UN (US) 1988 dir. Fred Walton
TV(US)
Curtiss, U.

I Sent a Letter to My Love
ATLANTIC (Fr) 1981
dir. Moshe Mizrahi
V
Rubens, B.

Ishi: The Last of his Tribe
LEWIS (US) 1978
dir. Robert Ellis Miller
TV(US)
Quinn, T. K. *Ishi in Two Worlds*

Island, The
UN (US) 1980 dir. Michael Ritchie
Benchley, P.

Island at the Top of the World, The
DISNEY (US) 1974
dir. Robert Stevenson
V
Cameron, I. *Lost Ones, The*

Island in the Sky
WAR (US) 1953 dir. William Wellman
Gann, E. K.

Island in the Sun
FOX (GB) 1957 dir. Robert Rossen
Waugh, A.

Island of Dr. Moreau, The
AIP (US) 1977 dir. Don Taylor
V
Wells, H. G.

Island of Lost Souls
PAR (US) 1932 dir. Erle C. Kenton
Wells, H. G. *Island of Dr. Moreau, The*

Island of the Blue Dolphins
UN (US) 1964 dir. James B. Clark
V
O'Dell, S.

Islands in the Stream
PAR (US) 1977 dir. Franklin Schaffner
V
Hemingway, E.

Isn't it Romantic?
PAR (US) 1948 dir. Norman Z. McLeod
Nolan, J. *Gather Rosebuds*

Is Paris Burning?
PAR (Fr/US) 1965 dir. René Clément
Collins, L. and Lapierre, D.

I Start Counting
UA (GB) 1969 dir. David Greene
Lindop, A. E.

Is Your Honeymoon Really Necessary?
ADELPHI (GB) 1953 dir. Maurice Elvey
Tidmarsh, E. V.
P

It
LORIMAR (US) 1989
dir. Tommy Lee Wallace
TVSe(US)
King, S.

I Take This Woman
PAR (US) 1931 dir. Marion Gering
Rinehart, M. R. *Lost Ecstasy*

It All Came True
WAR (US) 1940 dir. Lewis Seiler
Bromfield, L. *Better Than Life*

It Always Rains on Sundays
EAL (GB) 1947 dir. Robert Hamer
La Bern, A. J.

I Thank A Fool
MGM (GB) 1962 dir. Robert Stevens
Lindop, A. E.

It Happened one Christmas
UN TV (US) 1977 dir. Donald Wrye
TV(US)
Stern, P. V. D. *Greatest Gift, The*

It Happened One Night
COL (US) 1934 dir. Frank Capra
Adams, S. H. *Night Bus*

It Happens Every Thursday
UN (US) 1953 dir. Joseph Pevney
McIlvaine, J.

I, The Jury
UA (US) 1953 dir. Harry Essex
FOX (US) 1982 dir. Richard T. Heffron
V
Spillane, M.

It Pays to Advertise
PAR (US) 1931 dir. Frank Tuttle
Hackett, W.
P

It's Always Something
UN TV (US) 1990 dir. Richard Compton
TV(US)
Raab, S.

It's Good to be Alive
METRO (US) 1974 dir. Michael Landon
TV(US), V
Campanella, R.

It Shouldn't Happen to a Vet
EMI (GB) 1976 dir. Eric Till
V
Herriot, J. *All Things Bright and Beautiful*

It's Never too Late
ABP (GB) 1956 dir. Michael McCarthy
Douglas, F.
P

It's Tough to be Famous
IN (US) 1932 dir. Alfred E. Green
McCall, M. *Goldfish Bowl, The*

Ivanhoe
MGM (GB) 1952 dir. Richard Thorpe
V
COL (US/GB) 1982
dir. Douglas Canfield
TV(GB/US)
Scott, Sir W.

Ivy
UI (US) 1947 dir. Sam Wood
Lowndes, Mrs M. B. *Story of Ivy*

I Wake up Screaming
FOX (US) 1941
dir. H. Bruce Humberstone
GB title: Hot Spot
Fisher, S.

I Walk Alone
PAR (US) 1947 dir. Byron Haskin
Reeves, T. *Beggars are Coming to Town*
P

I Walk the Line
COL (US) 1970
dir. John Frankenheimer
V
Jones, M. *Exile, An*

I Want What I Want
CINERAMA (GB) 1972 dir. John Dexter
V
Brown, G.

I Was a Spy
GAU (GB) 1933 dir. Victor Saville
McKenna, M.

I was Monty's Double
ABP (GB) 1958 dir. John Guillermin
US title: Hell, Heaven and Hoboken
James, M. E. C.

I Went to the Dance
BRAZOS (US) 1989 dir. Leon Blank,
C. Strachwitz
Savoy, A. A.

Jackknife
CINEPLEX (US) 1989 dir. David Jones

Metcalfe, S. *Strange Snow*
P

Jack of all Trades
GAINS (GB) 1936 dir. Jack Hubert, Robert Stevenson

Vulpuis, P. *Youth at the Helm*
P

Jacobo Timerman: Prisoner Without a Name, Cell Without a Number
CHRYS YELL (US) 1983
dir. Linda Yellen
TV(US)

Timerman, J. *Prisoner Without a Name, Cell Without a Number*

Jake Spanner, Private Eye
FENADY (US) 1989 dir. Lee H. Katzin
TV(US)

Morse, L. A. *Old Dick, The*

Jalna
RKO (US) 1935 dir. John Cromwell

Roche, M. de la

Jamaica Inn
PAR (GB) 1939 dir. Alfred Hitchcock
V
HTV (GB) 1983
dir. Lawrence Gordon Clark
TV

Du Maurier, D.

Jamaica Run
PAR (US) 1953 dir. Lewis R. Foster

Murray, M.

James at 15
FOX TV (US) 1977 dir. Joseph Hardy
TV(US)

Wakefield, D.

Jane Eyre
MON (US) 1934 dir. Christy Cabanne
FOX (US) 1943 dir. Robert Stevenson
V
OMNIBUS (GB) 1971
dir. Delbert Mann
V
BBC (GB) 1984 dir. Julian Amyes
TV(GB)

Bronte, C.

Janie
WAR (US) 1944 dir. Michael Curtiz

Bentham, J. and Williams, H. V.
P

Jassy
GFD (GB) 1947 dir. Bernard Knowles

Lofts, N.

Java Head
ATP (GB) 1934 dir. J. Walter Ruben

Hergesheimer, J.

Jaws
UN (US) 1975 dir. Steven Spielberg
V

Benchley, P.

Jayne Mansfield Story, The
LAN (US) 1980 dir. Dick Lowry
TV(US)

Saxton, M. *Jayne Mansfield and the American Fifties*

Jazz Singer, The
WAR (US) 1953 dir. Michael Curtiz
EMI (US) 1980 dir. Richard Fleischer
V

Raphaelson, S. *Day of Atonement*
P

Jean de Florette
ORION (Fr) 1987 dir. Claude Berri
V

Pagnol, M.

Jeannie
TANSA (GB) 1941 dir. Harold French
US title: Girl in Distress

Stuart, A.
P

J. Edgar Hoover
RLC (US) 1987 dir. Robert Collins
TV(US)

Sullivan, W. G. and Brown, W. S.
My 30 Years in Hoover's FBI

Jekyll & Hyde
KING PHOENIX (US/GB) 1990
dir. David Wickes
TV(GB/US)

Stevenson, R. L. *Dr. Jekyll and Mr. Hyde*

Jennie Gerhardt
PAR (US) 1933 dir. Marion Gering

Dreiser, T.

Jennifer on my Mind
UA (US) 1971 dir. Noel Black

Simon, R. L. *Heir*

Jenny's War
HTV (US/GB) 1985 dir. Steven Gethers
Ch, TV(GB/US), V

Stoneley, J.

Jeremiah Johnson
WAR (US) 1972 dir. Sidney Pollack
V

Fisher, V.

Jessica
UA (Fr/It) 1961 dir. Jean Negulesco

Sandstrom, F. *Midwife of Pont Clery, The*

Jesus Christ Superstar
UN (US) 1973 dir. Norman Jewison
M, V

Webber, A. L. and Rice, T.
P

Jeux Interdits
R. DORFMANN (Fr) 1952
dir. René Clément

Boyer, F.

Jewel in the Crown, The
GRANADA (GB) 1984
dir. JimO'Brien/ChristopherMorahan
TVSe(GB), V

Scott, P. *Raj Quartet, The*

Jewel Robbery
WAR (US) 1932 dir. William Dieterle

Fodor, L.
P

Jew Süss
GAU (GB) 1934 dir. Lothar Mendes
US title: Power
TERRA (Ger) 1940 dir. Veit Harlan
V

Feutchwangler, L.

Jezebel
WAR (US) 1938 dir. William Wyler
V

Davis, D.
P

JFK
WAR (US) 1991 dir. Oliver Stone

Garrison, J. *On the Trail of the Assassins: My Investigation and Prosecution of the Murder of President Kennedy*

Marrs, J. *Crossfire: The Plot that Killed Kennedy*

Jigsaw
BL (GB) 1962 dir. Val Guest

Waugh, H. *Sleep Long My Love*

Jigsaw Man, The
J & M FILMS (GB) 1984
dir. Terence Young
V

Bennett, D.

Jimmy the Kid
NEW WORLD (US) 1982
dir. Gary Nelson
V

Westlake, D. E.

Joan of Arc
RKO (US) 1948 dir. Victor Fleming
V

Anderson, M. *Joan of Lorraine*
P

Joey Boy
BL (GB) 1965 dir. Frank Launder

Chapman, E.

John and Mary
FOX (US) 1969 dir. Peter Yates

Jones, M.

John and the Missus
CINEMA (Can) 1987
dir. Gordon Pinsent

Pinsent, G.

John Loves Mary
WAR (US) 1948 dir. David Butler

Krasna, N.
P

Johnny Angel
RKO (US) 1945 dir. Edwin L. Marin
V

Booth, C. G. *Mr. Angel Comes Aboard*

Johnny Belinda
WAR (US) 1948 dir. Jean Negulesco
V
MILBERG (US) 1958
dir. George Schaefer
TV(US)
LORIMAR (US) 1982 dir. Anthony Page
TV(US)

Harris, E.
P

Johnny Come Lately
CAGNEY (US) 1943
dir. William K. Howard
GB title: Johnny Vagabond

Bromfield, L. *McLeod's Folly*

Johnny Cool
UA (US) 1963 dir. William Asher

McPartland, J. *Kingdom of Johnny Cool, The*

Johnny Got His Gun
CINEMATION (US) 1971
dir. Dalton Trumbo
V

Trumbo, D.

Johnny Guitar
REP (US) 1953 dir. Nicholas Ray
V

Chanslor, R.

Johnny Handsome
TRI-STAR (US) 1989 dir. Walter Hill
V

Godey, J. *Three Worlds of Johnny
Handsome, The*

Johnny One-Eye
UA (US) 1950 dir. Robert Florey

Runyon, D.

Johnny on the Spot
FANCEY (GB) 1954
dir. Maclean Rogers

Cronin, M. *Paid in Full*

Johnny Tremain
DISNEY (US) 1957
dir. Robert Stevenson
Ch

Forbes, E.

Johnny, We Hardly Knew Ye
TALENT (US) 1977 dir. Gilbert Cates
TV(US)

O'Donnell, K. P., Powers, D. F. and
McCarthy, J.

Joker is Wild, The
PAR (US) 1957 dir. Charles Vidor

Cohn, A.

Jolly Bad Fellow, A
BL (GB) 1964 dir. Robert Hamer

Vulliamy, C. E. *Don Among the Dead
Men*

Jonathan Livingstone Seagull
PAR (US) 1973 dir. Hill Bartlett
V

Bach, R.

Joni
WORLDWIDE (US) 1980
dir. James F. Collier
V

Eareckson, J.

Jory
AVCO (US) 1973 dir. Jorge Fons
V

Bass, M. R.

Josepha
TRIUMPH (Fr) 1982
dir. Christopher Frank
V

Frank, C.

Joseph Andrews
UA (GB) 1977 dir. Tony Richardson
V

Fielding, H.

Joshua Then and Now
TCF (Can) 1985 dir. Ted Kotcheff
V

Richler, M.

Journey for Margaret
MGM (US) 1942 dir. W. S. van Dyke

White, W. L.

Journey into Fear
RKO (US) 1942
dir. Norman Foster/Orson Welles
V

Ambler, E.

Journey's End
TIFFANY (GB/US) 1930
dir. James Whale

Sherriff, R. C.
P

Journey to Shiloh
UI (US) 1966 dir. William Hale

Henry, W.

Journey to the Centre of the Earth
FOX (US) 1959 dir. Henry Levin
V
CANNON (US) 1989
dir. Rusty Lemorande
V
Verne, J.

Joy
UGC (Can/Fr) 1983 dir. Serge Bergon
V
Laurey, J.

Joy in the Morning
MGM (US) 1965 dir. Alex Segal
Smith, B.

Juarez
WAR (US) 1939 dir. William Dieterle
V
Harding, B. *Phantom Crown, The*

Jubal
COL (US) 1956 dir. Delmer Daves
V
Wellman, P. I. *Jubal Troop*

Jubilee Trail
REP (US) 1954 dir. Joseph Kane
Bristow, G.

Judge Dee and the Monastery Murders
ABC (US) 1974 dir. Jeremy Paul Kagan
TV(US)
Van Gulik, R. *The Haunted Monastery*

Judge Horton and the Scottsboro Boys
TOM (US) 1976 dir. Fielder Cook
TV(US)
Carter, D. T. *Scottsboro: A Tragedy of the American South*

Judgment at Nuremberg
UA (US) 1961 dir. Stanley Kramer
V
Mann, A.
P

Judgment in Berlin
NEW LINE (US) 1988 dir. Leo Penn
V
Stern, H. J.

Judgement in Stone, A
SCHULZ (Can) 1987 dir. Ousama Rawi
US title: The Housekeeper
V
Rendell, R.

Juggler, The
COL (US) 1953 dir. Edward Dmytryk
Blankfort, M.

Jules et Jim
SEDIF (Fr) 1962 dir. François Truffaut
V
Roche, H-P.

Julia
FOX (US) 1977 dir. Fred Zinnemann
V
Hellman, L. F. *Pentimento*

Julia Misbehaves
MGM (US) 1948 dir. Jack Conway
Sharp, M. *Nutmeg Tree, The*

Julius Caesar
MGM (US) 1953
dir. Joseph L. Mankiewicz
MGM (GB) 1969 dir. Stuart Burge
V
Shakespeare, W.
P

Jungle Book, The
KORDA (US) 1942 dir. Zoltan Korda,
André de Toth
V
DISNEY (US) 1967
dir. Wolfgang Reitherman
A, Ch, M, V
Kipling, R.

Junior Miss
FOX (US) 1945 dir. George Seaton
Benson, Mrs. S.

Juno and the Paycock
BI (GB) 1930 dir. Alfred Hitchcock
O'Casey, S.
P

Jupiter's Darling
MGM (US) 1954 dir. George Sidney
Sherwood, R. E. *Road to Rome, The*
P

Just Another Secret
BLAIR (US/GB) 1989
dir. Lawrence Gordon Clark
TV(GB/US)
Forsyth, F.

Just Ask for Diamond
FOX (GB) 1988 dir. Stephen Bayly
V
Horowitz, A. *Falcon's Malteser, The*

Just for You
PAR (US) 1952 dir. Elliot Nugent
Benet, S. V. *Famous*

Justine
FOX (US) 1969 dir. George Cukor
V
Durrell, L. *Alexandria Quartet, The*

Just Tell Me What You Want
WAR (US) 1980 dir. Sidney Lumet
V
Allen, J. P.

Just William
AB (GB) 1939 dir. Graham Cutts
Crompton, R.

Kaleidoscope
NBC (US) 1990 dir. Jud Taylor
TV(US)
Steel, D.

Kamikaze '89
TELECUL (Ger) 1983 dir. Wolf Gremm
V
Wahloo, P. *Murder on the 31st Floor*

Kamilla and the Thief
PENELOPE (Nor/GB) 1988
dir. Grete Salamonsen
Vinje, K.

Kanal
POLSKI (Pol) 1956 dir. Andrzej Wajda
V
Stawinski, J. *Kloakerne*

Kane and Abel
EMBASSY (US) 1985 dir. Buzz Kulik
TVSe(US), V
Archer, J.

Kangaroo
WORLD FILM (Aust) 1986
dir. Tim Burstall
V
Lawrence, D. H.

Kate Plus Ten
WAINWRIGHT (GB) 1938
dir. Reginald Denham
Wallace, E.

Kazan
COL (US) 1949 dir. Will Jason
Curwood, J. O.

Keep, The
PAR (GB) 1983 dir. Michael Mann
V
Wilson, F. P.

Keeper of the Bees
MON (US) 1935 dir. Christy Cabanne
Porter, G. S.

Keeper of the City
VIACOM (US) 1992 dir. Bobby Roth
TV(US)
Di Pego, G.

Keeper of the Flame
MGM (US) 1942 dir. George Cukor
Wylie, I. A. R.

Keepers of Youth
POWERS (GB) 1931
dir. Thomas Bentley
Ridley, A.
P

Keeping Secrets
FINNEGAN/PINCHUCK (US) 1991
dir. John Korty
TV(US)
Somers, S.

Keep Your Seats Please
ATP (GB) 1936 dir. Monty Banks
Ilf, E. and Petrov, E. *Twelve Chairs*
P

Kennedys of Massachusetts, The
ORION TV (US) 1990
dir. Lamont Johnson
TVSe(US)
Goodwin, D. K. *Fitzgeralds and the Kennedys, The*

Kennel Murder Case, The
WAR (US) 1933 dir. Michael Curtiz
V
Dine, S. S. van

Kent State
INTERPLAN (US) 1981
dir. James Goldstone
TV(US), V
Michener, J. A. *Kent State: What Happened and Why*

Kentuckian, The
UA (US) 1955 dir. Burt Lancaster
V
Holt, F. *Gabriel Horn, The*

Kentucky
FOX (US) 1938 dir. David Butler
Foote, J. T. *Look of Eagles, The*

Kermesse Heroique, La
TOBIS (Fr) 1935 dir. Jacques Feyder
Spaak, C.

Kes
UA (GB) 1969 dir. Ken Loach
V

Hines, B. *Kestrel for a Knave, A*

Key, The
WAR (US) 1934 dir. Michael Curtiz
Gore-Brown, R.
P

Key, The
COL (GB) 1958 dir. Carol Reed
Hartog, J. de *Stella*

Key, The
ENT (It) 1983 dir. Giovanni Tinto Brass
V
Tanizaki, J.

Key Exchange
FOX (US) 1985 dir. Barnet Kellman
V
Wade, K.
P

Key Largo
WAR (US) 1948 dir. John Huston
V
Anderson, M.
P

Keys of the Kingdom, The
FOX (US) 1944 dir. John M. Stahl
Cronin, A. J.

Key to Rebecca, The
TAFT (US) 1985 dir. David Hemmings
TVSe(US)
Follett, K.

Khartoum
UA (GB) 1966 dir. Basil Dearden
V
Caillou, A.

Kid for Two Farthings, A
LONDON (GB) 1955 dir. Carol Reed
Mankowitz, W.

Kid Galahad
WAR (US) 1937 dir. Michael Curtiz
UA (US) 1962 dir. Phil Karlson
M, V
Wallace, F.

Kidnapped
FOX (US) 1938 dir. Alfred L. Werker
V
DISNEY (GB) 1959
dir. Robert Stevenson
V
RANK (GB) 1971 dir. Delbert Mann
V
HTV (GB) 1979
TV(GB)
Stevenson, R. L.

Kidnapping of the President, The
CROWN (US) 1980
dir. George Mendelink
V
Templeton, C.

Killdozer
UN TV (US) 1974 dir. Jerry London
TV(US)
Sturgeon, T.

Killer Elite, The
UA (US) 1975 dir. Sam Peckinpah
V
Rostand, Robert

Killers, The
UN (US) 1946 dir. Robert Siodmak
UN (US) 1964 dir. Don Siegel
V
Hemingway, E.

Killers of Kilimanjaro, The
COL (GB) 1959 dir. Richard Thorpe
V

Hunter, J. A. & Mannix, D. P. *Tales of the African Frontier*

Killing, The
UA (US) 1956 dir. Stanley Kubrick
White, L. *Clean Break*

Killing Affair, A
HEMDALE (US) 1988
dir. David Saperstein
V

Houston, R. *Monday, Tuesday, Wednesday*

Killing Dad
PALACE (US) 1989 dir. Michael Austin
Quinn, A. *Berg*

Killing in a Small Town
INDIEPROD (US) 1990
dir. Stephen Gyllenhaal
TV(US)
Bloom, J. and Atkinson, J. *Evidence of Love*

Killing of Sister George, The
CINERAMA (US) 1967
dir. Robert Aldrich
V

Marcus, F.
P

Kill Off, The
CABRIOLET (US) 1990
dir. Maggie Greenwald
Thompson, J.

Kim
MGM (US) 1950 dir. Victor Saville
V
LF (GB) 1984 dir. John Davies
TVSe(GB)
Kipling, R.

Kind Hearts and Coronets
EAL (GB) 1949 dir. Robert Hamer
V

Horniman, R. *Noblesse Oblige*

Kind Lady
MGM (US) 1935 dir. George B. Seitz
MGM (US) 1951 dir. John Sturges
Chodorov, E.
P

Kind of Alaska, A
CENTRAL (GB) 1984 dir. Kenneth Ives
TV(GB)
Pinter, H.
P

Kind of Loving, A
AA (GB) 1962 dir. John Schlesinger
V

Barstow, S.

King and Country
WAR (GB) 1964 dir. Joseph Losey
Hodson, J. L. *Return to the Woods*
Wilson, J. *Hamp*
P

King and I, The
FOX (US) 1956 dir. Walter Lang
M, V

Landon, M. *Anna and the King of Siam*
Rogers, R. and Hammerstein II, O.
P

King Creole
PAR (US) 1958 dir. Michael Curtiz
V

Robbins, H. *Stone for Danny Fisher, A*

King David
PAR (US/GB) 1985
dir. Bruce Beresford
V

Bible *Samuel I & II: Chronicles I, Psalms of David*

King in Shadow
BL (Ger) 1961 dir. Harold Braun
Neumann, R. *Queen's Favourite, The*

King Lear
COL (Den/GB) 1970 dir. Peter Brook
V
GRANADA (GB) 1983
dir. Michael Elliott
TV(GB)
CANNON (US) 1988
dir. Jean-Luc Godard
Shakespeare, W.
P

King of the Damned
GAU (GB) 1935 dir. Walter Forde
Chancellor, J.
P

King of the Grizzlies
DISNEY (US) 1970 dir. Ron Kelly
V
Seton, E. T. *Biography of a Grizzly, The*

King of the Gypsies
PAR (US) 1978 dir. Frank Pierson
V
Maas, P.

King of the Khyber Rifles
FOX (US) 1954 dir. Henry King
Mundy, T.

King, Queen, Knave
WOLPER (US/Ger) 1972
dir. Jerzy Skolimowski
V
Nabokov, V.

King Ralph
UN (US) 1991 dir. David S. Ward
V
Williams, E. *Headlong*

King Rat
COL (US) 1965 dir. Bryan Forbes
V
Clavell, J.

King Richard and the Crusaders
WAR (US) 1954 dir. David Butler
Scott, Sir W. *Talisman, The*

King Richard II
M EVANS (US) 1954
dir. George Schaefer
TV(US)
Shakespeare, W.
P

Kings Go Forth
UA (US) 1958 dir. Delmer Daves
Brown, J. D.

King Solomon's Mines
GB (GB) 1937 dir. Robert Stevenson
MGM (US) 1950 dir. Compton Bennett
V
CANNON (US) 1985
dir. J. Lee Thompson
V
Haggard, Sir H. R.

King Solomon's Treasure
BARBER ROSE (Can/GB) 1979
dir. Alvin Rakoff
V
Haggard, Sir H. R. *Alan Quatermain*

King's Row
WAR (US) 1941 dir. Sam Wood
Bellamann, H.

King's Whore, The
J & M (GB) 1990 dir. Axel Corti
Tournier, J. *Jeanne de Luynes,*
Comtess de Verne

Kipps
FOX (GB) 1941 dir. Carol Reed
US title: Remarkable Mr Kipps, The
V
GRANADA TV (GB) 1960
TVSe(GB)
Wells, H. G.

Kismet
WAR (US) 1930 dir. John Francis Dillon
MGM (US) 1944 dir. William Dieterle
MGM (US) 1955 dir. Vincent Minnelli
M, V
Knoblock, E.
P

Kiss and Tell
COL (US) 1945 dir. Richard Wallace
Herbert, F. H.
P

Kiss Before Dying, A
UA (US) 1956 dir. Gerd Oswald
UN (US) 1991 dir. James Dearden
V
Levin, I.

Kiss Me Deadly
UA (US) 1955 dir. Robert Aldrich
Spillane, M.

Kiss Me Kate
MGM (US) 1953 dir. George Sidney
M
MILBERG (US) 1958 dir. George
Schaefer
TV(US), V
Shakespeare, W. *Taming of the
Shrew, The*
P
Spewack, S. and Spewack, B.
P

Kiss Me Stupid
UA (US) 1964 dir. Billy Wilder
Bonacci, A. *L'Oro della Fantasia*
P

Kiss of Fire
UN (US) 1955 dir. Joseph M. Newman
Lauritzen, J. *Rose and the Flame, The*

Kiss of the Spider Woman
ISLAND (US/Brazil) 1985
dir. Hector Babenco
V
Puig, M.

Kiss the Blood Off My Hands
UN (US) 1948 dir. Norman Foster
GB title: Blood on my Hands
Butler, G.

Kiss the Boys Goodbye
PAR (US) 1941 dir. Victor Schertzinger
Boothe, C.
P

Kiss Them for Me
FOX (US) 1957 dir. Stanley Donen
Wakeman, F. *Shore Leave*

Kiss Tomorrow Goodbye
WAR (US) 1950 dir. Gordon Douglas
V
McCoy, H.

Kitchen, The
BL (GB) 1961 dir. James Hill
Wesker, A.
P

Kitty
PAR (US) 1945 dir. Mitchell Leisen
Marshall, Mrs. R.

Kitty Foyle
RKO (US) 1940 dir. Sam Wood
V
Morley, C. D.

Klansman, The
PAR (US) 1974 dir. Terence Young
V
Huie, W. B.

Knack, The
UA (GB) 1965 dir. Richard Lester
Jellicoe, A.
P

Knave of Hearts
ABP (GB) 1954 dir. René Clément
US title: Lover Boy
Hemon, L. M. *Ripois and his Nemesis*

Knickerbocker Holiday
UN (US) 1944 dir. Harry Joe Brown
Irving, W. *Father Knickerbocker's
History of New York*

Knights of the Round Table
MGM (GB) 1954 dir. Richard Thorpe
V
Malory, Sir T. *Morte d'Arthur, Le*

**Knights of the Troubled
Order**
STUDIO (Pol) 1960
dir. Aleksander Ford
Sienkiewicz, H.

Knight Without Armour
UA (GB) 1937 dir. Jacques Feyder
V
Hilton, J.

Knockback
BBC (GB) 1985
TV(GB)
Adams, P. and Cooklin, S.

Knock on Any Door
COL (US) 1949 dir. Nicholas Ray
V
Motley, W.

Knots
CINEGATE (GB) 1975
dir. David I. Munro
Laing, R. D.

Kojak: The Belarus File
UN TV (US) 1985 dir. Robert Markowitz
TV(US), V
Loftus, J. *Belarus Secret, The*

Kojak: The Price of Justice
MCA/UN (US) 1987 dir. Alan Metzger
TV(US)
Uhnak, D. *Investigation, The*

Kotch
CINERAMA (US) 1971
dir. Jack Lemmon
Topkins, K.

Kramer vs Kramer
COL (US) 1979 dir. Robert Benton
V
Corman, A.

Kremlin Letter, The
FOX (US) 1970 dir. John Huston
V
Behn, N.

Kreutzer Sonata, The
FOR (Fr) 1938 dir. Charles Guichard
MOSFILM (USSR) 1987
dir. M. Schweitzer and S. Milkina
Tolstoy, L.

L

Laburnum Grove
ABP (GB) 1936 dir. Carol Reed

Priestley, J. B.
P

Lace
LORIMAR (US) 1984 dir. Billy Hale
TVSe(US), V

Conran, S.

Lacemaker, The
FR3 (Fr/It/Ger) 1977
dir. Claude Goretta
V

Laine, P.

Laddie
RKO (US) 1935 dir. George Stevens

Porter, G. S.

Ladies Club, The
NEW LINE (US) 1986 dir. A. K. Allen
V

Black, B., and Bishop, C. *Sisterhood*

Ladies in Love
FOX (US) 1936 dir. Edward H. Griffith

Bus-Fekete, L.
P

Ladies in Retirement
COL (US) 1941 dir. Charles Vidor

Percy, E. and Denham, R.
P

Lady and the Highwayman, The
GRADE (GB) 1989 dir. John Hough
TV(GB)

Cartland, B. *Cupid Rides Phillion*

Lady and the Monster, The
REP (US) 1944 dir. George Sherman
GB title: Lady and the Doctor, The

Siodmak, C. *Donovan's Brain*

Lady and the Tramp
DISNEY (US) 1955 dir. Hamilton Luske
A, V

Greene, W.

Lady Chatterley's Lover
COL (Fr) 1956 dir. Marc Allégret
CANNON (GB/Fr) 1981
dir. Just Jaeckin
V

Lawrence, D. H.

Lady Eve, The
PAR (US) 1941 dir. Preston Sturges
V

Hoffe, M.
P

Lady for a Day
COL (US) 1933 dir. Frank Capra

Runyon, D. *Madame la Gimp*

Lady Forgets, The
HILL (US) 1989 dir. Bradford May
TV(US)

Woolrich, C. *Black Curtain, The*

Lady from Shanghai, The
COL (US) 1948 dir. Orson Welles
V

King, S. *If I Die Before I Wake*

Lady in Cement
FOX (US) 1968 dir. Gordon Douglas
Albert, M. H.

Lady in the Car with Glasses and a Gun, The
COL (Fr/US) 1969 dir. Anatole Litvak
Japrisot, S.

Lady in the Dark, The
PAR (US) 1944 dir. Mitchell Leisen
Hart, M.
P

Lady in the Lake
MGM (US) 1946
dir. Robert Montgomery
Chandler, R.

Lady in the Morgue
UN (US) 1938 dir. Otis Garrett
GB title: Case of the Missing Blonde, The
Latimer, J.

Lady Killer
WAR (US) 1933 dir. Roy del Ruth
Shaffer, R. K. *Finger Man, The*

Lady L
MGM (Fr/It/US) 1965
dir. Peter Ustinov
Gary, R.

Lady Mislaid, A
ABP (GB) 1958 dir. David Macdonald
Horne, K.
P

Lady of Burlesque
STROMBERG (US) 1943
dir. William Wellman
GB title: Striptease Lady
V

Lee, G. R. *G-String Murders, The*

Lady of Scandal
MGM (US) 1930 dir. Sidney Franklin
Lonsdale, F. *High Road, The*
P

Lady of the House
METRO (US) 1978 dir. Ralph Norton,
Vincent Sherman
TV(US), V
Stanford, S.

Lady on a Train
UN (US) 1945 dir. Charles David
Charteris, L.

Lady Possessed
REP (US) 1952 dir. William Spier, Roy
Kellino
Kellino, P. *Del Palma*

Lady Sings the Blues
PAR (US) 1972 dir. Sidney J. Furie
V
Holiday, B.

Lady Surrenders, A
UN (US) 1930 dir. John Stahl
Erskine, J. *Sincerity*

Lady to Love, A
MGM (US) 1930 dir. Victor Seastrom
Howard, S. *They Knew What They Wanted*
P

Lady Vanishes, The
MGM (GB) 1938 dir. Alfred Hitchcock
RANK (GB) 1979 dir. Anthony Page
V

White, E. L. *Wheel Spins, The*

Lady who Wades in the Sea, The
PRESIDENT (Fr) 1991
dir. Laurent Heynemann

San-Antonio

Lady with a Lamp, The
BL (GB) 1951 dir. Herbert Wilcox
V

Berkeley, R.
P

Laguna Heat
WESTON (US) 1987 dir. Simon Langton
TV(US), V

Parker, T. J.

Lair of the White Worm, The
VESTRON (GB) 1988 dir. Ken Russell
V

Stoker, B.

Lamb
CANNON (GB) 1985 dir. Colin Gregg

MacLaverty, B.

Lamp Still Burns, The
TC (GB) 1943 dir. Maurice Elvey

Dickens, M. *One Pair of Feet*

Lancer Spy
FOX (US) 1937 dir. Gregory Ratoff

McKenna, M.

Landfall
AB (GB) 1949 dir. Ken Annakin

Shute, N.

Landlord, The
UA (US) 1970 dir. Hal Ashby

Hunter, K.

Land of Faraway, The
NORD/GORKY (Swe/USSR/Nor) 1988
dir. Vladimir Grammatikov
V

Lindgren, A. *Mio, My Son*

Land that Time Forgot, The
BL (GB) 1974 dir. Kevin Connor
V

Burroughs, E. R.

Lanigan's Rabbi
UN TV (US) 1976 dir. Lou Antonio
TV(US)

Kemelman, H. *Friday the Rabbi Slept Late*

Lantern Hill
DISNEY (US) 1990 dir. Kevin Sullivan
TV(US)

Montgomery, L. M. *Jane of Lantern Hill*

Larceny Inc.
WAR (US) 1942 dir. Lloyd Bacon

Perelman, L. and Perelman, S. J. *Night Before Christmas, The*
P

Lark, The
MILBERG (US) 1957
dir. George Schaefer
TV(US)

Anouilh, J.
P

Larry
TOM (US) 1974 dir. William A. Graham
TV(US), V

McQueen, Dr. R. *Larry: Case History of a Mistake*

Lash, The
IN (US) 1930 dir. Frank Lloyd

Bartlett, L. V. S. *Adios*

Lassie Come Home
MGM (US) 1943 dir. Fred M. Wilcox
Knight, E. M.

Last Angry Man, The
COL (US) 1959 dir. Daniel Mann
COL (US) 1974 dir. Jerrold Freedman
TV(US)
Green, G.

Last Chance, The
MGM (Switz) 1945
dir. Leopold Lindtberg
Schweizer, R.

Last Convertible, The
UN TV (US) 1979 dir. Sidney Hayers, Jo
Swerling, Jr., Gus Trikonis
TVSe(US)
Myrer, A.

Last Crop, The
CHANNEL 4 (GB) 1991
dir. Stephen Clayton
TV(GB)
Jolley, E.

Last Days of Patton, The
ENT PAR (US) 1986 dir. Delbert Mann
TV(US)
Farago, L.

Last Days of Pompeii, The
RKO (US) 1935 dir. Merian C. Cooper;
Ernest Schoedsack
V
COL (US) 1984 dir. Peter Hunt
TVSe(US), V
Lytton, 1st Baron

Last Detail, The
COL (US) 1973 dir. Hal Ashby
V
Ponicsan, D.

Last Embrace
UA (US) 1979 dir. Jonathan Demme
V
Bloom, M. T. *13th Man, The*

Last Emperor, The
NKL (China) 1988 dir. Li Han Hsiang
Li Shu Xian *Pu Yi and I; Pu Yi's Later Life; Pu Yi's Former Life*

Last Exit to Brooklyn
GUILD (Ger) 1989 dir. Ulrich Edel
Selby, Jr. H.

Last Flight, The
WAR (US) 1931 dir. William Dieterle
Saunders, J. M. *Single Lady*

Last Giraffe, The
WESTFALL PRODS (US) 1979
dir. Jack Couffer
TV(US)
Leslie-Melville, J. and Leslie-Melville, B. *Raising Daisy Rothschild*

Last Grenade, The
CINERAMA (GB) 1969
dir. Gordon Flemyng
Sherlock, J. *Ordeal of Major Grigsby, The*

Last Hard Man, The
FOX (US) 1976
dir. Andrew V. McLaglen
Garfield, B. *Gun Down*

Last Hunt, The
MGM (US) 1956 dir. Richard Brooks
Lott, M.

Last Hurrah, The
COL (US) 1958 dir. John Ford
V
COL (US) 1977 dir. Vincent Sherman
TV(US)
O'Connor, E.

Last Innocent Man, The
HBO (US) 1987 dir. Roger Spottiswoode
TV(US), V
Margolin, P. M.

Last Man on Earth, The
AIP (US/It) 1964 dir. Sidney Salkow
Matheson, R. *I Am Legend*

Last Man to Hang?, The
COL (GB) 1956 dir. Terence Fisher
Bullett, G. *Jury, The*

Last of Mrs Cheyney, The
MGM (US) 1929 dir. Sidney Franklin
MGM (US) 1937
dir. Richard Boleslawski
Lonsdale, F.
P

Last of Philip Banter, The
CINEVISTA (Sp) 1988
dir. Herve Hachuel
Franklin, J.

Last of the Belles
TITUS (US) 1974 dir. George Schlatter
TV(US)
Fitzgerald, F. S.

Last of the Mohicans, The
UA (US) 1936 dir. George B. Seitz
SCHICK SUNN (US) 1977
dir. James L. Conway
TV(US), V
Cooper, J. F.

Last of the Redmen
COL (US) 1947 dir. George Sherman
Cooper, J. F. *Last of the Mohicans, The*

Last of the Red Hot Lovers
PAR (US) 1972 dir. Gene Saks
V
Simon, N.
P

Last Page, The
EXCL (GB) 1952 dir. Terence Fisher
Chase, J. H.
P

Last Picture Show, The
COL (US) 1971 dir. Peter Bogdanovich
McMurtry, L.

Last Place on Earth, The
CENTRAL (GB) 1985
dir. Ferdinand Fairfax
TV(GB)
Huntford, R. *Scott and Amundsen*

Last Prostitute, The
BBK (US) 1991 dir. Lou Antonio
TV(US)
Borden, W. *Last Prostitute who Took Pride in her Work, The*
P

Last Safari, The
PAR (GB) 1967 dir. Henry Hathaway
Hanley, G. *Gilligan's Last Elephant*

Last Seance, The
GRANADA (GB) 1987
TV(GB)
Christie, A. *Hound of Hell, The*

Last Seen Wearing
CENTRAL (GB) 1989
dir. Edward Bennett
TV(GB)
Dexter, C.

Last Shot you Hear, The
FOX (GB) 1970 dir. Gordon Hessler
Fairchild, W. *Sound of Murder, The*
P

Last Summer
FOX (US) 1969 dir. Frank Perry
V
Hunter, E.

Last Sunset, The
UI (US) 1961 dir. Robert Aldrich
Rigsby, H. *Showdown at Crazy Horse*

Last Temptation of Christ, The
UN (US) 1988 dir. Martin Scorsese
V
Kazantzakis, N.

Last Time I Saw Paris, The
MGM (US) 1954 dir. Richard Brooks
V
Fitzgerald, F. S. *Babylon Revisited*

Last To Go, The
INTERSCOPE (US) 1991
dir. John Erman
TV(US)
Cooper, R. R.

Last Tycoon, The
PAR (US) 1976 dir. Elia Kazan
V
Fitzgerald, F. S.

Last Unicorn, The
SCHICK SUNN (US) 1982
dir. Jules Bass/ArthurRankinJr.
A, V
Beagle, P. S.

Last Valley, The
CINERAMA (GB) 1970
dir. James Clavell
V
Pick, J. B.

Last Warning, The
UN (US) 1938 dir. Albert S. Rogell
Latimer, J. *Dead Don't Care, The*

Last Wish
GROSSBART/BARNETT
PRODUCTIONS (US) 1992
dir. JeffBleckner
TV(US)
Rollin B.

Late Edwina Black, The
GFD (GB) 1951 dir. Maurice Elvey
Dinner, W. and Morum, W.
P

Late George Apley, The
FOX (US) 1946
dir. Joseph L. Mankiewicz
Marquand, J. P. *Within the Tides*

Late Great Planet Earth, The
ENT (US) 1979 dir. Robert Amram
V
Lindsay, H. and Carlson, C. C.

Laughing Anne
REP (GB) 1953 dir. Herbert Wilcox
Conrad, J. *Within the Tides*

Laughing Boy
MGM (US) 1934 dir. W. S. Van Dyke
LaFarge, O.

Laughing Policeman, The
TCF (US) 1973 dir. Stuart Rosenberg
GB title: Investigation of Murder, An
V
Sjowall, M. and Wahloo, P.

Laughter in the Dark
UA (GB/Fr) 1969 dir. Tony Richardson
Nabokov, V.

Laura
FOX (US) 1944 dir. Otto Preminger
V
Caspary, V.

Law and Disorder
BL (GB) 1957 dir. Charles Crichton
Roberts, D. *Smuggler's Circuit*

Law and Order
UN (US) 1932 dir. Edward L. Cahn
Burnett, W. R. *Saint Johnson*

Law and Order
PAR (US) 1976 dir. Marvin J. Chomsky
TV(US)
Uhnak, D.

Law and the Lady, The
MGM (US) 1951 dir. Edwin H. Knopf
Lonsdale, F. *Last of Mrs. Cheyney, The*
P

Lawless Street, A
COL (US) 1955 dir. Joseph H. Lewis
Ward, B. *Marshal of Medicine Bend, The*

Law of the Tropics
WAR (US) 1941 dir. Ray Enright
Hobart, A. T. *Oil for the Lamps of China*

Lawrence of Arabia
COL/BL (GB/US) 1962 dir. David Lean
V
Lawrence, T. E. *Seven Pillars of Wisdom*

Laxdale Hall
ABP (GB) 1952 dir. John Eldridge
US title: Scotch on the Rocks
Linklater, E.

League of Frightened Men, The
COL (US) 1937 dir. Alfred E. Green
Stout, R.

League of Gentlemen, The
RANK (GB) 1960 dir. Basil Dearden
V
Boland, J.

Learning Tree, The
WAR (US) 1969 dir. Gordon Parks
V
Parks, G.

Lease of Life
EAL (GB) 1954 dir. Charles Frend
Baker, F.

Leather Boys, The
BL (GB) 1963 dir. Sidney J. Furie
V
George, E.

Leathernecking
RKO (US) 1930 dir. Edward Cline
GB title: Present Arms
M
Fields, H., Rodgers and Hart
Present Arms
P

Leave Her to Heaven
FOX (US) 1945 dir. John M. Stahl
Williams, B. A.

Lectrice, La
ORION (Fr) 1989 dir. Michel Deville
Jean, R.

Left Hand of God, The
FOX (US) 1955 dir. Edward Dmytryk
V
Barrett, W. E.

Legend of Hell House, The
FOX (GB) 1973 dir. John Hough
V
Matheson, R. *Hell House*

Legend of Lobo, The
DISNEY (US) 1962 dir. James Algar
Ch, V
Seton, E. T. *Biography of a Grizzly and Other Animal Stories, The*

Legend of Sleepy Hollow, The
SCHICK SUNN (US) 1980
dir. Henning Schellerup
TV(US), V
Irving, W.

Legend of Suram Fortress, The
GRUZIA (USSR) 1985
dir. Sergei Paradjanov
Chonkadze, D.

Legend of the Holy Drinker
ART EYE (It) 1989 dir. Ermanno Olnu
Roth, J.

Legend of Walks Far Woman, The
EMI (US) 1982 dir. Mel Damski
TV(US), V
Stuart, C. *Walks Far Woman*

Lemon Drop Kid, The
PAR (US) 1951 dir. Sidney Lanfield
Runyon, D.

Lena: My 100 Children
GREENWALD (US) 1987 dir. Ed Sherin
TV(US)
Kuchler-Silberman, L *One Hundred Children*

Lenny
UA (US) 1974 dir. Bob Fosse
V
Barry, J.
P

Leona Helmsley: The Queen of Mean
FRIES (US) 1990 dir. Richard Michaels
TV(US)
Pierson, R. *Queen of Mean, The*

Léon Morin, Priest
ROME-PARIS (Fr/It) 1961
dir. Jean-Pierre Melville
Beck, B.

Leontyne
LEONTYNE/ITV (GB) 1990
dir. Richard Goodwin
TV(GB)
Goodwin, R.

Leopard, The
FOX (US/It) 1963 dir. Luchino Visconti
Lampedusa, G. de

Leopard in the Snow
ANGLO-CAN (GB/Can) 1977
dir. Gerry O'Hara
V
Mather, A.

Leopard Man, The
RKO (US) 1943 dir. Jacques Tourneur
V
Woolrich, C. *Black Alibi*

Les Misérables
UA (US) 1935 dir. Richard Boleslawski
FOX (US) 1952 dir. Lewis Milestone
ITC (GB) 1978 dir. Glenn Jordan
Hugo, V.

Less than Zero
FOX (US) 1987 dir. Marek Kanievska
V
Ellis, B.E.

Let It Ride
PAR (US) 1989 dir. Joe Pytka
Cronley, J. *Good Vibes*

Let No Man Write My Epitaph
COL (US) 1960 dir. Philip Leacock
Motley, W.

Let's Be Happy
ABP (GB) 1957 dir. Henry Levin
M
Stuart, A. *Jeannie*
P

Let's Do It Again
COL (US) 1953 dir. Alexander Hall
M
Richman, A. *Not so Long Ago*
P

Let's Face It
PAR (US) 1943 dir. Sidney Lanfield
Mitchell, N. and Medcraft, R.
Cradle Snatchers
P

Let's Kill Uncle
UI (US) 1966 dir. William Castle
O'Grady, R.

Let the People Sing
BN (GB) 1942 dir. John Baxter
Priestley, J. B.

Letter, The
PAR (US) 1929 dir. Jean de Limur
WAR (US) 1940 dir. William Wyler
V
WAR (US) 1982 dir. John Erman
TV(US)
Maugham, W. S.
P

Letter from an Unknown Woman
UI (US) 1948 dir. Max Ophuls
V
Zweig, S.

Letters from the Park
RTVE (Cuba) 1988
dir. Tomas Guttierez Alea
Marquez, G. G. *Love in the Time of Cholera*

Letter to Three Wives, A.
FOX (US) 1948
dir. Joseph L. Mankiewicz
V
FOX (US) 1985 dir. Larry Elikann
TV(US)
Klempner, J. *Letter to Five Wives*

Letting Go
ITC (US) 1985 dir. Jack Bender
TV(US)
Wanderer, Dr. Z. and Cabot, T.

Letty Lynton
MGM (US) 1932 dir. Clarence Brown
Lowndes, Mrs. M. B.

Liaisons Dangereuses, Les
MARCEAU (Fr) 1959 dir. Roger Vadim
de Laclos, P.

Libel
MGM (GB) 1959 dir. Anthony Asquith
Wooll, E.
P

Liberation of Lord Byron Jones, The
COL (US) 1970 dir. William Wyler
V
Ford, J. H.

Lie, The
SELVAGGIA (It) 1985
dir. Giovanni Soldati
Moravia, A. *L'Attention*

Liebelei
ELITE (Fr) 1932 dir. Max Ophuls
Schnitzler, A.
P

Lies My Father Told Me
COL (Can) 1975 dir. Jan Kadar
Allan, N.

Lies of the Twins
MCA TV (US) 1991 dir. Tim Hunter
TV(US)
Oates, J. C.

Life and Adventures of Nicholas Nickleby, The
PRIMETIME (GB) 1984
dir. Jim Goddard
TVSe(GB), V
Dickens, C. *Nicholas Nickleby*

Life and Loves of a She-Devil, The
BBC (GB) 1986 dir. Philip Saville
TVSe(GB)
Weldon, F.

Life Begins
WAR (US) 1932 dir. James Flood
GB title: Dream of Life
Axelson, M. M.
P

Life Begins at Eight Thirty
FOX (US) 1942 dir. Irving Pichel
GB title: Light of Heart, The
Williams, E. *Light of Heart, The*
P

Lifeforce
CANNON (US) 1985 dir. Tobe Hooper
V
Wilson, C. *Space Vampires*

Life for Ruth
RANK (GB) 1962 dir. Basil Dearden
US title: Condemned to Life
Green, J.
P

Life of Jimmy Dolan, The
WAR (US) 1933 dir. Archie Mayo
GB title: Kid's Last Fight, The
Millhauser, B. and Dix, B. M.
P

Life on a String
PBC (Ger/GB/China) 1991
dir. Chen Kaige
Tiesheng, S.

Life with Father
WAR (US) 1947 dir. Michael Curtiz
V
Day, C.
Lindsay, H. and Crouse, R.
P

Lift to the Scaffold
NEF (Fr) 1957 dir. Louis Malle
Calef, N.

Light at the Edge of the World, The
MGM (US/Sp) 1971
dir. Kevin Billington
V
Verne, J. *Lighthouse at the End of the World*

Light in the Forest, The
DISNEY (US) 1958
dir. Herschel Daugherty
V
Richter, C.

Light in the Piazza, The
MGM (GB) 1962 dir. Guy Green
Spencer, E.

Lightnin'
FOX (US) 1930 dir. Henry King
Bacon, F. and Smith, W.
P

Lightning Strikes Twice
WAR (US) 1951 dir. King Vidor

Echard, M. *Dark Fantastic*

Lightship, The
WAR (US) 1985 dir. Jerzy Skolimowski
V

Lenz, S. *Das Feuerschiff*

Light That Failed, The
PAR (US) 1939 dir. William Wellman

Kipling, R.

Light up the Sky
BL (GB) 1960 dir. Lewis Gilbert

Storey, R. *Touch it Light*
P

Light Years
MIRAMAX (Fr) 1988 dir. René Laloux
A, V

Andrevan, J-P. *Robots Against Gandahar*

Light Years Away
NEW YORKER (Fr) 1932
dir. Alain Tanner

Odier, D. *Voie Sauvage, La*

Like Mom, Like Me
CBS ENT (US) 1978
dir. Michael Pressman
TV(US)

Schwartz, S. *Like Mother, Like Me*

Like Normal People
FOX TV (US) 1979 dir. Harvey Hart
TV(US)

Meyers, R.

L'il Abner
PAR (US) 1959 dir. Melvin Frank
M

Mercer, J., dePaul, G., Panama. N. and Frank, M.
P

Lilacs in The Spring
REP (GB) 1954 dir. Herbert Wilcox
US title: Let's Make Up

Purcell, H. *Glorious Days, The*
P

Lili
MGM (US) 1952 dir. Charles Walters
V

Gallico, P.

Lili Marleen
ROXY (Ger) 1980
dir. Rainer Werner Fassbinder
V

Anderson, L. *Sky has Many Colours, The*

Lilies of the Field, The
UA (US) 1963 dir. Ralph Nelson
V

Barrett, W. E.

Liliom
FOX (US) 1930 dir. Frank Borzage

Molnar, F.
P

Lilith
COL (US) 1964 dir. Robert Rossen
V

Salamanca, J. R.

Limbo
UN (US) 1972 dir. Mark Robson

Silver, J.

Limbo Line, The
MONARCH (GB) 1968
dir. Samuel Gallen
V

Canning, V.

Linda
UN TV (US) 1973 dir. Jack Smight
TV(US)

MacDonald, J. D.

Lion, The
FOX (GB) 1962 dir. Jack Cardiff
Kessel, J.

Lionheart
CFF (GB) 1968 dir. Michael Forlong
Fullerton, A.

Lion is in The Streets, A
WAR (US) 1953 dir. Raoul Walsh
Langley, A. L.

Lion in Winter, The
AVCO (GB) 1968 dir. Anthony Harvey
V
Goldman, J.
P

Lion, The Witch and the Wardrobe, The
ITV (US/GB) 1978 dir. Bill Melendez
A, TVSe(GB/US), V
Lewis, C. S.

Liquidator, The
MGM (GB) 1965 dir. Jack Cardiff
V
Gardner, J.

Lisa, Bright and Dark
BANNER (US) 1973 dir. Jeannot Szwarc
Neufeld, J.

Lisbon Story, The
BN (GB) 1946 dir. Paul Stein
M
Purcell, H. and Parr-Davies, H.
P

List of Adrian Messenger, The
UI (US) 1963 dir. John Huston
V
Macdonald, P.

Little Ark, The
FOX (US) 1971 dir. James B. Clark
V
Hartog, J. de

Little Big Man
CIN CEN (US) 1970 dir. Arthur Penn
V
Berger, T.

Little Boy Lost
PAR (US) 1953 dir. George Seaton
Laski, M.

Little Caesar
WAR (US) 1930 dir. Mervyn Le Roy
V
Burnett, W. R.

Little Colonel
FOX (US) 1935 dir. David Butler
V
Johnson, A. F.

Little Dorrit
CANNON (GB) 1988
dir. Christine Edzard
Dickens, C.

Little Drummer Girl, The
WAR (US) 1984 dir. George Roy Hill
V
Le Carré, J.

Little Foxes, The
RKO (US) 1941 dir. William Wyler
V
MILBERG (US) 1956
dir. George Schaefer
TV(US)
Hellman, L. F.
P

Little Game, A
UN TV (US) 1971 dir. Paul Wendkos
TV(US)
Farrington, F.

Little Girl Who Lives Down The Lane, The
RANK (US/Fr/Can) 1976
dir. Nicolas Gessner
V

Koenig, L.

Little Gloria ... Happy at Last
METRO (US) 1983 dir. Waris Hussein
TVSe(US)

Goldsmith, B.

Little House on the Prairie
NBC ENT (US) 1974
dir. Michael Landon
TV(US), V

Wilder, L. I.

Little Hut, The
MGM (US) 1957 dir. Mark Robson
Roussin, A. & Mitford, N.
P

Little Kidnappers, The
DISNEY CH (US) 1990 dir. Don Shebib
Ch, TV(US)

Paterson, N. *Kidnappers, The*

Little Lord Fauntleroy
UA (US) 1936 dir. John Cromwell
V
ROSEMONT (GB) 1980 dir. Jack Gold
TV(GB)

Burnett, F. H.

Little Man, What Now?
UN (US) 1934 dir. Frank Borzage

Fallada, H.

Little Match Girl, The
NBC (US) 1987
dir. Michael Lindsay-Hogg
Ch, TV(US), V

Andersen, H. C.

Little Men
RKO (US) 1935 dir. Philip Rosen
V

Alcott, L. M.

Little Mermaid, The
DISNEY (US) 1989 dir. John Musker,
Ron Clements
A, Ch, V

Andersen, H. C.

Little Minister, The
RKO (US) 1934 dir. Richard Wallace
V

Barrie, Sir J. M.
P

Little Miss Marker
PAR (US) 1934 dir. Alexander Hall
GB title: Girl in Pawn, The
UN (US) 1980 dir. Walter Bernstein
V

Runyon, D.

Little Murders
FOX (US) 1971 dir. Alan Arkin
V

Feiffer, J.
P

Little Nellie Kelly
MGM (US) 1940 dir. Norman Taurog
M

Cohan, G. M.
P

Little Night Music, A
S&T (Austria/Ger) 1977
dir. Harold Prince
M, V

Wheeler, H., Sondheim, S.
P

Little Old New York
FOX (US) 1940 dir. Henry King

Young, R. J.
P

Little Prince, The
PAR (US) 1974 dir. Stanley Donen
M, V
Saint-Exupery de, A.

Little Princess, The
FOX (US) 1939 dir. Walter Lang
V
Burnett, F. H.

Little Romance, A
WAR (US) 1979 dir. George Roy Hill
V
Cauvin, P. *Blind Love*

Little Shepherd of Kingdom Come, The
FOX (US) 1961
dir. Andrew V. McLaglen
Fox, J.

Little Shop of Horrors
WAR (US) 1986 dir. Frank Oz
M, V
Ashman, H. and Menken, A.
P

Littlest Angel, The
OSTERMAN (US) 1969
dir. Walter C. Miller
TV(US), V
Tazewell, C.

Littlest Rebel, The
FOX (US) 1935 dir. David Butler
V
Peple, E.
P

Little Women
RKO (US) 1933 dir. George Cukor
MGM (US) 1948 dir. Mervyn Le Roy
V
UN (US) 1978 dir. David Lowell Rich
TVSe(US)
Alcott, L. M.

Little World of Don Camillo, The
LF (Fr/It) 1952 dir. Julien Duvivier
Guareschi, G.

Live Again, Die Again
UN TV (US) 1974 dir. Richard Colla
TV(US)
Sale, D. *Come to Mother*

Live and Let Die
UA (GB) 1973 dir. Guy Hamilton
V
Fleming, I.

Live Now, Pay Later
REGAL (GB) 1962 dir. Jay Lewis
Lindsay, J. *All on the Never-Never*

Lives of a Bengal Lancer
PAR (US) 1935 dir. Henry Hathaway
V
Brown, F. Y. *Bengal Lancer*

Living Daylights, The
MGM (GB) 1987 dir. John Glen
V
Fleming, I.

Living Free
COL (GB) 1972 dir. Jack Couffer
V
Adamson, J.

Living Proof: The Hank Williams, Jr. Story
TELECOM (US) 1983 dir. Dick Lowry
TV(US)
Williams, Jr., H. and Bane, M.
Living Proof

Lizzie
MGM (US) 1957 dir. Hugo Haas
Jackson, S. *Bird's Nest, The*

Lloyd's of London
FOX (US) 1936 dir. Henry King
Kenyon, C.

Lock up your Daughters
COL (GB) 1969 dir. Peter Coe
V
Miles, B.
P

Lodger, The
TWICKENHAM (GB) 1932
dir. Maurice Elvey
US title: Phantom Fiend, The
FOX (US) 1944 dir. John Brahm
Lowndes, Mrs. M. B.

Logan's Run
MGM (US) 1976 dir. Michael Anderson
V
Nolan, W. and Johnson, G.

Lola Montes
GAMMA (Fr/Ger) 1955
dir. Max Ophuls
V
Saint-Laurent, C.

Lolita
MGM (GB) 1962 dir. Stanley Kubrick
V
Nabokov, V.

Lolly Madonna XXX
MGM (US) 1973 dir. Richard C. Sarafian
GB title: Lolly-Madonna War, The
Grafton, S.

London Belongs to Me
UN (GB) 1948 dir. Sydney Gilliatt
US title: Dulcimer Street
THAMES TV (GB) 1977
dir. Raymond Menmuir
TVSe(GB)
Collins, N.

London by Night
MGM (US) 1937 dir. William Thiele
Scott, W. *Umbrella Man, The*
P

London Embassy, The
THAMES (GB) 1988
TV
Theroux, P.

London Nobody Knows, The
BL (GB) 1969 dir. Norman Cohen
Fletcher, G.

Loneliness of the Long Distance Runner, The
BL (GB) 1962 dir. Tony Richardson
Sillitoe, A.

Lonely are the Brave
UI (US) 1962 dir. David Miller
V
Abbey, E. *Brave Cowboy*

Lonely Guy, The
UN (US) 1984 dir. Arthur Hiller
V
Friedman, B. J. *Lonely Guy's Book of Life, The*

Lonely Hearts
TOHO (Jap) 1982 dir. Kon Ichikawa
McBain, E. *Lady, Lady, I Did It!*

Lonelyhearts
UA (US) 1958 dir. Vincent J. Donehue
West, N. *Miss Lonelyhearts*

Lonely Lady, The
UN (US) 1982 dir. Peter Sasdy
V
Robbins, H.

Lonely Passion of Judith Hearne, The
ISLAND/HANDMADE (GB) 1987
dir. Jack Clayton

Moore, B.

Lonely Profession, The
UN TV (US) 1979 dir. Douglas Heyes
TV(US)

Heyes, D. *Twelfth of Never, The*

Lonesome Dove
MOTOWN (US) 1989 dir. Simon Wincer
TVS(US)

McMurtry, L.

Lone Wolf Returns, The
COL (US) 1936
dir. Roy William McNeill

Vance, L. J.

Long and the Short and the Tall, The
WAR (GB) 1960 dir. Leslie Norman
US title: Jungle Fighters

Hall, W.
P

Long Day's Dying, The
PAR (GB) 1968 dir. Peter Collinson

White, A.

Long Day's Journey into Night
FOX (US) 1962 dir. Sidney Lumet
V

O'Neill, E. G.
P

Longest Day, The
FOX (US) 1962 dir. Ken Annakin,
AndrewMarton,Bernhard Wicki
V

Ryan, C.

Long Goodbye, The
UA (US) 1973 dir. Robert Altman
V

Chandler, R.

Long Gray Line, The
COL (US) 1955 dir. John Ford

Maher, M. and Campion, N. R.
Bringing up the Brass: My 55 Years at West Point

Long Haul, The
COL (GB) 1957 dir. Ken Hughes

Mills, M.

Long, Hot Summer, The
FOX (US) 1958 dir. Martin Ritt
V
L. HILL (US) 1985 dir. Stuart Cooper
TVSe(US)

Faulkner, W. *Hamlet, The*

Long, Long Trailer, The
MGM (US) 1954 dir. Vincente Minnelli

Twiss, C.

Long Lost Father
RICO (US) 1934
dir. Ernest B. Schoedsack

Stern, G. B.

Long Memory, The
GFD (GB) 1953 dir. Robert Hamer

Clewes, H.

Long Road Home
ROSEMONT (US) 1991 dir. John Korty

Taylor, R. B.

Long Ships, The
BL (GB/Yugo) 1963 dir. Jack Cardiff

Bengtsson, F.

Long Summer of George Adams, The
WAR TV (US) 1982 dir. Stuart Margolin
TV(US)
Hill, W.

Long Voyage Home, The
UA (US) 1940 dir. John Ford
V
O'Neill, E. G.
P

Long Wait, The
UA (US) 1954 dir. Victor Saville
Spillane, M.

Look Back in Anger
ABP (GB) 1959 dir. Tony Richardson
V
Osborne, J.
P

Looking for Miracles
DISNEY (US/Can) 1989
dir. Kevin Sullivan
Hotchner, A. E.

Looking for Mr Goodbar
PAR (US) 1987 dir. Richard Brooks
V
Rossner, J.

Looking Forward
MGM (US) 1933 dir. Clarence Brown
Anthony, C. L. *Service*
P

Looking Glass War, The
COL (GB) 1969 dir. Frank R. Pierson
V
Le Carré, J.

Loophole
B W (GB) 1981 dir. John Quested
V
Pollock, R.

Loose Change
UN TV (US) 1978 dir. Jules Irving
TVSe(US)
Davidson, S.

Loot
BL (GB) 1970 dir. Silvio Narizzano
V
Orton, J.
P

Lord Camber's Ladies
BI (GB) 1932 dir. Benn W. Levy
Vachell, H. A. *Case of Lady Camber, The*
P

Lord Edgware Dies
TWICKENHAM (GB) 1934
dir. Henry Edwards
Christie, A.

Lord Jim
COL (GB) 1964 dir. Richard Brooks
V
Conrad, J.

Lord Love A Duck
UA (US) 1966 dir. George Axelrod
Hine, A.

Lord of the Flies
BL (GB) 1963 dir. Peter Brooke
V
COL/PALACE (GB/US) 1990
dir. Harry Hook
Golding, W.

Lord of the Rings
UA (US) 1978 dir. Ralph Bakshi
A, V
Tolkien, J. R. R. *Fellowship of the Ring: Two Towers, The*

Lords of Discipline, The
PAR (US) 1983 dir. Franc Roddam
V

Conroy, P.

Lorna Doone
ATP (GB) 1934 dir. Basil Dean
COL (US) 1951 dir. Phil Karlson
THAMES (GB) 1990 dir. Alistair Grieve
TV

Blackmore, R. D.

Loser Takes All
BL (GB) 1956 dir. Ken Annakin

Greene, G.

Lost Command
COL (US) 1966 dir. Mark Robson
V

Larteguy, J. *Centurions, The*

Lost Continent, The
WAR (GB) 1968 dir. Michael Carreras

Wheatley, D. *Uncharted Seas*

Lost Empires
GRANADA (GB) 1985 dir. Alan Grint
TVSe(GB)

Priestley, J. B.

Lost Honor of Kathryn Beck, The
COMWORLD (US) 1984
dir. Simon Langton
TV(US)

Boll, H. *Lost Honor of Katharina Blum, The*

Lost Horizon
COL (US) 1937 dir. Frank Capra
V
COL (US) 1972 dir. Charles Jarrot
M

Hilton, J.

Lost in the Barrens
CBC (US/Can) 1991 dir. Michael Scott
TV(Can/US)

Mowat, F.

Lost Lady, A
WAR (US) 1934 dir. Alfred E. Green

Cather, W.

Lost Man, The
UN (US) 1969 dir. Robert Alan Arthur

Green, F. L.

Lost Moment, The
UN (US) 1947 dir. Martin Gabel
V

James, H. *Aspern Papers, The*

Lost Patrol
RKO (US) 1934 dir. John Ford

MacDonald, P. *Patrol*

Lost People, The
GFD (GB) 1949 dir. Bernard Knowles

Boland, B. *Cockpit*
P

Lost Weekend, The
PAR (US) 1945 dir. Billy Wilder
V

Jackson, C.

Lost World, The
FOX (US) 1960 dir. Irwin Allen

Doyle, Sir A. C.

Louisiana
CINEMAX (US) 1984
dir. Philippe de Broca
TVSe(US), V

Denuzière, M. *Louisiane; Fausse-Rivière*

Louisiana Purchase
PAR (US) 1941 dir. Irving Cummings
M
Ryskind, M.
P

Love Affair, A: The Eleanor and Lou Gehrig Story
FRIES (US) 1978 dir. Fielder Cook
TV(US), V
Gehrig, E. and Durso, J. *My Luke and I*

Love and Hate: A Marriage Made in Hell
CBC/BBC (US/Can/GB) 1991
dir. Francis Mankiewicz
TVSe(Can/US), TVSe(GB)
Siggins, M. *Canadian Tragedy, A*

Love Ban, The
BL (GB) 1973 dir. Ralph Thomas
Laffan, K. *It's a 2 ft 6 inch Above The Ground World*
P

Love Before Breakfast
UN (US) 1936 dir. Walter Lang
Baldwin, F. *Spinster Dinner*

Loved One, The
MGM (US) 1965 dir. Tony Richardson
Waugh, E.

Love for Lydia
LWT (GB) 1977
TVSe(GB)
Bates, H. E.

Love from a Stranger
UA (GB) 1937 dir. Rowland V. Lee
EAGLE LION (US) 1947
dir. Richard Whorf
GB title: Stranger Walked In, A
V
Vosper, F.
P

Love, Hate, Love
A. SPELLING (US) 1971
dir. George McCowan
TV(US)
Kaufman, L. *Color of Green*

Love in Germany, A
TRIUMPH (Ger) 1984
dir. Andrzej Wajda
V
Hochhuth, R. *Eine Liebe in Deutschland*

Love in the Afternoon
AA (US) 1957 dir. Billy Wilder
V
Arianet, C.

Love is a Ball
UA (US) 1963 dir. David Swift
GB title: All This and Money Too
Hardy, L. *Grand Duke and Mr. Pimm, The*

Love is a Many Splendoured Thing
FOX (US) 1955 dir. Henry King
V
Han Suyin. *Many Splendoured Thing, A*

Love is Never Silent
M. REES (US) 1985 dir. Joseph Sargent
TV(US)
Greenberg, J. *In This Sign*

Lovejoy
BBC (GB) 1990 dir. Ken Hannam and David Reynolds
TV(GB)
Gash, J.

Love Leads the Way
DISNEY CH (US) 1984
dir. Delbert Mann
TV(US), V
Frank, M. and Clark, B. *First Lady of the Seeing Eye*

Love Letters
PAR (US) 1945 dir. William Dieterle
Massie, C. *Pity my Simplicity*

Love Letters of a Star
UN (US) 1936 dir. Lewis R. Foster
King, R. *Case of the Constant God, The*

Lovely to Look At
MGM (US) 1952 dir. Mervyn LeRoy
M
Miller, A. D. *Gowns by Roberta*

Love Machine, The
COL (US) 1971 dir. Jack Haley Jr.
V
Susann, J.

Love me Tonight
PAR (US) 1932 dir. Rouben Mamoulian
M
Marchand, L. and Armont, P. *Tailor in the Château*
P

Love Nest
FOX (US) 1951 dir. Joseph Newman
Corbett, S.

Love on the Dole
BL (GB) 1941 dir. John Baxter
V
Greenwood, W.

Love Parade, The
PAR (US) 1929 dir. Ernst Lubitsch
M
Xaurof, L., and Chancel, J. *Prince Consort, The*
P

Lover, The
ITV (GB) 1963 dir. Joan Kemp-Welch
TV(GB)
Pinter, H.
P

Lovers of Lisbon, The
EGC (Fr) 1954 dir. Henri Verneuil
Kessel, J.

Love She Sought, The
ORION TV (US) 1990
dir. Joseph Sargent
TV(US)
Hassler, J. *Green Journey*

Loves of Carmen, The
COL (US) 1948 dir. Charles Vidor
V
Merimée, P. *Carmen*

Loves of Joanna Godden, The
GFD (GB) 1947 dir. Charles Frend
Smith, S. K. *Joanna Godden*

Love Story
GFD (GB) 1944 dir. Leslie Arliss
US title: Lady Surrenders, A
Drawbell, J. W. *Love and Forget*

Love Story
PAR (US) 1970 dir. Arthur Hiller
V
Segal, E.

Love Streams
CANNON (US) 1984
dir. John Cassavetes
V
Allan, T.
P

Love Under Fire
FOX (US) 1937 dir. George Marshall
Hackett, W.
P

Love with a Perfect Stranger
ATLANTIC/YTV (US/GB)
dir. Desmond Davis
TV(GB/US)
Wallace, P.

Lovey: A Circle of Children, Part II
TIME-LIFE (US) 1978 dir. Jud Taylor
TV(US), V
MacCracken, M. *Lovey, A Very Special Child*

Loving
COL (US) 1970 dir. Irvin Kershner
Ryan, J. M. *Brook Wilson Ltd*

Loving Couples
SANDREW (Swe) 1964
dir. Mai Zetterling
von Krusenstjerna, A. *Froknarna von Pahlen*

Loving Walter
FF (GB) 1986 dir. Stephen Frears
Cook, D. *Winter Doves*

Lovin' Molly
GALA (US) 1974 dir. Sidney Lumet
McMurtry, L. *Leaving Cheyenne*

Loyalties
AUT (GB) 1933 dir. Basil Dean
Galsworthy, J.
P

L-Shaped Room, The
BL (GB) 1962 dir. Bryan Forbes
Banks, L. R.

Luck of Ginger Coffey, The
BL (Can/US) 1964 dir. Irvin Kershner
Moore, B.

Luck of the Irish, The
FOX (US) 1948 dir. Henry Koster
Jones, G. P. and Jones, C. B. *There was a Little Man*

Lucky/Chances
NBC (US) 1990 dir. Buzz Kulik
TVSe(US)
Collins, J. *Lucky; Chances*

Lucky Jim
BL (GB) 1957 dir. John Boulting
V
Amis, K.

Lucky Stiff, The
UA (US) 1948 dir. Lewis R. Foster
Rice, C.

Lucy Gallant
PAR (US) 1955 dir. Robert Parrish
Cousins, M. *Life of Lucy Gallant, The*

Lunatic, The
ISLAND PICTURES (Fr) 1992
dir. Lol Creme
Winkler, A. C.

Lust for Gold
COL (US) 1949 dir. S. Sylvan Simon
Storm, B. *Thunder God's Gold*

Lust for Life
MGM (US) 1956 dir. Vincente Minnelli
Stone, I.

Luther
SEVEN KEYS (GB) 1973 dir. Guy Green
Osborne, J.
P

Luv
COL (US) 1967 dir. Clive Donner
V
Schisgal, M.
P

Luxury Liner
PAR (US) 1933 dir. Lothar Mendes
Kaus, G.

Lydia Bailey
FOX (US) 1952 dir. Jean Negulesco
Roberts, K.

McCabe and Mrs. Miller
WAR (US) 1971 dir. Robert Altman
V
Naughton, E. *McCabe*

Macabre
ABP (US) 1958 dir. William Castle
Durant, T. *Marble Forest*

MacArthur's Children
ORION (Jap) 1985
dir. Masahiro Shinoda
V
Alcu, Y.

Macbeth
REP (US) 1948 dir. Orson Welles
V
M. EVANS (US) 1954
dir. George Schaefer
TV(US), V
COMPASS (US) 1960
dir. George Schaefer
TV(US)
COL-WAR (GB) 1971
dir. Roman Polanski
V
Shakespeare, W.
P

McGuffin, The
BBC (GB) 1986
TV(GB)
Bowen, J.

Mackenna's Gold
COL (US) 1969 dir. J. Lee Thompson
V
Henry, W.

McKenzie Break, The
UA (GB) 1970 dir. Lamont Johnson
Shelley, S.

Mackintosh Man, The
COL-WAR (GB) 1973 dir. John Huston
V
Bagley, D. *Freedom Trap, The*

Macomber Affair, The
UA (US) 1947 dir. Zoltan Korda
Hemingway, E. *Short Happy Life of Francis Macomber, The*

Mack the Knife
21st CENTURY (US) 1989
dir. Menahem Golan
M
Brecht, B. and Weill, K. *Threepenny Opera, The*
P

McVicar
BW (GB) 1980 dir. Tom Clegg
V
McVicar, J. *McVicar by Himself*
P

Madame Bovary
MGM (US) 1949 dir. Vincente Minnelli
V
BBC (GB) 1975 dir. Rodney Bennett
TVSe(GB)
GOLDWYN (Fr) 1991
dir. Claude Chabrol
Flaubert, G.

Madame Butterfly
PAR (US) 1932 dir. Marion Gering
Belasco, D. & Long, J. L.
P

Madame Curie
MGM (US) 1943 dir. Mervyn Le Roy
Curie, E.

Madame Curie
BBC (GB) 1984
TV(GB)
Reid, R.

Madame De
FRANCO-LONDON (Fr/It) 1953
dir. Max Ophuls
US title: The Earrings of Madame De
deVilmorin, L.

Madame Sans-Gene
FOX (Fr/It/Sp) 1962
dir. Christian-Jaque
US/GB title: Madame
Sardou, V.
P

Madame Sousatzka
UN (GB) 1988 dir. John Schlesinger
V
Rubens, B.

Madame X
MGM (US) 1929 dir. John Barrymore
MGM (US) 1937
dir. James K. McGuiness
UN (US) 1965 dir. David Lowell Rich
V

UN (US) 1981 dir. Robert Ellis Miller
TV(US)
Bisson, A.
P

Madam Kitty
FOX (It/Fr/Ger) 1977
dir. Giovanni Tinto Brass
Norden, P.

Mad Death, The
BBC (GB) 1983 dir. Robert Young
TV(GB)
Slater, N.

Mad Genius, The
WAR (US) 1931 dir. Michael Curtiz
Brown, M. *Idol, The*
P

Madhouse
EMI (GB) 1974 dir. Jim Clark
Hall, A. *Devilday-Madhouse*

Madigan
UI (US) 1968 dir. Don Siegel
V
Dougherty, R. *Commissioner, The*

Madison Avenue
FOX (US) 1962 dir. Bruce Humberstone
Kirk, J. *Build-up Boys, The*

Mad Love
MGM (US) 1935 dir. Karl Freund
GB title: Hands of Orlac, The
Renard, M. *Hands of Orlac, The*

Madness of the Heart
TC (GB) 1949 dir. Charles Bennett
Sandstrom, F.

Madonna of the Seven Moons
GFD (GB) 1944 dir. Arthur Crabtree
Lawrence, M.

Mad Room, The
COL (US) 1969 dir. Bernard Girard
Denham, R. and Percy, E. *Ladies in Retirement*
P

Madwoman of Chaillot, The
WAR (GB) 1969 dir. Bryan Forbes
Girardoux, J.
P

Mafia Princess
GROUP W (US) 1986 dir. Robert Collins
TV(US)
Giancana, A. and Renner, T. C.
P

Magic
FOX (US) 1978
dir. Richard Attenborough
V
Goldman, W.

Magic Bow, The
GFD (GB) 1946 dir. Bernard Knowles
Komroff, M.

Magic Box, The
BL (GB) 1951 dir. John Boulting
V
Allister, R. *Friese-Greene*

Magic Christian, The
COMM (GB) 1969 dir. Joseph McGrath
V
Southern, T.

Magic Fire
REP (US) 1956 dir. William Dieterle
Harding, B.

Magic Flute, The
Swe TV (Swe) 1974
dir. Ingmar Bergman
M, TV(Swe), V
Mozart, W. A.

Magician of Lublin, The
RANK (Israel/Ger) 1979
dir. Menahem Golan
V
Singer, I. B.

Magic Mountain, The
SEITZ (Ger/Fr/It) 1982
dir. Hans Geissendoerfer
Mann, T.

Magic Moments
ATLANTIC/YTV (GB/US)
dir. Lawrence Gordon Clarke
TV(GB/US)
Roberts, N. *This Magic Moment*

Magic Toyshop, The
GRANADA TV (GB) 1987
dir. David Wheatley
TV(GB)
Carter, A.

Magnificent Ambersons, The
RKO (US) 1942 dir. Orson Welles
V
Tarkington, B.

Magnificent Obsession
UN (US) 1935 dir. John M. Stahl
V
UI (US) 1954 dir. Douglas Sirk
V
Douglas, L. C.

Magnificent Yankee, The
MGM (US) 1950 dir. John Sturges
COMPASS (US) 1965
dir. George Schaefer
TV(US)
Lavery, E.
P

Magus, The
FOX (GB) 1968 dir. Guy Green
Fowles, J.

Mahabharata, The
CHANNEL 4 (GB) 1990
dir. Peter Brook
Carrière, J-P.
P

Maids, The
ELY LANDAU (GB) 1974
dir. Christopher Miles
Genet, J.
P

Maigret Sets a Trap
JOLLY (Fr) 1957 dir. Jean Delannoy
Simenon, G.

Mains Sales, Les
RIVERS (Fr) 1951 dir. Fernand Rivers
Sartre, J-P.
P

Major Barbara
PASCAL (GB) 1941 dir. Gabriel Pascal/
Harold French/David Lean
V
Shaw, G. B.
P

Majority of One, A
WAR (US) 1961 dir. Mervyn Le Roy
Spiegelgass, L.
P

Make Haste to Live
REP (US) 1954 dir. William A. Seiter
Gordon, M. and Gordon, G.

Make me an Offer
BL (GB) 1954 dir. Cyril Frankel
Mankowitz, W.

Make me a Star
PAR (US) 1932 dir. William Beaudine
Wilson, H. L. *Merton of the Movies*

Make Mine Mink
RANK (GB) 1960 dir. Robert Asher
Coke, P. *Breath of Spring*
P

Make Way for a Lady
RKO (US) 1936 dir. David Burton
Jordan, E. G. *Daddy and I*

Make Way for Tomorrow
PAR (US) 1937 dir. Leo McCarey
Lawrence, J. *Years Are So Long, The*

Making It
FOX (US) 1971 dir. John Erman
Leigh, J. *What Can You Do?*

Makioka Sisters, The
R5/S8 (Jap) 1985 dir. Kon Ichikawa
Tanizaki, J.

Malachi's Cove
PENRITH (GB) 1973
dir. Henry Herbert
US title: Seaweed Children, The
Trollope, A.

Malarek
SVS/TELESCENE (Can) 1989
dir. Roger Cardinal
Malarek, V. *Hey, Malarek*

Male Animal, The
WAR (US) 1942 dir. Elliot Nugent
Thurber, J. and Nugent, E.
P

Malibu
COL (US) 1983 dir. E. W. Swackhamer
TVSe(US)
Murray, W.

Malice in Wonderland
ITC (US) 1985 dir. Gus Trikonis
TV(US)
Eells, G. *Hedda and Louella*

Mallens, The
GRANADA (GB) 1979
TVSe(GB)
Cookson, C.

Malone
ORION (US) 1987 dir. Harley Kokliss
V
Wingate, W. *Shotgun*

Maltese Falcon, The
WAR (US) 1941 dir. John Huston
V
Hammett, D.

Mambo Kings, The
WAR (US) 1992 dir. Arne Glimcher
Hijeulo, O. *Mambo Kings Play Songs of Love, The*

Mame
WAR (US) 1974 dir. Gene Saks
M, V
Dennis, P. *Auntie Mame*
Lawrence, J., Lee, R. E. and Herman, J.
P

Man, The
PAR (US) 1972 dir. Joseph Sargent
Wallace, I.

Man About the House, A
LF (GB) 1947 dir. Leslie Arliss
Young, F. B. and Perry, J.
P

Man About Town
FOX (US) 1932 dir. John Francis Dillon
Clift, D.

Man and Superman
MILBERG (US) 1956
dir. George Schaefer
TV(US)
Shaw, G. B.
P

Man at the Carlton Tower
AA (GB) 1961 dir. Robert Tronson
Wallace, E. *Man At The Carlton*

Man Called Horse, A
CIN CEN (US) 1970
dir. Elliot Silverstein
V
Johnson, D. M.

Man Called Intrepid, A
LORIMAR (GB) 1979 dir. Peter Carter
TVSe(GB)
Stevenson, W.

Man Called Noon, The
SCOTIA-BARBER (GB/Sp/It) 1973
dir. Peter Collinson
L'Amour, L.

Man Called Peter, A
FOX (US) 1955 dir. Henry Koster
V
Marshall, C.

Manchurian Candidate, The
UA (US) 1962 dir. John Frankenheimer
Condon, R.

Man Could Get Killed, A
UN (US) 1966 dir. Ronald Neame
Walker, D. E. *Diamonds are Danger*

Mandingo
PAR (US) 1975 dir. Richard Fleischer
V
Onstott, K.

Mandy
GFD (GB) 1952
dir. Alexander Mackendrick
US title: Crash of Silence, The
V

Lewis, H. *Day is Ours, This*

Maneaters are Loose!
MONA BBC TV (GB) 1984
dir. Timothy Galfos
TV(GB)

Willis, T. *Man-eater*

Man for all Seasons, A
COL (GB) 1966 dir. Fred Zinnemann
V
AGAMEMNON (US) 1988
dir. Charlton Heston
TV(US)

Bolt, R.
P

Man from Bitter Ridge, The
UN (US) 1955 dir. Jack Arnold

Raine, W. M. *Rawhide Justice*

Man from Dakota, The
MGM (US) 1940 dir. Leslie Fenton
GB title: Arouse and Beware

Kantor, M. *Arouse and Beware*

Man Hunt
FOX (US) 1941 dir. Fritz Lang

Household, G. *Rogue Male*

Manhunt for Claude Dallas
LONDON (US) 1986 dir. Jerry London
TV(US)

Long, J. *Outlaw: The True Story of Claude Dallas*

Manhunter, The
UN (US) 1976 dir. Don Taylor
TV(US)

Miller, W.

Manhunter
CANNON (US) 1986 dir. Michael Mann

Harris, T. *Red Dragon*

Manifesto
CANNON (Yugo) 1988
dir. Dusan Makajevev

Zola, E. *For a Night of Love*

Man I Married, The
TCF (US) 1940 dir. Irving Pichel

Shisgall, O. *Swastika*

Man in Grey, The
GFD (GB) 1943 dir. Leslie Arliss

Smith, Lady E.

Man in Half-Moon Street, The
PAR (US) 1944 dir. Ralph Murphy

Lyndon, B.
P

Man in Possession, The
MGM (US) 1931 dir. Sam Wood

Harwood, H. M.
P

Man Inside, The
COL (GB) 1958 dir. John Gilling

Graber, M. E.

Man in the Attic, The
FOX (US) 1953 dir. Hugo Fregonese

Lowndes, Mrs B. *Lodger, The*

Man in the Brown Suit, The
WAR TV (US) 1989 dir. Alan Grint
TV(US)

Christie, A.

Man in the Grey Flannel Suit, The
FOX (US) 1956 dir. Nunnally Johnson
V

Wilson, S.

Man in the Iron Mask, The
UA (US) 1939 dir. James Whale
ITC (US/GB) 1976 dir. Mike Newell
TV(GB/US), V
Dumas, A.

Man in the Middle
FOX (GB) 1963 dir. Guy Hamilton
Fast, H. *Winston Affair, The*

Man in the Mirror, The
WARDOUR (GB) 1936
dir. Maurice Elvey
Garrett, W.

Man in the Net, The
UA (US) 1958 dir. Michael Curtiz
Quentin, P.

Man in the Road, The
GN (GB) 1956 dir. Lance Comfort
Armstrong, A. *He was Found in the Road*

Manitou
ENT (US) 1978 dir. William Girdler
V
Masterton, G.

Man of Affairs
GAU (GB) 1937 dir. Herbert Mason
US title: *His Lordship*
Grant, N. *Nelson Touch, The*
P

Man of La Mancha
UA (US) 1972 dir. Arthur Hiller
M, V
Wasserman, D.
Cervantes, M. de *Don Quixote*
P

Man of the West
UA (US) 1958 dir. Anthony Mann
Brown, W. C. *Border Jumpers, The*

Man on a String
COL (US) 1960 dir. André de Toth
GB title: Confessions of a Counterspy
Morros, B. *My Ten Years as a Counter-Spy*

Man on Fire
TRI-STAR (It/Fr) 1987
dir. Elie Chouraqui
V
Quinnell, A. J.

Manon of the Spring
ORION (Fr) 1987 dir. Claude Berri
French title: Manon des Sources
V
Pagnol, M. *L'eau des Collines*

Man on the Eiffel Tower, The
BL (US) 1948 dir. Burgess Meredith
V
Simenon, G. *Battle of Nerves, A*

Man on the Roof, The
Svensk Film (Swe) 1976
dir. Bo Widenberg
Sjowall, M. and Wahloo, M. *Abominable Man, The*

Manproof
MGM (US) 1937 dir. Richard Thorpe
Lea, F. H. *Four Marys, The*

Man's Castle
COL (US) 1933 dir. Frank Borzage
Hazard, L.
P

Mansfield Park
BBC (GB) 1986 dir. David Giles
TVSe(GB), V
Austen, J.

Manslaughter
PAR (US) 1930 dir. George Abbott
Miller, A. D.

Man to Remember, A
RKO (US) 1938 dir. Garson Kanin
Haviland-Taylor, K. *Failure*

Mantrap
PAR (US) 1961 dir. Edmond O'Brien
Macdonald, J. P. *Taint of the Tiger*

Manuela
BL (GB) 1957 dir. Guy Hamilton
US title: Stowaway Girl
Woods, W.

Man Who Broke 1,000 Chains, The
JOURNEY (US) 1987 dir. Daniel Mann
TV(US), V
Burns, V. G.

Man Who Came Back, The
FOX (US) 1930 dir. Raoul Walsh
Goodman, J. E.
P

Man Who Came to Dinner, The
WAR (US) 1941 dir. William Keighley
UN (US) 1972 dir. Buzz Kulik
TV(US)
Kaufman, G. S. and Hart, M.
P

Man Who Could Cheat Death, The
PAR (GB) 1959 dir. Terence Fisher
Lyndon, B. *Man in Half-Moon Street, The*
P

Man Who Could Work Miracles, The
UA (GB) 1936 dir. Lothar Mendes
Wells, H. G.

Man Who Fell to Earth, The
BL (GB) 1976 dir. Nicholas Roeg
V
MGM/UA (US) 1987 dir. Robert J. Roth
TV(US)
Tevis, W.

Man Who had Power over Women, The
AVCO (GB) 1970 dir. John Krish
V
Williams, G.

Man Who Lived at The Ritz, The
HG (US) 1988 dir. Desmond Davis
TVSe(US)
Hotchner, A. E.

Man Who Loved Cat Dancing, The
MGM (US) 1973 dir. Richard Sarafian
V
Durham, M.

Man Who Loved Redheads, The
BL (GB) 1954 dir. Harold French
Rattigan, T. *Who is Sylvia?*
P

Man Who Mistook His Wife for a Hat, The
CHANNEL 4 (GB) 1988
dir. Christopher Rawlence
TV(GB)
Sacks, O.

Man Who Never Was, The
FOX (GB) 1955 dir. Ronald Neame
Montague, E. E. S.

Man Who Played God, The
WAR (US) 1932 dir. John G. Adolfi
GB title: Silent Voice, The
Goodman, J. E. *Silent Voice, The*
P

Man Who Understood Women
FOX (US) 1959 dir. Nunnally Johnson
Gary, R. *Colours of the Day, The*

Man Who Watched Trains Go By, The
EROS (GB) 1952 dir. Harold French
Simenon, G.

Man Who Would Be King, The
COL (US) 1975 dir. John Huston
V
Kipling, R.

Man with Bogart's Face, The
FOX (US) 1980 dir. Robert Day
V
Fenady, A. J.

Man Within, The
GFD (GB) 1947 dir. Bernard Knowles
US title: Smugglers, The
Greene, G.

Man with my Face, The
UA (US) 1951 dir. Edward J. Montague
Taylor, S. W.

Man Without A Country, The
ROSEMONT (US) 1973
dir. Delbert Mann
TV(US)
Hale, E. E.

Man Without A Star, The
UI (US) 1955 dir. King Vidor
V
Linford, D.

Man with the Golden Arm, The
UA (US) 1955 dir. Otto Preminger
V
Algren, N.

Man with the Golden Gun, The
UA (GB) 1974 dir. Guy Hamilton
V
Fleming, I.

Man with the Twisted Lip, The
GN (GB) 1951 dir. Richard M. Grey
Doyle, Sir A. C.

Man with Three Coffins, The
MWL (Kor) 1987 dir. Chang Ho Lee
Lee, J. *Wanderer Never Sleeps, Even on the Road, A*

Man With Two Faces, The
WAR (US) 1934 dir. Archie Mayo
Kaufman, G. S., and Woollcott, A. *Dark Tower, The*
P

Man, Woman and Child
PAR (US) 1983 dir. Dick Richards
V
Segal, E.

Mapp and Lucia
CHANNEL 4 (GB) 1985
dir. Donald McWhinnie
TVSe(GB)
Benson, E. F.
P

Maracaibo
PAR (US) 1958 dir. Cornel Wilde
Silliphant, S.

Marathon Man
PAR (US) 1976 dir. John Schlesinger
V
Goldman, W.

Marat/Sade
UA (GB) 1966 dir. Peter Brook
Weiss, P.
P

Marauders, The
MGM (US) 1955 dir. Gerald Mayer
Marcus, A.

Marcus-Nelson Murders, The
UN TV (US) 1973 dir. Joseph Sargent
TV(US)
Raab, S. *Justice in the Back Room*

Margaret Bourke-White
TNT (US) 1989 dir. Lawrence Schiller
TV(US)
Goldberg, V.

Margin for Error
FOX (US) 1943 dir. Otto Preminger
Boothe, C.
P

Maria Chapdelaine
ASTRAL (Fr) 1935 dir. Julien Duvivier
Canada (US) 1986 dir. Gilles Carle
Hemon, L.

Marie
MGM/UA (US) 1985
dir. Roger Donaldson
V
Maas, P. *Marie: A True Story*

Marie Antoinette
MGM (US) 1938 dir. W. S. Van Dyke
Zweig, S.

Marilyn: The Untold Story
SCHILLER (US) 1980 dir. Jack Arnold
TVSe(US)
Mailer, N. *Marilyn*

Marius
PAR (Fr) 1931 dir. Alexander Korda
V
Pagnol, M.
P

Marjorie Morningstar
WAR (US) 1958 dir. Irving Rapper
Wouk, H.

Mark, The
FOX (GB) 1961 dir. Guy Green
V
Israel, C. E.

Mark, I Love You
AUBREY (US) 1980
dir. Gunna Hellstrom
TV(US)
Painter, H. W.

Mark of Cain, The
TC (GB) 1948 dir. Brian Desmond Hurst
Shearing, J. *Airing in a Closed Carriage*

Mark of the Renegade
UI (US) 1951 dir. Hugo Fregonese
FOX (US) 1974 dir. Don McDougall
TV(US)
McCulley, J. *Curse of Capistrano, The*

Mark of Zorro, The
FOX (US) 1940 dir. Rouben Mamoulian
V
McCulley, J. *Curse of Capistrano, The*

Marlowe
MGM (US) 1969 dir. Paul Bogart
Chandler, R. *Little Sister, The*

Marnie
UI (US) 1964 dir. Alfred Hitchcock
V
Graham, W.

Marooned
COL (US) 1969 dir. John Sturges
V
Caidin, M.

Marriage is a Private Affair
MGM (US) 1944 dir. Robert Z. Leonard
Kelly, J.

Marriage of a Young Stockbroker, The
FOX (US) 1971 dir. Laurence Turman
Webb, C.

Marriage of Figaro, The
BBC (GB) 1990 dir. D. Bailey
M, TV(GB)
Beaumarchais, P. A. C. de
P
Mozart, W. A.

Marriage Playground, The
PAR (US) 1929 dir. Lothar Mendes
Wharton, E. *Children, The*

Married Man, A
LWT (GB) 1985 dir. Charles B. Jarrott
TVSe(GB)
Read, P. P.

Marry the Girl
WAR (US) 1937 dir. William McGann
Hope, E.

Martian Chronicles, The
NBC ENT (US/GB) 1980
dir. Michael Anderson
TVSe(GB/US), V
Bradbury, R.

Martians Go Home
TAURUS (US) 1990 dir. David Odell
Brown, F.

Marty
COL (US) 1955 dir. Delbert Mann
V
Chayefsky, P.
P

Marvin and Tige
CASTLE HILL (US) 1985
dir. Eric Weston
V
Glass, F.

Mary, Mary
WAR (US) 1963 dir. Mervyn Le Roy
Kerr, J.
P

Mary of Scotland
RKO (US) 1936 dir. John Ford
Anderson, M.
P

Mary Poppins
DISNEY (US) 1964
dir. Robert Stevenson
Ch, M, V
Travers, P. L.

Masada
UN TV (US) 1981 dir. Boris Sagal
GB title: Antagonists, The
TVSe(US), V
Gann, E. K. *Antagonists, The*

Maschenka
CLASART (GB) 1987
dir. John Goldschmidt
TVSe(GB)
Nabokov, V.

M*A*S*H
FOX (US) 1970 dir. Robert Altman
TVSe(US), V
Hooker, R. *MASH*

Mask of Dimitrios, The
WAR (US) 1944 dir. Jean Negulesco
Ambler, E.

Mask of Fu Manchu
MGM (US) 1932 dir. Charles Brabin,
Charles Vidor
Rohmer, S.

Masque of the Red Death, The
AA (GB) 1964 dir. Roger Corman
V
CONCORDE (US) 1989
dir. Larry Brand
Poe, E. A.

Masquerade
UA (GB) 1965 dir. Basil Dearden
Canning, V. *Castle Minerva*

Masquerader, The
GOLDWYN (US) 1933
dir. Richard Wallace
Thurston, K. C.

Massacre in Rome
GN (Fr/It) 1973
dir. George Pan Cosmatos
V
Katz, R. *Death in Rome*

Mass Appeal
UN (US) 1984 dir. Glenn Jordan
V
Davis, B. C.
P

Master of Ballantrae, The
WAR (US) 1953 dir. William Keighley
COL (US/GB) 1983 dir. Douglas Hickox
TVSe(GB/US)
Stevenson, R. L.

Master of Bankdam
ALL (GB) 1947 dir. Walter Forde
Armstrong, T. *Crowthers of Bankdam, The*

Master of the Game
ROSEMONT (US/GB) 1984
dir. Kevin Connor/Harvey Hart
TVSe(GB/US), V
Sheldon, S.

Master of the World
AA (US) 1961 dir. William Witney
V
Verne, J.

Matchmaker, The
PAR (US) 1958 dir. Joseph Anthony
Wilder, T.
P

Matilda
AIP (US) 1978 dir. Daniel Mann
V
Gallico, P.

Mating Game, The
MGM (US) 1959 dir. George Marshall
Bates, H. E. *Darling Buds of May, The*

Matter of Time, A
AIP (US/It) 1976 dir. Vincente Minnelli
V
Druon, M. *Film of Memory, The*

Matters of the Heart
MCA TV (US) 1990 dir. Michael Rhodes
TV(US)
Wersba, B. *Country of the Heart, The*

Matt Helm
COL TV (US) 1975 dir. Buzz Kulik
TV(US)
Hamilton, D.

Maurice
MI (GB) 1987 dir. James Ivory
V
Forster, E. M.

Maverick Queen, The
REP (US) 1956 dir. Joe Kane
V
Grey, Z.

Max and Helen
TNT (US) 1990 dir. Philip Saville
TV(US)
Wiesenthal, S. *Max and Helen: A Remarkable True Love Story*

Maxie
ORION (US) 1985 dir. Paul Aaron
V
Finney, J. *Marion's Wall*

Mayday at 40,000 Feet
WAR (US) 1976 dir. Robert Butler
TV(US)
Ferguson, A. *Jet Stream*

Mayerling
NERO (Fr) 1935 dir. Anatole Litvak
WAR (Fr/GB) 1968 dir. Terence Young
Anet, C.

May we Borrow Your Husband?
ITV (GB) 1986 dir. Bob Mahoney
TV(GB)
Greene, G.

Mazes and Monsters
P&G (US) 1982
dir. Steven Hilliard Stern
TV(US)
Jaffe, R.

Me and Him
NC/COL (Ger) 1989 dir. Doris Dorrie
Moravia, A. *Io e Lui*

Me and The Colonel
COL (US) 1958 dir. Peter Glenville
V
Werfel, F. *Jacobowsky and the Colonel*
P

Me and the Girls
BBC (GB) 1985 dir. Jack Gold
TV(GB), V
Coward, N.

Meanest Man in the World, The
FOX (US) 1943 dir. Sidney Lanfield
Cohan, G. M.
P

Mean Season, The
ORION (US) 1985 dir. Philip Borsos
V
Katzenbach, J. *In the Heat of the Summer*

Medal for the General, A
BN (GB) 1944 dir. Maurice Elvey
Ronald, J.

Medea
JANUS (It/Fr/Ger) 1970
dir. Pier Paolo Pasolini
V
Euripides
P

Medusa Touch, The
ITC (GB/Fr) 1978 dir. Jack Gold
V
Van Greenaway, P.

Meetings with Remarkable Men
ENT (GB) 1979 dir. Peter Brook
V
Gurdjieff, G. I.

Meet Me at the Fair
UN (US) 1952 dir. Douglas Sirk
Markey, G. *Great Companions, The*

Meet Me in St Louis
MGM (US) 1944 dir. Vincente Minnelli
M, V
Benson, Mrs. S.

Meet Me Tonight
GFD (GB) 1952 dir. Anthony Pelissier
Coward, N. *Red Peppers; Fumed Oak; Ways & Means*
P

Meet Mr Callaghan
EROS (GB) 1954 dir. Charles Saunders
Cheyney, P. *Urgent Hangman, The*

Meet Mr Lucifer
GFD (GB) 1953 dir. Anthony Pelissier
Ridley, A. *Beggar My Neighbour*
P

Meet Nero Wolfe
COL (US) 1936 dir. Herbert Biberman
Stout, R. *Fer de Lance*

Mélo
MK2 (Fr) 1986 dir. Alain Resnais
Bernstein, H.
P

Melody Lingers On, The
IN (US) 1935 dir. David Burton
Brentano, L.

Member of the Wedding, The
COL (US) 1952 dir. Fred Zinnemann
McCullers, C.

Memed my Hawk
EMI (GB) 1984 dir. Peter Ustinov
V
Kemal, Y.

Memoirs of a French Whore
Aidart (Fr) 1982 dir. Daniel Duval
Cordelier, J. *Life, The*

Memoirs of an Invisible Man
WARNER BROS. (US) 1992
dir. John Carpenter
Saint, H. F.

Memoirs of a Survivor
EMI (GB) 1981 dir. David Gladwell
V
Lessing, D.

Memories of Prison
REGINA (Port) 1989
dir. Nelson Pereira Dos Santos
Ramos, G.

Memories Never Die
UN TV (US) 1982 dir. Sandor Stern
TV(US)
Sherburne, Z. *Stranger in the House*

Memory of Eva Ryker, The
IRWIN ALLEN PRODS (US) 1980
dir. Walter Grauman
TV(US)
Stanwood, D. A.

Memphis
PROPAGANDA FILMS TV(US) 1992
dir. Yves Simoneau
TV(US)
Foote, S. *September, September*

Menace, The
COL (US) 1932 dir. Roy William Neill
Wallace, E. *Feathered Serpent*

Menace on the Mountain
DISNEY (US) 1970
dir. Vincent McEveety
V

Hancock, M. A.

Men Are Like That
PAR (US) 1930 dir. Frank Tuttle
Kelly, G. *Show-off, The*
P

Men are Such Fools
WAR (US) 1938 dir. Busby Berkeley
Baldwin, F.

Men in her Life
COL (US) 1941 dir. Gregory Ratoff
Smith, Lady E. *Ballerina*

Men in War
UA (US) 1957 dir. Anthony Mann
V

Praag, V. V. *Combat*

Men in White
MGM (US) 1934
dir. Richard Boleslawsky
Kingsley, S.
P

Men of Tomorrow
PAR (GB) 1932 dir. Leontine Sagan
Gibbs, A. H. *Young Apollo*
P

Men's Club, The
ATLANTIC (US) 1986 dir. Peter Medak
V

Michaels, L.

Menu for Murder
VON ZERNECK/SERTNER (US) 1990
dir. Larry Peerce
TV(US)
Wolzien, V.

Mephisto
MAFILM (Hun) 1981 dir. Istvan Szabo
Mann, K.

Mephisto Waltz, The
FOX (US) 1971 dir. Paul Wendkos
V

Stewart, F.

Mercenaries, The
MGM (GB) 1968 dir. Jack Cardiff
US title: Dark of the Sun
Smith, W. *Dark of the Sun*

Merchant of Venice, The
ATV (GB) 1974 dir. Jonathan Miller
TV(GB), V
Shakespeare, W.
P

Mermaids
ORION (US) 1990
dir. Richard Benjamin
V

Dann, P.

Merrill's Marauders
WAR (US) 1962 dir. Samuel Fuller
Ogburn, C. *Marauders, The*

Merry Christmas, Mr. Lawrence
UN (GB) 1983 dir. Nagisa Oshima
V

Post, Sir L. van der *Seed and the Sower, The*

Merry Widow, The
MGM (US) 1934 dir. Ernst Lubitsch
M
MGM (US) 1952 dir. Curtis Bernhardt
M
Lehar, F., Leon, V. and Stein, L.

Merton of the Movies
MGM (US) 1947 dir. Robert Alton
Wilson, H. L.

Message to Garcia, A
FOX (US) 1936 dir. George Marshall

Hubbard, E. and Rowan, A. S.

Messenger of Death
CANNON (US) 1988
dir. J. Lee Thompson

Burns, R. *Avenging Angels, The*

Mexican Hayride
UN (US) 1948 dir. Charles Barton

Fields, H. and Fields, D.
P

Miami Blues
ORION (US) 1990 dir. George Armitage
V

Willeford, C.

Michael and Mary
UN (GB) 1931 dir. Victor Saville

Milne, A. A.
P

Michael Kohlhaas
COL (Ger) 1980 dir. Volker Schlondorff

von Kleist, H.

Middle of the Night
COL (US) 1959 dir. Delbert Mann

Chayefsky, P.
P

Middle Watch
BI (GB) 1930 dir. Norman Walker
AB (GB) 1940 dir. Thomas Bentley

Hay, I. and Hall, S. K.
P

Midnight Cowboy
UA (US) 1969 dir. John Schlesinger

Herlihy, J. L.

Midnight Episode
COL (GB) 1950 dir. Gordon Parry

Simenon, G. *Monsieur La Souris*

Midnight Express
COL (GB) 1978 dir. Alan Parker
V

Hayes, B. and Hoffer, W.

Midnight Lace
UN (US) 1960 dir. David Miller
V
UN TV (US) 1981 dir. Ivan Nagy
TV(US)

Green, L. *Mathilda Shouted Fire*
P

Midnight Man, The
UN (US) 1974 dir. Roland Kibbee

Anthony, D. *Midnight Lady and the Mourning Man*

Midshipmaid, The
GB (GB) 1932 dir. Albert de Courville

Hay, I. and Hall, S. K.
P

Midshipman Easy
ATP (GB) 1935 dir. Carol Reed
US title: Men of the Sea

Marryat, F. *Mr. Midshipman Easy*

Midsummer Night's Dream, A
WAR (US) 1935 dir. Max Reinhardt
V
ITV (GB) 1964 dir. Joan Kemp-Welch
TV(GB)
COL (US) 1967 dir. Dan Eriksen
EAGLE (GB) 1968 dir. Peter Hall
V
MAINLINE (GB/Sp) 1985
dir. Celestino Corrado
V

Shakespeare, W.
P

Mighty Barnum, The
FOX (US) 1934 dir. Walter Lang

Fowler, G. and Meredyth, B.
P

Mighty Quinn, The
MGM (US) 1989 dir. Carl Schenkel
Carr, A. H. Z. *Finding Maubee*

Mikado, The
UN (GB) 1939 dir. Victor Scheitzinger
M, V
Gilbert, Sir W. S.; Sullivan, Sir A.
P

Milagro Beanfield War, The
UN (US) 1988 dir. Robert Redford
V
Nichols, J.

Mildred Pierce
WAR (US) 1945 dir. Michael Curtiz
V
Cain, J. M.

Millenium
FOX (US) 1989 dir. Michael Anderson
Varley, J. *Air Raid*

Millionairess, The
FOX (GB) 1960 dir. Anthony Asquith
Shaw, G. B.
P

Million Dollar Face, The
NEPHI-HAMNER (US) 1981
dir. Michael O'Herlihy
TV(US)
Wyse, L. *Kiss, Inc.*

Million Pound Note, The
GFD (GB) 1954 dir. Ronald Neame
US title: Man with a Million
V
Twain, M.

Mill on the Floss, The
STANDARD (GB) 1937 dir. Tim Whelan
V
Eliot, G.

Mill on the Po, The
LUX (It) 1949 dir. Alberto Lattuardo
Bacchelli, R.

Min and Bill
MGM (US) 1930 dir. George Hill
V
Moon, L. *Dark Star*

Mind of Mr. Reeder, The
RAYMOND (GB) 1936
dir. Jack Raymond
ITV (GB) 1969
TV(GB)
Wallace, E. *Mind of Mr J. G. Reeder, The*

Mind of Mr. Soames, The
COL (GB) 1970 dir. Alan Cooke
Maine, C. E.

Mind Reader, The
WAR (US) 1933 dir. Roy del Ruth
Cosby, V.

Mindwalk
ATLAS (US) 1991 dir. Bernt Capra
Capra, F. *Turning Point, The*

Mine Own Executioner
BI (GB) 1947 dir. Anthony Kimmins
V
Balchin, N.

Ministry of Fear
PAR (US) 1944 dir. Fritz Lang
Greene, G.

Miracle, The
WAR (US) 1959 dir. Irving Rapper
Vollmoeller, K.
P

Miracle in Milan
PDS (It) 1951 dir. Vittorio de Sica
V
Zavattini, C. *Toto il Buono*

Miracle in the Rain
WAR (US) 1956 dir. Rudolph Maté
Hecht, B.

Miracle Man, The
PAR (US) 1932 dir. Norman Z. McLeod
Packard, F. L.
P

Miracle of the Bells
PAR (US) 1948 dir. Irving Rapper
V
Janney, R.

Miracle of the White Stallions, The
DISNEY (US) 1963 dir. Arthur Hiller
GB title: Flight of the White Stallions, The
Podhajsky, A. *Dancing White Horses of Vienna, The*

Miracle on 34th Street
FOX (US) 1947 dir. George Seaton
GB title: Big Heart, The
V
TCF (US) 1973 dir. Fielder Cook
TV(US)
Davies, V.

Miracles for Sale
MGM (US) 1939 dir. Tod Browning
Rawson, C. *Death in a Top Hat*

Miracle Woman, The
COL (US) 1932 dir. Frank Capra
Riskin, R. and Meehan, J. *Bless You Sister*
P

Miracle Worker, The
UA (US) 1962 dir. Arthur Penn
V
KATZ-GALLIN (US) 1979 dir. Paul Aaron
TV(US), V
Gibson, W.
P

Mirage
UI (US) 1965 dir. Edward Dmytryk
V
Ericson, W.

Miranda
GFD (GB) 1947 dir. Ken Annakin
Blackmore, P.
P

Mirror Crack'd, The
EMI (GB) 1980 dir. Guy Hamilton
V
Christie, A. *Mirror Crack'd from Side to Side, The*

Mirrors
L. HILL (US) 1985 dir. Harry Winer
TV(US)
Lipton, J.

Misadventures of Mr. Wilt, The
GOLDWYN (US) 1990 dir. Michael Tuchner
Sharpe, T. *Wilt*

Misery
COL (US) 1990 dir. Rob Reiner
V
King, S.

Misfit Brigade, The
TRANSWORLD (US) 1988 dir. Gordon Hessler
Hassel, S. *Wheels of Terror*

Mishima
WAR (US) 1985 dir. Paul Schrader
V

Mishima, Y. *Runaway Horses; Temple of the Golden Pavilion*

Miss Firecracker
CORSAIR (US) 1989
dir. Thomas Schlammer
V

Henley, B. *Miss Firecracker Contest*
P

Missing
UN (US) 1982 dir. Costa-Gavras
V

Hauser, T. *Execution of Charles Horman, The*

Missing Pieces
TTC (US) 1983 dir. Mike Hodges
TV(US)
Alexander, K. *Private Investigation, A*

Mission of Danger
MGM (US) 1959 dir. George Waggner, Jacques Tourneur
Roberts, K. *Northwest Passage*

Mission to Moscow
WAR (US) 1943 dir. Michael Curtiz
Davies, J. E.

Miss Julie
LF (Swe) 1950 dir. Alf Sjoberg
TIGON (GB) 1972
dir. Robin Phillips & John Glenister
V

Strindberg, J. A.
P

Miss Sadie Thompson
COL (US) 1953 dir. Curtis Bernhardt
V

Maugham, W. S. *Rain*

Miss Susie Slagle's
PAR (US) 1946 dir. John Berry
Tucker, A.

Mister Buddwing
MGM (US) 1966 dir. Delbert Mann
GB title: Woman Without a Face
Hunter, E. *Buddwing*

Misterioso
BBC (GB) 1991 dir. John Glenister
TV(GB)
Plater, A.

Mistero Buffo
BBC (GB) 1990 dir. Don Coutts
TV(GB)
Fo, D.
P

Mister Quilp
EMI (GB) 1975 dir. Elliot Scott
Dickens, C. *Old Curiosity Shop, The*

Mister Roberts
WAR (US) 1955 dir. John Ford, Mervyn Le Roy
V

Heggen, T.

Mistral's Daughter
KRANTZ (Fr/Lux/US) 1986
dir. David Hickox, Kevin Connor
TVSe(Fr/Lux/US), V
Krantz, J.

Mistress Pamela
MGM-EMI (GB) 1973
dir. Jim O'Connolly
V

Richardson, S. *Pamela*

Misty
FOX (US) 1961 dir. James B. Clark
Henry, M. *Misty of Chincoteague*

Misunderstood
MGM/UA (US) 1984
dir. Jerry Schatzberg
V

Montgomery, F.

Mix me a Person
BL (GB) 1962 dir. Leslie Norman

Story, J. T.

Moby Dick
WAR (US) 1930 dir. Lloyd Bacon
WAR (GB) 1956 dir. John Huston
V

Melville, H.

Moderato Cantabile
R. J. LEVY (Fr/It) 1960 dir. Peter Brook

Duras, M.

Modern Hero, A
WAR (US) 1934 dir. G. W. Pabst

Bromfield, L.

Mog
LWT (GB) 1985 dir. Nic Phillips
TVSe(GB)

Tinniswood, P.

Mogambo
MGM (US) 1953 dir. John Ford
V

Collison, W. *Farewell to Women*
P

Molly Maguires, The
PAR (US) 1970 dir. Martin Ritt
V

Lewis, A. H. *Lament for Molly Maguires*

Moment of Danger
ABP (GB) 1960 dir. Laslo Benedek

MacKenzie, D.

Mom for Christmas, A
DISNEY (US) 1990 dir. George Miller
TV(US)

Dillon, B. *Mom by Magic, A*

Mommie Dearest
PAR (US) 1981 dir. Frank Perry
V

Crawford, C.

Mom, the Wolfman, and Me
TIME-LIFE (US) 1980
dir. Edmond A. Levy
TV(US)

Klein, N.

Moneychangers, The
PAR TV (US) 1976 dir. Boris Sagal
TVSe(US)

Hailey, A.

Money from Home
PAR (US) 1953 dir. George Marshall

Runyon, D.

Money, Power, Murder
CBS ENT (US) 1989 dir. Lee Philips
TV(US)

Lupica, M. *Dead Air*

Money Trap, The
MGM (US) 1966 dir. Burt Kennedy

White, L.

Mongo's Back in Town
CBS ENT (US) 1971
dir. Marvin J. Chomsky
TV(US)

Johnson, E. R.

Monkey Grip
PAV (Aust) 1982 dir. Ken Cameron
V

Garner, H.

Monkey House
ATLANTIS (US) 1991 dir. Paul Shapiro,
Gilbert Shilton, Allan King
TV(US)
Vonnegut, K. *Next Door; Euphio
Question, The; All the King's Men*

Monkey in Winter, A
CIPRA (Fr) 1962 dir. Henri Verneuil
Blondin, A.

Monkey on my Back
UA (US) 1957 dir. André de Toth
Brown, W.

Monkeys, Go Home!
DISNEY (US) 1967
dir. Andrew V. McLaglen
Wilkinson, G. R. *Monkeys, The*

Monkey Shines
ORION (US) 1988
dir. George A. Romero
V
Stewart, M.

Monocled Mutineer, The
BBC (GB) 1986
TVSe(GB)
Allison, W. and Fairley, J.

Monsieur Beaucaire
PAR (US) 1946 dir. George Marshall
Tarkington, B.

Monsieur Hire
ORION (Fr) 1989 dir. Patrice Leconte
Simenon, G. *Les fiancailles de M. Hire*

Monsignor
FOX (US) 1982 dir. Frank Perry
V
Leger, J. A. *Monsignore*

Monte Carlo
PAR (US) 1930 dir. Ernst Lubitsch
Tarkington, B. *Monsieur Beaucaire*

Monte Carlo
HIGHGATE (US) 1986
dir. Anthony Page
TVSe(US)
Sheppard, S.

Monte Walsh
CIN CEN (US) 1970
dir. William A. Fraker
V
Schaefer, J.

Month in the Country, A
EUSTON (GB) 1987 dir. Pat O'Connor
V
Carr, J. L.

Month in the Country, A
ITV (GB) 1955 dir. Robert Hamer
TV(GB)
BBC (GB) 1955 dir. Bill Hays
TV(GB)
PAR (US) 1985 dir. Quentin Lawrence
Turgenev, A.
P

Moon and Sixpence, The
UA (US) 1942 dir. Albert Lewin
Maugham, W. S.

Mooncussers, The
DISNEY (US) 1971 dir. James Neilson
V
Vinton, I. *Flying Ebony*

Moondial
BBC (GB) 1988
Ch, TVSe(GB)
Cresswell, H.

Moonfleet
MGM (US) 1955 dir. Fritz Lang
Faulkner, J. M.

Moon is Blue, The
UA (US) 1953 dir. Otto Preminger
V

Herbert, F. H.
P

Moon is Down, The
FOX (US) 1943 dir. Irving Pichel
Steinbeck, J.

Moon of the Wolf
FILMWAYS (US) 1972 dir. Daniel Petrie
TV(US)
Whitten, L. H.

Moonraker
UA (GB) 1979 dir. Lewis Gilbert
V

Fleming, I.

Moonraker, The
ABP (GB) 1958 dir. David MacDonald
Watkyn, A.
P

Moonshine War, The
MGM (US) 1970 dir. Richard Quine
Leonard, E.

Moon's Our Home, The
PAR (US) 1936 dir. William A. Seiter
V

Baldwin, F.

Moon-Spinners, The
DISNEY (GB) 1964 dir. James Neilson
V

Stewart, M.

Moontide
FOX (US) 1942 dir. Archie Mayo
Robertson, W.

Morals of Marcus, The
GB (GB) 1935 dir. Miles Mander

Locke, W. J. *Morals of Marcus Ordeyne, The*

Morgan — A Suitable Case for Treatment
BL (GB) 1966 dir. Karel Reisz
V

Mercer, D.
P

Morning After, The
WOLPER (US) 1974
dir. Richard T. Heffron
TV(US)
Weiner, J. B.

Morning Departure
GFD (GB) 1950 dir. Roy Baker
US title: Operation Disaster
Woollard, K.
P

Morning Glory
RKO (US) 1933 dir. Lowell Sherman
V

Akins, Z.
P

Morocco
PAR (US) 1930 dir. Josef von Sternberg
V

Vigny, B. *Amy Jolly*
P

Mortal Storm, The
MGM (US) 1940 dir. Frank Borzage
Bottome, P.

Moscow Nights
LF (GB) 1935 dir. Anthony Asquith
Benoit, P.

Mosquito Coast, The
WAR (US) 1986 dir. Peter Weir
V
Theroux, P.

Most Dangerous Man in the World, The
RANK (GB) 1969 dir. J. Lee Thompson
US title: Chairman, The
Kennedy, J. R. *The Chairman*

Mother Carey's Chickens
RKO (US) 1938 dir. Rowland V. Lee
Wiggin, K. D.

Mother Courage
ITV (GB) 1959
TV(GB)
Brecht, B.
P

Mother Didn't Tell Me
FOX (US) 1950 dir. Claude Binyon
Bard, M. *Doctor Wears Three Faces, The*

Mother Love
BBC (GB) 1989 dir. Simon Langton
TVSe(GB)
Taylor, D.

Mother Wore Tights
FOX (US) 1947 dir. Walter Lang
Young, M.

Moulin Rouge
FOX (US) 1934 dir. Sidney Lanfield
de Bri, L.
P

Moulin Rouge
UA (GB) 1952 dir. John Huston
V
La Mure, P.

Mountain, The
PAR (US) 1956 dir. Edward Dmytryk
Troyat, H.

Mountain Road, The
COL (US) 1960 dir. Delbert Mann
White, T. H.

Mountains of the Moon
TRI-STAR (US) 1990 dir. Bob Rafaelson
Harrison, W. *Burton and Speke*

Mourning Becomes Electra
RKO (US) 1947 dir. Dudley Nichols
O'Neill, E. G.
P

Mouse and the Child, The
SANRIO (US) 1978 dir. Fred Wolf,
Chuck Swenson
GB title: Extraordinary Adventures of
the Mouse and the Child, The
A, V
Hoban, R.

Mouse and the Woman, The
FACELIFT (GB) 1981 dir. Karl Francis
V
Thomas, D.

Mouse that Roared, The
COL (GB) 1959 dir. Jack Arnold
V
Wibberly, L.

Move
FOX (US) 1970 dir. Stuart Rosenberg
Lieber, J.

Moving Finger, The
BBC (GB) 1984 dir. Roy Boulting
TV(GB)
Christie, A.

Moving Targets
ACADEMY (Aust) 1987
dir. Chris Langman
V

Leopold, K. *When we Ran*

Moviola: The Scarlett O'Hara Wars
WAR TV (US) 1980 dir. John Erman
TV(US)

Kanin, G. *Moviola*

Moviola: The Silent Lovers
WAR TV (US) 1980 dir. John Erman
TV(US)

Kanin, G. *Moviola*

Moviola: This Year's Blonde
WAR TV (US) 1980 dir. John Erman
TV(US)

Kanin, G. *Moviola*

Mr. and Mrs. Bo Jo Jones
FOX TV (US) 1971 dir. Robert Day
TV(US)

Head, A.

Mr. and Mrs. Bridge
MIRAMAX (US) 1990 dir. James Ivory

Connell, E. S. *Mr Bridge; Mrs. Bridge*

Mr and Mrs. Edgehill
BBC (GB) 1985 dir. Gavin Miller
TV(GB), V

Coward, N.

Mr. and Mrs. North
MGM (US) 1941 dir. Robert B. Sinclair

Davis, O.
P

Mr. Belvedere Rings the Bell
FOX (US) 1951 dir. Henry Koster

McEnroe, R. E. *Silver Whistle, The*
P

Mr. Blandings Builds his Dream House
RKO (US) 1948 dir. H. C. Potter
V

Hodgins, E.

Mr. Deeds Goes to Town
COL (US) 1936 dir. Frank Capra

Kelland, C. B. *Opera Hat*

Mr. Denning Drives North
BL (GB) 1951 dir. Anthony Kimmins

Coppel, A.

Mr. Emmanuel
TC (GB) 1944 dir. Harold French
V

Golding, L.

Mr. Forbush and the Penguins
BL (GB) 1971 dir. Roy Boulting, Arne Sacksdorff

Billing, G.

Mr. Johnson
AVENUE (Aust) 1990
dir. Bruce Beresford

Carey, J.

Mr. Hobbs takes a Vacation
FOX (US) 1962 dir. Henry Koster
V

Streeter, E. *Hobbs' Vacation*

Mr. Moses
UA (GB) 1965 dir. Ronald Neame

Catto, M. *Mister Moses*

Mr. North
GOLDWYN (US) 1988
dir. Danny Huston
V

Wilder, T. *Theophilus North*

Mr. Peabody and the Mermaid
UN (US) 1948 dir. Irving Pichel
V

Jones, G. P. and Jones, C. B.
Peabody's Mermaid

Mr. Perrin and Mr. Traill
TC (GB) 1948 dir. Lawrence Huntington
Walpole, H.

Mr. Pye
CHANNEL 4 (GB) 1986
TVSe(GB)
Peake, M.

Mr. Skeffington
WAR (US) 1944 dir. Vincent Sherman
V
'Elizabeth'

Mr. Smith Goes To Washington
COL (US) 1939 dir. Frank Capra
V

Foster, L. R. *Gentleman From Montana, The*

Mr. Topaze
FOX (GB) 1961 dir. Peter Sellers
US title: I Like Money
Pagnol, M. *Topaze*
P

Mr. Winkle Goes to War
COL (US) 1944 dir. Alfred E. Green
GB title: Arms and the Woman
V
Pratt, T.

Mrs. Capper's Birthday
BBC (GB) 1985 dir. Mike Ockrent
TV(GB), V
Coward, N.

Mrs. Gibbons' Boys
BL (GB) 1962 dir. Max Varnel
Glickman, W. and Stein, J.
P

Mrs. Mike
UA (US) 1950 dir. Louis King
Freedman, B. and Freedman, N.

Mrs. Miniver
MGM (US) 1942 dir. William Wyler
Struther, J.

Mrs. Parkington
MGM (US) 1944 dir. Tom Garnett
Bromfield, L.

Mrs. Pollifax – Spy
UA (US) 1971 dir. Leslie Martinson
Gilman, D. *Unexpected Mrs. Pollifax, The*

Mrs. Pym of Scotland Yard
GN (GB) 1939 dir. Fred Elles
Morland, N.

Mrs. Wiggs of the Cabbage Patch
PAR (US) 1934 dir. Norman Taurog
PAR (US) 1942 dir. Ralph Murphy
Rice, A. H. and Flexner, A. C.

Mudlark, The
FOX (GB) 1950 dir. Jean Negulesco
Bonnet, T.

Muggable Mary: Street Cop
CBS ENT (US) 1982 dir. Sandor Stern
TV(US)
Glatzle, M.; Fiore, E. *Muggable Mary*

Murder
BI (GB) 1930 dir. Alfred Hitchcock
V
Dane, C. and Simpson, H. *Enter, Sir John*

Murder at the Gallop
MGM (GB) 1963 dir. George Pollock
Christie, A. *After the Funeral*

Murder at the Vicarage
BBC (GB) 1986 dir. Julian Amyes
TV(GB)
Christie, A.

Murder by the Book
ORION TV (US) 1987 dir. Mel Damski
TV(US)
Arrighi, M. *Alter Ego*

Murder by Proxy
EXCL (GB) 1955 dir. Terence Fisher
US title: Blackout
Nielson, H.

Murder C.O.D.
KUSHNER-LOCKE (US) 1990
dir. Alan Metzger
TV(US)
Paulsen, G. *Kill Fee*

Murderer's Row
BL (US) 1966 dir. Henry Levin
V
Hamilton, D.

Murder goes to College
PAR (US) 1937 dir. Charles Reisner
Steele, K.

Murder, Inc.
FOX (US) 1960 dir. Burt Balaban,
Stuart Rosenberg
Turkus, B. and Feder, S.

Murder in Coweta County
TELECOM (US) 1983 dir. Gary Nelson
TV(US)
Barnes, M. A.

Murder in Eden
BBC (GB) 1991 dir. Nicholas Renton
TV(GB)
McGinley, P. *Bogmail*

Murder in Texas
D. CLARK (US) 1981 dir. Billy Hale
TVSe(US), V
Kurth, A. *Prescription: Murder*

Murder in the Cathedral
FILM TRADERS (GB) 1951
dir. George Hoellering
Eliot, T. S.
P

Murder in the Family
FOX (GB) 1938 dir. Al Parker
Ronald, J.

Murder in Three Acts
WAR TV (US) 1986 dir. Gary Nelson
TV(US)
Christie, A.

Murder in Trinidad
FOX (US) 1934 dir. Louis King
Vandercook, J. W.

Murder is Announced, A
BBC (GB) 1985 dir. George Gallaccio
TV(GB)
BBC (GB) 1987 dir. David Giles
TVSe(GB)
Christie, A.

Murder is Easy
WAR (US) 1982 dir. Claude Whatham
TV(US)
Christie, A.

Murder Most Foul
MGM (GB) 1964 dir. George Pollock
Christie, A. *Mrs. McGinty's Dead*

Murder, My Sweet
RKO (US) 1944 dir. Edward Dmytryk
V

Chandler, R. *Farewell, My Lovely*

Murder of a Moderate Man
BBC (GB/It) 1985
TVSe(GB)

Howlett, J.

Murder of Dr. Harrigan
WAR (US) 1936 dir. Frank McDonald

Eberhart, M. G. *From this Dark Stairway*

Murder on The Orient Express
EMI (GB) 1974 dir. Sidney Lumet
V

Christie, A.

Murder Reported
COL (GB) 1957 dir. Charles Saunders

Chapman, R. *Murder for the Million*

Murder she Said
MGM (GB) 1961 dir. George Pollock

Christie, A. *4.50 from Paddington*

Murders in the Rue Morgue
UN (US) 1932 dir. Robert Florey
AIP (US) 1971 dir. Gordon Hessler
V
HALMI (US/GB) 1986
dir. Jeannot Szwarc
TV(GB/US)

Poe, E. A.

Murder with Mirrors
WAR (US) 1985 dir. Dick Lowry
TV(US)

Christie, A. *They Do it with Mirrors*

Murder Without Crime
ABP (GB) 1950 dir. J. Lee-Thompson

Thompson, J. L. *Double Error*
P

Murder Without Motive: The Edmund Perry Story
LEONARD HILL FILMS TV(US) 1992
dir. Kevin Hooks
TV(US)

Anson, R. A. *Best Intentions: The Education and Killing of Edmund Perry*

Murphy's Romance
COL (US) 1985 dir. Martin Ritt
V

Schott, M.

Murphy's War
PAR (GB) 1971 dir. Peter Yates
V

Catto, M.

Music in the Air
FOX (US) 1934 dir. Joe May
M

Hammerstein II, O. and Kern, J.
P

Music Lovers, The
UA (GB) 1970 dir. Ken Russell
V

Bowen, C. D., von Meck, B. *Beloved Friend*

Music Man, The
WAR (US) 1962 dir. Morton da Costa
M, V

Willson, M.

Mutiny on the Bounty
MGM (US) 1935 dir. Frank Lloyd
V
MGM (US) 1962 dir. Lewis Milestone
V

Nordhoff, J. N. and Hall, C.

Mutiny of the Elsinore
ARGYLE (GB) 1937 dir. Roy Lockwood

London, J.

My Brilliant Career
GUO (Aust) 1979 dir. Gillian Armstrong
V

Franklin, M.

My Brother Jonathan
AB (GB) 1947 dir. Harold French
BBC (GB) 1985
TVSe(GB)

Young, F. B.

My Brother's Wife
ADAM (US) 1989 dir. Jack Bender
TV(US)

Gurney, A. R. *Middle Ages, The*
P

My Cousin Rachel
FOX (US) 1952 dir. Henry Koster
NBC (US) 1984
TV(US)

Du Maurier, D.

My Darling Clementine
FOX (US) 1946 dir. John Ford
V

Lake, S. *Wyatt Earp, Frontier Marshal*

My Daughter Joy
BL (GB) 1950 dir. Gregory Ratoff
US title: Operation X

Nemirowsky, I. *David Golder*

My Death is a Mockery
ADELPHI (GB) 1952 dir. Tony Young

Baber, D.

My Fair Lady
WAR (US) 1964 dir. George Cukor
M, V

Shaw, G. B. *Pygmalion*
P

My Father, My Son
WEINTRAUB (US) 1988
dir. Jeff Bleckner
TV(US)

**Zumwalt, Jr., Admiral, E. and
Zumwalt III, E. R.**

My Father's Glory
GAU (Fr) 1991 dir. Yves Robert

Pagnol, M. *Gloire de Mon Père, La*

My Father's House
FILMWAYS (US) 1975 dir. Alex Segal
TV(US), V

Kunhardt, Jr., P.

My First Forty Years
TRI-STAR/COL (It) 1989
dir. Carlo Vanzina

di Meana, M. R.

My Forbidden Past
RKO (US) 1951 dir. Robert Stevenson
V

Banks, P. *Carriage Entrance*

My Friend Flicka
FOX (US) 1943 dir. Harold Schuster

O'Hara, M.

My Friend Ivan Lapshin
LENFILM (USSR) 1986
dir. Alexei Cherman

Cherman, Y.

My Gal Sal
FOX (US) 1942 dir. Irving Cummings

Dreiser, T. *My Brother Paul*

My Girl Tisa
IN (US) 1948 dir. Elliott Nugent

Prumbs, L. S. and Smith, S. B.
P

My Gun is Quick
UA (US) 1957 dir. George A. White
Spillane, M.

My Kidnapper, My Love
EMI (US) 1980 dir. Sam Wanamaker
TV(US)
Saul, O. *Dark Side of Love, The*

My Left Foot
PALACE (GB) 1989 dir. J. Sheridan
Brown, C.

My Life as a Dog
SVENSK (Swe) 1984
dir. Lasse Hallstrom
V
Jonsson, R.

My Lover, My Son
MGM (US/GB) 1970 dir. John Newland
Grierson, E. *Reputation for a Song*

My Mother's Castle
GAU (Fr) 1991 dir. Yves Robert
Pagnol, M. *Château de Ma Mère, Le*

My Name is Julia Ross
COL (US) 1945 dir. Joseph H. Lewis
Gilbert, A. *Woman in Red, The*

My Old Man
CBS ENT (US) 1979 dir. John Erman
TV(US), V
Hemingway, E.

My Own True Love
PAR (US) 1948 dir. Compton Bennett
Foldes, Y. *Make You a Fine Wife*

Myra Breckenridge
FOX (US) 1970 dir. Mike Sarne
V
Vidal, G.

My Reputation
WAR (US) 1946 dir. Curtis Bernhardt
Jaynes, C. *Instruct my Sorrows*

My Side of the Mountain
PAR (US/Can) 1969 dir. James B. Clark
George, J.

My Sister and I
GFD (GB) 1948 dir. Harold Huth
Bonett, E. *High Pavement*

My Sister Eileen
COL (US) 1942 dir. Alexander Hall
McKenney, R.

My Sister Eileen
COL (US) 1955 dir. Richard Quine
M
Fields, J. and Chodorov, J.
P

My Six Convicts
COL (US) 1952 dir. Hugo Fregonese
Wilson, D. P.

My Son, My Son
UA (US) 1940 dir. Charles Vidor
Spring, H.

Mysterious Affair at Styles
LWT (GB) 1990 dir. Roy Devenish
TV(GB)
Christie, A.

Mysterious Dr. Fu Manchu
PAR (US) 1929 dir. Rowland V. Lee
Rohmer, S.

Mysterious Island
COL (GB) 1962 dir. Cy Endfield
V
Verne, J.

Mystery Liner
MON (US) 1934 dir. William Nigh
Wallace, E. *Ghost of John Holling, The*

Mystery of Edwin Drood, The
UN (US) 1935 dir. Stuart Walker
Dickens, C.

Mystery of Marie Roget, The
UN (US) 1942 dir. Phil Rosen
Poe, E. A.

Mystery of Mr. X, The
MGM (US) 1934 dir. Edgar Selwyn
MacDonald, P. *X vs. Rex*

Mystery of the Wax Museum
WAR (US) 1933 dir. Michael Curtiz
V
Belden, C. S.
P

Mystic Warrior, The
WAR (US) 1984 dir. Richard T. Heffron
TVSe(US)
Hill, R. B. *Hanta Yo*

My Sweet Charlie
UN TV (US) 1970 dir. Lamont Johnson
TV(US), V
Westheimer, D.
P

My Wicked, Wicked Ways . . . The Legend of Errol Flynn
CBS ENT (US) 1985 dir. Don Taylor
TV(US), V
Flynn, E.

My Wife's Family
GB (GB) 1931 dir. Monty Banks
ABPC (GB) 1941 dir. Walter C. Mycroft
ABP (GB) 1956 dir. Gilbert Gunn
Duprez, F., Stephens, H., & Linton, H. B.
P

Naked and the Dead, The
RKO (US) 1958 dir. Raoul Walsh
V
Mailer, N.

Naked Civil Servant, The
THAMES (GB) 1975 dir. Jack Gold
TV(GB), V
Crisp, Q.

Naked Country, The
FILMWAYS (Aust) 1984
dir. Tim Burstall
V
West, M.

Naked Edge, The
UA (GB) 1961 dir. Michael Anderson
Ehrlich, M. *First Train to Babylon*

Naked Face, The
CANNON (US) 1984 dir. Bryan Forbes
V

Sheldon, S.

Naked Hours, The
COMPTON (It) 1964 dir. Marco Vicario

Moravia, A. *Appointment at the Beach*

Naked in the Sun
ALLIED (US) 1957 dir. R. John Hugh
V

Slaughter, F. G. *Warrior, The*

Naked Jungle, The
PAR (US) 1954 dir. Byron Haskin
V

Stephenson, C. *Leiningen Versus the Ants*

Naked Lunch
FOX (US) 1991 dir. David Cronenberg

Burroughs, W.

Naked Runner, The
WAR (GB) 1967 dir. Sidney J. Furie

Clifford, F.

Name of the Rose, The
FOX (US/Ger/It/Fr) 1987
dir. Jean-Jacques Annaud
V

Eco, U.

Nana
MGM (US) 1934 dir. Dorothy Arzner
GB title: Lady of the Boulevards
GALA (Fr/It) 1955 dir. Christian-Jacque
MINERVA (Swe) 1971 dir. Mac Ahlberg
CANNON (It) 1982 dir. Dan Wolman
V

Zola, E.

Nancy Steele is Missing
FOX (US) 1937 dir. George Marshall

Coe, C. F.

Nanny, The
WAR (GB) 1965 dir. Seth Holt
V

Piper, E.

Narrow Corner
WAR (US) 1933 dir. Alfred E. Green

Maugham, W. S.

Narrowing Circle, The
EROS (GB) 1955 dir. Charles Saunders

Symons, J.

Nasty Habits
SCOTIA-BARBER (GB) 1976
dir. Michael Lindsay-Hogg
US title: The Abbess
V

Spark, M. *Abbess of Crewe, The*

National Health, The
COL (GB) 1973 dir. Jack Gold
V

Nichols, P.
P

National Velvet
MGM (US) 1944 dir. Clarence Brown
V

Bagnold, E.

Native Son
CLASSIC (Arg) 1951 dir. Pierre Chenal
V
CINECOM (US) 1986
dir. Jerrold Freedman

Wright, R.

Natural, The
TRISTAR (US) 1984 dir. Barry Levinson
V

Malamud, B.

Nature of the Beast, The
FILM 4 (GB) 1988 dir. Franco Rosso

Howker, J.

Nazarin
BAR PON (Mex) 1958 dir. Luis Bunuel
V

Galdos, B. P.

Néa
NEW REALM (Fr/Ger) 1976
dir. Nelly Kaplan
US/GB title: Young Emanuelle
V

Arsan, E.

Nearly a Nasty Accident
BL (GB) 1961 dir. Don Chaffey
Stringer, D. *Touch Wood*
P

Necessity
B&E (US) 1988 dir. Michael Miller
TV(US)
Garfield, B.

Negatives
CRISPIN (GB) 1968 dir. Peter Medak
Everett, P.

Neighbors
COL (US) 1981 dir. John G. Avildsen
V

Berger, T.

Neither the Sea Nor the Sand
TIGON (GB) 1972 dir. Fred Burnley
V

Honeycombe, G.

Nemesis
BBC (GB) 1986 dir. David Tucker
TV(GB)
Christie, A.

Nero Wolfe
PAR TV (US) 1979 dir. Frank D. Gilroy
TV(US)
Stout, R. *Doorbell Rang, The*

Nest, The
CONCORDE (US) 1988
dir. Terence Winkless
V

Cantor, E.

Nest of Gentry
CORINTH (USSR) 1970
dir. Andrei Konchalovski
Turgenev, I. *House of the Gentle Folk*

Net, The
GFD (GB) 1953 dir. Anthony Asquith
Pudney, J.

Never a Dull Moment
RKO (US) 1950 dir. George Marshall
Swift, K. *Who Could Ask For Anything More*

Never a Dull Moment
DISNEY (US) 1967 dir. Jerry Paris
V

Godey, J.

Never Come Back
BBC (GB) 1990 dir. Joe Waters
TVSe(GB)
Mair, J.

Never Cry Wolf
DISNEY (US) 1983 dir. Carroll Ballard
V

Mowat, F.

Neverending Story, The
WAR (Ger/GB) 1984
dir. Wolfgang Petersen
Ch, V
Ende, M.

Neverending Story II: The Next Chapter, The
WAR (Ger) 1989 dir. George Miller
Ch
Ende, M. *Neverending Story, The*

Never Let Me Go
MGM (GB) 1953 dir. Delmer Daves

Bax, R. *Came the Dawn*

Never Love a Stranger
ABP (US) 1958 dir. Robert Stevens
V

Robbins, H.

Never Say Goodbye
UN (US) 1955 dir. Jerry Hopper

Pirandello, L. *Come Prima Meglio di Prima*
P

Never so Few
MGM (US) 1959 dir. John Sturges

Chamales, T.

Never Steal Anything Small
UN (US) 1958 dir. Charles Lederer
V

Mamoulian, R., and Anderson, M. *Devil's Hornpipe, The*
P

Never Take No for an Answer
INDEPENDENT (GB) 1951
dir. Maurice Cloche, Ralph Smart

Gallico, P. *Small Miracle, The*

Never the Twain Shall Meet
MGM (US) 1931 dir. W. S. van Dyke

Kyne, P. B.

Never Too Late
WAR (US) 1965 dir. Bud Yorkin

Long, S. A.
P

New Adventures of Pippi Longstocking, The
COL (US) 1988 dir. Ken Annakin
Ch, V

Lindgren, A.

New Centurions, The
COL (US) 1972 dir. Richard Fleischer
GB title: Precinct 45: Los Angeles Police
V

Wambaugh, J.

New Leaf, A
PAR (US) 1970 dir. Elaine May

Ritchie, J. *Green Heart, The*

New Morals for Old
MGM (US) 1932 dir. Charles Brabin

Druten, J. van *After All*
P

Nice Girl Like Me, A
AVCO (GB) 1969 dir. Desmond Davis
V

Piper, A. *Marry at Leisure*

Nice Work
BBC (GB) 1989 dir. C. Meraud
TVSe(GB)

Lodge, D.

Nicholas and Alexandra
COL (GB) 1971 dir. Franklin Schaffner
V

Massie, R. K.

Nicholas Nickleby
EAL (GB) 1947 dir. Alberto Cavalcanti
V

Dickens, C.

Night After Night
PAR (US) 1932 dir. Archie Mayo

Bromfield, L. *Single Night*

Night and the City
FOX (GB) 1950 dir. Jules Dassin

Kersh, G.

Nightbreaker
TNT (US) 1989 dir. Peter Markle
TV(US)
Rosenberg, H. *Atomic Soldiers*

Nightbreed
FOX (US) 1990 dir. Clive Barker
Barker, C. *Cabal*

Night Club Scandal
PAR (US) 1937 dir. Ralph Murphy
Rubin, D. *Riddle Me This*
P

Nightcomers, The
AVCO (GB) 1972 dir. Michael Winner
V
James, H. *Turn of the Screw, The*

Night Comes too Soon
BUTCHER (GB) 1948
dir. Denis Kavanagh
Lytton, B. *Haunted and the Haunters, The*
P

Night Digger, The
MGM (GB) 1971 dir. Alistair Reid
Cowley, J. *Nest in a Falling Tree*

Nightfall
COL (US) 1956 dir. Jacques Tourneur
Goodis, D.

Nightfall
CONCORDE (US) 1988
dir. Paul Mayersburg
V
Asimov, I.

Nightflyers
NEW CENTURY (US) 1987
dir. T. C. Blake
V
Martin, G. R. R.

Night Games
GALA (Swe) 1966 dir. Mai Zetterling
V
Zetterling, M.

Night Has a Thousand Eyes
PAR (US) 1948 dir. John Farrow
Woolrich, C.

Night has Eyes, The
ANGLO-AM 1952
Kennington, A.

Night in Paradise, A
UN (US) 1946 dir. Arthur Lubin
Hellman, G. S. *Peacock's Feather*

Night in the Life of Jimmy Reardon, A.
FOX (US) 1988 dir. William Richert
Richert, W. *Aren't you Even Gonna Kiss Me Goodbye*

Night Life of the Gods, The
UN (US) 1935 dir. Lowell Sherman
Smith, T.

Nightmare
UN (US) 1942 dir. Tim Whelan
MacDonald, P. *Escape*

Nightmare
UA (US) 1956 dir. Maxwell Shane
Woolrich, C.

Nightmare Alley
FOX (GB) 1947 dir. Edmund Goulding
Gresham, W.

Nightmare Man, The
BBC (US) 1981 dir. Douglas Camfield
TVSe(GB)
Wiltshire, D. *Child of Vodyanoi*

Nightmare Years, The
CONSOL (US) 1989 dir. Anthony Page
TV(US)

Shirer, W.

'Night, Mother
UN (US) 1986 dir. Tom Moore
V

Norman, M.
P

Night Must Fall
MGM (US) 1937 dir. Richard Thorpe
MGM (GB) 1964 dir. Karel Reisz

Williams, E.
P

Night Nurse
WAR (US) 1931 dir. William Wellman

Macy, D.

Night of January 16th, The
PAR (US) 1941 dir. William Clements

Rand, A.
P

Night of Courage
TITUS (US) 1987 dir. Elliot Silverstein
TV(US)

Williams, B. *In This Fallen City*
P

Night of the Big Heat
PLANET (GB) 1967 dir. Terence Fisher
V

Lymington, J.

Night of the Demon
COL (GB) 1957 dir. Jacques Tourneur
V

James, M. R. *Casting the Runes*

Night of the Eagle
IA (GB) 1961 dir. Sidney Hayers
US title: Burn, Witch, Burn

Leiber, F. *Conjure Wife*

Night of the Following Day, The
UN (US) 1969 dir. Hubert Cornfield

White, L. *Snatchers, The*

Night of the Fox
DOVE/ITC (US/GB) 1990
dir. Charles Jarrot
TVSe(GB/US)

Higgins, J.

Night of the Generals, The
COL/BL (GB) 1966 dir. Anatole Litvak
V

Hirst, H. H.

Night of the Hunter, The
UA (US) 1955 dir. Charles Laughton
V
KONIGSBERG/SANITSKY (US) 1991
dir. David Greene
TV(US)

Grubb, D.

Night of the Iguana, The
MGM (US) 1964 dir. John Huston
V

Williams, T.
P

Night of the Juggler
COL (US) 1980 dir. Robert Butler
V

McGivern, W. P.

Night of the Lepus
MGM (US) 1972 dir. William F. Claxton

Braddon, R. *Year of the Angry Rabbit, The*

Night Slaves
B. CROSBY (US) 1970 dir. Ted Post
TV(US)

Sohl, J.

Night They Raided Minsky's, The
UA (US) 1968 dir. William Friedkin
GB title: Night They Invented
Striptease, The
V

Barber, R.

Night to Remember, A
RANK (GB) 1957 dir. Roy Ward Baker
V

Lord, W.

Night Train to Munich
TCF (GB) 1940 dir. Carol Reed
V

Wellesley, G. *Report on a Fugitive*

Night unto Night
WAR (US) 1949 dir. Don Siegel

Wylie, P.

Night was our Friend
MONARCH (GB) 1951
dir. Michael Anderson

Pertwee, M.
P

Night Watch
AVCO (GB) 1973 dir. Brian G. Hutton
V

Fletcher, L.
P

Nightwing
COL (Neth) 1975 dir. Arthur Miller
V

Smith, M. C.

Night Without Stars
GFD (GB) 1951 dir. Anthony Pelissier
Graham, W.

Nijinsky
PAR (US) 1980 dir. Herbert Ross
V

Nijinsky, R.

Nikki, Wild Dog of the North
DISNEY (US) 1961 dir. Jack Couffer
V

Curwood, J. O. *Nomads of the North*

9½ Weeks
MGM/UA (US) 1986 dir. Adrian Lyne
V

McNeill, E.

Nine Girls
COL (US) 1944 dir. Leigh Jason
Pettit, W. H.
P

Nine Hours to Rama
FOX (GB) 1962 dir. Mark Robson
Wolpert, S.

Nine Lives
NORDS (NOR) 1959 dir. Arne Skouen
Howarth, D. *We Die Alone*

1915
BBC (GB/Australia) 1983
dir. Chris Thomson
TVSe (Aust/GB)
McDonald, R.

1984
ABP (GB) 1956 dir. Michael Anderson
BBC (GB) 1965
dir. Christopher Morahan
TV(GB)
BBC (GB) 1984 dir. Rudolph Cartier
TV(GB)
VIRGIN (GB) 1984 dir. Michael Radford
V

Orwell, G.

Ninth Configuration, The
LORIMAR (US) 1980
dir. William P. Blatty
V

Blatty, W.

Ninth Guest, The
COL (US) 1934 dir. Roy William Neill

Bristow, G.

92 in the Shade
UA (US) 1975 dir. Thomas McGuane
V

McGuane, T.

No Blade of Grass
MGM (GB) 1970 dir. Cornel Wilde
V

Christopher, J. *Death of Grass*

Noble House
DELAUR (US) 1988 dir. Gary Nelson
TVSe(US)

Clavell, J.

Nobody Runs Forever
RANK (GB) 1968 dir. Ralph Thomas
US title: High Commissioner, The

Cleary, J. *High Commissioner, The*

Nobody's Perfect
UN (US) 1978 dir. Alan Rafkin

Bosworth, A. R. *Crows of Edwina Hill, The*

Nobody's Perfekt
COL (US) 1981 dir. Peter Bonerz
V

Kenrick, T. *Two for the Price of One*

No Down Payment
FOX (US) 1957 dir. Martin Ritt

McPartland, J.

No Escape
PATHE (GB) 1936 dir. Norman Lee

Goodchild, G. and Witty, F. *No Exit*
P

No Hands on the Clock
PAR (US) 1941 dir. Frank McDonald

Homes, G.

No Highway
FOX (GB) 1951 dir. Henry Koster
US title: No Highway in the Sky

Shute, N.

Noh Mask Murders
TOEI (Jap) 1991 dir. Kon Ichikawa

Uchida, Y.

No Kidding
AA (GB) 1960 dir. Gerald Thomas
US title: Beware of Children

Anderson, V. *Beware of Children*

No Life King
NEW CENTURY (Jap) 1991
dir. Jun Ichikawa

Ito, S.

No Love for Johnnie
RANK (GB) 1960 dir. Ralph Thomas
V

Fienburgh, W.

No More Ladies
MGM (US) 1935
dir. Edward H. Griffith, George Cukor

Thomas, A. E.
P

No, My Darling Daughter
RANK (GB) 1961 dir. Ralph Thomas

Brooke, H. and Bannerman, K.
Handful of Tansy, A.
P

None but the Lonely Heart
RKO (US) 1944 dir. Clifford Odets
V

Llewellyn, R.

No No Nanette
WAR (US) 1930 dir. Clarence Badger
M
RKO (US) 1940 dir. Herbert Wilcox
M

Harbach, O., & Mandel, F.
P

Non Stop New York
GFD (GB) 1937 dir. Robert Stevenson

Attiwill, K. *Sky Steward*

No Orchids for Miss Blandish
ALL (GB) 1948 dir. St. John L. Clowes

Chase, J. H.

Noose
ABFC (GB) 1948
dir. Edmond T. Greville

Llewellyn, R.
P

No Place for Jennifer
ABP (GB) 1949 dir. Henry Cass

Hambledon, P. *No Difference to Me*

No Resting Place
ABP (GB) 1951 dir. Paul Rother

Niall, I.

Norman, Is That You?
MGM (US) 1976 dir. George Schlatter

Clark, R. and Bobrick, S.
P

No Room at the Inn
BN (GB) 1948 dir. Dan Birt

Temple, J.
P

No Room for the Groom
UI (US) 1952 dir. Douglas Sirk

Teilhet, D. L. *My True Love*

Northanger Abbey
BBC (GB) 1987 dir. Giles Foster
TV(GB)

Austen, J.

North and South
WAR (US) 1985 dir. Richard T. Heffron
TVSe(US)

Jakes, J.

North and South, Book II
WAR TV (US) 1986 dir. Kevin Connor
TVSe(US)

Jakes, J. *Love and War*

North Avenue Irregulars, The
DISNEY (US) 1978 dir. Bruce Bilson
GB title: Hill's Angels

Hill, Rev. A. F.

North Dallas Forty
PAR (US) 1979 dir. Ted Kotcheff
V

Gent, P.

Nor the Moon by Night
RANK (GB) 1958 dir. Ken Annakin
US title: Elephant Gun

Packer, J.

North Sea Hijack
CIC (GB) 1980 dir. Andrew V. McLaglen
US title: Ffolkes
V

Davies, J. *Esther, Ruth and Jennifer*

North to Alaska
FOX (US) 1960 dir. Henry Hathaway

Fodor, L. *Birthday Gift*
P

Northwest Mounted Police
PAR (US) 1940 dir. Cecil B de Mille

Fetherstonhaugh, R. C. *Royal Canadian Mounted Police*

Northwest Passage
MGM (US) 1940 dir. King Vidor
Roberts, K.

No Sad Songs for Me
COL (US) 1950 dir. Rudolph Maté
Southard, R.

No Sex Please — We're British
COL (GB) 1973 dir. Cliff Owen
V
Marriott, A. and Foot, A.
P

Not a Penny More, Not a Penny Less
BBC (GB) 1990 dir. Clive Donner
TVSe(GB)
Archer, J.

Not as a Stranger
UA (US) 1955 dir. Stanley Kramer
Thompson, M.

Nothin' But The Truth
PAR (US) 1941 dir. Elliott Nugent
Isham, F. S.

Nothing but the Night
FOX-RANK (GB) 1972 dir. Peter Sasdy
Blackburn, J.

Nothing Sacred
SELZNICK (US) 1937
dir. William Wellman
V
Street, James H. *Letter to the Editor*

No Time for Breakfast
BOURLA (Fr) 1980
dir. Jean-Louis Bertucelli
Loriot, N. *Cri, Un*

No Time for Comedy
WAR (US) 1940 dir. William Keighley
Behrman, S. N.
P

No Time for Sergeants
WAR (US) 1958 dir. Mervyn Le Roy
V
Hyman, M.

Not My Kid
FINNEGAN (US) 1985
dir. Michael Tuchner
TV(US), V
Polson, B.

Not Now Darling
MGM (GB) 1973 dir. Ray Cooney, David Croft
V
Cooney, R.
P

Not Quite Jerusalem
RANK (GB) 1985 dir. Lewis Gilbert
V
Kember, P.
P

No Trees in the Street
ABP (US) 1958 dir. J. Lee Thompson
V
Willis, T.
P

Not Without My Daughter
MGM (US) 1991 dir. Brian Gilbert
V
Mahmoody, B. and Hoffer, W.

Now and Forever
ABP (GB) 1955 dir. Mario Zampi
Delderfield, R. F. *Orchard Walls, The*
P

No Way Out
ORION (US) 1987 dir. Roger Donaldson
Fearing, K. *The Big Clock*

No Way to Treat a Lady
PAR (US) 1968 dir. Jack Smight
V
Goldman, W.

Now Barrabas was a Robber
WAR (GB) 1949 dir. Gordon Parry
Home, W. D. *Now Barrabas*

Nowhere to Go
EAL (GB) 1958 dir. Seth Holt
Mackenzie, D.

Nowhere to Run
MTM (US) 1978 dir. Richard Lang
TV(US)
Einstein, C. *Blackjack Hijack, The*

Now, Voyager
WAR (US) 1942 dir. Irving Rapper
V
Prouty, O.

Number Seventeen
BIP (GB) 1932 dir. Alfred Hitchcock
V
Farjeon, J. J.
P

Nun's Story, The
WAR (US) 1959 dir. Fred Zinnemann
V
Hulme, K.

Nurse
HALMI (US) 1980
dir. David Lowell Rich
TV(US)
Anderson, P.

Nurse Edith Cavell
RKO (US) 1939 dir. Herbert Wilcox
V
Berkeley, R. *Dawn*

Nursemaid Who Disappeared, The
WAR (GB) 1939 dir. Arthur Woods
MacDonald, P.

Nurse on Wheels
WAR (GB) 1963 dir. Gerald Thomas
Jones, J. *Nurse is a Neighbour*

Nurse's Secret, The
WAR (US) 1941 dir. Noel M. Smith
Rinehart, M. R. *Miss Pinkerton*

Nutcracker
ATLANTIC (US) 1986
dir. Carroll Ballard
M
Hoffman, E. T. A.

Nutcracker: Money, Madness and Murder
WAR TV (US) 1987 dir. Paul Bogart
TVSe(US)
Alexander, S. *Nutcracker: Money, Madness, Murder: A Family Album*

Nutcracker Prince, The
WAR (US) 1990 dir. Paul Schibli
A
Hoffman, E. T. A. *Nutcracker and the Mouseking, The*

Nuts
WAR (US) 1987 dir. Martin Ritt
V
Topor, T.
P

Oblomov
MOSFILM (USSR) 1981
dir. Nikita Milchalkov
V

Goncharov, I.

Obsession
GFD (GB) 1949 dir. Edward Dmytryk
US title: Hidden Room, The
V

Coppel, A. *Man About a Dog, A*
P

Occupe-toi d'Amélie
LUX (Fr) 1949 dir. Claude Autant-Lara

Feydeau, G.
P

October Man, The
GFD (GB) 1947 dir. Roy Baker
V

Ambler, E.

Odd Man Out
TC (GB) 1947 dir. Carol Reed
US title: Gang War
V

Green, F. L.

Odd Couple, The
PAR (US) 1968 dir. Gene Saks
V

Simon, N.
P

Odds Against Tomorrow
UA (US) 1959 dir. Robert Wise

McGivern, W.

Odessa File, The
COL (GB) 1974 dir. Ronald Neame
V

Forsyth, F.

Odette
BL (GB) 1950 dir. Herbert Wilcox
Tickell, J.

Oedipus the King
UI (GB) 1968 dir. Philip Saville

Sophocles
P

Oedipus Rex
HORIZON (It) 1947
dir. Pier Paolo Pasolini
V

Sophocles *Oedipus the King*
P

Offence, The
UA (GB) 1972 dir. Sidney Lumet
V

Hopkins, J. *This Story of Yours*
P

Of Human Bondage
RKO (US) 1934 dir. John Cromwell
WAR (US) 1946 dir. Edmund Goulding
MGM (GB) 1964 dir. Henry Hathaway
V

Maugham, W. S.

Of Human Hearts
MGM (US) 1938 dir. Clarence Brown
Morrow, H. *Benefits Forgot*

Of Mice and Men
UA (US) 1939 dir. Lewis Milestone
METROMEDIA (US) 1981
dir. Reza Badiyi
TV(US), V
Steinbeck, J.

Of Unknown Origin
WAR (Can) 1983
dir. George P. Cosmatos
V
Parker, C. G. *Visitor, The*

Oh Dad, Poor Dad ... Mama's Hung You In The Closet and I'm Feeling So Sad
PAR (US) 1966 dir. Richard Quine
Kopit, A.
P

Oh! God!
WAR (US) 1977 dir. Carl Reiner
V
Corman, A.

Oh! Men! Oh! Women!
FOX (US) 1957 dir. Nunnally Johnson
Chodorov, E.
P

Oh! What a Lovely War
PAR (GB) 1969
dir. Richard Attenborough
V
Chilton, C. and Littlewood, J. *Long, Long Trail, The*
P

Oil for the Lamps of China
WAR (US) 1935 dir. Mervyn Le Roy
Hobart, Mrs. A. T.

Oklahoma!
MAGNA (US) 1955 dir. Fred Zinnemann
M, V
Riggs, L. *Green Grow the Lilacs*
P
Rodgers, R. and Hammerstein, II, O.
P

Old Acquaintance
WAR (US) 1943 dir. Vincent Sherman
Druten, J. van
P

Old Curiosity Shop, The
BIP (GB) 1934 dir. Thomas Bentley
Dickens, C.

Old Dark House, The
UN (US) 1932 dir. James Whale
BL (GB) 1963 dir. William Castle
Priestley, J. B. *Benighted*

Old English
WAR (US) 1930 dir. Alfred E. Green
Galsworthy, J.
P

Old Gringo
COL (US) 1989 dir. Luis Puenzo
Fuentes, C. *Gringo Viejo*

Old Maid, The
WAR (US) 1939 dir. Edmund Goulding
V
Wharton, Mrs. E. N.

Old Man and the Sea, The
WAR (US) 1958 dir. John Sturges
STORKE PRODS (US) 1990
dir. Jud Taylor
TV(US)
Hemingway, E.

Old Men at the Zoo, The
BBC (GB) 1982 dir. Stuart Burge
TVSe(GB)
Wilson, A.

Old Yeller
DISNEY (US) 1957
dir. Robert Stevenson
V
Gipson, F. B.

Oliver!
COL (GB) 1968 dir. Carol Reed
M, V
Dickens, C. *Oliver Twist*

Oliver's Story
PAR (US) 1978 dir. John Korty
V
Segal, E.

Oliver Twist
CINEGUILD (GB) 1948 dir. David Lean
V
TRIDENT (US/GB) 1982
dir. Clive Donner
TV(US/GB)
BBC (GB) 1985
TVSe(GB)
Dickens, C.

Olivia
FDF (Fr) 1950 dir. Jacqueline Audry
'Olivia'

Omega Man, The
WAR (US) 1971 dir. Boris Sagar
V
Matheson, R. *I Am Legend*

On a Clear Day you can See Forever
PAR (US) 1970 dir. Vincente Minnelli
M, V
Lerner, A. J.
P

On Approval
FOX (GB) 1944 dir. Clive Brook
V
Lonsdale, F.
P

On Borrowed Time
MGM (US) 1939 dir. Harold S. Bucquet
MILBERG (US) 1957
dir. George Schaefer
TV(US)
Watkins, L. E.

Once a Crook
FOX (GB) 1941 dir. Herbert Mason
Price, E. and Attiwill, K.
P

Once a Jolly Swagman
WESSEX (GB) 1948 dir. Jack Lee
US title: Maniacs on Wheels
Slater, M.

Once an Eagle
UN TV (US) 1977 dir. E. W.
Swackhamer, Richard Michaels
TVSe(US)
Myrer, A.

Once in a Lifetime
UN (US) 1933 dir. Russell Mack
Hart, M. and Kaufman, G. S.
P

Once is not Enough
PAR (US) 1975 dir. Guy Green
V
Susann, J.

Once More My Darling
UI (US) 1949 dir. Robert Montgomery
Carson, R. *Come Be My Love*

Once More, With Feeling
COL (GB) 1960 dir. Stanley Donen
Kurnitz, H.
P

Once Upon a Time in America
WAR (US) 1984 dir. Sergio Leone
V

Aaronson, D. *Hoods, The*

On Dangerous Ground
RKO (US) 1951 dir. Nicholas Ray
Butler, G.

One Brief Summer
FOX (GB) 1969 dir. John MacKenzie
Tierney, H. *Valkyrie's Armour*
P

One Day in the Life of Ivan Denizovich
CINERAMA (GB) 1971
dir. Caspar Wrede
Solzhenitsyn, A.

One Deadly Summer
SNC (Fr) 1983 dir. Jean Becker
V
Japrisot, S.

One Desire
UI (US) 1955 dir. Jerry Hopper
Richter, C. *Tracy Cromwell*

One-Eyed Jacks
PAR (US) 1961 dir. Marlon Brando
V
Neider, C. *Authentic Death of Hendry Jones, The*

One Flew Over the Cuckoo's Nest
UA (US) 1975 dir. Milos Forman
V
Kesey, K.

One Foot in Heaven
WAR (US) 1941 dir. Irving Rapper
Spence, H.

One Hour With You
PAR (US) 1932 dir. George Cukor,
Ernst Lubitsch
M
Schmidt, L. *Only a Dream*
P

One Hundred and One Dalmatians
DISNEY (US) 1961
dir. Wolfgang Reitherman
A, Ch
Smith, D.

100 Rifles
FOX (US) 1969 dir. Tom Gries
V
MacLeod, R. *Californio, The*

One in a Million: The Ron LeFlore Story
EMI (US) 1978 dir. William A. Graham
TV(US), V
LeFlore, R. and Hawkins, J.
Breakout

One is a Lonely Number
MGM (US) 1972 dir. Mel Stuart
Morris, R.

One Man's Way
UA (US) 1964 dir. Denis Sanders
Gordon, A. *Minister to Millions*

One More River
UN (US) 1934 dir. James Whale
GB title: Over the River
Galsworthy, J. *Over the River*

One More Spring
FOX (US) 1935 dir. Henry King
Nathan, R.

One More Tomorrow
WAR (US) 1946 dir. Peter Godfrey

Barry, P. *Animal Kingdom, The*
P

One New York Night
MGM (US) 1935 dir. Jack Conway
GB title: Trunk Mystery, The

Carpenter E. C.
P

One Night in Lisbon
PAR (US) 1941 dir. Edward H. Griffith

Druten, J. van *There's Always Juliet*
P

One of my Wives is Missing
SPELLING-GOLDBERG (US) 1976
dir. Glenn Jordan
V

Thomas, R. *Trap for a Single Man*
P

One of our Dinosaurs is Missing
DISNEY (US) 1975
dir. Robert Stevenson
Ch, V

Forrest, D. *Great Dinosaur Robbery, The*

One of Those Things
RANK (Den) 1971 dir. Erik Balling

Bodelsen, A. *Hit, and Run, Run, Run*

One Police Plaza
CBS ENT (US) 1986 dir. Jerry Jameson
TV(US)

Caunitz, W. J.

One Shoe Makes it Murder
LORIMAR TV (US) 1982
dir. William Hale
TV(US), V

Bercovici, E. *So Little Cause for Caroline*

One Sunday Afternoon
PAR (US) 1933 dir. Stephen Roberts
WAR (US) 1948 dir. Raoul Walsh

Hagan, J.
P

One That Got Away, The
RANK (GB) 1957 dir. Roy Baker
V

Burt, K. and Leasor, J.

One Third of a Nation
PAR (US) 1939 dir. Dudley Murphy

Arent, A.
P

One Touch of Venus
UN (US) 1948 dir. William A. Seiter
V

Perelman, S. J. and Nash, O.
P

One, Two, Three
UA (US) 1961 dir. Billy Wilder
V

Molnar, F.
P

One Way Pendulum
UA (GB) 1964 dir. Peter Yates

Simpson, N. F.
P

One-Way Ticket
COL (US) 1935 dir. Herbert Biberman

Turner, E.

One Wild Oat
EROS (GB) 1951 dir. Charles Saunders

Sylvaine, V.
P

On Friday at 11
BL (Ger/Fr/It) 1961 dir. Alvin Rakoff

Chase, J. H. *World In My Pocket, The*

On Golden Pond
UN (US) 1981 dir. Mark Rydell
V

Thompson, E.
P

On Her Majesty's Secret Service
UA (GB) 1969 dir. Peter Hunt
V

Fleming, I.

Onion Field, The
AVCO (US) 1979 dir. Harold Becker
V

Wambaugh, J.

Onionhead
WAR (US) 1958 dir. Norman Taurog

Hill, W.

Only Game in Town, The
FOX (US) 1969 dir. George Stevens

Gilroy, F. D.
P

Only One Survived
CBS ENT (US) 1990 dir. Folco Quilici
TV(US)

Quilici, F. *Danger Adrift*

Only the Valiant
WAR (US) 1950 dir. Gordon Douglas
V

Warren, C. M.

Only Two Can Play
BL (GB) 1961 dir. Sidney Gilliat
V

Amis, K. *That Uncertain Feeling*

Only When I Larf
PAR (GB) 1968 dir. Basil Dearden
V

Deighton, L.

Only When I Laugh
COL (US) 1981 dir. Glenn Jordan
GB title: It Only Hurts When I Laugh
V

Simon, N. *Gingerbread Lady, The*
P

On Moonlight Bay
WAR (US) 1951 dir. Roy del Ruth
M

Tarkington, B. *Penrod*

On the Beach
UA (US) 1959 dir. Stanley Kramer
V

Shute, N.

On the Black Hill
CHANNEL 4 (GB) 1989
dir. Andrew Grieve
TV(GB)

Chatwin, B.

On the Fiddle
AA (GB) 1961 dir. Cyril Frankel
US title: Operation Snafu

Delderfield, R. F. *Stop at a Winner*

On the Night of the Fire
GFD (GB) 1939
dir. Brian Desmond Hurst
US title: Fugitive, The

Green, F. L.

On The Run
CFF (GB) 1969 dir. Pat Jackson
Ch, V

Bawden, N.

On the Waterfront
COL (US) 1954 dir. Elia Kazan
V

Schulberg, B. W.

On Valentine's Day
ANGELIKA (US) 1986 dir. Ken Harrison
V

Foote, H. *Valentine's Day*
P

On Wings of Eagles
TAFT (US) 1986
dir. Andrew V. McLaglen
TVSe(US)
Follett, K.

On Your Toes
WAR (US) 1939 dir. Ray Enright
Abbott, G.
P

Open Admissions
VIACOM (US) 1988 dir. Gus Trikonis
TV(US)
Lauro, S.
P

Opening Night
ITV (GB) 1978 dir. Brian McDuffie
TV(GB)
Marsh, N.

Opera do Malandro
AUSTRA/TF1 (Braz/Fr) 1986
dir. Ruy Guerra
Buarque, C.
P

Operation Amsterdam
RANK (GB) 1958
dir. Michael McCarthy
V

Walker, D. E. *Adventure in Diamonds*

Operation Daybreak
WAR (US) 1975 dir. Lewis Gilbert
V

Burgess, A. *Seven Men at Daybreak*

Operation Mad Ball
COL (US) 1957 dir. Richard Quine
Carter, A.
P

O Pioneers!
LORIMAR (US) 1992 dir. Glenn Jordan
TV(US)
Cather, W.

Opposite Sex, The
MGM (US) 1956 dir. David Miller
Boothe, C. *Women, The*
P

Optimists of Nine Elms, The
SCOTIA-BARBER (GB) 1973
dir. Anthony Simmons
V

Simmons, A.

Oranges are not the only Fruit
A&E/BBC (US/GB) 1990
dir. Beeban Kidron
TV(GB/US)
Winterson, J.

Orchid House, The
BBC (GB) 1991 dir. Harold Ove
TV(GB)
Allfrey, P. S.

Ordeal by Innocence
CANNON (GB) 1985
dir. Desmond Davis
V

Christie, A.

Orders are Orders
BL (GB) 1954 dir. David Paltenghi
V

Hay, I. and Armstrong, A. *Orders is Orders*
P

Orders is Orders
GAU (GB) 1933 dir. Walter Forde
Hay, I., & Armstrong, A.
P

Ordinary People
PAR (US) 1980 dir. Robert Redford
V
Guest, J.

Oregon Passage
ABP (US) 1958 dir. Paul Landres
Shirreffs, G. D. *Trails End*

Orient Express
FOX (US) 1934 dir. Paul Martin
Greene, G. *Stamboul Train*

Orphans
LORIMAR (US) 1987 dir. Alan J. Pakula
V
Kessler, L.
P

Orphée
A. PAULVÉÉ (Fr) 1949
dir. Jean Cocteau
Cocteau, J.
P

Orpheus Descending
NED (US) 1990 dir. Peter Hall
TV
Williams, T.
P

Oscar
TOUCH (US) 1991 dir. John Landis
V
Magnier, C.
P

Oscar, The
PAR (US) 1966 dir. Russel Rouse
V
Sale, R.

Osterman Weekend, The
FOX (US) 1983 dir. Sam Peckinpah
V
Ludlum, R.

Otello
CANNON (It) 1986 dir. Franco Zeffirelli
M, V
Verdi, G.

Othello
MERCURY (US/Fr) 1951
dir. Orson Welles
EAGLE (GB) 1965 dir. Stuart Burge
Shakespeare, W.
P

Othello the Black Commando
M B DIFF 1982
TV
Shakespeare, W. *Othello*
P

Other, The
FOX (US) 1972 dir. Robert Mulligan
V
Tryon, T.

Other Halves
OVINGHAM (GB) 1985 dir. John Laing
McCauley, S.

Other Man, The
UN TV (US) 1970 dir. Richard Colla
TV(US)
Lynn, M. *Mrs. Maitland's Affair*

Other People's Money
WAR (US) 1991 dir. Norman Jewison
Sterner, J.
P

Other Side of Midnight, The
FOX (US) 1977 dir. Charles Jarrott
V
Sheldon, S.

Other Side of the Mountain, The
UN (US) 1975 dir. Larry Peerce
GB title: Window to the Sky, A
V

Valens, E. G. *Long Way Up, A*

Otley
COL (GB) 1968 dir. Dick Clement
V

Waddell, M.

Our Betters
RKO (US) 1933 dir. George Cukor

Maugham, W. S.
P

Our Hearts Were Young and Gay
PAR (US) 1944 dir. Lewis Allen

Skinner, C. O. and Kimbrough, E.

Our Man in Havana
COL (GB) 1959 dir. Carol Reed

Greene, G.

Our Marriage
LFDP (Fr) 1985 dir. Valeria Sarimento

Tellado, C. *Mi Bodo Contigo*

Our Mother's House
MGM (GB) 1967 dir. Jack Clayton

Gloag, J.

Our Town
UA (US) 1940 dir. Sam Wood
V

Wilder, T. N.
P

Our Vines Have Tender Grapes
MGM (US) 1945 dir. Roy Rowland

Martin, G. V. *For Our Vines Have Tender Grapes*

Our Wife
COL (US) 1941 dir. John M. Stahl

Mearson, L. *Lillian Day*
P

Outback
NIT (Aus) 1970 dir. Ted Kotcheff

Cook, K. *Wake in Fright*

Outcast Lady
MGM (US) 1934 dir. Robert Z. Leonard
GB title: Woman of the World, A

Arlen, M. *Green Hat, The*

Outcast of the Islands, An
LF (GB) 1951 dir. Carol Reed

Conrad, J.

Outcasts of Poker Flat, The
RKO (US) 1937 dir. Christy Cabanne
FOX (US) 1952 dir. Joseph M. Newman

Harte, B.

Outfit, The
MGM (US) 1973 dir. John Flynn
V

Stark, R.

Outlaw Josey Wales, The
WAR (US) 1976 dir. Clint Eastwood
V

Carter, F. *Gone to Texas*

Out of Africa
UN (US) 1985 dir. Sidney Pollack
V

Dinesen, I.

Thurman, J. *Isak Dinesen*

Out of the Darkness
CFF (GB) 1985 dir. John Krish
Ch

Hoyland, J. *Ivy Garland, The*

Out of the Fog
WAR (US) 1941 dir. Anatole Litvak

Shaw, I. *Gentle People, The*
P

Out of the Past
RKO (US) 1947 dir. Jacques Tourneur
GB title: Build My Gallows High
V

Homes, G. *Build My Gallows High*

Out of the Shadows
KUSHNER-LOCKE/YTV (US/GB)
1988 dir. Willi Patterson
TV(GB/US)

Davidson, A.

Out on a Limb
ABC (US) 1987 dir. Robert Butler
TVSe(US)

MacLaine, S.

Outrage!
COL TV (US) 1986 dir. Walter Grauman
TV(US)

Denker, H.

Outsider, The
MGM (GB) 1931 dir. Harry Lachtman
ABPC (GB) 1939 dir. Paul Stein

Brandon, D.
P

Outsider, The
PAR (US) 1980 dir. Tony Luraschi

Leinster, C. *Heritage of Michael Flaherty, The*

Outsiders, The
WAR (US) 1983
dir. Francis Ford Coppola
V

Hinton, S. E.

Outward Bound
WAR (US) 1930 dir. Robert Milton

Vane, S.
P

Overboard
FAC-NEW (US) 1978 dir. John Newland
TV(US)

Searls, H.

Over 21
COL (US) 1945 dir. Alexander Hall

Gordon, R.
P

Owd Bob
BG (GB) 1938 dir. Robert Stevenson
US title: To the Victor

Olivant, A.

Owl and the Pussycat, The
COL (US) 1970 dir. Herbert Ross
V

Manhoff, B.
P

Ox-Bow Incident, The
FOX (US) 1943 dir. William Wellman
US title: Strange Incident
V

Clark, W. van T.

Oxbridge Blues
BBC (GB) 1984 dir. James Cellan Jones
TVSe(GB)

Raphael, F.

Pacific Destiny
BL (GB) 1956 dir. Wolf Rilla
Grimble, Sir A. *Pattern of Islands*

Pack, The
WAR (US) 1977 dir. Robert Clouse
V
Fisher, D.

Pack of Lies
HALMI (US) 1987 dir. Anthony Page
TV(US)
Whitemore, H.
P

Pad (And How to Use It), The
UI (US) 1966 dir. Brian C. Hutton
Shaffer, P. *Private Ear, The*
P

Paddy
FOX (Ireland) 1969 dir. Daniel Haller
V
Dunne, L. *Goodbye to the Hill*

Paddy the Next Best Thing
FOX (US) 1933 dir. Harry Lachman
Page, G.
P

Padre Padrone
RAI (It) 1977 dir. Paolo Taviani, Vittorio Taviani
V
Ledda, G.

Paganini Strikes Again
CFF (GB) 1973 dir. Gordon Gilbert
Ch
Lee, B.

Page Miss Glory
PAR (US) 1935 dir. Mervyn LeRoy
Schrank, J. and Dunning, P.
P

Paid
MGM (US) 1930 dir. Sam Wood
GB title: Within the Law
Veiller, B. *Within the Law*
P

Painted Veil, The
MGM (US) 1934
dir. Richard Boleslawski
Maugham, W. S.

Paint Your Wagon
PAR (US) 1969 dir. Joshua Logan
M, V
Lerner, A. J. and Loewe, F.
P

Pair of Briefs
RANK (GB) 1961 dir. Ralph Thomas
Brooke, H. and Bannerman, K. *How Say You?*
P

Pajama Game, The
WAR (US) 1957 dir. Stanley Donen
M, V
Bissell, R. P. *7½ Cents*

Pal Joey
COL (US) 1957 dir. George Sidney
M, V
O'Hara, J.

Palomino
NBC (US) 1991 dir. Michael Miller
TV(US)
Steel, D.

Panic in Needle Park, The
FOX (US) 1971 dir. Jerry Schatzberg
Mills, J.

Papa's Delicate Condition
PAR (US) 1963 dir. George Marshall
V
Griffith, C.

Paper Chase, The
FOX (US) 1973 dir. James Bridges
V
Osborn, J. J.

Paperhouse
VESTRON (GB) 1988 dir. Bernard Rose
Storr, C. *Marianne Dreams*

Paper Moon
PAR (US) 1973 dir. Peter Bogdanovich
V
Brown, J. D. *Addie Pray*

Paper Orchid
COL (GB) 1949 dir. Roy Baker
La Bern, A. J.

Papillon
COL (US) 1973 dir. Franklin Schaffner
V
Charrière, H.

Paradine Case, The
SELZNICK (US) 1947
dir. Alfred Hitchcock
V
Hichens, R.

Paradise for Three
MGM (US) 1938 dir. Edward Buzzell
Kastner, E. *Three Men in the Snow*

Paradise Postponed
THAMES (GB) 1986 dir. Alvin Rakoff
TVSe(GB)
Mortimer, J.

Parallax View, The
PAR (US) 1974 dir. Alan J. Pakula
V
Singer, L.

Parents Terribles, Les
SIRIUS (Fr) 1948 dir. Jean Cocteau
Cocteau, J.
P

Parent Trap, The
DISNEY (US) 1961 dir. David Swift
Ch, V
Kastner, E. *Lottie and Lisa*

Paris Blues
UA (US) 1961 dir. Martin Ritt
V
Flender, H.

Paris in Spring
PAR (US) 1935 dir. Lewis Milestone
Taylor, D.
P

Paris Interlude
MGM (US) 1934 dir. Edwin L. Marin
Perelman, S. J. and Perelman, L.
All Good Americans

Paris Trout
VIACOM (US) 1991
dir. Stephen Gyllenhaal
TV(US), V
Dexter, P.

Paris Underground
UA (US) 1945 dir. Gregory Ratoff
GB title: Madame Pimpernel
Shiber, Mrs. E.

Park is Mine, The
HBO (Can/US) 1985
dir. Steven Hilliard Stern
TV(US), V
Peters, S.

Parnell
MGM (US) 1937 dir. John M. Stahl
Schauffler, E.
P

Parrish
WAR (US) 1961 dir. Delmer Daves
Savage, M.

Parson of Panamint, The
PAR (US) 1941 dir. William McGann
Kyne, P. B.

Partners in Crime
AA (GB) 1961 dir. Peter Duffell
Wallace, E. *Man Who Knew, The*

Pascali's Island
AVENUE (GB) 1988 dir. James Dearden
V
Unsworth, B. *Idol Hunter, The*

Passage, The
HEMDALE (GB) 1978
dir. J. Lee Thompson
V
Nicolaysen, B. *Perilous Passage, The*

Passage from Hong Kong
WAR (US) 1941 dir. D. Ross Lederman
Biggers, E. D. *Agony Column*

Passage Home
GFD (GB) 1955 dir. Roy Baker
Armstrong, R.

Passage to India, A
COL-EMI (GB) 1984 dir. David Lean
V
Forster, E. M.

Passenger
KADR (Pol) 1963 dir. Andrzej Munk
Posmysz-Piasecka, Z.
P

Passengers, The
COL-WAR (Fr) 1977 dir. Serge Le Roy
Dwyer, K. R. *Shattered*

Passing of the Third Floor Back, The
GB (GB) 1935 dir. Berthold Viertel
Jerome, J. K.
P

Passionate Friends, The
CINEGUILD (GB) 1949 dir. David Lean
GB title: One Woman's Story
Wells, H. G.

Passionate Summer, The
RANK (US) 1958 dir. Rudolph Cartier
Mason, R. *Shadow and the Peak, The*

Passion Flower
MGM (US) 1930 dir. William de Mille
Norris, K.

Passport to Treason
EROS (GB) 1956 dir. Robert S. Baker
O'Brine, M.

Password is Courage, The
MGM (GB) 1962 dir. Andrew L. Stone
Castle, J.

Pastor Hall
UA (GB) 1940 dir. Roy Boulting
Toller, E.
P

Patch of Blue, A
MGM (US) 1965 dir. Guy Green
Kata, E. *Be Ready With Bells and Drums*

Pather Panchali
SAT. RAY (Ind) 1955 dir. Satyajit Ray
V
Bannerjee, B. B.

Paths of Glory
UA (US) 1957 dir. Stanley Kubrick
V
Cobb, H.

Patricia Neal Story, The
SCHILLER (US) 1981
dir. Antony Harvey & Anthony Page
TV(US)
Farrell, B. *Pat & Roald*

Patriots, The
COMPASS (US) 1963
dir. George Schaefer
TV(US)
Kingsley, S.
P

Patterns
UA (US) 1956 dir. Fielder Cook
GB title: Patterns of Power
Serling, R.
P

Patton
FOX (US) 1970 dir. Franklin Schaffner
GB title: Patton: Lust for Glory
V
Farago, L. *Patton: Ordeal & Triumph*

Patty Hearst
ATLANTIC (US) 1988
dir. Paul Schrader
V
Hearst, P. *Every Secret Thing*

Pawnbroker, The
PAR (US) 1964 dir. Sidney Lumet
V
Wallant, E. L.

Payment Deferred
MGM (US) 1932 dir. Lothar Mendel
Dell, J.
P

Payoff
VIACOM (US) 1991 dir. Stuart Cooper
TV(US)
Owen, R. T.

Payroll
AA (GB) 1960 dir. Sidney Hayers
Bickerton, D.

Pearl, The
RKO (US/Mex) 1948
dir. Emilio Fernandez
Steinbeck, J.

Pearl of Death, The
UN (US) 1944 dir. Roy William Neill
V
Doyle, Sir A. C. *Six Napoleons, The*

Peck's Bad Boy
FOX (US) 1934 dir. Edward Cline
Peck, G. W.

Peeper
FOX (US) 1975 dir. Peter Hyams
V

Laumer, K. *Deadfall*

Peg of Old Drury
WILCOX (GB) 1935 dir. Herbert Wilcox
Reade, C. and Taylor, T. *Masks and Faces*
P

Peg O' My Heart
MGM (US) 1933 dir. Robert Z. Leonard
Manners, J. H.
P

Pelle the Conqueror
CURZON (Den/Swe) 1988
dir. Bille August
Nexo, M. A.

Penelope
MGM (US) 1966 dir. Arthur Hiller
Cunningham, E. V.

Penguin Pool Murder, The
RKO (US) 1932 dir. George Marshall
Palmer, S.

Penn of Pennsylvania
BN (GB) 1941 dir. Lance Comfort
US title: The Courageous Mr. Penn
Vulliamy, C. E. *William Penn*

Penthouse, The
PAR (GB) 1967 dir. Peter Collinson
Forbes, J. S. *Meter Man, The*
P

Penthouse, The
GREEN-WHITE (US) 1989
dir. David Greene
TV(US)
Trevor, E.

People, The
METRO (USTV) 1972 dir. John Korty
V

Henderson, Z. *Pilgrimage*

People Against O'Hara, The
MGM (US) 1951 dir. John Sturges
Lipsky, E.

People Like Us
ITC (US) 1990 dir. Billy Hale
TVSe(US)
Dunne, D.

People That Time Forgot, The
BW (GB) 1977 dir. Kevin Connor
V

Burroughs, E. R.

People Will Talk
FOX (US) 1951
dir. Joseph L. Mankiewicz
Goetz, C. *Dr. Praetorius*
P

Pépé le Moko
PARIS (Fr) 1936 dir. Julian Duvivier
V

d'Ashelbe, R.

Percy
MGM-EMI (GB) 1971
dir. Ralph Thomas
V

Hitchcock, R.

Perfect Alibi, The
RKO (GB) 1931 dir. Basil Dean
Milne, A. A.
P

Perfect Marriage, The
PAR (US) 1946 dir. Lewis Allen
Raphaelson, S.
P

Perfect Murder, The
MI (Ind) 1990 dir. Zafar Hai
Keating, H. R. F.

Perfect Strangers
WAR (US) 1950 dir. Bretaigne Windust
GB title: Too Dangerous to Love
Hecht, B. and MacArthur, C. *Ladies and Gentlemen*
P

Perfect Tribute, The
P&G (US) 1991 dir. Jack Bender
TV(US)
Andrews, M. R.

Perfect Woman, The
GFD (GB) 1949 dir. Bernard Knowles
Geoffrey, W. and Mitchell, B.
P

Peril
TRIUMPH (Fr) 1985 dir. Michel DeVille
V
Belletto, R. *Sur la Terre Comme au Ciel*

Perilous Journey, A
REP (US) 1953 dir. R. G. Springsteen
Roe, V. *Golden Tide, The*

Period of Adjustment
MGM (US) 1962 dir. George Roy Hill
Williams, T.
P

Perri
DISNEY (US) 1957 dir. Ralph Wright
Ch, V
Salten, F.

Personal Affair
RANK (GB) 1953 dir. Anthony Pelissier
Storm, L.
P

Personal Property
MGM (US) 1937 dir. W. S. Van Dyke II
GB title: Man in Possession, The
Harwood, H. M. *Man in Possession, The*
P

Persons in Hiding
PAR (US) 1939 dir. Louis King
Hoover, J. E.

Persuasion
GRANADA TV (GB) 1969
dir. Howard Baker
TVSe(GB)
Austen, J.

Pete 'n Tillie
UN (US) 1972 dir. Martin Ritt
V
De Vries, P. *Witch's Milk*

Peter Ibbetson
PAR (US) 1935 dir. Henry Hathaway
Du Maurier, G.

Peter Lundy and the Medicine Hat Stallion
FRIENDLY (US) 1977
dir. Michael O'Herlihy
TV(US), V
Henry, M. *San Domingo, The Medicine Hat Stallion*

Peter Pan
DISNEY (US) 1953 dir. Ben Sharpsteen
A, V
NBC (US) 1955 dir. Michael Kidd
M, TV(US), V
ATV (GB) 1976 dir. Dwight Hemion
TV(GB)
Barrie, Sir J. M.; (and Leigh, C. Comden, B. and Green, A.1955 only)
P

Peter the Great
NBC ENT (US) 1986
dir. Marvin J. Chomsky,
Lawrence Shiller
TVSe(US)
Massie, R. K.

Peterville Diamond, The
WAR (GB) 1942 dir. Walter Forde
Fodor, L. *Jewel Robbery*
P

Petit Con
GOLDWYN (Fr) 1985
dir. Gerard Lauzier
V
Lauzier, G. *Souvenirs d'un Jeune Homme*

Petite Sirène, La
WA (Fr) 1984 dir. Roger Andrieux
Dangerfield, Y.

Petrified Forest, The
WAR (US) 1936 dir. Archie Mayo
V
Sherwood, R. E.
P

Pet Sematary
PAR (US) 1989 dir. Mary Lambert
V
King, S.

Petticoat Fever
MGM (US) 1936
dir. George Fitzmaurice
Reed, M.
P

Petulia
WAR (US) 1968 dir. Richard Lester
V
Haase, J. *Me and the Arch Kook Petulia*

Peyton Place
FOX (US) 1957 dir. Mark Robson
Metalious, G.

Phantom Lady
UN (US) 1944 dir. Robert Siodmak
Irish, W.

Phantom of the Opera, The
UN (US) 1943 dir. Arthur Lubin
V
UI (GB) 1962 dir. Terence Fisher
HALMI PRODS (US) 1983
dir. Robert Markowitz
TV(US)
21ST (US) 1989 dir. Dwight H. Little
SABAN/SCHERICK PRODS (US/Fr)
1990 dir. Tony Richardson
TV(US/Fr)
Leroux, G.

Phantom of the Rue Morgue
WAR (US) 1954 dir. Roy del Ruth
Poe, E. A. *Murders in the Rue Morgue*

Phantom Tollbooth, The
MGM (US) 1969 dir. Chuck Jones
A, V
Juster, N.

Philadelphia Experiment, The
NEW WORLD (US) 1984
dir. Stewart Raffill
V
Moore, W. I. and Berlitz, C.

Philadelphia Story, The
MGM (US) 1940 dir. George Cukor
V
Barry, P.
P

Physical Assault
TITAN (US) 1973
dir. William M. Bushnell
V

Kolpacoff, V. *Prisoners of Quai Dong, The*

Piaf — The Early Years
FOX (Fr) 1982 dir. Guy Casaril
Berteaut, S. *Piaf*

Piano for Mrs. Cimino, A
EMI (US) 1982 dir. George Schaefer
TV(US)
Oliphant, R.

Piccadilly Jim
MGM (US) 1936 dir. Robert Z. Leonard
Wodehouse, P. G.

Pickwick Papers, The
REN (GB) 1952 dir. Noel Langley
V
BBC (GB) 1985 dir. Brian Lighthill
TV(GB)
Dickens, C.

Picnic
COL (US) 1955 dir. Joshua Logan
V
Inge, W.
P

Picnic at Hanging Rock
AFC (Aust) 1975 dir. Peter Weir
Lindsay, J.

Picture of Dorian Gray, The
MGM (US) 1945 dir. Albert Lewin
V
CURTIS (US) 1973 dir. Glenn Jordan
TV(US)
Wilde, O.

Pieces of Dreams
UA (US) 1970 dir. Daniel Haller
Barrett, W. E. *Wine and the Music, The*

Pied Piper, The
SAG (GB) 1971 dir. Jacques Demy
Browning, R.

Pied Piper, The
FOX (US) 1942 dir. Irving Pichel
Shute, N.

Pigeon That Took Rome, The
PAR (US) 1962 dir. Melville Shavelson
Downes, D. *Easter Dinner, The*

Pilgrimage
FOX (US) 1933 dir. John Ford
Wylie, I. A. R.

Pillow to Post
WAR (US) 1945 dir. Vincent Sherman
Kohn, R. S. *Pillar to Post*
P

Pilot, The
SUMMIT (Can) 1981
dir. Cliff Robertson
Davis, R. P.

Pimpernel Smith
BN (GB) 1941 dir. Leslie Howard
V
Orczy, Baroness E. *Scarlet Pimpernel, The*

Pink Jungle, The
UI (US) 1968 dir. Delbert Mann
Williams, A. *Snake Water*

Pink String and Sealing Wax
EAL (GB) 1945 dir. Robert Hamer
Pertwee, R.
P

Pinky
FOX (US) 1949 dir. Elia Kazan
Sumner, C. R. *Quality*

Pinocchio
DISNEY (US) 1940 dir. Ben Sharpsteen
A, Ch, V
CANTO (US) 1968 dir. Sid Smith
TV(US)
Collodi, C.

Pirate, The
MGM (US) 1948 dir. Vincente Minnelli
M, V
Behrman, S. N.
P

Pirate, The
WAR TV (US) 1978
dir. Kenneth C. Annakin
TVSe(US)
Robbins, H.

Pirate Movie, The
FOX (Aus) 1982 dir. Ken Annakin
V
Sullivan, Sir A. and Gilbert, Sir W.
Pirates of Penzance, The
P

Pirates of Penzance, The
UN (GB) 1982 dir. Wilford Leach
M, V
Sullivan, Sir A. and Gilbert, Sir W.
P

Pit and the Pendulum, The
AA (US) 1961 dir. Roger Corman
V
FULL MOON (US) 1991
dir. Stuart Gordon
Poe, E. A.

Pitfall
UA (US) 1948 dir. André de Toth
Dratler, J.

Pit of Darkness
BUTCHER (GB) 1961
dir. Lance Comfort
McCutcheon, H. *To Dusty Death*

Pixote
UNIFILM (Port) 1981
dir. Hector Babenco
V
Lonzeiro, J. *Infancia dos Martos*

Place in the Sun, A
PAR (US) 1951 dir. George Stevens
V
Dreiser, T. *American Tragedy, An*

Place of One's Own, A
GFD (GB) 1945 dir. Bernard Knowles
Sitwell, Sir O.

Place To Go, A
BL (GB) 1963 dir. Basil Dearden
Fisher, M. *Bethnal Green*

Plague Dogs, The
NEPENTHE (GB) 1982
dir. Martin Rosen
A, V
Adams, R. G.

Plainsman, The
PAR (US) 1937 dir. Cecil B de Mille
V
Wilstach, F. *Wild Bill Hickok*

Planet of the Apes
FOX (US) 1968 dir. Franklin Schaffner
V
Boulle, P. *Monkey Planet*

Platoon Leader
CANNON (US) 1988 dir. Aaron Norris
V
McDonough, J. R.

Playboy of the Western World, The
FOUR PROVINCES (GB) 1962
dir. Brian Desmond Hurst
V

Synge, J. M.
P

Playground, The
JERAND (US) 1965 dir. Richard Hilliard

Sulzberger, C. *My Brother Death*

Playing for Time
SYZYGY (US) 1980 dir. Daniel Mann
TV(US), V

Fenelon, F.

Play it Again, Sam
PAR (US) 1972 dir. Herbert Ross
V

Allen, W.
P

Play it as it Lays
UN (US) 1972 dir. Frank Perry

Didion, J.

Plaza Suite
PAR (US) 1971 dir. Arthur Hiller
V
PAR (US) 1987 dir. Roger Beatty
TV(US)

Simon, N.
P

Please Don't Eat the Daisies
MGM (US) 1960 dir. Charles Walters

Kerr, J.

Please Turn Over
AA (GB) 1959 dir. Gerald Thomas

Thomas, B. *Book of the Month*
P

Pleasure of his Company, The
PAR (US) 1961 dir. George Seaton

Taylor, S. A. and Skinner, C. O.
P

Pleasures
COL TV (US) 1986 dir. Sharron Miller

Barbach, L.

Pleasure Seekers, The
FOX (US) 1964 dir. Jean Negulesco

Secondari, J. H. *Coins in the Fountain*

Plenty
FOX (US) 1985 dir. Fred Schepisi
V

Hare, D.
P

Plough and the Stars, The
RKO (US) 1936 dir. John Ford

O'Casey, S.
P

Plunder
WILCOX (GB) 1931 dir. Tom Walls

Travers, B.
P

Plunder of the Sun
WAR (US) 1953 dir. John Farrow

Dodge, D.

Plymouth Adventure, The
MGM (US) 1952 dir. Clarence Brown

Gebler, E.

Pocketful of Miracles
UA (US) 1961 dir. Frank Capra
V

Runyon, D. *Madame la Gimp*

Pocketful of Rye, A
BBC (GB) 1985 dir. Guy Slater
TV(GB), V
Christie, A.

Pocket Money
FA (US) 1972 dir. Stuart Rosenberg
V
Brown, J. P. S. *Jim Kane*

Poet's Pub
AQUILA (GB) 1949
dir. Frederick Wilson
Linklater, E.

Point Blank
MGM (US) 1967 dir. John Boorman
V
Stark, R.

Poirot: Peril at End House
LWT (GB) 1991 dir. Renny Rye
TV(GB)
Christie, A.

Poison Pen
AB (GB) 1939 dir. Paul Stein
Llewellyn, R.
P

Polly
DISNEY (US) 1989 dir. Debbie Allen
TV(US)
Porter, E. H. *Pollyanna*

Pollyanna
DISNEY (US) 1960 dir. David Swift
Ch, V
Porter, E. H.

Poor Cow
WAR (GB) 1967 dir. Ken Loach
V
Dunn, N.

Poor Little Rich Girl: The Barbara Hutton Story
ITC (US) 1987 dir. Charles Jarrot
TVSe(US)
Heymann, C. D. *Poor Little Rich Girl*

Pope of Greenwich Village, The
MGM/UA (US) 1984
dir. Stuart Rosenberg
V
Patrick, V.

Poppy
PAR (US) 1936
dir. A. Edward Sutherland
Donnelly, D.
P

Porgy and Bess
GOLDWYN (US) 1959
dir. Otto Preminger
M
Gershwin, G., Gershwin, I. and Heyward, D.
P
Heyward, D. and Heyward, D. *Porgy*
P

Pork Chop Hill
UA (US) 1959 dir. Lewis Milestone
V
Marshall, S. L. A.

Port Afrique
COL (GB) 1956 dir. Rudolph Maté
Dyer, B. V.

Porte des Lilas
FILMSONOR (Fr/It) 1957
dir. René Clair
Fallet, R. *Grande Ceinture, La*

Portia on Trial
REP (US) 1937 dir. George Nicholls, Jr.
Baldwin, F.

Portnoy's Complaint
WAR (US) 1972 dir. Ernest Lehman
V
Roth, P.

Portrait of a Marriage
BBC (GB) 1990 dir. Stephen Whittaker
TVSe(GB)
Nicolson, N.

Portrait of Clare
ABP (GB) 1950 dir. Lance Comfort
Young, F. B.

Portrait of Jennie
SELZNICK (US) 1948
dir. William Dieterle
GB title: Jennie
V
Nathan, R.

Portrait of the Artist as a Young Man
ULYSSES (GB) 1977 dir. Joseph Strick
V
Joyce, J.

Poseidon Adventure, The
FOX (US) 1972 dir. Ronald Neame
V
Gallico, P.

Possessed
MGM (US) 1931 dir. Clarence Brown
V
Selwyn, E. *Mirage, The*
P

Possessed
WAR (US) 1947 dir. Curtis Bernhardt
Weiman, R. *One Man's Secret*

Possession of Joel Delaney, The
SCOTIA-BARBER (US) 1971
dir. Waris Hussein
Stewart, R.

Postcards from the Edge
COL (US) 1990 dir. Mike Nichols
Fisher, C.

Postman Always Rings Twice, The
MGM (US) 1946 dir. Tay Garnett
PAR (US) 1981 dir. Bob Rafaelson
Cain, J. M.

Power, The
MGM (US) 1968 dir. Byron Haskin
Robinson, F.

Power and the Prize, The
MGM (US) 1956 dir. Henry Koster
Swiggett, H.

Pow Wow Highway
WAR (US) 1989 dir. Jonathan Wacks
Seals, D.

Prayer for the Dying, A
Goldwyn (GB) 1987 dir. Mike Hodges
V
Higgins, J.

Prelude to Fame
GFD (GB) 1950 dir. Fergus McDonell
Huxley, A. L. *Young Archimedes*

Premature Burial, The
AA (US) 1962 dir. Roger Corman
V
Poe, E. A.

Prescription: Murder
UN (US) 1968 dir. Richard Irving
TV(US)
Levinson, R. and Link, W.
P

Presenting Lily Mars
MGM (US) 1943 dir. Norman Taurog
M, V
Tarkington, B.

President's Lady, The
FOX (US) 1953 dir. Henry Levin
Stone, I. *Immortal Wife*

President's Mistress, The
KINGS RD (US) 1978
dir. John Llewellyn
TV(US), V
Anderson, P.

President's Plane is Missing, The
ABC (US) 1973 dir. Daryl Duke
TV(US)
Serling, R. J.

Press for Time
RANK (GB) 1966 dir. Robert Asher
V
McGill, A. *Yea, Yea, Yea*

Pressure Point
UA (US) 1962 dir. Hubert Cornfield
Lindner, R. *Fifty Minute Hour, The*

Prestige
RKO (US) 1932 dir. Tay Garnett
Hervey, H. *Lips of Steel*

Presumed Innocent
WAR (US) 1990 dir. Alan J. Pakula
Turow, S.

Pretty Maids All In A Row
MGM (US) 1971 dir. Roger Vadim
Pollini, F.

Pretty Poison
FOX (US) 1968 dir. Noel Black
V
Geller, S. *She Let Him Continue*

Pretty Polly
RANK (GB) 1967 dir. Guy Green
US title: Matter of Innocence, A
Coward, N. *Pretty Polly Barlow*

Price, The
TALENT (US) 1971 dir. Fielder Cook
TV(US)
Miller, A.
P

Price, The
CHANNEL 4 (GB) 1985 dir. Peter Smith
TVSe(GB)
Ransley, P.

Price of Silence, The
GN (GB) 1959 dir. Montgomery Tully
Meynell, L. *One Step From Murder*

Prick up your Ears
ZENITH (GB) 1986 dir. Stephen Frears
V
Lahr, J.

Pride and Extreme Prejudice
USA NET (US) 1990 dir. Ian Sharp
TV(US)
Forsyth, F.

Pride and Prejudice
MGM (US) 1940 dir. Robert Z. Leonard
V
BBC (GB) 1980 dir. Cyril Coke
TVSe(GB)
Austen, J.

Pride and the Passion, The
UA (US) 1957 dir. Stanley Kramer
V

Forester, C. S. *Gun, The*

Pride of the Marines
WAR (US) 1945 dir. Delmer Daves
GB title: Forever in Love

Butterfield, R. P. *Al Schmid, Marine*

Priest of Love
ENT (GB) 1981 dir. Christopher Miles
V

Moore, H. T.

Prime of Miss Jean Brodie, The
FOX (GB) 1969 dir. Ronald Neame
V
STV (GB) 1978 dir. Tina Wakerell
TV(GB)

Spark, M.

Prime Target
MGM/UA (US) 1989 dir. Robert Collins
TV(US)

O'Donnell, L. *No Business Being a Cop*

Primrose Path, The
RKO (US) 1940 dir. Gregory LaCava

Lincoln, V. *February Hill*

Prince and the Pauper, The
WAR (US) 1937 dir. William Keighley
V
DISNEY (US) 1961 dir. Don Chaffey
TV(US), V
WAR (PAN) 1977 dir. Richard Fleischer
US title: Crossed Swords

Twain, M.

Prince and the Showgirl, The
WAR (GB) 1957 dir. Laurence Olivier
V

Rattigan, T. *Sleeping Prince, The*
P

Prince of Central Park, The
LORIMAR (US) 1977 dir. Harvey Hart
TV(US)

Rhodes, E.

Prince of Foxes
FOX (US) 1949 dir. Henry King

Shellabarger, S.

Prince of Players
FOX (US) 1954 dir. Philip Dunne

Ruggles, E.

Prince of the City
ORION (US) 1981 dir. Sidney Lumet
V

Daley, R.

Prince of Tides, The
COL (US) 1991 dir. Barbra Streisand

Conroy, P.

Princess Bride, The
FOX (US) 1987 dir. Rob Reiner
V

Goldman, W.

Princess Comes Across, The
PAR (US) 1936 dir. William K. Howard

Rogger, L. L.

Princess Daisy
NBC ENT (US) 1984 dir. Waris Hussein
TVSe(US), V

Krantz, J.

Prince Who Was a Thief, The
UN (US) 1951 dir. Rudolph Maté

Dreiser, T.

Prisoner, The
COL (GB) 1955 dir. Peter Glenville

Boland, B.
P

Prisoner of Second Avenue, The
WAR (US) 1975 dir. Melvin Frank
V

Simon, N.
P

Prisoner of Zenda
UA (US) 1937 dir. John Cromwell
V
MGM (US) 1952 dir. Richard Thorpe
V
UN (US) 1979 dir. Richard Quine
BBC (GB) 1984
TV(GB)
Hope, A.

Private Affairs of Bel Ami, The
UA (US) 1947 dir. Albert Lewin
De Maupassant, G. *Bel Ami*

Private Angelo
ABP (GB) 1949 dir. Peter Ustinov
Linklater, E.

Private Battle, A
P&G (US) 1980
dir. Robert Michael Lewis
TV(US)
Ryan, C. and Ryan, K. M.

Private Lessons
J. FARLEY (US) 1981 dir. Alan Myerson
Greenburg, D. *Philly*

Private Life of Don Juan, The
LONDON (GB) 1934
dir. Alexander Korda
V

Bataille, H.
P

Private Lives
MGM (US) 1931 dir. Sidney Franklin
Coward, N.
P

Private Lives of Elizabeth and Essex, The
WAR (US) 1939 dir. Michael Curtiz
V

Anderson, M. *Elizabeth the Queen*
P

Privates on Parade
HANDMADE (GB) 1982
dir. Michael Blakemore
V

Nichols, P.
P

Private's Progress, A
BL (GB) 1956 dir. John Boulting
V

Hackney, A.

Private Worlds
PAR (US) 1935 dir. Gregory La Cava
Bottome, P.

Prize, The
MGM (US) 1963 dir. Mark Robson
Wallace, I.

Prize of Gold, A
COL (GB) 1955 dir. Mark Robson
Catto, M.

Prize of Peril, The
UGC (Fr/Yugo) 1983 dir. Yves Boisset
V

Sheckley, R.

Prizzi's Honor
FOX (US) 1985 dir. John Huston
V

Condon, R.

Professionals, The
COL (US) 1966 dir. Richard Brooks
V

O'Rourke, F. *Mule for the Marquesa, A*

Project X
PAR (US) 1968 dir. William Castle
Davies, L. P.

Promise, A
KT (Jap) 1987 dir. Yoshishige Yoshida
Sae, S. *Rojuko Kazoku*

Promise, The
COMM (GB) 1969 dir. Michael Hayes
Arbuzov, A.
P

Promise at Dawn
AVCO (US/Fr) 1970 dir. Jules Dassin
Gary, R. *Promisse de L'aube, La*
Taylor, S. *First Love*
P

Promised a Miracle
REP (US) 1988 dir. Stephen Gyllenhaal
TV(US)
Parker, L. and Tanner, D. *We Let Our Son Die*

Promise to Keep, A
WAR TV (US) 1990 dir. Rod Holcomb
TV(US)
Yarmolinsky, J. *Angels Without Wings*

Prospero's Books
FILM 4 (GB/Fr) 1991
dir. Peter Greenaway
Shakespeare, W. *Tempest, The*
P

Proud and Profane, The
PAR (US) 1956 dir. George Seaton
Crockett, L. H. *Magnificent Devils*

Proud Ones, The
FOX (US) 1956 dir. Robert D. Webb
Athanas, V.

Prudence and the Pill
FOX (GB) 1968 dir. Fielder Cook
V
Mills, H.
P

Psyche 59
BL (GB) 1964 dir. Alexander Singer
de Ligneris, F. *Psyche 63*

Psycho
UN (US) 1960 dir. A. Hitchcock
V
Bloch, R.

PT 109
WAR (US) 1963 dir. Leslie H. Martinson
V
Donovan, R. J. *PT109 — John F. Kennedy in World War II*

Public Defender
RKO (US) 1931 dir. J. Walter Ruben
Goodschild, G. *Splendid Crime, The*

Pumping Iron
CINEMA 51 (US) 1977
dir. George Butler
V
Gaines, C. and Butler, G.

Pumping Iron II
BLUE DOLPHIN (US) 1984
dir. George Butler
V
Gaines, C. and Butler, G. *Pumping Iron II: The Unprecedented Woman*

Pumpkin Eater, The
BL (GB) 1964 dir. Jack Clayton
Mortimer, P.

Puppet on a Chain
SCOTIA-BARBER (GB) 1970
dir. Geoffrey Reeve, Don Sharp
V
MacLean, A.

Purple Mask, The
UN (US) 1955 dir. Bruce Humberstone
Orczy, Baroness E. *Scarlet Pimpernel, The*

Purple Noon
HILLCREST (Fr) 1960
dir. René Clément
Highsmith, P. *Talented Mr. Ripley, The*

Purple Plain, The
GFD (GB) 1954 dir. Robert Parrish
V
Bates, H. E.

Pursuit of D. B. Cooper, The
UN (US) 1981 dir. Roger Spottiswoode
V
Reed, J. D. *Free Fall*

Pursuit
ABC (USTV) 1972 dir. Michael Crichton
Crichton, M. *Binary*

Pursuit of Happiness, The
PAR (US) 1934 dir. Alexander Hall
Langner, L. and Marshall, A.
P

Pursuit of Happiness, The
COL (US) 1971 dir. Robert Mulligan
V
Rogers, T.

Pushover
COL (US) 1954 dir. Richard Quine
Ballinger, W. *Rafferty*
Walsh, T. *Night Watch, The*

Pygmalion
MGM (GB) 1938 dir. Anthony Asquith
V
COMPASS (US) 1963
dir. George Schaefer
TV(US)
Shaw, G. B.
P

Q&A
TRI-STAR (US) 1990 dir. Sidney Lumet
Torres, E.

QB VII
COL (US) 1974 dir. Tom Gries
TVSe(US), V
Uris, L.

Quai Des Brumes
RAB (Fr) 1938 dir. Marcel Carné
MacOrlan, P.

Quai des Orfèvres
MAJ (Fr) 1947
dir. Henri-Georges Clouzot
Steeman, S-A. *Legitime Defense*

Quality Street
RKO (US) 1937 dir. George Stevens
Barrie, Sir J. M.
P

Quare Fellow, The
BL (GB) 1962 dir. Arthur Dreifuss
Behan, B.
P

Quartet
NEW WORLD (GB/Fr) 1981
dir. James Ivory

Rhys, J.

Quartet
GFD (GB) 1948
dir. Ralph Smart/Harold French/
Arthur Crabtree/Ken Annakin
V

Maugham, W. S. *Facts of Life, The;
Alien Corn, The; Kite, The;
Colonel'sLady, The*

Queen Bee
COL (US) 1955 dir. Ronald MacDougall

Lee, E.

Queenie
NEW WORLD (US) 1987
dir. Larry Peerce
TVSe(US)

Korda, M.

Queen of Spades, The
AB (GB) 1949 dir. Thorold Dickinson

Pushkin, A. S.

Queen of the Mob
PAR (US) 1940 dir. James Hogan

Hoover, J. E. *Persons in Hiding*

Querelle
TRIUMPH (Fr/Ger) 1983
dir. Rainer Werner Fassbinder
V

Genet, J. *Querelle de Brest*

Question of Honor, A
EMI (US) 1982 dir. Jud Taylor
TV(US), V

Grosso, S. and Rosenberg, P. *Point
Blank*

Quest for Fire
FOX (Can/Fr) 1982
dir. Jean-Jacques Annaud

Rosny, J. H.

Quick and the Dead, The
HBO (US) 1987 dir. Robert Day
TV(US), V

L'Amour, L.

Quick, Before it Melts
MGM (US) 1964 dir. Delbert Mann

Benjamin, P.

Quick Change
WAR (US) 1990 dir. Howard Franklin,
Bill Murray

Cronley, J.

Quiet American, The
UA (US) 1957 dir. Joseph L. Mankiewicz

Greene, G.

Quiet Days in Clichy
MIRACLE (Den) 1970
dir. Jens Jorgen Thorsen

Miller, H.

Quiet Duel, The
DAIEI (Jap) 1983 dir. Akira Kurosawa

Kikuta, K.
P

Quiet Earth, The
YEL (NZ) 1985 dir. Greg Murphy
TV

Madison, C.

Quiet Flows the Don
GORKI (USSR) 1958
dir. Sergei Gerasimov

Sholokhov, M. *And Quiet Flows the
Don*

Quiet Man, The
REP (US) 1952 dir. John Ford
V
Walsh, M. *Green Rushes*

Quiet Wedding
PAR (GB) 1941 dir. Anthony Asquith
McCracken, E.
P

Quiet Weekend
AB (GB) 1946 dir. Harold French
McCracken, E.
P

Quiller Memorandum, The
RANK (GB) 1966 dir. Michael Anderson
Trevor, E.

Quo Vadis
MGM (US) 1951 dir. Mervyn Le Roy
RAI (It) 1985
TVSe
Sienkiewicz, H.

Rabbit, Run
WAR (US) 1970 dir. Jack Smight
Updike, J.

Racers, The
FOX (US) 1955 dir. Henry Hathaway
GB title: Such Men are Dangerous
Ruesch, H. *Racer, The*

Rachel and the Stranger
RKO (US) 1948 dir. Norman Foster
V
Fast, H. *Rachel*

Rachel Papers, The
UA (GB) 1989 dir. Damian Harris
Amis, M.

Rachel, Rachel
WAR (US) 1968 dir. Paul Newman
V
Laurence, M. *Jest of God, A*

Racket, The
RKO (US) 1951 dir. John Cromwell
V
Cormack, B.
P

Raffles
UA (US) 1939 dir. Sam Wood
Hornung, E. W. *Raffles the Amateur Cracksman*

Rage in Harlem, A
MIRAMAX (US) 1991 dir. Bill Duke
Himes, C.

Rage in Heaven
MGM (US) 1941 dir. W. S. Van Dyke II
Hilton, J. *Dawn of Reckoning*

Rage of Angels
NBC (US) 1983 dir. Buzz Kulik
TVSe(US), V
Sequel (US) 1991 dir. Buzz Kulik
TV(US)
Sheldon, S.

Rage to Live, A
UA (US) 1965 dir. Walter Grauman
O'Hara, J.

Raging Bull
UA (US) 1980 dir. Martin Scorsese
V
La Motta, J.

Raging Moon, The
MGM (GB) 1970 dir. Bryan Forbes
V
Marshall, P.

Raging Tide, The
UI (US) 1951 dir. George Sherman
Gann, E. K. *Fiddler's Green*

Ragman's Daughter, The
FOX (GB) 1972 dir. Harold Becker
V
Sillitoe, A.

Ragtime
PAR (US) 1981 dir. Milos Forman
V
Doctorow, E. L.

Railway Children, The
MGM (GB) 1970 dir. Lionel Jeffries
Ch, V
Nesbit, E.

Rain
UA (US) 1932 dir. Lewis Milestone
V
Maugham, W. S.
P

Rainbow, The
VESTRON (GB) 1989 dir. Ken Russell
BBC (GB) 1989 dir. Stuart Burge
TVSe(GB)
Lawrence, D. H.

Rainbow
TEN-FOUR (US) 1978
dir. Jackie Cooper
TV(US), V
Finch, C.

Rainbow Drive
VIACOM (US) 1990 dir. Bobby Roth
TV(US)
Thorpe, R.

Rainmaker, The
PAR (US) 1956 dir. Joseph Anthony
Nash, N. R.
P

Rains Came, The
FOX (US) 1939 dir. Clarence Brown
Bromfield, L.

Rains of Ranchipur, The
FOX (US) 1955 dir. Jean Negulesco
Bromfield, L. *Rains Came, The*

Raintree County
MGM (US) 1957 dir. Edward Dmytryk
V
Lockridge, R.

Raise the Red Lantern
ORION (China) 1991 dir. Zhang Yimov
Tong, S. *Wives and Concubines*

Raise the Titanic
ITC (US) 1980 dir. Jerry Jameson
V
Cussler, C.

Raising a Riot
BL (GB) 1955 dir. Wendy Toye
Toombs, A.

Raisin in the Sun, A
COL (US) 1961 dir. Daniel Petrie
V
Hansberry, L.
P

Rally Round the Flag, Boys
FOX (US) 1958 dir. Leo McCarey
V
Shulman, M.

Rambling Rose
NEW LINE (US) 1991
dir. Martha Coolidge
Willingham, C.

Ramona
FOX (US) 1936 dir. Henry King
Jackson, Mrs. H. M.

Rampage
WAR (US) 1963 dir. Philip Carlson
Caillou, A.

Ramrod
UA (US) 1947 dir. André de Toth
Short, L.

Ran
Jap 1985 dir. Akira Kurosawa
Shakespeare, W. *King Lear*
P

Random Harvest
MGM (US) 1942 dir. Mervyn Le Roy
Hilton, J.

Rape, The
MIRACLE (Bel/Neth) 1973
dir. Fons Rademakers
V
Freeling, N. *Because of the Cats*

Rapture
FOX (US/Fr) 1965 dir. John Guillermin
Hastings, P. *Rapture in my Rags*

Rascal
DISNEY (US) 1969 dir. Norman Tokar
Ch, V
North, S. *Rascal, a Memoir of a Better Era*

Rat, The
RKO (GB) 1937 dir. Jack Raymond
Novello, I. and Collier, C.
P

Rat Race, The
PAR (US) 1960 dir. Robert Mulligan
Kanin, G.
P

Rattle of a Simple Man
WAR (GB) 1964 dir. Muriel Box
V
Dyer, C.
P

Razorback
WAR (Aust) 1984 dir. Russell Mulcahy
V
Brennan, P.

Razor's Edge, The
FOX (US) 1946 dir. Edmund Goulding
V
COL (US) 1984 dir. John Byrum
Maugham, W. S.

Reach for Glory
GALA (GB) 1962 dir. Philip Leacock
Rae, J. *Custard Boys, The*

Reach for the Sky
COL (GB) 1956 dir. Lewis Gilbert
V
Brickhill, P.

Reaching for the Sun
PAR (US) 1941 dir. William Wellman

Smitter, W. *F.O.B. Detroit*

Real Charlotte Somerville, The
YTV (GB) 1991 dir. Timothy Barry
TV(GB)

Ross, E. and Ross, M.

Real Glory, The
UA (US) 1939 dir. Henry Hathaway

Clifford, C.L.

Re-Animator
EMPIRE (US) 1985 dir. Stuart Gordon

Lovecraft, H. P. *Herbert West — The Re-Animator*

Reap the Wild Wind
PAR (US) 1942 dir. Cecil B. de Mille

Strabel, T.

Rearview Mirror
SCHICK SUNN (US) 1984
dir. Lou Antonio
TV(US)

Cooney, C. B.

Rear Window
PAR (US) 1954 dir. Alfred Hitchcock
V

Woolrich, C.

Reason for Living: The Jill Ireland Story
TEN-FOUR (US) 1991
dir. Michael Rhodes
TV(US)

Ireland, J. *Life Lines*

Rebecca
UA (US) 1940 dir. Alfred Hitchcock

Du Maurier, D.

Rebecca of Sunnybrook Farm
FOX (US) 1932 dir. Alfred Santell
FOX (US) 1938 dir. Allan Dwan
V

Wiggin, Mrs. K. D.

Rebel
MIRACLE (Aust) 1986
dir. Michael Jenkins
V

Herbert, B. *No Names . . . No Pack Drills*
P

Rebels, The
UN TV (US) 1979 dir. Russ Mayberry
TVSe(US)

Jakes, J.

Reckless Moment, The
COL (US) 1949 dir. Max Ophuls
V

Holding, Mrs. E. *Blank Wall, The*

Reckoning, The
COL (GB) 1969 dir. Jack Gold

Hall, P. *Harp That Once, The*

Red Alert
PAR (US) 1977 dir. William Hale
TV(US), V

King, H. *Paradigm Red*

Red Badge of Courage, The
MGM (US) 1951 dir. John Huston
V
M ARCH (US) 1981 dir. Don Taylor
TV(US)

Crane, S.

Redbeard
TOHO (Jap) 1965 dir. Akira Kurosawa

Yamamoto

Red Beret, The
COL (GB) 1953 dir. Terence Young
US title: Paratrooper
V
Saunders, H. St. G.

Red Canyon
UN (US) 1949 dir. George Sherman
Grey, Z. *Wildfire*

Red Danube, The
MGM (US) 1949 dir. George Sidney
Marshall, B. *Vespers in Vienna*

Red Dust
MGM (US) 1932 dir. Victor Fleming
V
Collison, W. *Farewell to Women*
P

Red Earth, White Earth
VIACOM (US) 1989 dir. David Greene
TV(US)
Weaver, W.

Red Headed Woman
MGM (US) 1932 dir. Jack Conway
Brush, K.

Red House, The
UA (US) 1947 dir. Delmer Daves
V
Chamberlain, G. A.

Red-Light Sting, The
UN TV (US) 1984 dir. Rod Holcomb
TV(US), V
Post, H. *Whorehouse Sting, The*

Red Pony, The
BL (US) 1949 dir. Lewis Milestone
V
UN (US) 1973 dir. Robert Totten
TV(US)
Steinbeck, J.

Red Riding Hood
CANNON (US) 1987 dir. Adam Brooks
Ch
Grimm, J. L. K. and Grimm, W. K.

Red River
UA (US) 1948 dir. Howard Hawks
V
Chase, B. *Chisolm Trail, The*

Red Sky at Morning
UN (US) 1971 dir. James Goldstone
Bradford, R.

Red Wagon
BIP (GB) 1935 dir. Paul Stein
Smith, Lady E.

Reflection of Fear
COL (US) 1973 dir. William A. Fraker
V
Forbes, S. *Go to thy Deathbed*

Reflections in a Golden Eye
WAR (US) 1967 dir. John Huston
V
McCullers, C.

Reflections of Murder
ABC (US) 1974 dir. John Badham
TV(US)
Boileau, P. & Narcejac, T. *Celle Qui N'Etait Plus*

Reilly, Ace of Spies
EUSTON (GB) 1983 dir. Jim Goddard
TVSe(GB), V
Lockhart, R. B.

Reincarnation of Peter Proud, The
AVCO (US) 1975 dir. J. Lee Thompson
V
Ehrlich, M.

Reivers, The
WAR (US) 1969 dir. Mark Rydell
V
Faulkner, W.

Relentless
CBS ENT (US) 1977 dir. Lee H. Katzin
TV(US)
Garfield, B.

Reluctant Debutante, The
MGM (US) 1958 dir. Vincente Minnelli
Home, W. D.
P

Reluctant Heroes
ABP (GB) 1951 dir. Jack Raymond
V
Morris, C.
P

Reluctant Widow, The
GFD (GB) 1950 dir. Bernard Knowles
Heyer, G.

Remains to be Seen
MGM (US) 1953 dir. Don Weis
Lindsay, H. and Crouse, R.
P

Remarkable Mr. Pennypacker, The
FOX (US) 1958 dir. Henry Levin
O'Brian, L.
P

Remember Last Night?
UN (US) 1936 dir. James Whale
Hobhouse, A. *Hangover Murders, The*

Remo Williams: The Adventure Begins
ORION (US) 1985 dir. Guy Hamilton
V
Murphy, W. and Sapir, R. *Destroyer, The*

Rendezvous
MGM (US) 1935 dir. William K. Howard
Yardley, H. O. *American Black Chamber, The*

Renegades
FOX (US) 1930 dir. Victor Fleming
Armandy, A.

Report to the Commissioner
UA (US) 1975 dir. Milton Katselas
GB title: Operation Undercover
V
Mills, J.

Reprisal
COL (US) 1956 dir. George Sherman
Gordon, A.

Requiem for a Heavyweight
COL (US) 1962 dir. Ralph Nelson
GB title: Blood Money
Serling, R.
P

Rescuers, The
DISNEY (US) 1977
dir. Wolfgang Reitherman
A, Ch
Sharp, M. *Rescuers, The, Miss Bianca*

Respectable Prostitute, The
MARCEAU (Fr) 1952
dir. Marcel Pagliero, Charles Brabant
Sartre, J-P.
P

Resurrection
UN (US) 1931 dir. Edwin Carewe
Tolstoy, L.

Return From the Ashes
UA (US) 1965 dir. J. Lee Thompson
Monteilhet, H.

Return from the River Kwai
RANK (GB) 1987
dir. Andrew V. McLaglen

Blair, J. and Blair, C.

Return of Don Camillo, The
MIRACLE (Fr/It) 1953
dir. Julien Duvivier

Guareschi, G. *Don Camillo and the Prodigal Son*

Return of Peter Grimm, The
RKO (US) 1935 dir. George Nicholls

Belasco, D.
P

Return of Sherlock Holmes
GRANADA (GB) 1988 dir. Michael Cox
TV(GB)

Doyle, Sir A. C.

Return of the Antelope, The
GRANADA (GB) 1987
Ch, TVSe(GB)

Hall, W.

Return of the Big Cat
DISNEY (US) 1974 dir. Tom Leetch

Dietz, L. *Year of the Big Cat, The*

Return of the Soldier, The
BW (GB) 1983 dir. Alan Bridges
V

West, R.

Return to Earth
KH (US) 1976 dir. Jud Taylor
TV(US), V

Aldrin, Jr., E. and Warga, W.

Return to Oz
DISNEY (US) 1985 dir. Walter Murch
V

Baum, L. F. *Marvellous Land of Oz, The; Ozma of Oz*

Return to Paradise
UA (US) 1953 dir. Mark Robson

Michener, J. A.

Return to Peyton Place
FOX (US) 1960 dir. Jose Ferrer

Metalious, G.

Return to the Blue Lagoon
COL (US) 1991 dir. William A. Graham

Stacpoole, H. D. *Garden of God, The*

Reuben, Reuben
FOX (US) 1983 dir. Robert Ellis Millet
V

De Vries, P.

Reunion
RANK (US/Fr/Ger) 1989
dir. Jerry Schatzberg

Uhlman, F.

Reunion in Vienna
MGM (US) 1933 dir. Sidney Franklin

Sherwood, R. E.
P

Revenge
CARLINER (US) 1971 dir. Jud Taylor
TV(US)

Davis, E.

Revenge
COL (US) 1990 dir. Tony Scott

Harrison, J.

Reversal of Fortune
WAR (US) 1990 dir. Barbet Schroeder

Dershowitz, A.

Revolt of Mamie Stover, The
FOX (US) 1956 dir. Raoul Walsh

Huie, W. B.

Revolutionary, The
UA (US) 1970 dir. Paul Williams
Koningsberger, H.

Reward, The
FOX (US) 1965 dir. Serge Bourgignon
Barrett, M.

Rhapsody
MGM (US) 1954 dir. Charles Vidor
Richardson, H. H. *Maurice Guest*

Rhapsody in August
ORION (Jap) 1991 dir. Akira Kurosawa
Murata, K. *Nabe-No-Kake*

Rhineman Exchange, The
UN TV (US) 1977 dir. Burt Kennedy
TVSe(US)
Ludlum, R.

Rhodes of Africa
GAU BRI (GB) 1936
dir. Berthold Viertes
US title: Rhodes
Millin, S. G. *Rhodes*

Rhubarb
PAR (US) 1951 dir. Allan Lubin
Smith, H. A.

Rich and Famous
MGM (US) 1981 dir. George Cukor
V
Druten, J. van *Old Acquaintance*
P

Rich and Strange
BIP (GB) 1931 dir. Alfred Hitchcock
US title: East of Shanghai
Collins, D.

Richard's Things
SOUTHERN (GB) 1980
dir. Anthony Harvey
V
Raphael, F.

Richard III
BL (GB) 1955 dir. Laurence Olivier
V
Shakespeare, W.
P

Rich Are Always With Us, The
WAR (US) 1932 dir. Alfred E. Green
Pettit, E.

Rich Man, Poor Girl
MGM (US) 1938 dir. Reinhold Schunzel
Ellis, E. *White Collars*
P

Rich Man, Poor Man
UN (US) 1976 dir. David Greene, Boris Sagal
TVSe(US)
Shaw, I.

Rich Man's Folly
PAR (US) 1931 dir. John Cromwell
Dickens, C. *Dombey and Son*

Rich Men, Single Women
A. SPELLING (US) 1990
dir. Elliot Silverstein
TV(US)
Beck, P. and Massman, P.

Richest Man in the World, The: The Story of Aristotle Onassis
KON/SAN (US) 1988 dir. Waris Hussein
TVSe(US)
Evans, P. *Ari: The Life and Time of Aristotle Onassis*

Riddle of the Sands, The
RANK (GB) 1979 dir. Tony Maylam
V

Childers, E.

Ride a Wild Pony
DISNEY (Aust) 1976 dir. Don Chaffey
V

Aldridge, J. *Sporting Proposition, A*

Ride Beyond Vengeance
COL (US) 1966 dir. Bernard McEveety

Dewlen, A. *Night of the Tiger, The*

Riders of the Purple Sage
FOX (US) 1931
dir. Hamilton MacFadden
FOX (US) 1941 dir. James Tinling

Grey, Z.

Ride the High Wind
BUTCHER (S. Africa) 1966
dir. David Millin

Harding, G. *North of Bushman's Rock*

Ride the Pink Horse
UI (US) 1947 dir. Robert Montgomery

Hughes, D. B.

Riding High
PAR (US) 1943 dir. George Marshall
GB title: Melody Inn

Montgomery, J. *Ready Money*
P

Rififi
PATHE (Fr) 1955 dir. Jules Dassin
V

Le Breton, A. *Monsieur Rififi*

Right Approach, The
FOX (US) 1961 dir. David Butler

Kanin, G.
P

Right Hand Man, The
UAA (Aust) 1987 dir. Di Drew
V

Peyton, K. M.

Right of Way
HBO Prem (US) 1983
dir. George Schaefer
TV(US), V

Lee, R.
P

Right Stuff, The
WAR (US) 1983 dir. Philip Kaufman
V

Wolfe, T.

Right to Live, The
WAR (US) 1935 dir. William Keighley
GB title: Sacred Flame, The

Maugham, W. S. *Sacred Flame, The*
P

Right to Love, The
PAR (US) 1930 dir. Richard Wallace

Glaspell, S. *Brook Adams*

Ring, The
UA (US) 1952 dir. Kurt Neumann

Shulman, I. *Cry Tough*

Ringer, The
REGENT (GB) 1952 dir. Guy Hamilton

Wallace, E.

Ring of Bright Water
RANK (GB) 1968 dir. Jack Couffer
V

Maxwell, G.

Rio Conchos
FOX (US) 1964 dir. Gordon Douglas
V

Huffaker, C. *Guns of Rio Conchos*

Riot
PAR (US) 1968 dir. Buzz Kulik
Elli, F.

Rise and Shine
FOX (US) 1941 dir. Allan Dwan
Thurber, J. *My Life and Hard Times*

Rising of the Moon, The
WAR (Ire) 1957 dir. John Ford
Gregory, Lady I. A.
McHugh, M. J. *Minute's Wait, A*
O'Connor, F. *Majesty of the Law, The*

Rita Hayworth: The Love Goddess
SUSSKIND (US) 1983
dir. James Goldstone
TV(US)
Kobal, J. *Rita Hayworth: The Time, the Place, and the Woman*

Rita, Sue and Bob Too
ORION (GB) 1987 dir. Alan Clarke
Dunbar, A.
P

Ritz, The
WAR (US) 1976 dir. Richard Lester
V
McNally, T.
P

Rivalry, The
DEFARIA (US) 1975 dir. Fielder Cook
TV(US)
Corwin, N.
P

River, The
UA (Ind) 1951 dir. Jean Renoir
V
Godden, R.

River Lady
UIN (US) 1948 dir. George Sherman
Branch, H.

River of Death
CANNON (US) 1988 dir. Steve Carver
V
MacLean, A.

River's End
WAR (US) 1930 dir. Michael Curtiz
Curwood, J. O.

Road Back, The
UN (US) 1937 dir. James Whale
Remarque, E. M.

Road House
GAU (GB) 1934 dir. Maurice Elvey
Hackett, W.
P

Road to Mecca, The
VIDEOVISION (US) 1992
dir. Athol Fugard
TV(US)
Fugard, A.
P

Road Show
H. ROACH (US) 1941
dir. Gordon Douglas
Hatch, E.

Road to Singapore
WAR (US) 1931 dir. Alfred E. Green
Pertwee, R. *Heat Wave*
P

Robert Kennedy and his Times
COL (US) 1985 dir. Marvin J. Chomsky
TVSe(US)
Schlesinger, Jr., A. M.

Robbery Under Arms
RANK (GB) 1957 dir. Jack Lee
Boldrewood, R.

Robe, The
FOX (US) 1953 dir. Henry Koster
V
Douglas, L. C.

Roberta
RKO (US) 1935 dir. William A. Seiter
M, V
Miller, A. D. *Gowns by Roberta*

Robinson Crusoe
BBC (GB) 1974 dir. James MacTaggart
TV(GB)
Defoe, D.

Rockabye
PEREGRINE (US) 1986
dir. Richard Michael
TV(US)
Koenig, L.

Rockabye
RADIO (US) 1932 dir. George Cukor
Bronder, L.
P

Rockets Galore
RANK (GB) 1958 dir. Michael Ralph
US title: Mad Little Island
Mackenzie, Sir C.

Rockets in the Dunes
RANK (GB) 1960
dir. William Hammond
Ch
Lamplugh, L

Rock Hudson
KON-SAN (US) 1990 dir. John Nicolella
TV
Gates, P. *My Husband, Rock Hudson*

Rocking Horse Winner, The
TC (GB) 1949 dir. Anthony Pelissier
V
Lawrence, D. H.

Rogue Cop
MGM (US) 1954 dir. Roy Rowland
McGivern, W. P.

Romance
MGM (US) 1930 dir. Clarence Brown
Sheldon, E.
P

Romance of a Horse Thief
ALLIED (Yugo) 1971
dir. Abraham Polonsky
Opatashu, D.

Romance of Rosy Ridge, The
MGM (US) 1947 dir. Roy Rowland
Kantor, M.

Romanoff and Juliet
UN (US) 1961 dir. Peter Ustinov
Ustinov, P.
P

Roman Spring of Mrs. Stone, The
WAR (GB/US) 1961 dir. José Quintero
V
Williams, T.

Romantic Comedy
MGM/UA (US) 1983 dir. Arthur Hiller
V
Slade, B.
P

Romantic Englishwoman, The
DIAL (GB) 1975 dir. Joseph Losey
V
Wiseman, T.

Romeo and Juliet
MGM (US) 1936 dir. George Cukor
GFD (GB) 1954 dir. Renato Castellani
V
PAR (GB) 1968 dir. Franco Zeffirelli
V

Shakespeare, W.
P

Ronde, La
S. GARDINE (Fr) 1950 dir. Max Ophuls
V
INTEROPA (Fr) 1964 dir. Roger Vadim

Schnitzler, A.
P

Rookery Nook
MGM (GB) 1930 dir. Tom Walls

Travers, B.
P

Room at the Top
BL (GB) 1958 dir. Jack Clayton
V

Braine, J.

Room for One More
WAR (US) 1952 dir. Norman Taurog

Rose, A. P.

Room Service
RKO (US) 1938 dir. William A. Seiter
V

Murray, J. and Boretz, A.
P

Room Upstairs, The
M. REES (US) 1987 dir. Stuart Margolin
TV(US)

Levinson, N.

Room With a View, A
GOLD (GB) 1985 dir. James Ivory
V

Forster, E. M.

Rooney
RANK (GB) 1958 dir. George Pollock

Cookson, C.

Roots
WOLPER (US) 1977
dirs. David Greene, Marvin,J.Chomsky,
John Erman, Gilbert Moses
TVSe(US),V

Haley, A.

Roots of Heaven, The
FOX (US) 1958 dir. John Huston

Gary, R.

Roots: The Next Generation
WAR TV (US) 1979 dirs. John Erman,
CharlesDubin,Georg Stanford Brown,
Lloyd Richards
TVSe(US)

Haley, A.

Rope
WAR (US) 1948 dir. Alfred Hitchcock
V

Hamilton, P.
P

Rosalie
MGM (US) 1937 dir. W. S. Van Dyke
M, V

McGuire, W. A. and Bolton, G.
P

Rose and the Jackal, The
S. White (US) 1990 dir. Jack Gold
TV(US)

Leech, M. *Reveille in Washington*

Rosary Murders, The
NEW LINE (US) 1987 dir. Fred Walton

Kienzle, W. X.

Roseanna McCoy
RKO (US) 1949 dir. Irving Reis

Hannum, A.

Rosebud
UA (US) 1975 dir. Otto Preminger
Hemingway, J. and Bonnecarrere, P.

Rose Marie
MGM (US) 1936 dir. W. S. Van Dyke
M, V
MGM (US) 1954 dir. Mervyn Le Roy
M
Harbach, O. and Hammerstein, II, O
P

Rosemary's Baby
PAR (US) 1968 dir. Roman Polanski
V
Levin, I.

Rosencrantz and Guildenstern are Dead
HOBO/CINECOM (US/GB) 1991 dir. Tom Stoppard
V
Stoppard, T.
P

Roses are for the Rich
PHOENIX (US) 1987 dir. Michael Miller
TVSe(US)
Lawson, J.

Rose Tattoo, The
PAR (US) 1955 dir. Daniel Mann
Williams, T.
P

Rosie
UN (US) 1967 dir. David Lowell Rich
Gordon, R.
P

Rosie: The Rosemary Clooney Story
FRIES (US) 1982 dir. Jackie Cooper
TV(US)
Clooney, R. and Strait, R. *This For Remembrance*

Rosie Dixon-Night Nurse
COL (GB) 1978 dir. Justin Cartwright
Dixon, R. *Confessions of a Night Nurse*

Rouge
ICA (HK) 1988 dir. Stanley Kwan
Pik-Wah, L.

Rouge et le Noir, Le
FRANCO-LONDON (Fr/It) 1954 dir. Claude Autant-Lara
Stendahl, H. B.

Rough and the Smooth, The
MGM (GB) 1959 dir. Robert Siodmak
US title: Portrait of a Sinner
Maugham, R.

Rough Cut
PAR (US) 1980 dir. Don Siegel
V
Lambert, D. *Touch the Lion's Paw*

Roughly Speaking
WAR (US) 1945 dir. Michael Curtiz
Pierson, Mrs. L.

Rough Night in Jericho
UN (US) 1967 dir. Arnold Laven
Albert, M. H. *Man in Black, The*

Rough Shoot
UA (GB) 1952 dir. Robert Parrish
US title: Shoot First
Household, G.

Rounders, The
MGM (US) 1965 dir. Burt Kennedy
Evans, M.

Roxanne
COL (US) 1987 dir. Fred Schepisi
V

Rostand, E. *Cyrano de Bergerac*
P

Roxanne: The Prize Pulitzer
QINTEX (US) 1989 dir. Richard Colla
TV(US)

Pulitzer, R.

Roxie Hart
FOX (US) 1942 dir. William A. Wellman

Watkins, M. *Chicago*
P

Royal Bed, The
RKO (US) 1931 dir. Lowell Sherman
V

Sherwood, R. E. *Queen's Husband, The*
P

Royal Family of Broadway, The
PAR (US) 1930 dir. George Cukor
GB title: Theatre Royal

Kaufman, G. S. and Ferber, E. *Royal Family, The*
P

Royal Flash
FOX RANK (GB) 1975
dir. Richard Lester
V

Fraser, G. M.

Royal Hunt of the Sun, The
RANK (GB) 1969 dir. Irving Lerner

Shaffer, P.
P

Royal Scandal, A
FOX (US) 1945 dir. Otto Preminger
GB title: Czarina

Biro, L. and Lengyel, M.
P

Ruddigore
GALA (GB) 1967 dir. Joy Batchelor
A, M

Gilbert, Sir W. S. and Sullivan, Sir A.
P

Ruggles of Red Gap
PAR (US) 1935 dir. Leo McCarey
V

Wilson, H. L.

Ruling Class, The
KEEP (GB) 1971 dir. Peter Medak
V

Barnes, P.
P

Rumble Fish
UN (US) 1983 dir. Francis Ford Coppola
V

Hinton, S. E.

Rumble on the Docks
COL (US) 1956 dir. Fred Sears

Paley, F.

Rumor of War, A
FRIES (US) 1980 dir. Richard T. Heffron
TVSe(US)

Caputo, P.

Rumpelstiltskin
CANNON (US) 1987 dir. David Irving
Ch, V

Grimm, J. L. K. and Grimm, W. K.

Rumpole of the Bailey
THAMES (GB) 1978
dir. Donald McWhinnie
TVSe(GB)

Mortimer, J.

Runaway Father
HEARST (US) 1991 dir. John Nicolella

Rashke, R.

Runaways, The
LORIMAR (US) 1974 dir. Harry Harris
TV(US)
Canning, V.

Run, Cougar, Run
DISNEY (US) 1972
dir. Michael Dmytryk
Murphy, R. *Mountain Lion, The*

Runestone, The
HYPERION PICTURES (US) 1992
dir. Willard Carroll
Rogers, M. E.

Runner Stumbles, The
SIMON (US) 1979 dir. Stanley Kramer
V
Stitt, M.
P

Running Man, The
COL (GB) 1963 dir. Carol Reed
Smith, S. *Ballad of the Running Man,
The*

Running Man, The
TRI-STAR (US) 1987
dir. Paul Michael Glaser
V
Bachman, R.

Running Scared
PAR (GB) 1972 dir. David Hemmings
V
McDonald, G.

Run Silent, Run Deep
UA (US) 1958 dir. Robert Wise
V
Beach, E. L.

Run Wild, Run Free
COL (GB) 1989 dir. Richard C. Sarafian
Rook, D. *White Colt, The*

Rush
MGM (US) 1991 dir. Lili Fini Zanuck
Wozencraft, K.

Russia House, The
MGM (US) 1990 dir. Fred Schepisi
V
Le Carré, J.

Russian Roulette
ITC (US) 1975 dir. Lon Lombardo
V
Ardies, T. *Kosygin is Coming*

**Russians are Coming, The
Russians are Coming, The**
UA (US) 1966 dir. Norman Jewison
V
Benchley, N. *Off-Islanders, The*

Russicum
TRI-STAR/Cecchi (It) 1989
dir. Pasquale Squitieri
Russo, E. *Martedì del Diavolo, Il*

Ruthless
EL (US) 1948 dir. Edgar G. Ulmer
Stoddart, D. *Prelude to Night*

St Ives
WAR (US) 1976 dir. J. Lee Thompson
V

Bleeck, O. *Procane Chronicle, The*

Sabotage
GB (GB) 1936 dir. Alfred Hitchcock
US title: Woman Alone, A
V

Conrad, J. *Secret Agent, The*

Saboteur, The
FOX (US) 1965 dir. Bernhard Wicki
Jeorg, W.

Sabrina
PAR (US) 1954 dir. Billy Wilder
GB title: Sabrina Fair
V

Taylor, S. *Sabrina Fair*
P

Sacketts, The
SHALAKO (US) 1979 dir. Robert Totten
TVSe(US), V

L'Amour, L. *Sackett; Daybreakers, The*

Sacred Flame, The
WAR (US) 1929 dir. Archie Mayo
Maugham, W. S.
P

Sacrifice of Youth
ART EYE (China) 1986
dir. Zhang Luanxin

Manling, Z. *There was that Beautiful Place*

Sail a Crooked Ship
COL (US) 1961 dir. Irving Brecher
Benchley, N.

Sailor Beware!
BL (GB) 1956 dir. Gordon Parry
US title: Panic in the Parlor
King, P. and Cary, F. L.
P

Sailor from Gibraltar, The
WOODFALL (GB) 1967
dir. Tony Richardson
Duras, M.

Sailor's Return, The
ARIEL (GB) 1978 dir. Jack Gold
Garnett, D.

Sailor Takes a Wife, The
MGM (US) 1945 dir. Richard Whorf
Erskine, C.
P

Sailor Who Fell From Grace With the Sea, The
FOX RANK (GB) 1976
dir. Lewis John Carlino
V

Mishima, Y. *Gogo no Eiko*

Saint in New York
RKO (US) 1938 dir. Ben Holmes
V

Charteris, L.

Saint Jack
NEW WORLD (US) 1979
dir. Peter Bogdanovich
V

Theroux, P.

Saint Joan
UA (GB) 1957 dir. Otto Preminger
V
COMPASS (US) 1967
dir. George Schaefer
TV(US)
Shaw, G. B.
P

Salamander, The
ITC (It/GB/US) 1981 dir. Peter Zinner
V

West, M.

Salem's Lot
WAR (US) 1979 dir. Tobe Hooper
TVSe(US), V
King, S.

Sally
WAR (US) 1930 dir. John Francis Dillon
M
Bolton, G., Kern, J. and Grey, C.
P

Sally in our Alley
ABP (GB) 1931 dir. Maurice Elvey
McEvoy, C. *Likes of 'er, The*

Salome
CANNON (Fr/It) 1987
dir. Claude d'Anna
Wilde, O.
P

Salome's Last Dance
VESTRON (GB) 1988 dir. Ken Russell
V

Wilde, O. *Salome*
P

Saloon Bar
EAL (GB) 1940 dir. Walter Forde
Harvey, F.
P

Salute John Citizen
BN (GB) 1942 dir. Maurice Elvey
V
Greenwood, R. *Mr. Bunting at War*

Salute the Toff
BUTCHER (GB) 1952
dir. Maclean Rogers
Creasey, J.

Salzburg Connection, The
FOX (US) 1972 dir. Lee H. Katzin
V
MacInnes, H.

Same Time, Next Year
UN (US) 1978 dir. Robert Mulligan
V
Slade, B.
P

Sammy Going South
BL (GB) 1963
dir. Alexander Mackendrick
US title: Boy Ten Feet Tall, A
Canaway, W. H.

Samson and Delilah
COMWORLD (US) 1984 dir. Lee Philips
TV(US), V
Linklater, E. *Husband of Delilah*

San Antone
REP (US) 1952 dir. Joe Kane
Carroll, C. *Golden Herd*

Sanctuary
FOX (US) 1960 dir. Tony Richardson
Faulkner, W.

Sanctuary of Fear
M. ARCH (US) 1979
dir. John Llewellyn Moxey
TV(US), V

Chesterton, G. K. *Father Brown, Detective*

Sanders of the River
UA (GB) 1935 dir. Zoltan Korda
US title: Bosambo
V

Wallace, E.

Sand Pebbles, The
FOX (US) 1966 dir. Robert Wise
V

McKenna, R.

Sands of the Kalahari
PAR (GB) 1965 dir. Cy Endfield
Mulvihill, W.

San Francisco Story, The
WAR (US) 1952 dir. Robert Parrish
Summers, R. A. *Vigilante*

Sangaree
PAR (US) 1953 dir. Edward Ludwig
Slaughter, F. G.

Santa Fe
COL (US) 1951 dir. Irving Pichel
Marshall, J. L.

Saraband for Dead Lovers
EL (GB) 1949 dir. Basil Dearden
Simpson, H.

Saracen Blade, The
COL (US) 1954 dir. William Castle
Yerby, F.

Sarah and Son
PAR (US) 1930 dir. Dorothy Arzner
Shea, T.

Sarah, Plain and Tall
SELF (US) 1991 dir. Glenn Jordan
TV(US)

MacLachlan, P.

Saratoga Trunk
WAR (US) 1945 dir. Sam Wood
Ferber, E.

Satan Bug, The
UA (US) 1965 dir. John Sturges
Stuart, I.

Satan Met a Lady
WAR (US) 1936 dir. William Dieterle
Hammett, D. *Maltese Falcon, The*

Saturday Island
RKO (GB) 1951 dir. Stuart Heisler
US title: Island of Desire
Brooke, H.

Saturday Night and Sunday Morning
BL (GB) 1960 dir. Karel Reisz
Sillitoe, A.

Saturday's Children
WAR (US) 1940 dir. Vincent Sherman
Anderson, M.
P

Saturday's Hero
COL (US) 1950 dir. David Miller
GB title: Idols in the Dust
Lampell, M. *Hero, The*

Savage, The
PAR (US) 1952 dir. George Marshall
Foreman, L. L. *Don Desperado*

Savage Innocents, The
RANK (Fr/It/GB) 1960
dir. Nicholas Ray
V

Ruesch, H. *Top of the World*

Savage Messiah
MGM-EMI (GB) 1972 dir. Ken Russell
Ede, H. S.

Savages
SPEL-GOLD (US) 1974 dir. Lee Katzin
TV(US)
White, R. *Death Watch*

Savage Sam
DISNEY (US) 1963 dir. Norman Tokar
V
Gipson, F.

Savage Wilderness
COL (US) 1956 dir. Anthony Mann
GB title: The Last Frontier
Emery, R. *Gilded Rooster, The*

Saving Grace
EMBASSY (US) 1986
dir. Robert M. Young
V
Gittelson, C.

Saxon Charm, The
UI (US) 1948 dir. Claude Binyon
Wakeman, F.

Sayonara
WAR (US) 1957 dir. Joshua Logan
V
Michener, J. A.

Scandalous John
DISNEY (US) 1971 dir. Robert Butler
V
Gardner, R. M.

Scandal Sheet
COL (US) 1952 dir. Phil Karlson
GB title: Dark Page, The
Fuller, S.

Scapegoat, The
MGM (GB) 1959 dir. Robert Hamer
Du Maurier, D.

Scaramouche
MGM (US) 1952 dir. George Sidney
V
Sabatini, R.

Scarecrow
OASIS (NZ) 1981 dir. Sam Pillsbury
Morrieson, H. M.

Scarface
UA (US) 1932 dir. Howard Hawks
V
Traili, A.

Scarlet and the Black, The
ITC (It/US) 1983 dir. Jerry London
TVSe(It/US), V
Gallagher, J. P. *Scarlet Pimpernel of the Vatican, The*

Scarlet Dawn
WAR (US) 1932 dir. William Dieterle
McCall, M. *Revolt*

Scarlet Letter, The
MAJ (US) 1934 dir. Robert G. Rignola
V
PBS (US) 1979 dir. Rick Hauser
TVSe(US)
Hawthorne, N.

Scarlet Pimpernel, The
UA (GB) 1934 dir. Harold Young
V
LONDON F.P. (US/GB) 1982
dir. Clive Donner
TVSe(GB/US)
Orczy, Baroness E.

Scarlet Street
UN (US) 1945 dir. Fritz Lang
V

de la Fouchardière, G. *Chienne, La*
P

Scattergood Baines
RKO (US) 1941 dir. Christy Cabanne
Kelland, C. B.

School for Scoundrels
WAR (GB) 1960 dir. Robert Namer
Potter, S. *Gamesmanship,
Oneupmanship, Lifemanship*

Scoop
LWT (GB) 1987 dir. Gavin Millar
TV(GB)
Waugh, E.

Scorpio Letters, The
MGM (US) 1967 dir. Richard Thorpe
V

Canning, V.

Scotland Yard
FOX (US) 1941 dir. Norman Foster
Clift, D.
P

Scream and Scream Again
AIP (GB) 1969 dir. Gordon Hessler
V

Saxon, P. *Disorientated Man, The*

Screaming Mimi
COL (US) 1958 dir. Gerd Oswald
Brown, F.

Screaming Woman, The
UN TV (US) 1972 dir. Jack Smight
TV(US)
Bradbury, R.

Scrooge
PAR (GB) 1935 dir. Henry Edwards
REN (GB) 1951
dir. Brian Desmond Hurst
V

FOX (GB) 1970 dir. Ronald Neame
M, V

Dickens, C. *Christmas Carol, A*

Scrooged
PAR (US) 1988 dir. Richard Donner
Dickens, C. *Christmas Carol, A*

Scruples
WAR (US) 1980 dir. Alan J. Levi
TVSe(US)
Krantz, J.

Scudda Hoo! Scudda Hay!
FOX (US) 1948 dir. F. Hugh Herbert
GB title: *Summer Lightning*
Chamberlain, G. A.

Sea Chase, The
WAR (US) 1955 dir. John Farrow
Geer, A.

Seagull, The
WAR (GB) 1969 dir. Sidney Lumet
Chekhov, A.
P

Seagulls over Sorrento
MGM (GB) 1954 dir. John Boulting and
Roy Boulting
US title: Crest of the Wave
Hastings, H.
P

Sea Hawk, The
WAR (US) 1940 dir. Michael Curtiz
V

Sabatini, R.

Sealed Verdict
PAR (US) 1948 dir. Lewis Allen
Shapiro, L.

Seal Morning
ITV (GB) 1986
TV
Farre, R.

Seance on a Wet Afternoon
RANK (GB) 1964 dir. Bryan Forbes
V
McShane, M.

Sea of Grass, The
MGM (US) 1947 dir. Elia Kazan
Richter, C. M.

Searchers, The
WAR (US) 1956 dir. John Ford
V
LeMay, A.

Search for Bridey Murphy, The
PAR (US) 1956 dir. Noel Langley
Bernstein, M.

Search for Beauty
PAR (US) 1934 dir. Erle C. Kenton
Gray, S. E. and Milton, P. R.
P

Searching Wind, The
PAR (US) 1946 dir. William Dieterle
Hellman, L. F.
P

Sea Shall Not Have Them, The
EROS (GB) 1954 dir. Lewis Gilbert
V
Harris, J.

Sea-Wife
FOX (GB) 1957 dir. Bob McNaught
V
Scott, J. M. *Sea Wyf and Biscuit*

Sea Wolf, The
FOX (US) 1930 dir. Alfred Santell
WAR (US) 1941 dir. Michael Curtiz
London, J.

Sea Wolves, The
RANK (GB/US/Switz) 1980
dir. Andrew McLaglen
V
Leasor, J. *Boarding Party*

Second Mrs. Tanqueray, The
VANDYKE (GB) 1952 dir. Dallas Bower
Pinero, Sir A. W.
P

Seconds
PAR (US) 1966 dir. John Frankenheimer
Ely, D.

Second Serve
LORIMAR (US) 1986 dir. Anthony Page
TV(US)
Richards, R., and Ames, J. *Renee Richards Story: The Second Serve, The*

Second Sight: A Love Story
TTC (US) 1984 dir. John Korty
TV(US)
Hocken, S. *Emma and I*

Second Time Around, The
FOX (US) 1961 dir. Vincent Sherman
Roberts, R. E. *Star in the West*

Secret Agent, The
GB 1936 dir. Alfred Hitchcock
V
Maugham, W. S. *Ashenden*

Secret Army, The
BBC (GB) 1979
TVSe(GB)
Brason, J.

Secret Beyond the Door, The
UI (US) 1948 dir. Fritz Lang
V
King, R.

Secret Bride, The
WAR (US) 1935 dir. William Dieterle
GB title: Concealment
Ide, L. *Concealment*
P

Secret Diary of Adrian Mole, Aged 13¾, The
THAMES (GB) 1985 dir. Peter Sasdy
TVSe(GB), V
Townsend, S.

Secret Garden, The
MGM (US) 1949 dir. Fred M. Wilcox
Ch, V
ROSEMONT (US) 1987 dir. Alan Grint
Ch, TV(US)
Burnett, F. H.

Secret Life of John Chapman, The
JOZAK (US) 1976 dir. David Lowell Rich
TV(US)
Coleman, J. R. *Blue Collar Journal*

Secret Life of Walter Mitty, The
RKO (US) 1947 dir. Norman Z. Macleod
V
Thurber, J.

Secret of N.I.M.H., The
MGM/UA (US) 1982 dir. Don Bluth
A, Ch, V
O'Brien, R. C. *Mrs Frisby and the Rats of N.I.M.H.*

Secret of Santa Vittoria, The
UA (US) 1969 dir. Stanley Kramer
Crichton, R.

Secret of Stamboul, The
HOB (GB) 1936 dir. Andrew Marton
Wheatley, D. *Eunuch of Stamboul, The*

Secret of St. Ives, The
COL (US) 1949 dir. Phil Rosen
Stevenson, R. L. *St. Ives*

Secret Places
RANK (GB) 1983 dir. Zelda Barron
V
Elliott, J.

Secret Servant, The
BBC (GB) 1985
TV(GB)
Lyall, G.

Secret Ways, The
RANK (US) 1961 dir. Phil Karlson
MacLean, A. *Last Frontier*

Secret Weapons
ITC (US) 1985 dir. Don Taylor
TV(US)
Lewis, D. *Sexpionage: The Exploitation of Sex by Soviet Intelligence*

Secret World of Polly Flint
Central (GB) 1987 dir. David Cobham
Ch, TVSe(GB)
Cresswell, H.

Seduction in Travis County, A
NEW WORLD (US) 1991
dir. George Kaczender
TV(US)
Meins, J. *Murder in Little Rock*

Seduction of Miss Leona, The
SCHERICK (US) 1980 dir. Joseph Hardy
TV(US)
Gundy, E. *Bliss*

Seed
UN (US) 1931 dir. John Stahl
Norris, C. G.

See Here, Private Hargrove
MGM (US) 1944 dir. Wesley Ruggles
Hargrove, M.

See How They Run
BL (GB) 1955 dir. Leslie Arliss
CHANNEL 4 (GB) 1984
TV(GB)
King, P.
P

See How They Run
UN TV (US) 1964 dir. David Lowell Rich
TV(US)
Blankfort, M. *Widow Makers, The*

Seekers, The
UN TV (US) 1979 dir. Sidney Hayers
TVSe(US)
Jakes, J.

Seizure: The Story of Kathy Morris
JOZAK (US) 1980 dir. Gerald Isenberg
TV(US)
Mee, Jr., C. L. *Seizure*

Selling Hitler
BBC (GB) 1991 dir. Anthony Reid
TV(GB)
Harris, R.

Semi-Tough
UA (US) 1977 dir. Michael Ritchie
V
Jenkins, D.

Send me No Flowers
UN (US) 1964 dir. Norman Jewison
V
Barrasch, N. and Moore, C.
P

Sensation
BIP (GB) 1936
dir. Brian Desmond Hurst
Dean, B. and Munro, G. *Murder Gang*
P

Sense of Guilt, A
BBC (GB) 1990
TVSe(GB)
Newman, A.

Sensitive, Passionate Man, A
FAC-NEW (US) 1977 dir. John Newland
TV(US)
Mahoney, B.

Sentinel, The
UN (US) 1977 dir. Michael Winner
V
Konvitz, J.

Senyora, La
ICA (Sp) 1987 dir. Jordi Cadenar
Mus, A.

Separate Peace, A
PAR (US) 1972 dir. Larry Peerce
V
Knowles, J.

Separate Tables
UA (US) 1958 dir. Delbert Mann
V
Rattigan, T.
P

Sequoia
MGM (US) 1935 dir. Chester Lyons
Hoyt, V. J. *Malibu, A Nature Story*

Serenade
WAR (US) 1956 dir. Anthony Mann
Cain, J. M.

Sergeant, The
WAR (US) 1968 dir. John Flynn

Murphy, D.

Serial
PAR (US) 1980 dir. Bill Persky
V

McFadden, C.

Serie Noire
GAU (Fr) 1979 dir. Alain Corneau

Thompson, J. *One Hell of a Woman*

Serious Charge
EROS (GB) 1959 dir. Terence Young

King, P.
P

Serpent, The
LA BOETIE (Fr/It/Ger) 1974
dir. Henri Verneuil

Nord, P.

Serpico
PAR (US) 1973 dir. Sidney Lumet
V

Maas, P.

Servant, The
WAR (GB) 1963 dir. Joseph Losey
V

Maugham, R.

Servant's Entrance
FOX (US) 1934 dir. Frank Lloyd

Boo, S.

Servants of Twilight, The
TRIMARK (US) 1991 dir. Jeffrey Obrow
TV(US)

Koontz, D. *Twilight*

Service of all the Dead
CENTRAL (GB) 1989
dir. Edward Bennett
TV(GB)

Dexter, C.

Seven Alone
HEMDALE (US) 1974 dir. Earl Bellamy
V

Morrow, H. *On to Oregon*

Seven Brides for Seven Brothers
MGM (US) 1954 dir. Stanley Donen
M, V

Benet, S. V. *Sobbin' Women, The*

Seven Cities of Gold
FOX (US) 1955 dir. Robert D. Webb
V

Ziegler, I. G. *Nine Days of Father Serra*

Seven Days in May
PAR (US) 1964 dir. John Frankenheimer
V

Knebel, F. and Bailey, C. W.

Seven Days' Leave
PAR (US) 1930 dir. Richard Wallace
GB title: Medals

Barrie, Sir J. M. *Old Lady Shows Her Medals, The*
P

Seven Faces of Dr. Lao, The
MGM (US) 1964 dir. George Pal
V

Finney, C. G.

Seven in Darkness
PAR TV (US) 1969 dir. Michael Caffey
TV(US)

Bishop, L. *Against Heaven's Hand*

Seven Keys to Baldpate
RKO (US) 1930 dir. Reginald Parker
RKO (US) 1935 dir. William Hamilton
RKO (US) 1947 dir. Lew Landers
Biggers, E. D.

Seven Minutes, The
FOX (US) 1971 dir. Russ Meyer
Wallace, I.

Seven Percent Solution, The
UN (US) 1976 dir. Herbert Ross
V
Meyer, N.

Seven Sinners
GAU (GB) 1937 dir. Albert de Courville
US title: Doomed Cargo
Ridley, A., and Merivale, B. *Wrecker, The*
P

Seventeen
PAR (US) 1940 dir. Louis King
Tarkington, B.

1776
COL (US) 1972 dir. Peter Hunt
M, V
Stone, P.
P

Seventh Avenue
UN TV (US) 1977 dir. Richard Irving,
Russ Mayberry
TVSe(US)
Bogner, N.

Seventh Cross, The
MGM (US) 1944 dir. Fred Zinnemann
Seghers, A.

7th Dawn, The
UA (GB) 1964 dir. Lewis Gilbert
Keon, M. *Durian Tree, The*

Seventh Heaven
FOX (US) 1937 dir. Henry King
Strong, A.
P

Seven Thieves
FOX (US) 1960 dir. Henry Hathaway
Catto, M. *Lions at the Kill*

Seventh Sin, The
MGM (US) 1957 dir. Ronald Neame
Maugham, W. S. *Painted Veil, The*

Seven Thunders
RANK (GB) 1957 dir. Hugo Fregonese
US title: Beasts of Marseilles, The
Croft-Cooke, R.

79 Park Avenue
UN (US) 1977 dir. Paul Wendkos
TVSe(US)
Robbins, H.

Seven Ways from Sundown
UI (US) 1960 dir. Harry Keller
Huffaker, C.

Seven Year Itch, The
FOX (US) 1955 dir. Billy Wilder
V
Axelrod, G.
P

Severed Head, A
COL (GB) 1970 dir. Dick Clement
Murdoch, I.

Sex and the Single Girl
WAR (US) 1964 dir. Richard Quine
Brown, H. G.

Sex and the Single Parent
TIME-LIFE (US) 1979
dir. Jackie Cooper
TV(US), V
Adams, J.

Sex Symbol, The
COL (US) 1974 dir. David Lowell Rich
TV(US), V
Bessie, A. *Symbol, The*

Shabby Tiger
GRANADA TV (GB) 1977
TVSe(GB)
Spring, H.

Shadow Box, The
SHADOW BOX (US) 1980
dir. Paul Newman
TV(US), V
Cristofer, M.
P

Shadowlands
BBC (Neth/GB) 1985
dir. Norman Stone
TV(GB)
Straub, P.

Shadow of Angels
ALB/ARTCO (Ger) 1983
dir. Daniel Schmid
Fassbinder, R. W.
P

Shadow of China
NEW LINE (US/Jap) 1991
dir. Mitsuo Yanagimachi
Nishiki, M. *Snake Head*

Shadow Over Elveron
UN TV (US) 1968 dir. James Goldstone
TV(US)
Kingsley, M.

Shadow Riders, The
COL TV (US) 1982
dir. Andrew V. McLaglen
TV(US)
L'Amour, L.

Shaft
MGM (US) 1971 dir. Gordon Parks
V
Tidyman, E.

Shaggy Dog, The
DISNEY (US) 1959 dir. Charles Barton
Ch, V
Salten, F. *Hound of Florence, The*

Shake Hands with the Devil
UA (Ire) 1959 dir. Michael Anderson
Conner, R.

Shalako
WAR (GB) 1968 dir. Edward Dmytryk
L'Amour, L.

Shane
PAR (US) 1953 dir. George Stevens
V
Schaefer, J. W.

Shanghai Gesture, The
IN (US) 1941 dir. Josef von Sternberg
V
Colton, J.
P

Shanghai Surprise
MGM (US) 1986 dir. Jim Goddard
V
Kenrick, T. *Faraday's Flowers*

Shangri-La
COMPASS (US) 1960
dir. George Schaefer
TV(US)
Hilton, J. *Lost Horizon*

Shape of Things to Come, The
BARBER DANN (Can) 1979
dir. George McGowan
V
Wells, H. G.

Share Out, The
AA (GB) 1962 dir. Gerald Glaister
Wallace, E. *Jack O'Judgement*

Sharky's Machine
WAR (US) 1981 dir. Burt Reynolds
V
Diehl, W.

Shattered
MGM-PATHE (US) 1991
dir. Wolfgang Petersen
Neely, R.

Shattered Dreams
CAROLCO (US) 1990 dir. Robert Iscove
TV(US)
Fedders, C. and Elliot, L.

Shattered Vows
RIVER CITY (US) 1984 dir. Jack Bender
TV(US)
Wong, Dr. M. G. *Nun: A Memoir*

She
RKO (US) 1935 dir. Irving Pichel
WAR (GB) 1965 dir. Robert Day
CONT (It) 1985 dir. Avi Nesher
Haggard, Sir H. R.

She-Devil
ORION (US) 1989 dir. Susan Seidelman
Weldon, F. *Life and Loves of a
She-Devil, The*

She Didn't Say No!
ABP (GB) 1958 dir. Cyril Frankel
Troy, U. *We Are Seven*

She Done Him Wrong
PAR (US) 1933 dir. Lowell Sherman
V
West, M. *Diamond Lil*
P

She Lives
ABC (US) 1973 dir. Stuart Hagmann
TV(US)
Neimark, P.

Shell Seekers, The
M. REES (US) 1989 dir. Waris Hussein
TV(US)
Pilcher, R.

She Loves Me Not
PAR (US) 1934 dir. Elliott Nugent
Lindsay, H.
P

Sheltering Sky, The
WAR (US) 1990
dir. Bernardo Bertolucci
Bowles, P.

Shepherd of the Hills, The
PAR (US) 1941 dir. Henry Hathaway
Wright, H. B.

Sherlock Holmes and the Voice of Terror
UN (US) 1942 dir. John Rawlins
V
Doyle, Sir A. C. *His Last Bow*

She Shall Have Murder
BL (GB) 1950 dir. Daniel Birt
Ames, D.

She's Working Her Way Through College
WAR (US) 1952
dir. Bruce Humberstone
Thurber, J. and Nugent, E. *Male
Animal, The*
P

Shining, The
WAR (GB) 1980 dir. Stanley Kubrick
V
King, S.

Shining Hour, The
MGM (US) 1938 dir. Frank Borzage
Winter, K.
P

Shining Season, A
COL TV (US) 1979 dir. Stuart Margolin
TV(US)
Buchanan, W.

Shining Through
FOX (US) 1992 dir. David Selzer
Isaacs, S.

Shining Victory
WAR (US) 1941 dir. Irving Rapper
Cronin, A. J. *Jupiter Laughs*
P

Shi No Toge
SHOCHIKU (Jap) 1990 dir. Kohei Oguri
Shimao, T.

Shipbuilders, The
BN (GB) 1944 dir. John Baxter
Blake, G.

Ship of Fools
COL (US) 1965 dir. Stanley Kramer
V
Porter, K. A.

Ship That Died of Shame, The
RANK (GB) 1955 dir. Basil Dearden
Monsarrat, N.

Shiralee, The
MGM (GB) 1957 dir. Leslie Norman
AUS (Aus) 1987 dir. Greg Ogilvie
TV(Aus)
Niland, D'A.

Shirley Valentine
PAR (GB) 1989 dir. Lewis Gilbert
V
Russell, W.
P

Shock to the System, A
MEDUSA (US) 1990 dir. Jan Egleson
Brett, S.

Shock Trauma
TELECOM (Can) 1982 dir. Eric Till
TV(Can)
Franklin, J. and Doelp, A.

Shock Treatment
WAR (US) 1964 dir. Denis Sanders
Van Atta, W.

Shoes of the Fisherman, The
MGM (US) 1968 dir. Michael Anderson
V
West, M. L.

Shogun
PAR (Jap/US) 1981 dir. Jerry London
TVSe(Jap/US), V
Clavell, J.

Shootdown
L. HILL (US) 1988
dir. Michael Pressman
TV(US)
Johnson, R. W.

Shooter
PAR TV (US) 1988 dir. Gary Nelson
TV(US)
Kennerly, D. H.

Shooting Party, The
MOSFILM (USSR) 1981
dir. Emil Loteanu
Chekhov, A.

Shooting Party, The
REEVE (GB) 1984 dir. Alan Bridges
V

Colegate, I.

Shootist, The
PAR (US) 1976 dir. Don Siegel
V

Swarthout, G.

Shootout
UN (US) 1971 dir. Henry Hathaway

James, W. *Lone Cowboy: My Life Story*

Shoot the Piano Player
PLEIADE (Fr) 1960
dir. François Truffaut
V

Goodis, D. *Down There*

Shop Around the Corner, The
MGM (US) 1940 dir. Ernst Lubitsch

Laszlo, N.
P

Shop at Sly Corner, The
BL (GB) 1946 dir. George King
US title: Code of Scotland Yard

Percy, E.
P

Shopworn Angel
MGM (US) 1938 dir. H. C. Potter

Burnet, D. *Private Pettigrew's Girl*
P

Short Cut to Hell
PAR (US) 1957 dir. James Cagney

Greene, G. *Gun For Sale, A*

Shout at the Devil
HEMDALE (GB) 1976 dir. Peter Hunt
V

Smith, W.

Showboat
UN (US) 1936 dir. James Whale
M

MGM (US) 1951 dir. George Sidney
this version also based on a play by
Kern, J. and Hammerstein II, O.
M, V

Ferber, E.

Showdown at Abilene
UN (US) 1956 dir. Charles Haas

Young, C. U. *Gun Shy*

Show-Off, The
MGM (US) 1934 dir. Charles Riesner

Kelly, G.
P

Show of Force, A
PAR (US) 1990 dir. Bruno Barreto

Nelson, A. *Murder Under Two Flags*

Shrike, The
UI (US) 1955 dir. José Ferrer

Kramm, J.
P

Shroud for a Nightingale
YTV (GB) 1984 dir. John Gorrie
TVSe(GB)

James, P. D.

Shuttered Room, The
WAR (GB) 1967 dir. David Greene

Lovecraft, H. P.

Sicilian, The
FOX (It/US) 1987 dir. Michael Cimino
V

Puzo, M.

Siddhartha
LOTUS (US) 1972 dir. Conrad Rooks

Hesse, H.

Sidelong Glances of a Pigeon Kicker, The
MGM (US) 1970 dir. John Dexter

Boyer, D.

Siesta
LORIMAR (US) 1987 dir. Mary Lambert
V

Chaplin, P.

Sign of Four, The
WW (GB) 1932 dir. Rowland V. Lee
EMBASSY (GB) 1983
dir. Desmond Davis
GRANADA (GB) 1988 dir. Michael Cox
TV(GB)

Doyle, Sir A. C.

Sign of the Cross, The
PAR (US) 1932 dir. Cecil B. de Mille

Barrett, W.
P

Sign of the Ram, The
COL (US) 1948 dir. John Sturges

Ferguson, M.

Signpost to Murder
MGM (US) 1964 dir. George Englund

Doyle, M.
P

Silas Marner
BBC (GB) 1985 dir. Giles Foster
TV(GB), V

Eliot, G.

Silence of the Lambs, The
ORION (US) 1991 dir. Jonathan Demme
V

Harris, T.

Silence of the North
UN (Can) 1981 dir. Allan Winton King
V

Fredrickson, O. and East, B.

Silencers, The
COL (US) 1966 dir. Phil Karlson

Hamilton, D.

Silent Dust
ABP (GB) 1947 dir. Lance Comfort

Pertwee, R. and Pertwee, M.
Paragon, The
P

Silent Enemy, The
ROMULUS (GB) 1958
dir. William Fairchild

Pugh, M. *Commander Crabb*

Silent Night, Lonely Night
UNTV (US) 1969 dir. Daniel Petrie
TV(US), V

Anderson, R.
P

Silent Partner, The
CAROLCO (Can) 1978 dir. Daryl Duke
V

Bodelsen, A. *Think of a Number*

Silent World of Nicholas Quinn
CENTRAL (GB) 1989
dir. Edward Bennett

Dexter, C.

Silk Stockings
MGM (US) 1957
dir. Rouben Mamoulian
M, V

Kaufman, G. S., McGrath, L. and Burrows, A.
P

Silver Bears
EMI (GB) 1978 dir. Ivan Passer
V

Erdman, P.

Silver Bullet
PAR (US) 1985 dir. Daniel Attias

King, S. *Cycle of the Werewolf*

Silver Chair, The
BBC (GB) 1990 dir. A. Kirby
Ch, TVSe(GB)

Lewis, C. S. *Prince Caspian and The Silver Chair*

Silver Chalice, The
WAR (US) 1954 dir. Victor Saville
V

Costain, T. B.

Silver Darlings, The
ALL (GB) 1947 dir. Clarence Elder, Clifford Evans

Gunn, N. M.

Simon and Laura
RANK (GB) 1955 dir. Muriel Box

Melville, A.
P

Since You Went Away
UA (US) 1944 dir. John Cromwell
V

Wilder, M. B.

Sinful Davey
UA (GB) 1969 dir. John Huston

Haggart, D. *Life of David Haggart, The*

Sinful Life, A
NEW LINE (US) 1989
dir. William Schreiner

Graham, M. *Just Like the Pom Pom Girls*
P

Singer Not the Song, The
RANK (GB) 1960 dir. Roy Baker
V

Lindop, A. E.

Sink the Bismarck
FOX (GB) 1960 dir. Lewis Gilbert

Forester, C. S. *Hunting the Bismarck*

Sinner's Holiday
WAR (US) 1930 dir. John G. Adolfi

Baumer, M. *Penny Arcade*
P

Sinner Take All
MGM (US) 1937 dir. Errol Taggart

Chambers, W. *Murder of a Wanton*

Sin of Madelon Claudet
MGM (US) 1931 dir. Edgar Selwyn

Knoblock, E. *Lullaby, The*
P

Sins
NEW WORLD (US) 1986
dir. Douglas Hickox
TVSe(US)

Gould, J.

Sins of Dorian Gray, The
RANKIN-BASS (US) 1983
dir. Tony Maylam
TV(US)

Wilde, O. *Picture of Dorian Gray, The*

Sins of Rachel Cade, The
WAR (US) 1960 dir. Gordon Douglas

Mercer, C. *Rachel Cade*

Sins of the Mother
CORAPEAKE (US) 1991
dir. John Patterson
TV(US)
Olsen, J. *Son*

Sirocco
COL (US) 1951 dir. Curtis Bernhardt
V

Kessel, J. *Coup de Grâce*

Sister Kenny
RKO (US) 1946 dir. Dudley Nichols
V

Kenny, E. and Ostenso, M. *And They Shall Walk*

Sisters, The
WAR (US) 1938 dir. Anatole Litvak

Brinig, M.

Sitter, The
FNM (US) 1991 dir. Rick Berger
TV(US)

Armstrong, C. *Mischief*

Sitting Pretty
FOX (US) 1948 dir. Walter Lang

Davenport, Mrs. G. *Belvedere*

Sitting Target
MGM (GB) 1972 dir. Douglas Hickox
V

Henderson, L.

Situation Hopeless But Not Serious
PAR (US) 1965 dir. Gottfried Reinhardt

Shaw, R. *Hiding Place, The*

Six Against the Rock
GAYLORD (US) 1987 dir. Paul Wendkos
TV(US)

Howard, C.

Six Bridges to Cross
UN (US) 1955 dir. Joseph Pevney

Dinneen, J. F. *They Stole $2.5 million and Got Away with it*

633 Squadron
UA (GB) 1964 dir. Walter Grauman

Smith, F. E.

Six Million Dollar Man, The
UN TV (US) 1973 dir. Richard Irving
TV(US)

Caidin, M. *Cyborg*

Six Weeks
UN (US) 1982 dir. Tony Bill
V

Stewart, F. M.

Skeezer
M. ARCH (US) 1982 dir. Peter H. Hunt
TV(US)

Yates, E. *Skeezer: Dog With a Mission*

Skin Game, The
BI (GB) 1931 dir. Alfred Hitchcock
V

Galsworthy, J.
P

Skin of our Teeth, The
GRANADA TV (GB) 1959
TV(GB)

Wilder, T.
P

Skyjacked
MGM (US) 1972 dir. John Guillermin
V

Harper, D. *Hijacked*

Skylark
PAR (US) 1941 dir. Mark Sandrich

Raphaelson, S.
P

Skyscraper Souls
MGM (US) 1932 dir. Edgar Selwyn

Baldwin, F. *Skyscraper*

Slapstick of Another Kind
LORIMAR (US) 1984 dir. Steven Paul
V

Vonnegut, K. *Slapstick*

Slate, Wyn and Me
HEMDALE (Aust) 1987
dir. Don McLennan

Savage, G. *Slate Wyn and Blanche McBride*

Slattery's Hurricane
FOX (US) 1949 dir. André de Toth

Wouk, H.

Slaughterhouse Five
UN (US) 1972 dir. George Roy Hill
V

Vonnegut, K.

Slaughter on 10th Avenue
UI (US) 1957 dir. Arnold Laven

Keating, W. J. and Carter, R. *Man Who Rocked the Boat, The*

Slave Ship
FOX (US) 1937 dir. Tay Garnett

King, G. S.

Slaves of New York
TRI-STAR (US) 1989 dir. James Ivory

Janowitz, T.

Slayground
UN/EMI (GB) 1983 dir. Terry Bedford
V

Stark, R.

Sleeping Beauty
DISNEY (US) 1959 dir. Clyde Geronomi
A, Ch
CANNON (US) 1987 dir. David Irving
Ch

Perrault, C.

Sleeping Car Murders, The
PECF (Fr) 1965 dir. Costa-Gavras

Japrisot, S.

Sleeping Tiger, The
INSIGNIA (GB) 1954 dir. Joseph Losey

Moiseiwitsch, M.

Sleeping with the Enemy
FOX (US) 1991 dir. Joseph Ruben
V

Price, N.

Sleep my Love
UA (US) 1948 dir. Douglas Sirk

Rosten, L.

Sleuth
FOX (GB) 1972
dir. Joseph L. Mankiewicz
V

Shaffer, A.
P

Slight Case of Murder, A
WAR (US) 1938 dir. Lloyd Bacon

Runyon, D. and Lindsay, H.
P

Slightly Honourable
UA (US) 1940 dir. Tay Garnett
V

Presnell, F. G. *Send Another Coffin*

Slightly Scarlet
RKO (US) 1956 dir. Allan Dwan
V

Cain, J. A.

Slow Burn
UN TV (US) 1986
dir. Matthew Chapman
TV(US), V

Lyons, A. *Castles Burning*

Slugs, The Movie
NEW WORLD (Sp) 1988 dir. J. P. Simon

Hutson, S.

Small Back Room, The
LF (GB) 1949 dir. Michael Powell,
Emeric Pressburger
US title: Hour of Glory

Balchin, N.

Small Killing, A
MOTOWN (US) 1981
dir. Steven Hilliard Stern
TV(US)

Barth, R. *Rag Bag Clan, The*

Small Miracle, The
LAN (US) 1983 dir. Jeannot Szwarc
TV(US)

Gallico, P.

Small Sacrifices
FRIES (US) 1989 dir. David Greene
TVSe(US)

Rule, A.

Small Town Girl
MGM (US) 1936
dir. William A. Wellmen

Williams, B. A.

Small Voice, The
BL (GB) 1948 dir. Fergus McDonell
US title: Hideout

Westerby, R.

Small World
GRANADA (GB) 1988
TV

Lodge, D.

Smash-up on Interstate 5
FILMWAYS (US) 1976
dir. John Llewellyn Moxey
TV(US)

Trevor, E. *Expressway*

Smiley
FOX (GB) 1955 dir. Anthony Kimmins

Raymond, M.

Smiley's People
BBC (GB) 1982 dir. Simon Langton
TVSe(GB)

Le Carré, J.

Smilin' Through
MGM (US) 1932 dir. Sidney Franklin
MGM (US) 1941 dir. Frank Borzage
V

Cowl, J. and Murfin, J.
P

Smoke
DISNEY (US) 1970
dir. Vincent McEveety
V

Corbin, W.

Smoky
FOX (US) 1946 dir. Louis King

James, W.

Smooth Talk
NEPENTHE (US) 1985
dir. Joyce Chopra
V

Oates, J. C. *Where are you Going,
Where have you Been?*

Smugglers, The
UN TV (US) 1968 dir. Norman Lloyd
TV(US)

Hely, E.

Snafu
COL (US) 1945 dir. Jack Moss
GB title: Welcome Home

Solomon, L. and Buchman, H.
P

Snake Pit, The
FOX (US) 1948 dir. Anatole Litvak

Ward, M. J.

Snowball Express
DISNEY (US) 1972 dir. Norman Tokar

O'Rear, F. and O'Rear, J. *Château Bon Vivant*

Snowbound
RKO (GB) 1948 dir. David MacDonald

Innes, H. *Lonely Skier, The*

Snow Goose, The
UN/BBC (US/GB) 1971
dir. Patrick Garland
TV(US/GB)

Gallico, P.

Snows of Kilimanjaro, The
FOX (US) 1952 dir. Henry King
V

Hemingway, E.

Snow Treasure
TIGON (US) 1968 dir. Irving Jacoby
V

McSwigan, M. *All Aboard for Freedom*

Snow White
CANNON (US) 1987 dir. Michael Berz
Ch

Grimm, J. L. K. and Grimm, W. K.

Snow White and the Seven Dwarfs
DISNEY (US) 1937 dir. David Hand
A

Grimm, J. L. K. and Grimm, W. K.

So Big
WAR (US) 1932 dir. William Wellman
WAR (US) 1953 dir. Robert Wise

Ferber, E.

Society Doctor
MGM (US) 1935 dir. George B. Seitz
GB title: After Eight Hours

Reeves, J. *Harbor, The*

So Dear to my Heart
DISNEY (US) 1948 dir. Harold Schuster
V

North, S.

So Ends our Night
UA (US) 1941 dir. John Cromwell

Remarque, E. M. *Flotsam*

So Evil My Love
PAR (GB) 1948 dir. Lewis Allen

Shearing, J. *For Her to See*

So Goes my Love
UN (US) 1946 dir. Frank Ryan
GB title: Genius in the Family, A

Maxim, H. P. *Genius in the Family, A*

Solar Crisis
SHOCHIKU (Jap) 1990
dir. Richard C. Sarafian

Kawata, T.

Soldier and the Lady, The
RKO (US) 1937 dir. George Nicholls, Jr.
GB title: Michael Strogoff

Verne, J. *Michael Strogoff*

Soldier Blue
AVCO (US) 1970 dir. Ralph Nelson
V

Olsen, T. V. *Arrow in the Sun*

Soldier in the Rain
WAR (US) 1963 dir. Ralph Nelson
V

Goldman, W.

Soldier of Fortune
FOX (US) 1955 dir. Edward Dmytryk
V

Gann, E. K.

Soldier's Story, A
COL (US) 1984 dir. Norman Jewison
V

Fuller, C. *Soldier's Play, A*
P

Soldiers Three
MGM (US) 1951 dir. Tay Garnett
Kipling, R.

Solid Gold Cadillac, The
COL (US) 1956 dir. Richard Quine
Teichman, H. and Kaufman, G. S.
P

Solitaire Man, The
MGM (US) 1933 dir. Jack Conway
Spewack, B. and Spewack, S.
P

Solitary Child, The
BL (GB) 1958 dir. Gerald Thomas
Bawden, N.

Solomon and Sheba
UA (US) 1959 dir. King Vidor
V

Wilbur, C.

So Long at the Fair
GFD (GB) 1950 dir. Terence Fisher
V

Thorne, A.

Somebody Up There Likes Me
MGM (US) 1956 dir. Robert Wise
Graziano, R.

Sombrero
MGM (US) 1953 dir. Norman Foster
Niggli, J. *Mexican Village*

Some Came Running
MGM (US) 1959 dir. Vincente Minnelli
Jones, J.

Some Kind of Hero
PAR (US) 1981 dir. Michael Pressman
V

Kirkwood, J.

Some Kind of Miracle
LORIMAR (US) 1979
dir. Jerrold Freedman
TV(US)

Willis, M. P. and Willis, J. *But There are Always Miracles*

Some Lie and Some Die
TVS (GB) 1990 dir. Neil Zeiger
TVSe
Rendell, R.

Someone at the Door
BIP (GB) 1936 dir. Herbert Brenon
Christie, D. and Christie, C.
P

Something for Everyone
NAT GEN (US) 1970 dir. Harold Prince
GB title: Black Flowers for the Bride
V

Kressing, H. *Cook, The*

Something of Value
MGM (US) 1957 dir. Richard Brooks
V

Ruark, R.

Something to Hide
AVCO (GB) 1973 dir. Alastair Reid
V

Monsarrat, N.

Something Wicked This Way Comes
DISNEY (US) 1983 dir. Jack Clayton
Ch, V

Bradbury, R.

Something Wild
UA (US) 1961 dir. Jack Garfein
V

Karmel, A. *Mary Ann*

Sometimes a Great Notion
UN (US) 1974 dir. Paul Newman
GB title: Never Give an Inch
V

Kesey, K.

Sometimes They Come Back
DELAUR (US) 1991
dir. Tom McLaughlin
TV(US)

King, S.

Somewhere in Time
UN (US) 1980 dir. Jeannot Szwarc
V

Matheson, R. *Bid Time Return*

Song of Bernadette, The
FOX (US) 1943 dir. Henry King
V

Werfel, F. V.

Song of Songs
PAR (US) 1933 dir. Rouben Mamoulian
Sheldon, E.
P

Song to Remember, A
COL (US) 1944 dir. Charles Vidor
V

Leslie, D. *Polonaise*

Son of Fury
TCF (US) 1942 dir. John Cromwell
Marshall, E. *Benjamin Blake*

Son of the Morning Star
REP (US) 1991 dir. Mike Robe
TVSe(US), V

Connell, E. S. *Son of the Morningstar: Custer and the Little Big Horn*

Son-Rise: A Miracle of Love
FILMWAYS (US) 1979 dir. Glenn Jordan
TV(US)

Kaufman, B. N. *Son-Rise*

Sons and Lovers
FOX (GB) 1960 dir. Jack Cardiff
Lawrence, D. H.

Sophia Loren — Her Own Story
EMI (US) 1980 dir. Mel Stuart
TV(US)

Hotchner, A. E. *Sophia Living and Loving: Her Own Story*

Sophie's Choice
UN/ITC (US) 1982 dir. Alan J. Pakula
V

Styron, W.

Sophisticated Gents, The
D. WILSON (US) 1981 dir. Harry Falk
TVSe(US)

Williams, J. A. *Junior Bachelor Society, The*

Sorcerer
UN (US) 1977 dir. William Friedkin
GB title: Wages of Fear

Arnaud, G. *Wages of Fear, The*

So Red the Rose
PAR (US) 1935 dir. King Vidor
Young, S.

Sorekara
TOEI (Jap) 1987 dir. Yoshimitsu Morita
Natsume, S.

Sorrell and Son
UA (GB) 1933 dir. Jack Raymond
YTV (GB) 1984 dir. Derek Bennett
TVSe(GB)

Deeping, W.

Sorry, Wrong Number
PAR (US) 1948 dir. Anatole Litvak
V
WIL. COURT (US) 1989
dir. Tony Wharmby
TV(US)
Fletcher, L.
P

So This is Love
WAR (US) 1953 dir. Gordon Douglas
GB title: Grace Moore Story, The
Moore, G. *You're Only Human Once*

So this is New York
UA (US) 1948 dir. Richard Fleischer
Lardner, R. W. *Big Town, The*

Sound and the Fury, The
FOX (US) 1959 dir. Martin Ritt
Faulkner, W.

Sounder
FOX (US) 1972 dir. Martin Ritt
V
Armstrong, W. H.

Sound of Music, The
FOX (US) 1965 dir. Robert Wise
M, V
Lindsay, H. and Crouse, R.
P
Trapp, M. A. *Story of the Trapp Family Singers, The*

Sounds from the Mountains
CORINTH (Jap) 1980 dir. Mikio Naruse
Kawabata, Y.

Soursweet
CIC (GB) 1988 dir. Mike Newell
Mo, T.

Southern Cross
G. REEVES (GB) 1983
TV(GB)
Coleman, T.

Southerner, The
UA (US) 1945 dir. Jean Renoir
V
Perry, G. S. *Hold Autumn in your Hands*

Southern Star, The
COL (GB/Fr) 1969 dir. Sidney Hayers
Verne, J. *Southern Star Mystery, The*

South Pacific
TODD AO (US) 1958 dir. Joshua Logan
M, V
Michener, J. P. *Tales from the South Pacific*
Rodgers, R., Hammerstein II, O., Logan, J. and Osborn, P.
P

South Riding
UA (GB) 1938 dir. Victor Saville
YTV (GB) 1974 dir. Alastair Reid
TVSe(GB)
Holtby, W.

South Sea Woman
WAR (US) 1953 dir. Arthur Lubin
Rankin, W. M.

Souvenir
CIC (GB) 1987 dir. Geoffrey Reeve
Hughes, D. *Pork Butcher, The*

So Well Remembered
RKO (GB) 1947 dir. Edward Dmytryk
Hilton, J.

Soylent Green
MGM (US) 1973 dir. Richard Fleischer
V

Harrison, H. *Make Room, Make Room!*

Space
PAR (US) 1985 dir. Joseph Sargent, Lee Phillips
TVSe(US)

Michener, J. A.

Spaceman and King Arthur, The
DISNEY (GB) 1979 dir. Russ Mayberry
US title: Unidentified Flying Oddball
V

Twain, M. *Connecticut Yankee in the Court of King Arthur, A*

Spanish Gardener, The
RANK (GB) 1956 dir. Philip Leacock
V

Cronin, A. J.

Spare the Rod
BL (GB) 1961 dir. Leslie Norman

Croft, M.

Sparkling Cyanide
WAR (US) 1983 dir. Robert Lewis
TV(US)

Christie, A.

Sparrows Can't Sing
WAR (GB) 1962 dir. Joan Littlewood

Lewis, S. *Sparrers Can't Sing*
P

Spartacus
UN (US) 1960 dir. Stanley Kubrick
V

Fast, H.

Spasms
PDC (Can) 1984 dir. William Fruet

Maryk, M. and Monahan, B. *Death Bite*

Speak Easily
MGM (US) 1932 dir. Edward Sedgwick

Kelland, C. B. *Footlights*

Spearfield's Daughter
FILMLINE (US) 1986
dir. Gilbert Shelton
TVSe(US)

Cleary, J.

Spellbound
PYRAMID (GB) 1940 dir. John Harlow
US title: Spell of Amy Nugent, The

Benson, R. *Necromancers, The*

Spellbound
UA (US) 1945 dir. Alfred Hitchcock
V

Beeding, F. *House of Dr. Edwards, The*

Spencer's Mountain
WAR (US) 1963 dir. Delmer Daves

Hamner, E.

Sphinx
WAR (US) 1981
dir. Franklin D. Schaffner
V

Cook, R.

Spider's Stratagem, The
RED FILM (It) 1970
dir. Bernardo Bertolucci

Borges, J. L. *Theme of the Traitor and the Hero, The*

Spider's Web, The
UA (GB) 1960 dir. Godfrey Grayson
BBC 2 (GB) 1985
TV(GB)

Christie, A.
P

Spikes Gang, The
UA (US) 1974 dir. Richard Fleischer

Tippette, G. *Bank Robber, The*

Spiral Road, The
UI (US) 1962 dir. Robert Mulligan

Hartog, J. de

Spiral Staircase, The
RKO (US) 1946 dir. Robert Siodmak
V
WAR (GB) 1975 dir. Peter Collinson
V

White, E. L. *Some Must Watch*

Spirit is Willing, The
PAR (US) 1967 dir. William Castle

Benchley, N. *Visitors, The*

Spirit of St. Louis, The
WAR (US) 1957 dir. Billy Wilder
V

Lindbergh, C. A. *We*

Spitfire
RKO (US) 1934 dir. John Cromwell
V

Vollmer, L. *Trigger*
P

Splendor
GOLDWYN (US) 1935
dir. Elliott Nugent

Crothers, R.
P

Split, The
MGM (US) 1968 dir. Gordon Flemyng
V

Stark, R. *Seventh, The*

Spoilers, The
PAR (US) 1930 dir. Edward Carew
UN (US) 1942 dir. Ray Enright
V
UN (US) 1955 dir. Jesse Hibbs

Beach, R.

Sporting Club, The
AVCO (US) 1971 dir. Larry Peerce
V

McGuane, T.

Sport of Kings, The
GAINS (GB) 1931 dir. Victor Saville

Hay, I.
P

Spring and Port Wine
AA (GB) 1970 dir. Peter Hammond

Naughton, B.
P

Spring in Park Lane
BL (GB) 1948 dir. Herbert Wilcox

Thomas, A. E. and Miller, A. D.
Come Out of the Kitchen
P

Spring Meeting
ABPC (GB) 1940 dir. Walter C. Mycroft

Farrell, M. J. and Perry, J.
P

Spy
WIL COURT (US) 1989
dir. Philip F. Messina
TV(US)

Garbo, N.

Spy Hunt
UN (US) 1950 dir. George Sherman
GB title: Panther's Moon

Canning, V. *Panther's Moon*

Spy in Black, The
COL (GB) 1939 dir. Michael Powell
US title: U-Boat 29
V

Clouston, J. S.

Spy Killer, The
ABC (US) 1969 dir. Roy Baker
TV(US)

Sangster, J. *Private I*

Spy of Napoleon
TWICKENHAM (GB) 1936
dir. Maurice Elvey
V

Orczy, Baroness E.

Spy Story
GALA (GB) 1976 dir. Lindsay Shonteff
V

Deighton, L.

Spy Who Came in from the Cold, The
PAR (GB) 1966 dir. Martin Ritt
V

Le Carré, J.

Spy Who Loved Me, The
UA (GB) 1977 dir. Lewis Gilbert
V

Fleming, I.

Square Dance
ISLAND (US) 1987 dir. Daniel Petrie
V

Hines, A.

Square Ring, The
GFD (GB) 1953 dir. Basil Dearden

Peterson, R.
P

Squaw Man, The
MGM (US) 1931 dir. Cecil B. deMille
GB title: White Man, The

Royle, E. M.
P

Squeaker, The
GAU BR (GB) 1937
dir. William K. Howard
US title: Murder on Diamond Row

Wallace, E.

Squeeze, The
WAR (GB) 1977 dir. Michael Apted
V

Craig, D.

Stagecoach
UA (US) 1939 dir. John Ford
V
FOX (US) 1966 dir. Gordon Douglas
HERITAGE (US) 1986 dir. Ted Post
TV(US), V

Haycox, E. *Stage to Lordsburg*

Stage Door
RKO (US) 1937 dir. Gregory La Cara
V

Kaufman, G. S. and Ferber, E.
P

Stage Fright
WAR (GB) 1950 dir. Alfred Hitchcock
V

Jepson, S. *Man Running*

Stage Struck
RKO (US) 1957 dir. Sidney Lumet
V

Akins, Z.
P

Staircase
FOX (US/Fr) 1969 dir. Stanley Donen

Dyer, C.
P

Staircase C
FILMS 7 (Fr) 1985
dir. Jean-Charles Tacchella
French title: Escalier C

Murail, E.

Stalag 17
PAR (US) 1953 dir. Billy Wilder
V

Bevan, D. and Trzcinski, E.
P

Stalker
(USSR) 1979 dir. Andrei Tarkovsky
Strugatsky, B., and Strugatsky, A.
Picnic by the Roadside

Stalking Moon, The
WAR (US) 1968 dir. Robert Mulligan
Olsen, T. V.

Stallion Road
WAR (US) 1947 dir. James V. Kern
Longstreet, S.

Stand by Me
COL (US) 1986 dir. Rob Reiner
V
King, S. *Body, The*

Stand by Your Man
GUBER-PETERS (US) 1981
dir. Jerry Jameson
TV(US)
Wynette, T. and Dew, J.

Stand up Virgin Soldiers
WAR (GB) 1977 dir. Norman Cohen
V
Thomas, L.

Stanley and Iris
MGM (US) 1990 dir. Martin Ritt
Barker, P. *Union Street*

Star 80
WAR (US) 1983 dir. Bob Fosse
V
Carpenter, T. *Death of a Playmate*

Starlight Hotel
REP (NZ) 1988 dir. Sam Pillsbury
V
Miller, G. H. *Dream Monger, The*

Star Quality
BBC (GB) 1985 dir. Alan Dosser
TVSe(GB)
Coward, N.

Stars and Bars
COL (US) 1988 dir. Pat O'Connor
V
Boyd, W.

Stars in my Crown
MGM (US) 1950 dir. Jacques Tourneur
Brown, J. D.

Stars Look Down, The
GN (GB) 1939 dir. Carol Reed
V
Cronin, A. J.

Star Spangled Girl, The
PAR (US) 1971 dir. Jerry Paris
Simon, N.
P

Starting Over
PAR (US) 1979 dir. Alan J. Pakula
V
Wakefield, D.

State Fair
FOX (US) 1933 dir. Henry King
FOX (US) 1945 dir. Walter Lang
M
FOX (US) 1962 dir. José Ferrer
M, V
Stong, P. D.

State of the Union
MGM (US) 1948 dir. Frank Capra
GB title: World and His Wife, The
V
Lindsay, H. and Crouse, R.
P

State Secret, The
BL (GB) 1950 dir. Sidney Gilliat
US title: Great Manhunt, The

Huggins, R. *Appointment with Fear*

Stationmaster's Wife, The
TELECUL (Ger) 1983
dir. Rainer Werner Fassbinder

Graf, O. M.

Station West
RKO (US) 1948 dir. Sidney Lanfield

Short, L.

Stay Away, Joe
MGM (US) 1968 dir. Peter Tewkesbury
V

Cushman, D.

Stay Hungry
UA (US) 1976 dir. Bob Rafaelson
V

Gaines, C.

Staying On
GRANADA (GB) 1980
dir. Silvio Narizzano/WarisHussein
TV(GB), V

Scott, P.

Stealing Heaven
FILM DALLAS (GB/Yugo) 1989
dir. Clive Donner
V

Meade, M.

Steamboat Round the Bend
FOX (US) 1935 dir. John Ford

Burman, B. L.

Steaming
NEW WORLD (GB) 1985
dir. Joseph Losey
V

Dunn, N.
P

Steel Magnolias
TRI-STAR (US) 1989 dir. Herbert Ross
V

Harling, R.
P

Stella
TOUCH (US) 1990 dir. John Erman

Prouty, O. *Stella Dallas*

Stella Dallas
UA (US) 1937 dir. King Vidor
V

Prouty, O.

Stepford Wives, The
CONTEM (US) 1975 dir. Bryan Forbes
V

Levin, I.

Step Lively
RKO (US) 1944 dir. Tim Whelan
V

Murray, J. and Boretz, A. *Room*
Service
P

Steppenwolf
CONTEM (US) 1974 dir. Fred Haines
V

Hesse, H.

Stepping Out
PAR (US) 1991 dir. Lewis Gilbert

Harris, R.
P

Sterile Cuckoo, The
PAR (US) 1969 dir. Alan J. Pakula
GB title: Pookie
V

Nicholson, J.

Stevie
FIRST (US/GB) 1978
dir. Robert Enders
Whitemore, H.
P

Stick
UN (US) 1985 dir. Burt Reynolds
V
Leonard, E.

Stiletto
AVCO (US) 1969 dir. Bernard Kowalski
V
Robbins, H.

Stillwatch
INTERSCOPE (US) 1987
dir. Rod Holcomb
TV(US)
Clark, M. H.

Stolen Airliner, The
BL (GB) 1955 dir. Don Sharp
Ch
Pudney, J. *Thursday Adventure*

Stolen Life, A
PAR (GB) 1939 dir. Paul Czinner
WAR (US) 1946 dir. Curtis Bernhardt
Benes, K. J.

Stone Fox
TAFT (US) 1987 dir. Harvey Hart
TV(US)
Gardiner, J. R.

Stone Killer, The
COL (US) 1973 dir. Michael Winner
V
Gardner, J. *Complete State of Death, A*

Stones for Ibarra
TITUS (US) 1988 dir. Jack Gold
TV(US)
Doerr, H.

Stopover Tokyo
FOX (US) 1957 dir. Richard L. Breen
V
Marquand, J. P.

Stop, You're Killing Me
WAR (US) 1952 dir. Roy del Ruth
Runyon, D. and Lindsay, H. *Slight Case of Murder, A*
P

Storm and Sorrow
HEARST (US) 1990 dir. Richard Colla
TV(US)
Craig, R. *Storm and Sorrow in the High High Pamirs*

Storm Fear
UA (US) 1955 dir. Cornel Wilde
Seeley, C.

Storm in a Teacup
LF (GB) 1937 dir. Ian Dalrymple, Victor Saville
V
Frank, B. *Sturm in Wasserglass*
P

Storm over the Nile
GFD (GB) 1955 dir. Terence Young
V
Mason, A. E. W. *Four Feathers, The*

Story of Dr. Wassell, The
PAR (US) 1944 dir. Cecil B. de Mille
Hilton, J.

Story of Esther Costello, The
COL (GB) 1957 dir. David Miller
US title: Golden Virgin, The
Monsarrat, N.

Story of G.I. Joe, The
UA (US) 1945 dir. William A. Wellman
Pyle, E. T.

Story of Gilbert and Sullivan, The
BL (GB) 1953 dir. Sidney Gilliatt

Baily, L. *Gilbert and Sullivan and Their World*

Story of Mankind, The
WAR (US) 1957 dir. Irwin Allen

Van Loon, H. W.

Story of O, The
NEW REALM (Fr) 1975 dir. Just Jaeckin
V

Réage, P.

Story of Temple Drake, The
PAR (US) 1933 dir. Stephen Roberts

Faulkner, W. *Sanctuary*

Story of the Beach Boys, The: Summer Dreams
L. HILL (USTV) 1990
dir. Michael Switzer
TV(US)

Gaines, S. *Heroes and Villains: The True Story of the Beach Boys*

Story of Women
NEW YORKER (Fr) 1989
dir. Claude Chabrol

Szpiner, F. *Affaire de Femmes, Une*

Stowaway to the Moon
FOX (US) 1975
dir. Andrew V. McLaglen
TV(US)

Shelton, W. R. *Stowaway to the Moon: The Camelot Odyssey*

Straight from the Heart
TELESCENE (Fr) 1990 dir. Lea Pool

Navarre, Y. *Kurwenal*

Straight, Place and Show
FOX (US) 1938 dir. David Butler
GB title: They're Off

Runyon, D., and Caesar, I.
P

Straight Time
WAR (US) 1978 dir. Ulu Grosbard
V

Bunker, E. *No Beast so Fierce*

Strange Affair, The
PAR (GB) 1968 dir. David Greene

Toms, B.

Strange Affair of Uncle Harry, The
UN (US) 1945 dir. Robert Siodmak
V

Job, T. *Uncle Harry*
P

Strange Boarders
GB (GB) 1938 dir. Herbert Mason

Oppenheim, E. P. *Strange Boarders of Paradise Crescent, The*

Strange Cargo
MGM (US) 1940
dir. Joseph L. Mankiewicz

Sale, R. *Not Too Narrow, Not Too Deep*

Strange Door, The
UI (US) 1951 dir. Joseph Pevney

Stevenson, R. L. *Sire of Maletroit's Door, The*

Strange Interlude
MGM (US) 1932 dir. Robert Z. Leonard
GB title: Strange Interval

O'Neill, E. G.
P

Strange Intruder
ABP (US) 1956 dir. Irving Rapper

Fowler, H. M. *Shades Will Not Vanish*

Strange One, The
COL (US) 1957 dir. Jack Garfein
GB title: End as a Man
Willingham, C. *End as a Man*

Stranger, The
PAR (Fr/It) 1967 dir. Luchino Visconti
Camus, A.

Stranger Came Home, The
EXCL (GB) 1954 dir. Terence Fisher
US title: Unholy Four, The
Sanders, G. *Stranger at Home*

Stranger in my Arms, A
UI (US) 1958 dir. Helmut Kautner
Wilder, R. *And Ride a Tiger*

Stranger in my Bed
TAFT (US) 1987 dir. Larry Elikann
TV(US)
Slater, B. and Leighton, F. S.

Stranger in our House
INTERPLAN (US) 1978 dir. Wes Craven
TV(US)
Duncan, L *Summer of Fear*

Stranger in the House
JARFID (GB) 1967 dir. Pierre Rouve
V
Simenon, G. *Strangers in the House*

Stranger in Town
EROS (GB) 1957 dir. George Pollock
Chittenden, F. *Uninvited, The*

Stranger is Watching, A
MGM/UA (US) 1982
dir. Sean Cunningham
V
Clark, M. H.

Strangers in Love
PAR (US) 1932 dir. Lothar Mendes
Locke, W. J. *Shorn Lamb, The*

Strangers in 7a, The
PALOMAR (US) 1972 dir. Paul Wendkos
TV(US)
Farrington, F.

Strangers May Kiss
MGM (US) 1931
dir. George Fitzmaurice
Parrott, U.

Strangers on a Train
WAR (US) 1951 dir. Alfred Hitchcock
V
Highsmith, P.

Strangers Return
MGM (US) 1933 dir. King Vidor
Stong, P. D.

Strangers When We Meet
COL (US) 1959 dir. Richard Quine
V
Hunter, E.

Strange Woman, The
UA (US) 1946 dir. Edgar G. Ulmer
Williams, B. A.

Strange World of Planet X, The
EROS (GB) 1958 dir. Gilbert Gunn
US title: Cosmic Monsters
Ray, R.

Strawberry Blonde, The
WAR (US) 1941 dir. Raoul Walsh
V
Hagan, J. *One Sunday Afternoon*
P

Strawberry Roan
BN (GB) 1944 dir. Maurice Elvey
Street, A. G.

Strawberry Statement, The
MGM (US) 1970 dir. Stuart Hagmann
V
Kunen, J. S.

Straw Dogs
CINERAMA (GB) 1971
dir. Sam Peckinpah
V
Williams, G. M. *Siege at Trencher's Farm, The*

Streamers
UA (US) 1983 dir. Robert Altman
V
Rabe, D.
P

Streetcar Named Desire, A
WAR (US) 1951 dir. Elia Kazan
V
PSO (US) 1984 dir. John Erman
TV(US)
Williams, T.
P

Street of Chance
PAR (US) 1942 dir. Jack Hively
Woolrich, C. *Black Curtain, The*

Street of Dreams
PHOENIX (US) 1988
dir. William A. Graham
TV(US)
Harris, T. *Good Night and Good Bye*

Street Scene
UA (US) 1931 dir. King Vidor
V
Rice, E.
P

Streets of San Francisco, The
WAR TV (US) 1972 dir. Walter Grauman
TV(US)
Weston, C. *Poor, Poor Ophelia*

Strictly Dishonourable
UN (US) 1931 dir. John Stahl
MGM (US) 1951 dir. Norman Panama, Melvin Frank
Sturges, P.
P

Strike It Rich
BRIT SCREEN (GB) 1990
dir. James Scott
Greene, G. *Loser Takes All*

Strike Me Pink
UA (US) 1936 dir. Norman Taurog
Kelland, C. B. *Dreamland*

Stripper, The
FOX (US) 1963 dir. Franklin Schaffner
GB title: Woman of Summer
V
Inge, W. *Loss of Roses, A*
P

Stroker Ace
UN/WAR (US) 1983 dir. Hal Needham
V
Neely, W. *Stand on It*

Strong Medicine
TELEPICS (US) 1986 dir. Guy Green
TVSe(US)
Hailey, A.

Stud, The
BW (GB) 1978 dir. Quentin Masters
V
Collins, J.

Stud Farm, The
HUNG (Hung) 1978 dir. Andras Kovacs
Gall, I.

Student Prince, The
MGM (US) 1954 dir. Richard Thorpe
M

Romberg, S.

Meyer-Foerster, W. *Old Heidelburg*
P

Studs Lonigan
UA (US) 1960 dir. Irving Lerner
V

LORIMAR (US) 1979
dir. James Goldstone
TVSe(US)

Farrell, J. T. *Young Manhood of Studs Lonigan, The*

Study in Scarlet, The
WW (US) 1933 dir. Edward L. Marin
V

Doyle, Sir A. C.

Study in Terror, A
COMPTON-TEKLI (GB) 1965
dir. James Hill
V

Queen, E.

Stunt Man, The
FOX (US) 1980 dir. Richard Rush
V

Brodeur, P.

Subject was Roses, The
MGM (US) 1968 dir. Ulu Grosbard

Gilroy, F. D.
P

Submarine Patrol
FOX (US) 1938 dir. John Ford

Milholland, R.

Subterraneans, The
MGM (US) 1960
dir. Ronald MacDougall

Kerouac, J.

Such Good Friends
PAR (US) 1972 dir. Otto Preminger

Gould, L.

Sudden Fear
RKO (US) 1952 dir. David Miller

Sherry, E.

Suddenly, Last Summer
COL (GB) 1959
dir. Joseph L. Mankiewicz
V

Williams, T.
P

Sudie & Simpson
HEARST (US) 1990
dir. Joan Tewkesbury
TV(US)

Carter, S. F. *Sudie*

Sugar Cane Alley
ORION (Fr) 1984 dir. Euzhan Palcy
V

Zobel, J. *Rue Cases Negres, La*

Sugarfoot
WAR (US) 1951 dir. Edward L. Marin

Kelland, C. B.

Suicide Club, The
ANGELIKA (US) 1988 dir. James Bruce

Stevenson, R. L.

Suicide's Wife, The
FAC-NEW (US) 1979 dir. John Newland
TV(US)

Madden, D.

Summer and Smoke
PAR (US) 1961 dir. Peter Glenville

Williams, T.
P

Summer Camp Nightmare
CONCORDE (US) 1987
dir. Bert C. Dragin
V

Butler, W. *Butterfly Revolution, The*

Summer Girl
LORIMAR (US) 1983
dir. Robert Michael Lewis
TV(US)

Crane, C.

Summer Heat
ATLANTIC (US) 1987
dir. Michie Gleason
V

Shivers, L. *Here to Get my Baby out of Jail*

Summer Holiday
MGM (US) 1948
dir. Rouben Mamoulian
M

O'Neill, E. G. *Ah Wilderness!*
P

Summer Lightning
CHANNEL 4 (GB) 1986
TV(GB)

Turgenev, I. *First Love*

Summer Magic
DISNEY (US) 1963 dir. James Neilson
V

Wiggin, K. D. *Mother Carey's Chickens*

Summer my Father Grew Up, The
SHAPIRO (US) 1991
dir. Michael Tuchner
TV(US)

Jennings, S. *Tooth of the Lion*
P

Summer of Fear
INTERPLAN (US) 1978 dir. Wes Craven
V

Duncan, L.

Summer of my German Soldier
HIGHGATE (US) 1978
dir. Michael Tuchner
TV(US), V

Greene, B.

Summer of the Seventeenth Doll, The
UA (US/Aust) 1959 dir. Leslie Norman

Lawler, R.
P

Summer Place, A
WAR (US) 1959 dir. Delmer Daves

Wilson, S.

Summer Storm
UA (US) 1944 dir. Douglas Sirk

Chekhov, A. *Shooting Party, The*

Summer Story, A
ITC/ATLANTIC (GB) 1988
dir. Piers Haggard

Galsworthy, J. *Apple Tree, The*

Summertime
UA (US) 1955 dir. David Lean
GB title: Summer Madness
V

Laurents, A *Time of the Cuckoo, The*
P

Summertree
WAR (US) 1971 dir. Anthony Newley

Cowen, R.
P

Summer with Monika
SVENSK (Swe) 1952
dir. Ingmar Bergman
V

Anders, P.

Sun also Rises, The
FOX (US) 1957 dir. Henry King
FOX (US) 1984 dir. James Goldstone
TVSe(US)

Hemingway, E.

Sunburn
HEMDALE (GB/US) 1979
dir. Richard C. Sarafian
V

Ellin, S. *Bind, The*

Sun Child
YTV (GB) 1988 dir. L. G. Clark
TV(GB)

Huth, A.

Sunday in New York
MGM (US) 1963 dir. Peter Tewkesbury

Krasna, N.
P

Sunday in the Country, A
MGM/UA (Fr) 1984
dir. Bertrand Tavernier
V

Bost, P. *Monsieur L'Admiral va Bientôt Mourir*

Sundays and Cybèle
TERRA (Fr) 1962 dir. Serge Bourgignon
V

Echasseriaux, B.

Sundown
UA (US) 1941 dir. Henry Hathaway
V

Lyndon, B.

Sundowners, The
WAR (GB/Aust) 1960
dir. Fred Zinnemann

Cleary, J.

Sunrise at Campobello
WAR (US) 1960 dir. Vincent J. Donehue
V

Schary, D.
P

Sunset Gang, The
AM PLAY (US) 1991 dir. Calvin Skaggs,
Tony Drazan
TVSe(US)

Adler, W.

Sunshine Boys, The
MGM (US) 1975 dir. Herbert Ross
V

Simon, N.
P

Sun Shines Bright, The
REP (US) 1953 dir. John Ford

Cobb, I. S. *Sun Shines Bright, The; Mob From Massac, The; Lord Provides, The*

Super Cops, The
MGM (US) 1974 dir. Gordon Parks
V

Whittemore, L. H.

Surprise Package
COL (GB) 1960 dir. Stanley Donen

Buchwald, A. *Gift From the Boys, A*

Surrender-Hell
AA (US) 1959 dir. John Barnwell

Harkins, P. *Blackburn's Headhunters*

Survive
STIGWOOD (Mex) 1976
dir. Rene Cardona
V

Blair, C.

Survivor, The
HEMDALE (Aust) 1981
dir. David Hemmings
V

Herbert, J.

Survive the Savage Sea
VON ZERNICK-SERTNER FILMS
TV(US) 1992 dir. Kevin James Dobson
Robertson, D.

Susana
PLEXUS (Sp) 1951 dir. Luis Bunuel
V

Reachi, M.

Susan and God
MGM (US) 1940 dir. George Cukor
GB title: Gay Mrs. Trexel, The
Crothers, R.
P

Susan Lenox, Her Fall and Rise
MGM (US) 1931 dir. Robert Z. Leonard
GB title: Rise of Helga, The
Graham, D.

Susan Slade
WAR (US) 1962 dir. Delmer Daves
Hume, D. *Sin of Susan Slade, The*

Suspect
BL (GB) 1960 dir. Roy Boulting
Balchin, N. *Sort of Traitor, A*

Suspect, The
UN (US) 1944 dir. Robert Siodmak
Ronald, J. *This Way Out*

Suspicion
RKO (US) 1941 dir. Alfred Hitchcock
V

Iles, F. *Before the Fact*

Suzy
MGM (US) 1936
dir. George Fitzmaurice
Gorman, H.

Svengali
WAR (US) 1931 dir. Archie Mayo
V
REN (GB) 1954 dir. William Alwyn
V
HALMI (US) 1983 dir. Anthony Harvey
TV(US)
Du Maurier, G. *Trilby*

Swallows and Amazons
EMI (GB) 1974 dir. Claude Whatham
Ch, V
Ransome, A.

Swamp Water
FOX (US) 1941 dir. Jean Renoir
GB title: Man Who Came Back, The
Bell, V.

Swan, The
MGM (US) 1956 dir. Charles Vidor
Molnar, F.
P

Swann in Love
GAU (Fr) 1984 dir. Volker Schlondorff
V

Proust, M. *Du Côté de chez Swann*

Swarm, The
WAR (US) 1978 dir. Irwin Allen
V
Herzog, A.

Sweeny Todd, the Demon Barber of Fleet Street
KING (GB) 1936 dir. George King
Dibdin-Pitt, G.
P

Sweet Bird of Youth
MGM (US) 1962 dir. Richard Brooks
KUSHNER-LOCKE (US) 1989
dir. Nicolas Roeg
TV(US)
Williams, T.
P

Sweet Charity
UN (US) 1969 dir. Robert Fosse
M, V
**Simon, N., Fields, D., and
Coleman, C.**
P

Sweet Country
CINEMA (US) 1987
dir. Michael Cacoyannis
Richards, C.

Sweet Hostage
BRUT (US) 1975 dir. Lee Phillips
TV(US)
Benchley, N. *Welcome to Xanadu*

Sweet Love, Bitter
FILM 2 (US) 1967 dir. Herbert Danska
Williams, J. *Night Song*

Sweet Ride, The
FOX (US) 1968 dir. Harvey Hart
Murray, W.

Sweet William
ITC (GB) 1980 dir. Claude Whatham
V
Bainbridge, B.

Swimmer, The
COL (US) 1968 dir. Frank Perry, Sidney Pollack
V
Cheever, J.

Swing High, Swing Low
PAR (US) 1937 dir. Mitchell Leisen
V
Walters, G. M. and Hopkins, A.
Burlesque
P

Swiss Family Robinson
RKO (US) 1940 dir. Edward Ludwig
V
DISNEY (GB) 1960 dir. Ken Annakin
V
FOX (US) 1975 dir. Harry Harris
TV(US)
Wyss, J. D.

Switching Channels
TRI-STAR (US) 1988 dir. Ted Kotcheff
V
Hecht, B. and MacArthur, C. *Front Page, The*
P

Sword and the Rose, The
DISNEY (GB) 1953 dir. Ken Annakin
V
Major, C. *When Knighthood was in Flower*

Sword in the Stone, The
DISNEY (US) 1963
dir. Wolfgang Reitherman
A, Ch, V
White, T. H. *Once and Future King, The*

Sword of Gideon
HBO (US/Can) 1986
dir. Michael Anderson
TV(US/Can)
Jones, G. *Vengeance*

Sworn to Silence
BLATT/SINGER (US) 1987
dir. Peter Levin
TV(US)
Alibrandi, T. and Armani, F. H.
Privileged Information

Sybil
LORIMAR (US) 1976 dir. Daniel Petrie
TVSe(US), V
Schreiber, F. R.

Sylvia
PAR (US) 1965 dir. Gordon Douglas
Cunningham, E. V.

Sylvia
ENT (NZ) 1985 dir. Michael Firth
V
Ashton-Warner, S. *Teacher, I Passed This Way*

Sylvia and the Ghost
ECRAN (Fr) 1944
dir. Claude Autant-Lara
V
Adam, A.
P

Sylvia Scarlett
RKO (US) 1935 dir. George Cukor
V
Mackenzie, Sir C.

Symphonie Pastorale, La
GIBE (Fr) 1946 dir. Jean Delannoy
Gide, A.

Symphony of Six Million
RKO (US) 1932 dir. Gregory LaCava
GB title: Melody of Life
Hurst, F.

Taffin
MGM/UA (GB) 1988
dir. Francis Megahy
V
Mallett, L.

Taggart
UI (US) 1965 dir. R. G. Springsteen
L'Amour, L.

Tagget
MCA TV (US) 1991
dir. Richard T. Heffron
TV(US)
Greenfield, I. A.

Tai-Pan
ORION (US) 1986 dir. Daryl Duke
V
Clavell, J.

Take, The
COL (US) 1974
dir. Robert Hartford-Davis
Newman, G. F. *Sir, You Bastard*

Take, The
MCA TV (US) 1990 dir. Leon Ichaso
TV(US)
Izzi, E.

Take a Giant Step
UA (US) 1959 dir. Philip Leacock

Peterson, L. S.
P

Take a Girl Like You
COL (GB) 1969 dir. Jonathan Miller
V

Amis, K.

Take Care of My Little Girl
FOX (US) 1951 dir. Jean Negulesco

Goodin, P.

Take Her, She's Mine
MGM (US) 1963 dir. Henry Koster

Ephron, P. and Ephron, H.
P

Take my Life
EL (GB) 1947 dir. Ronald Neame

Graham, W. and Taylor, V.

Taking of Pelham 123, The
UA (US) 1974 dir. Joseph Sargent
V

Godey, J.

Tale of Little Pig Robinson, The
TVS (GB) 1990 dir. Alan Bridges
TVSe(GB)

Potter, B.

Tale of Two Cities, A
MGM (US) 1935 dir. Jack Conway
V
RANK (GB) 1958 dir. Ralph Thomas
V
ROSEMONT (US/GB) 1980
dir. Jim Goddard
TV(GB/US)

Dickens, C.

Tales from the Darkside: the Movie
PAR (US) 1990 dir. John Harrison

Conan Doyle, Sir A. *Lot 27a*
King, S. *Cat From Hell*

Tales from the Vienna Woods
CINEMA 5 (Austria/Ger) 1981
dir. Maximilian Schell

von Horvath, O
P

Tales of Hoffman, The
BL (GB) 1951
dir. Michael Powell/EmericPressburger
M

Offenbach, J.

Tales of Ordinary Madness
(It/Fr) 1981 dir. Marco Ferri
V

Bukowski, C. *Erections, Ejaculations, Exhibitions and Tales of Ordinary Madness*

Tales of Terror
WAR (US) 1962 dir. Roger Corman
V

Poe, E. A. *Morella; Black Cat, The; Facts of the Case of Dr. Valdemar,The*

Talk About a Stranger
MGM (US) 1952 dir. David Bradley

Armstrong, C.

Talking Walls
NEW WORLD (US) 1987
dir. Stephen Verona
V

McGrady, M. *Motel Tapes, The*

Talk Radio
UN (US) 1988 dir. Oliver Stone

Bogosian, E.
P

Singular, S. *Talked to Death: The Life and Murder of Alan Berg*
P

Tall Headlines, The
GN (GB) 1952 dir. Terence Young

Lindop, A. E.

Tall Man Riding
WAR (US) 1955 dir. Lesley Selander

Fox, N. A.

Tall Men, The
FOX (US) 1955 dir. Raoul Walsh
V

Fisher, C.

Tall Story
WAR (US) 1960 dir. Joshua Logan

Nemerov, H. *Homecoming Game, The*

Talvisota
FINN (Fin) 1989 dir. Pekka Parikka

Tuuri, A.

Tamahine
WAR (GB) 1963 dir. Philip Leacock

Niklaus, T.

Tamango
SNEG (Fr) 1958 dir. John Berry

Merimée, P.

Tamarind Seed, The
SCOTIA-BARBER (GB) 1974
dir. Blake Edwards
V

Anthony, E.

Taming of the Shrew, The
M. EVANS (US) 1956
dir. George Schaefer
TV(US)
COL (US) 1967 dir. Franco Zeffirelli
V

Shakespeare, W.
P

Tammy and the Bachelor
UN (US) 1957 dir. Joseph Pevney
GB title: Tammy
V

Sumner, C. R.

Tap Roots
UI (US) 1948 dir. George Marshall

Street, J.

Taps
FOX (US) 1981 dir. Harold Becker
V

Freeman, D. *Father Sky*

Taras Bulba
UA (US) 1962 dir. J. Lee Thompson

Gogol, N.

Tarka the Otter
RANK (GB) 1979 dir. David Cobham
V

Williamson, H.

Tarnished Angels, The
UI (US) 1957 dir. Douglas Sirk

Faulkner, W. *Pylon*

Tarzan, The Ape Man
MGM (US) 1932 dir. W. S. VanDyke
V

Burroughs, E. R. *Tarzan of the Apes*

Taste for Death, A
YTV (GB) 1987
TVSe(GB)

James, P. D.

Taste of Excitement, A
MONARCH (GB) 1969 dir. Don Sharp
Healey, B. *Waiting for a Tiger*

Taste of Honey, A
Bryanston (GB) 1961
dir. Tony Richardson
Delaney, S.
P

Taxi!
WAR (US) 1931 dir. Roy del Ruth
Nicholson, K. *Blind Spot, The*
P

Tea and Sympathy
MGM (US) 1956 dir. Vincente Minnelli
Anderson, R.
P

Teahouse of the August Moon, The
MGM (US) 1956 dir. Daniel Mann
COMPASS (US) 1962
dir. George Schaefer
TV(US)
Sneider, V.
Patrick, J.
P

Tea in the Harem
M&R FILMS (Fr) 1986
dir. Mehdi Charef
Charef, M. *Thé au harem d'Archi Ahmen, Le*

Tears in the Rain
ATLANTIC/BL (US/GB) 1988
dir. Don Sharpe
TV(GB/US)
Wallace, P.

Teenage Rebel
FOX (US) 1956 dir. Edmund Goulding
Sommer, E.
P

Telefon
MGM (US) 1977 dir. Don Siegel
V
Wager, W.

Tell England
CAPITOL (GB) 1931
dir. Anthony Asquith, GeraldBarkas
US title: Battle of Gallipoli, The
Raymond, E.

Tell Me a Riddle
FILMWAYS (US) 1980 dir. Lee Grant
V
Olsen, T.

Tell me my Name
TALENT (US) 1977 dir. Delbert Mann
TV(US)
Carter, M.

Tell Me That You Love Me, Junie Moon
PAR (US) 1970 dir. Otto Preminger
Kellogg, M.

Tell-Tale Heart, The
ADELPHI (GB) 1953 dir. J. B. Williams
ABP (GB) 1960 dir. Ernest Morris
Poe, E. A.

Tell them Willie Boy is Here
UN (US) 1969 dir. Abraham Polonsky
V
Lawton, H. *Willie Boy*

Tempest
PAR (It/Fr/Yugo) 1958
dir. Alberto Lattuada
V
Pushkin, A. *Captain's Daughter, The*

Tempest, The
COMPASS (US) 1960
dir. George Schaefer
TV(US), V
MAINLINE (GB) 1980
dir. Derek Jarman
V

Shakespeare, W.
P

Temptation
UN (US) 1935 dir. Irving Pichel

Hichens, R. *Bella Donna*

Temptation Harbour
AB (GB) 1947 dir. Lance Comfort

Simenon, G. *Newhaven-Dieppe*

Temptation of Eileen Hughes, The
BBC (GB) 1988 dir. Trevor Powell
TV(GB)

Moore, B.

Tenant, The
PAR (Fr) 1976 dir. Roman Polanski
V

Topor, R.

Ten Days Wonder
HEMDALE (Fr) 1971
dir. Claude Chabrol

Queen, E.

Tenderfoot, The
DISNEY (US) 1964 dir. Byron Paul

Tevis, J. H. *Arizona in the 50's*

Tender is the Night
FOX (US) 1962 dir. Henry King
BBC/SHOWTIME (US/GB) 1985
dir. Robert Knights
TVSe(US/GB)

Fitzgerald, F. S.

Tender Trap, The
MGM (US) 1955 dir. Charles Walters

Shulman, M. and Smith, R. P.
P

Tendre Ennemie
WORLD (Fr) 1938 dir. Max Ophuls

Antoine, W. P. *L'Ennemie*
P

Ten Little Indians
ABP (GB) 1965 dir. George Pollock
V
CANNON (US) 1989
dir. Alan Birkinshaw

Christie, A. *Ten Little Niggers*

Ten Million Dollar Getaway, The
WIL COURT (US) 1991
dir. James A. Contner
TV(US)

Feiden, D.

Ten Minute Alibi
BL (GB) 1935 dir. Bernard Vorhaus

Armstrong, A.
P

Tennessee's Partner
RKO (US) 1955 dir. Allan Dwan
V

Harte, B.

Ten North Frederick
FOX (US) 1958 dir. Philip Dunne

O'Hara, J.

10 Rillington Place
COL (GB) 1970 dir. Richard Fleischer
V

Kennedy, L.

Ten Seconds to Hell
UA (US) 1959 dir. Robert Aldrich

Bachmann, L. *Phoenix, The*

Tension at Table Rock
RKO (US) 1956
dir. Charles Marquis Warren
V

Gruber, G. *Bitter Sage*

10.30 p.m. Summer
UA (US/Sp) 1966 dir. Jules Dassin

Duras, M. *10.30 p.m. on a Summer Night*

Tenth Man, The
ROSEMONT (US/GB) 1988
dir. Jack Gold
TV(GB/US)

Greene, G.

Tenth Month, The
HAMILTON (US) 1979
dir. Joan Tewkesbury
TV(US), V

Hobson, L. Z.

Term of Trial
WAR (GB) 1962 dir. Peter Glenville

Barlow, J.

Terms of Endearment
PAR (US) 1983 dir. James L. Brooks
V

McMurtry, L.

Terrible Beauty, A
UA (GB) 1960 dir. Tay Garnett

Roth, A.

Terronauts, The
EMBASSY (GB) 1967
dir. Montgomery Tully
V

Leinster, M. *Wailing Asteroid, The*

Terror, The
ALL (GB) 1938 dir. Richard Bird

Wallace, E.

Terror in the Sky
PAR TV (US) 1971
dir. Bernard L. Kowalski
TV(US)

Hailey, A. and Castle, J. *Runway Zero-Eight*

Terror on Highway 91
CBS (US) 1989 dir. Jerry Jameson
TV(US)

Sellers, S. *Terror on Highway 59*

Tess
COL (Fr/GB) 1981 dir. Roman Polanski
V

Hardy, T. *Tess of the d'Urbervilles*

Tess of the Storm Country
FOX (US) 1932 dir. Alfred Santell
FOX (US) 1961 dir. Paul Guilfoyle

White, G. M.

Testament
PAR (US) 1983 dir. Lynne Littman
V

Amen, C. *Last Testament, The*

Testimony of Two Men
UN TV (US) 1977 dir. Leo Penn,
Larry Yust
TVSe(US)

Caldwell, T.

Test of Love, A
UN (US) 1985 dir. Gil Brealey
V

Crossley, R., and McDonald, A.
Annie's Coming Out

Tex
DISNEY (US) 1982 dir. Tim Hunter
V

Hinton, S. E.

Texasville
COL (US) 1990 dir. Peter Bogdanovich

McMurtry, L.

Thanks for the Memory
PAR (US) 1938 dir. George Archainbaud

Goodrich, F., and Hackett, A. *Up Pops the Devil*
P

Thanksgiving Promise, The
DISNEY (US) 1986 dir. Beau Bridges
TV(US)

Yorgason, B. & Yorgason, B.
Chester, I Love You

Thank You, Jeeves
FOX (US) 1936
dir. Arthur Greville Collins

Wodehouse, P. G.

Thank You Mr. Moto
FOX (US) 1937 dir. Norman Foster

Marquand, J. P.

Thark
GB (GB) 1932 dir. Tom Walls

Travers, B.
P

That Certain Feeling
PAR (US) 1956 dir. Norman Panama, Melvin Frank

Kerr, J. and Brooke, E. *King of Hearts*
P

That Championship Season
CANNON (US) 1982 dir. Jason Miller
V

Miller, J.
P

That Cold Day in the Park
COMM (Can) 1969 dir. Robert Altman
V

Miles, R.

That Dangerous Age
LF (GB) 1948 dir. Gregory Ratoff
US title: If This Be Sin

Kennedy, M., Surgutchoff, I.
Autumn
P

That Darn Cat!
DISNEY (US) 1965
dir. Robert Stevenson
V

Gordon, M. and Gordon, G.
Undercover Cat

That Forsyte Woman
MGM (US) 1949 dir. Compton Bennett
GB title: Forsyte Saga, The

Galsworthy, J. *Man of Property, A*

That Hagen Girl
WAR (US) 1947 dir. Peter Godfrey

Kniepple, E.

That Lady
FOX (GB) 1955 dir. Terence Young

O'Brien, K.

That Obscure Object of Desire
GALAXIE (Fr/Sp) 1978 dir. Luis Bunuel
V

Louys, P. *Femme et le Pantin, Le*

That was then . . . This is now
PAR (US) 1985 dir. Christopher Cain
V

Hinton, S. E.

That Woman Opposite
MON (GB) 1957 dir. Compton Bennett

Carr, J. D. *Emperor's Snuffbox, The*

Theorem
AETOS (It) 1968 dir. Pier Paolo Pasolini

Pasolini, P. P.

There Goes the Bride
ENT (GB) 1980 dir. Terence Marcel

Cooney, R.
P

There Must be a Pony
COL TV (US) 1986 dir. Joseph Sargent
TV(US)

Kirkwood, J.

There's a Girl in my Soup
COL (GB) 1970 dir. Roy Boulting
V

Frisby, T.
P

There's Always Tomorrow
MGM (US) 1934 dir. Edward Sloman
UN (US) 1956 dir. Douglas Sirk

Parrot, U.

Thérèse
GALA (Fr) 1964 dir. Georges Franju

Mauriac, F. *Thérèse Desqueyroux*

There Shall Be No Night
MILBERG (US) 1956
dir. George Schaefer
TV(US)

Sherwood, R. E.
P

These Thousand Hills
FOX (US) 1958 dir. Richard Fleischer

Guthrie, Jr., A. B.

These Three
UA (US) 1936 dir. William Wyler
V

Hellman, L. F. *Children's Hour, The*
P

They Call it Murder
FOX (US) 1971 dir. Walter Grauman
TV(US)

Gardner, E. S. *D. A. Draws a Circle, The*

They Came to a City
EAL (GB) 1944 dir. Basil Dearden

Priestley, J. B.
P

They Came to Cordura
COL (US) 1959 dir. Robert Rossen
V

Swarthout, G.

They Drive by Night
WAR (GB) 1938 dir. Arthur Woods

Curtis, J.

They Drive by Night
WAR (US) 1940 dir. Raoul Walsh
GB title: Road to Frisco, The
V

Bezzerides, A. I. *Long Haul*

They Gave Him A Gun
MGM (US) 1937 dir. W. S. Van Dyke

Cowen, W. J.

They Knew Mr. Knight
GFD (GB) 1945 dir. Norman Walker

Whipple, D.

They Knew What They Wanted
RKO (US) 1940 dir. Garson Kanin
V

Howard, S. C.
P

They Live
UN (US) 1988 dir. John Carpenter
V

Nelson, R. *Eight O'Clock in the Morning*

They Made Me A Fugitive
WAR (GB) 1947 dir. Alberto Cavalcanti
US title: I Became a Criminal

Budd, J. *Convict has Escaped, A*

They Met in the Dark
RANK (GB) 1943 dir. Karel Lamac
Gilbert, A. *Vanishing Corpse, The*

They Might be Giants
UN (US) 1972 dir. Anthony Harvey
V
Goldman, J.
P

They're a Weird Mob
RANK (GB) 1966 dir. Michael Powell
V
Culotta, N.

They Shoot Horses, Don't They?
CINERAMA (US) 1969
dir. Sydney Pollack
V
McCoy, H.

They were Expendable
MGM (US) 1945 dir. John Ford
V
White, W. L.

They Were Sisters
GFD (GB) 1945 dir. Arthur Crabtree
Whipple, D.

They Won't Forget
WAR (US) 1937 dir. Mervyn Le Roy
Greene, W. *Death in the Deep South*

Thief
UA (US) 1981 dir. Michael Mann
GB title: Violent Street
V
Hohimer F. *Home Invaders, The*

Thief Who Came to Dinner, The
WAR (US) 1973 dir. Bud Yorkin
V
Smith, T. L.

Thieves' Highway
FOX (US) 1949 dir. Jules Dassin
Bezzerides, A. I. *Thieves' Market*

Thieves Like Us
UA (US) 1974 dir. Robert Altman
Anderson, E.

Thing, The
RKO (US) 1951 dir. Christian Nyby
GB title: Thing from Another World, The
UN (US) 1982 dir. John Carpenter
V
Campbell, J. W. *Who Goes There?*

Things to Come
UA (GB) 1936
dir. William Cameron Menzies
V
Wells, H. G. *Shape of Things to Come, The*

Thin Man, The
MGM (US) 1934 dir. W. S. Van Dyke
V
Hammett, D.

Thin Red Line, The
PLANET (US) 1964 dir. Andrew Marton
Jones, J.

Third Day, The
WAR (US) 1965 dir. Jack Smight
Hayes, J.

Third Degree Burn
HBO (US) 1989 dir. Roger Spottiswoode
TV(US)
Margolin, P. M.

Third Man, The
GFD (GB) 1949 dir. Carol Reed
V
Greene, G.

Third Man on the Mountain
DISNEY (GB) 1959 dir. Ken Annakin
Ch, V
Ullman, J. R. *Banner in the Sky*

Third Party Risk
EXCL (GB) 1955 dir. Daniel Birt
Bentley, N.

Third Voice, The
TCF (US) 1959 dir. Hubert Cornfield
Williams, C. *All the Way*

Thirteen at Dinner
WAR (US) 1985 dir. Lou Antonio
TV(US), V
Christie, A. *Lord Edgware Dies*

13 West Street
COL (US) 1962 dir. Philip Leacock
Brackett, L. *Tiger Amongst Us, The*

Thirty Day Princess
PAR (US) 1934 dir. Marion Gering
Kelland, C. B.

38: Vienna Before the Fall
SATEL/ALMARO (Ger) 1988
dir. Wolfgang Gluck
Torberg, F. *Auch das war Wein*

Thirty-Nine Steps, The
GB (GB) 1935 dir. Alfred Hitchcock
RANK (GB) 1959 dir. Ralph Thomas
V
RANK (GB) 1978 dir. Don Sharp
V
Buchan, J.

Thirty Seconds Over Tokyo
MGM (US) 1944 dir. Mervyn Le Roy
V
Lawson, T. and Considine, R.

This Above All
FOX (US) 1942 dir. Anatole Litvak
Knight, E. M.

This Angry Age
DELAUR (It) 1957 dir. René Clément
Duras, M. *Barrage contre le Pacifique, Un*

This Earth is Mine
UI (US) 1959 dir. Henry King
Hobart, A. T. *Cup and the Sword, The*

This Gun for Hire
PAR (US) 1942 dir. Frank Tuttle
V
BBK (US) 1991 dir. Lou Antonio
TV(US)
Greene, G. *Gun for Sale, A*

This Happy Breed
TC (GB) 1944 dir. David Lean
V
Coward, N.
P

This Happy Feeling
UN (US) 1958 dir. Blake Edwards
V
Herbert, F. H. *For Love or Money*
P

This Island Earth
UI (US) 1955 dir. Joseph Newman
V
Jones, R. F.

This is My Life
FOX (US) 1992 dir. Nora Ephron
Wolitzer, M. *This is Your Life*

This is My Street
WAR (GB) 1963 dir. Sidney Hayers
Maynard, N.

This is the Life
UN (US) 1943 dir. Felix Feist
M
Wray, F. and Lewis, S. *Angela is 22*
P

This Love of Ours
UI (US) 1945 dir. William Deiterle
Pirandello, L. *Come Prima Meglio di Prima*
P

This Man is Dangerous
RIALTO (GB) 1941
dir. Lawrence Huntington
Hume, D. *They Called Him Death*

This Man is Mine
RKO (US) 1934 dir. John Cromwell
Morrison, A. *Love Flies in the Window*
P

This Man is Mine
COL (GB) 1946 dir. Marcel Varnel
Beckwith, R. *Soldier for Christmas, A*

This Man Must Die
AA (Fr) 1970 dir. Claude Chabrol
Blake, N.

This Property is Condemned
PAR (US) 1966 dir. Sydney Pollack
V
Williams, T.
P

This Side of Heaven
MGM (US) 1934 dir. William K. Howard
Paradis, M.

This Sporting Life
RANK (GB) 1963 dir. Lindsay Anderson
V
Storey, D.

This was a Woman
FOX (GB) 1948 dir. Tim Whelan
Morgan, J.
P

This Woman is Mine
UN (US) 1941 dir. Frank Lloyd
Gabriel, G. W. *I, James Lewis*

Thorn Birds, The
WAR (US) 1979 dir. Daryl Duke
TVSe(US)
McCullough, C.

Those Calloways
DISNEY (US) 1964 dir. Norman Tokar
V
Annixter, P. *Swift Water*

Those Kids from Town
BN (GB) 1941 dir. Lance Comfort
Arlington, A. *These, Our Strangers*

Those were the Days
BIP (GB) 1934 dir. Thomas Bentley
Pinero, Sir A. W. *Magistrate, The*
P

Thousand Clowns, A
UA (US) 1965 dir. Fred Coe
V
Gardner, H.
P

Thousand Pieces of Gold
AM PLAY (US) 1990 dir. Nancy Kelly
McCunn, R. L.

1,000 Plane Raid, The
UA (GB) 1969 dir. Boris Sagal
Barker, R. *Thousand Plan, The*

Three
UA (GB) 1969 dir. James Salter
Shaw, I. *Then There Were Three*

Three Came Home
FOX (US) 1950 dir. Jean Negulesco
Keith, A.

Three Coins in the Fountain
FOX (US) 1954 dir. Jean Negulesco
Secondari, J. *Coins in the Fountain*

Three Comrades
MGM (US) 1938 dir. Frank Borzage
Remarque, E. M.

Three Cornered Moon
PAR (US) 1933 dir. Elliott Nugent
Tonkonogy, G.
P

Three Days of the Condor
PAR (US) 1975 dir. Sydney Pollack
V
Grady, J. *Six Days of the Condor*

Three Faces East
WAR (US) 1930 dir. Roy del Ruth
Kelly, A. P.
P

Three Faces of Eve, The
FOX (US) 1957 dir. Nunnally Johnson
Thigpen, C. H. and Cleckley, H. M.

3 for Bedroom C
INT (US) 1952 dir. Milton H. Bren
Lieberson, G.

Three for the Show
COL (US) 1955 dir. H. C. Potter
M
Maugham, W. S. *Home and Beauty*
P

Three Godfathers, The
MGM (US) 1936
dir. Richard Boleslawski
MGM (US) 1948 dir. John Ford
Kyne, P. B.

Three in the Attic
WAR (US) 1968 dir. Richard Wilson
V
Yafa, S. *Paxton Quigley's had the Course*

Three in the Cellar
AIP (US) 1970 dir. Theodore J. Flicker
V
Hall, A. *Late Boy Wonder, The*

Three Into Two Won't Go
UI (GB) 1969 dir. Peter Hall
Newman, A.

Three is a Family
UA (US) 1944 dir. Edward Ludwig
Ephron, P. and Ephron, H.
P

Three Lives of Thomasina, The
DISNEY (GB) 1963 dir. Don Chaffey
CH, V
Gallico, P. *Thomasina*

Three Men in a Boat
BL (GB) 1956 dir. Ken Annakin
Jerome, J. K.

Three Men on a Horse
WAR (US) 1936 dir. Mervyn LeRoy
Hudson, J. C. and Abbott, G.
P

Three Musketeers, The
RKO (US) 1935 dir. Rowland V Lee
V
FOX (US) 1939 dir. Allan Dwan
GB title: Singing Musketeer, The
MGM (US) 1948 dir. George Sidney
V
FOX-RANK (Panama) 1973
dir. Richard Lester
Dumas, A.

Three on a Date
ABC (US) 1978 dir. Bill Bixby
TV(US)
Buffington, S.

Three on a Spree
UA (GB) 1961 dir. Sidney J. Furie
McCutcheon, G. B. *Brewster's Millions*

Three Sailors and a Girl
WAR (US) 1953 dir. Roy del Ruth
M
Kaufman, G. S. *Butter and Egg Man, The*
P

Three Sisters
BL (GB) 1970 dir. Laurence Olivier
V
Chekhov, A.
P

Threesome
CBS ENT (US) 1984 dir. Lou Antonio
TV(US)
Gold, H. *Salt*

Three Strange Lives
FILM FORUM (Swe) 1980
dir. Ingmar Bergman
Tengroth, B.

Three Weird Sisters, The
BN (GB) 1948 dir. Dan Birt
Armstrong, C. *Case of the Three Weird Sisters, The*

Three Wise Fools
MGM (US) 1946 dir. Edward Buzzell
Strong, A.
P

Three Wishes for Jamie
COL TV (US) 1987
dir. Robert William Young
TV(US)
O'Neal, C.

Three Worlds of Gulliver, The
COL (US/Sp) 1959 dir. Jack Sher
V
Swift, J. *Gulliver's Travels*

Thumb Tripping
AVCO (US) 1972 dir. Quentin Masters
V
Mitchell, D.

Thunderball
UA (GB) 1965 dir. Terence Young
V
Fleming, I.

Thunderhead, Son of Flicka
FOX (US) 1945 dir. Louis King
O'Hara, M.

Thunder in the East
PAR (US) 1951 dir. Charles Vidor
Moorehead, A. *Rage of the Vulture*

Thunder in the Night
FOX (US) 1935 dir. George Archainbaud
Fodor, L. *Woman Lies, A*
P

Thunder on the Hill
UI (US) 1951 dir. Douglas Sirk
GB title: Bonaventure
Hastings, C. *Bonaventure*
P

Thunder Rock
MGM (GB) 1942 dir. Roy Boulting
Ardrey, R.
P

Thursday's Child
ABPC (GB) 1942 dir. Rodney Ackland
V

Macardle, D.

Thursday's Child
VIACOM (US) 1983
dir. David Lowell Rich
TV(US)

Poole, V.

Tiara Tahiti
RANK (GB) 1962
dir. William T. Kotcheff
V

Cotterell, G.

Ticket to Heaven
UA (US) 1981 dir. R. L. Thomas
V

Freed, J. *Moonwebs*

Tiger by the Tail
EROS (GB) 1955 dir. John Gilling

Mair, J. *Never Come Back*

Tiger in the Smoke
RANK (GB) 1956 dir. Roy Baker

Allingham, M.

Tiger Makes Out, The
COL (US) 1967 dir. Arthur Hiller

Schisgal, M. *Tiger, The*
P

Tigers Don't Cry
RANK (S. Africa) 1978
dir. Peter Collinson
V

Burmeister, J. *Running Scared*

Tiger's Tale, A
ATLANTIC (US) 1988
dir. Peter Douglas

Hannay, A. *Love and Other Natural Disasters*

Tiger Walks, A
DISNEY (US) 1964 dir. Norman Tokar
V

Niall, I.

Tight Spot
COL (US) 1955 dir. Phil Karlson

Kantor, L. *Dead Pigeon*
P

Till Death do us Part
SABAN/SCHERICK PRODS. 1992
dir. Yves Simoneau
TV(US)

Bugliosi, V.

Till the End of Time
RKO (US) 1946 dir. Edward Dmytryk
V

Busch, N. *They Dream of Home*

Till We Meet Again
PAR (US) 1944 dir. Frank Borzage

Maury, A.
P

Till We Meet Again
KRANTZ/YTV (US/GB) 1989
dir. Charles Jarrot
TVSe(GB/US)

Krantz, J.

Timberjack
REP (US) 1954 dir. Joe Kane

Cushman, D. *Ripper from Rawhide*

Time After Time
WAR (US) 1979 dir. Nicholas Meyer
V

Alexander, K. & Hayes, S.

Time for Killing, A
COL (US) 1967 dir. Phil Karlson
GB title: Long Ride Home, The

Wolford, N. and Wolford, S.
Southern Blade

Time Gentlemen, Please!
ABP (GB) 1952 dir. Lewis Gilbert
Minney, R. J. *Nothing to Lose*

Time Limit
UA (US) 1967 dir. Karl Malden
Denker, H., and Berkey, R.
P

Time Machine, The
MGM (US) 1960 dir. George Pal
V
SCHICK SUNN (US) 1978
dir. Henning Schellerup
TV(US)
Wells, H. G.

Time of Indifference
CONT (It/Fr) 1965
dir. Francesco Maselli
Moravia, A.

Time of Your Life, The
UA (US) 1948 dir. H. C. Potter
Saroyan, W.
P

Time Out of Mind
UN (US) 1947 dir. Robert Siodmak
Field, R.

Time Remembered
COMPASS (US) 1961
dir. George Schaefer
TV(US)
Anouilh, J.
P

Timestalkers
FRIES (US) 1987 dir. Michael Schultz
TV(US)
Brown, R. *Tintype, The*

Time to Live, A
ITC (US) 1985 dir. Rick Wallace
TV(US), V
Weisman, M-L. *Intensive Care*

Time to Love and a Time to Die, A
U-I (US) 1958 dir. Douglas Sirk
V
Remarque, E. M.

Time Without Pity
HARLEQUIN (GB) 1957
dir. Joseph Losey
Williams, E. *Someone Waiting*
P

Tin Drum, The
UA (Ger/Fr) 1979
dir. Volker Schlöndorff
V
Grass, G.

Tinker, Tailor, Soldier, Spy
BBC (GB) 1979 dir. Janet Irvin
TVSe(GB)
Le Carré, J.

Tip on a Dead Jockey
MGM (US) 1957 dir. Richard Thorpe
GB title: Time for Action
Shaw, I.

Tish
MGM (US) 1942 dir. S. Sylvan Simon
Rinehart, M. R. *Tish Marches On*

Titmuss Regained
ANGLIA (GB) 1991 dir. Michael Friend
TV
Mortimer, J.

Tobacco Road
FOX (US) 1941 dir. John Ford
Caldwell, E.
Kirkland, J.
P

Toby Tyler
DISNEY (US) 1959 dir. Charles Barton
V

Kaler, J. O.

To Catch a King
GAYLORD (US) 1984 dir. Clive Donner
TV(US)

Patterson, H.
V

To Catch a Thief
PAR (US) 1955 dir. Alfred Hitchcock
V

Dodge, D.

Today We Live
MGM (US) 1933 dir. Howard Hawks

Faulkner, W. *Turnabout*

To Dorothy, A Son
BL (GB) 1954 dir. Muriel Box
US title: Cash on Delivery

MacDougall, R.
P

To Find a Man
COL (US) 1971 dir. Buzz Kulik

Wilson, S. J.

To Have and Have Not
WAR (US) 1944 dir. Howard Hawks
V

Hemingway, E.

To Have and to Hold
LWT (GB) 1986
TVSe(GB)

Moggach, D.

To Heal a Nation
ORION TV (US) 1988
dir. Michael Pressman
TV(US)

Scruggs, J. C. and Swerdlow, J. L.

To Hell and Back
UI (US) 1955 dir. Jesse Hibbs
V

Murphy, A.

To Kill A Cop
COL TV (US) 1978 dir. Gary Nelson
TVSe(US)

Daley, R.

To Kill a Mockingbird
UI (US) 1962 dir. Robert Mulligan
V

Lee, H.

To Live and Die in L.A.
MGM/UA (US) 1985
dir. William Friedkin
V

Petievich, G.

Tomb of Ligeia, The
AIP (GB) 1964 dir. Roger Corman
V

Poe, E. A.

Tom Brown's Schooldays
RKO (US) 1940 dir. Robert Stevenson
REN (GB) 1951 dir. Gordon Parry
V

Hughes, T.

Tom Horn
WAR (US) 1980 dir. William Wiard
V

Horn, T. *Life of Tom Horn,
Government Scout & Interpreter*

Tom Jones
UA (GB) 1963 dir. Tony Richardson
V

Fielding, H. *History of Tom Jones, A
Foundling, The*

Tomorrow and Tomorrow
PAR (US) 1932 dir. Richard Wallace
Barry, P.
P

Tomorrow is Forever
RKO (US) 1946 dir. Irving Pichel
Bristow, G.

Tomorrow the World
UA (US) 1944 dir. Leslie Fenton
D'Usseau, A. and Gow, J. *Deep are the Roots*
P

Tom Sawyer
UA (US) 1973 dir. Don Taylor
M, V
UN (US) 1973 dir. James Neilson
TV(US)
Twain, M. *Adventures of Tom Sawyer, The*

Tom Thumb
MGM (GB) 1958 dir. George Pal
V
Grimm, J. L. K. and Grimm, W. K.

Tonight at 8.30
BBC (GB) 1991 dir. Joan Collins and Paul Annett
TV(GB)
Coward, N.
P

Tonight is Ours
PAR (US) 1933 dir. Stuart Walker
Coward, N. *Queen was in the Parlour, The*
P

Tonight or Never
GOLDWYN (US) 1931
dir. Mervyn LeRoy
Hatvany, L.
P

Tonight We Sing
FOX (US) 1953 dir. Mitchell Leisen
M
Hurok, S. and Goode, R. *Impressario*

Tonka
DISNEY (US) 1958 dir. Lewis R. Foster
V
Appel, D. *Comanche*

Tony Draws a Horse
GFD (GB) 1950
dir. John Paddy Carstairs
Storm, L.
P

Tony Rome
FOX (US) 1967 dir. Gordon Douglas
Albert, M. H. *Miami Mayhem*

Too Far to Go
ZOETROPE (US) 1982 dir. Fielder Cook
Updike, J.

Too Good to be True
NEWLAND-RAYNOR (US) 1988
dir. Christian I Nyby II
TV(US)
Williams, B. A. *Leave Her to Heaven*

Too Many Husbands
COL (US) 1940 dir. Wesley Ruggles
GB title: My Two Husbands
Maugham, W. S. *Home and Beauty*
P

Too Much, Too Soon
WAR (US) 1958 dir. Art Napoleon
Barrymore, D. and Frank, G.

Too Young to Go
RANK (GB) 1959 dir. Muriel Box
Shelley, E. *Pick Up Girl*
P

Topaz
UI (US) 1969 dir. Alfred Hitchcock
V
Uris, L.

Topaze
RKO (US) 1933
dir. Harry d'Abbabie d'Arrast
Pagnol, M.
P

Topkapi
UA (US) 1964 dir. Jules Dassin
V
Ambler, E. *Light of Day, The*

Topper
MGM (US) 1937
dir. Norman Z. MacLeod
V
PAPAZIAN (US) 1979
dir. Charles S. Dubin
TV(US)
Smith, T. *Jovial Ghosts, The*

Top Secret Affair
WAR (US) 1957 dir. H. C. Potter
GB title: Their Secret Affair
Marquand, J. P. *Melville Goodwin, USA*

To Race the Wind
GRAUMAN (US) 1980
dir. Walter Grauman
TV(US), V
Krents, H.

Torch Song Trilogy
NEW LINE (US) 1988 dir. Paul Bogart
Fierstein, H.
P

Torn Apart
CASTLE HILL (US) 1990
dir. Jack Fisher
Zeldis, C. *Forbidden Love, A*

Torrents of Spring
MILLIMETER (US) 1990
dir. Jerzy Skolimowski
V
Turgenev, I.

Tortilla Flat
MGM (US) 1942 dir. Victor Fleming
Steinbeck, J.

To Serve Them All My Days
BBC (GB) 1980 dir. Ronald Wilson
TVSe(GB)
Delderfield, R. F.

To Sir, With Love
COL (GB) 1966 dir. James Clavell
V
Braithwaite, E. R.

Total Recall
CAROLCO (US) 1990
dir. Paul Verhoeven
Dick, P. *We can Remember it for you Wholesale*

To the Devil, a Daughter
EMI (GB/Ger) 1976 dir. Peter Sykes
V
Wheatley, D.

To the Lighthouse
BBC (GB) 1983 dir. Colin Gregg
TV(GB), V
Woolf, V.

Touched by Love
COL (US) 1980 dir. Gus Trikonis
V
Canada, L. *To Elvis with Love*

Touch of Evil
UN (US) 1958 dir. Orson Welles
V
Masterson, W. *Badge of Evil*

Touch of Larceny, A
PAR (GB) 1959 dir. Guy Hamilton
Garve, A. *Megstone Plot, The*

Touch of Love, A
BL (GB) 1969 dir. Waris Hussein
US title: Thank You All Very Much
Drabble, M. *Millstone, The*

Tough Guys Don't Dance
CANNON (US) 1987
dir. Norman Mailer
V
Mailer, N.

Tourist
FOX (US) 1980 dir. Jeremy Summers
TV(US)
Green, G.

Tovarich
WAR (US) 1937 dir. Anatole Litvak
Deval, J.
P

Towering Inferno, The
COL-WAR (US) 1975
dir. John Gullermin, Irwin Allen
V
Stern, R. M. *Tower, The*
Scortia, T. N. and Robinson, F. M.
Glass Inferno, The

Town Like Alice, A
RANK (GB) 1956 dir. Jack Lee
US title: Rape of Malaya, The
V
AFC (Aust) 1981 dir. David Stevens
TVSe(Aust)
Shute, N.

Town Tamer
PAR (US) 1965 dir. Lesley Selander
Gruber, F.

Town Without Pity
UA (US/Switz) 1961
dir. Gottfried Reinhardt
Gregor, M. *Verdict, The*

Toys in the Attic
UA (US) 1963 dir. George Roy Hill
Hellman, L.
P

Toy Soldiers
TRI-STAR (US) 1991 dir. Daniel Petrie,
Jr.
Kennedy, W. P.

Track of the Cat
WAR (US) 1954 dir. William A. Wellman
Clark, W. van T.

Trader Horn
MGM (US) 1931 dir. W. S. Van Dyke
MGM (US) 1973 dir. Reza Badiyi
Lewis, E.

Trail of the Lonesome Pine, The
PAR (US) 1936 dir. Henry Hathaway
Fox, Jr., J.

Traitor's Gate
COL (GB) 1965 dir. Freddie Francis
Wallace, E.

Transplant
TIME-LIFE (US) 1979
dir. William A. Graham
TV(US)
Dossick, P.

Trapeze
UA (US) 1956 dir. Carol Reed
V
Catto, M. *Killing Frost, The*

Trapped in Silence
READER'S DIG (US) 1986
dir. Michael Tuchner
TV(US)

Hayden, T. *Murphy's Boy*

Traveller in Time, A
BBC (GB) 1978 dir. Dorothea Brooking
TVSe(GB)

Uttley, A.

Travellers by Night
TVS (GB) 1985
Ch, TVSe(GB)

Alcock, V.

Traveller's Joy
GFD (GB) 1949 dir. Ralph Thomas

Macrae, A.
P

Travelling North
VIEW PIC (Aust) 1986 dir. Carl Schultz
V

Williamson, D.
P

Travels with my Aunt
MGM (US) 1972 dir. George Cukor

Greene, G.

Travis McGee
HAJENO (US) 1983
dir. Andrew V. McLaglen
TV(US)

MacDonald, J. D. *Empty Copper Sea, The*

Tread Softly Stranger
ALDERDALE (GB) 1958
dir. Gordon Parry

Popplewell, J.
P

Treasure Hunt
BL (GB) 1952 dir. John Paddy Carstairs

Farrel, M. J. and Perry, J.
P

Treasure Island
MGM (US) 1934 dir. Victor Fleming
V
DISNEY (GB) 1950 dir. Byron Haskin
V
MGM-EMI (GB/Fr/Ger) 1971
dir. John Hough
V
AGAMEMNON FILMS (US) 1990
dir. Fraser Heston
TV(US)

Stevenson, R. L.

Treasure of Lost Canyon, The
UI (US) 1952 dir. Ted Tetzlaff

Stevenson, R. L. *Treasure of Franchard*

Treasure of Matecumbe
DISNEY (US) 1976
dir. Vincent McEveety
V

Taylor, R. L. *Journey to Matecumbe, A*

Treasure of the Golden Condor
FOX (US) 1953 dir. Delmer Daves

Marshall, E. *Jewel of Mahabar*

Treasure of the Sierra Madre, The
WAR (US) 1948 dir. John Huston
V

Traven, B.

Tree Grows in Brooklyn, A
FOX (US) 1945 dir. Elia Kazan
V
FOX (US) 1974 dir. Joseph Hardy
TV(US)

Smith, B.

Tree of Hands
GRANADA (GB) 1988 dir. Giles Foster

Rendell, R.

Trent's Last Case
BL (GB) 1952 dir. Herbert Wilcox

Bentley, E. C.

Trespasser, The
C. GREGG (GB) 1981 dir. Colin Gregg
V

Lawrence, D. H.

Trial
MGM (US) 1955 dir. Mark Robson

Mankiewicz, D. M.

Trial, The
BL (Fr/It/Ger) 1963 dir. Orson Welles
V
BBC (GB) 1986
TV(GB)

Kafka, F.

Trial of Vivienne Ware, The
FOX (US) 1932 dir. William K. Howard

Ellis, K. M.

Trial on the Road/Checkpoint
LENFILM (USSR) 1971
dir. Alexei German

German, Y.

Trials of Oscar Wilde, The
EROS (GB) 1960 dir. Ken Hughes
US title: Man with the Green Carnation,
The

Hyde, H. M.

Tribute
FOX (Can) 1980 dir. Bob Clark
V

Slade, B.
P

Trio
GFD (GB) 1950
dir. Ken Annakin/Harold French
V

Maugham, W. S. *Verge, The; Mr
Knowall; Sanitorium*

Triple Cross
AA (GB) 1967 dir. Terence Young
V

Owen, F. *Eddie Chapman Story, The*

Triple Echo
HEMDALE (GB) 1972
dir. Michael Apted
V

Bates, H. E.

Tripods, The
BBC (GB/US/Aust) 1984-5
dir. Graham Theakston, Christopher
Barry, Bob Blagden
TVSe(GB/US/Aust)

Christopher, J.

Trip to Bountiful, The
ISLAND (US) 1985 dir. Peter Masterson
V

Foote, H.
P

Triumph of Sherlock
Holmes, The
TWICKENHAM (GB) 1935
dir. Leslie Hiscott
V

Conan Doyle, Sir A. *Valley of Fear,
The*

Trojan Women, The
CINERAMA (US) 1971
dir. Michael Cacoyannis
V

Euripides
P

Tropic
ATV (GB) 1979 dir. Matthew Robinson
TVSe(GB)

Thomas, L. *Tropic of Ruislip, The*

Tropic of Cancer
PAR (US) 1970 dir. Joseph Strick
Miller, H.

Tropic Zone
PAR (US) 1952 dir. Lewis R. Foster
Gill, T. *Gentlemen of the Jungle*

Trottie True
TC (GB) 1949 dir. Brian Desmond Hurst
US title: Gay Lady, The
V

Brahms, C. and Simon, S. J.

Trouble for Two
MGM (US) 1936 dir. J. Walter Rubin
GB title: Suicide Club, The

Stevenson, R. L. *Suicide Club, The*

Trouble in Paradise
PAR (US) 1932 dir. Ernst Lubitsch
Aladar, L. *Honest Finder, The*

Trouble in the Glen
REP (GB) 1954 dir. Herbert Wilcox
V

Walsh, M.

Troubles
LWT (GB) 1989
dir. Christopher Morahan
TV(GB)

Farrell, J. G.

Trouble with Angels, The
COL (US) 1966 dir. Ida Lupino
V

Trahey, J. *Life with Mother Superior*

Trouble With Girls, The
MGM (US) 1969 dir. Peter Tewkesbury
V

Keene, D. and Babcock, D.
Chautauqua

Trouble with Harry, The
PAR (US) 1955 dir. Alfred Hitchcock
V

Story, J. T.

Trouble With Spies, The
HBO (US) 1987 dir. Burt Kennedy
V

Lovell, M. *Apple Pie in the Sky*

Trout, The
TRIUMPH (Fr) 1982 dir. Joseph Losey
Vailland, R. *Truite, La*

True as a Turtle
RANK (GB) 1957 dir. Wendy Toye
Coates, J.

True Confession
PAR (US) 1937 dir. Wesley Ruggles
Verneuil, L. and Berr, G. *Mon Crime*
P

True Confessions
UA (US) 1981 dir. Ulu Grosbard
V

Dunne, J. G.

True Grit
PAR (US) 1969 dir. Henry Hathaway
V

Portis, C.

Truth About Spring, The
UI (GB) 1964 dir. Richard Thorpe
deVere Stacpoole, H. D.

Try and Get Me
UA (US) 1951 dir. Cyril Endfield
GB title: Sound of Fury, The
Pagano, J. *Condemned, The*

Tumult
ATHENA (Den) 1970
dir. Hans Abramson
Allen, J. *Nu*

Tune in Tomorrow...
CINECOM (US) 1990 dir. Jon Amiel
Llosa, M. V. *Aunt Julia and the Scriptwriter*

Tunes of Glory
UA (GB) 1960 dir. Ronald Neame
V
Kennaway, J.

Tunnel, The
GAU (GB) 1935 dir. Maurice Elvey
US title: Transatlantic Tunnel
Kellerman, B.

Tunnel of Love, The
MGM (US) 1958 dir. Gene Kelly
De Vries, P.

Turnabout
UA (US) 1940 dir. Hal Roach
Smith, T.

Turn Back the Clock
NBC (US) 1989 dir. Larry Elikann
TV(US)
O'Farrell, W.

Turning Point of Jim Malloy, The
COL TV (US) 1975 dir. Frank D. Gilroy
TV(US)
O'Hara, J. *Doctor's Son, The*

Turn of the Screw
CURTIS (US) 1974 dir. Dan Curtis
TVSe(US), V
James, H.

Turn of the Tide
BN (GB) 1935 dir. Norman Walker
Walmsley, L. *Three Fevers*

Turn the Key Softly
GFD (GB) 1953 dir. Jack Lee
Brophy, J.

Turtle Diary
RANK (GB) 1985 dir. John Irvin
V
Hoban, R.

Tuttles of Tahiti, The
RKO (US) 1942 dir. Charles Vidor
V
Nordhoff, C. B. and Hall, J. N. *No More Gas*

TV Dante, A
CHANNEL 4 (GB) 1990
dir. Tom Phillips
TV(GB)
Dante Alighieri *Divina Commedia, La*

Twelfth Night
MILBERG (US) 1957 dir. David Greene
TV(US)
Shakespeare, W.
P

Twelve Angry Men
UA (US) 1957 dir. Sidney Lumet
Rose, R.
P

Twelve Chairs, The
UMC (US) 1970 dir. Mel Brooks
Ilf, E. and Petrov, E.
P

Twelve O'Clock High
FOX (US) 1949 dir. Henry King
V

Lay, B. and Bartlett, S.

Twentieth Century
COL (US) 1934 dir. Howard Hawks
Millholland, C. B. *Napoleon of Broadway*
P

Twenty-Four Hours of a Woman's Life
ABPC (GB) 1952 dir. Victor Saville
US title: Affair in Monte Carlo
Zweig, S.

29 Acacia Avenue
COL (GB) 1945 dir. Henry Cass
US title: Facts of Love, The
Constanduros, M. and Constanduros, D. *Acacia Avenue*
P

Twenty-One Days
LF (GB) 1937 dir. Basil Dean
V

Galsworthy, J. *First and the Last, The*
P

21 Hours at Munich
FILMWAYS (US) 1976
dir. William A. Graham
TV(US), V
Groussard, S. *Blood of Israel, The*

Twenty Plus Two
AA (US) 1962 dir. Joseph M. Newman
Gruber, F.

27th Day
COL (US) 1957 dir. William Asher
Mantley, J. *Joseph*

20,000 Leagues Under the Sea
DISNEY (US) 1954
dir. Richard Fleischer
V

Verne, J.

20,000 Years in Sing Sing
WAR (US) 1932 dir. Michael Curtiz
Lawes, L. E.

Twenty-Three Paces to Baker Street
FOX (US) 1956 dir. Henry Hathaway
MacDonald, P.

Twice Round the Daffodils
AA (GB) 1962 dir. Gerald Thomas
Cargill, P. and Beale, J. *Ring for Catty*
P

Twice Shy
DLT (US) 1989 dir. Deirdre Friel
TV(US)
Francis, D.

Twilight for the Gods
UN (US) 1958 dir. Joseph Pevney
Gann, E. K.

Twilight of Honor
MGM (US) 1963 dir. Boris Sagal
GB title: Charge is Murder, The
Dewlen, A.

Twilight's Last Gleaming
HEMDALE (US/Ger) 1977
dir. Robert Aldrich
V

Wager, W. *Viper Three*

Twinkle, Twinkle, 'Killer' Kane
UFD (US) 1980 dir. William Peter Blatty
Blatty, W. P.

Twisted Obsession
IVE (US) 1990 dir. Fernando Trueba

Frank, C. *Dream of the Mad Monkey, The*

Twister
VESTRON (US) 1990
dir. Michael Almereyda

Robison, M. *Oh!*

Twist of Fate
COL TV/HTV (US/GB) 1989
dir. Ian Sharp
TVSe(GB/US)

Fish, R. L. *Pursuit*

Twist of Sand, A
UA (GB) 1968 dir. Don Chaffey

Jenkins, G.

Two Against the World
WAR (US) 1936 dir. William McGann
GB title: Case of Mrs. Pembroke, The

Weitzenkorn, L. *Five-Star Final*
P

Two-Faced Woman
MGM (US) 1941 dir. George Cukor

Fulda, L.
P

Two Faces of Dr. Jekyll, The
HAMMER (GB) 1960
dir. Terence Fisher
US title: House of Fright

Stevenson, R. L. *Dr. Jekyll and Mr. Hyde*

Two for the Seesaw
UA (US) 1962 dir. Robert Wise

Gibson, W.
P

Two Gentlemen Sharing
PAR (GB) 1969 dir. Ted Kotcheff

Leslie, D. S.

Two in the Dark
RKO (US) 1936 dir. Ben Stoloff

Burgess, G.

Two Kinds of Love
CBS (US) 1983 dir. Jack Bender
TV(US), V

Mann, P. *There are Two Kinds of Terrible*

Two Kinds of Women
PAR (US) 1932 dir. William C. DeMille

Sherwood, R. E. *This is New York*
P

Two Left Feet
BL (GB) 1963 dir. Roy Baker

Leslie, D. S. *In My Solitude*

Two-Letter Alibi
BL (GB) 1962 dir. Robert Lynn

Garve, A. *Death and the Sky Above*

Two Loves
MGM (US) 1961 dir. Charles Walters
GB title: Spinster, The

Ashton-Warner, S. *Spinster*

Two Minute Warning
UN (US) 1976 dir. Larry Peerce

La Fontaine, G.

Two Mrs V. Carrolls, The
WAR (US) 1947 dir. Peter Godfrey

Vale, M.
P

Two Mrs. Grenvilles, The
LORIMAR (US) 1989 dir. John Erman
TVSe(US)

Dunne, D.

Two Rode Together
COL (US) 1961 dir. John Ford
V

Cooke, W. E.

Two Seconds
WAR (US) 1932 dir. Mervyn LeRoy
Lester, E.

2001, A Space Odyssey
MGM (GB) 1968 dir. Stanley Kubrick
V
Clarke, A. C. *Sentinel, The*

2010
MGM (US) 1984 dir. Peter Hyams
V
Clarke, A. C.

Two to Tango
CONCORDE (US/Arg) 1989
dir. Hector Olivera
V
Feinman, J. P. *Last Days of the Victim*

Two Weeks in Another Town
MGM (US) 1962 dir. Vincente Minnelli
Shaw, I.

Two Women
CHAMPION (It/Fr) 1960
dir. Vittorio de Sica
V
Moravia, A.

Two Worlds of Jennie Logan, The
FRIES (US) 1979 dir. Frank DeFelitta
TV(US)
Williams, D. *Second Sight*

Two Years Before the Mast
PAR (US) 1946 dir. John Farrow
Dana, R. H.

UFO Incident, The
UN TV (US) 1975 dir. Richard Colla
TV(US)
Fuller, J. G. *Interrupted Journey, The*

Ugly American, The
UI (US) 1962 dir. George England
V
Lederer, W. J. and Burdick, E. L.

Ugly Dachshund, The
DISNEY (US) 1965 dir. Norman Tokar
Stern, G. B.

Ultimate Imposter, The
UN TV (US) 1979 dir. Paul Stanley
TV(US), V
Zacha, Sr., W. T. *Capricorn Man, The*

Ulysses
ARCHWAY (It) 1954
dir. Mario Camerini
V
Homer *Odyssey, The*

Ulysses
BL (GB) 1967 dir. Joseph Strick
Joyce, J.

Unbearable Lightness of Being, The
ORION (US) 1988 dir. Philip Kaufman
Kundera, M.

Unchained
WAR (US) 1955 dir. Hall Bartlett
Scudder, K. J. *Prisoners are People*

Uncle Silas
TC (GB) 1947 dir. Charles Frank
US title: Inheritance, The
Le Fanu, S.

Uncle Tom's Cabin
TAFT (US) 1989 dir. Stan Lathan
TV(US)
Stowe, H. B.

Unconquered
PAR (US) 1947 dir. Cecil B. de Mille
Swanson, N. H.

Under Capricorn
WAR (GB) 1949 dir. Alfred Hitchcock
V
SOUTH AUSTRALIA FILM (Aust) 1983
dir. Rod Hardy
Simpson, H.

Undercover with the KKK
COL TV (US) 1979 dir. Barry Shear
TV(US)
Rowe, Jr., G. T. *My Years with the KKK*

Underground Man, The
PAR TV (US) 1974 dir. Paul Wendkos
TV(US)
MacDonald, R.

Under Milk Wood
RANK (GB) 1971 dir. Andrew Sinclair
V
Thomas, D.
P

Under My Skin
FOX (US) 1950 dir. Jean Negulesco
Hemingway, E. *My Old Man*

Under New Management
BUTCHER (GB) 1946
dir. John E. Blakeley
Jacob, N.

Under Satan's Sun
ERATO (Fr) 1987 dir. Maurice Pialat
Bernanos, G.

Undertow
CAPSTONE (US) 1991
dir. Thomas Mazziotti
Bell, N. *Raw Youth*
P

Under the Red Robe
FOX (GB) 1937 dir. Victor Sjostrom
V
Weyman, S.

Under the Volcano
UN (US) 1984 dir. John Huston
V
Lowry, M.

Under Two Flags
FOX (US) 1936 dir. Frank Lloyd
Ouida

Undying Monster, The
FOX (US) 1943 dir. John Brahm
GB title: Hammond Mystery, The
Kerrvish, J. D.

Uneasy Terms
BN (GB) 1948 dir. Vernon Sewell
Cheyney, P.

Unexpected Uncle
RKO (US) 1941 dir. Peter Godfrey
Hatch, E.

Unfaithful, The
WAR (US) 1947 dir. Vincent Sherman
Maugham, W. S. *Letter, The*
P

Unfinished Piece for Player Piano, An
MOSFILM (USSR) 1977
dir. Nikita Mikhalkov
V
Chekhov, A. *Platonov*

Unforgiven, The
UA (US) 1960 dir. John Huston
V
LeMay, A. *Siege at Dancing Bird, The*

Unguarded Hour, The
MGM (US) 1936 dir. Sam Wood
Fodor, L.
P

Unholy Matrimony
TAFT (US) 1988 dir. Jerrold Freedman
TV(US)
Dillman, J.

Uninvited, The
PAR (US) 1944 dir. Lewis Allen
V
Macardle, D. *Uneasy Freehold*

Union Station
PAR (US) 1950 dir. Rudolph Maté
V
Walsh, T. *Nightmare in Manhattan*

Unkindness of Ravens, An
TVS (GB) 1988 dir. John Gorrie
TV(GB)
Rendell, R.

Unseen, The
PAR (US) 1945 dir. Lewis Allen
White, E. L. *Her Heart in Her Throat*

Unsinkable Molly Brown, The
MGM (US) 1964 dir. Charles Walters
M, V
Morris, R. amd Willson, M.
P

Unspeakable Acts
LAN (US) 1990 dir. Linda Otto
TV(US)
Hollingsworth, J.

Unsuitable Job for a Woman, An
BOYD (GB) 1982 dir. Christopher Petit
V
James, P. D.

Unsuspected, The
WAR (US) 1947 dir. Michael Curtiz
Armstrong, C.

Untamed
PAR (US) 1940 dir. George Archainband
Lewis, S. *Mantrap*

Untamed
FOX (US) 1955 dir. Henry King
Moray, H.

Until They Sail
MGM (US) 1957 dir. Robert Wise
Michener, J. A. *Return to Paradise*

Up From the Beach
FOX (US) 1965 dir. Robert Parrish
Barr, G. *Epitaph for an Enemy*

Up Periscope
WAR (US) 1959 dir. Gordon Douglas
White, R.

Upstairs and Downstairs
RANK (GB) 1959 dir. Ralph Thomas
Thorn, R. S.

Up the Down Staircase
WAR (US) 1967 dir. Robert Mulligan
Kaufman, B.

Up the Garden Path
GRANADA (GB) 1990 dir. David Askey
TVSe(GB)
Limb, S.

Up the Junction
PAR (GB) 1967 dir. Peter Collinson
Dunn, N.

Up the Sandbox
WAR (US) 1973 dir. Irwin Kershner
V
Roiphe, A. R.

Users, The
A. SPELLING (US) 1978
dir. Joseph Hardy
TV(US), V
Haber, J.

Utz
BBC FILMS (GB/It/Ger) 1992
dir. George Sluizer
Chatwin, B.

Vagabond King, The
PAR (US) 1956 dir. Michael Curtiz
M
McCarthy, J. H.
Friml, R., Post, W. H. and Hooker, B.
P

Valachi Papers, The
CINEMA INT (Fr/It) 1972
dir. Terence Young
V
Maas, P.

Valdez is Coming
UA (US) 1971 dir. Edwin Sherin
V
Leonard, E.

Valentina
OFELIA (Sp) 1983
dir. Antonio José Betancor
Sender, R. J. *Days of Dawn*

Valentino
UA (GB) 1977 dir. Ken Russell
Steiger, B. and Mank, C.

Valentino Returns
VIDMARK/SKOURAS (US) 1989
dir. Paul Hoffman
Gardner, L. *Christ has Returned to Earth and Preaches Here Nightly*

Valiant is the Word for Carrie
RKO (US) 1936 dir. Wesley Ruggles
Benefield, B.

Valley of Decision, The
MGM (US) 1945 dir. Tay Garnett
Davenport, M.

Valley of Song
ABPC (GB) 1953 dir. Gilbert Gunn
Morgan, C. *Choir Practice*
P

Valley of the Dolls
FOX (US) 1967 dir. Mark Robson
V
Susann, J.

Valley of the Dolls 1981
FOX TV (US) 1981 dir. Walter Grauman
TVSe(US)
Susann, J. *Valley of the Dolls*

Valley of the Giants
WAR (US) 1938 dir. William Keighley
Kyne, P. B.

Valley of the Horses
PSO 1984
TV
Auel, J. M.

Valley of the Sun
RKO (US) 1942 dir. George Marshall
Kelland, C. B.

Valmont
ORION (GB) 1989 dir. Milos Forman
Laclos, P. de *Les liaisons dangéreuses*

Value for Money
RANK (GB) 1955 dir. Ken Annakin
Boothroyd, D.

Vanessa, Her Love Story
MGM (US) 1935 dir. William K. Howard
Walpole, Sir H.

Vanished
UN (US) 1971 dir. Buzz Kulik
TVSe(US)
Knebel, F.

Vanishing, The
INGRID (Swe) 1990 dir. George Sluizer
Krabbe, T. *Golden Egg, The*

Vanishing Act
LEVINSON-LINK (US) 1986
dir. David Greene
TV(US), V
Thomas, R. *Piège pour un homme seul*
P

Vanishing American, The
PAR (US) 1925 dir. George B. Seitz
V
Grey, Z.

Vanishing Virginian, The
MGM (US) 1941 dir. Frank Borzage
Williams, Mrs. R. *Father was a Handful*

Vanity Fair
HOL (US) 1932 dir. Chester M. Franklin
BBC (GB) 1988
TVSe(GB)
Thackeray, W. M.

Vanquished, The
PAR (US) 1953 dir. Edward Ludwig
Brown, K.

Vassa
IFEX (USSR) 1983 dir. Gleb Panfiluv
Gorky, M.
P

Vendetta
RKO (US) 1950 dir. Mel Ferrer
Merimée, P. *Columba*

Vendetta: Secrets of a Mafia Bride
TRIBUNE (US) 1991
dir. Stuart Margolin
TVSe(US)
Modignani, S. C. *Donna D'Onore*

Venetian Affair, The
MGM (US) 1966 dir. Jerry Thorpe
McInnes, H.

Venetian Bird
GFD (GB) 1952 dir. Ralph Thomas
US title: Assassin, The
Canning, V.

Vengeance
BL (GB/Ger) 1962 dir. Freddie Francis
Siodmak, C. *Donovan's Brain*

Vengeance is Mine
KINO (Jap) 1979 dir. Shohei Imamura
Saki, R.

Vengeance Valley
MGM (US) 1951 dir. Richard Thorpe
V
Short, L.

Venom
PAR (GB) 1982 dir. Piers Haggard
V
Scholefield, A.

Venus in Furs
COMM (GB/It/Ger) 1970
dir. Jess Franco
V
Sacher-Masoch, L. von

Verdict, The
WAR (US) 1946 dir. Don Siegel
Zangwill, I. *Big Bow Mystery, The*

Verdict
CCC (Fr/It) 1974 dir. André Cayatte
Coupon, H.

Verdict, The
FOX (US) 1982 dir. Sidney Lumet
V
Reed, B.

Veronico Cruz
BFI (Arg/GB) 1988 dir. Miguel Pereira
Ramos, F.

Vertigo
PAR (US) 1958 dir. Alfred Hitchcock
V
Boileau, P. and Narcejac, T. *Living and the Dead, The*

Very Missing Person, A
UN TV (US) 1972 dir. Russ Mayberry
TV(US)
Palmer, S., and Flora, F. *Hildegarde Withers Makes the Scene*

Very Moral Night, A
HUNG (Hun) 1977 dir. Karoly Makk
Hunyady, S. *House with the Red Light, The*

Vessel of Wrath
PAR (GB) 1938 dir. Erich Pommer
US title: Beachcomber, The
Maugham, W. S.

Vice Squad
UA (US) 1953 dir. Arnold Laven
GB title: Girl in Room 17, The
White, L. T. *Harness Bull*

Vice Versa
TC (GB) 1948 dir. Peter Ustinov
Anstey, F.

Vicki
FOX (US) 1953 dir. Harry Horner
Fisher, S. *I Wake Up Screaming*

Victoria Regina
COMPASS (US) 1961
dir. George Schaefer
TV(US), V
Housman, L.
P

Victoria the Great
RKO (GB) 1937 dir. Herbert Wilcox
Housman, L. *Victoria Regina*
P

Victors, The
BL (GB) 1963 dir. Carl Foreman
Baron, A *Human Kind, The*

Victory
PAR (US) 1940 dir. John Cromwell
Conrad, J.

View from Pompey's Head, The
FOX (US) 1955 dir. Philip Dunne
GB title: Secret Interlude
Basso, H.

View from the Bridge, A
TRANS (Fr) 1961 dir. Sidney Lumet
Miller, A.
P

Vigil in the Night
RKO (US) 1940 dir. George Stevens
Cronin, A. J.

Vikings, The
UA (US) 1958 dir. Richard Fleischer
V
Marshall, E. *Viking, The*

Village of the Damned
MGM (GB) 1960 dir. Wolf Rilla
V
Wyndham, J. *Midwich Cuckoos, The*

Village Tale, A
RKO (US) 1935 dir. John Cromwell
Strong, P.

Villain
EMI (GB) 1971 dir. Michael Tuchner
Barlow, J. *Burden of Proof, The*

Vintage, The
MGM (US) 1957 dir. Jeffrey Hayden
Keir, U.

Violators, The
RKO (US) 1957 dir. John Newland
Beckhardt, I. and Brown, W.

Violence at Noon
KINO (Jap) 1966 dir. Nagisa Oshima
Takeoa, T.

Violent Enemy, The
MONARCH (GB) 1969 dir. Don Sharp
Marlowe, H. *Candle for the Dead, A*

Violent Men, The
COL (US) 1955 dir. Rudolph Maté
GB title: Rough Company
Hamilton, D.

Violent Saturday
FOX (US) 1955 dir. Richard Fleischer
Heath, W. L.

Virgin and the Gypsy, The
LONDON SCR (GB) 1970
dir. Christopher Miles
Lawrence, D. H.

Virginian, The
PAR (US) 1929 dir. Victor Fleming
PAR (US) 1946 dir. Stuart Gilmore
V
Wister, O.

Virgin Island
BL (GB) 1958 dir. Pat Jackson
White, R. *Our Virgin Island*

Virgin Soldiers, The
COL (GB) 1969 dir. John Dexter
V
Thomas, L.

Virgin Witch
TIGON (GB) 1970 dir. Ray Austin
V
Vogel, K.

Virtuoso
BBC (GB) 1988 dir. Tony Smith
TV(GB)
Ogdon, B.

Vision Quest
WAR (US) 1985 dir. Harold Becker
V
Davis, T.

Visit, The
FOX (US) 1964 dir. Bernhard Wicki
Durrenmatt, F.
P

Visitors
BBC (GB) 1987 dir. Piers Haggard
TV(GB)
Potter, D. *Sufficient Carbohydrate*
P

Visit to a Small Planet
PAR (US) 1960 dir. Norman Taurog
Vidal, G.
P

Viva Zapata!
FOX (US) 1952 dir. Elia Kazan
V
Pinchon, E. *Zapata the Unconquerable*

V. I. Warshawski
HOLLYWOOD (US) 1991
dir. Jeff Kanew
Paretsky, S.

Voce Delle Lune, La
PENTA (It) 1990 dir. Federico Fellini
Cavazzini, E. *Poem of the Lunatics, The*

Voice of Bugle Ann, The
MGM (US) 1936 dir. Richard Thorpe
Kantor, M.

Voice of the Heart
PORTMAN (GB) 1989
dir. Tony Wharmby
TVSe(GB)
Bradford, B. T.

Voice of the Turtle
WAR (US) 1947 dir. Irving Rapper
Druten, J. van
P

Voices, The
BBC (GB) 1965 dir. Dennis Vance
TV(GB)
Crane, R. *Hero's Walk*

Voices
HEMDALE (GB) 1973
dir. Kevin Billington
V
Lortz, R. *Children of the Night*
P

Voices Within: The Lives of Truddi Chase
NEW WORLD TV (US) 1990
dir. Lamont Johnson
TVSe(US)
Chase, T. *When Rabbit Howls*

Volpone
SIRITZKY (Fr) 1947
dir. Maurice Tourneur

Jonson, B.
P

Voltaire
WAR (US) 1933 dir. John Adolfi

Gibbs, G. and Dudley, E. L.

Von Ryan's Express
FOX (US) 1965 dir. Mark Robson
V

Westheimer, D.

Voyage of the Damned
ITC (GB) 1976 dir. Stuart Rosenberg
V

Thomas, G. and Witts, M. M.

Vulture, The
YOSHA (Israel) 1981 dir. Yaky Yosha
Kaniuk, Y. *Last Jew, The*

Waco
PAR (US) 1966 dir. R. G. Springsteen
Sanford, H. and Lamb, M. *Emporia*

Wages of Fear
FDF (Fr/It) 1953
dir. Henri-Georges Clouzot
V

Arnaud, G.

Wait til the Sun Shines Nellie
FOX (US) 1952 dir. Henry King
Reyher, F.

Wait Until Dark
WAR (US) 1967 dir. Terence Young
V

Knott, F.
P

Wake Me When It's Over
FOX (US) 1960 dir. Mervyn Le Roy
Singer, H.

Wake of the Red Witch
REP (US) 1948 dir. Edward Ludwig
V

Roark, G.

Wake up and Live
FOX (US) 1937 dir. Sidney Lanfield
Brande, D.

Walkabout
FOX (Aust) 1971 dir. Nicholas Roeg
Marshall, J. V.

Walking Stick, The
MGM (GB) 1970 dir. Eric Till
Graham, W.

Walking Through the Fire
TIME-LIFE (US) 1979 dir. Robert Day
TV(US)
Lee, L.

Walk in the Spring Rain, A
COL (US) 1969 dir. Guy Green
V
Maddux, R.

Walk in the Sun, A
FOX (US) 1945 dir. Lewis Milestone
V
Brown, H. P. M.

Walk on the Wild Side, A
COL (US) 1962 dir. Edward Dmytryk
V
Algren, N.

Walk with Love and Death, A
FOX (US) 1969 dir. John Huston
Koningsberger, H.

Wall, The
TIME-LIFE (US) 1982
dir. Robert Markowitz
Hersey, J.

Wallenberg: A Hero's Story
PAR (US) 1985 dir. Lamont Johnson
TVSe(US)
Werbell, F. and Clarke, T. *Lost Hero: The Mystery of Raoul Wallenberg*

Wall of Noise
WAR (US) 1963 dir. Richard Wilson
Stein, D. M.

Walls of Jericho, The
FOX (US) 1948 dir. John M. Stahl
Wellman, P. I.

Waltzes from Vienna
GFD (GB) 1933 dir. Alfred Hitchcock
US title: Strauss's Great Waltz
Bolton, G.
P

Waltz of the Toreadors
RANK (GB) 1962 dir. John Guillermin
V
Anouilh, J.
P

Wanderers, The
ORION (US) 1979 dir. Philip Kaufman
V
Price, R.

Wandering Jew, The
OLY (GB) 1933 dir. Maurice Elvey
Thurston, E. T.
P

War and Love
CANNON (US/Israel) 1985
dir. Moshe Mizrahi
V
Eisner, J. P. *Survivor, The*

War and Peace
PAR (US/It) 1956 dir. King Vidor
V
MOSFILM (Russia) 1967
dir. Sergei Bondarchuk
Tolstoy, L.

War and Remembrance
LWT (US/GB) 1989 dir. Dan Curtis
TVSe(US/GB)
Wouk, H.

War Between the Tates, The
TALENT (US) 1977 dir. Lee Philips
TV(US), V
Lurie, A.

Ware Case, The
EAL (GB) 1938 dir. Robert Stevenson
Bancroft, G. P.
P

Warlock
FOX (US) 1959 dir. Edward Dmytryk
V
Hall, O.

War Lord, The
UN (US) 1965 dir. Franklin Schaffner
Stevens, L. *Lovers, The*
P

War Lover, The
COL (GB) 1962 dir. Philip Leacock
V
Hersey, J.

Warn London
BL (GB) 1934 dir. T. Hayes Hunter
Clift, D.

Warning Shot
PAR (US) 1966 dir. Buzz Kulik
Masterson, W. *711 — Officer Needs Help*

Warn That Man
AB (GB) 1942 dir. Laurence Huntington
Sylvaine, V.
P

Warning to Wantons
AQUILA (GB) 1949
dir. Donald B. Wilson
Mitchell, M.

War of the Roses, The
FOX (US) 1989 dir. Danny de Vito
V
Adler, W.

War of the Worlds
PAR (US) 1953 dir. Byron Haskin
V
Wells, H. G.

War Requiem
BBC (GB) 1989 dir. Derek Jarman
TV(GB)
Britten, B.

War Wagon, The
UI (US) 1967 dir. Burt Kennedy
Huffaker, C. *Badman*

Washington: Behind Closed Doors
PAR (US) 1977 dir. Gary Nelson
TVSe(US)
Ehrlichman, J. *Company, The*

Washington Masquerade
MGM (US) 1932 dir. Charles Brabin
GB title: Mad Masquerade
Bernstein, H. *Claw, The*
P

Watcher in the Woods
DISNEY (US) 1980 dir. John Hough
V
Randall, F. E.

Watchers
UN (US) 1988 dir. Jon Hess
V
Koontz, D.

Watch House, The
BBC (GB) 1990 dir. Ivan Keill
TV(GB)
Westall, R.

Watch it Sailor!
COL (GB) 1961 dir. Wolf Rilla
Cary, F. L. and King, P.
P

Watch on the Rhine
WAR (US) 1943 dir. Herman Shumlin
V

Hellman, L. F.
P

Water Babies, The
PROD (GB/Pol) 1978 dir. Lionel Jeffries
A, V

Kingsley, C.

Waterfront
GFD (GB) 1950 dir. Michael Anderson
US title: Waterfront Women

Brophy, J.

Water Gypsies, The
SDC (GB) 1932 dir. Maurice Elvey

Herbert, Sir A. P.

Waterloo Bridge
UN (US) 1931 dir. James Whale
MGM (US) 1940 dir. Mervyn Le Roy
V

Sherwood, R. E.
P

Watership Down
CIC (GB) 1978 dir. Martin Rosen
A, V

Adams, R.

Watusi
MGM (US) 1959 dir. Kurt Neumann

Haggard, Sir H. R. *King Solomon's Mines*

Way for a Sailor
MGM (US) 1930 dir. Sam Wood

Wetjen, A. R.

Way of a Gaucho
FOX (US) 1952 dir. Jacques Tourneur

Childs, H. *Gaucho*

Way to the Gold, The
FOX (US) 1957 dir. Robert D. Webb

Steele, W. D.

Wayward Bus, The
FOX (US) 1957 dir. Victor Vicas

Steinbeck, J.

Way West, The
UA (US) 1967 dir. Andrew V. McLaglen

Guthrie, Jr A. B.

Way We Were, The
COL (US) 1973 dir. Sydney Pollack

Laurents, A.

W. C. Fields and Me
UN (US) 1976 dir. Arthur Hiller

Monti, C. and Rice, C.

Weak and the Wicked, The
APB (GB) 1953 dir. J. Lee Thompson

Henry, J. *Who Lie in Gaol*

Weaker Sex, The
TC (GB) 1948 dir. Roy Baker

McCracken, E. *No Medals*
P

We Are Not Alone
WAR (US) 1939 dir. Edmund Goulding

Hilton, J.

Weather in the Streets, The
BBC (GB) 1984 dir. Gavin Millar
TV(GB), V

Lehman, R.

Wedding, The
TYNE-TEES (GB) 1984
dir. Gordon Flemyng
TV(GB)

Pritchett, V. S.

Weekend at Dunkirk
FOX (Fr/It) 1964 dir. Henri Verneuil

Merle, R. *Weekend à Zuydcoote*

Weekend at the Waldorf
MGM (US) 1945 dir. Robert Z. Leonard
M

Baum, V. *Grand Hotel*

Wee Willie Winkie
FOX (US) 1937 dir. John Ford
V

Kipling, R.

We Joined the Navy
WAR (GB) 1962 dir. Wendy Toye

Winton, J.

Welcome to Hard Times
MGM (US) 1967 dir. Burt Kennedy
GB title: Killer on a Horse

Doctorow, E. L.

Welcome to the Club
COL (US) 1970 dir. Walter Shenson

Wood, C. B.

We Live Again
UA (US) 1934 dir. Rouben Mamoulian

Tolstoy, L. *Resurrection*

Went the Day Well?
EAL (GB) 1942 dir. Alberto Cavalcanti
US title: Forty-Eight Hours

Greene, G.

We of the Never Never
AP (Aust) 1982 dir. Igor Auzins
V

Gunn, Mrs. A.

We're No Angels
PAR (US) 1955 dir. Michael Curtiz
V
PAR (US) 1989 dir. Neil Jordan

Husson, A. *My Three Angels*
P

We're Not Dressing
PAR (US) 1934 dir. Norman Taurog

Barrie, Sir J. M. *Admirable Crichton, The*
P

Western Union
FOX (US) 1941 dir. Fritz Lang

Grey, Z.

West Eleven
WAR (GB) 1963 dir. Michael Winner

Del Rivo, L. *Furnished Room, The*

West of the Pecos
RKO (US) 1934 dir. Phil Rosen
RKO (US) 1945 dir. Edward Killy

Grey, Z.

West Side Story
UA (US) 1961
dir. Robert Wise/Jerome Robbins
M, V

Laurents, A., Sondheim, S. and Bernstein, L.
P

Westward Passage
RKO (US) 1932 dir. Robert Milton

Barnes, M. A.

We The Living
SCALERA (It) 1942
dir. Goffredo Allessandrini

Rand, A.

We Think The World of You
CINECOM (GB) 1988 dir. Colin Gregg
V
Ackerley, J. R.

Wet Parade, The
MGM (US) 1932 dir. Victor Fleming
Sinclair, U.

We Were Dancing
MGM (GB) 1942 dir. Robert Z. Leonard
Coward, N. *Tonight at 8.30*
P

We Were Strangers
COL (US) 1949 dir. John Huston
Sylvester, R. *Rough Sketch*

Whale for the Killing, A
PLAYBOY (US) 1981
dir. Richard T. Heffron
TV(US), V
Mowat, F.

Whales of August, The
ALIVE (US) 1987 dir. Lindsay Anderson
V
Barry, D.
P

What a Life
PAR (US) 1939 dir. Theodore Reed
Goldsmith, C.
P

What-a-Mess
Central (GB)
A, TVSe(GB)
Muir, F.

What Became of Jack and Jill?
FOX (GB) 1971 dir. Bill Bain
Moody, L. *Ruthless Ones, The*

Whatever Happened to Aunt Alice?
PALOMAR (US) 1969 dir. Lee H. Katzin
V
Curtiss, U. *Forbidden Garden, The*

What Ever Happened to Baby Jane?
WAR (US) 1962 dir. Robert Aldrich
V
SPECTACOR (US) 1991
dir. David Greene
TV(US)
Farrell, H. *Baby Jane*

What Every Woman Knows
MGM (US) 1934 dir. Gregory La Cava
Barrie, Sir J. M.
P

What Mad Pursuit
BBC (GB) 1985 dir. Tony Smith
TV(GB), V
Coward, N.

What Price Glory?
FOX (US) 1952 dir. John Ford
V
Anderson, M. and Stallings, L.
P

What's a Nice Girl Like You . . .?
UN TV (US) 1971 dir. Jerry Paris
TV(US)
Cunningham, E. V. *Shirley*

Wheeler-Dealers
MGM (US) 1963 dir. Arthur Hiller
GB title: Separate Beds
Goodman, G. J. W. *Wheeler-Dealers, The*

Wheels
UN TV (US) 1978 dir. Jerry London
TVSe(US)
Hailey, A.

When Eight Bells Toll
RANK (GB) 1971 dir. Etienne Perier
MacLean, A.

When Hell was in Session
AUBREY-HAMNER (USTV) 1979
dir. Paul Krasny
TV(US), V
Denton, Jr., J. A. and Brandt, E.

When Ladies Meet
MGM (US) 1933 dir. Harry Beaumont
MGM (US) 1941 dir. Robert Z. Leonard
Crothers, R.
P

When Michael Calls
FOX (US) 1972 dir. Philip Leacock
TV(US)
Farris, J.

When my Baby Smiles at Me
FOX (US) 1948 dir. Walter Lang
Walters, G. M. and Hopkins, A.
Burlesque
P

When the Bough Breaks
TAFT (US) 1986 dir. Waris Hussein
TV(US)
Kellerman, J.

When the Boys Meet the Girls
MGM (US) 1965 dir. Alvin Ganzer
Bolton, G. and McGowan, J. *Girl Crazy*
P

When the Green Woods Laugh
YTV (GB) 1991 dir. Robert Tronson
TV
Bates, H. E.

When the Legends Die
FOX (US) 1972 dir. Stuart Millar
V
Borland, H.

When the Whales Came
FOX (GB) 1989 dir. Clive Rees
V
Morpurgo, M. *Why Whales Came*

When the Wind Blows
MELTDOWN (GB) 1987
dir. J. T. Murakami
A, V
Briggs, R.

When Time Ran Out
WAR (US) 1980 dir. James Goldstone
V
Thomas, G. and Witts, M. M. *Day the World Ended, The*

When Tomorrow Comes
UN (US) 1939 dir. John M. Stahl
Cain, J. A.

When we are Married
BN (GB) 1943 dir. Lance Comfort
Priestley, J. B.
P

When Worlds Collide
PAR (US) 1951 dir. Rudolph Maté
V
Balmer, E. and Wylie, P.

Where are the Children?
COL (US) 1986 dir. Bruce Malmuth
V
Clark, M. H.

Where Does it Hurt?
HEMDALE (US) 1971 dir. Rod Amateau
V
Amateau, R. and Robinson, B.
Operator, The

Where Eagles Dare
MGM (GB) 1969 dir. Brian G. Hutton
V
MacLean, A.

Where Love has Gone
PAR (US) 1964 dir. Edward Dmytryk
Robbins, H.

Where Pigeons Go To Die
WORLD (US) 1990 dir. Michael Landon
TV(US)
Campbell, R. W.

Where's Charley?
WAR (US) 1952 dir. David Butler
Thomas, B. *Charley's Aunt*
P

Where Sinners Meet
RKO (US) 1934 dir. J. Walter Ruben
Milne, A. A. *Dover Road, The*
P

Where's Poppa?
UA (US) 1970 dir. Carl Reiner
V
Klane, R.

Where the Boys Are
MGM (US) 1960 dir. Henry Levin
V
ITC (US) 1980 dir. Hy Averback
V
Swarthout, G.

Where the Hot Wind Blows
MGM (Fr/It) 1958 dir. Jules Dassin
V
Vailland, R.

Where the Lilies Bloom
UA (US) 1974 dir. William A. Graham
Cleaver, V. and Cleaver, B.

Where the Red Fern Grows
EMI (US) 1974 dir. Norman Tokar
V
Rawls, W.

Where There's A Will
EROS (GB) 1955 dir. Vernon Sewell
Delderfield, R. F.
P

Where the River Runs Black
MGM (US) 1986 dir. Christopher Cain
V
Kendall, D. *Lazaro*

Where the Sidewalk Ends
FOX (US) 1950 dir. Otto Preminger
Stuart, W. L. *Night Cry*

Where the Spies Are
MGM (GB) 1965 dir. Val Guest
V
Leasor, J. *Passport to Oblivion*

Where Were You When the Lights Went Out?
MGM (US) 1968 dir. Hy Averback
Magnier, C.
P

While I Live
DRYHURST (GB) 1947 dir. John Harlow
Bell, R. *This Same Garden*
P

While the City Sleeps
RKO (US) 1956 dir. Fritz Lang
V
Einstein, C. *Bloody Spur, The*

While the Patient Slept
IN (US) 1935 dir. Ray Enright
Eberhart, M. G.

While the Sun Shines
ABP (GB) 1947 dir. Anthony Asquith
Rattigan, T.
P

Whirlpool
FOX (US) 1949 dir. Otto Preminger
Endore, G. *Methinks the Lady*

Whisky Galore
EAL (GB) 1948
dir. Alexander MacKendrick
US title: Tight Little Island
V

Mackenzie, Sir C.

Whisperers, The
UA (GB) 1966 dir. Bryan Forbes
Nicolson, R. *Mrs. Ross*

Whispering Smith
PAR (US) 1948 dir. Leslie Fenton
Spearman, F. H.

Whistle Blower, The
HEMDALE (GB) 1987
dir. Simon Langton
V

Hale, J.

Whistle Down the Wind
RANK (GB) 1961 dir. Bryan Forbes
V

Bell, M. H.

Whistle Stop
UA (US) 1946 dir. Leonide Moguy
V

Wolff, M. M.

Whistling in the Dark
MGM (US) 1941 dir. S. Sylvan Simon
Gross, L. and Carpenter, E. C.
P

White Banners
WAR (US) 1938 dir. Edmund Goulding
Douglas, L. C.

White Buffalo, The
EMI (US) 1977 dir. J. Lee Thompson
Sale, R.

White Cargo
BI (GB) 1930 dir. J. D. Williams and A.
W. Barnes
MGM (US) 1942 dir. Richard Thorpe
Gordon, L.
P

White Cockatoo
WAR (US) 1935 dir. Alan Crosland
Eberhart, M. G.

White Corridors
GFD (GB) 1951 dir. Pat Jackson
Ashton, H. *Yeoman's Hospital*

White Dawn, The
PAR (US) 1974 dir. Philip Kaufman
V

Houston, J.

White Dog
PAR (US) 1982 dir. Samuel Fuller
Gary, R.

White Fang
FOX (US) 1936 dir. David Butler
FOX (It/Sp/Fr) 1974 dir. Lucio Fulci
DISNEY (US) 1991 dir. Randal Kleiser
London, J.

White Hot: The Mysterious Murder of Thelma Todd
NEWFELD-KEATING (US) 1991
dir. Paul Wendkos
TV(US)
Edmonds, A. *Hot Toddy*

White Hunter, Black Heart
WAR (US) 1990 dir. Clint Eastwood
Viertel, P.

White Lie
MCA TV (US) 1991 dir. Bill Condon
TV(US)
Charters, S. *Louisiana Black*

White Mischief
BBC-COL (GB) 1988
dir. Michael Radford
V
Fox, J.

White of the Eye
CANNON (GB) 1987
dir. Donald Cammell
V
Tracy, M. *Mrs. White*

White Palace
UN (US) 1990 dir. Luis Mandoki
V
Savan, G.

White Peak Farm
BBC (GB) 1988 dir. Andrew Morgan
Ch, TVSe
Doherty, B.

White Sister
MGM (US) 1933 dir. Victor Fleming
Crawford, E. M. & Hackett, W.
P

White Tower, The
RKO (US) 1950 dir. Ted Tetzlaff
V
Ullman, J. R.

White Unicorn, The
GFD (GB) 1947 dir. Bernard Knowles
US title: Bad Sister
Sandstrom, F. *Milk White Unicorn, The*

White Witch Doctor
FOX (US) 1953 dir. Henry Hathaway
Stinetorf, L. A.

Who?
BL (GB) 1974 dir. Jack Gold
US title: Man Without a Face
Budrys, A.

Who Framed Roger Rabbit?
TOUCH (US) 1988 dir. Robert Zemeckis
A, V
Wolf, G. K. *Who Censored Roger Rabbit?*

Who Goes There?
BL (GB) 1952 dir. Anthony Kimmins
US title: Passionate Sentry, The
Dighton, J.
P

Who has Seen the Wind
CINEMA WORLD (Can) 1980
dir. Allan King
Mitchell, W. O.

Who is Julia?
CBS ENT (US) 1986
dir. Walter Grauman
TV(US)
Harris, B. S.

Who is Killing the Great Chefs of Europe?
WAR (US) 1978 dir. Ted Kotcheff
GB title: Too Many Chefs
Lyons, N., and Lyons, I. *Someone is Killing the Great Chefs of Europe*

Who Killed the Cat?
GN (GB) 1966 dir. Montgomery Tully
Ridley, A. and Borer, M. *Tabitha*
P

Whole Town's Talking, The
COL (US) 1935 dir. John Ford
GB title: Passport to Fame
Burnett, W. R.

Whole Truth, The
COL (GB) 1958 dir. John Guillermin
Mackie, P.
P

Who'll Save Our Children?
TIME-LIFE (US) 1978
dir. George Schaefer
TV(US), V
Maddux, R. *Orchard Children, The*

Who'll Stop the Rain?
UA (US) 1978 dir. Karel Reisz
GB title: Dog Soldiers
V
Stone, R. *Dog Soldiers*

Whore
TRIMARK (GB) 1991 dir. Ken Russell
Hines, D. *Bondage*
P

Who's Afraid of Virginia Woolf?
WAR (US) 1966 dir. Mike Nichols
V
Albee, E.
P

Whose Life is it Anyway?
MGM (US) 1981 John Badham
V
Clark, B.
P

Who's Got the Action?
PAR (US) 1963 dir. Daniel Mann
Rose, A. *Four Horse Players are Missing*

Who Was That Lady?
COL (US) 1960 dir. George Sidney
Krasna, N. *Who Was That Lady I Saw You With?*
P

Why Didn't They Ask Evans?
LWT (GB) 1980 dir. John Davies, Tony Wharmby
TVSe(GB)
Christie, A.

Why Me?
LORIMAR (US) 1984 dir. Fielder Cook
TV(US)
Harmon, L. M.

Why Me?
TRIUMPH (US) 1990
dir. Gene Quintano
Westlake, D. E.

Why Not Stay for Breakfast?
ENT (GB) 1979 dir. Terence Martel
V
Stone, G. and Cooney, R.
P

Why Shoot the Teacher?
QUARTET (Can) 1976
dir. Silvio Narizzano
V
Braithwaite, M.

Why Would I Lie?
UA (US) 1980 dir. Larry Peerce
V
Hodges, H. *Fabricator, The*

Wicked Lady, The
GFD (GB) 1946 dir. Leslie Arliss
V
CANNON (GB) 1983
dir. Michael Winner
V
King-Hall, M. *Life and Death of the Wicked Lady Skelton, The*

Wicked Woman, A
MGM (US) 1934 dir. Charles Brabin
Austin, A.

Widow
LORIMAR (US) 1976
dir. J. Lee Thompson
TV(US)
Caine, L.

Wife Vs. Secretary
MGM (US) 1936 dir. Clarence Brown
Baldwin, F.

Wilby Conspiracy, The
UA (GB) 1975 dir. Ralph Nelson
V
Driscoll, P.

Wild Affair, The
BL (GB) 1965 dir. John Irish
Sansom, W. *Last Hours of Sandra Lee,*
The

Wild and the Willing, The
RANK (GB) 1962 dir. Ralph Thomas
US title: Young and Willing
Dobie, L. and Sloman, R. *Tinker, The*
P

Wild at Heart
GOLDWYN (US) 1990 dir. David Lynch
Gifford, B.

Wild Country, The
DISNEY (US) 1971 dir. Robert Totten
V
Moody, R. *Little Britches*

Wild Duck, The
ORION (GB) 1983 dir. Henri Safran
V
Ibsen, H.
P

Wild Geese, The
RANK (GB) 1978
dir. Andrew V. McLaglen
V
Carney, D.

Wild Geese II
UN (GB) 1985 dir. Peter Hunt
V
Carney, D. *Square Circle, The*

Wild Geese Calling
FOX (US) 1941 dir. John Brahm
White, S. E.

Wild Harvest
GN (US) 1961 dir. Jerry Baerwitz
Longstreet, S.

Wild in the Country
FOX (US) 1961 dir. Philip Dunne
V
Salamanca, J. R. *Lost Country, The*

Wild Man of Borneo, The
MGM (US) 1941 dir. Robert B. Sinclair
Mankiewicz, H. J., and Connelly, M.
P

Wild River
FOX (US) 1960 dir. Elia Kazan
Deal, B. *Dunbar's Cove*
Huie, W. B. *Mud on the Streets*

Wild Times
METRO (US) 1980
dir. Richard Compton
TVSe(US), V
Garfield, B.

Wild Women
A. SPELLING (US) 1970 dir. Don Taylor
TV(US), V
Forte, V. *Trailmakers, The*

Will Any Gentleman
ABP (GB) 1953 dir. Michael Anderson
Sylvaine, V.
P

Willard
CINERAMA (US) 1971 dir. Daniel Mann
V
Gilbert, S. *Ratman's Notebook*

Will: G. Gordon Liddy
SHAYNE (US) 1982
dir. Robert Lieberman
TV(US)
Liddy, G. G. *Will*

Will Success Spoil Rock Hunter?
FOX (US) 1957 dir. Frank Tashlin
GB title: Oh! For a Man!
Axelrod, G.
P

Will There Really Be A Morning?
ORION (US) 1983 dir. Fielder Cook
TV(US)
Farmer, F.

Willy Wonka and the Chocolate Factory
PAR (US) 1971 dir. Mel Stuart
Ch, V
Dahl, R. *Charlie and the Chocolate Factory*

Wilt
RANK (GB) 1989 dir. Michael Tuchner
Sharpe, T.

Wind Cannot Read, The
RANK (GB) 1958 dir. Ralph Thomas
Mason, R.

Windmills of the Gods
ITC (US) 1988 dir. Lee Philips
TVSe(US)
Sheldon, S.

Windom's Way
RANK (GB) 1957 dir. Ronald Neame
V
Ullman, J. R.

Winds of Jarrah, The
FILMCORP (Aust) 1983
dir. Mark Egerton
V
Dingwall, J. *House in the Timberwoods, The*

Winds of War, The
PAR (US) 1983 dir. Dan Curtis
TVSe(US)
Wouk, H.

Windwalker
PACIFIC (US) 1981 dir. Keith Merrill
V
Yorgason, B.

Winged Victory
FOX (US) 1944 dir. George Cukor
Hart, M.
P

Winnie
NBC (US) 1988 dir. John Korty
TV(US)
Bolnick, J. P. *Winnie: My Life in the Institution*

Winnie the Pooh and the Honey Tree
DISNEY (US) 1965
dir. Wolfgang Reitherman
A, V
Milne, A. A. *Winnie the Pooh*

Winslow Boy, The
IS (GB) 1945 dir. Anthony Asquith
V

Rattigan, T.
P

Winstanley
OTHER (GB) 1977
dir. Kevin Brownlow/Andrew Mollo

Caute, D. *Comrade Jacob*

Winter in Lisbon, The
JET (Sp) 1990 dir. José Antonio Zorrilla

Molina, A. M.

Winter Kills
AVCO (US) 1979 dir. William Richert
V

Condon, R.

Winter Meeting
WAR (US) 1948 dir. Bretaigne Windust

Vance, E.

Winter of our Discontent, The
LORIMAR (US) 1983 dir. Waris Hussein
TV(US)

Steinbeck, J.

Winter People
COL (US) 1989 dir. Ted Kotcheff
V

Ehle, J.

Winterset
RKO (US) 1936 dir. Alfred Santell
V
COMPASS (US) 1959
dir. George Schaefer
TV(US)

Anderson, M.
P

Winter's Tale, The
WAR (GB) 1968 dir. Frank Dunlop

Shakespeare, W.
P

Winter Tan, A
TELEFILM (Can) 1987 dir. Louise Clark

Holder, M. *Give Sorrow Words*

Wired
TAURUS (US) 1989 dir. Larry Peerce
V

Woodward, B.

Wise Blood
NEWLINE (US) 1980 dir. John Huston
V

O'Connor, F.

Witches, The
HAMMER (GB) 1966 dir. Cyril Frankel

Curtis, P. *Devil's Own, The*

Witches, The
WAR (US) 1990 dir. Nicolas Roeg

Dahl, R.

Witches of Eastwick, The
WAR (US) 1987 dir. George Miller
V

Updike, J.

Witches of Salem, The
FDF (Fr/Ger) 1957
dir. Raymond Rouleau

Miller, A. *Crucible, The*
P

Witchfinder General
TIGON (GB) 1968 dir. Michael Reeves
V

Bassett, R.

Witching Hour, The
PAR (US) 1934 dir. Henry Hathaway

Thomas, A.
P

Within the Law
MGM (US) 1939 dir. Gustav Machaty
Veiller, B.
P

Without Apparent Motive
VALORIA (Fr) 1971 dir. Philippe Labro
McBain, E. *Ten Plus One*

Without a Trace
FOX (US) 1983 dir. Stanley R. Jaffe
V
Gutcheon, B. *Still Missing*

Without Love
MGM (US) 1945 dir. Harold S. Bucquet
Barry, P.
P

Without Reservations
RKO (US) 1946 dir. Mervyn Le Roy
V
Allen, J. and Livingston, M. *Thanks God, I'll Take it From Here*

Without Warning: The James Brady Story
HBO (US) 1991
dir. Michael Toshiyuki Uno
TV(US)
Dickenson, M. *Thumbs Up: The Life and Courageous Comeback of White House Press Secretary Jim Brady*

Witness for the Prosecution
UA (US) 1957 dir. Billy Wilder
V
UATV (US) 1982 dir. Alan Gibson
TV(US)
Christie, A.
P

Wives and Lovers
PAR (US) 1963 dir. John Rich
Allen, J. P. *First Wife, The*
P

Wiz, The
DISNEY (US) 1978 dir. Sidney Lumet
M, V
Brown, W.
P
Baum, L. F. *Wonderful Wizard of Oz, The*
P

Wizard of Loneliness
SKOURAS (US) 1988 dir. Jenny Bowen
V
Nichols, J.

Wizard of Oz, The
MGM (US) 1939 dir. Victor Fleming
M, V
Baum, L. F. *Wonderful Wizard of Oz, The*

Wolfen
WAR (US) 1981 dir. Michael Wadleigh
V
Strieber, W.

Wolf Larsen
ABP (US) 1958 dir. Harman Jones
London, J. *Sea Wolf, The*

Wolf to the Slaughter
TVS (GB) 1988 dir. John Gorrie
TVSe(GB)
Rendell, R.

Wolves of Willoughby Chase, The
ZENITH (GB) 1988 dir. Stuart Orme
Aiken, J.

Woman Called Moses, A
H. JAFFE (US) 1978 dir. Paul Wendkos
TVSe(US)
Heidish, M.

Woman from the Provinces, A
OKO (Pol) 1987 dir. Andrzej Baranski
Sieminski, W.

Woman in a Dressing Gown
GODWIN (GB) 1957
dir. J. Lee Thompson
Willis, T.
P

Woman I Love, The
RKO (US) 1937 dir. Anatole Litvak
GB title: Woman Between, The
Kessel, J. *L'Equippage*

Woman in the Hall, The
GFD (GB) 1947 dir. Jack Lee
Stern, G. B.

Woman in the Window, The
RKO (US) 1944 dir. Fritz Lang
Wallis, J. H. *Once Off Guard*

Woman in White, The
WAR (US) 1948 dir. Peter Godfrey
Collins, W.

Woman Obsessed
FOX (US) 1959 dir. Henry Hathaway
Mantley, J. *Snow Birch, The*

Woman of Rome
MINERVA (It) 1954 dir. Luigi Zampa
V
Moravia, A.

Woman of Straw
UA (GB) 1964 dir. Basil Dearden
Arley, C.

Woman of Substance, A
OPT (US) 1984 dir. Don Sharp
TVSe(US), V
Bradford, B. T.

Woman of the Dunes, The
CONTEM (Jap) 1964
dir. Hiroshi Teshigahara
V
Abé, K. *Woman in the Dunes*

Woman on the Beach, The
RKO (US) 1947 dir. Jean Renoir
Wilson, M. *None so Blind*

Woman Rebels, A
RKO (US) 1936 dir. Mark Sandrich
V
Syrett, N. *Portrait of a Rebel*

Woman's Angle, A
ABP (GB) 1952 dir. Leslie Arliss
Feiner, R. *Three Cups of Coffee*

Woman's Face, A
MGM (US) 1941 dir. George Cukor
V
de Croisset, F. *Il était une fois*
P

Woman's Secret, A
RKO (US) 1949 dir. Nicholas Ray
Baum, V. *Mortgage on Life*

Woman's Vengeance, A
UN (US) 1947 dir. Zoltan Korder
Huxley, A. L. *Gioconda Smile, The*
P

Woman With No Name, The
ABP (GB) 1950 dir. Ladislas Vajda
Charles, T. *Happy Now I Go*

Women, The
MGM (US) 1939 dir. George Cukor
V
Booth, C.
P

Women in Love
UA (GB) 1969 dir. Ken Russell
V
Lawrence, D. H.

Women in White
UN TV (US) 1979 dir. Jerry London
TVSe(US)
Slaughter, F. G.

Women of Brewster Place, The
PHOENIX (US) 1989 dir. Donna Deitch
TVSe(US)
Naylor, G.

Women of Twilight
ROMULUS (GB) 1952
dir. Gordon Parry
US title: Twilight Women
Rayman, S.
P

Women's Room, The
WAR (US) 1980 dir. Glenn Jordan
TVSe(US)
French, M.

Wonder Bar
WAR (US) 1934 dir. Lloyd Bacon
M
Herczeg, G., Farkas, K., and Katscher, R.
P

Wonderful Country, The
UA (US) 1959 dir. Robert Parrish
Lea, T.

Wonderful World of the Brothers Grimm, The
MGM (US) 1962 dir. Henry Levin and George Pal
Ch
Grimm, J. L. K. and Grimm, W. K. *Dancing Princess, The; Cobbler & the Elves, The; Singing Bone, The*
Gerstner, H. *Die Bruder Grimm*

Wooden Horse, The
BL (GB) 1950 dir. Jack Lee
V
Williams, E.

Woof
CENTRAL (GB) 1990
dir. David Cobham
Ch, TVSe(GB)
Ahlberg, A.

Word, The
FRIES (US) 1978 dir. Richard Lang
TVSe(US)
Wallace, I.

Working Man, The
WAR (US) 1933 dir. John Adolfi
Franklin, E.

Work is a Four Letter Word
UI (GB) 1968 dir. Peter Hall
Livings, H. *Eh?*
P

World According to Garp, The
WAR (US) 1982 dir. George Roy Hill
V
Irving, J.

World in his Arms, The
UN (US) 1952 dir. Raoul Walsh
Beach, R.

World is Full of Married Men, The
NEW REALM (GB) 1979
dir. Robert Young
V

Collins, J.

World of Henry Orient, The
UA (US) 1964 dir. George Roy Hill
V

Johnson, N.

World of Suzie Wong, The
PAR (GB) 1960 dir. Richard Quine

Mason, R.

Worlds Apart
SCANLON (Israel) 1980
dir. Barbara Noble

Kollek, A. *Don't Ask Me If I Love*

World, The Flesh and the Devil, The
MGM (US) 1959
dir. Ronald MacDougall

Shiel, M. P. *Purple Cloud, The*

Worm's Eye View
ABP (GB) 1951 dir. Jack Raymond

Delderfield, R. F.
P

Worth Winning
FOX (US) 1989 dir. Will Mackenzie

Lewandowski, D.

Wrath of God, The
MGM (US) 1972 dir. Ralph Nelson

Graham, J.

Wrecking Crew, The
COL (US) 1968 dir. Phil Karlson
V

Hamilton, D.

Wreck of the Mary Deare, The
MGM (US) 1959 dir. Michael Anderson

Innes, H.

Written on the Wind
UN (US) 1956 dir. Douglas Sirk

Wilder, R.

Wrong Box, The
COL (GB) 1966 dir. Bryan Forbes
V

Stevenson, R. L. and Osbourne, L.

Wrong is Right
COL (US) 1982 dir. Richard Brooks
GB title: Man with the Deadly Lens, The
V

McCarry, C. *Deadly Angels, The*

WUSA
PAR (US) 1970 dir. Stuart Rosenberg

Stone, R. *Hall of Mirrors*

Wuthering Heights
UA (US) 1939 dir. William Wyler
MGM-EMI (GB) 1970 dir. Robert Fuest
V
PLEXUS (Sp) 1983 dir. Luis Bunuel

Bronte, E. J.

Wynne and Penkovsky
BBC (GB/US) 1984 dir. Paul Seed
TV(GB/US), V

Wynne, G. *Man from Moscow, A*

Yangtse Incident
BL (GB) 1957 dir. Michael Anderson
US title: Battle Hell
Earl, L.

Yankee Pasha
UI (US) 1954 dir. Joseph Pevney
Marshall, E.

Yank in Ermine, A
MON (GB) 1955 dir. Gordon Parry
Carstairs, J. P. *Solid! Said the Earl*

Yearling, The
MGM (US) 1946 dir. Clarence Brown
V
Rawlings, Mrs. M.

Year of Living Dangerously, The
MGM/UA (Aust) 1982 dir. Peter Weir
V
Koch, C. J.

Year of the Dragon
MGM/UA (US) 1985
dir. Michael Cimino
V
Daley, R.

Year of the Gun
TRIUMPH (US) 1991
dir. John Frankenheimer
Mewshaw, M.

Years Between, The
FOX (GB) 1946 dir. Compton Bennett
Du Maurier, D.
P

Yellow Canary, The
FOX (US) 1963 dir. Buzz Kulik
Masterson, W. *Evil Come, Evil Go*

Yellow Earth
GUANGXI (China) 1985 dir. Chen Kaige
Ke Lan *Echo in the Valley*

Yellow Jack
MGM (US) 1938 dir. George B. Seitz
Howard, S.
P

Yellow Sands
AB (GB) 1938 dir. Herbert Brenon
Phillpotts, E. & Phillpotts, A.
P

Yellowstone Kelly
WAR (US) 1959 dir. Gordon Douglas
Fisher, C.

Yellowthread Street
YTV (GB) 1990 dir. Ronald Graham
TVSe(GB)
Marshall, W.

Yellow Ticket, The
FOX (US) 1931 dir. Raoul Walsh
GB title: Yellow Passport, The
Morton, M.
P

Yen Family, The
FUJI (Jap) 1990 dir. Yojiro Takita
Tani, T. *Kimura Family, The*

Yentl
MGM/UA (US) 1983
dir. Barbra Streisand
M
Singer, I. B. *Yentl, the Yeshiva Boy*

Yes, Giorgio
MGM/UA (US) 1982
dir. Franklin Schaffner
V
Piper, A.

Yes, My Darling Daughter
WAR (US) 1939 dir. William Keighley
Reed, M. W.
P

Yesterday's Child
PAR TV (US) 1977 dir. Corey Allen,
Bob Rosenbaum
TV(US)
Disney, D. M. *Night of Clear Choice*

Yield to the Night
ABP (GB) 1956 dir. J. Lee Thompson
US title: Blonde Sinner
Henry, J.

You Can't Get Away with Murder
WAR (US) 1939 dir. Lewis Seiler
Lawes, L., and Finn, J. *Chalked Out*
P

You Can't Go Home Again
CBS ENT (US) 1979 dir. Ralph Nelson
TV(US)
Wolfe, T.

You Can't See Round Corners
UI (Aust) 1969 dir. David Cahill
Cleary, J.

You Can't Take it With You
COL (US) 1938 dir. Frank Capra
V
Kaufman, G. S. and Hart, M.
P

You'll Like My Mother
UN (US) 1972 dir. Lamont Johnson
Hintze, N. A.

You'll Never See Me Again
UN (US) 1973 dir. Jeannot Szwarc
TV(US)
Woolrich, C.

Young and Innocent
GFD (GB) 1937 dir. Alfred Hitchcock
US title: Girl was Young, A
V
Tey, J. *Shilling for Candles, A*

Young and Willing
UA (US) 1942 dir. Edward H. Griffith
V
Swann, F. *Out of the Frying Pan*
P

Young at Heart
WAR (US) 1954 dir. Gordon Douglas
V
Hurst, F.

Young Bess
MGM (US) 1953 dir. George Sidney
Irwin, M.

Young Billy Young
UA (US) 1969 dir. Burt Kennedy
Henry, W. *Who Rides with Wyatt?*

Youngblood Hawke
WAR (US) 1963 dir. Delmer Daves
Wouk, H.

Young Cassidy
MGM (GB) 1964
dir. Jack Cardiff/John Ford
O'Casey, S. *Mirror in my House*

Young Dr. Kildare
MGM (US) 1938 dir. Harold S. Bucquet
Brand, M.

Young Doctors, The
UA (US) 1961 dir. Phil Karlson
Hailey, A. *Final Diagnosis, The*

Youngest Profession, The
MGM (US) 1943 dir. Edward Buzzell
Day, L.

Young in Heart, The
SELZNICK (US) 1938
dir. Richard Wallace
Wylie, I. A. R. *Gay Banditti, The*

Young Joe, the Forgotten Kennedy
ABC (US) 1977 dir. Richard T. Heffron
TV(US)
Searls, H. *Lost Prince, The: Young Joe, The Forgotten Kennedy*

Young Lions, The
FOX (US) 1958 dir. Edward Dmytryk
V
Shaw, I.

Young Lovers, The
MGM (US) 1964 dir. Samuel Goldwyn, Jr.
Halevy, J.

Young Man with a Horn
WAR (US) 1950 dir. Michael Curtiz
GB title: Young Man of Music
V
Baker, D.

Young Philadelphians, The
WAR (US) 1959 dir. Vincent Sherman
GB title: City Jungle, The
V
Powell, R. *Philadelphian, The*

Young Pioneers
ABC (US) 1976 dir. Michael O'Herlihy
TV(US)
Lane, R. W.

Young Savages, The
UA (US) 1960 dir. John Frankenheimer
Hunter, E. *Matter of Conviction, A*

Young Visitors, The
CHANNEL 4 (GB) 1984 dir. James Hill
Ashford, D.

Young Warriors
UN (US) 1966 dir. John Peyser
V
Matheson, R. *Beardless Warriors*

Young Widow, The
UA (US) 1946 dir. Edwin L. Marin
Cushman, C. F.

Young Winston
COL-WAR (GB) 1972
dir. Richard Attenborough
V
Churchill, Sir W. S. *My Early Life*

Young Wives' Tale
ABP (GB) 1951 dir. Henry Cass
Jeans, R.
P

Young Woodley
BI (GB) 1929 dir. Thomas Bentley
Druten, J. van
P

You Only Live Twice
UA (GB) 1966 dir. Lewis Gilbert
V
Fleming, I.

You're a Big Boy Now
WAR (US) 1967
dir. Francis Ford Coppola
V
Benedictus, D.

You're Only Young Twice
ABP (GB) 1952 dir. Terry Gilbert
Bridie, J. *What Say They*
P

Your Money or Your Wife
BRENTWOOD (US) 1972
dir. Allen Reisner
TV(US)
Craig, J. *If You Want to See Your Wife Again*

Your Ticket is no Longer Valid
CAROLCO (Can) 1980
dir. George Kaczender
V
Gary, R.

Z
WAR (Fr/Alg) 1968 dir. Costa-Gavras
V
Vassilikos, V.

Zandy's Bride
WAR (US) 1974 dir. Jan Troell
Loss, L. B. *Stranger, The*

Zappa
IS (Den) 1984 dir. Bille August
Reuter, B.

Zarak
COL (GB) 1956 dir. Terence Young
Bevan, A. C. *Story of Zarak Khan, The*

Zaza
PAR (US) 1938 dir. George Cukor
Berton, P. and Simon, C.
P

Zastrozzi
CHANNEL 4 (GB) 1986
TV
Shelley, P. B.

Zazie Dans le Métro
CONNOISSEUR (Fr) 1960
dir. Louis Malle
Queneau, R.

Zoo 2000
BBC (GB) 1984
TV
Chertas, J.

Zoot Suit
UN (US) 1982 dir. Luis Valdez
Valdez, L.
P

Zorba the Greek
FOX (GB) 1964 dir. Michael Cacoyannis
V

Kazantzakis, N.

AUTHOR INDEX

Author's name —— **Spewack, B. and Spewack, S.**

Book or play title —— **Kiss Me Kate**

P —————————————————— Means adapted from a play

Name and location of publisher —— Various

MGM (US) 1953 dir. George Sidney ————— Film title (if different)

M, V —————————————————— Director's name

Studio name and country of origin —— MILBERG (US) 1958 dir. George Schaefer

TV (US) —————————————————— Date of release

GB title:

British, etc, title (if different) —————————————— Abbreviations as listed below

A = Animated film

Ch = Made for children

M = Based on a musical

TV (GB, US, etc) = Made for British, American, etc, television

TVSe = Made for television series or mini-series

V = Available on video

Aaronson, D.
Hoods, The
Once Upon a Time in America
WAR (US) 1984 dir. Sergio Leone
V

Abbey, E.
Brave Cowboy
University of New Mexico Press
(Albuquerque,NewMexico)
Lonely are the Brave
UI (US) 1962 dir. David Miller
V

Abbey, E.
Fire on the Mountain
University of New Mexico Press
(Albuquerque)
CARSON (US) 1981 dir. Donald Wrye
TV(US)

Abbot, A.
Murder of the Circus Queen, The
Collins
Circus Queen Murder
COL (US) 1933 dir. Roy William Neill

Abbott, G.
Boys from Syracuse, The
P
UN (US) 1940 dir. E. A. Sutherland
M

Abbott, G.
On Your Toes
P
WAR (US) 1939 dir. Ray Enright

Abbott, G. and Abrams, L.
Heat Lightning
P
Samuel French
WAR (US) 1934 dir. Mervyn Le Roy

Abé, K.
Woman in the Dunes
Knopf
Woman of the Dunes, The
CONTEM (Jap) 1964
dir. Hiroshi Teshigahara
V

Aberson, H. and Pearl, H.
Dumbo, the Flying Elephant
Dumbo
DISNEY (US) 1941 dir. Ben Sharpsteen
A, Ch, V

Ackerley, J. R.
We Think The World of You
Simon & Schuster
CINECOM (GB) 1988 dir. Colin Gregg
V

Adam, A.
Sylvia and the Ghost
P
ECRAN (Fr) 1944
dir. Claude Autant-Lara
V

Adamovich, A.
Story of Khatyn, The
Come and See
MOSFILM (USSR) 1985
dir. Elem Klimov

Adams, C.
Dangerous Days of Kiowa Jones, The
Doubleday
MGM (US) 1966 dir. Alex March
TV(US)

Adams, D.
Hitch-Hiker's Guide to the Galaxy, The
Harmony Books
BBC (GB) 1981 dir. Alan Bell
TVSe(GB)

Adams, J.
Sex and the Single Parent
TIME-LIFE (US) 1979
dir. Jackie Cooper
TV(US), V

Adams, P. and Cooklin, S.
Knockback
Duckworth
BBC (GB) 1985
TV(GB)

Adams, R.
Girl in a Swing, The
Knopf
J&M (GB/US) 1989 dir. Gordon Hessler

Adams, R.
Watership Down
Macmillan
CIC (GB) 1978 dir. Martin Rosen
A, V

Adams, R. G.
Plague Dogs, The
Knopf
NEPENTHE (GB) 1982
dir. Martin Rosen
A, V

Adams, S. H.
Gorgeous Hussy, The
Houghton, Mifflin Co. (Boston)
MGM (US) 1936 dir. Clarence Brown

Adams, S. H.
In Person
RKO (US) 1935 dir. William A. Seiter
V

Adams, S. H.
Night Bus
Longman
It Happened One Night
COL (US) 1934 dir. Frank Capra

Adamson, J.
Born Free
Pantheon Books
COL (GB) 1965 dir. James Hill
V

Adamson, J.
Living Free
Harcourt, Brace & World
COL (GB) 1972 dir. Jack Couffer
V

Adleman, R. H. and Walton, G.
Devil's Brigade, The
Chilton Books
UA (US) 1968 dir. Andrew V. MacLaglen

Adler, P.
House is Not a Home, A
Heinemann
PAR (US) 1964 dir. Russel Rouse

Adler, R. and Ross, J. Wallop, D
Year the Yankees Lost the Pennant, The
P
Damn Yankees
WAR (US) 1958 dir. George Abbott,
Stanley Donen
GB title: What Lola Wants
M, V

Adler, W.
Sunset Gang, The
Viking Press
AM PLAY (US) 1991 dir. Calvin Skaggs,
Tony Drazan
TVSe(US)

Adler, W.
War of the Roses, The
New American Library
FOX (US) 1989 dir. Danny de Vito
V

Agee, J.
Death in the Family, A
McDowell, Obolensky
All the Way Home
PAR (US) 1963 dir. Alex Segal
PAR (US) 1971 dir. Fred Coe
TV (US)

Ahlberg, A.
Woof
Viking Kestrel
CENTRAL (GB) 1990
dir. David Cobham
Ch, TVSe(GB)

Aiken, J.
Wolves of Willoughby Chase, The
Doubleday
ZENITH (GB) 1988 dir. Stuart Orme

Ainsworth, H.
Rookwood
Rittenhouse Press (Philadelphia)
Dick Turpin
STOLL-STAFFORD (GB) 1933
dir. Victor Hanbury, JohnStafford

Akae, B.
Irezumi: The Spirit of Tattoo
DAIEI (Jap) 1983
dir. Yoichi Takabayashi
V

Akins, Z.
Morning Glory
P
RKO (US) 1933 dir. Lowell Sherman
V

Akins, Z.
Stage Struck
P
Samuel French
RKO (US) 1957 dir. Sidney Lumet
V

Aladar, L.
Honest Finder, The
Trouble in Paradise
PAR (US) 1932 dir. Ernst Lubitsch

Albaret, C.
Monsieur Proust
McGraw-Hill
Celeste
PEL (W. Ger) 1981 dir. Percy Adlon

Albee, E.
Ballad of the Sad Café, The
P
Dramatists Play Service
MERCHANT IVORY/HOBO (US/GB)
1991 dir. Simon Callow

Albee, E.
Delicate Balance, A
P
Samuel French
SEVEN KEYS (US) 1975
dir. Tony Richardson

Albee, E.
Who's Afraid of Virginia Woolf?
P
Atheneum
WAR (US) 1966 dir. Mike Nichols
V

Albert, M. H.
Apache Rising
Muller

Duel at Diablo
UA (US) 1966 dir. Ralph Nelson

Albert, M. H.
Don is Dead, The
Coronet

UN (US) 1973 dir. Richard Fleischer
V

Albert, M. H.
Lady in Cement
FOX (US) 1968 dir. Gordon Douglas

Albert, M. H.
Man in Black, The
Rough Night in Jericho
UN (US) 1967 dir. Arnold Laven

Albert, M. H.
Miami Mayhem
Tony Rome
FOX (US) 1967 dir. Gordon Douglas

Albrand, M.
Desperate Moment
Chatto & Windus

GFD (GB) 1953 dir. Compton Bennett

Albrand, M.
Dishonoured
Random House

Captain Carey USA
PAR (US) 1950 dir. Mitchell Leisen
GB title: After Midnight

Alcock, V.
Travellers by Night
Delacorte Press

TVS (GB) 1985
Ch, TVSe(GB)

Alcott, L. M.
Little Men
Various

RKO (US) 1935 dir. Philip Rosen
V

Alcott, L. M.
Little Women
Various

RKO (US) 1933 dir. George Cukor
MGM (US) 1948 dir. Mervyn Le Roy
V
UN (US) 1978 dir. David Lowell Rich
TVSe(US)

Alcu, Y.
MacArthur's Children
ORION (Jap) 1985
dir. Masahiro Shinoda
V

Aldington, R.
All Men are Enemies
Heinemann

FOX (US) 1934 dir. George Fitzmaurice

Aldiss, B.
Frankenstein Unbound
Random House

TCF (US) 1990 dir. Roger Corman
V

Aldrich, B. S.
Silent Stars Go By, The
Gift of Love, The: A Christmas Story
TELECOM (US) 1983
dir. Delbert Mann
TV(US)

Aldrich, Mrs B.
Miss Bishop
Grosset & Dunlap

Cheers for Miss Bishop
PAR (US) 1941 dir. Tom Garnett
V

Aldridge, J.
Captive in the Land, A
Doubleday
GLORIA/GORKY (US/USSR) 1991
dir. John Berry

Aldridge, J.
Sporting Proposition, A
Ride a Wild Pony
DISNEY (Aust) 1976 dir. Don Chaffey
V

Aldrin, Jr., E. and Warga, W.
Return to Earth
Random House
KH (US) 1976 dir. Jud Taylor
TV(US), V

Alexander, K.
Private Investigation, A
Delacorte Press
Missing Pieces
TTC (US) 1983 dir. Mike Hodges
TV(US)

Alexander, K. & Hayes, S.
Time After Time
Delacorte Press
WAR (US) 1979 dir. Nicholas Meyer
V

Alexander, L.
Chronicles of Prydain, The
Summit Books
Black Cauldron, The
DISNEY (US) 1985 dirs. Ted Berman
and Richard Rich
A, Ch

Alexander, R.
Time Out for Ginger
P
Dramatists Play Service
Billie
UA (US) 1965 dir. Don Weis

Alexander, S.
Nutcracker: Money, Madness,
Murder: A Family Album
Doubleday
Nutcracker: Money, Madness and Murder
WAR TV (US) 1987 dir. Paul Bogart
TVSe(US)

Algren, N.
Man with the Golden Arm, The
Doubleday
UA (US) 1955 dir. Otto Preminger
V

Algren, N.
Walk on the Wild Side, A
Farrar, Straus & Cudahy
COL (US) 1962 dir. Edward Dmytryk
V

Ali, J.
Dark Days and Light Nights
P
Black Joy
WINCAST/WEST ONE (GB) 1977
dir. Anthony Simmons

Ali, M.
Greatest, The
COL-WAR (US/GB) 1977 dir. Tom Gries
V

Alibrandi, T. and Armani, F. H.
Privileged Information
Dodd, Mead
Sworn to Silence
BLATT/SINGER (US) 1987
dir. Peter Levin
TV(US)

Allan, N.
Lies My Father Told Me
New American Library
COL (Can) 1975 dir. Jan Kadar

Allan, T.
Love Streams
P

CANNON (US) 1984
dir. John Cassavetes
V

Allardice, J.
At War with the Army
P
Samuel French
PAR (US) 1951 dir. Hal Walker
V

Allen, H.
Anthony Adverse
Farrar & Rinehart
WAR (US) 1936 dir. Mervyn Le Roy
V

Allen, J. and Livingston, M.
Thanks God, I'll Take it From Here

Without Reservations
RKO (US) 1946 dir. Mervyn Le Roy
V

Allen, J.
Nu

Tumult
ATHENA (Den) 1970
dir. Hans Abramson

Allen, J. P.
First Wife, The
P

Wives and Lovers
PAR (US) 1963 dir. John Rich

Allen, J. P.
Just Tell Me What You Want
Dutton
WAR (US) 1980 dir. Sidney Lumet
V

Allen, W.
Don't Drink the Water
P
Samuel French
AVCO EMBASSY (US) 1969
dir. Howard Morris
V

Allen, W.
Play it Again, Sam
P
Samuel French
PAR (US) 1972 dir. Herbert Ross
V

Allfrey, P. S.
Orchid House, The
BBC (GB) 1991 dir. Harold Ove
TV(GB)

Allingham, M.
Tiger in the Smoke
Doubleday
RANK (GB) 1956 dir. Roy Baker

Allison, W. and Fairley, J.
Monocled Mutineer, The
BBC (GB) 1986
TVSe(GB)

Allister, R.
Friese-Greene
Marsland
Magic Box, The
BL (GB) 1951 dir. John Boulting
V

Altieri, Major J.
Darby's Rangers
WAR (US) 1957 dir. William Wellman
GB title: Young Invaders, The

Amado, J.
Dona Flor and her Two Husbands
Knopf
FD (Braz) 1977 dir. Bruno Barretto
V

Amado, J.
Gabriela, Clove and Cinnamon
Editora Record (Rio de Janeiro)
Gabriela
MGM/UA (Port) 1984
dir. Bruno Barreto
V

Amateau, R. and Robinson, B.
Operator, The
Where Does it Hurt?
HEMDALE (US) 1971 dir. Rod Amateau
V

Ambler, E.
Care of Time, The
Farrar, Straus & Giroux
ANGLIA (GB) (1990)
TV(GB)

Ambler, E.
Epitaph for a Spy
Doubleday
Hotel Reserve
RKO (GB) 1944 dir. Victor Hanbury

Ambler, E.
Journey into Fear
Knopf
RKO (US) 1942 dir. Norman Foster, Orson Welles
V

Ambler, E.
Light of Day, The
Knopf
Topkapi
UA (US) 1964 dir. Jules Dassin
V

Ambler, E.
Mask of Dimitrios, The
Ballantine Books
WAR (US) 1944 dir. Jean Negulesco

Ambler, E.
October Man, The
GFD (GB) 1947 dir. Roy Baker
V

Ambler, E.
Uncommon Danger
Hodder & Stoughton (London)
Background to Danger
WAR (US) 1943 dir. Raoul Walsh

Amen, C.
Last Testament, The
Testament
PAR (US) 1983 dir. Lynne Littman
V

Ames, D.
She Shall Have Murder
BL (GB) 1950 dir. Daniel Birt

Amis, K.
Green Man, The
Harcourt, Brace & World
BBC (GB) 1991 dir. Elijah Moshinsky
TV(GB)

Amis, K.
Lucky Jim
Doubleday
BL (GB) 1957 dir. John Boulting
V

Amis, K.
Take a Girl Like You
Gollancz (London)
COL (GB) 1969 dir. Jonathan Miller
V

Amis, K.
That Uncertain Feeling
Harcourt Brace
Only Two Can Play
BL (GB) 1961 dir. Sidney Gilliat
V

Amis, M.
Rachel Papers, The
Harmony Books
UA (GB) 1989 dir. Damian Harris

Anders, P.
Summer with Monika
SVENSK (Swe) 1952
dir. Ingmar Bergman
V

Andersen, H. C.
Emperor's New Clothes, The
Various
CANNON (US) 1987 dir. David Irving
Ch

Andersen, H. C.
Little Match Girl, The
Various
NBC (US) 1987
dir. Michael Lindsay-Hogg
Ch, TV(US), V

Andersen, H. C.
Little Mermaid, The
Various
DISNEY (US) 1989 dir. John Musker,
Ron Clements
A, Ch, M, V

Anderson, E.
Thieves Like Us
UA (US) 1974 dir. Robert Altman

Anderson, J.
Assault and Matrimony
Doubleday
NBC (US) 1987 dir. James Frawley
TV(US)

Anderson, L.
Sky has Many Colours, The
Lili Marleen
ROXY (Ger) 1980
dir. Rainer Werner Fassbinder
V

Anderson, M.
Anne of the Thousand Days
P
Dramatists Play Service
UN (GB) 1969 dir. Charles Jarrot
V

Anderson, M.
Barefoot in Athens
P
Sloane Associates
COMPASS (US) 1966
dir. George Schaefer
TV(US), V

Anderson, M.
Elizabeth the Queen
P
Samuel French
COMPASS (US) 1968
dir. George Schaefer
TV(US), V

Anderson, M.
Elizabeth the Queen
P
Samuel French
Private Lives of Elizabeth and Essex, The
WAR (US) 1939 dir. Michael Curtiz
V

Anderson, M.
Eve of St. Mark, The
P
W. Sloane Associates
FOX (US) 1944 dir. John M. Stahl

Anderson, M.
Joan of Lorraine
P
Dramatists Play Service
Joan of Arc
RKO (US) 1948 dir. Victor Fleming
V

Anderson, M.
Key Largo
P
Anderson House (Washington, D.C.)
WAR (US) 1948 dir. John Huston
V

Anderson, M.
Mary of Scotland
P
Samuel French
RKO (US) 1936 dir. John Ford

Anderson, M.
Saturday's Children
P
WAR (US) 1940 dir. Vincent Sherman

Anderson, M.
Winterset
P
Harcourt Brace
RKO (US) 1936 dir. Alfred Santell
V
COMPASS (US) 1959
dir. George Schaefer
TV(US)

Anderson, M. and Casella, A.
Death Takes a Holiday
P
Samuel French
PAR (US) 1934 dir. Mitchell Leisen
UN TV (US) 1971 dir. Robert Butler
TV(US)

Anderson, M. and Stallings, L.
What Price Glory?
P
Harcourt, Brace & Co.
FOX (US) 1952 dir. John Ford
V

Anderson, P.
Nurse
St. Martins Press
HALMI (US) 1980
dir. David Lowell Rich
TV(US)

Anderson, P.
President's Mistress, The
Simon & Schuster
KINGS RD (US) 1978
dir. John Llewellyn
TV(US), V

Anderson, R.
Silent Night, Lonely Night
P
Samuel French
UNTV (US) 1969 dir. Daniel Petrie
TV(US), V

Anderson, R.
Tea and Sympathy
P
Samuel French
MGM (US) 1956 dir. Vincente Minnelli

Anderson, R. W.
I Never Sang for my Father
P
Dramatists Play Service
COL (US) 1970 dir. Gilbert Cates
V

Anderson, V.
Beware of Children
No Kidding
AA (GB) 1960 dir. Gerald Thomas
US title: Beware of Children

Anderson, W. C.
Hurricane Hunters
Hurricane
METRO (US) 1974 dir. Jerry Jameson
TV(US)

Andrevan, J-P.
Robots Against Gandahar

Light Years
MIRAMAX (Fr) 1988 dir. René Laloux
A, V

Andrew, R. H.
Great Day in the Morning
Norton
RKO (US) 1955 dir. Jacques Tourneur
V

Andrews, M. R.
Perfect Tribute, The
C. Scribner's Sons
P&G (US) 1991 dir. Jack Bender
TV(US)

Andrews, V. C.
Flowers in the Attic
Pocket Books
NEW WORLD (US) 1987
dir. Jeffrey Bloom
V

Andrzejewski, J.
Ashes and Diamonds
POLSKI (Pol) 1958 dir. Andrzej Wajda
V

Anet, C.
Mayerling
NERO (Fr) 1935 dir. Anatole Litvak
WAR (Fr/GB) 1968 dir. Terence Young

Angelou, M.
I Know Why the Caged Bird Sings
Random House
TOMORROW INC. (US) 1979
dir. Fielder Cook
TV(US)

Angerson, W. C.
BAT 21
Prentice-Hall
TRI STAR (US) 1988 dir. Peter Markle
V

Annixter, P.
Swift Water

Those Calloways
DISNEY (US) 1964 dir. Norman Tokar
V

Anon.
Sir Gawain and the Green Knight
Various

Gawain and the Green Knight
THAMES (GB) 1990 dir. J. M. Phillips
TV(GB)

Anouilh, J.
Becket
P
Samuel French
PAR (GB) 1963 dir. Peter Glenville
V

Anouilh, J.
Lark, The
P
Random House
MILBERG (US) 1957
dir. George Schaefer
TV(US)

Anouilh, J.
Time Remembered
P
Samuel French
COMPASS (US) 1961
dir. George Schaefer
TV(US)

Anouilh, J.
Waltz of the Toreadors
P
Samuel French
RANK (GB) 1962 dir. John Guillermin
V

Anson, J.
Amityville Horror, The
Prentice-Hall
AIP (US) 1979 dir. Stuart Rosenberg
V

Anson, R. A.
Best Intentions: The Education and Killing of Edmund Perry
Random House

Murder Without Motive: The Edmund Perry Story
LEONARD HILL FILMS (US) 1992
dir. Kevin Hooks
TV(US)

Anstey, F.
Brass Bottle, The
Murray

RANK (US) 1964 dir. Harry Keller

Anstey, F.
Tinted Venus
Goddess of Love, The
NEW WORLD TV (US) 1988
dir. James Drake
TV(US)

Anstey, F.
Vice Versa
TC (GB) 1948 dir. Peter Ustinov

Anthelme, P.
I Confess
P
WAR (US) 1953 dir. Alfred Hitchcock
V

Anthony, C. L.
Service
P
Samuel French
Looking Forward
MGM (US) 1933 dir. Clarence Brown

Anthony, C.L.
Autumn Crocus
P
Samuel French
BI (GB) 1934 dir. Basil Dearden

Anthony, D.
Midnight Lady and the Mourning Man
Midnight Man, The
UN (US) 1974 dir. Roland Kibbee

Anthony, E.
Tamarind Seed, The
Dell Publishing Co.
SCOTIA-BARBER (GB) 1974
dir. Blake Edwards
V

Antoine, W. P.
L'Ennemie
P
Tendre Ennemie
WORLD (Fr) 1938 dir. Max Ophuls

Appel, B.
Fortress in the Rice
Bobbs-Merrill
Cry of Battle
WAR (US) 1964 dir. Irving Lerner
V

Appel, D.
Comanche
Tonka
DISNEY (US) 1958 dir. Lewis R. Foster
V

Arbuzov, A.
Promise, The
P
Oxford Univ. Press
COMM (GB) 1969 dir. Michael Hayes

Archard, M.
Alibi
CORONA (GB) 1942
dir. Brian Desmond Hirst

Archer, J.
First Among Equals
Simon & Schuster
ITV (GB) 1986
TV(GB)

Archer, J.
Kane and Abel
Simon & Schuster
EMBASSY (US) 1985 dir. Buzz Kulik
TVSe(US), V

Archer, J.
Not a Penny More, Not a Penny
Less
Doubleday
BBC (GB) 1990 dir. Clive Donner
TVSe(GB)

Archer, W.
Green Goddess, The
P
WAR (US) 1930 dir. Alfred E. Green

Archer, W.
Green Goddess, The
P
Samuel French
Adventure in Iraq
WAR (US) 1943 dir. D. Ross-Lederman

Ardies, T.
Kosygin is Coming
Russian Roulette
ITC (US) 1975 dir. Lon Lombardo
V

Ardrey, R.
Thunder Rock
P
Atheneum
MGM (GB) 1942 dir. Roy Boulting

Arent, A.
One Third of a Nation
P
PAR (US) 1939 dir. Dudley Murphy

Arianet, C.
Love in the Afternoon
AA (US) 1957 dir. Billy Wilder
V

Arjourni, J.
Happy Birthday, Turke!
SENATOR FILMS (Ger) 1992
dir. Dorris Dorrie

Arkell, R.
Charley Moon
BL (GB) 1956 dir. Guy Hamilton

Arlen, M.
Golden Arrow
P
WAR (US) 1936 dir. Alfred E. Green

Arlen, M.
Green Hat, The
Grosset & Dunlap
Outcast Lady
MGM (US) 1934 dir. Robert Z. Leonard
GB title: Woman of the World, A

Arley, C.
Woman of Straw
UA (GB) 1964 dir. Basil Dearden

Arlington, A.
These, Our Strangers
Those Kids from Town
BN (GB) 1941 dir. Lance Comfort

Armandy, A.
Renegades
FOX (US) 1930 dir. Victor Fleming

Armbrister, T.
Act of Vengeance
Saturday Review Press
LORIMAR (US) 1986
dir. John MacKenzie
TV(US)

Armont, P. and Gerbidon, M.
Coiffeur Pour Dames
P
HOCHE (Fr) 1952 dir. Jean Boyer
GB title: Artist with Ladies, An

Armstrong, A.
He was Found in the Road
Man in the Road, The
GN (GB) 1956 dir. Lance Comfort

Armstrong, A.
Ten Minute Alibi
P
BL (GB) 1935 dir. Bernard Vorhaus

Armstrong, C.
Case of the Three Weird Sisters, The
Three Weird Sisters, The
BN (GB) 1948 dir. Dan Birt

Armstrong, C.
Mischief
Coward-McCann
Don't Bother to Knock
FOX (US) 1952 dir. Roy Ward Baker
V

Armstrong, C.
Mischief
Coward-McCann
Sitter, The
FNM (US) 1991 dir. Rick Berger
TV(US)

Armstrong, C.
Talk About a Stranger
MGM (US) 1952 dir. David Bradley

Armstrong, C.
Unsuspected, The
Coward-McCann
WAR (US) 1947 dir. Michael Curtiz

Armstrong, R.
Passage Home
GFD (GB) 1955 dir. Roy Baker

Armstrong, T.
Crowthers of Bankdam, The
Master of Bankdam
ALL (GB) 1947 dir. Walter Forde

Armstrong, W. H.
Sounder
Harper & Row
FOX (US) 1972 dir. Martin Ritt
V

Arnaud, G.
Wages of Fear, The
Sorcerer
UN (US) 1977 dir. William Friedkin
GB title: Wages of Fear

Arnaud, G.
Wages of Fear
FDF (Fr/It) 1953
dir. Henri-Georges Clouzot
V

Arnold, E.
Blood Brother
Duell, Sloan & Pearce
Broken Arrow
FOX (US) 1950 dir. Delmer Daves
V

Arnold, E.
Commandos, The
First Comes Courage
COL (US) 1943 dir. Dorothy Arzner

Arnold, E.
Deep in my Heart
Duell, Sloan & Pearce
MGM (US) 1954 dir. Stanley Donen
M, V

Arnold, E.
Flight from Ashiya
Knopf
UA (US/Jap) 1963
dir. Michael Anderson

Arnow, A.
Dollmaker, The
Macmillan
IPC (US) 1984 dir. Daniel Petrie
TV(US), V

Arrighi, M.
Alter Ego
St. Martins Press
Murder by the Book
ORION TV (US) 1987 dir. Mel Damski
TV(US)

Arsan, E.
Emmanuelle
SF (Fr) 1975 dir. Just Jacklin
V

Arsan, E.
Néa
NEW REALM (Fr/Ger) 1976
dir. Nelly Kaplan
US/GB title: Young Emanuelle
V

Arthur, R. A.
Edge of the City
P
MGM (US) 1957 dir. Martin Ritt
GB title: Man is Ten Feet Tall, A

Arundel, E.
Persistent Warrior, The
Green Fingers
BN (GB) 1946 dir. John Harlow

Asche, O. and Norton, F.
Chu Chin Chow
P
GAU (GB) 1934 dir. Walter Forde
M

Ashford, D.
Young Visitors, The
Doran
CHANNEL 4 (GB) 1984 dir. James Hill

Ashman, H. and Menken, A.
Little Shop of Horrors
P
Samuel French
WAR (US) 1986 dir. Frank Oz
M, V

Ashton, H.
Yeoman's Hospital
White Corridors
GFD (GB) 1951 dir. Pat Jackson

Ashton-Warner, S.
Spinster
Simon & Schuster
Two Loves
MGM (US) 1961 dir. Charles Walters
GB title: Spinster

Ashton-Warner, S.
Teacher, I Passed This Way
Simon & Schuster;Knopf
Sylvia
ENT (NZ) 1985 dir. Michael Firth
V

Asimov, I.
Nightfall
Doubleday
CONCORDE (US) 1988
dir. Paul Mayersburg
V

Asinof, E.
Eight Men Out
ORION (US) 1988 dir. John Sayles
V

Asinof, E., Hinckle, W. & Turner, W.
Ten-Second Jailbreak, The
Holt, Rinehart & Winston
Breakout
COL (US) 1975 dir. Tom Gries
V

Athanas, V.
Proud Ones, The
FOX (US) 1956 dir. Robert D. Webb

Atkins, Z.
Greeks had a Word for Them, The
P
UA (US) 1932 dir. Lowell Sherman

Atkinson, E.
Greyfriar's Bobby
Harper

Challenge to Lassie
MGM (US) 1949 dir. Richard Thorpe

Atkinson, H.
Games, The
Simon & Schuster

FOX (GB) 1969 dir. Michael Winner
V

Attiwill, K.
Sky Steward

Non Stop New York
GFD (GB) 1937 dir. Robert Stevenson

Atwood, M.
Handmaid's Tale, The
Houghton, Mifflin Co. (Boston)

CINECOM (US) 1990
dir. Volker Schlondorff

Auel, J. M.
Clan of the Cave Bear, The
Crown Publishers

WAR (US) 1986 dir. Michael Chapman
V

Auel, J. M.
Valley of the Horses
Crown

PSO 1984
TV

Auque, R. and Forestier, P.
Hors La Vie

BAC (Fr/It/Bel) 1991
dir. Maroun Bagdadi

Austen, J.
Mansfield Park
Various

BBC (GB) 1986 dir. David Giles
TVSe(GB), V

Austen, J.
Northanger Abbey
Various

BBC (GB) 1987 dir. Giles Foster
TV(GB)

Austen, J.
Persuasion
Various

GRANADA TV (GB) 1969
dir. Howard Baker
TVSe(GB)

Austen, J.
Pride and Prejudice
Various

MGM (US) 1940 dir. Robert Z. Leonard
V
BBC (GB) 1980 dir. Cyril Coke
TVSe(GB)

Austin, A.
Wicked Woman, A
MGM (US) 1934 dir. Charles Brabin

Axelrod, G.
Goodbye Charlie
P
Samuel French

FOX (US) 1964 dir. Vincente Minnelli

Axelrod, G.
Seven Year Itch, The
P
Random House

FOX (US) 1955 dir. Billy Wilder
V

Axelrod, G.
Will Success Spoil Rock Hunter?
P
Samuel French

FOX (US) 1957 dir. Frank Tashlin
GB title: Oh! For a Man!

Axelson, M. M.
Life Begins
P
WAR (US) 1932 dir. James Flood
GB title: Dream of Life

Axelson, Mrs M. M.
Child is Born, A
P
Chadwell, Idaho
WAR (US) 1939 dir. Lloyd Bacon

Ayckbourn, A.
Chorus of Disapproval, A.
P
Samuel French
HOBO (GB) 1989 dir. Michael Winner

Ayres, H.
Common Touch, The
BN (GB) 1941 dir. John Baxter

B

Baber, D.
My Death is a Mockery
ADELPHI (GB) 1952 dir. Tony Young

Babson, M.
Bejewelled Death
Walker
Bejewelled
DISNEY CH (US/GB) 1991
dir. Terry Marcel
TV(GB/US)

Bacchelli, R.
Mill on the Po, The
Pantheon Books
LUX (It) 1949 dir. Alberto Lattuardo

Bach, R.
Jonathan Livingstone Seagull
Avon Books
PAR (US) 1973 dir. Hill Bartlett
V

Bachman, R.
Running Man, The
New American Library
TRI-STAR (US) 1987
dir. Paul Michael Glaser
V

Bachmann, L.
Kiss of Death
Devil Makes Three, The
MGM (US) 1952 dir. Andrew Marton

Bachmann, L.
Phoenix, The
Ten Seconds to Hell
UA (US) 1959 dir. Robert Aldrich

Bacon, F. and Smith, W.
Lightnin'
P
Samuel French
FOX (US) 1930 dir. Henry King

Bagley, D.
Freedom Trap, The
Doubleday
Mackintosh Man, The
COL-WAR (GB) 1973 dir. John Huston
V

Bagnold, E.
Chalk Garden, The
Random House
RANK (GB) 1963 dir. Ronald Neame
V

Bagnold, E.
National Velvet
Morrow
MGM (US) 1944 dir. Clarence Brown
V

Bailly, A.
Flame and the Flesh, The
MGM (US) 1954 dir. Richard Brooks

Baily, L.
Gilbert and Sullivan and Their World
Viking Press
Story of Gilbert and Sullivan, The
BL (GB) 1953 dir. Sidney Gilliatt

Bainbridge, B.
Dressmaker, The
George Braziller
FILM 4 (GB) 1988 dir. Jim O'Brien

Bainbridge, B.
Sweet William
G. Braziller
ITC (GB) 1980 dir. Claude Whatham
V

Baird, M. T.
Lesson in Love, A
Houghton, Mifflin Co. (Boston)
Circle of Two
BORDEAUX (Can) 1980
dir. Jules Dassin
V

Baker, C.
Ernest Hemingway: A Life Story
Scribners
Hemingway
WILSON (US) 1988
dir. Bernhard Sinkel
TVSe(US)

Baker, D.
Young Man with a Horn
Houghton, Mifflin Co. (Boston)
WAR (US) 1950 dir. Michael Curtiz
GB title: Young Man of Music
V

Baker, E.
Fine Madness, A
Putnam
WAR (US) 1966 dir. Irvin Kershner
V

Baker, F.
Lease of Life
EAL (GB) 1954 dir. Charles Frend

Baker, L.
Her Twelve Men
McGraw-Hill, N.Y.
MGM (US) 1954 dir. Robert Z. Leonard

Baker, T. and Jones, R.
Coffee, Tea or Me?
CBS ENT. (US) 1983
dir. Norman Panama
TV(US)

Balazs, J.
Hungarians
IFEX (Hun) 1981 dir. Zoltan Fabri

Balchin, N.
Mine Own Executioner
Collins (London)
Bl (GB) 1947 dir. Anthony Kimmins
V

Balchin, N.
Small Back Room, The
Doubleday

LF (GB) 1949 dir. Michael Powell,
Emeric Pressburger
US title: Hour of Glory

Balchin, N.
Sort of Traitor, A

Suspect
BL (GB) 1960 dir. Roy Boulting

Balderston, J. L.
Berkeley Square
P

Samuel French

FOX (US) 1933 dir. Frank Lloyd
MILBERG (US) 1959
dir. George Schaefer
TV(US)

Balderston, J. L.
Berkeley Square
P

Samuel French

House in the Square, The
FOX (GB) 1951 dir. Roy Baker
US title: I'll Never Forget You

Balderston, J. L. and Deane,
H.
Dracula
P

Samuel French

CIC (GB) 1979 dir. John Badham
V

Baldwin, F.
Beauty
Thorndike Press (Thorndike, Maine)

Beauty for Sale
MGM (US) 1933
dir. Richard Boleslawski

Baldwin, F.
Men are Such Fools

WAR (US) 1938 dir. Busby Berkeley

Baldwin, F.
Moon's Our Home, The
PAR (US) 1936 dir. William A. Seiter
V

Baldwin, F.
Portia on Trial
REP (US) 1937 dir. George Nicholls, Jr.

Baldwin, F.
Skyscraper
Skyscraper Souls
MGM (US) 1932 dir. Edgar Selwyn

Baldwin, F.
Spinster Dinner
Love Before Breakfast
UN (US) 1936 dir. Walter Lang

Baldwin, F.
Wife Vs. Secretary
MGM (US) 1936 dir. Clarence Brown

Baldwin, J.
Go Tell It On The Mountain
Dial Press

PRICE (US) 1985 dir. Stan Latham
TV

Ball, J.
In the Heat of the Night
V
Harper & Row

UA (US) 1967 dir. Norman Jewison
V

Ballard, J. G.
Empire of the Sun
Simon & Schuster

WAR (US) 1987 dir. Steven Spielberg
V

Ballinger, W. S.
Rafferty
Pushover
COL (US) 1954 dir. Richard Quine

Balmer, E. and Wylie, P.
When Worlds Collide
Lippincott (Philadelphia)
PAR (US) 1951 dir. Rudolph Maté
V

Balzac, H. de
Belle Noiseuse, La
Various
FR3 (Fr) 1991 dir. Jacques Rivette

Bancroft, G. P.
Ware Case, The
P
EAL (GB) 1938 dir. Robert Stevenson

Banks, L. R.
L-Shaped Room, The
Simon & Schuster
BL (GB) 1962 dir. Bryan Forbes

Banks, P.
Carriage Entrance
My Forbidden Past
RKO (US) 1951 dir. Robert Stevenson
V

Banks, P.
January Heights
Great Lie, The
WAR (US) 1941 dir. Edmund Goulding

Bannerjee, B. B.
Pather Panchali
Indiana University Press (Bloomington, Indiana)
SAT. RAY (Ind) 1955 dir. Satyajit Ray
V

Barak, M.
Enigma
Morrow
EMBASSY (GB/Fr) 1983
dir. Jeannot Szwarc
V

Barbach, L.
Pleasures
Doubleday
COL TV (US) 1986 dir. Sharron Miller

Barber, A.
Ghosts, The
Farrar, Straus & Girouy
Amazing Mr Blunden, The
HEMDALE (GB) 1972
dir. Lionel Jeffries
Ch, V

Barber, E.O.
Jenny Angel
Macmillan
Angel Baby
CONT DIS (US) 1960 dir. Paul Wendkos

Barber, R.
Night They Raided Minsky's, The
UA (US) 1968 dir. William Friedkin
GB title: Night They Invented Striptease, The
V

Bard, M.
Doctor Wears Three Faces, The
Mother Didn't Tell Me
FOX (US) 1950 dir. Claude Binyon

Bardawil, G.
Do You Like Women?
FRANCORITZ (Fr/It) 1964
dir. Jean Leon

Barfoot, J.
Dancing in the Dark
CAN BC (Can) 1986 dir. Leon Marr
V

Barillet, P. and Gredy, J-P.
Forty Carats
P
Samuel French
COL (US) 1973 dir. Milton Katselas

Barker, C.
Cabal
Poseidon Press
Nightbreed
FOX (US) 1990 dir. Clive Barker

Barker, C.
Hellbound Heart, The
Hellraiser
CINEMARQUE (GB) 1987
dir. Clive Barker
V

Barker, P.
Union Street
Putnam
Stanley and Iris
MGM (US) 1990 dir. Martin Ritt

Barker, R.
Thousand Plan, The
1,000 Plane Raid, The
UA (GB) 1969 dir. Boris Sagal

Barkley, D.
Freeway
Macmillan
NEW WORLD (US) 1988
dir. Francis Delia

Barlow, J.
Burden of Proof, The
Villain
EMI (GB) 1971 dir. Michael Tuchner

Barlow, J.
Term of Trial
Simon & Schuster
WAR (GB) 1962 dir. Peter Glenville

Barnes, J.
Evita: First Lady
Evita Peron
ZEPHYR (US) 1981
dir. Marvin Chomsky
TVSe(US)

Barnes, M. A.
Murder in Coweta County
T. Y. Crowell
TELECOM (US) 1983 dir. Gary Nelson
TV(US)

Barnes, M. A.
Westward Passage
Houghton, Mifflin Co. (Boston)
RKO (US) 1932 dir. Robert Milton

Barnes, P.
Ruling Class, The
P
Samuel French
KEEP (GB) 1971 dir. Peter Medak
V

Baron, A
Human Kind, The
Victors, The
BL (GB) 1963 dir. Carl Foreman

Barr, G.
Epitaph for an Enemy
Harper
Up From the Beach
FOX (US) 1965 dir. Robert Parrish

Barrasch, N. and Moore, C.
Send me No Flowers
P
Samuel French
UN (US) 1964 dir. Norman Jewison
V

Barrett, M.
Appointments in Zahrein
Pen
Escape from Zahrein
PAR (US) 1962 dir. Ronald Neame

Barrett, M.
Heroes of Yucca, The
Hale
Invincible Six, The
MOULIN ROUGE (US/Iran) 1970
dir. Jean Negulesco

Barrett, M.
Reward, The
FOX (US) 1965 dir. Serge Bourgignon

Barrett, W.
Sign of the Cross, The
P
PAR (US) 1932 dir. Cecil B. de Mille

Barrett, W. E.
Left Hand of God, The
Corgi
FOX (US) 1955 dir. Edward Dmytryk
V

Barrett, W. E.
Lilies of the Field, The
Doubleday
UA (US) 1963 dir. Ralph Nelson
V

Barrett, W. E.
Wine and the Music, The
Doubleday
Pieces of Dreams
UA (US) 1970 dir. Daniel Haller

Barrie, Sir J. M.
Admirable Crichton, The
P
Samuel French

COL (GB) 1957 dir. Lewis Gilbert
US title: Paradise Lagoon
COMPASS (US) 1968
dir. George Schaefer
TV(US)

Barrie, Sir J. M.
Admirable Crichton, The
P
Samuel French
We're Not Dressing
PAR (US) 1934 dir. Norman Taurog

Barrie, Sir J. M.
Alice Sit-by-the-Fire
P
Samuel French
Darling, How Could You
PAR (US) 1951 dir. Mitchell Leisen
GB title: Rendezvous

Barrie, Sir J. M.
Little Minister, The
P
Scribners
RKO (US) 1934 dir. Richard Wallace
V

Barrie, Sir J. M.
Old Lady Shows Her Medals, The
P
Samuel French
Seven Days' Leave
PAR (US) 1930 dir. Richard Wallace
GB title: Medals

Barrie, Sir J. M.
Quality Street
P
Samuel French
RKO (US) 1937 dir. George Stevens

Barrie, Sir J. M.
Rosalind
P
Forever Female
PAR (US) 1953 dir. Irving Rapper

Barrie, Sir J. M.
What Every Woman Knows
P
Samuel French
MGM (US) 1934 dir. Gregory La Cava

Barrie, Sir J. M.; (and Leigh, C. Comden, B. and Green, A.1955 only)
Peter Pan
P

DISNEY (US) 1953 dir. Ben Sharpsteen
A, V
NBC (US) 1955 dir. Michael Kidd
M, TV(US), V
ATV (GB) 1976 dir. Dwight Hemion
TV(GB)

Barringer, E. D.
Bowery to Bellevue
Norton, N.Y.

Girl in White, The
MGM (US) 1952 dir. John Sturges
GB title: So Bright the Flame

Barringer, M.
Inquest
P

CHARTER (GB) 1939 dir. Roy Boulting

Barrington, P.
Account Rendered
Barker

RANK (GB) 1957
dir. Peter Graham Scott

Barry, D.
Whales of August, The
P

ALIVE (US) 1987 dir. Lindsay Anderson
V

Barry, J.
Lenny
P
Random House, N.Y.

UA (US) 1974 dir. Bob Fosse
V

Barry, J.
Moi, Ma Soeur

Invitation au Voyage
TRIUMPH (Fr) 1983
dir. Peter Del Monte
V

Barry, P.
Animal Kingdom, The
P
Samuel French

RKO (US) 1932 dir. Edward H. Griffith
GB title: Woman in His House, The

Barry, P.
Animal Kingdom, The
P
Samuel French

One More Tomorrow
WAR (US) 1946 dir. Peter Godfrey

Barry, P.
Holiday
P
Samuel French

PATHE (US) 1930
dir. Edward H. Griffith
COL (US) 1938 dir. George Cukor
GB title: Free to Live
V

Barry, P.
Philadelphia Story, The
P
Samuel French

MGM (US) 1940 dir. George Cukor
V

Barry, P.
Philadelphia Story, The
P
Samuel French

High Society
MGM (US) 1956 dir. Charles Walters
M, V

Barry, P.
Tomorrow and Tomorrow
P
Samuel French

PAR (US) 1932 dir. Richard Wallace

Barry, P.
Without Love
P

MGM (US) 1945 dir. Harold S. Bucquet

Barrymore, D. and Frank, G.
Too Much, Too Soon
Holt
WAR (US) 1958 dir. Art Napoleon

Barstow, S.
Brother's Tale, A
Corgi
GRANADA (GB) 1983 dir. Les Chatfield
TVSe(GB)

Barstow, S.
Kind of Loving, A
AA (GB) 1962 dir. John Schlesinger
V

Barth, J.
End of the Road
ALLIED (US) 1970 dir. Aram Avakian
V

Barth, R.
Rag Bag Clan, The
Dial Press
Small Killing, A
MOTOWN (US) 1981
dir. Steven Hilliard Stern
TV(US)

Barthel, J.
Death in California, A.
Congdom & Lattes
LORIMAR (US) 1985 dir. Delbert Mann
TVSe(US)

Barthel, J.
Death in Canaan, A.
Dutton
WAR (US) 1978 dir. Tony Richardson
TV(US)

Bartlett, L. V. S.
Adios
Murray
Lash, The
IN (US) 1930 dir. Frank Lloyd

Bartolini, L.
Bicycle Thief, The
Macmillan
MGM (It) 1949 dir. Vittorio de Sica
V

Bass, M. R.
Jory
Putnam
AVCO (US) 1973 dir. Jorge Fons
V

Bass, R.
Emerald Illusion, The
Morrow
Code Name: Emerald
MGM/UA (US) 1985
dir. Jonathan Sanger
V

Bassani, G.
Garden of the Finzi-Continis, The
Harcourt, Brace, Jovanovich
DOCUMENTO (It/Ger) 1970
dir. Vittorio de Sica
V

Bassett, J.
Harm's Way
World Publishing
In Harm's Way
PAR (US) 1965 dir. Otto Preminger

Bassett, R.
Witchfinder General
TIGON (GB) 1968 dir. Michael Reeves
V

Bassing, E.
Home Before Dark
Longman
WAR (US) 1958 dir. Mervyn LeRoy

Basso, H.
View from Pompey's Head, The
Doubleday
FOX (US) 1955 dir. Philip Dunne
GB title: Secret Interlude

Bataille, H.
Private Life of Don Juan, The
P

LONDON (GB) 1934
dir. Alexander Korda
V

Bataille, M.
Christmas Tree, The
Murray

FOX (Fr/It) 1969 dir. Terence Young
V

Bates, H. E.
Breath of French Air, A
YTV (GB) 1991 dir. Robert Tronson
TV(GB)

Bates, H. E.
Darling Buds of May, The
Little, Brown (Boston)
YTV (GB) 1991 dir. Robert Tronson
TV(GB)

Bates, H. E.
Darling Buds of May, The
Little, Brown (Boston)
Mating Game, The
MGM (US) 1959 dir. George Marshall

Bates, H. E.
Dulcima
Penguin
EMI (GB) 1971 dir. Frank Nesbitt

Bates, H. E.
Love for Lydia
LWT (GB) 1977
TVSe(GB)

Bates, H. E.
Purple Plain, The
Little, Brown (Boston)
GFD (GB) 1954 dir. Robert Parrish
V

Bates, H. E.
Triple Echo
HEMDALE (GB) 1972
dir. Michael Apted
V

Bates, H. E.
When the Green Woods Laugh
YTV (GB) 1991 dir. Robert Tronson
TV

Battin, B. W.
Smithereens
Hell Hath No Fury
BAR-GENE (US) 1991
dir. Thomas J. Wright
TV(US)

Baum, L. F.
Marvellous Land of Oz, The; Ozma of Oz
Dutton; Dover
Return to Oz
DISNEY (US) 1985 dir. Walter Murch
V

Baum, L. F.
Wonderful Wizard of Oz, The
Various
Wizard of Oz, The
MGM (US) 1939 dir. Victor Fleming
M, V

Baum, L. F.
Wonderful Wizard of Oz, The
Various
Wiz, The
DISNEY (US) 1978 dir. Sidney Lumet
M, V

Baum, V.
Berlin Hotel
Doubleday
Hotel Berlin
WAR (US) 1945 dir. Peter Godfrey

Baum, V.
Grand Hotel
Grosset & Dunlap

MGM (US) 1932 dir. Edmund Goulding
V

Baum, V.
Grand Hotel
Grosset & Dunlap

Weekend at the Waldorf
MGM (US) 1945 dir. Robert Z. Leonard
M

Baum, V.
Mortgage on Life
Michael Joseph (London)

Woman's Secret, A
RKO (US) 1949 dir. Nicholas Ray

Baumer, M.
Penny Arcade
P

Sinner's Holiday
WAR (US) 1930 dir. John G. Adolfi

Bawden, N.
On The Run
Lippincott (Philadelphia)

CFF (GB) 1969 dir. Pat Jackson
Ch, V

Bawden, N.
Solitary Child, The

BL (GB) 1958 dir. Gerald Thomas

Bax, R.
Came the Dawn

Never Let Me Go
MGM (GB) 1953 dir. Delmer Daves

Bayer, W.
Switch
Linden Press

Doubletake
TITUS (US) 1985 dir. Jud Taylor
TVSe(US)

Beach, E. L.
Run Silent, Run Deep
Holt

UA (US) 1958 dir. Robert Wise
V

Beach, L.
Merry Andrew
P

Handy Andy
FOX (US) 1934 dir. David Butler

Beach, R.
Spoilers, The

PAR (US) 1930 dir. Edward Carew
UN (US) 1942 dir. Ray Enright
V
UN (US) 1955 dir. Jesse Hibbs

Beach, R.
World in his Arms, The

UN (US) 1952 dir. Raoul Walsh

Beach, R. E.
Don Careless
Hutchinson

Avengers, The
REP (US) 1950 dir. John Auer

Beagle, P. S.
Last Unicorn, The
Viking Press

SCHICK SUNN (US) 1982
dir. Jules Bass, Arthur Rankin Jr.
A, V

Beattie, A.
Chilly Scenes of Winter *also known as* **Head Over Heels**
Doubleday

UA (US) 1979 dir. Joan Micklin Silver
V

Beatty, D.
Cone of Silence
Secker & Warburg

BL (GB) 1960 dir. Charles Frend
US title: Trouble in the Sky

Beaumarchais, P. A. C.
Marriage of Figaro, The
P
Grund (Paris)
BBC (GB) 1990 dir. D. Bailey,
P. Hall
M, TV

Beaumont, C.
Intruder, The
Dark Harvest (Arlington Heights,
Illinois)
FILMGROUP (US) 1961
dir. Roger Corman
GB title: Stranger, The

Beck, B.
Léon Morin, Priest
ROME-PARIS (Fr/It) 1961
dir. Jean-Pierre Melville

Beck, P. and Massman, P.
Rich Men, Single Women
Delacorte Press
A. SPELLING (US) 1990
dir. Elliot Silverstein
TV(US)

Becker, S.
Covenant with Death, A
Atheneum
WAR (US) 1966 dir. Lamont Johnson

Beckhardt, I. and Brown, W.
Violators, The
Harcourt Brace
RKO (US) 1957 dir. John Newland

Beckles, G.
East of Piccadilly
ABPC (GB) 1940 dir. Harold Huth

Beckwith, R.
Boys in Brown
P
Marshall
GFD (GB) 1949 dir. Montgomery Tully

Beckwith, R.
Soldier for Christmas, A
This Man is Mine
COL (GB) 1946 dir. Marcel Varnel

Beeding, F.
House of Dr. Edwards, The
Spellbound
UA (US) 1945 dir. Alfred Hitchcock
V

Beeding, F.
Norwich Victims, The
Dead Men Tell No Tales
ALL (GB) 1938 dir. David MacDonald

Behan, B.
Quare Fellow, The
P
Samuel French
BL (GB) 1962 dir. Arthur Dreifuss

Behn, N.
Kremlin Letter, The
Simon & Schuster
FOX (US) 1970 dir. John Huston
V

Behrenberg, B.
**My Little Brother is Coming
Tomorrow**
Grambling's White Tiger
INTERPLAN (US) 1981
dir. Georg Stanford Brown
TV(US), V

Behrman, S. N.
Biography
P
Samuel French
Biography (of a Bachelor Girl)
MGM (US) 1935 dir. Edward H. Griffith

Behrman, S. N.
No Time for Comedy
P
Samuel French
WAR (US) 1940 dir. William Keighley

Behrman, S. N.
Pirate, The
P
Random House
MGM (US) 1948 dir. Vincente Minnelli
M, V

Behrman, S. N. and Logan, J.
Fanny
P
WAR (US) 1960 dir. Joshua Logan

Belasco, D.
Return of Peter Grimm, The
P
Dodd
RKO (US) 1935 dir. George Nicholls

Belasco, D. & Long, J. L.
Madame Butterfly
P
Scribners
PAR (US) 1932 dir. Marion Gering

Belden, C. S.
Mystery of the Wax Museum
P
WAR (US) 1933 dir. Michael Curtiz
V

Bell, M. H.
Whistle Down the Wind
Dutton
RANK (GB) 1961 dir. Bryan Forbes
V

Bell, N.
Raw Youth
P
Undertow
CAPSTONE (US) 1991
dir. Thomas Mazziotti

Bell, R.
This Same Garden
P
While I Live
DRYHURST (GB) 1947 dir. John Harlow

Bell, T.
All Brides are Beautiful
Grosset, N.Y.
From This Day Forward
RKO (US) 1946 dir. John Berry

Bell, V.
Swamp Water
Little, Brown (Boston)
FOX (US) 1941 dir. Jean Renoir
GB title: Man Who Came Back, The

Bellah, J. W.
Command, The
WAR (US) 1954 dir. David Butler

Bellah, J. W.
Dancing Lady
MGM (US) 1933 dir. Robert Z. Leonard
M, V

Bellah, J. W.
Massacre
Lion
Fort Apache
RKO (US) 1948 dir. John Ford
V

Bellamann, H.
King's Row
Simon & Schuster
WAR (US) 1941 dir. Sam Wood

Belletto, R.
Sur la Terre Comme au Ciel
Peril
TRIUMPH (Fr) 1985 dir. Michel DeVille
V

Bello, S.
Doing Life
St. Martin's Press
PHOENIX (US) 1986
dir. Gene Reynolds
TV(US)

Bemelmans, L.
Borrowed Christmas, A

Christmas Festival, A
COMPASS (US) 1959
dir. Albert McCleery
TV(US)

Ben Amitz, D.
I Don't Give a Damn

ROLL (Israel) 1988
dir. Shmuel Imberman
V

Benchley, N.
Off-Islanders, The
McGraw-Hill

Russians are Coming, The, Russians are Coming, The
UA (US) 1966 dir. Norman Jewison
V

Benchley, N.
Sail a Crooked Ship
McGraw-Hill

COL (US) 1961 dir. Irving Brecher

Benchley, N.
Visitors, The
McGraw-Hill

Spirit is Willing, The
PAR (US) 1967 dir. William Castle

Benchley, N.
Welcome to Xanadu
Atheneum

Sweet Hostage
BRUT (US) 1975 dir. Lee Phillips
TV(US)

Benchley, P.
Deep, The
Doubleday

COL-WAR (US) 1977 dir. Peter Yates
V

Benchley, P.
Island, The
Doubleday

UN (US) 1980 dir. Michael Ritchie

Benchley, P.
Jaws
Doubleday

UN (US) 1975 dir. Steven Spielberg
V

Benedictus, D.
You're a Big Boy Now
Dutton

WAR (US) 1967
dir. Francis Ford Coppola
V

Benefield, B.
Chicken-Wagon Family
Triangle Books, N.Y.

FOX (US) 1939 dir. Herbert I. Leeds

Benefield, B.
Valiant is the Word for Carrie

RKO (US) 1936 dir. Wesley Ruggles

Benes, K. J.
Stolen Life, A

PAR (GB) 1939 dir. Paul Czinner
WAR (US) 1946 dir. Curtis Bernhardt

Benet, S. V.
Famous

Just for You
PAR (US) 1952 dir. Elliot Nugent

Benet, S. V.
Sobbin' Women, The
Various

Seven Brides for Seven Brothers
MGM (US) 1954 dir. Stanley Donen
M, V

Benet, S.V.
Devil and Daniel Webster, The
Farrar & Rinehart

All that Money can Buy
RKO (US) 1941 dir. William Dieterle

Benford, T.
Hitler's Daughter
WIL COURT (US) 1990
dir. James A. Contner
TV(US)

Bengtsson, F.
Long Ships, The
Knopf
BL (GB/Yugo) 1963 dir. Jack Cardiff

Benjamin, P.
Quick, Before it Melts
Random House
MGM (US) 1964 dir. Delbert Mann

Benjamin, W.
Aaron Slick from Punkin Crick
P
PAR (US) 1952 dir. Claude Binyon
GB title: Marshmallow Moon

Bennett, A.
Anna of the Five Towns
Doran
BBC (GB) 1985
TVSe(GB)

Bennett, A.
Buried Alive
Brentano's
AIRTIME (GB) 1983
TVSe(GB)

Bennett, A.
Buried Alive
Brentano's
Holy Matrimony
PAR (US) 1943 dir. John Stahl

Bennett, A.
Buried Alive
Methuen
His Double Life
PAR (US) 1933 dir. Arthur Hopkins
V

Bennett, A.
Card, The
Eyre, Methuen & Company
GFD (GB) 1952 dir. Ronald Neame
US title: Promoter, The
V

Bennett, A.
Clayhanger
Dutton
ATV (GB) 1976 dir. John Davies, David Reid
TVSe(GB)

Bennett, A.
Mr Prohack
George H. Doran Co.
Dear Mr Prohack
GFD (GB) 1949 dir. Thornton Freeland

Bennett, C.
Blackmail
P
Rich & Cowan
BI (GB) 1929 dir. Alfred Hitchcock
V

Bennett, D.
Fly Away Home
P
Samuel French
Daughters Courageous
WAR (US) 1939 dir. Michael Curtiz

Bennett, D.
Jigsaw Man, The
Coward, McCann & Geoghegan
J & M FILMS (GB) 1984
dir. Terence Young
V

Bennett D. and White, I.
Fly Away Home
P
Samuel French
Always in My Heart
WAR (US) 1942 dir. Joe Graham

Bennett, J.
Catacombs
BL (GB) 1964 dir. Gordon Hessler
US title: Woman Who Wouldn't Die, The

Benoit, P.
Moscow Nights
LF (GB) 1935 dir. Anthony Asquith

Benson, E. F.
Mapp and Lucia
P
Heinemann (London)
CHANNEL 4 (GB) 1985
dir. Donald McWhinnie
TVSe(GB)

Benson, Mrs. S.
Junior Miss
Random House
FOX (US) 1945 dir. George Seaton

Benson, Mrs. S.
Meet Me in St Louis
Random House

MGM (US) 1944 dir. Vincente Minnelli
M, V

Benson, R.
Necromancers, The
Arno Press
Spellbound
PYRAMID (GB) 1940 dir. John Harlow
US title: Spell of Amy Nugent, The

Bentham, J. and Williams, H. V.
Janie
P
Samuel Fox
WAR (US) 1944 dir. Michael Curtiz

Bentley, E. C.
Trent's Last Case
Knopf
BL (GB) 1952 dir. Herbert Wilcox

Bentley, N.
Floating Dutchman, The
Joseph
AA (GB) 1953 dir. Vernon Sewell

Bentley, N.
Third Party Risk
EXCL (GB) 1955 dir. Daniel Birt

Bentley, P.
Inheritance
Macmillan
GRANADA (GB) 1967
TV(GB)

Bercovici, E.
So Little Cause for Caroline
Atheneum
One Shoe Makes it Murder
LORIMAR TV (US) 1982
dir. William Hale
TV(US), V

Berger, T.
Feud, The
Delacorte Press
CASTLE HILL (US) 1990 dir. Bill D'Elia

Berger, T.
Little Big Man
Dial Press
CIN CEN (US) 1970 dir. Arthur Penn
V

Berger, T.
Neighbors
Delacorte Press
COL (US) 1981 dir. John G. Avildsen
V

Berkeley, A.
Flight from Destiny
P
WAR (US) 1941 dir. Vincent Sherman

Berkeley, R.
Dawn

Nurse Edith Cavell
RKO (US) 1939 dir. Herbert Wilcox
V

Berkeley, R.
French Leave
P
French
AB (GB) 1930 dir. Jack Raymond

Berkeley, R.
Lady with a Lamp, The
P
Gollancz
BL (GB) 1951 dir. Herbert Wilcox
V

Berkman, T.
Cast a Giant Shadow
Doubleday
UA (US) 1966 dir. Melville Shavelson
V

Berna, P.
Hundred Million Frames, A
Pantheon Books

Horse Without a Head, The
DISNEY (GB) 1963 dir. Don Chaffey
Ch

Bernanos, G.
Diary of a Country Priest, The
Macmillan
GGT (Fr) 1950 dir. Robert Bresson
V

Bernanos, G.
Under Satan's Sun
Plon (Paris)
ERATO (Fr) 1987 dir. Maurice Pialat

**Bernstein, C. and
Woodward, R.**
All the President's Men
Simon & Schuster
WAR (US) 1976 dir. Alan J. Pakula
V

Bernstein, H.
Claw, The
P

Washington Masquerade
MGM (US) 1932 dir. Charles Brabin
GB title: Mad Masquerade

Bernstein, H.
Death is Part of the Process
Sinclair Browne
BBC (GB) 1986
TV(GB)

Bernstein, H.
Dreaming Lips
P
TRAFALGAR (GB) 1936
dir. Paul Czinner, Lee Garmes

Bernstein, H.
Mélo
P
MK2 (Fr) 1986 dir. Alain Resnais

Bernstein, M.
Search for Bridey Murphy, The
Doubleday
PAR (US) 1956 dir. Noel Langley

Berteaut, S.
Piaf
Harper & Row

Piaf— The Early Years
FOX (Fr) 1982 dir. Guy Casaril

Berton, P. and Simon, C.
Za Za
P
PAR (US) 1938 dir. George Cukor

Besier, R.
Barretts of Wimpole Street, The
P
Little, Brown (Boston)
MGM (US) 1934 dir. Sidney Franklin
MGM (US) 1956 dir. Sidney Franklin

Bessie, A.
Bread and a Stone
Hard Travelling
NEW WORLD (US) 1986
dir. Dan Bessie
V

Bessie, A.
Symbol, The
Random House
Sex Symbol, The
COL (US) 1974 dir. David Lowell Rich
TV(US), V

Bevan, A. C.
Story of Zarak Khan, The
Zarak
COL (GB) 1956 dir. Terence Young

Bevan, D. and Trzcinski, E.
Stalag 17
P
Dramatists Play Service
PAR (US) 1953 dir. Billy Wilder
V

Bezzerides, A. I.
Long Haul
They Drive by Night
WAR (US) 1940 dir. Raoul Walsh
GB title: Road to Frisco, The
V

Bezzerides, A. I.
Thieves' Market
Scribners
Thieves' Highway
FOX (US) 1949 dir. Jules Dassin

Bible
**Samuel I & II: Chronicles I,
Psalms of David**
Various
King David
PAR (US/GB) 1985
dir. Bruce Beresford
V

Bickerton, D.
Payroll
AA (GB) 1960 dir. Sidney Hayers

Bickham, J. M.
Apple Dumpling Gang, The
DISNEY (US) 1974 dir. Norman Tokar
CH, V

Biddle, C. D. and Crichton, K.
Happiest Millionaire, The
P
Sphere
DISNEY (US) 1967 dir. Norman Tokar
M, V

Biggers, E. D.
Agony Column
Grosset & Dunlap
Passage from Hong Kong
WAR (US) 1941 dir. D. Ross Lederman

Biggers, E. D.
Behind that Curtain
Grosset & Dunlap
FOX (US) 1929 dir. Irving Cummings

Biggers, E. D.
Black Camel
Crown Books
FOX (US) 1931
dir. Hamilton MacFadden

Biggers, E. D.
Charlie Chan Carries On
Buccaneer
FOX (US) 1931 dir. Hamilton McFadden

Biggers, E. D.
Seven Keys to Baldpate
Buccaneer Books
House of the Long Shadows, The
CANNON (GB) 1983 dir. Pete Walker
V

Biggers, E. D.
Seven Keys to Baldpate
Buccaneer Books

RKO (US) 1930 dir. Reginald Parker
RKO (US) 1935 dir. William Hamilton
RKO (US) 1947 dir. Lew Landers

Billing, G.
Mr. Forbush and the Penguins
Holt, Rinehart & Winston

BL (GB) 1971 dir. Roy Boulting, Arne Sacksdorff

Bingham, J.
Fragment of Fear
Panther

COL (GB) 1969 dir. Richard C. Sarafian
V

Bingham, S.
Charters and Caldicott
BBC

BBC (GB) 1985 dir. Julian Amyes
TVSe(GB)

Bird, S.
Boyfriend School, The
Doubleday

Don't Tell Her It's Me
HEMDALE (US) 1990
dir. Malcolm Mowbray

Birney, H.
Dice of God, The
Holt, N.Y.

Glory Guys
UA (US) 1965 dir. Arnold Laven

Biro, L.
Dark Journey
P

LONDON GBN (US) 1937
dir. Victor Saville

Biro, L.
Five Graves to Cairo
P

PAR (US) 1943 dir. Billy Wilder

Biro, L.
Hotel Imperial
P

PAR (US) 1939 dir. Robert Florey

Biro, L. and Lengyel, M.
Royal Scandal, A
P

FOX (US) 1945 dir. Otto Preminger
GB title: Czarina

Bishop, C.
Shadow Range
Macmillan

Cow Country
ABP (US) 1953 dir. Lesley Selander

Bishop, J.
FDR's Last Year
Morrow

FDR— The Last Year
TITUS PRODS (US) 1980
dir. Anthony Page
TV(US)

Bishop, L.
Against Heaven's Hand

Seven in Darkness
PAR TV (US) 1969 dir. Michael Caffey
TV(US)

Bissell, R. P.
7½ Cents
Little, Brown (Boston)

Pajama Game, The
WAR (US) 1957 dir. Stanley Donen
M, V

Bisson, A.
Madame X
P

MGM (US) 1929 dir. John Barrymore
MGM (US) 1937
dir. James K. McGuiness
UN (US) 1965 dir. David Lowell Rich
V
UN (US) 1981 dir. Robert Ellis Miller
TV(US)

Bizet, G.
Carmen
Dover Publishing
TRIUMPH (Fr) 1984 dir. Francesco Rosi

Black, B., and Bishop, C.
Sisterhood
Ladies Club, The
NEW LINE (US) 1986 dir. A. K. Allen
V

Black, I. S.
High Bright Sun, The
Hutchinson
RANK (GB) 1965 dir. Ralph Thomas
US title: McGuire Go Home

Black, I. S.
In the Wake of a Stranger
Dakers
BUTCHER (GB) 1959 dir. David Eady

Blackburn, J.
Nothing but the Night
FOX-RANK (GB) 1972 dir. Peter Sasdy

Blackburn, W. J.
Gaunt Women, The
Destiny of a Spy
UN TV (US) 1969 dir. Boris Sagal
TV(US)

Blackmore, P.
Miranda
P
GFD (GB) 1947 dir. Ken Annakin

Blackmore, R. D.
Lorna Doone
Dodd, Mead
ATP (GB) 1934 dir. Basil Dean
COL (US) 1951 dir. Phil Karlson
THAMES (GB) 1990 dir. Alistair Grieve
TV

Blair, C.
Survive
STIGWOOD (Mex) 1976
dir. Rene Cardona
V

Blair, J. and Blair, C.
Return from the River Kwai
Simon & Schuster
RANK (GB) 1987
dir. Andrew V. McLaglen

Blaisdell, A.
Nightmare
Gollancz
Fanatic
COL (GB) 1965 dir. Silvio Narizzano
US title: Die! Die! My Darling

Blake, G.
Shipbuilders, The
Lippincott (Philadelphia)
BN (GB) 1944 dir. John Baxter

Blake, M.
Dances with Wolves
Newmarket Press
ORION (US) 1990 dir. Kevin Costner
V

Blake, N.
This Man Must Die
AA (Fr) 1970 dir. Claude Chabrol

Blankenship, W. D.
Brotherly Love
Arbor House
CBS (US) 1985 dir. Jeff Bleckner
TV(US), V

Blankfort, M.
Juggler, The
Little, Brown (Boston)
COL (US) 1953 dir. Edward Dmytryk

Blankfort, M.
Widow Makers, The
Simon & Schuster

See How They Run
UN TV (US) 1964 dir. David Lowell Rich
TV(US)

Blasco-Ibanez, V.
Four Horsemen of the Apocalypse, The
Dutton

MGM (US) 1961 dir. Vincente Minnelli
V

Blatty, W. P.
Exorcist, The
Harper & Row

WAR (US) 1973 dir. William Friedkin
V

Blatty, W. P.
Legion
Simon & Schuster

Exorcist III, The
TCP (US) 1990 dir. William Peter Blatty

Blatty, W. P.
Ninth Configuration, The
Harper

LORIMAR (US) 1980
dir. William P. Blatty
V

Blatty, W. P.
Twinkle, Twinkle, 'Killer' Kane
Doubleday

FOX (US) 1980 dir. William Peter Blatty

Bleeck, O.
Procane Chronicle, The
Morrow

St Ives
WAR (US) 1976 dir. J. Lee Thompson
V

Bleier, R. and O'Neil, T.
Fighting Back
Stein & Day

MTM (US) 1980 dir. Robert Lieberman
TV(US)

Blixen, K.
Immortal Story
Random House

ORTF (Fr) 1968 dir. Orson Welles

Blixen, K. aka Dinesen, I.
Babette's Feast
DAN FI (Den) 1987 dir. Gabriel Axel

Bloch, R.
Psycho
UN (US) 1960 dir. A. Hitchcock
V

Bloch, R.
Psycho
Bates Motel
UN TV (US) 1987 dir. Richard Rothstein
TV(US)

Blochman, L. G.
Bombay Mail
UN (US) 1933 dir. Edwin L. Martin

Block, L.
Burglar
Random House

WAR (US) 1987 dir. Hugh Wilson
V

Block, L.
Stab in the Dark
Arbor House

8 Million Ways to Die
TRI-STAR (US) 1986 dir. Hal Ashby
V

Block, L.
Wild Calendar
World, N.Y.

Caught
MGM (US) 1948 dir. Max Ophuls
V

Blodgett, M.
Hero and the Terror
CANNON (US) 1988
dir. William Tanner

Blondin, A.
Monkey in Winter, A
CIPRA (Fr) 1962 dir. Henri Verneuil

Bloom, J. and Atkinson, J.
Evidence of Love
Texas Monthly Press (Austin, Texas)

Killing in a Small Town
INDIEPROD (US) 1990
dir. Stephen Gyllenhaal
TV(US)

Bloom, M. T.
13th Man, The
Star

Last Embrace
UA (US) 1979 dir. Jonathan Demme
V

Blume, J.
Forever
Bradbury Press (Scarsdale, New York)
EMI (US) 1978 dir. John Korty
TV(US)

Blythe, R.
Akenfield
Pantheon Books
ANGLIA (GB) 1975 dir. Peter Hall

Blyton, E.
Castle of Adventure
Macmillan
TVS (GB) 1990
Ch, TV(GB)

Blyton, E.
Five Have A Mystery to Solve
CFF (GB) 1964 dir. Ernest Morris
Ch

Blyton, E.
Five on a Treasure Island
Atheneum
BL (GB) 1957 dir. Gerald Landau
Ch

Boccaccio, G.
Decameron, The
Various

Decameron Nights
EROS (GB) 1952 dir. Hugo Fregonese
V

Boccaccio, G.
Decameron, The
Various
UA (It/Fr/W.Ger) 1970
dir. Pier Paolo Pasolini
V

Bodelsen, A.
Hit, and Run, Run, Run
One of Those Things
RANK (Den) 1971 dir. Erik Balling

Bodelsen, A.
Think of a Number
Silent Partner, The
CAROLCO (Can) 1978 dir. Daryl Duke
V

Boehm, D.
Employee's Entrance
P
WAR (US) 1933 dir. Roy del Ruth

Bogner, N.
Seventh Avenue
Coward-McCann
UN TV (US) 1977 dir. Richard Irving,
Russ Mayberry
TVSe(US)

Bogosian, E.
Talk Radio
P
Samuel French
UN (US) 1988 dir. Oliver Stone

Boileau, P. & Narcejac, T.
Celle Qui N'Etait Plus
Reflections of Murder
ABC (US) 1974 dir. John Badham
TV(US)

Boileau, P. and Narcejac, T.
Choice Cuts
Body Parts
PAR (US) 1991 dir. Eric Red

Boileau, P. and Narcejac, T.
Faces in the Dark
RANK (GB) 1960 dir. David Eady

Boileau, P. and Narcejac, T.
Living and the Dead, The
Washburn
Vertigo
PAR (US) 1958 dir. Alfred Hitchcock
V

Boileau, P. and Narcejac, T.
Woman Who Was, The
Diaboliques, Les
FILMSONOR (Fr) 1954
dir. Henri-Georges Clouzot
V

Boland, B.
Cockpit
P
Elek
Lost People, The
GFD (GB) 1949 dir. Bernard Knowles

Boland, B.
Prisoner, The
P
COL (GB) 1955 dir. Peter Glenville

Boland, J.
League of Gentlemen, The
RANK (GB) 1960 dir. Basil Dearden
V

Boldrewood, R.
Robbery Under Arms
RANK (GB) 1957 dir. Jack Lee

Boll, H.
Lost Honor of Katharina Blum, The
McGraw-Hill
Lost Honor of Kathryn Beck, The
COMWORLD (US) 1984
dir. Simon Langton
TV(US)

Bolnick, J. P.
Winnie: My Life in the Institution
St. Martin's Press
Winnie
NBC (US) 1988 dir. John Korty
TV(US)

Bolt, R.
Man for all Seasons, A
P
Samuel French
COL (GB) 1966 dir. Fred Zinnemann
V
AGAMEMNON (US) 1988
dir. Charlton Heston
TV(US)

Bolton, G.
Dark Angel, The
P
GOLDWYN (US) 1935
dir. Sidney Franklin

Bolton, G.
Waltzes from Vienna
P
GFD (GB) 1933 dir. Alfred Hitchcock
US title: Strauss's Great Waltz

Bolton, G., Kern, J. and Grey, C.
Sally
P
WAR (US) 1930 dir. John Francis Dillon
M

Bolton, G. and McGowan, J.
Girl Crazy
P
MGM (US) 1943 dir. Norman Taurog
M, V

Bolton, G. and McGowan, J.
Girl Crazy
P

When the Boys Meet the Girls
MGM (US) 1965 dir. Alvin Ganzer

Bolton, G., Wodehouse, P. G., Lindsay, H., Crouse, R.
Anything Goes
P
PAR (US) 1936 dir. Lewis Milestone
M
PAR (US) 1956 dir. Robert Lewis
M

Bombeck, E.
Grass is Always Greener over the Septic Tank, The
McGraw-Hill

J. HAMILTON (US) 1978
dir. Robert Day
TV(US), V

Bonacci, A.
L'Oro della Fantasia
P

Kiss Me Stupid
UA (US) 1964 dir. Billy Wilder

Bond, E.
Bingo
BBC (GB) 1990 dir. Don Taylor
TV(GB)

Bonestell, C. and Ley, W.
Conquest of Space
P
Sidgwick
PAR (US) 1955 dir. Byron Haskin
V

Bonett, E.
Girl Must Live, A
Miles
UN (GB) 1939 dir. Carol Reed

Bonett, E.
High Pavement
My Sister and I
GFD (GB) 1948 dir. Harold Huth

Bonner, C.
Legacy
Adam had Four Sons
COL (US) 1941 dir. Gregory Ratoff
V

Bonnet, T.
Mudlark, The
Doubleday
FOX (GB) 1950 dir. Jean Negulesco

Boo, S.
Servant's Entrance
FOX (US) 1934 dir. Frank Lloyd

Boom, C. Ten
Hiding Place, The
Bantam Books
WORLD WIDE (US) 1974
dir. James F. Collier
V

Booth, C. G.
General Died at Dawn, The
Bell
PAR (US) 1936 dir. Lewis Milestone

Booth, C. G.
Mr. Angel Comes Aboard

Johnny Angel
RKO (US) 1945 dir. Edwin L. Marin
V

Boothe, C.
Kiss the Boys Goodbye
P
Various
PAR (US) 1941 dir. Victor Schertzinger

Boothe, C.
Margin for Error
P
Random House
FOX (US) 1943 dir. Otto Preminger

Boothe, C.
Women, The
P
MGM (US) 1939 dir. George Cukor
V

Boothe, C.
Women, The
P
Opposite Sex, The
MGM (US) 1956 dir. David Miller

Boothe, E.
Ladies of the Mob
City Streets
PAR (US) 1931 dir. Rouben Mamoulian

Boothroyd, D.
Value for Money
RANK (GB) 1955 dir. Ken Annakin

Borden, M.
Action for Slander
Heinemann
UA (GB) 1938 dir. Tim Whelan
V

Borden, W.
Last Prostitute who Took Pride in her Work, The
P
Last Prostitute, The
BBK (US) 1991 dir. Lou Antonio
TV(US)

Borenstein, T.
Kofiko
Going Bananas
CANNON (US) 1988 dir. Boaz Davidson

Borges, J. L.
Theme of the Traitor and the Hero, The
Spider's Stratagem, The
RED FILM (It) 1970
dir. Bernardo Bertolucci

Borland, H.
When the Legends Die
Lippincott (Philadelphia)
FOX (US) 1972 dir. Stuart Millar
V

Born, N.
Circle of Deceit
BIOSKOP/ARTEMIS (Fr/W. Ger)
1981 dir. Volker Schlondorff

Bost, P.
Monsieur L'Admiral va Bientôt Mourir
Sunday in the Country, A
MGM/UA (Fr) 1984
dir. Bertrand Tavernier
V

Bosworth, A. R.
Crows of Edwina Hill, The
Harper
Nobody's Perfect
UN (US) 1978 dir. Alan Rafkin

Bottome, P.
Danger Signal
Faber
WAR (US) 1945 dir. Robert Florey

Bottome, P.
Heart of a Child
Putnam's
RANK (GB) 1958 dir. Clive Donner

Bottome, P.
Mortal Storm, The
Little, Brown (Boston)
MGM (US) 1940 dir. Frank Borzage

Bottome, P.
Private Worlds
Houghton, Mifflin Co. (Boston)
PAR (US) 1935 dir. Gregory La Cava

Boulle, P.
Bridge on the River Kwai, The
Vanguard
COL (GB) 1957 dir. David Lean
V

Boulle, P.
Monkey Planet
Vanguard Press
Planet of the Apes
FOX (US) 1968 dir. Franklin Schaffner
V

Bowen, C. D., von Meck, B.
Beloved Friend
Garden City Publishing Co. (Garden City, New York)
Music Lovers, The
UA (GB) 1970 dir. Ken Russell
V

Bowen, E.
Death of the Heart, The
Knopf
GRANADA (GB) 1985
TV(GB)

Bowen, J.
McGuffin, The
Atlantic Monthly Press
BBC (GB) 1986
TV(GB)

Bowles, P.
Sheltering Sky, The
New American Library
WAR (US) 1990
dir. Bernardo Bertolucci

Boyd, W.
Stars and Bars
Morrow
COL (US) 1988 dir. Pat O'Connor
V

Boyer, D.
Sidelong Glances of a Pigeon Kicker, The
MGM (US) 1970 dir. John Dexter

Boyer, F.
Jeux Interdits
R. DORFMANN (Fr) 1952
dir. René Clément

Boyle, K.
Maiden Maiden
Five Days One Summer
WAR (US) 1982 dir. Fred Zinnemann
V

Brackett, L.
Tiger Amongst Us, The
13 West Street
COL (US) 1962 dir. Philip Leacock

Bradbury, M.
History Man, The
Houghton, Mifflin Co. (Boston)
BBC (GB) 1981 dir. Robert Knights
TVSe(GB)

Bradbury, R.
Fahrenheit 451
Ballantine Books
UI (GB) 1966 dir. François Truffaut
V

Bradbury, R.
Foghorn, The
Doubleday

Beast From 20,000 Fathoms, The
WAR (US) 1953 dir. Eugene Lourie

Bradbury, R.
Illustrated Man, The
Doubleday

WAR (US) 1969 dir. Jack Smight
V

Bradbury, R.
Martian Chronicles, The
Doubleday

NBC ENT (US/GB) 1980
dir. Michael Anderson
TVSe(GB/US), V

Bradbury, R.
Screaming Woman, The

UN TV (US) 1972 dir. Jack Smight
TV(US)

Bradbury, R.
Something Wicked This Way Comes
Simon & Schuster

DISNEY (US) 1983 dir. Jack Clayton
Ch, V

Braddon, R.
Year of the Angry Rabbit, The
W. W. Norton

Night of the Lepus
MGM (US) 1972 dir. William F. Claxton

Bradford, B. T.
Act of Will
Doubleday

PORTMAN (US) 1989
TVSe(US), V

Bradford, B. T.
Hold the Dream
Doubleday

TAFT (GB) 1986 dir. Don Sharp
TVSe(GB), V

Bradford, B. T.
Voice of the Heart
Doubleday

PORTMAN (GB) 1989
dir. Tony Wharmby
TVSe(GB)

Bradford, B. T.
Woman of Substance, A
Doubleday

OPT (US) 1984 dir. Don Sharp
TVSe(US), V

Bradford, R.
Red Sky at Morning
Lippincott (Philadelphia)

UN (US) 1971 dir. James Goldstone

Bradlee, Jr, B.
Ambush Murders, The

FRIES (US) 1982
dir. Steven Hilliard Stern
TV(US)

Bradlee, Jr., B.
Guts and Glory: The Rise and Fall of Oliver North
D. I. Fine

Guts and Glory: The Oliver North Story
PAPAZIAN-HIRSCH (US) 1989
dir. Mike Robe
TVSe(US)

Bradley, M. H.
I Passed for White

WAR (US) 1960 dir. Fred M. Wilcox

Brady, L.
Edge of Doom

RKO (US) 1950 dir. Mark Robson
GB title: Stronger than Fear

Brahms, C. and Sherrin, N.
Beecham

YTV (GB) 1990 dir. Vernon Lawrence
TV(GB)

Brahms, C. and Simon, S. J.
Elephant is White, The
Joseph
Give Us the Moon
GFD (GB) 1944 dir. Val Guest

Brahms, C. and Simon, S. J.
No Nightingales
Joseph
Ghosts of Berkeley Square, The
BN (GB) 1947 dir. Vernon Sewell
V

Brahms, C. and Simon, S. J.
Trottie True
TC (GB) 1949 dir. Brian Desmond Hurst
US title: Gay Lady, The
V

Braine, J.
Room at the Top
Houghton, Mifflin Co. (Boston)
BL (GB) 1958 dir. Jack Clayton
V

Braithwaite, E. R.
To Sir, With Love
Prentice-Hall (Englewood Cliffs, New Jersey)
COL (GB) 1966 dir. James Clavell
V

Braithwaite, M.
Why Shoot the Teacher?
QUARTET (Can) 1976
dir. Silvio Narizzano
V

Brancati, V.
Bell'Antonio, Il
F. Ungar
CINA (It/Fr) 1960 dir. Piero Piccioni

Brancato, R. F.
Blinded by the Light
TIME-LIFE (US) 1980
dir. John A. Alonzo
TV(US), V

Branch, H.
River Lady
UIN (US) 1948 dir. George Sherman

Brand, C.
Green for Danger
University of California Press (Del Mar, California)
INDIVIDUAL (GB) 1946
dir. Sidney Gilliat
V

Brand, M.
Destry Rides Again
Gregg Press (Boston)
Destry
UI (US) 1954 dir. George Marshall

Brand, M.
Destry Rides Again
Gregg Press (Boston)
UN (US) 1939 dir. George Marshall
V

Brand, M.
Young Dr. Kildare
Dodd, Mead
MGM (US) 1938 dir. Harold S. Bucquet

Brande, D.
Wake up and Live
FOX (US) 1937 dir. Sidney Lanfield

Brandel, M.
Lizard's Tail, The
Hand, The
ORION/WAR (US) 1981
dir. Oliver Stone

Brandner, G.
Cameron's Closet
SVS (US) 1989 dir. Armand Mastroianni
V

Brandner, G.
Howling III
SQUARE (Aus) 1987 dir. Philippe Mora

Brandner, G.
Howling, The
Fawcett, N.Y.
AVCO (US) 1981 dir. Joe Dante
V

Brandner, G.
Walkers
From the Dead of Night
PHOENIX (US) 1989 dir. Paul Wendkos
TVSe(US)

Brandon, D.
Outsider, The
P
Samuel French
MGM (GB) 1931 dir. Harry Lachtman
ABPC (GB) 1939 dir. Paul Stein

Brashler, W.
Bingo Long Travelling All-Stars and Motor Kings, The
Harper & Row
UN (US) 1976 dir. John Badham
V

Brason, J.
Secret Army, The
BBC (GB) 1979
TVSe(GB)

Brawley, E.
Rap, The
Fast-Walking
PICKMAN (US) 1982
dir. James B. Harris
V

Brecht, B.
Galileo
P
Samuel French
CINEVISION (GB) 1975
dir. Joseph Losey

Brecht, B.
Herr Puntila and his Servant Matti
P
Samuel French
BAUERFILM (Austria) 1955
dir. Alberto Cavalcanti

Brecht, B.
Mother Courage
P
Samuel French
ITV (GB) 1959
TV(GB)

Brecht, B. and Weill, K.
Threepenny Opera, The
P
Grove Press
Mack the Knife
21st CENTURY (US) 1989
dir. Menahem Golan
M

Brennan, P.
Razorback
WAR (Aust) 1984 dir. Russell Mulcahy
V

Brent, J.
Few Days in Weasel Creek, A.
Seaview Books
WAR TV (US) 1981 dir. Dick Lowry
TV(US)

Brentano, L.
Melody Lingers On, The
IN (US) 1935 dir. David Burton

Breslin, H.
Bad Time at Honda
Muller
Bad Day at Black Rock
MGM (US) 1954 dir. John Sturges

Breslin, J.
Gang That Couldn't Shoot Straight, The
Viking Press
MGM (US) 1971 dir. James Goldstone

Brett, S.
Shock to the System, A
Scribners
MEDUSA (US) 1990 dir. Jan Egleson

Brewer, B.
Memory of Love
Rich & Gowan
In Name Only
RKO (US) 1939 dir. John Cromwell
V

Brewer, G. E. and Bloch, B.
Dark Victory
P
WAR (US) 1939 dir. Edmund Goulding
V
UN (US) 1976 dir. Robert Butler
TV(US)

Brickhill, P.
Dam Busters, The
Evans
ABP (GB) 1954 dir. Michael Anderson
V

Brickhill, P.
Great Escape, The
Ballantine Books
UA (US) 1963 dir. John Sturges
V

Brickhill, P.
Reach for the Sky
Norton
COL (GB) 1956 dir. Lewis Gilbert
V

Bridie, J.
It Depends what you Mean
P
Constable
Folly to be Wise
BL (GB) 1952 dir. Frank Launden

Bridie, J.
Sleeping Clergyman, A.
P
Constable (London)
Flesh and Blood
BL (GB) 1951 dir. Anthony Kimmins

Bridie, J.
What Say They
P
You're Only Young Twice
ABP (GB) 1952 dir. Terry Gilbert

Briggs, R.
When the Wind Blows
Schocken Books
MELTDOWN (GB) 1987
dir. J. T. Murakami
A, V

Brighouse, H.
Hobson's Choice
P
Samuel French
BL (GB) 1931 dir. Thomas Bentley
BL (GB) 1953 dir. David Lean
V
CBS ENT (US) 1983 dir. Gilbert Cates
TV(US)

Brinig, M.
Sisters, The
WAR (US) 1938 dir. Anatole Litvak

Brink, A.
Dry White Season, A
Penguin
MGM (US) 1989 dir. Euzhan Palcy

Brink, C. R.
Caddie Woodlawn
Macmillan
Caddie
HEMDALE (Aust) 1976
dir. Donald Crombie
V

Brinkley, W.
Don't Go Near the Water
Random House
MGM (US) 1957 dir. Charles Walters

Brinkman, B.
Ice House Heat Waves
P
Ice House
UPFRONT/CACTUS (US) 1989
dir. Eagle Pennell

Bristow, G.
Jubilee Trail
Thomas Y. Crowell
REP (US) 1954 dir. Joseph Kane

Bristow, G.
Ninth Guest, The
COL (US) 1934 dir. Roy William Neill

Bristow, G.
Tomorrow is Forever
RKO (US) 1946 dir. Irving Pichel

Britten, B.
War Requiem
BBC (GB) 1989 dir. Derek Jarman
TV(GB)

Brodeur, P.
Stunt Man, The
Atheneum
FOX (US) 1980 dir. Richard Rush
V

Bromfield, L.
Better Than Life
Cassell
It All Came True
WAR (US) 1940 dir. Lewis Seiler

Bromfield, L.
McLeod's Folly
Johnny Come Lately
CAGNEY (US) 1943
dir. William K. Howard
GB title: Johnny Vagabond

Bromfield, L.
Modern Hero, A
WAR (US) 1934 dir. G. W. Pabst

Bromfield, L.
Mrs. Parkington
Harper & Bros.
MGM (US) 1944 dir. Tom Garnett

Bromfield, L.
Rains Came, The
Harper & Bros.
FOX (US) 1939 dir. Clarence Brown

Bromfield, L.
Rains Came, The
Harper & Bros.
Rains of Ranchipur, The
FOX (US) 1955 dir. Jean Negulesco

Bromfield, L.
Single Night
Night After Night
PAR (US) 1932 dir. Archie Mayo

Bronder, L.
Rockabye
P
RADIO (US) 1932 dir. George Cukor

Bronte, C.
Jane Eyre
Various
MON (US) 1934 dir. Christy Cabanne
FOX (US) 1943 dir. Robert Stevenson
V
OMNIBUS (GB) 1971
dir. Delbert Mann
V
BBC (GB) 1984 dir. Julian Amyes
TV(GB)

Bronte, E. J.
Wuthering Heights
Various
UA (US) 1939 dir. William Wyler
MGM-EMI (GB) 1970 dir. Robert Fuest
V
PLEXUS (Sp) 1983 dir. Luis Bunuel

Brooke, H.
Saturday Island
RKO (GB) 1951 dir. Stuart Heisler
US title: Island of Desire

Brooke, H. and Bannerman, K.
All for Mary
P
Samuel French
RANK (GB) 1955 dir. Wendy Toye

Brooke, H. and Bannerman, K.
Handful of Tansy, A.
P
No, My Darling Daughter
RANK (GB) 1961 dir. Ralph Thomas

Brooke, H. and Bannerman, K.
How Say You?
P
Pair of Briefs
RANK (GB) 1961 dir. Ralph Thomas

Brookner, A.
Hotel du Lac
Pantheon
BBC (GB) 1986 dir. Giles Foster
TV(GB), V

Brooks, N.
Fragile Fox
P
Attack
UA (US) 1956 dir. Robert Aldrich

Brooks, R.
Brick Foxhole, The
Harper
Crossfire
RKO (US) 1947 dir. Edward Dmytryk
V

Brophy, J.
Day They Robbed the Bank of England, The
MGM (GB) 1959 dir. John Guillermin

Brophy, J.
Immortal Sergeant, The
Collins
FOX (US) 1943 dir. John Stahl
V

Brophy, J.
Turn the Key Softly
GFD (GB) 1953 dir. Jack Lee

Brophy, J.
Waterfront
GFD (GB) 1950 dir. Michael Anderson
US title: Waterfront Women

Brown, C.
My Left Foot
Faber & Faber
PALACE (GB) 1989 dir. J. Sheridan

Brown, F.
Martians Go Home
Ballantine Books
TAURUS (US) 1990 dir. David Odell

Brown, F.
Screaming Mimi
COL (US) 1958 dir. Gerd Oswald

Brown, F. Y.
Bengal Lancer
Viking Press
Lives of a Bengal Lancer
PAR (US) 1935 dir. Henry Hathaway
V

Brown, G.
I Want What I Want
Panther
CINERAMA (GB) 1972 dir. John Dexter
V

Brown, H.
Sound of Hunting, A
P
Knopf
Eight Iron Men
COL (US) 1952 dir. Edward Dmytryk

Brown, H.
Stars in their Courses, The
Knopf
El Dorado
PAR (US) 1966 dir. Howard Hawks
V

Brown, H. G.
Sex and the Single Girl
Random House
WAR (US) 1964 dir. Richard Quine

Brown, H. P. M.
Walk in the Sun, A
Knopf
FOX (US) 1945 dir. Lewis Milestone
V

Brown, J. D.
Addie Pray
Simon & Schuster
Paper Moon
PAR (US) 1973 dir. Peter Bogdanovich
V

Brown, J. D.
Kings Go Forth
Cassell
UA (US) 1958 dir. Delmer Daves

Brown, J. D.
Stars in my Crown
MGM (US) 1950 dir. Jacques Tourneur

Brown, J. E.
Incident at 125th Street
Doubleday
Incident in San Francisco
ABC TV (US) 1971 dir. Don Medford
TV(US)

Brown, J. P. S.
Jim Kane
Dial Press
Pocket Money
FA (US) 1972 dir. Stuart Rosenberg
V

Brown, K.
Vanquished, The
PAR (US) 1953 dir. Edward Ludwig

Brown, M.
Idol, The
P
Mad Genius, The
WAR (US) 1931 dir. Michael Curtiz

Brown, P. E.
Bad Man, The
P
Samuel French
MGM (US) 1940 dir. Richard Thorpe
GB title: Two Gun Cupid

Brown, R.
Tintype, The
Timestalkers
FRIES (US) 1987 dir. Michael Schultz
TV(US)

Brown, W.
Monkey on my Back
UA (US) 1957 dir. André de Toth

Brown, W.
Wiz, The
P
Samuel French
DISNEY (US) 1978 dir. Sidney Lumet
M, V

Brown, W. C.
Border Jumpers, The
Man of the West
UA (US) 1958 dir. Anthony Mann

Browne, G. A.
Green Ice
Delacorte Press
ITC (GB) 1981 dir. Ernest Day
V

Browne, G. A.
11 Harrowhouse
Arbor House
FOX (GB) 1974 dir. Aram Avakian
V

Browne, W.
Holly and the Ivy, The
P
Samuel French
BL (GB) 1952
dir. George More O'Ferrall

Browning, R.
Pied Piper, The
Harry Quitter (London)
SAG (GB) 1971 dir. Jacques Demy

Bruce, J. C.
Escape from Alcatraz
PAR (US) 1979 dir. Don Siegel
V

Brush, K.
Red Headed Woman
MGM (US) 1932 dir. Jack Conway

Bryan, C. D. B.
Friendly Fire
Putnam
M. ARCH (US) 1979 dir. David Greene
TV(US), V

Bryan, M.
Intent to Kill
Eyre & Spottiswoode
FOX (GB) 1958 dir. Jack Cardiff

Bryson, J.
Evil Angels
Summit Books
Cry in the Dark, A
CANNON (US) 1988 dir. Fred Schepisi
V

Buarque, C.
Opera do Malandro
P
AUSTRA/TF1 (Braz/Fr) 1986
dir. Ruy Guerra

Buchan, J.
Thirty-Nine Steps, The
G. H. Doran Co.
GB (GB) 1935 dir. Alfred Hitchcock
RANK (GB) 1959 dir. Ralph Thomas
V
RANK (GB) 1978 dir. Don Sharp
V

Buchanan, T.
Easy to Love
P
WAR (US) 1933 dir. William Keighley

Buchanan, W.
Shining Season, A
COL TV (US) 1979 dir. Stuart Margolin
TV(US)

Buchheim, L-G.
Boat, The
Knopf
COL (Ger) 1981 dir. Wolfgang Petersen
V

Buchwald, A.
Gift From the Boys, A
Surprise Package
COL (GB) 1960 dir. Stanley Donen

Buck, P.
China Sky
Blue Ribbon Books, N.Y.
RKO (US) 1945 dir. Ray Enright

Buck, P.
Devil Never Sleeps, The
Pan
FOX (GB) 1962 dir. Leo McCarey

Buck, P.
Dragon Seed
John Day Co.
MGM (US) 1944 dir. Jack Conway
V

Buck, P.
Good Earth, The
John Day Co.
MGM (US) 1937 dir. Sidney Franklin
V

Budd, J.
Convict has Escaped, A
They Made Me A Fugitive
WAR (GB) 1947 dir. Alberto Cavalcanti
US title: I Became a Criminal

Budrys, A.
Who?
V. Gollancz (London)
BL (GB) 1974 dir. Jack Gold
US title: Man Without a Face

Buffington, S.
Three on a Date
ABC (US) 1978 dir. Bill Bixby
TV(US)

Bugliosi, V.
Till Death do us Part
Norton
SABAN/SCHERICK PRODS. 1992
dir. Yves Simoneau
TV(US)

Bugliosi, V. and Gentry, C.
Helter Skelter
Norton
LORIMAR (US) 1976 dir. Tom Gries
TVSe(US), V

Bugliosi, V., and Henderson, B. B.
And the Sea will Tell
Norton
COL (US) 1991 dir. Tommy L. Wallace
TVSe(US)

Buhet, G.
Honey Siege, The
HTV (GB) 1988
Ch, TVSe(GB)

Bukowski, C.
Copulating Mermaid of Venice; Trouble with the Battery
Cold Moon
GAU (Fr) 1991 dir. Luc Besson, Andrée Martinez
French title: Lune Froide

Bukowski, C.
Erections, Ejaculations, Exhibitions and Tales of Ordinary Madness
Tales of Ordinary Madness
(It/Fr) 1981 dir. Marco Ferri
V

Bullett, G.
Jury, The
Garland Publishing
Last Man to Hang?, The
COL (GB) 1956 dir. Terence Fisher

Bunker, E.
No Beast so Fierce
Straight Time
WAR (US) 1978 dir. Ulu Grosbard
V

Bunyan, J.
Pilgrim's Progress
Various
Dangerous Journey
CHANNEL 4 (GB) 1985
TVSe (GB)

Burchard, P.
One Gallant Rush
St. Martin's Press

Glory
TRI-STAR (US) 1989 dir. Edward Zwick

Burdick, E. and Wheeler, H.
Fail Safe
McGraw-Hill

COL (US) 1963 dir. Sidney Lumet
V

Burger, G.
Baron Munchhausen

CESK (Czech) 1962 dir. Karel Zeman

Burgess, A.
Clockwork Orange, A
Norton

WAR (GB) 1971 dir. Stanley Kubrick
V

Burgess, A.
Seven Men at Daybreak
Dutton

Operation Daybreak
WAR (US) 1975 dir. Lewis Gilbert
V

Burgess, A.
Small Woman, The
Dutton

Inn of the Sixth Happiness, The
FOX (GB) 1958 dir. Mark Robson
V

Burgess, G.
Two in the Dark

RKO (US) 1936 dir. Ben Stoloff

Burke, J.
Echo of Barbara

RANK (GB) 1961 dir. Sidney Hayers

Burman, B. L.
Steamboat Round the Bend

FOX (US) 1935 dir. John Ford

Burmeister, J.
Running Scared
St. Martin's Press

Tigers Don't Cry
RANK (S. Africa) 1978
dir. Peter Collinson
V

Burnet, D.
Private Pettigrew's Girl
P

Shopworn Angel
MGM (US) 1938 dir. H. C. Potter

Burnett, F. H.
Little Lord Fauntleroy
Various

UA (US) 1936 dir. John Cromwell
V
ROSEMONT (GB) 1980 dir. Jack Gold
TV(GB)

Burnett, F. H.
Little Princess, The
Various

FOX (US) 1939 dir. Walter Lang
V

Burnett, F. H.
Secret Garden, The

MGM (US) 1949 dir. Fred M. Wilcox
Ch, V
ROSEMONT (US) 1987 dir. Alan Grint
Ch, TV(US)

Burnett, M. and Alison, J.
Everybody Comes to Rick's
P

Casablanca
WAR (US) 1943 dir. Michael Curtiz
V

Burnett, W. R.
Adobe Walls
Knopf

Arrowhead
PAR (US) 1953
dir. Charles Marquis Warren

Burnett, W. R.
Asphalt Jungle, The
Knopf
MGM (US) 1950 dir. John Huston
V

Burnett, W. R.
Asphalt Jungle, The
Knopf
Cairo
MGM (GB) 1963 dir. Wolf Rilla

Burnett, W. R.
Asphalt Jungle, The
Knopf
Cool Breeze
MGM (US) 1972 dir. Barry Pollack
V

Burnett, W. R.
Captain Lightfoot
Knopf
UI (US) 1955 dir. Douglas Sirk

Burnett, W. R.
Dance Hall
FOX (US) 1941 dir. Irving Pichel
V

Burnett, W. R.
Dark Command
Heinemann
REP (US) 1940 dir. Raoul Walsh
V

Burnett, W. R.
Dr. Socrates
WAR (US) 1935 dir. William Dieterle

Burnett, W. R.
High Sierra
Knopf
WAR (US) 1941 dir. Raoul Walsh
V

Burnett, W. R.
High Sierra
Knopf
I Died a Thousand Times
WAR (US) 1955 dir. Stuart Heisler

Burnett, W. R.
Iron Man
Heinemann
UN (US) 1931 dir. Tod Browning
UI (US) 1951 dir. Joseph Pevney
V

Burnett, W. R.
Little Caesar
Dial Press
WAR (US) 1930 dir. Mervyn Le Roy
V

Burnett, W. R.
Saint Johnson
Heinemann
Law and Order
UN (US) 1932 dir. Edward L. Cahn

Burnett, W. R.
Vanity Row
Corgi
Accused of Murder
REP (US) 1956 dir. Joe Kane

Burnett, W. R.
Whole Town's Talking, The
COL (US) 1935 dir. John Ford
GB title: Passport to Fame

Burnford, S.
Incredible Journey, The
Little, Brown (Boston)
DISNEY (US) 1963 dir. Fletcher Markle
A, Ch, V

Burnham, B.
Goodbye Mr Chips
P
MGM (GB) 1969 dir. Herbert Ross
M

Burns, O. A.
Cold Sassy Tree
Ticknor & Fields

TNT (US) 1989 dir. Joan Tewkesbury
TV(US)

Burns, R.
Avenging Angels, The
Viking Press

Messenger of Death
CANNON (US) 1988
dir. J. Lee Thompson

Burns, R. E.
I am a Fugitive from a Chain Gang
Paul

WAR (US) 1932 dir. Mervyn LeRoy
V

Burns, V. G.
Man Who Broke 1,000 Chains, The
JOURNEY (US) 1987 dir. Daniel Mann
TV(US), V

Burns, W. N.
Saga of Billy the Kid, The
Garden City Publishing Co. (Garden City)

Billy the Kid
MGM (US) 1930 dir. King Vidor
MGM (US) 1941 dir. David Millar

Burroughs, E. R.
At the Earth's Core
Doubleday

BL (GB) 1976 dir. Kevin Connor
V

Burroughs, E. R.
Land that Time Forgot, The
Various

BL (GB) 1974 dir. Kevin Connor
V

Burroughs, E. R.
People That Time Forgot, The
Doubleday

BW (GB) 1977 dir. Kevin Connor
V

Burroughs, E. R.
Tarzan of the Apes
Ballantine Books

Greystoke: The Legend of Tarzan, Lord of the Apes
WAR (GB) 1984 dir. Hugh Hudson
V

Burroughs, E. R.
Tarzan of the Apes
Ballantine Books

Tarzan, The Ape Man
MGM (US) 1932 dir. W. S. VanDyke
V

Burroughs, W.
Naked Lunch
Grove Press

FOX (US) 1991 dir. David Cronenberg

Burrows, A.
Cactus Flower
P
Samuel French

COL (US) 1969 dir. Gene Saks
V

Burrows, A.
Can Can
P

TCF (US) 1960 dir. Walter Lang
M, V

Burrows, A., Loesser, F. and Swerling, J.
Guys and Dolls
P

MGM (US) 1955
dir. Joseph L. Mankiewicz
M, V

Burrows, A., Weinstock, J., Gilbert, W. and Loesser, F.
How to Succeed in Business Without Really Trying

UA (US) 1967 dir. David Swift
M

Burt, K. and Leasor, J.
One That Got Away, The
RANK (GB) 1957 dir. Roy Baker
V

Burtis, T.
New Guinea Gold
Doubleday
Crosswinds
PAR (US) 1951 dir. Lewis R. Foster

Busch, N.
Duel in the Sun
W. H. Allen
MGM (US) 1946 dir. King Vidor
V

Busch, N.
Furies, The
PAR (US) 1950 dir. Anthony Mann

Busch, N.
They Dream of Home
Till the End of Time
RKO (US) 1946 dir. Edward Dmytryk
V

Busch, N.
We the O'Leary's
In Old Chicago
FOX (US) 1937 dir. Henry King

Bus-Fekete, L.
Birthday
P
Heaven Can Wait
FOX (US) 1943 dir. Ernst Lubitsch

Bus-Fekete, L.
Ladies in Love
P
FOX (US) 1936 dir. Edward H. Griffith

Bus-Fekete, L.
Lady Has a Heart, A
P
Baroness and the Butler, The
FOX (US) 1938 dir. Walter Lang

Butler, G.
Kiss the Blood Off My Hands
UN (US) 1948 dir. Norman Foster
GB title: Blood on my Hands

Butler, G.
On Dangerous Ground
RKO (US) 1951 dir. Nicholas Ray

Butler, W.
Butterfly Revolution, The
Ballantine Books
Summer Camp Nightmare
CONCORDE (US) 1987
dir. Bert C. Dragin
V

Butterfield, R. P.
Al Schmid, Marine
Pride of the Marines
WAR (US) 1945 dir. Delmer Daves
GB title: Forever in Love

Cahen, A.
Yekl

Hester Street
CONN (US) 1975
dir. Joan Micklin Silver
V

Caidin, M.
Cyborg

Six Million Dollar Man, The
UN TV (US) 1973 dir. Richard Irving
TV(US)

Caidin, M.
Marooned

Dutton
COL (US) 1969 dir. John Sturges
V

Caillou, A.
Cheetahs, The

World Publishers

Cheetah
DISNEY (US) 1989 dir. Jeff Blyth
Ch

Caillou, A.
Khartoum

W. H. Allen

UA (GB) 1966 dir. Basil Dearden
V

Caillou, A.
Rampage

Appleton-Century-Crofts

WAR (US) 1963 dir. Philip Carlson

Cain, J. A.
Slightly Scarlet

RKO (US) 1956 dir. Allan Dwan
V

Cain, J. A.
When Tomorrow Comes

UN (US) 1939 dir. John M. Stahl

Cain, J. M.
Butterfly

Random House, N.Y.

J & M (US) 1982 dir. Matt Cimber
V

Cain, J. M.
Double Indemnity

Knopf

PAR (US) 1944 dir. Billy Wilder
V
UN (US) 1973 dir. Jack Smight
TV(US)

Cain, J. M.
Mildred Pierce

Vintage Press

WAR (US) 1945 dir. Michael Curtiz
V

Cain, J. M.
Postman Always Rings Twice, The

Crown Publishing

MGM (US) 1946 dir. Tay Garnett
PAR (US) 1981 dir. Bob Rafaelson

Cain, J. M.
Postman Always Rings Twice, The
Grosset & Dunlap

Dernier Tournant, Le
LUX (Fr) 1939 dir. Pierre Chenal

Cain, J. M.
Serenade
Crown
WAR (US) 1956 dir. Anthony Mann

Caine, J.
Cold Room, The
Knopf
HBO PREM (US) 1984
dir. James Dearden
TV(US), V

Caine, L.
Widow
Morrow
LORIMAR (US) 1976
dir. J. Lee Thompson
TV(US)

Cairn, J.
Guy Named Joe, A
Hollywood Publications (London)
MGM (US) 1943 dir. Victor Fleming

Caldwell, A.
Flying Down to Rio
P
RKO (US) 1933 dir. Thornton Freeland
V

Caldwell, E.
Claudelle Inglish
WAR (US) 1961 dir. Gordon Douglas
GB title: Young and Eager

Caldwell, E.
God's Little Acre
The Modern Library
UA (US) 1958 dir. Anthony Mann
V

Caldwell, E.
Tobacco Road
FOX (US) 1941 dir. John Ford

Caldwell, T.
Captains and the Kings
Doubleday
UN TV (US) 1976 dir. Douglas Heyes,
Allen Reisner
TVSe(US)

Caldwell, T.
Testimony of Two Men
Doubleday
UN TV (US) 1977 dir. Leo Penn,
LarryYust
TVSe(US)

Calef, N.
Lift to the Scaffold
NEF (Fr) 1957 dir. Louis Malle

Cameron, I.
Lost Ones, The
W. Morrow
Island at the Top of the World, The
DISNEY (US) 1974
dir. Robert Stevenson
V

Camoletti, M.
Boeing-Boeing
P
Samuel French
PAR (US) 1965 dir. John Rich

Camp, W.
Idle on Parade
COL (GB) 1959 dir. John Gilling

Campanella, R.
It's Good to be Alive
Little, Brown (Boston)
METRO (US) 1974 dir. Michael Landon
TV(US), V

Campbell, G.
Cry for Happy
Harcourt, N.Y.

COL (US) 1961 dir. George Marshall

Campbell, J. W.
Who Goes There?
Hyperion Press (Westport, Connecticut)
Thing, The
RKO (US) 1951 dir. Christian Nyby
GB title: Thing from Another World,
The
UN (US) 1982 dir. John Carpenter
V

Campbell, Sir M.
Salute to the Gods
Cassell

Burn 'em up O'Connor
MGM (US) 1938 dir. Edward Sedgwick

Campbell, R. W.
Where Pigeons Go To Die
Rawson Associates

WORLD (US) 1990 dir. Michael Landon
TV(US)

Camus, A.
Stranger, The
Knopf

PAR (Fr/It) 1967 dir. Luchino Visconti

Canada, L.
To Elvis with Love
Touched by Love
COL (US) 1980 dir. Gus Trikonis
V

Canaway, W. H.
Sammy Going South
BL (GB) 1963
dir. Alexander Mackendrick
US title: Boy Ten Feet Tall, A

Canning, V.
Castle Minerva
Masquerade
UA (GB) 1965 dir. Basil Dearden

Canning, V.
Golden Salamander, The
GFD (GB) 1949 dir. Ronald Neame

Canning, V.
House of the Seven Flies, The
William Morrow
House of the Seven Hawks, The
MGM (GB) 1959 dir. Richard Thorpe

Canning, V.
Limbo Line, The
W. Sloane Associates

MONARCH (GB) 1968
dir. Samuel Gallen
V

Canning, V.
Panther's Moon
Spy Hunt
UN (US) 1950 dir. George Sherman
GB title: Panther's Moon

Canning, V.
Rainbird Pattern, The
Morrow
Family Plot
UN (US) 1976 dir. Alfred Hitchcock
V

Canning, V.
Runaways, The
Morrow

LORIMAR (US) 1974 dir. Harry Harris
TV(US)

Canning, V.
Scorpio Letters, The
MGM (US) 1967 dir. Richard Thorpe
V

Canning, V.
Venetian Bird
GFD (GB) 1952 dir. Ralph Thomas
US title: Assassin, The

Cantor, E.
Nest, The
CONCORDE (US) 1988
dir. Terence Winkless
V

Capon, P.
Murder at Shinglestrand
Ward Lock
Hidden Homicide
RANK (US) 1959 dir. Tony Yound

Capote, T.
Breakfast at Tiffany's
New American Library
PAR (US) 1961 dir. Blake Edwards
V

Capote, T.
In Cold Blood
Random House
COL (US) 1967 dir. Richard Brooks
V

Capote, T. and Cooper, W.
Glass House, The
TOM (US) 1972 dir. Tom Gries
TV(US), V

Capra, F.
Turning Point, The
Simon & Schuster
Mindwalk
ATLAS (US) 1991 dir. Bernt Capra

Caputo, P.
Rumor of War, A
Holt, Rinehart & Winston
FRIES (US) 1980 dir. Richard T. Heffron
TVSe(US)

Carey, J.
Mr. Johnson
Harper & Row
AVENUE (Aust) 1990
dir. Bruce Beresford

Carey, P.
Bliss
Faber
NSW (Aust) 1984 dir. Ray Lawrence
V

Cargill, P. and Beale, J.
Ring for Catty
P
Twice Round the Daffodils
AA (GB) 1962 dir. Gerald Thomas

Carleton, Mrs M. C.
Cry Wolf
Sun Dial, N.Y.
WAR (US) 1947 dir. Peter Godfrey
V

Carlile, C.
Honkytonk Man
Simon & Schuster
WAR (US) 1982 dir. Clint Eastwood
V

Carney, D.
Square Circle, The
Wild Geese II
UN (GB) 1985 dir. Peter Hunt
V

Carney, D.
Wild Geese, The
RANK (GB) 1978
dir. Andrew V. McLaglen
V

Carpenter, E. C.
One New York Night
P
MGM (US) 1935 dir. Jack Conway
GB title: Trunk Mystery, The

Carpenter, M.
Experiment Perilous
RKO (US) 1944 dir. Jacques Tourneur
V

Carpenter, T.
Death of a Playmate

Star 80
WAR (US) 1983 dir. Bob Fosse
V

Carr, A. H. Z.
Finding Maubee
Putnam

Mighty Quinn, The
MGM (US) 1989 dir. Carl Schenkel

Carr, J. D.
Emperor's Snuffbox, The
Harper & Bros.

That Woman Opposite
MON (GB) 1957 dir. Compton Bennett

Carr, J. L.
Month in the Country, A
St. Martins Press

EUSTON (GB) 1987 dir. Pat O'Connor
V

Carrière, J-P.
Mahabharata, The
P
Harper & Row

CHANNEL 4 (GB) 1990
dir. Peter Brook

Carroll, C.
Golden Herd

San Antone
REP (US) 1952 dir. Joe Kane

Carroll, G.
As the Earth Turns
Macmillan

WAR (US) 1934 dir. Alfred E. Green

Carroll, L.
Alice's Adventures in Wonderland
V
Various

FOX (GB) 1972 dir. William Sterling
A, Ch, V

Carroll, L.
Alice's Adventures in Wonderland
Various

Alice in Wonderland
PAR (US) 1933 dir. Norman Z. McLeod
Ch
DISNEY (US) 1951
dir. Clyde Geronomi, HamiltonLuske,
Wilfred Jackson
A, Ch
M. EVANS (US) 1955
dir. George Schaefer
TV (US)
COL TV (US) 1985 dir. Harry Harris
Ch, TV(US)

Carroll, L.
Alice's Adventures in Wonderland
Various

Alice
HEMDALE (Bel/Pol/GB) 1980
dir. Jerry Gruza
V

Carroll, S.
Big Hand for the Little Lady, A
P

WAR (US) 1966 dir. Fielder Cook
GB title: Big Deal at Dodge City

Cars, G. des
Brute, The
Little, Brown (Boston0

Green Scarf, The
BL (GB) 1954
dir. George More O'Ferrall

Carson, R.
Come Be My Love

Once More My Darling
UI (US) 1949 dir. Robert Montgomery

Carstairs, J. P.
Solid! Said the Earl

Yank in Ermine, A
MON (GB) 1955 dir. Gordon Parry

Carter, A.
Company of Wolves, The
Harper, N.Y.
PALACE (GB) 1984 dir. Neil Jordan
V

Carter, A.
Magic Toyshop, The
Simon & Schuster
GRANADA TV (GB) 1987
dir. David Wheatley
TV(GB)

Carter, A.
Operation Mad Ball
P
Samuel French
COL (US) 1957 dir. Richard Quine

Carter, D. T.
Scottsboro: A Tragedy of the American South
Louisiana State Univ. Press (Baton Rouge, Louisiana)
Judge Horton and the Scottsboro Boys
TOM (US) 1976 dir. Fielder Cook
TV(US)

Carter, F.
Gone to Texas
Delacorte Press
Outlaw Josey Wales, The
WAR (US) 1976 dir. Clint Eastwood
V

Carter, M.
Tell me my Name
Morrow
TALENT (US) 1977 dir. Delbert Mann
TV(US)

Carter, S. F.
Sudie
St. Martin's Press
Sudie & Simpson
HEARST (US) 1990
dir. Joan Tewkesbury
TV(US)

Cartland, B.
Cupid Rides Phillion
Lady and the Highwayman, The
GRADE (GB) 1989 dir. John Hough
TV(GB)

Cartland, B.
Duel of Hearts
TNT TV (US/GB) 1992 dir. John Hough
TV(US/GB)

Cartland, B.
Flame is Love, The
NBC ENT (US) 1979
dir. Michael O'Herlihy
TV(US), V

Cartland, B.
Ghost in Monte Carlo, A
GRADE (GB) 1990 dir. John Hough
TV(GB)

Cartland, B.
Hazard of Hearts, A
MGM (GB) 1987 dir. John Hough
TV(GB)

Cary, F. L. and King, P.
Watch it Sailor!
P
Samuel French
COL (GB) 1961 dir. Wolf Rilla

Cary, J.
Horse's Mouth, The
Harper
UA (GB) 1958 dir. Ronald Neame
V

Case, D.
Fengriffen
Hill & Wang
And Now the Screaming Starts
AMICUS (GB) 1973
dir. Roy Ward Baker
V

Caspary, V.
Bachelor in Paradise
Pan
MGM (US) 1961 dir. Jack Arnold

Caspary, V.
Bedelia
Houghton, Mifflin Co. (Boston)
GFD (GB) 1946 dir. Lance Comfort

Caspary, V.
Easy Living
PAR (US) 1937 dir. Mitchell Leisen

Caspary, V.
Girls, Les
MGM (US) 1957 dir. George Cukor
M, V

Caspary, V.
Laura
FOX (US) 1944 dir. Otto Preminger
V

Cassady, C.
Heart Beat
Creative Arts Book Co. (Berkeley,
California)
WAR (US) 1979 dir. John Byrum
V

Castle, J.
Password is Courage, The
Norton
MGM (GB) 1962 dir. Andrew L. Stone

Castleton, P. A.
Son of Robin Hood
Bandit of Sherwood Forest, The
COL (US) 1946
dir. George Sherman/Henry Levin

Cather, W.
Lost Lady, A
Knopf
WAR (US) 1934 dir. Alfred E. Green

Cather, W.
O Pioneers!
Penguin
LORIMAR (US) 1992 dir. Glenn Jordan
TV(US)

Cato, N.
All the Rivers Run
St. Martin's Press
Crawford (Aus) 1983 dir. George Miller,
Pino Amenta
TV(Aus)

Catto, M.
Devil at 4 O'Clock, The
Pan
COL (US) 1961 dir. Mervyn Le Roy
V

Catto, M.
Ferry to Hong Kong
RANK (GB) 1959 dir. Lewis Gilbert
V

Catto, M.
Fire Down Below
COL (GB) 1957 dir. Robert Parrish
V

Catto, M.
Hill in Korea, A
Hutchinson
BL (GB) 1956 dir. Julian Aymes
US title: Hell in Korea

Catto, M.
Killing Frost, The
Trapeze
UA (US) 1956 dir. Carol Reed
V

Catto, M.
Lions at the Kill
Seven Thieves
FOX (US) 1960 dir. Henry Hathaway

Catto, M.
Mister Moses
Morrow
Mr. Moses
UA (GB) 1965 dir. Ronald Neame

Catto, M.
Murphy's War
Simon & Schuster
PAR (GB) 1971 dir. Peter Yates
V

Catto, M.
Prize of Gold, A
COL (GB) 1955 dir. Mark Robson

Catton, B.
Blue and the Gray, The
COL TV (US) 1982
dir. Andrew McLaglen
TVSe(US), V

Caunitz, W. J.
One Police Plaza
Crown Publishing
CBS ENT (US) 1986 dir. Jerry Jameson
TV(US)

Caute, D.
Comrade Jacob
Pantheon Books
Winstanley
OTHER (GB) 1977
dir. Kevin Brownlow/Andrew Mollo

Cauvin, P.
Blind Love
J. C. Lattes (Paris)
Little Romance, A
WAR (US) 1979 dir. George Roy Hill
V

Cavanaugh, A.
Children are Gone, The
Simon & Schuster
Deadly Trap, The
NAT GEN (Fr/It) 1971
dir. René Clément
V

Cavazzini, E.
Poem of the Lunatics, The
Serpent's Tail (London)
Voce Delle Lune, La
PENTA (It) 1990 dir. Federico Fellini

Cecil, H.
Brothers in Law
Harper
BL (GB) 1957 dir. Ray Boulting

Cellini, B.
Infamous Life, An
Various
LC/CINEMAX (It/Fr/Ger) 1990
dir. Giacomo Battiato

Cervantes, M. de
Don Quixote
Various
VANDOR (Fr) 1933 dir. G. W. Pabst
LENFILM (USSR) 1957
dir. Grigori Kozintsev
V
EUSTON (GB) 1985
TV

Cervantes, M. de
Don Quixote
Various
Man of La Mancha
UA (US) 1972 dir. Arthur Hiller
M, V

Chais, P. H.
Six Weeks in August
Guess Who's Sleeping in my Bed?
ABC (US) 1973 dir. Theodore J. Flicker
TV(US)

Chamales, T.
Go Naked in the World
Deutsch
MGM (US) 1960
dir. Ronald MacDougall

Chamales, T.
Never so Few
MGM (US) 1959 dir. John Sturges

Chamberlain, G. A.
Phantom Filly, The

Home in Indiana
TCF (US) 1944 dir. Henry Hathaway

Chamberlain, G. A.
Red House, The

UA (US) 1947 dir. Delmer Daves
V

Chamberlain, G. A.
Scudda Hoo! Scudda Hay!

FOX (US) 1948 dir. F. Hugh Herbert
GB title: Summer Lightning

Chamberlain, G.A.
April Love
Crown Publishers

TCF (US) 1957 dir. Henry Levin

Chamberlain, W.
Company of Cowards, The
Harcourt Brace

Advance to the Rear
MGM (US) 1964 dir. George Marshall

Chamberlain, W.
Trumpets of Company K
Ballantine

Imitation General
MGM (US) 1958 dir. George Marshall

Chambers, W.
Murder of a Wanton

Sinner Take All
MGM (US) 1937 dir. Errol Taggart

Champion, B. and Powell, J.
Champion's Story: A Great Human Triumph
Coward, McCann & Geoghegan

Champions
Embassy (GB) 1983 dir. John Irvin
V

Chancellor, J.
King of the Damned
P

GAU (GB) 1935 dir. Walter Forde

Chandler, J. G.
Fire and Rain
Texas Monthly Press (Austin, Texas)

WIL COURT (US) 1989
dir. Jerry Jameson
TV(US)

Chandler, R.
Big Sleep, The
Knopf

WAR (US) 1946 dir. Howard Hawks
V
ITC (GB) 1977 dir. Michael Winner

Chandler, R.
Farewell, My Lovely
Vintage Books

RKO (US) 1944 dir. Edward Dmytryk
V
AVCO (US) 1975 dir. Dick Richards
V

Chandler, R.
Farewell, My Lovely
Vintage Press

Murder, My Sweet
RKO (US) 1944 dir. Edward Dmytryk
V

Chandler, R.
High Window, The
World Publishing

Brasher Doubloon, The
FOX (US) 1946 dir. John Brahm
GB title: High Window, The

Chandler, R.
Lady in the Lake
Vintage Books

MGM (US) 1946
dir. Robert Montgomery

Chandler, R.
Little Sister, The
Houghton, Mifflin Co. (Boston)
Marlowe
MGM (US) 1969 dir. Paul Bogart

Chandler, R.
Long Goodbye, The
Houghton, Mifflin Co. (Boston)
UA (US) 1973 dir. Robert Altman
V

Chanslor, R.
Ballad of Cat Ballou, The
Little, Brown
Cat Ballou
COL (US) 1965 dir. Eliot Silverstein
V

Chanslor, R.
Hazard
PAR (US) 1948 dir. George Marshall

Chanslor, R.
Johnny Guitar
REP (US) 1953 dir. Nicholas Ray
V

Chaplin, P.
Siesta
LORIMAR (US) 1987 dir. Mary Lambert
V

Chapman, E.
Joey Boy
Cassell
BL (GB) 1965 dir. Frank Launder

Chapman, J.
Dry Rot
P
English Theatre Guild
BL (GB) 1956 dir. Maurice Elvey

Chapman, R.
Behind the Headlines
Laurie
RANK (GB) 1956 dir. Charles Saunders

Chapman, R.
Murder for the Million
Murder Reported
COL (GB) 1957 dir. Charles Saunders

Chapman, R.
Winter Wears a Shroud
Laurie
Delavine Affair, The
MON (GB) 1954 dir. Douglas Pierce

Charef, M.
Thé au harem d'Archi Ahmen, Le
Tea in the Harem
M&R FILMS (Fr) 1986
dir. Mehdi Charef

Charles, T.
Happy Now I Go
Woman With No Name, The
ABP (GB) 1950 dir. Ladislas Vajda

Charles-Roux, E.
Dimenticare Palermo
B. Grasset (Paris)
PENTA (It/Fr) 1990 dir. Francesco Rosi

Charrière, H.
Papillon
Morrow
COL (US) 1973 dir. Franklin Schaffner
V

Charteris, L.
Lady on a Train
UN (US) 1945 dir. Charles David

Charteris, L.
Saint in New York
Magna Print Books
(Botton-By-Bowland, Lancashire)
RKO (US) 1938 dir. Ben Holmes
V

Charters, S.
Louisiana Black
Scribners

White Lie
MCA TV (US) 1991 dir. Bill Condon
TV(US)

Chase, B.
Chisolm Trail, The
Red River
UA (US) 1948 dir. Howard Hawks
V

Chase, J. H.
Eve
Gala (Fr/It) 1963 dir. Joseph Losey

Chase, J. H.
High Stakes
Jarrolds

I'll Get You For This
BL (GB) 1950 dir. Joseph M. Newman
US title: Lucky Nick Cain
V

Chase, J. H.
Last Page, The
P
French
EXCL (GB) 1952 dir. Terence Fisher

Chase, J. H.
No Orchids for Miss Blandish
Panther

Grissom Gang, The
CINERAMA (US) 1971
dir. Robert Aldrich
V

Chase, J. H.
No Orchids for Miss Blandish
Panther
ALL (GB) 1948 dir. St. John L. Clowes

Chase, J. H.
World In My Pocket, The
On Friday at 11
BL (Ger/Fr/It) 1961 dir. Alvin Rakoff

Chase, M.
Bernardine
P
Oxford University Press
FOX (US) 1957 dir. Henry Levin

Chase, M.
Harvey
P
Stein & Day
UN (US) 1950 dir. Henry Koster
TALENT ASS. (US) 1972
dir. Fielder Cook
TV(US)

Chase, T.
When Rabbit Howls
E. P. Dutton

Voices Within: The Lives of Truddi Chase
NEW WORLD TV (US) 1990
dir. Lamont Johnson
TVSe(US)

Chastain, T.
Death Stalk
D. WOLPER (US) 1975 dir. Robert Day
TV(US), V

Chatwin, B.
On the Black Hill
Viking Press
CHANNEL 4 (GB) 1989
dir. Andrew Grieve
TV(GB)

Chatwin, B.
Utz
Viking Press
BBC FILMS (GB/It/Ger) 1992
dir. George Sluizer

Chaucer, G.
Canterbury Tales, The
Various
UA (It/Fr) 1972 dir. Pier Paolo Pasolini
V

Chayefsky, P.
Altered States
Harper & Row
WAR (US) 1980 dir. Ken Russell
V

Chayefsky, P.
Bachelor Party, The
P
Simon & Schuster
UA (US) 1957 dir. Delbert Mann
V

Chayefsky, P.
Catered Affair, The
P
MGM (US) 1956 dir. Richard Brooks

Chayefsky, P.
Marty
P
Simon & Schuster
COL (US) 1955 dir. Delbert Mann
V

Chayefsky, P.
Middle of the Night
P
Samuel French
COL (US) 1959 dir. Delbert Mann

Cheever, J.
Swimmer, The
Ballantine Books
COL (US) 1968 dir. Frank Perry, Sidney Pollack
V

Chekhov, A.
Platonov
Coward-McCann
Unfinished Piece for Player Piano, An
MOSFILM (USSR) 1977
dir. Nikita Mikhalkov
V

Chekhov, A.
Seagull, The
P
Samuel French
WAR (GB) 1969 dir. Sidney Lumet

Chekhov, A.
Shooting Party, The
Various
MOSFILM (USSR) 1981
dir. Emil Loteanu

Chekhov, A.
Shooting Party, The
Summer Storm
UA (US) 1944 dir. Douglas Sirk

Chekhov, A.
Stories
Dark Eyes
EXCELSIOR (It) 1987
dir. Nikita Mikhalkov
V

Chekhov, A.
Three Sisters
P
Samuel French
BL (GB) 1970 dir. Laurence Olivier
V

Cherman, Y.
My Friend Ivan Lapshin
LENFILM (USSR) 1986
dir. Alexei Cherman

Chertas, J.
Zoo 2000
BBC (GB) 1984
TV(GB)

Chessman, C.
Cell 2455, Death Row
Greenwood Press
COL (US) 1955 dir. Fred F. Sears

Chesterton, G. K.
Blue Cross, The
Cassell

Father Brown
COL (GB) 1954 dir. Robert Hamer

Chesterton, G. K.
Father Brown, Detective
Dodd, Mead

Sanctuary of Fear
M. ARCH (US) 1979
dir. John Llewellyn Moxey
TV(US), V

Chesterton, G. K.
Wisdom of Father Brown, The
Penguin

Father Brown, Detective
PAR (US) 1935 dir. Edward Sedgwick
ATV (GB) 1974 dir. Robert Tronson
TVSe(GB)

Chetham-Strode, W.
Background
P
Samuel French

ABP (GB) 1953 dir. Daniel Birt
US title: Edge of Divorce

Chetwynd-Hayes, R.
**Elemental, The; Gate Crasher, The;
Act of Kindness, An; Door, The**
Fontana

From Beyond the Grave
EMI (GB) 1973 dir. Kevin Connor
V

Chevalier, G.
Clochemerle
Simon & Schuster

BLUE RIBBON (Fr) 1948
dir. Pierre Chénal

Cheyney, P.
Sinister Errand
Collins

Diplomatic Courier
FOX (US) 1952 dir. Henry Hathaway

Cheyney, P.
Uneasy Terms
BN (GB) 1948 dir. Vernon Sewell

Cheyney, P.
Urgent Hangman, The
Meet Mr Callaghan
EROS (GB) 1954 dir. Charles Saunders

Childers, E.
Riddle of the Sands, The
Dutton

RANK (GB) 1979 dir. Tony Maylam
V

Childress, A.
**Hero Ain't Nothing but a Sandwich,
A**
NEW WORLD (US) 1977
dir. Ralph Nelson

Childs, H.
Gaucho
Way of a Gaucho
FOX (US) 1952 dir. Jacques Tourneur

Chilton, C. and Littlewood, J.
Long, Long Trail, The
P
Methuen (London)

Oh! What a Lovely War
PAR (GB) 1969
dir. Richard Attenborough
V

Chittenden, F.
Uninvited, The
Stranger in Town
EROS (GB) 1957 dir. George Pollock

Chodorov, E.
Kind Lady
P
Samuel French

MGM (US) 1935 dir. George B. Seitz
MGM (US) 1951 dir. John Sturges

Chodorov, E.
Oh! Men! Oh! Women!
P
Samuel French
FOX (US) 1957 dir. Nunnally Johnson

Chonkadze, D.
Legend of Suram Fortress, The
GRUZIA (USSR) 1985
dir. Sergei Paradjanov

Chopin, K.
Awakening, The
Norton
End of August, The
QUARTET (US) 1981 dir. Bob Graham
V

Chopin, K.
Awakening, The
Norton
Grand Isle
TURNER (US) 1992 dir. Mary Lambert
TV(US)

Christian, T.C.
Baby Love
Cape
AVCO (GB) 1969 dir. Alistair Reid
V

Christie, A.
ABC Murders, The
Dodd, Mead
Alphabet Murders, The
MGM (GB) 1966 dir. Frank Tashlin

Christie, A.
After the Funeral
Dodd, Mead
Murder at the Gallop
MGM (GB) 1963 dir. George Pollock

Christie, A.
Appointment with Death
Ulverscroft (London)
CANNON (US) 1989
dir. Michael Winner
V

Christie, A.
At Bertram's Hotel
Dodd, Mead
BBC (GB) 1986 dir. Mary McMurray
TV(GB)

Christie, A.
Body in the Library, The
Dodd, Mead
BBC (GB) 1984 dir. George Gallaccio
TV(GB)

Christie, A.
Caribbean Mystery, A
Dodd, Mead
WAR (US) 1983 dir. Robert Lewis
TV(US)
BBC (GB) 1988 dir. Christopher Pettit
TV(GB)

Christie, A.
Dead Man's Folly
Dodd, Mead
WAR (US) 1986 dir. Clive Donner
TV(US)

Christie, A.
Death on the Nile
Dodd, Mead
EMI (GB) 1978 dir. John Guillermin
V

Christie, A.
Endless Night
Dodd, Mead
BL (GB) 1971 dir. Sidney Gilliat
V

Christie, A.
Evil Under the Sun
Collins
UN (GB) 1982 dir. Guy Hamilton
V

Christie, A.
Hound of Hell, The
Last Seance, The
GRANADA (GB) 1987
TV(GB)

Christie, A.
Lord Edgware Dies
Dodd, Mead

TWICKENHAM (GB) 1934
dir. Henry Edwards

Christie, A.
Lord Edgware Dies
Dodd, Mead

Thirteen at Dinner
WAR (US) 1985 dir. Lou Antonio
TV(US), V

Christie, A.
Man in the Brown Suit, The
Dodd, Mead

WAR TV (US) 1989 dir. Alan Grint
TV(US)

Christie, A.
Mirror Crack'd from Side to Side, The
Dodd, Mead

Mirror Crack'd, The
EMI (GB) 1980 dir. Guy Hamilton
V

Christie, A.
Moving Finger, The
Dodd, Mead

BBC (GB) 1984 dir. Roy Boulting
TV(GB)

Christie, A.
Mrs. McGinty's Dead
Dodd, Mead

Murder Most Foul
MGM (GB) 1964 dir. George Pollock

Christie, A.
Murder at the Vicarage
Dodd, Mead

BBC (GB) 1986 dir. Julian Amyes
TV(GB)

Christie, A.
Murder in Three Acts
Dodd, Mead

WAR TV (US) 1986 dir. Gary Nelson
TV(US)

Christie, A.
Murder is Announced, A
Dodd, Mead

BBC (GB) 1985 dir. George Gallaccio
TV(GB)
BBC (GB) 1987 dir. David Giles
TVSe(GB)

Christie, A.
Murder is Easy
Dodd, Mead

WAR (US) 1982 dir. Claude Whatham
TV(US)

Christie, A.
Murder on The Orient Express
Dodd, Mead

EMI (GB) 1974 dir. Sidney Lumet
V

Christie, A.
Mysterious Affair at Styles
Dodd, Mead

LWT (GB) 1990 dir. Roy Devenish
TV(GB)

Christie, A.
Nemesis
Dodd, Mead

BBC (GB) 1986 dir. David Tucker
TV(GB)

Christie, A.
Ordeal by Innocence
Dodd, Mead

CANNON (GB) 1985
dir. Desmond Davis
V

Christie, A.
Pocketful of Rye, A
Dodd, Mead

BBC (GB) 1985 dir. Guy Slater
TV(GB), V

Christie, A.
Poirot: Peril at End House
Dodd, Mead

LWT (GB) 1991 dir. Renny Rye
TV(GB)

Christie, A.
Sparkling Cyanide
WAR (US) 1983 dir. Robert Lewis
TV(US)

Christie, A.
Spider's Web, The
P
Samuel French

UA (GB) 1960 dir. Godfrey Grayson
BBC 2 (GB) 1985
TV(GB)

Christie, A.
Ten Little Niggers
Dodd, Mead

Ten Little Indians
ABP (GB) 1965 dir. George Pollock
V
CANNON (US) 1989
dir. Alan Birkinshaw

Christie, A.
Ten Little Niggers
Dodd, Mead

And Then There Were None
ABP (US) 1945 dir. René Clair
GB title: Ten Little Niggers
V
EMI (GB) 1974 dir. Peter Collinson

Christie, A.
They Do it with Mirrors
Dodd, Mead

Murder with Mirrors
WAR (US) 1985 dir. Dick Lowry
TV(US)

Christie, A.
Why Didn't They Ask Evans?
Dodd, Mead

LWT (GB) 1980 dir. John Davies, Tony
Wharmby
TVSe(GB)

Christie, A.
Witness for the Prosecution
P
Samuel French

UA (US) 1957 dir. Billy Wilder
V
UATV (US) 1982 dir. Alan Gibson
TV(US)

Christie, A.
4.50 from Paddington
Dodd, Mead

Murder she Said
MGM (GB) 1961 dir. George Pollock

Christie, D. and Christie, C.
Carrington, V. C.
P
Heinemann

BL (GB) 1954 dir. Anthony Asquith
US title: Court Martial
V

Christie, D. and Christie, C.
Grand National Night
P
Samuel French

REN (GB) 1953 dir. Bob McNaught
US title: Wicked Wife, The

Christie, D. and Christie, C.
Someone at the Door
P
BIP (GB) 1936 dir. Herbert Brenon

Christie, D. and Christie, P.
His Excellency
P
Elek

GFD (GB) 1951 dir. Robert Hamer

Christman, E.
Nice Italian Girl, A
Dodd, Mead

Black Market Baby
BRUT (US) 1977 dir. Robert Day
GB title: Don't Steal My Baby
TV(US)

Christopher, J.
Death of Grass
Simon & Schuster

No Blade of Grass
MGM (GB) 1970 dir. Cornel Wilde
V

Christopher, J.
Tripods, The
Dutton

BBC (GB/US/Aust) 1984-5
dir. Graham Theakston,
Christopher Barry, Bob Blagden
TVSe(GB/US/Aust)

Chu, L.
Eat a Bowl of Tea
COL (US) 1989 dir. Wayne Wang

Chubin, B.
Feet of the Snake, The
WELLER/MYERS (GB) 1985
TVSe(GB)

Churchill, Sir W. S.
My Early Life
Scribners

Young Winston
COL-WAR (GB) 1972
dir. Richard Attenborough
V

Churchill, Sir W.
Gathering Storm, The
BBC (GB/US) 1974 dir. Herbert Wise
TV(GB/US), V

Clancy, T.
Hunt for Red October, The
Naval Institute Press (Annapolis,
Maryland)
PAR (US) 1990 dir. John McTiernan

Clark, B.
Whose Life is it Anyway?
P
MGM (US) 1981 John Badham
V

Clark, M. H.
Cradle will Fall, The
Simon & Schuster
P&G PRODS (US) 1983
dir. J. Llewellyn Moxey
TV(US)

Clark, M. H.
Stillwatch
Simon & Schuster
INTERSCOPE (US) 1987
dir. Rod Holcomb
TV(US)

Clark, M. H.
Stranger is Watching, A
Simon & Schuster
MGM/UA (US) 1982
dir. Sean Cunningham
V

Clark, M. H.
Where are the Children?
Simon & Schuster
COL (US) 1986 dir. Bruce Malmuth
V

Clark, R. and Bobrick, S.
Norman, Is That You?
P
Samuel French
MGM (US) 1976 dir. George Schlatter

Clark, W. van T.
Ox-Bow Incident, The
Random House
FOX (US) 1943 dir. William Wellman
US title: Strange Incident
V

Clark, W. van T.
Track of the Cat
Random House
WAR (US) 1954 dir. William A. Wellman

Clarke, A. C.
Sentinel, The
Berkley Books
2001, A Space Odyssey
MGM (GB) 1968 dir. Stanley Kubrick
V

Clarke, A. C.
2010
Ballantine Books
MGM (US) 1984 dir. Peter Hyams
V

Clarke, D. H.
Housekeeper's Daughter, The
Laurie
UA (US) 1939 dir. Hal Roach

Clarke, D. H.
Impatient Virgin, The
Impatient Maiden
UN (US) 1932 dir. James Whale

Clarke, D. H.
Louis Beretti
Long
Born Reckless
FOX (US) 1930 dir. John Ford

Clarke, M.
For the Term of his Natural Life
FILMO (Aus) 1985 dir. Rob Stewart
TVSe(Aus)

Clauser, S.
Girl Named Sooner, A
FOX TV (US) 1975 dir. Delbert Mann
TV(US)

Clavell, J.
King Rat
Little, Brown (Boston)
COL (US) 1965 dir. Bryan Forbes
V

Clavell, J.
Noble House
Delacorte Press
DELAUR (US) 1988 dir. Gary Nelson
TVSe(US)

Clavell, J.
Shogun
Atheneum
PAR (Jap/US) 1981 dir. Jerry London
TVSe(Jap/US), V

Clavell, J.
Tai-Pan
Atheneum
ORION (US) 1986 dir. Daryl Duke
V

Cleary, J.
Green Helmet, The
Morrow
MGM (GB) 1960 dir. Michael Forlong

Cleary, J.
High Commissioner, The
Morrow
Nobody Runs Forever
RANK (GB) 1968 dir. Ralph Thomas
US title: High Commissioner, The

Cleary, J.
High Road to China
Morrow
WAR (US) 1983 dir. Brian G. Hutton
V

Cleary, J.
Spearfield's Daughter
FILMLINE (US) 1986
dir. Gilbert Shelton
TVSe(US)

Cleary, J.
Sundowners, The
Scribners
WAR (GB/Aust) 1960
dir. Fred Zinnemann

Cleary, J.
You Can't See Round Corners
UI (Aust) 1969 dir. David Cahill

Cleaver, V. and Cleaver, B.
Where the Lilies Bloom
Lippincott (Philadelphia)
UA (US) 1974 dir. William A. Graham

Clebert, J. P.
Blockhaus, Le
Blockhouse, The
GALACTUS (GB) 1973 dir. Clive Rees
V

Cleland, J.
Fanny Hill
Putnam
GALA (Ger) 1965 dir. Russ Meyer
BW (GB) 1983 dir. Gerry O'Hare
V

Clemente, G. W. and Stevens, K.
Cops are Robbers, The
Good Cops, Bad Cops
KUSHNER-LOCKE (US) 1990
dir. Paul Wendkos
TV(US)

Clewes, H.
Green Grow the Rushes
Lane
BL (GB) 1951 dir. Derek Twist

Clewes, H.
Long Memory, The
Macmillan
GFD (GB) 1953 dir. Robert Hamer

Clifford, C.L.
Real Glory, The
UA (US) 1939 dir. Henry Hathaway

Clifford, F.
Act of Mercy
Hamilton
Guns of Darkness
WAR (GB) 1962 dir. Anthony Asquith

Clifford, F.
Naked Runner, The
WAR (GB) 1967 dir. Sidney J. Furie

Clift, D.
Man About Town
Long
FOX (US) 1932 dir. John Francis Dillon

Clift, D.
Scotland Yard
P
FOX (US) 1941 dir. Norman Foster

Clift, D.
Warn London
BL (GB) 1934 dir. T. Hayes Hunter

Cloete, S.
Fiercest Heart, The
FOX (US) 1961 dir. George Sherman

Clooney, R. and Strait, R.
This For Remembrance
Simon & Schuster
Rosie: The Rosemary Clooney Story
FRIES (US) 1982 dir. Jackie Cooper
TV(US)

Clouston, J. S.
Spy in Black, The
COL (GB) 1939 dir. Michael Powell
US title: U-Boat 29
V

Clowes, St. J. L.
Dear Murderer
GFD (GB) 1947 dir. Arthur Crabtree

Coates, J.
True as a Turtle
RANK (GB) 1957 dir. Wendy Toye

Coates, R. M.
Wisteria Cottage
Gollancz
Edge of Fury
UA (US) 1958 dir. Robert Gurney,
Irving Lerner

Cobb, H.
Paths of Glory
University of Georgia Press
UA (US) 1957 dir. Stanley Kubrick
V

Cobb, I. S.
Sun Shines Bright, The; Mob From
Massac, The; Lord Provides, The
Sun Shines Bright, The
REP (US) 1953 dir. John Ford

Cochran, E.
Climax, The
P
UN (US) 1944 dir. George Waggner

Cochran, M.
And Deliver Us From Evil
Fugitive Among Us
ABC PRODS. (US) 1992
dir. Michael Toshiyuki Uno
TV(US)

Cockrell, F. M. and Cockrell, M.
Dark Waters
World, N.Y.
UA (US) 1944 dir. André de Toth
V

Cocteau, J.
Enfants Terribles, Les
Barnard Grasset (Paris)
MELVILLE (Fr) 1950
dir. Jean-Pierre Melville
V

Cocteau, J.
L'Amore
P
TEVERE (It) 1948
dir. Roberto Rossellini

Cocteau, J.
Orphée
P
Orion Press
A. PAULVÉ (Fr) 1949 dir. Jean Cocteau

Cocteau, J.
Parents Terribles, Les
P
Gallimard (Paris)
SIRIUS (Fr) 1948 dir. Jean Cocteau

Coe, C. F.
Nancy Steele is Missing
FOX (US) 1937 dir. George Marshall

Coetzee, J. M.
In the Heart of the Country
Dust
DASKA (Bel/Fr) 1985
dir. Marion Hansel
V

Coffee, L.
Weep No More
Cassell
Another Time, Another Place
PAR (GB) 1958 dir. Lewis Allen

Cohan, G. M.
Little Nellie Kelly
P

MGM (US) 1940 dir. Norman Taurog
M

Cohan, G. M.
Meanest Man in the World, The
P

FOX (US) 1943 dir. Sidney Lanfield

Cohn, A.
Joker is Wild, The
Random House

PAR (US) 1957 dir. Charles Vidor

Coke, P.
Breath of Spring
P

Samuel French

Make Mine Mink
RANK (GB) 1960 dir. Robert Asher

Cole, B.
Olimpia
Macmillan

Bobo, The
WAR (US) 1978 dir. Robert Parrish
V

Colegate, I.
Shooting Party, The
Viking Press

REEVE (GB) 1984 dir. Alan Bridges
V

Coleman, J.
At Mother's Request
Atheneum Publications

VISTA (US) 1987 dir. Michael Tuchner
TVSe(US)

Coleman, J. R.
Blue Collar Journal

Secret Life of John Chapman, The
JOZAK (US) 1976 dir. David Lowell Rich
TV(US)

Coleman, L.
Beulah Land
Doubleday

COL TV (US) 1980 dir. Virgil Vogel,
Harry Falk
TVSe(US)

Coleman, L.
Next of Kin
P

Hot Spell
PAR (US) 1958 dir. Daniel Mann

Coleman, T.
Southern Cross
G. REEVES (GB) 1983
TV(GB)

Colette
Gigi
Secker & Warburg (London)

(Fr) 1948 dir. Jacqueline Audry
MGM (US) 1958 dir. Vincente Minnelli
M, V

Colette
L'Ingenue Libertine
Various

CODO (Fr) 1950 dir. Jacqueline Audry

Collier, J. L.
Fires of Youth
Penguin

Danny Jones
CINERAMA (GB) 1972
dir. Jules Bricken
V

Collins, D.
Rich and Strange

BIP (GB) 1931 dir. Alfred Hitchcock
US title: East of Shanghai

Collins, D.
Sentimentalists, The
Little, Brown

His Woman
PAR (US) 1931 dir. Edward Sloman

Collins, J.
Bitch, The
Pan
BW (GB) 1979 dir. Gerry O'Hara
V

Collins, J.
Chances
NBC (US) 1990 dir. Buzz Kulik
TVSe(US)

Collins, J.
Hollywood Wives
WAR (US) 1985 dir. Robert Day
TVSe(US), V

Collins, J.
Lucky
Simon & Schuster
Lucky/Chances
NBC (US) 1990 dir. Buzz Kulik
TVSe(US)

Collins, J.
Stud, The
BW (GB) 1978 dir. Quentin Masters
V

Collins, J.
World is Full of Married Men, The
NEW REALM (GB) 1979
dir. Robert Young
V

Collins, L. and Lapierre, D.
Is Paris Burning?
Simon & Schuster
PAR (Fr/US) 1965 dir. René Clément

Collins, N.
London Belongs to Me
Collins
UN (GB) 1948 dir. Sydney Gilliatt
US title: Dulcimer Street
THAMES TV (GB) 1977
dir. Raymond Menmuir
TVSe(GB)

Collins, W.
Woman in White, The
American House (Mattituck, New York)
WAR (US) 1948 dir. Peter Godfrey

Collison, W.
Farewell to Women
P
Mogambo
MGM (US) 1953 dir. John Ford
V

Collison, W.
Farewell to Women
P
Red Dust
MGM (US) 1932 dir. Victor Fleming
V

Collodi, C.
Pinocchio
Dutton
DISNEY (US) 1940 dir. Ben Sharpsteen
A, Ch, V
CANTO (US) 1968 dir. Sid Smith
TV(US)

Colson, C.
Born Again
Chosen Books
AVCO (US) 1978 dir. Irving Rapper
V

Colton, J.
Shanghai Gesture, The
P
Boni & Liveright
IN (US) 1941 dir. Josef von Sternberg
V

Comden, B. and Green, A.
Bells are Ringing
P
Random House
MGM (US) 1960 dir. Vincente Minnelli
M, V

Compton, D.
Unsleeping Eye, The
Arrow, N.Y.

Deathwatch
CONTEM (Fr/Ger) 1979
dir. Bertrand Tavernier
V

Comstock, H. W.
Dr. X
P

WAR (US) 1932 dir. Michael Curtiz
V

Conchon, G.
L'Etat Sauvage
Cercle du Livre de France (Montreal)
FILMS 1966 (Fr) 1990 dir. Francis Girod

Conde, N.
Religion, The
New American Library

Believers, The
ORION (US) 1987 dir. John Schlesinger
V

Condon, R.
Manchurian Candidate, The
McGraw-Hill

UA (US) 1962 dir. John Frankenheimer

Condon, R.
Oldest Confession, The
Appleton-Century-Crofts

Happy Thieves, The
UA (US) 1962 dir. George Marshall

Condon, R.
Prizzi's Honor
Coward, McGann & Geoghegan
FOX (US) 1985 dir. John Huston
V

Condon, R.
Winter Kills
Dial Press
AVCO (US) 1979 dir. William Richert
V

Congwen, S.
Xiao, Xiao

Girl from Hunan, The
CHINA (China) 1986 dir. Xie Fei, U Lan

Connell, E. S.
Mr. Bridge; Mrs. Bridge
North Point Press (San Francisco)

Mr. and Mrs. Bridge
MIRAMAX (US) 1990 dir. James Ivory

Connell, E. S.
Son of the Morningstar: Custer and the Little Big Horn
North Point Press (San Francisco)

Son of the Morning Star
REP (US) 1991 dir. Mike Robe
TVSe(US), V

Connell, R. E.
Brother Orchid
WAR (US) 1940 dir. Lloyd Bacon

Connelly, M.
Green Pastures, The
P
Holt, Rinehart & Winston

WAR (US) 1936
dir. William Keighley/Marc Connelly
V
MILBERG (US) 1957
dir. George Schaefer
TV(US)

Conner, R.
Shake Hands with the Devil
UA (Ire) 1959 dir. Michael Anderson

Conners, B.
Applesauce
P
Samuel French

Brides are Like That
WAR (US) 1936 dir. William McGann

Conrad, J.
Within the Tides
Doubleday

Laughing Annie
REP (GB) 1953 dir. Herbert Wilcox

Conrad, J.
Lord Jim
Various

COL (GB) 1964 dir. Richard Brooks
V

Conrad, J.
Outcast of the Islands, An
Doubleday

LF (GB) 1951 dir. Carol Reed

Conrad, J.
Point of Honour, The
Fontana

Duellists, The
CIC (GB) 1977 dir. Ridley Scott
V

Conrad, J.
Secret Agent, The
Various

Sabotage
GB (GB) 1936 dir. Alfred Hitchcock
US title: Woman Alone, A
V

Conrad, J.
Secret Sharer, The
World Publishing

Face to Face
RKO (US) 1952 dir. John Brahm/
Bretaigne Windust

Conrad, J.
Victory
Sun Dial Press

PAR (US) 1940 dir. John Cromwell

Conran, S.
Lace
Simon & Schuster

LORIMAR (US) 1984 dir. Billy Hale
TVSe(US), V

Conroy, P.
Great Santini, The
Houghton, Mifflin Co. (Boston)

ORION (US) 1979
dir. Lewis John Carlino
V

Conroy, P.
Lords of Discipline, The
Houghton, Mifflin Co. (Boston)

PAR (US) 1983 dir. Franc Roddam
V

Conroy, P.
Prince of Tides, The
Houghton, Mifflin Co. (Boston)

COL (US) 1991 dir. Barbra Streisand

Conroy, P.
Water is Wide, The
Houghton, Mifflin Co. (Boston)

Conrack
FOX (US) 1974 dir. Martin Ritt
V

**Constanduros, M. and
Constanduros, D.**
Acacia Avenue
P

29 Acacia Avenue
COL (GB) 1945 dir. Henry Cass
US title: Facts of Love, The

Cook, D.
Winter Doves
Overlook Press (Woodstock, New York)

Loving Walter
FF (GB) 1986 dir. Stephen Frears

Cook, K.
Wake in Fright
St. Martin's Press

Outback
NIT (Aus) 1970 dir. Ted Kotcheff

Cook, R.
Coma
Little, Brown (Boston)
MGM (US) 1978 dir. Michael Crichton
V

Cook, R.
Sphinx
Macmillan
WAR (US) 1981
dir. Franklin D. Schaffner
V

Cooke, W. E.
Two Rode Together
COL (US) 1961 dir. John Ford
V

Cookson, C.
Black Candle, The
TYNE-TEES (GB) 1991
dir. Roy Battersby
TV(GB)

Cookson, C.
Black Velvet Gown, The
Summit Books
TYNE-TEES (GB) 1991
dir. Norman Stone
TV(GB)

Cookson, C.
Fifteen Streets, The
TYNE-TEES (GB) 1991
dir. David Wheatley
TV(GB)

Cookson, C.
Mallens, The
Dutton
GRANADA (GB) 1979
TVSe(GB)

Cookson, C.
Rooney
RANK (GB) 1958 dir. George Pollock

Coolen, A.
Doctor in the Village
NFM (Neth) 1958 dir. Fons Rademakers

Cooney, C. B.
Rearview Mirror
Random House
SCHICK SUNN (US) 1984
dir. Lou Antonio
TV(US)

Cooney, R.
Not Now Darling
P
Dramatists Play Service
MGM (GB) 1973 dir. Ray Cooney,
David Croft
V

Cooney, R.
There Goes the Bride
P
Samuel French
ENT (GB) 1980 dir. Terence Marcel

Coonts, S.
Flight of the Intruder
Naval Institute Press (Annapolis,
Maryland)
PAR (US) 1991 dir. John Milius

Cooper, J. F.
Deerslayer, The
Various
FOX (US) 1957 dir. Kurt Neumann
V
SCHICK SUNN (US) 1978
dir. Dick Friedenberg
TV(US), V

Cooper, J. F.
Last of the Mohicans, The
Various
UA (US) 1936 dir. George B. Scitz
SCHICK SUNN (US) 1977
dir. James L. Conway
TV(US), V

Cooper, J. F.
Last of the Mohicans, The
Various

Last of the Redmen
COL (US) 1947 dir. George Sherman

Cooper, R. R.
Last To Go, The
Harcourt, Brace, Jovanovich

INTERSCOPE (US) 1991
dir. John Erman
TV(US)

Cooper, S. and Cronyn, H.
Foxfire
P
Samuel French
M. REES (US) 1987 dir. Jud Taylor
TV(US)

Coppel, A.
Gazebo, The
MGM (US) 1959 dir. George Marshall

Coppel, A.
I Killed The Count
P
Samuel French
GN (GB) 1939 dir. Fred Zelnik

Coppel, A.
Man About a Dog, A
P

Obsession
GFD (GB) 1949 dir. Edward Dmytryk
US title: Hidden Room, The
V

Coppel, A.
Mr. Denning Drives North
BL (GB) 1951 dir. Anthony Kimmins

Corbett, J. J.
Roar of the Crowd, The
Gentleman Jim
WAR (US) 1942 dir. Raoul Walsh

Corbett, S.
Love Nest
FOX (US) 1951 dir. Joseph Newman

Corbin, W.
Smoke
DISNEY (US) 1970
dir. Vincent McEveety
V

Corcoran, J.
Bitter Harvest: Murder in the
Heartland
Viking Press

*In the Line of Duty: Manhunt in the
Dakotas*
P-K (US) 1991 dir. Dick Lowry
TV(US)

Cordelier, J.
Life, The
Viking Press

Memoirs of a French Whore
Aidart (Fr) 1982 dir. Daniel Duval

Corliss, A.
Summer Lightning
I Met My Love Again
WANGER (US) 1937 dir. Joshua Logan,
Arthur Ripley

Cormack, B.
Racket, The
P
Theatre Communications Group
RKO (US) 1951 dir. John Cromwell
V

Corman, A.
Kramer vs Kramer
Random House
COL (US) 1979 dir. Robert Benton
V

Corman, A.
Oh! God!
Simon & Schuster
WAR (US) 1977 dir. Carl Reiner
V

Cormier, R.
Chocolate War, The
Pantheon Books
MCEG (US) 1988 dir. Keith Gordon
V

Cormier, R.
I am the Cheese
Pantheon
ALMI (US) 1983 dir. Robert Jiras
V

Corrington, J. W.
Decoration Day
M. REES (US) 1990
dir. Robert Markowitz
TV(US)

Corwin, N.
Rivalry, The
P
Dramatists Play Service
DEFARIA (US) 1975 dir. Fielder Cook
TV(US)

Cory, D.
Deadfall
Walker Press
FOX (GB) 1968 dir. Bryan Forbes

Cosby, V.
Mind Reader, The
WAR (US) 1933 dir. Roy del Ruth

Costain, T. B.
Black Rose, The
Doubleday
FOX (US) 1950 dir. Henry Hathaway

Costain, T. B.
Silver Chalice, The
Doubleday
WAR (US) 1954 dir. Victor Saville
V

Cotler, G.
Bottletop Affair, The
Panther
Horizontal Lieutenant, The
MGM (US) 1962 dir. Richard Thorpe

Cotterell, G.
Tiara Tahiti
RANK (GB) 1962
dir. William T. Kotcheff
V

Coulter, S.
Embassy
Heinemann
HEMDALE (GB) 1972
dir. Gordon Hessler

Coupon, H.
Verdict
CCC (Fr/It) 1974 dir. André Cayatte

Cousins, M.
Life of Lucy Gallant, The
Lucy Gallant
PAR (US) 1955 dir. Robert Parrish

Cousins, N.
Anatomy of an Illness
Norton
CBS ENT. (US) 1984
dir. Richard Heffron
TV(US)

Coward, N.
Astonished Heart, The
P
Samuel French
GFD (GB) 1949 dir. Terence Fisher,
Anthony Darnborough

Coward, N.
Bitter Sweet
P
Chappell
UA (GB) 1933 dir. Herbert Wilcox
MGM (US) 1940 dir. W. S. Van Dyke II
M

Coward, N.
Blithe Spirit
P
Samuel French
CIN (GB) 1945 dir. David Lean
COMPASS (US) 1966
dir. George Schaefer
TV(US)

Coward, N.
Bon Voyage
BBC (GB) 1985 dir. Mike Vardy
TV(GB), V

Coward, N.
Cavalcade
P
Doubleday
FOX (US) 1932 dir. Frank Lloyd

Coward, N.
Design for Living
P
Doubleday
PAR (US) 1933 dir. Ernst Lubitsch

Coward, N.
Me and the Girls
Dutton
BBC (GB) 1985 dir. Jack Gold
TV(GB), V

Coward, N.
Mr and Mrs. Edgehill
Doubleday
BBC (GB) 1985 dir. Gavin Miller
TV(GB), V

Coward, N.
Mrs. Capper's Birthday
Dutton
BBC (GB) 1985 dir. Mike Ockrent
TV(GB), V

Coward, N.
Pretty Polly Barlow
Doubleday
Pretty Polly
RANK (GB) 1967 dir. Guy Green
US title: Matter of Innocence, A

Coward, N.
Private Lives
P
Samuel French
MGM (US) 1931 dir. Sidney Franklin

Coward, N.
Queen was in the Parlour, The
P
Tonight is Ours
PAR (US) 1933 dir. Stuart Walker

Coward, N.
Red Peppers; Fumed Oak; Ways & Means
P
Samuel French
Meet Me Tonight
GFD (GB) 1952 dir. Anthony Pelissier

Coward, N.
Star Quality
Dutton
BBC (GB) 1985 dir. Alan Dosser
TVSe(GB)

Coward, N.
Still Life
P
Samuel French
Brief Encounter
CIN (GB) 1945 dir. David Lean
V
ITC (US) 1974 dir. Alan Bridges
TV(US)

Coward, N.
This Happy Breed
P
Samuel French
TC (GB) 1944 dir. David Lean
V

Coward, N.
Tonight at 8.30
P
Doubleday
BBC (GB) 1991 dir. Joan Collins and
Paul Annett
TV(GB)

Coward, N.
Tonight at 8.30
P
Samuel French
We Were Dancing
MGM (GB) 1942 dir. Robert Z. Leonard

Coward, N.
What Mad Pursuit
Dutton
BBC (GB) 1985 dir. Tony Smith
TV(GB), V

Cowen, R.
Summertree
P
WAR (US) 1971 dir. Anthony Newley

Cowen, W. J.
They Gave Him A Gun
MGM (US) 1937 dir. W. S. Van Dyke

Cowl, J. and Murfin, J.
Smilin' Through
P
MGM (US) 1932 dir. Sidney Franklin
MGM (US) 1941 dir. Frank Borzage
V

Cowley, J.
Nest in a Falling Tree
Doubleday
Night Digger, The
MGM (GB) 1971 dir. Alistair Reid

Coxhead, E.
Friend in Need, The
Collins
Cry from the Streets, A.
EROS (GB) 1958 dir. Lewis Gilbert

Cozzens, J. G.
By Love Possessed
Harcourt, Brace
UA (US) 1961 dir. John Sturges

Cozzens, J. G.
Last Adam, The
Harcourt, Brace
Dr. Bull
FOX (US) 1933 dir. John Ford

Craig, D.
Squeeze, The
Stein & Day
WAR (GB) 1977 dir. Michael Apted
V

Craig, J.
If You Want to See Your Wife Again
Putnam
Your Money or Your Wife
BRENTWOOD (US) 1972
dir. Allen Reisner
TV(US)

Craig, R.
Storm and Sorrow in the High High Pamirs
Simon & Schuster
Storm and Sorrow
HEARST (US) 1990 dir. Richard Colla
TV(US)

Cram, M.
Tinfoil
Faithless
MGM (US) 1932 dir. Harry Beaumont

Cramer, R. W.
Babe: The Legend Comes to Life
Simon & Schuster
Babe Ruth
LYTTLE (US) 1991 dir. Mark Tinker
TV(US)

Crane, C.
Summer Girl
Dodd, Mead

LORIMAR (US) 1983
dir. Robert Michael Lewis
TV(US)

Crane, R.
Hero's Walk
Voices, The
BBC (GB) 1965 dir. Dennis Vance
TV(GB)

Crane, S.
Bride Comes to Yellow Sky, The
World Publishing

Face to Face
RKO (US) 1952
dir. John Brahm/Bretaigne Windust

Crane, S.
Red Badge of Courage, The
Various

MGM (US) 1951 dir. John Huston
V
M ARCH (US) 1981 dir. Don Taylor
TV(US)

Craven, F.
First Year, The
P
Samuel French

FOX (US) 1932 dir. William K. Howard

Craven, M.
I Heard the Owl Call My Name
Doubleday

TOMORROW INC. (US) 1973
dir. Daryl Duke
TV(US), V

Crawford, C.
Mommie Dearest
W. Morrow

PAR (US) 1981 dir. Frank Perry
V

Crawford, E. M. & Hackett, W.
White Sister
P

MGM (US) 1933 dir. Victor Fleming

Crawford, J.
Birch Interval
Houghton, Mifflin Co. (Boston)

GAMMA III (US) 1976
dir. Delbert Mann

Crawford, O.
Execution, The
St. Martin's Press

COMWORLD (US) 1985
dir. Paul Wendkos
TV(US), V

Creasey, J.
Gideon's Day
COL (GB) 1958 dir. John Ford
US title: Gideon of Scotland Yard

Creasey, J.
Hammer the Toff
Long

BUTCHER (GB) 1952
dir. Maclean Rogers

Creasey, J.
Salute the Toff
BUTCHER (GB) 1952
dir. Maclean Rogers

Cresswell, H.
Moondial
Macmillan

BBC (GB) 1988
Ch, TVSe(GB)

Cresswell, H.
Secret World of Polly Flint
Macmillan

Central (GB) 1987 dir. David Cobham
Ch, TVSe(GB)

Crichton, M.
Andromeda Strain, The
Knopf
UN (US) 1971 dir. Robert Wise
V

Crichton, M.
Binary
Knopf
Pursuit
ABC (USTV) 1972 dir. Michael Crichton

Crichton, M.
Great Train Robbery, The
Knopf
First Great Train Robbery, The
UA (GB) 1978 dir. Michael Crichton
V

Crichton, R.
Great Imposter, The
Random House
UI (US) 1961 dir. Robert Mulligan
V

Crichton, R.
Secret of Santa Vittoria, The
Simon & Schuster
UA (US) 1969 dir. Stanley Kramer

Crisp, Q.
Naked Civil Servant, The
Holt, Rinehart & Winston
THAMES (GB) 1975 dir. Jack Gold
TV(GB), V

Cristofer, M.
Shadow Box, The
P
Samuel French
SHADOW BOX (US) 1980
dir. Paul Newman
TV(US), V

Crockett, L. H.
Magnificent Devils
Proud and Profane, The
PAR (US) 1956 dir. George Seaton

Croft, M.
Spare the Rod
BL (GB) 1961 dir. Leslie Norman

Croft-Cooke, R.
Seven Thunders
RANK (GB) 1957 dir. Hugo Fregonese
US title: Beasts of Marseilles, The

Crompton, R.
Just William
Newnes
AB (GB) 1939 dir. Graham Cutts

Cronin, A. J.
Beyond this Place
Little, Brown (Boston)
REN (GB) 1959 dir. Jack Cardiff

Cronin, A. J.
Citadel, The
Little, Brown (Boston)
MGM (GB) 1938 dir. King Vidor
V
BBC (GB) 1983 dir. Peter Jefferies
TVSe(GB)

Cronin, A. J.
Grand Canary
Grosset & Dunlap
FOX (US) 1934 dir. Irving Cummings

Cronin, A. J.
Green Years, The
MGM (US) 1946 dir. Victor Saville

Cronin, A. J.
Hatter's Castle
Grosset & Dunlap
PAR (GB) 1941 dir. Lance Comfort

Cronin, A. J.
Jupiter Laughs
P
Little, Brown (Boston)
Shining Victory
WAR (US) 1941 dir. Irving Rapper

Cronin, A. J.
Keys of the Kingdom, The
Little, Brown (Boston)
FOX (US) 1944 dir. John M. Stahl

Cronin, A. J.
Spanish Gardener, The
Little, Brown (Boston)
RANK (GB) 1956 dir. Philip Leacock
V

Cronin, A. J.
Stars Look Down, The
Little, Brown (Boston)
GN (GB) 1939 dir. Carol Reed
V

Cronin, A. J.
Vigil in the Night
RKO (US) 1940 dir. George Stevens

Cronin, M.
Paid in Full
Museum Press
Johnny on the Spot
FANCEY (GB) 1954
dir. Maclean Rogers

Cronley, J.
Funny Farm
Atheneum
WAR (US) 1988 dir. George Roy Hill

Cronley, J.
Good Vibes
Doubleday
Let It Ride
PAR (US) 1989 dir. Joe Pytka

Cronley, J.
Quick Change
Doubleday
WAR (US) 1990 dir. Howard Franklin,
Bill Murray

Cross, B.
Half a Sixpence
P
PAR (GB) 1967 dir. George Sidney
M

Crossley, R.
Annie's Coming Out
Penguin
ENT (Aust) 1984 dir. Gil Brealey
V

Crossley, R., and McDonald, A.
Annie's Coming Out
Test of Love, A
UN (US) 1985 dir. Gil Brealey
V

Crothers, R.
As Husbands Go
P
Samuel French
FOX (US) 1934 dir. Hamilton McFadden

Crothers, R.
Old Lady 31
P
Brentano's
Captain is a Lady, The
MGM (US) 1940 dir. Robert Sinclair

Crothers, R.
Splendor
P
GOLDWYN (US) 1935
dir. Elliott Nugent

Crothers, R.
Susan and God
P
Random House
MGM (US) 1940 dir. George Cukor
GB title: Gay Mrs. Trexel, The

Crothers, R.
When Ladies Meet
P
Samuel French
MGM (US) 1933 dir. Harry Beaumont
MGM (US) 1941 dir. Robert Z. Leonard

Crowe, C.
Fast Times at Ridgemont High
Simon & Schuster
UN (US) 1982 dir. Amy Heckerling
V

Crowley, M.
Boys in the Band, The
P
Samuel French
WAR (US) 1970 dir. William Friedkin
V

Croy, H.
Family Honeymoon
Hurst & Bleckett
UN (US) 1948 dir. Claude Binyon

Croy, H.
Sixteen Hands
Hamilton
I'm From Missouri
PAR (US) 1939 dir. Theodore Reed

Cullinan, T.
Bedeviled, The
Putnam
Beguiled, The
UN (US) 1971 dir. Don Siegel
V

Culotta, N.
They're a Weird Mob
RANK (GB) 1966 dir. Michael Powell
V

Cunningham, E. V.
Penelope
Doubleday
MGM (US) 1966 dir. Arthur Hiller

Cunningham, E. V.
Sally
Face of Fear, The
Q. MARTIN (US) 1971
dir. George McCowan
TV(US)

Cunningham, E. V.
Shirley
What's a Nice Girl Like You . . .?
UN TV (US) 1971 dir. Jerry Paris
TV(US)

Cunningham, E. V.
Sylvia
Doubleday
PAR (US) 1965 dir. Gordon Douglas

Cunningham, J. M.
Tin Star, The
High Noon
UA (US) 1952 dir. Fred Zinnemann
V

Cunningham, J.
Hunter's Blood
CONCORDE (US) 1987
dir. Robert C. Hughes

Curie, E.
Madame Curie
Doubleday
MGM (US) 1943 dir. Mervyn Le Roy

Curran, R.
Haunted, The
St. Martin's Press
FOX TV (US) 1991 dir. Robert Mandel
TV(US)

Curtis, J.
They Drive by Night
WAR (GB) 1938 dir. Arthur Woods

Curtis, P.
Devil's Own, The
FOX (GB) 1967 dir. Cyril Frankel

Curtis, P.
Devil's Own, The

Witches, The
HAMMER (GB) 1966 dir. Cyril Frankel

Curtis, P.
You're Best Alone

Guilt is my Shadow
ABP (GB) 1950 dir. Roy Kellino

Curtiss, U.
Forbidden Garden, The
Dodd, Mead

Whatever Happened to Aunt Alice?
PALOMAR (US) 1969 dir. Lee H. Katzin
V

Curtiss, U.
I Saw What You Did

UN (US) 1965 dir. William Castle
UN (US) 1988 dir. Fred Walton
TV(US)

Curwood, J. O.
Back to God's Country

UN (US) 1953 dir. Joseph Pevney

Curwood, J. O.
God's Country and the Woman

WAR (US) 1936 dir. William Keighley

Curwood, J. O.
Grizzly King, The
Newmarket Press

Bear, The
TRI-STAR (Fr) 1989
dir. Jean-Jacques Annaud

Curwood, J. O.
Kazan
Grosset & Dunlap

COL (US) 1949 dir. Will Jason

Curwood, J. O.
Nomads of the North

Nikki, Wild Dog of the North
DISNEY (US) 1961 dir. Jack Couffer
V

Curwood, J. O.
River's End

WAR (US) 1930 dir. Michael Curtiz

Cusack, D.
Come in Spinner

BBC (GB) 1991 dir. Ray Marchand
TV(GB)

Cushman, C. F.
Young Widow, The

UA (US) 1946 dir. Edwin L. Marin

Cushman, D.
Ripper from Rawhide

Timberjack
REP (US) 1954 dir. Joe Kane

Cushman, D.
Stay Away, Joe
Viking Press

MGM (US) 1968 dir. Peter Tewkesbury
V

Cussler, C.
Raise the Titanic
Viking Press

ITC (US) 1980 dir. Jerry Jameson
V

Czeszko, B.
Generation

POLSKI (Pol) 1954 dir. Andrzej Wajda

Dahl, R.
Charlie and the Chocolate Factory
Knopf

Willy Wonka and the Chocolate Factory
PAR (US) 1971 dir. Mel Stuart
Ch, V

Dahl, R.
Danny the Champion of the World
Knopf
COL (GB) 1989 dir. Gavin Millar
Ch

Dahl, R.
Witches, The
Farrar, Straus & Giroux
WAR (US) 1990 dir. Nicolas Roeg

Dalby, L.
Geisha
University of California Press, Berkeley
American Geisha
INTERSCOPE (US) 1986
dir. Lee Philips
TV(US)

Daley, R.
Hands of a Stranger
Simon & Schuster
TAFT (US) 1987 dir. Larry Elikann
TV(US)

Daley, R.
Prince of the City
Houghton, Mifflin Co. (Boston)
ORION (US) 1981 dir. Sidney Lumet
V

Daley, R.
To Kill A Cop
Crown
COL TV (US) 1978 dir. Gary Nelson
TVSe(US)

Daley, R.
Year of the Dragon
Simon & Schuster
MGM/UA (US) 1985
dir. Michael Cimino
V

Dana, R. H.
Two Years Before the Mast
World Publishers
PAR (US) 1946 dir. John Farrow

Dane, C.
Bill of Divorcement, A
P
RKO (US) 1932 dir. George Cukor
RKO (US) 1940 dir. John Farrow
GB title: Never to Love
V

Dane, C. and Simpson, H.
Enter, Sir John
Farrar & Rinehart
Murder
BI (GB) 1930 dir. Alfred Hitchcock
V

Dangerfield, Y.
Petite Sirène, La
WA (Fr) 1984 dir. Roger Andrieux

Daninos, P.
Notebooks of Major Thompson, The
Knopf

Diary of Major Thompson, The
GALA (Fr) 1955 dir. Preston Sturges
US title: French They are a Funny Race,
The

Dann, P.
Mermaids
Ticknor & Fields
ORION (US) 1990
dir. Richard Benjamin
V

Dante Alighieri
La Divina Commedia
Various

A TV Dante
CHANNEL 4 (GB) 1990
dir. Tom Phillips
TV(GB)

Dante, N., Kirkwood, J. and Hamlisch, M.
Chorus Line, A
P
E. H. Morris
COL (US) 1985
dir. Richard Attenborough
M, V

Darlington, W.A.
Alf's Button
Alf's Button Afloat
GAINS (GB) 1938 dir. Marcel Varnel

Dart, I. R.
Beaches
Bantam Books
TOUCH (US) 1988 dir. Garry Marshall
V

d'Ashelbe, R.
Algiers
Pépé le Moko
WANGER (US) 1938 dir. John Cromwell

d'Ashelbe, R.
Pépé le Moko
PARIS (Fr) 1936 dir. Julian Duvivier
V

Dataller, R.
Steel Saraband
Hard Steel
GFD (GB) 1942 dir. Norman Walker

Davenport, M.
East Side, West Side
Scribners
MGM (US) 1949 dir. Mervyn Le Roy

Davenport, M.
Valley of Decision, The
Scribners
MGM (US) 1945 dir. Tay Garnett

Davenport, Mrs. G.
Belvedere
Sitting Pretty
FOX (US) 1948 dir. Walter Lang

Davidson, A.
Out of the Shadows
KUSHNER-LOCKE/YTV (US/GB)
1988 dir. Willi Patterson
TV(GB/US)

Davidson, B.
Indict and Convict
Harper & Row
UN TV (US) 1974 dir. Boris Sagal
TV(US)

Davidson, L.
Night Before Wenceslas, The
Harper
Hot Enough for June
RANK (GB) 1963 dir. Ralph Thomas

Davidson, S.
Loose Change
Doubleday
UN TV (US) 1978 dir. Jules Irving
TVSe(US)

Davies, H.
Here we go Round the Mulberry Bush
Coward, McCann & Geoghegan
UA (GB) 1967 dir. Clive Donner

Davies, H. H.
Girl from Tenth Avenue, The
P
WAR (US) 1935 dir. Alfred E. Green
GB title: Men on her Mind

Davies, J.
Esther, Ruth and Jennifer
North Sea Hijack
CIC (GB) 1980 dir. Andrew V. McLaglen
US title: Ffolkes
V

Davies, J. E.
Mission to Moscow
Garden City Publishing Co. (Garden City, New York)
WAR (US) 1943 dir. Michael Curtiz

Davies, L. P.
Alien, The
Doubleday
Groundstar Conspiracy, The
UN (US) 1972 dir. Lamont Johnson
V

Davies, L. P.
Project X
PAR (US) 1968 dir. William Castle

Davies, V.
Miracle on 34th Street
Harcourt Brace
FOX (US) 1947 dir. George Seaton
GB title: Big Heart, The
V
TCF (US) 1973 dir. Fielder Cook
TV(US)

Davis, B.
Full Fathom Fire
CONCORDE (US) 1990
dir. Carl Franklin

Davis, B. C.
Mass Appeal
P
Avon Books
UN (US) 1984 dir. Glenn Jordan
V

Davis, C. B.
Anointed, The
Adventure
MGM (US) 1945 dir. Victor Fleming

Davis, D. S.
Where the Dark Streets Go
Scribners
Broken Vows
R. HALMI (US) 1987 dir. Jud Taylor
TV(US)

Davis, D.
Jezebel
P
WAR (US) 1938 dir. William Wyler
V

Davis, E.
Me Two
All of Me
UN (US) 1984 dir. Carl Reiner
V

Davis, E.
Revenge
CARLINER (US) 1971 dir. Jud Taylor
TV(US)

Davis, O.
Mr. and Mrs. North
P
Samuel French
MGM (US) 1941 dir. Robert B. Sinclair

Davis, R. P.
Pilot, The
Morrow
SUMMIT (Can) 1981
dir. Cliff Robertson

Davis, T.
Vision Quest
Viking Press
WAR (US) 1985 dir. Harold Becker
V

Day, C.
Life with Father
P
Knopf
WAR (US) 1947 dir. Michael Curtiz
V

Day, L.
Youngest Profession, The
MGM (US) 1943 dir. Edward Buzzell

De Beauvoir, S.
Blood of Others, The
Knopf
HBO PREMIERE (Can/Fr) 1984
dir. Claude Chabrol
TV, V

de Bri, L.
Moulin Rouge
P
FOX (US) 1934 dir. Sidney Lanfield

de Croisset, F.
Il était une fois
P
Woman's Face, A
MGM (US) 1941 dir. George Cukor
V

De Felitta, F.
Audrey Rose
Putnam
UA (US) 1977 dir. Robert Wise
V

De Felitta, F.
Entity, The
Putnam
FOX (US) 1982 dir. Sidney J. Furie
V

De Frece, Lady
Recollections of Vesta Tilly
Hutchinson
After the Ball
BL (GB) 1957 dir. Compton Bennett

de Gouriadec, L.
Mort en fuite, La
Break the News
GFD (GB) 1938 dir. René Clair

de la Fouchardière, G.
Chienne, La
P
Scarlet Street
UN (US) 1945 dir. Fritz Lang
V

de la Fouchardière, G.
Chienne, La
BRAU (Fr) 1931 dir. Jean Renoir

de Laclos, P.
Liaisons Dangereuses, Les
Various
MARCEAU (Fr) 1959 dir. Roger Vadim

de Laclos, P.
Liaisons Dangereuses, Les
P
Dangerous Liaisons
WAR (US) 1988 dir. Stephen Frears
V

de Laclos, P.
Liaisons Dangereuses, Les
Various
Valmont
ORION (GB) 1989 dir. Milos Forman

de Ligneris, F.
Psyche 63
Psyche 59
BL (GB) 1964 dir. Alexander Singer

De Maupassant, G.
Bel Ami
Various

Private Affairs of Bel Ami, The
UA (US) 1947 dir. Albert Lewin

De Sade, Marquis
Justine
Grove Press

Cruel Passion
TARGET (GB) 1977 dir. Chris Boger

de Soto, J. M. V.
Infierno y la Brisa, El

Hail Hazana
STILLMAN (Sp) 1978
dir. Jose Maria Guttierez

De Villeneuve, Mme.
Beauty and the Beast
Various

LOPERT (Fr) 1947 dir. Jean Cocteau
V
PALM (US) 1976 dir. Fielder Cook
TV(US)
CANNON (US) 1987 dir. Eugene
Marner
DISNEY (US) 1991 dir. Gary Trousdale,
Kirk Wise
A, Ch, M

De Voto, B.
Across the Wide Missouri
Houghton, Mifflin Company (Boston)

MGM (US) 1951 dir. William Wellman

De Vries, P.
Let Me Count the Ways
Little, Brown (Boston)

How Do I Love Thee?
ABC (US) 1970 dir. Michael Gordon
V

De Vries, P.
Reuben, Reuben
Little, Brown (Boston)

FOX (US) 1983 dir. Robert Ellis Millet
V

De Vries, P.
Tunnel of Love, The
Little, Brown (Boston)

MGM (US) 1958 dir. Gene Kelly

De Vries, P.
Witch's Milk
Little, Brown (Boston)

Pete 'n Tillie
UN (US) 1972 dir. Martin Ritt
V

Deal, B.
Bluegrass
Doubleday

LAN (US) 1988 dir. Simon Wincer
TVSe(US)

Deal, B.
Dunbar's Cove

Wild River
FOX (US) 1960 dir. Elia Kazan

Deal, B. H.
Walls Came Tumbling Down, The
Doubleday

Friendships, Secrets and Lies
WAR TV (US) 1979
dir. Ann Zane Shanks, Marlena Laird
TV(US)

Dean, B. and Munro, G.
Murder Gang
P

Sensation
BIP (GB) 1936
dir. Brian Desmond Hurst

Dean, J.
Blind Ambition
Simon & Schuster

TIME-LIFE (US) 1979
dir. George Schaefer
TVSe(US)

Dean, M.
Mo: A Woman's View of Watergate
Simon & Schuster

Blind Ambition
TIME-LIFE (US) 1979
dir. George Schaefer
TVSe(US)

Dearsley, A. P.
Fly Away Peter
P
GFD (GB) 1948 dir. Charles Saunders

DeCapite, R.
Lost King, A
Harry and Son
ORION (US) 1984 dir. Paul Newman
V

Deeping, W.
Sorrell and Son
Knopf
UA (GB) 1933 dir. Jack Raymond
YTV (GB) 1984 dir. Derek Bennett
TVSe(GB)

Defoe, D.
Fortunes and Misfortunes of the Famous Moll Flanders, The
Various
Amorous Adventures of Moll Flanders, The
PAR (GB) 1965 dir. Terence Young

Defoe, D.
Robinson Crusoe
Various
Adventures of Robinson Crusoe, The
UA (Mex/US) 1954 dir. Luis Bunuel

Defoe, D.
Robinson Crusoe
Various
BBC (GB) 1974 dir. James MacTaggart
TV(GB)

Defoe, D.
Robinson Crusoe
Various
Crusoe
ISLAND (US) 1989 dir. Caleb Deschanel
V

Deford, F.
Alex: The Life of a Child
Viking Press
MANDY (US) 1986
dir. Robert Markowitz
TV (US)

Deford, F.
Everybody's All-American
WAR (US) 1988 dir. Taylor Hackford

Deighton, L.
Berlin Memorandum, The
Putnam
Funeral in Berlin
PAR (GB) 1966 dir. Guy Hamilton
V

Deighton, L.
Billion Dollar Brain
Putnam
UA (GB) 1967 dir. Ken Russell
V

Deighton, L.
Game Set and Match
GRANADA TV (GB) 1987
TV(GB)

Deighton, L.
Ipcress File, The
Simon & Schuster
RANK (GB) 1965 dir. Sidney J. Furie
V

Deighton, L.
Only When I Larf
Mysterious Press
PAR (GB) 1968 dir. Basil Dearden
V

Deighton, L.
Spy Story
Harcourt, Brace, Jovanovich
GALA (GB) 1976 dir. Lindsay Shonteff
V

Dekobra, M.
Hell is Sold Out
Laurie
EROS (GB) 1951 dir. Michael Anderson

Dekobra, M.
Sphinx has Spoken, The
Friends and Lovers
RKO (US) 1931 dir. Victor Schertzinger

Del Rivo, L.
Furnished Room, The
West Eleven
WAR (GB) 1963 dir. Michael Winner

Delacorta
Diva
Summit Books
GALAXIE (Fr) 1981
dir. Jean-Jacques Beineix
V

Delaney, S.
Taste of Honey, A
P
Grove Press
BRYANSTON (GB) 1961
dir. Tony Richardson

Delderfield, R. F.
All Over the Town
P
Simon & Schuster
RANK (GB) 1948 dir. Dereck Twist

Delderfield, R. F.
Bull Boys, The
P
Carry on Sergeant
AAM (GB) 1958 dir. Gerald Thomas

Delderfield, R. F.
Come Home Charlie and Face Them
Simon & Schuster
LWT (GB) 1990 dir. Roger Bamford
TV(GB)

Delderfield, R. F.
Glad Tidings
P
Samuel French
EROS (GB) 1953 dir. Wolf Rilla

Delderfield, R. F.
Orchard Walls, The
P
Now and Forever
ABP (GB) 1955 dir. Mario Zampi

Delderfield, R. F.
Stop at a Winner
Simon & Schuster
On the Fiddle
AA (GB) 1961 dir. Cyril Frankel
US title: Operation Snafu

Delderfield, R. F.
**There was a Fair Maid Dwelling;
Unjust Skies, The**
Hodder & Stoughton
Diana
BBC (GB) 1983 dir. David Tucker
TVSe(GB)

Delderfield, R. F.
To Serve Them All My Days
Simon & Schuster
BBC (GB) 1980 dir. Ronald Wilson
TVSe(GB)

Delderfield, R. F.
Where There's A Will
P
EROS (GB) 1955 dir. Vernon Sewell

Delderfield, R. F.
Worm's Eye View
P
ABP (GB) 1951 dir. Jack Raymond

Delibes, M.
Holy Innocents, The
Planeta (Barcelona)
GANESH (Sp) 1985 dir. Mario Camus
Spanish title: Los Santos Inocentes
V

Dell, F.
Bachelor Father
P
Casanova Brown
INTERNAT (US) 1944 dir. Sam Wood

Dell, J.
Payment Deferred
P
Samuel French
MGM (US) 1932 dir. Lothar Mendes

Delman, D.
Conspiracy of Terror
LORIMAR (US) 1975
dir. John Llewellyn Moxey
TV(US)

Delmar, V.
About Mrs. Leslie
Harcourt, Brace & Company
PAR (US) 1954 dir. Daniel Mann

Deming, R.
Careful Man, The
Drop Dead Darling
SEVEN ARTS (GB) 1966
dir. Ken Hughes
US title: Arrivederci Baby

Dempsey, J. and Dempsey, B. P.
Dempsey
Harper & Row
FRIES (US) 1983 dir. Gus Trikonis
TV(US)

Denham, R. and Percy, E.
Ladies in Retirement
P
Random House
Mad Room, The
COL (US) 1969 dir. Bernard Girard

Denker, H.
Outrage!
Morrow
COL TV (US) 1986 dir. Walter Grauman
TV(US)

Denker, H., and Berkey, R.
Time Limit
P
Samuel French
UA (US) 1967 dir. Karl Malden

Dennis, C.
Next-to-Last Train Ride, The
Macmillan
Finders Keepers
RANK (US) 1984 dir. Richard Lester
V

Dennis, P.
Auntie Mame
Vanguard Press
WAR (US) 1958 dir. Morton da Costa
V

Dennis, P.
Auntie Mame
Vanguard Press
Mame
WAR (US) 1974 dir. Gene Saks
M, V

Denton, Jr., J. A. and Brandt, E.
When Hell was in Session
Commission Press (Clover, South Carolina)
AUBREY-HAMNER (USTV) 1979
dir. Paul Krasny
TV(US), V

Denuzière, M.
Louisiane; Fausse-Rivière
Morrow

Louisiana
CINEMAX (US) 1984
dir. Philippe de Broca
TVSe(US), V

Dershowitz, A.
Reversal of Fortune
Random House
WAR (US) 1990 dir. Barbet Schroeder

desCars, G.
Brute, La
(Fr) 1987 dir. Claude Guillemot

Deval, J.
Her Cardboard Lover
P
MGM (US) 1942 dir. George Cukor

Deval, J.
Tovarich
P
Samuel French
WAR (US) 1937 dir. Anatole Litvak

deVere Stacpoole, H. D.
Truth About Spring, The
UI (GB) 1964 dir. Richard Thorpe

deVilmorin, L.
Madame De
J. Messner
FRANCO-LONDON (Fr/It) 1953
dir. Max Ophuls
US title: The Earrings of Madame De

DeVries, T.
Girl with the Red Hair, The
UA (Neth) 1983 dir. Ben Verbong

Dewlen, A.
Night of the Tiger, The
Ride Beyond Vengeance
COL (US) 1966 dir. Bernard McEveety

Dewlen, A.
Twilight of Honor
McGraw-Hill
MGM (US) 1963 dir. Boris Sagal
GB title: Charge is Murder, The

Dexter, C.
Dead of Jericho, The
St. Martin's Press
CENTRAL (GB) 1989
dir. Edward Bennett
TV(GB)

Dexter, C.
Last Seen Wearing
St. Martin's Press
CENTRAL (GB) 1989
dir. Edward Bennett
TV(GB)

Dexter, C.
Service of all the Dead
CENTRAL (GB) 1989
dir. Edward Bennett
TV(GB)

Dexter, C.
Silent World of Nicholas Quinn
St. Martin's Press
CENTRAL (GB) 1989
dir. Edward Bennett
TV(GB)

Dexter, P.
Paris Trout
Random House
VIACOM (US) 1991
dir. Stephen Gyllenhaal
TV(US), V

Di Donata, P.
Christ in Concrete
Bobbs-Merrill (Indianapolis)

Give Us This Day
GFD (GB) 1949 dir. Edward Dmytryk
US title: Salt to the Devil

di Meana, M. R.
My First Forty Years
TRI-STAR/COL (It) 1989
dir. Carlo Vanzina

Di Pego, G.
Keeper of the City
VIACOM (US) 1992 dir. Bobby Roth
TV(US)

Diamond, P.
Chicken Chronicles, The
Dell, N.Y.
AVCO (US) 1977 dir. Francis Simon
V

Dibdin-Pitt, G.
Sweeny Todd, the Demon Barber of
Fleet Street
P
Samuel French
KING (GB) 1936 dir. George King

Dibner, M.
Deep Six, The
Doubleday
WAR (US) 1958 dir. Rudolph Maté
V

Dick, P.
We can Remember it for you
Wholesale
Underwood/Miller (Los Angeles)
Total Recall
CAROLCO (US) 1990
dir. Paul Verhoeven

Dick, P. K.
Do Androids Dream of Electric
Sheep?
Doubleday
Blade Runner
WAR (US) 1982 dir. Ridley Scott
V

Dick, R. A.
Ghost and Mrs Muir, The
Harrap
FOX (US) 1947
dir. Joseph L. Mankiewicz

Dickens, C.
Bleak House
Various
BBC (GB) 1985 dir. Ross Devenish
TVSe(GB), V

Dickens, C.
Christmas Carol, A
Various
American Christmas Carol, An
SM HEM (US) 1979 dir. Eric Till
TV(US)

Dickens, C.
Christmas Carol, A
Various
MGM (US) 1938 dir. Edwin L. Marin
V
ENTERTAINMENT PARTNERS (US)
1984 dir. Clive Donner
TV(US), V

Dickens, C.
Christmas Carol, A
Various
Christmas Present, A
CHANNEL 4 (GB) 1985
TV(GB)

Dickens, C.
Christmas Carol, A
Various
Scrooged
PAR (US) 1988 dir. Richard Donner

Dickens, C.
Christmas Carol, A
Various

Scrooge
PAR (GB) 1935 dir. Henry Edwards
REN (GB) 1951
dir. Brian Desmond Hurst
V
FOX (GB) 1970 dir. Ronald Neame
M, V

Dickens, C.
David Copperfield
Various

MGM (US) 1935 dir. George Cukor
V
OMNIBUS (GB) 1970
dir. Delbert Mann
TV(GB), V
BBC (GB) 1986
TVSe(GB)

Dickens, C.
Dombey and Son
Various

BBC (GB) 1984
TVSe(GB)

Dickens, C.
Dombey and Son
Various

Rich Man's Folly
PAR (US) 1931 dir. John Cromwell

Dickens, C.
Great Expectations
Various

UN (US) 1934 dir. Stuart Walker
RANK/CINEGUILD (GB) 1946
dir. David Lean
V
SCOTIA BARBER/ITC (GB) 1974
dir. Joseph Hardy
V
PRIMETIME/HTV (GB/US) 1989
dir. Kevin Connor
TV(GB/US)

Dickens, C.
Hard Times
Various

GRANADA (GB) 1977 dir. John Irvin
TVSe(GB), V

Dickens, C.
Little Dorrit
Various

CANNON (GB) 1988
dir. Christine Edzard

Dickens, C.
Mystery of Edwin Drood, The
Various

UN (US) 1935 dir. Stuart Walker

Dickens, C.
Nicholas Nickleby
Various

EAL (GB) 1947 dir. Alberto Cavalcanti
V

Dickens, C.
Nicholas Nickleby
Various

*Life and Adventures of Nicholas
Nickleby, The*
PRIMETIME (GB) 1984
dir. Jim Goddard
TVSe(GB), V

Dickens, C.
Old Curiosity Shop, The
Various

BIP (GB) 1934 dir. Thomas Bentley

Dickens, C.
Old Curiosity Shop, The
Various

Mister Quilp
EMI (GB) 1975 dir. Elliot Scott

Dickens, C.
Oliver Twist
Various
CINEGUILD (GB) 1948 dir. David Lean
V
TRIDENT (US/GB) 1982
dir. Clive Donner
TV(US/GB)
BBC (GB) 1985
TVSe(GB)

Dickens, C.
Oliver Twist
Various
Oliver!
COL (GB) 1968 dir. Carol Reed
M, V

Dickens, C.
Pickwick Papers, The
Various
REN (GB) 1952 dir. Noel Langley
V
BBC (GB) 1985 dir. Brian Lighthill
TV(GB)

Dickens, C.
Tale of Two Cities, A
Various
MGM (US) 1935 dir. Jack Conway
V
RANK (GB) 1958 dir. Ralph Thomas
V
ROSEMONT (US/GB) 1980
dir. Jim Goddard
TV(GB/US)

Dickens, M.
One Pair of Feet
Lamp Still Burns, The
TC (GB) 1943 dir. Maurice Elvey

Dickenson, M.
**Thumbs Up: The Life and
Courageous Comeback of White
House Press Secretary Jim Brady**
Morrow
Without Warning: The James Brady Story
HBO (US) 1991
dir. Michael Toshiyuki Uno
TV(US)

Dickey, J.
Deliverance
Houghton, Mifflin Co. (Boston)
WAR (US) 1973 dir. John Boorman
V

Dickey, P.
Ghost Breakers, The
P
PAR (US) 1940 dir. George Marshall

Dickinson, P.
Changes, The
V. Gollancz
BBC (GB) 1975 dir. John Prowse
Ch, TV(GB)

Didion, J.
Play it as it Lays
Farrar, Straus & Giroux
UN (US) 1972 dir. Frank Perry

Diehl, W.
Sharky's Machine
Delacorte Press
WAR (US) 1981 dir. Burt Reynolds
V

Dietrich, W. and Thomas, B.
Howard: The Amazing Mr. Hughes
Amazing Howard Hughes, The
EMI TV (US) 1977
dir. William A. Graham
TVSe (US), V

Dietz, L.
Year of the Big Cat, The
Little, Brown (Boston)
Return of the Big Cat
DISNEY (US) 1974 dir. Tom Leetch

Dighton, J.
Happiest Days of Your Life, The
P
Samuel French
BL (GB) 1950 dir. Frank Launder

Dighton, J.
Who Goes There?
P
BL (GB) 1952 dir. Anthony Kimmins
US title: Passionate Sentry, The

Dijan, P.
372 Le Matin
Betty Blue
GAU (Fr) 1986 dir. Jean-Jacques Beineix
V

Dillman, J.
Unholy Matrimony
Macmillan
TAFT (US) 1988 dir. Jerrold Freedman
TV(US)

Dillon, B.
Mom by Magic, A
Lippincott (Philadelphia)
Mom for Christmas, A
DISNEY (US) 1990 dir. George Miller
TV(US)

Dineli, M.
Man, The
P
Beware My Lovely
RKO (US) 1952 dir. Harry Horner

Dinesen, I.
Out of Africa
Random House; Sierra Club Books
(San Francisco)
UN (US) 1985 dir. Sidney Pollack
V

Dingwall, J.
House in the Timberwoods, The
Winds of Jarrah, The
FILMCORP (Aust) 1983
dir. Mark Egerton
V

Dinneen, J. F.
They Stole $2.5 million and Got Away with it
Six Bridges to Cross
UN (US) 1955 dir. Joseph Pevney

Dinner, W. and Morum, W.
Late Edwina Black, The
P
Samuel French
GFD (GB) 1951 dir. Maurice Elvey

Disch, T. M.
Brave Little Toaster, The
Harper Row
HYP (US) 1989 dir. Jerry Rees
A

Disney, D. M.
Do not Fold, Spindle or Mutilate
Doubleday
L. RICH (US) 1971 dir. Ted Post
TV(US)

Disney, D. M.
Night of Clear Choice
Doubleday
Yesterday's Child
PAR TV (US) 1977 dir. Corey Allen,
Bob Rosenbaum
TV(US)

Disney, D. M.
Only Couples Need Apply
Doubleday
Betrayal
METRO (US) 1974 dir. Gordon Hessler
TV(US)

Divine, D.
Boy on a Dolphin, The
Macmillan
FOX (US) 1957 dir. Jean Negulesco

Dixon, R.
Confessions of a Night Nurse
Rosie Dixon-Night Nurse
COL (GB) 1978 dir. Justin Cartwright

Dobbs, M.
House of Cards
BBC (GB) 1991 dir. Paul Seed
TVSe(GB)

Dobie, L. and Sloman, R.
Tinker, The
P
Wild and the Willing, The
RANK (GB) 1962 dir. Ralph Thomas
US title: Young and Willing

Doblin, A.
Berlin Alexanderplatz
F. Ungar
TELECUL/CH 4 (Fr/GB) 1985
dir. RainerWernerFassbinder
TVSe(Fr/GB)

Doctorow, E. L.
Billy Bathgate
Random House
TOUCH (US) 1991 dir. Robert Benton

Doctorow, E. L.
Book of Daniel, The
Random House
Daniel
PAR (GB) 1983 dir. Sidney Lumet
V

Doctorow, E. L.
Ragtime
Random House
PAR (US) 1981 dir. Milos Forman
V

Doctorow, E. L.
Welcome to Hard Times
Random House
MGM (US) 1967 dir. Burt Kennedy
GB title: Killer on a Horse

Dodge, D.
Plunder of the Sun
Random House
WAR (US) 1953 dir. John Farrow

Dodge, D.
To Catch a Thief
PAR (US) 1955 dir. Alfred Hitchcock
V

Dodge, M. M.
Hans Brinker, or the Silver Skates
World Publishing
MILBERG (US) 1957 dir. Sidney Lumet
TV(US)

Dodson, K.
Away All Boats
Little, Brown (Boston)
UI (US) 1956 dir. Joseph Pevney
V

Doerr, H.
Stones for Ibarra
Viking Press
TITUS (US) 1988 dir. Jack Gold
TV(US)

Doherty, B.
White Peak Farm
Methuen (London)
BBC (GB) 1988 dir. Andrew Morgan
Ch, TVSe(GB)

Donnelly, D.
Poppy
P
PAR (US) 1936
dir. A. Edward Sutherland

Donoso, J.
Hell Without Limits
E. P. Dutton

AZTECA (Mex) 1978
dir. Arturo Ripstein

Donovan, R. J.
PT109— John F. Kennedy in World War II
McGraw-Hill

PT 109
WAR (US) 1963 dir. Leslie H. Martinson
V

Dorner, M.
Nightmare
McGraw-Hill

Don't Touch My Daughter
P-K (US) 1991 dir. John Pasquin
TV(US)

Dorris, M.
Broken Cord, The
Harper & Row

UNTV (US) 1992 dir. Ken Olin

Doss, H.
Family Nobody Wanted, The

UN TV (US) 1975 dir. Ralph Senensky
TV(US)

Dossick, P.
Transplant
Viking Press

TIME-LIFE (US) 1979
dir. William A. Graham
TV(US)

Dostoevski, F.
Brothers Karamazov, The
Various

MGM (US) 1957 dir. Richard Brooks
V
(USSR) 1980 dir. Ivan Pyriev

Dostoevski, F.
Crime and Punishment
Various

COL (US) 1935 dir. Josef von Sternberg
GAU (Fr) 1935 dir. Pierre Chenal
AA (US) 1958 dir. Denis Sanders

Dostoevski, F.
Eternal Husband, The
Various

L'Homme au Chapeau Rond
ALCINA (Fr) 1946 dir. Pierre Billon

Dostoevski, F.
Gambler, The
Various

LENFILM (USSR) 1982
dir. Alexei Batalov

Dostoevski, F.
Great Gambler
Macmillan

Great Sinner, The
MGM (US) 1949 dir. Robert Siodmak

Dougherty, R.
Commissioner, The
Hart-Davis

Madigan
UI (US) 1968 dir. Don Siegel
V

Douglas, C.
Houseman's Tale, A
Taplinger Publishing Co.

BBC (GB) 1985
TV(GB)

Douglas, F.
It's Never too Late
P
Evans

ABP (GB) 1956 dir. Michael McCarthy

Douglas, L. C.
Big Fisherman, The
Houghton, Mifflin Co. (Boston)

CENT (US) 1959 dir. Frank Borzage

Douglas, L. C.
Disputed Passage
Houghton, Mifflin Co. (Boston)
PAR (US) 1939 dir. Frank Borzage

Douglas, L. C.
Green Light, The
Davies
WAR (US) 1937 dir. Frank Borzage

Douglas, L. C.
Magnificent Obsession
Houghton, Mifflin Co. (Boston)
UN (US) 1935 dir. John M. Stahl
V
UI (US) 1954 dir. Douglas Sirk
V

Douglas, L. C.
Robe, The
Houghton, Mifflin Co. (Boston)
FOX (US) 1953 dir. Henry Koster
V

Douglas, L. C.
White Banners
Houghton, Mifflin Co. (Boston)
WAR (US) 1938 dir. Edmund Goulding

Douglas, M.
Dealing: or The Berkeley-to-Boston-Forty-Brick-Lost-Bag-Blues
WAR (US) 1972 dir. Paul Williams

Downes, D.
Easter Dinner, The
Pigeon That Took Rome, The
PAR (US) 1962 dir. Melville Shavelson

Downs, R. C. S.
Peoples
Bobbs-Merrill (Indianapolis)
Billy: Portrait of a Street Kid
CARLINER (US) 1977
dir. Steven Gethers
TV(US), V

Doyle, M.
Signpost to Murder
P
MGM (US) 1964 dir. George Englund

Doyle, Sir A. C.
Adventure of the Five Orange Pips
Murray
House of Fear
UN (US) 1945 dir. Roy William Neill
V

Doyle, Sir A. C.
Adventures of Sherlock Holmes, The
Harper & Row
FOX (US) 1939 dir. Alfred Werker
GB title: Sherlock Holmes
GRANADA (GB) 1984 dir. Paul Annett
TVSe(GB),V

Doyle, Sir A. C.
Cat From Hell
Tales from the Darkside: the Movie
PAR (US) 1990 dir. John Harrison

Doyle, Sir A. C.
Exploits of Brigadier Gerard, The
Murray (London)
Adventures of Gerard, The
UA (GB) 1970 dir. Jerzy Skolimowski

Doyle, Sir A. C.
His Last Bow
Various
Sherlock Holmes and the Voice of Terror
UN (US) 1942 dir. John Rawlins
V

Doyle, Sir A. C.
Hound of the Baskervilles, The
Various

ID (GB) 1932 dir. V. G. Gundrey
FOX (US) 1939 dir. Sidney Lawfield
UA (GB) 1959 dir. Terence Fisher
UN (US) 1972 dir. Barry Crane
TV(US)
HEMDALE (GB) 1977
dir. Paul Morrissey
V
EMBASSY (GB) 1983
dir. Douglas Hickox

Doyle, Sir A. C.
Lost World, The
Various

FOX (US) 1960 dir. Irwin Allen

Doyle, Sir A. C.
Man with the Twisted Lip, The
Various

GN (GB) 1951 dir. Richard M. Grey

Doyle, Sir A. C.
Return of Sherlock Holmes
Various

GRANADA (GB) 1988 dir. Michael Cox
TV(GB)

Doyle, Sir A. C.
Sign of Four, The
Samuel French

WW (GB) 1932 dir. Rowland V. Lee
EMBASSY (GB) 1983
dir. Desmond Davis
GRANADA (GB) 1988 dir. Michael Cox
TV(GB)

Doyle, Sir A. C.
Six Napoleons, The
Pearl of Death, The
UN (US) 1944 dir. Roy William Neill
V

Doyle, Sir A. C.
Study in Scarlet, The
Various

WW (US) 1933 dir. Edward L. Marin
V

Doyle, Sir A. C.
Valley of Fear, The
Various

Triumph of Sherlock Holmes, The
TWICKENHAM (GB) 1935
dir. Leslie Hiscott
V

Drabble, M.
Millstone, The
Morrow

Touch of Love, A
BL (GB) 1969 dir. Waris Hussein
US title: Thank You All Very Much

Dratler, J.
Pitfall
Thomas Y. Crowell

UA (US) 1948 dir. André de Toth

Drawbell, J. W.
Love and Forget
Collins

Love Story
GFD (GB) 1944 dir. Leslie Arliss
US title: Lady Surrenders, A

Dreiser, T.
American Tragedy, An
New American Library

PAR (US) 1931 dir. Josef von Sternberg

Dreiser, T.
American Tragedy, An
New American Library

Place in the Sun, A
PAR (US) 1951 dir. George Stevens
V

Dreiser, T.
Jennie Gerhardt
World Publishing

PAR (US) 1933 dir. Marion Gering

Dreiser, T.
My Brother Paul
Boni & Liveright
My Gal Sal
FOX (US) 1942 dir. Irving Cummings

Dreiser, T.
Prince Who Was a Thief, The
World Publishing Co.
UN (US) 1951 dir. Rudolph Maté

Dreiser, T.
Sister Carrie
Viking Press
Carrie
PAR (US) 1952 dir. William Wyler

Drexler, R.
To Smithereens
New American Library
Below the Belt
ATLANTIC (US) 1982
dir. Robert Fowler
V

Driscoll, P.
Wilby Conspiracy, The
Lippincott (Philadelphia)
UA (GB) 1975 dir. Ralph Nelson
V

Drought, J.
Gypsy Moths, The
MGM (US) 1969
dir. John Frankenheimer

Drummond, J. D.
But for These Men
Elmfield Press
Heroes of the Telemark
RANK (GB) 1965 dir. Anthony Mann
V

Druon, M.
Film of Memory, The
Scribners
Matter of Time, A
AIP (US/It) 1976 dir. Vincente Minnelli
V

Drury, A.
Advise and Consent
Doubleday
COL (US) 1962 dir. Otto Preminger

Druten, J. van
After All
P
G. P. Putnam's Sons
New Morals for Old
MGM (US) 1932 dir. Charles Brabin

Druten, J. van
Behold We Live
P
Gollancz
If I Were Free
RKO (US) 1933 dir. Elliot Nugent

Druten, J. van
Bell, Book and Candle
P
Dramatists Play Service
COL (US) 1958 dir. Richard Quine
V

Druten, J. van
I am a Camera
P
Dramatists Play Service
BL (GB) 1955 dir. Henry Cornelius
V

Druten, J. van
I am a Camera
P
Dramatists Play Service
Cabaret
CINERAMA (US) 1972 dir. Bob Fosse
M, V

Druten, J. van
I Remember Mama
P
Dramatists Play Service
RKO (US) 1948 dir. George Stevens
V

Druten, J. van
London Wall
P
Gallancz
After Office Hours
BI (GB) 1935 dir. Thomas Bentley

Druten, J. van
Old Acquaintance
P
Samuel French
WAR (US) 1943 dir. Vincent Sherman

Druten, J. van
Old Acquaintance
P
Samuel French
Rich and Famous
MGM (US) 1981 dir. George Cukor
V

Druten, J. van
There's Always Juliet
P
Samuel French
One Night in Lisbon
PAR (US) 1941 dir. Edward H. Griffith

Druten, J. van
Voice of the Turtle
P
Random House
WAR (US) 1947 dir. Irving Rapper

Druten, J. van
Young Woodley
P
Samuel French
BI (GB) 1929 dir. Thomas Bentley

Du Maurier, D.
Birds, The
Doubleday
UN (US) 1963 dir. Alfred Hitchcock
V

Du Maurier, D.
Don't Look Now
Doubleday
BL (GB) 1973 dir. Nicolas Roeg
V

Du Maurier, D.
Frenchman's Creek
R. Bentley (Cambridge, Massachusetts)
PAR (US) 1944 dir. Mitchell Leisen

Du Maurier, D.
Hungry Hill
Doubleday
TC (GB) 1947 dir. Brian Desmond Hurst

Du Maurier, D.
Jamaica Inn
Doubleday
PAR (GB) 1939 dir. Alfred Hitchcock
V
HTV (GB) 1983
dir. Lawrence Gordon Clark
TV

Du Maurier, D.
My Cousin Rachel
Doubleday
FOX (US) 1952 dir. Henry Koster
NBC (US) 1984
TV(US)

Du Maurier, D.
Rebecca
Doubleday
UA (US) 1940 dir. Alfred Hitchcock

Du Maurier, D.
Scapegoat, The
Doubleday
MGM (GB) 1959 dir. Robert Hamer

Du Maurier, D.
Years Between, The
P
Doubleday
FOX (GB) 1946 dir. Compton Bennett

Du Maurier, G.
Peter Ibbetson
Heritage Press
PAR (US) 1935 dir. Henry Hathaway

Du Maurier, G.
Trilby
Harper
Svengali
WAR (US) 1931 dir. Archie Mayo
V
REN (GB) 1954 dir. William Alwyn
V
HALMI (US) 1983 dir. Anthony Harvey
TV(US)

Duffy, C. T. and Jennings, D.
San Quentin Story, The
Doubleday
Duffy of San Quentin
WAR (US) 1954 dir. Walter Doniger

Duffy, M.
Gor Saga, The
Viking Press
First Born
BBC (GB) 1988 dir. Philip Saville
TVSe(GB)

Duke, P. and Turan, K.
My Name is Anna: The Autobiography of Patty Duke
Bantam Books
Call me Anna
FINNEGAN (US) 1990
dir. Gilbert Cates
TV(US)

Dulay, C.
Chanel Solitaire
Quadrangle
GARDENIA (Fr/GB) 1981
dir. George Kaczender
V

Dumas, A.
Black Tulip, The
Various
CINERAMA (Fr) 1963
dir. Christian Jacque
V

Dumas, A.
Companions of Jehu, The
Various
Fighting Guardsman, The
COL (US) 1945 dir. Henry Levin

Dumas, A.
Count of Monte Cristo, The
UA (US) 1934 dir. Rowland V. Lee
ROSEMONT (GB) 1975
dir. David Greene
TV(GB)
(Fr/GB) 1987 dir. D. de la Patellière
TV(Fr/GB)

Dumas, A.
Deux Frères
Various
Corsican Brothers, The
UA (US) 1942 dir. Gregory Ratoff
ROSEMONT (US) 1985 dir. Ian Sharp
TV(US), V

Dumas, A.
Man in the Iron Mask, The
Various
UA (US) 1939 dir. James Whale
ITC (US/GB) 1976 dir. Mike Newell
TV(GB/US), V

Dumas, A.
Man in the Iron Mask, The
Various
Fifth Musketeer, The
SASCH WIEN FILMS (Austria) 1978
dir. Ken Annakin
V

Dumas, A.
Memoirs of a Physician
Black Magic
UA (US) 1949 dir. Gregory Ratoff

Dumas, A.
Three Musketeers, The
Various

RKO (US) 1935 dir. Rowland V Lee
V
FOX (US) 1939 dir. Allan Dwan
GB title: Singing Musketeer, The
MGM (US) 1948 dir. George Sidney
V
FOX-RANK (Panama) 1973
dir. Richard Lester

Dumas, A.
Three Musketeers, The

Four Musketeers, The
FOX-RANK (Pan/Sp) 1974
dir. Richard Lester
V

Dumas, A. fils
Dame aux Camélias, La
Various

Camille
MGM (US) 1936 dir. George Cukor
ROSEMONT (US/GB) 1984
dir. Desmond Davis
TV(GB/US), V

Dunbar, A.
Rita, Sue and Bob Too
P
Methuen

ORION (GB) 1987 dir. Alan Clarke

Duncan, A.
It's a Vet's Life
Joseph

In the Doghouse
RANK (GB) 1961 dir. Darcy Conyers

Duncan, I.
My Life
Boni & Liveright

Isadora
UI (GB) 1969 dir. Karel Reisz
US title: Loves of Isadora, The
V

Duncan, L.
Summer of Fear
Little, Brown (Boston)

INTERPLAN (US) 1978 dir. Wes Craven
V

Duncan, L
Summer of Fear
Little, Brown (Boston)

Stranger in our House
INTERPLAN (US) 1978 dir. Wes Craven
TV(US)

Dunn, N.
Poor Cow

WAR (GB) 1967 dir. Ken Loach
V

Dunn, N.
Steaming
P
Samuel French

NEW WORLD (GB) 1985
dir. Joseph Losey
V

Dunn, N.
Up the Junction
Lippincott (Philadelphia)

PAR (GB) 1967 dir. Peter Collinson

Dunne, D.
Inconvenient Woman, An
Crown Publishers

ABC (US) 1991 dir. Larry Elikann
TVSe(US)

Dunne, D.
People Like Us
Crown Publishing Co.

ITC (US) 1990 dir. Billy Hale
TVSe(US)

Dunne, D.
Two Mrs. Grenvilles, The
Crown Publishers

LORIMAR (US) 1989 dir. John Erman
TVSe(US)

Dunne, J. G.
True Confessions
Dutton
UA (US) 1981 dir. Ulu Grosbard
V

Dunne, L.
Goodbye to the Hill
Houghton, Mifflin Co. (Boston)
Paddy
FOX (Ireland) 1969 dir. Daniel Haller
V

Dunning, P. and Abbott, G.
Broadway
P
Samuel French
UN (US) 1942 dir. Seiter, W. A.

Duprez, F., Stephens, H., & Linton, H. B.
My Wife's Family
P
GB (GB) 1931 dir. Monty Banks
ABPC (GB) 1941 dir. Walter C. Mycroft
ABP (GB) 1956 dir. Gilbert Gunn

Duran, M.
Liberté Provisoire
P
He Stayed for Breakfast
COL (US) 1940 dir. Alexander Hall

Durang, C.
Beyond Therapy
P
Samuel French
NEW WORLD (US) 1987
dir. Robert Altman
V

Durant, T.
Marble Forest
Wingate
Macabre
ABP (US) 1958 dir. William Castle

Duras, M.
Barrage contre le Pacifique, Un
Gallimard (Paris)
This Angry Age
DELAUR (It) 1957 dir. René Clément

Duras, M.
Moderato Cantabile
Grove Press
R. J. LEVY (Fr/It) 1960 dir. Peter Brook

Duras, M.
Sailor from Gibraltar, The
WOODFALL (GB) 1967
dir. Tony Richardson

Duras, M.
10.30 p.m. on a Summer Night
J. Calder (London)
10.30 p.m. Summer
UA (US/Sp) 1966 dir. Jules Dassin

Durham, M.
Man Who Loved Cat Dancing, The
Harcourt, Brace, Jovanovich
MGM (US) 1973 dir. Richard Sarafian
V

Durrell, L.
Alexandria Quartet, The
Dutton
Justine
FOX (US) 1969 dir. George Cukor
V

Durrenmatt, F.
Judge and his Hangman, The
Continuum Publishing Co.
End of the Game
TCF (US/Ger) 1976
dir. Maximilian Schell

Durrenmatt, F.
Visit, The
P
Samuel French
FOX (US) 1964 dir. Bernhard Wicki

D'Usseau, A. and Gow, J.
Deep are the Roots
P
Samuel French
Tomorrow the World
UA (US) 1944 dir. Leslie Fenton

Dutton, G.
Queen Emma of the South Seas
Emma: Queen of the South Seas
FRIES (US) 1988 dir. Bryan Forbes
TVSe(US)

Dwyer, K. R.
Shattered
Random House
Passengers, The
COL-WAR (Fr) 1977 dir. Serge Le Roy

Dyer, B. V.
Port Afrique
Harper
COL (GB) 1956 dir. Rudolph Maté

Dyer, C.
Rattle of a Simple Man
P
Samuel French
WAR (GB) 1964 dir. Muriel Box
V

Dyer, C.
Staircase
P
Samuel French
FOX (US/Fr) 1969 dir. Stanley Donen

Dyer, G.
Fog Over Frisco
WAR (US) 1934 dir. William Dieterle

E

Eareckson, J.
Joni
Zondervan Pub. House (Grand Rapids, Michigan)
WORLDWIDE (US) 1980
dir. James F. Collier
V

Earl, L.
Yangtse Incident
Knopf
BL (GB) 1957 dir. Michael Anderson
US title: Battle Hell

Eastlake, W.
Castle Keep
Simon & Schuster
COL (US) 1969 dir. Sydney Pollack

Eastwood, J.
Mark of the Leopard
Beyond Mombasa
COL (GB) 1955 dir. George Marshall

Eberhart, M. G.
From this Dark Stairway
Murder of Dr. Harrigan
WAR (US) 1936 dir. Frank McDonald

Eberhart, M. G.
While the Patient Slept
IN (US) 1935 dir. Ray Enright

Eberhart, M. G.
White Cockatoo
WAR (US) 1935 dir. Alan Crosland

Echard, M.
Dark Fantastic
Invincible Press
Lightning Strikes Twice
WAR (US) 1951 dir. King Vidor

Echasseriaux, B.
Sundays and Cybèle
TERRA (Fr) 1962 dir. Serge Bourgignon
V

Eco, U.
Name of the Rose, The
Harcourt, Brace, Jovanovich
FOX (US/Ger/It/Fr) 1987
dir. Jean-Jacques Annaud
V

Ede, H. S.
Savage Messiah
Gordon Fraser (London)
MGM-EMI (GB) 1972 dir. Ken Russell

Edens, O.
Heart & Hand
Collins
House Divided, A
UN (US) 1932 dir. William Wyler

Edmonds, A.
Hot Toddy
Morrow
White Hot: The Mysterious Murder of Thelma Todd
NEWFELD-KEATING (US) 1991
dir. Paul Wendkos
TV(US)

Edmonds, W. D.
Chad Hanna
Little, Brown (Boston)
FOX (US) 1940 dir. Henry King

Edmonds, W. D.
Drums Along the Mohawk
Little, Brown (Boston)
FOX (US) 1939 dir. John Ford
V

Edmonds, W. D.
Rome Haul
Triangle Books, N.Y.
Farmer Takes a Wife, The
FOX (US) 1935 dir. Victor Fleming
FOX (US) 1953 dir. Henry Levin
M

Edwards, A.
Haunted Summer
Coward, McCann & Geoghegan
CANNON (US) 1988 dir. Ivan Passer
V

Eells, G.
Hedda and Louella
Putnam
Malice in Wonderland
ITC (US) 1985 dir. Gus Trikonis
TV(US)

Egan, M.
Dominant Sex, The
P
Gollancz
AB (GB) 1937 dir. Herbert Brenon

Egleton, C.
Seven Days to a Killing
Coward, McCann & Geoghegan
Black Windmill, The
PAR (GB) 1974 dir. Don Siegel
V

Ehle, J.
Winter People
Harper & Row
COL (US) 1989 dir. Ted Kotcheff
V

Ehrlich, J.
Gun and the Pulpit, The
CINE TV (US) 1974 dir. Daniel Petrie
TV(US)

Ehrlich, M.
First Train to Babylon
Harper
Naked Edge, The
UA (GB) 1961 dir. Michael Anderson

Ehrlich, M.
Reincarnation of Peter Proud, The
Bobbs-Merrill (Indianapolis)
AVCO (US) 1975 dir. J. Lee Thompson
V

Ehrlichman, J.
Company, The
Simon & Schuster
Washington: Behind Closed Doors
PAR (US) 1977 dir. Gary Nelson
TVSe(US)

Einstein, C.
Blackjack Hijack, The
Nowhere to Run
MTM (US) 1978 dir. Richard Lang
TV(US)

Einstein, C.
Bloody Spur, The
While the City Sleeps
RKO (US) 1956 dir. Fritz Lang
V

Eisner, J. P.
Survivor, The
Morrow
War and Love
CANNON (US/Israel) 1985
dir. Moshe Mizrahi
V

Elder, L. and Streshinsky, S.
And I Alone Survived
Dutton
OSL (US) 1978 dir. William Graham
TV(US), V

Elder, R. and Elder, S.
Crash
FRIES (US) 1978 dir. Barry Shear
TV(US)

Elfman, B.
Girls of Huntington House, The
Houghton, Mifflin Co. (Boston)
LORIMAR (US) 1973 dir. Alf Kjellin
TV(US)

Eliot, G.
Mill on the Floss, The
Various
STANDARD (GB) 1937 dir. Tim Whelan
V

Eliot, G.
Silas Marner
Various
BBC (GB) 1985 dir. Giles Foster
TV(GB), V

Eliot, T. S.
Murder in the Cathedral
P
Samuel French
FILM TRADERS (GB) 1951
dir. George Hoellering

'Elizabeth'
Enchanted April
RKO (US) 1935 dir. Harry Beaumont

'Elizabeth'
Mr. Skeffington
Doubleday
WAR (US) 1944 dir. Vincent Sherman
V

Elkin, S.
The Bailbondsman
Alex and the Gypsy
TCF (US) 1976 dir. John Korty

Elkind, M.
Internecine Project, The
MACLEAN (GB) 1974 dir. Ken Hughes
V

Elli, F.
Riot
Coward-McCann
PAR (US) 1968 dir. Buzz Kulik

Ellin, S.
Bind, The
Random House

Sunburn
HEMDALE (GB/US) 1979
dir. Richard C. Sarafian
V

Ellin, S.
Dreadful Summit
Simon & Schuster
Big Night, The
UA (US) 1951 dir. Joseph Losey

Ellin, S.
House of Cards
Random House
UN (US) 1968 dir. John Guillerman

Elliot, J.
Buttercup Chain, The
Panther
COL (GB) 1969 dir. Robert Ellis Miller

Elliott, J.
Secret Places
St. Martin's Press
RANK (GB) 1983 dir. Zelda Barron
V

Elliott, S.
Signs of Life
Ticknor & Fields
Careful, He Might Hear You
SYME (Aust) 1983 dir. Carl Schultz
V

Ellis, B.E.
Less than Zero
Simon & Schuster
FOX (US) 1987 dir. Marek Kanievska
V

Ellis, E.
White Collars
P
Rich Man, Poor Girl
MGM (US) 1938 dir. Reinhold Schunzel

Ellis, K. M.
Trial of Vivienne Ware, The
FOX (US) 1932 dir. William K. Howard

Ellison, J. W.
Double Standard
FRIES (US) 1988 dir. Louis Rudolph
TV (US)

Ellroy, J.
Blood on the Moon
Mysterious Press
Cop
ATLANTIC (US) 1988
dir. James B. Harris
V

Ellsberg, E.
Pigboats
Hell Below
MGM (US) 1933 dir. Jack Conway

Ely, D.
Seconds
Pantheon Books
PAR (US) 1966 dir. John Frankenheimer

Emery, R.
Gilded Rooster, The
Savage Wilderness
COL (US) 1956 dir. Anthony Mann
GB title: The Last Frontier

Emmons, D. G.
Sacajawea of the Shoshones
Far Horizons, The
PAR (US) 1955 dir. Rudolph Maté

Ende, M.
Neverending Story, The
Doubleday
WAR (Ger/GB) 1984
dir. Wolfgang Petersen
Ch, V

Ende, M.
Neverending Story, The
Doubleday
Neverending Story II: The Next Chapter, The
WAR (Ger) 1989 dir. George Miller
Ch

Endore, G.
Methinks the Lady
Duell, Sloan & Pearce
Whirlpool
FOX (US) 1949 dir. Otto Preminger

Endore, G.
Werewolf of Paris, The
Long
Curse of the Werewolf, The
RANK (GB) 1961 dir. Terence Fisher
V

England, B.
Conduct Unbecoming
P
Samuel French
BL (GB) 1975 dir. Michael Anderson
V

England, B.
Figures in a Landscape
CINECREST (GB) 1970
dir. Joseph Losey

Engstrandt, S. D.
Beyond the Forest
Cape
WAR (US) 1949 dir. King Vidor

Ephron, N.
Heartburn
Knopf
PAR (US) 1986 dir. Mike Nichols

Ephron, P. and Ephron, H.
Take Her, She's Mine
P
Samuel French
MGM (US) 1963 dir. Henry Koster

Ephron, P. and Ephron, H.
Three is a Family
P
UA (US) 1944 dir. Edward Ludwig

Epstein, S.
Eye of the Beholder
Comeback, The
CBS ENT (US) 1989
dir. Jerrold Freedman
TV(US)

Erdman, P.
Silver Bears
Scribners
EMI (GB) 1978 dir. Ivan Passer
V

Ericson, W.
Mirage
UI (US) 1965 dir. Edward Dmytryk
V

Erskine, C.
Sailor Takes a Wife, The
P
MGM (US) 1945 dir. Richard Whorf

Erskine, J.
Sincerity
Bobbs-Merrill (Indianapolis)
Lady Surrenders, A
UN (US) 1930 dir. John Stahl

Erskine, L. Y.
Renfrew's Long Trail
Danger Ahead
MON (GB) 1940 dir. Ralph Staub

Ertz, S.
In the Cool of the Day
Harper
MGM (US) 1962 dir. Robert Stevens

Ervine, St. J. G.
Boyd's Shop
P
Macmillan
RANK (GB) 1960 dir. Henry Cass

Etons, U.
Angel Dusted
NRW (US) 1981 dir. Dick Lowry
TV(US)

Euripides
Iphighenia
P
Various
UA (Greece) 1978
dir. Michael Cacoyannis
V

Euripides
Medea
P
Samuel French
JANUS (It/Fr/Ger) 1970
dir. Pier Paolo Pasolini
V

Euripides
Trojan Women, The
P
Various
CINERAMA (US) 1971
dir. Michael Cacoyannis
V

Evans, E.
Branded
Various
PAR (US) 1950 dir. Rudolph Maté

Evans, E.
Wishing Well
P
Samuel French
Happiness of Three Women, The
ADELPHI (GB) 1954 dir. Maurice Elvey

Evans, M.
Rounders, The
Doubleday
MGM (US) 1965 dir. Burt Kennedy

Evans, P.
Ari: The Life and Time of Aristotle
Onassis
Summit Books
*Richest Man in the World, The: The
Story of Aristotle Onassis*
KON/SAN (US) 1988 dir. Waris Hussein
TVSe(US)

Everett, P.
Negatives
Simon & Schuster
CRISPIN (GB) 1968 dir. Peter Medak

Everett, P.
Walk Me to the Distance
Ticknor & Fields
Follow Your Heart
NBC (US) 1990 dir. Noel Nosseck
TV(US)

Fabian, R.
Fabian of the Yard
EROS (GB) 1954
dir. Edward Thommen,
Anthony Beauchamp

Fairchild, W.
Do Not Disturb
P
FOX (US) 1965 dir. Ralph Levy

Fairchild, W.
Sound of Murder, The
P
Samuel French
Last Shot you Hear, The
FOX (GB) 1970 dir. Gordon Hessler

Fallada, H.
Little Man, What Now?
Simon & Schuster
UN (US) 1934 dir. Frank Borzage

Fallet, R.
Grande Ceinture, La
Porte des Lilas
FILMSONOR (Fr/It) 1957
dir. René Clair

Fante, J.
Full of Life
Black Sparrow Press (Santa Rosa,
California)
COL (US) 1956 dir. Richard Quine

Farago, L.
Last Days of Patton, The
McGraw-Hill
ENT PAR (US) 1986 dir. Delbert Mann
TV(US)

Farago, L.
Patton: Ordeal & Triumph
I. Obolensky
Patton
FOX (US) 1970 dir. Franklin Schaffner
GB title: Patton: Lust for Glory
V

Farjeon, J. J.
Number Seventeen
P
BIP (GB) 1932 dir. Alfred Hitchcock
V

Farley, W.
Black Stallion, The
Random House
UA (US) 1979 dir. Carroll Ballard
Ch, V

Farley, W.
Black Stallion Returns, The
MGM (US) 1983 dir. Robert Dalva
Ch, V

Farmer, F.
Will There Really Be A Morning?
Putnam
ORION (US) 1983 dir. Fielder Cook
TV(US)

494

Farnol, J.
Amateur Gentlemen, The
Sampson Low
UA (GB) 1936 dir. Thornton Freeland

Farre, R.
Seal Morning
ITV (GB) 1986
TV

Farrell, B.
Pat & Roald
Random House
Patricia Neal Story, The
SCHILLER (US) 1981
dir. Antony Harvey & Anthony Page
TV(US)

Farrell, H.
Baby Jane
W. J. Black
What Ever Happened to Baby Jane?
WAR (US) 1962 dir. Robert Aldrich
V
SPECTACOR (US) 1991
dir. David Greene
TV(US)

Farrell, H.
How Awful About Allan
Holt, Rinehart & Winston
A. SPELLING (US) 1970
dir. Curtis Harrington
TV(US)

Farrell, J. G.
Troubles
Knopf
LWT (GB) 1989
dir. Christopher Morahan
TV(GB)

Farrell, J. T.
Young Manhood of Studs Lonigan, The
World Publishing
Studs Lonigan
UA (US) 1960 dir. Irving Lerner
V
LORIMAR (US) 1979
dir. James Goldstone
TVSe(US)

Farrell, M. J. and Perry, J.
Spring Meeting
P
ABPC (GB) 1940 dir. Walter C. Mycroft

Farrell, M. J. and Perry, J.
Treasure Hunt
P
BL (GB) 1952 dir. John Paddy Carstairs

Farrere, C.
Battle, The
Putnam
GAU (Fr) 1934 dir. Nicolas Farkas

Farrington, F.
Little Game, A
UN TV (US) 1971 dir. Paul Wendkos
TV(US)

Farrington, F.
Strangers in 7a, The
PALOMAR (US) 1972 dir. Paul Wendkos
TV(US)

Farris, J.
Fury, The
Playboy Press (Chicago)
FOX (US) 1978 dir. Brian De Palma
V

Farris, J.
Harrison High
Dell
Because They're Young
COL (US) 1960 dir. Paul Wendkos

Farris, J.
Ramey

Greatest Gift, The
UN TV (US) 1974 dir. Boris Sagal
TV(US)

Farris, J.
When Michael Calls

FOX (US) 1972 dir. Philip Leacock
TV(US)

Fassbinder, R. W.
Shadow of Angels
P

ALB/ARTCO (Ger) 1983
dir. Daniel Schmid

Fast, H.
April Morning
Crown Publishers

S GOLD TV (US) 1988
dir. Delbert Mann
TV(US)

Fast, H.
Freedom Road
Duell, Sloan & Pearce

BRAUN (US) 1980 dir. Jan Kadar
TVSe(US), V

Fast, H.
Immigrants, The
Houghton, Mifflin Co. (Boston)

UN (US) 1978 dir. Alan J. Levi
TVSe(US)

Fast, H.
Rachel
Crown Publishing

Rachel and the Stranger
RKO (US) 1948 dir. Norman Foster
V

Fast, H.
Spartacus
Crown Publishers

UN (US) 1960 dir. Stanley Kubrick
V

Fast, H.
Winston Affair, The
Crown

Man in the Middle
FOX (GB) 1963 dir. Guy Hamilton

Fauchois, R.
Boudu Sauvé des Eaux
P

M. SIMON (Fr) 1932 dir. Jean Renoir
V

Fauchois, R.
Boudu Sauvé des Eaux
P

Down and Out in Beverly Hills
TOUCH (US) 1986 dir. Paul Mazursky
V

Faulk, J. H.
Fear on Trial
Simon & Schuster

LAN (US) 1975 dir. Lamont Johnson
TV(US)

Faulkner, J. M.
Moonfleet
Little, Brown (Boston)

MGM (US) 1955 dir. Fritz Lang

Faulkner, W.
Hamlet, The
Random House

Long, Hot Summer, The
FOX (US) 1958 dir. Martin Ritt
V
L. HILL (US) 1985 dir. Stuart Cooper
TVSe(US)

Faulkner, W.
Intruder in the Dust
Random House

MGM (US) 1949 dir. Clarence Brown

Faulkner, W.
Pylon
Viking Press

Tarnished Angels, The
UI (US) 1957 dir. Douglas Sirk

Faulkner, W.
Reivers, The
Random House
WAR (US) 1969 dir. Mark Rydell
V

Faulkner, W.
Sanctuary
Random House
FOX (US) 1960 dir. Tony Richardson

Faulkner, W.
Sanctuary
Viking Press
Story of Temple Drake, The
PAR (US) 1933 dir. Stephen Roberts

Faulkner, W.
Sound and the Fury, The
Random House
FOX (US) 1959 dir. Martin Ritt

Faulkner, W.
Turnabout
Random House
Today We Live
MGM (US) 1933 dir. Howard Hawks

Fearing, K.
Big Clock, The
Harcourt, Brace
PAR (US) 1947 dir. John Farrow

Fearing, K.
The Big Clock
Harcourt, Brace
No Way Out
ORION (US) 1987 dir. Roger Donaldson

Fedders, C. and Elliot, L.
Shattered Dreams
Dell Publishing
CAROLCO (US) 1990 dir. Robert Iscove
TV(US)

Feiden, D.
Ten Million Dollar Getaway, The
WIL COURT (US) 1991
dir. James A. Contner
TV(US)

Feifer, G.
Girl from Petrovka, The
Viking Press
UN (US) 1974 dir. Robert Ellis Miller
V

Feiffer, J.
Little Murders
P
Samuel French
FOX (US) 1971 dir. Alan Arkin
V

Feiner, R.
Three Cups of Coffee
Woman's Angle, A
ABP (GB) 1952 dir. Leslie Arliss

Feinman, J. P.
Last Days of the Victim
Two to Tango
CONCORDE (US/Arg) 1989
dir. Hector Olivera
V

Fenady, A. J.
Man with Bogart's Face, The
H. Regnery Co. (Chicago)
FOX (US) 1980 dir. Robert Day
V

Fenelon, F.
Playing for Time
Bantam Books
SYZYGY (US) 1980 dir. Daniel Mann
TV(US), V

Fenton, E.
Golden Doors, The
Escapade in Florence
DISNEY (US) 1962 dir. Steve Previn
Ch, V

Ferber, E.
Cimarron
Doubleday

RKO (US) 1930 dir. Wesley Ruggles
MGM (US) 1960 dir. Anthony Mann

Ferber, E.
Come and Get It
Doubleday

UA (US) 1936
dir. Howard Hawks/William A. Wellman
V

Ferber, E.
Giant
Doubleday

WAR (US) 1956 dir. George Stevens
V

Ferber, E.
Ice Palace
Doubleday

WAR (US) 1960 dir. Vincent Sherman
V

Ferber, E.
Saratoga Trunk
Doubleday

WAR (US) 1945 dir. Sam Wood

Ferber, E.
Showboat
Doubleday

UN (US) 1936 dir. James Whale
M
MGM (US) 1951 dir. George Sidney
M, V

Ferber, E.
So Big
Doubleday

WAR (US) 1932 dir. William Wellman
WAR (US) 1953 dir. Robert Wise

Ferguson, A.
Jet Stream
Morrow

Mayday at 40,000 Feet
WAR (US) 1976 dir. Robert Butler
TV(US)

Ferguson, M.
Sign of the Ram, The
COL (US) 1948 dir. John Sturges

Fernandez, G.
Vietnam Trilogy
P

Cease Fire
CINEWORLD (US) 1985
dir. David Nutter
V

Ferris, P.
Detective, The
Weidenfeld

BBC (GB) 1985 dir. Don Leaver
TVSe(GB)

Ferris, W.
Across 110th Street
Harper, N.Y.

UA (US) 1972 dir. Barry Shear
V

Fest, J.
Hitler: A Career
Harcourt, Brace, Jovanovich

GTO (Ger) 1987
dir. Christian Herrendoerfer,
Joachim C. Fest
V

Fetherstonhaugh, R. C.
Royal Canadian Mounted Police
Carrick & Evans

Northwest Mounted Police
PAR (US) 1940 dir. Cecil B de Mille

Feutchwangler, L.
Jew Süss
M. Secker (London)
GAU (GB) 1934 dir. Lothar Mendes
US title: Power
TERRA (Ger) 1940 dir. Veit Harlan
V

Feydeau, G.
Flea in her Ear, A
P
Samuel French
FOX (US/Fr) 1968 dir. Jacques Charon

Feydeau, G.
Occupe-toi d'Amélie
P
LUX (Fr) 1949 dir. Claude Autant-Lara

**Feydeau, G. and
Desvallieres, M.**
Hotel Paradiso
P
Samuel French
MGM (US) 1966 dir. Peter Glenville

Fidler, K.
Flash the Sheepdog
CFF (US) 1967 dir. Laurence Henson
Ch

Field, H. and Mierzenski, S.
Angry Harvest
CCC (Ger) 1986 dir. Agneiszka Holland
V

Field, R.
All This and Heaven Too
Macmillan
WAR (US) 1940 dir. Anatole Litvak
V

Field, R.
And Now Tomorrow
Collins
PAR (US) 1944 dir. Irving Pichel

Field, R.
Time Out of Mind
Macmillan
UN (US) 1947 dir. Robert Siodmak

Fielding, H.
History of Tom Jones, A Foundling,
The
Various
Tom Jones
UA (GB) 1963 dir. Tony Richardson
V

Fielding, H.
History of Tom Jones, A Foundling,
The
Bawdy Adventures of Tom Jones, The
UN (GB) 1976 dir. Cliff Owen
M, V

Fielding, H.
Joseph Andrews
Various
UA (GB) 1977 dir. Tony Richardson
V

Fields, H.
Dubarry was a Lady
P
MGM (US) 1943 dir. Roy de Ruth
M

Fields, H.
Hit the Deck
P
Samuel French
MGM (US) 1955 dir. Roy Rowland
M

Fields, H. and Fields, D.
Annie Get Your Gun
P
MGM (US) 1950 dir. George Sidney
M

Fields, H. and Fields, D.
Mexican Hayride
P
UN (US) 1948 dir. Charles Barton

Fields, H., Rodgers and Hart
Present Arms
P

Leathernecking
RKO (US) 1930 dir. Edward Cline
GB title: Present Arms
M

Fields, J.
Doughgirls, The
P
Random House
WAR (US) 1944 dir. James V. Kern

Fields, J. and Chodorov, J.
Anniversary Waltz
P
Random House
Happy Anniversary
UA (US) 1959 dir. David Miller

Fields, J. and Chodorov, J.
My Sister Eileen
P
Random House
COL (US) 1955 dir. Richard Quine
M

Fienburgh, W.
No Love for Johnnie
RANK (GB) 1960 dir. Ralph Thomas
V

Fierstein, H.
Torch Song Trilogy
P
Samuel French
NEW LINE (US) 1988 dir. Paul Bogart

Finch, C.
Rainbow
Grosset & Dunlap
TEN-FOUR (US) 1978
dir. Jackie Cooper
TV(US), V

Finch, M.
Dentist in the Chair
Ace
REN (GB) 1960 dir. Don Chaffey

Finney, C. G.
Seven Faces of Dr. Lao, The
MGM (US) 1964 dir. George Pal
V

Finney, J.
Assault on a Queen
Simon & Schuster
PAR (US) 1966 dir. Jack Donohue

Finney, J.
Body Snatchers, The
Dell
Invasion of the Body Snatchers, The
ALLIED (US) 1956 dir. Don Siegel
UA (US) 1978 dir. Philip Kaufman
V

Finney, J.
Five Against the House
COL (US) 1955 dir. Phil Karlson

Finney, J.
Good Neighbour Sam
Eyre & Spottiswoode (London)
COL (US) 1964 dir. David Swift
V

Finney, J.
House of Numbers
Eyre & Spottiswoode
MGM (US) 1957 dir. Russell Rouse

Finney, J.
Marion's Wall
Simon & Schuster
Maxie
ORION (US) 1985 dir. Paul Aaron
V

Fish, R. L.
Pursuit
Doubleday
Twist of Fate
COL TV/HTV (US/GB) 1989
dir. Ian Sharp
TVSe(GB/US)

Fisher, B. and Marx, A.
Impossible Years, The
P
Samuel French
MGM (US) 1968 dir. Michael Gordon

Fisher, C.
Postcards from the Edge
Simon & Schuster
COL (US) 1990 dir. Mike Nichols

Fisher, C.
Tall Men, The
Houghton, Mifflin Co. (Boston)
FOX (US) 1955 dir. Raoul Walsh
V

Fisher, C.
Yellowstone Kelly
WAR (US) 1959 dir. Gordon Douglas

Fisher, D.
Pack, The
Putnam
WAR (US) 1977 dir. Robert Clouse
V

Fisher, M.
Bethnal Green
Holt, Rinehart & Winston
Place To Go, A
BL (GB) 1963 dir. Basil Dearden

Fisher, S.
I Wake up Screaming
Hale
FOX (US) 1941
dir. H. Bruce Humberstone
GB title: Hot Spot

Fisher, S.
I Wake Up Screaming
Vicki
FOX (US) 1953 dir. Harry Horner

Fisher, S. G.
Destination Tokyo
WAR (US) 1943 dir. Delmer Daves
V

Fisher, V.
Jeremiah Johnson
Four Square Books
WAR (US) 1972 dir. Sidney Pollack
V

Fitch, C.
Beau Brummell
P
J. Lane
MGM (GB) 1954 dir. Curtis Bernhardt

Fitzgerald, F. S.
Babylon Revisited
Scribners
Last Time I Saw Paris, The
MGM (US) 1954 dir. Richard Brooks
V

Fitzgerald, F. S.
Great Gatsby, The
Scribners
PAR (US) 1949 dir. Elliot Nugent
PAR (US) 1974 dir. Jack Clayton
V

Fitzgerald, F. S.
Last of the Belles
TITUS (US) 1974 dir. George Schlatter
TV(US)

Fitzgerald, F. S.
Last Tycoon, The
Scribners
PAR (US) 1976 dir. Elia Kazan
V

Fitzgerald, F. S.
Tender is the Night
Scribner,s

FOX (US) 1962 dir. Henry King
BBC/SHOWTIME (US/GB) 1985
dir. Robert Knights
TVSe(US/GB)

Fitz-Simons, F.
Bright Leaf
Rinehart, N.Y.

WAR (US) 1950 dir. Michael Curtiz

Flagg, F.
Fried Green Tomatoes at the Whistle Stop Cafe
Random House

Fried Green Tomatoes
UN (US) 1991 dir. Jon Avnet

Flaubert, G.
Madame Bovary
Various

MGM (US) 1949 dir. Vincente Minnelli
V
BBC (GB) 1975 dir. Rodney Bennett
TVSe(GB)
GOLDWYN (Fr) 1991
dir. Claude Chabrol

Flavin, M.
One Way Out
P
Samuel French, N.Y.

Convicted
COL (US) 1950 dir. Henry Levin

Fleetwood, H.
Order of Death, The

Corrupt
NEW LINE (It) 1983 dir. Robert Faenza
V

Fleischman, A. S.
Blood Alley
Corgi

WAR (US) 1955 dir. William Wellman

Fleischman, A. S.
Yellowleg
Muller

Deadly Companions, The
WAR (US) 1961 dir. Sam Peckinpah
V

Fleischman, S.
By the Great Horn Spoon
Penguin

Adventures of Bullwhip Griffin, The
DISNEY (US) 1965 dir. James Neilson
V

Fleming, B.
Colonel Effingham's Raid
Duell, Sloan & Pearce

FOX (US) 1945 dir. Irving Pichel
GB title: Man of the Hour
V

Fleming, I.
Casino Royale
Macmillan

COL (GB) 1967 dir. John Huston
V

Fleming, I.
Chitty, Chitty Bang Bang
Random House

UA (GB) 1968 dir. Ken Hughes
Ch, V

Fleming, I.
Diamonds are Forever
Jonathan Cape

UA (GB) 1971 dir. Guy Hamilton
V

Fleming, I.
Dr No
New American Library

UA (GB) 1962 dir. Terence Young
V

Fleming, I.
From Russia With Love
New American Library
UA (GB) 1963 dir. Terence Young
V

Fleming, I.
Goldfinger
New American Library
UA (GB) 1964 dir. Guy Hamilton
V

Fleming, I.
Live and Let Die
Cape
UA (GB) 1973 dir. Guy Hamilton
V

Fleming, I.
Living Daylights, The
New American Library
MGM (GB) 1987 dir. John Glen
V

Fleming, I.
Man with the Golden Gun, The
New American Library
UA (GB) 1974 dir. Guy Hamilton
V

Fleming, I.
Moonraker
Macmillan
UA (GB) 1979 dir. Lewis Gilbert
V

Fleming, I.
On Her Majesty's Secret Service
New American Library
UA (GB) 1969 dir. Peter Hunt
V

Fleming, I.
Spy Who Loved Me, The
Viking Press
UA (GB) 1977 dir. Lewis Gilbert
V

Fleming, I.
Thunderball
Viking Press
UA (GB) 1965 dir. Terence Young
V

Fleming, I.
You Only Live Twice
New American Library
UA (GB) 1966 dir. Lewis Gilbert
V

Flender, H.
Paris Blues
UA (US) 1961 dir. Martin Ritt
V

Fletcher, G.
London Nobody Knows, The
BL (GB) 1969 dir. Norman Cohen

Fletcher, L.
Blindfold
UI (US) 1965 dir. Philip Dunne

Fletcher, L.
Night Watch
P
Random House
AVCO (GB) 1973 dir. Brian G. Hutton
V

Fletcher, L.
Sorry, Wrong Number
P
Dramatists Play Service
PAR (US) 1948 dir. Anatole Litvak
V
WIL. COURT (US) 1989
dir. Tony Wharmby
TV(US)

Flexner, J. T.
George Washington II: The Forging
of a Nation
Little, Brown, (Boston)
MGM/UA TV (US) 1986
dir. William A. Graham
TVSe(US)

Flexner, J. T.
George Washington
Little, Brown (Boston)
MGM TV (US) 1984 dir. Buzz Kulik
TVSe(US)

Flynn, E.
My Wicked, Wicked Ways . . . The
Legend of Errol Flynn
Putnam
CBS ENT (US) 1985 dir. Don Taylor
TV(US), V

Fo, D.
Mistero Buffo
P
Bertani (Verona)
BBC (GB) 1990 dir. Don Coutts
TV(GB)

Fodor, L.
Birthday Gift
P
North to Alaska
FOX (US) 1960 dir. Henry Hathaway

Fodor, L.
Blondie White
P
Footsteps in the Dark
WAR (US) 1941 dir. Lloyd Bacon

Fodor, L.
Jewel Robbery
P
Samuel French
WAR (US) 1932 dir. William Dieterle

Fodor, L.
Jewel Robbery
P
Peterville Diamond, The
WAR (GB) 1942 dir. Walter Forde

Fodor, L.
Unguarded Hour, The
P
MGM (US) 1936 dir. Sam Wood

Fodor, L.
Woman Lies, A
P
Thunder in the Night
FOX (US) 1935 dir. George Archainbaud

Fogle, J.
Drugstore Cowboy
Delta Fiction
AVENUE (US) 1989 dir. Gus van Sant

Foldes, Y.
Golden Ear-Rings
W. Morrow
PAR (US) 1947 dir. Mitchell Leisen

Foldes, Y.
Make You a Fine Wife
My Own True Love
PAR (US) 1948 dir. Compton Bennett

Follett, K.
Eye of the Needle
Arbor House
UA (GB) 1981 dir. Richard Marquand
V

Follett, K.
Key to Rebecca, The
Morrow
TAFT (US) 1985 dir. David Hemmings
TVSe(US)

Follett, K.
On Wings of Eagles
Morrow
TAFT (US) 1986
dir. Andrew V. McLaglen
TVSe(US)

Fontaine, R. L.
Happy Time, The
Random House
COL (US) 1952 dir. Richard Fleischer

Fontane, T.
Fontane Effi Briest
TANGO (W Ger) 1974
dir. Rainer Werner Fassbinder

Foote, H.
Chase, The
COL (US) 1966 dir. Arthur Penn
V

Foote, H.
Travelling Lady, The
P
Baby, The Rain Must Fall
COL (US) 1965 dir. Robert Mulligan
V

Foote, H.
Trip to Bountiful, The
P
ISLAND (US) 1985 dir. Peter Masterson
V

Foote, H.
Valentine's Day
P
Grove Press
On Valentine's Day
ANGELIKA (US) 1986 dir. Ken Harrison
V

Foote, J. T.
Look of Eagles, The
Appleton-Century-Croft
Kentucky
FOX (US) 1938 dir. David Butler

Foote, S.
September, September
Random House
Memphis
PROPAGANDA FILMS TV(US) 1992
dir. Yves Simoneau
TV(US)

Forbes, C.
Avalanche Express
Samuel French
FOX (Eire) 1979 dir. Mark Robson
V

Forbes, E.
Johnny Tremain
Houghton, Mifflin Co. (Boston)
DISNEY (US) 1957
dir. Robert Stevenson
Ch

Forbes, J. S.
Meter Man, The
P
Penthouse, The
PAR (GB) 1967 dir. Peter Collinson

Forbes, M.
Hollow Triumph
Martin
EL (US) 1948 dir. Steve Sekely

Forbes, R.
Fourth Brother, The
China
PAR (US) 1943 dir. John Farrow

Forbes, S.
Go to thy Deathbed
Reflection of Fear
COL (US) 1973 dir. William A. Fraker
V

Ford, B. and Chase, C.
Times Of My Life, The
Harper & Row
Betty Ford Story, The
WAR TV (US) 1987 dir. David Greene
TV(US)

Ford, J. H.
Liberation of Lord Byron Jones, The
Little, Brown (Boston)
COL (US) 1970 dir. William Wyler
V

Foreman, L. L.
Don Desperado
Savage, The
PAR (US) 1952 dir. George Marshall

Foreman, L. L.
Road to San Jacinto
Dutton, N.Y.
Arrow in the Dust
ABP (US) 1954 dir. Lesley Selander

Forest, J-C.
Barbarella
PAR (Fr/It) 1967 dir. Roger Vadim
V

Forester, C. S.
African Queen, The
The Modern Library
ROMULUS (US/GB) 1951
dir. John Houston
V

Forester, C. S.
Brown on 'Resolution'
GB (GB) 1935 dir. Walter Forde
US title: Born for Glory

Forester, C. S.
Captain Hornblower, R. N.
Little, Brown (Boston)
Captain Horatio Hornblower, R. N.
WAR (GB) 1951 dir. Raoul Walsh

Forester, C. S.
Gun, The
Bodley Head (London)
Pride and the Passion, The
UA (US) 1957 dir. Stanley Kramer
V

Forester, C. S.
Hunting the Bismarck
Sink the Bismarck
FOX (GB) 1960 dir. Lewis Gilbert

Forrest, A. J.
Interpol
Wingate
COL (GB) 1957 dir. John Gilling
US title: Pickup Alley

Forrest, D.
Great Dinosaur Robbery, The
One of our Dinosaurs is Missing
DISNEY (US) 1975
dir. Robert Stevenson
Ch, V

Forrester, L.
Girl Called Fathom, A
Fathom
FOX (GB) 1967 dir. Leslie Martinson

Forster, E. M.
Howards' End
Knopf
MERCHANT IVORY (GB) 1992
dir. James Ivory

Forster, E. M.
Maurice
Norton
MI (GB) 1987 dir. James Ivory
V

Forster, E. M.
Passage to India, A
Harcourt Brace
COL-EMI (GB) 1984 dir. David Lean
V

Forster, E. M.
Room With a View, A
Putnam
GOLD (GB) 1985 dir. James Ivory
V

Forster, M.
Georgy Girl
Secker & Warburg
COL (GB) 1966 dir. Silvio Narizzano
V

Forsyth, F.
Casualty of War, A
BLAIR (US) 1990 dir. Tom Clegg
TV(GB/US)

Forsyth, F.
Day of the Jackal, The
Viking Press
UN (Fr/GB) 1973 dir. Fred Zinnemann
V

Forsyth, F.
Dogs of War, The
Viking Press
UA (GB) 1980 dir. John Irvin
V

Forsyth, F.
Fourth Protocol, The
Viking Press
RANK (GB) 1987 dir. John MacKenzie
V

Forsyth, F.
In No Comebacks
Viking Press
Cry of the Innocent
NBC ENT. (US) 1980
dir. Michael O'Herlihy
V

Forsyth, F.
Just Another Secret
BLAIR (US/GB) 1989
dir. Lawrence Gordon Clark
TV(GB/US)

Forsyth, F.
Odessa File, The
Viking Press
COL (GB) 1974 dir. Ronald Neame
V

Forsyth, F.
Pride and Extreme Prejudice
USA NET (US) 1990 dir. Ian Sharp
TV(US)

Forte, V.
Trailmakers, The
Wild Women
A. SPELLING (US) 1970 dir. Don Taylor
TV(US), V

Fossey, D.
Gorillas in the Mist
Houghton, Mifflin Co. (Boston)
WAR/UN (US) 1988 dir. Michael Apted
V

Foster, L. R.
Gentleman From Montana, The
Mr. Smith Goes To Washington
COL (US) 1939 dir. Frank Capra
V

Fowler, G. and Meredyth, B.
Mighty Barnum, The
P
FOX (US) 1934 dir. Walter Lang

Fowler, G.
Beau James
Viking Press
PAR (US) 1957 dir. Melville Shavelson

Fowler, H. M.
Shades Will Not Vanish
Morrow
Strange Intruder
ABP (US) 1956 dir. Irving Rapper

Fowles, J.
Collector, The
Little, Brown (Boston)
BL (US) 1965 dir. William Wyler
V

Fowles, J.
Ebony Tower, The
Little, Brown (Boston)
GRANADA (GB) 1984
dir. Robert Knights
TV(GB), V

Fowles, J.
French Lieutenant's Woman, The
Little, Brown (Boston)
UA (GB) 1981 dir. Karel Reisz
V

Fowles, J.
Magus, The
Little, Brown (Boston)
FOX (GB) 1968 dir. Guy Green

Fox, J.
Little Shepherd of Kingdom Come, The
Grosset & Dunlap
FOX (US) 1961
dir. Andrew V. McLaglen

Fox, J.
White Mischief
Random House
BBC-COL (GB) 1988
dir. Michael Radford
V

Fox, Jr., J.
Trail of the Lonesome Pine, The
Grosset & Dunlap
PAR (US) 1936 dir. Henry Hathaway

Fox, N. A.
Roughshod
Gunsmoke
UN (US) 1953 dir. Nathan Juran

Fox, N. A.
Tall Man Riding
WAR (US) 1955 dir. Lesley Selander

Fox, P.
Desperate Characters
Harcourt, Brace & World
ITC (US) 1971 dir. Frank D. Gilroy
V

Foxman, S.
Classified Love
CBS ENT (US) 1986 dir. Don Taylor
TV(US)

Frame, J.
Angel at My Table, An
Braziller
FINE LINE (Aus) 1991
dir. Jane Campion

France, A.
Crime of Sylvester Bonnard, The
John Lane Co.
Chasing Yesterday
RKO (US) 1935 dir. George Nicholls, Jr.

Francis, D.
Blood Sport
Harper & Row
DLT (US) 1989 dir. Harvey Hart
TV(US)

Francis, D.
Dead Cert
Harper & Row
UA (GB) 1974 dir. Tony Richardson

Francis, D.
In the Frame
Harper & Row
DLT (US) 1989 dir. Wigbert Wicker
TV(US)

Francis, D.
Twice Shy
Putnam
DLT (US) 1989 dir. Deirdre Friel
TV(US)

Frank, A.
Anne Frank: The Diary of a Young Girl
Doubleday
Diary of Anne Frank, The
FOX (US) 1959 dir. George Stevens
V
FOX (US) 1980 dir. Boris Sagal
TV(US)
BBC (GB) 1988
TVSe(GB)

Frank, B.
Cervantes
PRISMA (Sp/It/Fr) 1968
dir. Vincent Sherman

Frank, B.
Sturm in Wasserglass
P
Storm in a Teacup
LF (GB) 1937 dir. Ian Dalrymple, Victor Saville
V

Frank, C.
Dream of the Mad Monkey, The
Twisted Obsession
IVE (US) 1990 dir. Fernando Trueba

Frank, C.
Josepha
TRIUMPH (Fr) 1982
dir. Christopher Frank
V

Frank, C.
L'Année des Meduses
AT (Fr) 1987 dir. Christopher Frank
V

Frank, G.
Boston Strangler, The
Cape
FOX (US) 1968 dir. Richard Fleischer
V

Frank, L.
Carl and Anna
Desire Me
MGM (US) 1947 dir. George Cukor

Frank, M. and Clark, B.
First Lady of the Seeing Eye
Love Leads the Way
DISNEY CH (US) 1984
dir. Delbert Mann
TV(US), V

Frank, P.
Hold Back The Night
Lippincott (Philadelphia)
ABP (US) 1956 dir. Allan Dwan

Frankau, G.
Christopher Strong
Hutchinson
RKO (US) 1933 dir. Dorothy Arzner
V

Franke, C. and Crane, M.
Bombshell
P
MGM (US) 1933 dir. Victor Fleming
GB title: Blonde Bombshell

Franken, R.
Another Language
P
Samuel French
MGM (US) 1933 dir. Edward H. Griffith

Franken, R.
Claudia and David
W. H. Allen
FOX US 1946 dir. Walter Lang

Franken, R.
Claudia
Farrar & Rinehart
FOX (US) 1943 dir. Edmund Goulding

Franklin, E.
Working Man, The
WAR (US) 1933 dir. John Adolfi

Franklin, J.
Last of Philip Banter, The
CINEVISTA (Sp) 1988
dir. Herve Hachuel

Franklin, J. and Doelp, A.
Shock Trauma
TELECOM (Can) 1982 dir. Eric Till
TV(Can)

Franklin, M.
My Brilliant Career
St. Martin's Press
GUO (Aust) 1979 dir. Gillian Armstrong
V

Franzero, C. M.
Life and Times of Cleopatra, The
Redman
Cleopatra
FOX (US) 1963
dir. Joseph L. Mankiewicz
V

Fraser, G. M.
Royal Flash
Knopf
FOX RANK (GB) 1975
dir. Richard Lester
V

Fraser, N.
Eva Peron
Evita Peron
ZEPHYR (US) 1981
dir. Marvin Chomsky
TVSe(US)

Frazee, S.
Desert Guns
World, N.Y.
Gold of the Seven Saints
WAR (US) 1961 dir. Gordon Douglas

Frede, R.
Interns, The
Random House
COL (US) 1962 dir. David Swift

Fredrickson, O. and East, B.
Silence of the North
Crown Publishers
UN (Can) 1981 dir. Allan Winton King
V

Freed, J.
Moonwebs
Ticket to Heaven
UA (US) 1981 dir. R. L. Thomas
V

Freedman, B. and Freedman, N.
Mrs. Mike
Coward-McCann
UA (US) 1950 dir. Louis King

Freedman, D.
Mendel Inc.
P
Heart of New York
WAR (US) 1932 dir. Mervyn LeRoy

Freeling, N.
Because of the Cats
Harper & Row
Rape, The
MIRACLE (Bel/Neth) 1973
dir. Fons Rademakers
V

Freeling, N.
Love in Amsterdam
Caroll & Graf
Amsterdam Affair
LIP/TRIO/GROUP W (GB) 1968
dir. Gerry O'Hara
V

Freeman, D.
Father Sky
Morrow
Taps
FOX (US) 1981 dir. Harold Becker
V

Freeman, L. and Roy, J.
Betrayal
Stein & Day
EMI TV (US) 1978 dir. Paul Wendkos
TV(US), V

Freemantle, B.
Charlie M
Doubleday
Charlie Muffin
EUSTON (GB) 1979 dir. Jack Gold
V

French, M.
Women's Room, The
Summit Books
WAR (US) 1980 dir. Glenn Jordan
TVSe(US)

Friedman, B. J.
Change of Plan, A
Heartbreak Kid, The
FOX (US) 1972 dir. Elaine May
V

Friedman, B. J.
Lonely Guy's Book of Life, The
Lonely Guy, The
UN (US) 1984 dir. Arthur Hiller
V

Friml, R., Post, W. H. and Hooker, B.
Vagabond King, The
P
Samuel French
PAR (US) 1956 dir. Michael Curtiz
M

Frings, Mrs. K.
Hold Back The Dawn
Duell, Sloan & Pearce
PAR (US) 1941 dir. Mitchell Leisen

Frisby, T.
There's a Girl in my Soup
P
Samuel French
COL (GB) 1970 dir. Roy Boulting
V

Fuentes, C.
Gringo Viejo
Farrar, Straus & Giroux
Old Gringo
COL (US) 1989 dir. Luis Puenzo

Fugard, A.
Road to Mecca, The
P
Theatres Communications Group
VIDEOVISION (US) 1992
dir. Athol Fugard
TV(US)

Fuhmann, F.
Kamaraden
Duped Till Doomsday
DEFA (Ger) 1957 dir. Kurt Jung-Alsen

Fukazawa, S.
Ballad of Narayama
ROEI (Jap) 1983 dir. Shohei Imamura

Fulda, L.
Two-Faced Woman
P
MGM (US) 1941 dir. George Cukor

Fuller, C.
Soldier's Play, A
P
Samuel French
Soldier's Story, A
COL (US) 1984 dir. Norman Jewison
V

Fuller, J. G.
Ghost of Flight 401, The
Putnam
PAR TV (US) 1978
dir. Steven Hilliard Stern
TV(US)

Fuller, J. G.
Interrupted Journey, The
Dial Press

UFO Incident, The
UN TV (US) 1975 dir. Richard Colla
TV(US)

Fuller, S.
Scandal Sheet
COL (US) 1952 dir. Phil Karlson
GB title: Dark Page, The

Fullerton, A.
Lionheart
Norton
CFF (GB) 1968 dir. Michael Forlong

Fulop-Miller, R.
Triumph
Great Moment, The
PAR (US) 1944 dir. Preston Sturges

G

Gabriel, G. W.
I, James Lewis
This Woman is Mine
UN (US) 1941 dir. Frank Lloyd

Gaddis, T. E.
Birdman of Alcatraz
Aeonian Press
UA (US) 1961 dir. John Frankenheimer

Gage, N.
Eleni
Random House
WAR (US) 1985 dir. Peter Yates
V

Gaines, C.
Stay Hungry
UA (US) 1976 dir. Bob Rafaelson
V

Gaines, C. and Butler, G.
Pumping Iron
Simon & Schuster
CINEMA 51 (US) 1977
dir. George Butler
V

Gaines, C. and Butler, G.
Pumping Iron II: The Unprecedented Woman
Pumping Iron II
BLUE DOLPHIN (US) 1984
dir. George Butler
V

Gaines, E. J.
Autobiography of Miss Jane Pittman, The
Bantam Books
TOM (US) 1974 dir. John Korty
TV(US), V

Gaines, E. J.
Gathering of Old Men, A
Knopf
CONSOL (US) 1987
dir. Volker Schlondorff
TV(US)

Gaines, R.
Final Night
Heinemann
Front Page Story
BL (GB) 1953 dir. Gordon Parry

Gaines, S.
Heroes and Villains: The True Story of the Beach Boys
New American Library

Story of the Beach Boys, The: Summer Dreams
L. HILL (USTV) 1990
dir. Michael Switzer
TV(US)

Galante, P.
Berlin Wall, The

Freedom Fighter
COL TV (US/GB) 1987
dir. Desmond Davis
TV(GB/US)

Galdos, B. P.
Nazarin
BAR PON (Mex) 1958 dir. Luis Bunuel
V

Gale, R. P. and Hauser, T.
Final Warning: The Legacy of Chernobyl
Warner Books

Chernobyl: The Final Warning
CAROLCO (US/USSR) 1991
dir. Anthony Page
TV(US/USSR)

Gall, I.
Stud Farm, The
HUNG (Hung) 1978 dir. Andras Kovacs

Gallagher, J. P.
Scarlet Pimpernel of the Vatican, The

Scarlet and the Black, The
ITC (It/US) 1983 dir. Jerry London
TVSe(It), V

Gallagher, S.
Chimera
Anglia (GB) 1991 dir. Nicholas Gillott
TV(GB)

Gallagher, T.
Monogamist, The

Family Man, The
TIME-LIFE (US) 1979 dir. Glenn Jordan
TV(US), V

Gallico, P.
Hand of Mary Constable, The
Doubleday

Daughter of the Mind
FOX (US) 1969 dir. Walter Grauman
TV(US)

Gallico, P.
Lili
MGM (US) 1952 dir. Charles Walters
V

Gallico, P.
Matilda
Coward-McCann

AIP (US) 1978 dir. Daniel Mann
V

Gallico, P.
Poseidon Adventure, The
Coward-McCann

FOX (US) 1972 dir. Ronald Neame
V

Gallico, P.
Small Miracle, The
Doubleday

Never Take No for an Answer
INDEPENDENT (GB) 1951
dir. Maurice Cloche, Ralph Smart

Gallico, P.
Small Miracle, The
M. Joseph (London)

LAN (US) 1983 dir. Jeannot Szwarc
TV(US)

Gallico, P.
Snow Goose, The
Knopf

UN/BBC (US/GB) 1971
dir. Patrick Garland
TV(US/GB)

Gallico, P.
Thomasina
Doubleday

Three Lives of Thomasina, The
DISNEY (GB) 1963 dir. Don Chaffey
Ch, V

Gallico, P.
Trial by Terror
Knopf

Assignment Paris
COL (US) 1952 dir. Robert Parrish

Galsworthy, J.
Apple Tree, The
Scribners

Summer Story, A
ITC/ATLANTIC (GB) 1988
dir. Piers Haggard

Galsworthy, J.
Escape
P
Samuel French

RKO (GB) 1930 dir. Basil Dean
FOX (US) 1948
dir. Joseph L. Mankiewicz

Galsworthy, J.
First and the Last, The
P

Twenty-One Days
LF (GB) 1937 dir. Basil Dean
V

Galsworthy, J.
Forsyte Saga, The
Scribners

BBC (GB) 1967 dir. David Giles
TVSe(GB), V

Galsworthy, J.
Loyalties
P
Samuel French

AUT (GB) 1933 dir. Basil Dean

Galsworthy, J.
Man of Property, A
Scribners

That Forsyte Woman
MGM (US) 1949 dir. Compton Bennett
GB title: Forsyte Saga, The

Galsworthy, J.
Old English
P
Scribners

WAR (US) 1930 dir. Alfred E. Green

Galsworthy, J.
Over the River
Scribners

One More River
UN (US) 1934 dir. James Whale
GB title: Over the River

Galsworthy, J.
Skin Game, The
P
Samuel French

BI (GB) 1931 dir. Alfred Hitchcock
V

Gann, E. K.
Antagonists, The
Simon & Schuster

Masada
UN TV (US) 1981 dir. Boris Sagal
GB title: Antagonists, The
TVSe(US), V

Gann, E. K.
Blaze of Noon
H. Holt & Company

PAR (US) 1947 dir. John Farrow

Gann, E. K.
Fate is the Hunter
Simon & Schuster

FOX (US) 1964 dir. Ralph Nelson

Gann, E. K.
Fiddler's Green
William Sloane Associates

Raging Tide, The
UI (US) 1951 dir. George Sherman

Gann, E. K.
High and the Mighty, The
Sloane

WAR (US) 1954 dir. William Wellman

Gann, E. K.
Island in the Sky
Joseph

WAR (US) 1953 dir. William Wellman

Gann, E. K.
Soldier of Fortune
W. Sloane Associates

FOX (US) 1955 dir. Edward Dmytryk
V

Gann, E. K.
Twilight for the Gods
Sloane

UN (US) 1958 dir. Joseph Pevney

Gann, E.
Aviator, The
Arbor House

MGM/UA (US) 1985 dir. George Miller
V

Garbo, N.
Spy
WIL COURT (US) 1989
dir. Philip F. Messina
TV(US)

Garden, J.
All on a Summer's Day
Joseph

Double Confession
ABP (GB) 1950 dir. Ken Annakin

Gardiner, J. R.
Stone Fox
Crowell

TAFT (US) 1987 dir. Harvey Hart
TV(US)

Gardner, E. S.
Case of the Caretaker's Cat, The
Cassell

Case of the Black Cat, The
WAR (US) 1936 dir. William McGann

Gardner, E. S.
Case of the Curious Bride, The
Cassell

WAR (US) 1935 dir. Michael Curtiz

Gardner, E. S.
Case of the Howling Dog, The
Grosset, N.Y.

WAR (US) 1934 dir. Alan Crosland

Gardner, E. S.
Case of the Lucky Legs, The
Hammond

WAR (US) 1935 dir. Archie Mayo

Gardner, E. S.
Case of the Stuttering Bishop, The
WAR (US) 1937 dir. William Clemens

Gardner, E. S.
Case of the Velvet Claws, The
WAR (US) 1936 dir. William Clemens

Gardner, E. S.
D. A. Draws a Circle, The
They Call it Murder
FOX (US) 1971 dir. Walter Grauman
TV(US)

Gardner, H.
Goodbye People, The
P
Samuel French

EMBASSY (US) 1984 dir. Herb Gardner
V

Gardner, H.
Thousand Clowns, A
P
Samuel French
UA (US) 1965 dir. Fred Coe
V

Gardner, J.
Complete State of Death, A
Stone Killer, The
COL (US) 1973 dir. Michael Winner
V

Gardner, J.
Liquidator, The
Viking Press
MGM (GB) 1965 dir. Jack Cardiff
V

Gardner, L.
Christ has Returned to Earth and Preaches Here Nightly
Valentino Returns
VIDMARK/SKOURAS (US) 1989
dir. Paul Hoffman

Gardner, L.
Fat City
Farrar. Straus & Giroux
COL (US) 1972 dir. John Huston
V

Gardner, R. M.
Scandalous John
DISNEY (US) 1971 dir. Robert Butler
V

Gare, N.
Fringe Dwellers, The
OZFILMS (Aus) 1986
dir. Bruce Beresford

Garfield, B.
Death Wish
McKay Co.
CANNON (US) 1974
dir. Michael Winner
V

Garfield, B.
Fear in a Handful of Dust
Fleshburn
CROWN (US) 1984 dir. George Gage
V

Garfield, B.
Gun Down
Dell, N.Y.
Last Hard Man, The
FOX (US) 1976
dir. Andrew V. McLaglen

Garfield, B.
Hopscotch
Lippincott (Philadelphia)
AVCO (US) 1980 dir. Ronald Neame
V

Garfield, B.
Necessity
St. Martins Press
B&E (US) 1988 dir. Michael Miller
TV(US)

Garfield, B.
Relentless
World Publishing
CBS ENT (US) 1977 dir. Lee H. Katzin
TV(US)

Garfield, B.
Wild Times
Simon & Schuster
METRO (US) 1980
dir. Richard Compton
TVSe(US), V

Garfield, L.
Black Jack
Partheon Books
ENT (GB) 1979 dir. Kenneth Loach
V

Garner, H.
Monkey Grip
Seaview Books
PAV (Aust) 1982 dir. Ken Cameron
V

Garnett, D.
Sailor's Return, The
ARIEL (GB) 1978 dir. Jack Gold

Garrett, W.
Man in the Mirror, The
WARDOUR (GB) 1936
dir. Maurice Elvey

Garrison, J.
On the Trail of the Assassins: My Investigation and Prosecution of the Murder of President Kennedy
Sheridan Press

JFK
WAR (US) 1991 dir. Oliver Stone
V

Garstin, C.
China Seas
Chatto & Windus
MGM (US) 1935 dir. Tay Garnett
V

Garth, D.
Four Men and a Prayer
FOX (US) 1938 dir. John Ford

Garve, A.
Death and the Sky Above
Two-Letter Alibi
BL (GB) 1962 dir. Robert Lynn

Garve, A.
Megstone Plot, The
Harper
Touch of Larceny, A
PAR (GB) 1959 dir. Guy Hamilton

Gary, R.
Clair de Femme
Cercle du Nouveau Livre (Paris)
GAU (Fr/It/Ger) 1979 dir. Costa-Gavras

Gary, R.
Colours of the Day, The
Joseph
Man Who Understood Women
FOX (US) 1959 dir. Nunnally Johnson

Gary, R.
Lady L
Simon & Schuster
MGM (Fr/It/US) 1965
dir. Peter Ustinov

Gary, R.
Promisse de L'aube, La
P
Gallimard (Paris); Harper
Promise at Dawn
AVCO (US/Fr) 1970 dir. Jules Dassin

Gary, R.
Roots of Heaven, The
Simon & Schuster
FOX (US) 1958 dir. John Huston

Gary, R.
White Dog
World Publishers
PAR (US) 1982 dir. Samuel Fuller

Gary, R.
Your Ticket is no Longer Valid
G. Braziller
CAROLCO (Can) 1980
dir. George Kaczender
V

Gash, J.
Lovejoy
BBC (GB) 1990 dir. Ken Hannam and David Reynolds
TV(GB)

Gaskell, J.
All Neat in Black Stockings
Houghton & Stoughton
WAR (GB) 1968
dir. Christopher Morahan

Gaskin, C.
File on Devlin, The
COMPASS (US) 1969
dir. George Schaefer
TV(US)

Gates, P.
My Husband, Rock Hudson
Doubleday
Rock Hudson
KON-SAN (US) 1990 dir. John Nicolella
TV(US)

Gates, T.
Cloud Waltzing
Harlequin
AVV/YTV (US/GB) 1987
dir. Gordon Flemyng
TV(GB/US)

Gaulden, R.
Five Card Stud
PAR (US) 1968 dir. Henry Hathaway
V

Gay, J.
Beggar's Opera, The
P
Samuel French
BL (GB) 1952 dir. Peter Brook
M, V

Gay, J.
Beggar's Opera, The
P
Samuel French
BARRANDOV (Czech) 1991
dir. Jiri Menzel

Gazzo, M. V.
Hatful of Rain, A
P
Samuel French
FOX (US) 1957 dir. Fred Zinnemann

Gebler, E.
Plymouth Adventure, The
Doubleday
MGM (US) 1952 dir. Clarence Brown

Gebler, E.
Shall I Eat You Now?
P
Pan
Hoffman
ABP (GB) 1970 dir. Alvin Rackoff
V

Geer, A.
Sea Chase, The
WAR (US) 1955 dir. John Farrow

Gegauff, P.
La Clé de la Rue Saint Nicolas
À Double Tour
PARIS/PANI (Fr/It) 1959
dir. Claude Chabrol

Gehrig, E. and Durso, J.
My Luke and I
Crowell
Love Affair, A: The Eleanor and Lou Gehrig Story
FRIES (US) 1978 dir. Fielder Cook
TV(US), V

Gelber, J.
Connection, The
P
Grove Press
CONT (US) 1961 dir. Shirley Clarke
V

Geller, S.
She Let Him Continue
Pretty Poison
FOX (US) 1968 dir. Noel Black
V

Genet, J.
Balcony, The
P
Samuel French
BL (US) 1963 dir. Joseph Strick

Genet, J.
Maids, The
P
Samuel French
ELY LANDAU (GB) 1974
dir. Christopher Miles

Genet, J.
Querelle de Brest
Grove Press
Querelle
TRIUMPH (Fr/Ger) 1983
dir. Rainer Werner Fassbinder
V

Gent, P.
North Dallas Forty
Morrow
PAR (US) 1979 dir. Ted Kotcheff
V

Geoffrey, W. and Mitchell, B.
Perfect Woman, The
P
GFD (GB) 1949 dir. Bernard Knowles

George, E.
Leather Boys, The
Blond
BL (GB) 1963 dir. Sidney J. Furie
V

George, J.
My Side of the Mountain
Dutton
PAR (US/Can) 1969 dir. James B. Clark

George, P.
Red Alert
Gregg Press
Dr Strangelove; Or How I Learned to Stop Worrying and Love the Bomb
COL (GB) 1963 dir. Stanley Kubrick
V

German, Y.
Trial on the Road/Checkpoint
LENFILM (USSR) 1971
dir. Alexei German

Gershe, L
Butterflies are Free
P
Samuel French
COL (US) 1972 dir. Milton Katselas
V

Gershwin, G. and Gershwin, I.
Porgy
Doubleday
P
Porgy and Bess
Gershwin Publishing Corp.
GOLDWYN (US) 1959
dir. Otto Preminger
M

Gerstner, H.
The Die Bruder Grimm
Wonderful World of the Brothers Grimm, The
MGM (US) 1962 dir. Henry Levin and George Pal
Ch

Geyer, S.
By Candlelight
P
UN (US) 1933 dir. James Whale

Giancana, A. and Renner, T. C.
Mafia Princess
P
Morrow
GROUP W (US) 1986 dir. Robert Collins
TV(US)

Gibbs, A. H.
Young Apollo
P
Men of Tomorrow
PAR (GB) 1932 dir. Leontine Sagan

Gibbs, G. and Dudley, E. L.
Voltaire
WAR (US) 1933 dir. John Adolfi

Gibson, W.
Cobweb, The
MGM (US) 1955 dir. Vincente Minnelli

Gibson, W.
Miracle Worker, The
P
Samuel French
UA (US) 1962 dir. Arthur Penn
V
KATZ-GALLIN (US) 1979
dir. Paul Aaron
TV(US), V

Gibson, W.
Two for the Seesaw
P
Samuel French
UA (US) 1962 dir. Robert Wise

Gide, A.
Symphonie Pastorale, La
Gallimard (Paris)
GIBE (Fr) 1946 dir. Jean Delannoy

Gielgud, V. H.
Death at Broadcasting House
Rich & Cowan
PHOENIX (GB) 1934
dir. Reginald Denham

Gies, M. and Gold, A. L.
Anne Frank Remembered: The Story of the Woman Who Helped To Hide the Frank Family
Simon & Schuster
Attic, The: Hiding of Anne Frank, The
TELECOM/YTV (US/GB) 1988
dir. John Erman
TV(GB/US)

Gifford, B.
Wild at Heart
Grove Press
GOLDWYN (US) 1990 dir. David Lynch

Gifford, T.
Glendower Legacy, The
Putnam
Dirty Tricks
FILMPLAN (Can) 1980 dir. Alvin Rakoff
V

Gignoux, R.
Le Fruit Vert
P
Between Us Girls
UN (US) 1942 dir. Henry Koster

Gilbert, A.
Vanishing Corpse, The
They Met in the Dark
RANK (GB) 1943 dir. Karel Lamac

Gilbert, A.
Woman in Red, The
My Name is Julia Ross
COL (US) 1945 dir. Joseph H. Lewis

Gilbert, E.
Hot Nocturne
P
Blues in the Night
WAR (US) 1941 dir. Anatole Litvak

Gilbert, M.
Death has Deep Roots
Harper
Guilty?
GN (GB) 1956 dir. Edmund Greville

Gilbert, M.
Death in Captivity
Hodder & Stoughton
Danger Within
BL (GB) 1958 dir. Don Chaffey
US title: Breakout

Gilbert, S.
Ratman's Notebook
Willard
CINERAMA (US) 1971 dir. Daniel Mann
V

Gilbert, Sir W. S. and Sullivan, Sir A.
Mikado, The
P
Samuel French
UN (GB) 1939 dir. Victor Scheitzinger
M, V

Gilbert, Sir W. S. and Sullivan, Sir A.
Pirates of Penzance, The
P
Various
UN (GB) 1982 dir. Wilford Leach
M, V

Gilbert, Sir W. S. and Sullivan, Sir A.
Pirates of Penzance, The
P
Various

Pirate Movie, The
FOX (Aus) 1982 dir. Ken Annakin
V

Gilbert, Sir W. S. and Sullivan, Sir A.
Ruddigore
P
GALA (GB) 1967 dir. Joy Batchelor
A, M

Gilbreth, Jr., F. B. and Carey, E.
Belles on Their Toes
Crowell
FOX (US) 1952 dir. Henry Levin

Gilbreth, Jr., F. B. and Carey, E. G.
Cheaper by the Dozen
Crowell
FOX (US) 1950 dir. Walter Lang

Gilden, K. B.
Hurry Sundown
Doubleday
PAR (US) 1967 dir. Otto Preminger

Gill, T.
Gentlemen of the Jungle
Tropic Zone
PAR (US) 1952 dir. Lewis R. Foster

Gillham, B.
Place to Hide, A
Deutsch
Break Out
CFTF (GB) 1984 dir. Frank Godwin
Ch

Gillies, J.
Cash on Demand
P
COL (GB) 1963 dir. Quentin Lawrence

Gilman, D.
Unexpected Mrs. Pollifax, The
Doubleday
Mrs. Pollifax – Spy
UA (US) 1971 dir. Leslie Martinson

Gilman, P.
Diamond Head
COL (US) 1962 dir. Guy Green
V

Gilpatric, G.
Action in the North Atlantic
Dutton
WAR (US) 1943 dir. Lloyd Bacon

Gilroy, F. D.
From Noon Till Three
Doubleday
UA (US) 1976 dir. Frank D. Gilroy
V

Gilroy, F. D.
Only Game in Town, The
P
Samuel French
FOX (US) 1969 dir. George Stevens

Gilroy, F. D.
Subject was Roses, The
P
Samuel French
MGM (US) 1968 dir. Ulu Grosbard

Ginsbury, N.
First Gentleman, The
P
COL (GB) 1948 dir. Alberto Cavalcanti
US title: Affairs of a Rogue

Giono, J.
Angele
INTERAMA (FR) 1934
dir. Marcel Pagnol

Giono, J.
Harvest
North Point Press (San Francisco)
M. PAGNOL (Fr) 1937
dir. Marcel Pagnol
V

Giono, J.
Jean le Bleu
Fasquelle (Paris)
Femme du Boulanger, La
PAGNOL (Fr) 1938 dir. Marcel Pagnol

Giovanni, J.
Hole, The
PLAY ART (Fr/It) 1959
dir. Jacques Becker

Giovanni, P.
Crucifer of Blood
P
Samuel French
AGAMEMNON (US) 1991
dir. Fraser Heston
TV(US)

Gipson, F. B.
Circles Round the Wagon
Hound-Dog Man
FOX (US) 1959 dir. Don Siegel

Gipson, F. B.
Old Yeller
Harper
DISNEY (US) 1957
dir. Robert Stevenson
V

Gipson, F.
Savage Sam
Harper
DISNEY (US) 1963 dir. Norman Tokar
V

Girardoux, J.
Madwoman of Chaillot, The
P
Hill & Wang
WAR (GB) 1969 dir. Bryan Forbes

Gittelson, C.
Saving Grace
EMBASSY (US) 1986
dir. Robert M. Young
V

Glasgow, E.
In This Our Life
Harcourt Brace & Co.
WAR (US) 1942 dir. John Huston

Glaspell, S.
Brook Adams
Right to Love, The
PAR (US) 1930 dir. Richard Wallace

Glass, F.
Marvin and Tige
St. Martin's Press
CASTLE HILL (US) 1985
dir. Eric Weston
V

Glatzle, M. and Fiore, E.
Muggable Mary
Muggable Mary: Street Cop
CBS ENT (US) 1982 dir. Sandor Stern
TV(US)

Glemser, B.
Girl on a Wing
Macdonald

Come Fly with Me
MGM (US) 1963 dir. Henry Levin

Glickman, W. and Stein, J.
Mrs. Gibbons' Boys
P
Samuel French

BL (GB) 1962 dir. Max Varnel

Glitman, R. M.
Ruling Passion, The

High Price of Passion, The
TAFT (US) 1986 dir. Larry Elikann
TV(US)

Gloag, J.
Our Mother's House
Simon & Schuster

MGM (GB) 1967 dir. Jack Clayton

Godden, R.
Battle of Villa Fiorita, The
Viking Press

WAR (GB) 1964 dir. Delmer Daves
US title: Affair at the Villa Fiorita

Godden, R.
Black Narcissus
Little, Brown (Boston)

ARC (GB) 1946 dir. Michael Powell
V

Godden, R.
Episode of Sparrows, An
Viking Press

Innocent Sinners
RANK (US) 1957 dir. Philip Leacock

Godden, R.
Fugue in Time, A
Macmillan

Enchantment
RKO (US) 1948 dir. Irving Reis

Godden, R.
Greengage Summer, The
Viking Press

RANK (GB) 1961 dir. Lewis Gilbert
US title: Loss of Innocence

Godden, R.
In this House of Brede
Viking Press

TOMORROW (US) 1975
dir. George Schaefer
TV(US), V
CHANNEL 4 (GB) 1984
TV(GB)

Godden, R.
River, The
Viking Press

UA (Ind) 1951 dir. Jean Renoir
V

Godey, J.
Never a Dull Moment
Simon & Schuster

DISNEY (US) 1967 dir. Jerry Paris
V

Godey, J.
Taking of Pelham 123, The
Putnam

UA (US) 1974 dir. Joseph Sargent
V

Godey, J.
Three Worlds of Johnny Handsome, The
Random House

Johnny Handsome
TRI-STAR (US) 1989 dir. Walter Hill
V

Goetz, C.
Dr. Praetorius
P

People Will Talk
FOX (US) 1951
dir. Joseph L. Mankiewicz

Gogol, N. V.
Inspector General, The
P
Samuel French
WAR (US) 1949 dir. Henry Koster
V

Gogol, N.
Taras Bulba
Knopf
UA (US) 1962 dir. J. Lee Thompson

Gold, H.
Salt
Dial Press
Threesome
CBS ENT (US) 1984 dir. Lou Antonio
TV(US)

Goldberg, Dr. M.
Critical List, The
MTM INC (US) 1978 dir. Lou Antonio
TVSe(US)

Goldberg, V.
Margaret Bourke-White
Harper & Row
TNT (US) 1989 dir. Lawrence Schiller
TV(US)

Golden, J., and Strange, H.
After Tomorrow
P
FOX (US) 1932 dir. Frank Borzage

Golding, L.
Mr. Emmanuel
Viking Press
TC (GB) 1944 dir. Harold French
V

Golding, W.
Lord of the Flies
Coward-McCann
BL (GB) 1963 dir. Peter Brooke
V
COL/PALACE (GB/US) 1990
dir. Harry Hook

Goldman, J.
Lion in Winter, The
P
Samuel French
AVCO (GB) 1968 dir. Anthony Harvey
V

Goldman, J.
They Might be Giants
P
UN (US) 1972 dir. Anthony Harvey
V

Goldman, W.
Soldier in the Rain
WAR (US) 1963 dir. Ralph Nelson
V

Goldman, W.
Casual Sex
P
Casual Sex?
UN (US) 1988 dir. Genevieve Robert
V

Goldman, W.
Heat
Warner Books
NEW CENTURY (US) 1987
dir. Dick Richards
V

Goldman, W.
Magic
Delacorte Press
FOX (US) 1978
dir. Richard Attenborough
V

Goldman, W.
Marathon Man
Delacorte Press
PAR (US) 1976 dir. John Schlesinger
V

Goldman, W.
No Way to Treat a Lady
Harcourt Brace & World
PAR (US) 1968 dir. Jack Smight
V

Goldman, W.
Princess Bride, The
Ballantine Books
FOX (US) 1987 dir. Rob Reiner
V

Goldsmith, B.
Little Gloria ... Happy at Last
Knopf
METRO (US) 1983 dir. Waris Hussein
TVSe(US)

Goldsmith, C.
Father was a Fullback
P
FOX (US) 1949 dir. John M. Stahl

Goldsmith, C.
What a Life
P
PAR (US) 1939 dir. Theodore Reed

Goldsmith, M. M.
Detour
PRC (US) 1946 dir. Edgar G. Ulmer

Golon, S.
Angelique
Lippincott (Philadelphia)
FRANCOS (Fr/W.Ger/It) 1964
dir. Bernard Borderie

Goncharov, I.
Oblomov
Russkii iazyk (Moscow0
MOSFILM (USSR) 1981
dir. Nikita Milchalkov
V

Goodchild, G. and Witty, F.
No Exit
P
No Escape
PATHE (GB) 1936 dir. Norman Lee

Goodhart, W.
Generation
P
Samuel French
AVCO (US) 1969 dir. George Schaefer
GB title: Time for Giving, A
V

Goodin, P.
Take Care of My Little Girl
FOX (US) 1951 dir. Jean Negulesco

Goodis, D.
Burglar, The
Vintage Books
COL (US) 1957 dir. Paul Wendkos

Goodis, D.
Burglar, The
Vintage Books
Burglars, The
COL (Fr/It) 1971 dir. Henri Verneuill
V

Goodis, D.
Dark Passage
World, N.Y.
WAR (US) 1947 dir. Delmer Daves
V

Goodis, D.
Down There
Black Lizard Books (Berkeley, California)
Shoot the Piano Player
PLEIADE (Fr) 1960
dir. François Truffaut
V

Goodis, D.
Nightfall
Vintage Books
COL (US) 1956 dir. Jacques Tourneur

Goodman, G. J. W.
Wheeler-Dealers, The

Wheeler-Dealers
MGM (US) 1963 dir. Arthur Hiller
GB title: Separate Beds

Goodman, J. E.
Man Who Came Back, The
P

FOX (US) 1930 dir. Raoul Walsh

Goodman, J. E.
Silent Voice, The
P

Man Who Played God, The
WAR (US) 1932 dir. John G. Adolfi
GB title: Silent Voice, The

Goodrich, F., and Hackett, A.
Up Pops the Devil
P

Thanks for the Memory
PAR (US) 1938 dir. George Archainbaud

Goodschild, G.
Splendid Crime, The

Public Defender
RKO (US) 1931 dir. J. Walter Ruben

Goodwin, D. K.
Fitzgeralds and the Kennedys, The
Simon & Schuster

Kennedys of Massachusetts, The
ORION TV (US) 1990
dir. Lamont Johnson
TVSe(US)

Goodwin, R.
Leontyne

LEONTYNE/ITV (GB) 1990
dir. Richard Goodwin
TV(GB)

Gordon, A.
Minister to Millions

One Man's Way
UA (US) 1964 dir. Denis Sanders

Gordon, A.
Reprisal

COL (US) 1956 dir. George Sherman

Gordon, B.
I'm Dancing as Fast as I Can
Harper & Row

PAR (US) 1982 dir. Jack Hofsiss
V

Gordon, L.
White Cargo
P

BI (GB) 1930 dir. J. D. Williams,
A. W. Barnes
MGM (US) 1942 dir. Richard Thorpe

Gordon, M. and Gordon G.
Case File F.B.I.

Down 3 Dark Streets
UA (US) 1954 dir. Arnold Laven

Gordon, M. and Gordon, G.
Make Haste to Live
Doubleday, N. Y.

REP (US) 1954 dir. William A. Seiter

Gordon, M. and Gordon, G.
Operation Terror

Experiment in Terror
COL (US) 1962 dir. Blake Edwards
GB title: The Grip of Fear
V

Gordon, M. and Gordon, G.
Undercover Cat
Doubleday

That Darn Cat!
DISNEY (US) 1965
dir. Robert Stevenson
V

Gordon, R.
Captain's Table, The
Michael Joseph

RANK (GB) 1958 dir. Jack Lee
V

Gordon, R.
Doctor in the House
Harcourt, Brace
GFD (GB) 1954 dir. Ralph Thomas
V

Gordon, R.
Over 21
P
COL (US) 1945 dir. Alexander Hall

Gordon, R.
Rosie
P
UN (US) 1967 dir. David Lowell Rich

Gordon, R.
Years Ago
P
Viking
Actress, The
MGM (US) 1953 dir. George Cukor

Gore-Brown, R.
Key, The
P
WAR (US) 1934 dir. Michael Curtiz

Gores, J.
Hammett
WAR (US) 1982 dir. Wim Wenders
V

Gorky, M.
Bas-Fonds, Les
P
Metheun
ALB (Fr) 1936 dir. Jean Renoir

Gorky, M.
Vassa
P
IFEX (USSR) 1983 dir. Gleb Panfiluv

Gorman, H.
Suzy
MGM (US) 1936
dir. George Fitzmaurice

Gosling, P.
Fair Game
Coward, McCann & Geoghegan
Cobra
WAR (US) 1986 dir. G. P. Cosmatos
V

Gottlieb, P.
Agency
Sphere
CAROLCO (Can) 1981
dir. George Kaczender
V

Goudge, E.
Green Dolphin Street
Coward-McCann
MGM (US) 1947 dir. Victor Saville
V

Gould, H.
Cocktail
St. Martin's Press
TOUCH (US) 1988
dir. Roger Donaldson
V

Gould, J.
Sins
New American Library
NEW WORLD (US) 1986
dir. Douglas Hickox
TVSe(US)

Gould, L.
Such Good Friends
Random House
PAR (US) 1972 dir. Otto Preminger

Gouzenko, I.
This was my Choice
Dent
Iron Curtain
FOX (US) 1948 dir. William Wellman

Graber, M. E.
Man Inside, The
COL (GB) 1958 dir. John Gilling

Graczyk, E.
Come Back to the Five and Dime, Jimmy Dean, Jimmy Dean
P
Samuel French
SANDCASTLE (US) 1982
dir. Robert Altman
V

Grady, J.
Six Days of the Condor
Norton
Three Days of the Condor
PAR (US) 1975 dir. Sydney Pollack
V

Graeme, B.
Suspense
Face in the Night
GN (GB) 1956 dir. Lance Comfort

Graf, O. M.
Stationmaster's Wife, The
TELECUL (Ger) 1983
dir. Rainer Werner Fassbinder

Grafton, S.
Lolly Madonna XXX
MGM (US) 1973 dir. Richard C. Sarafian
GB title: Lolly-Madonna War, The

Graham, C.
Bordertown
WAR (US) 1934 dir. Archie Mayo

Graham, D.
Susan Lenox, Her Fall and Rise
MGM (US) 1931 dir. Robert Z. Leonard
GB title: Rise of Helga, The

Graham, J.
Wrath of God, The
MGM (US) 1972 dir. Ralph Nelson

Graham, M.
Just Like the Pom Pom Girls
P
Sinful Life, A
NEW LINE (US) 1989
dir. William Schreiner

Graham, R. L. and Gill, D.
Dove, The
Harper & Row
EMI (US) 1974 dir. Charles Jarrot
V

Graham, S. and Frank, G.
Beloved Infidel
Holt
FOX (US) 1959 dir. Henry King

Graham, W.
Forgotten Story, The
HTV (GB) 1982
TV(GB)

Graham, W.
Fortune is a Woman
Doubleday
COL (GB) 1956 dir. Sidney Gilliatt
US title: She Played with Fire

Graham, W.
Marnie
Doubleday
UI (US) 1964 dir. Alfred Hitchcock
V

Graham, W.
Night Without Stars
GFD (GB) 1951 dir. Anthony Pelissier

Graham, W.
Walking Stick, The
Doubleday
MGM (GB) 1970 dir. Eric Till

Graham, W. and Taylor, V.
Take my Life
Doubleday
EL (GB) 1947 dir. Ronald Neame

Granger, K. R. G.
Ten Against Caesar
Gun Fury
COL (US) 1953 dir. Raoul Walsh
V

Grant, N.
Dusty Ermine
P
TWICKENHAM (GB) 1938
dir. Bernard Vorhaus

Grant, N.
Nelson Touch, The
P
Man of Affairs
GAU (GB) 1937 dir. Herbert Mason
US title: *His Lordship*

Grass, G.
Tin Drum, The
Pantheon Books
UA (Ger/Fr) 1979
dir. Volker Schlöndorff
V

Graves, R.
I, Claudius
Methuen
BBC (GB) 1976 dir. Herbert Wise
TVSe(GB), V

Gray, M. and Gallo, M.
For Those I Loved
Little, Brown (Boston)
GALA (Can/Fr) 1983 dir. Robert Enrico
V
BBC (GB) 1991 dir. Robert R. Enrico
TV(GB)

Gray, S.
Butley
P
Samuel French
Seven Kings (GB/US) 1973
dir. Harold Pinter

Gray, S. E. and Milton, P. R.
Search for Beauty
P
PAR (US) 1934 dir. Erle C. Kenton

Graziano, R.
Somebody Up There Likes Me
Simon & Schuster
MGM (US) 1956 dir. Robert Wise

Green, F. L.
Lost Man, The
Joseph
UN (US) 1969 dir. Robert Alan Arthur

Green, F. L.
Odd Man Out
Reynal & Hitchcock
TC (GB) 1947 dir. Carol Reed
US title: Gang War
V

Green, F. L.
On the Night of the Fire
GFD (GB) 1939
dir. Brian Desmond Hurst
US title: Fugitive, The

Green, G.
Hostage Heart, The
MGM (US) 1977 dir. Bernard McEverty
TV(US)

Green, G.
Last Angry Man, The
Scribners
COL (US) 1959 dir. Daniel Mann
COL (US) 1974 dir. Jerrold Freedman
TV(US)

Green, G.
Tourist
Doubleday
FOX (US) 1980 dir. Jeremy Summers
TV(US)

Green, J.
Life for Ruth
P

RANK (GB) 1962 dir. Basil Dearden
US title: Condemned to Life

Green, J.
Murder Mistaken
P
Evans

Cast a Dark Shadow
EROS (GB) 1955 dir. Lewis Gilbert

Green, L.
Mathilda Shouted Fire
P

Midnight Lace
UN (US) 1960 dir. David Miller
V
UN TV (US) 1981 dir. Ivan Nagy
TV(US)

Green, P.
House of Connelly, The
P
Samuel French

Carolina
FOX (US) 1934 dir. Henry King
GB title: House of Connelly

Greenberg, J.
I Never Promised you a Rose Garden
Holt, Rinehart & Winston

NEW WORLD (US) 1977
dir. Anthony Page
V

Greenberg, J.
In This Sign
Holt, Rinehart & Winston

Love is Never Silent
M. REES (US) 1985 dir. Joseph Sargent
TV(US)

Greenburg, D.
Nanny, The
Macmillan

Guardian, The
UN (US) 1990 dir. William Friedkin

Greenburg, D.
Philly
Private Lessons
J. FARLEY (US) 1981 dir. Alan Myerson

Greene, B.
Summer of my German Soldier
Bantam Books

HIGHGATE (US) 1978
dir. Michael Tuchner
TV(US), V

Greene, G.
Across the Bridge
Heinemann

RANK (GB) 1957 dir. Ken Annakin
V

Greene, G.
Basement Room, The
Penguin

Fallen Idol, The
FOX (GB) 1948 dir. Carol Reed
US title: Lost Illusion, The
V

Greene, G.
Brighton Rock
Penguin

AB (GB) 1947 dir. John Boulting
US title: Young Scarface
V

Greene, G.
Comedians, The
Viking Press

MGM (US/Fr) 1967 dir. Peter Glenville

Greene, G.
Confidential Agent
Viking Press

WAR (US) 1945 dir. Herman Shumlin

Greene, G.
Doctor Fisher of Geneva
Simon & Schuster

BBC (GB) 1984
dir. Michael Lindsay-Hogg
TV(GB)

Greene, G.
End of the Affair, The
Penguin

COL (GB) 1954 dir. Edward Dmytryk

Greene, G.
England Made Me
Heinemann (London)

HEMDALE (GB) 1972 dir. Peter Duffell

Greene, G.
Gun For Sale, A
Heinemann (London)

Short Cut to Hell
PAR (US) 1957 dir. James Cagney

Greene, G.
Gun for Sale, A
Viking Press

This Gun for Hire
PAR (US) 1942 dir. Frank Tuttle
V
BBK (US) 1991 dir. Lou Antonio
TV(US)

Greene, G.
Heart of the Matter
Viking Press

BL (GB) 1953
dir. George More O'Ferrall

Greene, G.
Honorary Consul, The
Simon & Schuster

PAR (GB) 1983 dir. John Mackenzie
US title: Beyond the Limit
V

Greene, G.
Human Factor, The
Simon & Schuster

RANK (GB) 1979 dir. Otto Preminger
V

Greene, G.
Loser Takes All
Viking Press

BL (GB) 1956 dir. Ken Annakin

Greene, G.
Loser Takes All
Viking Press

Strike It Rich
BRIT SCREEN (GB) 1990
dir. James Scott

Greene, G.
Man Within, The
Doubleday

GFD (GB) 1947 dir. Bernard Knowles
US title: Smugglers, The

Greene, G.
May we Borrow Your Husband?
Viking Press

ITV (GB) 1986 dir. Bob Mahoney
TV(GB)

Greene, G.
Ministry of Fear
Viking Press

PAR (US) 1944 dir. Fritz Lang

Greene, G.
Our Man in Havana
Viking Press

COL (GB) 1959 dir. Carol Reed

Greene, G.
Power and the Glory, The
Viking Press

Fugitive, The
RKO (US) 1947 dir. John Ford
V

Greene, G.
Quiet American, The
Viking Press

UA (US) 1957 dir. Joseph L. Mankiewicz

Greene, G.
Stamboul Train
Orient Express
FOX (US) 1934 dir. Paul Martin

Greene, G.
Tenth Man, The
Simon & Schuster

ROSEMONT (US/GB) 1988
dir. Jack Gold
TV(GB/US)

Greene, G.
Third Man, The
Viking Press

GFD (GB) 1949 dir. Carol Reed
V

Greene, G.
Travels with my Aunt
Viking Press

MGM (US) 1972 dir. George Cukor

Greene, G.
Went the Day Well?

EAL (GB) 1942 dir. Alberto Cavalcanti
US title: Forty-Eight Hours

Greene, S.
Boy who Drank Too Much, The
Viking Press

MTM (US) 1980 dir. Jerrold Freedman
TV(US)

Greene, W.
Death in the Deep South
Stacpole

They Won't Forget
WAR (US) 1937 dir. Mervyn Le Roy

Greene, W.
Lady and the Tramp
Various

DISNEY (US) 1955 dir. Hamilton Luske
A, V

Greenfield, I. A.
Tagget

MCA TV (US) 1991
dir. Richard T. Heffron
TV(US)

Greenwald, H.
Call Girl, The
Ballantine Books

Girl of the Night
WAR (US) 1960 dir. Joseph Cates

Greenwood, R.
Mr. Bunting at War

Salute John Citizen
BN (GB) 1942 dir. Maurice Elvey
V

Greenwood, W.
Cure for Love, The
P
French

BL (GB) 1949 dir. Robert Donat

Greenwood, W.
Love on the Dole

BL (GB) 1941 dir. John Baxter
V

Gregor, M.
Bridge, The

FONO (W. Ger) 1959
dir. Bernhard Wicki

Gregor, M.
Verdict, The
Random House

Town Without Pity
UA (US/Switz) 1961
dir. Gottfried Reinhardt

Gregory, Lady I. A.
Rising of the Moon, The
Putnam

WAR (Ire) 1957 dir. John Ford

Grendel, F.
Ceremony, The

UA (US/Sp) 1963 dir. Laurence Harvey

Gresham, W.
Nightmare Alley

FOX (GB) 1947 dir. Edmund Goulding

Grey, Z.
Desert Gold
W. J. Black

PAR (US) 1936 dir. James Hogan
V

Grey, Z.
Fighting Caravans
W. J. Black

PAR (US) 1931 dir. Otto Brower, David
Burton
V

Grey, Z.
Forlorn River
W. J. Black

PAR (US) 1937 dir. Charles Barton

Grey, Z.
Maverick Queen, The
W. J. Black

REP (US) 1956 dir. Joe Kane
V

Grey, Z.
Riders of the Purple Sage
W. J. Black

FOX (US) 1931
dir. Hamilton MacFadden
FOX (US) 1941 dir. James Tinling

Grey, Z.
Twin Sombreros
W. J. Black

Gunfighters
COL (US) 1947 dir. George Waggner

Grey, Z.
Vanishing American, The
W. J. Black

PAR (US) 1925 dir. George B. Seitz
V

Grey, Z.
West of the Pecos
Grosset & Dunlap

RKO (US) 1934 dir. Phil Rosen
RKO (US) 1945 dir. Edward Killy

Grey, Z.
Western Union
W. J. Black

FOX (US) 1941 dir. Fritz Lang

Grey, Z.
Wildfire
G. K. Hall

Red Canyon
UN (US) 1949 dir. George Sherman

Grierson, E.
Reputation for a Song

My Lover, My Son
MGM (US/GB) 1970 dir. John Newland

Griffith, C.
Papa's Delicate Condition
Houghton Mifflin Co. (Boston)

PAR (US) 1963 dir. George Marshall
V

Grimble, Sir A.
Pattern of Islands, A

Pacific Destiny
BL (GB) 1956 dir. Wolf Rilla

Grimm, J. L. K. and Grimm, W. K.
Dancing Princess, The; Cobbler & the Elves, The; Singing Bone, The
Various
Wonderful World of the Brothers Grimm, The
MGM (US) 1962 dir. Henry Levin, George Pal
Ch

Grimm, J. L. K. and Grimm, W. K.
Hansel and Gretel
Various
CANNON (US) 1987 dir. Len Talan
Ch, V

Grimm, J. L. K. and Grimm, W. K.
Red Riding Hood
Various
CANNON (US) 1987 dir. Adam Brooks
Ch

Grimm, J. L. K. and Grimm, W. K.
Rumpelstiltskin
Various
CANNON (US) 1987 dir. David Irving
Ch, V

Grimm, J. L. K. and Grimm, W. K.
Snow White
Various
CANNON (US) 1987 dir. Michael Berz
Ch

Grimm, J. L. K. and Grimm, W. K.
Snow White and the Seven Dwarfs
Various
DISNEY (US) 1937 dir. David Hand
A

Grimm, J. L. K. and Grimm, W. K.
Tom Thumb
Various
MGM (GB) 1958 dir. George Pal
V

Groom, W.
As Summers Die
Summit Books
TELEPIC (US) 1986
dir. Jean-Claude Tramont
TV(US)

Gross, L.
Last Jews in Berlin, The
Simon & Schuster
Forbidden
ENT (GB/Ger) 1984 dir. Anthony Page
TV(GB)

Gross, L. and Carpenter, E. C.
Whistling in the Dark
P
MGM (US) 1941 dir. S. Sylvan Simon

Grossbach, R.
Easy and Hard Ways Out
Harper's Magazine Press
Best Defense
PAR (US) 1984 dir. Willard Huyck

Grossman, B.
Bachelor Flat
P
TCF (US) 1961 dir. Frank Tashlin

Grossman, V.
City of Bardish, A
Commissar
GORKY (USSR) 1988
dir. Alexander Askoldov

Grosso, S. and Rosenberg, P.
Point Blank
Grosset & Dunlap

Question of Honor, A
EMI (US) 1982 dir. Jud Taylor
TV(US), V

Groussard, S.
Blood of Israel, The

21 Hours at Munich
FILMWAYS (US) 1976
dir. William A. Graham
TV(US), V

Grubb, D.
Fools Paradise
Hodder & Stoughton

Fools Parade
COL (US) 1971
dir. Andrew V. McLaglen
GB title: Dynamite Man from Glory Jail

Grubb, D.
Night of the Hunter, The
Harper

UA (US) 1955 dir. Charles Laughton
V
KONIGSBERG/SANITSKY (US) 1991
dir. David Greene
TV(US)

Gruber, F.
Buffalo Grass

Big Land, The
WAR (US) 1957 dir. Gordon Douglas
GB title: Stampeded
V

Gruber, F.
Town Tamer
PAR (US) 1965 dir. Lesley Selander

Gruber, F.
Twenty Plus Two
AA (US) 1962 dir. Joseph M. Newman

Gruber, G.
Bitter Sage

Tension at Table Rock
RKO (US) 1956
dir. Charles Marquis Warren
V

Guareschi, G.
Don Camillo and the Prodigal Son

Return of Don Camillo, The
MIRACLE (Fr/It) 1953
dir. Julien Duvivier

Guareschi, G.
Don Camillo's Last Round
Rizzoli (Italy) 1955
dir. Carmine Guareschi

Guareschi, G.
Little World of Don Camillo, The
Pellegrini & Cudahy

LF (Fr/It) 1952 dir. Julien Duvivier

Guest, J.
Ordinary People
Viking Press

PAR (US) 1980 dir. Robert Redford
V

Guido, B.
Fall, The
ARG SONO (Arg) 1958
dir. Leopoldo Torre Nilsson

Guido, B.
House of the Angel, The
ARG SONO (Arg) 1957
dir. Leopoldo Torre Nilsson

Guimard, P.
Choses de la Vie, Les
LIRA/FIDA (Fr/It) 1969
dir. Claude Sautet

Gulick, B.
Hallelujah Trail, The
UA (US) 1965 dir. John Sturges

Gulick, W.
Bend of the Snake
Houghton, Mifflin Co. (Boston)
Bend of the River
UI (US) 1952 dir. Anthony Mann
GB title: Where the River Bends
V

Gundy, E.
Bliss
Viking Press
Seduction of Miss Leona, The
SCHERICK (US) 1980 dir. Joseph Hardy
TV(US)

Gunn, J. E.
Deadlier than the Male
Born to Kill
RKO (US) 1947 dir. Robert Wise
GB title: Lady of Deceit
V

Gunn, Mrs. A.
We of the Never Never
AP (Aust) 1982 dir. Igor Auzins
V

Gunn, N.
Blood Hunt
BBC (GB) 1986
TV(GB)

Gunn, N. M.
Silver Darlings, The
ALL (GB) 1947 dir. Clarence Elder,
Clifford Evans

Gunther, J.
Death Be Not Proud
Modern Library
WESTFALL (US) 1975 dir. Donald Wrye
TV(US), V

Gurdjieff, G. I.
Meetings with Remarkable Men
Dutton
ENT (GB) 1979 dir. Peter Brook
V

Gurney, A. R.
Middle Ages, The
P
Avon Books
My Brother's Wife
ADAM (US) 1989 dir. Jack Bender
TV(US)

Gutcheon, B.
Still Missing
Putnam
Without a Trace
FOX (US) 1983 dir. Stanley R. Jaffe
V

Guthrie, A. B.
Big Sky, The
Houghton, Mifflin Co. (Boston)
RKO (US) 1952 dir. Howard Hawks
V

Guthrie, Jr., A. B.
These Thousand Hills
Houghton, Mifflin Co. (Boston)
FOX (US) 1958 dir. Richard Fleischer

Guthrie, Jr., A. B.
Way West, The
W. Sloane Associates
UA (US) 1967 dir. Andrew V. McLaglen

Guthrie, W.
Bound for Glory
E. P. Dutton
UA (US) 1976 dir. Hal Ashby
V

Gwaltney, F. I.
Day the Century Ended, The
Secker & Warburg
Between Heaven and Hell
FOX (US) 1956 dir. Richard Fleischer

Haase, J.
Erasmus with Freckles
Simon & Schuster

Dear Brigitte
FOX (US) 1965 dir. Henry Koster
V

Haase, J.
Me and the Arch Kook Petulia
Coward, McCann

Petulia
WAR (US) 1968 dir. Richard Lester
V

Haber, J.
Users, The
Delacorte Press

A. SPELLING (US) 1978
dir. Joseph Hardy
TV(US), V

Hackett, W.
Espionage
P
MGM (US) 1937 dir. Kurt Neumann

Hackett, W.
It Pays to Advertise
P
Samuel French
PAR (US) 1931 dir. Frank Tuttle

Hackett, W.
Love Under Fire
P
FOX (US) 1937 dir. George Marshall

Hackett, W.
Road House
P
GAU (GB) 1934 dir. Maurice Elvey

Hackney, A.
Private Life
I'm All Right Jack
BL (GB) 1959 dir. John Boulting
V

Hackney, A.
Private's Progress, A
BL (GB) 1956 dir. John Boulting
V

Haedrich, M.
Crack in the Mirror
W. H. Allen
FOX (US) 1960 dir. Richard Fleischer

Hagan, J.
One Sunday Afternoon
P
Samuel French
PAR (US) 1933 dir. Stephen Roberts
WAR (US) 1948 dir. Raoul Walsh

Hagan, J.
One Sunday Afternoon
P
Samuel French
Strawberry Blonde, The
WAR (US) 1941 dir. Raoul Walsh
V

Haggard, Sir H. R.
Alan Quatermain
Various

Allan Quatermain and the Lost City of Gold
CANNON (US) 1987 dir. Gary Nelson
V

Haggard, Sir H. R.
Alan Quatermain
Various

King Solomon's Treasure
BARBER ROSE (Can/GB) 1979
dir. Alvin Rakoff
V

Haggard, Sir H. R.
King Solomon's Mines
Various

GB (GB) 1937 dir. Robert Stevenson
MGM (US) 1950 dir. Compton Bennett
V
CANNON (US) 1985
dir. J. Lee Thompson
V

Haggard, Sir H. R.
King Solomon's Mines
Various

Watusi
MGM (US) 1959 dir. Kurt Neumann

Haggard, Sir H. R.
She
Various

RKO (US) 1935 dir. Irving Pichel
WAR (GB) 1965 dir. Robert Day
CONT (It) 1985 dir. Avi Nesher

Haggart, D.
Life of David Haggart, The

Sinful Davey
UA (GB) 1969 dir. John Huston

Hailey, A.
Airport
Doubleday

UN (US) 1970 dir. George Seaton
V

Hailey, A.
Airport
Doubleday

International Airport
A. SPELLING (US) 1985
dir. Charles Dubin, Don Chaffey
TV(US)

Hailey, A.
Final Diagnosis, The
Doubleday

Young Doctors, The
UA (US) 1961 dir. Phil Karlson

Hailey, A.
Hotel
Doubleday

WAR (US) 1967 dir. Richard Quine
V

Hailey, A.
Moneychangers, The
Doubleday

PAR TV (US) 1976 dir. Boris Sagal
TVSe(US)

Hailey, A.
Strong Medicine
Doubleday

TELEPICS (US) 1986 dir. Guy Green
TVSe(US)

Hailey, A.
Wheels
Doubleday

UN TV (US) 1978 dir. Jerry London
TVSe(US)

Hailey, A. and Castle, J.
Runway Zero-Eight
Doubleday

Terror in the Sky
PAR TV (US) 1971
dir. Bernard L. Kowalski
TV(US)

Haines, W. W.
Command Decision
Little, Brown (Boston)
MGM (US) 1948 dir. Sam Wood

Halbert, F. and Halbert, S.
Bitter Harvest
FRIES (US) 1981 dir. Roger Young
TV(US)

Hale, E. E.
Man Without A Country, The
Heritage Press
ROSEMONT (US) 1973
dir. Delbert Mann
TV(US)

Hale, J.
Whistle Blower, The
Atheneum
HEMDALE (GB) 1987
dir. Simon Langton
V

Halevy, J.
Young Lovers, The
Simon & Schuster
MGM (US) 1964 dir. Samuel Goldwyn,
Jr.

Haley, A.
Roots: The Next Generation
Doubleday
WAR TV (US) 1979 dirs. John Erman,
Charles Dubin, Georg Stanford Brown,
Lloyd Richards
TVSe(US)

Haley, A.
Roots
Doubleday
WOLPER (US) 1977
dirs. David Greene, Marvin J. Chomsky,
John Erman, Gilbert Moses
TVSe(US),V

Hall, A.
Devilday-Madhouse
Madhouse
EMI (GB) 1974 dir. Jim Clark

Hall, A.
Late Boy Wonder, The
Three in the Cellar
AIP (US) 1970 dir. Theodore J. Flicker
V

Hall, J.
Ask Agamemnon
Atheneum
Goodbye Gemini
CINDERAMA (GB) 1970
dir. Alan Gibson

Hall, O.
Downhill Racers
Viking Press
Downhill Racer
PAR (US) 1969 dir. Michael Ritchie
V

Hall, O.
Warlock
Viking Press
FOX (US) 1959 dir. Edward Dmytryk
V

Hall, P.
Harp That Once, The
Reckoning, The
COL (GB) 1969 dir. Jack Gold

Hall, W.
Long and the Short and the Tall, The
P
Theatre Arts Books
WAR (GB) 1960 dir. Leslie Norman
US title: Jungle Fighters

Hall, W.
Return of the Antelope, The
Bodley Head (London)
GRANADA (GB) 1987
Ch, TVSe(GB)

Halliday, M.
Cat and Mouse
Hodder & Stoughton
EROS (GB) 1958 dir. Paul Rotha
V

Hambledon, P.
No Difference to Me
No Place for Jennifer
ABP (GB) 1949 dir. Henry Cass

Hamill, P.
Flesh and Blood
Random House
PAR TV (US) 1979 dir. Jud Taylor
TVSe(US)

Hamill, P.
Gift, The
PAR TV (US) 1979 dir. Don Taylor
TV(US)

Hamilton, C.
His Majesty the King
Exile, The
UN (US) 1948 dir. Max Ophuls

Hamilton, D.
Ambushers, The
COL (US) 1967 dir. Harry Levin
V

Hamilton, D.
Big Country, The
Wingate
UA (US) 1958 dir. William Wyler
V

Hamilton, D.
Five Steps to Danger
UA (US) 1956 dir. Henry S. Kesler

Hamilton, D.
Matt Helm
COL TV (US) 1975 dir. Buzz Kulik
TV(US)

Hamilton, D.
Murderer's Row
BL (US) 1966 dir. Henry Levin
V

Hamilton, D.
Silencers, The
COL (US) 1966 dir. Phil Karlson

Hamilton, D.
Violent Men, The
COL (US) 1955 dir. Rudolph Maté
GB title: Rough Company

Hamilton, D.
Wrecking Crew, The
COL (US) 1968 dir. Phil Karlson
V

Hamilton, H.
Banjo on my Knee
TCF (US) 1936 dir. John Cromwell

Hamilton, N., Casey, R. and Shute, J.
Return Engagement
P
Fools for Scandal
WAR (US) 1938 dir. Mervyn LeRoy

Hamilton, P.
Angel Street
P
Stein & Day
Gaslight
BN (GB) 1939 dir. Thorold Dickinson
US title: Angel Street
MGM (US) 1944 dir. George Cukor
GB title: Murder in Thornton Square, The
V

Hamilton, P.
Hangover Square
Random House
FOX (US) 1945 dir. John Brahm

Hamilton, P.
Rope
P
Samuel French
WAR (US) 1948 dir. Alfred Hitchcock
V

Hamilton, P.
Street Has a Thousand Eyes, The
Constable
Bitter Harvest
RANK (GB) 1963
dir. Peter Graham Scott
V

Hammerstein II, O. and Kern, J.
Music in the Air
P
FOX (US) 1934 dir. Joe May
M

Hammett, D.
Dain Curse, The
Cassell
POLL (US) 1978 dir. E. W. Swackhamer
TVSe(US), V

Hammett, D.
Glass Key, The
Knopf
PAR (US) 1935 dir. Frank Tuttle
PAR (US) 1942 dir. Stuart Heisler

Hammett, D.
Maltese Falcon, The
Knopf
WAR (US) 1941 dir. John Huston
V

Hammett, D.
Maltese Falcon, The
Knopf
Satan Met a Lady
WAR (US) 1936 dir. William Dieterle

Hammett, D.
Thin Man, The
Knopf
MGM (US) 1934 dir. W. S. Van Dyke
V

Hamner, E.
Spencer's Mountain
WAR (US) 1963 dir. Delmer Daves

Hamner, Jr., E.
Homecoming, The – A Christmas Story
Random House
LORIMAR (US) 1974 dir. Fielder Cook
TV(US), V

Hampton, C.
Liaisons Dangereuses, Les
P
Various
Dangerous Liaisons
WAR (US) 1988 dir. Stephen Frears
V

Han Suyin.
Many Splendoured Thing, A
Little, Brown (Boston)
Love is a Many Splendoured Thing
FOX (US) 1955 dir. Henry King
V

Hancock, M. A.
Menace on the Mountain
DISNEY (US) 1970
dir. Vincent McEveety
V

Hanff, H.
84 Charing Cross Road
Grossman
COL (US/GB) 1987 dir. David Jones
V

Hanley, C.
Love From Everybody
Don't Bother to Knock
WAR (GB) 1961 dir. Cyril Frankel
US title: Why Bother to Knock

Hanley, G.
Gilligan's Last Elephant
Collins

Last Safari, The
PAR (GB) 1967 dir. Henry Hathaway

Hannay, A.
Love and Other Natural Disasters
Little, Brown (Boston)

Tiger's Tale, A
ATLANTIC (US) 1988
dir. Peter Douglas

Hannum, A.
Roseanna McCoy
RKO (US) 1949 dir. Irving Reis

Hansberry, L.
Raisin in the Sun, A
P
Samuel French
COL (US) 1961 dir. Daniel Petrie
V

Harbach, O., & Mandel, F.
No No Nanette
P
WAR (US) 1930 dir. Clarence Badger
M
RKO (US) 1940 dir. Herbert Wilcox
M

Harbach, O. and Hammerstein, II, O
Rose Marie
P
MGM (US) 1936 dir. W. S. Van Dyke
M, V
MGM (US) 1954 dir. Mervyn Le Roy
M

Harbach, O., Schwab, L. and Mandel, F.
Desert Song
P
Samuel French
WAR (US) 1943 dir. Robert Florey
M
WAR (US) 1953
dir. Bruce Humberstone
M

Harburg, E. Y. and Saidy, F.
Finian's Rainbow
P
WAR (US) 1968
dir. Francis Ford Coppola
M, V

Harding, B.
Magic Fire
Bobbs-Merrill (Indianapolis)
REP (US) 1956 dir. William Dieterle

Harding, B.
Phantom Crown, The
Blue Ribbon Books

Juarez
WAR (US) 1939 dir. William Dieterle
V

Harding, G.
North of Bushman's Rock

Ride the High Wind
BUTCHER (S. Africa) 1966
dir. David Millin

Hardy, J. B.
Everything is Thunder
GB (GB) 1936 dir. Milton Rosmer

Hardy, L.
Grand Duke and Mr. Pimm, The
Harper

Love is a Ball
UA (US) 1963 dir. David Swift
GB title: All This and Money Too

Hardy, S.
Forbidden Valley
Macaulay, N.Y.

UN (US) 1938 dir. Wyndham Gittens

Hardy, T.
Far from the Madding Crowd
Knopf

WAR (GB) 1967 dir. John Schlesinger
V

Hardy, T.
Tess of the d'Urbervilles
Various

Tess
COL (Fr/GB) 1981 dir. Roman Polanski
V

Hare, D.
Plenty
P
Samuel French

FOX (US) 1985 dir. Fred Schepisi
V

Harel, I.
House on Garibaldi Street, The
Viking Press

ITC (US) 1979 dir. Peter Collinson
TV(US), V

Hargreaves, Sir G.
Atlantis, The Lost Continent
P

MGM (US) 1961 dir. George Pal

Hargrove, M.
Girl He Left Behind, The
Viking Press, N.Y.

WAR (US) 1956 dir. David Butler

Hargrove, M.
See Here, Private Hargrove
MGM (US) 1944 dir. Wesley Ruggles

Harker, H.
Goldenrod
Random House

TALENT (US) 1977 dir. Harvey Hart
TV(US), V

Harkins, P.
Blackburn's Headhunters
Norton

Surrender-Hell
AA (US) 1959 dir. John Barnwell

Harling, R.
Steel Magnolias
Fireside Theatre
P

TRI-STAR (US) 1989 dir. Herbert Ross
V

Harmon, L. M.
Why Me?
Stein & Day

LORIMAR (US) 1984 dir. Fielder Cook
TV(US)

Harper, D.
Hijacked

Skyjacked
MGM (US) 1972 dir. John Guillermin
V

Harragan, B. L.
Games Mother Never Taught You
Rawson Associates

CBS ENT (US) 1982 dir. Lee Philips
TV(US)

Harris, A.
Follow the Widower

Heads or Tails
CASTLE HILL (Fr) 1983
dir. Robert Enrico

Harris, B. S.
Who is Julia?
CBS ENT (US) 1986
dir. Walter Grauman
TV(US)

Harris, C.
I'd Climb the Highest Mountain
FOX (US) 1951 dir. Henry King

Harris, E.
Johnny Belinda
P
Samuel French
WAR (US) 1948 dir. Jean Negulesco
V
MILBERG (US) 1958
dir. George Schaefer
TV(US)
LORIMAR (US) 1982 dir. Anthony Page
TV(US)

Harris, F.
On the Trail: My Reminiscences as a Cowboy
C. Boni

Cowboy
COL (US) 1957 dir. Delmer Daves

Harris, J.
Sea Shall Not Have Them, The
EROS (GB) 1954 dir. Lewis Gilbert
V

Harris, M.
Bang the Drum Slowly
Knopf
PAR (US) 1973 dir. John Hancock
V

Harris, M.
Hatter Fox
Random House

Girl Called Hatter Fox, The
EMI (US) 1977 dir. George Schaefer
TV (US)

Harris, R.
Selling Hitler
Pantheon Books

BBC (GB) 1991 dir. Anthony Reid
TV(GB)

Harris, R.
Stepping Out
P
Samuel French
PAR (US) 1991 dir. Lewis Gilbert

Harris, T.
Black Sunday
Putnam
PAR (US) 1977 dir. John Frankenheimer
V

Harris, T.
Good Night and Good Bye
Delacorte Press

Street of Dreams
PHOENIX (US) 1988
dir. William A. Graham
TV(US)

Harris, T.
Red Dragon
Putnam

Manhunter
CANNON (US) 1986 dir. Michael Mann

Harris, T.
Silence of the Lambs, The
St. Martin's Press

ORION (US) 1991 dir. Jonathan Demme
V

Harrison, H.
Make Room, Make Room!
Gregg Press

Soylent Green
MGM (US) 1973 dir. Richard Fleischer
V

Harrison, J.
Revenge
COL (US) 1990 dir. Tony Scott

Harrison, W.
Burton and Speke
St. Martins Press

Mountains of the Moon
TRI-STAR (US) 1990 dir. Bob Rafaelson

Hart, M.
Act One
Random House
WAR (US) 1963 dir. Dore Schary

Hart, M.
Christopher Blake
P
Random House
Decision of Christopher Blake, The
WAR (US) 1948 dir. Peter Godfrey

Hart, M.
Lady in the Dark, The
P
Dramatists Play Service
PAR (US) 1944 dir. Mitchell Leisen

Hart, M.
The Cellist
P
Connecting Rooms
TELSTAR (GB) 1969
dir. Franklin Gollings
V

Hart, M.
Winged Victory
P
Random House
FOX (US) 1944 dir. George Cukor

Hart, M. and Kaufman, G. S.
Once in a Lifetime
P
Samuel French
UN (US) 1933 dir. Russell Mack

Harte, B.
Luck of Roaring Camp, The;
Outcasts of Poker Flat, The
Houghton, Mifflin Company (Boston);
New American Library
California Gold Rush
TAFT (US) 1981 dir. Jack Hively
TV(US), V

Harte, B.
Outcasts of Poker Flat, The
Heritage Press
RKO (US) 1937 dir. Christy Cabanne
FOX (US) 1952 dir. Joseph M. Newman

Harte, B.
Tennessee's Partner
Houghton, Mifflin Co. (Boston)
RKO (US) 1955 dir. Allan Dwan
V

Hartley, L. P.
Go-Between, The
Knopf
EMI (GB) 1970 dir. Joseph Losey
V

Hartley, L. P.
Hireling, The
Rinehart
COL (GB) 1973 dir. Alan Bridges
V

Hartmann, N. M.
Game for Vultures
Pan
NEWLINE (GB) 1979 dir. James Fargo
V

Hartog, J. de
Four-Poster, The
P
Random House
COL (GB) 1952 dir. Irving Reis

Hartog, J. de
Inspector, The
Atheneum
FOX (GB) 1962 dir. Philip Dunne
US title: Lisa

Hartog, J. de
Little Ark, The
Harper
FOX (US) 1971 dir. James B. Clark
V

Hartog, J. de
Spiral Road, The
Harper
UI (US) 1962 dir. Robert Mulligan

Hartog, J. de
Stella
Putnam, N.Y.
Key, The
COL (GB) 1958 dir. Carol Reed

Harvey, F.
Saloon Bar
P
EAL (GB) 1940 dir. Walter Forde

Harvey, W. F.
Beast with Five Fingers, The
Dutton
WAR (US) 1946 dir. Robert Florey
V

Harwood, H. M.
Cynara
P
E. Benn Ltd. (London)
GOLDWYN (US) 1933 dir. King Vidor

Harwood, H. M.
Iron Duke, The
P
GAU BR (GB) 1935 dir. Victor Saville
V

Harwood, H. M.
Man in Possession, The
P
MGM (US) 1931 dir. Sam Wood

Harwood, H. M.
Man in Possession, The
P
Personal Property
MGM (US) 1937 dir. W. S. Van Dyke II
GB title: Man in Possession, The

Harwood, R.
Dresser, The
P
COL (GB) 1983 dir. Peter Yates
V

Hasford, G.
The Short Timers
Knopf
Full Metal Jacket
WB (US) 1987 dir. Stanley Kubrick
V

Hassel, S.
Wheels of Terror
Misfit Brigade, The
TRANSWORLD (US) 1988
dir. Gordon Hessler

Hassler, J.
Green Journey
Morrow
Love She Sought, The
ORION TV (US) 1990
dir. Joseph Sargent
TV(US)

Hastings, C.
Bonaventure
P
Thunder on the Hill
UI (US) 1951 dir. Douglas Sirk
GB title: Bonaventure

Hastings, H.
Seagulls over Sorrento
P
MGM (GB) 1954 dir. John Boulting,
Roy Boulting
US title: Crest of the Wave

Hastings, P.
Rapture in my Rags
Rapture
FOX (US/Fr) 1965 dir. John Guillermin

Hastings, Sir P.
Blind Goddess, The
P
Samuel French
FOX (GB) 1947 dir. Harold French

Hatch, E.
Road Show
H. ROACH (US) 1941
dir. Gordon Douglas

Hatch, E.
Unexpected Uncle
RKO (US) 1941 dir. Peter Godfrey

Hatch, E.
Year of the Horse, The
Crown, N.Y.
Horse in the Grey Flannel Suit, The
DISNEY (US) 1968 dir. Norman Tokar
Ch, V

Hatvany, L.
Tonight or Never
P
GOLDWYN (US) 1931
dir. Mervyn LeRoy

Hauser, T.
Execution of Charles Horman, The
Harcourt, Brace, Jovanovich
Missing
UN (US) 1982 dir. Costa-Gavras
V

Havel, V.
Beggar's Opera, The
BARRANDOV (Czech) 1991
dir. Jiri Menzel
P

Haviland-Taylor, K.
Failure
Man to Remember, A
RKO (US) 1938 dir. Garson Kanin

Hawkins, J. and Hawkins, W.
Floods of Fear
Eyre & Spottiswoode
RANK (GB) 1958 dir. Charles Crichton

Hawksworth, H. and Schwarz, T.
Five of Me, The
FARREN (US) 1981 dir. Paul Wendkos
TV(US)

Hawley, C.
Cash McCall
WAR (US) 1960 dir. Joseph Pevney

Hawley, C.
Executive Suite
Houghton, Mifflin Co. (Boston)
MGM (US) 1954 dir. Robert Wise

Hawthorne, N.
House of the Seven Gables
Various
UN (US) 1940 dir. Joe May

Hawthorne, N.
Scarlet Letter, The
MAJ (US) 1934 dir. Robert G. Rignola
V
PBS (US) 1979 dir. Rick Hauser
TVSe(US)

Hay, I.
Bachelor Born
P
Samuel French
Housemaster
ABPC (GB) 1938 dir. Herbert Brenon

Hay, I.
Sport of Kings, The
P
GAINS (GB) 1931 dir. Victor Saville

Hay, I., and Armstrong, A.
Orders is Orders
P
GAU (GB) 1933 dir. Walter Forde

Hay, I. and Armstrong, A.
Orders is Orders
P

Orders are Orders
BL (GB) 1954 dir. David Paltenghi
V

Hay, I. and Hall, S. K.
Middle Watch
P
Samuel French

BI (GB) 1930 dir. Norman Walker
AB (GB) 1940 dir. Thomas Bentley

Hay, I. and Hall, S. K.
Midshipmaid, The
P

GB (GB) 1932 dir. Albert de Courville

Hay, I. and King-Hall, S.
Off the Record
P
Samuel French

Carry on, Admiral
REN (GB) 1957 dir. Val Guest

Haycox, E.
Bugles in the Afternoon
Gregg Press (Boston)

WAR (US) 1952 dir. Roy Rowland
V

Haycox, E.
Canyon Passage
G. K. Hall

UN (US) 1946 dir. Jacques Tourneur

Haycox, E.
Stage to Lordsburg
Lorrimer Publishing Ltd. (London)

Stagecoach
UA (US) 1939 dir. John Ford
V
FOX (US) 1966 dir. Gordon Douglas
HERITAGE (US) 1986 dir. Ted Post
TV(US), V

Hayden, T.
Murphy's Boy
Putnam

Trapped in Silence
READER'S DIG (US) 1986
dir. Michael Tuchner
TV(US)

Hayes, A.
Girl on the Via Flaminia, The
Harper

Act of Love
UA (US) 1954 dir. Anatole Litvak

Hayes, B. and Hoffer, W.
Midnight Express
Dutton

COL (GB) 1978 dir. Alan Parker
V

Hayes, D.
Comedy Man, The
Abelard-Schuman

BL (GB) 1964 dir. Alvin Rakoff

Hayes, J.
Desperate Hours, The
Random House

PAR (US) 1955 dir. William Wyler
MGM (US) 1990 dir. Michael Cimino
V

Hayes, J.
Third Day, The
McGraw-Hill

WAR (US) 1965 dir. Jack Smight

Hayes, K. and Lazzarino, A.
Broken Promise
Putnam

EMI TV (US) 1981 dir. Don Taylor
TV(US)

Hayes, M. and Hayes, J. A.
Bon Voyage

DISNEY (US) 1962 dir. James Neilson
V

Hayes, N.
Dildo Cay
Davies

Bahama Passage
PAR (US) 1941 dir. Edward H. Griffith

Hayward, B.
Haywire
Knopf

WAR (US) 1980 dir. Michael Tuchner
TV(US)

Hazard, L.
Man's Castle
P

COL (US) 1933 dir. Frank Borzage

Head, A.
Mr. and Mrs. Bo Jo Jones
Putnam

FOX TV (US) 1971 dir. Robert Day
TV(US)

Healey, B.
Waiting for a Tiger

Taste of Excitement, A
MONARCH (GB) 1969 dir. Don Sharp

Hearn, M. P.
Dreamer of Oz, The: L. Frank Baum Story

ADAM (US) 1990 dir. Jack Bender
TV(US)

Hearst, P.
Every Secret Thing
Doubleday

Patty Hearst
ATLANTIC (US) 1988
dir. Paul Schrader
V

Heath, W. L.
Violent Saturday

FOX (US) 1955 dir. Richard Fleischer

Hebden, M.
Eye-witness
Harrap

Eyewitness
MGM (GB) 1970 dir. John Hough
US title: Sudden Terror

Hechler, K.
Bridge at Remagen, The
Ballantine

UA (US) 1969 dir. John Guillermin
V

Hecht, B.
Florentine Dagger, The
Harrap

WAR (US) 1935 dir. Robert Florey

Hecht, B.
Gaily, Gaily
Elek Books (London)

UA (US) 1969 dir. Norman Jewison
GB title: Chicago, Chicago

Hecht, B.
I Hate Actors!

GALAXY (Fr) 1988
dir. Gerald Krawczyk

Hecht, B.
Miracle in the Rain
Knopf

WAR (US) 1956 dir. Rudolph Maté

Hecht, B. and MacArthur, C.
Front Page, The
P
Samuel French

UA (US) 1931 dir. Lewis Miles
U-I (US) 1974 dir. Billy Wilder
V

Hecht, B. and MacArthur, C.
Front Page, The
P
Samuel French

His Girl Friday
COL (US) 1940 dir. Howard Hawks
V

Hecht, B. and MacArthur, C.
Front Page, The
P
Samuel French
Switching Channels
TRI-STAR (US) 1988 dir. Ted Kotcheff
V

Hecht, B. and MacArthur, C.
Ladies and Gentlemen
P
Samuel French
Perfect Strangers
WAR (US) 1950 dir. Bretaigne Windust
GB title: Too Dangerous to Love

Heggen, T.
Mister Roberts
Random House
WAR (US) 1955 dir. John Ford, Mervyn
Le Roy
V

Heidish, M.
Woman Called Moses, A
Houghton, Mifflin Co. (Boston)
H. JAFFE (US) 1978 dir. Paul Wendkos
TVSe(US)

Helias, P-J.
Horse of Pride, The
Plon (Paris)
FILM FORUM (Fr) 1980
dir. Claude Chabrol
V

Heller, J.
Catch-22
Simon & Schuster
PAR (US) 1970 dir. Mike Nichols
V

Hellman, G. S.
Peacock's Feather
Night in Paradise, A
UN (US) 1946 dir. Arthur Lubin

Hellman, L. F.
Another Part of the Forest
P
Dramatists Play Service
UN (US) 1948 dir. Michael Gordon

Hellman, L. F.
Children's Hour, The
P
Dramatists Play Service
These Three
UA (US) 1936 dir. William Wyler
V

Hellman, L. F.
Children's Hour, The
P
Dramatists Play Service
UA (US) 1961 dir. William Wyler
GB title: Loudest Whispers, The

Hellman, L. F.
Little Foxes, The
P
Dramatists Play Service
RKO (US) 1941 dir. William Wyler
V
MILBERG (US) 1956
dir. George Schaefer
TV(US)

Hellman, L. F.
Pentimento
Little, Brown (Boston)
Julia
FOX (US) 1977 dir. Fred Zinnemann
V

Hellman, L. F.
Searching Wind, The
P
Little, Brown (Boston)
PAR (US) 1946 dir. William Dieterle

Hellman, L. F.
Toys in the Attic
P
Dramatists Play Service
UA (US) 1963 dir. George Roy Hill

Hellman, L. F.
Watch on the Rhine
P
Dramatists Play Service
WAR (US) 1943 dir. Herman Shumlin
V

Helseth, H. E.
Chair for Martin Rome, The
Dodd, N.Y.
Cry of the City
FOX (US) 1948 dir. Robert Siodmak

Helvick, J.
Beat the Devil
Boardman
ROMULUS (GB) 1953 dir. John Huston
V

Hely, E.
Smugglers, The
UN TV (US) 1968 dir. Norman Lloyd
TV(US)

Hembert, G.
House of Rothschild, The
P
FOX (US) 1934 dir. Alfred Werker

Hemingway, E.
Farewell to Arms, A
Scribners
PAR (US) 1932 dir. Frank Borzage
V
FOX (US) 1957 dir. Charles Vidor
V

Hemingway, E.
For Whom the Bell Tolls
Scribners
PAR (US) 1943 dir. Sam Wood
V

Hemingway, E.
Islands in the Stream
Scribners
PAR (US) 1977 dir. Franklin Schaffner
V

Hemingway, E.
Killers, The
Scribners
UN (US) 1946 dir. Robert Siodmak
UN (US) 1964 dir. Don Siegel
V

Hemingway, E.
My Old Man
CBS ENT (US) 1979 dir. John Erman
TV(US), V

Hemingway, E.
My Old Man
Under My Skin
FOX (US) 1950 dir. Jean Negulesco

Hemingway, E.
Old Man and the Sea, The
Scribners
WAR (US) 1958 dir. John Sturges
STORKE PRODS (US) 1990
dir. Jud Taylor
TV(US)

Hemingway, E.
Short Happy Life of Francis Macomber, The
Scribners
Macomber Affair, The
UA (US) 1947 dir. Zoltan Korda

Hemingway, E.
Snows of Kilimanjaro, The
Scribners
FOX (US) 1952 dir. Henry King
V

Hemingway, E.
Sun also Rises, The
Scribners
FOX (US) 1957 dir. Henry King
FOX (US) 1984 dir. James Goldstone
TVSe(US)

Hemingway, E.
To Have and Have Not
Scribners

WAR (US) 1944 dir. Howard Hawks
V

Hemingway, E.
To Have and Have Not
Scribners

Breaking Point, The
WAR (US) 1950 dir. Michael Curtiz

Hemingway, E.
To Have and Have Not
Scribners

Gun Runners, The
UA (US) 1958 dir. Don Siegel

**Hemingway, J. and
Bonnecarrere, P.**
Rosebud
Morrow

UA (US) 1975 dir. Otto Preminger

Hemon, L.
M. Ripois and his Nemesis
Allen & Unwin

Knave of Hearts
ABP (GB) 1954 dir. René Clément
US title: Lover Boy

Hemon, L.
Maria Chapdelaine
Macmillan

ASTRAL (Fr) 1935 dir. Julien Duvivier
Canada (US) 1986 dir. Gilles Carle

Hen, Jozef
Boxer and Death, The
(Czech/Ger) 1962 dir. Peter Solan
V

Henderson, L.
Sitting Target
MGM (GB) 1972 dir. Douglas Hickox
V

Henderson, Z.
Pilgrimage
Gregg Press

People, The
METRO (USTV) 1972 dir. John Korty
V

Henley, B.
Crimes of the Heart
P
Viking Press

DELAUR (US) 1986
dir. Bruce Beresford
V

Henley, B.
Miss Firecracker Contest
P
Dramatists Play Service

Miss Firecracker
CORSAIR (US) 1989
dir. Thomas Schlamme
V

Henrich, W.
Cross of Iron
Bobbs-Merrill (Indianapolis)

AVCO (GB/Ger) 1977
dir. Sam Peckinpah

Henry, H.
Jackdaws Strut
Bought
WAR (US) 1931 dir. Archie Mayo

Henry, J.
Who Lie in Gaol
Weak and the Wicked, The
APB (GB) 1953 dir. J. Lee Thompson

Henry, J.
Yield to the Night
ABP (GB) 1956 dir. J. Lee Thompson
US title: Blonde Sinner

Henry, M.
Misty of Chincoteague
Rand-McNally (Chicago)
Misty
FOX (US) 1961 dir. James B. Clark

Henry, M.
San Domingo, The Medicine Hat Stallion
Rand McNally (Chicago)
Peter Lundy and the Medicine Hat Stallion
FRIENDLY (US) 1977
dir. Michael O'Herlihy
TV(US), V

Henry, W.
Journey to Shiloh
Random House
UI (US) 1966 dir. William Hale

Henry, W.
Mackenna's Gold
Random House
COL (US) 1969 dir. J. Lee Thompson
V

Henry, W.
Who Rides with Wyatt?
Random House
Young Billy Young
UA (US) 1969 dir. Burt Kennedy

Henstell, D.
Friend
Deadly Friend
WAR (US) 1986 dir. Wes Craven
V

Herbert, B.
No Names . . . No Pack Drills
P
Rebel
MIRACLE (Aust) 1986
dir. Michael Jenkins
V

Herbert, F.
Dune
Chilton Books
UN (US) 1984 dir. David Lynch
V

Herbert, F. H.
For Love or Money
P
This Happy Feeling
UN (US) 1958 dir. Blake Edwards
V

Herbert, F. H.
Kiss and Tell
P
Longman
COL (US) 1945 dir. Richard Wallace

Herbert, F. H.
Moon is Blue, The
P
Random House
UA (US) 1953 dir. Otto Preminger
V

Herbert, J.
Deadly Eyes
WAR (US) 1983 dir. Robert Clouse
V

Herbert, J.
Fortune and Men's Eyes
P
Samuel French
MGM (US/Can) 1971 dir. Harvey Hart

Herbert, J.
Survivor, The
HEMDALE (Aust) 1981
dir. David Hemmings
V

Herbert, Sir A. P.
House by the River
REP (US) 1950 dir. Fritz Lang

Herbert, Sir A. P.
Water Gypsies, The
Doubleday

SDC (GB) 1932 dir. Maurice Elvey

Herczeg, G., Farkas, K., and Katscher, R.
Wonder Bar
P

WAR (US) 1934 dir. Lloyd Bacon
M

Hergesheimer, J.
Java Head
Knopf

ATP (GB) 1934 dir. J. Walter Ruben

Herlihy, J. L. and Noble, W.
Blue Denim
P
Samuel French

TCF (US) 1959 dir. Philip Dunne
GB title: Blue Jeans

Herlihy, J. L.
All Fall Down
Dutton

MGM (US) 1961
dir. John Frankenheimer

Herlihy, J. L.
Midnight Cowboy
Simon & Schuster

UA (US) 1969 dir. John Schlesinger

Herman, V.
Coming Out of the Ice
Harcourt, Brace, Jovanovich

KONIGSBERG (US) 1982
dir. Waris Hussein
TV(US), V

Hermann, K. and Rieck, H.
Christiane F
Arlington

FOX (Ger) 1981 dir. Ulrich Edel
V

Herriot, J.
All Things Bright and Beautiful
St. Martin's Press

It Shouldn't Happen to a Vet
EMI (GB) 1976 dir. Eric Till
V

Herriot, J.
If Only They Could Talk; It Shouldn't Happen to a Vet; Lord God Made Them All, The
G. K. Hall, Boston

All Creatures Great and Small
EMI (GB) 1974 dir. Claude Whatham
TVSe(GB), V

Hersey, J.
Wall, The
Knopf

TIME-LIFE (US) 1982
dir. Robert Markowitz

Hersey, J.
War Lover, The
Knopf

COL (GB) 1962 dir. Philip Leacock
V

Hersey, J. R.
Bell for Adano, A
Knopf

FOX (US) 1945 dir. Henry King
Hayward (US) 1967 dir. Mel Ferber
TV(US)

Herts, B. R.
Grand Slam
WAR (US) 1933 dir. William Dieterle

Hervey, H.
Lips of Steel
Prestige
RKO (US) 1932 dir. Tay Garnett

Herzog, A.
Swarm, The
Simon & Schuster

WAR (US) 1978 dir. Irwin Allen
V

Hesse, H.
Siddhartha
New Directions
LOTUS (US) 1972 dir. Conrad Rooks

Hesse, H.
Steppenwolf
Holt, Rinehart & Winston
CONTEM (US) 1974 dir. Fred Haines
V

Heth, E. H.
Any Number Can Play
MGM (US) 1949 dir. Mervyn Le Roy

Heyer, G.
Reluctant Widow, The
Putnam
GFD (GB) 1950 dir. Bernard Knowles

Heyes, D.
Twelfth of Never, The
Lonely Profession, The
UN TV (US) 1979 dir. Douglas Heyes
TV(US)

Heym, S.
Hostages
PAR (US) 1943 dir. Frank Tuttle

Heymann, C. D.
Poor Little Rich Girl
Carol Publishing Group
Poor Little Rich Girl: The Barbara Hutton Story
ITC (US) 1987 dir. Charles Jarrot
TVSe(US)

Heyward, D. and Heyward, D.
Porgy
P
Doubleday
Porgy and Bess
GOLDWYN (US) 1959
dir. Otto Preminger
M

Hichens, R.
Bella Donna
Temptation
UN (US) 1935 dir. Irving Pichel

Hichens, R.
Belladonna
Heinemann
OLY (GB) 1934 dir. Robert Milton

Hichens, R.
Garden of Allah, The
Grosset & Dunlap
UA (US) 1936 dir. Richard Boleslawski
V

Hichens, R.
Paradine Case, The
Doubleday
SELZNICK (US) 1947
dir. Alfred Hitchcock
V

Higgins, G. V.
Friends of Eddie Coyle, The
Knopf
PAR (US) 1973 dir. Peter Yates

Higgins, J.
Confessional
Stein & Day
HG/GRANADA (US) 1990
dir. Gordon Flemyng
TVSe(GB/US)

Higgins, J.
Eagle has Landed, The
Holt, Rinehart & Winston
ITC (GB) 1976 dir. John Sturges
V

Higgins, J.
Night of the Fox
Simon & Schuster
DOVE/ITC (US/GB) 1990
dir. Charles Jarrot
TVSe(GB/US)

Higgins, J.
Prayer for the Dying, A
Holt, Rinehart & Winston

Goldwyn (GB) 1987 dir. Mike Hodges
V

Highsmith, P.
Dites-Lui que Je L'Aime
Harper

ART EYE (Fr) 1977 dir. Claude Miller
GB title: This Sweet Sickness
US title: Tell Her I Love Her

Highsmith, P.
Edith's Diary
Simon & Schuster

ZDF (W Ger) 1986
dir. Hans W. Geissendoerfer

Highsmith, P.
Glass Cell, The
SOLARIS (Ger) 1981
dir. Hans C. Geissendoerfer

Highsmith, P.
Ripley's Game
Knopf

American Friend, The
CINEGATE (W. Ger) 1977
dir. Wim Wenders
V

Highsmith, P.
Strangers on a Train
WAR (US) 1951 dir. Alfred Hitchcock
V

Highsmith, P.
Talented Mr. Ripley, The
Coward-McCann

Purple Noon
HILLCREST (Fr) 1960
dir. René Clément

Hijeulo, O.
Mambo Kings Play Songs of Love, The
Farrar, Straus & Giroux

Mambo Kings, The
WAR (US) 1992 dir. Arne Glimcher

Hill, R. B.
Hanta Yo
Doubleday

Mystic Warrior, The
WAR (US) 1984 dir. Richard T. Heffron
TVSe(US)

Hill, R. L.
Evil That Men Do, The
TRI-STAR (US) 1984
dir. J. Lee Thompson
V

Hill, Rev. A. F.
North Avenue Irregulars, The
Cowles

DISNEY (US) 1978 dir. Bruce Bilson
GB title: Hill's Angels

Hill, W.
Long Summer of George Adams, The
McKay

WAR TV (US) 1982 dir. Stuart Margolin
TV(US)

Hill, W.
Onionhead
D. McKay Co.

WAR (US) 1958 dir. Norman Taurog

Hilton, J.
Dawn of Reckoning
Rage in Heaven
MGM (US) 1941 dir. W. S. Van Dyke II

Hilton, J.
Goodbye Mr Chips
Doubleday

MGM (GB) 1939 dir. Sam Wood
V

MGM (GB) 1969 dir. Herbert Ross
M

Hilton, J.
Knight Without Armour
Grosset & Dunlap

UA (GB) 1937 dir. Jacques Feyder
V

Hilton, J.
Lost Horizon
Morrow

COL (US) 1937 dir. Frank Capra
V

COL (US) 1972 dir. Charles Jarrot
M

Hilton, J.
Lost Horizon
Morrow

Shangri-La
COMPASS (US) 1960
dir. George Schaefer
TV(US)

Hilton, J.
Random Harvest
Little, Brown (Boston)

MGM (US) 1942 dir. Mervyn Le Roy

Hilton, J.
So Well Remembered
Little, Brown (Boston)

RKO (GB) 1947 dir. Edward Dmytryk

Hilton, J.
Story of Dr. Wassell, The
Little, Brown (Boston)

PAR (US) 1944 dir. Cecil B. de Mille

Hilton, J.
We Are Not Alone
Little, Brown (Boston)

WAR (US) 1939 dir. Edmund Goulding

Himes, C.
Cotton Comes to Harlem
Putnam

UA (US) 1969 dir. Ossie Davis

Himes, C.
Heat's On, The
Putnam

Come Back Charleston Blue
WAR (US) 1972 dir. Mark Warren

Himes, C.
Rage in Harlem, A
Vintage Books

MIRAMAX (US) 1991 dir. Bill Duke

Hine, A.
Lord Love A Duck
Atheneum Press, N.Y.

UA (US) 1966 dir. George Axelrod

Hines, A.
Square Dance
Harper & Row

ISLAND (US) 1987 dir. Daniel Petrie
V

Hines, B.
Kestrel for a Knave, A
Joseph

Kes
UA (GB) 1969 dir. Ken Loach
V

Hines, D.
Bondage
P

Whore
TRIMARK (GB) 1991 dir. Ken Russell

Hinton, S. E.
Outsiders, The
Viking Press

WAR (US) 1983
dir. Francis Ford Coppola
V

Hinton, S. E.
Rumble Fish
Delacorte Press
UN (US) 1983 dir. Francis Ford Coppola
V

Hinton, S. E.
Tex
Delacorte Press
DISNEY (US) 1982 dir. Tim Hunter
V

Hinton, S. E.
That was then . . . This is now
Viking Press
PAR (US) 1985 dir. Christopher Cain
V

Hintze, N. A.
You'll Like My Mother
UN (US) 1972 dir. Lamont Johnson

Hintze, N.
Aloha Means Goodbye
Random House
UN TV (US) 1974 dir. David Lowell Rich
TV(US)

Hirschfeld, B.
Aspen
Bantam Books
UN TV (US) 1977 dir. Douglas Heyes
TVSe(US)

Hirst, H. H.
Night of the Generals, The
COL/BL (GB) 1966 dir. Anatole Litvak
V

Hitchcock, R.
Percy
Dodd, Mead
MGM-EMI (GB) 1971
dir. Ralph Thomas
V

Hitchens, D. and Hitchens, B.
Fool's Gold
Bande à Part
ANOUCHKA/ORSAY (Fr) 1964
dir. Jean-Luc Godard

Hjortsberg, W.
Falling Angel
Harcourt, Brace, Jovanovich
Angel Heart
TRI-STAR (US) 1987 dir. Alan Parker
V

Hoban, R.
Mouse and the Child, The
Harper & Row
SANRIO (US) 1978 dir. Fred Wolf,
Chuck Swenson
GB title: Extraordinary Adventures of
the Mouse and the Child, The
A, V

Hoban, R.
Turtle Diary
Random House
RANK (GB) 1985 dir. John Irvin
V

Hobart, A. T.
Cup and the Sword, The
This Earth is Mine
UI (US) 1959 dir. Henry King

Hobart, A. T.
Oil for the Lamps of China
Bobbs-Merrill (Indianapolis)
Law of the Tropics
WAR (US) 1941 dir. Ray Enright

Hobart, Mrs. A. T.
Oil for the Lamps of China
Bobbs-Merrill (Indianapolis)
WAR (US) 1935 dir. Mervyn Le Roy

Hobhouse, A.
Hangover Murders, The
Remember Last Night?
UN (US) 1936 dir. James Whale

Hobson, L. Z.
Consenting Adult
Doubleday
STARGER (US) 1985 dir. Gilbert Cates
TV(US)

Hobson, L. Z.
Gentleman's Agreement
Simon & Schuster
FOX (US) 1947 dir. Elia Kazan

Hobson, L. Z.
Tenth Month, The
Dell
HAMILTON (US) 1979
dir. Joan Tewkesbury
TV(US), V

Hochhuth, R.
Eine Liebe in Deutschland
Little, Brown (Boston)
Love in Germany, A
TRIUMPH (Ger) 1984
dir. Andrzej Wajda
V

Hocken, S.
Emma and I
Second Sight: A Love Story
TTC (US) 1984 dir. John Korty
TV(US)

Hodges, H.
Fabricator, The
Crown Publishers
Why Would I Lie?
UA (US) 1980 dir. Larry Peerce
V

Hodgins, E.
Mr. Blandings Builds his Dream House
Simon & Schuster
RKO (US) 1948 dir. H. C. Potter
V

Hodson, J. L.
Return to the Woods
King and Country
WAR (GB) 1964 dir. Joseph Losey

Hoffe, M.
Daybreak
GFD (GB) 1946 dir. Compton Bennett

Hoffe, M.
Lady Eve, The
P
PAR (US) 1941 dir. Preston Sturges
V

Hoffman, E. T. A.
Nutcracker and the Mouseking, The
A. Whitman & Co. (Chicago)
Nutcracker Prince, The
WAR (US) 1990 dir. Paul Schibli
A

Hoffman, E. T. A.
Nutcracker
Crown Publishers
ATLANTIC (US) 1986
dir. Carroll Ballard
M

Hoffman, W. H.
As Is
P
Vintage Books
BRANDMAN (US) 1986
dir. Michael Lindsay-Hogg
TV(US)

Hohimer F.
Home Invaders, The
Thief
UA (US) 1981 dir. Michael Mann
GB title: Violent Street
V

Holden, A.
Witness, The
Bedroom Window, The
DELAUR (US) 1987 dir. Curtis Hanson

Holder, M.
Give Sorrow Words
Winter Tan, A
TELEFILM (Can) 1987 dir. Louise Clark

Holding, Mrs. E.
Blank Wall, The
Reckless Moment, The
COL (US) 1949 dir. Max Ophuls
V

Holdridge, D.
Death of a Common Man
Hale
End of the River, The
GFD (GB) 1947 dir. Derek Twist

Holiday, B.
Lady Sings the Blues
Doubleday
PAR (US) 1972 dir. Sidney J. Furie
V

Holland, I.
Bump in the Night
Doubleday
RHI (US) 1991 dir. Karen Arthur
TV(US)

Holland, M.
Fallen Angel
Dutton, N.Y.
FOX (US) 1945 dir. Otto Preminger

Hollander, X.
Happy Hooker, The
Crown Publishing
SCOTIA BARBER (US) 1975
dir. Nicholas Sgarro
V

Holles, R.
Siege of Battersea, The
Joseph
Guns at Batasi
FOX (GB) 1964 dir. John Guillermin

Hollingsworth, J.
Unspeakable Acts
Contemporary Books
LAN (US) 1990 dir. Linda Otto
TV(US)

Holmes, J. C.
Best Foot Forward
P
MGM (US) 1943 dir. Edward Buzzell
M, V

Holt, F.
Gabriel Horn, The
Various
Kentuckian, The
UA (US) 1955 dir. Burt Lancaster
V

Holtby, W.
South Riding
Macmillan
UA (GB) 1938 dir. Victor Saville
YTV (GB) 1974 dir. Alastair Reid
TVSe(GB)

Holzer, H.
Murder in Amityville
Amityville II: The Possession
ORION (US) 1982
dir. Damiano Damiani
V

Home, W. D.
Chiltern Hundreds, The
P
Samuel French
TC (GB) 1949 dir. John Paddy Carstairs

Home, W. D.
Now Barrabas
Longmans, Green
Now Barrabas was a Robber
WAR (GB) 1949 dir. Gordon Parry

Home, W. D.
Reluctant Debutante, The
P
Samuel French
MGM (US) 1958 dir. Vincente Minnelli

Homer
Odyssey, The
Various
Ulysses
ARCHWAY (It) 1954
dir. Mario Camerini
V

Homes, G.
Build My Gallows High
Against all Odds
COL (US) 1984 dir. Taylor Hackford
V

Homes, G.
Build My Gallows High
Out of the Past
RKO (US) 1947 dir. Jacques Tourneur
GB title: Build My Gallows High
V

Homes, G.
Forty Whacks
Grosset, N.Y.
Crime by Night
WAR (US) 1944 dir. William Clemens

Homes, G.
No Hands on the Clock
PAR (US) 1941 dir. Frank McDonald

Honeycombe, G.
Neither the Sea Nor the Sand
TIGON (GB) 1972 dir. Fred Burnley
V

Honma, Y.
Family Game, The
TOHO (Jap) 1983
dir. Yoshimitsu Morita
V

Hooke, N. W.
Darkness I Leave You
Gypsy and the Gentleman, The
RANK (GB) 1957 dir. Joseph Losey

Hooke, N. W.
Deadly Record
AA (GB) 1959 dir. Lawrence Huntington

Hooker, R.
MASH
Morrow
M*A*S*H
FOX (US) 1970 dir. Robert Altman
TVSe(US), V

Hoover, J. E.
Persons in Hiding
Little, Brown (Boston)
PAR (US) 1939 dir. Louis King

Hoover, J. E.
Persons in Hiding
Little, Brown (Boston)
Illegal Traffic
PAR (US) 1938 dir. Louis King

Hoover, J. E.
Persons in Hiding
Little, Brown (Boston)
Queen of the Mob
PAR (US) 1940 dir. James Hogan

Hope, A.
Prisoner of Zenda
Heritage Press
UA (US) 1937 dir. John Cromwell
V
MGM (US) 1952 dir. Richard Thorpe
V
UN (US) 1979 dir. Richard Quine
BBC (GB) 1984
TV(GB)

Hope, E.
Marry the Girl
WAR (US) 1937 dir. William McGann

Hopkins, J.
This Story of Yours
P

Offence, The
UA (GB) 1972 dir. Sidney Lumet
V

Hopwood, A.
Gold Diggers, The
P

Gold Diggers of Broadway
WAR (US) 1939 dir. Roy del Ruth

Horgan, P.
Distant Trumpet, A.
Farrar, Straus & Cudahy

WAR (US) 1964 dir. Raoul Walsh

Horn, T.
Life of Tom Horn, Government Scout & Interpreter
University of Oklahoma Press
(Norman, Oklahoma)

Tom Horn
WAR (US) 1980 dir. William Wiard
V

Horne, K.
Fools Rush In
P

RANK (GB) 1949
dir. John Paddy Carstairs

Horne, K.
Lady Mislaid, A
P

ABP (GB) 1958 dir. David Macdonald

Horniman, R.
Bellamy the Magnificent

Bedtime Story, A
PAR (US) 1933 dir. Norman Taurog

Horniman, R.
Noblesse Oblige

Kind Hearts and Coronets
EAL (GB) 1949 dir. Robert Hamer
V

Hornung, E. W.
Raffles the Amateur Cracksman
St. Martin's Press

Raffles
UA (US) 1939 dir. Sam Wood

Horowitz, A.
Falcon's Malteser, The
Diamond's Edge
KINGS (US) 1990 dir. Stephen Bayly

Horowitz, A.
Falcon's Malteser, The
Just Ask for Diamond
FOX (GB) 1988 dir. Stephen Bayly
V

Horowitz, S.
Calling Dr. Horowitz
Bad Medicine
TCF (US) 1985 dir. Harvey Miller
V

Horton, S.
Billionaire Boys Club, The
St. Martin's Press

ITC (US) 1987 dir. Marvin Chomsky
TVSe(US)

Hossein, R. and Dard, F.
Caviar Rouge, Le
GALAXY (Fr/Switz) 1988
dir. Robert Hossein

Hotchner, A. E.
Looking for Miracles
Harper & Row

DISNEY (US/Can) 1989
dir. Kevin Sullivan

Hotchner, A. E.
Man Who Lived at The Ritz, The
Weidenfeld & Nicolson (London)

HG (US) 1988 dir. Desmond Davis
TVSe(US)

Hotchner, A. E.
Sophia Living and Loving, Her Own Story
Morrow

Sophia Loren— Her Own Story
EMI (US) 1980 dir. Mel Stuart
TV(US)

Hough, E.
North of 36
D. Appleton & Co.

Conquering Horde
PAR (US) 1931 dir. Edward Sloman

Hough, R.
Captain Bligh and Mr Christian
E. P. Dutton

Bounty, The
ORION (GB) 1984 dir. Roger Donaldson
V

Houghton, S.
Hindle Wakes
P
J. W. Luce (Boston)

GB (GB) 1931 dir. Victor Saville
MON (GB) 1952 dir. Arthur Crabtree

Household, G.
Brandy for the Parson
Little, Brown (Boston)

MGM (GB) 1952 dir. John Eldridge

Household, G.
Dance of the Dwarfs
Little, Brown (Boston)

DOVE (Phil/US) 1982 dir. Gus Trikonis
V

Household, G.
Rogue Male
Little, Brown (Boston)

Man Hunt
FOX (US) 1941 dir. Fritz Lang

Household, G.
Rough Shoot
Little, Brown (Boston)

UA (GB) 1952 dir. Robert Parrish
US title: Shoot First

Household, G.
Watcher in the Shadows
Little, Brown (Boston)

Deadly Harvest
CBS ENT (US) 1972
dir. Michael O'Herlihy
TV(US), V

Housman, L.
Consider Your Verdict
P
CHARTER (GB) 1938 dir. Roy Boulting

Housman, L.
Victoria Regina
P
Scribners

COMPASS (US) 1961
dir. George Schaefer
TV(US), V

Housman, L.
Victoria Regina
P
Scribners

Victoria the Great
RKO (GB) 1937 dir. Herbert Wilcox

Houston, J.
White Dawn, The
Harcourt, Brace, Jovanovich

PAR (US) 1974 dir. Philip Kaufman
V

Houston, R.
Monday, Tuesday, Wednesday

Killing Affair, A
HEMDALE (US) 1988
dir. David Saperstein
V

Howard, C.
Six Against the Rock
Dial Press
GAYLORD (US) 1987 dir. Paul Wendkos
TV(US)

Howard, C.
The Arm
Big Town, The
COL (US) 1987 dir. Ben Bolt
V

Howard, E. J.
After Julius
Viking Press
YTV (GB) 1979
TV(GB)

Howard, E. J.
Getting it Right
Viking Press
MEDUSA (US) 1989 dir. Randal Kleiser

Howard, H.
Assignment 'K'
Collins
COL (GB) 1968 dir. Val Guest

Howard, L.
Blind Date
Longman
RANK (GB) 1959 dir. Joseph Losey
US title: Chance Meeting
V

Howard, S.
Late Christopher Bean, The
P
Samuel French
Christopher Bean
MGM (US) 1933 dir. Sam Wood

Howard, S.
They Knew What They Wanted
P
Samuel French
Lady to Love, A
MGM (US) 1930 dir. Victor Seastrom

Howard, S.
They Knew What They Wanted
P
Samuel French
RKO (US) 1940 dir. Garson Kanin
V

Howard, S.
Yellow Jack
P
Harcourt, Brace & Co.
MGM (US) 1938 dir. George B. Seitz

Howarth, D.
We Die Alone
Macmillan
Nine Lives
NORDS (NOR) 1959 dir. Arne Skouen

Howe, G. L.
Call it Treason
Decision Before Dawn
FOX (US) 1951 dir. Anatole Litvak

Howker, J.
Nature of the Beast, The
Greenwillow Books
FILM 4 (GB) 1988 dir. Franco Rosso

Howlett, J.
Murder of a Moderate Man
St. Martins Press
BBC (GB/It) 1985
TVSe(GB)

Hoyland, J.
Ivy Garland, The
Out of the Darkness
CFF (GB) 1985 dir. John Krish
Ch

Hoyt, V. J.
Malibu, A Nature Story
Lothrop, Lee & Shepard (Boston)
Sequoia
MGM (US) 1935 dir. Chester Lyons

Hrabal, B.
Closely Watched Trains
Simon & Schuster
CESK (Czech) 1966 dir. Jiri Menzel
V

Hubbard, E. and Rowan, A. S.
Message to Garcia, A
Thomas Y. Crowell
FOX (US) 1936 dir. George Marshall

Hubler, R. G.
I've Got Mine
Beachhead
UA (US) 1954 dir. Stuart Heisler

Huch, R.
Der Letste Sommer
Guardian Angel, The
SANDREW (Swe) 1990
dir. Suzanne Osten

Huckaby, E. P.
Crisis at Central High
TIME-LIFE (US) 1981
dir. Lamont Johnson
TV(US), V

Hudson, J.
Case of Need, A
World Publishing Co.
Carey Treatment, The
MGM (US) 1972 dir. Blake Edwards
V

Hudson, J. C. and Abbott, G.
Three Men on a Horse
P
Dramatists Play Service
WAR (US) 1936 dir. Mervyn LeRoy

Hudson, W. H.
Green Mansions
Various
MGM (US) 1959 dir. Mel Ferrer

Huffaker, C.
Badman
War Wagon, The
UI (US) 1967 dir. Burt Kennedy

Huffaker, C.
Flaming Lance
Simon & Schuster
Flaming Star
FOX (US) 1960 dir. Don Siegel
V

Huffaker, C.
Guns of Rio Conchos
Thorndike Press (Thorndike, Maine)
Rio Conchos
FOX (US) 1964 dir. Gordon Douglas
V

Huffaker, C.
Nobody Loves a Drunken Indian
McCay
Flap
WAR (US) 1970 dir. Carol Reed
GB title: Last Warrior, The

Huffaker, C.
Seven Ways from Sundown
UI (US) 1960 dir. Harry Keller

Huggins, R.
Appointment with Fear
State Secret, The
BL (GB) 1950 dir. Sidney Gilliat
US title: Great Manhunt, The

Huggins, R.
Double Take, The
I Love Trouble
COL (US) 1948 dir. S. Sylvan Simon

Hughes, D.
Pork Butcher, The
Souvenir
CIC (GB) 1987 dir. Geoffrey Reeve

Hughes, D. B.
Fallen Sparrow, The
RKO (US) 1943 dir. Richard Wallace

Hughes D. B.
In a Lonely Place
Doubleday
COL (US) 1950 dir. Nicholas Ray
V

Hughes, D. B.
Ride the Pink Horse
Collier
UI (US) 1947 dir. Robert Montgomery

Hughes, D. B.
Ride the Pink Horse
Collier
Hanged Man, The
UN (US) 1964 dir. Don Siegel
TV(US)

Hughes, R.
High Wind in Jamaica, A
The Modern Library
FOX (GB) 1965
dir. Alexander Mackendrick

Hughes, T.
Tom Brown's Schooldays
Rand McNally (Chicago)
RKO (US) 1940 dir. Robert Stevenson
REN (GB) 1951 dir. Gordon Parry
V

Hugo, V.
Les Misérables
Various
UA (US) 1935 dir. Richard Boleslawski
FOX (US) 1952 dir. Lewis Milestone
ITC (GB) 1978 dir. Glenn Jordan

Hugo, V.
Notre Dame de Paris
Various
Hunchback of Notre Dame, The
RKO (US) 1939 dir. William Dieterle
V
RANK (Fr/It) 1956 dir. Jean Delannoy
BBC (GB) 1977 dir. Alan Cooke
TV(GB)
COL (US/GB) 1982
dir. Michael Tuchner
TV(GB/US)

Huie, W. B.
Americanization of Emily, The
Dutton Press
MGM (US) 1964 dir. Arthur Hiller

Huie, W. B.
Execution of Private Slovik, The
Delacorte Press
UN TV (US) 1974 dir. Lamont Johnson
TV(US)

Huie, W. B.
Klansman, The
Delacorte Press
PAR (US) 1974 dir. Terence Young
V

Huie, W. B.
Mud on the Streets
Wild River
FOX (US) 1960 dir. Elia Kazan

Huie, W. B.
Revolt of Mamie Stover, The
Duell, Sloan & Pearce
FOX (US) 1956 dir. Raoul Walsh

Hulme, K.
Nun's Story, The
Little, Brown (Boston)
WAR (US) 1959 dir. Fred Zinnemann
V

Hume, D.
Sin of Susan Slade, The
Susan Slade
WAR (US) 1962 dir. Delmer Daves

Hume, D.
They Called Him Death
This Man is Dangerous
RIALTO (GB) 1941
dir. Lawrence Huntington

Humphrey, W.
Home from the Hill
Knopf
MGM (US) 1959 dir. Vincente Minnelli
V

Hunt, I.
Across Five Aprils
Follett Publishing Co. (Chicago)
LCA (US) 1990 dir. Kevin Meyer
TV(US)

Hunter, E.
Blackboard Jungle, The
Arbor House
MGM (US) 1955 dir. Richard Brooks

Hunter, E.
Buddwing
Simon & Schuster
Mister Buddwing
MGM (US) 1966 dir. Delbert Mann
GB title: Woman Without a Face

Hunter, E.
Chisholms, The
Harper & Row
LAN (US) 1979 dir. Mel Stuart
TVSe(US)

Hunter, E.
Every Little Crook and Nanny
Doubleday
MGM (US) 1972 dir. Cy Howard

Hunter, E.
Last Summer
Doubleday
FOX (US) 1969 dir. Frank Perry
V

Hunter, E.
Matter of Conviction, A
Young Savages, The
UA (US) 1960 dir. John Frankenheimer

Hunter, E.
Strangers When We Meet
Simon & Schuster
COL (US) 1959 dir. Richard Quine
V

Hunter, H.
Bengal Tiger
Bengal Brigade
UI (US) 1954 dir. Laslo Benedek
GB title: Bengal Rifles

Hunter, J. A. & Mannix, D. P.
Tales of the African Frontier
Harper
Killers of Kilimanjaro, The
COL (GB) 1959 dir. Richard Thorpe
V

Hunter, J. D.
Blue Max, The
Dutton
FOX (US) 1966 dir. John Guillermin
V

Hunter, K.
Landlord, The
Scribners
UA (US) 1970 dir. Hal Ashby

Huntford, R.
Scott and Amundsen
Putnam
Last Place on Earth, The
CENTRAL (GB) 1985
dir. Ferdinand Fairfax
TV(GB)

Hunyady, S.
House with the Red Light, The

Very Moral Night, A
HUNG (Hun) 1977 dir. Karoly Makk

Hurlbut, G. and Logan, J.
Higher and Higher
P

RKO (US) 1943 dir. Tim Whelan
M, V

Hurok, S. and Goode, R.
Impressario
Random House

Tonight We Sing
FOX (US) 1953 dir. Mitchell Leisen
M

Hurst, F.
Anatomy of Me
Doubleday

Imitation of Life
UN (US) 1934 dir. John Stahl
UN (US) 1959 dir. Douglas Sirk
V

Hurst, F.
Back Street
Cosmopolitan

UN (US) 1932 dir. John M. Stahl
UN (US) 1941 dir. Robert Stevenson
UN (US) 1961 dir. David Miller
V

Hurst, F.
Five and Ten
MGM (US) 1931 dir. Robert Z. Leonard
GB title: Daughter of Luxury

Hurst, F.
Humoresque
Harper
WAR (US) 1946 dir. Jean Negulesco

Hurst, F.
Sister Act
Four Daughters
WAR (US) 1938 dir. Michael Curtiz

Hurst, F.
Symphony of Six Million
RKO (US) 1932 dir. Gregory LaCava
GB title: Melody of Life

Hurst, F.
Young at Heart
WAR (US) 1954 dir. Gordon Douglas
V

Husson, A.
My Three Angels
P

We're No Angels
PAR (US) 1955 dir. Michael Curtiz
V
PAR (US) 1989 dir. Neil Jordan

Hutchinson, A. S. M.
If Winter Comes
Little, Brown (Boston)
MGM (US) 1948 dir. Victor Saville

Huth, A.
Sun Child
YTV (GB) 1988 dir. L. G. Clark
TV(GB)

Hutson, S.
Eff Off
Corgi

Class of Miss MacMichael, The
GALA (GB) 1978 dir. Silvio Narizzano
V

Hutson, S.
Slugs, The Movie
NEW WORLD (Sp) 1988 dir. J. P. Simon

Hutton, M. G.
Happy Family, The
P
Deane
APEX (GB) 1952 dir. Muriel Box
US title: Mr. Lord Says No

Huxley, A. L.
Gioconda Smile, The
P
Chatto & Windus (London)
Woman's Vengeance, A
UN (US) 1947 dir. Zoltan Korder

Huxley, A. L.
Young Archimedes
Doran
Prelude to Fame
GFD (GB) 1950 dir. Fergus McDonell

Huxley, A.
Ape and Essence
Chatto & Windus (London)
BBC (GB) 1966 dir. David Benedictus
TV(GB)

Huxley, A.
Brave New World
Harper & Row
UN (US) 1980 dir. D. B. Brinckerhoff
TV

Huxley, A.
Devils of Loudon, The
Harper & Row
Devils, The
WAR (GB) 1971 dir. Ken Russell
V

Hyams, J.
Bogie
New American Library
FRIES (US) 1980 dir. Vincent Sherman
TV(US)

Hyde, H. M.
Trials of Oscar Wilde, The
Dover
EROS (GB) 1960 dir. Ken Hughes
US title: Man with the Green Carnation, The

Hyman, M.
No Time for Sergeants
Random House
WAR (US) 1958 dir. Mervyn Le Roy
V

Hynd, A.
Betrayal from the East
McBride, N.Y.
RKO (US) 1945 dir. William Beake

Ibanez, V. B.
Blood and Sand
F. Ungar Publishing Co.
FOX (US) 1941 dir. Rouben Mamoulian

Ibsen, H.
Doll's House, A
P
Samuel French
COMPASS (US) 1959
dir. George Schaefer
TV(US), V
BL (GB) 1973 dir. Patrick Garland
V

Ibsen, H.
Enemy of the People, An
P
Samuel French
ENT (US) 1978 dir. George Schaefer
V

Ibsen, H.
Enemy of the People, An
P
Samuel French
Ganashatru
ELECTRIC (Ind) 1989 dir. Satyajit Ray

Ibsen, H.
Hedda Gabler
P
Samuel French
Hedda
SCOTIA BARBER (GB) 1977
dir. Trevor Nunn
V

Ibsen, H.
Wild Duck, The
P
Samuel French
ORION (GB) 1983 dir. Henri Safran
V

Ibuse, M.
Black Rain
Kodansha International
ART EYE (Jap) 1988
dir. Shohei Imamura

Ide, L.
Concealment
P
Secret Bride, The
WAR (US) 1935 dir. William Dieterle
GB title: Concealment

Idell, A. E.
Centennial Summer
Henry Holt & Company
FOX (GB) 1946 dir. Otto Preminger

Iles, F.
Before the Fact
Gregg Press
Suspicion
RKO (US) 1941 dir. Alfred Hitchcock
V

Ilf, E. and Petrov, E.
Twelve Chairs, The
P
Random House
UMC (US) 1970 dir. Mel Brooks

Ilf, E. and Petrov, E.
Twelve Chairs
P
Random House
Keep Your Seats Please
ATP (GB) 1936 dir. Monty Banks

Ingalls, R.
End of Tragedy, The
Simon & Schuster
Dead on the Money
INDIEPROD (US) 1991
dir. Mark Cullingham
TV(US)

Inge, W.
Bus Stop
P
Random House
FOX (US) 1956 dir. Joshua Logan
V

Inge, W.
Loss of Roses, A
P
Stripper, The
FOX (US) 1963 dir. Franklin Schaffner
GB title: Woman of Summer
V

Inge, W.
Picnic
P
Random House
COL (US) 1955 dir. Joshua Logan
V

Inge, W.
Come Back, Little Sheba
P
Samuel French
PAR (US) 1952 dir. Daniel Mann
GRANADA (US) 1977
dir. Silvio Narizzano
TV(GB/US)

Inge, W. M.
Dark at the Top of the Stairs, The
P
Dramatists Play Service
WAR (US) 1960 dir. Delbert Mann

Inman, R.
Home Fires Burning
Little, Brown (Boston)
M. REES (US) 1989 dir. Glenn Jordan
TV(US)

Innaurato, A.
Gemini
P
Dramatists Play Service
Happy Birthday, Gemini
UA (US) 1980 dir. Richard Benner

Innes, H.
Campbell's Kingdom
Knopf
RANK (GB) 1957 dir. Ralph Thomas
V

Innes, H.
Lonely Skier, The
Snowbound
RKO (GB) 1948 dir. David MacDonald

Innes, H.
White South, The
Collins (London)
Hell Below Zero
COL (GB) 1954 dir. Mark Robson

Innes, H.
Wreck of the Mary Deare, The
Knopf
MGM (US) 1959 dir. Michael Anderson

Innes, M.
Christmas at Candleshoe
Penguin
Candleshoe
DISNEY (GB) 1977 dir. Norman Tokar
V

Ireland, J.
Life Lines
Warner Books

Reason for Living: The Jill Ireland Story
TEN-FOUR (US) 1991
dir. Michael Rhodes
TV(US)

Irish, W.
Bride Wore Black, The
UA (Fr/It) 1967 dir. François Truffaut

Irish, W.
Deadline at Dawn
Lippincott (Philadelphia)
RKO (US) 1946 dir. Harold Clurman
V

Irish, W.
I Married A Dead Man
I Married A Shadow
IS (Fr) 1983 dir. Robin Davis

Irish, W.
Phantom Lady
Collier & Son
UN (US) 1944 dir. Robert Siodmak

Irvine, L.
Castaway
Random House
VIRGIN (GB) 1986 dir. Nicolas Roeg
V

Irving, H. R.
Bohunk
P
Black Fury
WAR (US) 1935 dir. Michael Curtiz
V

Irving, J.
Hotel New Hampshire, The
Dutton
ORION (US) 1984 dir. Tony Richardson
V

Irving, J.
World According to Garp, The
E. P. Dutton
WAR (US) 1982 dir. George Roy Hill
V

Irving, W.
Father Knickerbocker's History of New York
Various
Knickerbocker Holiday
UN (US) 1944 dir. Harry Joe Brown

Irving, W.
Legend of Sleepy Hollow, The
Various
SCHICK SUNN (US) 1980
dir. Henning Schellerup
TV(US), V

Irwin, M.
Young Bess
Harcourt, Brace & Co.
MGM (US) 1953 dir. George Sidney

Isaacs, S.
Compromising Positions
Times Books
PAR (US) 1985 dir. Frank Perry
V

Isaacs, S.
Shining Through
Harper & Row
FOX (US) 1992 dir. David Selzer

Isham, F. S.
Nothin' But The Truth
PAR (US) 1941 dir. Elliott Nugent

Israel, C. E.
Mark, The
Macmillan
FOX (GB) 1961 dir. Guy Green
V

Ito, S.
No Life King
NEW CENTURY (Jap) 1991
dir. Jun Ichikawa

Iwaszkiewicz, J.
Devil and the Nun, The
KADR (Pol) 1960
dir. Jerzy Kawalerowicz

Izzi, E.
Take, The
St. Martin's Press
MCA TV (US) 1990 dir. Leon Ichaso
TV(US)

Jacks, J.
Murder on the Wild Side
Fawcett, N.Y.

Black Eye
WAR (US) 1974 dir. Jack Arnold

Jackson, C.
Lost Weekend, The
Farrar & Rinehart
PAR (US) 1945 dir. Billy Wilder
V

Jackson, F.
Bishop Misbehaves, The
P
Samuel French
MGM (US) 1935 dir. E. A. Dupont
GB title: Bishop's Misadventures, The

Jackson, Mrs. H. M.
Ramona
Grosset & Dunlap
FOX (US) 1936 dir. Henry King

Jackson, S.
Bird's Nest, The
Farrar, Straus & Young
Lizzie
MGM (US) 1957 dir. Hugo Haas

Jackson, S.
Haunting of Hill House, The
Viking Press
Haunting, The
MGM (GB) 1963 dir. Robert Wise
V

Jacob, N.
Under New Management
BUTCHER (GB) 1946
dir. John E. Blakeley

Jacobs, J. and Casey, W.
Grease
P
Samuel French
PAR (US) 1978 dir. Randal Kleiser
M

Jacobs, W. W.
Interruption, The
Methuen
Footsteps in the Fog
COL (GB) 1955 dir. Arthur Lubin

Jaffe, R.
Best of Everything, The
Cape
FOX (US) 1959 dir. Jean Negulesco

Jaffe, R.
Mazes and Monsters
Delacorte Press

P&G (US) 1982
dir. Steven Hilliard Stern
TV(US)

Jakes, J.
Bastard, The
UN TV (US) 1978 dir. Lee Katzin
TVSe(US)

Jakes, J.
Love and War
Harcourt, Brace, Jovanovich
North and South, Book II
WAR TV (US) 1986 dir. Kevin Connor
TVSe(US)

Jakes, J.
North and South
Harcourt, Brace, Jovanovich
WAR (US) 1985 dir. Richard T. Heffron
TVSe(US)

Jakes, J.
Rebels, The
Harcourt, Brace, Jovanovich
UN TV (US) 1979 dir. Russ Mayberry
TVSe(US)

Jakes, J.
Seekers, The
Pyramid Books
UN TV (US) 1979 dir. Sidney Hayers
TVSe(US)

James, H.
Aspern Papers, The
Doubleday
Aspern
CONN (Port) 1981
dir. Eduardo de Gregorion

James, H.
Aspern Papers, The
Doubleday
Lost Moment, The
UN (US) 1947 dir. Martin Gabel
V

James, H.
Bostonians, The
Various
RANK (GB) 1984 dir. James Ivory
V

James, H.
Daisy Miller
Various
PAR (US) 1974 dir. Peter Bogdanovich
V

James, H.
Europeans, The
Various
GB (GB) 1979 dir. James Ivory
V

James, H.
Turn of the Screw, The
New American Library
Nightcomers, The
AVCO (GB) 1972 dir. Michael Winner
V

James, H.
Turn of the Screw, The
Various
Innocents, The
FOX (GB) 1961 dir. Jack Clayton

James, H.
Turn of the Screw
Scribners
CURTIS (US) 1974 dir. Dan Curtis
TVSe(US), V

James, H.
Washington Square
The Modern Library
Heiress, The
PAR (US) 1949 dir. William Wyler
V

James, M. E. C.
I was Monty's Double
Rider
ABP (GB) 1958 dir. John Guillermin
US title: Hell, Heaven and Hoboken

James, M. R.
Casting the Runes
Night of the Demon
COL (GB) 1957 dir. Jacques Tourneur
V

James, P. D.
Black Tower, The
Scribners
ANGLIA (GB) 1985
TVSe(GB)

James, P. D.
Cover Her Face
Scribners
ANGLIA (GB) 1985
TVSe(GB)

James, P. D.
Death of an Expert Witness
Scribners
ANGLIA (GB) 1983 dir. Herbert Wise
TVSe(GB)

James, P. D.
Shroud for a Nightingale
Scribners
YTV (GB) 1984 dir. John Gorrie
TVSe(GB)

James, P. D.
Taste for Death, A
Knopf
YTV (GB) 1987
TVSe(GB)

James, P. D.
Unsuitable Job for a Woman, An
Scribners
BOYD (GB) 1982 dir. Christopher Petit
V

James, W.
Lone Cowboy: My Life Story
Scribners
Shootout
UN (US) 1971 dir. Henry Hathaway

James, W.
Smoky
Scribners
FOX (US) 1946 dir. Louis King

Janeway, Mrs E.
Daisy Kenyon
Doubleday
FOX (US) 1947 dir. Otto Preminger

Janney, R.
Miracle of the Bells
Prentice-Hall
PAR (US) 1948 dir. Irving Rapper
V

Janos, V.
I Married an Angel
P
MGM (US) 1942 dir. W. S. Van Dyke
M

Janowitz, T.
Slaves of New York
Crown
TRI-STAR (US) 1989 dir. James Ivory

Janus, C. G.
Miss 4th of July, Goodbye
Goodbye, Miss 4th of July
FINNEGAN/PINCHUK (US) 1988
dir. George Miller
TV(US)

Japrisot, S.
Lady in the Car with Glasses and a
Gun, The
Simon & Schuster
COL (Fr/US) 1969 dir. Anatole Litvak

Japrisot, S.
One Deadly Summer
Harcourt, Brace, Jovanovich
SNC (Fr) 1983 dir. Jean Becker
V

Japrisot, S.
Sleeping Car Murders, The
PECF (Fr) 1965 dir. Costa-Gavras

Jaynes, C.
Instruct my Sorrows
My Reputation
WAR (US) 1946 dir. Curtis Bernhardt

Jean, R.
Lectrice, La
ORION (Fr) 1989 dir. Michel Deville

Jeans, R.
Young Wives' Tale
P
ABP (GB) 1951 dir. Henry Cass

Jellicoe, A.
Knack, The
P
Samuel French
UA (GB) 1965 dir. Richard Lester

Jenkins, D.
Baja Oklahoma
Atheneum
HBO (US) 1988 dir. Bobby Roth
TV(US)

Jenkins, D.
Dead Solid Perfect
Atheneum
HBO (US) 1988 dir. Bobby Roth
TV(US)

Jenkins, D.
Semi-Tough
New American Library
UA (US) 1977 dir. Michael Ritchie
V

Jenkins, G.
Twist of Sand, A
Viking Press
UA (GB) 1968 dir. Don Chaffey

Jennings, S.
Tooth of the Lion
P
Summer my Father Grew Up, The
SHAPIRO (US) 1991
dir. Michael Tuchner
TV(US)

Jennings, W. D.
Cowboys, The
Stein & Day
WAR (US) 1972 dir. Mark Rydell
V

Jeorg, W.
Saboteur, The
FOX (US) 1965 dir. Bernhard Wicki

Jepson, S.
Man Running
Stage Fright
WAR (GB) 1950 dir. Alfred Hitchcock
V

Jerome, H.
Conquest
P
MGM (US) 1937 dir. Clarence Brown
GB title: Marie Walewska

Jerome, J. K.
Passing of the Third Floor Back,
The
P
Samuel French
GB (GB) 1935 dir. Berthold Viertel

Jerome, J. K.
Three Men in a Boat
J. M. Dent (London)
BL (GB) 1956 dir. Ken Annakin

Jessup, R.
Chuka
Jenkins
PAR (US) 1967 dir. Gordon Douglas

Jessup, R.
Cincinnati Kid, The
Little, Brown (Boston)
MGM (US) 1965 dir. Norman Jewison
V

Jessup, R.
Deadly Duo
Boardman
UA (US) 1962 dir. Reginald Le Borg

Jhabvala, R. P.
Heat and Dust
Harper & Row
UN/ENT (GB) 1983 dir. James Ivory
V

Job, T.
Uncle Harry
P
Samuel French
Strange Affair of Uncle Harry, The
UN (US) 1945 dir. Robert Siodmak
V

Johnson, A. F.
Little Colonel
Various
FOX (US) 1935 dir. David Butler
V

Johnson, D. M.
Hanging Tree, The
Deutsch
WAR (US) 1958 dir. Delmer Daves

Johnson, D. M.
Man Called Horse, A
Deutsch
CIN CEN (US) 1970
dir. Elliot Silverstein
V

Johnson, E. R.
Mongo's Back in Town
CBS ENT (US) 1971
dir. Marvin J. Chomsky
TV(US)

Johnson, N.
World of Henry Orient, The
UA (US) 1964 dir. George Roy Hill
V

Johnson, R. and McCormick, M.
Too Dangerous to be at Large
Dangerous Company
FINNEGAN (US) 1982
dir. Lamont Johnson
TV(US)

Johnson, R. W.
Shootdown
Penguin
L. HILL (US) 1988
dir. Michael Pressman
TV(US)

Johnston, J.
The Old Jest
Doubleday
Dawning, The
TVS (GB) 1988 dir. Robert Knights
TVSe(GB)

Johnston, V.
Howling in the Woods, A
G. K. Hall (Boston)
UN (US) 1971 dir. Daniel Petrie
TV(US)

Jolley, E.
Last Crop, The
CHANNEL 4 (GB) 1991
dir. Stephen Clayton
TV(GB)

Jones, D. C.
Court Martial of George Amstrong Custer, The
Scribners
HALLMARK (US) 1977
dir. Glenn Jordan
TV(US)

Jones, D. F.
Colossus
Putnam
Forbin Project, The
UN (US) 1970 dir. Joseph Sargent
GB title: Colossus, the Forbin Project

Jones, G.
Vengeance
Sword of Gideon
HBO (US/Can) 1986
dir. Michael Anderson
TV(US/Can)

Jones, G. P. and Jones, C. B.
Peabody's Mermaid
Random House
Mr. Peabody and the Mermaid
UN (US) 1948 dir. Irving Pichel
V

Jones, G. P. and Jones, C. B.
There was a Little Man
Random House, N.Y.
Luck of the Irish, The
FOX (US) 1948 dir. Henry Koster

Jones, J.
From Here to Eternity
Scribners
COL (US) 1953 dir. Fred Zinnemann
V
COL (US) 1979 dir. Buzz Kulik
TVSe(US)

Jones, J.
Nurse is a Neighbour
Nurse on Wheels
WAR (GB) 1963 dir. Gerald Thomas

Jones, J.
Some Came Running
Scribners
MGM (US) 1959 dir. Vincente Minnelli

Jones, J.
Thin Red Line, The
Scribners
PLANET (US) 1964 dir. Andrew Marton

Jones, M.
Exile, An
Deutsch
I Walk the Line
COL (US) 1970
dir. John Frankenheimer
V

Jones, M.
John and Mary
Cape
FOX (US) 1969 dir. Peter Yates

Jones, R. F.
This Island Earth
Shasta Publishers (Chicago)
UI (US) 1955 dir. Joseph Newman
V

Jones, R.
Acorn People, The
Abingdon
NBC ENT (US) 1981
dir. Joan Tewkesbury
TV(US), V

Jones, T. and Schmidt, H.
Fantasticks, The
P
Applause Theatre Books Publishers
COMPASS (US) 1964
dir. George Schaefer
M, TV(US)

Jonson, B.
Volpone
P
Various
SIRITZKY (Fr) 1947
dir. Maurice Tourneur

Jonsson, R.
My Life as a Dog
Farrar, Straus & Giroux
SVENSK (Swe) 1984
dir. Lasse Hallstrom
V

Jordan, E. G.
Daddy and I
Grosset, N. Y.
Make Way for a Lady
RKO (US) 1936 dir. David Burton

Jorgensen, C.
Christine Jorgensen Story, The
P. S. Eriksson
UA (US) 1970 dir. Irving Rapper

Josselin, J. F.
Few Days With Me, A
GALAXY (Fr) 1989 dir. Claude Sautet

Joyce, J.
Dead, The
VESTRON (US) 1987 dir. John Huston
V

Joyce, J.
Portrait of the Artist as a Young
Man
Viking Press
ULYSSES (GB) 1977 dir. Joseph Strick
V

Joyce, J.
Ulysses
Modern Library
BL (GB) 1967 dir. Joseph Strick

Judson, W.
Cold River
Mason & Lipscomb
PACIFIC (US) 1982 dir. Fred G. Sullivan
V

Juster, N.
Phantom Tollbooth, The
Random House
MGM (US) 1969 dir. Chuck Jones
A, V

Kafka, F.
Amerika
Schocken Books
Class Relations
ART EYE (Ger/Fr) 1983
dir. Jean Marie Straub, Daniele Huillet

Kafka, F.
Trial, The
Schocken Books
Insurance Man, The
BBC (GB) 1986
TV(GB)

Kafka, F.
Trial, The
Various
BL (Fr/It/Ger) 1963 dir. Orson Welles
V
BBC (GB) 1986
TV(GB)

Kaler, J. O.
Toby Tyler
Harper
DISNEY (US) 1959 dir. Charles Barton
V

Kandel, A.
City for Conquest
WAR (US) 1940 dir. Anatole Litvak
V

Kandel, A.
Hot Money
P
High Pressure
WAR (US) 1932 dir. Mervyn Le Roy

Kanin, F.
Goodbye, My Fancy
P
WAR (US) 1951 dir. Vincent Sherman

Kanin, G.
Born Yesterday
P
Dramatists Play Service
COL (US) 1950 dir. George Cukor
V
MILBERG (US) 1956 dir. Garson Kanin
TV (US)

Kanin, G.
Moviola
Simon & Schuster
Moviola: The Scarlett O'Hara Wars
WAR TV (US) 1980 dir. John Erman
TV(US)

Kanin, G.
Moviola
Simon & Schuster
Moviola: The Silent Lovers
WAR TV (US) 1980 dir. John Erman
TV(US)

Kanin, G.
Moviola
Simon & Schuster
Moviola: This Year's Blonde
WAR TV (US) 1980 dir. John Erman
TV(US)

Kanin, G.
Rat Race, The
P
Dramatists Play Service
PAR (US) 1960 dir. Robert Mulligan

Kanin, G.
Right Approach, The
P
FOX (US) 1961 dir. David Butler

Kaniuk, Y.
Last Jew, The
Vulture, The
YOSHA (Israel) 1981 dir. Yaky Yosha

Kantor, L.
Dead Pigeon
P
Samuel French
Tight Spot
COL (US) 1955 dir. Phil Karlson

Kantor, M.
Arouse and Beware
Coward-McCann
Man from Dakota, The
MGM (US) 1940 dir. Leslie Fenton
GB title: Arouse and Beware

Kantor, M.
Gentle Annie
MGM (US) 1944 dir. Andrew Marton

Kantor, M.
Glory for Me
Coward-McCann
Best Years of Our Lives, The
GOLDWYN (US) 1946
dir. William Wyler
V

Kantor, M.
God and My Country
World Publishing
Follow Me Boys!
DISNEY (US) 1966 dir. Norman Tokar
V

Kantor, M.
Gun Crazy
Coward-McCann, N.Y.
Deadly is the Female
UA (US) 1949 dir. Joseph Lewis

Kantor, M.
Happy Land
Coward-McCann
FOX (US) 1943 dir. Irving Pichel

Kantor, M.
Romance of Rosy Ridge, The
Coward-McCann
MGM (US) 1947 dir. Roy Rowland

Kantor, M.
Voice of Bugle Ann, The
Coward-McCann
MGM (US) 1936 dir. Richard Thorpe

Karmel, A.
Mary Ann
Something Wild
UA (US) 1961 dir. Jack Garfein
V

Kastle, H.
Cross Country
Delacorte
NEW WORLD (Can) 1983
dir. Paul Lynch
V

Kastner, E.
Emil and the Detectives
UFA (Ger) 1931 dir. Gerhard Lamprecht
Ch
DISNEY (US) 1964
dir. Peter Tewkesbury
Ch, V

Kastner, E.
Fabian
UA (Ger) 1982 dir. Wolf Gremm

Kastner, E.
Lottie and Lisa
Little, Brown (Boston)
Parent Trap, The
DISNEY (US) 1961 dir. David Swift
Ch, V

Kastner, E.
Three Men in the Snow
Paradise for Three
MGM (US) 1938 dir. Edward Buzzell

Kata, E.
Be Ready With Bells and Drums
St. Martin's Press
Patch of Blue, A
MGM (US) 1965 dir. Guy Green

Katcha, V.
Eye for an Eye, An
UGC (Fr/It) 1956 dir. André Cayatte

Katcham, V.
Hameçon, The
Hook, The
MGM (US) 1962 dir. George Seaton

Katkov, N.
Blood and Orchids
LORIMAR (US) 1986 dir. Jerry Thorpe
TVSe(US)

Katz, R.
Death in Rome
Macmillan
Massacre in Rome
GN (Fr/It) 1973
dir. George Pan Cosmatos
V

Katz, W.
Death Dreams
D. CLARK (US) 1991
dir. Martin Donovan
TV(US)

Katzenbach, J.
In the Heat of the Summer
Atheneum
Mean Season, The
ORION (US) 1985 dir. Philip Borsos
V

Kaufelt, D.
Six Months With an Older Woman
Putnam
In Love With an Older Woman
FRIES (US) 1982 dir. Jack Bender
TV(US)

Kaufman, B. N.
Son-Rise
Harper & Row
Son-Rise: A Miracle of Love
FILMWAYS (US) 1979 dir. Glenn Jordan
TV(US)

Kaufman, B.
Up the Down Staircase
Prentice-Hall
WAR (US) 1967 dir. Robert Mulligan

Kaufman, G. S.
The Butter and Egg Man
P
Samuel French
Angel from Texas, An
WAR (US) 1940 dir. Ray Enright

Kaufman, G. S.
Butter and Egg Man, The
P
Samuel French
Three Sailors and a Girl
WAR (US) 1953 dir. Roy del Ruth
M

Kaufman, G. S. and Connelly, M.
Dulcy
P
Samuel French
MGM (US) 1940 dir. S. Sylvan Simon

Kaufman, G. S. and Dayton, K.
First Lady
P
WAR (US) 1937 dir. Stanley Logan

Kaufman, G. S., Dietz, H. and Schwarz, A.
Bandwagon, The
P
Dancing in the Dark
FOX (US) 1949 dir. Irving Reis

Kaufman, G. S. and Ferber, E.
Dinner at Eight
P
Samuel French
MGM (US) 1933 dir. George Cukor
V
TNT (US) 1989 dir. Ron Lagomarsino
TV(US)

Kaufman, G. S. and Ferber, E.
Royal Family, The
P
Samuel French
Royal Family of Broadway, The
PAR (US) 1930 dir. George Cukor
GB title: Theatre Royal

Kaufman, G. S. and Ferber, E.
Stage Door
P
Dramatists Play Service
RKO (US) 1937 dir. Gregory La Cava
V

Kaufman, G. S. and Hart, M.
George Washington Slept Here
P
The Modern Library
WAR (US) 1942 dir. William Keighley

Kaufman, G. S. and Hart, M.
Man Who Came to Dinner, The
P
Random House
WAR (US) 1941 dir. William Keighley
UN (US) 1972 dir. Buzz Kulik
TV(US)

Kaufman, G. S. and Hart, M.
You Can't Take it With You
P
Random House
COL (US) 1938 dir. Frank Capra
V

Kaufman, G. S., McGrath, L. and Burrows, A.
Silk Stockings
P
MGM (US) 1957
dir. Rouben Mamoulian
M, V

Kaufman, G. S., and Woollcott, A.
Dark Tower, The
P
Random House
Man With Two Faces, The
WAR (US) 1934 dir. Archie Mayo

Kaufman, L.
Color of Green
Holt
Love, Hate, Love
A. SPELLING (US) 1971
dir. George McCowan
TV(US)

Kaufman, S.
Diary of a Mad Housewife
Penguin
UI (US) 1970 dir. Frank Perry
V

Kaus, G.
Dark Angel
Cassell
Her Sister's Secret
PRC (US) 1946 dir. Edgar G. Ulmer

Kaus, G.
Luxury Liner
Cassell
PAR (US) 1933 dir. Lothar Mendes

Kawabata, Y.
Sounds from the Mountains
Knopf
CORINTH (Jap) 1980 dir. Mikio Naruse

Kawata, T.
Solar Crisis
SHOCHIKU (Jap) 1990
dir. Richard C. Sarafian

Kaye, M. M.
Far Pavilions, The
St. Martin's Press
GOLD (GB) 1983 dir. Peter Duffell
TVSe(GB), V

Kazan, E.
America, America
Stein & Day
WAR (US) 1964 dir. Elia Kazan
GB title: Anatolian Smile, The

Kazan, E.
Arrangement, The
Stein & Day
WAR (US) 1969 dir. Elia Kazan
V

Kazantzakis, N.
Last Temptation of Christ, The
Simon & Schuster
UN (US) 1988 dir. Martin Scorsese
V

Kazantzakis, N.
The Greek Passion
Simon & Schuster
He Who Must Die
KASSLER (Fr/It) 1957 dir. Jules Dassin

Kazantzakis, N.
Zorba the Greek
Simon & Schuster
FOX (GB) 1964 dir. Michael Cacoyannis
V

Ke Lan
Echo in the Valley
Yellow Earth
GUANGXI (China) 1985 dir. Chen Kaige

Keane, C.
Hunter, The
Arbor House
PAR (US) 1980 dir. Buzz Kulik
V

Keane, J. B.
Field, The
P
AVENUE (GB) 1990 dir. Jim Sheridan

Keating, H. R. F.
Perfect Murder, The
Dutton
MI (Ind) 1990 dir. Zafar Hai

Keating, W. J. and Carter, R.
Man Who Rocked the Boat, The
Slaughter on 10th Avenue
UI (US) 1957 dir. Arnold Laven

Keefe, F. L.
Interpreter, The
Before Winter Comes
COL (GB) 1968 dir. J. Lee Thompson

Keene, D. and Babcock, D.
Chautauqua
Putnam
Trouble With Girls, The
MGM (US) 1969 dir. Peter Tewkesbury
V

Keir, U.
Vintage, The
MGM (US) 1957 dir. Jeffrey Hayden

Keith, A.
Three Came Home
Little, Brown (Boston)
FOX (US) 1950 dir. Jean Negulesco

Kelland, C. B.
Arizona
Harper & Bros.

COL (US) 1940 dir. Wesley Ruggles

Kelland, C. B.
Dreamland
Harper

Strike Me Pink
UA (US) 1936 dir. Norman Taurog

Kelland, C. B.
Footlights
Speak Easily
MGM (US) 1932 dir. Edward Sedgwick

Kelland, C. B.
Opera Hat
Mr. Deeds Goes to Town
COL (US) 1936 dir. Frank Capra

Kelland, C. B.
Scattergood Baines
RKO (US) 1941 dir. Christy Cabanne

Kelland, C. B.
Sugarfoot
Harper & Bros.

WAR (US) 1951 dir. Edward L. Marin

Kelland, C. B.
Thirty Day Princess
PAR (US) 1934 dir. Marion Gering

Kelland, C. B.
Valley of the Sun
Harper & Bros.

RKO (US) 1942 dir. George Marshall

Kellerman, B.
Tunnel, The
GAU (GB) 1935 dir. Maurice Elvey
US title: Transatlantic Tunnel

Kellerman, J.
When the Bough Breaks
Atheneum

TAFT (US) 1986 dir. Waris Hussein
TV(US)

Kellino, P.
Del Palma
Dutton

Lady Possessed
REP (US) 1952 dir. William Spier, Roy Kellino

Kellock, H.
Houdini
Heinemann

PAR (US) 1953 dir. George Marshall

Kellogg, M.
Tell Me That You Love Me, Junie Moon
Farrar, Straus & Giroux

PAR (US) 1970 dir. Otto Preminger

Kelly, A. P.
British Intelligence
P

WAR (US) 1940 dir. Terry Morse
GB title: Enemy Agent

Kelly, A. P.
Three Faces East
P
Samuel French

WAR (US) 1930 dir. Roy del Ruth

Kelly, G.
Craig's Wife
P
Samuel French

COL (US) 1936 dir. Dorothy Arzner
V

Kelly, G.
Craig's Wife
P
Samuel French

Harriet Craig
COL (US) 1950 dir. Vincent Sherman

Kelly, G.
Show-Off, The
P
Samuel French
MGM (US) 1934 dir. Charles Riesner

Kelly, G.
Show-off, The
P
Samuel French
Men Are Like That
PAR (US) 1930 dir. Frank Tuttle

Kelly, G.
The Torch Bearers
P
Samuel French
Doubting Thomas
FOX (US) 1935 dir. David Butler

Kelly, J.
Marriage is a Private Affair
Cassell
MGM (US) 1944 dir. Robert Z. Leonard

Kelly, M. T.
Dream Like Mine, A
Clearcut
TELEFILM (Can) 1991
dir. Richard Bugajski

Kemal, Y.
Memed my Hawk
Pantheon Books
EMI (GB) 1984 dir. Peter Ustinov
V

Kember, P.
Not Quite Jerusalem
P
Methuen (London)
RANK (GB) 1985 dir. Lewis Gilbert
V

Kemelman, H.
Friday the Rabbi Slept Late
Crown Publishers
Lanigan's Rabbi
UN TV (US) 1976 dir. Lou Antonio
TV(US)

Kempinski, T.
Duet for One
P
Samuel French
CANNON (GB) 1987
dir. Andrei Konchalovsky
V

Kendall, D.
Lazaro
Where the River Runs Black
MGM (US) 1986 dir. Christopher Cain
V

Kendrick, B. H. and W. H. Allen
Bright Victory
UI (US) 1951 dir. Mark Robson
GB title: Lights Out

Kendrick, B. H.
Odour of Violets
Methuen
Eyes in the Night
MGM (US) 1942 dir. Fred Zinnemann

Keneally, T.
Chant of Jimmie Blacksmith, The
Viking Press
FOX (Aust) 1979 dir. Fred Schepisi
V

Kennaway, J.
Household Ghosts
Atheneum
Country Dance
MGM (GB) 1969 dir. J. Lee Thompson

Kennaway, J.
Tunes of Glory
Harper
UA (GB) 1960 dir. Ronald Neame
V

Kennedy, A.
Domino Principle, The
Viking Press
ITC (US) 1977 dir. Stanley Kramer
V

Kennedy, J. R.
The Chairman
Most Dangerous Man in the World, The
RANK (GB) 1969 dir. J. Lee Thompson
US title: Chairman, The

Kennedy, L.
10 Rillington Place
Simon & Schuster
COL (GB) 1970 dir. Richard Fleischer
V

Kennedy, M., Surgutchoff, I.
Autumn
P
That Dangerous Age
LF (GB) 1948 dir. Gregory Ratoff
US title: If This Be Sin

Kennedy, M.
Constant Nymph, The
Doubleday
GAU (GB) 1933 dir. Basil Dean
WAR (US) 1943 dir. Edmund Goulding

Kennedy, M.
Escape Me Never
P
Heinemann
UA (GB) 1935 dir. Paul Czinner
WAR (US) 1947 dir. Peter Godfrey

Kennedy, W. P.
Toy Soldiers
St. Martin's Press
TRI-STAR (US) 1991 dir. Daniel Petrie, Jr.

Kennedy, W.
Ironweed
Viking Press
TRI-STAR (US) 1987 dir. Hector Babenco
V

Kennerly, D. H.
Shooter
Newsweek Books
PAR TV (US) 1988 dir. Gary Nelson
TV(US)

Kennington, A.
Night has Eyes, The
ANGLO-AM 1952

Kenny, E. and Ostenso, M.
And They Shall Walk
Dodd, Mead
Sister Kenny
RKO (US) 1946 dir. Dudley Nichols
V

Kenrick, T.
Faraday's Flowers
Doubleday
Shanghai Surprise
MGM (US) 1986 dir. Jim Goddard
V

Kenrick, T.
Two for the Price of One
Bobbs-Merrill (Indianapolis)
Nobody's Perfekt
COL (US) 1981 dir. Peter Bonerz
V

Kenward, A. R.
Proof Thru' the Night
P
Samuel French
Cry Havoc
MGM (US) 1943 dir. Richard Thorpe

Kenyon, C.
Lloyd's of London
FOX (US) 1936 dir. Henry King

Keon, M.
Durian Tree, The
7th Dawn, The
UA (GB) 1964 dir. Lewis Gilbert

Kerouac, J.
Subterraneans, The
Deutsch (London)
MGM (US) 1960
dir. Ronald MacDougall

Kerr, G.
Cottage to Let
P
GFD (GB) 1941 dir. Anthony Asquith
US title: Bombsight Stolen

Kerr, J.
Mary, Mary
P
Doubleday
WAR (US) 1963 dir. Mervyn Le Roy

Kerr, J.
Please Don't Eat the Daisies
Doubleday
MGM (US) 1960 dir. Charles Walters

Kerr, J. and Brooke, E.
King of Hearts
P
Doubleday
That Certain Feeling
PAR (US) 1956 dir. Norman Panama,
Melvin Frank

Kerrvish, J. D.
Undying Monster, The
FOX (US) 1943 dir. John Brahm
GB title: Hammond Mystery, The

Kersh, G.
Night and the City
Simon & Schuster
FOX (GB) 1950 dir. Jules Dassin

Kesey, K.
One Flew Over the Cuckoo's Nest
Viking Press
UA (US) 1975 dir. Milos Forman
V

Kesey, K.
Sometimes a Great Notion
V
Viking Press
UN (US) 1974 dir. Paul Newman
GB title: Never Give an Inch
V

Kessel, J.
Belle de Jour
Barker
CURZON (Fr/It) 1967 dir. Luis Bunuel

Kessel, J.
Coup de Grâce
Sirocco
COL (US) 1951 dir. Curtis Bernhardt
V

Kessel, J.
Horsemen, The
Farrar, Straus & Giroux
COL (US) 1970
dir. John Frankenheimer
V

Kessel, J.
L'Equippage
Gallimard (Paris)
Woman I Love, The
RKO (US) 1937 dir. Anatole Litvak
GB title: Woman Between, The

Kessel, J.
Lion, The
Knopf
FOX (GB) 1962 dir. Jack Cardiff

Kessel, J.
Lovers of Lisbon, The
EGC (Fr) 1954 dir. Henri Verneuil

Kesselring, J. O.
Arsenic and Old Lace
P
Dramatists Play Service
WAR (US) 1944 dir. Frank Capra
V
COMPASS (US) 1962
dir. George Schaefer
TV(US)

Kessler, L.
Orphans
P
Samuel French
LORIMAR (US) 1987 dir. Alan J. Pakula
V

Kesson, J.
Another Time, Another Place
Chatto & Windus
CINEGATE (GB) 1983
dir. Michael Radford
V

Ketron, L.
Fresh Horses
P
WEINTRAUB (US) 1988
dir. David Anspaugh
V

Key, A.
Escape to Witch Mountain
Westminster Press (Philadelphia)
DISNEY (US) 1974 dir. John Hough
Ch, V

Key, T.
Digby— The Biggest Dog in the World
Piccolo
RANK (GB) 1973 dir. Joseph McGrath
Ch, V

Keyes, D.
Flowers for Algernon
Harcourt, Brace & World
Charly
CINERAMA (US) 1968
dir. Ralph Nelson
V

Keyhoe, D. E.
Flying Saucers from Outer Space
Hutchinson
Earth v. The Flying Saucers
COL (US) 1956 dir. Fred F. Sears
V

Kienzle, W. X.
Rosary Murders, The
Andrews & McMeel (Kansas City)
NEW LINE (US) 1987 dir. Fred Walton

Kikuchi, K.
Gate of Hell
DAIEI (Jap) 1953
dir. Teinosuke Kinugasa
V

Kikuta, K.
Quiet Duel, The
P
DAIEI (Jap) 1983 dir. Akira Kurosawa

Kimmins, A.
Amorous Prawn, The
P
Samuel French
BL (GB) 1962 dir. Anthony Kimmins
US title: Playgirl and the War Minister, The

Kinder, G.
Victim: The Other Side of Murder
Delacorte Press
Aftermath: A Test of Love
COL (US) 1991 dir. Glenn Jordan
TV (US)

King, F.
Ghoul, The
GAU (GB) 1933 dir. T. Hayes Hunter

King, G. S.
Slave Ship
FOX (US) 1937 dir. Tay Garnett

King, H.
Paradigm Red
Bobbs-Merrill (Indianapolis)
Red Alert
PAR (US) 1977 dir. William Hale
TV(US), V

King, L. L. and Masterson, P.
Best Little Whorehouse in Texas
P
Samuel French
UN (US) 1982 dir. Colin Higgins
M, V

King, P.
On Monday Next
P
Samuel French
Curtain Up
GFD (GB) 1952 dir. Ralph Smart
V

King, P.
See How They Run
P
Samuel French
BL (GB) 1955 dir. Leslie Arliss
CHANNEL 4 (GB) 1984
TV(GB)

King, P.
Serious Charge
P
EROS (GB) 1959 dir. Terence Young

King, P. and Cary, F. L.
Sailor Beware!
P
Samuel French
BL (GB) 1956 dir. Gordon Parry
US title: Panic in the Parlor

King, R.
Case of the Constant God, The
Love Letters of a Star
UN (US) 1936 dir. Lewis R. Foster

King, R.
Secret Beyond the Door, The
UI (US) 1948 dir. Fritz Lang
V

King, S.
Body, The
Stand by Me
COL (US) 1986 dir. Rob Reiner
V

King, S.
Carrie
New American Library
UA (US) 1976 dir. Brian de Palma
V

King, S.
Cat From Hell
Tales from the Darkside: The Movie
PAR (US) 1990 dir. John Harrison

King, S.
Children of the Corn
NEW WORLD (US) 1984
dir. Fritz Kiersch

King, S.
Christine
Viking Press
COL (US) 1983 dir. John Carpenter
V

King, S.
Cujo
Viking Press
WAR (US) 1982 dir. Lewis Teague
V

King, S.
Cycle of the Werewolf
Silver Bullet
PAR (US) 1985 dir. Daniel Attias

King, S.
Dead Zone, The
Viking Press
PAR (US) 1983 dir. David Cronenberg
V

King, S.
Firestarter
Viking Press
UN (US) 1984 dir. Mark L. Lester
V

King, S.
Graveyard Shift
PAR (US) 1990 dir. Ralph S. Singleton

King, S.
If I Die Before I Wake
Lady from Shanghai, The
COL (US) 1948 dir. Orson Welles
V

King, S.
It
Viking Press
LORIMAR (US) 1989
dir. Tommy Lee Wallace
TVSe(US)

King, S.
Misery
Viking Press
COL (US) 1990 dir. Rob Reiner
V

King, S.
Pet Sematary
Doubleday
PAR (US) 1989 dir. Mary Lambert
V

King, S.
Salem's Lot
Doubleday
WAR (US) 1979 dir. Tobe Hooper
TVSe(US), V

King, S.
Shining, The
Doubleday
WAR (GB) 1980 dir. Stanley Kubrick
V

King, S.
Sometimes They Come Back
DELAUR (US) 1991
dir. Tom McLaughlin
TV(US)

King-Hall, M.
Life and Death of the Wicked Lady
Skelton, The
Rinehart
Wicked Lady, The
GFD (GB) 1946 dir. Leslie Arliss
V
CANNON (GB) 1983
dir. Michael Winner
V

Kingman, L. and Green, G.
His Majesty O'Keefe
Hale
WAR (GB) 1954 dir. Byron Haskin

Kingsley, C.
Water Babies, The
Dodd, Mead
PROD (GB/Pol) 1978 dir. Lionel Jeffries
A, V

Kingsley, M.
Shadow Over Elveron
UN TV (US) 1968 dir. James Goldstone
TV(US)

Kingsley, S.
Dead End
P
UA (US) 1937 dir. William Wyler
V

Kingsley, S.
Detective Story
P
Dramatists Play Service
PAR (US) 1951 dir. William Wyler

Kingsley, S.
Men in White
P
Samuel French
MGM (US) 1934
dir. Richard Boleslawsky

Kingsley, S.
Patriots, The
P
Random House
COMPASS (US) 1963
dir. George Schaefer
TV(US)

Kinsella, W. P.
Shoeless Joe
Houghton, Mifflin Co. (Boston)
Field of Dreams
UN (US) 1989 dir. Phil A. Robinson

Kipling, R.
Captains Courageous
Various
MGM (US/GB) 1937
dir. Victor Fleming
V
ROSEMONT (US) 1977
dir. Harvey Hart
TV(GB/US)

Kipling, R.
Jungle Book, The
Various
KORDA (US) 1942 dir. Zoltan Korda,
André de Toth
DISNEY (US) 1967
dir. Wolfgang Reitherman
A, Ch, M, V

Kipling, R.
Kim
Various
MGM (US) 1950 dir. Victor Saville
V
LF (GB) 1984 dir. John Davies
TVSe(GB)

Kipling, R.
Light That Failed, The
Various
PAR (US) 1939 dir. William Wellman

Kipling, R.
Man Who Would Be King, The
Doubleday
COL (US) 1975 dir. John Huston
V

Kipling, R.
Soldiers Three
Various
MGM (US) 1951 dir. Tay Garnett

Kipling, R.
Toomai of the Elephants
Various
Elephant Boy
UA (GB) 1937 dir. Robert Flaherty,
Zoltan Korda
V

Kipling, R.
Wee Willie Winkie
Various
FOX (US) 1937 dir. John Ford
V

Kirk, J.
Build-up Boys, The
Hart-Davis
Madison Avenue
FOX (US) 1962 dir. Bruce Humberstone

Kirkbride, R.
Girl Named Tamiko, A
Pan
PAR (US) 1962 dir. John Sturges

Kirkland, J.
Tobacco Road
P
Samuel French
FOX (US) 1941 dir. John Ford

Kirkwood, J.
Some Kind of Hero
PAR (US) 1981 dir. Michael Pressman
V

Kirkwood, J.
There Must be a Pony
COL TV (US) 1986 dir. Joseph Sargent
TV(US)

Kirstein, L.
Lay this Laurel
St. Martin's Press
Glory
TRI-STAR (US) 1989 dir. Edward Zwick

Kjelgaard, J. A.
Big Red
Holiday House
DISNEY (US) 1962 dir. Norman Tokar
A, Ch, V

Klaben, H. and Day, B.
Hey, I'm Alive!
FRIES (US) 1975 dir. Lawrence Schiller
TV(US)

Klane, R.
Fire Sale
FOX (US) 1977 dir. Alan Arkin

Klane, R.
Where's Poppa?
Random House
UA (US) 1970 dir. Carl Reiner
V

Kleiman, D.
Deadly Silence, A.
Atlantic Monthly Press
R. GREENWALD (US) 1989
dir. John Patterson
TV(US)

Klein, A.
Counterfeit Traitor, The
Holt
PAR (US) 1962 dir. George Seaton

Klein, N.
Mom, the Wolfman, and Me
Pantheon Books
TIME-LIFE (US) 1980
dir. Edmond A. Levy
TV(US)

Klempner, J.
Letter to Five Wives
Scribners
Letter to Three Wives, A.
FOX (US) 1948
dir. Joseph L. Mankiewicz
V
FOX (US) 1985 dir. Larry Elikann
TV(US)

Kluge, P. F.
Eddie and the Cruisers
EMBASSY (US) 1983
dir. Martin Davidson
V

Knebel, F. and Bailey, C. W.
Seven Days in May
Harper & Row
PAR (US) 1964 dir. John Frankenheimer
V

Knebel, F.
Vanished
Doubleday
UN (US) 1971 dir. Buzz Kulik
TVSe(US)

Kniepple, E.
That Hagen Girl
WAR (US) 1947 dir. Peter Godfrey

Knight, E. M.
Lassie Come Home
Various
MGM (US) 1943 dir. Fred M. Wilcox

Knight, E. M.
This Above All
Harper & Bros.
FOX (US) 1942 dir. Anatole Litvak

Knoblock, E.
Kismet
P
G. H. Doran
WAR (US) 1930 dir. John Francis Dillon
MGM (US) 1944 dir. William Dieterle
MGM (US) 1955 dir. Vincent Minnelli
M, V

Knoblock, E.
Lullaby, The
P
Sin of Madelon Claudet
MGM (US) 1931 dir. Edgar Selwyn

Knoll, H. H.
Cabin in the Cotton
WAR (US) 1932 dir. Michael Curtiz

Knott, F.
Dial 'M' for Murder
P
WAR (US) 1954 dir. Alfred Hitchcock
MILBERG (US) 1958
dir. George Schaefer
TIME-LIFE PRODS (US) 1981
dir. Boris Sagal
TV(US)

Knott, F.
Wait Until Dark
P
Dramatists Play Service
WAR (US) 1967 dir. Terence Young
V

Knowles, J.
Separate Peace, A
Bantam Books
PAR (US) 1972 dir. Larry Peerce
V

Kobal, J.
Rita Hayworth: The Time, the Place, and the Woman
Norton
Rita Hayworth: The Love Goddess
SUSSKIND (US) 1983
dir. James Goldstone
TV(US)

Kober, A.
Having Wonderful Time
P
Random House
RKO (US) 1938 dir. Alfred Santell
V

Koch, C. J.
Year of Living Dangerously, The
St. Martin's Press
MGM/UA (Aust) 1982 dir. Peter Weir
V

Koda, A.
Flowing
East-West (Jap) 1956 dir. Mikio Naruse

Koenig, L.
Little Girl Who Lives Down The Lane, The
Souvenir
RANK (US/Fr/Can) 1976
dir. Nicolas Gessner
V

Koenig, L.
Rockabye
St. Martin's Press
PEREGRINE (US) 1986
dir. Richard Michael
TV(US)

Kohn, B. G.
Best Man Wins, The
COL (US) 1934 dir. Erle C. Kenton
V

Kohn, R. S.
Pillar to Post
P
Pillow to Post
WAR (US) 1945 dir. Vincent Sherman

Kohner, F.
Gidget Goes to New York
Gidget Grows Up
COL TV (US) 1969 dir. James Sheldon
TV(US)

Kohner, F.
Gidget
Putnam
COL (US) 1959 dir. Paul Wendkos
V

Kolb, K.
Couch Trip, The
ORION (US) 1988 dir. Michael Ritchie
V

Kolb, K.
Getting Straight
Barrie & Rockhill
COL (US) 1970 dir. Richard Rush
V

Kollek, A.
Don't Ask Me If I Love
Worlds Apart
SCANLON (Israel) 1980
dir. Barbara Noble

Kolpacoff, V.
Prisoners of Quai Dong, The
New American Library
Physical Assault
TITAN (US) 1973
dir. William M. Bushnell
V

Komroff, M.
Magic Bow, The
Harper & Bros.
GFD (GB) 1946 dir. Bernard Knowles

Konig, H.
Death of a Schoolboy
NEUE STUDIO (Austria) 1991
dir. Peter Patzak

Konig, J.
David
KINO (W.Ger) 1982 dir. Peter Lilienthal

Konigsburg, E. L.
Father's Arcane Daughter
Atheneum
Caroline?
B&E (US) 1990 dir. Joseph Sargent
TV(US)

Konigsburg, E. L.
From the Mixed-up Files of Mrs Basil E. Frankwester
Atheneum
Hideaways, The
UA (US) 1973 dir. Fielder Cook
V

Koningsberger, H.
Revolutionary, The
Farrar, Straus & Giroux
UA (US) 1970 dir. Paul Williams

Koningsberger, H.
Walk with Love and Death, A
Simon & Schuster
FOX (US) 1969 dir. John Huston

Konvitz, J.
Sentinel, The
UN (US) 1977 dir. Michael Winner
V

Koontz, D.
Demon Seed
Bantam, Toronto
MGM (US) 1977 dir. Donald Cammell
V

Koontz, D.
Face of Fear, The
WAR TV (US) 1990 dir. Farhad Mann
TV(US)

Koontz, D.
Twilight
Servants of Twilight, The
TRIMARK (US) 1991 dir. Jeffrey Obrow
TV(US)

Koontz, D.
Watchers
Putnam
UN (US) 1988 dir. Jon Hess
V

Kopit, A.
Indians
P
Samuel French
Buffalo Bill and the Indians
UA (US) 1976 dir. Robert Altman
V

Kopit, A.
Oh Dad, Poor Dad ... Mama's Hung You In The Closet and I'm Feeling So Sad
P
PAR (US) 1966 dir. Richard Quine

Korda, M.
Queenie
Simon & Schuster
NEW WORLD (US) 1987
dir. Larry Peerce
TVSe(US)

Kosinski, J.
Being There
Harcourt, Brace, Jovanovich
LORIMAR (US) 1979 dir. Hal Ashby
V

Kovic, R.
Born on the Fourth of July
McGraw-Hill
UN (US) 1989 dir. Oliver Stone

Kozniewski, K.
Five Boys from Barska Street
POLSKI (Pol) 1953 dir. Aleksander Ford

Krabbe, T.
Golden Egg, The
Vanishing, The
INGRID (Swe) 1990 dir. George Sluizer

Kramm, J.
Shrike, The
P
Random House
UI (US) 1955 dir. José Ferrer

Krantz, J.
I'll Take Manhattan
Crown
S. KRANTZ (US) 1987
dir. Douglas Hickox, Richard Michaels
TVSe(US)

Krantz, J.
Mistral's Daughter
Crown Publishing
KRANTZ (Fr/Lux/US) 1986
dir. David Hickox, Kevin Connor
TVSe(Fr/Lux/US), V

Krantz, J.
Princess Daisy
Crown Publishing
NBC ENT (US) 1984 dir. Waris Hussein
TVSe(US), V

Krantz, J.
Scruples
Crown Publishing
WAR (US) 1980 dir. Alan J. Levi
TVSe(US)

Krantz, J.
Till We Meet Again
Crown Publishers
KRANTZ/YTV (US/GB) 1989
dir. Charles Jarrot
TVSe(GB/US)

Krasna, N.
Dear Ruth
P
Gollancz
PAR (US) 1947 dir. William D. Russell

Krasna, N.
John Loves Mary
P
WAR (US) 1948 dir. David Butler

Krasna, N.
Kind Sir
P
Dramatists Play Service
Indiscreet
WAR (GB) 1958 dir. Stanley Donen
V
REPUBLIC (US) 1988
dir. Richard Michaels
TV(US)

Krasna, N.
Small Miracle
P
Samuel French
Four Hours to Kill
PAR (US) 1935 dir. Mitchell Leisen

Krasna, N.
Sunday in New York
P
Random House
MGM (US) 1963 dir. Peter Tewkesbury

Krasna, N.
Who Was That Lady I Saw You
With?
P
Random House
Who Was That Lady?
COL (US) 1960 dir. George Sidney

Krause, C. A.
Guyana Massacre: The Eyewitness
Account
Guyana Tragedy: The Story of Jim Jones
KONIGSBERG (US) 1980
dir. William A. Graham
TVSe(US), V

Krents, H.
To Race the Wind
Putnam
GRAUMAN (US) 1980
dir. Walter Grauman
TV(US), V

Kressing, H.
Cook, The
Random House
Something for Everyone
NAT GEN (US) 1970 dir. Harold Prince
GB title: Black Flowers for the Bride
V

Krumgold, J.
And Now Miguel
Crowell
UI (US) 1965 dir. James B. Clark

Kuchler-Silberman, L
One Hundred Children
Doubleday
Lena: My 100 Children
GREENWALD (US) 1987 dir. Ed Sherin
TV(US)

Kummer, C.
Good Gracious Annabelle
P
Annabelle's Affairs
FOX (US) 1931 dir. Alfred Werker

Kundera, M.
Unbearable Lightness of Being, The
Harper & Row

ORION (US) 1988 dir. Philip Kaufman

Kunen, J. S.
Strawberry Statement, The
Random House

MGM (US) 1970 dir. Stuart Hagmann
V

Kunhardt, Jr., P.
My Father's House
Random House

FILMWAYS (US) 1975 dir. Alex Segal
TV(US), V

Kurnitz, H.
Once More, With Feeling
P
Random House

COL (GB) 1960 dir. Stanley Donen

Kurth, A.
Prescription: Murder

Murder in Texas
D. CLARK (US) 1981 dir. Billy Hale
TVSe(US), V

Kurth, P.
Anastasia: The Riddle of Anna Anderson
Little, Brown (Boston)

Anastasia: The Mystery of Anna
TELECOM (US) 1986
dir. Marvin Chomsky
TVSe(US)

Kutagawa, R. A.
In the Grove

Iron Maze
TRANS-TOKYO (US/Jap) 1991
dir. Hiroaki Yoshida

Kyne, P. B.
Never the Twain Shall Meet

MGM (US) 1931 dir. W. S. van Dyke

Kyne, P. B.
Parson of Panamint, The
PAR (US) 1941 dir. William McGann

Kyne, P. B.
Three Godfathers, The

Hell's Heroes
UN (US) 1930 dir. William Wyler

Kyne, P. B.
Three Godfathers, The

MGM (US) 1936
dir. Richard Boleslawski
MGM (US) 1948 dir. John Ford

Kyne, P. B.
Valley of the Giants
Doubleday

WAR (US) 1938 dir. William Keighley

Kytle, R.
Last Voyage of the Valhalla

Desperate Voyage
WIZAN (US) 1980
dir. Michael O'Herlihy
TV(US)

L

La Bern, A. J.
Goodbye Piccadilly, Farewell Leicester Square
Pan
Frenzy
RANK (GB) 1971 dir. Alfred Hitchcock
V

La Bern, A. J.
It Always Rains on Sundays
EAL (GB) 1947 dir. Robert Hamer

La Bern, A. J.
Night Darkens the Streets
Good-Time Girl
GFD (GB) 1948 dir. David MacDonald

La Bern, A. J.
Paper Orchid
COL (GB) 1949 dir. Roy Baker

La Fontaine, G.
Flashpoint
Mayflower
TRI-STAR (US) 1984
dir. William Tannen
V

La Fontaine, G.
Two Minute Warning
UN (US) 1976 dir. Larry Peerce

La Motta, J.
Raging Bull
UA (US) 1980 dir. Martin Scorsese
V

La Mure, P.
Moulin Rouge
Random House
UA (GB) 1952 dir. John Huston
V

La Rochhelle, P. D.
Feu Follet, Le
ARCO (Fr/It) 1963 dir. Louis Malle

Laborde, J.
Lesser of Two Evils, The
Investigation
QUARTET (Fr) 1978 dir. Etienne Perier
V

Lacey, R.
Ford: The Man and the Machine
LANTANA (US) 1987 dir. Allan Eastman
TVSe(US)

LaFarge, O.
Laughing Boy
Houghton, Mifflin Co. (Boston)
MGM (US) 1934 dir. W. S. Van Dyke

Laferrière, D.
Comment faire l'amour avec un nègre sans se fatiguer
How to Make Love to a Negro Without Getting Tired
ANGELIKA (Fr) 1990
dir. Jacques Benoit

Laffan, K.
It's a 2 ft 6 inch Above The Ground
World
P
Faber
Love Ban, The
BL (GB) 1973 dir. Ralph Thomas

Lagerkvist, P.
Barabbas
Random House
COL (It) 1962 dir. Richard Fleischer
V

Lahr, J.
Prick up your Ears
Knopf
ZENITH (GB) 1986 dir. Stephen Frears
V

Laine, P.
Lacemaker, The
FR3 (Fr/It/Ger) 1977
dir. Claude Goretta
V

Laing, R. D.
Knots
Vintage Books
CINEGATE (GB) 1975
dir. David I. Munro

Lake, S.
Wyatt Earp, Frontier Marshall
Houghton, Mifflin Co. (Boston)
Frontier Marshall
FOX (US) 1933 dir. Lew Seiler
FOX (US) 1939 dir. Allan Dwan

Lake, S.
Wyatt Earp, Frontier Marshal
Houghton, Mifflin Co. (Boston)
My Darling Clementine
FOX (US) 1946 dir. John Ford
V

Lam, N. and Burke, I.
China Cry
PENLAND (US) 1990
dir. James F. Collier

Lambert, D.
Touch the Lion's Paw
Saturday Review Press
Rough Cut
PAR (US) 1980 dir. Don Siegel
V

Lambert, G.
Inside Daisy Clover
Viking Press
WAR (US) 1965 dir. Robert Mulligan

L'Amour, L.
Broken Gun, The
Cancel My Reservation
MGM-EMI (US) 1972 dir. Paul Bogart

L'Amour, L.
Burning Hills, The
Bantam Books
WAR (US) 1956 dir. Stuart Heisler
GB title: Apache Territory

L'Amour, L.
Catlow
Ulverscroft (London)
MGM (GB) 1971 dir. Sam Wanamaker
V

L'Amour, L.
Conagher
Bantam Books
IMAGINE (US) 1991
dir. Reynaldo Villalobos
TV(US)

L'Amour, L.
Down the Long Hills
Bantam Books
DISNEY CH (US) 1986
dir. Burt Kennedy
TV(US)

L'Amour, L.
East of Sumatra
UI (US) 1953 dir. Budd Boetticher

L'Amour, L.
Guns of the Timberland
Ulverscroft (Leicester)
WAR (US) 1960 dir. Robert D. Webb
V

L'Amour, L.
Heller With A Gun
Heller in Pink Tights
PAR (US) 1960 dir. George Cukor
V

L'Amour, L.
Hondo
Fawcett Books
WAR (US) 1953 dir. John Farrow

L'Amour, L.
Man Called Noon, The
Corgi
SCOTIA-BARBER (GB/Sp/It) 1973
dir. Peter Collinson

L'Amour, L.
Quick and the Dead, The
Bantam Books
HBO (US) 1987 dir. Robert Day
TV(US), V

L'Amour, L.
Sackett; Daybreakers, The
Bantam Books
Sacketts, The
SHALAKO (US) 1979 dir. Robert Totten
TVSe(US), V

L'Amour, L.
Shadow Riders, The
G. K. Hall (Boston)
COL TV (US) 1982
dir. Andrew V. McLaglen
TV(US)

L'Amour, L.
Shalako
WAR (GB) 1968 dir. Edward Dmytryk

L'Amour, L.
Taggart
Bantam Books
UI (US) 1965 dir. R. G. Springsteen

Lampedusa, G. de
Leopard, The
Pantheon
FOX (US/It) 1963 dir. Luchino Visconti

Lampell, M.
Hero, The
Saturday's Hero
COL (US) 1950 dir. David Miller
GB title: Idols in the Dust

Lamplugh, L
Rockets in the Dunes
RANK (GB) 1960
dir. William Hammond
Ch

Landon, C.
Ice Cold in Alex
W. Sloane Associates
ABP (GB) 1958 dir. J. Lee Thompson
US title: Desert Attack
V

Landon, M.
Anna and the King of Siam
John Day Company
FOX (US) 1946 dir. John Cromwell

Lane, K.
Gambit
Hodder & Stoughton
UI (US) 1966 dir. Ronald Neame
V

Lane, R. W.
Young Pioneers
McGraw-Hill
ABC (US) 1976 dir. Michael O'Herlihy
TV(US)

Lang, D.
Casualties of War
McGraw-Hill
COL (US) 1989 dir. Brian de Palma

Langelaan, G.
Fly, The
FOX (US) 1958 dir. Kurt Neumann
FOX (US) 1986 dir. David Cronenberg
V

Langley, A. L.
Lion is in The Streets, A
McGraw-Hill
WAR (US) 1953 dir. Raoul Walsh

Langley, N.
Little Lambs Eat Ivy
P
Samuel French
Father's Doing Fine
ABP (GB) 1952 dir. Henry Cass

Langner, L. and Marshall, A.
Pursuit of Happiness, The
P
Samuel French
PAR (US) 1934 dir. Alexander Hall

Lansburg, O.
Dear John
Random House
SANDREW (Swe) 1964
dir. Lars Magnus Lindgren

Lapierre, D.
City of Joy
Doubleday
TRI-STAR (US) 1992 dir. Roland Joffe

Lardner, R.
Alibi Ike
WAR (US) 1935 dir. Ray Enright

Lardner, R.
Big Town, The
Scribners
So this is New York
UA (US) 1948 dir. Richard Fleischer

Lardner, R.
Champion
Scribners
UA (US) 1949 dir. Mark Robson
V

Larner, J.
Drive, He Said
Delacorte Press
COL (US) 1970 dir. Jack Nicholson

Larsen, R. W.
Bundy: The Deliberate Stranger
Prentice-Hall
Deliberate Stranger, The
LORIMAR (US) 1986
dir. Marvin Chomsky
TVSe(US)

Larteguy, J.
Centurions, The
Dutton
Lost Command
COL (US) 1966 dir. Mark Robson
V

Larusso, II, L.
Wheelbarrow Closers
P
Samuel French
Closer, The
ION (US) 1990 dir. Dimitri Logothetis

Lash, J. P.
Eleanor and Franklin
Norton
TALENT (US) 1976 dir. Daniel Petrie
TVSe(US)

Lash, J. P.
Eleanor and Franklin
Norton

Eleanor and Franklin: The White House Years
TALENT (US) 1977 dir. Daniel Petrie
TV(US)

Lash, J. P.
Helen and Teacher
Delacorte Press

Helen Keller— The Miracle Continues
FOX TV (US) 1984 dir. Alan Gibson
TV(US)

Laski, M.
Little Boy Lost
Houghton, Mifflin Co. (Boston)

PAR (US) 1953 dir. George Seaton

Laszlo, N.
Shop Around the Corner, The
P

MGM (US) 1940 dir. Ernst Lubitsch

Laszlo, N.
Shop Around the Corner, The
P

In the Good Old Summertime
MGM (US) 1949 dir. Robert Z. Leonard
M, V

Latimer, J.
Dead Don't Care, The
Methuen

Last Warning, The
UN (US) 1938 dir. Albert S. Rogell

Latimer, J.
Lady in the Morgue
Methuen

UN (US) 1938 dir. Otis Garrett
GB title: Case of the Missing Blonde, The

Laumer, K.
Deadfall
Doubleday

Peeper
FOX (US) 1975 dir. Peter Hyams
V

Launder, F. and Gilliat, S.
Meet a Body
P
French

Green Man, The
BL (GB) 1956 dir. Robert Day
V

Laurence, M.
Jest of God, A
Knopf

Rachel, Rachel
WAR (US) 1968 dir. Paul Newman
V

Laurents, A., Sondheim, S. and Bernstein, L.
West Side Story
P
Random House

UA (US) 1961
dir. Robert Wise/Jerome Robbins
M, V

Laurents, A.
Home of the Brave
P

UA (US) 1949 dir. Mark Robson
V

Laurents, A.
Gypsy
P

WAR (US) 1962 dir. Mervyn Le Roy
M, V

Laurents, A.
Time of the Cuckoo, The
P

Summertime
UA (US) 1955 dir. David Lean
GB title: Summer Madness
V

Laurents, A.
Way We Were, The
Harper & Row

COL (US) 1973 dir. Sydney Pollack

Laurey, J.
Joy
W. H. Allen

UGC (Can/Fr) 1983 dir. Serge Bergon
V

Lauritzen, J.
Rose and the Flame, The

Kiss of Fire
UN (US) 1955 dir. Joseph M. Newman

Lauro, S.
Open Admissions
P
Samuel French

VIACOM (US) 1988 dir. Gus Trikonis
TV(US)

Lauzier, G.
Souvenirs d'un Jeune Homme

Petit Con
GOLDWYN (Fr) 1985
dir. Gerard Lauzier
V

Lavallee, D.
Event One Thousand
Coronet

Gray Lady Down
UN (US) 1978 dir. David Greene
V

Lavery, E.
Magnificent Yankee, The
P
Samuel French

MGM (US) 1950 dir. John Sturges
COMPASS (US) 1965
dir. George Schaefer
TV(US)

Lavery, E. G.
First Legion, The
P
Samuel French

UA (US) 1951 dir. Douglas Sirk
V

Lavin, N. and Thorp, M.
Hop Dog, The
OUP

Adventure in the Hopfields
ABP (GB) 1954 dir. John Guillermin

Lawes, L., and Finn, J.
Chalked Out
P

You Can't Get Away with Murder
WAR (US) 1939 dir. Lewis Seiler

Lawes, L. E.
Invisible Stripes
WAR (US) 1939 dir. Lloyd Bacon

Lawes, L. E.
20,000 Years in Sing Sing
WAR (US) 1932 dir. Michael Curtiz

Lawler, R.
Summer of the Seventeenth Doll, The
P
Samuel French

UA (US/Aust) 1959 dir. Leslie Norman

Lawlor, H.
What Beckoning Ghost

Dominique
GRAND PRIZE (GB) 1978
dir. Michael Anderson

Lawrence, D. H.
Captain's Doll, The
Penguin
BBC (GB) 1982
TV(GB)

Lawrence, D. H.
Fox, The
Heinemann
WAR (US/Can) 1967 dir. Mark Rydell

Lawrence, D. H.
Kangaroo
Viking Press
WORLD FILM (Aust) 1986
dir. Tim Burstall
V

Lawrence, D. H.
Lady Chatterley's Lover
Modern Library
COL (Fr) 1956 dir. Marc Allégret
CANNON (GB/Fr) 1981
dir. Just Jaeckin
V

Lawrence, D. H.
Rainbow, The
Penguin
VESTRON (GB) 1989 dir. Ken Russell
BBC (GB) 1989 dir. Stuart Burge
TVSe(GB)

Lawrence, D. H.
Rocking Horse Winner, The
Viking Press
TC (GB) 1949 dir. Anthony Pelissier
V

Lawrence, D. H.
Sons and Lovers
Viking Press
FOX (GB) 1960 dir. Jack Cardiff

Lawrence, D. H.
Trespasser, The
C. GREGG (GB) 1981 dir. Colin Gregg
V

Lawrence, D. H.
Virgin and the Gypsy, The
Knopf
LONDON SCR (GB) 1970
dir. Christopher Miles

Lawrence, D. H.
Women in Love
Modern Library
UA (GB) 1969 dir. Ken Russell
V

Lawrence, D. H. and Skinner, M. L.
Boy in the Bush, The
Cambridge University Press
(Cambridge)
CHANNEL 4 (GB) 1984
dir. Rob Stewart
TV(GB)

Lawrence, H. L.
Children of Light, The
Macdonald
Damned, The
BL (GB) 1961 dir. Joseph Losey
US title: These Are The Damned

Lawrence, J.
Years Are So Long, The
Stokes
Make Way for Tomorrow
PAR (US) 1937 dir. Leo McCarey

Lawrence, J. and Lee, R. E.
First Monday in October
P
Samuel French
PAR (US) 1981 dir. Ronald Neame
V

Lawrence, J. and Lee, R. E.
Inherit the Wind
P
Random House
UA (US) 1960 dir. Stanley Kramer
V
COMPASS (US) 1965
dir. George Schaefer
TV(US)
VINCENT (US) 1988 dir. David Greene
TV(US)

Lawrence, J., Lee, R. E. and Herman, J.
Mame
P
Random House
WAR (US) 1974 dir. Gene Saks
M, V

Lawrence, M.
Madonna of the Seven Moons
GFD (GB) 1944 dir. Arthur Crabtree

Lawrence, T. E.
Seven Pillars of Wisdom
Doubleday
Lawrence of Arabia
COL/BL (GB/US) 1962 dir. David Lean
V

Lawson, J.
Roses are for the Rich
PHOENIX (US) 1987 dir. Michael Miller
TVSe(US)

Lawson, T. and Considine, R.
Thirty Seconds Over Tokyo
Random House
MGM (US) 1944 dir. Mervyn Le Roy
V

Lawton, H.
Willie Boy
Paisano Press (Balboat Island, California)
Tell them Willie Boy is Here
UN (US) 1969 dir. Abraham Polonsky
V

Lay, B. and Bartlett, S.
Twelve O'Clock High
FOX (US) 1949 dir. Henry King
V

Le Breton, A.
Monsieur Rififi
Hachette (Paris)
Rififi
PATHE (Fr) 1955 dir. Jules Dassin
V

Le Carré, J.
Call for the Dead
Walker Press
Deadly Affair, The
COL (GB) 1966 dir. Sidney Lumet
V

Le Carré, J.
Little Drummer Girl, The
Knopf
WAR (US) 1984 dir. George Roy Hill
V

Le Carré, J.
Looking Glass War, The
Coward-McCann
COL (GB) 1969 dir. Frank R. Pierson
V

Le Carré, J.
Russia House, The
Knopf
MGM (US) 1990 dir. Fred Schepisi
V

Le Carré, J.
Smiley's People
Knopf
BBC (GB) 1982 dir. Simon Langton
TVSe(GB)

Le Carré, J.
Spy Who Came in from the Cold, The
Coward-McCann
PAR (GB) 1966 dir. Martin Ritt
V

Le Carré, J.
Tinker, Tailor, Soldier, Spy
Knopf

BBC (GB) 1979 dir. Janet Irvin
TVSe(GB)

Le Fanu, S.
Uncle Silas

TC (GB) 1947 dir. Charles Frank
US title: Inheritance, The

Le Fanu, S.
Uncle Silas
Dark Angel, The
BBC (GB) 1991 dir. Peter Hammond
TV(GB)

Lea, F. H.
Four Marys, The
Manproof
MGM (US) 1937 dir. Richard Thorpe

Lea, T.
Brave Bulls, The
Little, Brown (Boston)

COL (US) 1951 dir. Robert Rossen

Lea, T.
Confessions from a Holiday Camp
Sphere

COL (GB) 1977 dir. Norman Cohen
V

Lea, T.
Confessions of a Driving Instructor
Sphere

COL (GB) 1976 dir. Norman Cohen
V

Lea, T.
Confessions of a Pop Performer
Futura

COL (GB) 1975 dir. Norman Cohen
V

Lea, T.
Confessions of a Window Cleaner
Sphere

COL (GB) 1974 dir. Val Guest
V

Lea, T.
Wonderful Country, The
Little, Brown (Boston)

UA (US) 1959 dir. Robert Parrish

Lear, M. W.
Heartsounds
Simon & Schuster

EMBASSY (US) 1984 dir. Glenn Jordan
TV(US)

Lear, P.
Goldengirl
Doubleday

AVCO (US) 1979 dir. Joseph Sargent
TV(US), V

Leasor, J.
Boarding Party
Sea Wolves, The
RANK (GB/US/Switz) 1980
dir. Andrew McLaglen
V

Leasor, J.
Passport to Oblivion
Lippincott (Philadelphia)
Where the Spies Are
MGM (GB) 1965 dir. Val Guest
V

Leasor, J.
Who Killed Sir Harry Oakes?
Houghton, Mifflin Co. (Boston)
Eureka!
MGM/UA (GB/US) 1982
dir. Nicolas Roeg
V

LeBlanc, M. and de Croisset, F.
Arsene Lupin
P
Houghton, Mifflin Company (Boston)
MGM (US) 1932 dir. Jack Conway

Ledda, G.
Padre Padrone
Urizen Books
RAI (It) 1977 dir. Paolo Taviani, Vittorio Taviani
V

Lederer, W. J. and Burdick, E. L.
Ugly American, The
Norton
UI (US) 1962 dir. George England
V

Lee, B.
Paganini Strikes Again
CFF (GB) 1973 dir. Gordon Gilbert
Ch

Lee, C. Y.
Flower Drum Song
Farrar, Straus & Cudahy
UI (US) 1961 dir. Henry Koster
M, V

Lee, E.
Queen Bee
COL (US) 1955 dir. Ronald MacDougall

Lee, G. R.
Gypsy
Harper; Random House
WAR (US) 1962 dir. Mervyn LeRoy
M, V

Lee, G. R.
G-String Murders, The
Lady of Burlesque
STROMBERG (US) 1943
dir. William Wellman
GB title: Striptease Lady
V

Lee, H.
To Kill a Mockingbird
Lippincott (Philadelphia)
UI (US) 1962 dir. Robert Mulligan
V

Lee, J.
Career
P
Samuel French
PAR (US) 1959 dir. Joseph Anthony

Lee, J.
Wanderer Never Sleeps, Even on the Road, A
Man with Three Coffins, The
MWL (Kor) 1987 dir. Lee Chang Ho

Lee, L.
Sweet Poison
Along Came a Spider
FOX TV (US) 1970 dir. Lee H. Katzin
TV(US)

Lee, L.
Walking Through the Fire
Dutton
TIME-LIFE (US) 1979 dir. Robert Day
TV(US)

Lee, R.
Right of Way
P
HBO Prem (US) 1983
dir. George Schaefer
TV(US), V

Leech, M.
Reveille in Washington
Harper & Bros.

Rose and the Jackal, The
S. White (US) 1990 dir. Jack Gold
TV(US)

LeFlore, R. and Hawkins, J.
Breakout
Harper & Row

One in a Million: The Ron LeFlore Story
EMI (US) 1978 dir. William A. Graham
TV(US), V

Leger, J. A.
Monsignore

Monsignor
FOX (US) 1982 dir. Frank Perry
V

Lehar, F., Leon, V. and Stein, L.
Merry Widow, The
Samuel French

MGM (US) 1934 dir. Ernst Lubitsch
M
MGM (US) 1952 dir. Curtis Bernhardt
M

Lehman, E.
French Atlantic Affair, The
Atheneum

MGM TV (US) 1979 dir. Douglas Heyes
TVSe(US)

Lehman, R.
Weather in the Streets, The
BBC (GB) 1984 dir. Gavin Millar
TV(GB), V

Leiber, F.
Conjure Wife
Gregg Press

Night of the Eagle
IA (GB) 1961 dir. Sidney Hayers
US title: Burn, Witch, Burn

Leigh, J.
What Can You Do?
Panther

Making It
FOX (US) 1971 dir. John Erman

Leimbach, M.
Dying Young
Doubleday

TCF (US) 1991 dir. Joel Schumacher

Leinster, C.
Heritage of Michael Flaherty, The

Outsider, The
PAR (US) 1980 dir. Tony Luraschi

Leinster, M.
Wailing Asteroid, The

Terronauts, The
EMBASSY (GB) 1967
dir. Montgomery Tully
V

LeMay, A.
Searchers, The
Harper

WAR (US) 1956 dir. John Ford
V

LeMay, A.
Siege at Dancing Bird, The

Unforgiven, The
UA (US) 1960 dir. John Huston
V

LeMay, A.
Useless Cowboy, The

Along Came Jones
UA (US) 1945 dir. Stuart Heisler
V

Lengyel, M.
Angel
P

PAR (US) 1937 dir. Ernest Lubitsch

Lengyel, M.
The Czarina
P

Catherine the Great
KORDA (GB) 1934 dir. Paul Czinner
V

Lennart, I.
Funny Girl
P

COL (US) 1968 dir. William Wyler
M, V

Lenz, S.
Das Feuerschiff
Various

Lightship, The
WAR (US) 1985 dir. Jerzy Skolimowski
V

Leonard, E.
Big Bounce, The
Armchair Detective Library

WAR (US) 1969 dir. Alex March

Leonard, E.
Cat Chaser
Arbor House

VESTRON (US) 1989 dir. Abel Ferrara

Leonard, E.
Glitz
Arbor House

LORIMAR (US) 1988 dir. Sandor Stern
TV(US)

Leonard, E.
Hombre
Armchair Detective Library

FOX (US) 1967 dir. Martin Ritt
V

Leonard, E.
Moonshine War, The
Doubleday

MGM (US) 1970 dir. Richard Quine

Leonard, E.
Stick
Arbor House

UN (US) 1985 dir. Burt Reynolds
V

Leonard, E.
Valdez is Coming
UA (US) 1971 dir. Edwin Sherin
V

Leonard, E.
52 Pick-Up
Avon, N.Y.

Ambassador, The
CANNON (US) 1984
dir. J. Lee Thompson
V

Leonard, E.
52 Pick-Up
CANNON (US) 1986
dir. John Frankenheimer
V

Leonard, H.
Big Birthday, The
P

Broth of a Boy
E. DALTON (Eire) 1958
dir. George Pollack

Leonard, H.
Da
P
Samuel French

FILM DALLAS (US) 1988
dir. Matt Clarke
V

Leopold, K.
When we Ran

Moving Targets
ACADEMY (Aust) 1987
dir. Chris Langman
V

LePere, G.
Never Pass This Way Again
Adler & Adler
Dark Holiday
ORION TV (US) 1989 dir. Lou Antonio
TV(US)

Lerner, A. J.
On a Clear Day you can See Forever
P
PAR (US) 1970 dir. Vincente Minnelli
M, V

Lerner, A. J. and Loewe, F.
Brigadoon
P
Sam Fox (London)
MGM (US) 1954 dir. Vincente Minnelli
M, V

Lerner, A. J. and Loewe, F.
Camelot
P
Random House
WAR (US) 1967 dir. Joshua Logan
M, V

Lerner, A. J. and Loewe, F.
Paint Your Wagon
P
Coward-McCann
PAR (US) 1969 dir. Joshua Logan
M, V

Leroux, G.
Phantom of the Opera, The
Various
UN (US) 1943 dir. Arthur Lubin
V
UI (GB) 1962 dir. Terence Fisher
HALMI PRODS (US) 1983
dir. Robert Markowitz
TV(US)
21ST (US) 1989 dir. Dwight H. Little
SABAN/SCHERICK PRODS (US/Fr)
1990 dir. Tony Richardson
TV(US/Fr)

Leslie, D.
Polonaise
Song to Remember, A
COL (US) 1944 dir. Charles Vidor
V

Leslie, D. S.
In My Solitude
Two Left Feet
BL (GB) 1963 dir. Roy Baker

Leslie, D. S.
Two Gentlemen Sharing
PAR (GB) 1969 dir. Ted Kotcheff

Leslie, R. F.
Bears and I, The
DISNEY (US) 1974
dir. Bernard McEveety
Ch, V

Leslie-Melville, J. and Leslie-Melville, B.
Raising Daisy Rothschild
Simon & Schuster
Last Giraffe, The
WESTFALL PRODS (US) 1979
dir. Jack Couffer
TV(US)

Lessing, D.
Grass is Singing, The
Popular Library
MAINLINE (Zam/Swe) 1981
dir. Michael Raeburn

Lessing, D.
Memoirs of a Survivor
Knopf
EMI (GB) 1981 dir. David Gladwell
V

Lester, E.
Two Seconds
WAR (US) 1932 dir. Mervyn LeRoy

Leven, J.
Creator
Coward, McCann & Geoghegan
UN (US) 1985 dir. Ivan Passer
V

Levenkron, S.
Best Little Girl in the World, The
Contemporary Books (Chicago)
A. SPELLING (US) 1981
dir. Sam O'Steen
TV(US)

Levi, C.
Christ Stopped At Eboli
Farrar, Straus
ART EYE (It/Fr) 1979
dir. Francesco Rosi
V

Levin, I.
Boys from Brazil, The
Random House
ITC (US/GB) 1978
dir. Franklin Shaffner
V

Levin, I.
Critic's Choice
P
Random House
WAR (US) 1963 dir. Don Weis

Levin, I.
Deathtrap
P
Random House
WAR (US) 1982 dir. Sidney Lumet

Levin, I.
Dr. Cook's Garden
P
PAR TV (US) 1971 dir. Ted Post
TV(US)

Levin, I.
Kiss Before Dying, A
Joseph
UA (US) 1956 dir. Gerd Oswald
UN (US) 1991 dir. James Dearden
V

Levin, I.
Rosemary's Baby
Random House
PAR (US) 1968 dir. Roman Polanski
V

Levin, I.
Stepford Wives, The
Random House
CONTEM (US) 1975 dir. Bryan Forbes
V

Levin, M.
Compulsion
Simon & Schuster
FOX (US) 1959 dir. Richard Fleischer

Levinson, N.
Room Upstairs, The
Simon & Schuster
M. REES (US) 1987 dir. Stuart Margolin
TV(US)

Levinson, R. and Link, W.
Prescription: Murder
P
UN (US) 1968 dir. Richard Irving
TV(US)

Levoy, M.
Alan and Naomi
Harper & Row
Triton Films (US) 1992
dir. Sterling van Wagenen

Levy, B. W.
Evergreen
P
GAU (GB) 1934 dir. Victor Saville
M

Levy, E.
Beast Within, The
Arbor House
MGM/UA (US) 1982 dir. Philippe Mora
V

Lewandowski, D.
Worth Winning
FOX (US) 1989 dir. Will Mackenzie

Lewis, A.
Gideon's Trumpet
Random House
WORLDVISION (US) 1980
dir. Robert Collins
TV(US), V

Lewis, A. H.
Lament for Molly Maguires
Molly Maguires, The
PAR (US) 1970 dir. Martin Ritt
V

Lewis, C. S.
Lion, The Witch and the Wardrobe, The
Macmillan
ITV (US/GB) 1978 dir. Bill Melendez
A, TVSe(GB/US), V

Lewis, C. S.
Prince Caspian and The Silver Chair
Silver Chair, The
BBC (GB) 1990 dir. A. Kirby
Ch, TVSe(GB)

Lewis, D.
Sexpionage: The Exploitation of Sex by Soviet Intelligence
Secret Weapons
ITC (US) 1985 dir. Don Taylor
TV(US)

Lewis, E.
Trader Horn
Library Guild of America
MGM (US) 1931 dir. W. S. Van Dyke
MGM (US) 1973 dir. Reza Badiyi

Lewis, H.
Day is Ours, This
Macdonald
Mandy
GFD (GB) 1952
dir. Alexander Mackendrick
US title: Crash of Silence, The
V

Lewis, M.
Great Balls of Fire
Quill
ORION (US) 1989 dir. Jim McBride

Lewis, O.
Children of Sanchez, The
Random House
HALL BARTLETT (US/Mex) 1978
dir. Hall Bartlett
V

Lewis, S.
Ann Vickers
RKO (US) 1933 dir. John Cromwell
V

Lewis, S.
Arrowsmith
Harcourt, Brace & World
UA (US) 1931 dir. John Ford
V

Lewis, S.
Babbit
Various
WAR (US) 1934 dir. William Keighley

Lewis, S.
Cass Timberlane
Random House
MGM (US) 1947 dir. George Sidney

Lewis, S.
Dodsworth
Harcourt, Brace & Co.
UA (US) 1936 dir. William Wyler
V

Lewis, S.
Elmer Gantry
New American Library
UA (US) 1960 dir. Richard Brooks
V

Lewis, S.
Main Street
Harcourt, Brace & World
I Married a Doctor
WAR (US) 1936 dir. Archie Mayo

Lewis, S.
Mantrap
Untamed
PAR (US) 1940 dir. George Archainband

Lewis, S.
Sparrers Can't Sing
P
Sparrows Can't Sing
WAR (GB) 1962 dir. Joan Littlewood

Lewis, T.
Jack's Return Home
Get Carter
MGM (GB) 1971 dir. Mike Hodges

Li Shu Xian
Pu Yi and I; Pu Yi's Later Life; Pu Yi's Former Life
Last Emperor, The
NKL (China) 1988 dir. Li Han Hsiang

Liddy, G. G.
Will
St. Martin's Press
Will: G. Gordon Liddy
SHAYNE (US) 1982
dir. Robert Lieberman
TV(US)

Lieber, J.
Move
FOX (US) 1970 dir. Stuart Rosenberg

Lieberman, H.
Crawlspace
David McKay
TITUS (US) 1972 dir. Joan Newland
TV(US)

Lieberson, G.
3 for Bedroom C
INT (US) 1952 dir. Milton H. Bren

Li-Eng, S.
Dark Night
GOODYEAR (Tai/HK) 1986
dir. Fred Tan

Lilar, S.
Confession Anonyme, La
Benvenuta
NI (Bel/Fr) 1982 dir. André Delvaux

Limb, S.
Up the Garden Path
GRANADA (GB) 1990 dir. David Askey
TVSe(GB)

Lincoln, V.
February Hill
Primrose Path, The
RKO (US) 1940 dir. Gregory LaCava

Lindbergh, C. A.
We
G. P. Putnam's Sons
Spirit of St. Louis, The
WAR (US) 1957 dir. Billy Wilder
V

Lindgren, A.
Mio, My Son
Viking Press
Land of Faraway, The
NORD/GORKY (Swe/USSR/Nor) 1988
dir. Vladimir Grammatikov
V

Lindgren, A.
New Adventures of Pippi
Longstocking, The
Viking Press
COL (US) 1988 dir. Ken Annakin
Ch, V

Lindner, R.
Fifty Minute Hour, The
Bantam Books
Pressure Point
UA (US) 1962 dir. Hubert Cornfield

Lindop, A. E.
I Start Counting
UA (GB) 1969 dir. David Greene

Lindop, A. E.
I Thank A Fool
Cassells
MGM (GB) 1962 dir. Robert Stevens

Lindop, A. E.
Singer Not the Song, The
Appleton-Century-Crofts
RANK (GB) 1960 dir. Roy Baker
V

Lindop, A. E.
Tall Headlines, The
GN (GB) 1952 dir. Terence Young

Lindquist, D.
Berlin, Tunnel 21
FILMWAYS (US) 1981
dir. Richard Michaels
TV(US), V

Lindsay, H.
She Loves Me Not
P
PAR (US) 1934 dir. Elliott Nugent

Lindsay, H. and Carlson, C. C.
Late Great Planet Earth, The
Zondervan (Grand Rapids, Michigan)
ENT (US) 1979 dir. Robert Amram
V

Lindsay, H. and Crouse, R.
Call me Madam
P
TCF (US) 1953 dir. Walter Lang
M

Lindsay, H. and Crouse, R.
Life with Father
P
Stein & Day
WAR (US) 1947 dir. Michael Curtiz
V

Lindsay, H. and Crouse, R.
Remains to be Seen
P
Random House
MGM (US) 1953 dir. Don Weis

Lindsay, H. and Crouse, R.
Sound of Music, The
P
Random House
FOX (US) 1965 dir. Robert Wise
M, V

Lindsay, H. and Crouse, R.
State of the Union
P
Dramatists Play Service
MGM (US) 1948 dir. Frank Capra
GB title: World and His Wife, The
V

Lindsay, J.
All on the Never-Never
Live Now, Pay Later
REGAL (GB) 1962 dir. Jay Lewis

615

Lindsay, J.
Picnic at Hanging Rock
Penguin Books
AFC (Aust) 1975 dir. Peter Weir

Lindsay, N.
Age of Consent
Laurie
COL (Aust) 1969 dir. Michael Powell
V

Lindsey, R.
Falcon and the Snowman, The
Simon & Schuster
ORION (US) 1985 dir. John Schlesinger

Linford, D.
Man Without A Star, The
Morrow, N.Y.
UI (US) 1955 dir. King Vidor
V

Ling, P. S.
Strange Tales of Liao Zhai
Chinese Ghost Story II
GORDON (China) 1990
dir. Ching Siu-Tung

Linklater, E.
Husband of Delilah
Harcourt, Brace & World
Samson and Delilah
COMWORLD (US) 1984 dir. Lee Philips
TV(US), V

Linklater, E.
Laxdale Hall
Cape
ABP (GB) 1952 dir. John Eldridge
US title: Scotch on the Rocks

Linklater, E.
Poet's Pub
J. Cape & H. Smith
AQUILA (GB) 1949
dir. Frederick Wilson

Linklater, E.
Private Angelo
J. Cape (London)
ABP (GB) 1949 dir. Peter Ustinov

Lippold, E.
House with the Heavy Doors, The
Fiancée, The
(Ger) 1984 dir. Gunter Reisch, Gunther Rucker

Lipscombe, W. P. and Minney, R. J.
Clive of India
P
Gollancz
FOX (US) 1935 dir. Richard Boleslawski

Lipsky, E.
People Against O'Hara, The
MGM (US) 1951 dir. John Sturges

Lipton, J.
Mirrors
St. Martins Press
L. HILL (US) 1985 dir. Harry Winer
TV(US)

Lispector, C.
Hour of the Star, The
Carcenet (Manchester)
RAIZ (Braz) 1987 dir. Suzana Amaral

List, J. A.
Day the Loving Stopped, The
MONASH-ZEITMAN (US) 1981
dir. Delbert Mann
TV(US)

List, S.
Nobody Makes Me Cry
Between Friends
HBO (US) 1983 dir. Lou Antonio
V

Littell, R.
Amateur, The
Simon & Schuster
FOX (Can) 1982 dir. Charles Jarrot
V

Livings, H.
Eh?
P
Dramatists Play Service
Work is a Four Letter Word
UI (GB) 1968 dir. Peter Hall

Llewellyn, R.
How Green Was My Valley
Macmillan
FOX (US) 1941 dir. John Ford

Llewellyn, R.
None but the Lonely Heart
Macmillan
RKO (US) 1944 dir. Clifford Odets
V

Llewellyn, R.
Noose
P
ABFC (GB) 1948
dir. Edmond T. Greville

Llewellyn, R.
Poison Pen
P
AB (GB) 1939 dir. Paul Stein

Llosa, M. V.
Aunt Julia and the Scriptwriter
Farrar, Straus & Giroux
Tune in Tomorrow...
CINECOM (US) 1990 dir. Jon Amiel

Llosa, M. V.
City and the Dogs, The
INCA (Peru) 1985
dir. Francisco J. Lombardi
V

Locke, W. J.
Beloved Vagabond, The
Lane
COL (GB) 1936 dir. Curtis Bernhardt

Locke, W. J.
Morals of Marcus Ordeyne, The
John Lane Co.
Morals of Marcus, The
GB (GB) 1935 dir. Miles Mander

Locke, W. J.
Shorn Lamb, The
Strangers in Love
PAR (US) 1932 dir. Lothar Mendes

Lockhart, R. B.
Reilly, Ace of Spies
Stein & Day
EUSTON (GB) 1983 dir. Jim Goddard
TVSe(GB), V

Lockhart, Sir. R. H. B.
Memoirs of a British Agent
Putnam
British Agent
WAR (US) 1934 dir. Michael Curtiz

Lockridge, R.
Raintree County
Houghton, Mifflin Co. (Boston)
MGM (US) 1957 dir. Edward Dmytryk
V

Lockwood, C. A. and Adamson, H. C.
Hellcats of the Sea
Hellcats of the Navy
COL (US) 1957 dir. Nathan Juran
V

Lodge, D.
Nice Work
Secker & Warburg (London)
BBC (GB) 1989 dir. C. Meraud
TVSe(GB)

Lodge, D.
Small World
Macmillan
GRANADA (GB) 1988
TV(GB)

Lofting, H.
Doctor Dolittle
Lippincott (Philadelphia)
FOX (US) 1967 dir. Richard Fleischer
Ch, M, V

Lofts, N.
Jassy
GFD (GB) 1947 dir. Bernard Knowles

Loftus, J.
Belarus Secret, The
Knopf
Kojak: The Belarus File
UN TV (US) 1985 dir. Robert Markowitz
TV(US), V

Logan, J. and Heggen, T.
Mister Roberts
P
Houghton, Mifflin Co. (Boston)
Ensign Pulver
WAR (US) 1964 dir. Joshua Logan

London, A. and London, L.
On Trial
L'Aveu
CORONA (Fr) 1970 dir. Costa-Gavras

London, J.
Call of the Wild
Various
UA (US) 1935 dir. William Wellman
MASSFILMS (GB/Fr/It/Ger) 1972
dir. Ken Annakin
V
FRIES (US) 1976 dir. Jerry Jameson
TV(US)

London, J.
Martin Eden
Macmillan
Adventures of Martin Eden, The
COL (US) 1942 dir. Sidney Salkow

London, J.
Mexican, The
Fighter, The
UA (US) 1952 dir. Herbert Kline
V

London, J.
Mutiny of the Elsinore
Grosset & Dunlap
ARGYLE (GB) 1937 dir. Roy Lockwood

London, J.
Sea Wolf, The
Various
FOX (US) 1930 dir. Alfred Santell
WAR (US) 1941 dir. Michael Curtiz

London, J.
Sea Wolf, The
Various
Wolf Larsen
ABP (US) 1958 dir. Harman Jones

London, J.
White Fang
Various
FOX (US) 1936 dir. David Butler
FOX (It/Sp/Fr) 1974 dir. Lucio Fulci
DISNEY (US) 1991 dir. Randal Kleiser

London, J. and Fish, R.
Assassination Bureau, The
Ameron House
PAR (GB) 1969 dir. Basil Dearden

Long, J.
Outlaw: The True Story of Claude Dallas
Morrow
Manhunt for Claude Dallas
LONDON (US) 1986 dir. Jerry London
TV(US)

Long, S. A.
Never Too Late
P
Samuel French
WAR (US) 1965 dir. Bud Yorkin

Longstreet, S.
Gay Sisters, The
Random House
WAR (US) 1942 dir. Irving Rapper

Longstreet, S.
Stallion Road
Sun Dial Press
WAR (US) 1947 dir. James V. Kern

Longstreet, S.
Wild Harvest
GN (US) 1961 dir. Jerry Baerwitz

Longyear, B.
Enemy Mine
FOX (US) 1986 dir. Wolfgang Petersen
V

Lonsdale, F.
Aren't We All?
P
Samuel French
PAR (GB) 1932
dir. Harry Lachman & Rudolf Maté

Lonsdale, F.
High Road, The
P
Collins
Lady of Scandal
MGM (US) 1930 dir. Sidney Franklin

Lonsdale, F.
Last of Mrs Cheyney, The
P
Collins
MGM (US) 1929 dir. Sidney Franklin
MGM (US) 1937
dir. Richard Boleslawski

Lonsdale, F.
Last of Mrs. Cheyney, The
P
Collins
Law and the Lady, The
MGM (US) 1951 dir. Edwin H. Knopf

Lonsdale, F.
On Approval
P
Samuel French
FOX (GB) 1944 dir. Clive Brook
V

Lonzeiro, J.
Infancia dos Martos
Pixote
UNIFILM (Port) 1981
dir. Hector Babenco
V

Loos, A.
But Gentlemen Marry Brunettes
Boni & Liveright
Gentlemen Marry Brunettes
UA (US) 1955 dir. Richard Sale

Loos, A.
Gentlemen Prefer Blondes
Boni & Liveright
FOX (US) 1953 dir. Howard Hawks
V

Loraine, P.
Break in the Circle
Morrow
EXC (GB) 1955 dir. Val Guest

Loraine, P.
Day of the Arrow
Collins
Eye of the Devil
MGM (GB) 1967 dir. J. Lee Thompson

Loraine, P.
Dublin Nightmare
RANK (GB) 1957 dir. John Pomeroy

Lorca, F. G.
Blood Wedding
P
Samuel French
LIBRA (Sp) 1981 dir. Carlos Saura
V

Lorca, F. G.
House of Bernada Alba, The
P
Losada (Buenos Aires)
GALA (Sp) 1990 dir. Mario Camus
CHANNEL 4 (GB) 1992
dir. Nuria Espert and StuartBurge
TV(GB)

Lord, G.
Fortress
HBO PREM (US) 1985
dir. Arch Nicholson
TV(US), V

Lord, W.
Night to Remember, A
Ameron House
RANK (GB) 1957 dir. Roy Ward Baker
V

Loriot, N.
Cri, Un
B. Grasset (Paris)
No Time for Breakfast
BOURLA (Fr) 1980
dir. Jean-Louis Bertucelli

Lortz, R.
Children of the Night
P
Voices
HEMDALE (GB) 1973
dir. Kevin Billington
V

Loss, L. B.
Stranger, The
Warner Books
Zandy's Bride
WAR (US) 1974 dir. Jan Troell

Lothar, E.
Angel with the Trumpet, The
Doubleday
BL (GB) 1949 dir. Anthony Bushell

Lothar, E.
Clairvoyant, The
Secker
GB (GB) 1935 dir. Maurice Elvey
V

Lothar, E.
Mills of God, The
Secker
Act of Murder, An
UN (US) 1948 dir. Michael Gordon

Lothar, R. and Adler, H.
Red Cat, The
P
Folies Bergère
FOX (US) 1935 dir. Roy del Ruth
GB title: Man from the Folies Bergère, The

Lott, M.
Last Hunt, The
Houghton, Mifflin Co. (Boston)
MGM (US) 1956 dir. Richard Brooks

Louys, P.
Femme et le Pantin, La
Gallimard (Paris)
Devil is a Woman, The
PAR (US) 1935 dir. Josef von Sternberg

Louys, P.
Femme et le Pantin, La
Gallimard (Paris)
That Obscure Object of Desire
GALAXIE (Fr/Sp) 1978 dir. Luis Bunuel
V

Lovecraft, H. P.
Case of Charles Dexter, The
Panther
Haunted Palace, The
AMERICAN (US) 1963
dir. Roger Corman

Lovecraft, H. P.
Color Out of Space, The
Die, Monster, Die!
AIP (US/GB) 1965 dir. Daniel Haller

Lovecraft, H. P.
From Beyond
EMPIRE (US) 1986 dir. Stuart Gordon
V

Lovecraft, H. P.
Herbert West— The Re-Animator
Bride of Re-Animator
WILDSTREET (US) 1991
dir. Brian Yuzna

Lovecraft, H. P.
Herbert West— The Re-Animator
Re-Animator
EMPIRE (US) 1985 dir. Stuart Gordon

Lovecraft, H. P.
Shuttered Room, The
Arkham House (Sauk City, Wisconsin)
Dunwich Horror, The
AMERICAN (US) 1970
dir. Daniel Haller
V

Lovecraft, H. P.
Shuttered Room, The
WAR (GB) 1967 dir. David Greene

Lovell, M.
Apple Pie in the Sky
Doubleday
Trouble With Spies, The
HBO (US) 1987 dir. Burt Kennedy
V

Lowden, D.
Bellman and True
Holt, Rinehart & Winston
HANDMADE (GB) 1987
dir. Richard Loncraine
V

Lowndes, M. B.
Lodger, The
Longmans, Green
Man in the Attic, The
FOX (US) 1953 dir. Hugo Fregonese

Lowndes, Mrs. M. B.
Letty Lynton
Benn
MGM (US) 1932 dir. Clarence Brown

Lowndes, Mrs. M. B.
Lodger, The
Longmans, Green
TWICKENHAM (GB) 1932
dir. Maurice Elvey
US title: Phantom Fiend, The
FOX (US) 1944 dir. John Brahm

Lowndes, Mrs. M. B.
Story of Ivy
Somerset Books
Ivy
UI (US) 1947 dir. Sam Wood

Lowry, M.
Under the Volcano
Lippincott (Philadelphia)
UN (US) 1984 dir. John Huston
V

Ludlum, R.
Bourne Identity, The
R. Marek Publishers
WAR TV (US) 1988 dir. Roger Young
TVSe(US)

Ludlum, R.
Holcroft Covenant, The
R. Marek Publishers
UN (GB) 1985 dir. John Frankenheimer
V

Ludlum, R.
Osterman Weekend, The
World Publishing Co.
FOX (US) 1983 dir. Sam Peckinpah
V

Ludlum, R.
Rhineman Exchange, The
Dial Press
UN TV (US) 1977 dir. Burt Kennedy
TVSe(US)

Lukas, J. A.
Common Ground
Knopf
LORIMAR TV (US) 1990
dir. Michael Newell
TVSe(US)

Lund, D.
Eric
Lippincott (Philadelphia)
LORIMAR (US) 1975
dir. James Goldstone
TV(US)

Lupica, M.
Dead Air
Villard Books
Money, Power, Murder
CBS ENT (US) 1989 dir. Lee Philips
TV(US)

Lurie, A.
War Between the Tates, The
Random House
TALENT (US) 1977 dir. Lee Philips
TV(US), V

Lyall, G.
Secret Servant, The
Viking Press
BBC (GB) 1985
TV(GB)

Lymington, J.
Night of the Big Heat
PLANET (GB) 1967 dir. Terence Fisher
V

Lyndon, B.
Amazing Dr. Clitterhouse, The
P
Samuel French
WAR (US) 1938 dir. Anatole Litvak

Lyndon, B.
Man in Half-Moon Street, The
P
PAR (US) 1944 dir. Ralph Murphy

Lyndon, B.
Man in Half-Moon Street, The
P
Man Who Could Cheat Death, The
PAR (GB) 1959 dir. Terence Fisher

Lyndon, B.
Sundown
UA (US) 1941 dir. Henry Hathaway
V

Lynn, L. and Vecsey, G.
Coal Miner's Daughter
Henry Regnery Co.
UN (US) 1980 dir. Michael Apted
V

Lynn, M.
Mrs. Maitland's Affair
Other Man, The
UN TV (US) 1970 dir. Richard Colla
TV(US)

Lyon, D.
Tentacles
Harper, N.Y.
House on Telegraph Hill, The
FOX (US) 1951 dir. Robert Wise

Lyons, A.
Castles Burning
Holt, Rinehart & Winston
Slow Burn
UN TV (US) 1986
dir. Matthew Chapman
TV(US), V

Lyons, N., and Lyons, I.
Someone is Killing the Great Chefs of Europe
Harcourt, Brace, Jovanovich
Who is Killing the Great Chefs of Europe?
WAR (US) 1978 dir. Ted Kotcheff
GB title: Too Many Chefs

Lytton, B.
Haunted and the Haunters, The
P
Farrar, Straus & Giroux
Night Comes too Soon
BUTCHER (GB) 1948
dir. Denis Kavanagh

Lytton, 1st Baron
Last Days of Pompeii, The
Various
RKO (US) 1935 dir. Merian C. Cooper,
Ernest Schoedsack
COL (US) 1984 dir. Peter Hunt
TVSe(US), V

Maas, P.
King of the Gypsies
Viking Press
PAR (US) 1978 dir. Frank Pierson
V

Maas, P.
Marie: A True Story
Random House
Marie
MGM/UA (US) 1985
dir. Roger Donaldson
V

Maas, P.
Serpico
Viking Press
PAR (US) 1973 dir. Sidney Lumet
V

Maas, P.
Valachi Papers, The
Putnam
CINEMA INT (Fr/It) 1972
dir. Terence Young
V

Macardle, D.
Thursday's Child
ABPC (GB) 1942 dir. Rodney Ackland
V

Macardle, D.
Uneasy Freehold
Uninvited, The
PAR (US) 1944 dir. Lewis Allen
V

Macaulay, D.
Cathedral
Houghton, Mifflin Co. (Boston)
UNICORN 1984
TV(GB)

McBain, E.
Blood Relatives
Random House
FILMCORD (Can/Fr) 1981
dir. Claude Chabrol

McBain, E.
Fuzz
Hamilton
UA (US) 1972 dir. Richard A. Colla
V

McBain, E.
King's Ransom, The
High and Low
TOHO (Jap) 1963 dir. Akira Kurosawa

McBain, E.
Lady, Lady, I Did It!
Simon & Schuster

Lonely Hearts
TOHO (Jap) 1982 dir. Kon Ichikawa

McBain, E.
Ten Plus One
Simon & Schuster

Without Apparent Motive
VALORIA (Fr) 1971 dir. Philippe Labro

McCall, M.
Goldfish Bowl, The
Paul

It's Tough to be Famous
IN (US) 1932 dir. Alfred E. Green

McCall, M.
Revolt

Scarlet Dawn
WAR (US) 1932 dir. William Dieterle

McCarry, C.
Deadly Angels, The

Wrong is Right
COL (US) 1982 dir. Richard Brooks
GB title: Man with the Deadly Lens, The
V

McCarthy, J. H.
Fighting O'Flynn, The
UN (US) 1949 dir. Arthur Pierson

McCarthy, J. H.
If I Were King
Heinemann
PAR (US) 1938 dir. Frank Lloyd

McCarthy, J. H.
Vagabond King, The
PAR (US) 1956 dir. Michael Curtiz
M

McCarthy, M.
Group, The
Harcourt, Brace & World
UA (US) 1966 dir. Sidney Lumet
V

McCauley, S.
Other Halves
Penguin
OVINGHAM (GB) 1985 dir. John Laing

McCoy, H.
Bad for Each Other
COL (US) 1954 dir. Irving Rapper

McCoy, H.
Kiss Tomorrow Goodbye
Random House
WAR (US) 1950 dir. Gordon Douglas
V

McCoy, H.
They Shoot Horses, Don't They?
Simon & Schuster
CINERAMA (US) 1969
dir. Sydney Pollack
V

McCracken, E.
No Medals
P

Weaker Sex, The
TC (GB) 1948 dir. Roy Baker

McCracken, E.
Quiet Wedding
P
PAR (GB) 1941 dir. Anthony Asquith

McCracken, E.
Quiet Wedding
P

Happy is the Bride
BL (GB) 1957 dir. Roy Boulting

McCracken, E.
Quiet Weekend
P

AB (GB) 1946 dir. Harold French

MacCracken, M.
Circle of Children, A
Lippincott (Philadelphia)

FOX (US) 1977 dir. Don Taylor
TV(US), V

MacCracken, M.
Lovey, A Very Special Child
Lippincott (Philadelphia)

Lovey: A Circle of Children, Part II
TIME-LIFE (US) 1978 dir. Jud Taylor
TV(US), V

McCrum, R.
In the Secret State
Simon & Schuster

BBC (GB) 1985
TV(GB)

McCullers, C.
Ballad of the Sad Café, The
Houghton, Mifflin Co. (Boston)

MERCHANT IVORY/HOBO (US/GB)
1991 dir. Simon Callow

McCullers, C.
Heart is a Lonely Hunter, The
Houghton, Mifflin Co. (Boston)

WAR (US) 1968 dir. Robert Ellis Miller
V

McCullers, C.
Member of the Wedding, The
Houghton, Mifflin Co. (Boston)

COL (US) 1952 dir. Fred Zinnemann

McCullers, C.
Reflections in a Golden Eye
Houghton, Mifflin Co. (Boston)

WAR (US) 1967 dir. John Huston
V

McCulley, J.
Curse of Capistrano, The
Grosset, N.Y.

Mark of the Renegade
UI (US) 1951 dir. Hugo Fregonese
FOX (US) 1974 dir. Don McDougall
TV(US)

McCulley, J.
Curse of Capistrano, The
Grosset, N.Y.

Mark of Zorro, The
FOX (US) 1940 dir. Rouben Mamoulian
V

McCullough, C.
Indecent Obsession, An
Harper & Row

PBL (Aus) 1985 dir. Lex Marinos
V

McCullough, C.
Thorn Birds, The
Harper & Row

WAR (US) 1979 dir. Daryl Duke
TVSe(US)

McCunn, R. L.
Thousand Pieces of Gold
Design Enterprises of San Francisco
(SanFrancisco,California)

AM PLAY (US) 1990 dir. Nancy Kelly

McCutcheon, G. B.
Brewster's Millions
H. S Stone & Co. (Chicago)

UA (US) 1945 dir. Allan Dwan
BRITISH & DOMINION (GB) 1935
dir. Thornton Freeland
UN (US) 1985 dir. Walter Hill
V

McCutcheon, G. B.
Brewster's Millions
H. S. Stone & Co. (Chicago)

Three on a Spree
UA (GB) 1961 dir. Sidney J. Furie

McCutcheon, H.
To Dusty Death

Pit of Darkness
BUTCHER (GB) 1961
dir. Lance Comfort

MacDermot, G., Ragni, G. and Rado, J.
Hair
P
Pocket Books
UA (US) 1979 dir. Milos Forman
M, V

Macdonald, B.
Egg and I, The
Lippincott (Philadelphia)
UN (US) 1947 dir. Chester Erskine
V

McDonald, G.
Fletch
Bobbs-Merrill (Indianapolis)
UIP (US) 1985 dir. Michael Ritchie
V

McDonald, G.
Running Scared
PAR (GB) 1972 dir. David Hemmings
V

MacDonald, J. D.
Condominium
Lippincott (Philadelphia)
UN TV (US) 1980 dir. Sidney Hayers
TVSe(US)

MacDonald, J. D.
Darker than Amber
Lippincott (Philadelphia)
FOX (US) 1970 dir. Robert Clouse

MacDonald, J. D.
Empty Copper Sea, The
Lippincott (Philadelphia)
Travis McGee
HAJENO (US) 1983
dir. Andrew V. McLaglen
TV(US)

MacDonald, J. D.
Executioners, The
Simon & Schuster
Cape Fear
UI (US) 1962 dir. J. Lee Thompson
V
UN (US) 1991 dir. Martin Scorsese

MacDonald, J. D.
Girl, The Gold Watch and Everything, The
PAR TV (US) 1980 dir. William Wiard
TV(US)

MacDonald, J. D.
Linda
UN TV (US) 1973 dir. Jack Smight
TV(US)

Macdonald, J. P.
Taint of the Tiger
Pan
Mantrap
PAR (US) 1961 dir. Edmond O'Brien

MacDonald, P.
Escape
Doubleday
Nightmare
UN (US) 1942 dir. Tim Whelan

MacDonald, P.
List of Adrian Messenger, The
Penguin
UI (US) 1963 dir. John Huston
V

MacDonald, P.
Nursemaid Who Disappeared, The
WAR (GB) 1939 dir. Arthur Woods

MacDonald, P.
Patrol
Collins
Lost Patrol
RKO (US) 1934 dir. John Ford

MacDonald, P.
Twenty-Three Paces to Baker Street
FOX (US) 1956 dir. Henry Hathaway

MacDonald, P.
X vs Rex
Hour of Thirteen, The
MGM (GB) 1952 dir. Harold French

MacDonald, P.
X vs. Rex
Mystery of Mr. X, The
MGM (US) 1934 dir. Edgar Selwyn

MacDonald, R.
Blue City
Hill & Co. (Boston)
PAR (US) 1986 dir. Michelle Manning

Macdonald, R.
Drowning Pool, The
Fontana
WAR (US) 1975 dir. Stuart Rosenberg
V

Macdonald, R.
Moving Target, The
Knopf
Harper
WAR (US) 1966 dir. Jack Smight
GB title: Moving Target, The
V

Macdonald, R.
Three Roads, The
Double Negative
QUADRANT (Can) 1980
dir. George Bloomfield

MacDonald, R.
Underground Man, The
Knopf
PAR TV (US) 1974 dir. Paul Wendkos
TV(US)

McDonald, R.
1915
G. Braziller
BBC (GB/Australia) 1983
dir. Chris Thomson
TVSe (Aust/GB)

McDonough, J. R.
Platoon Leader
Presidio Press (Novato, California)
CANNON (US) 1988 dir. Aaron Norris
V

MacDougall, R.
Escapade
P
Constable
EROS (GB) 1955 dir. Philip Leacock

MacDougall, R.
Gentle Gunman, The
P
Elek
GFD (GB) 1952 dir. Basil Dearden

MacDougall, R.
To Dorothy, A Son
P
Samuel French
BL (GB) 1954 dir. Muriel Box
US title: Cash on Delivery

McEnroe, R. E.
Silver Whistle, The
P
Mr. Belvedere Rings the Bell
FOX (US) 1951 dir. Henry Koster

McEvoy, C.
Likes of 'er, The
Sally in our Alley
ABP (GB) 1931 dir. Maurice Elvey

McEwan, I.
Comfort of Strangers, The
Simon & Schuster
SOVEREIGN (US/It) 1990
dir. Paul Schrader

McFadden, C.
Serial
Knopf
PAR (US) 1980 dir. Bill Persky
V

McGill, A.
Yea, Yea, Yea
Press for Time
RANK (GB) 1966 dir. Robert Asher
V

McGinley, P.
Bogmail
Ticknor & Fields
Murder in Eden
BBC (GB) 1991 dir. Nicholas Renton
TV(GB)

McGinley, P.
Goosefoot
Fantasist, The
BLUE DOLPHIN (Ire) 1987
dir. Robin Hardy

McGinniss, J.
Blind Faith
Thorndike Press (Thorndike, Maine)
NBC (US) 1990 dir. Paul Wendkos
TVSe(US)

McGinniss, J.
Fatal Vision
Putnam
NBC ENT (US) 1984 dir. David Greene
TVSe(US), V

McGivern, W. P.
Big Heat, The
Dodd, Mead
COL (US) 1953 dir. Fritz Lang
V

McGivern, W. P.
Caper of the Golden Bulls, The
Dodd, Mead
EMBASSY (US) 1966 dir. Russel Rouse
GB title: Carnival of Thieves
V

McGivern, W. P.
Darkest Hour
Collins
Hell on Frisco Bay
WAR (US) 1955 dir. Frank Tuttle
V

McGivern, W. P.
Night of the Juggler
Putnam
COL (US) 1980 dir. Robert Butler
V

McGivern, W. P.
Rogue Cop
Dodd, Mead
MGM (US) 1954 dir. Roy Rowland

McGivern, W.
Odds Against Tomorrow
UA (US) 1959 dir. Robert Wise

McGovern, J.
Fraulein
Calder
FOX (US) 1957 dir. Henry Koster

McGrady, M.
Motel Tapes, The
Talking Walls
NEW WORLD (US) 1987
dir. Stephen Verona
V

McGrath, J.
Blood Red Roses
CHANNEL 4 (GB) 1987
TVSe(GB)

McGrath, J.
Events whilst Guarding the Bofors Gun
P
Methuen
Bofors Gun, The
RANK (GB) 1968 dir. Jack Gold

McGuane, T.
Sporting Club, The
Simon & Schuster
AVCO (US) 1971 dir. Larry Peerce
V

McGuane, T.
92 in the Shade
Farrar, Straus & Giroux
UA (US) 1975 dir. Thomas McGuane
V

McGuire, W. A. and Bolton,
G.
Rosalie
P
MGM (US) 1937 dir. W. S. Van Dyke
M, V

McHugh, J.
Minute's Wait, A
Rising of the Moon
WAR (Ire) 1957 dir. John Ford

McIlvaine, J.
It Happens Every Thursday
McRae-Smith
UN (US) 1953 dir. Joseph Pevney

McIlvanney, W.
Big Man, The
Morrow
PALACE (GB) 1990 dir. David Leland

MacIlwraith, W.
Anniversary, The
P
Samuel French
WAR (GB) 1968 dir. Roy Ward Baker

McInerney, J.
Bright Lights, Big City
Vintage Contemporaries
MGM/UA (US) 1988 dir. James Bridges
V

MacInnes, C.
Absolute Beginners
Farrar, Straus & Giroux
VIRGIN (GB) 1985 dir. Julien Temple
V

MacInnes, H.
Above Suspicion
Little, Brown (Boston)
MGM (US) 1943 dir. Richard Thorpe

MacInnes, H.
Assignment in Brittany
Little, Brown (Boston)
MGM (US) 1943 dir. Jack Conway

MacInnes, H.
Salzburg Connection, The
Harcourt, Brace & World
FOX (US) 1972 dir. Lee H. Katzin
V

McInnes, H.
Venetian Affair, The
Harcourt, Brace & World
MGM (US) 1966 dir. Jerry Thorpe

McKay, C.
Banjo
Big Fella
FORTUNE (GB) 1937 dir. J. E. Wills

Macken, W.
Flight of the Doves
Macmillan
COL (US) 1971 dir. Ralph Nelson
V

McKenna, M.
I Was a Spy
Jarrolds
GAU (GB) 1933 dir. Victor Saville

McKenna, M.
Lancer Spy
FOX (US) 1937 dir. Gregory Ratoff

McKenna, R.
Sand Pebbles, The
Harper & Row
FOX (US) 1966 dir. Robert Wise
V

McKenney, R.
My Sister Eileen
Harcourt, Brace & World
COL (US) 1942 dir. Alexander Hall

MacKenzie, D.
Moment of Danger
ABP (GB) 1960 dir. Laslo Benedek

Mackenzie, D.
Nowhere to Go
EAL (GB) 1958 dir. Seth Holt

MacKenzie, Sir C.
Carnival
Various
RANK (GB) 1946 dir. Stanley Haynes

Mackenzie, Sir C.
Carnival
Various
Dance Pretty Lady
BI (GB) 1932 dir. Anthony Asquith

Mackenzie, Sir C.
Rockets Galore
RANK (GB) 1958 dir. Michael Ralph
US title: Mad Little Island

Mackenzie, Sir C.
Sylvia Scarlett
RKO (US) 1935 dir. George Cukor
V

Mackenzie, Sir C.
Whisky Galore
EAL (GB) 1948
dir. Alexander MacKendrick
US title: Tight Little Island
V

Mackie, P.
Whole Truth, The
P
COL (GB) 1958 dir. John Guillermin

McKie, R.
Heroes, The
TVS FILMS (Aus) 1990
dir. Donald Crombie
TV(Aus)

MacLachlan, P.
Sarah, Plain and Tall
Harper & Row
SELF (US) 1991 dir. Glenn Jordan
TV(US)

MacLaine, S.
Out on a Limb
Bantam Books
ABC (US) 1987 dir. Robert Butler
TVSe(US)

MacLaverty, B.
Cal
G. Braziller
WAR (GB) 1984 dir. Pat O'Connor
V

MacLaverty, B.
Lamb
G. Braziller
CANNON (GB) 1985 dir. Colin Gregg

MacLean, A.
Bear Island
Doubleday
COL (Can/GB) 1979 dir. Don Sharp
V

MacLean, A.
Breakheart Pass
Doubleday
UA (US) 1975 dir. Tom Gries
V

MacLean, A.
Caravan to Vaccares
Doubleday
RANK (GB/Fr) 1974
dir. Geoffrey Reeve
V

MacLean, A.
Fear is the Key
Collins
EMI (GB) 1972 dir. Michael Tuchner
V

MacLean, A.
Force 10 from Navarone
Doubleday
COL (GB) 1978 dir. Guy Hamilton
V

MacLean, A.
Golden Rendezvous
Collins
RANK (US) 1977 dir. Ashley Lazarus
V

MacLean, A.
Guns of Navarone, The
Doubleday
COL (GB) 1961 dir. J. Lee Thompson
V

MacLean, A.
Ice Station Zebra
Doubleday
MGM (US) 1968 dir. John Sturges
V

MacLean, A.
Last Frontier
Secret Ways, The
RANK (US) 1961 dir. Phil Karlson

MacLean, A.
Puppet on a Chain
Doubleday
SCOTIA-BARBER (GB) 1970
dir. Geoffrey Reeve, Don Sharp
V

MacLean, A.
River of Death
Doubleday
CANNON (US) 1988 dir. Steve Carver
V

MacLean, A.
When Eight Bells Toll
Doubleday
RANK (GB) 1971 dir. Etienne Perier

MacLean, A.
Where Eagles Dare
Doubleday
MGM (GB) 1969 dir. Brian G. Hutton
V

MacLean, H.
In Broad Daylight
Harper & Row
NEW WORLD (US) 1991
dir. James Steven Sadwith
TV(US)

McLellan, C. M. S. and Morton, H.
Belle of New York, The
P
Samuel French
MGM (US) 1952 dir. Charles Walters
M, V

McLendon, J.
Eddie Macon's Run
UN (US) 1983 dir. Jeff Kane
V

MacLeod, R.
Appaloosa, The
Walker Press
UN (US) 1968 dir. Sidney J. Furie
GB title: Southwest to Sonora
V

MacLeod, R.
Californio, The
Curley Publishing (South Yarmouth, Massachusetts)
100 Rifles
FOX (US) 1969 dir. Tom Gries
V

McMahon, T. P.
Issue of the Bishop's Blood, The
Doubleday
Abduction of St. Anne
Q. MARTIN (US) 1975 dir. Harry Falk
TV(US), V

McMurtry, L.
Horseman, Pass By
Harper
Hud
PAR (US) 1963 dir. Martin Ritt
V

McMurtry, L.
Last Picture Show, The
Simon & Schuster
COL (US) 1971 dir. Peter Bogdanovich

McMurtry, L.
Leaving Cheyenne
Harper & Row
Lovin' Molly
GALA (US) 1974 dir. Sidney Lumet

McMurtry, L.
Lonesome Dove
Simon & Schuster
MOTOWN (US) 1989 dir. Simon Wincer
TVS(US)

McMurtry, L.
Terms of Endearment
Simon & Schuster
PAR (US) 1983 dir. James L. Brooks
V

McMurtry, L.
Texasville
Simon & Schuster
COL (US) 1990 dir. Peter Bogdanovich

McNally, T.
Frankie and Johnny in the Clair de Lune
P
Plume
Frankie and Johnny
PAR (US) 1991 dir. Garry Marshall

McNally, T.
Ritz, The
P
Samuel French
WAR (US) 1976 dir. Richard Lester
V

McNeile, H. C.
Sapper
Bulldog Drummond
GOLDWYN (US) 1929
dir. F. Richard Jones
V

McNeill, E.
9½ Weeks
Berkley Publishing
MGM/UA (US) 1986 dir. Adrian Lyne
V

McNeill, J.
Child in the House
Hodder & Stoughton
EROS (GB) 1956 dir. C. Baker Endfield

McNulty, F.
Burning Bed, The
Harcourt, Brace, Jovanovich
TA (US) 1984 dir. Robert Greenwald
TV(US), V

McNulty, J. L.
Third Avenue, New York
Easy Come, Easy Go
PAR (US) 1947 dir. John Farrow

MacOrlan, P.
Quai Des Brumes
RAB (Fr) 1938 dir. Marcel Carné

McPartland, J.
Kingdom of Johnny Cool, The
Johnny Cool
UA (US) 1963 dir. William Asher

McPartland, J.
No Down Payment
FOX (US) 1957 dir. Martin Ritt

McQueen, Dr. R.
Larry: Case History of a Mistake
Larry
TOM (US) 1974 dir. William A. Graham
TV(US), V

Macrae, A.
Traveller's Joy
P
GFD (GB) 1949 dir. Ralph Thomas

McShane, M.
Passing of Evil, The
Cassell
Grasshopper, The
NGL (US) 1969 dir. Jerry Paris

McShane, M.
Seance on a Wet Afternoon
RANK (GB) 1964 dir. Bryan Forbes
V

McSwigan, M.
All Aboard for Freedom
Snow Treasure
TIGON (US) 1968 dir. Irving Jacoby
V

McTaggart, L.
Baby Brokers, The
Born to be Sold
SAMUELS (US) 1981
dir. Burt Brinckerhoff
TV(US)

McVeigh, S.
Grand Central Murder
Houghton, Mifflin Co. (Boston)
MGM (US) 1942 dir. S. Sylvan Simon

McVicar, J.
McVicar by Himself
P
McVicar
BW (GB) 1980 dir. Tom Clegg
V

Macy, D.
Night Nurse
WAR (US) 1931 dir. William Wellman

Madden, W.
Suicide's Wife, The
Bobbs-Merrill (Indianapolis)
FAC-NEW (US) 1979 dir. John Newland
TV(US)

Maddux, R.
Orchard Children, The
Who'll Save Our Children?
TIME-LIFE (US) 1978
dir. George Schaefer
TV(US), V

Maddux, R.
Walk in the Spring Rain, A
Dell Publishing Co.
COL (US) 1969 dir. Guy Green
V

Madison, C.
Quiet Earth, The
YEL (NZ) 1985 dir. Greg Murphy
TV(NZ)

Maeterlinck, M.
Blue Bird, The
P
Dodd, Mead
FOX (US) 1940 dir. Walter Lane
FOX (US/Rus) 1976 dir. George Cukor
V

Magnier, C.
Oscar
P
TOUCH (US) 1991 dir. John Landis
V

Magnier, C.
Where Were You When the Lights Went Out?
P
MGM (US) 1968 dir. Hy Averback

Magorian, M.
Back Home
Harper & Row
DISNEY (US) 1990 dir. Piers Haggard
TV(US)

Mahan, P. W.
Doctor, You've got to be Kidding
MGM (US) 1967 dir. Peter Tewkesbury

Maher, M. and Campion, N. R.
Bringing up the Brass: My 55 Years at West Point
McKay
Long Gray Line, The
COL (US) 1955 dir. John Ford

Mahmoody, B. and Hoffer, W.
Not Without My Daughter
St. Martin's Press
MGM (US) 1991 dir. Brian Gilbert
V

Mahoney, B.
Sensitive, Passionate Man, A
FAC-NEW (US) 1977 dir. John Newland
TV(US)

Maier, W.
Pleasure Island
Wingate
Girls of Pleasure Island, The
PAR (US) 1953
dir. F. Hugh Herbert & Alvin Ganzer

Mailer, N.
American Dream, An
Dial Press
WAR (US) 1966 dir. Robert Gist
GB title: See You in Hell, Darling
V

Mailer, N.
Executioner's Song, The
Little, Brown (Boston)
FCI (US) 1982 dir. Lawrence Schiller
TVSe(US), V

Mailer, N.
Marilyn
Grosset & Dunlap
Marilyn: The Untold Story
SCHILLER (US) 1980 dir. Jack Arnold
TVSe(US)

Mailer, N.
Naked and the Dead, The
Rinehart
RKO (US) 1958 dir. Raoul Walsh
V

Mailer, N.
Tough Guys Don't Dance
Random House
CANNON (US) 1987
dir. Norman Mailer
V

Maine, C. E.
Mind of Mr. Soames, The
COL (GB) 1970 dir. Alan Cooke

Mair, J.
Never Come Back
BBC (GB) 1990 dir. Joe Waters
TVSe(GB)

Mair, J.
Never Come Back
Tiger by the Tail
EROS (GB) 1955 dir. John Gilling

Majerus, J.
Grandpa and Frank
Lippincott (Philadelphia)

Home to Stay
TIME-LIFE INC. (US) 1978
dir. Delbert Mann
TV(US), V

Major, C.
When Knighthood was in Flower
Grosset & Dunlap

Sword and the Rose, The
DISNEY (GB) 1953 dir. Ken Annakin
V

Malamud, B.
Angel Levine, The
Farrar, Straus & Giroux

UA (US) 1970 dir. Jan Kadar

Malamud, B.
Fixer, The
Farrar, Straus & Giroux

MGM (US) 1969
dir. John Frankenheimer

Malamud, B.
Natural, The
Farrar, Straus & Giroux

TRISTAR (US) 1984 dir. Barry Levinson
V

Malarek, V.
Hey, Malarek

Malarek
SVS/TELESCENE (Can) 1989
dir. Roger Cardinal

Mallett, L.
Taffin

MGM/UA (GB) 1988
dir. Francis Megahy
V

Mallory, J.
Sweet Aloes
P

Give Me Your Heart
WAR (US) 1936 dir. Archie Mayo
GB title: Sweet Aloes

Malory, Sir T.
Morte d'Arthur, Le
Various

Excalibur
ORION (US) 1981 dir. John Boorman

Malory, Sir T.
Morte d'Arthur, Le
Various

Knights of the Round Table
MGM (GB) 1954 dir. Richard Thorpe
V

Mamet, D.
Sexual Perversity in Chicago
P
Samuel French

About Last Night . . .
TRI-STAR (US) 1986 dir. Edward Zwick
V

Mamoulian, R., and Anderson, M.
Devil's Hornpipe, The
P

Never Steal Anything Small
UN (US) 1958 dir. Charles Lederer
V

Mandiargues, A. P. de
Motocyclette, La
Greenwood Press

Girl on a Motorcycle
BL (GB/Fr) 1968 dir. Jack Cardiff
US title: Naked Under Leather
V

Manhoff, B.
Owl and the Pussycat, The
P
Samuel French
COL (US) 1970 dir. Herbert Ross
V

Mankiewicz, D. M.
Trial
MGM (US) 1955 dir. Mark Robson

Mankiewicz, H. J., and Connelly, M.
Wild Man of Borneo, The
P
MGM (US) 1941 dir. Robert B. Sinclair

Mankowitz, W.
Expresso Bongo
BL (GB) 1959 dir. Val Guest
M

Mankowitz, W.
Kid for Two Farthings, A
Andre Deutsch (London)
LONDON (GB) 1955 dir. Carol Reed

Mankowitz, W.
Make me an Offer
Dutton
BL (GB) 1954 dir. Cyril Frankel

Manley, W. F.
Wild Waves
Big Broadcast, The
PAR (US) 1932 dir. Frank Tuttle

Manling, Z.
There was that Beautiful Place
Sacrifice of Youth
ART EYE (China) 1986
dir. Zhang Luanxin

Mann, A.
Judgment at Nuremberg
P
UA (US) 1961 dir. Stanley Kramer
V

Mann, H.
Professor Unrath
F. Ungar Publishing Co.
Blue Angel, The
PAR (Ger) 1930 dir. Josef von Sternberg
FOX (US) 1959 dir. Edward Dmytryk
V

Mann, K.
Mephisto
Random House
MAFILM (Hun) 1981 dir. Istvan Szabo

Mann, P.
There are Two Kinds of Terrible
Doubleday
Two Kinds of Love
CBS (US) 1983 dir. Jack Bender
TV(US), V

Mann, R.
Foreign Body
ORION (GB) 1986 dir. Ronald Neame

Mann, T.
Confessions of Felix Krull, The
Knopf
FILMAUFBAU (Ger) 1958
dir. Kurt Hoffman
V

Mann, T.
Death in Venice
Vintage Books
WAR (It) 1971 dir. Luchino Visconti
V

Mann, T.
Doktor Faustus
Knopf
SAFIR (Ger) 1982 dir. Franz Seitz

Mann, T.
Magic Mountain, The
Heritage Press
SEITZ (Ger/Fr/It) 1982
dir. Hans Geissendoerfer

Manners, J. H.
Peg O' My Heart
P
Samuel French
MGM (US) 1933 dir. Robert Z. Leonard

Mannix, D.
Fox and the Hound, The
Dutton
DISNEY (US) 1981 dir. Art Stevens
A, Ch

Mantley, J.
27th Day
COL (US) 1957 dir. William Asher

Mantley, J.
Snow Birch, The
Woman Obsessed
FOX (US) 1959 dir. Henry Hathaway

Marasco, R.
Burnt Offerings
Delacorte Press
UA (US) 1976 dir. Dan Curtis
V

Marasco, R.
Child's Play
P
Samuel French
PAR (US) 1972 dir. Sidney Lumet
V

Marceau, F.
Bonne Soupe, La
P
BELSTAR (Fr/It) 1963
dir. Robert Thomas

March, W.
Bad Seed, The
Hamilton
WAR (US) 1956 dir. Mervyn Le Roy
V
WAR (US) 1985 dir. Paul Wendkos
TV(US)

Marchand, L. and Armont, P.
Tailor in the Château
P
Love me Tonight
PAR (US) 1932 dir. Rouben Mamoulian
M

Marchant, W.
Desk Set, The
P
Samuel French
TCF (US) 1957 dir. Walter Lang
GB title: His Other Woman

Marcin, M.
Cheating Cheaters
P
UN (US) 1934 dir. Richard Thorpe

Marcus, A.
Marauders, The
MGM (US) 1955 dir. Gerald Mayer

Marcus, F.
Killing of Sister George, The
P
Samuel French
CINERAMA (US) 1967
dir. Robert Aldrich
V

Margolin, P. M.
Last Innocent Man, The
Little, Brown (Boston)
HBO (US) 1987 dir. Roger Spottiswoode
TV(US), V

Margolin, P. M.
Third Degree Burn
HBO (US) 1989 dir. Roger Spottiswoode
TV(US)

Markey, G.
Great Companions, The
Meet Me at the Fair
UN (US) 1952 dir. Douglas Sirk

Markfield, W.
To an Early Grave
Bye Bye Braverman
WAR (US) 1968 dir. Sidney Lumet

Marks, L.
Girl who Couldn't Quit, The
P
Samuel French
MON (GB) 1950 dir. Norman Lee

Markson, D.
Ballad of Dingus Magee, The
Bobbs-Merrill (Indianapolis)
Dirty Dingus Magee
MGM (US) 1970 dir. Burt Kennedy
V

Markstein, G.
Tiptoe Boys, The
Final Option, The
MGM/UA (GB) 1983 dir. Ian Sharp
V

Marlowe, C.
Edward II
P
Various
WORK TITLE (GB) 1991
dir. Derek Jarman

Marlowe, C.
Tragical History of Doctor Faustus
P
Various
Doctor Faustus
COL (GB) 1967 dir. Richard Burton,
Neville Coghill
V

Marlowe, D.
Dandy in Aspic, A.
G. P. Putnam's Sons
COL (GB) 1968 dir. Anthony Mann

Marlowe, D.
Echos of Celandine
Disappearance, The
CINEGATE (GB/Can) 1977
dir. Stuart Cooper
V

Marlowe, H.
Candle for the Dead, A
Violent Enemy, The
MONARCH (GB) 1969 dir. Don Sharp

Marquand, J. P.
B.F.'s Daughter
Viking Press
MGM (US) 1948 dir. Robert Z. Leonard

Marquand, J. P.
H.M. Pulham, Esq
Little, Brown (Boston)
MGM (US) 1940 dir. King Vidor

Marquand, J. P.
Melville Goodwin, USA
Little, Brown (Boston)
Top Secret Affair
WAR (US) 1957 dir. H. C. Potter
GB title: Their Secret Affair

Marquand, J. P.
Stopover Tokyo
Little, Brown (Boston)
FOX (US) 1957 dir. Richard L. Breen
V

Marquand, J. P.
Thank You Mr. Moto
Curtis Publishing Co. (Indianapolis)
FOX (US) 1937 dir. Norman Foster

Marquand, J. P.
Within the Tides
Little, Brown (Boston)
Late George Apley, The
FOX (US) 1946
dir. Joseph L. Mankiewicz

Marquez, G. G.
Chronicle of a Death Foretold
Knopf
ITAL/MEDIA (It/Fr) 1987
dir. Francesco Rosi
V

Marquez, G. G.
Love in the Time of Cholera
Knopf
Letters from the Park
RTVE (Cuba) 1988
dir. Tomas Guttierez Alea

Marquis, D.
Old Soak, The
P
Good Old Soak
MGM (US) 1937 dir. J. Walter Ruben

Marriott, A. and Foot, A.
No Sex Please— We're British
P
Samuel French
COL (GB) 1973 dir. Cliff Owen
V

Marrs, J.
Crossfire: The Plot that Killed
Kennedy
Carrol and Graf
JFK
WAR (US) 1991 dir. Oliver Stone

Marryat, F.
Mr. Midshipman Easy
Dutton
Midshipman Easy
ATP (GB) 1935 dir. Carol Reed
US title: Men of the Sea

Marsh, N.
Artists in Crime
Aeonian Press
BBC (GB) 1990 dir. Silvio Narizzano
TV(GB)

Marsh, N.
Died in the Wool
ITV (GB) 1978 dir. Brian McDuffie
TVSe(GB)

Marsh, N.
Opening Night
ITV (GB) 1978 dir. Brian McDuffie
TV(GB)

Marshall, B.
Vespers in Vienna
Red Danube, The
MGM (US) 1949 dir. George Sidney

Marshall, C.
Man Called Peter, A
McGraw-Hill
FOX (US) 1955 dir. Henry Koster
V

Marshall, E.
Benjamin Blake
Son of Fury
TCF (US) 1942 dir. John Cromwell

Marshall, E.
Jewel of Mahabar
Treasure of the Golden Condor
FOX (US) 1953 dir. Delmer Daves

Marshall, E.
Viking, The
Vikings, The
UA (US) 1958 dir. Richard Fleischer
V

Marshall, E.
Yankee Pasha
Farrar, Straus
UI (US) 1954 dir. Joseph Pevney

Marshall, J. L.
Santa Fe
Random House
COL (US) 1951 dir. Irving Pichel

Marshall, J. V.
River Ran out of Eden, A
Morrow
Golden Seal, The
GOLDWYN (US) 1983 dir. Frank Zuniga
V

Marshall, J. V.
Walkabout
Doubleday
FOX (Aust) 1971 dir. Nicholas Roeg

Marshall, Mrs. R.
Kitty
World Publishing
PAR (US) 1945 dir. Mitchell Leisen

Marshall, P.
Raging Moon, The
Bobbs-Merrill (Indianapolis)
MGM (GB) 1970 dir. Bryan Forbes
V

Marshall, R.
Bixby Girls, The
Heinemann
All the Fine Young Cannibals
MGM (US) 1960 dir. Michael Anderson

Marshall, S. L. A.
Pork Chop Hill
Morrow
UA (US) 1959 dir. Lewis Milestone
V

Marshall, W.
Yellowthread Street
Holt, Rinehart & Winston
YTV (GB) 1990 dir. Ronald Graham
TVSe(GB)

Martin, C.
I'll Be Seeing You
SELZNICK (US) 1944
dir. William Dieterle

Martin, G.
Living Arrows
Between Two Women
J. AVNET (US) 1986 dir. Jon Avnet
TV(US)

Martin, G. R. R.
Nightflyers
NEW CENTURY (US) 1987
dir. T. C. Blake
V

Martin, G. V.
For Our Vines Have Tender Grapes
Grosset & Dunlap
Our Vines Have Tender Grapes
MGM (US) 1945 dir. Roy Rowland

Marton, G. and Meray, T.
Catch me a Spy
Harper & Row
RANK (GB) 1971 dir. Dick Clement
V

Maryk, M. and Monahan, B.
Death Bite
Spasms
PDC (Can) 1984 dir. William Fruet

Maschwitz, E.
Balalaika
P
MGM (US) 1939 dir. Reinhold Schunzel

Masefield, J.
Box of Delights, The
Macmillan
BBC 1984 dir. Renny Rye
Ch, TVSe(GB), V

Mason, A. E. W.
At the Villa Rose
Hodder & Stoughton
AB (GB) 1939 dir. Walter Summers
US title: House of Mystery

Mason, A. E. W.
Drum, The
UA (GB) 1938 dir. Zoltan Korda
US title: Drums

Mason, A. E. W.
Fire Over England
Hodder & Stoughton
UA (GB) 1937 dir. William K. Howard
V

Mason, A. E. W.
Four Feathers, The
Doubleday
Storm over the Nile
GFD (GB) 1955 dir. Terence Young
V

Mason, A. E. W.
Four Feathers, The
Macmillan
PAR (US) 1929 dir. Lothar Mendes
UA (GB) 1939 dir. Zoltan Korda
V
ROSEMONT (GB) 1978 dir. Don Sharp
TV(GB), V

Mason, A. E. W.
House of the Arrow, The
C. Scribners Sons
AB (GB) 1930 dir. Leslie Hiscott
AB (GB) 1940 dir. Harold French
ABP (GB) 1953 dir. Michael Anderson

Mason, B. A.
In Country
Harper & Row
WAR (US) 1989 dir. Norman Jewison
V

Mason, H.
Photo Finish
Joseph
Follow that Horse!
WAR (GB) 1959 dir. Alan Bromly

Mason, R.
Shadow and the Peak, The
Macmillan
Passionate Summer, The
RANK (US) 1958 dir. Rudolph Cartier

Mason, R.
Wind Cannot Read, The
RANK (GB) 1958 dir. Ralph Thomas

Mason, R.
World of Suzie Wong, The
PAR (GB) 1960 dir. Richard Quine

Massie, C.
Corridor of Mirrors
GFD (GB) 1948 dir. Terence Young

Massie, C.
Pity my Simplicity
Methuen
Love Letters
PAR (US) 1945 dir. William Dieterle

Massie, R. K.
Nicholas and Alexandra
Atheneum
COL (GB) 1971 dir. Franklin Schaffner
V

Massie, R. K.
Peter the Great
Knopf
NBC ENT (US) 1986
dir. Marvin J. Chomsky,
Lawrence Shiller
TVSe(US)

Masters, J.
Bhowani Junction
Viking Press
MGM (GB) 1955 dir. George Cukor

Masters, J.
Deceivers, The
Viking Press
MERCHANT IVORY (GB/Ind) 1988
dir. Nicholas Meyer

Masterson, W.
All Through the Night
W. H. Allen

Cry in the Night, A
WAR (US) 1956 dir. Frank Tuttle
V

Masterson, W.
Badge of Evil

Touch of Evil
UN (US) 1958 dir. Orson Welles
V

Masterson, W.
Death of Me Yet, The
A. SPELLING (US) 1971
dir. John Llewellyn Moxey
TV(US)

Masterson, W.
Evil Come, Evil Go

Yellow Canary, The
FOX (US) 1963 dir. Buzz Kulik

Masterson, W.
711— Officer Needs Help

Warning Shot
PAR (US) 1966 dir. Buzz Kulik

Masterton, G.
Manitou
Pinnacle, N.Y.

ENT (US) 1978 dir. William Girdler
V

Mastrosimone, W.
Extremities
P
Samuel French

ATLANTIC (US) 1986
dir. Robert M. Young
V

Mastrosimone, W.
Nanawatai
P
Samuel French

Beast, The
COL (US) 1988 dir. Kevin Reynolds

Mather, A.
Leopard in the Snow
Mills & Boon

ANGLO-CAN (GB/Can) 1977
dir. Gerry O'Hara
V

Matheson, R.
Beardless Warriors
Little, Brown (Boston)

Young Warriors
UN (US) 1966 dir. John Peyser
V

Matheson, R.
Bid Time Return

Somewhere in Time
UN (US) 1980 dir. Jeannot Szwarc
V

Matheson, R.
Hell House
Corgi

Legend of Hell House, The
FOX (GB) 1973 dir. John Hough
V

Matheson, R.
I Am Legend
Bantam, N.Y.

Last Man on Earth, The
AIP (US/It) 1964 dir. Sidney Salkow

Matheson, R.
I Am Legend

Omega Man, The
WAR (US) 1971 dir. Boris Sagal
V

Matheson, R.
Ride the Nightmare

Cold Sweat
CORONA/FAIRFILM (It/Fr) 1974
dir. Terence Young
V

Matheson, R.
Shrinking Man, The
Gregg Press

Incredible Shrinking Man, The
UN (US) 1957 dir. Jack Arnold
V

Matthiessen, P.
At Play in the Fields of the Lord
Bantam Books

UN (US) 1991 dir. Hector Babenco

Maugham, R.
Line on Ginger
Chapman & Hall

Intruder, The
BL (GB) 1953 dir. Guy Hamilton
V

Maugham, R.
Rough and the Smooth, The
Harcourt, Brace

MGM (GB) 1959 dir. Robert Siodmak
US title: Portrait of a Sinner

Maugham, R.
Servant, The
WAR (GB) 1963 dir. Joseph Losey
V

Maugham W. S.
Adorable Julia

ETOILE (Austria/Fr) 1962
dir. Alfred Weidenmann
GB title: Seduction of Julia, The

Maugham, W. S.
Ant and the Grasshopper, The;
Winter Cruise; Gigolo and Gigolette
Heinemann

Encore
GFD (GB) 1951 dir. Harold French, Pat
Jackson, Anthony Pellissier
V

Maugham, W. S.
Ashenden
Doubleday

Secret Agent, The
(GB) 1936 dir. Alfred Hitchcock
V

Maugham, W. S.
Christmas Holiday
Doubleday

UN (US) 1944 dir. Robert Siodmak

Maugham, W. S.
Facts of Life, The; Alien Corn, The;
Kite, The; Colonel's Lady, The
Doubleday

Quartet
GFD (GB) 1948
dir. Ralph Smart/Harold French/
Arthur Crabtree/Ken Annakin
V

Maugham, W. S.
Home and Beauty
P
Doubleday

Three for the Show
COL (US) 1955 dir. H. C. Potter
M

Maugham, W. S.
Home and Beauty
P
Doubleday

Too Many Husbands
COL (US) 1940 dir. Wesley Ruggles
GB title: My Two Husbands

Maugham, W. S.
Hour Before the Dawn, The
Doubleday

PAR (US) 1944 dir. Frank Tuttle

Maugham, W. S.
Letter, The
P
George H. Doran Co.

Unfaithful, The
WAR (US) 1947 dir. Vincent Sherman

Maugham, W. S.
Letter, The
P
George H. Doran Co.
PAR (US) 1929 dir. Jean de Limur
WAR (US) 1940 dir. William Wyler
V
WAR (US) 1982 dir. John Erman
TV(US)

Maugham, W. S.
Moon and Sixpence, The
Doubleday
UA (US) 1942 dir. Albert Lewin

Maugham, W. S.
Narrow Corner
Doubleday
WAR (US) 1933 dir. Alfred E. Green

Maugham, W. S.
Of Human Bondage
Doubleday
RKO (US) 1934 dir. John Cromwell
WAR (US) 1946 dir. Edmund Goulding
MGM (GB) 1964 dir. Henry Hathaway
V

Maugham, W. S.
Our Betters
P
Heinemann (London)
RKO (US) 1933 dir. George Cukor

Maugham, W. S.
Painted Veil, The
G. H. Doran
MGM (US) 1934
dir. Richard Boleslawski

Maugham, W. S.
Painted Veil, The
Heinemann
Seventh Sin, The
MGM (US) 1957 dir. Ronald Neame

Maugham, W. S.
Rain
P
Heinemann
UA (US) 1932 dir. Lewis Milestone
V

Maugham, W. S.
Rain
Doubleday
Miss Sadie Thompson
COL (US) 1953 dir. Curtis Bernhardt
V

Maugham, W. S.
Razor's Edge, The
Heinemann
FOX (US) 1946 dir. Edmund Goulding
V
COL (US) 1984 dir. John Byrum

Maugham, W. S.
Sacred Flame, The
P
Doubleday
WAR (US) 1929 dir. Archie Mayo

Maugham, W. S.
Sacred Flame, The
P
Doubleday
Right to Live, The
WAR (US) 1935 dir. William Keighley
GB title: Sacred Flame, The

Maugham, W. S.
Stories
Flotsam and Jetsam
ATV (GB) 1960
TV(GB)

Maugham, W. S.
Verge, The; Mr Knowall; Sanitorium
Doubleday
Trio
GFD (GB) 1950
dir. Ken Annakin/Harold French
V

Maugham, W. S.
Vessel of Wrath
Doubleday
PAR (GB) 1938 dir. Erich Pommer
US title: Beachcomber, The

Maugham, W.S.
Vessel of Wrath
Beachcomber, The
GFD (GB) 1954 dir. Muriel Box

Maurette, M. and Bolton, G.
Anastasia
P
Samuel French
FOX (GB) 1956 dir. Anatole Litvak
V
COMPASS (US) 1967
dir. George Schaefer
TV(US)

Mauriac, F.
Thérèse Desqueyroux
B. Grasset (Paris)
Thérèse
GALA (Fr) 1964 dir. Georges Franju

Maurois, A.
Edward VII and his Times
Entente Cordiale
FLORA (Fr) 1939 dir. Marcel l'Herbier

Maury, A.
Till We Meet Again
P
PAR (US) 1944 dir. Frank Borzage

Maxfield, H. S.
Legacy of a Spy
Harper
Double Man, The
WAR (GB) 1967 dir. Franklin Schaffner
V

Maxim, H. P.
Genius in the Family, A
Harper
So Goes my Love
UN (US) 1946 dir. Frank Ryan
GB title: Genius in the Family, A

Maxwell, G.
Ring of Bright Water
Dutton
RANK (GB) 1968 dir. Jack Couffer
V

Mayer, E. J.
Firebrand
P
Samuel French
Affairs of Cellini, The
FOX (US) 1934 dir. Gregory La Cava

Maynard, N.
This is My Street
WAR (GB) 1963 dir. Sidney Hayers

Mayo, J.
Hammerhead
Heinemann
COL (GB) 1968 dir. David Miller

Mayse, A.
Desperate Search
Harrap
MGM (US) 1952 dir. Joseph Lewis

Mead, S.
How to Succeed in Business Without Really Trying
Simon & Schuster
UA (US) 1967 dir. David Swift
M

Meade, M.
Stealing Heaven
Morrow
FILM DALLAS (GB/Yugo) 1989
dir. Clive Donner
V

Mearson, L.
Lillian Day
P

Our Wife
COL (US) 1941 dir. John M. Stahl

Medoff, M.
Children of a Lesser God
P
Dramatists Play Service
PAR (US) 1986 dir. Randa Haines
V

Mee, Jr., C. L.
Seizure

Seizure: The Story of Kathy Morris
JOZAK (US) 1980 dir. Gerald Isenberg
TV(US)

Meehan, T.
Annie
P
Macmillan
COL (US) 1982 dir. John Huston
M, V

Meins, J.
Murder in Little Rock
St. Martin's Press

Seduction in Travis County, A
NEW WORLD (US) 1991
dir. George Kaczender
TV(US)

Meldal-Johnson, T.
Always

Déjà Vu
CANNON (GB) 1985
dir. Anthony Richmond

Melville, A.
Castle in the Air
P
Samuel French
ABP (GB) 1952 dir. Henry Cass

Melville, A.
Simon and Laura
P
RANK (GB) 1955 dir. Muriel Box

Melville, H.
Billy Budd
Various
AAL (GB) 1962 dir. Peter Ustinov
V

Melville, H.
Moby Dick
Various
WAR (US) 1930 dir. Lloyd Bacon
WAR (GB) 1956 dir. John Huston
V

Melville, H.
Typee
Grosset & Dunlap
Enchanted Island
WAR (US) 1958 dir. Allan Dwan
V

Mercer, C.
Rachel Cade

Sins of Rachel Cade, The
WAR (US) 1960 dir. Gordon Douglas

Mercer, D.
In Two Minds
P
Family Life
EMI (GB) 1971 dir. Ken Loach
V

Mercer, D.
Morgan – A Suitable Case for Treatment
P
BL (GB) 1966 dir. Karel Reisz
V

Mercer, J., dePaul, G., Panama. N. and Frank, M.
L'il Abner
P
PAR (US) 1959 dir. Melvin Frank
M

Mergendahl, C.
Bramble Bush
Muller
WAR (US) 1960 dir. Daniel Petrie

Merimée, P.
Carmen
Various
TRIUMPH (Fr) 1984 dir. Francesco Rosi
V

Merimée, P.
Carmen
Various
First Name: Carmen
IS (Fr) 1984 dir. Jean-Luc Godard

Merimée, P.
Carmen
Various
Loves of Carmen, The
COL (US) 1948 dir. Charles Vidor
V

Merimée, P.
Columba
Oxford University Press
Vendetta
RKO (US) 1950 dir. Mel Ferrer

Merimée, P.
Tamango
Oxford University Press (London)
SNEG (Fr) 1958 dir. John Berry

Merle, R.
Day of the Dolphin, The
Weidenfeld
AVCO (US) 1973 dir. Mike Nichols
V

Merle, R.
Weekend à Zuydcoote
Knopf
Weekend at Dunkirk
FOX (Fr/It) 1964 dir. Henri Verneuil

Merritt, A.
Burn, Witch, Burn
Devil Doll, The
MGM (US) 1936 dir. Tod Browning
V

Metalious, G.
Peyton Place
J. Messner
FOX (US) 1957 dir. Mark Robson

Metalious, G.
Return to Peyton Place
FOX (US) 1960 dir. Jose Ferrer

Metcalfe, S.
Strange Snow
P
Samuel French
Jackknife
CINEPLEX (US) 1989 dir. David Jones

Mewshaw, M.
Year of the Gun
Atheneum
TRIUMPH (US) 1991
dir. John Frankenheimer

Meyer, N.
Seven Percent Solution, The
Dutton
UN (US) 1976 dir. Herbert Ross
V

Meyer-Foerster, W.
Old Heidelburg
P
Student Prince, The
MGM (US) 1954 dir. Richard Thorpe
M

Meyers, R.
Like Normal People
McGraw-Hill
FOX TV (US) 1979 dir. Harvey Hart
TV(US)

Meynell, L.
Breaking Point, The
Collins
BUTCHER (GB) 1961
dir. Lance Comfort

Meynell, L.
House in Marsh Road, The
P
Samuel French
GN (GB) 1960 dir. Montgomery Tully

Meynell, L.
One Step From Murder
Price of Silence, The
GN (GB) 1959 dir. Montgomery Tully

Michael, J.
Deceptions
Poseidon Press
COL (US) 1985 dir. Robert Chenault
TVSe(US)

Michaels, B.
Ammie, Come Home
Meredith Press
House That Would Not Die, The
A. SPELLING (US) 1980 dir. J. L. Moxey
TV(US)

Michaels, L.
Men's Club, The
Farrar, Straus & Giroux
ATLANTIC (US) 1986 dir. Peter Medak
V

Michener, J. A.
Bridges at Toko-Ri, The
Random House
PAR (US) 1954 dir. Mark Robson
V

Michener, J. A.
Caravans
Random House
BORDEAUX (US/Iran) 1978
dir. James Fargo
V

Michener, J. A.
Centennial
Random House
UN TV (US) 1979 dir. Virgil Vogel,
PaulKrasny,Harry Falk, Bernard
McEveety
TVSe(US)

Michener, J. A.
Dynasty
PARADINE TV (US) 1976
dir. Lee Philips
TV(US)

Michener, J. A.
Hawaii
Random House
UA (US) 1966 dir. George Roy Hill
V

Michener, J. A.
Kent State: What Happened and Why
Random House
Kent State
INTERPLAN (US) 1981
dir. James Goldstone
TV(US), V

Michener, J. A.
Return to Paradise
Random House
UA (US) 1953 dir. Mark Robson

Michener, J. A.
Return to Paradise
Random House
Until They Sail
MGM (US) 1957 dir. Robert Wise

Michener, J. A.
Sayonara
Random House
WAR (US) 1957 dir. Joshua Logan
V

Michener, J. A.
Space
Random House
PAR (US) 1985 dir. Joseph Sargent, Lee Phillips
TVSe(US)

Michener, J. P.
Tales from the South Pacific
P
Macmillan
South Pacific
TODD AO (US) 1958 dir. Joshua Logan
M, V

Middleton, G. and Thomas, A. E.
Big Pond, The
P
PAR (US) 1930 dir. Hobart Henley

Miles, B.
Lock up your Daughters
P
Samuel French
COL (GB) 1969 dir. Peter Coe
V

Miles, R.
That Cold Day in the Park
COMM (Can) 1969 dir. Robert Altman
V

Milholland, R.
Submarine Patrol
FOX (US) 1938 dir. John Ford

Millar, R.
Frieda
P
EAL (GB) 1947 dir. Basil Dearden

Miller, A.
All My Sons
P
Dramatists Play Service
UI (US) 1948 dir. Irving Reis
BBC (GB) 1990 dir. Jack O'Brien
TV(GB)

Miller, A.
Crucible, The
P
Viking Press
Witches of Salem, The
FDF (Fr/Ger) 1957
dir. Raymond Rouleau

Miller, A.
Death of a Salesman
P
Dramatists Play Service
COL (US) 1951 dir. Laslo Benedek
PUNCH (US) 1985
dir. Volker Schlondorff
TV(US), V

Miller, A.
Price, The
P
Viking Press
TALENT (US) 1971 dir. Fielder Cook
TV(US)

Miller, A.
View from the Bridge, A
P
Viking Press
TRANS (Fr) 1961 dir. Sidney Lumet

Miller, A. D.
Gowns by Roberta
Lovely to Look At
MGM (US) 1952 dir. Mervyn LeRoy
M

Miller, A. D.
Gowns by Roberta
Roberta
RKO (US) 1935 dir. William A. Seiter
M, V

Miller, A. D.
Manslaughter
Dodd, N.Y.
PAR (US) 1930 dir. George Abbott

Miller, A.D.
And One Was Wonderful
Methuen
MGM (US) 1940 dir. Robert Sinclair

Miller, A. D. and Thomas, A. E.
Come out of the Kitchen
P
Samuel French
Honey
PAR (US) 1930 dir. Wesley Ruggles

Miller, A. D. and Thomas, A. E.
Come out of the Kitchen
P
Samuel French
Spring in Park Lane
BL (GB) 1948 dir. Herbert Wilcox

Miller, G. H.
Dream Monger, The
Starlight Hotel
REP (NZ) 1988 dir. Sam Pillsbury
V

Miller, H.
Quiet Days in Clichy
Grove Press
MIRACLE (Den) 1970
dir. Jens Jorgen Thorsen

Miller, H.
Tropic of Cancer
Grove Press
PAR (US) 1970 dir. Joseph Strick

Miller, I.
Burning Bridges
Putnam
LORIMAR TV (US) 1990
dir. Sheldon Larry
TV(US)

Miller, J.
That Championship Season
P
Dramatists Play Service
CANNON (US) 1982 dir. Jason Miller
V

Miller, S.
Good Mother, The
Harper & Row
TOUCH (US) 1988 dir. Leonard Nimoy
V

Miller, W.
Cool World, The
Secker & Warburg
WISEMAN (US) 1963
dir. Shirley Clarke
V

Miller, W.
Manhunter, The
UN (US) 1976 dir. Don Taylor
TV(US)

Millhauser, B. and Dix, B. M.
Life of Jimmy Dolan, The
P
WAR (US) 1933 dir. Archie Mayo
GB title: Kid's Last Fight, The

Millholland, C. B.
Napoleon of Broadway
P
Twentieth Century
COL (US) 1934 dir. Howard Hawks

Milligan, S.
Adolf Hitler — My Part in his
Downfall
Joseph
UA (GB) 1972 dir. Norman Cohen

Milligan, S. and Antrobus, J.
Bed Sitting Room, The
P
UA (GB) 1969 dir. Richard Lester

Millin, S. G.
Rhodes
Chatto & Windus (London)
Rhodes of Africa
GAU BRI (GB) 1936
dir. Berthold Viertes
US title: Rhodes

Mills, H.
Prudence and the Pill
P
FOX (GB) 1968 dir. Fielder Cook
V

Mills, J.
Panic in Needle Park, The
Farrar, Straus & Giroux
FOX (US) 1971 dir. Jerry Schatzberg

Mills, J.
Report to the Commissioner
Farrar, Straus & Giroux
UA (US) 1975 dir. Milton Katselas
GB title: Operation Undercover
V

Mills, M.
Long Haul, The
Pan
COL (GB) 1957 dir. Ken Hughes

Milne, A. A.
Dover Road, The
P
Where Sinners Meet
RKO (US) 1934 dir. J. Walter Ruben

Milne, A. A.
Four Days Wonder
Dutton
UN (US) 1936 dir. Sidney Salkow

Milne, A. A.
Michael and Mary
P
Chatto & Windus (London)
UN (GB) 1931 dir. Victor Saville

Milne, A. A.
Perfect Alibi, The
P
Samuel French
RKO (GB) 1931 dir. Basil Dean

Milne, A. A.
Winnie the Pooh
Dutton
Winnie the Pooh and the Honey Tree
DISNEY (US) 1965
dir. Wolfgang Reitherman
A, V

Minahan, J.
Great Diamond Robbery, The
Norton
Diamond Trap, The
COL TV (US) 1988 dir. Don Taylor
TV(US)

Minney, R. J.
Carve Her Name with Pride
Newnes
RANK (GB) 1958 dir. Lewis Gilbert
V

Minney, R. J.
Nothing to Lose
Time Gentlemen, Please!
ABP (GB) 1952 dir. Lewis Gilbert

Mirbeau, O.
Diary of a Chambermaid, The
B. BOGEAUS (US) 1946
dir. Jean Renoir
V

Mishima, Y.
Gogo no Eiko
Perigee Books

Sailor Who Fell From Grace With the Sea, The
FOX RANK (GB) 1976
dir. Lewis John Carlino
V

Mishima, Y.
Runaway Horses; Temple of the Golden Pavilion
Knopf

Mishima
WAR (US) 1985 dir. Paul Schrader
V

Mitchell, D.
Thumb Tripping
Little, Brown (Boston)

AVCO (US) 1972 dir. Quentin Masters
V

Mitchell, D., Mitchell, C., Ofshe, R.
Light on Synanon, The
Seaview Books

Attack on Fear
TOM (US) 1984 dir. Mel Damski
TV(US)

Mitchell, J.
Another Country
P
Samuel French

GOLD (GB) 1984 dir. Marek Kanievska
V

Mitchell, J.
Red File for Callan, A
Simon & Schuster

Callan
EMI (GB) 1974 dir. Don Sharp
V

Mitchell, M.
Gone with the Wind
Macmillan

MGM (US) 1939 dir. Victor Fleming
V

Mitchell, M.
Warning to Wantons
AQUILA (GB) 1949
dir. Donald B. Wilson

Mitchell, N. and Medcraft, R.
Cradle Snatchers
P

Let's Face It
PAR (US) 1943 dir. Sidney Lanfield

Mitchell, P.
Act of Love
Knopf
PAR TV (US) 1980 dir. Jud Taylor
TV(US)

Mitchell, W. O.
Who has Seen the Wind
CINEMA WORLD (Can) 1980
dir. Allan King

Mitford, N.
Blessing, The
Random House

Count Your Blessings
MGM (US) 1959 dir. Jean Negulesco

Mitra, N. M.
Big City, The
R. D. BANSAL (Ind) 1963
dir. Satyajit Ray

Mo, T.
Soursweet
Random House

CIC (GB) 1988 dir. Mike Newell

Moberg, V.
Emigrants, The
SVENSK (Swe) 1970 dir. Jan Troell

Modignani, S. C.
Donna D'Onore

Vendetta: Secrets of a Mafia Bride
TRIBUNE (US) 1991
dir. Stuart Margolin
TVSe(US)

Moggach, D.
To Have and to Hold
E. P. Dutton
LWT (GB) 1986
TVSe(GB)

Moiseiwitsch, M.
Sleeping Tiger, The
INSIGNIA (GB) 1954 dir. Joseph Losey

Molin, L.
Bomb, The
CHANNEL 4 (Ger) 1987
dir. H. C. Gorlitz

Molina, A. M.
Winter in Lisbon, The
JET (Sp) 1990 dir. José Antonio Zorrilla

Molnar, F.
Girl from Trieste, The
P

Bride Wore Red, The
MGM (US) 1937 dir. Dorothy Arzner

Molnar, F.
Good Fairy, The
P
R. Long & R. R. Smith

UN (US) 1935 dir. William Wyler
HALLMARK (US) 1956
dir. George Schaefer
TV(US)

Molnar, F.
Great Love
P

Double Wedding
MGM (US) 1937 dir. Richard Thorpe

Molnar, F.
Guardsman, The
P
Samuel French
MGM (US) 1931 dir. Sidney Franklin

Molnar, F.
Guardsman, The
P
Samuel French
Chocolate Soldier, The
MGM (US) 1941 dir. Roy Del Ruth
M

Molnar, F.
Liliom
P
Samuel French
FOX (US) 1930 dir. Frank Borzage

Molnar, F.
Liliom
P
Samuel French
Carousel
TCF (US) 1956 dir. Henry King
M

Molnar, F.
Olympia
P
Garden City Publishing Co. (Garden City, New York)
His Glorious Night
MGM (US) 1929 dir. Lionel Barrymore
GB title: Breath of Scandal

Molnar, F.
Olympia
P
Garden City Publishing Co. (Garden City, NY)
Breath of Scandal, A.
PAR (US) 1960 dir. Michael Curtiz and Mario Russo
V

Molnar, F.
One, Two, Three
P

UA (US) 1961 dir. Billy Wilder
V

Molnar, F.
Swan, The
P

Garden City Publishing Co. (Garden City, New York)

MGM (US) 1956 dir. Charles Vidor

Monaghan, J.
Last of the Badmen
Bad Men of Tombstone
ABP (US) 1949 dir. Kurt Neumann

Monks, J. and Finklehoffe, F. F.
Brother Rat
P

Random House, N.Y.

FOX (US) 1938 dir. William Keighley

Monks, J. and Finklehoffe, F. F.
Brother Rat
P

Random House, N.Y.

About Face
WAR (US) 1952 dir. Roy del Ruth

Monro, R.
French Mistress, A
P

French

BL (GB) 1960 dir. Roy Boulting

Monsarrat, N.
Cruel Sea, The
Knopf

GFD (GB) 1952 dir. Charles Frend
V

Monsarrat, N.
Ship That Died of Shame, The
W. Sloane Associates

RANK (GB) 1955 dir. Basil Dearden

Monsarrat, N.
Something to Hide
Morrow

AVCO (GB) 1973 dir. Alastair Reid
V

Monsarrat, N.
Story of Esther Costello, The
Knopf

COL (GB) 1957 dir. David Miller
US title: Golden Virgin, The

Montague, E. E. S.
Man Who Never Was, The
Lippincott (Philadelphia)

FOX (GB) 1955 dir. Ronald Neame

Monteilhet, H.
Return From the Ashes
Simon & Schuster

UA (US) 1965 dir. J. Lee Thompson

Montgomery, F.
Misunderstood

MGM/UA (US) 1984
dir. Jerry Schatzberg
V

Montgomery, J.
Ready Money
P

Riding High
PAR (US) 1943 dir. George Marshall
GB title: Melody Inn

Montgomery, J. H.
Irene
P

RKO (US) 1940 dir. Herbert Wilcox

Montgomery, L. M.
Anne of Green Gables
Grosset & Dunlap

RKO (US) 1934 dir. George Nicholls
SULLIVAN (GB) 1985
TVSe(GB), V

Montgomery, L. M.
Anne of Windy Willows
Harrap (London)

Anne of Windy Poplars
RKO (US) 1940 dir. Jack Hively

Montgomery, L. M.
Jane of Lantern Hill
Various

Lantern Hill
DISNEY (US) 1990 dir. Kevin Sullivan
TV(US/Can)

Monti, C. and Rice, C.
W. C. Fields and Me
Prentice-Hall (Englewood Cliffs, New Jersey)

UN (US) 1976 dir. Arthur Hiller

Moody, L.
Ruthless Ones, The

What Became of Jack and Jill?
FOX (GB) 1971 dir. Bill Bain

Moody, R.
Little Britches
Norton

Wild Country, The
DISNEY (US) 1971 dir. Robert Totten
V

Moon, L.
Dark Star

Min and Bill
MGM (US) 1930 dir. George Hill
V

Mooney, M. M.
Hindenburg, The
Dodd, Mead

UN (US) 1975 dir. Robert Wise
V

Moorcock, M.
Final Programme, The
Allison & Busby (London)

MGM-EMI (GB) 1973 dir. Robert Fuest
US title: Last Days of Man on Earth,
The
V

Moore, B.
Black Robe
Dutton

ALLIANCE (Can/Aust) 1991
dir. Bruce Beresford

Moore, B.
Catholics
Holt, Rinehart & Winston

Glazier (US) 1973 dir. Jack Gold
TV(US), V

Moore, B.
Cold Heaven
Holt, Rinehart & Winston

HEMDALE (US) 1992 dir. Nicolas Roeg

Moore, B.
Lonely Passion of Judith Hearne, The
ISLAND/HANDMADE (GB) 1987
dir. Jack Clayton

Moore, B.
Luck of Ginger Coffey, The
Little, Brown (Boston)

BL (Can/US) 1964 dir. Irvin Kershner

Moore, B.
Temptation of Eileen Hughes, The
Farrar, Straus & Giroux

BBC (GB) 1988 dir. Trevor Powell
TV(GB)

Moore, D. T.
Gymkata
MGM/UA (US) 1985 dir. Robert Clouse
V

Moore, G.
Esther Waters
Oxford University Press
WESSEX (GB) 1948 dir. Jan Dalrymple

Moore, G.
You're Only Human Once
So This is Love
WAR (US) 1953 dir. Gordon Douglas
GB title: Grace Moore Story, The

Moore, H. T.
Priest of Love
Farrar, Straus & Giroux
ENT (GB) 1981 dir. Christopher Miles
V

Moore, R.
Dubai
Doubleday
ACI (US) 1980
TVSe(US)

Moore, R.
French Connection, The
Little, Brown (Boston)
FOX (US) 1971 dir. William Friedkin
V

Moore, R.
Green Berets, The
Crown Publishers
WAR (US) 1968
dir. John Wayne/Ray Kellogg
V

Moore, R.
Spoonhandle
W. Morrow
Deep Waters
FOX (US) 1948 dir. Henry King

Moore, W. I. and Berlitz, C.
Philadelphia Experiment, The
Grosset & Dunlap
NEW WORLD (US) 1984
dir. Stewart Raffill
V

Moorehead, A.
Rage of the Vulture
Thunder in the East
PAR (US) 1951 dir. Charles Vidor

Moorhouse, F.
Americans, Baby, The; Electrical Experience, The
Coca-Cola Kid, The
CINECOM (Aus) 1985
dir. Dusan Makevejev
V

Moorhouse, F.
Everlasting Secret Family and Other Secrets, The
Everlasting Secret Family, The
FGH (Aus) 1989 dir. Michael Thornhill

Morante, E.
Arturo's Island
Knopf
MGM (It) 1962 dir. Damiano Damiani

Morante, E.
History
Knopf
SACIS (It) 1988 dir. Luigi Comencina

Moravia, A.
Appointment at the Beach
Naked Hours, The
COMPTON (It) 1964 dir. Marco Vicario

Moravia, A.
Conformist, The
Farrar, Straus & Young
CURZON (It/Fr/W.Ger) 1969
dir. Bernardo Bertolucci

Moravia, A.
Empty Canvas, The
Farrar, Straus & Cudahy
CC (It/Fr) 1964 dir. Damiano Damiani
V

Moravia, A.
Io e Lui
Farrar, Straus & Giroux
Me and Him
NC/COL (Ger) 1989 dir. Doris Dorrie

Moravia, A.
L'Attention
Woodhills, N.Y.
Lie, The
SELVAGGIA (It) 1985
dir. Giovanni Soldati

Moravia, A.
Time of Indifference
Farrar, Straus & Young
CONT (It/Fr) 1965
dir. Francesco Maselli

Moravia, A.
Two Women
CHAMPION (It/Fr) 1960
dir. Vittorio de Sica
V

Moravia, A.
Woman of Rome
Secker & Warburg (London)
MINERVA (It) 1954 dir. Luigi Zampa
V

Moray, H.
Untamed
FOX (US) 1955 dir. Henry King

Morell, D.
First Blood
Pan
ORION (US) 1982 dir. Ted Kotcheff
V

Morell, P.
Diamond Jim
Simon & Schuster
UN (US) 1935 dir. A. Edward Sutherland

Morey, W.
Kavik the Wolf Dog
Dutton
Courage of Kavik, the Wolf Dog, The
PANTHEON (US) 1980 dir. Peter Carter
TV(US)

Morgan, A.
Great Man, The
Dutton, N.Y.
UI (US) 1956 dir. Jose Ferrer

Morgan, C.
Burning Glass, The
ATV (GB) 1956 dir. Cyril Coke
TV(GB)
ATV (GB) 1960 dir. David Boisseau
TV(GB)

Morgan, C.
Choir Practice
P
Valley of Song
ABPC (GB) 1953 dir. Gilbert Gunn

Morgan, C.
Fountain, The
RKO (US) 1934 dir. John Cromwell

Morgan, G.
Albert RN
P
DIAL (GB) 1953 dir. Lewis Gilbert
US title: Break to Freedom

Morgan, J.
This was a Woman
P
FOX (GB) 1948 dir. Tim Whelan

Morgan, K. S.
Past Forgetting
Simon & Schuster
Ike
ABC (US) 1979 dir. Melville Shavelson,
Boris Sagal
TVSe(US), V

Morier, J. J.
Adventures of Hajji Baba of Ispahan
Heritage Press
Adventures of Hajji Baba, The
FOX (US) 1954 dir. Don Weis

Morland, N.
Mrs. Pym of Scotland Yard
GN (GB) 1939 dir. Fred Elles

Morley, C. D.
Kitty Foyle
Lippincott (Philadelphia0
RKO (US) 1940 dir. Sam Wood
V

Morley, R. and Langley, N.
Edward, My Son
P
Random House
MGM (GB) 1949 dir. George Cukor

Morley, W.
Gentle Ben
Gentle Giant, The
PAR (US) 1967 dir. James Neilson
Ch, V

Morpurgo, M.
Friend or Foe
V
CFF (GB) 1982 dir. John Krish
Ch, V

Morpurgo, M.
Why Whales Came
Scholastic Inc.
When the Whales Came
FOX (GB) 1989 dir. Clive Rees
V

Morrell, D.
Brotherhood of the Rose
St. Martin's Press
NBC (US) 1989 dir. Marvin Chomsky
TVSe(US)

Morrieson, H. M.
Scarecrow
OASIS (NZ) 1981 dir. Sam Pillsbury

Morrieson, R. H.
Came a Hot Friday
ORION (NZ) 1985 dir. Ian Mune
V

Morris, C.
Reluctant Heroes
P
ABP (GB) 1951 dir. Jack Raymond
V

Morris, D. R.
All Hands on Deck
TCF (US) 1961 dir. Norman Taurog
M

Morris, R.
One is a Lonely Number
MGM (US) 1972 dir. Mel Stuart

Morris, R. and Willson, M.
Unsinkable Molly Brown, The
P
Putnam
MGM (US) 1964 dir. Charles Walters
M, V

Morris, W.
Good Old Boy: A Delta Summer
Good Old Boy
DISNEY CH (US) 1988
dir. Tom G. Robertson
TV(US)

Morrison, A.
Love Flies in the Window
P
This Man is Mine
RKO (US) 1934 dir. John Cromwell

Morros, B.
My Ten Years as a Counter-Spy

Man on a String
COL (US) 1960 dir. André de Toth
GB title: Confessions of a Counterspy

Morrow, H.
Benefits Forgot

Of Human Hearts
MGM (US) 1938 dir. Clarence Brown

Morrow, H.
On to Oregon

Seven Alone
HEMDALE (US) 1974 dir. Earl Bellamy
V

Morse, L. A.
Old Dick, The
Avon Books

Jake Spanner, Private Eye
FENADY (US) 1989 dir. Lee H. Katzin
TV(US)

Mortimer, J.
Dock Brief, The
P
Samuel French

MGM (GB) 1962 dir. James Hill
US title: Trial & Error

Mortimer, J.
Paradise Postponed
Penguin

THAMES (GB) 1986 dir. Alvin Rakoff
TVSe(GB)

Mortimer, J.
Rumpole of the Bailey
Penguin

THAMES (GB) 1978
dir. Donald McWhinnie
TVSe(GB)

Mortimer, J.
Titmuss Regained
Viking Press

ANGLIA (GB) 1991 dir. Michael Friend
TV(GB)

Mortimer, P.
Pumpkin Eater, The
McGraw-Hill

BL (GB) 1964 dir. Jack Clayton

Morton, M.
Yellow Ticket, The
P

FOX (US) 1931 dir. Raoul Walsh
GB title: Yellow Passport, The

Mosel, T.
Dear Heart
Obolensky, N.Y.

WAR (US) 1964 dir. Delbert Mann

Mosley, L.
Cat and the Mice, The
Barker

Foxhole in Cairo
BL (GB) 1960 dir. John Moxey
V

Mosley, N.
Accident
Hodder & Stoughton

MON (GB) 1967 dir. Joseph Losey
V

Moss, W. S.
Ill Met By Moonlight
Macmillan

RANK (GB) 1956 dir. Michael Powell/
Emeric Pressburger
US title: Night Ambush
V

Motley, W.
Knock on Any Door
Appleton-Century-Croft

COL (US) 1949 dir. Nicholas Ray
V

Motley, W.
Let No Man Write My Epitaph
Random House

COL (US) 1960 dir. Philip Leacock

Mowat, F.
Lost in the Barrens
CBC (US/Can) 1991 dir. Michael Scott
TV(Can/US)

Mowat, F.
Never Cry Wolf
Thorndike Press (Thorndike, Maine)
DISNEY (US) 1983 dir. Carroll Ballard
V

Mowat, F.
Whale for the Killing, A
Little, Brown (Boston)
PLAYBOY (US) 1981
dir. Richard T. Heffron
TV(US), V

Moyzisch, L. C.
Operation Cicero
Readers Union (London)
Five Fingers
FOX (US) 1952
dir. Joseph L. Mankiewicz

Mozart, W. A.
Magic Flute, The
Various
Swe TV (Swe) 1974
dir. Ingmar Bergman
M, TV(Swe), V

Mozart, W. A.
Marriage of Figaro, The
Various
BBC (GB) 1990 dir. D. Bailey and
Peter Hall
M, TV(GB)

Muir, F.
What-a-Mess
Central (GB)
A, TVSe(GB)

Mukoda, K.
Buddies
TOHO/SHOCHIKU (Jap) 1990
dir. Yasuo Furuhata

Mulford, C. E.
Hopalong Cassidy
Aeonian Library
PAR (US) 1935 dir. Howard Bretherton

Mulisch, H.
Assault, The
Pantheon Books
CANNON (Neth) 1986
dir. Fons Rademakers

Mullin, C.
Error of Judgment: The
Birmingham Bombings
Chatto & Windus (London)
Investigation, The: Inside a Terrorist Bombing
GRANADA (US/GB) 1990
dir. Mike Beckham
TV(GB/US)

Mulvihill, W.
Sands of the Kalahari
PAR (GB) 1965 dir. Cy Endfield

Mundy, T.
King of the Khyber Rifles
Bobbs-Merrill (Indianapolis, Indiana)
FOX (US) 1954 dir. Henry King

Munro, J.
Innocent Bystanders
Knopf
SCOTIA-BARBER (GB) 1972
dir. Peter Collinson

Murail, E.
Staircase C
FILMS 7 (Fr) 1985
dir. Jean-Charles Tacchella
French title: Escalier C

Murata, K.
Nabe-No-Kake
Rhapsody in August
ORION (Jap) 1991 dir. Akira Kurosawa

Murdoch, I.
Bell, The
Viking Press
BBC (GB) 1982 dir. Barry Davis
TV(GB)

Murdoch, I.
Severed Head, A
COL (GB) 1970 dir. Dick Clement

Murger, H.
Scènes de la Vie Bohème
Dodd, Mead
Bohemian Life
FILMS A2/PYRAMIDE PRODS. (Fr)
1992 dir. Aki Kaurismaki

Murphy, A.
To Hell and Back
H. Holt
UI (US) 1955 dir. Jesse Hibbs
V

Murphy, D.
Sergeant, The
WAR (US) 1968 dir. John Flynn

Murphy, R.
Mountain Lion, The
Run, Cougar, Run
DISNEY (US) 1972
dir. Michael Dmytryk

Murphy, W. and Sapir, R.
Destroyer, The
Remo Williams: The Adventure Begins
ORION (US) 1985 dir. Guy Hamilton
V

Murray, J. and Boretz, A.
Room Service
P
Random House
RKO (US) 1938 dir. William A. Seiter
V

Murray, J. and Boretz, A.
Room Service
P
Random House
Step Lively
RKO (US) 1944 dir. Tim Whelan
V

Murray, M.
Jamaica Run
PAR (US) 1953 dir. Lewis R. Foster

Murray, W.
Malibu
Coward, McCann & Geoghegan
COL (US) 1983 dir. E. W. Swackhamer
TVSe(US)

Murray, W.
Sweet Ride, The
FOX (US) 1968 dir. Harvey Hart

Mus, A.
Senyora, La
ICA (Sp) 1987 dir. Jordi Cadenar

Myers, E.
Mrs Christopher
Chapman & Hall
Blackmailed
GFD (US) 1950 dir. Marc Allégret

Myrer, A.
Big War, The
Appleton-Century-Crofts
In Love and War
FOX (US) 1958 dir. Philip Dunne

Myrer, A.
Last Convertible, The
Putnam
UN TV (US) 1979 dir. Sidney Hayers,
Jo Swerling, Jr., Gus Trikonis
TVSe(US)

Myrer, A.
Once an Eagle
Holt, Rinehart & Winston

UN TV (US) 1977
dir. E. W. Swackhamer,
Richard Michaels
TVSe(US)

Nabokov, V.
Despair
Putnam

GALA (Ger) 1978
dir. Rainer Werner Fassbinder
V

Nabokov, V.
King, Queen, Knave
McGraw-Hill

WOLPER (US/Ger) 1972
dir. Jerzy Skolimowski
V

Nabokov, V.
Laughter in the Dark
Bobbs-Merrill (Indianapolis)

UA (GB/Fr) 1969 dir. Tony Richardson

Nabokov, V.
Lolita
Putnam

MGM (GB) 1962 dir. Stanley Kubrick
V

Nabokov, V.
Maschenka
Ardis (Ann Arbor, Michigan)

CLASART (GB) 1987
dir. John Goldschmidt
TVSe(GB)

Nakamura, I.
Empire of Passion

PARIS/OSHIMA (Jap) 1980
dir. Magisa Oshima

Nash, N. R.
Rainmaker, The
P
Samuel French

PAR (US) 1956 dir. Joseph Anthony

Nason, D. and Etchison, B.
Celebration Family

VS/S (US) 1987 dir. Robert Day
TV(US)

Nathan, R.
In Barley Fields
Constable

Bishop's Wife, The
RKO (US) 1947 dir. Henry Koster
V

Nathan, R.
One More Spring
Knopf

FOX (US) 1935 dir. Henry King

Nathan, R.
Portrait of Jennie
Knopf
SELZNICK (US) 1948
dir. William Dieterle
GB title: Jennie
V

Nathanson, E. M.
Dirty Dozen, The
Random House
MGM (US) 1967 dir. Robert Aldrich
V

Natsume, S.
I am a Cat
Coward, McCann & Geoghagen
TOHO (Jap) 1982 dir. Kenichi Kawa

Natsume, S.
Sorekara
Louisiana State Univ. Press (Baton
Rouge, Louisiana)
TOEI (Jap) 1987 dir. Yoshimitsu Morita

Naughton, B.
Alfie
P
Samuel French
PAR (GB) 1966 dir. Lewis Gilbert
V

Naughton, B.
All in Good Time
P
Samuel French
Family Way, The
BL (GB) 1966 dir. Roy Boulting

Naughton, B.
Spring and Port Wine
P
Samuel French
AA (GB) 1970 dir. Peter Hammond

Naughton, E.
McCabe
Macmillan
McCabe and Mrs. Miller
WAR (US) 1971 dir. Robert Altman
V

Navarre, Y.
Kurwenal
Straight from the Heart
TELESCENE (Fr) 1990 dir. Lea Pool

Naylor, G.
Women of Brewster Place, The
Viking Press
PHOENIX (US) 1989 dir. Donna Deitch
TVSe(US)

Neely, R.
Innocents with Dirty Hands
Star
FOX-RANK (Fr/It/Ger) 1975
dir. Claude Chabrol

Neely, R.
Shattered
Random House
MGM-PATHE (US) 1991
dir. Wolfgang Petersen

Neely, W.
Stand on It
Stroker Ace
UN/WAR (US) 1983 dir. Hal Needham
V

Neider, C.
Authentic Death of Hendry Jones, The
One-Eyed Jacks
PAR (US) 1961 dir. Marlon Brando
V

Neimark, P.
She Lives
ABC (US) 1973 dir. Stuart Hagmann
TV(US)

Nelson, A.
Murder Under Two Flags
Tichnor & Fields

Show of Force, A
PAR (US) 1990 dir. Bruno Barreto

Nelson, R.
Eight O'Clock in the Morning

They Live
UN (US) 1988 dir. John Carpenter
V

Nemerov, H.
Homecoming Game, The
Simon & Schuster

Tall Story
WAR (US) 1960 dir. Joshua Logan

Nemirowsky, I.
David Golder

My Daughter Joy
BL (GB) 1950 dir. Gregory Ratoff
US title: Operation X

Nesbit, E.
Five Children And It
Dell

BBC (GB) 1991 dir. Marian Fox
Ch, TVSe(GB)

Nesbit, E.
Railway Children, The
Various

MGM (GB) 1970 dir. Lionel Jeffries
Ch, V

Neufeld, J.
Lisa, Bright and Dark
S. G. Phillips

BANNER (US) 1973 dir. Jeannot Szwarc

Neumann, R.
Queen's Favourite, The
Gollancz

King in Shadow
BL (Ger) 1961 dir. Harold Braun

Nevin, D.
Dream West

SCHICK SUNN (US) 1986
dir. Dick Lowry
TVSe(US)

Newman, A.
Bouquet of Barbed Wire
Doubleday

LWT (GB) 1976 dir. Tony Wharmby
TVSe(GB), V

Newman, A.
Sense of Guilt, A

BBC (GB) 1990
TVSe(GB)

Newman, A.
Three Into Two Won't Go

UI (GB) 1969 dir. Peter Hall

Newman, B.
Battle of the VI

MAY-SEW (GB) 1958 dir. Vernon Sewell
US title: Unseen Heroes

Newman, G. F.
Sir, You Bastard

Take, The
COL (US) 1974
dir. Robert Hartford-Davis

Nexo, M. A.
Pelle the Conqueror
H. Holt & Co.

CURZON (Den/Swe) 1988
dir. Bille August

Niall, I.
No Resting Place
Knopf

ABP (GB) 1951 dir. Paul Rother

Niall, I.
Tiger Walks, A
Morrow

DISNEY (US) 1964 dir. Norman Tokar
V

Nichols, A.
Abie's Irish Rose
P
Samuel French
UA (US) 1952 dir. Edward A. Sutherland

Nichols, A.
Give me a Sailor
P
PAR (US) 1938 dir. Elliott Nugent

Nichols, B.
Evensong
P
Doubleday
GAU (GB) 1934 dir. Victor Saville

Nichols, J.
Milagro Beanfield War, The
Holt, Rinehart & Winston
UN (US) 1988 dir. Robert Redford
V

Nichols, J.
Wizard of Loneliness, The
Putnam
SKOURAS (US) 1988 dir. Jenny Bowen
V

Nichols, P.
Day in the Death of Joe Egg, A
P
Grove Press
COL (GB) 1971 dir. Peter Medak
V

Nichols, P.
National Health, The
P
Samuel French
COL (GB) 1973 dir. Jack Gold
V

Nichols, P.
Privates on Parade
P
Samuel French
HANDMADE (GB) 1982
dir. Michael Blakemore
V

Nicholson, J.
Sterile Cuckoo, The
D. McKay
PAR (US) 1969 dir. Alan J. Pakula
GB title: Pookie
V

Nicholson, K.
Barker, The
P
Samuel French
Diamond Horseshoe
FOX (US) 1945 dir. George Seaton

Nicholson, K.
Blind Spot, The
P
Taxi!
WAR (US) 1931 dir. Roy del Ruth

Nicolaysen, B.
Perilous Passage, The
Playboy Press (Chicago)
Passage, The
HEMDALE (GB) 1978
dir. J. Lee Thompson
V

Nicolson, M.
House of a Thousand Candles, The
REP (US) 1936 dir. Arthur Lubin

Nicolson, N.
Portrait of a Marriage
Atheneum
BBC (GB) 1990 dir. Stephen Whittaker
TVSe(GB)

Nicolson, R.
Mrs. Ross

Whisperers, The
UA (GB) 1966 dir. Bryan Forbes

Nielson, H.
Murder by Proxy

EXCL (GB) 1955 dir. Terence Fisher
US title: Blackout

Niggli, J.
Mexican Village
University of North Carolina Press
(Chapel Hill, North Carolina)

Sombrero
MGM (US) 1953 dir. Norman Foster

Nijinsky, R.
Nijinsky
Simon & Schuster
PAR (US) 1980 dir. Herbert Ross
V

Niklaus, T.
Tamahine
WAR (GB) 1963 dir. Philip Leacock

Niland, D'A.
Shiralee, The
Angus & Robertson (London)

MGM (GB) 1957 dir. Leslie Norman
AUS (Aus) 1987 dir. Greg Ogilvie
TV(Aus)

Niles, B.
Condemned to Devil's Island
Cape

Condemned
UA (US) 1929 dir. Wesley Ruggles

Nimmo, J.
Emlyn's Moon

HTV (GB) 1990 dir. Pennant Roberts
Ch, TVSe(GB)

Nin, A.
Henry and June
Harcourt, Brace, Jovanovich

UN (US) 1990 dir. Philip Kaufman

Nishiki, M.
Snake Head

Shadow of China
NEW LINE (US/Jap) 1991
dir. Mitsuo Yanagimachi

Noble, H.
Woman with a Sword
Doubleday

Drums in the Deep South
RKO (GB) 1952
dir. William Cameron Menzies
V

Noel, S.
House of Secrets
Deutsch

RANK (GB) 1956 dir. Guy Green
US title: Triple Deception

Nolan, F.
Algonquin Project, The
Morrow, N.Y.

Brass Target
UN (US) 1978 dir. John Hough
V

Nolan, J.
Gather Rosebuds

Isn't it Romantic?
PAR (US) 1948 dir. Norman Z. McLeod

Nolan, W. and Johnson, G.
Logan's Run
Gollancz

MGM (US) 1976 dir. Michael Anderson
V

Nord, P.
Serpent, The
LA BOETIE (Fr/It/Ger) 1974
dir. Henri Verneuil

Norden, P.
Madam Kitty
FOX (It/Fr/Ger) 1977
dir. Giovanni Tinto Brass

Nordhoff, C. B. and Hall, J. N.
Botany Bay
Little, Brown (Boston)
PAR (US) 1952 dir. John Farrow
V

Nordhoff, C. B. and Hall, J. N.
Hurricane, The
Little, Brown (Boston)
UA (US) 1937 dir. John Ford
ITC (US) 1979 dir. Jan Troell
V

Nordhoff, C. B. and Hall, J. N.
High Barbaree
MGM (US) 1947 dir. Jack Conway

Nordhoff, C. B. and Hall, J. N.
Mutiny on the Bounty
Little, Brown (Boston)
MGM (US) 1935 dir. Frank Lloyd
V
MGM (US) 1962 dir. Lewis Milestone
V

Nordhoff, C. B. and Hall, J. N.
No More Gas
Little, Brown (Boston)
Tuttles of Tahiti, The
RKO (US) 1942 dir. Charles Vidor
V

Norman, J.
Tarnsman of Gor
Ballantine Books
Gor
CANNON (US) 1989 dir. Fritz Kiersch

Norman, M.
'Night, Mother
P
Dramatists Play Service
UN (US) 1986 dir. Tom Moore
V

Norris, C. G.
Seed
UN (US) 1931 dir. John Stahl

Norris, K.
Passion Flower
MGM (US) 1930 dir. William de Mille

North, S.
Rascal, a Memoir of a Better Era
Dutton
Rascal
DISNEY (US) 1969 dir. Norman Tokar
Ch, V

North, S.
So Dear to my Heart
Doubleday
DISNEY (US) 1948 dir. Harold Schuster
V

Norton, M.
Bed-Knob and Broomstick
Harcourt, Brace
Bedknobs and Broomsticks
DISNEY (US) 1971
dir. Robert Stevenson
Ch, V

Norton, M.
Borrowers, The
Harcourt, Brace, Jovanovich
FOX TV (US) 1973 dir. Walter C. Miller
Ch, TV(US)

Novello, I.
Dancing Years, The
ABPC (GB) 1949 dir. Harold French
ATV (GB) 1979
TV(GB)

Novello, I.
Glamorous Night
P
ABP (GB) 1937
dir. Brian Desmond Hurst
M

Novello, I.
I Lived With You
P
GB (GB) 1933 dir. Maurice Elvey

Novello, I.
Truth Game, The
P
Samuel French, N.Y.
But the Flesh is Weak
MGM (US) 1932 dir. Jack Conway

Novello, I. and Collier, C.
Rat, The
P
RKO (GB) 1937 dir. Jack Raymond

O

Oates, J. C.
Lies of the Twins
Dutton
MCA TV (US) 1991 dir. Tim Hunter
TV(US)

Oates, J. C.
Where are you Going, Where have you Been?
Fawcett Publishers (Greenwich, Connecticut)
Smooth Talk
NEPENTHE (US) 1985
dir. Joyce Chopra
V

O'Brian, L.
Remarkable Mr. Pennypacker, The
P
Samuel French
FOX (US) 1958 dir. Henry Levin

O'Brien, D.
Two of a Kind: The Hillside Stranglers
New American Library
Case of the Hillside Stranglers, The
FRIES (US) 1989 dir. Steven Gethers
TV(US)

O'Brien, E.
Country Girls, The
Knopf
LONDON (GB) 1983
dir. Desmond Davis
V

O'Brien, E.
Lonely Girl, The
Cape
Girl With Green Eyes
UA (GB) 1964 dir. Desmond Davis
V

O'Brien, K.
That Lady
Heinemann (London)
FOX (GB) 1955 dir. Terence Young

O'Brien, R. C.
Mrs Frisby and the Rats of N.I.M.H.
Atheneum

Secret of N.I.M.H., The
MGM/UA (US) 1982 dir. Don Bluth
A, Ch, V

O'Brine, M.
Passport to Treason
EROS (GB) 1956 dir. Robert S. Baker

O'Casey, S.
Juno and the Paycock
P
Samuel French
BI (GB) 1930 dir. Alfred Hitchcock

O'Casey, S.
Mirror in my House
Young Cassidy
MGM (GB) 1964
dir. Jack Cardiff/John Ford

O'Casey, S.
Plough and the Stars, The
P
Samuel French
RKO (US) 1936 dir. John Ford

O'Connell, T.
Face Behind the Mask, The
P
COL (US) 1941 dir. Robert Florey

O'Connor, E.
Irishman, The
S AUST (Aust) 1978
dir. Donald Crombie
V

O'Connor, E.
Last Hurrah, The
Little, Brown (Boston)
COL (US) 1958 dir. John Ford
V
COL (US) 1977 dir. Vincent Sherman
TV(US)

O'Connor, F.
Majesty of the Law, The
Knopf

Rising of the Moon, The
WAR (Ire) 1957 dir. John Ford
V

O'Connor, F.
Wise Blood
Harcourt Brace
NEWLINE (US) 1980 dir. John Huston
V

O'Connor, G.
Darlings of the Gods
THAMES (GB) 1991
dir. Catherine Millar
TVSe(GB)

O'Dell, S.
Island of the Blue Dolphins
Houghton, Mifflin Co. (Boston)
UN (US) 1964 dir. James B. Clark
V

Odets, C.
Big Knife, The
P
Dramatists Play Service
UA (US) 1955 dir. Robert Aldrich

Odets, C.
Clash by Night
P
Random House
RKO (US) 1952 dir. Fritz Lang
V

Odets, C.
Country Girl, The
P
Dramatists Play Service
PAR (US) 1954 dir. George Seaton
V
PAR (US) 1974 dir. Paul Bogart
TV(US)

Odets, C.
Golden Boy
P
Gollancz
COL (US) 1939 dir. Rouben Mamoulian
V

Odier, D.
Voie Sauvage, La
Light Years Away
NEW YORKER (Fr) 1932
dir. Alain Tanner

Odlum, J.
Each Dawn I Die
Various
WAR (US) 1939 dir. William Keighley
V

O'Donnell, J. P.
Bunker, The
Houghton, Mifflin Company (Boston)
TIME-LIFE (US) 1981
dir. George Schaefer
TV(US)

O'Donnell, K. P., Powers, D. F. and McCarthy, J.
Johnny, We Hardly Knew Ye
Little, Brown (Boston)
TALENT (US) 1977 dir. Gilbert Cates
TV(US)

O'Donnell, L.
No Business Being a Cop
Putnam
Prime Target
MGM/UA (US) 1989 dir. Robert Collins
TV(US)

O'Donnell, Jr., L.
Deadly Force: The Story of How a Badge Can Become a License to Kill
Morrow
Case of Deadly Force, A
TELECOM (US) 1986
dir. Michael Miller
TV(US)

O'Farrell, W.
Turn Back the Clock
NBC (US) 1989 dir. Larry Elikann
TV(US)

Offenbach, J.
Tales of Hoffman, The
Various
BL (GB) 1951 dir. Michael Powell/
Emeric Pressburger
M

O'Flaherty, L.
Informer, The
Cape (London)
RKO (US) 1935 dir. John Ford
V

Ogburn, C.
Marauders, The
Harper
Merrill's Marauders
WAR (US) 1962 dir. Samuel Fuller

Ogden, D.
Halfway House, The
P
EAL (GB) 1944 dir. Basil Dearden

Ogdon, B.
Virtuoso
BBC (GB) 1988 dir. Tony Smith
TV(GB)

O'Grady, R.
Let's Kill Uncle
Longman
UI (US) 1966 dir. William Castle

O'Hara, J.
Butterfield 8
Harcourt
MGM (US) 1960 dir. Daniel Mann

O'Hara, J.
Doctor's Son, The
Random House
Turning Point of Jim Malloy, The
COL TV (US) 1975 dir. Frank D. Gilroy
TV(US)

O'Hara, J.
From the Terrace
Random House
FOX (US) 1960 dir. Mark Robson

O'Hara, J.
Pal Joey
Random House
COL (US) 1957 dir. George Sidney
M, V

O'Hara, J.
Rage to Live, A
Random House
UA (US) 1965 dir. Walter Grauman

O'Hara, J.
Ten North Frederick
Random House
FOX (US) 1958 dir. Philip Dunne

O'Hara, M.
Green Grass of Wyoming
FOX (US) 1949 dir. Louis King

O'Hara, M.
My Friend Flicka
Lippincott (Philadelphia)
FOX (US) 1943 dir. Harold Schuster

O'Hara, M.
Thunderhead, Son of Flicka
Lippincott (Philadelphia)
FOX (US) 1945 dir. Louis King

Oliphant, R.
Piano for Mrs. Cimino, A
Prentice-Hall (Englewood Cliffs, New Jersey)
EMI (US) 1982 dir. George Schaefer
TV(US)

Olivant, A.
Owd Bob
BG (GB) 1938 dir. Robert Stevenson
US title: To the Victor

'Olivia'
Olivia
FDF (Fr) 1950 dir. Jacqueline Audry

Olsen, J.
Son
Dell Publishing
Sins of the Mother
CORAPEAKE (US) 1991
dir. John Patterson
TV(US)

Olsen, T. V.
Arrow in the Sun
Soldier Blue
AVCO (US) 1970 dir. Ralph Nelson
V

Olsen, T. V.
Stalking Moon, The
Doubleday
WAR (US) 1968 dir. Robert Mulligan

Olsen, T.
Tell Me a Riddle
Delacorte Press
FILMWAYS (US) 1980 dir. Lee Grant
V

Olshan, J.
Clara's Heart
Arbor House
WB (US) 1988 dir. Robert Mulligan

O'Neal, C.
Three Wishes for Jamie
Knightsbridge Publishers
COL TV (US) 1987
dir. Robert William Young
TV(US)

O'Neill, E. G.
Ah, Wilderness
P
Samuel French
MGM (US) 1935 dir. Clarence Brown
M. ALBERG (US) 1959
dir. Robert Mulligan
TV(US)

O'Neill, E. G.
Ah Wilderness!
P
Samuel French
Summer Holiday
MGM (US) 1948
dir. Rouben Mamoulian
M

O'Neill, E. G.
Anna Christie
P
The Modern Library
MGM (US) 1930 dir. Clarence Brown
V

O'Neill, E. G.
Desire Under the Elms
P
Vintage Books
PAR (US) 1958 dir. Delbert Mann

O'Neill, E. G.
Emperor Jones, The
P
Vintage Books
UA (US) 1933 dir. Dudley Murphy
V

O'Neill, E. G.
Hairy Ape, The
P
The Modern Library
UA (US) 1944 dir. Alfred Santell

O'Neill, E. G.
Iceman Cometh, The
P
Random House
AFT (US) 1973 dir. John Frankenheimer

O'Neill, E. G.
Long Day's Journey into Night
P
Yale University Press (New Haven, Connecticut)
FOX (US) 1962 dir. Sidney Lumet
V

O'Neill, E. G.
Long Voyage Home, The
P
The Modern Library
UA (US) 1940 dir. John Ford
V

O'Neill, E. G.
Mourning Becomes Electra
P
H. Liveright
RKO (US) 1947 dir. Dudley Nichols

O'Neill, E. G.
Strange Interlude
P
H. Liveright
MGM (US) 1932 dir. Robert Z. Leonard
GB title: Strange Interval

Onstott, K.
Drum
Pan
PAR (US) 1976 dir. Steve Carver
V

Onstott, K.
Mandingo
Pan
PAR (US) 1975 dir. Richard Fleischer
V

O-Oka, Shohei
Fires on the Plain
DAIEI (Jap) 1959 dir. Kon Ichikawa
V

Opatashu, D.
Romance of a Horse Thief
ALLIED (Yugo) 1971
dir. Abraham Polonsky

Oppenheim, E. P.
Amazing Quest of Mr Ernest Bliss, The
Hodder & Stoughton

Amazing Quest of Ernest Bliss, The
KLEMENT (GB) 1936 dir. Alfred Zeisler
US title: Romance & Riches

Oppenheim, E. P.
Great Impersonation, The
P. F. Collier

UN (US) 1935 dir. Alan Crosland
UN (US) 1942 dir. John Rawlins

Oppenheim, E. P.
Strange Boarders of Paradise Crescent, The

Strange Boarders
GB (GB) 1938 dir. Herbert Mason

Orczy, Baroness E.
Elusive Pimpernel, The
Various

BL (GB) 1950 dir. Michael Powell

Orczy, Baroness E.
Emperor's Candlesticks, The
Various

MGM (US) 1937
dir. George Fitzmaurice

Orczy, Baroness E.
Scarlet Pimpernel, The

UA (GB) 1934 dir. Harold Young
V
LONDON F.P. (US/GB) 1982
dir. Clive Donner
TVSe(GB/US)

Orczy, Baroness E.
Scarlet Pimpernel, The
Various

Pimpernel Smith
BN (GB) 1941 dir. Leslie Howard
V

Orczy, Baroness E.
Scarlet Pimpernel, The
Various

Purple Mask, The
UN (US) 1955 dir. Bruce Humberstone

Orczy, Baroness E.
Spy of Napoleon
Various

TWICKENHAM (GB) 1936
dir. Maurice Elvey
V

O'Rear, F. and O'Rear, J.
Château Bon Vivant
Macmillan

Snowball Express
DISNEY (US) 1972 dir. Norman Tokar

Orgel, D.
Devil in Vienna, The
Dial Press

Friendship in Vienna, A
DISNEY CH (US) 1988
dir. Arthur Allan Seidelman
TV(US)

O'Rourke, F.
Bravados, The
Heinemann

FOX (US) 1958 dir. Henry King
V

O'Rourke, F.
Great Bank Robbery, The
Sphere

WAR (US) 1969 dir. Hy Averback

O'Rourke, F.
Mule for the Marquesa, A
Morrow

Professionals, The
COL (US) 1966 dir. Richard Brooks
V

Orton, J.
Entertaining Mr. Sloane
P
Samuel French
PAR (GB) 1969 dir. Douglas Hickox
V

Orton, J.
Loot
P
Simon French
BL (GB) 1970 dir. Silvio Narizzano
V

Orwell, G.
Animal Farm
New American Library
ABP (GB) 1955 dir. John Halas and Joy Batchelor
A,V

Orwell, G.
1984
Harcourt, Brace, Jovanovich
ABP (GB) 1956 dir. Michael Anderson
BBC (GB) 1965
dir. Christopher Morahan
TV(GB)
BBC (GB) 1984 dir. Rudolph Cartier
TV(GB)
VIRGIN (GB) 1984 dir. Michael Radford
V

Osada, A.
Children of Hiroshima
Putnam
KEL (Jap) 1952 dir. Kaneto Shindo

Osborn, J. J.
Paper Chase, The
Houghton, Mifflin, Co. (Boston)
FOX (US) 1973 dir. James Bridges
V

Osborne, H.
Shore Leave
Hit the Deck
MGM (US) 1955 dir. Roy Rowland
M

Osborne, H. and Scott, A.
Shore Leave
P
Follow the Fleet
RKO (US) 1936 dir. Mark Sandrich
M, V

Osborne, J.
Entertainer, The
P
Criterion
BL (GB) 1960 dir. Tony Richardson
RSO FILMS (US) 1976 dir. Donald Wrye
TV(US)

Osborne, J.
Inadmissible Evidence
P
Grove Press
PAR (GB) 1968 dir. Anthony Page

Osborne, J.
Look Back in Anger
P
Faber & Faber (London)
ABP (GB) 1959 dir. Tony Richardson
V

Osborne, J.
Luther
P
Criterion Books
SEVEN KEYS (GB) 1973 dir. Guy Green

Otokichi, M.
Actor's Revenge, An
DAIEI (Jap) 1963 dir. Kon Ichikawa

Ouida
Dog of Flanders, A
Lippincott (Philadelphia)
FOX (US) 1959 dir. James B. Clark
V

Ouida
Under Two Flags
FOX (US) 1936 dir. Frank Lloyd

Oursler, F.
Great Jasper, The
RKO (US) 1933 dir. J. Walter Ruben

Oursler, F.
Greatest Story Ever Told, The
Doubleday
UA (US) 1965 dir. George Stevens
V

Overholser, W. D.
Cast a Long Shadow
Doubleday
UA (US) 1959 dir. Thomas Carr

Owen, F.
Eddie Chapman Story, The
J. Messner
Triple Cross
AA (GB) 1967 dir. Terence Young
V

Owen, G.
Ballad of the Flim-Flam Man, The
Crown Publishers
Flim-Flam Man, The
FOX (US) 1967 dir. Irvin Kershner
V

Owen, R. T.
Payoff
VIACOM (US) 1991 dir. Stuart Cooper
TV(US)

Packard, F. L.
Miracle Man, The
P
PAR (US) 1932 dir. Norman Z. McLeod

Packer, J.
Nor the Moon by Night
Lippincott (Philadelphia)
RANK (GB) 1958 dir. Ken Annakin
US title: Elephant Gun

Paez, J. L.
Dona Herlinda and her Son
CLASA (Mex) 1986 dir. J. H. Hermosillo
V

Pagano, J.
Condemned, The
Try and Get Me
UA (US) 1951 dir. Cyril Endfield
GB title: Sound of Fury, The

Page, E.
Tree of Liberty, The
Collins
Howards of Virginia, The
COL (US) 1940 dir. Frank Lloyd
GB title: Tree of Liberty, The
V

Page, G.
Paddy the Next Best Thing
P
Samuel French
FOX (US) 1933 dir. Harry Lachman

Page, T.
Hephaestus Plague, The
Putnam
Bug
PAR (US) 1975 dir. Jeannot Szwarc
V

Pagnol, M.
Château de Ma Mère, Le
My Mother's Castle
GAU (Fr) 1991 dir. Yves Robert

Pagnol, M.
Gloire de Mon Père, La
North Point Press (San Francisco)
My Father's Glory
GAU (Fr) 1991 dir. Yves Robert

Pagnol, M.
Jean de Florette
North Point Press (San Francisco)
ORION (Fr) 1987 dir. Claude Berri
V

Pagnol, M.
L'eau des Collines
Manon of the Spring
ORION (Fr) 1987 dir. Claude Berri
French title: Manon des Sources
V

Pagnol, M.
Marius
P
Fasquelle (Paris)
PAR (Fr) 1931 dir. Alexander Korda
V

Pagnol, M.
Topaze
P
Barron's Educational Series (Great Neck, New York)
RKO (US) 1933
dir. Harry d'Abbabie d'Arrast

Pagnol, M.
Topaze
P
Barron's Educational Series (Great Neck, N.Y.)
Mr. Topaze
FOX (GB) 1961 dir. Peter Sellers
US title: I Like Money

Paige, L. and Lipman, D.
Maybe I'll Pitch Forever
Don't Look Back
TBA (US) 1981 dir. Richard Colla
TV(US)

Painter, H. W.
Mark, I Love You
AUBREY (US) 1980
dir. Gunna Hellstrom
TV(US)

Palgi Y.
Great Wind Cometh, A
Hanna's War
CANNON (US) 1988
dir. Menahem Golan
V

Paley, F.
Rumble on the Docks
COL (US) 1956 dir. Fred Sears

Palin, M. and Jones, T.
Secrets
P
Consuming Passions
GOLDWYN (GB) 1988 dir. Giles Foster
V

Palmer, S.
Penguin Pool Murder, The
RKO (US) 1932 dir. George Marshall

Palmer, S., and Flora, F.
Hildegarde Withers Makes the Scene
Random House
Very Missing Person, A
UN TV (US) 1972 dir. Russ Mayberry
TV(US)

Papashvily, G. and Papashvily, H.
Anything Can Happen
Harper
PAR (US) 1952 dir. George Seaton

Parades, A.
With a Pistol in His Hand
Ballad of Gregorio Cortez, The
EMBASSY (US) 1983
dir. Robert M. Young
V

Paradis, M.
This Side of Heaven
MGM (US) 1934 dir. William K. Howard

Paretsky, S.
V. I. Warshawski
HOLLYWOOD (US) 1991
dir. Jeff Kanew

Paris, R-M.
Camille Claudel
Seaver Books
GAU BR (Fr) 1989 dir. Bruno Nuytten

Parker, C. G.
Visitor, The
Of Unknown Origin
WAR (Can) 1983
dir. George P. Cosmatos
V

Parker, G.
Translation of a Savage, The
Methuen
Behold my Wife
PAR (US) 1934 dir. Mitchell Leisen

Parker, L. and Tanner, D.
We Let Our Son Die
Promised a Miracle
REP (US) 1988 dir. Stephen Gyllenhaal
TV(US)

Parker, L. N.
Disraeli
P
WAR (US) 1929 dir. Alfred E. Green

Parker, T. J.
Laguna Heat
St. Martin's Press
WESTON (US) 1987 dir. Simon Langton
TV(US), V

Parks, G.
Learning Tree, The
Harper & Row
WAR (US) 1969 dir. Gordon Parks
V

Parks, L.R.
My Thirty Years Backstairs at the White House
Fleet
Backstairs at the White House
FRIENDLY PRODS (US) 1979
dir. Michael O'Herlihy
TVSe(US)

Parrish, A.
All Kneeling
Benn
Born to be Bad
RKO (US) 1950 dir. Nicholas Ray
V

Parrot, U.
There's Always Tomorrow
MGM (US) 1934 dir. Edward Sloman
UN (US) 1956 dir. Douglas Sirk

Parrott, U.
Ex-Wife
New American Library
Divorcee, The
MGM (US) 1930 dir. Robert Z. Leonard

Parrott, U.
Strangers May Kiss
MGM (US) 1931
dir. George Fitzmaurice

Pascal, E.
Marriage Bed, The
Allen & Unwin
Husband's Holiday
PAR (US) 1931 dir. Robert Milton

Pasolini, P. P.
Theorem
Garzanti (Milan)
AETOS (It) 1968 dir. Pier Paolo Pasolini

Pasternak, B.
Doctor Zhivago
Pantheon
MGM (US) 1965 dir. David Lean
V

Paterson, N.
Kidnappers, The
Little Kidnappers, The
DISNEY CH (US) 1990 dir. Don Shebib
Ch, TV(US)

Paton, A.
Cry, The Beloved Country
Scribners
BL (GB) 1951 dir. Zoltan Korda

Patrick, J.
Hasty Heart, The
P
Random House
ABP (GB) 1949 dir. Vincent Sherman

Patrick, J.
Teahouse of the August Moon, The
P
Dramatists Play Service
MGM (US) 1956 dir. Daniel Mann
COMPASS (US) 1962
dir. George Schaefer
TV(US)

Patrick, V.
Family Business
Poseidon Press
TRI-STAR (US) 1989 dir. Sidney Lumet

Patrick, V.
Pope of Greenwich Village, The
Harper & Row
MGM/UA (US) 1984
dir. Stuart Rosenberg
V

Patten, L. B.
Death of a Gunfighter
J. Curley & Ass. (South Yarmouth, Massachusetts)
UI (US) 1969 dir. Robert Totten, Don Siegel
V

Patterson, H.
To Catch a King
V
Stein & Day
GAYLORD (US) 1984 dir. Clive Donner
TV(US)

Patterson, J.
Virgin
McGraw-Hill
Child of Darkness, Child of Light
WIL COURT (US) 1991
dir. Marina Sargenti
TV(US)

Patton, F. G.
Good Morning, Miss Dove
Dodd, Mead
FOX (US) 1955 dir. Henry Koster

Paulsen, G.
Hatchet
Bradbury Press
Cry in the Wild, A
CONCORDE (US) 1990
dir. Mark Griffiths

Paulsen, G.
Kill Fee
D. I. Fine
Murder C.O.D.
KUSHNER-LOCKE (US) 1990
dir. Alan Metzger
TV(US)

Paulton, E.
Money by Wire
P
Get Off My Foot
WAR (GB) 1935 dir. William Beaudine

Payne, L.
Nose on my Face, The
Hodder & Stoughton

Girl in the Headlines, The
BL (GB) 1963 dir. Michael Truman
US title: Model Murder Case, The

Payne, S.
Black Aces
Wright & Brown
UN (US) 1937 dir. Buck Jones

Peach, L. D.
Great Mr. Handel, The
RANK (GB) 1942 dir. Norman Walker

Peake, M.
Mr. Pye
Overlook Press
CHANNEL 4 (GB) 1986
TVSe(GB)

Pearce, D.
Cool Hand Luke
Scribners
WAR (US) 1967 dir. Stuart Rosenberg
V

Pearson, J.
Life of Ian Fleming, The
McGraw-Hill

Goldeneye
ANGLIA (GB) 1990 dir. Don Boyd
TV(GB)

Pearson, W.
Fever in the Blood, A
Macmillan
WAR (US) 1960 dir. Vincent Sherman

Peck, G. W.
Peck's Bad Boy
Thompson & Thomas (Chicago)
FOX (US) 1934 dir. Edward Cline

Peck, R.
Don't Look and it Won't Hurt
Simon & Schuster

Gas, Food and Lodging
IRS (US) 1992 dir. Allison Anders

Peck, R.
Father Figure
Viking Press
TIME-LIFE (US) 1980 dir. Jerry London
TV(US), V

Peck, R. H.
Are You In The House Alone
Viking Press
FRIES PRODS (US) 1978
dir. Walter Grauman
M, TV(US), V

Peple, E. H.
Beloved Bachelor, The
P
PAR (US) 1931 dir. Lloyd Corrigan

Peple, E.
Littlest Rebel, The
P
FOX (US) 1935 dir. David Butler
V

Percival, D.
Girlfriend
P
Girl/Boy
HEMDALE (GB) 1971 dir. Bob Kellett

Percy, E.
Shop at Sly Corner, The
P
BL (GB) 1946 dir. George King
US title: Code of Scotland Yard

Percy, E. and Denham, R.
Ladies in Retirement
P
Random House
COL (US) 1941 dir. Charles Vidor

679

Perelman, L. and Perelman, S. J.
Night Before Christmas, The
P

Larceny Inc.
WAR (US) 1942 dir. Lloyd Bacon

Perelman, S. J. and Nash, O.
One Touch of Venus
P
Little, Brown (Boston)
UN (US) 1948 dir. William A. Seiter
V

Perelman, S. J. and Perelman, L.
All Good Americans
Paris Interlude
MGM (US) 1934 dir. Edwin L. Marin

Perkins, K.
Desert Voices
Desert Pursuit
ABP (US) 1952 dir. George Blair

Perrault, C.
Sleeping Beauty
Various

DISNEY (US) 1959 dir. Clyde Geronomi
A, Ch
CANNON (US) 1987 dir. David Irving
Ch

Perrin, S. and Balzer, G.
Are You With It?
P
Various

UN (US) 1948 dir. Jack Hively
M

Perry, G.
Bluebell
BBC (GB) 1986
TVSe(GB)

Perry, G. S.
Hold Autumn in your Hands
Southerner, The
UA (US) 1945 dir. Jean Renoir
V

Pertwee, M.
Don't Just Lie There, Say Something
P
Samuel French
RANK (GB) 1973 dir. Bob Kellet
V

Pertwee, M.
Night was our Friend
P
MONARCH (GB) 1951
dir. Michael Anderson

Pertwee, R. and Pertwee, M.
Paragon, The
P
Silent Dust
ABP (GB) 1947 dir. Lance Comfort

Pertwee, R.
Heat Wave
P
Road to Singapore
WAR (US) 1931 dir. Alfred E. Green

Pertwee, R.
Pink String and Sealing Wax
P
Samuel French
EAL (GB) 1945 dir. Robert Hamer

Peters, S.
Fourth War, The
CANNON (US) 1990
dir. John Frankenheimer

Peters, S.
Park is Mine, The
Doubleday
HBO (Can/US) 1985
dir. Steven Hilliard Stern
TV(US), V

Peterson, J.
Here Come the Littles
ATLANTIC (US) 1985
dir. Bernard Deyries
A, V

Peterson, L. S.
Take a Giant Step
P
Samuel French
UA (US) 1959 dir. Philip Leacock

Peterson, R.
Square Ring, The
P
GFD (GB) 1953 dir. Basil Dearden

Petievich, G.
To Live and Die in L.A.
Arbor House
MGM/UA (US) 1985
dir. William Friedkin
V

Petrakis, H. M.
Dream of Kings, A
D. McKay Co.
WAR (US) 1969 dir. Daniel Mann

Petronius
Satyricon
Various
Fellini Satyricon
UA (It) 1969 dir. Federico Fellini
V

Pettit, E.
Rich Are Always With Us, The
WAR (US) 1932 dir. Alfred E. Green

Pettit, W. H.
Nine Girls
P
COL (US) 1944 dir. Leigh Jason

Peyton, K. M.
Flambards
World Publications
YTV (GB) 1979
TVSe(GB)

Peyton, K. M.
Right Hand Man, The
Oxford University Press
UAA (Aust) 1987 dir. Di Drew
V

Phillips, M.
Blood Rights
St. Martin's Press
BBC (GB) 1991 dir. Leslie Manning
TV(GB)

Phillips, M.
Pick up Sticks
Michael Joseph
Cherry Picker, The
FOX-RANK (GB) 1974 dir. Peter Curran
V

Phillpotts, E. & Phillpotts, A.
Yellow Sands
P
AB (GB) 1938 dir. Herbert Brenon

Philpotts, E.
Farmer's Wife, The
P
Samuel French
AB (GB) 1940 dir. Norman Lee

Pick, J. B.
Last Valley, The
Sphere
CINERAMA (GB) 1970
dir. James Clavell
V

Pielmeier, J.
Agnes of God
P
Samuel French
COL (US) 1985 dir. Norman Jewison
V

Pierson, Mrs. L.
Roughly Speaking
Simon & Schuster
WAR (US) 1945 dir. Michael Curtiz

Pierson, R.
Queen of Mean, The
Bantam Books
Leona Helmsley: The Queen of Mean
FRIES (US) 1990 dir. Richard Michaels
TV(US)

Pike, R. L.
Mute Witness
Doubleday
Bullitt
WAR (US) 1968 dir. Peter Yates
V

Pik-Wah, L.
Rouge
ICA (HK) 1988 dir. Stanley Kwan

Pilcher, R.
Shell Seekers, The
St. Martin's Press
M. REES (US) 1989 dir. Waris Hussein
TV(US)

Pileggi, N.
Wiseguy: Life in A Mafia Family
Simon & Schuster
Goodfellas
WAR (US) 1990 dir. Martin Scorsese

Pilkington, R.
Nepomuk of the River
Macmillan
Golden Head, The
CINERAMA (US/Hun) 1965
dir. Richard Thorpe

Pilling, A.
Henry's Leg
Viking Kestrel
TVS (GB) 1990 dir. Michael Kerrigan
TVSe(GB), V

Pinchon, E.
Zapata the Unconquerable
Viva Zapata!
FOX (US) 1952 dir. Elia Kazan
V

Pinero, Sir A. W.
Enchanted Cottage, The
P
W. H. Baker Co. (Boston)
RKO (US) 1945 dir. John Cromwell

Pinero, Sir A. W.
Magistrate, The
P
Methuen
Those were the Days
BIP (GB) 1934 dir. Thomas Bentley

Pinero, Sir A. W.
Second Mrs. Tanqueray, The
P
Methuen
VANDYKE (GB) 1952 dir. Dallas Bower

Pinsent, G.
John and the Missus
CINEMA (Can) 1987
dir. Gordon Pinsent

Pinter, H.
Betrayal
P
Dramatists Play Service
VIRGIN (GB) 1982 dir. David Jones
V

Pinter, H.
Birthday Party, The
P
Samuel French
CINERAMA (GB) 1968
dir. William Friedkin
V
BBC (GB) 1988
TV(GB)

Pinter, H.
Caretaker, The
P
Dramatists Play Service
BL (GB) 1963 dir. Clive Donner
US title: Guest, The

Pinter, H.
Homecoming, The
P
Grove Press
SEVEN KEYS (GB) 1973 dir. Peter Hall

Pinter, H.
Kind of Alaska, A
P
Dramatists Play Service
CENTRAL (GB) 1984 dir. Kenneth Ives
TV(GB)

Pinter, H.
Lover, The
P
Grove Press
ITV (GB) 1963 dir. Joan Kemp-Welch
TV(GB)

Pinto, M.
Pensamientos
El
NACIONAL (Mex) 1952
dir. Luis Bunuel

Piper, A.
Marry at Leisure
Nice Girl Like Me, A
AVCO (GB) 1969 dir. Desmond Davis
V

Piper, A.
Yes, Giorgio
MGM/UA (US) 1982
dir. Franklin Schaffner
V

Piper, E.
Bunny Lake is Missing
Harper
COL (GB) 1965 dir. Otto Preminger

Piper, E.
Nanny, The
Atheneum
WAR (GB) 1965 dir. Seth Holt
V

Pirandello, L.
As You Desire Me
P
Samuel French
MGM (US) 1932
dir. George Fitzmaurice

Pirandello, L.
Come Prima Meglio di Prima
P
Never Say Goodbye
UN (US) 1955 dir. Jerry Hopper

Pirandello, L.
Come Prima Meglio di Prima
P
This Love of Ours
UI (US) 1945 dir. William Deiterle

Pirandello, L.
L'Homme de Nulle Part
CG (Fr) 1987 dir. Pierre Chenal

Pirro, U.
Five Branded Women
PAR (It/US) 1960 dir. Martin Ritt

Plain, B.
Evergreen
Delacorte Press
METRO (US) 1985 dir. Fielder Cook
TVSe(US)

Plater, A.
Misterioso
BBC (GB) 1991 dir. John Glenister
TV(GB)

Plath, S.
Bell Jar, The
Harper
AVCO (US) 1979 dir. Larry Peerce
V

Platt, K.
Boy Who Could Make Himself Disappear, The
Baxter!
EMI (GB) 1972 dir. Lionel Jeffries
Ch

Podhajsky, A.
Dancing White Horses of Vienna, The
Doubleday
Miracle of the White Stallions, The
DISNEY (US) 1963 dir. Arthur Hiller
GB title: Flight of the White Stallions, The

Poe, E. A.
Fall of the House of Usher, The
Various
TAFT (US) 1982 dir. James Conway
TV(US)

Poe, E. A.
Fall of the House of Usher, The
Various
House of Usher, The
AIP (US) 1960 dir. Roger Corman
GB title: Fall of the House of Usher, The
21st CENTURY (US) 1988
dir. Alan Birkinshaw
V

Poe, E. A.
Haunting of Morella, The
Various
CONCORDE (US) 1990
dir. Jim Wynorski

Poe, E. A.
Masque of the Red Death, The
Various
AA (GB) 1964 dir. Roger Corman
V
CONCORDE (US) 1989
dir. Larry Brand

Poe, E. A.
Morella; Black Cat, The; Facts of the Case of Dr. Valdemar,The
Various
Tales of Terror
WAR (US) 1962 dir. Roger Corman
V

Poe, E. A.
Murders in the Rue Morgue
Various
UN (US) 1932 dir. Robert Florey
AIP (US) 1971 dir. Gordon Hessler
V
HALMI (US/GB) 1986
dir. Jeannot Szwarc
TV(GB/US)

Poe, E. A.
Murders in the Rue Morgue
Various
Phantom of the Rue Morgue
WAR (US) 1954 dir. Roy del Ruth

Poe, E. A.
Mystery of Marie Roget, The
UN (US) 1942 dir. Phil Rosen

Poe, E. A.
Pit and the Pendulum, The
Various
AA (US) 1961 dir. Roger Corman
V
FULL MOON (US) 1991
dir. Stuart Gordon

Poe, E. A.
Premature Burial, The
Various
AA (US) 1962 dir. Roger Corman
V

Poe, E. A.
Tell-Tale Heart, The
Various
ADELPHI (GB) 1953 dir. J. B. Williams
ABP (GB) 1960 dir. Ernest Morris

Poe, E. A.
Tomb of Ligeia, The
Various
AIP (GB) 1964 dir. Roger Corman
V

Poiret, J.
Cage Aux Folles, La
P
UA (Fr/It) 1978 dir. Edouard Molinaro
V

Pollini, F.
Pretty Maids All In A Row
MGM (US) 1971 dir. Roger Vadim

Pollock, R.
Loophole
Dutton
B W (GB) 1981 dir. John Quested
V

Polson, B.
Go Toward the Light
CORAPEAKE (US) 1988 dir. Mike Robe
TV(US)

Polson, B.
Not My Kid
Arbor House
FINNEGAN (US) 1985
dir. Michael Tuchner
TV(US), V

Ponicsan, D.
Cinderella Liberty
Harper & Row
FOX (US) 1974 dir. Mark Rydell

Ponicsan, D.
Last Detail, The
New American Library
COL (US) 1973 dir. Hal Ashby
V

Poole, V.
Thursday's Child
Little, Brown (Boston)
VIACOM (US) 1983
dir. David Lowell Rich
TV(US)

Popkin, Z.
Death of Innocence, A
Lippincott (Philadelphia)
CARLINER (US) 1971
dir. Paul Wendkos
TV

Popplewell, J.
Tread Softly Stranger
P
ALDERDALE (GB) 1958
dir. Gordon Parry

Porter, E. H.
Pollyanna
Dell Publishing
DISNEY (US) 1960 dir. David Swift
Ch, V

Porter, E. H.
Pollyanna
Dell Publishing
Polly
DISNEY (US) 1989 dir. Debbie Allen
TV(US)

Porter, G. S.
Freckles
Grosset & Dunlap
RKO (US) 1935 dir. Edward Killy
FOX (US) 1960 dir. Harry Spalding

Porter, G. S.
Girl of the Limberlost, A
Grosset & Dunlap

MON (US) 1934 dir. Christy Cabanne
FREEDOM PRODS. (US) 1990
dir. Burt Brinckerhoff
TV(US)

Porter, G. S.
Keeper of the Bees
Hutchinson

MON (US) 1935 dir. Christy Cabanne

Porter, G. S.
Laddie
Doubleday

RKO (US) 1935 dir. George Stevens

Porter, K. A.
Ship of Fools
Little, Brown (Boston)

COL (US) 1965 dir. Stanley Kramer
V

Porter, R.
Chrysalis
P

All of Me
PAR (US) 1934 dir. James Flood

Portis, C.
True Grit
Simon & Schuster

PAR (US) 1969 dir. Henry Hathaway
V

Posmysz-Piasecka, Z.
Passenger
P

KADR (Pol) 1963 dir. Andrzej Munk

Post, H.
Whorehouse Sting, The

Red-Light Sting, The
UN TV (US) 1984 dir. Rod Holcomb
TV(US), V

Post, Sir L. van der
Seed and the Sower, The
Morrow

Merry Christmas, Mr. Lawrence
UN (GB) 1983 dir. Nagisa Oshima
V

Potok, C.
Chosen, The
CONTEM (US) 1981
dir. Jeremy Paul Kagan
V

Potter, B.
Tale of Little Pig Robinson, The
D. McKay Co.

TVS (GB) 1990 dir. Alan Bridges
TVSe(GB)

Potter, D.
Brimstone and Treacle
P

NAMARA (GB) 1982
dir. Richard Loncraine
V

Potter, D.
Sufficient Carbohydrate
P
Faber & Faber (London)

Visitors
BBC (GB) 1987 dir. Piers Haggard
TV(GB)

Potter, S.
Gamesmanship, Oneupmanship, Lifemanship
Holt, Rinehart & Winston

School for Scoundrels
WAR (GB) 1960 dir. Robert Namer

Powell, D.
Hello Sister

FOX (US) 1933 dir. Erich von Stroheim

Powell, M.
Graf Spee

Battle of the River Plate, The
RANK (GB) 1956 dir. Michael Powell
and Emeric Pressburger
US title: Pursuit of the Graf Spee
V

Powell, R.
Philadelphian, The
Scribners

Young Philadelphians, The
WAR (US) 1959 dir. Vincent Sherman
GB title: City Jungle, The
V

Powell, R.
Pioneer Go Home
Hodder & Stoughton

Follow that Dream
UA (US) 1962 dir. Gordon Douglas
V

Powers, A. and Misenheimer, M.
Framed
Pinnacle

PAR (US) 1975 dir. Phil Karlson
V

Powers, F. G. and Gentry, C.
Operation Overflight
Holt, Rinehart & Winston

*Francis Gary Powers: The True Story of
the U-2 Spy Incident*
FRIES (US) 1976 dir. Delbert Mann
TV(US), V

Praag, V. V.
Combat

Men in War
UA (US) 1957 dir. Anthony Mann
V

Pratt, T.
Barefoot Mailman, The
COL (US) 1951 dir. Earl McEvoy

Pratt, T.
Incredible Mr. Limpet, The
WAR (US) 1964 dir. Arthur Lubin
A

Pratt, T.
Mr. Winkle Goes to War
COL (US) 1944 dir. Alfred E. Green
GB title: Arms and the Woman
V

Preedy, G.
General Crack
Dodd, Mead
WAR (US) 1930 dir. Alan Crosland

Presley, P. and Harman, S.
Elvis and Me
Putnam
NEW WORLD TV (US) 1988
dir. Larry Peerce
TVSe(US)

Presnell, F. G.
Send Another Coffin

Slightly Honourable
UA (US) 1940 dir. Tay Garnett
V

Pressburger, E.
Killing a Mouse on Sunday

Behold a Pale Horse
COL (US) 1964 dir. Fred Zinnemann
V

Price, E.
Red for Danger

Blondes for Danger
WILCOX (GB) 1938 dir. Jack Raymond

Price, E. and Attiwill, K.
Once a Crook
P
FOX (GB) 1941 dir. Herbert Mason

Price, N.
Sleeping with the Enemy
Berkley Publishers
FOX (US) 1991 dir. Joseph Ruben
V

Price, R.
Bloodbrothers
Houghton, Mifflin Company (Boston)
WAR (US) 1978 dir. Robert Mulligan
V

Price, R.
Wanderers, The
ORION (US) 1979 dir. Philip Kaufman
V

Priestley, J. B.
Benighted
Old Dark House, The
UN (US) 1932 dir. James Whale
BL (GB) 1963 dir. William Castle

Priestley, J. B.
Dangerous Corner
P
RKO (US) 1934 dir. Phil Rosen

Priestley, J. B.
Good Companions, The
Harper & Bros.
GAU (GB) 1932 dir. Victor Saville
ABP (GB) 1956 dir. J. Lee Thompson

Priestley, J. B.
Inspector Calls, An
P
Harper
BL (GB) 1954 dir. Guy Hamilton
V

Priestley, J. B.
Laburnum Grove
P
Samuel French
ABP (GB) 1936 dir. Carol Reed

Priestley, J. B.
Let the People Sing
Harper & Bros.
BN (GB) 1942 dir. John Baxter

Priestley, J. B.
Lost Empires
Little, Brown (Boston)
GRANADA (GB) 1985 dir. Alan Grint
TVSe(GB)

Priestley, J. B.
They Came to a City
P
EAL (GB) 1944 dir. Basil Dearden

Priestley, J. B.
When we are Married
P
Samuel French
BN (GB) 1943 dir. Lance Comfort

Prince, P.
Good Father, The
FILM 4 (GB) 1986 dir. Mike Newell

Pritchett, V. S.
Wedding, The
Random House
TYNE-TEES (GB) 1984
dir. Gordon Flemyng
TV(GB)

Prochnau, W.
Trinity's Child
Putnam
By Dawn's Early Light
HBO (US) 1990 dir. Jack Sholder
TV (US)

Procter, M.
Hell is a City
WAR (GB) 1959 dir. Val Guest

Proffitt, N.
Gardens of Stone
Carroll & Graf
TRI-STAR (US) 1987
dir. Francis Ford Coppola
V

Prokosch, F.
City of Shadows
Chatto & Windus
Conspirators, The
WAR (US) 1944 dir. Jean Negulesco

Proust, M.
Du Côté de chez Swann
Modern Library
Swann in Love
GAU (Fr) 1984 dir. Volker Schlondorff
V

Prouty, O.
Now, Voyager
Sun Dial Press
WAR (US) 1942 dir. Irving Rapper
V

Prouty, O.
Stella Dallas
Houghton, Mifflin Co. (Boston)
UA (US) 1937 dir. King Vidor
V

Prouty, O.
Stella Dallas
Houghton, Mifflin Co. (Boston)
Stella
TOUCH (US) 1990 dir. John Erman

Prumbs, L. S. and Smith, S. B.
My Girl Tisa
P
IN (US) 1948 dir. Elliott Nugent

Przybyszewska, S.
Danton Affair, The
P
Danton
GAU/TFI (Fr/Pol) 1982
dir. Andrzej Wajda

Puccini, G.
Bohème, La
Various
NEW YORKER/ERATO (Fr/It) 1989
dir. Leo Conencini
M

Pudney, J.
Net, The
GFD (GB) 1953 dir. Anthony Asquith

Pudney, J.
Thursday Adventure
Stolen Airliner, The
BL (GB) 1955 dir. Don Sharp
Ch

Pugh, M.
Commander Crabb
Silent Enemy, The
ROMULUS (GB) 1958
dir. William Fairchild

Puig, M.
Kiss of the Spider Woman
Knopf
ISLAND (US/Brazil) 1985
dir. Hector Babenco
V

Pulitzer, R.
Roxanne: The Prize Pulitzer
Villard Books
QINTEX (US) 1989 dir. Richard Colla
TV(US)

Purcell, H.
Glorious Days, The
P
Lilacs in The Spring
REP (GB) 1954 dir. Herbert Wilcox
US title: Let's Make Up

Purcell, H. and Parr-Davies, H.
Lisbon Story, The
P
BN (GB) 1946 dir. Paul Stein
M

Purdy, J.
In a Shallow Grave
Arbor House
SKOURAS (US) 1988
dir. Kenneth Bowser

Pushkin, A. S.
Queen of Spades, The
Knopf
AB (GB) 1949 dir. Thorold Dickinson

Pushkin, A.
Captain's Daughter, The
Viking Press
Tempest
PAR (It/Fr/Yugo) 1958
dir. Alberto Lattuada
V

Puzo, M.
Fortunate Pilgrim, The
NBC (US) 1988 dir. Stuart Cooper
TVSe(US)

Puzo, M.
Godfather, The
Putnam
PAR (US) 1972
dir. Francis Ford Coppola
V

Puzo, M.
Godfather, The
Putnam
Godfather Part II, The
PAR (US) 1974
dir. Francis Ford Coppola
V

Puzo, M.
Sicilian, The
Simon & Schuster
FOX (It/US) 1987 dir. Michael Cimino
V

Pyle, E. T.
Story of G.I. Joe, The
UA (US) 1945 dir. William A. Wellman

Pyle, H.
Men of Iron
Harper
Black Shield of Falworth, The
UI (US) 1954 dir. Rudolph Maté

Queen, E.
Cat of Many Tales
Ellery Queen: Don't Look Behind You
UN TV (US) 1971 dir. Barry Shear
TV(US)

Queen, E.
Fourth Side of the Triangle, The
Morrow
Ellery Queen: Too Many Suspects
UN TV (US) 1975 dir. David Greene
TV(US)

Queen, E.
Study in Terror, A
COMPTON-TEKLI (GB) 1965
dir. James Hill
V

Queen, E.
Ten Days Wonder
HEMDALE (Fr) 1971
dir. Claude Chabrol

Quefflec, H.
Recteur de l'Ile de Sein, Un
Dieu à Besoin des Hommes
TRANS (Fr) 1950 dir. Jean Delannoy

Queneau, R.
Zazie Dans le Métro
Gallimard (Paris)
CONNOISSEUR (Fr) 1960
dir. Louis Malle

Quentin, P.
Fatal Woman
Simon & Schuster
Black Widow
FOX (US) 1954 dir. Nunnally Johnson

Quentin, P.
Man in the Net, The
UA (US) 1958 dir. Michael Curtiz

Quignard, P.
Every Morning of the World
BAC FILMS (Fr) 1992 dir. Alan Corneau

Quilici, F.
Danger Adrift
Only One Survived
CBS ENT (US) 1990 dir. Folco Quilici
TV(US)

Quinn, A.
Berg
Killing Dad
PALACE (US) 1989 dir. Michael Austin

Quinn, T. K.
Ishi in Two Worlds
University of California Press
(Berkeley, California)
Ishi: The Last of his Tribe
LEWIS (US) 1978
dir. Robert Ellis Miller
TV(US)

Quinn, T. K.
Ishi in Two Worlds
University of California Press
(Berkeley, California)
Ishi: The Last of his Tribe
LEWIS (US) 1978
dir. Robert Ellis Miller
TV(US)

Quinnell, A. J.
Man on Fire
Morrow
TRI-STAR (It/Fr) 1987
dir. Elie Chouraqui
V

Raab, S.
Ariana
UN TV (US) 1989 dir. Paul Krasny
TV(US)

Raab, S.
It's Always Something
UN TV (US) 1990 dir. Richard Compton
TV(US)

Raab, S.
Justice in the Back Room
Marcus-Nelson Murders, The
UN TV (US) 1973 dir. Joseph Sargent
TV(US)

Rabe, D.
Streamers
P
Samuel French
UA (US) 1983 dir. Robert Altman
V

Radiguet, R.
Devil in the Flesh
Calder & Boyars (Boston)
TRANS (Fr) 1947
dir. Claude Autant-Lara
ORION (It/Fr) 1987
dir. Marco Bellocchio
V

Rae, J.
Custard Boys, The
Holt-Davies
FOREST HALL (GB) 1979
dir. Colin Finbow

Rae, J.
Custard Boys, The
Reach for Glory
GALA (GB) 1962 dir. Philip Leacock

Raine, W. M.
Rawhide Justice
Hodder & Stoughton
Man from Bitter Ridge, The
UN (US) 1955 dir. Jack Arnold

Ramati, A.
Assisi Underground, The
Stein & Day
CANNON (GB) 1985
dir. Alexander Ramati
V

Ramati, A.
Beyond the Mountains
Penguin
Desperate Ones, The
AMERICAN (Sp/US) 1968
dir. Alexander Ramati
V

Ramos, F.
Veronico Cruz
BFI (Arg/GB) 1988 dir. Miguel Pereira

Ramos, G.
Memories of Prison
REGINA (Port) 1989
dir. Nelson Pereira Dos Santos

Rand, A.
Fountainhead, The
Bobbs-Merrill (Indianapolis)
WAR (US) 1949 dir. King Vidor
V

Rand, A.
Night of January 16th, The
P
World Publishing Co.
PAR (US) 1941 dir. William Clements

Rand, A.
We The Living
Random House
SCALERA (It) 1942
dir. Goffredo Allessandrini

Randall, B.
Fan, The
PAR (US) 1981 dir. Edward Bianchi
V

Randall, F. E.
Watcher in the Woods
DISNEY (US) 1980 dir. John Hough
V

Rankin, W. M.
South Sea Woman
WAR (US) 1953 dir. Arthur Lubin

Ransley, P.
Price, The
CHANNEL 4 (GB) 1985 dir. Peter Smith
TVSe(GB)

Ransome, A.
Swallows and Amazons
Jonathan Cape (London)
EMI (GB) 1974 dir. Claude Whatham
Ch, V

Raphael, F.
Oxbridge Blues
Cape (London)
BBC (GB) 1984 dir. James Cellan Jones
TVSe(GB)

Raphael, F.
Richard's Things
Bobbs-Merrill (Indianapolis)
SOUTHERN (GB) 1980
dir. Anthony Harvey
V

Raphaelson, S.
Accent on Youth
P
Samuel French
But Not For Me
PAR (US) 1959 dir. Walter Lang

Raphaelson, S.
Accent on Youth
P
PAR (US) 1935 dir. Wesley Ruggles

Raphaelson, S.
Day of Atonement
P
Samuel French
Jazz Singer, The
WAR (US) 1953 dir. Michael Curtiz
EMI (US) 1980 dir. Richard Fleischer
V

Raphaelson, S.
Hilda Crane
P
Random House
FOX (US) 1956 dir. Philip Dunne

Raphaelson, S.
Perfect Marriage, The
P
Dramatists Play Service
PAR (US) 1946 dir. Lewis Allen

Raphaelson, S.
Skylark
P
PAR (US) 1941 dir. Mark Sandrich

Rascovich, M.
Bedford Incident, The
Atheneum
COL (GB) 1965 dir. James B. Harris
V

Rashke, R.
Escape from Sobibor
Houghton, Mifflin Co. (Boston)
ZENITH (US) 1987 dir. Jack Gold
TV(US)

Rashke, R.
Runaway Father
Harcourt, Brace, Jovanovich
HEARST (US) 1991 dir. John Nicolella

Raspe, R. E.
Twelve Adventures of the Celebrated Baron Munchausen
Deutsch (London)
Adventures of Baron Munchausen, The
COL (GB) 1988 dir. Terry Gilliam
V

Rattigan, T.
Bequest to the Nation
P
Dramatic Publishing Co. (Chicago)
UN (GB) 1973 dir. James Cellan Jones

Rattigan, T.
Browning Version, The
P
Samuel French
GFD (GB) 1951 dir. Anthony Asquith
V

Rattigan, T.
Deep Blue Sea, The
P
Random House
FOX (GB) 1955 dir. Anatole Litvak

Rattigan, T.
French Without Tears
P
Samuel French
PAR (GB) 1939 dir. Anthony Asquith

Rattigan, T.
Separate Tables
P
Samuel French
UA (US) 1958 dir. Delbert Mann
V

Rattigan, T.
Sleeping Prince, The
P
Random House
Prince and the Showgirl, The
WAR (GB) 1957 dir. Laurence Olivier
V

Rattigan, T.
While the Sun Shines
P
Samuel French
ABP (GB) 1947 dir. Anthony Asquith

Rattigan, T.
Who is Sylvia?
P
H. Hamilton (London)
Man Who Loved Redheads, The
BL (GB) 1954 dir. Harold French

Rattigan, T.
Winslow Boy, The
P
Dramatists Play Service
IS (GB) 1945 dir. Anthony Asquith
V

Rau, M. and Rau, N.
I'm Giving Them Up For Good
Cold Turkey
UA (US) 1970 dir. Norman Lear

Raven, S.
Doctors Wear Scarlet
Simon & Schuster
Incense for the Damned
GN (GB) 1970
dir. Robert Hartford-Davis

Rawlings, Mrs. M.
Yearling, The
Scribners
MGM (US) 1946 dir. Clarence Brown
V

Rawlings, M. K.
Cross Creek
Scribners
UN (US) 1983 dir. Martin Ritt
V

Rawls, W.
Where the Red Fern Grows
Doubleday
EMI (US) 1974 dir. Norman Tokar
V

Rawson, C.
Death in a Top Hat
Gregg Press
Miracles for Sale
MGM (US) 1939 dir. Tod Browning

Ray, R.
Strange World of Planet X, The
EROS (GB) 1958 dir. Gilbert Gunn
US title: Cosmic Monsters

Rayman, S.
Women of Twilight
P
ROMULUS (GB) 1952
dir. Gordon Parry
US title: Twilight Women

Raymond, E.
Berg, The
P
Benn
Atlantic
BI (GB) 1929 dir. E. A. Dupont

Raymond, E.
For Them That Trespass
ABP (GB) 1949 dir. Alberto Cavalcanti

Raymond, E.
Tell England
CAPITOL (GB) 1931
dir. Anthony Asquith, GeraldBarkas
US title: Battle of Gallipoli, The

Raymond, M.
Smiley
FOX (GB) 1955 dir. Anthony Kimmins

Rayner, D. A.
Escort
Kimber
Enemy Below, The
FOX (US) 1957 dir. Dick Powell

Reachi, M.
Susana
PLEXUS (Sp) 1951 dir. Luis Bunuel
V

Read, P. P.
Married Man, A
Lippincott (Philadelphia)
LWT (GB) 1985 dir. Charles B. Jarrott
TVSe(GB)

Reade, C. and Taylor, T.
Masks and Faces
P
Peg of Old Drury
WILCOX (GB) 1935 dir. Herbert Wilcox

Réage, P.
Return to the Château
Fruits of Passion
(Fr/Jap) 1982 dir. Shuji Terayama

Réage, P.
Story of O, The
NEW REALM (Fr) 1975 dir. Just Jaeckin
V

Rebeta-Burditt, J.
Cracker Factory, The
EMI (US) 1979 dir. Burt Brinckerhoff
TV(US), V

Reddin, K.
Another Shore
EAL (GB) 1948 dir. Charles Crichton

Redon, J.
Eyes Without A Face
CH ELYSEE (Fr/It) 1959
dir. George Franju

Reed, B.
Verdict, The
Simon & Schuster
FOX (US) 1982 dir. Sidney Lumet
V

Reed, J. D.
Free Fall
Delacorte Press
Pursuit of D. B. Cooper, The
UN (US) 1981 dir. Roger Spottiswoode
V

Reed, M.
Petticoat Fever
P
Samuel French
MGM (US) 1936
dir. George Fitzmaurice

Reed, M. W.
Yes, My Darling Daughter
P
Samuel French
WAR (US) 1939 dir. William Keighley

Reese, J.
Looters, The
Charley Varrick
UN (US) 1973 dir. Don Siegel
V

Reeves, J.
Harbor, The
Society Doctor
MGM (US) 1935 dir. George B. Seitz
GB title: After Eight Hours

Reeves, T.
Beggars are Coming to Town
P
I Walk Alone
PAR (US) 1947 dir. Byron Haskin

Reid, R.
Madame Curie
BBC (GB) 1984
TV(GB)

Reid, R. P.
Colditz Story, The
Lippincott (Philadelphia)
BL (GB) 1954 dir. Guy Hamilton
V

Reilly, R. T.
Red Hugh, Prince of Donegal
Farrar, Straus & Giroux
Fighting Prince of Donegal, The
DISNEY (GB) 1966
dir. Michael O'Herlihy
V

Reiner, C.
Enter Laughing
P
Samuel French
COL (US) 1967 dir. Carl Reiner
V

Remarque, E. M.
All Quiet on the Western Front
Little, Brown (Boston)
UN (US) 1930 dir. Lewis Milestone
V
M ARCH (US) 1979 dir. Delbert Mann
TV(US), V

Remarque, E. M.
Arch of Triumph
Appleton, Century
UA (US) 1948 dir. Lewis Milestone
HTV (GB) 1984 dir. Waris Hussein
TV(GB), V

Remarque, E. M.
Flotsam

So Ends our Night
UA (US) 1941 dir. John Cromwell

Remarque, E. M.
Heaven has no Favourites
Harcourt, Brace & World

Bobby Deerfield
WAR (US) 1977 dir. Sydney Pollack
V

Remarque, E. M.
Road Back, The
Little, Brown (Boston)

UN (US) 1937 dir. James Whale

Remarque, E. M.
Three Comrades
Little, Brown (Boston)

MGM (US) 1938 dir. Frank Borzage

Remarque, E. M.
Time to Love and a Time to Die, A
Harcourt Brace

U-I (US) 1958 dir. Douglas Sirk
V

Renard, M.
Hands of Orlac, The

Mad Love
MGM (US) 1935 dir. Karl Freund
GB title: Hands of Orlac, The

Rendell, R.
Affair in Mind, An

BBC (GB) 1988 dir. Clive Luke
TV(GB)

Rendell, R.
Judgement in Stone, A
Doubleday

SCHULZ (Can) 1987 dir. Ousama Rawi
US title: The Housekeeper
V

Rendell, R.
Some Lie and Some Die
Doubleday

TVS (GB) 1990 dir. Neil Zeiger
TVSe

Rendell, R.
Tree of Hands
Pantheon Books

GRANADA (GB) 1988 dir. Giles Foster

Rendell, R.
Unkindness of Ravens, An
Pantheon Books

TVS (GB) 1988 dir. John Gorrie
TV(GB)

Rendell, R.
Wolf to the Slaughter
Doubleday

TVS (GB) 1988 dir. John Gorrie
TV(GB)

Resko, J.
Reprieve

Convicts Four
ALLIED (US) 1962 dir. Millard Kaufman
GB title: Reprieve

Resnik, M.
Any Wednesday
P
Stein & Day

WAR (US) 1966 dir. Robert Ellis Miller
GB title: Bachelor Girl Apartment
V

Resnik, M.
Girl in the Turquoise Bikini, The
Transworld

How Sweet It Is
WAR (US) 1968 dir. Jerry Paris

Reuben, D.
Everything you Ever Wanted to Know about Sex but were Afraid to Ask
D. McKay Co.
UA (US) 1972 dir. Woody Allen
V

Reuter, B.
Zappa
IS (Den) 1984 dir. Bille August

Reve, G.
Fourth Man, The
VER NED (Neth) 1984
dir. Paul Verhoeven
V

Reyher, F.
Wait til the Sun Shines Nellie
FOX (US) 1952 dir. Henry King

Rhodes, E. M.
Pasco Por Aqui
Houghton, Mifflin Co. (Boston)
Four Faces West
UA (US) 1948 dir. Alfred E. Green
V

Rhodes, E.
Prince of Central Park, The
Coward, McCann & Geoghegan
LORIMAR (US) 1977 dir. Harvey Hart
TV(US)

Rhys, J.
Quartet
Harper & Row
NEW WORLD (GB/Fr) 1981
dir. James Ivory

Ricardei, M. and Dubois, W.
I Loved You Wednesday
P
TCF (US) 1933 dir. Henry King,
William Cameron Menzies

Rice, A. H. and Flexner, A. C.
Mrs. Wiggs of the Cabbage Patch
Appleton-Century
PAR (US) 1934 dir. Norman Taurog
PAR (US) 1942 dir. Ralph Murphy

Rice, C.
Having Wonderful Crime
RKO (US) 1945 dir. Eddie Sutherland

Rice, C.
Home Sweet Homicide
Simon & Schuster
FOX (US) 1946 dir. Lloyd Bacon

Rice, C.
Lucky Stiff, The
World, N.Y.
UA (US) 1948 dir. Lewis R. Foster

Rice, E.
Adding Machine, The
P
Samuel French
RANK (GB) 1968 dir. Jerome Epstein

Rice, E.
Counsellor at Law
P
Samuel French
UN (US) 1933 dir. William Wyler

Rice, E.
Dream Girl
P
Hill & Wang
PAR (US) 1947 dir. Mitchell Leisen
M. EVANS (US) 1955
dir. George Schaefer
TV(US)

Rice, E.
Street Scene
P
Samuel French
UA (US) 1931 dir. King Vidor
V

Rich, M.
Bare Essence
WAR TV (US) 1982 dir. Walter Grauman
TVSe(US)

Richards, C.
Sweet Country
Harcourt, Brace, Jovanovich
CINEMA (US) 1987
dir. Michael Cacoyannis

Richards, L. E.
Captain January
FOX (US) 1936 dir. David Butler
Ch, V

Richards, R., and Ames, J.
**Renee Richards Story, The: The
Second Serve**
Stein & Day
Second Serve
LORIMAR (US) 1986 dir. Anthony Page
TV(US)

Richardson, H. H.
Getting of Wisdom, The
W. W. Norton
TEDDERWICK (Aus) 1979
dir. Bruce Beresford
V

Richardson, H. H.
Maurice Guest
Duffield
Rhapsody
MGM (US) 1954 dir. Charles Vidor

Richardson, S.
Pamela
Various
Mistress Pamela
MGM-EMI (GB) 1973
dir. Jim O'Connolly
V

Richer, C.
Tikoyo and his Shark
Beyond the Reef
UN (US) 1981 dir. Frank C. Clark

Richert, W.
**Aren't you Even Gonna Kiss Me
Goodbye**
Night in the Life of Jimmy Reardon, A.
FOX (US) 1988 dir. William Richert

Richler, M.
**Apprenticeship of Duddy Kravitz,
The**
Little, Brown (Boston)
RANK (Can) 1974 dir. Ted Kotcheff
V

Richler, M.
Joshua Then and Now
Knopf
TCF (Can) 1985 dir. Ted Kotcheff
V

Richman, A.
Awful Truth, The
P
COL (US) 1937 dir. Leo McCarey

Richman, A.
Not so Long Ago
P
Samuel French, N.Y.
Let's Do It Again
COL (US) 1953 dir. Alexander Hall
M

Richter, C.
Awakening Land, The
Knopf
WAR TV (US) 1978 dir. Boris Sagal
TVSe(US)

Richter, C.
Light in the Forest, The
Knopf
DISNEY (US) 1958
dir. Herschel Daugherty
V

Richter, C.
Tracy Cromwell
Knopf
One Desire
UI (US) 1955 dir. Jerry Hopper

Richter, C. M.
Sea of Grass, The
Franklin Watts, Inc.
MGM (US) 1947 dir. Elia Kazan

Ridley, A.
Beggar My Neighbour
P
Meet Mr Lucifer
GFD (GB) 1953 dir. Anthony Pelissier

Ridley, A.
Easy Money
P
GFD (GB) 1948 dir. Bernard Knowles

Ridley, A.
Ghost Train, The
P
Samuel French
GFD (GB) 1931 dir. Walter Forde
GFD (GB) 1941 dir. Walter Forde
V

Ridley, A.
Keepers of Youth
P
Benn
POWERS (GB) 1931
dir. Thomas Bentley

Ridley, A. and Borer, M.
Tabitha
P
Who Killed the Cat?
GN (GB) 1966 dir. Montgomery Tully

Ridley, A., and Merivale, B.
Wrecker, The
P
Seven Sinners
GAU (GB) 1937 dir. Albert de Courville
US title: Doomed Cargo

Rigby, R. and Allen, R. S.
Hill, The
P
MGM (GB) 1965 dir. Sidney Lumet

Riggs, L.
Green Grow the Lilacs
P
Oklahoma!
MAGNA (US) 1955 dir. Fred Zinnemann
M, V

Rigsby, H.
Showdown at Crazy Horse
Last Sunset, The
UI (US) 1961 dir. Robert Aldrich

Riley, L.
Personal Appearance
P
Samuel French
Go West Young Man
PAR (US) 1936 dir. Henry Hathaway

Riley, W.
Peter Pettinger
Agitator, The
BRIT NAT (GB) 1944 dir. John Harlow

Rimmer, R. H.
Harrad Experiment, The
Bantam Books
CINERAMA (US) 1973 dir. Ted Post
V

Rinehart, M. R.
Bat, The
P
Samuel French
ALLIED (US) 1959 dir. Crane Wilbur
V

Rinehart, M. R.
Bat, The
P
Samuel French
Bat Whispers, The
UA (US) 1930 dir. Roland West

Rinehart, M. R.
Lost Ecstasy
Doran, N.Y.

I Take This Woman
PAR (US) 1931 dir. Marion Gering

Rinehart, M. R.
Miss Pinkerton
Rinehart

Nurse's Secret, The
WAR (US) 1941 dir. Noel M. Smith

Rinehart, M. R.
Tish Marches On
Rinehart

Tish
MGM (US) 1942 dir. S. Sylvan Simon

Riskin, R. and Meehan, J.
Bless You Sister
P

Miracle Woman, The
COL (US) 1932 dir. Frank Capra

Ritchie, J.
Green Heart, The

New Leaf, A
PAR (US) 1970 dir. Elaine May

Roark, G.
Fair Wind to Java
Falcon Press

REP (US) 1952 dir. Joseph Kane
V

Roark, G.
Wake of the Red Witch
Little, Brown (Boston)

REP (US) 1948 dir. Edward Ludwig
V

Robb, J.
Punitive Action
Hamilton

Desert Sands
UA (US) 1955 dir. Lesley Selander

Robbins, C.
Air America
Putnam

TRI-STAR (US) 1990
dir. Roger Spottiswoode

Robbins, H.
Adventurers, The
Blond

PAR (US) 1970 dir. Lewis Gilbert

Robbins, H.
Betsy, The
Pocket Press

UA (US) 1978 dir. Daniel Petrie
V

Robbins, H.
Carpetbaggers, The
Simon & Schuster

PAR (US) 1964 dir. Edward Dmytryk
V

Robbins, H.
Dream Merchants, The

COL TV (US) 1980
dir. Vincent Sherman
TVSe(US)

Robbins, H.
Lonely Lady, The
Simon & Schuster

UN (US) 1982 dir. Peter Sasdy
V

Robbins, H.
Never Love a Stranger

ABP (US) 1958 dir. Robert Stevens
V

Robbins, H.
Pirate, The
Simon & Schuster

WAR TV (US) 1978
dir. Kenneth C. Annakin
TVSe(US)

Robbins, H.
Stiletto
AVCO (US) 1969 dir. Bernard Kowalski
V

Robbins, H.
Stone for Danny Fisher, A
Knopf
King Creole
PAR (US) 1958 dir. Michael Curtiz
V

Robbins, H.
Where Love has Gone
Simon & Schuster
PAR (US) 1964 dir. Edward Dmytryk

Robbins, H.
79 Park Avenue
Knopf
UN (US) 1977 dir. Paul Wendkos
TVSe(US)

Robbins, T.
Spurs
Freaks
MGM (US) 1932 dir. Tod Browning
V

Roberts, C. E. B.
Don Chicago
BN (GB) 1945 dir. Maclean Rogers

Roberts, D.
Smuggler's Circuit
Methuen
Law and Disorder
BL (GB) 1957 dir. Charles Crichton

Roberts, E. B. and Cavett, F. M.
Forsaking All Others
P
MGM (US) 1934 dir. W. S. Van Dyke

Roberts, E. M.
Great Meadow, The
Cape
MGM (US) 1931 dir. Charles Brabin

Roberts, K.
Captain Caution
Doubleday
UA (US) 1940 dir. Richard Wallace
V

Roberts, K.
Lydia Bailey
Doubleday
FOX (US) 1952 dir. Jean Negulesco

Roberts, K.
Northwest Passage
Doubleday
MGM (US) 1940 dir. King Vidor

Roberts, K.
Northwest Passage
Doubleday
Mission of Danger
MGM (US) 1959 dir. George Waggner,
Jacques Tourneur

Roberts, N.
This Magic Moment
Harlequin
Magic Moments
ATLANTIC/YTV (GB/US)
dir. Lawrence Gordon Clarke
TV(GB/US)

Roberts, R. E.
Star in the West
Second Time Around, The
FOX (US) 1961 dir. Vincent Sherman

Robertson, D.
Greatest Thing That Almost Never Happened, The
Putnam
FRIES (US) 1977 dir. Gilbert Moses
TV(US)

Robertson, D.
Survive the Savage Sea
Praeger
VON ZERNICK-SERTNER FILMS
(US) 1992 dir. Kevin James Dobson
TV(US)

Robertson, E. A.
Four Frightened People
PAR (US) 1934 dir. Cecil B. de Mille

Robertson, W.
Moontide
FOX (US) 1942 dir. Archie Mayo

Robeson, K.
Doc Savage— Man of Bronze
Corgi
WAR (US) 1975 dir. Michael Anderson
V

Robinson, F.
Power, The
Lippincott (Philadelphia)
MGM (US) 1968 dir. Byron Haskin

Robinson, H. M.
Cardinal, The
Simon & Schuster
COL (US) 1963 dir. Otto Preminger
V

Robinson, H. M.
Perfect Round, The
Americana
CROWN (US) 1983 dir. David Carradine
V

Robinson, J. S.
Bedtime Story
Random House
Cry for Love, A
FRIES/SACKS (US) 1980
dir. Paul Wendkos
TV(US)

Robinson, M.
Housekeeping
Farrar, Straus & Giroux
COL (US) 1987 dir. Bill Forsyth
V

Robison, M.
Oh!
Godine
Twister
VESTRON (US) 1990
dir. Michael Almereyda

Robles, E.
Cela S'Appelle L'Aurore
MARCEAU/LAE (Fr/It) 1955
dir. Luis Bunuel

Roche, A. S.
Case Against Mrs Ames, The
Melrose
PAR (US) 1936 dir. William A. Seiter

Roche, H-P.
Jules et Jim
SEDIF (Fr) 1962 dir. François Truffaut
V

Roche, M. de la
Jalna
Little, Brown (Boston)
RKO (US) 1935 dir. John Cromwell

Rock, P.
Extraordinary Seaman, The
Souvenir Press
MGM (US) 1969
dir. John Frankenheimer

Rodgers, M.
Freaky Friday
Harper & Row
DISNEY (US) 1976 dir. Gary Nelson
Ch, V

Rodgers, R. and Hammerstein, II, O.
King and I, The
FOX (US) 1956 dir. Walter Lang
M, V

Rodgers, R. and Hammerstein, II, O.
Oklahoma!
P
Random House
MAGNA (US) 1955 dir. Fred Zinnemann
M, V

Rodgers, R., Hammerstein II, O., Logan, J. and Osborn, P.
South Pacific
P
Random House
TODD AO (US) 1958 dir. Joshua Logan
M, V

Roe, V.
Golden Tide, The
Perilous Journey, A
REP (US) 1953 dir. R. G. Springsteen

Roffey, J.
Hostile Witness
P
Samuel French
UA (GB) 1968 dir. Ray Milland

Rogers, M. E.
Runestone, The
HYPERION PICTURES (US) 1992
dir. Willard Carroll

Rogers, T.
Pursuit of Happiness, The
New American Library
COL (US) 1971 dir. Robert Mulligan
V

Rogger, L. L.
Princess Comes Across, The
PAR (US) 1936 dir. William K. Howard

Rohan, C.
Delinquents, The
Penguin
GR UN (Aust) 1990 dir. Chris Thomson

Rohmer, S.
Daughter of Fu Manchu
Daughter of the Dragon
PAR (US) 1931 dir. Lloyd Corrigan

Rohmer, S.
Drums of Fu Manchu
Cassell
REP (US) 1940
dir. William Witney/John English
V

Rohmer, S.
Mask of Fu Manchu
Thorndike Press (Thorndike, Maine)
MGM (US) 1932 dir. Charles Brabin,
Charles Vidor

Rohmer, S.
Mysterious Dr. Fu Manchu
PAR (US) 1929 dir. Rowland V. Lee

Roiphe, A. R.
Up the Sandbox
Simon & Schuster
WAR (US) 1973 dir. Irwin Kershner
V

Rollin, B.
First You Cry
Lippincott (Philadelphia)
MTM (US) 1978 dir. George Schaefer
TV(US)

Rollin B.
Last Wish
Simon & Schuster
GROSSBART/BARNETT
PRODUCTIONS (US) 1992
dir. JeffBleckner
TV(US)

Roman, E.
After the Trial
Death Sentence
SPELLING-GOLDBERG (US) 1974
dir. E. W. Swackhamer
TV(US), V

Romberg, S.
Student Prince, The
MGM (US) 1954 dir. Richard Thorpe
M

Ronald, J.
Medal for the General, A
BN (GB) 1944 dir. Maurice Elvey

Ronald, J.
Murder in the Family
FOX (GB) 1938 dir. Al Parker

Ronald, J.
This Way Out
Suspect, The
UN (US) 1944 dir. Robert Siodmak

Rook, D.
Ballad of the Belstone Fox, The
Hodder & Stoughton
Belstone Fox, The
RANK (GB) 1973 dir. James Hill
V

Rook, D.
White Colt, The
Dutton
Run Wild, Run Free
COL (GB) 1989 dir. Richard C. Sarafian

Rooney, P.
Captain Boycott
INDIVIDUAL (GB) 1947
dir. Frank Launder

Roos, K.
To Save His Life
Dodd, Mead
Dead Men Tell No Tales
FOX (US) 1971 dir. Walter Grauman
TV(US)

Root, L.
Cabin in the Sky
P
MGM (US) 1943 dir. Vincente Minnelli
M, V

Ropes, B.
Forty-Second Street
WAR (US) 1933 dir. Lloyd Bacon
M, V

Rorick, I. S.
Mr and Mrs Cugat
Jarrolds
Are Husbands Necessary?
PAR (US) 1942 dir. Norman Taurog

Rose, A.
Four Horse Players are Missing
Who's Got the Action?
PAR (US) 1963 dir. Daniel Mann

Rose, A. P.
Room for One More
Houghton, Mifflin Co. (Boston)
WAR (US) 1952 dir. Norman Taurog

Rose, R.
Crime in the Streets
P
AA (US) 1956 dir. Don Siegel

Rose, R.
Twelve Angry Men
P
UA (US) 1957 dir. Sidney Lumet

Rosenbaum, E.
Taste of my own Medicine, A
Random House
Doctor, The
TOUCH (US) 1991 dir. Randa Haines

Rosenberg, H.
Atomic Soldiers
Beacon Press (Boston)
Nightbreaker
TNT (US) 1989 dir. Peter Markle
TV(US)

Rosenberg, P.
Contract on Cherry Street
Crowell
COL TV (US) 1977
dir. William A. Grahan
TV(US)

Rosny, J. H.
Quest for Fire
Pantheon Books
FOX (Can/Fr) 1982
dir. Jean-Jacques Annaud

Ross, E. and Ross, M.
Real Charlotte Somerville, The
YTV (GB) 1991 dir. Timothy Barry
TV(GB)

Ross, K.
Breaker Morant
P
S. AUST (Aust) 1980
dir. Bruce Beresford
V

Ross, S.
He Ran All The Way
Farrar, N.Y.
UA (US) 1951 dir. John Berry

Rossi, N.
Glass Full of Snow, A
CIN IT (It) 1988 dir. Florestano Vancini

Rossner, J.
Looking for Mr Goodbar
Simon & Schuster
PAR (US) 1987 dir. Richard Brooks
V

Rostand, E.
Cyrano de Bergerac
P
Samuel French
Roxanne
COL (US) 1987 dir. Fred Schepisi
V

Rostand, E.
Cyrano de Bergerac
P
UA (US) 1950 dir. Michael Gordon
V
COMPASS (US) 1962
dir. George Schaefer
TV(US)
UGC (Fr) 1990 dir. Jean-Paul Rappeneau

Rostand, M.
L'Homme Que J'ai Tué
P
Broken Lullaby
PAR (US) 1931 dir. Ernst Lubitsch

Rostand, Robert
Killer Elite, The
Delacorte Press
UA (US) 1975 dir. Sam Peckinpah
V

Rosten, L.
Captain Newman, M.D.
Harper
UI (US) 1963 dir. David Miller
V

Rosten, L.
Sleep my Love
UA (US) 1948 dir. Douglas Sirk

Roth, A.
Terrible Beauty, A
Farrar, Straus & Cudahy
UA (GB) 1960 dir. Tay Garnett

Roth, J.
Legend of the Holy Drinker
ART EYE (It) 1989 dir. Ermanno Olnu

Roth, L., Frank, G.
I'll Cry Tomorrow
F. Fell
MGM (US) 1955 dir. Daniel Mann
V

Roth, P.
Goodbye Columbus
Bantam Books
PAR (US) 1969 dir. Larry Peerce
V

Roth, P.
Portnoy's Complaint
Random House
WAR (US) 1972 dir. Ernest Lehman
V

Rothenberg, M. and White, M.
David
Revell
ITC (US) 1988 dir. John Erman
TV(US)

Rouland, J-P and Olivier, C.
Tendre Poulet
Dear Inspector
ARIANE/MONDEX (Fr) 1977
dir. Philippe de Broca

Roussin, A. & Mitford, N.
Little Hut, The
P
Random House
MGM (US) 1957 dir. Mark Robson

Rouverol, A.
Skidding
P
Samuel French
Family Affair, A
MGM (US) 1937 dir. George B. Seitz

Rowe, Jr., G. T.
My Years with the KKK
Undercover with the KKK
COL TV (US) 1979 dir. Barry Shear
TV(US)

Royle, E. M.
Squaw Man, The
P
MGM (US) 1931 dir. Cecil B. deMille
GB title: White Man, The

Ruark, R.
Something of Value
Doubleday
MGM (US) 1957 dir. Richard Brooks
V

Rubens, B.
I Sent a Letter to My Love
St. Martin's Press
ATLANTIC (Fr) 1981
dir. Moshe Mizrahi
V

Rubens, B.
Madame Sousatzka
UN (GB) 1988 dir. John Schlesinger
V

Rubin, D.
Riddle Me This
P
Samuel French
Guilty as Hell
PAR (US) 1932 dir. Erle C. Kenton

Rubin, D.
Riddle Me This
P
Samuel French
Night Club Scandal
PAR (US) 1937 dir. Ralph Murphy

Rubin, T. I.
Lisa and David
Macmillan
David and Lisa
BL (US) 1963 dir. Frank Perry
V

Ruesch, H.
Racer, The
Racers, The
FOX (US) 1955 dir. Henry Hathaway
GB title: Such Men are Dangerous

Ruesch, H.
Top of the World
Savage Innocents, The
RANK (Fr/It/GB) 1960
dir. Nicholas Ray
V

Ruggles, E.
Prince of Players
Norton
FOX (US) 1954 dir. Philip Dunne

Rule, A.
Small Sacrifices
New American Library
FRIES (US) 1989 dir. David Greene
TVSe(US)

Rule, J.
Desert of the Heart
Desert Hearts
MGM (US) 1986 dir. Donna Deitch
V

Runyon, D.
Bloodhounds of Broadway
Morrow
FOX (US) 1952 dir. Harmon Jones
COL (US) 1989 dir. Howard Brookner

Runyon, D.
Guys and Dolls
Penguin
MGM (US) 1955
dir. Joseph L. Mankiewicz
M, V

Runyon, D.
Johnny One-Eye
Morrow
UA (US) 1950 dir. Robert Florey

Runyon, D.
Lemon Drop Kid, The
Morrow
PAR (US) 1951 dir. Sidney Lanfield

Runyon, D.
Little Miss Marker
Morrow
PAR (US) 1934 dir. Alexander Hall
GB title: Girl in Pawn, The
UN (US) 1980 dir. Walter Bernstein
V

Runyon, D.
Little Pinks
Big Street, The
RKO (US) 1942 dir. Irving Reis
V

Runyon, D.
Madame la Gimp
Morrow
Lady for a Day
COL (US) 1933 dir. Frank Capra

Runyon, D.
Madame la Gimp
Morrow
Pocketful of Miracles
UA (US) 1961 dir. Frank Capra
V

Runyon, D.
Money from Home
Morrow
PAR (US) 1953 dir. George Marshall

Runyon, D., and Caesar, I.
Straight, Place and Show
P
FOX (US) 1938 dir. David Butler
GB title: They're Off

Runyon, D. and Lindsay, H.
Slight Case of Murder, A
P
Theatre Communications Group
WAR (US) 1938 dir. Lloyd Bacon

Runyon, D. and Lindsay, H.
Slight Case of Murder, A
P
Theatre Communications Group
Stop, You're Killing Me
WAR (US) 1952 dir. Roy del Ruth

Russell, R.
Incubus, The
Sphere
NEW REALM (Can) 1982
dir. John Hough
V

Russell, S. M.
Lamp is Heavy, A
Angus & Robertson
Feminine Touch, The
RANK (GB) 1956 dir. Pat Jackson

Russell, W.
Educating Rita
P
Samuel French
RANK (GB) 1983 dir. Lewis Gilbert
V

Russell, W.
Shirley Valentine
P
Samuel French
PAR (GB) 1989 dir. Lewis Gilbert
V

Russo, E.
Martedì del Diavolo, Il
Russicum
TRI-STAR/Cecchi (It) 1989
dir. Pasquale Squitieri

Ryan, C.
Bridge Too Far, A
Simon & Schuster
UA (GB/US) 1977
dir. Richard Attenborough
V

Ryan, C.
Longest Day, The
Simon & Schuster
FOX (US) 1962 dir. Ken Annakin,
AndrewMarton,Bernhard Wicki
V

Ryan, C. and Ryan, K. M.
Private Battle, A
Simon & Schuster
P&G (US) 1980
dir. Robert Michael Lewis
TV(US)

Ryan, J. M.
Brook Wilson Ltd
Hodder Fawcett
Loving
COL (US) 1970 dir. Irvin Kershner

Ryan, P.
How I Won the War
Morrow
UA (GB) 1967 dir. Richard Lester
V

Ryck, F.
Family Business
EUROPEAN (Fr) 1987 dir. Costa-Gavras

Ryskind, M.
Louisiana Purchase
P
PAR (US) 1941 dir. Irving Cummings
M

Ryskind, M. and Kaufman, G.S.
Animal Crackers
P
Samuel French
PAR (US) 1930 dir. Victor Heerman
V

Ryton, R.
Crown Matrimonial
P
TALENT (US) 1974 dir. Alan Bridges
TV(US)

Saba, U.
Ernesto
Carcanet (Manchester)
CLESI (It) 1978 dir. Salvatore Samperi
V

Sabatini, R.
Black Swan, The
Hutchinson
FOX (US) 1942 dir. Henry King

Sabatini, R.
Captain Blood Returns
Captain Pirate
COL (US) 1952 dir. Ralph Murphy
GB title: Captain Blood, Fugitive

Sabatini, R.
Captain Blood
Houghton, Mifflin Co. (Boston)
WAR (US) 1935 dir. Michael Curtiz
V

Sabatini, R.
Fortunes of Captain Blood, The
Grosset & Dunlap
COL (US) 1950 dir. Gordon Douglas

Sabatini, R.
Scaramouche
Houghton, Mifflin Co. (Boston)
MGM (US) 1952 dir. George Sidney
V

Sabatini, R.
Sea Hawk, The
WAR (US) 1940 dir. Michael Curtiz
V

Sacher-Masoch, L. von
Venus in Furs
COMM (GB/It/Ger) 1970
dir. Jess Franco
V

Sackler, H.
Great White Hope, The
P
Samuel French
FOX (US) 1970 dir. Martin Ritt
V

Sacks, O.
Awakenings
Vintage Books
COL (US) 1990 dir. Penny Marshall
V

Sacks, O.
Man Who Mistook His Wife for a Hat, The
Harper & Row
CHANNEL 4 (GB) 1988
dir. Christopher Rawlence
TV(GB)

Sackville-West, V.
All Passion Spent
Doubleday
BBC (GB) 1986
TV(GB)

Sadleir, M.
Fanny by Gaslight
Appleton-Century
GFD (GB) 1944 dir. Anthony Asquith
US title: Man of Evil
V
BBC (GB) 1981 dir. Peter Jefferies
TVSe(GB)

Sae, S.
Rojuko Kazoku
Promise, A
KT (Jap) 1987 dir. Yoshishige Yoshida

Sagan, F.
Aimez-vous Brahms?
Murray
Goodbye Again
UA (US) 1961 dir. Anatole Litvak

Sagan, F.
Bonjour Tristesse
Dutton
COL (GB) 1957 dir. Otto Preminger
V

Sagan, F.
Certain Smile, A.
Dutton
FOX (US) 1958 dir. Jean Negulesco

Sagan, F.
Chamade, La
Dutton
ARIANE (Fr) 1969 dir. Alain Cavalier
US title: Heartkeeper, The

Saint, H. F.
Memoirs of an Invisible Man
Atheneum
WARNER BROS. (US) 1992
dir. John Carpenter

St. John, A. R.
Final Verdict
Doubleday
Final Verdict, The
TURNER (US) 1991 dir. Jack Fisk
TV(US)

St. John, A. R.
Free Soul, A
MGM (US) 1931 dir. Clarence Brown

St. John, A. R.
Girl Who Had Everything, The
MGM (US) 1953 dir. Richard Thorpe

St. John L. Cloowes
Dear Murderer
GFD (GB) 1947 dir. Arthur Crabtree

Saint-Exupery de, A.
Little Prince, The
Reynal & Hitchcock
PAR (US) 1974 dir. Stanley Donen
M, V

Saint-Laurent, C.
Caroline Chérie
GAU (Fr) 1951 dir. Richard Pottier

Saint-Laurent, C.
Lola Montes
GAMMA (Fr/Ger) 1955
dir. Max Ophuls
V

Saki, R.
Vengeance is Mine
KINO (Jap) 1979 dir. Shohei Imamura

Salamanca, J. R.
Lilith
Simon & Schuster
COL (US) 1964 dir. Robert Rossen
V

Salamanca, J. R.
Lost Country, The
Wild in the Country
FOX (US) 1961 dir. Philip Dunne
V

Sale, D.
Come to Mother
Live Again, Die Again
UN TV (US) 1974 dir. Richard Colla
TV(US)

Sale, R.
Not Too Narrow, Not Too Deep
Strange Cargo
MGM (US) 1940
dir. Joseph L. Mankiewicz

Sale, R.
Oscar, The
Simon & Schuster
PAR (US) 1966 dir. Russel Rouse
V

Sale, R.
White Buffalo, The
Simon & Schuster
EMI (US) 1977 dir. J. Lee Thompson

Salerno, S.
Deadly Blessing
Bed of Lies
WOLPER TV(US) 1992
dir. William A. Graham

Salten, F.
Bambi
Grosset & Dunlap
DISNEY (US) 1942 dir. David Hand
A, Ch, V

Salten, F.
Florian
Cape
MGM (US) 1940 dir. Edwin L. Marin

Salten, F.
Hound of Florence, The
Shaggy Dog, The
DISNEY (US) 1959 dir. Charles Barton
Ch, V

Salten, F.
Perri
Bobbs-Merrill (Indianapolis)
DISNEY (US) 1957 dir. Ralph Wright
Ch, V

Salter, J.
Hunters, The
Harper
FOX (US) 1958 dir. Dick Powell

San-Antonio
Lady who Wades in the Sea, The
Fleuve Noir (Paris)
PRESIDENT (Fr) 1991
dir. Laurent Heynemann

Sanders, G.
Stranger at Home
Stranger Came Home, The
EXCL (GB) 1954 dir. Terence Fisher
US title: Unholy Four, The

Sanders, L.
Anderson Tapes, The
Putnam
COL (US) 1971 dir. Sidney Lumet
V

Sanders, L.
First Deadly Sin, The
Putnam
CIC (US) 1980 dir. Brian G. Hutton
V

Sandler, S.
Crossing Delancey
P
Samuel French
WAR (US) 1988 dir. Joan Micklin Silver
V

Sandoz, M.
Cheyenne Autumn
McGraw-Hill
WAR (US) 1964 dir. John Ford

Sands, L.
Deadlock
P
English Theatre
Another Man's Poison
EROS (GB) 1951 dir. Irving Rapper

Sandstrom, F.
Madness of the Heart
Cassell
TC (GB) 1949 dir. Charles Bennett

Sandstrom, F.
Midwife of Pont Clery, The
Ace
Jessica
UA (Fr/It) 1961 dir. Jean Negulesco

Sandstrom, F.
Milk White Unicorn, The
White Unicorn, The
GFD (GB) 1947 dir. Bernard Knowles
US title: Bad Sister

Sanford, H. and Lamb, M.
Emporia
Waco
PAR (US) 1966 dir. R. G. Springsteen

Sangster, J.
Foreign Exchange
ABC (US) 1970 dir. Roy Baker
TV(US)

Sangster, J.
Private I
Norton
Spy Killer, The
ABC (US) 1969 dir. Roy Baker
TV(US)

Sansom, W.
Last Hours of Sandra Lee, The
Wild Affair, The
BL (GB) 1965 dir. John Irish

Saperstein, D.
Cocoon
Thorndike Press (Thorndike, Maine)
FOX (US) 1985 dir. Ron Howard
V

Sardou, V.
Madame Sans-Gene
P
Albin Michel (Paris)
FOX (Fr/It/Sp) 1962
dir. Christian-Jaque
US/GB title: Madame

Saroyan, W.
Human Comedy, The
Harcourt Brace & Co.
MGM (US) 1943 dir. Clarence Brown
V

Saroyan, W.
Time of Your Life, The
P
Samuel French
UA (US) 1948 dir. H. C. Potter

Sartre, J-P.
Condemned of Altona, The
P
Knopf
FOX (Fr/It) 1962 dir. Vittorio di Sica

Sartre, J-P.
Huis Clos
P
Samuel French
MARCEAU (Fr) 1954
dir. Jacqueline Audry

Sartre, J-P.
Mains Sales, Les
P
Gallimard (Paris)
RIVERS (Fr) 1951 dir. Fernand Rivers

Sartre, J-P.
Respectable Prostitute, The
P
Gallimard (Paris)
MARCEAU (Fr) 1952
dir. Marcel Pagliero, Charles Brabant

Saul, J.
Cry for the Strangers
MGM (US) 1982 dir. Peter Medak
TV(US)

Saul, O.
Dark Side of Love, The
Harper & Row
My Kidnapper, My Love
EMI (US) 1980 dir. Sam Wanamaker
TV(US)

Saunders, H. St. G.
Red Beret, The
COL (GB) 1953 dir. Terence Young
US title: Paratrooper
V

Saunders, J. M.
Devil Dogs of the Air
WAR (US) 1935 dir. Lloyd Bacon

Saunders, J. M.
Single Lady
Last Flight, The
WAR (US) 1931 dir. William Dieterle

Savage, G.
Slate Wyn and Blanche McBride
Slate, Wyn and Me
HEMDALE (Aust) 1987
dir. Don McLennan

Savage, M.
Parrish
Simon & Schuster
WAR (US) 1961 dir. Delmer Daves

Savan, G.
White Palace
Bantam Books
UN (US) 1990 dir. Luis Mandoki
V

Savoir, A.
Bluebeard's Eighth Wife
P
PAR (US) 1938 dir. Ernst Lubitsch

Savory, G.
George and Margaret
P
Samuel French
WAR (GB) 1940 dir. George King

Savoy, A. A.
I Went to the Dance
BRAZOS (US) 1989 dir. Leon Blank, C.
Strachwitz

Saxon, L.
LaFitte the Pirate
The Century Company
Buccaneer, The
PAR (US) 1937 dir. Cecil B. de Mille
PAR (US) 1958 dir. Anthony Quinn
V

Saxon, P.
Disorientated Man, The
Scream and Scream Again
AIP (GB) 1969 dir. Gordon Hessler
V

Saxton, M.
Jayne Mansfield and the American Fifties
Houghton, Mifflin Co. (Boston)
Jayne Mansfield Story, The
LAN (US) 1980 dir. Dick Lowry
TV(US)

Sayers, D. L.
Busman's Honeymoon
Kent State University Press (Kent, Ohio)
MGM (GB) 1940 dir. Arthur Woods
US title: Haunted Honeymoon
BBC (GB) 1988
TVSe(GB)

Sayers, G. and Silverman, A.
I am Third
Brian's Song
COL TV (US) 1971 dir. Buzz Kulik
TV(US), V

Schaefer, J. W.
Shane
Houghton, Mifflin Co. (Boston)
PAR (US) 1953 dir. George Stevens
V

Schaefer, J.
Monte Walsh
Houghton, Mifflin Co. (Boston)
CIN CEN (US) 1970
dir. William A. Fraker
V

Schary, D.
Sunrise at Campobello
P
Random House
WAR (US) 1960 dir. Vincent J. Donehue
V

Schauffler, E.
Parnell
P
MGM (US) 1937 dir. John M. Stahl

Schisgal, M.
Luv
P
Dodd, Mead
COL (US) 1967 dir. Clive Donner
V

Schisgal, M.
Tiger, The
P
Dramatists Play Service
Tiger Makes Out, The
COL (US) 1967 dir. Arthur Hiller

Schlesinger, Jr., A. M.
Robert Kennedy and his Times
Houghton, Mifflin Co. (Boston)
COL (US) 1985 dir. Marvin J. Chomsky
TVSe(US)

Schmidt, L.
Only a Dream
P
One Hour With You
PAR (US) 1932 dir. George Cukor,
Ernst Lubitsch
M

Schnitzler, A.
Liebelei
P
ELITE (Fr) 1932 dir. Max Ophuls

Schnitzler, A.
Ronde, La
P
Samuel French
S. GARDINE (Fr) 1950 dir. Max Ophuls
V
INTEROPA (Fr) 1964 dir. Roger Vadim

Schoendoerffer, P.
Crabe Tambour, Le
Coward, McCann & Geoghegan
AMLF (Fr) 1977
dir. Pierre Schoendoerffer

Schoendoerffer, P.
Farewell to the King
Stein & Day
ORION (US) 1989 dir. John Milius

Scholefield, A.
Venom
PAR (GB) 1982 dir. Piers Haggard
V

Schott, M.
Murphy's Romance
Harper & Row
COL (US) 1985 dir. Martin Ritt
V

Schrank, J. and Dunning, P.
Page Miss Glory
P
Samuel French
PAR (US) 1935 dir. Mervyn LeRoy

Schreiber, F. R.
Sybil
H. Regnery (Chicago)
LORIMAR (US) 1976 dir. Daniel Petrie
TVSe(US), V

Schulberg, B. W.
Harder They Fall
Random House
COL (US) 1956 dir. Mark Robson
V

Schulberg, B. W.
On the Waterfront
Random House
COL (US) 1954 dir. Elia Kazan
V

Schulberg, B. W.
Your Arkansas Traveller
Random House
Face in the Crowd, A
WAR (US) 1957 dir. Elia Kazan
V

Schulman, A.
Hole in the Head, A
P
Samuel French
UA (US) 1959 dir. Frank Capra

Schwartz, S.
Like Mother, Like Me
Like Mom, Like Me
CBS ENT (US) 1978
dir. Michael Pressman
TV(US)

Schweizer, R.
Last Chance, The
Drummond & Secker
MGM (Switz) 1945
dir. Leopold Lindtberg

Sciascia, L.
The Context
Illustrious Corpses
PEA/LAA (It) 1976 dir. Francesco Rosi

Scortia, T. N. and Robinson, F. M.
Glass Inferno, The
Doubleday
Towering Inferno, The
COL-WAR (US) 1975
dir. John Gullermin, Irwin Allen
V

Scortia, T. N. and Robinson, F. M.
Gold Crew, The
Warner Books
Fifth Missile, The
MGM/UA TV (US) 1986
dir. Larry Peerce
TV(US)

Scott, A. and Haight, G.
Goodbye Again
P
Samuel French
Honeymoon for Three
WAR (US) 1941 dir. Lloyd Bacon

Scott, A.
Great Man's Whiskers, The
P

UN TV (US) 1973 dir. Philip Leacock
TV(US)

Scott, J. M.
Sea Wyf and Biscuit
Sea Wife
FOX (GB) 1957 dir. Bob McNaught
V

Scott, P.
Raj Quartet, The
Jewel in the Crown, The
GRANADA (GB) 1984 dir. Jim O'Brien/
Christopher Morahan
TVSe(GB), V

Scott, P.
Staying On
Morrow
GRANADA (GB) 1980
dir. Silvio Narizzano/WarisHussein
TV(GB), V

Scott, R. L.
God is my Co-Pilot
Hodder & Stoughton
WAR (US) 1945 dir. Robert Florey

Scott, W.
Umbrella Man, The
P
London by Night
MGM (US) 1937 dir. William Thiele

Scott, Sir W.
Ivanhoe
Various
MGM (GB) 1952 dir. Richard Thorpe
V
COL (US/GB) 1982
dir. Douglas Canfield
TV(GB/US)

Scott, Sir W.
Quentin Durward
Various
Adventures of Quentin Durward, The
MGM (GB) 1955 dir. Richard Thorpe
US title: Quentin Durward

Scott, Sir W.
Talisman, The
Various
King Richard and the Crusaders
WAR (US) 1954 dir. David Butler

Scruggs, J. C. and Swerdlow, J. L.
To Heal a Nation
Harper & Row
ORION TV (US) 1988
dir. Michael Pressman
TV(US)

Scudder, K. J.
Prisoners are People
Unchained
WAR (US) 1955 dir. Hall Bartlett

Seals, D.
Pow Wow Highway
WAR (US) 1989 dir. Jonathan Wacks

Searls, H.
Crowded Sky, The
Harper
WAR (US) 1960 dir. Joseph Pevney

Searls, H.
Lost Prince, The: Young Joe, The Forgotten Kennedy
World Publishing Co.
Young Joe, the Forgotten Kennedy
ABC (US) 1977 dir. Richard T. Heffron
TV(US)

Searls, H.
Overboard
Norton
FAC-NEW (US) 1978 dir. John Newland
TV(US)

Seaton, G.
Cockeyed Miracle, The
P
MGM (US) 1946 dir. S. Sylvan Simon

Secondari, J.
Coins in the Fountain
Lippincott (Philadelphia)
Three Coins in the Fountain
FOX (US) 1954 dir. Jean Negulesco

Secondari, J. H.
Coins in the Fountain
Lippincott (Philadelphia)
Pleasure Seekers, The
FOX (US) 1964 dir. Jean Negulesco

Seeley, C.
Storm Fear
Holt
UA (US) 1955 dir. Cornel Wilde

Seff, M. and Wilson, F.
Blessed Event
P
WAR (US) 1932 dir. Roy del Ruth

Segal, E.
Love Story
Harper & Row
PAR (US) 1970 dir. Arthur Hiller
V

Segal, E.
Man, Woman and Child
Harper & Row
PAR (US) 1983 dir. Dick Richards
V

Segal, E.
Oliver's Story
Harper & Row
PAR (US) 1978 dir. John Korty
V

Segall, H.
For Heaven's Sake
P
FOX (US) 1950 dir. George Seaton

Segall, H.
Halfway to Heaven
P
Heaven Can Wait
PAR (US) 1978 dir. Warren Beatty,
Buck Henry
V

Segall, H.
Halfway to Heaven
P
Here Comes Mr. Jordan
COL (US) 1941 dir. Alexander Hall
V

Seghers, A.
Seventh Cross, The
Little, Brown (Boston)
MGM (US) 1944 dir. Fred Zinnemann

Selby, Jr. H.
Last Exit to Brooklyn
Grove Press
GUILD (Ger) 1989 dir. Ulrich Edel

Selinko, A.
Desirée
Morrow
FOX (US) 1954 dir. Henry Koster
V

Sellers, S.
Terror on Highway 59
Terror on Highway 91
CBS (US) 1989 dir. Jerry Jameson
TV(US)

Sellier, Jr., C. E.
Capture of Grizzly Adams, The
TAFT (US) 1982 dir. Don Kessler
TV(US)

Selwyn, E.
Barbarian, The
P

MGM (US) 1933 dir. Sam Wood
GB title: Night in Cairo, A

Selwyn, E.
Mirage, The
P

Possessed
MGM (US) 1931 dir. Clarence Brown
V

Semple, L.
Golden Fleecing, The
P

Samuel French

Honeymoon Machine, The
MGM (US) 1961 dir. Richard Thorpe

Sender, R. J.
Days of Dawn

Valentina
OFELIA (Sp) 1983
dir. Antonio José Betancor

Senesh, H.
Diaries of Hannah Senesh, The

Hannah's War
CANNON (US) 1988
dir. Menahem Golan
V

Serling, R. J.
President's Plane is Missing, The
Doubleday

ABC (US) 1973 dir. Daryl Duke
TV(US)

Serling, R.
Patterns
P

Simon & Schuster

UA (US) 1956 dir. Fielder Cook
GB title: Patterns of Power

Serling, R.
Requiem for a Heavyweight
P

Samuel French

COL (US) 1962 dir. Ralph Nelson
GB title: Blood Money

Seton, A.
Dragonwyck
Houghton, Mifflin Co. (Boston)

FOX (US) 1946
dir. Joseph L. Mankiewicz

Seton, A.
Foxfire
Ulverscroft (London)

UI (US) 1955 dir. Joseph Pevney

Seton, E. T.
Biography of a Grizzly and Other Animal Stories, The
Rand McNally (Chicago)

Legend of Lobo, The
DISNEY (US) 1962 dir. James Algar
Ch, V

Seton, E. T.
Biography of a Grizzly, The
Rand McNally (Chicago)

King of the Grizzlies
DISNEY (US) 1970 dir. Ron Kelly
V

Seward, F. A.
Gold for the Caesars
Redman

MGM (US) 1964 dir. Andre de Toth

Sewell, A.
Black Beauty

FOX (US) 1946 dir. Max Nosseck
TIGON (GB) 1971 dir. James Hill
UN (US) 1978 dir. Daniel Haller
Ch, TVSe(US)

Seymour, G.
Glory Boys, The
Random House
YTV (GB) 1984 dir. Michael Ferguson
TV(GB), V

Seymour, G.
Harry's Game
Random House
YTV (GB) 1982
dir. Lawrence Gordon Clark
TVSe(GB), V

Seymour, H.
Infernal Idol
Avon, N.Y.
Craze
EMI (GB) 1973 dir. Freddie Francis
V

Shadbolt, M.
Among the Cinders
NEW WORLD (US) 1985
dir. Rolf Haedrich
V

Shaffer, A.
Sleuth
P
Samuel French
FOX (GB) 1972
dir. Joseph L. Mankiewicz
V

Shaffer, P.
Amadeus
P
Samuel French
ORION (US) 1984 dir. Milos Forman
V

Shaffer, P.
Equus
P
Samuel French
UA (GB) 1977 dir. Sidney Lumet
V

Shaffer, P.
Five Finger Exercise
P
Harcourt Brace
COL (US) 1962 dir. Delbert Mann

Shaffer, P.
Private Ear, The
P
Samuel French
Pad (And How to Use It), The
UI (US) 1966 dir. Brian C. Hutton

Shaffer, P.
Public Eye, The
P
Samuel French
Follow Me
UN (GB) 1972 dir. Carol Reed
US title: Public Eye, The

Shaffer, P.
Royal Hunt of the Sun, The
P
Samuel French
RANK (GB) 1969 dir. Irving Lerner

Shaffer, R. K.
Finger Man, The
Lady Killer
WAR (US) 1933 dir. Roy del Ruth

Shagan, S.
Formula, The
Morrow
MGM (US) 1980 dir. John G. Avildsen
V

Shakespeare, W.
Antony and Cleopatra
P
Various
RANK (GB) 1972 dir. Charlton Heston
V
ITV (GB) 1974 dir. Jon Scoffield

Shakespeare, W.
As You Like It
P
Various
FOX (GB) 1936 dir. Paul Czinner
V

Shakespeare, W.
Comedy of Errors, The
P
Various
Boys from Syracuse, The
UN (US) 1940 dir. E. A. Sutherland
M

Shakespeare, W.
Hamlet
P
Various
TC (GB) 1948 dir. Laurence Olivier
M. EVANS (US) 1953
dir. Albert McCleery
TV(US)
CLASSIC (USSR) 1964
dir. Grigori Kozintsev
V
COL (GB) 1969 dir. Tony Richardson
V
ATV/UN (GB/US) 1970 dir. Peter Wood
TV(GB/US)
WAR/GUILD (US/GB) 1990
dir. Franco Zeffirelli
V

Shakespeare, W.
Henry V
P
Various
TC (GB) 1944 dir. Laurence Olivier
V
RENAISSANCE (GB) 1989
dir. Kenneth Branagh

Shakespeare, W.
Julius Caesar
P
Various
MGM (US) 1953
dir. Joseph L. Mankiewicz
MGM (GB) 1969 dir. Stuart Burge
V

Shakespeare, W.
King Lear
P
Various
COL (Den/GB) 1970 dir. Peter Brook
V
GRANADA (GB) 1983
dir. Michael Elliott
TV(GB)
CANNON (US) 1988
dir. Jean-Luc Godard

Shakespeare, W.
King Lear
P
Various
Ran
Jap 1985 dir. Akira Kurosawa

Shakespeare, W.
King Richard II
P
Various
M EVANS (US) 1954
dir. George Schaefer
TV(US)

Shakespeare, W.
Macbeth
P
Various
REP (US) 1948 dir. Orson Welles
V
M. EVANS (US) 1954
dir. George Schaefer
TV(US), V
COMPASS (US) 1960
dir. George Schaefer
TV(US)
COL-WAR (GB) 1971
dir. Roman Polanski
V

Shakespeare, W.
Merchant of Venice, The
P
Various
ATV (GB) 1974 dir. Jonathan Miller
TV(GB), V

Shakespeare, W.
Midsummer Night's Dream, A
P
Various
WAR (US) 1935 dir. Max Reinhardt
V
ITV (GB) 1964 dir. Joan Kemp-Welch
TV(GB)
COL (US) 1967 dir. Dan Eriksen
EAGLE (GB) 1968 dir. Peter Hall
V
MAINLINE (GB/Sp) 1985
dir. Celestino Corrado
V

Shakespeare, W.
Othello
P
Various
MERCURY (US/Fr) 1951
dir. Orson Welles
EAGLE (GB) 1965 dir. Stuart Burge

Shakespeare, W.
Othello
P
Various
Othello the Black Commando
M B DIFF 1982
TV

Shakespeare, W.
Richard III
P
Various
BL (GB) 1955 dir. Laurence Olivier
V

Shakespeare, W.
Romeo and Juliet
P
Various
MGM (US) 1936 dir. George Cukor
GFD (GB) 1954 dir. Renato Castellani
V
PAR (GB) 1968 dir. Franco Zeffirelli
V

Shakespeare, W.
Taming of the Shrew, The
P
Various
M. EVANS (US) 1956
dir. George Schaefer
TV(US)
COL (US) 1967 dir. Franco Zeffirelli
V

Shakespeare, W.
Taming of the Shrew, The
P
Various
Kiss Me Kate
MGM (US) 1953 dir. George Sidney
M, V
MILBERG (US) 1958
dir. George Schaefer
TV(US)

Shakespeare, W.
Tempest, The
P
Various
COMPASS (US) 1960
dir. George Schaefer
TV(US), V
MAINLINE (GB) 1958
dir. Derek Jarman
V

Shakespeare, W.
Tempest, The
P
Various
Prospero's Books
FILM 4 (GB/Fr) 1991
dir. Peter Greenaway

Shakespeare, W.
Twelfth Night
P
Various
MILBERG (US) 1957 dir. David Greene
TV(US)

Shakespeare, W.
Winter's Tale, The
P
Various
WAR (GB) 1968 dir. Frank Dunlop

Shankar
Company Limited
CHILRANGALI (Ind) 1971
dir. Satyajit Ray
V

Shannon, E.
**Desperados: Latin Drug Lords, US
Lawmen and the War America
Can't Win**
Viking Press
Drug Wars: The Camarena Story
ZZY INC. (US) 1990 dir. Brian Gibson
TVSe(US)

Shannon, R.
Fabulous Ann Medlock
Adventures of Captain Fabian, The
REP (US) 1951 dir. William Marshall
V

Shapiro, L.
Sealed Verdict
PAR (US) 1948 dir. Lewis Allen

Shapiro, L.
Sixth of June, The
Doubleday
D-Day the Sixth of June
FOX (US) 1956 dir. Henry Koster
V

Sharp, D.
Conflict of Wings
Putnam, N.Y.
BL (GB) 1953 dir. John Eldridge
US title: Fuss Over Feathers

Sharp, M.
Britannia Mews
Little, Brown (Boston)
TCF (GB) 1948 dir. Jean Negulesco
US title: Forbidden Street, The

Sharp, M.
Cluny Brown
Little, Brown (Boston)
FOX (US) 1946 dir. Ernst Lubitsch

Sharp, M.
Nutmeg Tree, The
Little, Brown (Boston)
Julia Misbehaves
MGM (US) 1948 dir. Jack Conway

Sharp, M.
Rescuers, The, Miss Bianca
Little, Brown (Boston)
Rescuers, The
DISNEY (US) 1977
dir. Wolfgang Reitherman
A, Ch

Sharpe, T.
Blott on the Landscape
Secker & Warburg (London)
BBC (GB) 1985 dir. Roger Bamford
TVSe(GB)

Sharpe, T.
Wilt
Secker & Warburg (London)
RANK (GB) 1989 dir. Michael Tuchner

Sharpe, T.
Wilt
Secker & Warburg (London)
Misadventures of Mr. Wilt, The
GOLDWYN (US) 1990
dir. Michael Tuchner

Shaw, C.
Heaven Knows Mr. Allison
Muller
FOX (US) 1957 dir. John Huston

Shaw, G. B.
Androcles and the Lion
P
Samuel French
RKO (US) 1952 dir. Chester Erskine
V

Shaw, G. B.
Arms And The Man
P
Samuel French
WARDOUR (GB) 1932 dir. Cecil Lewis
ARGENT (GB) 1982
TV(GB)

Shaw, G. B.
Arms and the Man
P
Samuel French
Helden
SOKAL/GOLDBAUM (Ger) 1959
dir. Franz Peter Wirth

Shaw, G. B.
Caesar and Cleopatra
P
Samuel French
RANK (GB) 1945 dir. Gabriel Pascal
V
TALENT ASS. (US) 1976
dir. James Cellan Jones
TV(US)

Shaw, G. B.
Captain Brassbound's Conversion
P
Samuel French
COMPASS (US) 1960
dir. George Schaefer
TV(US)

Shaw, G. B.
Devil's Disciple, The
P
Samuel French
M. EVANS (US) 1955
dir. George Schaefer
TV(US)
UA (GB) 1959 dir. Guy Hamilton

Shaw, G. B.
Doctor's Dilemma, The
P
Samuel French
MGM (GB) 1958 dir. Anthony Asquith

Shaw, G. B.
Great Catherine
P
Samuel French
WAR (GB) 1968 dir. Gordon Flemyng

Shaw, G. B.
How He Lied to Her Husband
P
Samuel French
BI (GB) 1931 dir. Cecil Lewis

Shaw, G. B.
Major Barbara
P
Samuel French
PASCAL (GB) 1941
dir. Gabriel Pascal/Harold French/David
Lean
V

Shaw, G. B.
Man and Superman
P
Samuel French
MILBERG (US) 1956
dir. George Schaefer
TV(US)

Shaw, G. B.
Millionairess, The
P
Samuel French
FOX (GB) 1960 dir. Anthony Asquith

Shaw, G. B.
Pygmalion
P
Samuel French
MGM (GB) 1938 dir. Anthony Asquith
V
COMPASS (US) 1963
dir. George Schaefer
TV(US)

Shaw, G. B.
Pygmalion
P
Samuel French
My Fair Lady
WAR (US) 1964 dir. George Cukor
M, V

Shaw, G. B.
Saint Joan
P
Samuel French
UA (GB) 1957 dir. Otto Preminger
V
COMPASS (US) 1967
dir. George Schaefer
TV(US)

Shaw, I.
Beggarman, Thief
Delacorte Press
UN TV (US) 1979 dir. Lawrence Doheny
TVSe(US)

Shaw, I.
Evening in Byzantium
Delacorte Press
UN TV (US) 1978 dir. Jerry London
TVSe(US)

Shaw, I.
Gentle People, The
P
Random House
Out of the Fog
WAR (US) 1941 dir. Anatole Litvak

Shaw, I.
In the French Style
Delacorte Press
COL (US/Fr) 1963 dir. Robert Parrish

Shaw, I.
Rich Man, Poor Man
Delacorte Press
UN (US) 1976 dir. David Greene, Boris Sagal
TVSe(US)

Shaw, I.
Then There Were Three
Delacorte Press
Three
UA (GB) 1969 dir. James Salter

Shaw, I.
Tip on a Dead Jockey
Random House
MGM (US) 1957 dir. Richard Thorpe
GB title: Time for Action

Shaw, I.
Two Weeks in Another Town
Random House
MGM (US) 1962 dir. Vincente Minnelli

Shaw, I.
Young Lions, The
Random House
FOX (US) 1958 dir. Edward Dmytryk
V

Shaw, R.
Hiding Place, The
Situation Hopeless But Not Serious
PAR (US) 1965 dir. Gottfried Reinhardt

Shea, T.
Sarah and Son
PAR (US) 1930 dir. Dorothy Arzner

Shearing, J.
Airing in a Closed Carriage
Harper & Bros.
Mark of Cain, The
TC (GB) 1948 dir. Brian Desmond Hurst

Shearing, J.
Blanche Fury
Heinemann
CIN (GB) 1948 dir. Marc Allégret

Shearing, J.
For Her to See
So Evil My Love
PAR (GB) 1948 dir. Lewis Allen

Sheckley, R.
Game of X, The
Sphere
Condorman
DISNEY (US) 1981 dir. Charles Jarrot
V

Sheckley, R.
Immortality, Inc.
Holt, Rinehart & Winston
Freejack
Warner Bros. (US) 1992
dir. Geoff Murphy

Sheckley, R.
Prize of Peril, The
UGC (Fr/Yugo) 1983 dir. Yves Boisset
V

Sheean, V.
Personal History
Doubleday
Foreign Correspondent
UA (US) 1940 dir. Alfred Hitchcock
V

Sheldon, E.
Song of Songs
P
PAR (US) 1933 dir. Rouben Mamoulian

Sheldon, E.
Romance
P
MGM (US) 1930 dir. Clarence Brown

Sheldon, E. and Barnes, M. A.
Dishonoured Lady
P
MARS (US) 1947 dir. Robert Stevenson
V

Sheldon, S.
Bloodline
Morrow
PAR (US) 1979 dir. Terence Young
V

Sheldon, S.
If Tomorrow Comes
Morrow
CBS ENT (US) 1986 dir. Jerry London
TVSe(US)

Sheldon, S.
Master of the Game
W. Morrow
ROSEMONT (US/GB) 1984
dir. Kevin Connor/Harvey Hart
TVSe(GB/US), V

Sheldon, S.
Naked Face, The
Morrow
CANNON (US) 1984 dir. Bryan Forbes
V

Sheldon, S.
Other Side of Midnight, The
Morrow
FOX (US) 1977 dir. Charles Jarrott
V

Sheldon, S.
Rage of Angels
Morrow
NBC (US) 1983 dir. Buzz Kulik
TVSe(US), V
Sequel (US) 1991 dir. Buzz Kulik
TV(US)

Sheldon, S.
Windmills of the Gods
Morrow
ITC (US) 1988 dir. Lee Philips
TVSe(US)

Shellabarger, S.
Captain from Castille
Little, Brown (Boston)
FOX (US) 1947 dir. Henry King

Shellabarger, S.
Prince of Foxes
Little, Brown (Boston)
FOX (US) 1949 dir. Henry King

Shelley, E.
Pick Up Girl
P
Too Young to Go
RANK (GB) 1959 dir. Muriel Box

Shelley, Mrs M. W.
Frankenstein
Various
UN (US) 1931 dir. James Whale
DAN CURTIS PRODS (US) 1973
dir. Glenn Jordan
TV(US), V

Shelley, Mrs M. W.
Frankenstein
Various
Curse of Frankenstein, The
WAR (GB) 1957 dir. Terence Fisher
V

Shelley, Mrs M. W.
Frankenstein
Various
Frankenstein: The True Story
UN TV (US) 1973 dir. Jack Smight
TVSe(US)

Shelley, P. B.
Zastrozzi
CHANNEL 4 (GB) 1986
TV(GB)

Shelley, S.
McKenzie Break, The
Sphere
UA (GB) 1970 dir. Lamont Johnson

Shelton, W. R.
Stowaway to the Moon: The
Camelot Odyssey
Doubleday
Stowaway to the Moon
FOX (US) 1975
dir. Andrew V. McLaglen
TV(US)

Shem, S.
House of God, The
R. Marek Publishing
UA (US) 1984 dir. Donald Wrye

Shepard, S.
Fool for Love
P
Bantam Books
CANNON (US) 1985 dir. Robert Altman
V

Shepherd, J.
In God We Trust, All Others Pay
Cash
Doubleday
Christmas Story, A
MGM/UA (US) 1983 dir. Bob Clark
V

Sheppard, S.
Monte Carlo
Summit Books
HIGHGATE (US) 1986
dir. Anthony Page
TVSe(US)

Sherburne, Z.
Stranger in the House
Memories Never Die
UN TV (US) 1982 dir. Sandor Stern
TV(US)

Sherlock, J.
Ordeal of Major Grigsby, The
Morrow
Last Grenade, The
CINERAMA (GB) 1969
dir. Gordon Flemyng

Sherriff, R. C.
Home at Seven
P
Samuel French
BL (GB) 1952 dir. Ralph Richardson
US title: Murder on Monday

Sherriff, R. C.
Journey's End
P
Samuel French
Aces High
EMI (GB/Fr) 1976 dir. Jack Gold
V

Sherriff, R. C.
Journey's End
P
Samuel French
TIFFANY (GB/US) 1930
dir. James Whale

Sherry, E.
Sudden Fear
RKO (US) 1952 dir. David Miller

Sherry, G.
Black Limelight
P
ABPC (GB) 1938 dir. Paul Stein

Sherwin, D. and Howlett, J.
Crusaders
Sphere
If . . .
PAR (GB) 1968 dir. Lindsay Anderson
V

Sherwood, R. E.
Abe Lincoln of Illinois
P
Scribners
Abe Lincoln in Illinois
RKO (US) 1940 dir. John Cromwell
V
COMPASS (US) 1964
dir. George Schaefer
TV(US)

Sherwood, R. E.
Idiot's Delight
P
Fireside Theatre (Garden City, New York)
MGM (US) 1939 dir. Clarence Brown
V

Sherwood, R. E.
Petrified Forest, The
P
C. Scribners Sons
Escape in the Desert
WAR (US) 1945 dir. Edward A. Blatt

Sherwood, R. E.
Petrified Forest, The
P
C. Scribners Sons
WAR (US) 1936 dir. Archie Mayo
V

Sherwood, R. E.
Queen's Husband, The
P
Scribners
Royal Bed, The
RKO (US) 1931 dir. Lowell Sherman
V

Sherwood, R. E.
Reunion in Vienna
P
MGM (US) 1933 dir. Sidney Franklin

Sherwood, R. E.
Road to Rome, The
P
Samuel French
Jupiter's Darling
MGM (US) 1954 dir. George Sidney

Sherwood, R. E.
There Shall Be No Night
P
Scribners
MILBERG (US) 1956
dir. George Schaefer
TV(US)

Sherwood, R. E.
This is New York
P
Scribners
Two Kinds of Women
PAR (US) 1932 dir. William C. DeMille

Sherwood, R. E.
Waterloo Bridge
P

UN (US) 1931 dir. James Whale
MGM (US) 1940 dir. Mervyn Le Roy
V

Sherwood, R. E.
Waterloo Bridge
P
Gaby
MGM (US) 1956 dir. Curtis Bernhardt

Shevelove, B. and Gelbart, L.
Funny Thing Happened on the Way to the Forum, A
P
Dodd, Mead
UA (GB) 1966 dir. Richard Lester
V

Shiber, Mrs. E.
Paris Underground
Scribners
UA (US) 1945 dir. Gregory Ratoff
GB title: Madame Pimpernel

Shiel, M. P.
Purple Cloud, The
Chatto & Windus (London)
World, The Flesh and the Devil, The
MGM (US) 1959
dir. Ronald MacDougall

Shimao, T.
Shi No Toge
SHOCHIKU (Jap) 1990 dir. Kohei Oguri

Shirer, W.
Nightmare Years, The
Simon & Schuster
CONSOL (US) 1989 dir. Anthony Page
TV(US)

Shirk, A.
Ape, The
P
MON (US) 1940 dir. William Nigh
V

Shirreffs, G. D.
Trails End
Oregon Passage
ABP (US) 1958 dir. Paul Landres

Shisgall, O.
Swastika
Man I Married, The
TCF (US) 1940 dir. Irving Pichel

Shivers, L.
Here to Get my Baby out of Jail
Random House
Summer Heat
ATLANTIC (US) 1987
dir. Michie Gleason
V

Sholokhov, M.
And Quiet Flows the Don
Knopf
Quiet Flows the Don
GORKI (USSR) 1958
dir. Sergei Gerasimov

Shores, D.
Daddy's Dyin' . . . Who's Got the Will?
P
Samuel French
MGM/UA (US) 1990 dir. Jack Fisk

Short, L.
Albuquerque
PAR (US) 1948 dir. Ray Enright

Short, L.
Ambush
Collins
MGM (US) 1949 dir. Sam Wood

Short, L.
Coroner Creek
Collins
COL (US) 1948 dir. Ray Enright

Short, L.
Gunman's Choice

Blood on the Moon
RKO (US) 1948 dir. Robert Wise
V

Short, L.
Ramrod
Thorndike Press
UA (US) 1947 dir. André de Toth

Short, L.
Station West
RKO (US) 1948 dir. Sidney Lanfield

Short, L.
Vengeance Valley
MGM (US) 1951 dir. Richard Thorpe
V

Shulman, I.
Amboy Dukes, The
Doubleday
City Across The River
UI (US) 1949 dir. Maxwell Shane

Shulman, I.
Children of the Dark
Holt, N.Y.
Cry Tough
UA (US) 1959 dir. Paul Stanley

Shulman, I.
Cry Tough
Ring, The
UA (US) 1952 dir. Kurt Neumann

Shulman, I.
Harlow
Random House
PAR (US) 1965 dir. Gordon Douglas
V

Shulman, M.
Rally Round the Flag, Boys
Doubleday
FOX (US) 1958 dir. Leo McCarey
V

Shulman, M. and Smith, R. P.
Tender Trap, The
P
Random House
MGM (US) 1955 dir. Charles Walters

Shulman, N.B.
What? . . . Dead Again?
Legacy Publishing Co. (Baton Rouge, Louisiana)
Doc Hollywood
WAR (US) 1991
dir. Michael Caton-Jones

Shute, N.
Landfall
Morrow
AB (GB) 1949 dir. Ken Annakin

Shute, N.
No Highway
Morrow
FOX (GB) 1951 dir. Henry Koster
US title: No Highway in the Sky

Shute, N.
On the Beach
W. Morrow
UA (US) 1959 dir. Stanley Kramer
V

Shute, N.
Pied Piper, The
Morrow
FOX (US) 1942 dir. Irving Pichel

Shute, N.
Pied Piper, The
W. Morrow & Co.
Crossing to Freedom
TELECOM/GRANADA (GB/US) 1990
dir. Norman Stone
TV(GB/US)

Shute, N.
Town Like Alice, A
Morrow
RANK (GB) 1956 dir. Jack Lee
US title: Rape of Malaya, The
V
AFC (Aust) 1981 dir. David Stevens
TVSe(Aust)

Siddons, A. R.
Heartbreak Hotel
Heart of Dixie
ORION (US) 1989 dir. Martin Davidson

Sidley, M.
Five Little Peppers and How They Grew
Grosset & Dunlap
COL (US) 1939 dir. Charles Barton

Sieminski, W.
Woman from the Provinces, A
OKO (Pol) 1987 dir. Andrzej Baranski

Sienkiewicz, H.
Deluge, The
Hippocrene Books
POLSKI (Pol) 1974 dir. Jerzy Hoffman

Sienkiewicz, H.
Knights of the Troubled Order
STUDIO (Pol) 1960
dir. Aleksander Ford

Sienkiewicz, H.
Quo Vadis
Grosset & Dunlap
MGM (US) 1951 dir. Mervyn Le Roy
RAI (It) 1985
TVSe(It)

Sierra, G. and Sierra M.
Cradle Song, The
P
E. P. Dutton
M. EVANS (US) 1956
dir. George Schaefer
TV(US)
COMPASS (US) 1960
dir. George Schaefer
TV(US)

Siggins, M.
Canadian Tragedy, A
Love and Hate: A Marriage Made in Hell
CBC/BBC (US/Can/GB) 1991
dir. Francis Mankiewicz
TVSe(Can/US/GB)

Silliphant, S.
Maracaibo
Farrar, Straus
PAR (US) 1958 dir. Cornel Wilde

Sillitoe, A.
General, The
Knopf
Counterpoint
UI (US) 1968 dir. Ralph Nelson

Sillitoe, A.
Loneliness of the Long Distance Runner, The
Knopf
BL (GB) 1962 dir. Tony Richardson

Sillitoe, A.
Ragman's Daughter, The
Knopf
FOX (GB) 1972 dir. Harold Becker
V

Sillitoe, A.
Saturday Night and Sunday Morning
Knopf
BL (GB) 1960 dir. Karel Reisz

Silver, J.
Limbo
Viking Press
UN (US) 1972 dir. Mark Robson

Silverman, A.
Foster and Laurie
Little, Brown (Boston)
FRIES (US) 1975
dir. John Llewellyn Moxey
TV(US)

Simenon, G.
Act of Passion
Routledge
Forbidden Fruit
CAMEO-POLY (Fr) 1952
dir. Henri Verneuil

Simenon, G.
Battle of Nerves, A
Man on the Eiffel Tower, The
BL (US) 1948 dir. Burgess Meredith
V

Simenon, G.
Betty
MK2 (Fr) 1992 dir. Claude Chabrol

Simenon, G.
Bottom of the Bottle, The
TCF (US) 1956 dir. Henry Hathaway
GB title: Beyond the River

Simenon, G.
Brothers Rico, The
Harcourt, Brace & World
COL (US) 1957 dir. Phil Karlson

Simenon, G.
Brothers Rico, The
Harcourt, Brace & World
Family Rico, The
CBS (US) 1972 dir. Paul Wendkos
TV(US)

Simenon, G.
En Cas de Malheur
UCIL (Fr/It) 1958
dir. Claude Autant-Lara

Simenon, G.
Les fiançailles de M. Hire
Harcourt, Brace, Jovanovich
Monsieur Hire
ORION (Fr) 1989 dir. Patrice Leconte

Simenon, G.
Locataire, La
L'Etoile du Nord
UA (Fr) 1982
dir. Pierre Granier-Deferre

Simenon, G.
Maigret Sets a Trap
Harcourt, Brace, Jovanovich
JOLLY (Fr) 1957 dir. Jean Delannoy

Simenon, G.
Man Who Watched Trains Go By, The
Harcourt, Brace, Jovanovich
EROS (GB) 1952 dir. Harold French

Simenon, G.
Monsieur La Souris
Harcourt, Brace, Jovanovich
Midnight Episode
COL (GB) 1950 dir. Gordon Parry

Simenon, G.
Newhaven-Dieppe
Temptation Harbour
AB (GB) 1947 dir. Lance Comfort

Simenon, G.
Strangers in the House
Stranger in the House
JARFID (GB) 1967 dir. Pierre Rouve
V

Simmons, A.
Optimists of Nine Elms, The
Methuen (London)
SCOTIA-BARBER (GB) 1973
dir. Anthony Simmons
V

Simon, N.
Barefoot in the Park
P
Random House
PAR (US) 1967 dir. Gene Saks
V

Simon, N.
Biloxi Blues
P
Random House
UN (US) 1988 dir. Mike Nichols
V

Simon, N.
Brighton Beach Memoirs
P
Samuel French
UN (US) 1986 dir. Gene Saks
V

Simon, N.
California Suite
P
Samuel French
COL (US) 1975 dir. Herbert Ross
V

Simon, N.
Chapter Two
P
Random House
COL (US) 1979 dir. Robert Moore
V

Simon, N.
Come Blow Your Horn
P
Samuel French
PAR (US) 1963 dir. Bud Yorkin

Simon, N.
Gingerbread Lady, The
P
Samuel French
Only When I Laugh
COL (US) 1981 dir. Glenn Jordan
GB title: It Only Hurts When I Laugh
V

Simon, N.
I Ought to be in Pictures
P
Samuel French
TCF (US) 1982 dir. Herbert Ross
V

Simon, N.
Last of the Red Hot Lovers
P
Samuel French
PAR (US) 1972 dir. Gene Saks
V

Simon, N.
Odd Couple, The
P
Samuel French
PAR (US) 1968 dir. Gene Saks
V

Simon, N.
Plaza Suite
P
Samuel French
PAR (US) 1971 dir. Arthur Hiller
V
PAR (US) 1987 dir. Roger Beatty
TV(US)

Simon, N.
Prisoner of Second Avenue, The
P
Samuel French
WAR (US) 1975 dir. Melvin Frank
V

Simon, N.
Star Spangled Girl, The
P
Dramatists Play Service
PAR (US) 1971 dir. Jerry Paris

Simon, N.
Sunshine Boys, The
P
Samuel French
MGM (US) 1975 dir. Herbert Ross
V

Simon, N., Fields, D. and Coleman, C.
Sweet Charity
P
Random House
UN (US) 1969 dir. Robert Fosse
M, V

Simon, R. L.
Big Fix, The
Pocket Books, N.Y.
UN (US) 1978 dir. Jeremy Paul Kagan
V

Simon, R. L.
Heir
Macdonald
Jennifer on my Mind
UA (US) 1971 dir. Noel Black

Simpson, H.
Saraband for Dead Lovers
EL (GB) 1949 dir. Basil Dearden

Simpson, H.
Under Capricorn
WAR (GB) 1949 dir. Alfred Hitchcock
V
SOUTH AUSTRALIA FILM (Aust) 1983
dir. Rod Hardy

Simpson, N. F.
One Way Pendulum
P
Samuel French
UA (GB) 1964 dir. Peter Yates

Sinclair, H.
Horse Soldiers, The
Harper
UA (US) 1959 dir. John Ford
V

Sinclair, U.
Gnome-Mobile, The
Laurie
DISNEY (US) 1967
dir. Robert Stevenson
Ch, V

Sinclair, U.
Wet Parade, The
Farrar & Rinehart
MGM (US) 1932 dir. Victor Fleming

Singer, H.
Wake Me When It's Over
FOX (US) 1960 dir. Mervyn Le Roy

Singer, I. B.
Enemies, A Love Story
Farrar, Straus & Giroux
FOX (US) 1989 dir. Paul Mazursky

Singer, I. B.
Magician of Lublin, The
Noonday Press
RANK (Israel/Ger) 1979
dir. Menahem Golan
V

Singer, I. B.
Yentl, the Yeshiva Boy
Farrar, Straus & Giroux
Yentl
MGM/UA (US) 1983
dir. Barbra Streisand
M

Singer, L.
Parallax View, The
Doubleday
PAR (US) 1974 dir. Alan J. Pakula
V

Singular, S.
Talked to Death: The Life and Murder of Alan Berg
Beech Tree Books

Talk Radio
UN (US) 1988 dir. Oliver Stone

Siodmak, C.
Donovan's Brain
UA (US) 1953 dir. Felix Feist
V

Siodmak, C.
Donovan's Brain

Lady and the Monster, The
REP (US) 1944 dir. George Sherman
GB title: Lady and the Doctor, The

Siodmak, C.
Donovan's Brain

Vengeance
BL (GB/Ger) 1962 dir. Freddie Francis

Siodmak, C.
Hauser's Memory
Putnam

UN (US) 1970 dir. Boris Sagal
TV(US)

Sitwell, Sir O.
Place of One's Own, A
Duckworth (London)

GFD (GB) 1945 dir. Bernard Knowles

Sjowall, M. and Wahloo, M.
Abominable Man, The

Man on the Roof, The
Svensk Film (Swe) 1976
dir. Bo Widenberg

Sjowall, M. and Wahloo, P.
Laughing Policeman, The

TCF (US) 1973 dir. Stuart Rosenberg
GB title: Investigation of Murder, An
V

Skinner, C. O. and Kimbrough, E.
Our Hearts Were Young and Gay
Dodd, Mead

PAR (US) 1944 dir. Lewis Allen

Slade, B.
Romantic Comedy
P
Samuel French

MGM/UA (US) 1983 dir. Arthur Hiller
V

Slade, B.
Same Time, Next Year
P
Samuel French

UN (US) 1978 dir. Robert Mulligan
V

Slade, B.
Tribute
P
Samuel French

FOX (Can) 1980 dir. Bob Clark
V

Slater, B. and Leighton, F. S.
Stranger in my Bed
Arbor House

TAFT (US) 1987 dir. Larry Elikann
TV(US)

Slater, H.
Conspirator
Lehmann

MGM (GB) 1949 dir. Victor Saville

Slater, M.
Once a Jolly Swagman

WESSEX (GB) 1948 dir. Jack Lee
US title: Maniacs on Wheels

Slater, N.
Mad Death, The

BBC (GB) 1983 dir. Robert Young
TV(GB)

Slaughter, F. G.
Doctor's Wives
Doubleday
COL (US) 1971 dir. George Schaefer
V

Slaughter, F. G.
Sangaree
PAR (US) 1953 dir. Edward Ludwig

Slaughter, F. G.
Warrior, The
Naked in the Sun
ALLIED (US) 1957 dir. R. John Hugh
V

Slaughter, F. G.
Women in White
Doubleday
UN TV (US) 1979 dir. Jerry London
TVSe(US)

Sloane, W.
Edge of Running Water, The
Farrar & Rinehart
Devil Commands, The
COL (US) 1941 dir. Edward Dmytryk

Slowacki, J.
Mazepa
Blanche
TELEPRESSE (Fr) 1971
dir. Walerian Borowczyk

Small, G. R.
Mittelmann's Hardware
Finding the Way Home
MGM/UA TV (US) 1991
dir. Rob Holcomb
TV(US)

Smith, B.
Joy in the Morning
Harper & Row
MGM (US) 1965 dir. Alex Segal

Smith, B.
Tree Grows in Brooklyn, A
Harper & Bros.
FOX (US) 1945 dir. Elia Kazan
V
FOX (US) 1974 dir. Joseph Hardy
TV(US)

Smith, D.
Call it a Day
P
Samuel French
WAR (US) 1937 dir. Archie Mayo

Smith, D.
Dear Octopus
P
Samuel French
GFD (GB) 1943 dir. Harold French
US title: Randolph Family, The

Smith, D.
One Hundred and One Dalmatians
DISNEY (US) 1961
dir. Wolfgang Reitherman
A, Ch

Smith, F. E.
633 Squadron
UA (GB) 1964 dir. Walter Grauman

Smith, H. A.
Rhubarb
Doubleday
PAR (US) 1951 dir. Allan Lubin

Smith, Lady E.
Ballerina
Men in her Life
COL (US) 1941 dir. Gregory Ratoff

Smith, Lady E.
Caravan
BL (GB) 1946 dir. Arthur Crabtree

Smith, Lady E.
Man in Grey, The
GFD (GB) 1943 dir. Leslie Arliss

Smith, Lady E.
Red Wagon
BIP (GB) 1935 dir. Paul Stein

Smith, M.
Gypsy in Amber
Putnam
Art of Crime, The
UN TV (US) 1975 dir. Richard Irving
TV(US)

Smith, M. C.
Gorky Park
Random House
ORION (GB) 1983 dir. Michael Apted
V

Smith, M. C.
Nightwing
Norton
COL (Neth) 1975 dir. Arthur Miller
V

Smith, P.
Angel City
FAC-NEW (US) 1980 dir. Philip Leacock
TV(US)

Smith, S.
Ballad of the Running Man, The
Harper
Running Man, The
COL (GB) 1963 dir. Carol Reed

Smith, S. K.
Joanna Godden
Dial Press
Loves of Joanna Godden, The
GFD (GB) 1947 dir. Charles Frend

Smith, T.
Jovial Ghosts, The
Topper
MGM (US) 1937
dir. Norman Z. MacLeod
V
PAPAZIAN (US) 1979
dir. Charles S. Dubin
TV(US)

Smith, T.
Night Life of the Gods, The
UN (US) 1935 dir. Lowell Sherman

Smith, T.
The Passionate Witch
Sun Dial Press
I Married a Witch
UA (US) 1942 dir. René Clair
V

Smith, T.
Turnabout
Doubleday
UA (US) 1940 dir. Hal Roach

Smith, T. L.
Thief Who Came to Dinner, The
Doubleday
WAR (US) 1973 dir. Bud Yorkin
V

Smith, W.
Dark of the Sun
Mercenaries, The
MGM (GB) 1968 dir. Jack Cardiff
US title: Dark of the Sun

Smith, W.
Gold Mine
Heinemann
Gold
HEMDALE (GB) 1974 dir. Peter Hunt

Smith, W.
Shout at the Devil
HEMDALE (GB) 1976 dir. Peter Hunt
V

Smitter, W.
F.O.B. Detroit
Reaching for the Sun
PAR (US) 1941 dir. William Wellman

Sneider, V.
Teahouse of the August Moon, The
Putnam

MGM (US) 1956 dir. Daniel Mann
COMPASS (US) 1962
dir. George Schaefer
TV(US)

Soderberg, H.
Gertrud
P

PATHE (Den) 1966 dir. C. T. Dreyer
V

Sohl, J.
Night Slaves

B. CROSBY (US) 1970 dir. Ted Post
TV(US)

Sohmer, S.
Favorite Son
Bantam Books

NBC (US) 1988 dir. Jeff Bleckner
TVSe(US)

Solomon, L. and Buchman, H.
Snafu
P

COL (US) 1945 dir. Jack Moss
GB title: Welcome Home

Solzhenitsyn, A.
One Day in the Life of Ivan Denizovich
Bantam Books

CINERAMA (GB) 1971
dir. Caspar Wrede

Somers, P.
Beginner's Luck
Collins

Desperate Man, The
AA (GB) 1959 dir. Peter Maxwell

Somers, S.
Keeping Secrets
Warner Books

FINNEGAN/PINCHUCK (US) 1991
dir. John Korty
TV(US)

Somerville, E. and Ross, M.
Experiences of an Irish RM
Dent

CHANNEL 4 (GB) 1982
TVSe(GB)

Sommer, E.
Teenage Rebel
P

FOX (US) 1956 dir. Edmund Goulding

Sophocles
Electra
P
Various

UA (Greece) 1962
dir. Michael Cacoyannis

Sophocles
Oedipus the King
P
Various

UI (GB) 1968 dir. Philip Saville

Sophocles
Oedipus the King
P
Various

Oedipus Rex
HORIZON (It) 1947
dir. Pier Paolo Pasolini
V

Sorino, O.
Funny Dirty Little War
CINEVISTA (Sp) 1986
dir. Hector Olivera
V

Soutar, A.
Devil's Triangle
Almost Married
FOX (US) 1932
dir. W. Cameron Menzies

Southard, R.
No Sad Songs for Me
COL (US) 1950 dir. Rudolph Maté

Southern, T.
Magic Christian, The
Random House
COMM (GB) 1969 dir. Joseph McGrath
V

Southern, T. and Hoffenberg, M.
Candy
Putnam
CINERAMA (US) 1968
dir. Christian Marquand

Spaak, C.
Kermesse Heroique, La
TOBIS (Fr) 1935 dir. Jacques Feyder

Spark, M.
Abbess of Crewe, The
Viking Press
Nasty Habits
SCOTIA-BARBER (GB) 1976
dir. Michael Lindsay-Hogg
US title: The Abbess
V

Spark, M.
Prime of Miss Jean Brodie, The
Lippincott (Philadelphia)
FOX (GB) 1969 dir. Ronald Neame
V
STV (GB) 1978 dir. Tina Wakerell
TV(GB)

Spearman, F. H.
Whispering Smith
PAR (US) 1948 dir. Leslie Fenton

Speer, A.
Inside the Third Reich
Macmillan
ABC (US) 1982 dir. Marvin J. Chomsky
TVSe(US), V

Spence, H.
One Foot in Heaven
McGraw-Hill
WAR (US) 1941 dir. Irving Rapper

Spence, R.
Gorilla, The
P
FOX (US) 1939 dir. Allan Dwan
V

Spencer, E.
Light in the Piazza, The
McGraw-Hill
MGM (GB) 1962 dir. Guy Green

Spencer, L.
Fulfillment, The
Fulfillment of Mary Gray, The
INDIAN NECK (US) 1989
dir. Piers Haggard
TV(US)

Spencer, S.
Endless Love
Knopf
UN (US) 1981 dir. Franco Zeffirelli
V

Spewack B. and Spewack, S.
Boy Meets Girl
P
Dramatists Play Service
WAR (US) 1938 dir. Lloyd Bacon

Spewack B. and Spewack, S.
Kiss Me Kate
P
MGM (US) 1953 dir. George Sidney
M, V
MILBERG (US) 1958
dir. George Schaefer
TV(US)

Spewack, B. and Spewack, S.
Solitaire Man, The
P
Samuel French
MGM (US) 1933 dir. Jack Conway

Spiegelgass, L.
Majority of One, A
P
Samuel French
WAR (US) 1961 dir. Mervyn Le Roy

Spillane, M.
Girl Hunters, The
FOX (GB) 1963 dir. Roy Rowland
V

Spillane, M.
I, The Jury
Barker
UA (US) 1953 dir. Harry Essex
FOX (US) 1982 dir. Richard T. Heffron
V

Spillane, M.
Kiss Me Deadly
New American Library
UA (US) 1955 dir. Robert Aldrich

Spillane, M.
Long Wait, The
Barker
UA (US) 1954 dir. Victor Saville

Spillane, M.
My Gun is Quick
New American Library
UA (US) 1957 dir. George A. White

Spring, H.
Fame is the Spur
Viking Press
TC (GB) 1947 dir. Roy Boulting
BBC (GB) 1982 dir. David Giles
TVSe(GB)

Spring, H.
My Son, My Son
Viking Press
UA (US) 1940 dir. Charles Vidor

Spring, H.
Shabby Tiger
GRANADA TV (GB) 1977
TVSe(GB)

Spyri, J.
Heidi
Various
FOX (US) 1937 dir. Allan Dwan
V
NBC (US) 1968 dir. Delbert Mann
TV(US)
BBC (GB) 1974
dir. June Wyndham-Davies
TVSe(GB)

Spyri, J.
Heidi
Various
Heidi's Song
HANNA-BARBERA (US) 1982
dir. Robert Taylor
A, V

Stacpoole, H. D.
Blue Lagoon, The
GFD (GB) 1949 dir. Frank Launder
COL (US) 1980 dir. Randal Kleiser
V

Stacpoole, H. D.
Garden of God, The
Return to the Blue Lagoon
COL (US) 1991 dir. William A. Graham

Stadley, P.
Autumn of a Hunter
Deadly Hunt, The
FOUR STAR (US) 1971
dir. John Newland
TV(US)

Stahl, B.
Blackbeard's Ghost
Houghton, Mifflin, Co. (Boston)
DISNEY (US) 1968
dir. Robert Stevenson
V, Ch

Standish, R.
Elephant Walk
Macmillan
PAR (US) 1954 dir. William Dieterle

Stanford, S.
Lady of the House
Putnam
METRO (US) 1978 dir. Ralph Norton,
Vincent Sherman
TV(US), V

Stanton, W.
Golden Evenings of Summer, The
Lancer, N.Y.
Charley and the Angel
DISNEY (US) 1974
dir. Vincent McEveety
V

Stanwood, D. A.
Memory of Eva Ryker, The
Coward, McCann & Geoghegan
IRWIN ALLEN PRODS (US) 1980
dir. Walter Grauman
TV(US)

Stark, R.
Outfit, The
Gregg Press
MGM (US) 1973 dir. John Flynn
V

Stark, R.
Point Blank
Schocken Books
MGM (US) 1967 dir. John Boorman
V

Stark, R.
Seventh, The
Gregg Press
Split, The
MGM (US) 1968 dir. Gordon Flemyng
V

Stark, R.
Slayground
Random House
UN/EMI (GB) 1983 dir. Terry Bedford
V

Starr, B. and Perry, H.
Blaze Starr: My Life as Told to Huey Perry
Blaze
TOUCHSTONE (US) 1989
dir. Ron Shelton

Starr, J.
Corpse Came C.O.D., The
COL (US) 1947 dir. Henry Levin

Stawinski, J. S.
Eroica
KADR (Pol) 1957 dir. Andrzej Munk

Stawinski, J.
Kloakerne
Kanal
POLSKI (Pol) 1956 dir. Andrzej Wajda
V

Stead, C.
For Love Alone
Harcourt Brace
WARRANTY (Aus) 1986
dir. Stephen Wallace
V

Steel, D.
Changes
Delacorte Press
NBC (US) 1991 dir. Charles Jarrot
TV(US)

Steel, D.
Crossings
Delacorte Press
A. SPELLING (US) 1986
dir. Karen Arthur
TVSe(US)

Steel, D.
Daddy
Delacorte Press
NBC (US) 1991 dir. Michael Miller

Steel, D.
Fine Things
Delacorte Press
NBC (US) 1990 dir. Tom Moore
TV(US)

Steel, D.
Kaleidoscope
Delacorte Press
NBC (US) 1990 dir. Jud Taylor
TV(US)

Steel, D.
Palomino
NBC (US) 1991 dir. Michael Miller
TV(US)

Steele, K.
Murder goes to College
PAR (US) 1937 dir. Charles Reisner

Steele, W. D.
Way to the Gold, The
Doubleday
FOX (US) 1957 dir. Robert D. Webb

Steeman, S-A.
Legitime Defense
Quai des Orfèvres
MAJ (Fr) 1947
dir. Henri-Georges Clouzot

Steiger, B. and Mank, C.
Valentino
UA (GB) 1977 dir. Ken Russell

Stein, B.
Ludes
Boost, The
HEMDALE (US) 1988
dir. Harold Becker

Stein, D. M.
Wall of Noise
Crown
WAR (US) 1963 dir. Richard Wilson

Stein, J.
Fiddler on the Roof
P
UA (US) 1971 dir. Norman Jewison
M, V

Steinbeck, J.
Cannery Row
Viking Press
MGM (US) 1982 dir. David S. Ward
V

Steinbeck, J.
East of Eden
Viking Press
WAR (US) 1954 dir. Elia Kazan
V
NEUFELD PRODS (US) 1980
dir. Harvey Hart
TVSe(US)

Steinbeck, J.
Grapes of Wrath, The
Viking Press
FOX (US) 1940 dir. John Ford
V

Steinbeck, J.
Moon is Down, The
Viking Press
FOX (US) 1943 dir. Irving Pichel

Steinbeck, J.
Of Mice and Men
The Modern Library
UA (US) 1939 dir. Lewis Milestone
METROMEDIA (US) 1981
dir. Reza Badiyi
TV(US), V

Steinbeck, J.
Pearl, The
Viking Press
RKO (US/Mex) 1948
dir. Emilio Fernandez

Steinbeck, J.
Red Pony, The
Viking Press
BL (US) 1949 dir. Lewis Milestone
V
UN (US) 1973 dir. Robert Totten
TV(US)

Steinbeck, J.
Tortilla Flat
Modern Library
MGM (US) 1942 dir. Victor Fleming

Steinbeck, J.
Wayward Bus, The
Viking Press
FOX (US) 1957 dir. Victor Vicas

Steinbeck, J.
Winter of our Discontent, The
Viking Press
LORIMAR (US) 1983 dir. Waris Hussein
TV(US)

Stendahl, H. B.
Rouge et le Noir, Le
Garnier-Flammarion (Paris)
FRANCO-LONDON (Fr/It) 1954
dir. Claude Autant-Lara

Stephenson, C.
Leiningen Versus the Ants
Naked Jungle, The
PAR (US) 1954 dir. Byron Haskin
V

Sterling, T.
Evil of the Day, The
Penguin
Honey Pot, The
UA (US) 1966 dir. Joseph L. Mankiewicz

Stern, D.
Francis
Farrar, N.Y.
UI (US) 1949 dir. Arthur Lubin

Stern, G. B.
Long Lost Father
RICO (US) 1934
dir. Ernest B. Schoedsack

Stern, G. B.
Ugly Dachshund, The
Books for Library Press (Freeport, New York)
DISNEY (US) 1965 dir. Norman Tokar

Stern, G. B.
Woman in the Hall, The
GFD (GB) 1947 dir. Jack Lee

Stern, H. J.
Judgment in Berlin
Universe Books
NEW LINE (US) 1988 dir. Leo Penn
V

Stern, P. V. D.
Greatest Gift, The
It Happened one Christmas
UN TV (US) 1977 dir. Donald Wrye
TV(US)

Stern, R.M.
Tower, The
McKay
Towering Inferno, The
COL-WAR (US) 1975
dir. John Gullermin, Irwin Allen
V

Sterner, J.
Other People's Money
P
Samuel French
WAR (US) 1991 dir. Norman Jewison

Stevens, L.
Lovers, The
P
Samuel French
War Lord, The
UN (US) 1965 dir. Franklin Schaffner

Stevens, W. R.
Deadly Intentions
GREEN-EPSTEIN (US) 1985
dir. Noel Black
TVSe(US)

Stevenson, J. and Stevenson, P.
Counterattack
P
COL (US) 1945 dir. Zoltan Korda
GB title: One Against Seven

Stevenson, R. L.
Black Arrow
COL (US) 1948 dir. Gordon Douglas
GB title: Black Arrow Strikes, The
TOWER (US) 1985 dir. John Hough
TV(US/GB), V

Stevenson, R. L.
Body Snatcher, The
Various
RKO (US) 1945 dir. Robert Wise
V

Stevenson, R. L.
Dr Jekyll and Mr Hyde
Various
PAR (US) 1931 dir. Rouben Mamoulian
MGM (US) 1941 dir. Victor Fleming
V

Stevenson, R. L.
Dr. Jekyll and Mr. Hyde
Various
Jekyll & Hyde
KING PHOENIX (US/GB) 1990
dir. David Wickes
TV(GB/US)

Stevenson, R. L.
Dr. Jekyll and Mr. Hyde
Various
Two Faces of Dr. Jekyll, The
HAMMER (GB) 1960
dir. Terence Fisher
US title: House of Fright

Stevenson, R. L.
Ebb Tide
Scribners
PAR (US) 1937 dir. James Hogan

Stevenson, R. L.
Ebb Tide
Various
Adventure Island
PAR (US) 1947 dir. Peter Stewart

Stevenson, R. L.
Kidnapped
Various
FOX (US) 1938 dir. Alfred L. Werker
V
DISNEY (GB) 1959
dir. Robert Stevenson
V
RANK (GB) 1971 dir. Delbert Mann
V
HTV (GB) 1979
TV(GB)

Stevenson, R. L.
Master of Ballantrae, The
Various
WAR (US) 1953 dir. William Keighley
COL (US/GB) 1983 dir. Douglas Hickox
TVSe(GB/US)

Stevenson, R. L.
St. Ives
Various
Secret of St. Ives, The
COL (US) 1949 dir. Phil Rosen

Stevenson, R. L.
Sire of Maletroit's Door, The
Various
Strange Door, The
UI (US) 1951 dir. Joseph Pevney

Stevenson, R. L.
Suicide Club, The
Doubleday
ANGELIKA (US) 1988 dir. James Bruce

Stevenson, R. L.
Suicide Club, The
Doubleday
Trouble for Two
MGM (US) 1936 dir. J. Walter Rubin
GB title: Suicide Club, The

Stevenson, R. L.
Treasure Island
Various
MGM (US) 1934 dir. Victor Fleming
V
DISNEY (GB) 1950 dir. Byron Haskin
V
MGM-EMI (GB/Fr/Ger) 1971
dir. John Hough
V
AGAMEMNON FILMS (US) 1990
dir. Fraser Heston
TV(US)

Stevenson, R. L.
Treasure of Franchard
Various
Treasure of Lost Canyon, The
UI (US) 1952 dir. Ted Tetzlaff

Stevenson, R. L. and Osbourne, L.
Wrong Box, The
Scribners
COL (GB) 1966 dir. Bryan Forbes
V

Stevenson, W.
Man Called Intrepid, A
Harcourt, Brace, Jovanovich
LORIMAR (GB) 1979 dir. Peter Carter
TVSe(GB)

Stewart, D. O.
Mr and Mrs Haddock Abroad
Finn and Hattie
PAR (US) 1930 dir. Norman Taurog,
Norman McLeod

Stewart, F. M.
Ellis Island
Telepics (US) 1984 dir. Jerry London
TVSe(US)

Stewart, F. M.
Six Weeks
Arbor House
UN (US) 1982 dir. Tony Bill
V

Stewart, F.
Mephisto Waltz, The
Coward-McCann
FOX (US) 1971 dir. Paul Wendkos
V

Stewart, M.
Bye Bye Birdie
P
Morris
COL (US) 1963 dir. George Sidney
M, V

Stewart, M.
Monkey Shines
Freundlich Books
ORION (US) 1988
dir. George A. Romero
V

Stewart, M.
Moon-Spinners, The
Morrow
DISNEY (GB) 1964 dir. James Neilson
V

Stewart, M. and Herman, J.
Hello Dolly
FOX (US) 1969 dir. Gene Kelly
M, V

Stewart, R.
Desert Town
World, N.Y.
Desert Fury
PAR (US) 1947 dir. Lewis Allen

Stewart, R.
Possession of Joel Delaney, The
Little, Brown (Boston)
SCOTIA-BARBER (US) 1971
dir. Waris Hussein

Stinetorf, L. A.
White Witch Doctor
FOX (US) 1953 dir. Henry Hathaway

Stitt, M.
Runner Stumbles, The
P
J. T. White (Clifton, New Jersey)
SIMON (US) 1979 dir. Stanley Kramer
V

Stockdale, J. and Stockdale, S.
In Love and War
Harper & Row
TA (US) 1987 dir. Paul Aaron
TV(US)

Stoddart, D.
Prelude to Night
Ruthless
EL (US) 1948 dir. Edgar G. Ulmer

Stoker B.
Dracula
Samuel French
CIC (GB) 1979 dir. John Badham
V

Stoker, B.
Dracula
Various
UN (US) 1931 dir. Tod Browning
V
UI (GB) 1958 dir. Terence Fisher
US title: House of Dracula
EMI (It) 1973 dir. Paul Morrissey
UN (US) 1974 dir. Dan Curtis
TV (US), V

Stoker, B.
Dracula's Guest
Jarrold's
Dracula's Daughter
UN (US) 1936 dir. Lambert Hillyer
V

Stoker, B.
Jewel of the Seven Stars
Various
Blood from the Mummy's Tomb
MGM-EMI (GB) 1971 dir. Seth Holt
V

Stoker, B.
Jewel of the Seven Stars
Various
Awakening, The
EMI (GB) 1980 dir. Mike Newell
V

Stoker, B.
Lair of the White Worm, The
Various
VESTRON (GB) 1988 dir. Ken Russell
V

Stokes, S.
Court Circular
Joseph
I Believe in You
EAL (GB) 1952 dir. Basil Dearden

Stokes, S.
Isadora Duncan, An Intimate Portrait
Pan

Isadora
UI (GB) 1969 dir. Karel Reisz
US title: Loves of Isadora, The
V

Stone, G. and Cooney, R.
Why Not Stay for Breakfast?
P
Samuel French
ENT (GB) 1979 dir. Terence Martel
V

Stone, I.
Agony and the Ecstacy, The
Doubleday
FOX (US) 1965 dir. Carol Reed
V

Stone, I.
Immortal Wife
Doubleday
President's Lady, The
FOX (US) 1953 dir. Henry Levin

Stone, I.
Lust for Life
Doubleday
MGM (US) 1956 dir. Vincente Minnelli

Stone, Mrs G.
Bitter Tea of General Yen, The
Bobbs-Merrill (Indianapolis)
COL (US) 1932 dir. Frank Capra

Stone, P.
1776
P
COL (US) 1972 dir. Peter Hunt
M, V

Stone, R.
Dog Soldiers
Houghton, Mifflin Co. (Boston)
Who'll Stop the Rain?
UA (US) 1978 dir. Karel Reisz
GB title: Dog Soldiers
V

Stone, R.
Hall of Mirrors
Houghton, Mifflin Co. (Boston)
WUSA
PAR (US) 1970 dir. Stuart Rosenberg

Stoneley, J.
Jenny's War
HTV (US/GB) 1985 dir. Steven Gethers
Ch, TV(GB/US), V

Stong, P. D.
Career
Grosset, N.Y.
RKO (US) 1939 dir. Leigh Jason

Stong, P. D.
State Fair
The Century
FOX (US) 1933 dir. Henry King
FOX (US) 1945 dir. Walter Lang
M
FOX (US) 1962 dir. José Ferrer
M, V

Stong, P. D.
Strangers Return
MGM (US) 1933 dir. King Vidor

Stoppard, T.
Rosencrantz and Guildenstern are Dead
P
Samuel French
HOBO/CINECOM (US/GB) 1991
dir. Tom Stoppard
V

Storey, D.
In Celebration
P
Random House
SEVEN KEYS (GB) 1974
dir. Lindsay Anderson

Storey, D.
This Sporting Life
Macmillan
RANK (GB) 1963 dir. Lindsay Anderson
V

Storey, R.
Touch it Light
P
Samuel French
Light up the Sky
BL (GB) 1960 dir. Lewis Gilbert

Storm, B.
Thunder God's Gold
Lust for Gold
COL (US) 1949 dir. S. Sylvan Simon

Storm, L.
Great Day
Lane
RKO (GB) 1945 dir. Lance Comfort

Storm, L.
Personal Affair
P
RANK (GB) 1953 dir. Anthony Pelissier

Storm, L.
Tony Draws a Horse
P
GFD (GB) 1950
dir. John Paddy Carstairs

Storr, C.
Marianne Dreams
Faber & Faber (London)
Paperhouse
VESTRON (GB) 1988 dir. Bernard Rose

Story, J. T.
Mix me a Person
BL (GB) 1962 dir. Leslie Norman

Story, J. T.
Trouble with Harry, The
PAR (US) 1955 dir. Alfred Hitchcock
V

Stout, D.
Carolina Skeletons
Mysterious Press
KUSHNER-LOCKE (US) 1991
dir. John Erman
TV (US)

Stout, R.
Doorbell Rang, The
Viking Press
Nero Wolfe
PAR TV (US) 1979 dir. Frank D. Gilroy
TV(US)

Stout, R.
Fer de Lance
Viking Press
Meet Nero Wolfe
COL (US) 1936 dir. Herbert Biberman

Stout, R.
League of Frightened Men, The
COL (US) 1937 dir. Alfred E. Green

Stowe, H. B.
Uncle Tom's Cabin
Viking Press
TAFT (US) 1989 dir. Stan Lathan
TV(US)

Strabel, T.
Reap the Wild Wind
PAR (US) 1942 dir. Cecil B. de Mille

Straker, J. F.
Hell is Empty
Harrap
RANK (Czech/GB) 1967
dir. John Ainsworth, Bernard Knowles
V

Straub, P.
Ghost Story
Coward, McCann & Geoghegan
UN (US) 1981 dir. John Irvin
V

Straub, P.
Julia
Putnam
Full Circle
PAR (GB/Can) 1976
dir. Richard Loncraine

Straub, P.
Shadowlands
BBC (Neth/GB) 1985
dir. Norman Stone
TV(Neth/GB)

Streatfeild, N.
Aunt Clara
Collins
BL (GB) 1954 dir. Anthony Kimmins

Street, A. G.
Strawberry Roan
BN (GB) 1944 dir. Maurice Elvey

Street, J.
Tap Roots
Dial Press
UI (US) 1948 dir. George Marshall

Street, J. H.
Goodbye, My Lady
WAR (US) 1956 dir. William Wellman

Street, J. H.
Letter to the Editor
Nothing Sacred
SELZNICK (US) 1937
dir. William Wellman
V

Streeter, E.
Father of the Bride
Simon & Schuster
MGM (US) 1950 dir. Vincente Minnelli
V
DISNEY (US) 1991 dir. Charles Shyer

Streeter, E.
Hobbs' Vacation
Mr. Hobbs takes a Vacation
FOX (US) 1962 dir. Henry Koster
V

Streiber, W.
Communion
Beech Tree Books
NEW LINE (US) 1989
dir. Philippe Mora

Streuvels, S.
Flaxfield, The
Sun & Moon Press (Los Angeles)
COURIER (Bel/Neth) 1983
dir. Jan Gruyaert

Strieber, W.
Hunger, The
Morrow
MGM/UA (US) 1983 dir. Tony Scott
V

Strieber, W.
Wolfen
Morrow
WAR (US) 1981 dir. Michael Wadleigh
V

Strindberg, A.
Dance of Death, The
P
Samuel French
PAR (GB) 1968 dir. David Giles

Strindberg, A.
Father, The
P
Samuel French
BBC (GB) 1985
TV(GB)

Strindberg, J. A.
Miss Julie
P
Samuel French
LF (Swe) 1950 dir. Alf Sjoberg
TIGON (GB) 1972 dir. Robin Phillips,
John Glenister
V

Stringer, D.
Touch Wood
P
Nearly a Nasty Accident
BL (GB) 1961 dir. Don Chaffey

Strode, W. S.
Guinea Pig, The
P
S. Low, Marston & Co. (London)
PILGRIM-PATHE (GB) 1948
dir. Roy Boulting
US title: Outsider, The

Strong, A.
Seventh Heaven
P
FOX (US) 1937 dir. Henry King

Strong, A.
Three Wise Fools
P
Samuel French
MGM (US) 1946 dir. Edward Buzzell

Strong, L. A. G.
Brothers, The
Gollancz
GFD (GB) 1947 dir. David MacDonald

Strong, P.
Village Tale, A
RKO (US) 1935 dir. John Cromwell

Strueby, K.
General Goes Too Far, The
High Command, The
ABFD (GB) 1936 dir. Thorold Dickinson
V

Strugatsky, B., and Strugatsky, A.
Picnic by the Roadside
Macmillan
Stalker
(USSR) 1979 dir. Andrei Tarkovsky

Struther, J.
Mrs. Miniver
Harcourt Brace
MGM (US) 1942 dir. William Wyler

Stryzkowski, J.
Austeria
POLSKI (Pol) 1988
dir. Jerzy Kawaterowicz

Stuart, A.
Jeannie
P
Samuel French
Let's Be Happy
ABP (GB) 1957 dir. Henry Levin
M

Stuart, A.
Jeannie
P
Samuel French
TANSA (GB) 1941 dir. Harold French
US title: Girl in Distress

Stuart, C.
Walks Far Woman
Dial Press
Legend of Walks Far Woman, The
EMI (US) 1982 dir. Mel Damski
TV(US), V

Stuart, I.
Satan Bug, The
UA (US) 1965 dir. John Sturges

Stuart, W. L.
Night Cry

Where the Sidewalk Ends
FOX (US) 1950 dir. Otto Preminger

Sturgeon, T.
Killdozer

UN TV (US) 1974 dir. Jerry London
TV(US)

Sturges, P.
Strictly Dishonourable
P
Samuel French

UN (US) 1931 dir. John Stahl
MGM (US) 1951 dir. Norman Panama,
Melvin Frank

Styron, W.
Sophie's Choice
Random House

UN/ITC (US) 1982 dir. Alan J. Pakula
V

Sullivan, T. and Gill, D.
If You Could See What I Can Hear
Harper & Row

SCHICK SUNN (US) 1982 dir. Eric Till
V

Sullivan, W. G. and Brown, W. S.
My 30 Years in Hoover's FBI

J. Edgar Hoover
RLC (US) 1987 dir. Robert Collins
TV(US)

Sulzberger, C.
My Brother Death

Playground, The
JERAND (US) 1965 dir. Richard Hilliard

Summers, R. A.
Vigilante

San Francisco Story, The
WAR (US) 1952 dir. Robert Parrish

Sumner, C. R.
Quality

Pinky
FOX (US) 1949 dir. Elia Kazan

Sumner, C. R.
Tammy and the Bachelor

UN (US) 1957 dir. Joseph Pevney
GB title: Tammy
V

Sundman, P. O.
Flight of the Eagle
Pantheon Books

SUMMIT (Swe) 1983 dir. Jan Troell
V

Susann, J.
Love Machine, The
Simon & Schuster

COL (US) 1971 dir. Jack Haley Jr.
V

Susann, J.
Once is not Enough
Morrow

PAR (US) 1975 dir. Guy Green
V

Susann, J.
Valley of the Dolls
Random House

FOX (US) 1967 dir. Mark Robson
V

Susann, J.
Valley of the Dolls
Random House

Valley of the Dolls 1981
FOX TV (US) 1981 dir. Walter Grauman
TVSe(US)

Swann, F.
Out of the Frying Pan
P
Samuel French

Young and Willing
UA (US) 1942 dir. Edward H. Griffith
V

Swanson, N. H.
First Rebel, The
Grosset

Allegheny Uprising
RKO (US) 1939 dir. William A. Seiter
GB title: First Rebel, The
V

Swanson, N. H.
Unconquered
Doubleday
PAR (US) 1947 dir. Cecil B. de Mille

Swarthout, G.
Bless the Beasts and Children
Doubleday
COL (US) 1971 dir. Stanley Kramer
V

Swarthout, G.
Melodeon, The
Doubleday

Christmas to Remember, A
ENGLUND (US) 1978
dir. George Englund
TV(US), V

Swarthout, G.
Shootist, The
Doubleday
PAR (US) 1976 dir. Don Siegel
V

Swarthout, G.
They Came to Cordura
Random House
COL (US) 1959 dir. Robert Rossen
V

Swarthout, G.
Where the Boys Are
Random House
MGM (US) 1960 dir. Henry Levin
V
ITC (US) 1980 dir. Hy Averback
V

Swift, J.
Gulliver's Travels
Various

PAR (US) 1939 dir. Dave Fleischer
EMI (GB) 1976 dir. Peter Hunt
A, V

Swift, J.
Gulliver's Travels
Various

Three Worlds of Gulliver, The
COL (US/Sp) 1959 dir. Jack Sher
V

Swift, K.
Who Could Ask For Anything More

Never a Dull Moment
RKO (US) 1950 dir. George Marshall

Swiggett, H.
Power and the Prize, The
MGM (US) 1956 dir. Henry Koster

Sylvaine, V.
Aren't Men Beasts!
P
Jenkins
AB (GB) 1937 dir. Graham Cutts

Sylvaine, V.
As Long As They're Happy
P
Samuel French
GFD (GB) 1955 dir. J. Lee Thompson

Sylvaine, V.
One Wild Oat
P
EROS (GB) 1951 dir. Charles Saunders

Sylvaine, V.
Warn That Man
P
AB (GB) 1942 dir. Laurence Huntington

Sylvaine, V.
Will Any Gentleman
P
ABP (GB) 1953 dir. Michael Anderson

Sylvester, R.
Big Boodle, The
UA (US) 1957 dir. Richard Wilson
GB title: Night in Havana

Sylvester, R.
Rough Sketch
We Were Strangers
COL (US) 1949 dir. John Huston

Symons, J.
Narrowing Circle, The
Harper
EROS (GB) 1955 dir. Charles Saunders

Synge, J. M.
Playboy of the Western World, The
P
Samuel French
FOUR PROVINCES (GB) 1962
dir. Brian Desmond Hurst
V

Syrett, N.
Portrait of a Rebel
Woman Rebels, A
RKO (US) 1936 dir. Mark Sandrich
V

Szekely, H.
School of Drama
P
Dramatic School
MGM (US) 1938 dir. Robert B. Sinclair, Jr.

Szekely, H. and Stemmple, R. A.
Desire
P
PAR (US) 1936 dir. Frank Borzage

Szpiner, F.
Affaire de Femmes, Une
Story of Women
NEW YORKER (Fr) 1989
dir. Claude Chabrol

Tagore, R.
Home and the World, The
NFC (Ind) 1985 dir. Satyajit Ray
V

Takeoa, T.
Violence at Noon
KINO (Jap) 1966 dir. Nagisa Oshima

Takeyama, M.
Burmese Harp, The
C. E. Tuttle Co. (Rutland, Vermont)
NIKKATSU (Jap) 1956
dir. Kon Ichikawa
V

Talese, G.
Honor Thy Father
World Publishing
METRO (US) 1973 dir. Paul Wendkos
TVSe(US), V

Tani, T.
Kimura Family, The
Yen Family, The
FUJI (Jap) 1990 dir. Yojiro Takita

Tanizaki, J.
Buddhist Cross, The
Putnam, N.Y.
Berlin Affair, The
CANNON (It/Ger) 1985
dir. Liliana Cavani
V

Tanizaki, J.
Key, The
Perigee Books
ENT (It) 1983 dir. Giovanni Tinto Brass
V

Tanizaki, J.
Makioka Sisters, The
Knopf
R5/S8 (Jap) 1985 dir. Kon Ichikawa

Tannenbaum, R. K. and Rosenberg, P.
Badge of the Assassin
E. P. Dutton
BLATT/SINGER (US) 1985
dir. Mel Damski
TV(US)

Tarkington, B.
Alice Adams
Macmillan
RKO (US) 1933 dir. George Stevens

Tarkington, B.
Magnificent Ambersons, The
Arbor House
RKO (US) 1942 dir. Orson Welles
V

Tarkington, B.
Monsieur Beaucaire
Doubleday
PAR (US) 1946 dir. George Marshall

Tarkington, B.
Monsieur Beaucaire
Doubleday
Monte Carlo
PAR (US) 1930 dir. Ernst Lubitsch

Tarkington, B.
Penrod
Doubleday
By the Light of the Silvery Moon
WAR (US) 1953 dir. David Butler

Tarkington, B.
Penrod
Doubleday
On Moonlight Bay
WAR (US) 1951 dir. Roy del Ruth
M

Tarkington, B.
Presenting Lily Mars
Doubleday
MGM (US) 1943 dir. Norman Taurog
M, V

Tarkington, B.
Seventeen
Grosset & Dunlap
PAR (US) 1940 dir. Louis King

Tarloff, F.
Guide for the Married Man, The
FOX (US) 1967 dir. Gene Kelly
V

Tate, S.
Fuzzy Pink Nightgown, The
Harper, N.Y.
UA (US) 1957 dir. Norman Taurog

Taylor, B.
Godsend, The
CANNON (US) 1980
dir. Gabrielle Beaumont
V

Taylor, D.
Mother Love
G. P. Putnam's Sons
BBC (GB) 1989 dir. Simon Langton
TVSe(GB)

Taylor, D.
Paris in Spring
P
PAR (US) 1935 dir. Lewis Milestone

Taylor, J.
Asking for It
St. Martin's Press
Invasion of Privacy, An
EMBASSY TV (US) 1983
dir. Mel Damski
TV(US)

Taylor, K.
Address Unknown
Simon & Schuster
COL (US) 1944
dir. William Cameron Menzies

Taylor, R.
Chicken Every Sunday
McGraw-Hill
FOX (US) 1948 dir. George Seaton

Taylor, R. B.
Long Road Home
H. Holt
ROSEMONT (US) 1991 dir. John Korty

Taylor, R. L.
Journey to Matecumbe, A
McGraw-Hill
Treasure of Matecumbe
DISNEY (US) 1976
dir. Vincent McEveety
V

Taylor, R. L.
Travels of Jaimie McPheeters, The
Doubleday
Guns of Diablo
MGM (US) 1964 dir. Boris Sagal
V

Taylor, S.
Avanti!
P
UA (US) 1972 dir. Billy Wilder
V

Taylor, S.
Sabrina Fair
P
Random House
Sabrina
PAR (US) 1954 dir. Billy Wilder
GB title: Sabrina Fair
V

Taylor, S. A.
First Love
P
Harper
Promise at Dawn
AVCO (US/Fr) 1970 dir. Jules Dassin

Taylor, S. A.
Happy Time, The
P
COL (US) 1952 dir. Richard Fleischer

Taylor, S. A. and Skinner, C. O.
Pleasure of his Company, The
P
Random House
PAR (US) 1961 dir. George Seaton

Taylor, S. W.
Man with my Face, The
Hodder & Stoughton
UA (US) 1951 dir. Edward J. Montague

Tazewell, C.
Littlest Angel, The
Children's Press (Chicago)
OSTERMAN (US) 1969
dir. Walter C. Miller
TV(US), V

Tebelak, J. M.
Godspell
P
COL (US) 1973 dir. David Greene
M

Teichman, H. and Kaufman, G. S.
Solid Gold Cadillac, The
P
Random House
COL (US) 1956 dir. Richard Quine

Teilhet, D. L.
My True Love
No Room for the Groom
UI (US) 1952 dir. Douglas Sirk

Teilhet, D.
Fearmakers, The
PACEMAKER (US) 1958
dir. Jacques Tourneur

Telfer, D.
Caretakers, The
Simon & Schuster
UA (US) 1963 dir. Hall Bartlett
GB title: Borderlines

Tellado, C.
Mi Bodo Contigo
Our Marriage
LFDP (Fr) 1985 dir. Valeria Sarimento

Temple, J.
No Room at the Inn
P
Samuel French
BN (GB) 1948 dir. Dan Birt

Temple, W. F.
Four-Sided Triangle
Long
HAMMER (GB) 1952
dir. Terence Fisher

Templeton, C.
Kidnapping of the President, The
Simon & Schuster
CROWN (US) 1980
dir. George Mendelink
V

Tengroth, B.
Three Strange Lives
FILM FORUM (Swe) 1980
dir. Ingmar Bergman

Terasaki, G.
Bridge to the Sun
University of North Carolina Press
(Chapel Hill)
MGM (Fr/US) 1961 dir. Etienne Périer

Terrot, C.
Alligator Named Daisy, An
RANK (GB) 1955 dir. J. Lee Thompson

Terrot, C.
Angel Who Pawned Her Harp, The
Collins
BL (GB) 1954 dir. Alan Bromly

Tevis, J. H.
Arizona in the 50's
Tenderfoot, The
DISNEY (US) 1964 dir. Byron Paul

Tevis, W.
Colour of Money, The
Warner Books
DISNEY (US) 1986 dir. Martin Scorcese
V

Tevis, W.
Hustler, The
Harper
FOX (US) 1961 dir. Robert Rossen
V

Tevis, W.
Man Who Fell to Earth, The
Avon Books
BL (GB) 1976 dir. Nicholas Roeg
V
MGM/UA (US) 1987 dir. Robert J. Roth
TV(US)

Tey, J.
Brat Farrar
Macmillan
PHILCO (US) 1950 dir. Gordon Duff
TV(US)
BBC (GB) 1986
TVSe(GB)

Tey, J.
Franchise Affair, The
P. Davies (London)
ABP (GB) 1951
dir. Lawrence Hurtington
BBC (GB) 1988
TVSe(GB)

Tey, J.
Shilling for Candles, A
Young and Innocent
GFD (GB) 1937 dir. Alfred Hitchcock
US title: Girl was Young, A
V

Thackeray, W. M.
Barry Lyndon
Various
WAR/HAWK (GB) 1975
dir. Stanley Kubrick
V

Thackeray, W. M.
Vanity Fair
Various
Becky Sharp
RKO (US) 1935 dir. Rouben Mamoulian
V

Thackeray, W. M.
Vanity Fair
HOL (US) 1932 dir. Chester M. Franklin
BBC (GB) 1988
TVSe(GB)

Thayer, T.
Call Her Savage
Long
PAR (US) 1932 dir. John Francis Dillon

Thayer, T.
One Woman
Fame is the Name of the Game
UN TV (US) 1966 dir. Stuart Rosenberg
TV(US)

Theroux, P.
Half Moon Street
Houghton, Mifflin Co. (Boston)
RKO (US) 1986 dir. Bob Swaim
V

Theroux, P.
London Embassy, The
Houghton, Mifflin Co. (Boston)
THAMES (GB) 1988
TV(GB)

Theroux, P.
Mosquito Coast, The
Houghton, Mifflin Co. (Boston)
WAR (US) 1986 dir. Peter Weir
V

Theroux, P.
Saint Jack
Houghton, Mifflin Co.
NEW WORLD (US) 1979
dir. Peter Bogdanovich
V

Thiele, C.
Blue Fin
Harper & Row
S. AUS (Aus) 1978 dir. Carl Schultz
V

Thigpen, C. H. and Cleckley, H. M.
Three Faces of Eve, The
McGraw-Hill
FOX (US) 1957 dir. Nunnally Johnson

Thomas, A.
Witching Hour, The
P
PAR (US) 1934 dir. Henry Hathaway

Thomas, A. E.
No More Ladies
P
MGM (US) 1935
dir. Edward H. Griffith, George Cukor

Thomas, B.
Book of the Month
P
Please Turn Over
AA (GB) 1959 dir. Gerald Thomas

Thomas, B.
Bud and Lou
Lippincott (Philadelphia)
BANNER (US) 1978
dir. Robert C. Thompson
TV(US)

Thomas, B.
Charley's Aunt
P
Samuel French
FOX (US) 1941 dir. Archie Mayo
GB title: Charley's American Aunt
V

Thomas, B.
Charley's Aunt
P
Samuel French
Where's Charley?
WAR (US) 1952 dir. David Butler

Thomas, B.
Shooting Star
P
Deane
Great Game, The
ADELPHI (GB) 1952 dir. Maurice Elvey

Thomas, C.
Firefox
G. K. Hall (Boston)
WAR (US) 1982 dir. Clint Eastwood
V

Thomas, D.
Mouse and the Woman, The
FACELIFT (GB) 1981 dir. Karl Francis
V

Thomas, D.
Under Milk Wood
P
Samuel French
RANK (GB) 1971 dir. Andrew Sinclair
V

Thomas, G. and Witts, M. M.
Day the Bubble Burst, The
Doubleday
FOX (US) 1982 dir. Joseph Hardy
TV(US)

Thomas, G. and Witts, M. M.
Day the World Ended, The
Stein & Day
When Time Ran Out
WAR (US) 1980 dir. James Goldstone
V

Thomas, G. and Witts, M. M.
Enola Gay
Stein & Day

VIACOM (US) 1980
dir. David Lowell Rich
TV(US), V

Thomas, G. and Witts, M. M.
Voyage of the Damned
Stein & Day

ITC (GB) 1976 dir. Stuart Rosenberg
V

Thomas, L.
Dangerous Davies — The Last Detective

INNER CIRCLE (GB) 1980
dir. Val Guest
V

Thomas, L.
Stand up Virgin Soldiers

WAR (GB) 1977 dir. Norman Cohen
V

Thomas, L.
Tropic of Ruislip, The

Tropic
ATV (GB) 1979 dir. Matthew Robinson
TVSe(GB)

Thomas, L.
Virgin Soldiers, The

COL (GB) 1969 dir. John Dexter
V

Thomas, P.
Spy, The

Defector, The
PECF (Fr/W.Ger) 1966 dir. Raoul Levy

Thomas, R.
Piège Pour un Homme Seul
P

Honeymoon with a Stranger
TCF (US) 1969 dir. John Peyser
TV(US)

Thomas, R.
Piège pour un homme seul
P

Vanishing Act
LEVINSON-LINK (US) 1986
dir. David Greene
TV(US), V

Thomas, R.
Trap for a Single Man
P

One of my Wives is Missing
SPELLING-GOLDBERG (US) 1976
dir. Glenn Jordan
V

Thomas, W. V.
Anzio
Holt, Rinehart & Winston

PAN (It) 1968 dir. Edward Dmytryk
GB title: Battle for Anzio, The
V

Thompson, E.
On Golden Pond
P
Dodd, Mead
UN (US) 1981 dir. Mark Rydell
V

Thompson, J. L.
Double Error
P

Murder Without Crime
ABP (GB) 1950 dir. J. Lee Thompson

Thompson, J.
After Dark, My Sweet
Vintage Books

AVENUE (US) 1990 dir. James Foley

Thompson, J.
Getaway, The

CINERAMA (US) 1972
dir. Sam Peckinpah
V

Thompson, J.
Grifters, The
MIRAMAX (US) 1990
dir. Stephen Frears

Thompson, J.
Kill Off, The
D. I. Fine
CABRIOLET (US) 1990
dir. Maggie Greenwald

Thompson, J.
One Hell of a Woman
Serie Noire
GAU (Fr) 1979 dir. Alain Corneau

Thompson, J.
POP: 1280
Vintage Books
Coup de Torchon
FT (Fr) 1981 dir. Bertrand Tavernier
GB title: Clean Slate

Thompson, M.
Not as a Stranger
Scribners
UA (US) 1955 dir. Stanley Kramer

Thompson, T.
Celebrity
Doubleday
NBC (US) 1984 dir. Paul Wendkos
TVSe(US), V

Thompson, T.
Death of Richie, The
H. JAFFE (US) 1977 dir. Paul Wendkos
TV(US), V

Thorn, R. S.
Full Treatment, The
Heinemann
COL (GB) 1960 dir. Val Guest
US title: Stop Me Before I Kill

Thorn, R. S.
Upstairs and Downstairs
RANK (GB) 1959 dir. Ralph Thomas

Thornburg, N.
Cutter and Bone
Little, Brown (Boston)
UA (US) 1981 dir. Ivan Passer
GB title: Cutter's Way
V

Thorndike, R.
Christoper Syn
Abelard-Schuman
Dr. Syn, Alias the Scarecrow
DISNEY (US) 1962 dir. James Neilson
V

Thorndike, R.
Christopher Syn
Abelard-Schuman
Dr Syn
GAU (GB) 1937 dir. Roy. William Neill
V

Thorne, A.
Baby and the Battleship, The
Heinemann
BL (GB) 1956 dir. Jay Lewis
V

Thorne, A.
So Long at the Fair
GFD (GB) 1950 dir. Terence Fisher
V

Thorp, R.
Detective, The
Dial Press
FOX (US) 1968 dir. Gordon Douglas
V

Thorp, R.
Die Hard
FOX (US) 1988 dir. John McTiernan
V

Thorpe, R.
Rainbow Drive
Summit Books
VIACOM (US) 1990 dir. Bobby Roth
TV(US)

Thurber, J.
Catbird Seat, The

Battle of the Sexes, The
PROM (GB) 1960 dir. Charles Crichton

Thurber, J.
My Life and Hard Times
Harper & Bros.

Rise and Shine
FOX (US) 1941 dir. Allan Dwan

Thurber, J.
Secret Life of Walter Mitty, The
RKO (US) 1947 dir. Norman Z. Macleod
V

Thurber, J. and Nugent, E.
Male Animal, The
P
Samuel French
WAR (US) 1942 dir. Elliot Nugent

Thurber, J. and Nugent, E.
Male Animal, The
P
Samuel French
She's Working Her Way Through College
WAR (US) 1952
dir. Bruce Humberstone

Thurman, J.
Isak Dinesen
Sierra Club Books (San Francisco)
Out of Africa
UN (US) 1985 dir. Sidney Pollack
V

Thurston, E. T.
Wandering Jew, The
P
OLY (GB) 1933 dir. Maurice Elvey

Thurston, K. C.
Masquerader, The
Harper & Bros.
GOLDWYN (US) 1933
dir. Richard Wallace

Thynne, A.
Carry Cot, The

Blue Blood
MIQ (GB) 1973 dir. Andrew Sinclair
V

Tickell, J.
Appointment with Venus
Doubleday
GFD (GB) 1951 dir. Ralph Thomas
US title: Island Rescue

Tickell, J.
Hand and the Flower, The
Hodder & Stoughton
Day to Remember, A
GFD (GB) 1953 dir. Ralph Thomas

Tickell, J.
Odette
BL (GB) 1950 dir. Herbert Wilcox

Tidmarsh, E. V.
Is Your Honeymoon Really
Necessary?
P
Deane
ADELPHI (GB) 1953 dir. Maurice Elvey

Tidyman, E.
Dummy
Little, Brown (Boston)
WAR TV (US) 1979 dir. Frank Perry
TV(US)

Tidyman, E.
Shaft
MGM (US) 1971 dir. Gordon Parks
V

Tierney, H.
Valkyrie's Armour
P
One Brief Summer
FOX (GB) 1969 dir. John MacKenzie

Tiesheng, S.
Life on a String
PBC (Ger/GB/China) 1991
dir. Chen Kaige

Tilsley, F.
Mutiny
Reynal
H.M.S. Defiant
COL (GB) 1962 dir. Lewis Gilbert
US title: Damn the Defiant

Timerman, J.
Prisoner Without a Name, Cell Without a Number
Knopf
Jacobo Timerman: Prisoner Without a Name, Cell Without a Number
CHRYS YELL (US) 1983
dir. Linda Yellen
TV(US)

Tinkle, J. L.
Thirteen Days to Glory: The Seige of the Alamo
Alamo: 13 Days to Glory, The
FRIES (US) 1987 dir. Burt Kennedy
TV(US)

Tinniswood, P.
Mog
LWT (GB) 1985 dir. Nic Phillips
TVSe(GB)

Tippette, G.
Bank Robber, The
Spikes Gang, The
UA (US) 1974 dir. Richard Fleischer

Titus, E.
Basil of Baker Street
Whittlesey House
Great Mouse Detective, The
DISNEY (US) 1986
dir. Burny Mattinson
A, Ch

Toby, M.
Courtship of Eddie's Father, The
Random House
MGM (US) 1963 dir. Vincente Minnelli

Tolkien, J. R. R.
Fellowship of the Ring: Two Towers, The
Houghton, Mifflin Co. (Boston)
Lord of the Rings
UA (US) 1978 dir. Ralph Bakshi
A, V

Toller, E.
Pastor Hall
P
Random House
UA (GB) 1940 dir. Roy Boulting

Tolstoy, L.
Anna Karenina
Various
MGM (US) 1935 dir. Clarence Brown
BL (GB) 1947 dir. Julien Duvivier
RASTAR (US) 1985 dir. Simon Langton
TV(GB/US)

Tolstoy, L.
False Note, The
L'Argent
EOS (Switz/Fr) 1983
dir. Robert Bresson

Tolstoy, L.
Father Sergius
Various
MOSFILM (USSR) 1978
dir. Igor Talankin

Tolstoy, L.
Kreutzer Sonata, The
Various
FOR (Fr) 1938 dir. Charles Guichard
MOSFILM (USSR) 1987
dir. M. Schweitzer and S. Milkina

Tolstoy, L.
Resurrection
Various
UN (US) 1931 dir. Edwin Carewe

Tolstoy, L.
Resurrection
Various
We Live Again
UA (US) 1934 dir. Rouben Mamoulian

Tolstoy, L.
War and Peace
Various
PAR (US/It) 1956 dir. King Vidor
V
MOSFILM (Russia) 1967
dir. Sergei Bondarchuk

Toms, B.
Strange Affair, The
PAR (GB) 1968 dir. David Greene

Tong, S.
Wives and Concubines
Raise the Red Lantern
ORION (China) 1991 dir. Zhang Yimov

Tonkonogy, G.
Three Cornered Moon
P
Samuel French
PAR (US) 1933 dir. Elliott Nugent

Toombs, A.
Raising a Riot
T. Y. Crowell Co.
BL (GB) 1955 dir. Wendy Toye

Topkins, K.
Kotch
McGraw-Hill
CINERAMA (US) 1971
dir. Jack Lemmon

Topor, R.
Tenant, The
Doubleday
PAR (Fr) 1976 dir. Roman Polanski
V

Topor, T.
Nuts
P
Samuel French
WAR (US) 1987 dir. Martin Ritt
V

Torberg, F.
Auch das war Wein
38: Vienna Before the Fall
SATEL/ALMARO (Ger) 1988
dir. Wolfgang Gluck

Torres, E.
Q&A
Dial Press
TRI-STAR (US) 1990 dir. Sidney Lumet

Totheroh, D.
Deep Valley
WAR (US) 1947 dir. Jean Negulesco

Tournier, J.
Jeanne de Luynes, Comtess de Verne
Mercure de France (Paris)
King's Whore, The
J & M (GB) 1990 dir. Axel Corti

Townsend, S.
Secret Diary of Adrian Mole, Aged 13¾, The
THAMES (GB) 1985 dir. Peter Sasdy
TVSe(GB), V

Tracy, D.
Criss Cross
Constable
UI (US) 1949 dir. Robert Siodmak
V

Tracy, M.
Mrs. White
White of the Eye
CANNON (GB) 1987
dir. Donald Cammell
V

Trahey, J.
Life with Mother Superior
Farrar, Straus & Cudahy
Trouble with Angels, The
COL (US) 1966 dir. Ida Lupino
V

Traili, A.
Scarface
UA (US) 1932 dir. Howard Hawks
V

Tranter, F.
Courtneys of Curzon Street, The
BL (GB) 1947 dir. Herbert Wilcox
US title: Courtney Affair, The

Tranter, N.
Bridal Path, The
Hodder & Stoughton
BL (GB) 1959 dir. Frank Launder

Trapp, M. A.
Story of the Trapp Family Singers, The
P
Lippincott (Philadelphia)
Sound of Music, The
FOX (US) 1965 dir. Robert Wise

Traven, B.
Bridge in the Jungle, The
Knopf
UA (US/Mexico) 1970
dir. Pancho Kohner

Traven, B.
Treasure of the Sierra Madre, The
Knopf
WAR (US) 1948 dir. John Huston
V

Traver, R.
Anatomy of a Murder
St. Martin's Press
COL (US) 1959 dir. Otto Preminger
V

Travers, B.
Banana Ridge
P
Samuel French
ABP (GB) 1941 dir. Walter C. Mycroft

Travers, B.
Cuckoo in the Nest, A
P
Samuel French
GB (GB) 1938 dir. Tom Walls

Travers, B.
Cuckoo in the Nest, A
P
Samuel French
Fast and Loose
GFD (GB) 1954 dir. Gordon Parry

Travers, B.
Dirty Work
P
Samuel French
GAU (GB) 1934 dir. Tom Walls

Travers, B.
Plunder
P
Samuel French
WILCOX (GB) 1931 dir. Tom Walls

Travers, B.
Rookery Nook
P
Samuel French
MGM (GB) 1930 dir. Tom Walls

Travers, B.
Thark
P
Samuel French
GB (GB) 1932 dir. Tom Walls

Travers, P. L.
Mary Poppins
Harcourt, Brace & World

DISNEY (US) 1964
dir. Robert Stevenson
Ch, M, V

Tregaskis, R. W.
Guadalcanal Diary
Random House

FOX (US) 1943 dir. Lewis Seiler

Trenhaile, J.
Man Called Kyril, A
St. Martin's Press

Codename: Kyril
INCITO/HTV (US/GB) 1988
dir. Ian Sharp
TV(GB/US)

Trevanian
Eiger Sanction, The
Crown Publishers

UN (US) 1975 dir. Clint Eastwood
V

Treves, Sir F.
Elephant Man and Other Reminiscences, The
Holt

Elephant Man, The
PAR (GB) 1980 dir. David Lynch

Trevor, E.
Big Pick-Up, The
Macmillan

Dunkirk
MGM (GB) 1958 dir. Leslie Norman

Trevor, E.
Expressway

Smash-up on Interstate 5
FILMWAYS (US) 1976
dir. John Llewellyn Moxey
TV(US)

Trevor, E.
Flight of the Phoenix, The
Harper & Row

FOX (US) 1965 dir. Robert Aldrich
V

Trevor, E.
Penthouse, The
GREEN-WHITE (US) 1989
dir. David Greene
TV(US)

Trevor, E.
Pillars of Midnight, The
Heinemann

80,000 Suspects
RANK (GB) 1963 dir. Val Guest

Trevor, E.
Quiller Memorandum, The
Simon & Schuster

RANK (GB) 1966 dir. Michael Anderson

Trevor, W.
Ballroom of Romance, The
Penguin

BBC (GB) 1980 dir. Patrick O'Connor
TV

Trevor, W.
Children of Dynmouth, The
Viking Press

BBC (GB) 1987 dir. Peter Hammond
TV(GB)

Trevor, W.
Fools of Fortune
Viking Press

PALACE (GB) 1990 dir. Pat O'Connor

Trollope, A.
Barchester Towers: Warden, The
Various

Barchester Chronicles, The
BBC (GB) 1982 dir. David Giles
TVSe(GB)

Trollope, A.
Malachi's Cove
PENRITH (GB) 1973
dir. Henry Herbert
US title: Seaweed Children, The

Troy, U.
We Are Seven
She Didn't Say No!
ABP (GB) 1958 dir. Cyril Frankel

Troyat, H.
Mountain, The
Simon & Schuster
PAR (US) 1956 dir. Edward Dmytryk

Truesdell, J.
Be Still My Love
Boardman
Accused, The
PAR (US) 1948 dir. William Dieterle
V

Trumbo, D.
Johnny Got His Gun
Lippincott (Philadelphia)
CINEMATION (US) 1971
dir. Dalton Trumbo
V

Truscott IV, L. K.
Dress Gray
WAR TV (US) 1986 dir. Glenn Jordan
TVSe(US)

Tryon, T.
Crowned Heads
Knopf
Fedora
MAINLINE (Ger/Fr) 1978
dir. Billy Wilder
V

Tryon, T.
Harvest Home
Knopf
Dark Secret of Harvest Home, The
UN TV (US) 1978 dir. Leo Penn
TVSe(US), V

Tryon, T.
Other, The
Knopf
FOX (US) 1972 dir. Robert Mulligan
V

Tucker, A.
Miss Susie Slagle's
PAR (US) 1946 dir. John Berry

Tully, J.
Beggars of Life
Chatto & Windus
PAR (US) 1928 dir. William Wellman

Tunis, J. R.
Hard, Fast and Beautiful
RKO (US) 1951 dir. Ida Lupino

Turgenev, A.
Month in the Country, A
P
Samuel French
ITV (GB) 1955 dir. Robert Hamer
TV(GB)
BBC (GB) 1955 dir. Bill Hays
TV(GB)
PAR (US) 1985 dir. Quentin Lawrence

Turgenev, I.
First Love
Bradda Books (London)
Summer Lightning
CHANNEL 4 (GB) 1986
TV(GB)

Turgenev, I.
House of the Gentle Folk
Macmillan
Nest of Gentry
CORINTH (USSR) 1970
dir. Andrei Konchalovski

Turgenev, I.
Torrents of Spring
Farrar, Straus & Cudahy
MILLIMETER (US) 1990
dir. Jerzy Skolimowski
V

Turkus, B. and Feder, S.
Murder, Inc.
Farrar, Straus & Young
FOX (US) 1960 dir. Burt Balaban,
Stuart Rosenberg

Turnbull, M.
Looking After Sandy
Bad Little Angel
MGM (US) 1939 dir. William Thiele

Turner, D.
Semi Detached
P
All the Way Up
GRANADA/EMI (GB) 1970
dir. James MacTaggart

Turner, E.
One-Way Ticket
COL (US) 1935 dir. Herbert Biberman

Turney, C.
Other One, The
Holt
Back from the Dead
FOX (US) 1957
dir. Charles Marquis Warren

Turow, S.
Burden of Proof, The
Farrar, Straus & Giroux
ABC Prods. TVS(US) 1992
dir. Mike Robe

Turow, S.
Presumed Innocent
Farrar, Straus & Giroux
WAR (US) 1990 dir. Alan J. Pakula

Tuuri, A.
Talvisota
FINN (Fin) 1989 dir. Pekka Parikka

Twain, M.
**Adventures of Huckleberry Finn,
The**
Various
MGM (US) 1960 dir. Michael Curtiz
V
TAFT (US) 1981 dir. Jack B. Hively
TV(US)

Twain, M.
**Adventures of Huckleberry Finn,
The**
Various
Huckleberry Finn
PAR (US) 1931 dir. Norman Taurog
MGM (US) 1939 dir. Richard Thorpe
V
UA (US) 1974 dir. J. Lee Thompson
M, V
ABC (US) 1975 dir. Robert Totten
TV(US)

Twain, M.
Adventures of Tom Sawyer, The
Various
UA (US) 1938 dir. Norman Taurog
V

Twain, M.
Adventures of Tom Sawyer, The
Various
Tom Sawyer
UA (US) 1973 dir. Don Taylor
M, V
UN (US) 1973 dir. James Neilson
TV(US)

Twain, M.
**Connecticut Yankee at the Court of
King Arthur, A**
Various
Connecticut Yankee, A.
FOX (US) 1931 dir. David Butler

Twain, M.
Connecticut Yankee at the Court of King Arthur, A
Various

Connecticut Yankee in King Arthur's Court, A
PAR (US) 1948 dir. Tay Garnett
GB title: Yankee in King Arthur's Court, A
M, V
CONSOL (US) 1989 dir. Mel Damski
TV(US)

Twain, M.
Connecticut Yankee at the Court of King Arthur, A
Various

Spaceman and King Arthur, The
DISNEY (GB) 1979 dir. Russ Mayberry
US title: Unidentified Flying Oddball
V

Twain, M.
Million Pound Note, The
Various

GFD (GB) 1954 dir. Ronald Neame
US title: Man with a Million
V

Twain, M.
Prince and the Pauper, The
Various

WAR (US) 1937 dir. William Keighley
V
DISNEY (US) 1961 dir. Don Chaffey
TV(US), V
WAR (PAN) 1977 dir. Richard Fleischer
US title: Crossed Swords

Tweed, T. F.
Rinehard

Gabriel Over the White House
MGM (US) 1933 dir. Gregory LaCava

Twiss, C.
Long, Long Trailer, The
Crowell, N.Y.

MGM (US) 1954 dir. Vincente Minnelli

Tyler, A.
Accidental Tourist, The
Knopf

WAR (US) 1988 dir. Lawrence Kasdan
V

Tyler, P.
Garden of Cucumbers, A
Random House

Fitzwilly
UA (US) 1967 dir. Delbert Mann
GB title: Fitzwilly Strikes Back

Uchida, Y.
Noh Mask Murders
TOEI (Jap) 1991 dir. Kon Ichikawa

Uhlman, F.
Reunion
Farrar, Straus & Giroux

RANK (US/Fr/Ger) 1989
dir. Jerry Schatzberg

Uhnak, D.
Bait, The
Simon & Schuster
ABC (US) 1973 dir. Leonard Horn
TV(US)

Uhnak, D.
False Witness
Simon & Schuster
NEW WORLD TV (US) 1989
dir. Arthur Allan Seidelman
TV(US)

Uhnak, D.
Investigation, The
Simon & Schuster
Kojak: The Price of Justice
MCA/UN (US) 1987 dir. Alan Metzger
TV(US)

Uhnak, D.
Law and Order
Simon & Schuster
PAR (US) 1976 dir. Marvin J. Chomsky
TV(US)

Uhnak, D.
Ledger, The
J. Curley & Ass. (South Yarmouth,
Massachusetts)
Get Christy Love!
WOLPER (US) 1974
dir. William A. Graham
TV(US)

Uhry, A.
Driving Miss Daisy
P
Theatre Communications Group
WAR (US) 1989 dir. Bruce Beresford

Ullman, J. R.
White Tower, The
Lippincott (Philadelphia)
RKO (US) 1950 dir. Ted Tetzlaff
V

Ullman, J. R.
Banner in the Sky
Lippincott (Philadelphia)
Third Man on the Mountain
DISNEY (GB) 1959 dir. Ken Annakin
Ch, V

Ullman, J. R.
Windom's Way
Lippincott (Philadelphia)
RANK (GB) 1957 dir. Ronald Neame
V

Unekis, R.
Chase, The
Walker, N.Y.
Dirty Mary, Crazy Larry
FOX (US) 1974 dir. John Hough
V

Unsworth, B.
Idol Hunter, The
Simon & Schuster
Pascali's Island
AVENUE (GB) 1988 dir. James Dearden
V

Updike, J.
Rabbit, Run
Knopf
WAR (US) 1970 dir. Jack Smight

Updike, J.
Too Far to Go
Fawcett Crest
ZOETROPE (US) 1982 dir. Fielder Cook

Updike, J.
Witches of Eastwick, The
Knopf
WAR (US) 1987 dir. George Miller
V

Uris, L.
Angry Hills, The
Random House
MGM (GB) 1959 dir. Robert Aldrich

Uris, L.
Battle Cry
WAR (US) 1954 dir. Raoul Walsh
V

Uris, L.
Exodus
Doubleday
UA (US) 1960 dir. Otto Preminger
V

Uris, L.
QB VII
Doubleday
COL (US) 1974 dir. Tom Gries
TVSe(US), V

Uris, L.
Topaz
McGraw-Hill
UI (US) 1969 dir. Alfred Hitchcock
V

Ustinov, P.
Romanoff and Juliet
P
Random House
UN (US) 1961 dir. Peter Ustinov

Uttley, A.
Traveller in Time, A
Viking Press
BBC (GB) 1978 dir. Dorothea Brooking
TVSe(GB)

Vachell, H. A.
Case of Lady Camber, The
P
Samuel French
Lord Camber's Ladies
BI (GB) 1932 dir. Benn W. Levy

Vailland, R.
Truite, La
Trout, The
TRIUMPH (Fr) 1982 dir. Joseph Losey

Vailland, R.
Where the Hot Wind Blows
MGM (Fr/It) 1958 dir. Jules Dassin
V

Valdez, L.
Zoot Suit
P
UN (US) 1982 dir. Luis Valdez

Vale, M.
Two Mrs V. Carrolls, The
P
WAR (US) 1947 dir. Peter Godfrey

Valens, E. G.
Long Way Up, A
Harper & Row
Other Side of the Mountain, The
UN (US) 1975 dir. Larry Peerce
GB title: Window to the Sky, A
V

Valin, J.
Final Notice
Dodd, Mead
SHARMHILL (US) 1989
dir. Steven Hilliard Stern
TV(US)

Valme and Terzolli
Bankers Also Have Souls
P

Gift, The
GOLDWYN (Fr) 1983 dir. Michel Lang
V

Van Atta, W.
Shock Treatment
WAR (US) 1964 dir. Denis Sanders

van der Meersch, M.
Bodies and Souls
Pilot Press

Doctor and the Girl, The
MGM (US) 1949 dir. Curtis Bernhardt

van Dine, S. S.
Bishop Murder Case, The
Scribners
MGM (US) 1930 dir. Nick Grinde and
David Burton

van Dine, S. S.
Casino Murder Case, The
MGM (US) 1935 dir. Edwin Marin

van Dine, S. S.
Gracie Allen Murder Case, The
PAR (US) 1939 dir. Alfred E. Green

van Dine, S. S.
Kennel Murder Case, The
Cassell
WAR (US) 1933 dir. Michael Curtiz
V

van Dine, S. S.
Kennel Murder Case, The
Gregg Press (Boston)
Calling Philco Vance
WAR (US) 1939 dir. William Clemens

Van Greenaway, P.
Medusa Touch, The
ITC (GB/Fr) 1978 dir. Jack Gold
V

Van Gulik, R.
The Haunted Monastery
Scribners

Judge Dee and the Monastery Murders
ABC (US) 1974 dir. Jeremy Paul Kagan
TV(US)

Van Loon, H. W.
Story of Mankind, The
Boni & Liveright
WAR (US) 1957 dir. Irwin Allen

van Slyke, H.
Best Place To Be, The
Doubleday
R. HUNTER (US) 1979 dir. David Miller
TVSe(US)

Vance, E.
Escape
Collins
MGM (US) 1940 dir. Mervyn Le Roy

Vance, E.
Winter Meeting
WAR (US) 1948 dir. Bretaigne Windust

Vance, J. H.
Bad Ronald
LORIMAR (US) 1974 dir. Buzz Kulik
TV(US)

Vance, L. J.
Lone Wolf Returns, The
COL (US) 1936
dir. Roy William McNeill

Vandercook, J. W.
Murder in Trinidad
FOX (US) 1934 dir. Louis King

Vane, S.
Outward Bound
P
Samuel French
WAR (US) 1930 dir. Robert Milton

Vane, S.
Outward Bound
P

Between Two Worlds
WAR (US) 1944 dir. Edward A. Blatt

Varley, J.
Air Raid
Berkley Books
Millenium
FOX (US) 1989 dir. Michael Anderson

Vasquez-Figueroa, A.
Ebano
Plaza & James (Barcelona)
Ashanti
COL (Switz) 1979 dir. Richard Fleischer

Vassilikos, V.
Z
Farrar, Straus & Giroux
WAR (Fr/Alg) 1968 dir. Costa-Gavras
V

Veber, F.
Buddy Buddy
P
MGM (US) 1981 dir. Billy Wilder
V

Veiller, B.
Within the Law
P
MGM (US) 1939 dir. Gustav Machaty

Veiller, B.
Within the Law
P
Paid
MGM (US) 1930 dir. Sam Wood
GB title: Within the Law

Verdi, G.
Otello
Various
CANNON (It) 1986 dir. Franco Zeffirelli
M, V

Verne, J.
Around the World in Eighty Days
Grosset & Dunlap
UA (US) 1956 dir. Michael Anderson,
Kevin McClory
HARMONY GOLD (US) 1989
dir. Buzz Kulik
TVSe(US), V

Verne, J.
Captain Grant's Children
Various
In Search of the Castaways
DISNEY (GB) 1961
dir. Robert Stevenson
Ch, V

Verne, J.
Five Weeks in a Balloon
Various
FOX (US) 1962 dir. Irwin Allen
V

Verne, J.
From the Earth to the Moon
Various
WAR (US) 1958 dir. Byron Haskin
V

Verne, J.
Journey to the Centre of the Earth
Various
FOX (US) 1959 dir. Henry Levin
V
CANNON (US) 1989
dir. Rusty Lemorande
V

Verne, J.
Lighthouse at the End of the World
Light at the Edge of the World, The
MGM (US/Sp) 1971
dir. Kevin Billington
V

Verne, J.
Master of the World
Various
AA (US) 1961 dir. William Witney
V

Verne, J.
Michael Strogoff
Various
Soldier and the Lady, The
RKO (US) 1937 dir. George Nicholls, Jr.
GB title: Michael Strogoff

Verne, J.
Mysterious Island
COL (GB) 1962 dir. Cy Endfield
V

Verne, J.
Southern Star Mystery, The
Various
Southern Star, The
COL (GB/Fr) 1969 dir. Sidney Hayers

Verne, J.
20,000 Leagues Under the Sea
DISNEY (US) 1954
dir. Richard Fleischer
V

Verneuil, L.
Jealousy
P
Samuel French
Deception
WAR (US) 1946 dir. Irving Rapper
V

Verneuil, L. and Berr, G.
Mon Crime
P
True Confession
PAR (US) 1937 dir. Wesley Ruggles

Very, P.
Goupi Mains Rouges
MINERVA (Fr) 1943
dir. Jacques Becker
US title: It Happened at the Inn

Vickers, R.
Girl in the News, The
FOX (GB) 1940 dir. Carol Reed

Vidal, G.
Best Man, The
P
Little, Brown (Boston)
UA (US) 1964 dir. Franklin Schaffner

Vidal, G.
Lincoln
Random House
Gore Vidal's Lincoln
FINNEGAN/PINCHUK (US) 1988
dir. Lamont Johnson
TVSe(US)

Vidal, G.
Myra Breckenridge
Little, Brown (Boston)
FOX (US) 1970 dir. Mike Sarne
V

Vidal, G.
Visit to a Small Planet
P
Little, Brown (Boston)
PAR (US) 1960 dir. Norman Taurog

Vidalie, A.
Heaven Fell That Night
IENA (Fr/It) 1958 dir. Roger Vadim

Viertel, P.
White Hunter, Black Heart
Doubleday
WAR (US) 1990 dir. Clint Eastwood

Vigny, B.
Amy Jolly
P
Morocco
PAR (US) 1930 dir. Josef von Sternberg
V

Vinje, K.
Kamilla and the Thief
PENELOPE (Nor/GB) 1988
dir. Grete Salamonsen

Vinton, I.
Flying Ebony
Mooncussers, The
DISNEY (US) 1971 dir. James Neilson
V

Viola, C. G.
Prico
Children Are Watching Us, The
MAGLI (It) 1942 dir. Vittorio de Sica
V

Vivant, D.
Point de Lendemain
Amants, Les
NEF (Fr) 1958 dir. Louis Malle

Vizinczey, S.
In Praise of Older Women
Atlantic Monthly Press
ASTRAL (Can) 1977
dir. George Kaczender
V

Vogel, K.
Virgin Witch
TIGON (GB) 1970 dir. Ray Austin
V

Vollmer, L.
Trigger
P
Spitfire
RKO (US) 1934 dir. John Cromwell
V

Vollmoeller, K.
Miracle, The
P
WAR (US) 1959 dir. Irving Rapper

von Horvath, O
Tales from the Vienna Woods
P
CINEMA 5 (Austria/Ger) 1981
dir. Maximilian Schell

von Kleist, H.
Michael Kohlhaas
Continuum
COL (Ger) 1980 dir. Volker Schlondorff

von Krusenstjerna, A.
Froknarna von Pahlen
Loving Couples
SANDREW (Swe) 1964
dir. Mai Zetterling

Vonnegut, K.
Happy Birthday, Wanda Jane
P
Samuel French
COL (US) 1971 dir. Mark Robson

Vonnegut, K.
**Next Door; Euphio Question, The;
All the King's Men**
Monkey House
ATLANTIS (US) 1991 dir. Paul Shapiro,
Gilbert Shilton, Allan King
TV(US)

Vonnegut, K.
Slapstick
Delacorte Press
Slapstick of Another Kind
LORIMAR (US) 1984 dir. Steven Paul
V

Vonnegut, K.
Slaughterhouse Five
Delacorte Press
UN (US) 1972 dir. George Roy Hill
V

Vosper, F.
Love from a Stranger
P

UA (GB) 1937 dir. Rowland V. Lee
EAGLE LION (US) 1947
dir. Richard Whorf
GB title: Stranger Walked In, A
V

Votler, G.
The Cipher

Arabesque
UN (US) 1966 dir. Stanley Donen
V

Vulliamy, C. E.
Don Among the Dead Men
Joseph

Jolly Bad Fellow, A
BL (GB) 1964 dir. Robert Hamer

Vulliamy, C. E.
William Penn
C. Scribner's Sons

Penn of Pennsylvania
BN (GB) 1941 dir. Lance Comfort
US title: The Courageous Mr. Penn

Vulpuis, P.
Youth at the Helm
P

Jack of all Trades
GAINS (GB) 1936 dir. Jack Hubert,
Robert Stevenson

Waddell, M.
Otley
Stein & Day

COL (GB) 1968 dir. Dick Clement
V

Wade, K.
Key Exchange
P

FOX (US) 1985 dir. Barnet Kellman
V

Wagenheim, K.
Babe Ruth, His Life and Legend
Simon & Schuster

Babe Ruth
LYTTLE (US) 1991 dir. Mark Tinker
TV(US)

Wager, W.
Telefon
Macmillan

MGM (US) 1977 dir. Don Siegel
V

Wager, W.
Viper Three
Macmillan

Twilight's Last Gleaming
HEMDALE (US/Ger) 1977
dir. Robert Aldrich
V

Wager, W.
58 Minutes
Macmillan

Die Hard 2
FOX (US) 1990 dir. Renny Harlin

Wagoner, D.
Escape Artist, The
Farrar, Straus & Giroux
ORION (US) 1982 dir. Caleb Deschanel
V

Wahloo, P.
Murder on the 31st Floor
Knopf
Kamikaze '89
TELECUL (Ger) 1983 dir. Wolf Gremm
V

Wainwright, J.
Brainwash
St. Martin's Press
Inquisitor, The
GALA (Fr) 1981 dir. Claude Miller

Wakatsuki, J. and Houston, J. D.
Farewell to Manzanar
Houghton, Mifflin Co. (Boston)
UN TV (US) 1976 dir. John Korty
TV(US)

Wakefield, D.
James at 15
FOX TV (US) 1977 dir. Joseph Hardy
TV(US)

Wakefield, D.
Starting Over
Delacorte Press
PAR (US) 1979 dir. Alan J. Pakula
V

Wakefield, G.
Counsel's Opinion
P
KORDA (GB) 1933 dir. Allan Dwan

Wakefield, G.
Counsel's Opinion
P
Divorce of Lady X, The
LONDON (GB) 1938 dir. Tim Whelan
V

Wakeman, F.
Hucksters, The
Rinehart
MGM (US) 1947 dir. Jack Conway

Wakeman, F.
Saxon Charm, The
UI (US) 1948 dir. Claude Binyon

Wakeman, F.
Shore Leave
Farras, N.Y.
Kiss Them for Me
FOX (US) 1957 dir. Stanley Donen

Walker, A.
Colour Purple, The
Harcourt, Brace, Jovanovich
WAR (US) 1986 dir. Steven Spielberg
V

Walker, D.
Geordie
Houghton, Mifflin Co. (Boston)
BL (GB) 1955 dir. Frank Launder
US title: Wee Geordie

Walker, D.
Harry Black and the Tiger
FOX (GB) 1958 dir. Hugo Fregonese
US title: Harry Black

Walker, D. E.
Adventure in Diamonds
W. W. Norton
Operation Amsterdam
RANK (GB) 1958
dir. Michael McCarthy
V

Walker, D. E.
Diamonds are Danger
Evans
Man Could Get Killed, A
UN (US) 1966 dir. Ronald Neame

Walker, G.
Case History

Damned Don't Cry, The
WAR (US) 1950 dir. Vincent Sherman

Walker, G.
Cruising
W. H. Allen

LORIMAR (US) 1980
dir. William Friedkin
V

Wall, M.
Amongst Barbarians
BBC (GB) 1990 dir. Jane Howell
TV(GB)

Wallace, E.
Calendar, The
GFD (GB) 1948 dir. Arthur Crabtree

Wallace, E.
Case of the Frightened Lady, The
BL (GB) 1940 dir. George King
US title: Frightened Lady, The

Wallace, E.
Case of the Frightened Lady, The
Frightened Lady, The
BL (GB) 1932 dir. T. Hayes Hunter

Wallace, E.
Crimson Circle, The
Hodder & Stoughton

NEW ERA (GB) 1929 dir. Fred Zelnick
WAINRIGHT (GB) 1936
dir. Reginald Denham

Wallace, E.
Daffodil Mystery, The
Ward Lock

Devil's Daffodil, The
BL (GB) 1962 dir. Akos Rathony

Wallace, E.
Feathered Serpent
Doubleday

Menace, The
COL (US) 1932 dir. Roy William Neill

Wallace, E.
Fellowship of the Frog, The
Chivers Press (Trowbridge)

Frog, The
WILCOX (GB) 1937 dir. Jack Raymond

Wallace, E.
Four Just Men, The
EAL (GB) 1939 dir. Walter Forde
US title: Secret Four, The

Wallace, E.
Ghost of John Holling, The

Mystery Liner
MON (US) 1934 dir. William Nigh

Wallace, E.
Jack O'Judgement

Share Out, The
AA (GB) 1962 dir. Gerald Glaister

Wallace, E.
Kate Plus Ten
Ward Lock

WAINRIGHT (GB) 1938
dir. Reginald Denham

Wallace, E.
Lone House Mystery, The

Attempt to Kill
AA (GB) 1961 dir. Royston Murray

Wallace, E.
Man At The Carlton
Hodder & Stoughton

Man at the Carlton Tower
AA (GB) 1961 dir. Robert Tronson

Wallace, E.
Man Who Knew, The

Partners in Crime
AA (GB) 1961 dir. Peter Duffell

Wallace, E.
Mind of Mr J. G. Reeder, The

Mind of Mr. Reeder, The
RAYMOND (GB) 1936
dir. Jack Raymond
ITV (GB) 1969
TV(GB)

Wallace, E.
On The Spot
P

Dangerous to Know
PAR (US) 1938 dir. Robert Florey

Wallace, E.
Ringer, The
A. L. Burt Co.

Gaunt Stranger, The
NORTHWOOD (GB) 1938
dir. Walter Forde
US title: Phantom Strikes, The

Wallace, E.
Ringer, The
REGENT (GB) 1952 dir. Guy Hamilton

Wallace, E.
Sanders of the River
UA (GB) 1935 dir. Zoltan Korda
US title: Bosambo
V

Wallace, E.
Squeaker, The
GAU BR (GB) 1937
dir. William K. Howard
US title: Murder on Diamond Row

Wallace, E.
Terror, The
ALL (GB) 1938 dir. Richard Bird

Wallace, E.
Traitor's Gate
COL (GB) 1965 dir. Freddie Francis

Wallace, F.
Kid Galahad
Hale

WAR (US) 1937 dir. Michael Curtiz
UA (US) 1962 dir. Phil Karlson
M, V

Wallace, I.
Chapman Report, The
Cassell

WAR (US) 1962 dir. George Cukor

Wallace, I.
Man, The
Fawcett

PAR (US) 1972 dir. Joseph Sargent

Wallace, I.
Prize, The
Simon & Schuster

MGM (US) 1963 dir. Mark Robson

Wallace, I.
Seven Minutes, The
Simon & Schuster

FOX (US) 1971 dir. Russ Meyer

Wallace, I.
Word, The
Simon & Schuster

FRIES (US) 1978 dir. Richard Lang
TVSe(US)

Wallace, L.
Ben Hur
Harper

MGM (US) 1926 dir. Fred Niblo
MGM (US) 1959 dir. William Wyler
V

Wallace, P.
Dreams Lost, Dreams Found
Harlequin

ATLANTIC/YTV (US/GB) 1987
dir. Willi Patterson
TV(GB/US)

Wallace, P.
Love with a Perfect Stranger
Harlequin
ATLANTIC/YTV (US/GB)
dir. Desmond Davis
TV(GB/US)

Wallace, P.
Tears in the Rain
Harlequin
ATLANTIC/BL (US/GB) 1988
dir. Don Sharpe
TV(GB/US)

Wallach, I.
Muscle Beach
Gollancz

Don't Make Waves
MGM (US) 1967
dir. Alexander Mackendrick

Wallant, E. L.
Pawnbroker, The
Harcourt, Brace & World
PAR (US) 1964 dir. Sidney Lumet
V

Waller, L.
Hide in Plain Sight
Delacorte Press
UA (US) 1980 dir. James Caan
V

Wallis, A. J. and Blair, C. E.
Thunder Above
Jarrolds

Beyond the Curtain
RANK (GB) 1960 dir. Compton Bennett

Wallis, J. H.
Once Off Guard
Woman in the Window, The
RKO (US) 1944 dir. Fritz Lang

Wallop, D.
Year the Yankees Lost the Pennant, The
Norton
Damn Yankees
WAR (US) 1958 dir. George Abbott,
Stanley Donen
GB title: What Lola Wants
M, V

Walmsley, L.
Three Fevers
Turn of the Tide
BN (GB) 1935 dir. Norman Walker

Walpole, H.
Mr. Perrin and Mr. Traill
G. Doran
TC (GB) 1948 dir. Lawrence
Huntington

Walpole, Sir H.
Vanessa, Her Love Story
Doubleday
MGM (US) 1935 dir. William K. Howard

Walsh, M.
Green Rushes
Quiet Man, The
REP (US) 1952 dir. John Ford
V

Walsh, M.
Trouble in the Glen
Lippincott (Philadelphia)
REP (GB) 1954 dir. Herbert Wilcox
V

Walsh, T.
Night Watch, The
Pushover
COL (US) 1954 dir. Richard Quine

Walsh, T.
Nightmare in Manhattan
Union Station
PAR (US) 1950 dir. Rudolph Maté
V

Waltari, M.
Egyptian, The
Putnam
FOX (US) 1954 dir. Michael Curtiz

Walter, E.
Easiest Way, The
P
Dodd, N.Y.
MGM (US) 1931 dir. Jack Conway

Walters, G. M. and Hopkins, A.
Burlesque
P
Samuel French
Swing High, Swing Low
PAR (US) 1937 dir. Mitchell Leisen
V

Walters, G. M. and Hopkins, A.
Burlesque
P
Samuel French
When my Baby Smiles at Me
FOX (US) 1948 dir. Walter Lang

Walton, T.
Inside Moves
Doubleday
BARBER (US) 1980 dir. Richard Donner
V

Wambaugh, J.
Black Marble, The
Delacorte Press
AVCO EMBASSY (US) 1980
dir. Harold Becker
V

Wambaugh, J.
Blue Knight, The
Little, Brown
LORIMAR (US) 1973 dir. Robert Butler
TVSe(US)

Wambaugh, J.
Choirboys, The
Delacorte Press
LORIMAR (US) 1977 dir. Robert Aldrich
V

Wambaugh, J.
Echoes in the Darkness
W. Morrow
NEW WORLD TV (US) 1987
dir. Glenn Jordan
TVSe(US)

Wambaugh, J.
Glitter Dome, The
W. Morrow
HBO (US) 1984 dir. Stuart Margolin
TV(US), V

Wambaugh, J.
New Centurions, The
W. Morrow
COL (US) 1972 dir. Richard Fleischer
GB title: Precinct 45: Los Angeles Police
V

Wambaugh, J.
Onion Field, The
Delacorte Press
AVCO (US) 1979 dir. Harold Becker
V

Wanderer, Dr. Z. and Cabot, T.
Letting Go
ITC (US) 1985 dir. Jack Bender
TV(US)

Ward, B.
Marshal of Medicine Bend, The
Hodder & Stoughton
Lawless Street, A
COL (US) 1955 dir. Joseph H. Lewis

Ward, M. J.
Snake Pit, The
Exposition Press
FOX (US) 1948 dir. Anatole Litvak

Ward, R.
Cattle Annie and Little Britches
Morrow

UN (US) 1981 dir. Lamont Johnson
V

Ware, H.
Come Fill the Cup
WAR (US) 1951 dir. Gordon Douglas

Warner, D.
Death of a Snout

Informers, The
RANK (GB) 1963 dir. Ken Annakin
US title: Underworld Informers

Warner, R.
Aerodrome, The
OUP

BBC (GB) 1983 dir. Giles Foster
TV(GB), V

Warren, C. E. T. and Benson, J.
Above us the Waves
Harrap

GFD (GB) 1955 dir. Ralph Thomas
V

Warren, C. M.
Only the Valiant
WAR (US) 1950 dir. Gordon Douglas
V

Warren, F. B.
Face at the Window
P

PENNANT (GB) 1939 dir. George King

Warren, R. P.
Band of Angels
Random House

WAR (US) 1957 dir. Raoul Walsh

Warren, R.P.
All the King's Men
Harcourt Brace

COL (US) 1949 dir. Robert Rossen
V

Warwick, J.
Blind Alley
P
Samuel French

COL (US) 1939 dir. Charles Vidor

Wasserman, D.
Man of La Mancha
P
Random House

UA (US) 1972 dir. Arthur Hiller
M, V

Waterhouse, K
Billy Liar
Norton

WAR (GB) 1963 dir. John Schlesinger
V

Watkins, L. E.
On Borrowed Time

MGM (US) 1939 dir. Harold S. Bucquet
MILBERG (US) 1957
dir. George Schaefer
TV(US)

Watkins, M.
Chicago
P
Samuel French

Roxie Hart
FOX (US) 1942 dir. William A. Wellman

Watkyn, A.
For Better, For Worse
P
Elek

ABP (GB) 1954 dir. J. Lee Thompson
V

Watkyn, A.
Moonraker, The
P
ABP (GB) 1958 dir. David MacDonald

Watson, C.
Miss Lonelyhearts 4122
Crooked Hearts, The
LORIMAR (US) 1972 dir. Jay Sandrich
TV(US)

Waugh, A.
Guy Renton, A London Story
Farrar, Straus
Circle of Deception
FOX (GB) 1960 dir. Jack Lee

Waugh, A.
Island in the Sun
Farrar, Straus & Cudahy
FOX (GB) 1957 dir. Robert Rossen

Waugh, E.
Brideshead Revisited
Little, Brown (Boston)
GRANADA (GB) 1981
dir. Charles Sturridge
TVSe(GB), V

Waugh, E.
Decline and Fall
Farrar
Decline and Fall ... of a Birdwatcher
FOX (GB) 1968 dir. John Karsh

Waugh, E.
Handful of Dust, A
Chapman & Hall (London)
NEW LINE (GB) 1988
dir. Charles Sturridge
V

Waugh, E.
Loved One, The
Little, Brown (Boston)
MGM (US) 1965 dir. Tony Richardson

Waugh, E.
Scoop
LWT (GB) 1987 dir. Gavin Millar
TV(GB)

Waugh, H.
Sleep Long My Love
Carroll & Graf
Jigsaw
BL (GB) 1962 dir. Val Guest

Wead, F.
Ceiling Zero
P
WAR (US) 1935 dir. Howard Hawks

Weaver, G.
Count a Lonely Cadence
Cadence
New Line (US) 1990 dir. Martin Sheen

Weaver, W.
Red Earth, White Earth
Simon & Schuster
VIACOM (US) 1989 dir. David Greene
TV(US)

Webb, C.
Graduate, The
New American Library
UA (US) 1967 dir. Mike Nichols
V

Webb, C.
Marriage of a Young Stockbroker, The
Lippincott (Philadelphia)
FOX (US) 1971 dir. Laurence Turman

Webb, M.
Gone to Earth
J. Cape (London)
BL (GB) 1950
dir. Michael Powell/Emeril Pressburger
US title: Wild Heart, The

Webber, A. L. and Rice, T.
Jesus Christ Superstar
P
Leeds Music Corp.
UN (US) 1973 dir. Norman Jewison
M, V

Webster, J.
Daddy Long Legs
Hawthorne Books
FOX (US) 1931 dir. Alfred Santell
FOX (US) 1955 dir. Jean Negulesco
M

Weidman, J.
House of Strangers
FOX (US) 1949
dir. Joseph L. Mankiewicz

Weidman, J.
I Can Get It For You Wholesale
Simon & Schuster
FOX (US) 1951 dir. Michael Gordon
GB title: This is My Affair

Weiman, R.
One Man's Secret
Possessed
WAR (US) 1947 dir. Curtis Bernhardt

Weiner, J. B.
Morning After, The
Delacorte Press
WOLPER (US) 1974
dir. Richard T. Heffron
TV(US)

Weisman, M-L.
Intensive Care
Random House
Time to Live, A
ITC (US) 1985 dir. Rick Wallace
TV(US), V

Weiss, P.
Marat/Sade
P
Atheneum
UA (GB) 1966 dir. Peter Brook

Weitzenkorn, L.
Five Star Final
P
WAR (US) 1931 dir. Mervyn LeRoy

Weitzenkorn, L.
Five-Star Final
P
Two Against the World
WAR (US) 1936 dir. William McGann
GB title: Case of Mrs. Pembroke, The

Weldon, F.
Life and Loves of a She-Devil, The
Pantheon
BBC (GB) 1986 dir. Philip Saville
TVSe(GB)

Weldon, F.
Life and Loves of a She-Devil, The
Pantheon Books
She-Devil
ORION (US) 1989 dir. Susan Seidelman

Wellard, J.
Action of the Tiger
MGM (GB) 1957 dir. Terence Young

Wellesley, G.
Report on a Fugitive
Night Train to Munich
TCF (GB) 1940 dir. Carol Reed
V

Wellman, P. I.
Bronco Apache
Apache
UA (US) 1954 dir. Robert Aldrich
V

Wellman, P. I.
Comancheros, The
Doubleday
FOX (US) 1961 dir. Michael Curtiz
V

Wellman, P. I.
Iron Mistress, The
Doubleday

WAR (US) 1952 dir. Gordon Douglas

Wellman, P. I.
Jubal Troop
Grosset, N.Y.

Jubal
COL (US) 1956 dir. Delmer Daves
V

Wellman, P. I.
Walls of Jericho, The
Lippincott (Philadelphia)

FOX (US) 1948 dir. John M. Stahl

Wells, H. G.
Door in the Wall, The
M. Kennerly

ABP (GB) 1956 dir. Glenn H. Alvey, Jr.

Wells, H. G.
First Men in the Moon
Bobbs-Merrill (Indianapolis)

Col (GB) 1963 dir. Nathan Juran

Wells, H. G.
History of Mr. Polly, The
Duffield

GFD (GB) 1949 dir. Anthony Pelissier

Wells, H. G.
Invisible Man, The
Various

UN (US) 1933 dir. James Whale
V
UN (US) 1975 dir. Robert Michael Lewis
TV(US)
BBC (GB) 1984 dir. Brian Lightill
TV(GB)

Wells, H. G.
Invisible Man, The
Heritage Press

Gemini Man
UN TV (US) 1976 dir. Alan J. Levi
TV(US)

Wells, H. G.
Island of Dr. Moreau, The
Various

Island of Lost Souls
PAR (US) 1932 dir. Erle C. Kenton

Wells, H. G.
Island of Dr. Moreau, The
Various

AIP (US) 1977 dir. Don Taylor
V

Wells, H. G.
Kipps

FOX (GB) 1941 dir. Carol Reed
US title: Remarkable Mr Kipps, The
V
GRANADA TV (GB) 1960
TVSe(GB)

Wells, H. G.
Kipps

Half a Sixpence
PAR (GB) 1967 dir. George Sidney
M

Wells, H. G.
Man Who Could Work Miracles, The
Crescent Press (London)

UA (GB) 1936 dir. Lothar Mendes

Wells, H. G.
Passionate Friends, The
Harper

CINEGUILD (GB) 1949 dir. David Lean
GB title: One Woman's Story

Wells, H. G.
Shape of Things to Come, The
Various

BARBER DANN (Can) 1979
dir. George McGowan
V

Wells, H. G.
Shape of Things to Come, The
Various

Things to Come
UA (GB) 1936
dir. William Cameron Menzies
V

Wells, H. G.
Time Machine, The
Various

MGM (US) 1960 dir. George Pal
V
SCHICK SUNN (US) 1978
dir. Henning Schellerup
TV(US)

Wells, H. G.
Valley of the Ants, The
Various

Empire of the Ants
AIP (US) 1977 dir. Bert I. Gordon
V

Wells, H. G.
War of the Worlds
Various

·PAR (US) 1953 dir. Byron Haskin
V

Wells, L. E.
Day of the Outlaw, The
UA (US) 1958 dir. André de Toth

Werbell, F. and Clarke, T.
Lost Hero: The Mystery of Raoul
Wallenberg
McGraw-Hill

Wallenberg: A Hero's Story
PAR (US) 1985 dir. Lamont Johnson
TVSe(US)

Werfel, F.
Forty Days of Musa Dagh
Aeonian (Mattituck, New York)

HIGH INV (US/Tur) 1987
dir. Sarky Mouradia
V

Werfel, F.
Jacobowsky and the Colonel
P
Random House

Me and The Colonel
COL (US) 1958 dir. Peter Glenville
V

Werfel, F. V.
Song of Bernadette, The
Viking Press

FOX (US) 1943 dir. Henry King
V

Wersba, B.
Country of the Heart, The
Atheneum

Matters of the Heart
MCA TV (US) 1990 dir. Michael Rhodes
TV(US)

Wesker, A.
Kitchen, The
P
Samuel French

BL (GB) 1961 dir. James Hill

West, J.
Friendly Persuasion
Harcourt, Brace & Co.

MGM (US) 1956 dir. WIlliam Wyler
V
AA (US) 1975 dir. Joseph Sargent
TV(US)

West, M.
Devil's Advocate, The
Morrow

RANK (Ger) 1977 dir. Guy Green

West, M.
Diamond Lil
P

She Done Him Wrong
PAR (US) 1933 dir. Lowell Sherman
V

West, M.
Naked Country, The
Morrow

FILMWAYS (Aust) 1984
dir. Tim Burstall
V

West, M.
Salamander, The
Morrow

ITC (It/GB/US) 1981 dir. Peter Zinner
V

West, M. L.
Big Story, The
Heinemann

Crooked Road, The
GALA (GB/Yugo) 1964 dir. Don Chaffey

West, M. L.
Shoes of the Fisherman, The
Morrow

MGM (US) 1968 dir. Michael Anderson
V

West, N.
Day of the Locust, The

PAR (US) 1975 dir. John Schlesinger
V

West, N.
Miss Lonelyhearts
Farrar, Straus & Cudahy

Lonelyhearts
UA (US) 1958 dir. Vincent J. Donehue

West, R.
Return of the Soldier, The
Dial Press

BW (GB) 1983 dir. Alan Bridges
V

West, S.
Amos
Rawson Associates

BRYNA (US) 1985 dir. Michael Tuchner
TV(US), V

Westall, R.
Watch House, The
Greenwillow Books

BBC (GB) 1990 dir. Ivan Keill
TV(GB)

Westerby, R.
Small Voice, The

BL (GB) 1948 dir. Fergus McDonell
US title: Hideout

Westheimer, D.
My Sweet Charlie
P
Samuel French

UN TV (US) 1970 dir. Lamont Johnson
TV(US), V

Westheimer, D.
Von Ryan's Express
Doubleday

FOX (US) 1965 dir. Mark Robson
V

Westlake, D. E.
Bank Shot, The
Simon & Schuster

UA (US) 1974 dir. Gower Champion
V

Westlake, D. E.
Busy Body, The
Random House

PAR (US) 1967 dir. William Castle

Westlake, D. E.
Hot Rock, The
Simon & Schuster

TCF (US) 1972 dir. Peter Yates
GB title: How to Steal a Diamond in
Four Uneasy Lessons

Westlake, D. E.
Jimmy the Kid
M. Evans

NEW WORLD (US) 1982
dir. Gary Nelson
V

Westlake, D. E.
Why Me?
Viking Press
TRIUMPH (US) 1990
dir. Gene Quintano

Weston, C.
Poor, Poor Ophelia
Random House
Streets of San Francisco, The
WAR TV (US) 1972 dir. Walter Grauman
TV(US)

Weston, J.
Hail, Hero!
CIN CEN (US) 1969 dir. David Miller

Wetjen, A. R.
Way for a Sailor
MGM (US) 1930 dir. Sam Wood

Weverka, R. and Sellier, Jr., C.
Hangar 18
SCHICK SUNN (US) 1980
dir. James L. Conway
V

Weyman, S.
Under the Red Robe
FOX (GB) 1937 dir. Victor Sjostrom
V

Wharton, E.
Age of Innocence
Appleton
RKO (US) 1934 dir. Philip Moeller

Wharton, E.
Children, The
Scribners
Marriage Playground, The
PAR (US) 1929 dir. Lothar Mendes

Wharton, E. N.
Old Maid, The
Doubleday
WAR (US) 1939 dir. Edmund Goulding
V

Wharton, W.
Birdy
Knopf
TRI-STAR (US) 1984 dir. Alan Parker
V

Wharton, W.
Dad
Knopf
UN (US) 1989 dir. Gary D. Goldberg

Wheatley, D.
Devil Rides Out, The
Hutchinson
ABP (GB) 1971 dir. Terence Fisher
US title: Devil's Bride, The

Wheatley, D.
Eunuch of Stamboul, The
Secret of Stamboul, The
HOB (GB) 1936 dir. Andrew Marton

Wheatley, D.
Forbidden Territory
Hutchinson
GAU (GB) 1934 dir. Phil Rosen

Wheatley, D.
To the Devil, a Daughter
EMI (GB/Ger) 1976 dir. Peter Sykes
V

Wheatley, D.
Uncharted Seas
Hutchinson
Lost Continent, The
WAR (GB) 1968 dir. Michael Carreras

Wheeler, H., Sondheim, S.
Little Night Music, A
P
Applause Theatre Books
S&T (Austria/Ger) 1977
dir. Harold Prince
M, V

Whipple, D.
They Knew Mr. Knight
GFD (GB) 1945 dir. Norman Walker

Whipple, D.
They Were Sisters
GFD (GB) 1945 dir. Arthur Crabtree

White, A.
Long Day's Dying, The
Hodder & Stoughton
PAR (GB) 1968 dir. Peter Collinson

White, E. B.
Charlotte's Web
Harper
SCOTIA-BARBER (US) 1972
dir. Charles A. Nichols
A, Ch, V

White, E. L.
Her Heart in Her Throat
Unseen, The
PAR (US) 1945 dir. Lewis Allen

White, E. L.
Some Must Watch
Spiral Staircase, The
RKO (US) 1946 dir. Robert Siodmak
V
WAR (GB) 1975 dir. Peter Collinson
V

White, E. L.
Wheel Spins, The
Harper
Lady Vanishes, The
MGM (GB) 1938 dir. Alfred Hitchcock
RANK (GB) 1979 dir. Anthony Page
V

White, G. M.
Tess of the Storm Country
FOX (US) 1932 dir. Alfred Santell
FOX (US) 1961 dir. Paul Guilfoyle

White, L.
Clean Break
Boardman
Killing, The
UA (US) 1956 dir. Stanley Kubrick

White, L.
Money Trap, The
MGM (US) 1966 dir. Burt Kennedy

White, L.
Snatchers, The
Night of the Following Day, The
UN (US) 1969 dir. Hubert Cornfield

White, L. T.
Harness Bull
Vice Squad
UA (US) 1953 dir. Arnold Laven
GB title: Girl in Room 17, The

White, R.
Death Watch
Savages
SPEL-GOLD (US) 1974 dir. Lee Katzin
TV(US)

White, R.
Our Virgin Island
Virgin Island
BL (GB) 1958 dir. Pat Jackson

White, R.
Up Periscope
Doubleday
WAR (US) 1959 dir. Gordon Douglas

White, S. E.
Wild Geese Calling
Doubleday
FOX (US) 1941 dir. John Brahm

White, T. H.
Mountain Road, The
W. Sloane Associates
COL (US) 1960 dir. Delbert Mann

White, T. H.
Once and Future King, The
Putnam
Camalot
WAR (US) 1967 dir. Joshua Logan
M, V

White, T. H.
Once and Future King, The
Putnam
Sword in the Stone, The
DISNEY (US) 1963
dir. Wolfgang Reitherman
A, Ch, V ·

White, W. L.
Journey for Margaret
Harcourt, Brace & Co.
MGM (US) 1942 dir. W. S. van Dyke

White, W. L.
They were Expendable
Harcourt, Brace & Co.
MGM (US) 1945 dir. John Ford
V

Whitehead, D.
Attack on Terror: The FBI Against
The Ku Klux Klan in Mississippi
Funk & Wagnalls
*Attack on Terror: The FBI Versus The
Ku Klux Klan*
WAR TV (US) 1975
dir. Marvin Chomsky
TVSe(US)

Whitehead, D.
FBI Story, The
Random House
WAR' (US) 1959 dir. Mervyn LeRoy
V

Whitemore, H.
Pack of Lies
P
Samuel French
HALMI (US) 1987 dir. Anthony Page
TV(US)

Whitemore, H.
Stevie
P
Samuel French
FIRST (US/GB) 1978
dir. Robert Enders

Whitman, S. E.
Captain Apache
BENMAR (US/Sp) 1971
dir. Alexander Singer
V

Whittemore, L. H.
Super Cops, The
Stein & Day
MGM (US) 1974 dir. Gordon Parks
V

Whitten, L. H.
Moon of the Wolf
FILMWAYS (US) 1972 dir. Daniel Petrie
TV(US)

Whittington, H.
Desire in the Dust
TCF (US) 1960 dir. William F. Claxton

Wibberley, L.
Hands of Cormac Joyce, The
CRAWFORD PRODS (US) 1972
dir. Fielder Cook
TV(US)

Wibberly, L.
Mouse that Roared, The
Little, Brown (Boston)
COL (GB) 1959 dir. Jack Arnold
V

Wicker, T.
Time to Die, A
Bodley Head
Attica
ABC (US) 1980 dir. Marvin J. Chomsky
TV(US),V

Wiesenthal, S.
Max and Helen: A Remarkable
True Love Story
Morrow
Max and Helen
TNT (US) 1990 dir. Philip Saville
TV(US)

Wiggin, K. D.
Mother Carey's Chickens
Houghton, Mifflin Co. (Boston)
RKO (US) 1938 dir. Rowland V. Lee

Wiggin, K. D.
Mother Carey's Chickens
Houghton, Mifflin Co. (Boston)
Summer Magic
DISNEY (US) 1963 dir. James Neilson
V

Wiggin, Mrs. K. D.
Rebecca of Sunnybrook Farm
Houghton, Mifflin Co. (Boston)
FOX (US) 1932 dir. Alfred Santell
FOX (US) 1938 dir. Allan Dwan
V

Wilbur, C.
Solomon and Sheba
UA (US) 1959 dir. King Vidor
V

Wilde, H. and Eunson, D.
Guest in the House
P
Samuel French
UA (US) 1944 dir. John Brahm
V

Wilde, O.
Canterville Ghost, The
MGM (US) 1943 dir. Jules Dassin
HTV (GB/US) 1986 dir. Paul Bogart
TV(GB/US), V

Wilde, O.
Ideal Husband, An
P
Doubleday
BL (GB) 1948 dir. Alexander Korda
V

Wilde, O.
Importance of Being Earnest, The
P
Samuel French
RANK/GFD (GB) 1952
dir. Anthony Asquith
V

Wilde, O.
Lady Windemere's Fan
P
Samuel French
Fan, The
FOX (US) 1949 dir. Otto Preminger
GB title: Lady Windemere's Fan

Wilde, O.
Lord Arthur Savile's Crime
Doubleday
Flesh and Fantasy
UN (US) 1943 dir. Julien Duvivier

Wilde, O.
Picture of Dorian Gray, The
Various
MGM (US) 1945 dir. Albert Lewin
V
CURTIS (US) 1973 dir. Glenn Jordan
TV(US)

Wilde, O.
Picture of Dorian Gray, The
Unicorn Press

Dorian Gray
AIP (It/Ger) 1970
dir. Massimo Dallamano
V

Wilde, O.
Picture of Dorian Gray, The
Various

Sins of Dorian Gray, The
RANKIN-BASS (US) 1983
dir. Tony Maylam
TV(US)

Wilde, O.
Salome
P
Methuen (London)
CANNON (Fr/It) 1987
dir. Claude d'Anna

Wilde, O.
Salome
P
Methuen (London)
Salome's Last Dance
VESTRON (GB) 1988 dir. Ken Russell
V

Wilder, L. I.
Little House on the Prairie
Harper
NBC ENT (US) 1974
dir. Michael Landon
TV(US), V

Wilder, M. B.
Since You Went Away
McGraw-Hill
UA (US) 1944 dir. John Cromwell
V

Wilder, R.
And Ride a Tiger
Stranger in my Arms, A
UI (US) 1958 dir. Helmut Kautner

Wilder, R.
Flamingo Road
WAR (US) 1949 dir. Michael Curtiz

Wilder, R.
Written on the Wind
Putnam
UN (US) 1956 dir. Douglas Sirk

Wilder, T.
Bridge of San Luis Rey, The
Grosset & Dunlap
UA (US) 1944 dir. Rowland V. Lee
V

Wilder, T.
Matchmaker, The
P
Samuel French
PAR (US) 1958 dir. Joseph Anthony

Wilder, T.
Matchmaker, The
P
Samuel French
Hello Dolly
FOX (US) 1969 dir. Gene Kelly
M, V

Wilder, T.
Our Town
P
Samuel French
UA (US) 1940 dir. Sam Wood
V

Wilder, T.
Skin of our Teeth, The
P
Samuel French
GRANADA TV (GB) 1959
TV(GB)

Wilder, T.
Theophilus North
Harper & Row

Mr. North
GOLDWYN (US) 1988
dir. Danny Huston
V

Wilk, M.
Don't Raise the Bridge, Lower the River
Macmillan

BL (GB) 1967 dir. Jerry Paris
V

Wilkerson, D.
Cross and the Switchblade, The
Random House

FOX (US) 1970 dir. Don Murray
V

Wilkins, V.
King Reluctant, A
Cape

Dangerous Exile
RANK (GB) 1957
dir. Brian Desmond Hurst

Wilkinson, G. R.
Monkeys, The

Monkeys, Go Home!
DISNEY (US) 1967
dir. Andrew V. McLaglen

Willard, J.
Cat and the Canary, The
P
Samuel French

Cat Creeps, The
UN (US) 1930 dir. Rupert Julian

Willard, J.
Cat and the Canary, The
P
Samuel French

PAR (US) 1939 dir. Elliot Nugent
GALA (GB) 1978 dir. Radley Metzger
V

Willeford, C.
Cockfighter
Crown, N.Y.

EMI (US) 1974 dir. Monte Hellman
V

Willeford, C.
Miami Blues
St. Martin's Press

ORION (US) 1990 dir. George Armitage
V

Williams, A.
Snake Water
Harper & Row

Pink Jungle, The
UI (US) 1968 dir. Delbert Mann

Williams, B.
Earl of Chicago
Harrap

MGM (US) 1940 dir. Richard Thorpe

Williams, B.
In This Fallen City
P

Night of Courage
TITUS (US) 1987 dir. Elliot Silverstein
TV(US)

Williams, B. A.
Leave Her to Heaven
Houghton, Mifflin Co. (Boston)

FOX (US) 1945 dir. John M. Stahl

Williams, B. A.
Leave Her to Heaven
Houghton, Mifflin Co. (Boston)

Too Good to be True
NEWLAND-RAYNOR (US) 1988
dir. Christian I Nyby II
TV(US)

Williams, B. A.
Small Town Girl

MGM (US) 1936
dir. William A. Wellmen

Williams, B. A.
Strange Woman, The
Houghton, Mifflin Co. (Boston)
UA (US) 1946 dir. Edgar G. Ulmer

Williams, B.A.
All The Brothers were Valiant
MGM (US) 1953 dir. Richard Thorpe

Williams, C.
All the Way
Third Voice, The
TCF (US) 1959 dir. Hubert Cornfield

Williams, C.
Dead Calm
WAR (Aus) 1989 dir. Philip Noyce

Williams, C.
Hell Hath no Fury
Hot Spot, The
ORION (US) 1990 dir. Dennis Hopper

Williams, C.
Long Saturday Night, The
Confidentially Yours
IS (Fr) 1984 dir. François Truffaut
V

Williams, C.
Long Saturday Night, The
Finally, Sunday
FILMS A2 (Fr) 1983
dir. François Truffaut

Williams, C.
Wrong Venus, The
Don't Just Stand There
UN (US) 1967 dir. Ron Winston

Williams, D.
Second Sight
Simon & Schuster
Two Worlds of Jennie Logan, The
FRIES (US) 1979 dir. Frank DeFelitta
TV(US)

Williams, E.
Corn is Green, The
P
Random House
WAR (US) 1945 dir. Irving Rapper
V
M. EVANS (US) 1956
dir. George Schaefer
TV(US)
WAR (US) 1979 dir. George Cukor
TV(US)

Williams, E.
Headlong
Viking Press
King Ralph
UN (US) 1991 dir. David S. Ward
V

Williams, E.
Light of Heart, The
P
Life Begins at Eight Thirty
FOX (US) 1942 dir. Irving Pichel
GB title: Light of Heart, The

Williams, E.
Night Must Fall
P
Samuel French
MGM (US) 1937 dir. Richard Thorpe
MGM (GB) 1964 dir. Karel Reisz

Williams, E.
Someone Waiting
P
Time Without Pity
HARLEQUIN (GB) 1957
dir. Joseph Losey

Williams, E.
Wooden Horse, The
Harper
BL (GB) 1950 dir. Jack Lee
V

Williams, G.
Man Who had Power over Women, The
Stein & Day
AVCO (GB) 1970 dir. John Krish
V

Williams, G. M.
Siege at Trencher's Farm, The
Straw Dogs
CINERAMA (GB) 1971
dir. Sam Peckinpah
V

Williams, H. and Williams, M.
Grass is Greener, The
P
Samuel French
UI (GB) 1960 dir. Stanley Donen
V

Williams, J.
Night Song
Collins
Sweet Love, Bitter
FILM 2 (US) 1967 dir. Herbert Danska

Williams, J. A.
Junior Bachelor Society, The
Doubleday
Sophisticated Gents, The
D. WILSON (US) 1981 dir. Harry Falk
TVSe(US)

Williams, Jr., H. and Bane, M.
Living Proof
Putnam
Living Proof: The Hank Williams, Jr. Story
TELECOM (US) 1983 dir. Dick Lowry
TV(US)

Williams, Mrs. R.
Father was a Handful
Vanishing Virginian, The
MGM (US) 1941 dir. Frank Borzage

Williams, N.
Class Enemy
P
Samuel French
SFB (Ger) 1984 dir. Peter Stein

Williams, T.
Baby Doll
P
Secker & Warburg
WAR (US) 1956 dir. Elia Kazan
V

Williams, T.
Cat on a Hot Tin Roof
P
Dramatists Play Service
MGM (US) 1958 dir. Richard Brooks
V
GRANADA TV (GB) 1976
dir. Robert Moore
TV(GB/US)

Williams, T.
Glass Menagerie, The
P
Dramatists Play Service
WAR (US) 1950 dir. Irving Rapper
TALENT (US) 1973
dir. Anthony Harvey
TV(US)
CINEPLEX (US) 1987 dir. Paul Newman
V

Williams, T.
Milk Train Doesn't Stop Here Anymore, The
P
Dramatists Play Service
Boom!
UI (GB) 1968 dir. Joseph Losey

Williams, T.
Night of the Iguana, The
P
New American Library
MGM (US) 1964 dir. John Huston
V

Williams, T.
Orpheus Descending
P
Dramatists Play Service
NED (US) 1990 dir. Peter Hall
TV(US)

Williams, T.
Orpheus Descending
P
Dramatists Play Service
Fugitive Kind, The
UA (US) 1960 dir. Sidney Lumet
V

Williams, T.
Period of Adjustment
P
Dramatists Play Service
MGM (US) 1962 dir. George Roy Hill

Williams, T.
Roman Spring of Mrs. Stone, The
New Directions
WAR (GB/US) 1961 dir. José Quintero
V

Williams, T.
Rose Tattoo, The
P
Dramatists Play Service
PAR (US) 1955 dir. Daniel Mann

Williams, T.
Streetcar Named Desire, A
P
Dramatists Play Service
WAR (US) 1951 dir. Elia Kazan
V
PSO (US) 1984 dir. John Erman
TV(US)

Williams, T.
Suddenly, Last Summer
P
New Directions
COL (GB) 1959
dir. Joseph L. Mankiewicz
V

Williams, T.
Summer and Smoke
P
Dramatists Play Service
PAR (US) 1961 dir. Peter Glenville

Williams, T.
Sweet Bird of Youth
P
New Directions
MGM (US) 1962 dir. Richard Brooks
KUSHNER-LOCKE (US) 1989
dir. Nicolas Roeg
TV(US)

Williams, T.
This Property is Condemned
P
PAR (US) 1966 dir. Sydney Pollack
V

Williams, V.
Clubfoot
Hodder & Stoughton
Crouching Beast, The
OLY (GB) 1935 dir. Victor Hanbury

Williams, W.
Ada Dallas
Ada
MGM (US) 1961 dir. Daniel Mann

Williamson, D.
Don's Party
Double Head (Aust) 1976
dir. Bruce Beresford

Williamson, D.
Travelling North
P
VIEW PIC (Aust) 1986 dir. Carl Schultz
V

Williamson, H.
Tarka the Otter
Beacon Press (Boston)
RANK (GB) 1979 dir. David Cobham
V

Willingham, C.
End as a Man
Vanguard Press

Strange One, The
COL (US) 1957 dir. Jack Garfein
GB title: End as a Man

Willingham, C.
Rambling Rose
Delacorte Press

NEW LINE (US) 1991
dir. Martha Coolidge

Willis, M. P. and Willis, J.
But There are Always Miracles
Viking Press

Some Kind of Miracle
LORIMAR (US) 1979
dir. Jerrold Freedman
TV(US)

Willis, T.
Hot Summer Night
P

Flame in the Streets
RANK (GB) 1961 dir. Roy Baker

Willis, T.
Man-eater
Morrow

Maneaters are Loose!
MONA BBC TV (GB) 1984
dir. Timothy Galfos
TV(GB)

Willis, T.
No Trees in the Street
P

ABP (US) 1958 dir. J. Lee Thompson
V

Willis, T.
Woman in a Dressing Gown
P

GODWIN (GB) 1957
dir. J. Lee Thompson

Willson, M.
Music Man, The
Putnam

WAR (US) 1962 dir. Morton da Costa
M, V

Wilson, A.
Old Men at the Zoo, The
Secker & Warburg (London)

BBC (GB) 1982 dir. Stuart Burge
TVSe(GB)

Wilson, C.
Empty Saddles
Ward Lock

UN (US) 1937 dir. Les Selander

Wilson, C.
Space Vampires
Random House

Lifeforce
CANNON (US) 1985 dir. Tobe Hooper
V

Wilson, D. P.
My Six Convicts
Rinehart

COL (US) 1952 dir. Hugo Fregonese

Wilson, F. P.
Keep, The
Morrow

PAR (GB) 1983 dir. Michael Mann
V

Wilson, H. L.
Bunker Bean
Lane

RKO (US) 1936
dir. William Hamilton/Edward Kelly

Wilson, H. L.
Merton of the Movies
Doubleday

MGM (US) 1947 dir. Robert Alton

Wilson, H. L.
Merton of the Movies
Doubleday

Make me a Star
PAR (US) 1932 dir. William Beaudine

Wilson, H. L.
Ruggles of Red Gap
Grosset

PAR (US) 1935 dir. Leo McCarey
V

Wilson, H. L.
Ruggles of Red Gap

Fancy Pants
PAR (US) 1950 dir. George Marshall

Wilson, J.
Hamp

King and Country
WAR (GB) 1964 dir. Joseph Losey

Wilson, J. R.
Pack, The
Heinemann

Behind the Mask
BL (GB) 1958 dir. Brian Desmond Hurst

Wilson, M.
None so Blind

Woman on the Beach, The
RKO (US) 1947 dir. Jean Renoir

Wilson, S.
Boy Friend, The
P

MGM (GB) 1971 dir. Ken Russell
M, V

Wilson, S.
Man in the Grey Flannel Suit, The
Simon & Schuster

FOX (US) 1956 dir. Nunnally Johnson
V

Wilson, S.
Summer Place, A
Simon & Schuster

WAR (US) 1959 dir. Delmer Daves

Wilson, S. J.
To Find a Man

COL (US) 1971 dir. Buzz Kulik

Wilstach, F.
Wild Bill Hickok

Plainsman, The
PAR (US) 1937 dir. Cecil B de Mille
V

Wiltshire, D.
Child of Vodyanoi

Nightmare Man, The
BBC (US) 1981 dir. Douglas Camfield
TVSe(GB)

Wingate, W.
Shotgun

Malone
ORION (US) 1987 dir. Harley Kokliss
V

Winkler, A. C.
Lunatic, The

ISLAND PICTURES (Fr) 1992
dir. Lol Creme

Winsor, K.
Forever Amber
Macmillan

FOX (US) 1947 dir. Otto Preminger

Winter, K.
Shining Hour, The
P
Samuel French

MGM (US) 1938 dir. Frank Borzage

Winterson, J.
Oranges are not the only Fruit
Pandora Press
A&E/BBC (US/GB) 1990
dir. Beeban Kidron
TV(GB/US)

Winton, J.
We Joined the Navy
WAR (GB) 1962 dir. Wendy Toye

Wiseman, T.
Romantic Englishwoman, The
Putnam
DIAL (GB) 1975 dir. Joseph Losey
V

Wister, O.
Virginian, The
Dodd, Mead
PAR (US) 1929 dir. Victor Fleming
PAR (US) 1946 dir. Stuart Gilmore
V

Wodehouse, P. G.
Code of the Woosters
Central (GB) 1991 dir. Simon Langton
TV(GB)

Wodehouse, P. G.
Damsel in Distress, A
Jenkins
RKO (US) 1937 dir. George Stevens
M, V

Wodehouse, P. G.
Girl on the Boat, The
H. Jenkins (London)
UA (GB) 1962 dir. Henry Kaplan

Wodehouse, P. G.
Piccadilly Jim
H. Jenkins (London)
MGM (US) 1936 dir. Robert Z. Leonard

Wodehouse, P. G.
Thank You, Jeeves
FOX (US) 1936
dir. Arthur Greville Collins

Wohl, B.
Cold Wind in August
Mayflower
UA (US) 1961 dir. Alexander Singer

Wolaston, N.
Eclipse
GALA (GB) 1976 dir. Simon Perry

Wolf, G. K.
Who Censored Roger Rabbit?
St. Martin's Press
Who Framed Roger Rabbit?
TOUCH (US) 1988 dir. Robert Zemeckis
A, V

Wolfe, T.
Bonfire of the Vanities, The
Farrar, Straus & Giroux
WAR (US) 1990 dir. Brian De Palma
V

Wolfe, T.
Right Stuff, The
Farrar, Straus & Giroux
WAR (US) 1983 dir. Philip Kaufman
V

Wolfe, T.
You Can't Go Home Again
Harper & Row
CBS ENT (US) 1979 dir. Ralph Nelson
TV(US)

Wolfe, W.
Ask Any Girl
Hammond
MGM (US) 1959 dir. Charles Walters

Wolfe, W.
If a Man Answers
UN (US) 1962 dir. Henry Levin

Wolfert, I.
American Guerilla in the Philippines, An
Simon & Schuster
TCF (US) 1950 dir. Fritz Lang
GB title: I Shall Return

Wolfert, I.
Tucker's People
Gollancz
Force of Evil
MGM (US) 1948 dir. Abraham Polonsky
V

Wolff, M. M.
Whistle Stop
UA (US) 1946 dir. Leonide Moguy
V

Wolff, R.
Abdication, The
P
WAR (GB) 1974 dir. A. Harvey

Wolford, N. and Wolford, S.
Southern Blade
Time for Killing, A
COL (US) 1967 dir. Phil Karlson
GB title: Long Ride Home, The

Wolitzer, M.
This is Your Life
Crown Publishing
This is My Life
FOX (US) 1992 dir. Nora Ephron

Wolpert, S.
Nine Hours to Rama
Random House
FOX (GB) 1962 dir. Mark Robson

Wolzien, V.
Menu for Murder
VON ZERNECK/SERTNER (US) 1990
dir. Larry Peerce
TV(US)

Wong, Dr. M. G.
Nun: A Memoir
Harcourt, Brace, Jovanovich
Shattered Vows
RIVER CITY (US) 1984 dir. Jack Bender
TV(US)

Wood, B. & Geasland, J.
Twins
Putnam
Dead Ringers
FOX (Can) 1988 dir. David Cronenberg
V

Wood, C. B.
Welcome to the Club
COL (US) 1970 dir. Walter Shenson

Wood, D. and Dempster, D.
Narrow Margin, The
McGraw-Hill
Battle of Britain
UA (GB) 1969 dir. Guy Hamilton
V

Wood, Mrs H.
East Lynne
Various
Ex-Flame
Tiffany (US) 1930 dir. Victor Halperin

Wood, Mrs. H.
East Lynne
FOX (US) 1931 dir. Frank Lloyd

Woods, D.
Biko
Vintage Books
Cry Freedom
UN (GB) 1987
dir. Richard Attenborough
V

Woods, S.
Chiefs
Norton
HIGHGATE (US) 1983
dir. Jerry London
TVSe(US)

Woods, S.
Grass Roots
Simon & Schuster
JBS PRODS. (US) 1992
dir. Jerry London
TVSe(US)

Woods, W.
Manuela
Hart-Davis
BL (GB) 1957 dir. Guy Hamilton
US title: Stowaway Girl

Woods, W. H.
Edge of Darkness
Grosset, N.Y.
WAR (US) 1943 dir. Lewis Milestone

Woodward, B. and Bernstein, C.
Final Days, The
Simon & Schuster
SAMUELS (US) 1989
dir. Richard Pearce
TV(US)

Woodward, B.
Wired
Simon & Schuster
TAURUS (US) 1989 dir. Larry Peerce
V

Woodward, W. E.
Evelyn Prentice
MGM (US) 1934 dir. William K. Howard

Woolcott, A. and Kaufman, G. S.
Dark Tower, The
P
Random House
WAR (GB) 1943 dir. John Harlow

Woolf, V.
To the Lighthouse
Harcourt, Brace & World
BBC (GB) 1983 dir. Colin Gregg
TV(GB), V

Wooll, E.
Libel
P
Samuel French
MGM (GB) 1959 dir. Anthony Asquith

Woollard, K.
Morning Departure
P
GFD (GB) 1950 dir. Roy Baker
US title: Operation Disaster

Woolrich, C.
Black Alibi
Ballantine Books
Leopard Man, The
RKO (US) 1943 dir. Jacques Tourneur
V

Woolrich, C.
Black Angel
Ballantine Books
UN (US) 1946 dir. Roy William Neill

Woolrich, C.
Black Curtain, The
Ballantine Books
Lady Forgets, The
HILL (US) 1989 dir. Bradford May
TV(US)

Woolrich, C.
Black Curtain, The
Ballantine Books
Street of Chance
PAR (US) 1942 dir. Jack Hively

Woolrich, C.
Black Path of Fear, The
Ballantine Books
Chase, The
NERO (US) 1947 dir. Arthur Ripley

Woolrich, C.
Bride in Black, The
NEW WORLD (US) 1990
dir. James Goldstone
TV(US)

Woolrich, C.
I'm Dangerous Tonight
MCA TV (US) 1990 dir. Tobe Hooper
TV(US)

Woolrich, C.
Night Has a Thousand Eyes
Farrar & Rinehart
PAR (US) 1948 dir. John Farrow

Woolrich, C.
Nightmare
UA (US) 1956 dir. Maxwell Shane

Woolrich, C.
Rear Window
PAR (US) 1954 dir. Alfred Hitchcock
V

Woolrich, C.
You'll Never See Me Again
UN (US) 1973 dir. Jeannot Szwarc
TV(US)

Worker, D., and Worker, B.
Escape
San Francisco Book Company (San Francisco)
H. JAFFE (US) 1980
dir. Robert Michael Lewis
TV(US)

Wortman, E.
Almost Too Late
Anything to Survive
SABAN/SCHERICK (US) 1990
dir. Zale Dalen
TV(US)

Wouk, H.
Caine Mutiny Court-Martial, The
P
Samuel French
MALTESE (US) 1988
dir. Robert Altman
TV(US)

Wouk, H.
Caine Mutiny, The
Doubleday
COL (US) 1954 dir. Edward Dmytryk
V

Wouk, H.
Marjorie Morningstar
Doubleday
WAR (US) 1958 dir. Irving Rapper

Wouk, H.
Slattery's Hurricane
FOX (US) 1949 dir. André de Toth

Wouk, H.
War and Remembrance
Little, Brown (Boston)
LWT (US/GB) 1989 dir. Dan Curtis
TVSe(US/GB)

Wouk, H.
Winds of War, The
PAR (US) 1983 dir. Dan Curtis
TVSe(US)

Wouk, H.
Youngblood Hawke
Doubleday
WAR (US) 1963 dir. Delmer Daves

Wozencraft, K.
Rush
Random House
MGM (US) 1991 dir. Lili Fini Zanuck

Wray, F. and Lewis, S.
Angela is 22
P
This is the Life
UN (US) 1943 dir. Felix Feist
M

Wren, P. C.
Beau Geste
Lippincott (Philadelphia)
PAR (US) 1939 dir. William A. Wellman
V
UI (US) 1966 dir. Douglas Heyes
V
BBC (GB) 1984
TVSe(GB)

Wren, P. C.
Beau Ideal
Murray
RKO (US) 1931 dir. Herbert Brenon

Wright, H. B.
Shepherd of the Hills, The
PAR (US) 1941 dir. Henry Hathaway

Wright, R.
Native Son
Harper
CLASSIC (Arg) 1951 dir. Pierre Chenal
V
CINECOM (US) 1986
dir. Jerrold Freedman

Wyden, P.
Day One: Before Hiroshima and After
Simon & Schuster
Day One
A. SPELLING (US) 1989
dir. Joseph Sargent
TV(US)

Wylie, I. A. R.
Gay Banditti, The
Young in Heart, The
SELZNICK (US) 1938
dir. Richard Wallace

Wylie, I. A. R.
Keeper of the Flame
Random House
MGM (US) 1942 dir. George Cukor

Wylie, I. A. R.
Pilgrimage
FOX (US) 1933 dir. John Ford

Wylie, P.
Night unto Night
Farrar & Rinehart
WAR (US) 1949 dir. Don Siegel

Wyndham, J.
Chocky
Ballantine Books
THAMES (GB) 1984 dir. Chris Hodson
Ch, TVSe(GB), V

Wyndham, J.
Day of the Triffids, The
Doubleday
RANK (GB) 1962 dir. Steve Sekely
V
BBC (GB) 1982 dir. Ken Hannam
TVSe(GB)

Wyndham, J.
Midwich Cuckoos, The
M. Joseph (London)
Village of the Damned
MGM (GB) 1960 dir. Wolf Rilla
V

Wynette, T. and Dew, J.
Stand by Your Man
Simon & Schuster
GUBER-PETERS (US) 1981
dir. Jerry Jameson
TV(US)

Wynne, G.
Man from Moscow, A
Atheneum
Wynne and Penkovsky
BBC (GB/US) 1984 dir. Paul Seed
TV(GB/US), V

Wynne, P.
Little Flat in the Temple, A
Devotion
RKO (US) 1931 dir. Robert Milton

Wyse, L.
Kiss, Inc.
Doubleday

Million Dollar Face, The
NEPHI-HAMNER (US) 1981
dir. Michael O'Herlihy
TV(US)

Wyss, J. D.
Swiss Family Robinson
Various

RKO (US) 1940 dir. Edward Ludwig
V
DISNEY (GB) 1960 dir. Ken Annakin
V
FOX (US) 1975 dir. Harry Harris
TV(US)

Xaurof, L., and Chancel, J.
Prince Consort, The
P

Love Parade, The
PAR (US) 1929 dir. Ernst Lubitsch
M

Yafa, S.
Paxton Quigley's had the Course

Three in the Attic
WAR (US) 1968 dir. Richard Wilson
V

Yallop, D.
Beyond Reasonable Doubt
Hodder & Stoughton

J & M (NZ) 1980 dir. John Laing
V

Yamada, T.
Discarnates, The

SHOCHIKU (Jap) 1989
dir. Nobuhiko Obayashi

Yamamoto
Redbeard
TOHO (Jap) 1965 dir. Akira Kurosawa

Yamazaki, T.
Family, The
PUBLIC (Jap) 1974
dir. Karei Naru Ichikozo

Yardley, H. O.
American Black Chamber, The
Faber & Faber (London)
Rendezvous
MGM (US) 1935 dir. William K. Howard

Yarmolinsky, J.
Angels Without Wings
Houghton, Mifflin Co. (Boston)
Promise to Keep, A
WAR TV (US) 1990 dir. Rod Holcomb
TV(US)

Yates, E.
Skeezer: Dog With a Mission
Skeezer
M. ARCH (US) 1982 dir. Peter H. Hunt
TV(US)

Yerby, F.
Foxes of Harrow, The
Dial Press
FOX (US) 1947 dir. John M. Stahl

Yerby, F.
Golden Hawk, The
Heinemann
COL (US) 1952 dir. Sidney Salkow

Yerby, F.
Saracen Blade, The
COL (US) 1954 dir. William Castle

Yordan, P.
Anna Lucasta
P
Random House
COL UA(US) 1949 dir. Irving Rapper
UA (US) 1958 dir. Arnold Laven

Yordan, P.
Man of the West
Deutsch
Gun Glory
MGM (US) 1957 dir. Roy Rowland

Yorgason, B. & Yorgason, B.
Chester, I Love You
Thanksgiving Promise, The
DISNEY (US) 1986 dir. Beau Bridges
TV(US)

Yorgason, B.
Windwalker
PACIFIC (US) 1981 dir. Keith Merrill
V

York, A.
Eliminator, The
Hutchinson
Danger Route
UA (GB) 1967 dir. Seth Holt

Young, C. U.
Gun Shy
Showdown at Abilene
UN (US) 1956 dir. Charles Haas

Young, D.
Rommel, The Desert Fox
Harper
Desert Fox, The
FOX (US) 1951 dir. Henry Hathaway
GB title: Rommel, Desert Fox
V

Young, F. B.
My Brother Jonathan
Knopf
AB (GB) 1947 dir. Harold French
BBC (GB) 1985
TVSe(GB)

Young, F. B.
Portrait of Clare
Heinemann (London)
ABP (GB) 1950 dir. Lance Comfort

Young, F. B. and Perry, J.
Man About the House, A
P
Heinemann
LF (GB) 1947 dir. Leslie Arliss

Young, J. R.
Behind the Rising Sun
RKO (US) 1943 dir. Edward Dmytryk
V

Young, K.
Ravine, The
Pan
Assault
RANK (GB) 1971 dir. Sidney Hayers
V

Young, M.
Mother Wore Tights
FOX (US) 1947 dir. Walter Lang

Young, R. J.
Checkers
P
FOX (US) 1937
dir. H. Bruce Humberstone

Young, R. J.
Little Old New York
P
FOX (US) 1940 dir. Henry King

Young, S.
So Red the Rose
PAR (US) 1935 dir. King Vidor

Zacha, Sr., W. T.
Capricorn Man, The
Ultimate Imposter, The
UN TV (US) 1979 dir. Paul Stanley
TV(US), V

Zackel, F.
Cocaine and Blue Eyes
COL TV (US) 1983
dir. E. W. Swackhamer
TV(US)

Zaharias, B. D. and Paxton, H.
This Life I've Led: My Autobiography
Barnes
Babe
MGM TV (US) 1975 dir. Buzz Kulik
TV(US)

Zalazny, R.
Damnation Alley
Putnam
FOX (US) 1977 dir. Jack Smight
V

Zangwill, I.
Big Bow Mystery, The
Greenhill Books (London)
Verdict, The
WAR (US) 1946 dir. Don Siegel

Zavattini, C.
Toto il Buono
Miracle in Milan
PDS (It) 1951 dir. Vittorio de Sica
V

Zeldis, C.
Forbidden Love, A
Torn Apart
CASTLE HILL (US) 1990
dir. Jack Fisher

Zetterling, M.
Night Games
Coward-McCann
GALA (Swe) 1966 dir. Mai Zetterling
V

Ziegler, I. G.
Nine Days of Father Serra
Seven Cities of Gold
FOX (US) 1955 dir. Robert D. Webb
V

Ziemer, G.
Education for Death
Constable
Hitler's Children
RKO (US) 1943 dir. Edward Dmytryk
V

Zindel, P.
Effect of Gamma Rays on Man-in-the-Moon Marigolds, The
P
Harper & Row
FOX-RANK (US) 1972 dir. Paul Newman

Zobel, J.
Rue Cases Negres, La
Sugar Cane Alley
ORION (Fr) 1984 dir. Euzhan Palcy
V

Zola, E.
Bête Humaine, La
Fasquelle (Paris)
PARIS (Fr) 1938 dir. Jean Renoir
V

Zola, E.
For a Night of Love
Shakespeare House
Manifesto
CANNON (Yugo) 1988
dir. Dusan Makajevev

Zola, E.
Kill, The
Arrow
Game is Over, The
COL (Fr/It) 1967 dir. Roger Vadim
V

Zola, E.
La Bête Humaine
Fasquelle (Paris)
Human Desire
COL (US) 1954 dir. Fritz Lang

Zola, E.
L'Assommoir
Penguin
Gervaise
CLCC (Fr) 1956 dir. René Clément
V

Zola, E.
Nana
Various
MGM (US) 1934 dir. Dorothy Arzner
GB title: Lady of the Boulevards
GALA (Fr/It) 1955 dir. Christian-Jacque
MINERVA (Swe) 1971 dir. Mac Ahlberg
CANNON (It) 1982 dir. Dan Wolman
V

Zuckmayer, C.
Devil's General, The
P
RYAL (W Ger) 1955 dir. Helmut Kautner

Zumwalt, Jr., Admiral, E. and Zumwalt III, E. R.
My Father, My Son
Macmillan
WEINTRAUB (US) 1988
dir. Jeff Bleckner
TV(US)

Zweig, A.
Case of Sergeant Grischa, The
Penguin
RKO (US) 1930 dir. Herbert Brenon

Zweig, S.
Beware of Pity
Harmony Books
TC (GB) 1946 dir. Maurice Elvey

Zweig, S.
Brennendes Geheimnis
E. P. Dutton
Burning Secret
VESTRON (GB/Ger) 1988
dir. Andrew Birkin
V

Zweig, S.
Letter from an Unknown Woman
Viking Press
UI (US) 1948 dir. Max Ophuls
V

Zweig, S.
Marie Antoinette
Viking Press
MGM (US) 1938 dir. W. S. Van Dyke

Zweig, S.
Twenty-Four Hours of a Woman's Life
ABPC (GB) 1952 dir. Victor Saville
US title: Affair in Monte Carlo

CHANGE OF ORIGINAL
─────TITLE INDEX─────

Book or play title ——— **Taming of the Shrew, The** ——— Film title

Author's name ——— Shakespeare, W.
Kiss Me Kate ——— Director's name

Studio name, location ——— MGM (US) 1953 dir. George Sidney
and release date ——— MILBERG (US) 1958 dir. George Schaefer
GB title:

British, etc, title
(if different)

A = Animated film

Ch = Made for children

M = Based on a musical

TV (GB, US, etc) = Made for British,
American, etc, television
TVSe = Made-for-television series or
mini-series
V = Available on video

Abbess of Crewe, The
Spark, M.

Nasty Habits
SCOTIA-BARBER (GB) 1976
dir. Michael Lindsay-Hogg
US title: The Abbess

ABC Murders, The
Christie, A.

Alphabet Murders, The
MGM (GB) 1966 dir. Frank Tashlin

Abe Lincoln of Illinois
Sherwood, R. E.

Abe Lincoln in Illinois
RKO (US) 1940 dir. John Cromwell
COMPASS (US) 1964
dir. George Schaefer

Abominable Man, The
Sjowall, M. and Wahloo, M.

Man on the Roof, The
Svensk Film (Swe) 1976
dir. Bo Widenberg

Acacia Avenue
Constanduros, M. and Constanduros, D.

29 Acacia Avenue
COL (GB) 1945 dir. Henry Cass
US title: Facts of Love, The

Accent on Youth
Raphaelson, S.

But Not For Me
PAR (US) 1959 dir. Walter Lang

Act of Mercy
Clifford, F.

Guns of Darkness
WAR (GB) 1962 dir. Anthony Asquith

Act of Passion
Simenon, G.

Forbidden Fruit
CAMEO-POLY (Fr) 1952
dir. Henri Verneuil

Ada Dallas
Williams, W.

Ada
MGM (US) 1961 dir. Daniel Mann

Addie Pray
Brown, J. D.

Paper Moon
PAR (US) 1973 dir. Peter Bogdanovich

Adios
Bartlett, L. V. S.

Lash, The
IN (US) 1930 dir. Frank Lloyd

Admirable Crichton, The
Barrie, Sir J. M.

We're Not Dressing
PAR (US) 1934 dir. Norman Taurog

Adobe Walls
Burnett, W. R.

Arrowhead
PAR (US) 1953
dir. Charles Marquis Warren

Adventure in Diamonds
Walker, D. E.

Operation Amsterdam
RANK (GB) 1958
dir. Michael McCarthy

Adventure of the Five Orange Pips
Doyle, Sir A. C.

House of Fear
UN (US) 1945 dir. Roy William Neill

Adventures of Hajji Baba of Ispahan
Morier, J. J.

Adventures of Hajji Baba, The
FOX (US) 1954 dir. Don Weis

Adventures of Huckleberry Finn, The
Twain, M.

Huckleberry Finn
PAR (US) 1931 dir. Norman Taurog
MGM (US) 1939 dir. Richard Thorpe
UA (US) 1974 dir. J. Lee Thompson
ABC (US) 1975 dir. Robert Totten

Adventures of Tom Sawyer, The
Twain, M.

Tom Sawyer
UA (US) 1973 dir. Don Taylor
UN (US) 1973 dir. James Neilson

Affaire de Femmes, Une
Szpiner, F.

Story of Women
NEW YORKER (Fr) 1989
dir. Claude Chabrol

After All
Druten, J. van

New Morals for Old
MGM (US) 1932 dir. Charles Brabin

After the Funeral
Christie, A.

Murder at the Gallop
MGM (GB) 1963 dir. George Pollock

After the Trial
Roman, E.

Death Sentence
SPELLING-GOLDBERG (US) 1974
dir. E. W. Swackhamer

Against Heaven's Hand
Bishop, L.

Seven in Darkness
PAR TV (US) 1969 dir. Michael Caffey

Agony Column
Biggers, E. D.

Passage from Hong Kong
WAR (US) 1941 dir. D. Ross Lederman

Ah Wilderness!
O'Neill, E. G.

Summer Holiday
MGM (US) 1948
dir. Rouben Mamoulian

Aimez-vous Brahms?
Sagan, F.

Goodbye Again
UA (US) 1961 dir. Anatole Litvak

Air Raid
Varley, J.

Millenium
FOX (US) 1989 dir. Michael Anderson

Airing in a Closed Carriage
Shearing, J.

Mark of Cain, The
TC (GB) 1948 dir. Brian Desmond Hurst

Airport
Hailey, A.

International Airport
A. SPELLING (US) 1985
dir. Charles Dubin, Don Chaffey

Al Schmid, Marine
Butterfield, R. P.

Pride of the Marines
WAR (US) 1945 dir. Delmer Daves
GB title: Forever in Love

Alan Quatermain
Haggard, Sir H. R.

King Solomon's Treasure
BARBER ROSE (Can/GB) 1979
dir. Alvin Rakoff

Alexandria Quartet, The
Durrell, L.

Justine
FOX (US) 1969 dir. George Cukor

Alf's Button
Darlington, W.A.

Alf's Button Afloat
GAINS (GB) 1938 dir. Marcel Varnel

Algonquin Project, The
Nolan, F.

Brass Target
UN (US) 1978 dir. John Hough

Alice Sit-by-the-Fire
Barrie, Sir J. M.

Darling, How Could You
PAR (US) 1951 dir. Mitchell Leisen
GB title: Rendezvous

Alice's Adventures in Wonderland
Carroll, L.

Alice in Wonderland
PAR (US) 1933 dir. Norman Z. McLeod
DISNEY (US) 1951
dir. Clyde Geronomi, HamiltonLuske,
Wilfred Jackson
M. EVANS (US) 1955
dir. George Schaefer
COL TV (US) 1985 dir. Harry Harris

Alice's Adventures in Wonderland
Carroll, L.

Alice
HEMDALE (Bel/Pol/GB) 1980
dir. Jerry Gruza

Alien, The
Davies, L. P.

Groundstar Conspiracy, The
UN (US) 1972 dir. Lamont Johnson

All Aboard for Freedom
McSwigan, M.

Snow Treasure
TIGON (US) 1968 dir. Irving Jacoby

All Brides are Beautiful
Bell, T.

From This Day Forward
RKO (US) 1946 dir. John Berry

All Good Americans
Perelman, S. J. and Perelman, L.

Paris Interlude
MGM (US) 1934 dir. Edwin L. Marin

All in Good Time
Naughton, B.

Family Way, The
BL (GB) 1966 dir. Roy Boulting

All Kneeling
Parrish, A.

Born to be Bad
RKO (US) 1950 dir. Nicholas Ray

All on a Summer's Day
Garden, J.

Double Confession
ABP (GB) 1950 dir. Ken Annakin

All on the Never-Never
Lindsay, J.

Live Now, Pay Later
REGAL (GB) 1962 dir. Jay Lewis

All the Way
Williams, C.

Third Voice, The
TCF (US) 1959 dir. Hubert Cornfield

All Things Bright and Beautiful
Herriot, J.

It Shouldn't Happen to a Vet
EMI (GB) 1976 dir. Eric Till

All Through the Night
Masterson, W.

Cry in the Night, A
WAR (US) 1956 dir. Frank Tuttle

Allan Quatermain
Haggard, H. R.

Allan Quatermain and the Lost City of Gold
CANNON (US) 1987 dir. Gary Nelson

Almost Too Late
Wortman, E.

Anything to Survive
SABAN/SCHERICK (US) 1990
dir. Zale Dalen

Alter Ego
Arrighi, M.

Murder by the Book
ORION TV (US) 1987 dir. Mel Damski

Always
Meldal-Johnson, T.

Déjà Vu
CANNON (GB) 1985
dir. Anthony Richmond

Amazing Quest of Mr Ernest Bliss, The
Oppenheim, E. P.

Amazing Quest of Ernest Bliss, The
KLEMENT (GB) 1936 dir. Alfred Zeisler
US title: Romance & Riches

Amboy Dukes, The
Shulman, I.

City Across The River
UI (US) 1949 dir. Maxwell Shane

American Black Chamber, The
Yardley, H. O.

Rendezvous
MGM (US) 1935 dir. William K. Howard

American Tragedy, An
Dreiser, T.

Place in the Sun, A
PAR (US) 1951 dir. George Stevens

Americans, Baby, The; Electrical Experience, The
Moorhouse, F.

Coca-Cola Kid, The
CINECOM (Aus) 1985
dir. Dusan Makevejev

Amerika
Kafka, F.

Class Relations
ART EYE (Ger/Fr) 1983
dir. Jean Marie Straub/Daniele Huillet

Ammie, Come Home
Michaels, B.

House That Would Not Die, The
A. SPELLING (US) 1980 dir. J. L. Moxey

Amy Jolly
Vigny, B.

Morocco
PAR (US) 1930 dir. Josef von Sternberg

Anastasia: The Riddle of Anna Anderson
Kurth, P.

Anastasia: The Mystery of Anna
TELECOM (US) 1986
dir. Marvin Chomsky

Anatomy of Me
Hurst, F.

Imitation of Life
UN (US) 1934 dir. John Stahl
UN (US) 1959 dir. Douglas Sirk

And Deliver Us From Evil
Cochran, M.

Fugitive Among Us
ABC PRODS TV (US) 1992
dir. Michael Toshiyuki Uno

And Quiet Flows the Don
Sholokhov, M.

Quiet Flows the Don
GORKI (USSR) 1958
dir. Sergei Gerasimov

And Ride a Tiger
Wilder, R.

Stranger in my Arms, A
UI (US) 1958 dir. Helmut Kautner

And They Shall Walk
Kenny, E. and Ostenso, M.

Sister Kenny
RKO (US) 1946 dir. Dudley Nichols

Angel Street
Hamilton, P.

Gaslight
BN (GB) 1939 dir. Thorold Dickinson
US title: Angel Street
MGM (US) 1944 dir. George Cukor
GB title: Murder in Thornton Square,
The

Angela is 22
Wray, F. and Lewis, S.

This is the Life
UN (US) 1943 dir. Felix Feist

Angels Without Wings
Yarmolinsky, J.

Promise to Keep, A
WAR TV (US) 1990 dir. Rod Holcomb

Animal Kingdom, The
Barry, P.

One More Tomorrow
WAR (US) 1946 dir. Peter Godfrey

Anna and the King of Siam
Landon, M.

King and I, The
FOX (US) 1956 dir. Walter Lang

Anne Frank Remembered: The Story of the Woman Who Helped To Hide the Frank Family
Gies, M. and Gold, A. L.

Attic, The: The Hiding of Anne Frank
TELECOM/YTV (US/GB) 1988
dir. John Erman

Anne Frank: The Diary of a Young Girl
Frank, A.

Diary of Anne Frank, The
FOX (US) 1959 dir. George Stevens
FOX (US) 1980 dir. Boris Sagal
BBC (GB) 1988

Anne of Windy Willows
Montgomery, L. M.

Anne of Windy Poplars
RKO (US) 1940 dir. Jack Hively

Annie's Coming Out
Crossley, R., and McDonald, A.

Test of Love, A
UN (US) 1985 dir. Gil Brealey

Anniversary Waltz
Fields, J. and Chodorov, J.

Happy Anniversary
UA (US) 1959 dir. David Miller

Anointed, The
Davis, C. B.

Adventure
MGM (US) 1945 dir. Victor Fleming

Ant and the Grasshopper, The; Winter Cruise; Gigolo and Gigolette
Maugham, W. S.

Encore
GFD (GB) 1951 dir. Harold French, Pat Jackson, Anthony Pellissier

Antagonists, The
Gann, E. K.

Masada
UN TV (US) 1981 dir. Boris Sagal
GB title: Antagonists, The

Apache Rising
Albert, M. H.

Duel at Diablo
UA (US) 1966 dir. Ralph Nelson

Apple Pie in the Sky
Lovell, M.

Trouble With Spies, The
HBO (US) 1987 dir. Burt Kennedy

Apple Tree, The
Galsworthy, J.

Summer Story, A
ITC/ATLANTIC (GB) 1988 dir. Piers Haggard

Applesauce
Conners, B.

Brides are Like That
WAR (US) 1936 dir. William McGann

Appointment at the Beach
Moravia, A.

Naked Hours, The
COMPTON (It) 1964 dir. Marco Vicario

Appointment with Fear
Huggins, R.

State Secret, The
BL (GB) 1950 dir. Sidney Gilliat
US title: Great Manhunt, The

Appointments in Zahrein
Barrett, M.

Escape from Zahrein
PAR (US) 1962 dir. Ronald Neame

Aren't you Even Gonna Kiss Me Goodbye
Richert, W.

Night in the Life of Jimmy Reardon, A.
FOX (US) 1988 dir. William Richert

Ari: The Life and Time of Aristotle Onassis
Evans, P.

Richest Man in the World, The: The Story of Aristotle Onassis
KON/SAN (US) 1988 dir. Waris Hussein

Arizona in the 50's
Tevis, J. H.

Tenderfoot, The
DISNEY (US) 1964 dir. Byron Paul

Arm, The
Howard, C.

Big Town, The
COL (US) 1987 dir. Ben Bolt

Arms and the Man
Shaw, G. B.

Helden
SOKAL/GOLDBAUM (Ger) 1959 dir. Franz Peter Wirth

Arouse and Beware
Kantor, M.

Man from Dakota, The
MGM (US) 1940 dir. Leslie Fenton
GB title: Arouse and Beware

Arrow in the Sun
Olsen, T. V.

Soldier Blue
AVCO (US) 1970 dir. Ralph Nelson

Ashenden
Maugham, W. S.
Secret Agent, The
(GB) 1936 dir. Alfred Hitchcock

Ask Agamemnon
Hall, J.
Goodbye Gemini
CINDERAMA (GB) 1970
dir. Alan Gibson

Asking for It
Taylor, J.
Invasion of Privacy, An
EMBASSY TV (US) 1983
dir. Mel Damski

Aspern Papers, The
James, H.
Aspern
CONN (Port) 1981
dir. Eduardo de Gregorion

Aspern Papers, The
James, H.
Lost Moment, The
UN (US) 1947 dir. Martin Gabel

Asphalt Jungle, The
Burnett, W. R.
Cairo
MGM (GB) 1963 dir. Wolf Rilla

Asphalt Jungle, The
Burnett, W. R.
Cool Breeze
MGM (US) 1972 dir. Barry Pollack

L'Assommoir
Zola, E.
Gervaise
CLCC (Fr) 1956 dir. René Clément

Atomic Soldiers
Rosenberg, H.
Nightbreaker
TNT (US) 1989 dir. Peter Markle

Attack on Terror: The FBI Against The Ku Klux Klan in Mississippi
Whitehead, D.
Attack on Terror: The FBI Versus The Ku Klux Klan
WAR TV (US) 1975
dir. Marvin Chomsky

L'Attention
Moravia, A.
Lie, The
SELVAGGIA (It) 1985
dir. Giovanni Soldati

Auch das war Wein
Torberg, F.
38: Vienna Before the Fall
SATEL/ALMARO (Ger) 1988
dir. Wolfgang Gluck

Aunt Julia and the Scriptwriter
Llosa, M. V.
Tune in Tomorrow...
CINECOM (US) 1990 dir. Jon Amiel

Auntie Mame
Dennis, P.
Mame
WAR (US) 1974 dir. Gene Saks

Authentic Death of Hendry Jones, The
Neider, C.
One-Eyed Jacks
PAR (US) 1961 dir. Marlon Brando

Autumn of a Hunter
Stadley, P.
Deadly Hunt, The
FOUR STAR (US) 1971
dir. John Newland

Autumn
Kennedy, M., Surgutchoff, I.

That Dangerous Age
LF (GB) 1948 dir. Gregory Ratoff
US title: If This Be Sin

Avenging Angels, The
Burns, R.

Messenger of Death
CANNON (US) 1988
dir. J. Lee Thompson

Awakening, The
Chopin, K.

End of August, The
QUARTET (US) 1981 dir. Bob Graham

Awakening, The
Chopin, K.

Grand Isle
TURNER (US) 1992 dir. Mary Lambert

B

Babe: The Legend Comes to Life
Cramer, R. W.

Babe Ruth
LYTTLE (US) 1991 dir. Mark Tinker

Babe Ruth, His Life and Legend
Wagenheim, K.

Babe Ruth
LYTTLE (US) 1991 dir. Mark Tinker

Baby Brokers, The
McTaggart, L.

Born to be Sold
SAMUELS (US) 1981
dir. Burt Brinckerhoff

Baby Jane
Farrell, H.

What Ever Happened to Baby Jane?
WAR (US) 1962 dir. Robert Aldrich
SPECTACOR (US) 1991
dir. David Greene

Babylon Revisited
Fitzgerald, F. S.

Last Time I Saw Paris, The
MGM (US) 1954 dir. Richard Brooks

Bachelor Born
Hay, I.

Housemaster
ABPC (GB) 1938 dir. Herbert Brenon

Bachelor Father
Dell, F.

Casanova Brown
INTERNAT (US) 1944 dir. Sam Wood

Bad Time at Honda
Breslin, H.

Bad Day at Black Rock
MGM (US) 1954 dir. John Sturges

Badge of Evil
Masterson, W.

Touch of Evil
UN (US) 1958 dir. Orson Welles

Badman
Huffaker, C.
War Wagon, The
UI (US) 1967 dir. Burt Kennedy

Bailbondsman, The
Elkin, S.
Alex and the Gypsy
TCF (US) 1976 dir. John Korty

Ballad of Cat Ballou, The
Chanslor, R.
Cat Ballou
COL (US) 1965 dir. Eliot Silverstein

Ballad of Dingus Magee, The
Markson, D.
Dirty Dingus Magee
MGM (US) 1970 dir. Burt Kennedy

Ballad of the Belstone Fox, The
Rook, D.
Belstone Fox, The
RANK (GB) 1973 dir. James Hill

Ballad of the Flim-Flam Man, The
Owen, G.
Flim-Flam Man, The
FOX (US) 1967 dir. Irvin Kershner

Ballad of the Running Man, The
Smith, S.
Running Man, The
COL (GB) 1963 dir. Carol Reed

Ballerina
Smith, Lady E.
Men in her Life
COL (US) 1941 dir. Gregory Ratoff

Bandwagon, The
Kaufman, G. S., Dietz, H. and Schwarz, A.
Dancing in the Dark
FOX (US) 1949 dir. Irving Reis

Banjo
McKay, C.
Big Fella
FORTUNE (GB) 1937 dir. J. E. Wills

Bank Robber, The
Tippette, G.
Spikes Gang, The
UA (US) 1974 dir. Richard Fleischer

Bankers Also Have Souls
Valme and Terzolli
Gift, The
GOLDWYN (Fr) 1983 dir. Michel Lang

Banner in the Sky
Ullman, J. R.
Third Man on the Mountain
DISNEY (GB) 1959 dir. Ken Annakin

Barchester Towers: Warden, The
Trollope, A.
Barchester Chronicles, The
BBC (GB) 1982 dir. David Giles

Barker, The
Nicholson, K.
Diamond Horseshoe
FOX (US) 1945 dir. George Seaton

Barrage contre le Pacifique, Un
Duras, M.
This Angry Age
DELAUR (It) 1957 dir. René Clément

Basement Room, The
Greene, G.

Fallen Idol, The
FOX (GB) 1948 dir. Carol Reed
US title: Lost Illusion, The

Basil of Baker Street
Titus, E.

Great Mouse Detective, The
DISNEY (US) 1986
dir. Burny Mattinson

Bat, The
Rinehart, M. R.

Bat Whispers, The
UA (US) 1930 dir. Roland West

Battle of Nerves, A
Simenon, G.

Man on the Eiffel Tower, The
BL (US) 1948 dir. Burgess Meredith

Be Ready With Bells and Drums
Kata, E.

Patch of Blue, A
MGM (US) 1965 dir. Guy Green

Be Still My Love
Truesdell, J.

Accused, The
PAR (US) 1948 dir. William Dieterle

Beardless Warriors
Matheson, R.

Young Warriors
UN (US) 1966 dir. John Peyser

Beauty
Baldwin, F.

Beauty for Sale
MGM (US) 1933
dir. Richard Boleslawski

Because of the Cats
Freeling, N.

Rape, The
MIRACLE (Bel/Neth) 1973
dir. Fons Rademakers

Bedeviled, The
Cullinan, T.

Beguiled, The
UN (US) 1971 dir. Don Siegel

Bed-Knob and Broomstick
Norton, M.

Bedknobs and Broomsticks
DISNEY (US) 1971
dir. Robert Stevenson

Bedtime Story
Robinson, J. S.

Cry for Love, A
FRIES/SACKS (US) 1980
dir. Paul Wendkos

Before the Fact
Iles, F.

Suspicion
RKO (US) 1941 dir. Alfred Hitchcock

Beggar My Neighbour
Ridley, A.

Meet Mr Lucifer
GFD (GB) 1953 dir. Anthony Pelissier

Beggars are Coming to Town
Reeves, T.

I Walk Alone
PAR (US) 1947 dir. Byron Haskin

Beginner's Luck
Somers, P.

Desperate Man, The
AA (GB) 1959 dir. Peter Maxwell

Behold We Live
Druten, J. van

If I Were Free
RKO (US) 1933 dir. Elliot Nugent

Bejewelled Death
Babson, M.
Bejewelled
DISNEY CH (US/GB) 1991
dir. Terry Marcel

Bel Ami
De Maupassant, G.
Private Affairs of Bel Ami, The
UA (US) 1947 dir. Albert Lewin

Belarus Secret, The
Loftus, J.
Kojak: The Belarus File
UN TV (US) 1985 dir. Robert Markowitz

Bella Donna
Hichens, R.
Temptation
UN (US) 1935 dir. Irving Pichel

Bellamy the Magnificent
Horniman, R.
Bedtime Story, A
PAR (US) 1933 dir. Norman Taurog

Beloved Friend
Bowen, C. D., von Meck, B.
Music Lovers, The
UA (GB) 1970 dir. Ken Russell

Belvedere
Davenport, Mrs. G.
Sitting Pretty
FOX (US) 1948 dir. Walter Lang

Bend of the Snake
Gulick, W.
Bend of the River
UI (US) 1952 dir. Anthony Mann
GB title: Where the River Bends

Benefits Forgot
Morrow, H.
Of Human Hearts
MGM (US) 1938 dir. Clarence Brown

Bengal Lancer
Brown, F. Y.
Lives of a Bengal Lancer
PAR (US) 1935 dir. Henry Hathaway

Bengal Tiger
Hunter, H.
Bengal Brigade
UI (US) 1954 dir. Laslo Benedek
GB title: Bengal Rifles

Benighted
Priestley, J. B.
Old Dark House, The
UN (US) 1932 dir. James Whale
BL (GB) 1963 dir. William Castle

Benjamin Blake
Marshall, E.
Son of Fury
TCF (US) 1942 dir. John Cromwell

Berg, The
Raymond, E.
Atlantic
BI (GB) 1929 dir. E. A. Dupont

Berg
Quinn, A.
Killing Dad
PALACE (US) 1989 dir. Michael Austin

Berkeley Square
Balderston, J. L.
House in the Square, The
FOX (GB) 1951 dir. Roy Baker
US title: I'll Never Forget You

Berlin Hotel
Baum, V.
Hotel Berlin
WAR (US) 1945 dir. Peter Godfrey

Berlin Memorandum, The
Deighton, L.
Funeral in Berlin
PAR (GB) 1966 dir. Guy Hamilton

Berlin Wall, The
Galante, P.
Freedom Fighter
COL TV (US/GB) 1987
dir. Desmond Davis

Best Intentions: The Education and Killing of Edmund Perry
Anson, R. A.
Murder Without Motive: The Edmund Perry Story
LEONARD HILL FILMS (US) 1992
dir. Kevin Hooks

La Bête Humaine
Zola, E.
Human Desire
COL (US) 1954 dir. Fritz Lang

Bethnal Green
Fisher, M.
Place To Go, A
BL (GB) 1963 dir. Basil Dearden

Better Than Life
Bromfield, L.
It All Came True
WAR (US) 1940 dir. Lewis Seiler

Beware of Children
Anderson, V.
No Kidding
AA (GB) 1960 dir. Gerald Thomas
US title: Beware of Children

Beyond the Mountains
Ramati, A.
Desperate Ones, The
AMERICAN (Sp/US) 1968
dir. Alexander Ramati

Bid Time Return
Matheson, R.
Somewhere in Time
UN (US) 1980 dir. Jeannot Szwarc

Big Birthday, The
Leonard, H.
Broth of a Boy
E. DALTON (Eire) 1958
dir. George Pollack

Big Bow Mystery, The
Zangwill, I.
Verdict, The
WAR (US) 1946 dir. Don Siegel

Big Clock, The
Fearing, K.
No Way Out
ORION (US) 1987 dir. Roger Donaldson

Big Pick-Up, The
Trevor, E.
Dunkirk
MGM (GB) 1958 dir. Leslie Norman

Big Story, The
West, M. L.
Crooked Road, The
GALA (GB/Yugo) 1964 dir. Don Chaffey

Big Town, The
Lardner, R. W.
So this is New York
UA (US) 1948 dir. Richard Fleischer

Big War, The
Myrer, A.
In Love and War
FOX (US) 1958 dir. Philip Dunne

Biko
Woods, D.
Cry Freedom
UN (GB) 1987
dir. Richard Attenborough

Binary
Crichton, M.
Pursuit
ABC (USTV) 1972 dir. Michael Crichton

Bind, The
Ellin, S.
Sunburn
HEMDALE (GB/US) 1979
dir. Richard C. Sarafian

Biography of a Grizzly and Other Animal Stories, The
Seton, E. T.
Legend of Lobo, The
DISNEY (US) 1962 dir. James Algar

Biography of a Grizzly, The
Seton, E. T.
King of the Grizzlies
DISNEY (US) 1970 dir. Ron Kelly

Biography
Behrman, S. N.
Biography (of a Bachelor Girl)
MGM (US) 1935 dir. Edward H. Griffith

Bird's Nest, The
Jackson, S.
Lizzie
MGM (US) 1957 dir. Hugo Haas

Birthday Gift
Fodor, L.
North to Alaska
FOX (US) 1960 dir. Henry Hathaway

Birthday
Bus-Fekete, L.
Heaven Can Wait
FOX (US) 1943 dir. Ernst Lubitsch

Bitter Harvest: Murder in the Heartland
Corcoran, J.
In the Line of Duty: Manhunt in the Dakotas
P-K (US) 1991 dir. Dick Lowry

Bitter Sage
Gruber, G.
Tension at Table Rock
RKO (US) 1956
dir. Charles Marquis Warren

Bixby Girls, The
Marshall, R.
All the Fine Young Cannibals
MGM (US) 1960 dir. Michael Anderson

Black Alibi
Woolrich, C.
Leopard Man, The
RKO (US) 1943 dir. Jacques Tourneur

Black Curtain, The
Woolrich, C.
Lady Forgets, The
HILL (US) 1989 dir. Bradford May

Black Curtain, The
Woolrich, C.
Street of Chance
PAR (US) 1942 dir. Jack Hively

Black Path of Fear, The
Woolrich, C.
Chase, The
NERO (US) 1947 dir. Arthur Ripley

Blackburn's Headhunters
Harkins, P.
Surrender-Hell
AA (US) 1959 dir. John Barnwell

Blackjack Hijack, The
Einstein, C.
Nowhere to Run
MTM (US) 1978 dir. Richard Lang

Blank Wall, The
Holding, Mrs. E.
Reckless Moment, The
COL (US) 1949 dir. Max Ophuls

Blaze Starr: My Life as Told to Huey Perry
Starr, B. and Perry, H.
Blaze
TOUCHSTONE (US) 1989
dir. Ron Shelton

Bless You Sister
Riskin, R. and Meehan, J.
Miracle Woman, The
COL (US) 1932 dir. Frank Capra

Blessing, The
Mitford, N.
Count Your Blessings
MGM (US) 1959 dir. Jean Negulesco

Blind Love
Cauvin, P.
Little Romance, A
WAR (US) 1979 dir. George Roy Hill

Blind Spot, The
Nicholson, K.
Taxi!
WAR (US) 1931 dir. Roy del Ruth

Bliss
Gundy, E.
Seduction of Miss Leona, The
SCHERICK (US) 1980 dir. Joseph Hardy

Blockhaus, Le
Clebert, J. P.
Blockhouse, The
GALACTUS (GB) 1973 dir. Clive Rees

Blondie White
Fodor, L.
Footsteps in the Dark
WAR (US) 1941 dir. Lloyd Bacon

Blood Brother
Arnold, E.
Broken Arrow
FOX (US) 1950 dir. Delmer Daves

Blood of Israel, The
Groussard, S.
21 Hours at Munich
FILMWAYS (US) 1976
dir. William A. Graham

Blood on the Moon
Ellroy, J.
Cop
ATLANTIC (US) 1988
dir. James B. Harris

Bloody Spur, The
Einstein, C.
While the City Sleeps
RKO (US) 1956 dir. Fritz Lang

Blue Collar Journal
Coleman, J. R.
Secret Life of John Chapman, The
JOZAK (US) 1976 dir. David Lowell Rich

Blue Cross, The
Chesterton, G. K.
Father Brown
COL (GB) 1954 dir. Robert Hamer

Boarding Party
Leasor, J.
Sea Wolves, The
RANK (GB/US/Switz) 1980
dir. Andrew McLaglen

Bodies and Souls
van der Meersch, M.
Doctor and the Girl, The
MGM (US) 1949 dir. Curtis Bernhardt

Body Snatchers, The
Finney, J.
Invasion of the Body Snatchers, The
ALLIED (US) 1956 dir. Don Siegel
UA (US) 1978 dir. Philip Kaufman

Body, The
King, S.
Stand by Me
COL (US) 1986 dir. Rob Reiner

Bogmail
McGinley, P.
Murder in Eden
BBC (GB) 1991 dir. Nicholas Renton

Bohunk
Irving, H. R.
Black Fury
WAR (US) 1935 dir. Michael Curtiz

Bonaventure
Hastings, C.
Thunder on the Hill
UI (US) 1951 dir. Douglas Sirk
GB title: Bonaventure

Bondage
Hines, D.
Whore
TRIMARK (GB) 1991 dir. Ken Russell

Book of Daniel, The
Doctorow, E. L.
Daniel
PAR (GB) 1983 dir. Sidney Lumet

Book of the Month
Thomas, B.
Please Turn Over
AA (GB) 1959 dir. Gerald Thomas

Border Jumpers, The
Brown, W. C.
Man of the West
UA (US) 1958 dir. Anthony Mann

Borrowed Christmas, A
Bemelmans, L.
Christmas Festival, A
COMPASS (US) 1959
dir. Albert McCleery

Bottletop Affair, The
Cotler, G.
Horizontal Lieutenant, The
MGM (US) 1962 dir. Richard Thorpe

Boudu Sauvé des Eaux
Fauchois, R.
Down and Out in Beverly Hills
TOUCH (US) 1986 dir. Paul Mazursky

Bowery to Bellevue
Barringer, E. D.
Girl in White, The
MGM (US) 1952 dir. John Sturges
GB title: So Bright the Flame

Boy Who Could Make Himself Disappear, The
Platt, K.
Baxter!
EMI (GB) 1972 dir. Lionel Jeffries

Boyfriend School, The
Bird, S.
Don't Tell Her It's Me
HEMDALE (US) 1990
dir. Malcolm Mowbray

Brainwash
Wainwright, J.
Inquisitor, The
GALA (Fr) 1981 dir. Claude Miller

Brave Cowboy
Abbey, E.
Lonely are the Brave
UI (US) 1962 dir. David Miller

Bread and a Stone
Bessie, A.
Hard Travelling
NEW WORLD (US) 1986
dir. Dan Bessie

Breakout
LeFlore, R. and Hawkins, J.
One in a Million: The Ron LeFlore Story
EMI (US) 1978 dir. William A. Graham

Breath of Spring
Coke, P.
Make Mine Mink
RANK (GB) 1960 dir. Robert Asher

Brennendes Geheimnis
Zweig, S.
Burning Secret
VESTRON (GB/Ger) 1988
dir. Andrew Birkin

Brewster's Millions
McCutcheon, G. B.
Three on a Spree
UA (GB) 1961 dir. Sidney J. Furie

Brick Foxhole, The
Brooks, R.
Crossfire
RKO (US) 1947 dir. Edward Dmytryk

Bride Comes to Yellow Sky, The
Crane, S.
Face to Face
RKO (US) 1952
dir. John Brahm/Bretaigne Windust

Bringing up the Brass: My 55 Years at West Point
Maher, M. and Campion, N. R.
Long Gray Line, The
COL (US) 1955 dir. John Ford

Broken Gun, The
L'Amour, L.
Cancel My Reservation
MGM-EMI (US) 1972 dir. Paul Bogart

Bronco Apache
Wellman, P. I.
Apache
UA (US) 1954 dir. Robert Aldrich

Brook Adams
Glaspell, S.
Right to Love, The
PAR (US) 1930 dir. Richard Wallace

Brook Wilson Ltd
Ryan, J. M.
Loving
COL (US) 1970 dir. Irvin Kershner

Brother Rat
Monks, J. and Finklehoffe, F. F.
About Face
WAR (US) 1952 dir. Roy del Ruth

Brothers Rico, The
Simenon, G.
Family Rico, The
CBS (US) 1972 dir. Paul Wendkos

Brute, The
des Cars, G.
Green Scarf, The
BL (GB) 1954
dir. George More O'Ferrall

Buddhist Cross, The
Tanizaki, J.
Berlin Affair, The
CANNON (It/Ger) 1985
dir. Liliana Cavani

Buddwing
Hunter, E.
Mister Buddwing
MGM (US) 1966 dir. Delbert Mann
GB title: Woman Without a Face

Buffalo Grass
Gruber, F.
Big Land, The
WAR (US) 1957 dir. Gordon Douglas
GB title: Stampeded

Build My Gallows High
Homes, G.
Against all Odds
COL (US) 1984 dir. Taylor Hackford

Build My Gallows High
Homes, G.
Out of the Past
RKO (US) 1947 dir. Jacques Tourneur
GB title: Build My Gallows High

Build-up Boys, The
Kirk, J.
Madison Avenue
FOX (US) 1962 dir. Bruce Humberstone

Bull Boys, The
Delderfield, R. F.
Carry on Sergeant
AAM (GB) 1958 dir. Gerald Thomas

Bundy: The Deliberate Stranger
Larsen, R. W.
Deliberate Stranger, The
LORIMAR (US) 1986
dir. Marvin Chomsky

Burden of Proof, The
Barlow, J.
Villain
EMI (GB) 1971 dir. Michael Tuchner

Burglar, The
Goodis, D.
Burglars, The
COL (Fr/It) 1971 dir. Henri Verneuill

Buried Alive
Bennett, A.
His Double Life
PAR (US) 1933 dir. Arthur Hopkins

Buried Alive
Bennett, A.
Holy Matrimony
PAR (US) 1943 dir. John Stahl

Burlesque
Walters, G. M. and Hopkins, A.
Swing High, Swing Low
PAR (US) 1937 dir. Mitchell Leisen

Burlesque
Walters, G. M. and Hopkins, A.
When my Baby Smiles at Me
FOX (US) 1948 dir. Walter Lang

Burn, Witch, Burn
Merritt, A.
Devil Doll, The
MGM (US) 1936 dir. Tod Browning

Burton and Speke
Harrison, W.
Mountains of the Moon
TRI-STAR (US) 1990 dir. Bob Rafaelson

But for These Men
Drummond, J. D.
Heroes of the Telemark
RANK (GB) 1965 dir. Anthony Mann

But Gentlemen Marry Brunettes
Loos, A.
Gentlemen Marry Brunettes
UA (US) 1955 dir. Richard Sale

But There are Always Miracles

Willis, M. P. and Willis, J.

Some Kind of Miracle
LORIMAR (US) 1979
dir. Jerrold Freedman

Butter and Egg Man, The

Kaufman, G. S.

Angel from Texas, An
WAR (US) 1940 dir. Ray Enright

Butter and Egg Man, The

Kaufman, G. S.

Three Sailors and a Girl
WAR (US) 1953 dir. Roy del Ruth

Butterfly Revolution, The

Butler, W.

Summer Camp Nightmare
CONCORDE (US) 1987
dir. Bert C. Dragin

By the Great Horn Spoon

Fleischman, S.

Adventures of Bullwhip Griffin, The
DISNEY (US) 1965 dir. James Neilson

Cabal

Barker, C.

Nightbreed
FOX (US) 1990 dir. Clive Barker

Caddie Woodlawn

Brink, C. R.

Caddie
HEMDALE (Aust) 1976
dir. Donald Crombie

Californio, The

MacLeod, R.

100 Rifles
FOX (US) 1969 dir. Tom Gries

Call for the Dead

Le Carré, J.

Deadly Affair, The
COL (GB) 1966 dir. Sidney Lumet

Call Girl, The

Greenwald, H.

Girl of the Night
WAR (US) 1960 dir. Joseph Cates

Call it Treason

Howe, G. L.

Decision Before Dawn
FOX (US) 1951 dir. Anatole Litvak

Calling Dr. Horowitz

Horowitz, S.

Bad Medicine
TCF (US) 1985 dir. Harvey Miller

Came the Dawn

Bax, R.

Never Let Me Go
MGM (GB) 1953 dir. Delmer Daves

Canadian Tragedy, A
Siggins, M.
Love and Hate: A Marriage Made in Hell
CBC/BBC (US/Can/GB) 1991
dir. Francis Mankiewicz

Candle for the Dead, A
Marlowe, H.
Violent Enemy, The
MONARCH (GB) 1969 dir. Don Sharp

Capricorn Man, The
Zacha, Sr., W. T.
Ultimate Imposter, The
UN TV (US) 1979 dir. Paul Stanley

Captain Bligh and Mr Christian
Hough, R.
Bounty, The
ORION (GB) 1984 dir. Roger Donaldson

Captain Blood Returns
Sabatini, R.
Captain Pirate
COL (US) 1952 dir. Ralph Murphy
GB title: Captain Blood, Fugitive

Captain Grant's Children
Verne, J.
In Search of the Castaways
DISNEY (GB) 1961
dir. Robert Stevenson

Captain Hornblower, R. N.
Forester, C. S.
Captain Horatio Hornblower, R. N.
WAR (GB) 1951 dir. Raoul Walsh

Captain's Daughter, The
Pushkin, A.
Tempest
PAR (It/Fr/Yugo) 1958
dir. Alberto Lattuada

Careful Man, The
Deming, R.
Drop Dead Darling
SEVEN ARTS (GB) 1966
dir. Ken Hughes
US title: Arrivederci Baby

Carl and Anna
Frank, L.
Desire Me
MGM (US) 1947 dir. George Cukor

Carmen
Merimée, P.
First Name: Carmen
IS (Fr) 1984 dir. Jean-Luc Godard

Carmen
Merimée, P.
Loves of Carmen, The
COL (US) 1948 dir. Charles Vidor

Carnival
Mackenzie, Sir C.
Dance Pretty Lady
BI (GB) 1932 dir. Anthony Asquith

Carriage Entrance
Banks, P.
My Forbidden Past
RKO (US) 1951 dir. Robert Stevenson

Carry Cot, The
Thynne, A.
Blue Blood
MIQ (GB) 1973 dir. Andrew Sinclair

Case File F.B.I.
Gordon, M. and Gordon, G.
Down 3 Dark Streets
UA (US) 1954 dir. Arnold Laven

Case History
Walker, G.
Damned Don't Cry, The
WAR (US) 1950 dir. Vincent Sherman

Case of Charles Dexter, The
Lovecraft, H. P.
Haunted Palace, The
AMERICAN (US) 1963
dir. Roger Corman

Case of Lady Camber, The
Vachell, H. A.
Lord Camber's Ladies
BI (GB) 1932 dir. Benn W. Levy

Case of Need, A
Hudson, J.
Carey Treatment, The
MGM (US) 1972 dir. Blake Edwards

Case of the Caretaker's Cat, The
Gardner, E. S.
Case of the Black Cat, The
WAR (US) 1936 dir. William McGann

Case of the Constant God, The
King, R.
Love Letters of a Star
UN (US) 1936 dir. Lewis R. Foster

Case of the Frightened Lady, The
Wallace, E.
Frightened Lady, The
BL (GB) 1932 dir. T. Hayes Hunter

Case of the Three Weird Sisters, The
Armstrong, C.
Three Weird Sisters, The
BN (GB) 1948 dir. Dan Birt

Casting the Runes
James, M. R.
Night of the Demon
COL (GB) 1957 dir. Jacques Tourneur

Castle Minerva
Canning, V.
Masquerade
UA (GB) 1965 dir. Basil Dearden

Castles Burning
Lyons, A.
Slow Burn
UN TV (US) 1986
dir. Matthew Chapman

Casual Sex
Goldman, W.
Casual Sex?
UN (US) 1988 dir. Genevieve Robert

Cat and the Canary, The
Willard, J.
Cat Creeps, The
UN (US) 1930 dir. Rupert Julian

Cat and the Mice, The
Mosley, L.
Foxhole in Cairo
BL (GB) 1960 dir. John Moxey

Cat From Hell
King, S.
Tales from the Darkside: the Movie
PAR (US) 1990 dir. John Harrison

Cat of Many Tales
Queen, E.
Ellery Queen: Don't Look Behind You
UN TV (US) 1971 dir. Barry Shear

Catbird Seat, The
Thurber, J.
Battle of the Sexes, The
PROM (GB) 1960 dir. Charles Crichton

Celle Qui N'Etait Plus
Boileau, P. & Narcejac, T.
Reflections of Murder
ABC (US) 1974 dir. John Badham

Cellist, The
Hart, M.
Connecting Rooms
TELSTAR (GB) 1969
dir. Franklin Gollings

Centurions, The
Larteguy, J.
Lost Command
COL (US) 1966 dir. Mark Robson

Chair for Martin Rome, The
Helseth, H. E.
Cry of the City
FOX (US) 1948 dir. Robert Siodmak

Chairman, The
Kennedy, J. R.
Most Dangerous Man in the World, The
RANK (GB) 1969 dir. J. Lee Thompson
US title: Chairman, The

Chalked Out
Lawes, L., and Finn, J.
You Can't Get Away with Murder
WAR (US) 1939 dir. Lewis Seiler

Champion's Story: A Great Human Triumph
Champion, B. and Powell, J.
Champions
Embassy (GB) 1983 dir. John Irvin

Chances
Collins, J.
Lucky/Chances
NBC (US) 1990 dir. Buzz Kulik

Change of Plan, A
Friedman, B. J.
Heartbreak Kid, The
FOX (US) 1972 dir. Elaine May

Charley's Aunt
Thomas, B.
Where's Charley?
WAR (US) 1952 dir. David Butler

Charlie and the Chocolate Factory
Dahl, R.
Willy Wonka and the Chocolate Factory
PAR (US) 1971 dir. Mel Stuart

Charlie M
Freemantle, B.
Charlie Muffin
EUSTON (GB) 1979 dir. Jack Gold

Chase, The
Unekis, R.
Dirty Mary, Crazy Larry
FOX (US) 1974 dir. John Hough

Château Bon Vivant
O'Rear, F. and O'Rear, J.
Snowball Express
DISNEY (US) 1972 dir. Norman Tokar

Château de Ma Mère, Le
Pagnol, M.
My Mother's Castle
GAU (Fr) 1991 dir. Yves Robert

Chautauqua
Keene, D. and Babcock, D.
Trouble With Girls, The
MGM (US) 1969 dir. Peter Tewkesbury

Cheetahs, The
Caillou, A.
Cheetah
DISNEY (US) 1989 dir. Jeff Blyth

Chester, I Love You
Yorgason, B. & Yorgason, B.
Thanksgiving Promise, The
DISNEY (US) 1986 dir. Beau Bridges

Chicago
Watkins, M.
Roxie Hart
FOX (US) 1942 dir. William A. Wellman

Chienne, La
de la Fouchardière, G.

Scarlet Street
UN (US) 1945 dir. Fritz Lang

Child of Vodyanoi
Wiltshire, D.

Nightmare Man, The
BBC (US) 1981 dir. Douglas Camfield

Children, The
Wharton, E.

Marriage Playground, The
PAR (US) 1929 dir. Lothar Mendes

Children are Gone, The
Cavanaugh, A.

Deadly Trap, The
NAT GEN (Fr/It) 1971
dir. René Clément

Children of the Dark
Shulman, I.

Cry Tough
UA (US) 1959 dir. Paul Stanley

Children of the Light, The
Lawrence, H. L.

Damned, The
BL (GB) 1961 dir. Joseph Losey
US title: These Are The Damned

Children of the Night
Lortz, R.

Voices
HEMDALE (GB) 1973
dir. Kevin Billington

Children's Hour, The
Hellman, L. F.

These Three
UA (US) 1936 dir. William Wyler

Chisolm Trail, The
Chase, B.

Red River
UA (US) 1948 dir. Howard Hawks

Choice Cuts
Boileau, P. and Narcejac, T.

Body Parts
PAR (US) 1991 dir. Eric Red

Choir Practice
Morgan, C.

Valley of Song
ABPC (GB) 1953 dir. Gilbert Gunn

Christ has Returned to Earth and Preaches Here Nightly
Gardner, L.

Valentino Returns
VIDMARK/SKOURAS (US) 1989
dir. Paul Hoffman

Christ in Concrete
Di Donata, P.

Give Us This Day
GFD (GB) 1949 dir. Edward Dmytryk
US title: Salt to the Devil

Christmas at Candleshoe
Innes, M.

Candleshoe
DISNEY (GB) 1977 dir. Norman Tokar

Christmas Carol, A
Dickens, C.

American Christmas Carol, An
SM HEM (US) 1979 dir. Eric Till

Christmas Carol, A
Dickens, C.

Christmas Present, A
CHANNEL 4 (GB) 1985

Christmas Carol, A
Dickens, C.

Scrooged
PAR (US) 1988 dir. Richard Donner

Christmas Carol, A
Dickens, C.

Scrooge
PAR (GB) 1935 dir. Henry Edwards
REN (GB) 1951
dir. Brian Desmond Hurst
FOX (GB) 1970 dir. Ronald Neame

Christopher Blake
Hart, M.

Decision of Christopher Blake, The
WAR (US) 1948 dir. Peter Godfrey

Christopher Syn
Thorndike, R.

Dr Syn
GAU (GB) 1937 dir. Roy. William Neill

Christopher Syn
Thorndike, R.

Dr. Syn, Alias the Scarecrow
DISNEY (US) 1962 dir. James Neilson

Chronicles of Prydain, The
Alexander, L.

Black Cauldron, The
DISNEY (US) 1985 dirs. Ted Berman
and Richard Rich

Chrysalis
Porter, R.

All of Me
PAR (US) 1934 dir. James Flood

Cipher, The
Votler, G.

Arabesque
UN (US) 1966 dir. Stanley Donen

Circles Round the Wagon
Gipson, F. B.

Hound-Dog Man
FOX (US) 1959 dir. Don Siegel

City of Bardish, A
Grossman, V.

Commissar
GORKY (USSR) 1988
dir. Alexander Askoldov

City of Shadows
Prokosch, F.

Conspirators, The
WAR (US) 1944 dir. Jean Negulesco

Claw, The
Bernstein, H.

Washington Masquerade
MGM (US) 1932 dir. Charles Brabin
GB title: Mad Masquerade

Clé de la Rue Saint Nicolas, La
Gegauff, P.

À Double Tour
PARIS/PANI (Fr/It) 1959
dir. Claude Chabrol

Clean Break
White, L.

Killing, The
UA (US) 1956 dir. Stanley Kubrick

Clubfoot
Williams, V.

Crouching Beast, The
OLY (GB) 1935 dir. Victor Hanbury

Cockpit
Boland, B.

Lost People, The
GFD (GB) 1949 dir. Bernard Knowles

Coins in the Fountain
Secondari, J. H.

Pleasure Seekers, The
FOX (US) 1964 dir. Jean Negulesco

Coins in the Fountain
Secondari, J.

Three Coins in the Fountain
FOX (US) 1954 dir. Jean Negulesco

Color of Green
Kaufman, L.

Love, Hate, Love
A. SPELLING (US) 1971
dir. George McCowan

Color Out of Space, The
Lovecraft, H. P.

Die, Monster, Die!
AIP (US/GB) 1965 dir. Daniel Haller

Colossus
Jones, D. F.

Forbin Project, The
UN (US) 1970 dir. Joseph Sargent
GB title: Colossus, the Forbin Project

Colours of the Day, The
Gary, R.

Man Who Understood Women
FOX (US) 1959 dir. Nunnally Johnson

Columba
Merimée, P.

Vendetta
RKO (US) 1950 dir. Mel Ferrer

Comanche
Appel, D.

Tonka
DISNEY (US) 1958 dir. Lewis R. Foster

Combat
Praag, V. V.

Men in War
UA (US) 1957 dir. Anthony Mann

Come Be My Love
Carson, R.

Once More My Darling
UI (US) 1949 dir. Robert Montgomery

Come Out of the Kitchen
Miller, A. D. and Thomas, A. E.

Honey
PAR (US) 1930 dir. Wesley Ruggles

Come Out of the Kitchen
Thomas, A. E. and Miller, A. D.

Spring in Park Lane
BL (GB) 1948 dir. Herbert Wilcox

Come Prima Meglio di Prima
Pirandello, L.

Never Say Goodbye
UN (US) 1955 dir. Jerry Hopper

Come Prima Meglio di Prima
Pirandello, L.

This Love of Ours
UI (US) 1945 dir. William Deiterle

Come to Mother
Sale, D.

Live Again, Die Again
UN TV (US) 1974 dir. Richard Colla

Comedy of Errors, The
Shakespeare, W.

Boys from Syracuse, The
UN (US) 1940 dir. E. A. Sutherland

Commander Crabb
Pugh, M.

Silent Enemy, The
ROMULUS (GB) 1958
dir. William Fairchild

Commandos, The
Arnold, E.

First Comes Courage
COL (US) 1943 dir. Dorothy Arzner

Comment faire l'amour avec un nègre sans se fatiguer
Laferrière, D.

How to Make Love to a Negro Without Getting Tired
ANGELIKA (Fr) 1990
dir. Jacques Benoit

Commissioner, The
Dougherty, R.

Madigan
UI (US) 1968 dir. Don Siegel

Companions of Jehu, The
Dumas, A.

Fighting Guardsman, The
COL (US) 1945 dir. Henry Levin

Company of Cowards, The
Chamberlain, W.

Advance to the Rear
MGM (US) 1964 dir. George Marshall

Company, The
Ehrlichman, J.

Washington: Behind Closed Doors
PAR (US) 1977 dir. Gary Nelson

Complete State of Death, A
Gardner, J.

Stone Killer, The
COL (US) 1973 dir. Michael Winner

Comrade Jacob
Caute, D.

Winstanley
OTHER (GB) 1977
dir. Kevin Brownlow/Andrew Mollo

Concealment
Ide, L.

Secret Bride, The
WAR (US) 1935 dir. William Dieterle
GB title: Concealment

Condemned, The
Pagano, J.

Try and Get Me
UA (US) 1951 dir. Cyril Endfield
GB title: Sound of Fury, The

Condemned to Devil's Island
Niles, B.

Condemned
UA (US) 1929 dir. Wesley Ruggles

Confession Anonyme La
Lilar, S.

Benvenuta
NI (Bel/Fr) 1982 dir. André Delvaux

Confessions of a Night Nurse
Dixon, R.

Rosie Dixon-Night Nurse
COL (GB) 1978 dir. Justin Cartwright

Conjure Wife
Leiber, F.

Night of the Eagle
IA (GB) 1961 dir. Sidney Hayers
US title: Burn, Witch, Burn

Connecticut Yankee at the Court of King Arthur, A
Twain, M.

Connecticut Yankee, A.
FOX (US) 1931 dir. David Butler

Connecticut Yankee at the Court of King Arthur, A
Twain, M.

Connecticut Yankee in King Arthur's Court, A
PAR (US) 1948 dir. Tay Garnett
GB title: Yankee in King Arthur's Court, A
CONSOL (US) 1989 dir. Mel Damski

Connecticut Yankee in the Court of King Arthur, A
Twain, M.
Spaceman and King Arthur, The
DISNEY (GB) 1979 dir. Russ Mayberry
US title: Unidentified Flying Oddball

Context, The
Sciascia, L.
Illustrious Corpses
PEA/LAA (It) 1976 dir. Francesco Rosi

Convict has Escaped, A
Budd, J.
They Made Me A Fugitive
WAR (GB) 1947 dir. Alberto Cavalcanti
US title: I Became a Criminal

Cook, The
Kressing, H.
Something for Everyone
NAT GEN (US) 1970 dir. Harold Prince
GB title: Black Flowers for the Bride

Cops are Robbers, The
Clemente, G. W. and Stevens, K.
Good Cops, Bad Cops
KUSHNER-LOCKE (US) 1990
dir. Paul Wendkos

Copulating Mermaid of Venice; Trouble with the Battery
Bukowski, C.
Cold Moon
GAU (Fr) 1991 dir. Luc Besson, André Martinez
French title: Lune Froide

Counsel's Opinion
Wakefield, G.'
Divorce of Lady X, The
LONDON (GB) 1938 dir. Tim Whelan

Count a Lonely Cadence
Weaver, G.
Cadence
New Line (US) 1990 dir. Martin Sheen

Country of the Heart, The
Wersba, B.
Matters of the Heart
MCA TV (US) 1990 dir. Michael Rhodes

Coup de Grâce
Kessel, J.
Sirocco
COL (US) 1951 dir. Curtis Bernhardt

Court Circular
Stokes, S.
I Believe in You
EAL (GB) 1952 dir. Basil Dearden

Cradle Snatchers
Mitchell, N. and Medcraft, R.
Let's Face It
PAR (US) 1943 dir. Sidney Lanfield

Craig's Wife
Kelly, G.
Harriet Craig
COL (US) 1950 dir. Vincent Sherman

Cri, Un
Loriot, N.
No Time for Breakfast
BOURLA (Fr) 1980
dir. Jean-Louis Bertucelli

Crime of Sylvester Bonnard, The
France, A.
Chasing Yesterday
RKO (US) 1935 dir. George Nicholls, Jr.

Crossfire: The Plot that killed Kennedy
Marrs, J.
JFK
WAR (US) 1991 dir. Oliver Stone

Crowned Heads
Tryon, T.
Fedora
MAINLINE (Ger/Fr) 1978
dir. Billy Wilder

Crows of Edwina Hill, The
Bosworth, A. R.
Nobody's Perfect
UN (US) 1978 dir. Alan Rafkin

Crowthers of Bankdam, The
Armstrong, T.
Master of Bankdam
ALL (GB) 1947 dir. Walter Forde

Crucible, The
Miller, A.
Witches of Salem, The
FDF (Fr/Ger) 1957
dir. Raymond Rouleau

Crusaders
Sherwin, D. and Howlett, J.
If . . .
PAR (GB) 1968 dir. Lindsay Anderson

Cry Tough
Shulman, I.
Ring, The
UA (US) 1952 dir. Kurt Neumann

Cuckoo in the Nest, A
Travers, B.
Fast and Loose
GFD (GB) 1954 dir. Gordon Parry

Cup and the Sword, The
Hobart, A. T.
This Earth is Mine
UI (US) 1959 dir. Henry King

Cupid Rides Phillion
Cartland, B.
Lady and the Highwayman, The
GRADE (GB) 1989 dir. John Hough

Curse of Capistrano, The
McCulley, J.
Mark of the Renegade
UI (US) 1951 dir. Hugo Fregonese
FOX (US) 1974 dir. Don McDougall

Curse of Capistrano, The
McCulley, J.
Mark of Zorro, The
FOX (US) 1940 dir. Rouben Mamoulian

Custard Boys, The
Rae, J.
Reach for Glory
GALA (GB) 1962 dir. Philip Leacock

Cyborg
Caidin, M.
Six Million Dollar Man, The
UN TV (US) 1973 dir. Richard Irving

Cycle of the Werewolf
King, S.
Silver Bullet
PAR (US) 1985 dir. Daniel Attias

Cyrano de Bergerac
Rostand, E.
Roxanne
COL (US) 1987 dir. Fred Schepisi

Czarina, The
Lengyel, M.
Catherine the Great
KORDA (GB) 1934 dir. Paul Czinner

D. A. Draws a Circle, The
Gardner, E. S.

They Call it Murder
FOX (US) 1971 dir. Walter Grauman

Daddy and I
Jordan, E. G.

Make Way for a Lady
RKO (US) 1936 dir. David Burton

Daffodil Mystery, The
Wallace, E.

Devil's Daffodil, The
BL (GB) 1962 dir. Akos Rathony

Dame aux Camélias, La
Dumas, A. fils

Camille
MGM (US) 1936 dir. George Cukor
ROSEMONT (US/GB) 1984
dir. Desmond Davis

Dancing Princess, The; Cobbler & the Elves, The; Singing Bone, The
Grimm, J. L. K. and Grimm, W. K.

Wonderful World of the Brothers Grimm, The
MGM (US) 1962 dir. Henry Levin and George Pal

Dancing White Horses of Vienna, The
Podhajsky, A.

Miracle of the White Stallions, The
DISNEY (US) 1963 dir. Arthur Hiller
GB title: Flight of the White Stallions, The

Danger Adrift
Quilici, F.

Only One Survived
CBS ENT (US) 1990 dir. Folco Quilici

Danton Affair, The
Przybyszewska, S.

Danton
GAU/TFI (Fr/Pol) 1982
dir. Andrzej Wajda

Dark Angel
Kaus, G.

Her Sister's Secret
PRC (US) 1946 dir. Edgar G. Ulmer

Dark Days and Light Nights
Ali, J.

Black Joy
WINCAST/WEST ONE (GB) 1977
dir. Anthony Simmons

Dark Fantastic
Echard, M.

Lightning Strikes Twice
WAR (US) 1951 dir. King Vidor

Dark of the Sun
Smith, W.

Mercenaries, The
MGM (GB) 1968 dir. Jack Cardiff
US title: Dark of the Sun

Dark Side of Love, The
Saul, O.

My Kidnapper, My Love
EMI (US) 1980 dir. Sam Wanamaker

Dark Star
Moon, L.
Min and Bill
MGM (US) 1930 dir. George Hill

Dark Tower, The
Kaufman, G. S., and Woollcott, A.
Man With Two Faces, The
WAR (US) 1934 dir. Archie Mayo

Darkest Hour
McGivern, W. P.
Hell on Frisco Bay
WAR (US) 1955 dir. Frank Tuttle

Darkness I Leave You
Hooke, N. W.
Gypsy and the Gentleman, The
RANK (GB) 1957 dir. Joseph Losey

Darling Buds of May, The
Bates, H. E.
Mating Game, The
MGM (US) 1959 dir. George Marshall

Das Feuerschiff
Lenz, S.
Lightship, The
WAR (US) 1985 dir. Jerzy Skolimowski

Daughter of Fu Manchu
Rohmer, S.
Daughter of the Dragon
PAR (US) 1931 dir. Lloyd Corrigan

David Golder
Nemirowsky, I.
My Daughter Joy
BL (GB) 1950 dir. Gregory Ratoff
US title: Operation X

Dawn
Berkeley, R.
Nurse Edith Cavell
RKO (US) 1939 dir. Herbert Wilcox

Dawn of Reckoning
Hilton, J.
Rage in Heaven
MGM (US) 1941 dir. W. S. Van Dyke II

Day is Ours, This
Lewis, H.
Mandy
GFD (GB) 1952
dir. Alexander Mackendrick
US title: Crash of Silence, The

Day of Atonement
Raphaelson, S.
Jazz Singer, The
WAR (US) 1953 dir. Michael Curtiz
EMI (US) 1980 dir. Richard Fleischer

Day of the Arrow
Loraine, P.
Eye of the Devil
MGM (GB) 1967 dir. J. Lee Thompson

Day One: Before Hiroshima and After
Wyden, P.
Day One
A. SPELLING (US) 1989
dir. Joseph Sargent

Day the Century Ended, The
Gwaltney, F. I.
Between Heaven and Hell
FOX (US) 1956 dir. Richard Fleischer

Day the World Ended, The
Thomas, G. and Witts, M. M.
When Time Ran Out
WAR (US) 1980 dir. James Goldstone

Days of Dawn
Sender, R. J.
Valentina
OFELIA (Sp) 1983
dir. Antonio José Betancor

Dead Air
Lupica, M.
Money, Power, Murder
CBS ENT (US) 1989 dir. Lee Philips

Dead Don't Care, The
Latimer, J.
Last Warning, The
UN (US) 1938 dir. Albert S. Rogell

Dead Pigeon
Kantor, L.
Tight Spot
COL (US) 1955 dir. Phil Karlson

Deadfall
Laumer, K.
Peeper
FOX (US) 1975 dir. Peter Hyams

Deadlier than the Male
Gunn, J. E.
Born to Kill
RKO (US) 1947 dir. Robert Wise
GB title: Lady of Deceit

Deadlock
Sands, L.
Another Man's Poison
EROS (GB) 1951 dir. Irving Rapper

Deadly Angels, The
McCarry, C.
Wrong is Right
COL (US) 1982 dir. Richard Brooks
GB title: Man with the Deadly Lens, The

Deadly Blessing
Salerno, S.
Bed of Lies
WOLPER TV(US) 1992
dir. William A. Graham

Deadly Force: The Story of How a Badge Can Become a License to Kill
O'Donnell, Jr., L.
Case of Deadly Force, A
TELECOM (US) 1986
dir. Michael Miller

Death and the Sky Above
Garve, A.
Two-Letter Alibi
BL (GB) 1962 dir. Robert Lynn

Death Bite
Maryk, M. and Monahan, B.
Spasms
PDC (Can) 1984 dir. William Fruet

Death has Deep Roots
Gilbert, M.
Guilty?
GN (GB) 1956 dir. Edmund Greville

Death in a Top Hat
Rawson, C.
Miracles for Sale
MGM (US) 1939 dir. Tod Browning

Death in Captivity
Gilbert, M.
Danger Within
BL (GB) 1958 dir. Don Chaffey
US title: Breakout

Death in Rome
Katz, R.
Massacre in Rome
GN (Fr/It) 1973
dir. George Pan Cosmatos

Death in the Deep South
Greene, W.
They Won't Forget
WAR (US) 1937 dir. Mervyn Le Roy

Death in the Family, A
Agee, J.

All the Way Home
PAR (US) 1963 dir. Alex Segal
PAR (US) 1971 dir. Fred Coe

Death of a Common Man
Holdridge, D.

End of the River, The
GFD (GB) 1947 dir. Derek Twist

Death of a Playmate
Carpenter, T.

Star 80
WAR (US) 1983 dir. Bob Fosse

Death of a Snout
Warner, D.

Informers, The
RANK (GB) 1963 dir. Ken Annakin
US title: Underworld Informers

Death of Grass
Christopher, J.

No Blade of Grass
MGM (GB) 1970 dir. Cornel Wilde

Death Watch
White, R.

Savages
SPEL-GOLD (US) 1974 dir. Lee Katzin

Decameron, The
Boccaccio, G.

Decameron Nights
EROS (GB) 1952 dir. Hugo Fregonese

Decline and Fall
Waugh, E.

Decline and Fall . . . of a Birdwatcher
FOX (GB) 1968 dir. John Karsh

Deep are the Roots
D'Usseau, A. and Gow, J.

Tomorrow the World
UA (US) 1944 dir. Leslie Fenton

Del Palma
Kellino, P.

Lady Possessed
REP (US) 1952 dir. William Spier, Roy Kellino

Der Letste Sommer
Huch, R.

Guardian Angel, The
SANDREW (Swe) 1990
dir. Suzanne Osten

Desert Guns
Frazee, S.

Gold of the Seven Saints
WAR (US) 1961 dir. Gordon Douglas

Desert of the Heart
Rule, J.

Desert Hearts
MGM (US) 1986 dir. Donna Deitch

Desert Town
Stewart, R.

Desert Fury
PAR (US) 1947 dir. Lewis Allen

Desert Voices
Perkins, K.

Desert Pursuit
ABP (US) 1952 dir. George Blair

Desperados: Latin Drug Lords, US Lawmen and the War America Can't win
Shannon, E.

Drug Wars: The Camarena Story
ZZY INC. (US) 1990 dir. Brian Gibson

Destroyer, The
Murphy, W. and Sapir, R.

Remo Williams: The Adventure Begins
ORION (US) 1985 dir. Guy Hamilton

Destry Rides Again
Brand, M.
Destry
UI (US) 1954 dir. George Marshall

Deux Frères
Dumas, A.
Corsican Brothers, The
UA (US) 1942 dir. Gregory Ratoff
ROSEMONT (US) 1985 dir. Ian Sharp

Devil and Daniel Webster, The
Benet, S.V.
All that Money can Buy
RKO (US) 1941 dir. William Dieterle

Devil in Vienna, The
Orgel, D.
Friendship in Vienna, A
DISNEY CH (US) 1988
dir. Arthur Allan Seidelman

Devilday-Madhouse
Hall, A.
Madhouse
EMI (GB) 1974 dir. Jim Clark

Devil's Hornpipe, The
Mamoulian, R., and Anderson, M.
Never Steal Anything Small
UN (US) 1958 dir. Charles Lederer

Devils of Loudon, The
Huxley, A.
Devils, The
WAR (GB) 1971 dir. Ken Russell

Devil's Own, The
Curtis, P.
Witches, The
HAMMER (GB) 1966 dir. Cyril Frankel

Devil's Triangle
Soutar, A.
Almost Married
FOX (US) 1932
dir. W. Cameron Menzies

Diamond Lil
West, M.
She Done Him Wrong
PAR (US) 1933 dir. Lowell Sherman

Diamonds are Danger
Walker, D. E.
Man Could Get Killed, A
UN (US) 1966 dir. Ronald Neame

Diaries of Hannah Senesh, The
Senesh, H.
Hanna's War
CANNON (US) 1988
dir. Menahem Golan

Dice of God, The
Birney, H.
Glory Guys
UA (US) 1965 dir. Arnold Laven

Die Bruder Grimm
Gerstner, H.
Wonderful World of the Brothers Grimm, The
MGM (US) 1962 dir. Henry Levin,
George Pal

Dildo Cay
Hayes, N.
Bahama Passage
PAR (US) 1941 dir. Edward H. Griffith

Dishonoured
Albrand, M.
Captain Carey USA
PAR (US) 1950 dir. Mitchell Leisen
GB title: After Midnight

Disorientated Man, The
Saxon, P.
Scream and Scream Again
AIP (GB) 1969 dir. Gordon Hessler

Divina Commedia, La
Dante Alighieri
TV Dante, A
CHANNEL 4 (GB) 1990
dir. Tom Phillips

Do Androids Dream of Electric Sheep?
Dick, P. K.
Blade Runner
WAR (US) 1982 dir. Ridley Scott

Doctor Wears Three Faces, The
Bard, M.
Mother Didn't Tell Me
FOX (US) 1950 dir. Claude Binyon

Doctor's Son, The
O'Hara, J.
Turning Point of Jim Malloy, The
COL TV (US) 1975 dir. Frank D. Gilroy

Doctors Wear Scarlet
Raven, S.
Incense for the Damned
GN (GB) 1970
dir. Robert Hartford-Davis

Dog Soldiers
Stone, R.
Who'll Stop the Rain?
UA (US) 1978 dir. Karel Reisz
GB title: Dog Soldiers

Dombey and Son
Dickens, C.
Rich Man's Folly
PAR (US) 1931 dir. John Cromwell

Don Among the Dead Men
Vulliamy, C. E.
Jolly Bad Fellow, A
BL (GB) 1964 dir. Robert Hamer

Don Camillo and the Prodigal Son
Guareschi, G.
Return of Don Camillo, The
MIRACLE (Fr/It) 1953
dir. Julien Duvivier

Don Careless
Beach, R. E.
Avengers, The
REP (US) 1950 dir. John Auer

Don Desperado
Foreman, L. L.
Savage, The
PAR (US) 1952 dir. George Marshall

Don Quixote
Cervantes, M. de
Man of La Mancha
UA (US) 1972 dir. Arthur Hiller

Donna D'Onore
Modignani, S. C.
Vendetta: Secrets of a Mafia Bride
TRIBUNE (US) 1991
dir. Stuart Margolin

Donovan's Brain
Siodmak, C.
Lady and the Monster, The
REP (US) 1944 dir. George Sherman
GB title: Lady and the Doctor, The

Donovan's Brain
Siodmak, C.
Vengeance
BL (GB/Ger) 1962 dir. Freddie Francis

Don't Ask Me If I Love
Kollek, A.
Worlds Apart
SCANLON (Israel) 1980
dir. Barbara Noble

Don't Look and it Won't Hurt
Peck, R.
Gas, Food and Lodging
IRS (US) 1992 dir. Allison Anders

Doorbell Rang, The
Stout, R.
Nero Wolfe
PAR TV (US) 1979 dir. Frank D. Gilroy

Double Error
Thompson, J. L.
Murder Without Crime
ABP (GB) 1950 dir. J. Lee-Thompson

Double Take, The
Huggins, R.
I Love Trouble'
COL (US) 1948 dir. S. Sylvan Simon

Dover Road, The
Milne, A. A.
Where Sinners Meet
RKO (US) 1934 dir. J. Walter Ruben

Down There
Goodis, D.
Shoot the Piano Player
PLEIADE (Fr) 1960
dir. François Truffaut

Downhill Racers
Hall, O.
Downhill Racer
PAR (US) 1969 dir. Michael Ritchie

Dr. Jekyll and Mr. Hyde
Stevenson, R. L.
Jekyll & Hyde
KING PHOENIX (US/GB) 1990
dir. David Wickes

Dr. Jekyll and Mr. Hyde
Stevenson, R. L.
Two Faces of Dr. Jekyll, The
HAMMER (GB) 1960
dir. Terence Fisher
US title: House of Fright

Dr. Praetorius
Goetz, C.
People Will Talk
FOX (US) 1951
dir. Joseph L. Mankiewicz

Dracula's Guest
Stoker, B.
Dracula's Daughter
UN (US) 1936 dir. Lambert Hillyer

Dreadful Summit
Ellin, S.
Big Night, The
UA (US) 1951 dir. Joseph Losey

Dream Like Mine, A
Kelly, M. T.
Clearcut
TELEFILM (Can) 1991
dir. Richard Bugajski

Dream Monger, The
Miller, G. H.
Starlight Hotel
REP (NZ) 1988 dir. Sam Pillsbury

Dream of the Mad Monkey, The
Frank, C.
Twisted Obsession
IVE (US) 1990 dir. Fernando Trueba

Dreamland
Kelland, C. B.
Strike Me Pink
UA (US) 1936 dir. Norman Taurog

Du Côté de chez Swann
Proust, M.
Swann in Love
GAU (Fr) 1984 dir. Volker Schlondorff

Dumbo, the Flying Elephant
Aberson, H. and Pearl, H.
Dumbo
DISNEY (US) 1941 dir. Ben Sharpsteen

Dunbar's Cove
Deal, B.
Wild River
FOX (US) 1960 dir. Elia Kazan

Durian Tree, The
Keon, M.
7th Dawn, The
UA (GB) 1964 dir. Lewis Gilbert

E

East Lynne
Wood, Mrs H.
Ex-Flame
Tiffany (US) 1930 dir. Victor Halperin

Easter Dinner, The
Downes, D.
Pigeon That Took Rome, The
PAR (US) 1962 dir. Melville Shavelson

Easy and Hard Ways Out
Grossbach, R.
Best Defense
PAR (US) 1984 dir. Willard Huyck

L'Eau des Collines
Pagnol, M.
Manon of the Spring
ORION (Fr) 1987 dir. Claude Berri
French title: Manon des Sources

Ebano
Vasquez-Figueroa, A.
Ashanti
COL (Switz) 1979 dir. Richard Fleischer

Ebb Tide
Stevenson, R. L.
Adventure Island
PAR (US) 1947 dir. Peter Stewart

Echo in the Valley
Ke Lan
Yellow Earth
GUANGXI (China) 1985 dir. Chen Kaige

Echos of Celandine
Marlowe, D.
Disappearance, The
CINEGATE (GB/Can) 1977
dir. Stuart Cooper

Eddie Chapman Story, The
Owen, F.
Triple Cross
AA (GB) 1967 dir. Terence Young

Edge of Running Water, The
Sloane, W.
Devil Commands, The
COL (US) 1941 dir. Edward Dmytryk

Education for Death
Ziemer, G.

Hitler's Children
RKO (US) 1943 dir. Edward Dmytryk

Edward VII and his Times
Maurois, A.

Entente Cordiale
FLORA (Fr) 1939 dir. Marcel l'Herbier

Eff Off
Hutson, S.

Class of Miss MacMichael, The
GALA (GB) 1978 dir. Silvio Narizzano

Eh?
Livings, H.

Work is a Four Letter Word
UI (GB) 1968 dir. Peter Hall

Eight O'Clock in the Morning
Nelson, R.

They Live
UN (US) 1988 dir. John Carpenter

Eine Liebe in Deutschland
Hochhuth, R.

Love in Germany, A
TRIUMPH (Ger) 1984
dir. Andrzej Wajda

Eleanor and Franklin
Lash, J. P.

Eleanor and Franklin: The White House Years
TALENT (US) 1977 dir. Daniel Petrie

Elemental, The; Gate Crasher, The; Act of Kindness, An; Door, The
Chetwynd-Hayes, R.

From Beyond the Grave
EMI (GB) 1973 dir. Kevin Connor

Elephant is White, The
Brahms, C. and Simon, S. J.

Give Us the Moon
GFD (GB) 1944 dir. Val Guest

Elephant Man and Other Reminiscences, The
Treves, Sir F.

Elephant Man, The
PAR (GB) 1980 dir. David Lynch

Eliminator, The
York, A.

Danger Route
UA (GB) 1967 dir. Seth Holt

Elizabeth the Queen
Anderson, M.

Private Lives of Elizabeth and Essex, The
WAR (US) 1939 dir. Michael Curtiz

Emerald Illusion, The
Bass, R.

Code Name: Emerald
MGM/UA (US) 1985
dir. Jonathan Sanger

Emma and I
Hocken, S.

Second Sight: A Love Story
TTC (US) 1984 dir. John Korty

Emperor's Snuffbox, The
Carr, J. D.

That Woman Opposite
MON (GB) 1957 dir. Compton Bennett

Emporia
Sanford, H. and Lamb, M.

Waco
PAR (US) 1966 dir. R. G. Springsteen

Empty Copper Sea, The
MacDonald, J. D.

Travis McGee
HAJENO (US) 1983
dir. Andrew V. McLaglen

End as a Man
Willingham, C.

Strange One, The
COL (US) 1957 dir. Jack Garfein
GB title: End as a Man

End of Tragedy, The
Ingalls, R.

Dead on the Money
INDIEPROD (US) 1991
dir. Mark Cullingham

Enemy of the People, An
Ibsen, H.

Ganashatru
ELECTRIC (Ind) 1989 dir. Satyajit Ray

L'Ennemie
Antoine, W. P.

Tendre Ennemie
WORLD (Fr) 1938 dir. Max Ophuls

Enter, Sir John
Dane, C. and Simpson, H.

Murder
BI (GB) 1930 dir. Alfred Hitchcock

Episode of Sparrows, An
Godden, R.

Innocent Sinners
RANK (US) 1957 dir. Philip Leacock

Epitaph for a Spy
Ambler, E.

Hotel Reserve
RKO (GB) 1944 dir. Victor Hanbury

Epitaph for an Enemy
Barr, G.

Up From the Beach
FOX (US) 1965 dir. Robert Parrish

L'Equippage
Kessel, J.

Woman I Love, The
RKO (US) 1937 dir. Anatole Litvak
GB title: Woman Between, The

Erasmus with Freckles
Haase, J.

Dear Brigitte
FOX (US) 1965 dir. Henry Koster

Erections, Ejaculations, Exhibitions and Tales of Ordinary Madness
Bukowski, C.

Tales of Ordinary Madness
(It/Fr) 1981 dir. Marco Ferri

Ernest Hemingway: A Life Story
Baker, C.

Hemingway
WILSON (US) 1988
dir. Bernhard Sinkel

Error of Judgment: The Birmingham Bombings
Mullin, C.

Investigation, The: Inside a Terrorist Bombing
GRANADA (US/GB) 1990
dir. Mike Beckham

Escape
MacDonald, P.

Nightmare
UN (US) 1942 dir. Tim Whelan

Escort
Rayner, D. A.

Enemy Below, The
FOX (US) 1957 dir. Dick Powell

Esther, Ruth and Jennifer
Davies, J.

North Sea Hijack
CIC (GB) 1980 dir. Andrew V. McLaglen
US title: Ffolkes

Eternal Husband, The
Dostoevski, F.

L'Homme au Chapeau Rond
ALCINA (Fr) 1946 dir. Pierre Billon

847

Eunuch of Stamboul, The
Wheatley, D.

Secret of Stamboul, The
HOB (GB) 1936 dir. Andrew Marton

Eva Peron
Fraser, N.

Evita Peron
ZEPHYR (US) 1991
dir. Marvin Chomsky

Event One Thousand
Lavallee, D.

Gray Lady Down
UN (US) 1978 dir. David Greene

Events whilst Guarding the Bofors Gun
McGrath, J.

Bofors Gun, The
RANK (GB) 1968 dir. Jack Gold

Everlasting Secret Family and Other Secrets, The
Moorhouse, F.

Everlasting Secret Family, The
FGH (Aus) 1989 dir. Michael Thornhill

Every Secret Thing
Hearst, P.

Patty Hearst
ATLANTIC (US) 1988
dir. Paul Schrader

Everybody Comes to Rick's
Burnett, M. and Alison, J.

Casablanca
WAR (US) 1943 dir. Michael Curtiz

Evidence of Love
Bloom, J. and Atkinson, J.

Killing in a Small Town
INDIEPROD (US) 1990
dir. Stephen Gyllenhaal

Evil Angels
Bryson, J.

Cry in the Dark, A
CANNON (US) 1988 dir. Fred Schepisi

Evil Come, Evil Go
Masterson, W.

Yellow Canary, The
FOX (US) 1963 dir. Buzz Kulik

Evil of the Day, The
Sterling, T.

Honey Pot, The
UA (US) 1966 dir. Joseph L. Mankiewicz

Evita: First Lady
Barnes, J.

Evita Peron
ZEPHYR (US) 1991
dir. Marvin Chomsky

Execution of Charles Horman, The
Hauser, T.

Missing
UN (US) 1982 dir. Costa-Gavras

Executioners, The
MacDonald, J. D.

Cape Fear
UI (US) 1962 dir. J. Lee Thompson
UN (US) 1991 dir. Martin Scorsese

Exile, An
Jones, M.

I Walk the Line
COL (US) 1970
dir. John Frankenheimer

Exploits of Brigadier Gerard, The
Doyle, Sir A. C.

Adventures of Gerard, The
UA (GB) 1970 dir. Jerzy Skolimowski

Expressway
Trevor, E.
Smash-up on Interstate 5
FILMWAYS (US) 1976
dir. John Llewellyn Moxey

Ex-Wife
Parrott, U.
Divorcee, The
MGM (US) 1930 dir. Robert Z. Leonard

Eye of the Beholder
Epstein, S.
Comeback, The
CBS ENT (US) 1989
dir. Jerrold Freedman

Eye-witness
Hebden, M.
Eyewitness
MGM (GB) 1970 dir. John Hough
US title: Sudden Terror

F.O.B. Detroit
Smitter, W.
Reaching for the Sun
PAR (US) 1941 dir. William Wellman

Fabricator, The
Hodges, H.
Why Would I Lie?
UA (US) 1980 dir. Larry Peerce

Fabulous Ann Medlock
Shannon, R.
Adventures of Captain Fabian, The
REP (US) 1951 dir. William Marshall

Facts of Life, The; Alien Corn, The; Kite, The; Colonel's Lady, The
Maugham, W. S.
Quartet
GFD (GB) 1948
dir. Ralph Smart/Harold French/
Arthur Crabtree/Ken Annakin

Failure
Haviland-Taylor, K.
Man to Remember, A
RKO (US) 1938 dir. Garson Kanin

Fair Game
Gosling, P.
Cobra
WAR (US) 1986 dir. G. P. Cosmatos

Falcon's Malteser, The
Horowitz, A.
Diamond's Edge
KINGS (US) 1990 dir. Stephen Bayly

Falcon's Malteser, The
Horowitz, A.
Just Ask for Diamond
FOX (GB) 1988 dir. Stephen Bayly

Fall of the House of Usher, The
Poe, E. A.

House of Usher, The
AIP (US) 1960 dir. Roger Corman
GB title: Fall of the House of Usher, The
21st CENTURY (US) 1988
dir. Alan Birkinshaw

Falling Angel
Hjortsberg, W.

Angel Heart
TRI-STAR (US) 1987 dir. Alan Parker

False Note, The
Tolstoy, L.

L'Argent
EOS (Switz/Fr) 1983
dir. Robert Bresson

Famous
Benet, S. V.

Just for You
PAR (US) 1952 dir. Elliot Nugent

Faraday's Flowers
Kenrick, T.

Shanghai Surprise
MGM (US) 1986 dir. Jim Goddard

Farewell, My Lovely
Chandler, R.

Murder, My Sweet
RKO (US) 1944 dir. Edward Dmytryk

Farewell to Women
Collison, W.

Mogambo
MGM (US) 1953 dir. John Ford

Farewell to Women
Collison, W.

Red Dust
MGM (US) 1932 dir. Victor Fleming

Fatal Woman
Quentin, P.

Black Widow
FOX (US) 1954 dir. Nunnally Johnson

Father Brown, Detective
Chesterton, G. K.

Sanctuary of Fear
M. ARCH (US) 1979
dir. John Llewellyn Moxey

Father Knickerbocker's History of New York
Irving, W.

Knickerbocker Holiday
UN (US) 1944 dir. Harry Joe Brown

Father Sky
Freeman, D.

Taps
FOX (US) 1981 dir. Harold Becker

Father was a Handful
Williams, Mrs. R.

Vanishing Virginian, The
MGM (US) 1941 dir. Frank Borzage

Father's Arcane Daughter
Konigsburg, E. L.

Caroline?
B&E (US) 1990 dir. Joseph Sargent

FDR's Last Year
Bishop, J.

FDR— The Last Year
TITUS PRODS (US) 1980
dir. Anthony Page

Fear in a Handful of Dust
Garfield, B.

Fleshburn
CROWN (US) 1984 dir. George Gage

Feathered Serpent
Wallace, E.

Menace, The
COL (US) 1932 dir. Roy William Neill

February Hill
Lincoln, V.
Primrose Path, The
RKO (US) 1940 dir. Gregory LaCava

Fellowship of the Frog, The
Wallace, E.
Frog, The
WILCOX (GB) 1937 dir. Jack Raymond

Fellowship of the Ring: Two Towers, The
Tolkien, J. R. R.
Lord of the Rings
UA (US) 1978 dir. Ralph Bakshi

Femme et le Pantin, La
Louys, P.
Devil is a Woman, The
PAR (US) 1935 dir. Josef von Sternberg

Femme et le Pantin, Le
Louys, P.
That Obscure Object of Desire
GALAXIE (Fr/Sp) 1978 dir. Luis Bunuel

Fengriffen
Case, D.
And Now the Screaming Starts
AMICUS (GB) 1973
dir. Roy Ward Baker

Fer de Lance
Stout, R.
Meet Nero Wolfe
COL (US) 1936 dir. Herbert Biberman

Les fiancailles de M. Hire
Simenon, G.
Monsieur Hire
ORION (Fr) 1989 dir. Patrice Leconte

Fiddler's Green
Gann, E. K.
Raging Tide, The
UI (US) 1951 dir. George Sherman

Fifty Minute Hour, The
Lindner, R.
Pressure Point
UA (US) 1962 dir. Hubert Cornfield

52 Pick-Up
Leonard, E.
Ambassador, The
CANNON (US) 1984
dir. J. Lee Thompson

58 Minutes
Wager, W.
Die Hard 2
FOX (US) 1990 dir. Renny Harlin

Film of Memory, The
Druon, M.
Matter of Time, A
AIP (US/It) 1976 dir. Vincente Minnelli

Final Diagnosis, The
Hailey, A.
Young Doctors, The
UA (US) 1961 dir. Phil Karlson

Final Night
Gaines, R.
Front Page Story
BL (GB) 1953 dir. Gordon Parry

Final Verdict
St. John, A. R.
Final Verdict, The
TURNER (US) 1991 dir. Jack Fisk

Final Warning: The Legacy of Chernobyl
Gale, R. P. and Hauser, T.
Chernobyl: The Final Warning
CAROLCO (US/USSR) 1991
dir. Anthony Page

Finding Maubee
Carr, A. H. Z.
Mighty Quinn, The
MGM (US) 1989 dir. Carl Schenkel

Finger Man, The
Shaffer, R. K.

Lady Killer
WAR (US) 1933 dir. Roy del Ruth

Fire Band
Mayer, E. J.

Affairs of Cellini, The
FOX (US) 1934 dir. Gregory La Cava

Fires of Youth
Collier, J. L.

Danny Jones
CINERAMA (GB) 1972
dir. Jules Bricken

First and the Last, The
Galsworthy, J.

Twenty-One Days
LF (GB) 1937 dir. Basil Dean

First Lady of the Seeing Eye
Frank, M. and Clark, B.

Love Leads the Way
DISNEY CH (US) 1984
dir. Delbert Mann

First Love
Taylor, S.

Promise at Dawn
AVCO (US/Fr) 1970 dir. Jules Dassin

First Love
Turgenev, I.

Summer Lightning
CHANNEL 4 (GB) 1986

First Rebel, The
Swanson, N. H.

Allegheny Uprising
RKO (US) 1939 dir. William A. Seiter
GB title: First Rebel, The

First Train to Babylon
Ehrlich, M.

Naked Edge, The
UA (GB) 1961 dir. Michael Anderson

First Wife, The
Allen, J. P.

Wives and Lovers
PAR (US) 1963 dir. John Rich

Fitzgeralds and the Kennedys, The
Goodwin, D. K.

Kennedys of Massachusetts, The
ORION TV (US) 1990
dir. Lamont Johnson

Five-Star Final
Weitzenkorn, L.

Two Against the World
WAR (US) 1936 dir. William McGann
GB title: Case of Mrs. Pembroke, The

Flaming Lance
Huffaker, C.

Flaming Star
FOX (US) 1960 dir. Don Siegel

Flotsam
Remarque, E. M.

So Ends our Night
UA (US) 1941 dir. John Cromwell

Flowers for Algernon
Keyes, D.

Charly
CINERAMA (US) 1968
dir. Ralph Nelson

Fly Away Home
Bennett D. and White, I.

Always in My Heart
WAR (US) 1942 dir. Joe Graham

Fly Away Home
Bennett, D.

Daughters Courageous
WAR (US) 1939 dir. Michael Curtiz

Flying Ebony
Vinton, I.
Mooncussers, The
DISNEY (US) 1971 dir. James Neilson

Flying Saucers from Outer Space
Keyhoe, D. E.
Earth v. The Flying Saucers
COL (US) 1956 dir. Fred F. Sears

Foghorn, The
Bradbury, R.
Beast From 20,000 Fathoms, The
WAR (US) 1953 dir. Eugene Lourie

Follow the Widower
Harris, A.
Heads or Tails
CASTLE HILL (Fr) 1983
dir. Robert Enrico

Fool's Gold
Hitchens, D. and Hitchens, B.
Bande à Part
ANOUCHKA/ORSAY (Fr) 1964
dir. Jean-Luc Godard

Fools Paradise
Grubb, D.
Fools Parade
COL (US) 1971
dir. Andrew V. McLaglen
GB title: Dynamite Man from Glory Jail

Footlights
Kelland, C. B.
Speak Easily
MGM (US) 1932 dir. Edward Sedgwick

For a Night of Love
Zola, E.
Manifesto
CANNON (Yugo) 1988
dir. Dusan Makajevev

For Her to See
Shearing, J.
So Evil My Love
PAR (GB) 1948 dir. Lewis Allen

For Love or Money
Herbert, F. H.
This Happy Feeling
UN (US) 1958 dir. Blake Edwards

For Our Vines Have Tender Grapes
Martin, G. V.
Our Vines Have Tender Grapes
MGM (US) 1945 dir. Roy Rowland

Forbidden Garden, The
Curtiss, U.
Whatever Happened to Aunt Alice?
PALOMAR (US) 1969 dir. Lee H. Katzin

Forbidden Love, A
Zeldis, C.
Torn Apart
CASTLE HILL (US) 1990
dir. Jack Fisher

Fortress in the Rice
Appel, B.
Cry of Battle
WAR (US) 1964 dir. Irving Lerner

Fortunes and Misfortunes of the Famous Moll Flanders, The
Defoe, D.
Amorous Adventures of Moll Flanders, The
PAR (GB) 1965 dir. Terence Young

Forty Whacks
Homes, G.
Crime by Night
WAR (US) 1944 dir. William Clemens

4.50 from Paddington
Christie, A.
Murder she Said
MGM (GB) 1961 dir. George Pollock

Four Feathers, The
Mason, A. E. W.
Storm over the Nile
GFD (GB) 1955 dir. Terence Young

Four Horse Players are Missing
Rose, A.
Who's Got the Action?
PAR (US) 1963 dir. Daniel Mann

Four Marys, The
Lea, F. H.
Manproof
MGM (US) 1937 dir. Richard Thorpe

Fourth Brother, The
Forbes, R.
China
PAR (US) 1943 dir. John Farrow

Fourth Side of the Triangle, The
Queen, E.
Ellery Queen: Too Many Suspects
UN TV (US) 1975 dir. David Greene

Fragile Fox
Brooks, N.
Attack
UA (US) 1956 dir. Robert Aldrich

Frankenstein
Shelley, Mrs M. W.
Curse of Frankenstein, The
WAR (GB) 1957 dir. Terence Fisher

Frankenstein
Shelley, Mrs M. W.
Frankenstein: The True Story
UN TV (US) 1973 dir. Jack Smight

Frankie and Johnny in the Clair de Lune
McNally, T.
Frankie and Johnny
PAR (US) 1991 dir. Garry Marshall

Free Fall
Reed, J. D.
Pursuit of D. B. Cooper, The
UN (US) 1981 dir. Roger Spottiswoode

Freedom Trap, The
Bagley, D.
Mackintosh Man, The
COL-WAR (GB) 1973 dir. John Huston

Friday the Rabbi Slept Late
Kemelman, H.
Lanigan's Rabbi
UN TV (US) 1976 dir. Lou Antonio

Fried Green Tomatoes at the Whistle Stop Cafe
Flagg, F.
Fried Green Tomatoes
UN (US) 1991 dir. Jon Avnet

Friend in Need, The
Coxhead, E.
Cry from the Streets, A.
EROS (GB) 1958 dir. Lewis Gilbert

Friend
Henstell, D.
Deadly Friend
WAR (US) 1986 dir. Wes Craven

Friese-Greene
Allister, R.
Magic Box, The
BL (GB) 1951 dir. John Boulting

Froknarna von Pahlen
von Krusenstjerna, A.

Loving Couples
SANDREW (Swe) 1964
dir. Mai Zetterling

From the Mixed-up Files of Mrs Basil E. Frankwester
Konigsburg, E. L.

Hideaways, The
UA (US) 1973 dir. Fielder Cook

From this Dark Stairway
Eberhart, M. G.

Murder of Dr. Harrigan
WAR (US) 1936 dir. Frank McDonald

Front Page, The
Hecht, B. and MacArthur, C.

His Girl Friday
COL (US) 1940 dir. Howard Hawks

Front Page, The
Hecht, B. and MacArthur, C.

Switching Channels
TRI-STAR (US) 1988 dir. Ted Kotcheff

Fruit Vert, Le
Gignoux, R.

Between Us Girls
UN (US) 1942 dir. Henry Koster

Fugue in Time, A
Godden, R.

Enchantment
RKO (US) 1948 dir. Irving Reis

Fulfillment, The
Spencer, L.

Fulfillment of Mary Gray, The
INDIAN NECK (US) 1989
dir. Piers Haggard

Furnished Room, The
Del Rivo, L.

West Eleven
WAR (GB) 1963 dir. Michael Winner

Gabriel Horn, The
Holt, F.

Kentuckian, The
UA (US) 1955 dir. Burt Lancaster

Gabriela, Clove and Cinnamon
Amado, J.

Gabriela
MGM/UA (Port) 1984
dir. Bruno Barreto

Game of X, The
Sheckley, R.

Condorman
DISNEY (US) 1981 dir. Charles Jarrot

Gamesmanship, Oneupmanship, Lifemanship
Potter, S.

School for Scoundrels
WAR (GB) 1960 dir. Robert Namer

Garden of Cucumbers, A
Tyler, P.

Fitzwilly
UA (US) 1967 dir. Delbert Mann
GB title: Fitzwilly Strikes Back

Garden of God, The
Stacpoole, H. D.

Return to the Blue Lagoon
COL (US) 1991 dir. William A. Graham

Gather Rosebuds
Nolan, J.

Isn't it Romantic?
PAR (US) 1948 dir. Norman Z. McLeod

Gaucho
Childs, H.

Way of a Gaucho
FOX (US) 1952 dir. Jacques Tourneur

Gaunt Women, The
Blackburn, W. J.

Destiny of a Spy
UN TV (US) 1969 dir. Boris Sagal

Gay Banditti, The
Wylie, I. A. R.

Young in Heart, The
SELZNICK (US) 1938
dir. Richard Wallace

Geisha
Dalby, L.

American Geisha
INTERSCOPE (US) 1986
dir. Lee Philips

Gemini
Innaurato, A.

Happy Birthday, Gemini
UA (US) 1980 dir. Richard Benner

General Goes Too Far, The
Strueby, K.

High Command, The
ABFD (GB) 1936 dir. Thorold Dickinson

General, The
Sillitoe, A.

Counterpoint
UI (US) 1968 dir. Ralph Nelson

Genius in the Family, A
Maxim, H. P.

So Goes my Love
UN (US) 1946 dir. Frank Ryan
GB title: Genius in the Family, A

Gentle Ben
Morley, W.

Gentle Giant, The
PAR (US) 1967 dir. James Neilson

Gentle People, The
Shaw, I.

Out of the Fog
WAR (US) 1941 dir. Anatole Litvak

Gentleman From Montana, The
Foster, L. R.

Mr. Smith Goes To Washington
COL (US) 1939 dir. Frank Capra

Gentlemen of the Jungle
Gill, T.

Tropic Zone
PAR (US) 1952 dir. Lewis R. Foster

Ghost of John Holling, The
Wallace, E.

Mystery Liner
MON (US) 1934 dir. William Nigh

Ghosts, The
Barber, A.

Amazing Mr Blunden, The
HEMDALE (GB) 1972
dir. Lionel Jeffries

Gidget Goes to New York
Kohner, F.

Gidget Grows Up
COL TV (US) 1969 dir. James Sheldon

Gift From the Boys, A
Buchwald, A.
Surprise Package
COL (GB) 1960 dir. Stanley Donen

**Gilbert and Sullivan and
Their World**
Baily, L.
Story of Gilbert and Sullivan, The
BL (GB) 1953 dir. Sidney Gilliatt

Gilded Rooster, The
Emery, R.
Savage Wilderness
COL (US) 1956 dir. Anthony Mann
GB title: The Last Frontier

Gilligan's Last Elephant
Hanley, G.
Last Safari, The
PAR (GB) 1967 dir. Henry Hathaway

Gingerbread Lady, The
Simon, N.
Only When I Laugh
COL (US) 1981 dir. Glenn Jordan
GB title: It Only Hurts When I Laugh

Gioconda Smile, The
Huxley, A. L.
Woman's Vengeance, A
UN (US) 1947 dir. Zoltan Korder

Girl Called Fathom, A
Forrester, L.
Fathom
FOX (GB) 1967 dir. Leslie Martinson

Girl Crazy
Bolton, G. and McGowan, J.
When the Boys Meet the Girls
MGM (US) 1965 dir. Alvin Ganzer

Girl from Trieste, The
Molnar, F.
Bride Wore Red, The
MGM (US) 1937 dir. Dorothy Arzner

**Girl in the Turquoise Bikini,
The**
Resnik, M.
How Sweet It Is
WAR (US) 1968 dir. Jerry Paris

Girl on a Wing
Glemser, B.
Come Fly with Me
MGM (US) 1963 dir. Henry Levin

Girl on the Via Flaminia, The
Hayes, A.
Act of Love
UA (US) 1954 dir. Anatole Litvak

Girlfriend
Percival, D.
Girl/Boy
HEMDALE (GB) 1971 dir. Bob Kellett

Give Sorrow Words
Holder, M.
Winter Tan, A
TELEFILM (Can) 1987 dir. Louise Clark

Glass Inferno, The
Stein, R. M., Scortia, T. N. and
Robinson, F. M.
Towering Inferno, The
COL-WAR (US) 1975
dir. John Gullermin, Irwin Allen

Glendower Legacy, The
Gifford, T.
Dirty Tricks
FILMPLAN (Can) 1980 dir. Alvin Rakoff

Gloire de Mon Père, La
Pagnol, M.
My Father's Glory
GAU (Fr) 1991 dir. Yves Robert

Glorious Days, The
Purcell, H.

Lilacs in The Spring
REP (GB) 1954 dir. Herbert Wilcox
US title: Let's Make Up

Glory for Me
Kantor, M.

Best Years of Our Lives, The
GOLDWYN (US) 1946
dir. William Wyler

Go to thy Deathbed
Forbes, S.

Reflection of Fear
COL (US) 1973 dir. William A. Fraker

God and My Country
Kantor, M.

Follow Me Boys!
DISNEY (US) 1966 dir. Norman Tokar

Godfather, The
Puzo, M.

Godfather Part II, The
PAR (US) 1974
dir. Francis Ford Coppola

Gogo no Eiko
Mishima, Y.

Sailor Who Fell From Grace With the Sea, The
FOX RANK (GB) 1976
dir. Lewis John Carlino

Gold Crew, The
Scortia, T. N. and Robinson, F. M.

Fifth Missile, The
MGM/UA TV (US) 1986
dir. Larry Peerce

Gold Diggers, The
Hopwood, A.

Gold Diggers of Broadway
WAR (US) 1939 dir. Roy del Ruth

Gold Mine
Smith, W.

Gold
HEMDALE (GB) 1974 dir. Peter Hunt

Golden Doors, The
Fenton, E.

Escapade in Florence
DISNEY (US) 1962 dir. Steve Previn

Golden Egg, The
Krabbe, T.

Vanishing, The
INGRID (Swe) 1990 dir. George Sluizer

Golden Evenings of Summer, The
Stanton, W.

Charley and the Angel
DISNEY (US) 1974
dir. Vincent McEveety

Golden Fleecing, The
Semple, L.

Honeymoon Machine, The
MGM (US) 1961 dir. Richard Thorpe

Golden Herd
Carroll, C.

San Antone
REP (US) 1952 dir. Joe Kane

Golden Tide, The
Roe, V.

Perilous Journey, A
REP (US) 1953 dir. R. G. Springsteen

Goldfish Bowl, The
McCall, M.

It's Tough to be Famous
IN (US) 1932 dir. Alfred E. Green

Gone to Texas
Carter, F.

Outlaw Josey Wales, The
WAR (US) 1976 dir. Clint Eastwood

Good Gracious Annabelle
Kummer, C.
Annabelle's Affairs
FOX (US) 1931 dir. Alfred Werker

Good Night and Good Bye
Harris, T.
Street of Dreams
PHOENIX (US) 1988
dir. William A. Graham

Good Old Boy: A Delta Summer
Morris, W.
Good Old Boy
DISNEY CH (US) 1988
dir. Tom G. Robertson

Good Vibes
Cronley, J.
Let It Ride
PAR (US) 1989 dir. Joe Pytka

Goodbye Again
Scott, A. and Haight, G.
Honeymoon for Three
WAR (US) 1941 dir. Lloyd Bacon

Goodbye Piccadilly, Farewell Leicester Square
La Bern, A. J.
Frenzy
RANK (GB) 1971 dir. Alfred Hitchcock

Goodbye to the Hill
Dunne, L.
Paddy
FOX (Ireland) 1969 dir. Daniel Haller

Goosefoot
McGinley, P.
Fantasist, The
BLUE DOLPHIN (Ire) 1987
dir. Robin Hardy

Gor Saga, The
Duffy, M.
First Born
BBC (GB) 1988 dir. Philip Saville

Gowns by Roberta
Miller, A. D.
Lovely to Look At
MGM (US) 1952 dir. Mervyn LeRoy

Gowns by Roberta
Miller, A. D.
Roberta
RKO (US) 1935 dir. William A. Seiter

Graf Spee
Powell, M.
Battle of the River Plate, The
RANK (GB) 1956 dir. Michael Powell
and Emeric Pressburger
US title: Pursuit of the Graf Spee

Grand Duke and Mr. Pimm, The
Hardy, L.
Love is a Ball
UA (US) 1963 dir. David Swift
GB title: All This and Money Too

Grand Hotel
Baum, V.
Weekend at the Waldorf
MGM (US) 1945 dir. Robert Z. Leonard

Grande Ceinture, La
Fallet, R.
Porte des Lilas
FILMSONOR (Fr/It) 1957
dir. René Clair

Grandpa and Frank
Majerus, J.
Home to Stay
TIME-LIFE INC. (US) 1978
dir. Delbert Mann

Great Companions, The
Markey, G.
Meet Me at the Fair
UN (US) 1952 dir. Douglas Sirk

Great Diamond Robbery, The
Minahan, J.
Diamond Trap, The
COL TV (US) 1988 dir. Don Taylor

Great Dinosaur Robbery, The
Forrest, D.
One of our Dinosaurs is Missing
DISNEY (US) 1975
dir. Robert Stevenson

Great Gambler
Dostoevski, F.
Great Sinner, The
MGM (US) 1949 dir. Robert Siodmak

Great Love
Molnar, F.
Double Wedding
MGM (US) 1937 dir. Richard Thorpe

Great Train Robbery, The
Crichton, M.
First Great Train Robbery, The
UA (GB) 1978 dir. Michael Crichton

Great Wind Cometh, A
Palgi, Y.
Hanna's War
CANNON (US) 1988
dir. Menahem Golan

Greatest Gift, The
Stern, P. V. D.
It Happened one Christmas
UN TV (US) 1977 dir. Donald Wrye

Greek Passion, The
Kazantzakis, N.
He Who Must Die
KASSLER (Fr/It) 1957 dir. Jules Dassin

Green Goddess, The
Archer, W.
Adventure in Iraq
WAR (US) 1943 dir. D. Ross-Lederman

Green Grows the Lilacs
Riggs, L.
Oklahoma!
MAGNA (US) 1955 dir. Fred Zinneman

Green Hat, The
Arlen, M.
Outcast Lady
MGM (US) 1934 dir. Robert Z. Leonard
GB title: Woman of the World, A

Green Heart, The
Ritchie, J.
New Leaf, A
PAR (US) 1970 dir. Elaine May

Green Journey
Hassler, J.
Love She Sought, The
ORION TV (US) 1990
dir. Joseph Sargent

Green Rushes
Walsh, M.
Quiet Man, The
REP (US) 1952 dir. John Ford

Greyfriar's Bobby
Atkinson, E.
Challenge to Lassie
MGM (US) 1949 dir. Richard Thorpe

Gringo Viejo
Fuentes, C.
Old Gringo
COL (US) 1989 dir. Luis Puenzo

Grizzly King, The
Curwood, J. O.
Bear, The
TRI-STAR (Fr) 1989
dir. Jean-Jacques Annaud

G-String Murders, The
Lee, G. R.

Lady of Burlesque
STROMBERG (US) 1943
dir. William Wellman
GB title: Striptease Lady

Guardsman, The
Molnar, F.

Chocolate Soldier, The
MGM (US) 1941 dir. Roy Del Ruth

Gulliver's Travels
Swift, J.

Three Worlds of Gulliver, The
COL (US/Sp) 1959 dir. Jack Sher

Gun Crazy
Kantor, M.

Deadly is the Female
UA (US) 1949 dir. Joseph Lewis

Gun Down
Garfield, B.

Last Hard Man, The
FOX (US) 1976
dir. Andrew V. McLaglen

Gun For Sale, A
Greene, G.

Short Cut to Hell
PAR (US) 1957 dir. James Cagney

Gun for Sale, A
Greene, G.

This Gun for Hire
PAR (US) 1942 dir. Frank Tuttle
BBK (US) 1991 dir. Lou Antonio

Gun Shy
Young, C. U.

Showdown at Abilene
UN (US) 1956 dir. Charles Haas

Gun, The
Forester, C. S.

Pride and the Passion, The
UA (US) 1957 dir. Stanley Kramer

Gunman's Choice
Short, L

Blood on the Moon
RKO (US) 1948 dir. Robert Wise

Guns of Rio Conchos
Huffaker, C.

Rio Conchos
FOX (US) 1964 dir. Gordon Douglas

Guts and Glory: The Rise and Fall of Oliver North
Bradlee, Jr., B.

Guts and Glory: The Oliver North Story
PAPAZIAN-HIRSCH (US) 1989
dir. Mike Robe

Guy Renton, A London Story
Waugh, A.

Circle of Deception
FOX (GB) 1960 dir. Jack Lee

Guyana Massacre: The Eyewitness Account
Krause, C. A.

Guyana Tragedy: The Story of Jim Jones
KONIGSBERG (US) 1980
dir. William A. Graham

Gypsy in Amber
Smith, M.

Art of Crime, The
UN TV (US) 1975 dir. Richard Irving

Halfway to Heaven
Segall, H.
Heaven Can Wait
PAR (US) 1978 dir. Warren Beatty,
Buck Henry

Halfway to Heaven
Segall, H.
Here Comes Mr. Jordan
COL (US) 1941 dir. Alexander Hall

Hall of Mirrors
Stone, R.
WUSA
PAR (US) 1970 dir. Stuart Rosenberg

Hameçon, The
Katcham, V.
Hook, The
MGM (US) 1962 dir. George Seaton

Hamlet, The
Faulkner, W.
Long, Hot Summer, The
FOX (US) 1958 dir. Martin Ritt
L. HILL (US) 1985 dir. Stuart Cooper

Hamp
Wilson, J.
King and Country
WAR (GB) 1964 dir. Joseph Losey

Hand and the Flower, The
Tickell, J.
Day to Remember, A
GFD (GB) 1953 dir. Ralph Thomas

Hand of Mary Constable, The
Gallico, P.
Daughter of the Mind
FOX (US) 1969 dir. Walter Grauman

Handful of Tansy, A.
Brooke, H. and Bannerman, K.
No, My Darling Daughter
RANK (GB) 1961 dir. Ralph Thomas

Hands of Orlac, The
Renard, M.
Mad Love
MGM (US) 1935 dir. Karl Freund
GB title: Hands of Orlac, The

Hangover Murders, The
Hobhouse, A.
Remember Last Night?
UN (US) 1936 dir. James Whale

Hanta Yo
Hill, R. B.
Mystic Warrior, The
WAR (US) 1984 dir. Richard T. Heffron

Happy Now I Go
Charles, T.
Woman With No Name, The
ABP (GB) 1950 dir. Ladislas Vajda
COL (US) 1952 dir. Richard Fleischer

Harbor, The
Reeves, J.
Society Doctor
MGM (US) 1935 dir. George B. Seitz
GB title: After Eight Hours

Harm's Way
Bassett, J.

In Harm's Way
PAR (US) 1965 dir. Otto Preminger

Harness Bull
White, L. T.

Vice Squad
UA (US) 1953 dir. Arnold Laven
GB title: Girl in Room 17, The

Harp That Once, The
Hall, P.

Reckoning, The
COL (GB) 1969 dir. Jack Gold

Harrison High
Farris, J.

Because They're Young
COL (US) 1960 dir. Paul Wendkos

Harvest Home
Tryon, T.

Dark Secret of Harvest Home, The
UN TV (US) 1978 dir. Leo Penn

Hatchet
Paulsen, G.

Cry in the Wild, A
CONCORDE (US) 1990
dir. Mark Griffiths

Hatter Fox
Harris, M.

Girl Called Hatter Fox, The
EMI (US) 1977 dir. George Schaefer

Haunted and the Haunters, The
Lytton, B.

Night Comes too Soon
BUTCHER (GB) 1948
dir. Denis Kavanagh

Haunted Monastery, The
Van Gulik, R.

Judge Dee and the Monastery Murders
ABC (US) 1974 dir. Jeremy Paul Kagan

Haunting of Hill House, The
Jackson, S.

Haunting, The
MGM (GB) 1963 dir. Robert Wise

He was Found in the Road
Armstrong, A.

Man in the Road, The
GN (GB) 1956 dir. Lance Comfort

Headlong
Williams, E.

King Ralph
UN (US) 1991 dir. David S. Ward

Heart & Hand
Edens, O.

House Divided, A
UN (US) 1932 dir. William Wyler

Heartbreak Hotel
Siddons, A. R.

Heart of Dixie
ORION (US) 1989 dir. Martin Davidson

Heat Wave
Pertwee, R.

Road to Singapore
WAR (US) 1931 dir. Alfred E. Green

Heat's On, The
Himes, C.

Come Back Charleston Blue
WAR (US) 1972 dir. Mark Warren

Heaven has no Favourites
Remarque, E. M.

Bobby Deerfield
WAR (US) 1977 dir. Sydney Pollack

Hedda and Louella
Eells, G.

Malice in Wonderland
ITC (US) 1985 dir. Gus Trikonis

Hedda Gabler
Ibsen, H.

Hedda
SCOTIA BARBER (GB) 1977
dir. Trevor Nunn

Heidi
Spyri, J.

Heidi's Song
HANNA-BARBERA (US) 1982
dir. Robert Taylor

Heir
Simon, R. L.

Jennifer on my Mind
UA (US) 1971 dir. Noel Black

Helen and Teacher
Lash, J. P.

Helen Keller— The Miracle Continues
FOX TV (US) 1984 dir. Alan Gibson

Hell Hath no Fury
Williams, C.

Hot Spot, The
ORION (US) 1990 dir. Dennis Hopper

Hell House
Matheson, R.

Legend of Hell House, The
FOX (GB) 1973 dir. John Hough

Hellbound Heart, The
Barker, C.

Hellraiser
CINEMARQUE (GB) 1987
dir. Clive Barker

Hellcats of the Sea
Lockwood, C. A. and Adamson, H. C.

Hellcats of the Navy
COL (US) 1957 dir. Nathan Juran

Heller With A Gun
L'Amour, L.

Heller in Pink Tights
PAR (US) 1960 dir. George Cukor

Hephaestus Plague, The
Page, T.

Bug
PAR (US) 1975 dir. Jeannot Szwarc

Her Heart in Her Throat
White, E. L.

Unseen, The
PAR (US) 1945 dir. Lewis Allen

Herbert West— The Re-Animator
Lovecraft, H. P.

Bride of Re-Animator
WILDSTREET (US) 1991
dir. Brian Yuzna

Herbert West— The Re-Animator
Lovecraft, H. P.

Re-Animator
EMPIRE (US) 1985 dir. Stuart Gordon

Here to Get my Baby out of Jail
Shivers, L.

Summer Heat
ATLANTIC (US) 1987
dir. Michie Gleason

Heritage of Michael Flaherty, The
Leinster, C.

Outsider, The
PAR (US) 1980 dir. Tony Luraschi

Hero, The
Lampell, M.

Saturday's Hero
COL (US) 1950 dir. David Miller
GB title: Idols in the Dust

Heroes and Villains: The True Story of the Beach Boys
Gaines, S.
Story of the Beach Boys, The: Summer Dreams
L. HILL (USTV) 1990
dir. Michael Switzer

Heroes of Yucca, The
Barrett, M.
Invincible Six, The
MOULIN ROUGE (US/Iran) 1970
dir. Jean Negulesco

Hero's Walk
Crane, R.
Voices, The
BBC (GB) 1965 dir. Dennis Vance

Hey, Malarek
Malarek, V.
Malarek
SVS/TELESCENE (Can) 1989
dir. Roger Cardinal

Hiding Place, The
Shaw, R.
Situation Hopeless But Not Serious
PAR (US) 1965 dir. Gottfried Reinhardt

High Commissioner, The
Cleary, J.
Nobody Runs Forever
RANK (GB) 1968 dir. Ralph Thomas
US title: High Commissioner, The

High Pavement
Bonett, E.
My Sister and I
GFD (GB) 1948 dir. Harold Huth

High Road, The
Lonsdale, F.
Lady of Scandal
MGM (US) 1930 dir. Sidney Franklin

High Sierra
Burnett, W. R.
I Died a Thousand Times
WAR (US) 1955 dir. Stuart Heisler

High Stakes
Chase, J. H.
I'll Get You For This
BL (GB) 1950 dir. Joseph M. Newman
US title: Lucky Nick Cain

High Window, The
Chandler, R.
Brasher Doubloon, The
FOX (US) 1946 dir. John Brahm
GB title: High Window, The

Hijacked
Harper, D.
Skyjacked
MGM (US) 1972 dir. John Guillermin

Hildegarde Withers Makes the Scene
Palmer, S., and Flora, F.
Very Missing Person, A
UN TV (US) 1972 dir. Russ Mayberry

His Last Bow
Doyle, Sir A. C.
Sherlock Holmes and the Voice of Terror
UN (US) 1942 dir. John Rawlins

His Majesty the King
Hamilton, C.
Exile, The
UN (US) 1948 dir. Max Ophuls

History of Tom Jones, A Foundling, The
Fielding, H.
Bawdy Adventures of Tom Jones, The
UN (GB) 1976 dir. Cliff Owen

History of Tom Jones, A Foundling, The
Fielding, H.

Tom Jones
UA (GB) 1963 dir. Tony Richardson

Hit, and Run, Run, Run
Bodelsen, A.

One of Those Things
RANK (Den) 1971 dir. Erik Balling

Hobbs' Vacation
Streeter, E.

Mr. Hobbs takes a Vacation
FOX (US) 1962 dir. Henry Koster

Hold Autumn in your Hands
Perry, G. S.

Southerner, The
UA (US) 1945 dir. Jean Renoir

Home and Beauty
Maugham, W. S.

Three for the Show
COL (US) 1955 dir. H. C. Potter

Home and Beauty
Maugham, W. S.

Too Many Husbands
COL (US) 1940 dir. Wesley Ruggles
GB title: My Two Husbands

Home Invaders, The
Hohimer F.

Thief
UA (US) 1981 dir. Michael Mann
GB title: Violent Street

Homecoming Game, The
Nemerov, H.

Tall Story
WAR (US) 1960 dir. Joshua Logan

L'Homme Que J'ai Tué
Rostand, M.

Broken Lullaby
PAR (US) 1931 dir. Ernst Lubitsch

Honest Finder, The
Aladar, L.

Trouble in Paradise
PAR (US) 1932 dir. Ernst Lubitsch

Hoods, The
Aaronson, D.

Once Upon a Time in America
WAR (US) 1984 dir. Sergio Leone

Hop Dog, The
Lavin, N. and Thorp, M.

Adventure in the Hopfields
ABP (GB) 1954 dir. John Guillermin

Horseman, Pass By
McMurtry, L.

Hud
PAR (US) 1963 dir. Martin Ritt

Hot Money
Kandel, A.

High Pressure
WAR (US) 1932 dir. Mervyn LeRoy

Hot Nocturne
Gilbert, E.

Blues in the Night
WAR (US) 1941 dir. Anatole Litvak

Hot Summer Night
Willis, T.

Flame in the Streets
RANK (GB) 1961 dir. Roy Baker

Hot Toddy
Edmonds, A.

White Hot: The Mysterious Murder of Thelma Todd
NEWFELD-KEATING (US) 1991
dir. Paul Wendkos

Hound of Florence, The
Salten, F.

Shaggy Dog, The
DISNEY (US) 1959 dir. Charles Barton

Hound of Hell, The
Christie, A.
Last Seance, The
GRANADA (GB) 1987

House in the Timberwoods, The
Dingwall, J.
Winds of Jarrah, The
FILMCORP (Aust) 1983
dir. Mark Egerton

House of Connelly, The
Green, P.
Carolina
FOX (US) 1934 dir. Henry King
GB title: House of Connelly

House of Dr. Edwards, The
Beeding, F.
Spellbound
UA (US) 1945 dir. Alfred Hitchcock

House of the Gentle Folk
Turgenev, I.
Nest of Gentry
CORINTH (USSR) 1970
dir. Andrei Konchalovski

House of the Seven Flies, The
Canning, V.
House of the Seven Hawks, The
MGM (GB) 1959 dir. Richard Thorpe

House with the Heavy Doors, The
Lippold, E.
Fiancée, The
(Ger) 1984 dir. Gunter Reisch, Gunther Rucker

House with the Red Light, The
Hunyady, S.
Very Moral Night, A
HUNG (Hun) 1977 dir. Karoly Makk

Household Ghosts
Kennaway, J.
Country Dance
MGM (GB) 1969 dir. J. Lee Thompson

How Say You?
Brooke, H. and Bannerman, K.
Pair of Briefs
RANK (GB) 1961 dir. Ralph Thomas

Howard: The Amazing Mr. Hughes
Dietrich, W. and Thomas, B.
Amazing Howard Hughes, The
EMI TV (US) 1977
dir. William A. Graham

Human Kind, The
Baron, A
Victors, The
BL (GB) 1963 dir. Carl Foreman

Hundred Million Frames, A
Berna, P.
Horse Without a Head, The
DISNEY (GB) 1963 dir. Don Chaffey

Hunting the Bismarck
Forester, C. S.
Sink the Bismarck
FOX (GB) 1960 dir. Lewis Gilbert

Hurricane Hunters
Anderson, W. C.
Hurricane
METRO (US) 1974 dir. Jerry Jameson

Husband of Delilah
Linklater, E.
Samson and Delilah
COMWORLD (US) 1984 dir. Lee Philips

I

I am a Camera
Druten, J. van
Cabaret
CINERAMA (US) 1972 dir. Bob Fosse

I Am Legend
Matheson, R.
Last Man on Earth, The
AIP (US/It) 1964 dir. Sidney Salkow

I Am Legend
Matheson, R.
Omega Man, The
WAR (US) 1971 dir. Boris Sagal

I am Third
Sayers, G. and Silverman, A.
Brian's Song
COL TV (US) 1971 dir. Buzz Kulik

I, James Lewis
Gabriel, G. W.
This Woman is Mine
UN (US) 1941 dir. Frank Lloyd

I Married A Dead Man
Irish, W.
I Married A Shadow
IS (Fr) 1983 dir. Robin Davis

I Wake Up Screaming
Fisher, S.
Vicki
FOX (US) 1953 dir. Harry Horner

Ice House Heat Waves
Brinkman, B.
Ice House
UPFRONT/CACTUS (US) 1989
dir. Eagle Pennell

Idol, The
Brown, M.
Mad Genius, The
WAR (US) 1931 dir. Michael Curtiz

Idol Hunter, The
Unsworth, B.
Pascali's Island
AVENUE (GB) 1988 dir. James Dearden

Idyll of Miss Sarah Brown, The
Runyon, D.
Guys and Dolls
MGM (US) 1955
dir. Joseph L. Mankiewicz

If I Die Before I Wake
King, S.
Lady from Shanghai, The
COL (US) 1948 dir. Orson Welles

If Only They Could Talk; It Shouldn't Happen to a Vet; Lord God Made Them All, The
Herriot, J.
All Creatures Great and Small
EMI (GB) 1974 dir. Claude Whatham
BBC (GB) 1980

If You Want to See Your Wife Again
Craig, J.

Your Money or Your Wife
BRENTWOOD (US) 1972
dir. Allen Reisner

Il était une fois
de Croisset, F.

Woman's Face, A
MGM (US) 1941 dir. George Cukor

I'm Giving Them Up For Good
Rau, M. and Rau, N.

Cold Turkey
UA (US) 1970 dir. Norman Lear

Immortal Wife
Stone, I.

President's Lady, The
FOX (US) 1953 dir. Henry Levin

Immortality, Inc.
Sheckley, R.

Freejack
Warner Bros. (US) 1992
dir.Geoff Murphy

Impatient Virgin, The
Clarke, D. H.

Impatient Maiden
UN (US) 1932 dir. James Whale

Impressario
Hurok, S. and Goode, R.

Tonight We Sing
FOX (US) 1953 dir. Mitchell Leisen

In Barley Fields
Nathan, R.

Bishop's Wife, The
RKO (US) 1947 dir. Henry Koster

In God We Trust, All Others Pay Cash
Shepherd, J.

Christmas Story, A
MGM/UA (US) 1983 dir. Bob Clark

In My Solitude
Leslie, D. S.

Two Left Feet
BL (GB) 1963 dir. Roy Baker

In No Comebacks
Forsyth, F.

Cry of the Innocent
NBC ENT. (US) 1980
dir. Michael O'Herlihy

In the Grove
Kutagawa, R. A.

Iron Maze
TRANS-TOKYO (US/Jap) 1991
dir. Hiroaki Yoshida

In the Heart of the Country
Coetzee, J. M.

Dust
DASKA (Bel/Fr) 1985
dir. Marion Hansel

In the Heat of the Summer
Katzenbach, J.

Mean Season, The
ORION (US) 1985 dir. Philip Borsos

In This Fallen City
Williams, B.

Night of Courage
TITUS (US) 1987 dir. Elliot Silverstein

In This Sign
Greenberg, J.

Love is Never Silent
M. REES (US) 1985 dir. Joseph Sargent

In Two Minds
Mercer, D.
Family Life
EMI (GB) 1971 dir. Ken Loach

Incident at 125th Street
Brown, J. E.
Incident in San Francisco
ABC TV (US) 1971 dir. Don Medford

Indians
Kopit, A.
Buffalo Bill and the Indians
UA (US) 1976 dir. Robert Altman

Infancia dos Martos
Lonzeiro, J.
Pixote
UNIFILM (Port) 1981
dir. Hector Babenco

Infernal Idol
Seymour, H.
Craze
EMI (GB) 1973 dir. Freddie Francis

Infierno y la Brisa, El
de Soto, J. M. V.
Hail Hazana
STILLMAN (Sp) 1978
dir. Jose Maria Guttierez

Instruct my Sorrows
Jaynes, C.
My Reputation
WAR (US) 1946 dir. Curtis Bernhardt

Intensive Care
Weisman, M-L.
Time to Live, A
ITC (US) 1985 dir. Rick Wallace

Interpreter, The
Keefe, F. L.
Before Winter Comes
COL (GB) 1968 dir. J. Lee Thompson

Interrupted Journey, The
Fuller, J. G.
UFO Incident, The
UN TV (US) 1975 dir. Richard Colla

Interruption, The
Jacobs, W. W.
Footsteps in the Fog
COL (GB) 1955 dir. Arthur Lubin

Investigation, The
Uhnak, D.
Kojak: The Price of Justice
MCA/UN (US) 1987 dir. Alan Metzger

Invisible Man, The
Wells, H. G.
Gemini Man
UN TV (US) 1976 dir. Alan J. Levi

Io e Lui
Moravia, A.
Me and Him
NC/COL (Ger) 1989 dir. Doris Dorrie

Isadora Duncan, An Intimate Portrait
Stokes, S.
Isadora
UI (GB) 1969 dir. Karel Reisz
US title: Loves of Isadora, The

Ishi in Two Worlds
Quinn, T. K.
Ishi: The Last of his Tribe
LEWIS (US) 1978
dir. Robert Ellis Miller

Island of Dr. Moreau, The
Wells, H. G.
Island of Lost Souls
PAR (US) 1932 dir. Erle C. Kenton

Issue of the Bishop's Blood, The
McMahon, T. P.

Abduction of St. Anne
Q. MARTIN (US) 1975 dir. Harry Falk

It Depends what you Mean
Bridie, J.

Folly to be Wise
BL (GB) 1952 dir. Frank Launden

It's a Vet's Life
Duncan, A.

In the Doghouse
RANK (GB) 1961 dir. Darcy Conyers

It's a 2 ft 6 inch Above The Ground World
Laffan, K.

Love Ban, The
BL (GB) 1973 dir. Ralph Thomas

I've Got Mine
Hubler, R. G.

Beachhead
UA (US) 1954 dir. Stuart Heisler

Ivy Garland, The
Hoyland, J.

Out of the Darkness
CFF (GB) 1985 dir. John Krish

Jack O'Judgement
Wallace, E.

Share Out, The
AA (GB) 1962 dir. Gerald Glaister

Jackdaws Strut
Henry, H.

Bought
WAR (US) 1931 dir. Archie Mayo

Jack's Return Home
Lewis, T.

Get Carter
MGM (GB) 1971 dir. Mike Hodges

Jacobowsky and the Colonel
Werfel, F.

Me and The Colonel
COL (US) 1958 dir. Peter Glenville

Jane of Lantern Hill
Montgomery, L. M.

Lantern Hill
DISNEY (US/Can) 1990
dir. Kevin Sullivan

January Heights
Banks, P.

Great Lie, The
WAR (US) 1941 dir. Edmund Goulding

Jayne Mansfield and the American Fifties
Saxton, M.

Jayne Mansfield Story, The
LAN (US) 1980 dir. Dick Lowry

Jealousy
Verneuil, L.

Deception
WAR (US) 1946 dir. Irving Rapper

Jean le Bleu
Giono, J.
Femme du Boulanger, La
PAGNOL (Fr) 1938 dir. Marcel Pagnol

Jeanne de Luynes, Comtess de Verne
Tournier, J.
King's Whore, The
J & M (GB) 1990 dir. Axel Corti

Jeannie
Stuart, A.
Let's Be Happy
ABP (GB) 1957 dir. Henry Levin

Jenny Angel
Barber, E.O.
Angel Baby
CONT DIS (US) 1960 dir. Paul Wendkos

Jest of God, A
Laurence, M.
Rachel, Rachel
WAR (US) 1968 dir. Paul Newman

Jet Stream
Ferguson, A.
Mayday at 40,000 Feet
WAR (US) 1976 dir. Robert Butler

Jewel of Mahabar
Marshall, E.
Treasure of the Golden Condor
FOX (US) 1953 dir. Delmer Daves

Jewel of the Seven Stars
Stoker, B.
Awakening, The
EMI (GB) 1980 dir. Mike Newell

Jewel of the Seven Stars
Stoker, B.
Blood from the Mummy's Tomb
MGM-EMI (GB) 1971 dir. Seth Holt

Jewel Robbery
Fodor, L.
Peterville Diamond, The
WAR (GB) 1942 dir. Walter Forde

Jim Kane
Brown, J. P. S.
Pocket Money
FA (US) 1972 dir. Stuart Rosenberg

Joan of Lorraine
Anderson, M.
Joan of Arc
RKO (US) 1948 dir. Victor Fleming

Joanna Godden
Smith, S. K.
Loves of Joanna Godden, The
GFD (GB) 1947 dir. Charles Frend

Journey to Matecumbe, A
Taylor, R. L.
Treasure of Matecumbe
DISNEY (US) 1976
dir. Vincent McEveety

Journey's End
Sherriff, R. C.
Aces High
EMI (GB/Fr) 1976 dir. Jack Gold

Jovial Ghosts, The
Smith, T.
Topper
MGM (US) 1937
dir. Norman Z. MacLeod
PAPAZIAN (US) 1979
dir. Charles S. Dubin

Jubal Troop
Wellman, P. I.
Jubal
COL (US) 1956 dir. Delmer Daves

Judge and his Hangman, The
Durrenmatt, F.

End of the Game
TCF (US/Ger) 1976
dir. Maximilian Schell

Julia
Straub, P.

Full Circle
PAR (GB/Can) 1976
dir. Richard Loncraine

Junior Bachelor Society, The
Williams, J. A.

Sophisticated Gents, The
D. WILSON (US) 1981 dir. Harry Falk

Jupiter Laughs
Cronin, A. J.

Shining Victory
WAR (US) 1941 dir. Irving Rapper

Jury, The
Bullett, G.

Last Man to Hang?, The
COL (GB) 1956 dir. Terence Fisher

Just Like the Pom Pom Girls
Graham, M.

Sinful Life, A
NEW LINE (US) 1989
dir. William Schreiner

Justice in the Back Room
Raab, S.

Marcus-Nelson Murders, The
UN TV (US) 1973 dir. Joseph Sargent

Justine
De Sade, Marquis

Cruel Passion
TARGET (GB) 1977 dir. Chris Boger

Kamaraden
Fuhmann, F.

Duped Till Doomsday
DEFA (Ger) 1957 dir. Kurt Jung-Alsen

Kavik the Wolf Dog
Morey, W.

Courage of Kavik, the Wolf Dog, The
PANTHEON (US) 1980 dir. Peter Carter

Kennel Murder Case, The
van Dine, S. S.

Calling Philco Vance
WAR (US) 1939 dir. William Clemens

Kent State: What Happened and Why
Michener, J. A.

Kent State
INTERPLAN (US) 1981
dir. James Goldstone

Kestrel for a Knave, A
Hines, B.

Kes
UA (GB) 1969 dir. Ken Loach

Kidnappers, The
Paterson, N.

Little Kidnappers, The
DISNEY CH (US) 1990 dir. Don Shebib

Kill Fee
Paulsen, G.
Murder C.O.D.
KUSHNER-LOCKE (US) 1990
dir. Alan Metzger

Kill, The
Zola, E.
Game is Over, The
COL (Fr/It) 1967 dir. Roger Vadim

Killing a Mouse on Sunday
Pressburger, E.
Behold a Pale Horse
COL (US) 1964 dir. Fred Zinnemann

Killing Frost, The
Catto, M.
Trapeze
UA (US) 1956 dir. Carol Reed

Kimura Family, The
Tani, T.
Yen Family, The
FUJI (Jap) 1990 dir. Yojiro Takita

Kind Sir
Krasna, N.
Indiscreet
WAR (GB) 1958 dir. Stanley Donen
REPUBLIC (US) 1988
dir. Richard Michaels

King Lear
Shakespeare, W.
Ran
Jap 1985 dir. Akira Kurosawa

King of Hearts
Kerr, J. and Brooke, E.
That Certain Feeling
PAR (US) 1956 dir. Norman Panama,
Melvin Frank

King Reluctant, A
Wilkins, V.
Dangerous Exile
RANK (GB) 1957
dir. Brian Desmond Hurst

King Solomon's Mines
Haggard, Sir H. R.
Watusi
MGM (US) 1959 dir. Kurt Neumann

Kingdom of Johnny Cool, The
McPartland, J.
Johnny Cool
UA (US) 1963 dir. William Asher

King's Ransom, The
McBain, E.
High and Low
TOHO (Jap) 1963 dir. Akira Kurosawa

Kipps
Wells, H. G.
Half a Sixpence
TPAR (GB) 1967 dir. George Sidney

Kiss, Inc.
Wyse, L.
Million Dollar Face, The
NEPHI-HAMNER (US) 1981
dir. Michael O'Herlihy

Kiss of Death
Bachmann, L.
Devil Makes Three, The
MGM (US) 1952 dir. Andrew Marton

Kloakerne
Stawinski, J.
Kanal
POLSKI (Pol) 1956 dir. Andrzej Wajda

Kofiko
Borenstein, T.
Going Bananas
CANNON (US) 1988 dir. Boaz Davidson

Kosygin is Coming
Ardies, T.

Russian Roulette
ITC (US) 1975 dir. Lov Lombardo

Kurwenal
Navarre, Y.

Straight from the Heart
TELESCENE (Fr) 1990 dir. Lea Pool

Ladies and Gentlemen
Hecht, B. and MacArthur, C.

Perfect Strangers
WAR (US) 1950 dir. Bretaigne Windust
GB title: Too Dangerous to Love

Ladies in Retirement
Denham, R. and Percy, E.

Mad Room, The
COL (US) 1969 dir. Bernard Girard

Ladies of the Mob
Boothe, E.

City Streets
PAR (US) 1931 dir. Rouben Mamoulian

Lady Has a Heart, A
Bus-Fekete, L.

Baroness and the Butler, The
FOX (US) 1938 dir. Walter Lang

Lady, Lady, I Did It!
McBain, E.

Lonely Hearts
TOHO (Jap) 1982 dir. Kon Ichikawa

Lady Windemere's Fan
Wilde, O.

Fan, The
FOX (US) 1949 dir. Otto Preminger
GB title: Lady Windemere's Fan

LaFitte the Pirate
Saxon, L.

Buccaneer, The
PAR (US) 1937 dir. Cecil B. de Mille
PAR (US) 1958 dir. Anthony Quinn

Lament for Molly Maguires
Lewis, A. H.

Molly Maguires, The
PAR (US) 1970 dir. Martin Ritt

Lamp is Heavy, A
Russell, S. M.

Feminine Touch, The
RANK (GB) 1956 dir. Pat Jackson

Larry: Case History of a Mistake
McQueen, Dr. R.

Larry
TOM (US) 1974 dir. William A. Graham

Last Adam, The
Cozzens, J. G.

Dr. Bull
FOX (US) 1933 dir. John Ford

Last Days of the Victim
Feinman, J. P.

Two to Tango
CONCORDE (US/Arg) 1989
dir. Hector Olivera

Last Frontier
MacLean, A.
Secret Ways, The
RANK (US) 1961 dir. Phil Karlson

Last Hours of Sandra Lee, The
Sansom, W.
Wild Affair, The
BL (GB) 1965 dir. John Irish

Last Jew, The
Kaniuk, Y.
Vulture, The
YOSHA (Israel) 1981 dir. Yaky Yosha

Last Jews in Berlin, The
Gross, L.
Forbidden
ENT (GB/Ger) 1984 dir. Anthony Page

Last of Mrs. Cheyney, The
Lonsdale, F.
Law and the Lady, The
MGM (US) 1951 dir. Edwin H. Knopf

Last of the Badmen
Monaghan, J.
Bad Men of Tombstone
ABP (US) 1949 dir. Kurt Neumann

Last of the Mohicans, The
Cooper, J. F.
Last of the Redmen
COL (US) 1947 dir. George Sherman

Last Prostitute who Took Pride in her Work, The
Borden, W.
Last Prostitute, The
BBK (US) 1991 dir. Lou Antonio

Last Testament, The
Amen, C.
Testament
PAR (US) 1983 dir. Lynne Littman

Last Voyage of the Valhalla
Kytle, R.
Desperate Voyage
WIZAN (US) 1980
dir. Michael O'Herlihy

Late Boy Wonder, The
Hall, A.
Three in the Cellar
AIP (US) 1970 dir. Theodore J. Flicker

Late Christopher Bean, The
Howard, S.
Christopher Bean
MGM (US) 1933 dir. Sam Wood

Lay this Laurel
Kirstein, L.
Glory
TRI-STAR (US) 1989 dir. Edward Zwick

Lazaro
Kendall, D.
Where the River Runs Black
MGM (US) 1986 dir. Christopher Cain

Leave Her to Heaven
Williams, B. A.
Too Good to be True
NEWLAND-RAYNOR (US) 1988
dir. Christian I Nyby II

Leaving Cheyenne
McMurtry, L.
Lovin' Molly
GALA (US) 1974 dir. Sidney Lumet

Ledger, The
Uhnak, D.
Get Christy Love!
WOLPER (US) 1974
dir. William A. Graham

Legacy
Bonner, C.
Adam had Four Sons
COL (US) 1941 dir. Gregory Ratoff

Legacy of a Spy
Maxfield, H. S.
Double Man, The
WAR (GB) 1967 dir. Franklin Schaffner

Legion
Blatty, W. P.
Exorcist III, The
FOX (US) 1990 dir. William Peter Blatty

Legitime Defense
Steeman, S-A.
Quai des Orfèvres
MAJ (Fr) 1947
dir. Henri-Georges Clouzot

Leiningen Versus the Ants
Stephenson, C.
Naked Jungle, The
PAR (US) 1954 dir. Byron Haskin

Lesser of Two Evils, The
Laborde, J.
Investigation
QUARTET (Fr) 1978 dir. Etienne Perier

Lesson in Love, A
Baird, M. T.
Circle of Two
BORDEAUX (Can) 1980
dir. Jules Dassin

Let Me Count the Ways
De Vries, P.
How Do I Love Thee?
ABC (US) 1970 dir. Michael Gordon

Letter, The
Maugham, W. S.
Unfaithful, The
WAR (US) 1947 dir. Vincent Sherman

Letter to Five Wives
Klempner, J.
Letter to Three Wives, A.
FOX (US) 1948
dir. Joseph L. Mankiewicz
FOX (US) 1985 dir. Larry Elikann

Letter to the Editor
Street, James H.
Nothing Sacred
SELZNICK (US) 1937
dir. William Wellman

Liaisons Dangereuses, Les
Hampton, C.
Dangerous Liaisons
WAR (US) 1988 dir. Stephen Frears

Liaisons Dangereuses, Les
de Laclos, P.
Dangerous Liaisons
WAR (US) 1988 dir. Stephen Frears

Liberté Provisoire
Duras, M.
He Stayed for Breakfast
COL (US) 1940 dir. Alexander Hall

Life and Death of the Wicked Lady Skelton, The
King-Hall, M.
Wicked Lady, The
GFD (GB) 1946 dir. Leslie Arliss
CANNON (GB) 1983
dir. Michael Winner

Life and Loves of a She-Devil, The
Weldon, F.
She-Devil
ORION (US) 1989 dir. Susan Seidelman

Life and Times of Cleopatra, The
Franzero, C. M.
Cleopatra
FOX (US) 1963
dir. Joseph L. Mankiewicz

Life Lines
Ireland, J.
Reason for Living: The Jill Ireland Story
TEN-FOUR (US) 1991
dir. Michael Rhodes

Life of David Haggart, The
Haggart, D.
Sinful Davey
UA (GB) 1969 dir. John Huston

Life of Ian Fleming, The
Pearson, J.
Goldeneye
ANGLIA (GB) 1990 dir. Don Boyd

Life of Lucy Gallant, The
Cousins, M.
Lucy Gallant
PAR (US) 1955 dir. Robert Parrish

Life of Tom Horn, Government Scout & Interpreter
Horn, T.
Tom Horn
WAR (US) 1980 dir. William Wiard

Life, The
Cordelier, J.
Memoirs of a French Whore
Aidart (Fr) 1982 dir. Daniel Duval

Life with Mother Superior
Trahey, J.
Trouble with Angels, The
COL (US) 1966 dir. Ida Lupino

Light of Day, The
Ambler, E.
Topkapi
UA (US) 1964 dir. Jules Dassin

Light of Heart, The
Williams, E.
Life Begins at Eight Thirty
FOX (US) 1942 dir. Irving Pichel
GB title: Light of Heart, The

Light on Synanon, The
Mitchell, D., Mitchell, C., Ofshe, R.
Attack on Fear
TOM (US) 1984 dir. Mel Damski

Lighthouse at the End of the World
Verne, J.
Light at the Edge of the World, The
MGM (US/Sp) 1971
dir. Kevin Billington

Like Mother, Like Me
Schwartz, S.
Like Mom, Like Me
CBS ENT (US) 1978
dir. Michael Pressman

Likes of 'er, The
McEvoy, C.
Sally in our Alley
ABP (GB) 1931 dir. Maurice Elvey

Liliom
Molnar, F.
Carousel
TCF (US) 1956 dir. Henry King

Lillian Day
Mearson, L.
Our Wife
COL (US) 1941 dir. John M. Stahl

Lincoln
Vidal, G.
Gore Vidal's Lincoln
FINNEGAN/PINCHUK (US) 1988
dir. Lamont Johnson

Line on Ginger
Maugham, R.
Intruder, The
BL (GB) 1953 dir. Guy Hamilton

Lions at the Kill
Catto, M.
Seven Thieves
FOX (US) 1960 dir. Henry Hathaway

Lips of Steel
Hervey, H.
Prestige
RKO (US) 1932 dir. Tay Garnett

Lisa and David
Rubin, T. I.
David and Lisa
BL (US) 1963 dir. Frank Perry

Little Britches
Moody, R.
Wild Country, The
DISNEY (US) 1971 dir. Robert Totten

Little Flat in the Temple, A
Wynne, P.
Devotion
RKO (US) 1931 dir. Robert Milton

Little Lambs Eat Ivy
Langley, N.
Father's Doing Fine
ABP (GB) 1952 dir. Henry Cass

Little Pinks
Runyon, D.
Big Street, The
RKO (US) 1942 dir. Irving Reis

Little Sister, The
Chandler, R.
Marlowe
MGM (US) 1969 dir. Paul Bogart

Living and the Dead, The
Boileau, P. and Narcejac, T.
Vertigo
PAR (US) 1958 dir. Alfred Hitchcock

Living Arrows
Martin, G.
Between Two Women
J. AVNET (US) 1986 dir. Jon Avnet

Living Proof
Williams, Jr., H. and Bane, M.
Living Proof: The Hank Williams, Jr. Story
TELECOM (US) 1983 dir. Dick Lowry

Lizard's Tail, The
Brandel, M.
Hand, The
ORION/WAR (US) 1981
dir. Oliver Stone

Locataire, La
Simenon, G.
L'Etoile du Nord
UA (Fr) 1982
dir. Pierre Granier-Deferre

Lodger, The
Lowndes, Mrs B.
Man in the Attic, The
FOX (US) 1953 dir. Hugo Fregonese

London Wall
Druten, J. van
After Office Hours
BI (GB) 1935 dir. Thomas Bentley

Lone Cowboy: My Life Story
James, W.
Shootout
UN (US) 1971 dir. Henry Hathaway

Lone House Mystery, The
Wallace, E.

Attempt to Kill
AA (GB) 1961 dir. Royston Murray

Lonely Girl, The
O'Brien, E.

Girl With Green Eyes
UA (GB) 1964 dir. Desmond Davis

Lonely Guy's Book of Life, The
Friedman, B. J.

Lonely Guy, The
UN (US) 1984 dir. Arthur Hiller

Lonely Skier, The
Innes, H.

Snowbound
RKO (GB) 1948 dir. David MacDonald

Long Haul
Bezzerides, A. I.

They Drive by Night
WAR (US) 1940 dir. Raoul Walsh
GB title: Road to Frisco, The

Long, Long Trail, The
Chilton, C. and Littlewood, J.

Oh! What a Lovely War
PAR (GB) 1969
dir. Richard Attenborough

Long Saturday Night, The
Williams, C.

Confidentially Yours
IS (Fr) 1984 dir. François Truffaut

Long Saturday Night, The
Williams, C.

Finally, Sunday
FILMS A2 (Fr) 1983
dir. François Truffaut

Long Way Up, A
Valens, E. G.

Other Side of the Mountain, The
UN (US) 1975 dir. Larry Peerce
GB title: Window to the Sky, A

Look of Eagles, The
Foote, J. T.

Kentucky
FOX (US) 1938 dir. David Butler

Looking After Sandy
Turnbull, M.

Bad Little Angel
MGM (US) 1939 dir. William Thiele

Looters, The
Reese, J.

Charley Varrick
UN (US) 1973 dir. Don Siegel

Lord Arthur Savile's Crime
Wilde, O.

Flesh and Fantasy
UN (US) 1943 dir. Julien Duvivier

Lord Edgware Dies
Christie, A.

Thirteen at Dinner
WAR (US) 1985 dir. Lou Antonio

Loser Takes All
Greene, G.

Strike It Rich
BRIT SCREEN (GB) 1990
dir. James Scott

Loss of Roses, A
Inge, W.

Stripper, The
FOX (US) 1963 dir. Franklin Schaffner
GB title: Woman of Summer

Lost Country, The
Salamanca, J. R.

Wild in the Country
FOX (US) 1961 dir. Philip Dunne

Lost Ecstasy
Rinehart, M. R.
I Take This Woman
PAR (US) 1931 dir. Marion Gering

Lost Hero: The Mystery of Raoul Wallenberg
Werbell, F. and Clarke, T.
Wallenberg: A Hero's Story
PAR (US) 1985 dir. Lamont Johnson

Lost Honor of Katharina Blum, The
Boll, H.
Lost Honor of Kathryn Beck, The
COMWORLD (US) 1984
dir. Simon Langton

Lost Horizon
Hilton, J.
Shangri-La
COMPASS (US) 1960
dir. George Schaefer

Lost King, A
DeCapite, R.
Harry and Son
ORION (US) 1984 dir. Paul Newman

Lost Ones, The
Cameron, I.
Island at the Top of the World, The
DISNEY (US) 1974
dir. Robert Stevenson

Lost Prince, The: Young Joe, The Forgotten Kennedy
Searls, H.
Young Joe, the Forgotten Kennedy
ABC (US) 1977 dir. Richard T. Heffron

Lot 27a
Doyle, Sir A. C.
Tales from the Darkside: The Movie
PAR (US) 1990 dir. John Harrison

Lottie and Lisa
Kastner, E.
Parent Trap, The
DISNEY (US) 1961 dir. David Swift

Louis Beretti
Clarke, D. H.
Born Reckless
FOX (US) 1930 dir. John Ford

Louisiana Black
Charters, S.
White Lie
MCA TV (US) 1991 dir. Bill Condon

Louisiane; Fausse-Rivière
Denuzière, M.
Louisiana
CINEMAX (US) 1984
dir. Philippe de Broca

Love and Forget
Drawbell, J. W.
Love Story
GFD (GB) 1944 dir. Leslie Arliss
US title: Lady Surrenders, A

Love and Other Natural Disasters
Hannay, A.
Tiger's Tale, A
ATLANTIC (US) 1988
dir. Peter Douglas

Love and War
Jakes, J.
North and South, Book II
WAR TV (US) 1986 dir. Kevin Connor

Love Flies in the Window
Morrison, A.
This Man is Mine
RKO (US) 1934 dir. John Cromwell

Love From Everybody
Hanley, C.

Don't Bother to Knock
WAR (GB) 1961 dir. Cyril Frankel
US title: Why Bother to Knock

Love in Amsterdam
Freeling, N.

Amsterdam Affair
LIP/TRIO/GROUP W (GB) 1968
dir. Gerry O'Hara

Love in the Time of Cholera
Marquez, G. G.

Letters from the Park
RTVE (Cuba) 1988
dir. Tomas Guttierez Alea

Lovers, The
Stevens, L.

War Lord, The
UN (US) 1965 dir. Franklin Schaffner

Lovey, A Very Special Child
MacCracken, M.

Lovey: A Circle of Children, Part II
TIME-LIFE (US) 1978 dir. Jud Taylor

Luck of Roaring Camp, The; Outcasts of Poker Flat, The
Harte, B.

California Gold Rush
TAFT (US) 1981 dir. Jack Hively

Lucky
Collins, J.

Lucky/Chances
NBC (US) 1990 dir. Buzz Kulik

Ludes
Stein, B.

Boost, The
HEMDALE (US) 1988
dir. Harold Becker

Lullaby, The
Knoblock, E.

Sin of Madelon Claudet
MGM (US) 1931 dir. Edgar Selwyn

M

M. Ripois and his Nemesis
Hemon, L.

Knave of Hearts
ABP (GB) 1954 dir. René Clément
US title: Lover Boy

McCabe
Naughton, E.

McCabe and Mrs. Miller
WAR (US) 1971 dir. Robert Altman

McLeod's Folly
Bromfield, L.

Johnny Come Lately
CAGNEY (US) 1943
dir. William K. Howard
GB title: Johnny Vagabond

McVicar by Himself
McVicar, J.

McVicar
BW (GB) 1980 dir. Tom Clegg

Madame la Gimp
Runyon, D.
Lady for a Day
COL (US) 1933 dir. Frank Capra

Madame la Gimp
Runyon, D.
Pocketful of Miracles
UA (US) 1961 dir. Frank Capra

Magistrate, The
Pinero, Sir A. W.
Those were the Days
BIP (GB) 1934 dir. Thomas Bentley

Magnificent Devils
Crockett, L. H.
Proud and Profane, The
PAR (US) 1956 dir. George Seaton

Maiden Maiden
Boyle, K.
Five Days One Summer
WAR (US) 1982 dir. Fred Zinnemann

Main Street
Lewis, S.
I Married a Doctor
WAR (US) 1936 dir. Archie Mayo

Majesty of the Law, The
O'Connor, F.
Rising of the Moon, The
WAR (Ire) 1957 dir. John Ford

Make Room, Make Room!
Harrison, H.
Soylent Green
MGM (US) 1973 dir. Richard Fleischer

Make You a Fine Wife
Foldes, Y.
My Own True Love
PAR (US) 1948 dir. Compton Bennett

Male Animal, The
Thurber, J. and Nugent, E.
She's Working Her Way Through College
WAR (US) 1952
dir. Bruce Humberstone

Malibu, A Nature Story
Hoyt, V. J.
Sequoia
MGM (US) 1935 dir. Chester Lyons

Maltese Falcon, The
Hammett, D.
Satan Met a Lady
WAR (US) 1936 dir. William Dieterle

Mambo Kings Play Songs of Love, The
Hijeulo, O.
Mambo Kings, The
WAR (US) 1992 dir. Arne Glimcher

Man About a Dog, A
Coppel, A.
Obsession
GFD (GB) 1949 dir. Edward Dmytryk
US title: Hidden Room, The

Man At The Carlton
Wallace, E.
Man at the Carlton Tower
AA (GB) 1961 dir. Robert Tronson

Man Called Kyril, A
Trenhaile, J.
Codename: Kyril
INCITO/HTV (US/GB) 1988
dir. Ian Sharp

Man from Moscow, A
Wynne, G.
Wynne and Penkovsky
BBC (GB/US) 1984 dir. Paul Seed

Man in Black, The
Albert, M. H.
Rough Night in Jericho
UN (US) 1967 dir. Arnold Laven

Man in Half-Moon Street, The
Lyndon, B.
Man Who Could Cheat Death, The
PAR (GB) 1959 dir. Terence Fisher

Man in Possession, The
Harwood, H. M.
Personal Property
MGM (US) 1937 dir. W. S. Van Dyke II
GB title: Man in Possession, The

Man in the Iron Mask, The
Dumas, A.
Fifth Musketeer, The
SASCH WIEN FILMS (Austria) 1978
dir. Ken Annakin

Man of Property, A
Galsworthy, J.
That Forsyte Woman
MGM (US) 1949 dir. Compton Bennett
GB title: Forsyte Saga, The

Man of the West
Yordan, P.
Gun Glory
MGM (US) 1957 dir. Roy Rowland

Man Running
Jepson, S.
Stage Fright
WAR (GB) 1950 dir. Alfred Hitchcock

Man, The
Dineli, M.
Beware My Lovely
RKO (US) 1952 dir. Harry Horner

Man Who Knew, The
Wallace, E.
Partners in Crime
AA (GB) 1961 dir. Peter Duffell

Man Who Rocked the Boat, The
Keating, W. J. and Carter, R.
Slaughter on 10th Avenue
UI (US) 1957 dir. Arnold Laven

Man-eater
Willis, T.
Maneaters are Loose!
MONA BBC TV (GB) 1984
dir. Timothy Galfos

Mantrap
Lewis, S.
Untamed
PAR (US) 1940 dir. George Archainband

Many Splendoured Thing, A
Han Suyin.
Love is a Many Splendoured Thing
FOX (US) 1955 dir. Henry King

Marauders, The
Ogburn, C.
Merrill's Marauders
WAR (US) 1962 dir. Samuel Fuller

Marble Forest
Durant, T.
Macabre
ABP (US) 1958 dir. William Castle

Marianne Dreams
Storr, C.
Paperhouse
VESTRON (GB) 1988 dir. Bernard Rose

Marie: A True Story
Maas, P.
Marie
MGM/UA (US) 1985
dir. Roger Donaldson

Marilyn
Mailer, N.
Marilyn: The Untold Story
SCHILLER (US) 1980 dir. Jack Arnold

Marion's Wall
Finney, J.
Maxie
ORION (US) 1985 dir. Paul Aaron

Mark of the Leopard
Eastwood, J.
Beyond Mombasa
COL (GB) 1955 dir. George Marshall

Marriage Bed, The
Pascal, E.
Husband's Holiday
PAR (US) 1931 dir. Robert Milton

Marry at Leisure
Piper, A.
Nice Girl Like Me, A
AVCO (GB) 1969 dir. Desmond Davis

Marshal of Medicine Bend, The
Ward, B.
Lawless Street, A
COL (US) 1955 dir. Joseph H. Lewis

Martedì del Diavolo, Il
Russo, E.
Russicum
TRI-STAR/Cecchi (It) 1989
dir. Pasquale Squitieri

Martin Eden
London, J.
Adventures of Martin Eden, The
COL (US) 1942 dir. Sidney Salkow

Marvellous Land of Oz, The; Ozma of Oz
Baum, L. F.
Return to Oz
DISNEY (US) 1985 dir. Walter Murch

Mary Ann
Karmel, A.
Something Wild
UA (US) 1961 dir. Jack Garfein

MASH
Hooker, R.
*M*A*S*H*
FOX (US) 1970 dir. Robert Altman

Masks and Faces
Reade, C. and Taylor, T.
Peg of Old Drury
WILCOX (GB) 1935 dir. Herbert Wilcox

Massacre
Bellah, J. W.
Fort Apache
RKO (US) 1948 dir. John Ford

Matchmaker
Wilder, T.
Hello Dolly
FOX (US) 1969 dir. Gene Kelly

Mathilda Shouted Fire
Green, L.
Midnight Lace
UN (US) 1960 dir. David Miller
UN TV (US) 1981 dir. Ivan Nagy

Matter of Conviction, A
Hunter, E.
Young Savages, The
UA (US) 1960 dir. John Frankenheimer

Maurice Guest
Richardson, H. H.
Rhapsody
MGM (US) 1954 dir. Charles Vidor

Max and Helen: A Remarkable True Love Story
Wiesenthal, S.
Max and Helen
TNT (US) 1990 dir. Philip Saville

Maybe I'll Pitch Forever
Paige, L. and Lipman, D.

Don't Look Back
TBA (US) 1981 dir. Richard Colla

Mazepa
Slowacki, J.

Blanche
TELEPRESSE (Fr) 1971
dir. Walerian Borowczyk

Me and the Arch Kook Petulia
Haase, J.

Petulia
WAR (US) 1968 dir. Richard Lester

Me Two
Davis, E.

All of Me
UN (US) 1984 dir. Carl Reiner

Meet a Body
Launder, F. and Gilliat, S.

Green Man, The
BL (GB) 1956 dir. Robert Day

Megstone Plot, The
Garve, A.

Touch of Larceny, A
PAR (GB) 1959 dir. Guy Hamilton

Melodeon, The
Swarthout, G.

Christmas to Remember, A
ENGLUND (US) 1978
dir. George Englund

Melville Goodwin, USA
Marquand, J. P.

Top Secret Affair
WAR (US) 1957 dir. H. C. Potter
GB title: Their Secret Affair

Memoirs of a British Agent
Lockhart, Sir. R. H. B.

British Agent
WAR (US) 1934 dir. Michael Curtiz

Memoirs of a Physician
Dumas, A.

Black Magic
UA (US) 1949 dir. Gregory Ratoff

Memory of Love
Brewer, B.

In Name Only
RKO (US) 1939 dir. John Cromwell

Men of Iron
Pyle, H.

Black Shield of Falworth, The
UI (US) 1954 dir. Rudolph Maté

Mendel Inc.
Freedman, D.

Heart of New York
WAR (US) 1932 dir. Mervyn LeRoy

Merry Andrew
Beach, L.

Handy Andy
FOX (US) 1934 dir. David Butler

Merton of the Movies
Wilson, H. L.

Make me a Star
PAR (US) 1932 dir. William Beaudine

Meter Man, The
Forbes, J. S.

Penthouse, The
PAR (GB) 1967 dir. Peter Collinson

Methinks the Lady
Endore, G.

Whirlpool
FOX (US) 1949 dir. Otto Preminger

Mexican, The
London, J.
Fighter, The
UA (US) 1952 dir. Herbert Kline

Mexican Village
Niggli, J.
Sombrero
MGM (US) 1953 dir. Norman Foster

Mi Bodo Contigo
Tellado, C.
Our Marriage
LFDP (Fr) 1985 dir. Valeria Sarimento

Miami Mayhem
Albert, M. H.
Tony Rome
FOX (US) 1967 dir. Gordon Douglas

Michael Strogoff
Verne, J.
Soldier and the Lady, The
RKO (US) 1937 dir. George Nicholls, Jr.
GB title: Michael Strogoff

Middle Ages, The
Gurney, A. R.
My Brother's Wife
ADAM (US) 1989 dir. Jack Bender

Midnight Lady and the Mourning Man
Anthony, D.
Midnight Man, The
UN (US) 1974 dir. Roland Kibbee

Midwich Cuckoos, The
Wyndham, J.
Village of the Damned
MGM (GB) 1960 dir. Wolf Rilla

Midwife of Pont Clery, The
Sandstrom, F.
Jessica
UA (Fr/It) 1961 dir. Jean Negulesco

Milk Train Doesn't Stop Here Anymore, The
Williams, T.
Boom!
UI (GB) 1968 dir. Joseph Losey

Milk White Unicorn, The
Sandstrom, F.
White Unicorn, The
GFD (GB) 1947 dir. Bernard Knowles
US title: Bad Sister

Mills of God, The
Lothar, E.
Act of Murder, An
UN (US) 1948 dir. Michael Gordon

Millstone, The
Drabble, M.
Touch of Love, A
BL (GB) 1969 dir. Waris Hussein
US title: Thank You All Very Much

Mind of Mr J. G. Reeder, The
Wallace, E.
Mind of Mr. Reeder, The
RAYMOND (GB) 1936
dir. Jack Raymond
ITV (GB) 1969

Minister to Millions
Gordon, A.
One Man's Way
UA (US) 1964 dir. Denis Sanders

Minute's Wait, A
McHugh, M. J.
Rising of the Moon, The
WAR (Ire) 1957 dir. John Ford

Mio, My Son
Lindgren, A.
Land of Faraway, The
NORD/GORKY (Swe/USSR/Nor) 1988
dir. Vladimir Grammatikov

Mirage, The
Selwyn, E.

Possessed
MGM (US) 1931 dir. Clarence Brown

Mirror Crack'd from Side to Side, The
Christie, A.

Mirror Crack'd, The
EMI (GB) 1980 dir. Guy Hamilton

Mirror in my House
O'Casey, S.

Young Cassidy
MGM (GB) 1964
dir. Jack Cardiff/John Ford

Mischief
Armstrong, C.

Don't Bother to Knock
FOX (US) 1952 dir. Roy Ward Baker

Mischief
Armstrong, C.

Sitter, The
FNM (US) 1991 dir. Rick Berger

Miss Bishop
Aldrich, Mrs B.

Cheers for Miss Bishop
PAR (US) 1941 dir. Tom Garnett

Miss Firecracker Contest
Henley, B.

Miss Firecracker
CORSAIR (US) 1989
dir. Thomas Schlamme

Miss Lonelyhearts 4122
Watson, C.

Crooked Hearts, The
LORIMAR (US) 1972 dir. Jay Sandrich

Miss Lonelyhearts
West, N.

Lonelyhearts
UA (US) 1958 dir. Vincent J. Donehue

Miss Pinkerton
Rinehart, M. R.

Nurse's Secret, The
WAR (US) 1941 dir. Noel M. Smith

Miss 4th of July, Goodbye
Janus, C. G.

Goodbye, Miss 4th of July
FINNEGAN/PINCHUK (US) 1988
dir. George Miller

Mister Moses
Catto, M.

Mr. Moses
UA (GB) 1965 dir. Ronald Neame

Mister Roberts
Logan, J. and Heggen, T.

Ensign Pulver
WAR (US) 1964 dir. Joshua Logan

Misty of Chincoteague
Henry, M.

Misty
FOX (US) 1961 dir. James B. Clark

Mittelmann's Hardware
Small, G. R.

Finding the Way Home
MGM/UA TV (US) 1991
dir. Rob Holcomb

Mo: A Woman's view of Watergate
Dean, M.

Blind Ambition
TIME-LIFE (US) 1979 dir. George Schaefer

Moi, Ma Soeur
Barry, J.

Invitation au Voyage
TRIUMPH (Fr) 1983
dir. Peter Del Monte

Mom by Magic, A
Dillon, B.
Mom for Christmas, A
DISNEY (US) 1990 dir. George Miller

Mon Crime
Verneuil, L. and Berr, G.
True Confession
PAR (US) 1937 dir. Wesley Ruggles

Monday, Tuesday, Wednesday
Houston, R.
Killing Affair, A
HEMDALE (US) 1988
dir. David Saperstein

Money by Wire
Paulton, E.
Get Off My Foot
WAR (GB) 1935 dir. William Beaudine

Monkey Planet
Boulle, P.
Planet of the Apes
FOX (US) 1968 dir. Franklin Schaffner

Monkeys, The
Wilkinson, G. R.
Monkeys, Go Home!
DISNEY (US) 1967
dir. Andrew V. McLaglen

Monogamist, The
Gallagher, T.
Family Man, The
TIME-LIFE (US) 1979 dir. Glenn Jordan

Monsieur Beaucaire
Tarkington, B.
Monte Carlo
PAR (US) 1930 dir. Ernst Lubitsch

Monsieur La Souris
Simenon, G.
Midnight Episode
COL (GB) 1950 dir. Gordon Parry

Monsieur L'Admiral va Bientôt Mourir
Bost, P.
Sunday in the Country, A
MGM/UA (Fr) 1984
dir. Bertrand Tavernier

Monsieur Proust
Albaret, C.
Celeste
PEL (W. Ger) 1981 dir. Percy Adlon

Monsieur Rififi
Le Breton, A.
Rififi
PATHE (Fr) 1955 dir. Jules Dassin

Monsignore
Leger, J. A.
Monsignor
FOX (US) 1982 dir. Frank Perry

Moonwebs
Freed, J.
Ticket to Heaven
UA (US) 1981 dir. R. L. Thomas

Morals of Marcus Ordeyne, The
Locke, W. J.
Morals of Marcus, The
GB (GB) 1935 dir. Miles Mander

Morella; Black Cat, The; Facts of the Case of Dr. Valdemar,The
Poe, E. A.
Tales of Terror
WAR (US) 1962 dir. Roger Corman

Mort en fuite, La
de Gouriadec, L.
Break the News
GFD (GB) 1938 dir. René Clair

Morte d'Arthur, Le
Malory, Sir T.
Excalibur
ORION (US) 1981 dir. John Boorman

Morte d'Arthur, Le
Malory, Sir T.
Knights of the Round Table
MGM (GB) 1954 dir. Richard Thorpe

Mortgage on Life
Baum, V.
Woman's Secret, A
RKO (US) 1949 dir. Nicholas Ray

Motel Tapes, The
McGrady, M.
Talking Walls
NEW WORLD (US) 1987
dir. Stephen Verona

Mother Carey's Chickens
Wiggin, K. D.
Summer Magic
DISNEY (US) 1963 dir. James Neilson

Motocyclette, La
Mandiargues, A. P. de
Girl on a Motorcycle
BL (GB/Fr) 1968 dir. Jack Cardiff
US title: Naked Under Leather

Mountain Lion, The
Murphy, R.
Run, Cougar, Run
DISNEY (US) 1972
dir. Michael Dmytryk

Moving Target, The
Macdonald, R.
Harper
WAR (US) 1966 dir. Jack Smight
GB title: Moving Target, The

Moviola
Kanin, G.
Moviola: The Scarlett O'Hara Wars
WAR TV (US) 1980 dir. John Erman

Moviola
Kanin, G.
Moviola: The Silent Lovers
WAR TV (US) 1980 dir. John Erman

Moviola
Kanin, G.
Moviola: This Year's Blonde
WAR TV (US) 1980 dir. John Erman

Mr. Angel Comes Aboard
Booth, C. G.
Johnny Angel
RKO (US) 1945 dir. Edwin L. Marin

Mr. Bridge; Mrs. Bridge
Connell, E. S.
Mr. and Mrs. Bridge
MIRAMAX (US) 1990 dir. James Ivory

Mr. Bunting at War
Greenwood, R.
Salute John Citizen
BN (GB) 1942 dir. Maurice Elvey

Mr. and Mrs. Cugat
Rorick, I. S.
Are Husbands Necessary?
PAR (US) 1942 dir. Norman Taurog

Mr. and Mrs. Haddock Abroad
Stewart, D. O.
Finn and Hattie
PAR (US) 1930 dir. Norman Taurog,
Norman McLeod

Mr. Midshipman Easy
Marryat, F.
Midshipman Easy
ATP (GB) 1935 dir. Carol Reed
US title: Men of the Sea

Mr Prohack
Bennett, A.
Dear Mr Prohack
GFD (GB) 1949 dir. Thornton Freeland

Mrs. McGinty's Dead
Christie, A.
Murder Most Foul
MGM (GB) 1964 dir. George Pollock

Mrs. Maitland's Affair
Lynn, M.
Other Man, The
UN TV (US) 1970 dir. Richard Colla

Mrs Christopher
Myers, E.
Blackmailed
GFD (US) 1950 dir. Marc Allégret

Mrs. Frisby and the Rats of N.I.M.H.
O'Brien, R. C.
Secret of N.I.M.H., The
MGM/UA (US) 1982 dir. Don Bluth

Mrs. Ross
Nicolson, R.
Whisperers, The
UA (GB) 1966 dir. Bryan Forbes

Mrs. White
Tracy, M.
White of the Eye
CANNON (GB) 1987
dir. Donald Cammell

Mud on the Streets
Huie, W. B.
Wild River
FOX (US) 1960 dir. Elia Kazan

Muggable Mary
Glatzle, M.; Fiore, E.
Muggable Mary: Street Cop
CBS ENT (US) 1982 dir. Sandor Stern

Mule for the Marquesa, A
O'Rourke, F.
Professionals, The
COL (US) 1966 dir. Richard Brooks

Murder at Shinglestrand
Capon, P.
Hidden Homicide
RANK (US) 1959 dir. Tony Yound

Murder for the Million
Chapman, R.
Murder Reported
COL (GB) 1957 dir. Charles Saunders

Murder Gang
Dean, B. and Munro, G.
Sensation
BIP (GB) 1936
dir. Brian Desmond Hurst

Murder in Amityville
Holzer, H.
Amityville II: The Possession
ORION (US) 1982
dir. Damiano Damiani

Murder in Little Rock
Meins, J.
Seduction in Travis County, A
NEW WORLD (US) 1991
dir. George Kaczender

Murder Mistaken
Green, J.
Cast a Dark Shadow
EROS (GB) 1955 dir. Lewis Gilbert

Murder of a Wanton
Chambers, W.
Sinner Take All
MGM (US) 1937 dir. Errol Taggart

Murder of the Circus Queen, The
Abbot, A.

Circus Queen Murder
COL (US) 1933 dir. Roy William Neill

Murder on the Wild Side
Jacks, J.

Black Eye
WAR (US) 1974 dir. Jack Arnold

Murder on the 31st Floor
Wahloo, P.

Kamikaze '89
TELECUL (Ger) 1983 dir. Wolf Gremm

Murder Under Two Flags
Nelson, A.

Show of Force, A
PAR (US) 1990 dir. Bruno Barreto

Murders in the Rue Morgue
Poe, E. A.

Phantom of the Rue Morgue
WAR (US) 1954 dir. Roy del Ruth

Murphy's Boy
Hayden, T.

Trapped in Silence
READER'S DIG (US) 1986
dir. Michael Tuchner

Muscle Beach
Wallach, I.

Don't Make Waves
MGM (US) 1967
dir. Alexander Mackendrick

Mute Witness
Pike, R. L.

Bullitt
WAR (US) 1968 dir. Peter Yates

Mutiny
Tilsley, F.

H.M.S. Defiant
COL (GB) 1962 dir. Lewis Gilbert
US title: Damn the Defiant

My Brother Death
Sulzberger, C.

Playground, The
JERAND (US) 1965 dir. Richard Hilliard

My Brother Paul
Dreiser, T.

My Gal Sal
FOX (US) 1942 dir. Irving Cummings

My Early Life
Churchill, Sir W. S.

Young Winston
COL-WAR (GB) 1972
dir. Richard Attenborough

My Husband, Rock Hudson
Gates, P.

Rock Hudson
KON-SAN (US) 1990 dir. John Nicolella

My Life
Duncan, I.

Isadora
UI (GB) 1969 dir. Karel Reisz
US title: Loves of Isadora, The

My Life and Hard Times
Thurber, J.

Rise and Shine
FOX (US) 1941 dir. Allan Dwan

My Little Brother is Coming Tomorrow
Behrenberg, B.

Grambling's White Tiger
INTERPLAN (US) 1981
dir. Georg Stanford Brown

My Luke and I
Gehrig, E. and Durso, J.

Love Affair, A: The Eleanor and Lou Gehrig Story
FRIES (US) 1978 dir. Fielder Cook

My Name is Anna: The Autobiography of Patty Duke
Duke, P. and Turan, K.

Call me Anna
FINNEGAN (US) 1990
dir. Gilbert Cates

My Old Man
Hemingway, E.

Under My Skin
FOX (US) 1950 dir. Jean Negulesco

My Ten Years as a Counter-Spy
Morros, B.

Man on a String
COL (US) 1960 dir. André de Toth
GB title: Confessions of a Counterspy

My Thirty Years Backstairs at the White House
Parks, L.R.

Backstairs at the White House
FRIENDLY PRODS (US) 1979
dir. Michael O'Herlihy

My Three Angels
Husson, A.

We're No Angels
PAR (US) 1955 dir. Michael Curtiz
PAR (US) 1989 dir. Neil Jordan

My True Love
Teilhet, D. L.

No Room for the Groom
UI (US) 1952 dir. Douglas Sirk

My Years with the KKK
Rowe, Jr., G. T.

Undercover with the KKK
COL TV (US) 1979 dir. Barry Shear

My 30 Years in Hoover's FBI
Sullivan, W. G. and Brown, W. S.

J. Edgar Hoover
RLC (US) 1987 dir. Robert Collins

Nabe-No-Kake
Murata, K.

Rhapsody in August
ORION (Jap) 1991 dir. Akira Kurosawa

Nanawatai
Mastrosimone, W.

Beast, The
COL (US) 1988 dir. Kevin Reynolds

Nanny, The
Greenburg, D.

Guardian, The
UN (US) 1990 dir. William Friedkin

Napoleon of Broadway
Millholland, C. B.

Twentieth Century
COL (US) 1934 dir. Howard Hawks

Narrow Margin, The
Wood, D. and Dempster, D.
Battle of Britain
UA (GB) 1969 dir. Guy Hamilton

Necromancers, The
Benson, R.
Spellbound
PYRAMID (GB) 1940 dir. John Harlow
US title: Spell of Amy Nugent, The

Nelson Touch, The
Grant, N.
Man of Affairs
GAU (GB) 1937 dir. Herbert Mason
US title: His Lordship

Nepomuk of the River
Pilkington, R.
Golden Head, The
CINERAMA (US/Hun) 1965
dir. Richard Thorpe

Nest in a Falling Tree
Cowley, J.
Night Digger, The
MGM (GB) 1971 dir. Alistair Reid

Never Come Back
Mair, J.
Tiger by the Tail
EROS (GB) 1955 dir. John Gilling

Never Pass This Way Again
LePere, G.
Dark Holiday
ORION TV (US) 1989 dir. Lou Antonio

Neverending Story, The
Ende, M.
Neverending Story II: The Next Chapter, The
WAR (Ger) 1989 dir. George Miller

New Guinea Gold
Burtis, T.
Crosswinds
PAR (US) 1951 dir. Lewis R. Foster

Newhaven-Dieppe
Simenon, G.
Temptation Harbour
AB (GB) 1947 dir. Lance Comfort

Next Door; Euphio Question, The; All the King's Men
Vonnegut, K.
Monkey House
ATLANTIS (US) 1991 dir. Paul Shapiro, Gilbert Shilton, Allan King

Next of Kin
Coleman, L.
Hot Spell
PAR (US) 1958 dir. Daniel Mann

Next-to-Last Train Ride, The
Dennis, C.
Finders Keepers
RANK (US) 1984 dir. Richard Lester

Nice Italian Girl, A
Christman, E.
Black Market Baby
BRUT (US) 1977 dir. Robert Day
GB title: Don't Steal My Baby

Nicholas Nickleby
Dickens, C.
Life and Adventures of Nicholas Nickleby, The
PRIMETIME (GB) 1984
dir. Jim Goddard

Night Before Christmas, The
Perelman, L. and Perelman, S. J.
Larceny Inc.
WAR (US) 1942 dir. Lloyd Bacon

Night Before Wenceslas, The
Davidson, L.
Hot Enough for June
RANK (GB) 1963 dir. Ralph Thomas

Night Bus
Adams, S. H.
It Happened One Night
COL (US) 1934 dir. Frank Capra

Night Cry
Stuart, W. L.
Where the Sidewalk Ends
FOX (US) 1950 dir. Otto Preminger

Night Darkens the Streets
La Bern, A. J.
Good-Time Girl
GFD (GB) 1948 dir. David MacDonald

Night of Clear Choice
Disney, D. M.
Yesterday's Child
PAR TV (US) 1977 dir. Corey Allen,
Bob Rosenbaum

Night of the Tiger, The
Dewlen, A.
Ride Beyond Vengeance
COL (US) 1966 dir. Bernard McEveety

Night Song
Williams, J.
Sweet Love, Bitter
FILM 2 (US) 1967 dir. Herbert Danska

Night Watch, The
Walsh, T.
Pushover
COL (US) 1954 dir. Richard Quine

Nightmare
Blaisdell, A.
Fanatic
COL (GB) 1965 dir. Silvio Narizzano
US title: Die! Die! My Darling

Nightmare
Dorner, M.
Don't Touch My Daughter
P-K (US) 1991 dir. John Pasquin

Nightmare in Manhattan
Walsh, T.
Union Station
PAR (US) 1950 dir. Rudolph Maté

Nine Days of Father Serra
Ziegler, I. G.
Seven Cities of Gold
FOX (US) 1955 dir. Robert D. Webb

No Beast so Fierce
Bunker, E.
Straight Time
WAR (US) 1978 dir. Ulu Grosbard

No Business Being a Cop
O'Donnell, L.
Prime Target
MGM/UA (US) 1989 dir. Robert Collins

No Difference to Me
Hambledon, P.
No Place for Jennifer
ABP (GB) 1949 dir. Henry Cass

No Exit
Goodchild, G. and Witty, F.
No Escape
PATHE (GB) 1936 dir. Norman Lee

No Medals
McCracken, E.
Weaker Sex, The
TC (GB) 1948 dir. Roy Baker

No More Gas
Nordhoff, C. B. and Hall, J. N.
Tuttles of Tahiti, The
RKO (US) 1942 dir. Charles Vidor

No Names . . . No Pack Drills
Herbert, B.
Rebel
MIRACLE (Aust) 1986
dir. Michael Jenkins

No Nightingales
Brahms, C. and Simon, S. J.
Ghosts of Berkeley Square, The
BN (GB) 1947 dir. Vernon Sewell

No Orchids for Miss Blandish
Chase, J. H.
Grissom Gang, The
CINERAMA (US) 1971
dir. Robert Aldrich

Noblesse Oblige
Horniman, R.
Kind Hearts and Coronets
EAL (GB) 1949 dir. Robert Hamer

Nobody Loves a Drunken Indian
Huffaker, C.
Flap
WAR (US) 1970 dir. Carol Reed
GB title: Last Warrior, The

Nobody Makes Me Cry
List, S.
Between Friends
HBO (US) 1983 dir. Lou Antonio

Nomads of the North
Curwood, J. O.
Nikki, Wild Dog of the North
DISNEY (US) 1961 dir. Jack Couffer

None so Blind
Wilson, M.
Woman on the Beach, The
RKO (US) 1947 dir. Jean Renoir

North of Bushman's Rock
Harding, G.
Ride the High Wind
BUTCHER (S. Africa) 1966
dir. David Millin

North of 36
Hough, E.
Conquering Horde
PAR (US) 1931 dir. Edward Sloman

Northwest Passage
Roberts, K.
Mission of Danger
MGM (US) 1959 dir. George Waggner,
Jacques Tourneur

Norwich Victims, The
Beeding, F.
Dead Men Tell No Tales
ALL (GB) 1938 dir. David MacDonald

Nose on my Face, The
Payne, L.
Girl in the Headlines, The
BL (GB) 1963 dir. Michael Truman
US title: Model Murder Case, The

Not so Long Ago
Richman, A.
Let's Do It Again
COL (US) 1953 dir. Alexander Hall

Not Too Narrow, Not Too Deep
Sale, R.
Strange Cargo
MGM (US) 1940
dir. Joseph L. Mankiewicz

Notebooks of Major Thompson, The
Daninos, P.
Diary of Major Thompson, The
GALA (Fr) 1955 dir. Preston Sturges
US title: French They are a Funny Race, The

Nothing to Lose
Minney, R. J.

Time Gentlemen, Please!
ABP (GB) 1952 dir. Lewis Gilbert

Notre Dame de Paris
Hugo, V.

Hunchback of Notre Dame, The
RKO (US) 1939 dir. William Dieterle
RANK (Fr/It) 1956 dir. Jean Delannoy
BBC (GB) 1977 dir. Alan Cooke
COL (US/GB) 1982
dir. Michael Tuchner

Now Barrabas
Home, W. D.

Now Barrabas was a Robber
WAR (GB) 1949 dir. Gordon Parry

Nun: A Memoir
Wong, Dr. M. G.

Shattered Vows
RIVER CITY (US) 1984 dir. Jack Bender

Nurse is a Neighbour
Jones, J.

Nurse on Wheels
WAR (GB) 1963 dir. Gerald Thomas

Nutcracker and the Mouseking, The
Hoffman, E. T. A.

Nutcracker Prince, The
WAR (US) 1990 dir. Paul Schibli

Nutcracker: Money, Madness, Murder: A Family Album
Alexander, S.

Nutcracker: Money, Madness and Murder
WAR TV (US) 1987 dir. Paul Bogart

Nutmeg Tree, The
Sharp, M.

Julia Misbehaves
MGM (US) 1948 dir. Jack Conway

Nu
Allen, J.

Tumult
ATHENA (Den) 1970
dir. Hans Abramson

Odour of Violets
Kendrick, B. H.

Eyes in the Night
MGM (US) 1942 dir. Fred Zinnemann

Odyssey, The
Homer

Ulysses
ARCHWAY (It) 1954
dir. Mario Camerini

Oedipus the King
Sophocles

Oedipus Rex
HORIZON (It) 1947
dir. Pier Paolo Pasolini

Off the Record
Hay, I. and King-Hall, S.

Carry on, Admiral
REN (GB) 1957 dir. Val Guest

Off-Islanders, The
Benchley, N.
Russians are Coming, The Russians are Coming, The
UA (US) 1966 dir. Norman Jewison

Oh!
Robison, M.
Twister
VESTRON (US) 1990
dir. Michael Almereyda

Oil for the Lamps of China
Hobart, A. T.
Law of the Tropics
WAR (US) 1941 dir. Ray Enright

Old Acquaintance
Druten, J. van
Rich and Famous
MGM (US) 1981 dir. George Cukor

Old Curiosity Shop, The
Dickens, C.
Mister Quilp
EMI (GB) 1975 dir. Elliot Scott

Old Dick, The
Morse, L. A.
Jake Spanner, Private Eye
FENADY (US) 1989 dir. Lee H. Katzin

Old Heidelburg
Meyer-Foerster, W.
Student Prince, The
MGM (US) 1954 dir. Richard Thorpe

Old Jest, The
Johnston, J.
Dawning, The
TVS (GB) 1988 dir. Robert Knights

Old Lady Shows Her Medals, The
Barrie, Sir J. M.
Seven Days' Leave
PAR (US) 1930 dir. Richard Wallace
GB title: Medals

Old Lady 31
Crothers, R.
Captain is a Lady, The
MGM (US) 1940 dir. Robert Sinclair

Old Soak, The
Marquis, D.
Good Old Soak
MGM (US) 1937 dir. J. Walter Ruben

Oldest Confession, The
Condon, R.
Happy Thieves, The
UA (US) 1962 dir. George Marshall

Olimpia
Cole, B.
Bobo, The
WAR (US) 1978 dir. Robert Parrish

Oliver Twist
Dickens, C.
Oliver!
COL (GB) 1968 dir. Carol Reed

Olympia
Molnar, F.
Breath of Scandal, A.
PAR (US) 1960 dir. Michael Curtiz and Mario Russo

Olympia
Molnar, F.
His Glorious Night
MGM (US) 1929 dir. Lionel Barrymore
GB title: Breath of Scandal

On Monday Next
King, P.
Curtain Up
GFD (GB) 1952 dir. Ralph Smart

On The Spot
Wallace, E.
Dangerous to Know
PAR (US) 1938 dir. Robert Florey

On the Trail: My Reminiscences as a Cowboy
Harris, F.
Cowboy
COL (US) 1957 dir. Delmer Daves

On the Trail of the Assassins: My Investigation and Prosecution of the Murder of President Kennedy
Garrison, J.
JFK
WAR (US) 1991 dir. Oliver Stone

On to Oregon
Morrow, H.
Seven Alone
HEMDALE (US) 1974 dir. Earl Bellamy

On Trial
London, A. and London, L.
L'Aveu
CORONA (Fr) 1970 dir. Costa-Gavras

Once and Future King, The
White, T. H.
Camelot
WAR (US) 1967 dir. Joshua Logan

Once and Future King, The
White, T. H.
Sword in the Stone, The
DISNEY (US) 1963
dir. Wolfgang Reitherman

Once Off Guard
Wallis, J. H.
Woman in the Window, The
RKO (US) 1944 dir. Fritz Lang

One Gallant Rush
Burchard, P.
Glory
TRI-STAR (US) 1989 dir. Edward Zwick

One Hell of a Woman
Thompson, J.
Serie Noire
GAU (Fr) 1979 dir. Alain Corneau

One Hundred Children
Kuchler-Silberman, L
Lena: My 100 Children
GREENWALD (US) 1987 dir. Ed Sherin

One Man's Secret
Weiman, R.
Possessed
WAR (US) 1947 dir. Curtis Bernhardt

One Pair of Feet
Dickens, M.
Lamp Still Burns, The
TC (GB) 1943 dir. Maurice Elvey

One Step From Murder
Meynell, L.
Price of Silence, The
GN (GB) 1959 dir. Montgomery Tully

One Sunday Afternoon
Hagan, J.
Strawberry Blonde, The
WAR (US) 1941 dir. Raoul Walsh

One Way Out
Flavin, M.
Convicted
COL (US) 1950 dir. Henry Levin

One Woman
Thayer, T.

Fame is the Name of the Game
UN TV (US) 1966 dir. Stuart Rosenberg

Only a Dream
Schmidt, L.

One Hour With You
PAR (US) 1932 dir. George Cukor,
Ernst Lubitsch

Only Couples Need Apply
Disney, D. M.

Betrayal
METRO (US) 1974 dir. Gordon Hessler

Opera Hat
Kelland, C. B.

Mr. Deeds Goes to Town
COL (US) 1936 dir. Frank Capra

Operation Cicero
Moyzisch, L. C.

Five Fingers
FOX (US) 1952
dir. Joseph L. Mankiewicz

Operation Overflight
Powers, F. G. and Gentry, C.

*Francis Gary Powers: The True Story of
the U-2 Spy Incident*
FRIES (US) 1976 dir. Delbert Mann

Operation Terror
Gordon M. and Gordon, G.

Experiment in Terror
COL (US) 1962 dir. Blake Edwards
GB title: The Grip of Fear

Operator, The
Amateau, R. and Robinson, B.

Where Does it Hurt?
HEMDALE (US) 1971 dir. Rod Amateau

Orchard Children, The
Maddux, R.

Who'll Save Our Children?
TIME-LIFE (US) 1978
dir. George Schaefer

Orchard Walls, The
Delderfield, R. F.

Now and Forever
ABP (GB) 1955 dir. Mario Zampi

Ordeal of Major Grigsby, The
Sherlock, J.

Last Grenade, The
CINERAMA (GB) 1969
dir. Gordon Flemyng

Order of Death, The
Fleetwood, H.

Corrupt
NEW LINE (It) 1983 dir. Robert Faenza

Orders is Orders
Hay, I. and Armstrong, A.

Orders are Orders
BL (GB) 1954 dir. David Paltenghi

L'Oro della Fantasia
Bonacci, A.

Kiss Me Stupid
UA (US) 1964 dir. Billy Wilder

Orpheus Descending
Williams, T.

Fugitive Kind, The
UA (US) 1960 dir. Sidney Lumet

Othello
Shakespeare, W.

Othello the Black Commando
M B DIFF 1982

Other One, The
Turney, C.

Back from the Dead
FOX (US) 1957
dir. Charles Marquis Warren

Our Virgin Island
White, R.

Virgin Island
BL (GB) 1958 dir. Pat Jackson

Out of the Frying Pan
Swann, F.

Young and Willing
UA (US) 1942 dir. Edward H. Griffith

Outlaw: The True Story of Claude Dallas
Long, J.

Manhunt for Claude Dallas
LONDON (US) 1986 dir. Jerry London

Outward Bound
Vane, S.

Between Two Worlds
WAR (US) 1944 dir. Edward A. Blatt

Over the River
Galsworthy, J.

One More River
UN (US) 1934 dir. James Whale
GB title: Over the River

Pack, The
Wilson, J. R.

Behind the Mask
BL (GB) 1958 dir. Brian Desmond Hurst

Paco Por Aqui
Rhodes, E. M.

Four Faces West
UA (US) 1948 dir. Alfred E. Green

Paid in Full
Cronin, M.

Johnny on the Spot
FANCEY (GB) 1954
dir. Maclean Rogers

Painted Veil, The
Maugham, W. S.

Seventh Sin, The
MGM (US) 1957 dir. Ronald Neame

Pamela
Richardson, S.

Mistress Pamela
MGM-EMI (GB) 1973
dir. Jim O'Connolly

Panther's Moon
Canning, V.

Spy Hunt
UN (US) 1950 dir. George Sherman
GB title: Panther's Moon

Paradigm Red
King, H.
Red Alert
PAR (US) 1977 dir. William Hale

Paragon, The
Pertwee, R. and Pertwee, M.
Silent Dust
ABP (GB) 1947 dir. Lance Comfort

Passing of Evil, The
McShane, M.
Grasshopper, The
NGL (US) 1969 dir. Jerry Paris

Passionate Witch, The
Smith, T.
I Married a Witch
UA (US) 1942 dir. René Clair

Passport to Oblivion
Leasor, J.
Where the Spies Are
MGM (GB) 1965 dir. Val Guest

Past Forgetting
Morgan, K. S.
Ike
ABC (US) 1979 dir. Melville Shavelson,
Boris Sagal

Pat & Roald
Farrell, B.
Patricia Neal Story, The
SCHILLER (US) 1981
dir. Antony Harvey & Anthony Page

Patrol
MacDonald, P.
Lost Patrol
RKO (US) 1934 dir. John Ford

Pattern of Islands, A
Grimble, Sir A.
Pacific Destiny
BL (GB) 1956 dir. Wolf Rilla

Patton: Ordeal & Triumph
Farago, L.
Patton
FOX (US) 1970 dir. Franklin Schaffner
GB title: Patton: Lust for Glory

Paxton Quigley's had the Course
Yafa, S.
Three in the Attic
WAR (US) 1968 dir. Richard Wilson

Peabody's Mermaid
Jones, G. P. and Jones, C. B.
Mr. Peabody and the Mermaid
UN (US) 1948 dir. Irving Pichel

Peacock's Feather
Hellman, G. S.
Night in Paradise, A
UN (US) 1946 dir. Arthur Lubin

Penny Arcade
Baumer, M.
Sinner's Holiday
WAR (US) 1930 dir. John G. Adolfi

Penrod
Tarkington, B.
By the Light of the Silvery Moon
WAR (US) 1953 dir. David Butler

Penrod
Tarkington, B.
On Moonlight Bay
WAR (US) 1951 dir. Roy del Ruth

Pensamientos
Pinto, M.
El
NACIONAL (Mex) 1952
dir. Luis Bunuel

Pentimento
Hellman, L. F.
Julia
FOX (US) 1977 dir. Fred Zinnemann

Peoples
Downs, R. C. S.
Billy: Portrait of a Street Kid
CARLINER (US) 1977
dir. Steven Gethers

Pépé le Moko
d'Ashelbe, R.
Algiers
WANGER (US) 1938 dir. John Cromwell

Perfect Round, The
Robinson, H. M.
Americana
CROWN (US) 1983 dir. David Carradine

Perilous Passage, The
Nicolaysen, B.
Passage, The
HEMDALE (GB) 1978
dir. J. Lee Thompson

Persistent Warrior, The
Arundel, E.
Green Fingers
BN (GB) 1946 dir. John Harlow

Personal Appearance
Riley, L.
Go West Young Man
PAR (US) 1936 dir. Henry Hathaway

Personal History
Sheean, V.
Foreign Correspondent
UA (US) 1940 dir. Alfred Hitchcock

Persons in Hiding
Hoover, J. E.
Illegal Traffic
PAR (US) 1938 dir. Louis King

Persons in Hiding
Hoover, J. E.
Queen of the Mob
PAR (US) 1940 dir. James Hogan

Peter Pettinger
Riley, W.
Agitator, The
BRIT NAT (GB) 1944 dir. John Harlow

Petrified Forest, The
Sherwood, R. E.
Escape in the Desert
WAR (US) 1945 dir. Edward A. Blatt

Phantom Crown, The
Harding, B.
Juarez
WAR (US) 1939 dir. William Dieterle

Phantom Filly, The
Chamberlain, G. A.
Home in Indiana
TCF (US) 1944 dir. Henry Hathaway

Philadelphia Story, The
Barry, P.
High Society
MGM (US) 1956 dir. Charles Walters

Philadelphian, The
Powell, R.
Young Philadelphians, The
WAR (US) 1959 dir. Vincent Sherman
GB title: City Jungle, The

Philly
Greenburg, D.
Private Lessons
J. FARLEY (US) 1981 dir. Alan Myerson

Phoenix, The
Bachmann, L.
Ten Seconds to Hell
UA (US) 1959 dir. Robert Aldrich

Photo Finish
Mason, H.
Follow that Horse!
WAR (GB) 1959 dir. Alan Bromly

Piaf
Berteaut, S.
Piaf — The Early Years
FOX (Fr) 1982 dir. Guy Casaril

Pick Up Girl
Shelley, E.
Too Young to Go
RANK (GB) 1959 dir. Muriel Box

Pick up Sticks
Phillips, M.
Cherry Picker, The
FOX-RANK (GB) 1974 dir. Peter Curran

Picnic by the Roadside
Strugatsky, B., and Strugatsky, A.
Stalker
(USSR) 1979 dir. Andrei Tarkovsky

Picture of Dorian Gray, The
Wilde, O.
Dorian Gray
AIP (It/Ger) 1970
dir. Massimo Dallamano

Picture of Dorian Gray, The
Wilde, O.
Sins of Dorian Gray, The
RANKIN-BASS (US) 1983
dir. Tony Maylam

Pied Piper, The
Shute, N.
Crossing to Freedom
TELECOM/GRANADA (GB/US) 1990
dir. Norman Stone

Piège Pour un Homme Seul
Thomas, R.
Honeymoon with a Stranger
TCF (US) 1969 dir. John Peyser

Piège Pour un Homme Seul
Thomas, R.
Vanishing Act
LEVINSON-LINK (US) 1986
dir. David Greene

Pigboats
Ellsberg, E.
Hell Below
MGM (US) 1933 dir. Jack Conway

Pilgrimage
Henderson, Z.
People, The
METRO (USTV) 1972 dir. John Korty

Pilgrim's Progress
Bunyan, J.
Dangerous Journey
CHANNEL 4 (GB) 1985

Pillar to Post
Kohn, R. S.
Pillow to Post
WAR (US) 1945 dir. Vincent Sherman

Pillars of Midnight, The
Trevor, E.
80,000 Suspects
RANK (GB) 1963 dir. Val Guest

Pioneer Go Home
Powell, R.
Follow that Dream
UA (US) 1962 dir. Gordon Douglas

Pirates of Penzance, The
Sullivan, Sir A. and Gilbert, Sir W.
Pirate Movie, The
FOX (Aus) 1982 dir. Ken Annakin

Pity my Simplicity
Massie, C.
Love Letters
PAR (US) 1945 dir. William Dieterle

Place to Hide, A
Gillham, B.
Break Out
CFTF (GB) 1984 dir. Frank Godwin

Platonov
Chekhov, A.
Unfinished Piece for Player Piano, An
MOSFILM (USSR) 1977
dir. Nikita Mikhalkov

Pleasure Island
Maier, W.
Girls of Pleasure Island, The
PAR (US) 1953
dir. F. Hugh Herbert & Alvin Ganzer

Poem of the Lunatics, The
Cavazzini, E.
Voce Delle Lune, La
PENTA (It) 1990 dir. Federico Fellini

Point Blank
Grosso, S. and Rosenberg, P.
Question of Honor, A
EMI (US) 1982 dir. Jud Taylor

Point de Lendemain
Vivant, D.
Amants, Les
NEF (Fr) 1958 dir. Louis Malle

Point of Honour, The
Conrad, J.
Duellists, The
CIC (GB) 1977 dir. Ridley Scott

Pollyanna
Porter, E. H.
Polly
DISNEY (US) 1989 dir. Debbie Allen

Polonaise
Leslie, D.
Song to Remember, A
COL (US) 1944 dir. Charles Vidor

Poor Little Rich Girl
Heymann, C. D.
Poor Little Rich Girl: The Barbara Hutton Story
ITC (US) 1987 dir. Charles Jarrot

Poor, Poor Ophelia
Weston, C.
Streets of San Francisco, The
WAR TV (US) 1972 dir. Walter Grauman

POP: 1280
Thompson, J.
Coup de Torchon
FT (Fr) 1981 dir. Bertrand Tavernier
GB title: Clean Slate

Porgy
Heyward, D. and Heyward, D.
Porgy and Bess
GOLDWYN (US) 1959
dir. Otto Preminger

Pork Butcher, The
Hughes, D.
Souvenir
CIC (GB) 1987 dir. Geoffrey Reeve

Portrait of a Rebel
Syrett, N.
Woman Rebels, A
RKO (US) 1936 dir. Mark Sandrich

Postman Always Rings Twice, The
Cain, J. M.
Dernier Tournant, Le
LUX (Fr) 1939 dir. Pierre Chenal

Power and the Glory, The
Greene, G.
Fugitive, The
RKO (US) 1947 dir. John Ford

Prelude to Night
Stoddart, D.
Ruthless
EL (US) 1948 dir. Edgar G. Ulmer

Prescription: Murder
Kurth, A.
Murder in Texas
D. CLARK (US) 1981 dir. Billy Hale

Present Arms
Fields, H., Rodgers and Hart
Leathernecking
RKO (US) 1930 dir. Edward Cline
GB title: Present Arms

Pretty Polly Barlow
Coward, N.
Pretty Polly
RANK (GB) 1967 dir. Guy Green
US title: Matter of Innocence, A

Prico
Viola, C. G.
Children Are Watching Us, The
MAGLI (It) 1942 dir. Vittorio de Sica

Prince Caspian and The Silver Chair
Lewis, C. S.
Silver Chair, The
BBC (GB) 1990 dir. A. Kirby

Prince Consort, The
Xaurof, L., and Chancel, J.
Love Parade, The
PAR (US) 1929 dir. Ernst Lubitsch

Prisoner Without a Name, Cell Without a Number
Timerman, J.
Jacobo Timerman: Prisoner Without a Name, Cell Without a Number
CHRYS-YELL (US) 1983
dir. Linda Yellen

Prisoners are People
Scudder, K. J.
Unchained
WAR (US) 1955 dir. Hall Bartlett

Prisoners of Quai Dong, The
Kolpacoff, V.
Physical Assault
TITAN (US) 1973
dir. William M. Bushnell

Private Ear, The
Shaffer, P.
Pad (And How to Use It), The
UI (US) 1966 dir. Brian C. Hutton

Private Investigation, A
Alexander, K.
Missing Pieces
TTC (US) 1983 dir. Mike Hodges

Private I
Sangster, J.
Spy Killer, The
ABC (US) 1969 dir. Roy Baker

Private Life
Hackney, A.
I'm All Right Jack
BL (GB) 1959 dir. John Boulting

Private Pettigrew's Girl
Burnet, D.
Shopworn Angel
MGM (US) 1938 dir. H. C. Potter

Privileged Information
Alibrandi, T. and Armani, F. H.
Sworn to Silence
BLATT/SINGER (US) 1987
dir. Peter Levin

Procane Chronicle, The
Bleeck, O.
St Ives
WAR (US) 1976 dir. J. Lee Thompson

Professor Unrath
Mann, H.
Blue Angel, The
PAR (Ger) 1930 dir. Josef von Sternberg
FOX (US) 1959 dir. Edward Dmytryk

Promisse de L'aube, La
Gary, R.
Promise at Dawn
AVCO (US/Fr) 1970 dir. Jules Dassin

Proof Thru' the Night
Kenward, A. R.
Cry Havoc
MGM (US) 1943 dir. Richard Thorpe

Psyche 63
de Ligneris, F.
Psyche 59
BL (GB) 1964 dir. Alexander Singer

Psycho
Bloch, R.
Bates Motel
UN TV (US) 1987 dir. Richard Rothstein

PT109— John F. Kennedy in World War II
Donovan, R. J.
PT 109
WAR (US) 1963 dir. Leslie H. Martinson

Pu Yi and I; Pu Yi's Later Life; Pu Yi's Former Life
Li Shu Xian
Last Emperor, The
NKL (China) 1988 dir. Li Han Hsiang

Public Eye, The
Shaffer, P.
Follow Me
UN (GB) 1972 dir. Carol Reed
US title: Public Eye, The

Pumping Iron II: The Unprecedented Woman
Gaines, C. and Butler, G.
Pumping Iron II
BLUE DOLPHIN (US) 1984
dir. George Butler

Punitive Action
Robb, J.
Desert Sands
UA (US) 1955 dir. Lesley Selander

Purple Cloud, The
Shiel, M. P.
World, The Flesh and the Devil, The
MGM (US) 1959
dir. Ronald MacDougall

Pursuit
Fish, R. L.
Twist of Fate
COL TV/HTV (US/GB) 1989
dir. Ian Sharp

Pygmalion
Shaw, G. B.
My Fair Lady
WAR (US) 1964 dir. George Cukor

Pylon
Faulkner, W.
Tarnished Angels, The
UI (US) 1957 dir. Douglas Sirk

Q

Quality
Sumner, C. R.
Pinky
FOX (US) 1949 dir. Elia Kazan

Queen Emma of the South Seas
Dutton, G.
Emma: Queen of the South Seas
FRIES (US) 1988 dir. Bryan Forbes

Queen of Mean, The
Pierson, R.
Leona Helmsley: The Queen of Mean
FRIES (US) 1990 dir. Richard Michaels

Queen was in the Parlour, The
Coward, N.
Tonight is Ours
PAR (US) 1933 dir. Stuart Walker

Queen's Favourite, The
Neumann, R.
King in Shadow
BL (Ger) 1961 dir. Harold Braun

Queen's Husband, The
Sherwood, R. E.
Royal Bed, The
RKO (US) 1931 dir. Lowell Sherman

Quentin Durward
Scott, Sir W.
Adventures of Quentin Durward, The
MGM (GB) 1955 dir. Richard Thorpe
US title: Quentin Durward

Querelle de Brest
Genet, J.
Querelle
TRIUMPH (Fr/Ger) 1983
dir. Rainer Werner Fassbinder

Quiet Wedding
McCracken, E.
Happy is the Bride
BL (GB) 1957 dir. Roy Boulting

Racer, The
Ruesch, H.

Racers, The
FOX (US) 1955 dir. Henry Hathaway
GB title: Such Men are Dangerous

Rachel Cade
Mercer, C.

Sins of Rachel Cade, The
WAR (US) 1960 dir. Gordon Douglas

Rachel
Fast, H.

Rachel and the Stranger
RKO (US) 1948 dir. Norman Foster

Rafferty
Ballinger, W.

Pushover
COL (US) 1954 dir. Richard Quine

Raffles the Amateur Cracksman
Hornung, E. W.

Raffles
UA (US) 1939 dir. Sam Wood

Rag Bag Clan, The
Barth, R.

Small Killing, A
MOTOWN (US) 1981
dir. Steven Hilliard Stern

Rage of the Vulture
Moorehead, A.

Thunder in the East
PAR (US) 1951 dir. Charles Vidor

Rainbird Pattern, The
Canning, V.

Family Plot
UN (US) 1976 dir. Alfred Hitchcock

Rains Came, The
Bromfield, L.

Rains of Ranchipur, The
FOX (US) 1955 dir. Jean Negulesco

Rain
Maugham, W. S.

Miss Sadie Thompson
COL (US) 1953 dir. Curtis Bernhardt

Raising Daisy Rothschild
Leslie-Melville, J. and Leslie-Melville, B.

Last Giraffe, The
WESTFALL PRODS (US) 1979
dir. Jack Couffer

Raj Quartet, The
Scott, P.

Jewel in the Crown, The
GRANADA (GB) 1984
dir. JimO'Brien/ChristopherMorahan

Ramey
Farris, J.

Greatest Gift, The
UN TV (US) 1974 dir. Boris Sagal

Rap, The
Brawley, E.

Fast-Walking
PICKMAN (US) 1982
dir. James B. Harris

Rapture in my Rags
Hastings, P.

Rapture
FOX (US/Fr) 1965 dir. John Guillermin

Rascal, a Memoir of a Better Era
North, S.

Rascal
DISNEY (US) 1969 dir. Norman Tokar

Ratman's Notebook
Gilbert, S.

Willard
CINERAMA (US) 1971 dir. Daniel Mann

Ravine, The
Young, K.

Assault
RANK (GB) 1971 dir. Sidney Hayers

Raw Youth
Bell, N.

Undertow
CAPSTONE (US) 1991
dir. Thomas Mazziotti

Rawhide Justice
Raine, W. M.

Man from Bitter Ridge, The
UN (US) 1955 dir. Jack Arnold

Ready Money
Montgomery, J.

Riding High
PAR (US) 1943 dir. George Marshall
GB title: Melody Inn

Recollections of Vesta Tilly
De Frece, Lady

After the Ball
BL (GB) 1957 dir. Compton Bennett

Recteur de l'Ile de Sein, Un
Quefflec, H.

Dieu à Besoin des Hommes
TRANS (Fr) 1950 dir. Jean Delannoy

Red Alert
George, P.

Dr Strangelove; Or How I Learned to Stop Worrying and Love the Bomb
COL (GB) 1963 dir. Stanley Kubrick

Red Cat, The
Lothar, R. and Adler, H.

Folies Bergère
FOX (US) 1935 dir. Roy del Ruth
GB title: Man from the Folies Bergère, The

Red Dragon
Harris, T.

Manhunter
CANNON (US) 1986 dir. Michael Mann

Red File for Callan, A
Mitchell, J.

Callan
EMI (GB) 1974 dir. Don Sharp

Red for Danger
Price, E.

Blondes for Danger
WILCOX (GB) 1938 dir. Jack Raymond

Red Hugh, Prince of Donegal
Reilly, R. T.

Fighting Prince of Donegal, The
DISNEY (GB) 1966
dir. Michael O'Herlihy

Red Peppers; Fumed Oak; Ways & Means
Coward, N.

Meet Me Tonight
GFD (GB) 1952 dir. Anthony Pelissier

Religion, The
Conde, N.

Believers, The
ORION (US) 1987 dir. John Schlesinger

Renee Richards Story, The
Richards, R., and Ames, J.
Second Serve
LORIMAR (US) 1986 dir. Anthony Page

Renfrew's Long Trail
Erskine, L. Y.
Danger Ahead
MON (GB) 1940 dir. Ralph Staub

Report on a Fugitive
Wellesley, G.
Night Train to Munich
TCF (GB) 1940 dir. Carol Reed

Reprieve
Resko, J.
Convicts Four
ALLIED (US) 1962 dir. Millard Kaufman
GB title: Reprieve

Reputation for a Song
Grierson, E.
My Lover, My Son
MGM (US/GB) 1970 dir. John Newland

Rescuers, The: Miss Bianca
Sharp, M.
Rescuers, The
DISNEY (US) 1977
dir. Wolfgang Reitherman

Resurrection
Tolstoy, L.
We Live Again
UA (US) 1934 dir. Rouben Mamoulian

Return Engagement
Hamilton, N., Casey, R. and Shute, J.
Fools for Scandal
WAR (US) 1938 dir. Mervyn LeRoy

Return to Paradise
Michener, J. A.
Until They Sail
MGM (US) 1957 dir. Robert Wise

Return to the Château
Réage, P.
Fruits of Passion
(Fr/Jap) 1982 dir. Shuji Terayama

Return to the Woods
Hodson, J. L.
King and Country
WAR (GB) 1964 dir. Joseph Losey

Reveille in Washington
Leech, M.
Rose and the Jackal, The
S. White (US) 1990 dir. Jack Gold

Revolt
McCall, M.
Scarlet Dawn
WAR (US) 1932 dir. William Dieterle

Rhodes
Millin, S. G.
Rhodes of Africa
GAU BRI (GB) 1936
dir. Berthold Viertes
US title: Rhodes

Riddle Me This
Rubin, D.
Guilty as Hell
PAR (US) 1932 dir. Erle C. Kenton

Riddle Me This
Rubin, D.
Night Club Scandal
PAR (US) 1937 dir. Ralph Murphy

Ride the Nightmare
Matheson, R.
Cold Sweat
CORONA/FAIRFILM (It/Fr) 1974
dir. Terence Young

Ride the Pink Horse
Hughes, D. B.
Hanged Man, The
UN (US) 1964 dir. Don Siegel

Rinehard
Tweed, T. F.

Gabriel Over the White House
MGM (US) 1933 dir. Gregory LaCava

Ring for Catty
Cargill, P. and Beale, J.

Twice Round the Daffodils
AA (GB) 1962 dir. Gerald Thomas

Ringer, The
Wallace, E.

Gaunt Stranger, The
NORTHWOOD (GB) 1938
dir. Walter Forde
US title: Phantom Strikes, The

Ripley's Game
Highsmith, P.

American Friend, The
CINEGATE (W. Ger) 1977
dir. Wim Wenders

Ripper from Rawhide
Cushman, D.

Timberjack
REP (US) 1954 dir. Joe Kane

Rita Hayworth: The Time, the Place, and the Woman
Kobal, J.

Rita Hayworth: The Love Goddess
SUSSKIND (US) 1983
dir. James Goldstone

River Ran out of Eden, A
Marshall, J. V.

Golden Seal, The
GOLDWYN (US) 1983 dir. Frank Zuniga

Road to Rome, The
Sherwood, R. E.

Jupiter's Darling
MGM (US) 1954 dir. George Sidney

Road to San Jacinto
Foreman, L. L.

Arrow in the Dust
ABP (US) 1954 dir. Lesley Selander

Roar of the Crowd, The
Corbett, J. J.

Gentleman Jim
WAR (US) 1942 dir. Raoul Walsh

Robinson Crusoe
Defoe, D.

Adventures of Robinson Crusoe, The
UA (Mex/US) 1954 dir. Luis Bunuel

Robinson Crusoe
Defoe, D.

Crusoe
ISLAND (US) 1989 dir. Caleb Deschanel

Robots Against Gandahar
Andrevan, J-P.

Light Years
MIRAMAX (Fr) 1988 dir. René Laloux

Rogue Male
Household, G.

Man Hunt
FOX (US) 1941 dir. Fritz Lang

Rojuko Kazoku
Sae, S.

Promise, A
KT (Jap) 1987 dir. Yoshishige Yoshida

Rome Haul
Edmonds, W. D.

Farmer Takes a Wife, The
FOX (US) 1935 dir. Victor Fleming
FOX (US) 1953 dir. Henry Levin

Rommel, The Desert Fox
Young, D.

Desert Fox, The
FOX (US) 1951 dir. Henry Hathaway
GB title: Rommel, Desert Fox

Rookwood
Ainsworth, H.

Dick Turpin
STOLL-STAFFORD (GB) 1933
dir. Victor Hanbury, John Stafford

Room Service
Murray, J. and Boretz, A.

Step Lively
RKO (US) 1944 dir. Tim Whelan

Rosalind
Barrie, Sir J. M.

Forever Female
PAR (US) 1953 dir. Irving Rapper

Rose and the Flame, The
Lauritzen, J.

Kiss of Fire
UN (US) 1955 dir. Joseph M. Newman

Rough Sketch
Sylvester, R.

We Were Strangers
COL (US) 1949 dir. John Huston

Roughshod
Fox, N. A.

Gunsmoke
UN (US) 1953 dir. Nathan Juran

Royal Canadian Mounted Police
Fetherstonhaugh, R. C.

Northwest Mounted Police
PAR (US) 1940 dir. Cecil B de Mille

Royal Family, The
Kaufman, G. S. and Ferber, E.

Royal Family of Broadway, The
PAR (US) 1930 dir. George Cukor
GB title: Theatre Royal

Rue Cases Negres, La
Zobel, J.

Sugar Cane Alley
ORION (Fr) 1984 dir. Euzhan Palcy

Ruggles of Red Gap
Wilson, H. L.

Fancy Pants
PAR (US) 1950 dir. George Marshall

Ruling Passion, The
Glitman, R. M.

High Price of Passion, The
TAFT (US) 1986 dir. Larry Elikann

Runaway Horses; Temple of the Golden Pavilion
Mishima, Y.

Mishima
WAR (US) 1985 dir. Paul Schrader

Running Scared
Burmeister, J.

Tigers Don't Cry
RANK (S. Africa) 1978
dir. Peter Collinson

Runway Zero-Eight
Hailey, A. and Castle, J.

Terror in the Sky
PAR TV (US) 1971
dir. Bernard L. Kowalski

Ruthless Ones, The
Moody, L.

What Became of Jack and Jill?
FOX (GB) 1971 dir. Bill Bain

S

Sabrina Fair
Taylor, S.
Sabrina
PAR (US) 1954 dir. Billy Wilder
GB title: Sabrina Fair

Sacajawea of the Shoshones
Emmons, D. G.
Far Horizons, The
PAR (US) 1955 dir. Rudolph Maté

Sackett; Daybreakers, The
L'Amour, L.
Sacketts, The
SHALAKO (US) 1979 dir. Robert Totten

Sacred Flame, The
Maugham, W. S.
Right to Live, The
WAR (US) 1935 dir. William Keighley
GB title: Sacred Flame, The

Saga of Billy the Kid, The
Burns, W. N.
Billy the Kid
MGM (US) 1930 dir. King Vidor
MGM (US) 1941 dir. David Millar

St. Ives
Stevenson, R. L.
Secret of St. Ives, The
COL (US) 1949 dir. Phil Rosen

Saint Johnson
Burnett, W. R.
Law and Order
UN (US) 1932 dir. Edward L. Cahn

Sally
Cunningham, E. V.
Face of Fear, The
Q. MARTIN (US) 1971
dir. George McCowan

Salome
Wilde, O.
Salome's Last Dance
VESTRON (GB) 1988 dir. Ken Russell

Salt
Gold, H.
Threesome
CBS ENT (US) 1984 dir. Lou Antonio

Salute to the Gods
Campbell, Sir M.
Burn 'em up O'Connor
MGM (US) 1938 dir. Edward Sedgwick

Samuel I & II: Chronicles I, Psalms of David
Bible
King David
PAR (US/GB) 1985
dir. Bruce Beresford

San Domingo, The Medicine Hat Stallion
Henry, M.
Peter Lundy and the Medicine Hat Stallion
FRIENDLY (US) 1977
dir. Michael O'Herlihy

San Quentin Story, The
Duffy, C. T. and Jennings, D.
Duffy of San Quentin
WAR (US) 1954 dir. Walter Doniger

Sanctuary
Faulkner, W.
Story of Temple Drake, The
PAR (US) 1933 dir. Stephen Roberts

Sapper
McNeile, H. C.
Bulldog Drummond
GOLDWYN (US) 1929
dir. F. Richard Jones

Satyricon
Petronius
Fellini Satyricon
UA (It) 1969 dir. Federico Fellini

Scarlet Pimpernel of the Vatican, The
Gallagher, J. P.
Scarlet and the Black, The
ITC (It/US) 1983 dir. Jerry London

Scarlet Pimpernel, The
Orczy, Baroness E.
Pimpernel Smith
BN (GB) 1941 dir. Leslie Howard

Scarlet Pimpernel, The
Orczy, Baroness E.
Purple Mask, The
UN (US) 1955 dir. Bruce Humberstone

Scènes de la Vie Bohème
Murger, H.
Bohemian Life
FILMS A2/PYRAMIDE PRODS. (Fr)
1992 dir. Aki Kaurismaki

School of Drama
Szekely, H.
Dramatic School
MGM (US) 1938 dir. Robert B. Sinclair, Jr.

Scott and Amundsen
Huntford, R.
Last Place on Earth, The
CENTRAL (GB) 1985
dir. Ferdinand Fairfax

Scottsboro: A Tragedy of the American South
Carter, D. T.
Judge Horton and the Scottsboro Boys
TOM (US) 1976 dir. Fielder Cook

Sea Wolf, The
London, J.
Wolf Larsen
ABP (US) 1958 dir. Harman Jones

Sea Wyf and Biscuit
Scott, J. M.
Sea-Wife
FOX (GB) 1957 dir. Bob McNaught

Second Sight
Williams, D.
Two Worlds of Jennie Logan, The
FRIES (US) 1979 dir. Frank DeFelitta

Secret Agent, The
Conrad, J.
Sabotage
GB (GB) 1936 dir. Alfred Hitchcock
US title: Woman Alone, A

Secret Sharer, The
Conrad, J.
Face to Face
RKO (US) 1952
dir. John Brahm/Bretaigne Windust

Secrets
Palin, M. and Jones, T.
Consuming Passions
GOLDWYN (GB) 1988 dir. Giles Foster

Seed and the Sower, The
Post, Sir L. van der
Merry Christmas, Mr. Lawrence
UN (GB) 1983 dir. Nagisa Oshima

Seizure
Mee, Jr., C. L.
Seizure: The Story of Kathy Morris
JOZAK (US) 1980 dir. Gerald Isenberg

Semi Detached
Turner, D.
All the Way Up
GRANADA/EMI (GB) 1970
dir. James MacTaggart

Send Another Coffin
Presnell, F. G.
Slightly Honourable
UA (US) 1940 dir. Tay Garnett

Sentimentalists, The
Collins, D.
His Woman
PAR (US) 1931 dir. Edward Sloman

Sentinel, The
Clarke, A. C.
2001, A Space Odyssey
MGM (GB) 1968 dir. Stanley Kubrick

September, September
Foote, S.
Memphis
PROPAGANDA FILMS TV(US) 1992
dir. Yves Simoneau

Service
Anthony, C. L.
Looking Forward
MGM (US) 1933 dir. Clarence Brown

Seven Days to a Killing
Egleton, C.
Black Windmill, The
PAR (GB) 1974 dir. Don Siegel

Seven Keys to Baldpate
Biggers, E. D.
House of the Long Shadows, The
CANNON (GB) 1983 dir. Pete Walker

Seven Men at Daybreak
Burgess, A.
Operation Daybreak
WAR (US) 1975 dir. Lewis Gilbert

Seven Pillars of Wisdom
Lawrence, T. E.
Lawrence of Arabia
COL/BL (GB/US) 1962 dir. David Lean

Seventh, The
Stark, R.
Split, The
MGM (US) 1968 dir. Gordon Flemyng

7½ Cents
Bissell, R. P.
Pajama Game, The
WAR (US) 1957 dir. Stanley Donen

711— Officer Needs Help
Masterson, W.
Warning Shot
PAR (US) 1966 dir. Buzz Kulik

**Sexpionage: The Exploitation
of Sex by Soviet Intelligence**
Lewis, D.
Secret Weapons
ITC (US) 1985 dir. Don Taylor

Sexual Perversity in Chicago
Mamet, D.
About Last Night . . .
TRI-STAR (US) 1986 dir. Edward Zwick

Shades Will Not Vanish
Fowler, H. M.

Strange Intruder
ABP (US) 1956 dir. Irving Rapper

Shadow and the Peak, The
Mason, R.

Passionate Summer, The
RANK (US) 1958 dir. Rudolph Cartier

Shadow Range
Bishop, C.

Cow Country
ABP (US) 1953 dir. Lesley Selander

Shall I Eat You Now?
Gebler, E.

Hoffman
ABP (GB) 1970 dir. Alvin Rackoff

Shape of Things to Come, The
Wells, H. G.

Things to Come
UA (GB) 1936
dir. William Cameron Menzies

Shattered
Dwyer, K. R.

Passengers, The
COL-WAR (Fr) 1977 dir. Serge Le Roy

She Let Him Continue
Geller, S.

Pretty Poison
FOX (US) 1968 dir. Noel Black

Shilling for Candles, A
Tey, J.

Young and Innocent
GFD (GB) 1937 dir. Alfred Hitchcock
US title: Girl was Young, A

Shirley
Cunningham, E. V.

What's a Nice Girl Like You . . .?
UN TV (US) 1971 dir. Jerry Paris

Shoeless Joe
Kinsella, W. P.

Field of Dreams
UN (US) 1989 dir. Phil A. Robinson

Shooting Party, The
Chekhov, A.

Summer Storm
UA (US) 1944 dir. Douglas Sirk

Shooting Star
Thomas, B.

Great Game, The
ADELPHI (GB) 1952 dir. Maurice Elvey

Shop Around the Corner, The
Laszlo, N.

In the Good Old Summertime
MGM (US) 1949 dir. Robert Z. Leonard

Shore Leave
Osborne, H.

Hit the Deck
MGM (US) 1955 dir. Roy Rowland

Shore Leave
Osborne, H. and Scott, A.

Follow the Fleet
RKO (US) 1936 dir. Mark Sandrich

Shore Leave
Wakeman, F.

Kiss Them for Me
FOX (US) 1957 dir. Stanley Donen

Shorn Lamb, The
Locke, W. J.

Strangers in Love
PAR (US) 1932 dir. Lothar Mendes

Short Happy Life of Francis Macomber, The
Hemingway, E.

Macomber Affair, The
UA (US) 1947 dir. Zoltan Korda

Short Timers, The
Hasford, G.
Full Metal Jacket
WB (US) 1987 dir. Stanley Kubrick

Shotgun
Wingate, W.
Malone
ORION (US) 1987 dir. Harley Kokliss

Showdown at Crazy Horse
Rigsby, H.
Last Sunset, The
UI (US) 1961 dir. Robert Aldrich

Show-off, The
Kelly, G.
Men Are Like That
PAR (US) 1930 dir. Frank Tuttle

Shrinking Man, The
Matheson, R.
Incredible Shrinking Man, The
UN (US) 1957 dir. Jack Arnold

Shuttered Room, The
Lovecraft, H. P.
Dunwich Horror, The
AMERICAN (US) 1970
dir. Daniel Haller

Siege at Dancing Bird, The
LeMay, A.
Unforgiven, The
UA (US) 1960 dir. John Huston

Siege at Trencher's Farm, The
Williams, G. M.
Straw Dogs
CINERAMA (GB) 1971
dir. Sam Peckinpah

Siege of Battersea, The
Holles, R.
Guns at Batasi
FOX (GB) 1964 dir. John Guillermin

Signs of Life
Elliott, S.
Careful, He Might Hear You
SYME (Aust) 1983 dir. Carl Schultz

Silent Stars Go By, The
Aldrich, B. S.
Gift of Love, The: A Christmas Story
TELECOM (US) 1983
dir. Delbert Mann

Silent Voice, The
Goodman, J. E.
Man Who Played God, The
WAR (US) 1932 dir. John G. Adolfi
GB title: Silent Voice, The

Silver Whistle, The
McEnroe, R. E.
Mr. Belvedere Rings the Bell
FOX (US) 1951 dir. Henry Koster

Sin of Susan Slade, The
Hume, D.
Susan Slade
WAR (US) 1962 dir. Delmer Daves

Sincerity
Erskine, J.
Lady Surrenders, A
UN (US) 1930 dir. John Stahl

Single Lady
Saunders, J. M.
Last Flight, The
WAR (US) 1931 dir. William Dieterle

Single Night
Bromfield, L.
Night After Night
PAR (US) 1932 dir. Archie Mayo

Sinister Errand
Cheyney, P.
Diplomatic Courier
FOX (US) 1952 dir. Henry Hathaway

Sir Gawain and the Green Knight
Anon.
Gawain and the Green Knight
THAMES (GB) 1990 dir. J. M. Phillips

Sir, You Bastard
Newman, G. F.
Take, The
COL (US) 1974
dir. Robert Hartford-Davis

Sire of Maletroit's Door, The
Stevenson, R. L.
Strange Door, The
UI (US) 1951 dir. Joseph Pevney

Sister Act
Hurst, F.
Four Daughters
WAR (US) 1938 dir. Michael Curtiz

Sister Carrie
Dreiser, T.
Carrie
PAR (US) 1952 dir. William Wyler

Sisterhood
Black, B., and Bishop, C.
Ladies Club, The
NEW LINE (US) 1986 dir. A. K. Allen

Six Days of the Condor
Grady, J.
Three Days of the Condor
PAR (US) 1975 dir. Sydney Pollack

Six Months With an Older Woman
Kaufelt, D.
In Love With an Older Woman
FRIES (US) 1982 dir. Jack Bender

Six Napoleons, The
Doyle, Sir A. C.
Pearl of Death, The
UN (US) 1944 dir. Roy William Neill

Six Weeks in August
Chais, P. H.
Guess Who's Sleeping in my Bed?
ABC (US) 1973 dir. Theodore J. Flicker

Sixteen Hands
Croy, H.
I'm From Missouri
PAR (US) 1939 dir. Theodore Reed

Sixth of June, The
Shapiro, L.
D-Day the Sixth of June
FOX (US) 1956 dir. Henry Koster

Skeezer: Dog With a Mission
Yates, E.
Skeezer
M. ARCH (US) 1982 dir. Peter H. Hunt

Skidding
Rouverol, A.
Family Affair, A
MGM (US) 1937 dir. George B. Seitz

Sky has Many Colours, The
Anderson, L.
Lili Marleen
ROXY (Ger) 1980
dir. Rainer Werner Fassbinder

Sky Steward
Attiwill, K.
Non Stop New York
GFD (GB) 1937 dir. Robert Stevenson

Skyscraper
Baldwin, F.
Skyscraper Souls
MGM (US) 1932 dir. Edgar Selwyn

Slapstick
Vonnegut, K.

Slapstick of Another Kind
LORIMAR (US) 1984 dir. Steven Paul

Slate Wyn and Blanche McBride
Savage, G.

Slate, Wyn and Me
HEMDALE (Aust) 1987
dir. Don McLennan

Sleep Long My Love
Waugh, H.

Jigsaw
BL (GB) 1962 dir. Val Guest

Sleeping Clergyman, A.
Bridie, J.

Flesh and Blood
BL (GB) 1951 dir. Anthony Kimmins

Sleeping Prince, The
Rattigan, T.

Prince and the Showgirl, The
WAR (GB) 1957 dir. Laurence Olivier

Slight Case of Murder, A
Runyon, D. and Lindsay, H.

Stop, You're Killing Me
WAR (US) 1952 dir. Roy del Ruth

Small Miracle, The
Gallico, P.

Never Take No for an Answer
INDEPENDENT (GB) 1951
dir. Maurice Cloche, Ralph Smart

Small Miracle
Krasna, N.

Four Hours to Kill
PAR (US) 1935 dir. Mitchell Leisen

Small Woman, The
Burgess, A.

Inn of the Sixth Happiness, The
FOX (GB) 1958 dir. Mark Robson

Smithereens
Battin, B. W.

Hell Hath No Fury
BAR-GENE (US) 1991
dir. Thomas J. Wright

Smuggler's Circuit
Roberts, D.

Law and Disorder
BL (GB) 1957 dir. Charles Crichton

Snake Head
Nishiki, M.

Shadow of China
NEW LINE (US/Jap) 1991
dir. Mitsuo Yanagimachi

Snake Water
Williams, A.

Pink Jungle, The
UI (US) 1968 dir. Delbert Mann

Snatchers, The
White, L.

Night of the Following Day, The
UN (US) 1969 dir. Hubert Cornfield

Snow Birch, The
Mantley, J.

Woman Obsessed
FOX (US) 1959 dir. Henry Hathaway

So Little Cause for Caroline
Bercovici, E.

One Shoe Makes it Murder
LORIMAR TV (US) 1982
dir. William Hale

Sobbin' Women, The
Benet, S. V.

Seven Brides for Seven Brothers
MGM (US) 1954 dir. Stanley Donen

Soldier for Christmas, A
Beckwith, R.

This Man is Mine
COL (GB) 1946 dir. Marcel Varnel

Soldier's Play, A
Fuller, C.

Soldier's Story, A
COL (US) 1984 dir. Norman Jewison

Solid! Said the Earl
Carstairs, J. P.

Yank in Ermine, A
MON (GB) 1955 dir. Gordon Parry

Some Must Watch
White, E. L.

Spiral Staircase, The
RKO (US) 1946 dir. Robert Siodmak
WAR (GB) 1975 dir. Peter Collinson

Someone is Killing the Great Chefs of Europe
Lyons, N., and Lyons, I.

Who is Killing the Great Chefs of Europe?
WAR (US) 1978 dir. Ted Kotcheff
GB title: Too Many Chefs

Someone Waiting
Williams, E.

Time Without Pity
HARLEQUIN (GB) 1957
dir. Joseph Losey

Son
Olsen, J.

Sins of the Mother
CORAPEAKE (US) 1991
dir. John Patterson

Son of Robin Hood
Castleton, P. A.

Bandit of Sherwood Forest, The
COL (US) 1946
dir. George Sherman/Henry Levin

Son of the Morningstar: Custer and the Little Big Horn
Connell, E. S.

Son of the Morning Star
REP (US) 1991 dir. Mike Robe

Son-Rise
Kaufman, B. N.

Son-Rise: A Miracle of Love
FILMWAYS (US) 1979 dir. Glenn Jordan

Sophia Living and Loving: Her Own Story
Hotchner, A. E.

Sophia Loren— Her Own Story
EMI (US) 1980 dir. Mel Stuart

Sort of Traitor, A
Balchin, N.

Suspect
BL (GB) 1960 dir. Roy Boulting

Sound of Hunting, A
Brown, H.

Eight Iron Men
COL (US) 1952 dir. Edward Dmytryk

Sound of Murder, The
Fairchild, W.

Last Shot you Hear, The
FOX (GB) 1970 dir. Gordon Hessler

Southern Blade
Wolford, N. and Wolford, S.

Time for Killing, A
COL (US) 1967 dir. Phil Karlson
GB title: Long Ride Home, The

Southern Star Mystery, The
Verne, J.

Southern Star, The
COL (GB/Fr) 1969 dir. Sidney Hayers

Souvenirs d'un Jeune Homme
Lauzier, G.

Petit Con
GOLDWYN (Fr) 1985
dir. Gerard Lauzier

Space Vampires
Wilson, C.

Lifeforce
CANNON (US) 1985 dir. Tobe Hooper

Sparrers Can't Sing
Lewis, S.

Sparrows Can't Sing
WAR (GB) 1962 dir. Joan Littlewood

Sphinx has Spoken, The
Dekobra, M.

Friends and Lovers
RKO (US) 1931 dir. Victor Schertzinger

Spinster
Ashton-Warner, S.

Two Loves
MGM (US) 1961 dir. Charles Walters

Spinster Dinner
Baldwin, F.

Love Before Breakfast
UN (US) 1936 dir. Walter Lang

Splendid Crime, The
Goodschild, G.

Public Defender
RKO (US) 1931 dir. J. Walter Ruben

Spoonhandle
Moore, R.

Deep Waters
FOX (US) 1948 dir. Henry King

Sporting Proposition, A
Aldridge, J.

Ride a Wild Pony
DISNEY (Aust) 1976 dir. Don Chaffey

Spurs
Robbins, T.

Freaks
MGM (US) 1932 dir. Tod Browning

Spy, The
Thomas, P.

Defector, The
PECF (Fr/W.Ger) 1966 dir. Raoul Levy

Square Circle, The
Carney, D.

Wild Geese II
UN (GB) 1985 dir. Peter Hunt

Stab in the Dark
Block, L.

8 Million Ways to Die
TRI-STAR (US) 1986 dir. Hal Ashby

Stage to Lordsburg
Haycox, E.

Stagecoach
UA (US) 1939 dir. John Ford
FOX (US) 1966 dir. Gordon Douglas
HERITAGE (US) 1986 dir. Ted Post

Stamboul Train
Greene, G.

Orient Express
FOX (US) 1934 dir. Paul Martin

Stand on It
Neely, W.

Stroker Ace
UN/WAR (US) 1983 dir. Hal Needham

Star in the West
Roberts, R. E.

Second Time Around, The
FOX (US) 1961 dir. Vincent Sherman

Stars in their Courses, The
Brown, H.

El Dorado
PAR (US) 1966 dir. Howard Hawks

Steel Saraband
Dataller, R.

Hard Steel
GFD (GB) 1942 dir. Norman Walker

Stella Dallas
Prouty, O.
Stella
TOUCH (US) 1990 dir. John Erman

Stella
Hartog, J. de
Key, The
COL (GB) 1958 dir. Carol Reed

Still Life
Coward, N.
Brief Encounter
CIN (GB) 1945 dir. David Lean
ITC (US) 1974 dir. Alan Bridges

Still Missing
Gutcheon, B.
Without a Trace
FOX (US) 1983 dir. Stanley R. Jaffe

Stone for Danny Fisher, A
Robbins, H.
King Creole
PAR (US) 1958 dir. Michael Curtiz

Stop at a Winner
Delderfield, R. F.
On the Fiddle
AA (GB) 1961 dir. Cyril Frankel
US title: Operation Snafu

Stories
Chekhov, A.
Dark Eyes
EXCELSIOR (It) 1987
dir. Nikita Mikhalkov

Stories
Maugham, W. S.
Flotsam and Jetsam
ATV (GB) 1960

Storm and Sorrow in the High High Pamirs
Craig, R.
Storm and Sorrow
HEARST (US) 1990 dir. Richard Colla

Story of Ivy
Lowndes, Mrs M. B.
Ivy
UI (US) 1947 dir. Sam Wood

Story of Khatyn, The
Adamovich, A.
Come and See
MOSFILM (USSR) 1985
dir. Elem Klimov

Story of the Trapp Family Singers, The
Trapp, M. A.
Sound of Music, The
FOX (US) 1965 dir. Robert Wise

Story of Zarak Khan, The
Bevan, A. C.
Zarak
COL (GB) 1956 dir. Terence Young

Stowaway to the Moon: The Camelot Odyssey
Shelton, W. R.
Stowaway to the Moon
FOX (US) 1975
dir. Andrew V. McLaglen

Strange Boarders of Paradise Crescent, The
Oppenheim, E. P.
Strange Boarders
GB (GB) 1938 dir. Herbert Mason

Strange Snow
Metcalfe, S.
Jackknife
CINEPLEX (US) 1989 dir. David Jones

Strange Tales of Liao Zhai
Ling, P. S.

Chinese Ghost Story II
GORDON (China) 1990
dir. Ching Siu-Tung

Stranger at Home
Sanders, G.

Stranger Came Home, The
EXCL (GB) 1954 dir. Terence Fisher
US title: Unholy Four, The

Stranger in the House
Sherburne, Z.

Memories Never Die
UN TV (US) 1982 dir. Sandor Stern

Stranger, The
Loss, L. B.

Zandy's Bride
WAR (US) 1974 dir. Jan Troell

Strangers in the House
Simenon, G.

Stranger in the House
JARFID (GB) 1967 dir. Pierre Rouve

Street Has a Thousand Eyes, The
Hamilton, P.

Bitter Harvest
RANK (GB) 1963
dir. Peter Graham Scott

Sturm in Wasserglass
Frank, B.

Storm in a Teacup
LF (GB) 1937 dir. Ian Dalrymple, Victor Saville

Sudie
Carter, S. F.

Sudie & Simpson
HEARST (US) 1990
dir. Joan Tewkesbury

Sufficient Carbohydrate
Potter, D.

Visitors
BBC (GB) 1987 dir. Piers Haggard

Suicide Club, The
Stevenson, R. L.

Trouble for Two
MGM (US) 1936 dir. J. Walter Rubin
GB title: Suicide Club, The

Summer Lightning
Corliss, A.

I Met My Love Again
WANGER (US) 1937 dir. Joshua Logan, Arthur Ripley

Summer of Fear
Duncan, L

Stranger in our House
INTERPLAN (US) 1978 dir. Wes Craven

Sun Shines Bright, The; Mob From Massac, The; LordProvides, The
Cobb, I. S.

Sun Shines Bright, The
REP (US) 1953 dir. John Ford

Sur la Terre Comme au Ciel
Belletto, R.

Peril
TRIUMPH (Fr) 1985 dir. Michel DeVille

Survivor, The
Eisner, J. P.

War and Love
CANNON (US/Israel) 1985
dir. Moshe Mizrahi

Suspense
Graeme, B.

Face in the Night
GN (GB) 1956 dir. Lance Comfort

Swastika
Shisgall, O.

Man I Married, The
TCF (US) 1940 dir. Irving Pichel

Sweet Aloes
Mallory, J.

Give Me Your Heart
WAR (US) 1936 dir. Archie Mayo
GB title: Sweet Aloes

Sweet Poison
Lee, L.

Along Came a Spider
FOX TV (US) 1970 dir. Lee H. Katzin

Swift Water
Annixter, P.

Those Calloways
DISNEY (US) 1964 dir. Norman Tokar

Switch
Bayer, W.

Doubletake
TITUS (US) 1985 dir. Jud Taylor

Symbol, The
Bessie, A.

Sex Symbol, The
COL (US) 1974 dir. David Lowell Rich

Tabitha
Ridley, A. and Borer, M.

Who Killed the Cat?
GN (GB) 1966 dir. Montgomery Tully

Tailor in the Château
Marchand, L. and Armont, P.

Love me Tonight
PAR (US) 1932 dir. Rouben Mamoulian

Taint of the Tiger
Macdonald, J. P.

Mantrap
PAR (US) 1961 dir. Edmond O'Brien

Talented Mr. Ripley, The
Highsmith, P.

Purple Noon
HILLCREST (Fr) 1960
dir. René Clément

Tales from the South Pacific
Michener, J. A.

South Pacific
TODD AO (US) 1958 dir. Joshua Logan

Tales of the African Frontier
Hunter, J. A. & Mannix, D. P.

Killers of Kilimanjaro, The
COL (GB) 1959 dir. Richard Thorpe

Talisman, The
Scott, Sir W.

King Richard and the Crusaders
WAR (US) 1954 dir. David Butler

Talked to Death: The Life and Murder of Alan Berg
Singular, S.

Talk Radio
UN (US) 1988 dir. Oliver Stone

Taming of the Shrew, The
Shakespeare, W.

Kiss me Kate
MGM (US) 1953 dir. George Sidney
MILBERG (US) 1958
dir. George Schaefer

Tarnsman of Gor
Norman, J.

Gor
CANNON (US) 1989 dir. Fritz Kiersch

Tarzan of the Apes
Burroughs, E. R.

Greystoke: The Legend of Tarzan, Lord of the Apes
WAR (GB) 1984 dir. Hugh Hudson

Tarzan of the Apes
Burroughs, E. R.

Tarzan, The Ape Man
MGM (US) 1932 dir. W. S. VanDyke

Taste of my own Medicine, A
Rosenbaum, E.

Doctor, The
TOUCH (US) 1991 dir. Randa Haines

Teacher, I Passed This Way
Ashton-Warner, S.

Sylvia
ENT (NZ) 1985 dir. Michael Firth

Tempest, The
Shakespeare, W.

Prospero's Books
FILM 4 (GB/Fr) 1991
dir. Peter Greenaway

Ten Against Caesar
Granger, K. R. G.

Gun Fury
COL (US) 1953 dir. Raoul Walsh

Ten Little Niggers
Christie, A.

And Then There Were None
ABP (US) 1945 dir. René Clair
GB title: Ten Little Niggers
EMI (GB) 1974 dir. Peter Collinson

Ten Little Niggers
Christie, A.

Ten Little Indians
ABP (GB) 1965 dir. George Pollock
CANNON (US) 1989
dir. Alan Birkinshaw

Ten Plus One
McBain, E.

Without Apparent Motive
VALORIA (Fr) 1971 dir. Philippe Labro

Tendre Poulet
Rouland, J-P and Olivier, C.

Dear Inspector
ARIANE/MONDEX (Fr) 1977
dir. Philippe de Broca

Ten-Second Jailbreak, The
Asinof, E., Hinckle, W. & Turner, W.

Breakout
COL (US) 1975 dir. Tom Gries

10.30 p.m. on a Summer Night
Duras, M.

10.30 p.m. Summer
UA (US/Sp) 1966 dir. Jules Dassin

Tentacles
Lyon, D.

House on Telegraph Hill, The
FOX (US) 1951 dir. Robert Wise

Terror on Highway 59
Sellers, S.

Terror on Highway 91
CBS (US) 1989 dir. Jerry Jameson

Tess of the d'Urbervilles
Hardy, T.
Tess
COL (Fr/GB) 1981 dir. Roman Polanski

Thanks God, I'll Take it From Here
Allen, J. and Livingston, M.
Without Reservations
RKO (US) 1946 dir. Mervyn Le Roy

That Uncertain Feeling
Amis, K.
Only Two Can Play
BL (GB) 1961 dir. Sidney Gilliat

Thé au harem d'Archi Ahmen, Le
Charef, M.
Tea in the Harem
M&R FILMS (Fr) 1986
dir. Mehdi Charef

Theme of the Traitor and the Hero, The
Borges, J. L.
Spider's Stratagem, The
RED FILM (It) 1970
dir. Bernardo Bertolucci

Then There Were Three
Shaw, I.
Three
UA (GB) 1969 dir. James Salter

Theophilus North
Wilder, T.
Mr. North
GOLDWYN (US) 1988
dir. Danny Huston

There are Two Kinds of Terrible
Mann, P.
Two Kinds of Love
CBS (US) 1983 dir. Jack Bender

There was a Fair Maid Dwelling: The Unjust Skies
Delderfield, R. F.
Diana
BBC (GB) 1983 dir. David Tucker

There was a Little Man
Jones, G. P. and Jones, C. B.
Luck of the Irish, The
FOX (US) 1948 dir. Henry Koster

There was that Beautiful Place
Manling, Z.
Sacrifice of Youth
ART EYE (China) 1986
dir. Zhang Luanxin

There's Always Juliet
Druten, J. van
One Night in Lisbon
PAR (US) 1941 dir. Edward H. Griffith

Thérèse Desqueyroux
Mauriac, F.
Thérèse
GALA (Fr) 1964 dir. Georges Franju

These, Our Strangers
Arlington, A.
Those Kids from Town
BN (GB) 1941 dir. Lance Comfort

They Called Him Death
Hume, D.
This Man is Dangerous
RIALTO (GB) 1941
dir. Lawrence Huntington

They Do it with Mirrors
Christie, A.
Murder with Mirrors
WAR (US) 1985 dir. Dick Lowry

They Dream of Home
Busch, N.
Till the End of Time
RKO (US) 1946 dir. Edward Dmytryk

They Knew What They Wanted
Howard, S.
Lady to Love, A
MGM (US) 1930 dir. Victor Seastrom

They Stole $2.5 million and Got Away with it
Dinneen, J. F.
Six Bridges to Cross
UN (US) 1955 dir. Joseph Pevney

Thieves' Market
Bezzerides, A. I.
Thieves' Highway
FOX (US) 1949 dir. Jules Dassin

Think of a Number
Bodelsen, A.
Silent Partner, The
CAROLCO (Can) 1978 dir. Daryl Duke

Third Avenue, New York
McNulty, J. L.
Easy Come, Easy Go
PAR (US) 1947 dir. John Farrow

Thirteen Days to Glory: The Seige of the Alamo
Tinkle, J. L.
Alamo: 13 Days to Glory, The
FRIES (US) 1987 dir. Burt Kennedy

13th Man, The
Bloom, M. T.
Last Embrace
UA (US) 1979 dir. Jonathan Demme

This For Remembrance
Clooney, R. and Strait, R.
Rosie: The Rosemary Clooney Story
FRIES (US) 1982 dir. Jackie Cooper

This is New York
Sherwood, R. E.
Two Kinds of Women
PAR (US) 1932 dir. William C. DeMille

This is Your Life
Wolitzer, M.
This is My Life
FOX (US) 1992 dir. Nora Ephron

This Life I've Led: My Autobiography
Zaharias, B. D. and Paxton, H.
Babe
MGM TV (US) 1975 dir. Buzz Kulik

This Magic Moment
Roberts, N.
Magic Moments
ATLANTIC/YTV (GB/US)
dir. Lawrence Gordon Clarke

This Same Garden
Bell, R.
While I Live
DRYHURST (GB) 1947 dir. John Harlow

This Story of Yours
Hopkins, J.
Offence, The
UA (GB) 1972 dir. Sidney Lumet

This was my Choice
Gouzenko, I.
Iron Curtain
FOX (US) 1948 dir. William Wellman

This Way Out
Ronald, J.
Suspect, The
UN (US) 1944 dir. Robert Siodmak

Thomasina
Gallico, P.

Three Lives of Thomasina, The
DISNEY (GB) 1963 dir. Don Chaffey

Thousand Plan, The
Barker, R.

1,000 Plane Raid, The
UA (GB) 1969 dir. Boris Sagal

Three Cups of Coffee
Feiner, R.

Woman's Angle, A
ABP (GB) 1952 dir. Leslie Arliss

Three Fevers
Walmsley, L.

Turn of the Tide
BN (GB) 1935 dir. Norman Walker

Three Godfathers, The
Kyne, P. B.

Hell's Heroes
UN (US) 1930 dir. William Wyler

Three Men in the Snow
Kastner, E.

Paradise for Three
MGM (US) 1938 dir. Edward Buzzell

Three Musketeers, The
Dumas, A.

Four Musketeers, The
FOX-RANK (Pan/Sp) 1974
dir. Richard Lester

Three Roads, The
Macdonald, R.

Double Negative
QUADRANT (Can) 1980
dir. George Bloomfield

Three Worlds of Johnny Handsome, The
Godey, J.

Johnny Handsome
TRI-STAR (US) 1989 dir. Walter Hill

372 Le Matin
Dijan, P.

Betty Blue
GAU (Fr) 1986 dir. Jean-Jacques Beineix

Threepenny Opera, The
Brecht, B. and Weill, K.

Mack the Knife
21st CENTURY (US) 1989
dir. Menahem Golan

Thumbs Up: The Life and Courageous Comeback of White House Press Secretary Jim Brady
Dickenson, M.

Without Warning: The James Brady Story
HBO (US) 1991
dir. Michael Toshiyuki Uno

Thunder Above
Wallis, A. J. and Blair, C. E.

Beyond the Curtain
RANK (GB) 1960 dir. Compton Bennett

Thunder God's Gold
Storm, B.

Lust for Gold
COL (US) 1949 dir. S. Sylvan Simon

Thursday Adventure
Pudney, J.

Stolen Airliner, The
BL (GB) 1955 dir. Don Sharp

Tiger Amongst Us, The
Brackett, L.

13 West Street
COL (US) 1962 dir. Philip Leacock

Tiger, The
Schisgal, M.

Tiger Makes Out, The
COL (US) 1967 dir. Arthur Hiller

Tikoyo and his Shark
Richer, C.
Beyond the Reef
UN (US) 1981 dir. Frank C. Clark

Time of the Cuckoo, The
Laurents, A
Summertime
UA (US) 1955 dir. David Lean
GB title: Summer Madness

Time Out for Ginger
Alexander, R.
Billie
UA (US) 1965 dir. Don Weis

Time to Die, A
Wicker, T.
Attica
ABC (US) 1980 dir. Marvin J. Chomsky

Times Of My Life, The
Ford, B. and Chase, C.
Betty Ford Story, The
WAR TV (US) 1987 dir. David Greene

Tin Star, The
Cunningham, J. M.
High Noon
UA (US) 1952 dir. Fred Zinnemann

Tinfoil
Cram, M.
Faithless
MGM (US) 1932 dir. Harry Beaumont

Tinker, The
Dobie, L. and Sloman, R.
Wild and the Willing, The
RANK (GB) 1962 dir. Ralph Thomas
US title: Young and Willing

Tinted Venus
Anstey, F.
Goddess of Love, The
NEW WORLD TV (US) 1988
dir. James Drake

Tintype, The
Brown, R.
Timestalkers
FRIES (US) 1987 dir. Michael Schultz

Tiptoe Boys, The
Markstein, G.
Final Option, The
MGM/UA (GB) 1983 dir. Ian Sharp

Tish Marches On
Rinehart, M. R.
Tish
MGM (US) 1942 dir. S. Sylvan Simon

To an Early Grave
Markfield, W.
Bye Bye Braverman
WAR (US) 1968 dir. Sidney Lumet

To Dusty Death
McCutcheon, H.
Pit of Darkness
BUTCHER (GB) 1961
dir. Lance Comfort

To Elvis with Love
Canada, L.
Touched by Love
COL (US) 1980 dir. Gus Trikonis

To Have and Have Not
Hemingway, E.
Breaking Point, The
WAR (US) 1950 dir. Michael Curtiz

To Have and Have Not
Hemingway, E.
Gun Runners, The
UA (US) 1958 dir. Don Siegel

To Save His Life
Roos, K.
Dead Men Tell No Tales
FOX (US) 1971 dir. Walter Grauman

To Smithereens
·Drexler, R.

Below the Belt
ATLANTIC (US) 1982
dir. Robert Fowler

Tonight at 8.30
Coward, N.

We Were Dancing
MGM (GB) 1942 dir. Robert Z. Leonard

Too Dangerous to be at Large
Johnson, R. and McCormick, M.

Dangerous Company
FINNEGAN (US) 1982
dir. Lamont Johnson

Toomai of the Elephants
Kipling, R.

Elephant Boy
UA (GB) 1937 dir. Robert Flaherty,
Zoltan Korda

Tooth of the Lion
Jennings, S.

Summer my Father Grew Up, The
SHAPIRO (US) 1991
dir. Michael Tuchner

Top of the World
Ruesch, H.

Savage Innocents, The
RANK (Fr/It/GB) 1960
dir. Nicholas Ray

Topaze
Pagnol, M.

Mr. Topaze
FOX (GB) 1961 dir. Peter Sellers
US title: I Like Money

Torch Bearers, The
Kelly, G.

Doubting Thomas
FOX (US) 1935 dir. David Butler

Toto il Buono
Zavattini, C.

Miracle in Milan
PDS (It) 1951 dir. Vittorio de Sica

Touch it Light
Storey, R.

Light up the Sky
BL (GB) 1960 dir. Lewis Gilbert

Touch the Lion's Paw
Lambert, D.

Rough Cut
PAR (US) 1980 dir. Don Siegel

Touch Wood
Stringer, D.

Nearly a Nasty Accident
BL (GB) 1961 dir. Don Chaffey

Tower, The
Stein, R. M., Scortia, T.N. and
Robinson, F. M.

Towering Inferno, The
COL-WAR (US) 1975
dir. John Guillermin, Irwin Allen

Tracy Cromwell
Richter, C.

One Desire
UI (US) 1955 dir. Jerry Hopper

Tragical History of Doctor Faustus
Marlowe, C.

Doctor Faustus
COL (GB) 1967 dir. Richard Burton,
Neville Coghill

Trailmakers, The
Forte, V.

Wild Women
A. SPELLING (US) 1970 dir. Don Taylor

Trails End
Shirreffs, G. D.

Oregon Passage
ABP (US) 1958 dir. Paul Landres

Translation of a Savage, The
Parker, G.

Behold my Wife
PAR (US) 1934 dir. Mitchell Leisen

Trap for a Single Man
Thomas, R.

One of my Wives is Missing
SPELLING-GOLDBERG (US) 1976
dir. Glenn Jordan

Travelling Lady, The
Foote, H.

Baby, The Rain Must Fall
COL (US) 1965 dir. Robert Mulligan

Travels of Jaimie McPheeters, The
Taylor, R. L.

Guns of Diablo
MGM (US) 1964 dir. Boris Sagal

Treasure of Franchard
Stevenson, R. L.

Treasure of Lost Canyon, The
UI (US) 1952 dir. Ted Tetzlaff

Tree of Liberty, The
Page, E.

Howards of Virginia, The
COL (US) 1940 dir. Frank Lloyd
GB title: Tree of Liberty, The

Trial by Terror
Gallico, P.

Assignment Paris
COL (US) 1952 dir. Robert Parrish

Trial, The
Kafka, F.

Insurance Man, The
BBC (GB) 1986

Trigger
Vollmer, L.

Spitfire
RKO (US) 1934 dir. John Cromwell

Trilby
Du Maurier, G.

Svengali
WAR (US) 1931 dir. Archie Mayo
REN (GB) 1954 dir. William Alwyn
HALMI (US) 1983 dir. Anthony Harvey

Trinity's Child
Prochnau, W.

By Dawn's Early Light
HBO (US) 1990 dir. Jack Sholder

Triumph
Fulop-Miller, R.

Great Moment, The
PAR (US) 1944 dir. Preston Sturges

Tropic of Ruislip, The
Thomas, L.

Tropic
ATV (GB) 1979 dir. Matthew Robinson

Truite, La
Vailland, R.

Trout, The
TRIUMPH (Fr) 1982 dir. Joseph Losey

Trumpets of Company K
Chamberlain, W.

Imitation General
MGM (US) 1958 dir. George Marshall

Truth Game, The
Novello, I.

But the Flesh is Weak
MGM (US) 1932 dir. Jack Conway

Tucker's People
Wolfert, I.

Force of Evil
MGM (US) 1948 dir. Abraham Polonsky

Turn of the Screw, The
James, H.
Innocents, The
FOX (GB) 1961 dir. Jack Clayton

Turn of the Screw, The
James, H.
Nightcomers, The
AVCO (GB) 1972 dir. Michael Winner

Turnabout
Faulkner, W.
Today We Live
MGM (US) 1933 dir. Howard Hawks

Turning Point, The
Capra, F.
Mindwalk
ATLAS (US) 1991 dir. Bernt Capra

Twelfth of Never, The
Heyes, D.
Lonely Profession, The
UN TV (US) 1979 dir. Douglas Heyes

Twelve Adventures of the Celebrated Baron Munchausen
Raspe, R. E.
Adventures of Baron Munchausen, The
COL (GB) 1988 dir. Terry Gilliam

Twelve Chairs
Ilf, E. and Petrov, E.
Keep Your Seats Please
ATP (GB) 1936 dir. Monty Banks

Twilight
Koontz, D.
Servants of Twilight, The
TRIMARK (US) 1991 dir. Jeffrey Obrow

Twin Sombreros
Grey, Z.
Gunfighters
COL (US) 1947 dir. George Waggner

Twins
Wood, B. & Geasland, J.
Dead Ringers
FOX (Can) 1988 dir. David Cronenberg

Two for the Price of One
Kenrick, T.
Nobody's Perfekt
COL (US) 1981 dir. Peter Bonerz

Two of a Kind: The Hillside Stranglers
O'Brien, D.
Case of the Hillside Stranglers, The
FRIES (US) 1989 dir. Steven Gethers

Typee
Melville, H.
Enchanted Island
WAR (US) 1958 dir. Allan Dwan

Umbrella Man, The
Scott, W.
London by Night
MGM (US) 1937 dir. William Thiele

Uncharted Seas
Wheatley, D.
Lost Continent, The
WAR (GB) 1968 dir. Michael Carreras

Uncle Harry
Job, T.
Strange Affair of Uncle Harry, The
UN (US) 1945 dir. Robert Siodmak

Uncle Silas
Le Fanu, S.
Dark Angel, The
BBC (GB) 1991 dir. Peter Hammond

Uncommon Danger
Ambler, E.
Background to Danger
WAR (US) 1943 dir. Raoul Walsh

Undercover Cat
Gordon, M. and Gordon, G.
That Darn Cat!
DISNEY (US) 1965
dir. Robert Stevenson

Uneasy Freehold
Macardle, D.
Uninvited, The
PAR (US) 1944 dir. Lewis Allen

Unexpected Mrs. Pollifax, The
Gilman, D.
Mrs. Pollifax–Spy
UA (US) 1971 dir. Leslie Martinson

Uninvited, The
Chittenden, F.
Stranger in Town
EROS (GB) 1957 dir. George Pollock

Union Street
Barker, P.
Stanley and Iris
MGM (US) 1990 dir. Martin Ritt

Unsleeping Eye, The
Compton, D.
Deathwatch
CONTEM (Fr/Ger) 1979
dir. Bertrand Tavernier

Up Pops the Devil
Goodrich, F., and Hackett, A.
Thanks for the Memory
PAR (US) 1938 dir. George Archainbaud

Urgent Hangman, The
Cheyney, P.
Meet Mr Callaghan
EROS (GB) 1954 dir. Charles Saunders

Useless Cowboy, The
LeMay, A.
Along Came Jones
UA (US) 1945 dir. Stuart Heisler

Valentine's Day
Foote, H.

On Valentine's Day
ANGELIKA (US) 1986 dir. Ken Harrison

Valkyrie's Armour
Tierney, H.

One Brief Summer
FOX (GB) 1969 dir. John MacKenzie

Valley of Fear, The
Conan Doyle, Sir A.

Triumph of Sherlock Holmes, The
TWICKENHAM (GB) 1935
dir. Leslie Hiscott

Valley of the Ants, The
Wells, H. G.

Empire of the Ants
AIP (US) 1977 dir. Bert I. Gordon

Valley of the Dolls
Susann, J.

Valley of the Dolls 1981
FOX TV (US) 1981 dir. Walter Grauman

Vanishing Corpse, The
Gilbert, A.

They Met in the Dark
RANK (GB) 1943 dir. Karel Lamac

Vanity Fair
Thackeray, W. M.

Becky Sharp
RKO (US) 1935 dir. Rouben Mamoulian

Vanity Row
Burnett, W. R.

Accused of Murder
REP (US) 1956 dir. Joe Kane

Vengeance
Jones, G.

Sword of Gideon
HBO (US/Can) 1986
dir. Michael Anderson

Verdict, The
Gregor, M.

Town Without Pity
UA (US/Switz) 1961
dir. Gottfried Reinhardt

Verge, The; Mr Knowall; Sanitorium
Maugham, W. S.

Trio
GFD (GB) 1950
dir. Ken Annakin/Harold French

Vespers in Vienna
Marshall, B.

Red Danube, The
MGM (US) 1949 dir. George Sidney

Vessel of Wrath
Maugham, W.S.

Beachcomber, The
GFD (GB) 1954 dir. Muriel Box

Victim: The Other Side of Murder
Kinder, G.

Aftermath: A Test of Love
COL (US) 1991 dir. Glenn Jordan

Victoria Regina
Housman, L.

Victoria the Great
RKO (GB) 1937 dir. Herbert Wilcox

Vietnam Trilogy
Fernandez, G.

Cease Fire
CINEWORLD (US) 1985
dir. David Nutter

Vigilante
Summers, R. A.

San Francisco Story, The
WAR (US) 1952 dir. Robert Parrish

Viking, The
Marshall, E.

Vikings, The
UA (US) 1958 dir. Richard Fleischer

Viper Three
Wager, W.

Twilight's Last Gleaming
HEMDALE (US/Ger) 1977
dir. Robert Aldrich

Virgin
Patterson, J.

Child of Darkness, Child of Light
WIL COURT (US) 1991
dir. Marina Sargenti

Visitor, The
Parker, C. G.

Of Unknown Origin
WAR (Can) 1983
dir. George P. Cosmatos

Visitors, The
Benchley, N.

Spirit is Willing, The
PAR (US) 1967 dir. William Castle

Voie Sauvage, La
Odier, D.

Light Years Away
NEW YORKER (Fr) 1932
dir. Alain Tanner

Wages of Fear, The
Arnaud, G.

Sorcerer
UN (US) 1977 dir. William Friedkin
GB title: Wages of Fear

Wailing Asteroid, The
Leinster, M.

Terronauts, The
EMBASSY (GB) 1967
dir. Montgomery Tully

Waiting for a Tiger
Healey, B.

Taste of Excitement, A
MONARCH (GB) 1969 dir. Don Sharp

Wake in Fright
Cook, K.

Outback
NIT (Aus) 1970 dir. Ted Kotcheff

Walk Me to the Distance
Everett, P.

Follow Your Heart
NBC (US) 1990 dir. Noel Nosseck

Walkers
Brandner, G.

From the Dead of Night
PHOENIX (US) 1989 dir. Paul Wendkos

Walks Far Woman
Stuart, C.

Legend of Walks Far Woman, The
EMI (US) 1982 dir. Mel Damski

Walls Came Tumbling Down, The
Deal, B. H.

Friendships, Secrets and Lies
WAR TV (US) 1979
dir. Ann Zane Shanks, Marlena Laird

Wanderer Never Sleeps, Even on the Road, A
Lee, J.

Man with Three Coffins, The
MWL (Kor) 1987 dir. Chang-Ho Lee

Warrior, The
Slaughter, F. G.

Naked in the Sun
ALLIED (US) 1957 dir. R. John Hugh

Washington Square
James, H.

Heiress, The
PAR (US) 1949 dir. William Wyler

Watcher in the Shadows
Household, G.

Deadly Harvest
CBS ENT (US) 1972
dir. Michael O'Herlihy

Water is Wide, The
Conroy, P.

Conrack
FOX (US) 1974 dir. Martin Ritt

Waterloo Bridge
Sherwood, R. E.

Gaby
MGM (US) 1956 dir. Curtis Bernhardt

We
Lindbergh, C. A.

Spirit of St. Louis, The
WAR (US) 1957 dir. Billy Wilder

We Are Seven
Troy, U.

She Didn't Say No!
ABP (GB) 1958 dir. Cyril Frankel

We can Remember it for you Wholesale
Dick, P.

Total Recall
CAROLCO (US) 1990
dir. Paul Verhoeven

We Die Alone
Howarth, D.

Nine Lives
NORDS (NOR) 1959 dir. Arne Skouen

We Let Our Son Die
Parker, L. and Tanner, D.

Promised a Miracle
REP (US) 1988 dir. Stephen Gyllenhaal

We the O'Leary's
Busch, N.

In Old Chicago
FOX (US) 1937 dir. Henry King

Weekend à Zuydcoote
Merle, R.
Weekend at Dunkirk
FOX (Fr/It) 1964 dir. Henri Verneuil

Weep No More
Coffee, L.
Another Time, Another Place
PAR (GB) 1958 dir. Lewis Allen

Welcome to Xanadu
Benchley, N.
Sweet Hostage
BRUT (US) 1975 dir. Lee Phillips

Werewolf of Paris, The
Endore, G.
Curse of the Werewolf, The
RANK (GB) 1961 dir. Terence Fisher

What? . . . Dead Again?
Shulman, N.B.
Doc Hollywood
WAR (US) 1991
dir. Michael Caton-Jones

What Beckoning Ghost
Lawlor, H.
Dominique
GRAND PRIZE (GB) 1978
dir. Michael Anderson

What Can You Do?
Leigh, J.
Making It
FOX (US) 1971 dir. John Erman

What Say They
Bridie, J.
You're Only Young Twice
ABP (GB) 1952 dir. Terry Gilbert

Wheel Spins, The
White, E. L.
Lady Vanishes, The
MGM (GB) 1938 dir. Alfred Hitchcock
RANK (GB) 1979 dir. Anthony Page

Wheelbarrow Closers
Larusso, II, L.
Closer, The
ION (US) 1990 dir. Dimitri Logothetis

Wheeler-Dealers, The
Goodman, G. J. W.
Wheeler-Dealers
MGM (US) 1963 dir. Arthur Hiller
GB title: Separate Beds

Wheels of Terror
Hassel, S.
Misfit Brigade, The
TRANSWORLD (US) 1988
dir. Gordon Hessler

When Knighthood was in Flower
Major, C.
Sword and the Rose, The
DISNEY (GB) 1953 dir. Ken Annakin

When Rabbit Howls
Chase, T.
Voices Within: The Lives of Truddi Chase
NEW WORLD TV (US) 1990
dir. Lamont Johnson

When we Ran
Leopold, K.
Moving Targets
ACADEMY (Aust) 1987
dir. Chris Langman

Where are you Going, Where have you Been?
Oates, J. C.
Smooth Talk
NEPENTHE (US) 1985
dir. Joyce Chopra

Where the Dark Streets Go
Davis, D. S.
Broken Vows
R. HALMI (US) 1987 dir. Jud Taylor

White Collars
Ellis, E.
Rich Man, Poor Girl
MGM (US) 1938 dir. Reinhold Schunzel

White Colt, The
Rook, D.
Run Wild, Run Free
COL (GB) 1989 dir. Richard C. Sarafian

White South, The
Innes, H.
Hell Below Zero
COL (GB) 1954 dir. Mark Robson

Who Censored Roger Rabbit?
Wolf, G. K.
Who Framed Roger Rabbit?
TOUCH (US) 1988 dir. Robert Zemeckis

Who Could Ask For Anything More
Swift, K.
Never a Dull Moment
RKO (US) 1950 dir. George Marshall

Who Goes There?
Campbell, J. W.
Thing, The
RKO (US) 1951 dir. Christian Nyby
GB title: Thing from Another World, The
UN (US) 1982 dir. John Carpenter

Who is Sylvia?
Rattigan, T.
Man Who Loved Redheads, The
BL (GB) 1954 dir. Harold French

Who Killed Sir Harry Oakes?
Leasor, J.
Eureka!
MGM/UA (GB/US) 1982
dir. Nicolas Roeg

Who Lie in Gaol
Henry, J.
Weak and the Wicked, The
APB (GB) 1953 dir. J. Lee Thompson

Who Rides with Wyatt?
Henry, W.
Young Billy Young
UA (US) 1969 dir. Burt Kennedy

Who Was That Lady I Saw You With?
Krasna, N.
Who Was That Lady?
COL (US) 1960 dir. George Sidney

Whorehouse Sting, The
Post, H.
Red-Light Sting, The
UN TV (US) 1984 dir. Rod Holcomb

Why Whales Came
Morpurgo, M.
When the Whales Came
FOX (GB) 1989 dir. Clive Rees

Widow Makers, The
Blankfort, M.
See How They Run
UN TV (US) 1964 dir. David Lowell Rich

Wild Bill Hickok
Wilstach, F.
Plainsman, The
PAR (US) 1937 dir. Cecil B de Mille

Wild Calendar
Block, L.
Caught
MGM (US) 1948 dir. Max Ophuls

Wild Waves
Manley, W. F.
Big Broadcast, The
PAR (US) 1932 dir. Frank Tuttle

Wildfire
Grey, Z.
Red Canyon
UN (US) 1949 dir. George Sherman

Will
Liddy, G. G.
Will: G. Gordon Liddy
SHAYNE (US) 1982
dir. Robert Lieberman

William Penn
Vulliamy, C. E.
Penn of Pennsylvania
BN (GB) 1941 dir. Lance Comfort
US title: The Courageous Mr. Penn

Willie Boy
Lawton, H.
Tell them Willie Boy is Here
UN (US) 1969 dir. Abraham Polonsky

Wilt
Sharpe, T.
Misadventures of Mr. Wilt, The
GOLDWYN (US) 1990
dir. Michael Tuchner

Wine and the Music, The
Barrett, W. E.
Pieces of Dreams
UA (US) 1970 dir. Daniel Haller

Winnie: My Life in the Institution
Bolnick, J. P.
Winnie
NBC (US) 1988 dir. John Korty

Winnie the Pooh
Milne, A. A.
Winnie the Pooh and the Honey Tree
DISNEY (US) 1965
dir. Wolfgang Reitherman

Winston Affair, The
Fast, H.
Man in the Middle
FOX (GB) 1963 dir. Guy Hamilton

Winter Doves
Cook, D.
Loving Walter
FF (GB) 1986 dir. Stephen Frears

Winter Wears a Shroud
Chapman, R.
Delavine Affair, The
MON (GB) 1954 dir. Douglas Pierce

Wisdom of Father Brown, The
Chesterton, G. K.
Father Brown, Detective
PAR (US) 1935 dir. Edward Sedgwick
ATV (GB) 1974 dir. Robert Tronson

Wiseguy: Life in A Mafia Family
Pileggi, N.
Goodfellas
WAR (US) 1990 dir. Martin Scorsese

Wishing Well
Evans, E.
Happiness of Three Women, The
ADELPHI (GB) 1954 dir. Maurice Elvey

Wisteria Cottage
Coates, R. M.
Edge of Fury
UA (US) 1958 dir. Robert Gurney,
Irving Lerner

Witch's Milk
De Vries, P.
Pete 'n Tillie
UN (US) 1972 dir. Martin Ritt

With a Pistol in His Hand
Parades, A.
Ballad of Gregorio Cortez, The
EMBASSY (US) 1983
dir. Robert M. Young

Within the Law
Veiller, B.
Paid
MGM (US) 1930 dir. Sam Wood
GB title: Within the Law

Within the Tides
Conrad, J.
Laughing Anne
REP (GB) 1953 dir. Herbert Wilcox

Within the Tides
Marquand, J. P.
Late George Apley, The
FOX (US) 1946
dir. Joseph L. Mankiewicz

Witness, The
Holden, A.
Bedroom Window, The
DELAUR (US) 1987 dir. Curtis Hanson

Wives and Concubines
Tong, S.
Raise the Red Lantern
ORION (China) 1991 dir. Zhang Yimov

Woman in Red, The
Gilbert, A.
My Name is Julia Ross
COL (US) 1945 dir. Joseph H. Lewis

Woman in the Dunes
Abé, K.
Woman of the Dunes, The
CONTEM (Jap) 1964
dir. Hiroshi Teshigahara

Woman Lies, A
Fodor, L.
Thunder in the Night
FOX (US) 1935 dir. George Archainbaud

Woman Who Was, The
Boileau, P. and Narcejac, T.
Diaboliques, Les
FILMSONOR (Fr) 1954
dir. Henri-Georges Clouzot

Woman with a Sword
Noble, H.
Drums in the Deep South
RKO (GB) 1952
dir. William Cameron Menzies

Women, The
Boothe, C.
Opposite Sex, The
MGM (US) 1956 dir. David Miller

Wonderful Wizard of Oz, The
Baum, L. F.
Wiz
DISNEY (US) 1978 dir. Sidney Lumet

Wonderful Wizard of Oz, The
Baum, L. F.
Wizard of Oz, The
MGM (US) 1939 dir. Victor Fleming

World In My Pocket, The
Chase, J. H.
On Friday at 11
BL (Ger/Fr/It) 1961 dir. Alvin Rakoff

Wrecker, The
Ridley, A., and Merivale, B.
Seven Sinners
GAU (GB) 1937 dir. Albert de Courville
US title: Doomed Cargo

Wrong Venus, The
Williams, C.
Don't Just Stand There
UN (US) 1967 dir. Ron Winston

Wyatt Earp, Frontier Marshall
Lake, S.

Frontier Marshall
FOX (US) 1933 dir. Lew Seiler
FOX (US) 1939 dir. Allan Dwan

Wyatt Earp, Frontier Marshal
Lake, S.

My Darling Clementine
FOX (US) 1946 dir. John Ford

X vs Rex
MacDonald, P.

Hour of Thirteen, The
MGM (GB) 1952 dir. Harold French

X vs. Rex
MacDonald, P.

Mystery of Mr. X, The
MGM (US) 1934 dir. Edgar Selwyn

Xiao, Xiao
Congwen, S.

Girl from Hunan, The
CHINA (China) 1986 dir. Xie Fei, U Lan

Yea, Yea, Yea
McGill, A.

Press for Time
RANK (GB) 1966 dir. Robert Asher

Year of the Angry Rabbit, The
Braddon, R.

Night of the Lepus
MGM (US) 1972 dir. William F. Claxton

Year of the Big Cat, The
Dietz, L.

Return of the Big Cat
DISNEY (US) 1974 dir. Tom Leetch

Year of the Horse, The
Hatch, E.

Horse in the Grey Flannel Suit, The
DISNEY (US) 1968 dir. Norman Tokar

Year the Yankees Lost the Pennant, The
Wallop, D

Damn Yankees
WAR (US) 1958 dir. George Abbott,
Stanley Donen
GB title: What Lola Wants

Years Ago
Gordon, R.

Actress, The
MGM (US) 1953 dir. George Cukor

Years Are So Long, The
Lawrence, J.

Make Way for Tomorrow
PAR (US) 1937 dir. Leo McCarey

Yekl
Cahen, A.

Hester Street
CONN (US) 1975
dir. Joan Micklin Silver

Yellowleg
Fleischman, A. S.

Deadly Companions, The
WAR (US) 1961 dir. Sam Peckinpah

Yentl, the Yeshiva Boy
Singer, I. B.

Yentl
MGM/UA (US) 1983
dir. Barbra Streisand

Yeoman's Hospital
Ashton, H.

White Corridors
GFD (GB) 1951 dir. Pat Jackson

Young Apollo
Gibbs, A. H.

Men of Tomorrow
PAR (GB) 1932 dir. Leontine Sagan

Young Archimedes
Huxley, A. L.

Prelude to Fame
GFD (GB) 1950 dir. Fergus McDonell

Young Manhood of Studs Lonigan, The
Farrell, J. T.

Studs Lonigan
UA (US) 1960 dir. Irving Lerner
LORIMAR (US) 1979
dir. James Goldstone

Your Arkansas Traveller
Schulberg, B. W.

Face in the Crowd, A
WAR (US) 1957 dir. Elia Kazan

You're Best Alone
Curtis, P.

Guilt is my Shadow
ABP (GB) 1950 dir. Roy Kellino

You're Only Human Once
Moore, G.

So This is Love
WAR (US) 1953 dir. Gordon Douglas
GB title: Grace Moore Story, The

Youth at the Helm
Vulpuis, P.

Jack of all Trades
GAINS (GB) 1936 dir. Jack Hubert,
Robert Stevenson

Zapata the Unconquerable
Pinchon, E.
Viva Zapata!
FOX (US) 1952 dir. Elia Kazan

Musicals Index

Little Nellie Kelly
Little Night Music, A
Little Prince, The
Little Shop of Horrors
Lost Horizon
Louisiana Purchase
Lovely to Look At
Love Me Tonight
Love Parade, The
Mack the Knife
Magic Flute, The
Mame
Man of La Mancha
Marriage of Figaro, The
Mary Poppins
Meet Me In St. Louis
Merry Widow
Mikado, The
Music in the Air
Music Man, The
My Fair Lady
My Sister Eileen
No No Nanette
Nutcracker
Oklahoma!
Oliver!
On a Clear Day You Can See
  Forever
One Hour With You
On Moonlight Bay
Otello
Paint Your Wagon
Pajama Game, The
Pal Joey

Pirate, The
Pirates of Penzance, The
Porgy and Bess
Presenting Lily Mars
Roberta
Rosalie
Rose Marie
Ruddigore
Sally
Scrooge
Seven Brides for Seven Brothers
1776
Showboat
Silk Stockings
Sound of Music, The
South Pacific
State Fair
Student Prince, The
Summer Holiday
Sweet Charity
Tales of Hoffman
This is the Life
Three for the Show
Three Sailors and a Girl
Tom Sawyer
Tonight We Sing
Unsinkable Molly Brown, The
Vagabond King, The
Week-end at the Waldorf
Wiz, The
Wizard of Oz, The
Wonder Bar
Yentl

Made-for-TV index:
_____ films, mini-series and serials _____

Detective, The
Diana
Diary of Anne Frank, The
Died in the Wool
Dombey and Son
Doubletake
Dream Merchants, The
Dream West
Dress Gray
Drug Wars: The Camarena Story
Dubai
East of Eden
Echoes in the Darkness
Eleanor and Franklin
Ellis Island
Elvis and Me
Emlyn's Moon
Emma: Queen of the South Seas
Evening in Byzantium
Evergreen
Evita Peron
Executioner's Song, The
Experiences of an Irish RM
Fame is the Spur
Fanny by Gaslight
Far Pavilions
Fatal Vision
Father Brown, Detective
Favorite Son
Feet of the Snake, The
First Born
Flambards
Flesh and Blood
Ford: The Man and the Machine
Forsyte Saga, the
For the Term of his Natural Life
Fortunate Pilgrim, The
Franchise Affair, The
Frankenstein: The True Story
Freedom Road
French Atlantic Affair, The
From the Dead of Night
George Washington

George Washington II: The Forging
   of a Nation
Gore Vidal's Lincoln
Guts and Glory: The Rise and Fall
   of Oliver North
Guyana Tragedy: The Story of Jim
   Jones
Hard Times
Harry's Game
Heidi
Helter Skelter
Hemingway
Henry's Leg
History Man, The
Hitch-Hiker's Guide to the Galaxy,
   The
Hold the Dream
Hollywood Wives
Honor thy Father
House of Cards
I Claudius
If Tomorrow Comes
Ike
I'll Take Manhattan
Immigrants, The
Inconvenient Woman, An
Inside the Third Reich
It
Jewel in the Crown, The
Kane and Abel
Kennedys of Massachusetts, The
Key to Rebecca, The
Kim
Kipps
Lace
Last Convertible, The
Last Days of Pompeii, The
Life and Adventures of Nicholas
   Nickleby, The
Life and Loves of a She-Devil
Lion, the Witch and the Wardrobe,
   The
Little Gloria – Happy at Last
Little Women

Scarlet Pimpernel, The
Scruples
Secret Army, The
Secret Diary of Adrian Mole, Aged 13¾, The
Secret World of Polly Flint, The
Seekers, The
Sense of Guilt, A
Seventh Avenue
79 Park Avenue
Shabby Tiger
Shogun
Shroud for a Nightingale
Sins
Small Sacrifices
Smiley's People
Some Lie and Some Die
Son of the Morning Star
Sophisticated Gents, The
Sorrell and Son
South Riding
Space
Spearfield's Daughter
Star Quality
Strong Medicine
Studs Lonigan
Sun Also Rises, The
Sunset Gang, The
Sweet Hostage
Sybil
Taste for Death, A
Tender is the Night
Testimony of Two Men
Thorn Birds, The
Till We Meet Again
To Have and to Hold

To Kill a Cop
To Serve Them All My Days
Town Like Alice, A
Traveller in Time, A
Tripods, The
Tropic
Turn of the Screw
Twist of Fate
Two Mrs. Grenvilles, The
Up the Garden Path
Valley of the Dolls
Vanished
Vanity Fair
Vendetta: Secrets of a Mafia Bride
Voices Within: The Lives of Truddi Chase
Wallenberg: A Hero's Story
War and Remembrance
Washington: Behind Closed Doors
What-a-Mess
Wheels
When the Bough Breaks
White Peak Farm
Why Didn't They Ask Evans?
Wild Times
Windmills of the Gods
Winds of War, The
Woman Called Moses, A
Woman of Substance, A
Women's Room, The
Women in White
Women of Brewster Place, The
Woof
Word, The
Yellowthread Street

Animated films index

Production and
_____ Distribution Companies _____

Since this book was first published, many companies originally listed now no longer exist. Changes of ownership have also occurred. The publishers would be pleased to hear from anyone who can supply further information

AA	Anglo-American
AAI	Anglo-Allied
AAm	Anglo Amalgamated
A & E	Arts and Entertainment
AB	Associated British
ABC	ABC Circle Films
ABC TV	ABC Television
	1330 Avenue of the Americas, New York NY 10019
ABFD	
ABP	
ABPC	
ACADEMY	
ACI	American Communications Industries
ADAM	Adam Productions
ADELPHI	
AETOS	
AFC	Australian Film Commission
AFT	American Film Theatre
AGAMEMNON	Agamemnon Films
AIDART	
AIP	American International Productions
AIRTIME	
ALB	Albatross
ALCINA	
ALIVE	Alive Films
	8271 Melrose Avenue, Los Angeles, CA 90046
ALL	
ALDERDALE	
ALLIANCE	Alliance Comm.
ALLIED	Allied Artists
ALMARO	Almaro Film
ALMI	
ALP	
AMERICAN	American Int
AMICUS	
AMLF	
AM PLAY	American Playhouse

ANGELIKA	Angelika Films
	1974 Broadway, 4th Floor, New York, NY 10023
ANGLE	Angle Films
ANGLIA	Anglia Television
	Anglia House, Norwich, Norfolk
ANGLO-AM	Anglo-American
ANOUCHKA	
AP	Adams Packer
A. PAULYE	
APEX	
AQUILA	
ARC	
ARCHWAY	
ARCO	
ARGENT	
ARG SONO	Argentine Sono
ARGYLE	
ARIANE	
ARIEL	Ariel Productions
	162-170 Wardour Street, London W1
ARTCO	Artcofilm SA
ARTEMIS	
ART EYE	Artificial Eye Film Company
	211 Camden High Street, London NW1 7BT
A. SPELLING	*see* Spelling
ASTRAL	Astral Films
AT	AT Films
ATHENA	
ATLANTIS	
ATLAS	Atlas Productions
ATP	
ATV	
ATLANTIC	Atlantic Entertainment
AUBREY	Aubrey Company
AUBREY-HAMNER	
AUS	Australia Television
AUSTRA	
AUT	
AVCO	AVCO Embassy
AVENUE	Avenue Entertainment
	12100 Wilshire Boulevard, Suite 1650, Los Angeles, CA 90024
AVV	Atlantic Video Ventures
AZTECA	Azteca Films
B & E	Barry and Enright
BAC	Bac Films
BANNER	Banner Associates
BARBER	
BARBER DANN	
BARBER ROSE	
BAR-GENE	Bar-Gene Productions

BAR PON
BARRANDOV
BAUERFILM
BBC   British Broadcasting Corporation
BBK   BBK Productions
B. BOGEAUS   Benedict Bogeaus
B. CROSBY   Bing Crosby Productions
BELSTAR
BENMAR
BFI   BFI Productions
              29 Rathbone Street, London W1P 1AG

BG
BI
BIOSKOP
BIP
BL
BLAIR   Blair Ent
BLATT   Daniel Blatt Productions
BLUE DOLPHIN Blue Dolphin Films, via Glenbuck Films
              15-17 Old Compton Street, London W1V 6JR

BLUE RIBBON
BN
BORDEAUX   Bordeaux Films
              22 Soho Square, London W1V 5FJ

BOURLA
BOYD   Boyd's Co. Film Productions
              9 Great Newport Street, London WC2H 7JA
BRANDMAN   Brandman Productions
BRAU   Braunberger-Richebe
BRAUN
BRAZOS
BRENTWOOD
BRETON
BRYNA
BRUT   Brut Productions
BW   Brent Walker Films
              Knightsbridge House, Knightsbridge, London SW7 1RB

BRIT NAT
BRIT SCREEN
BRYANSTON
BUTCHER

CABRIOLET   Cabriolet Films
CACTUS
CAGNEY   Cagney Productions
CAMEO-POLY
CAN BC
CANNON   Cannon Films
CAPSTONE   Capstone Films
CARLINER   Mark Carliner Productions
CAROLCO   Carolco Pictures
              8800 Sunset Boulevard, Los Angeles, CA 90048

CARSON	Carson Productions
CAPITOL	
CASTLE HILL	Castle Hill Productions
	116 N. Robertson, Suite 701, Los Angeles, CA 90048
CBC	Canadian Broadcasting Corporation
CBS ENT	CBS Entertainment
	7800 Beverly Boulevard, Los Angeles, CA 90036
CC	
CCC	CCC Filmkunst
CECCHI	Cecchi Gori
CENT	Centurion
CENTRAL	Central Independent Television
	Central House, Broad Street, Birmingham
CESK	Ceskoslovensky Film
CFF	
CFTF	
CG	Cinema Guild
C. GREGG	Colin Gregg
CH ELYSEE	Champs Elysée
CHAMPION	
CHANNEL 4	Channel Four Television Company
	60 Charlotte Street, London W1
CHARTER	
CHILRANGALI	
CHINA	China Film
CHRYS-YELL	Chrysalis-Yellen
CIC	
CIN	
CINA	Cina del Duca
CIN CEN	Cinema Center
CINECOM	Cinecom International Films
	1250 Broadway, New York, NY 10001
CINEGATE	
CINEGUILD	
CINEMA	Cinema Group
CINEMA INT	
CINEMA 5	
CINEMA 51	
CINEMARQUE	
CINEMATION	
CINEMAX	
CINEPLEX	
CINERAMA	
CINETV	Cinetelevision
CINEVISION	
CINEVISTA	Cinevista, Inc.
	353 W. 39th Street, New York, NY 10018
CINEWORLD	
CIN IT	Cinema Italia
CIN WORLD	Cinema World
CIPRA	
CLASA	

CLASART	
CLASSIC	Classic Cinemas
CLCC	
CLESI	Clesi Cinematografica
CODO	Codo-Cinema
COL	Columbia Pictures
	10202 W. Washington Boulevard, Culver City, CA 90232
COL TV	Columbia Television (*see* COL)
COMM	Commonwealth
COMPASS	Compass Film Productions
	3rd Floor, 18-19 Warwick Street, London W1R 5RB
COMPTON	
COMPTON-TEKLI	
COMWORLD	Comworld Productions
CONCORDE	Concorde Pictures
	11600 San Vicente Boulevard, Los Angeles, CA 90049
CONN	Connoisseur
CONSOL	Consolidated Ent
CONT	Continental
CONT DIS	
CONTEM	Contemporary
CORAPEAKE	Corapeake Productions
CORINTH	
CORONA	Films Corona
CORSAIR	Corsair Pictures
	1640 S. Sepulveda Boulevard, Suite 210, Los Angeles, CA 90025
COURIER	
CRAWFORD	Crawford Productions
CRISPIN	
CROWN	
CURTIS	Curtis Productions
CURZON	
DAIEI	Daiei Films
DAN FI	Danish FI
DASKA	DASKA Films
D. CLARK	Dick Clark Productions
DEFA	
DEFARIA	
DELAUR	DeLaurentiis
DIAL	
DISNEY	Disney Productions
	500 S. Buena Vista, Burbank, CA 91521
DISNEY CH	Disney Channel
DLT	DLT Ent.
DOCUMENTO	
DOUBLE HEAD	
DOVE	
DRYHURST	
D. WILSON	Daniel Wilson Productions
D. WOLPER	David Wolper Productions

EAGLE	
EAL	Ealing
EAST-WEST	
ECRAN	Ecran Français
E. DALTON	Emmet Dalton
EGC	
EL	
ELECTRIC	Electric Pictures
ELITE	
ELY LANDAU	
EMBASSY	Embassy Films
EMBASSY TV	
EMI	EMI Films
EMI TV	EMI Television, a division of EMI Films
EMPIRE	
ENGLUND	George Englund Ent.
ENT	Enterprise
ENT PAR	Entertainment Partners
EOS	
ERATO	Erato Films
EROS	
ETOILE	
EUROPEAN	European Classics
EUSTON	Euston Films
	365 Euston Road, London NW1 3AR
EXCALIBUR	Excalibur Films via Glenbuck Films
EXCELSIOR	
EXCL	Exclusive
FA	First Artists
FAC-NEW	Factor-Newland Productions
FAIRFILM	
FANCEY	
FARREN	
FCI	Film Communication Inc.
FD	
FDF	Films de France
FENADY	
FF	Film Forum
FGH	
FI	First Ind.
FIDA	
FILMAUFBAU	
FILMCORP	
FILM DALLAS	
FILM FORUM	
FILM 2	
FILM 4	
FILMLINE	
FILMO	
FILMPLAN	
FILMS A2	

FILMS 1966
FILMS 7
FILMSONOR
FILM TRADERS
FILMWAYS
FINE LINE
FINN   Finn Kimo
FINNEGAN   Finnegan Associates
FIRST   First Artists
FLORA   Flora Films
FNM   FNM Films
FONO
FOR   Forrestier-Parant
FOREST HALL
FORTUNE
FOUR STAR
FOX   20th Century Fox
                        PO Box 900, Beverly Hills, CA 90213
FOX TV   20th Century Fox Television Company
                        PO Box 900, Beverly Hills, CA 90213
FR3
FRANCO-LONDON
FRANCORITZ
FRANCOS
FRIENDLY   Fred Friendly Productions
FRIES   Charles Fries Entertainment
                        6922 Hollywood Boulevard, 12th Floor, Hollywood,
                        CA 90028
FT   Films de la Tour
FUJI
FULL MOON   Full Moon Entertainment

GAINS   Gainsborough
GALA
GALACTUS
GALAXIE
GALAXY   Galaxy International
GAMMA
GAMMA III
GANESH
GARDENIA
GAU   Gaumont
GAU BR   Gaumont British
GAYLORD   Gaylord Productions
GFD
GGT
GIBE   Films Gibe
GLAZIER   Glazier Productions
GLORIA   Gloria Productions
GN
GODWIN
GOLD   Goldcrest Films and Television
                        7-12 Noel Street, London W1Y 3PB

GOLDBAUM	
GOLDBERG	
GOLDWYN	Samuel Goldwyn Company
	10203 Santa Monica Boulevard, Suite 500, Los Angeles, CA 90067
GOODYEAR	Goodyear Movie Company
GORDON	Gordon Films
GORKI	
GORKY	Gorky Film Studios
GRADE	Grade Company
GRANADA	Granada Television
	Granada TV Centre, Manchester
GRAND PRIZE	
GRAUMAN	
GREEN-EPSTEIN	Green-Epstein Productions
GREENWALD	Robert Greenwald Productions
GREEN-WHITE	Green-White Productions
G. REEVES	Geoff Reeves
GROUP W	
GR UN	Greater Union Dist
GRUZIA	Gruziafilm
GTO	via Glenbuck Films
GAUNGXI	
GUBER-PETERS	Guber-Peters Entertainment
GUILD	
GUO	
HAJENO	Hajeno Productions
HALL BARTLET	
HALLMARK	Hallmark Hall of Fame
HALMI	Robert Halmi Productions
HAMILTON	Hamilton Productions
HAMMER	Hammer Film Productions
	Cannon Elstree Studios, Borehamwood, Herts WD6 1JG
HANDMADE	HandMade Films
	26 Cadogan Square, London SW1X 0JP
HANNA-BARBERA	Hanna-Barbera Productions
HARLEQUIN	
HAWK	
HBO	HBO Pictures
	2049 Century Park East, Los Angeles, CA 90067
HBO PREM	*see* HBO
HEARST	Hearst Entertainment
HEMDALE	Hemdale Film Corporation
	1118 N. Wetherly Drive, Los Angeles, CA 90069
HERITAGE	
HG	Harmony Gold
HIGHGATE	Highgate Pictures
HIGH INV	
HILL	Hill Films
HILLCREST	
H. JAFFE	Henry Jaffe Entertainment

HOBO	
HOL	
HOLLYWOOD	Hollywood Pictures (*see* DISNEY)
HORIZON	
H. ROACH	Hal Roach
HTV	Harlech Television
	HTV Wales, Television Centre, Cardiff CF5 6XJ
HUNG	Hungarofilm
HYP	Hyperion
IA	
I. ALLEN	Irwin Allen Productions
ICA	
IENA	
IFEX	International Film Exchange
IMAGINE	Imagine Television
IN	
INCA	Inca Films
INCITO	Incito Productions
INDEPENDENT	
INDIAN NECK	Indian Neck Ent
INDIEPROD	Indieprod Company
INDIVIDUAL	
INGRID	Ingrid Productions
INNER CIRCLE	Inner Circle Films
INSIGNIA	
INT	
INTERAMA	
INTERNAT	
INTEROPA	
INTERPLAN	Interplanetary Productions
INTERSCOPE	Interscope Communications
	10900 Wilshire Boulevard, Apt. 1400, Los Angeles, CA 90024
ION	Ion Pictures
IPC	IPC Films
IS	International Spectrafilm
ISLAND	Island Films
	4 Kensington Park Gardens, London W11 3HB
ITAL	
ITC	ITC Entertainment
	45 Seymour Street, London W1
ITV	Independent Television
IVE	
J & M	J & M Films
JANUS	
JARFID	
J. AVNET	Jon Avnet Company
JERAND	Jerand Films
JET	Jet Films
J. FARLEY	Jensen Farley Pictures

J. HAMILTON	Joe Hamilton Productions
JOLLY	Jolly Films
JOURNEY	Journey Ent
JOZAK	Jozak Company
KADR	
KASSLER	
KATZ-GALLIN	
KEEP	
KEL	Kendai Eiga Lyokai
KH	King-Hitzig Productions
KING	
KING PHOENIX	King Phoenix Ent
KINGS	Kings Road
KINO	
KLEMENT	
KONIGSBERG	Konigsberg Company
KON-SAN	Konigsberg-Sanitsky Company
KORDA	
KRANTZ	Steve Krantz Productions
KT	Kinema Tokyo
KUSHNER-LOCKE	Kushner-Locke Company
LAA	Les Artistes Associés
LA BOETIE	Films La Boetie
LAE	Laetitia
LAN	Landsburg Company
LANTANA	Lantana Productions
LC	Leader Cinematografica
LCA	LCA Productions
LENFILM	
LEONTYNE	
LEWIS	Lewis Productions
LF	
LFDP	Les Films du Passage
L. HILL	Leonard Hill Films
LIBRA	
LIP	
LIRA	
LONDON	London Film Productions
	44a Floral Street, London WC2E 9DA
LONDON SCR	London Screenplays
LOPERT	
LORIMAR	Lorimar Telepictures Inc
LOTUS	
L. RICH	Lee Rich Productions
LUX	
LWT	London Weekend Television
	London Television Centre, Upper Ground, SE1 9LT
LYTTLE	Lyttle Productions
M & R	M & R Films

MACLEAN
MAFILM
MAGLI   Franco Magli
MAGNA
MAINLINE   Mainline Films
MAJ   Majestic
MALTESE   Maltese Productions
MANDY   Mandy Films
MARCEAU   Films Marceau
M. ARCH   Marble Arch
MARS
MASSFILMS
MAY-SEW   Maynard-Sewell
MB DIFF   MB Diffusion
MCA TV
MCEG
MEDIA
MEDUSA
MELTDOWN
MELVILLE
METRO   Metromedia Producers Corporation
M. EVANS   Maurice Evans Productions
MGM   MGM 1000 W. Washington Boulevard, Culver City CA 90232
MGM TV   *see* MGM
MGM-PATHE   *see* MGM
MI   Merchant Ivory Productions
        34 South Molton Street, London W1Y 2BP

MILBERG
MILLIMETER
MINERVA   Minerva International
MIQ   Mallard-Impact-Quadrant
MIRACLE   Miracle Films
MIRAMAX   Miramax Films
        18 E. 48th Street, Suite 1601, New York, NY 10017

MK2
MON   Monogram
MONA   Mona Productions
MONARCH
MONASH-ZEITMAN Monash-Zeitman Productions
MONDEX
MOSFILM   Moscow Films
MOTOWN   Motown Productions
MOULIN ROUGE
M. PAGNOL   *see* Pagnol
M. REES   Marian Rees Associates
M. SIMON   Michel Simon
MTM   MTM Enterprises
MWL   Myung-Won Lee
MYERS

NACIONAL
NAMARA

NAT GEN	National General
NBC	NBC Productions
NBC ENT	NBC Entertainment
	3000 W. Alameda Avenue, Burbank, CA 91523
NC	Nieue Constantin
NED	Nederlander
NEF	Nouvelles Editions de Films
NEPENTHE	
NEPHI-HAMNER	Nephi-Hamner Productions
NERO	Nero Films
NEUE STUDIO	Neue Studio Film *GmbH*
NEW CENTURY	
NEW ERA	
NEWFELD-KEATING	Newfeld-Keating Productions
NEWLAND-RAYNOR	Newland-Raynor Productions
NEW LINE	New Line Cinema
	578 8th Avenue, 16th Floor, New York, NY 10018
NEW REALM	
NEW WORLD TV	*see* New World
NEW YORKER	New Yorker Films
	16 W. 61st Street, New York, NY 10023
NFC	National Film Corporation
NFM	Nationale Filmproductie Maatschapp
NGL	National General Lectures
NI	Nouvelle Imagerie
NIKKATSU	
NIT	
NKL	New Kwun Lun Films
NORD	Nordisk Tonefilm
NORDS	Nordsjfilm
NORTHWOOD	
NRW	NRW Features
NSW	New South Wales
OASIS	
OFELIA	Ofelia Films
OKO	Oko Film
OLY	
OMNIBUS	Omnibus Productions
OPT	Operation Prime Time
ORION	Orion Pictures Corp.
	1888 Century Park East, Los Angeles, CA 90067
ORSAY	
ORTF	
OSHIMA	Oshima Productions
OSL	
OSTERMAN	
OTHER	The Other Cinema
OZFILMS	

P & G	Procter and Gamble Productions
PACEMAKER	
PACIFIC	
PAGNOL	Marcel Pagnol
PAIZ	
PALACE	Palace Productions
	16-17 Wardour Mews, London W1V 3FF
PALM	Palm Productions
PALOMAR	Palomar Productions
PAN	Panavision
PANI	Panitalia
PANTHEON	Pantheon Productions
PAPAZIAN	Papazian Productions
PAPAZIAN-HIRSCH	Papazian-Hirsch Entertainment
PAR	Paramount Pictures Corporation
	5555 Melrose Avenue, Hollywood, CA 90038
PARADINE TV	
PARIS	Paris Films
PAR TV	Paramount Pictures Television
PASCAL	
PATHE	Pathe News
PAV	Pavilion Films
PBC	Pandora-Beijing-China Film Company
PBL	PBL Australia
PDC	Producers Distribution Company
PDS	
PEA	
PECF	
PEL	Pelemele
PENELOPE	Penelope Film
PENLAND	
PENNANT	
PENRITH	
PENTA	
PEREGRINE	Peregrine Ent
PHILCO	
PHOENIX	Phoenix Entertainment
PICKMAN	
PILGRIM-PATHE	
PINCHUK	
P-K	Patchett-Kaufman
PLANET	
PLAY-ART	
PLAYBOY	Playboy Productions
PLEIADE	Films de la Pleiade
PLEXUS	
POLL	Poll Productions
POLSKI	Film Polski
PORTMAN	Portman Productions
	159-165 Great Portland Street, London W1N 6NR
POWERS	
PRC	

PRESIDENT	President Films
PRICE	
PRIMETIME	Primetime Television
	Seymour Mews House, Seymour Mews, Wigmore Street, London W1H 9PE
PRISMA	
PROD	Producer Associates
PROM	Prometheus
PSO	Producers Sales Organization
PUBLIC	
PUNCH	Punch Productions
PYRAMID	
Q. MARTIN	Quinn Martin
QUADRANT	
QUARTET	
QINTEX	Qintex Entertainment
R5	
RAB	Rabinovitch
RADIO	
RAI	
RAIZ	
RANK	
RANKIN-BASS	
R. D. BANSAL	
R. DORFMANN	
READER'S DIG	Reader's Digest Entertainment
RED FILM	
REEVE	Reeve and Partners Film Company
	Panton House, Panton Street, Haymarket, London SW1Y 4EN
REGAL	
REGINA	Regina Films
REGENT	Regent Productions
	Regent House, 235 Regent Street, London W1A 2JT
REN	
RENAISSANCE	
REP	Republic
R. GREENWALD	*see* Greenwald
R. HALMI	*see* Halmi
RHI	RHI Entertainment
R. HUNTER	Ross Hunter Productions
RIALTO	
RICO	
RIVER CITY	River City Productions
RIVERS	
RIZZOLI	
R. J. LEVY	
RKO	RKO Productions International
	33 Dover Street, London W1X 3RA
RLC	RLC Productions

ROEI
ROLL   Roll Film
ROME-PARIS   Rome-Paris Films
ROMULUS
ROSEMONT   Rosemont Productions
ROXY
RTVE
RYAL

S8
S & T
SABAN   Saban Productions
SACIS
SACKS   Alan Sacks Productions
SAFIR
SAG   Sagittarius
SAMUELS   Samuels Productions
SANDCASTLE
SANDREW
SANITSKY
SANRIO
SASCH WIEN
SATEL
SAT. RAY
S. AUST   South Australia Film Corporation
SCALERA   Scalera Films
SCANLON
SCHERICK   Scherick Associates
SCHICK SUNN   Schick Sunn Classics
SCHILLER
SCHULZ
SCOTIA-BARBER
SDC
SEDIF
SELF   Self Productions
SELVAGGIA
SELZNICK
SERTNER
SEVEN ARTS
SEVEN KEYS
SEVEN KINGS
SF
SFB
S. GARDINE
S. GOLD   Samuel Goldwyn Television
SHADOW BOX   Shadow Box Films
SHALAKO   Shalako Entertainment
SHAPIRO   Shapiro Productions
SHARMHILL
SHAYNE   Shayne Company
SHOCHIKU   Shochiku-Fuji

SHOWTIME	Showtime
	10 Universal City Plaza, 31st Floor, Universal City, CA 91608
SIMON	Simon Productions
SINGER	
SIRITZKY	
SIRIUS	
SKOURAS	Skouras Pictures
S. KRANTZ	*see* KRANTZ
SNC	
SM-HEM	Smith-Hemion
SOKAL	
SOLARIS	
SOUTHERN	Southern Pictures
SOVEREIGN	
SPECTACOR	
SPEL-GOLD	Spelling-Goldberg
SPELLING	Aaron Spelling Productions
	5700 Wilshire Boulevard, 5th Floor, Los Angeles, CA 90036
SQUARE	Square Pictures
STANDARD	
STARGER	Starger Company
STIGWOOD	Robert Stigwood Organization
	118-120 Wardour Street, London W1V 4BT
STILLMAN	Stillman International
STOLL-STAFFORD	
STROMBERG	
STUDIO	Studio Unit
SULLIVAN	Sullivan Films
SUMMIT	
SUSSKIND	Susskind Company
SVENSK	Svensk Film
SVS	
SWE TV	Swedish TV
S. WHITE	*see* White
SYME	
SYZYGY	Syzygy Productions
TA	Tisch-Avnet Productions
TAFT	Taft International
TALENT	Talent Associates
TANGO	
TANSA	
TARGET	
TAURUS	Taurus Entertainment
	2545 Hempstead Turnpike, East Meadow, NY 11554
TBA	TBA Productions
TC	
TCF	*see* Fox
TCF TV	*see* Fox TV
TEDDERWICK	

TELECOM	Telecom Ent
TELECUL	Teleculture
TELEFILM	Telefilm Canada
TELEPICS	Telepictures
TELEPRESSE	
TELESCENE	Les Films Telescene
TELSTAR	
TEN-FOUR	Ten-Four Productions
TERRA	
TEVERE	Tevere Film
TFI	
THAMES	Thames Television
	Thames Television House, 306-316 Euston Road, London NW1
TIFFANY	
TIGON	
TIME-LIFE	Time-Life Productions
TITAN	
TITUS	Titus Productions
TNT	Turner Network Television
	1875 Century Park East, Los Angeles, CA 90067
TOBIS	
TODD AO	
TOEI	
TOHO	
TOM	Tomorrow Ent
TOUCH	Touchstone Films
	500 S. Buena Vista, Burbank, CA 91521
TOWER	Tower Productions
TRAFALGAR	
TRANS	Transcontinental
TRANS-TOKYO	Trans-Tokyo Corporation
TRANS WORLD	Trans World International
	The Pier House, Strand on the Green, London W4 3NN
TRIDENT	
TRIMARK	
TRIO	
TRI-STAR	Tri -Star Pictures
	10202 W. Washington Boulevard, Culver City, CA 90232
TRIUMPH	
TTC	TTC Productions
TURNER	Turner Pictures (*see* TNT)
TRIMARK	
TVS	Television South, Television Centre, Southampton, Hants.
TVS FILMS	
21ST CENTURY	21st Century Film Corporation
	7000 W. 3rd Street, Los Angeles, CA 90048
21ST FILM	
TWICKENHAM	
TYNE-TEES	Tyne-Tees Television
	The Television Centre, City Road, Newcastle upon Tyne

UA	United Artists
UAA	
UCIL	
UFA	
UFD	
UGC	
UI	Universal International
UIP	
ULYSSES	Ulysses Film
UMC	
UN	Universal Studios
	100 Universal City Plaza, Universal City, CA 91608
UNIFILM	
UN TV	Universal Television
UNICORN	Unicorn Organisation
	Pottery Lane Studios, 34a Pottery Lane, Holland Park,
	London W11 4LZ
UPFRONT	Upfront Films
USA NET	USA Network
	1230 Avenue of the Americas, 8th Floor, New York,
	NY 10020
VALORIA	
VANDYKE	
VER NED	
VESTRON	
VIACOM	Viacom Productions
	10 Universal City Plaza, Universal City, CA 91608
VIDMARK	
VIEW PICS	View Pictures
VINCENT	Vincent Pictures
VIRGIN	
VISTA	Vista Organization Productions
VON ZERNECK	
VSS	Von Serneck/Samuels Productions
WA	World Artists
WAINWRIGHT	
WANGER	Walter Wanger
WAR	Warner Bros
	4000 Warner Boulevard, Burbank, CA 91522
WAR TV	Warner Bros. Television
WARDOUR	Wardour Motion Pictures
	11 Wardour Mews, London W1
WARRANTY	
WEINTRAUB	Weintraub Productions
WELLER	
WESSEX	
WESTFALL	Westfall Productions
WESTON	Weston Productions
WEST ONE	
WHITE	Steve White Productions

WIL COURT	Wilshire Court Productions
WILCOX	
WILDSTREET	Wildstreet Pictures
WILSON	
WINCAST	
WISEMAN	
WIZAN	
WOLPER	Wolper Productions
WOODFALL	
WORK TITLE	Working Title
WORLD	World International
WORLD FILM	
WORLDVISION	Worldvision Ent
WORLD WIDE	World Wide Films
WW	
YEL	Yellowthread
YOSHA	Yosha Productions
YTV	Yorkshire Television
	The Television Centre, Leeds
ZDF	
ZENITH	Zenith Productions
	8 Great Titchfield Street, London W1P 7AA
ZEPHYR	
ZEOTROPE	Zeotrope
	93 Union Road, London SW4 6JD
ZZY	ZZY Inc

Further information might be available from:
British Film Institute,
127 Charing Cross Road, London WC2H 0EA

British Film & Television Producers Association Ltd.,
162 Wardour Street, London W1V 4AB

Academy of Motion Picture Arts and Sciences
Margaret Herrick Library
333 S. La Cienega, Beverly Hills, CA 90211